SAMPSON & TINDALL'S

TEXAS
FAMILY CODE ANNOTATED

WITH RELATED STATE AND FEDERAL STATUTES
AND ACCOMPANYING CD–ROM

ANNOTATIONS BY
JOHN J. SAMPSON
HARRY L. TINDALL
ANGELA PENCE ENGLAND
STEPHANIE STEVENS

AUGUST 2011 EDITION

WEST®
A Thomson Reuters business

Mat #: 40952618

ISBN: 978-0-314-92257-1

Dedication for the 21st Edition

The 2011 Edition of *Sampson & Tindall's Texas Family Code Annotated* is dedicated to:

Justice Frank G. Evans, III

Justice Evans served as both Justice and Chief Justice of the Houston First Court of Appeals from 1973 until his retirement in 1991. He is recognized as the Father of Alternative Dispute Resolution in Texas and was the principal advocate for the Texas ADR legislation in 1987. No piece of legislation has changed the practice of family law anymore than this act. In the two dozen years since ADR arrived in Texas, mediation, collaboration, and arbitration have become commonplace in our state.

Justice Evans has also taught mediation for years at the South Texas College of Law. The law school has named the Frank Evans Center for Conflict Resolution in his honor.

We proudly dedicate this edition to Justice Evans in recognition of his outstanding public service.

*

The Authors

John J. Sampson is the William Benjamin Wynne Professor of Law at the University of Texas School of Law, where he has taught since 1970. He was the editor of the *State Bar Family Law Section Report* from 1976 to 2007, and a legislative advisor to both Legislative Committees and the Family Law Council since 1975. Professor Sampson served as co-reporter or reporter for the Uniform Interstate Family Support Act, National Conference of Commissioners on Uniform State Laws, from 1990 to the present. From 1997 through 2002, he was the reporter for the revision of the Uniform Parentage Act. Since 2002 he has served as a member of U.S. State Dept. Delegations, first in 2002 to Central America, and every year from 2003 through 2007 to The Hague, Netherlands, for multilateral negotiations to draft the new maintenance convention for international child support enforcement.

Harry L. Tindall is a founding member of Tindall & England, P.C., Houston, Texas. He currently serves as Chair of the Joint Editorial Board—Family Law, a joint project of the American Bar Association, American Academy of Matrimonial Lawyers, and the National Conference of Commissioners on Uniform State Laws. He is also a Texas Commissioner, National Conference of Commissioners on Uniform State Laws (1995–Present), where he served as Chair of the drafting committee for the Uniform Parentage Act (2002) and Vice-Chair of the Uniform Collaborative Law Act (2010). He is currently a member of the Board of Trustees, Collaborative Law Institute of Texas and the Board of Directors, International Academy of Collaborative Professionals.

Angela Pence England is a board certified family law attorney in Houston, Texas, where she is a shareholder with the firm of Tindall & England, P.C., and an adjunct professor at South Texas College of Law. She currently serves on the Family Law Council, State Bar of Texas and has served as Chair of the Burta Rhoads Raborn Family Law Inn of Court, Chair of the Collaborative Law Section of the Houston Bar Association, and Chair of the Gulf Coast Family Law Specialists.

Stephanie Stevens is a Clinical Professor of Law at St. Mary's School of Law where she serves as supervising attorney of the Criminal Justice Clinic. She teaches juvenile law and is an examiner for Texas Board of Legal Specialization for Juvenile Law Certification.

Guest Commentators

Charles G. Childress, Clinical Professor, Children's Rights Clinic, University of Texas School of Law (Retired).

Gay Cox, Attorney, Dallas, Texas.

Honorable David Farr, Attorney, Judge, 312th District Court, Houston, Texas.

Diana Friedman, Attorney, Dallas, Texas.

Honorable J. Andrew Hathcock, Associate Judge, Travis County; Former Associate Judge, Child Protection Court of Central Texas.

Alicia Gray Key, Director, Child Support Division, Attorney General of Texas; Former Administrative Director, Texas Office of Court Administration.

Jeana A. Lungwitz, Clinical Professor of Law, Domestic Violence Clinic, University of Texas School of Law.

H. Patrick Sullivan, Director of Federal Policy Analysis, Child Support Enforcement, Office of the Attorney General.

Preface By The Authors

The August 2011 Edition of *Sampson & Tindall's Texas Family Code Annotated*, our 21st annual edition, reports the actions of the 82nd Legislature through the end of the Regular and First Called Sessions (2011).

The 2011 legislative amendments and additions are reported in a manner to allow the bench and bar to see at a glance exactly what the legislature enacted, amended and repealed. New statutory language is in **boldfaced type** and deleted language is shown [~~struck through~~].

As in previous editions, new case citations have been added this year, along with an update of yearly CLE and law review articles. Previous editions of Sampson & Tindall's Texas Family Code Annotated should be retained to determine legislative histories of Family Code sections, as well as citations to older cases and CLE materials.

The BIG NEWS for the August 2011 Edition is the improvements to the 2010 CD-ROM, which now provides the full legislative histories of the Family Code sections, the full text of the Texas Rules of Civil Procedure and the Texas Rules of Evidence, additional CLE materials and leading cases, with complimentary hypertext linking to Westlaw to access the full text of the more than 1,600 cases.

Texas attorneys involved in family law practice encounter a wide variety of issues involving an enormous spectrum of law other than that contained in the Texas Family Code, including a wide variety of state and federal law. Beginning with our first edition in 1981, this publication has recognized this truism by including selected provisions from other Texas Codes and the United States Code, a.k.a. U.S.C. or U.S.C.A. Interestingly, as the Family Code grew to its present massive proportions the space devoted to other law diminished in order to limit the size of the book to a reasonable degree. Over the years, that has been something of a losing battle. The time has come to take more dramatic action for the benefit of our readers.

Luckily modern technology has been on our doorstep for the past few years, but we have not taken full advantage of the world of electronic delivery of information. We hope the following decision is but the first step in reducing the bulk of the print version of SAMPSON & TINDALL'S TEXAS FAMILY CODE ANNOTATED, while increasing the overall utility of the entire package.

On the ACCOMPANYING CD-ROM the editors are pleased to provide selected materials directly related to Family Law issues from:

McGEHEE'S TEXAS CIVIL PRACTICE & REMEDIES CODE ANNOTATED (2010), by Diane Feiler McGehee, of council with the Houston firm of McGehee, Chang, Barnes;

KINKEADE & MCCOLLOCH'S TEXAS PENAL CODE ANNOTATED (2010-2011), by The Honorable Ed Kinkeade, U.S. District Judge for the Northern District of Texas, and S. Michael McColloch of McColl & McColloch, Dallas;

JOHANSON'S TEXAS PROBATE CODE ANNOTATED (2011), by Professor Stanley M. Johanson, Fannie Coplin Regents Chair at the School of Law, University of Texas at Austin; and

BEYER'S TEXAS PROPERTY CODE ANNOTATED (2011), by Professor Gerry W. Beyer, Governor Preston E. Smith Regents Professor of Law the Texas Tech School of Law.

In addition, we have greatly expanded our selection of Related Federal Law. Examine our choices and please let us know how we can better advance the statutory knowledge of Texas family law attorneys.

We are especially grateful to Joyce C. Sampson of Austin for her continued dedication to helping produce this book on time. Finally, we acknowledge the great assistance of our Attorney Editor Christy Klancher and Principal Publishing Specialist Janice Scholz of Thomson Reuters.

John J. Sampson
University of Texas School of Law
727 Dean Keeton Street
Austin, Texas 78705
Telephone: (512) 232–1267
Fax: (512) 471–6988
E-mail: jsampson@law.utexas.edu

Harry L. Tindall
Tindall & England PC
1330 Post Oak Blvd., Suite 1550
Houston, Texas 77056–3081
Telephone: (713) 622–8733
Fax: (713) 622–8744
E-mail: htindall@tindallengland.com

All statutory references, author commentary, legal articles, case citations and other references in this publication are through:

—Legislation—

82nd Texas Legislature, Regular and First Called Sessions (2011), for legislation affecting the Texas Family Code

82nd Texas Legislature, Regular Session (2011), for legislation affecting related Texas Codes

112th Congress, First Session, Public Law 112–20

—CLE Materials—

2011 Advanced Family Law Course [Adv. Fam. L.]

2011 Marriage Dissolution Institute [Marriage Dissolution]

2011 U.T. Family Law on the Front Lines [U.T. Fam. L. Front Lines]

2011 U.T. Parent-Child Relationship [U.T. Parent-Child Rel.]

—Cases—

339 S.W.3d (May 2011)

www.supreme.courts.state.tx.us (June 2011)

2011 WL 2465455

130 S.Ct. (July 2010)

*

Table of Contents

TEXAS FAMILY CODE

TITLE 1: The Marriage Relationship

Subtitle A: Marriage

Subtitle B: Property Rights and Liabilities

Subtitle C: Dissolution of Marriage

TITLE 4: Protective Orders and Family Violence

Subtitle A. General Provisions

Subtitle B. Protective Orders

Subtitle C. Reporting Family Violence

TITLE 5: The Parent–Child Relationship and the Suit Affecting the Parent–Child Relationship

Subtitle A. General Provisions

★★★

FOLLOWING MATERIALS ARE ON THE ACCOMPANYING CD-ROM

TEXAS CONSTITUTION AND RELATED TEXAS LAW

Texas Constitution of 1876

Texas Civil Practice and Remedies Code

Texas Code of Criminal Procedure

Texas Government Code

Texas Penal Code

Texas Probate Code

Texas Property Code

★★★

RELATED FEDERAL LAW

Page

Special Immigrant Juvenile Status (SIJS)

Military Retirement and Insurance. Benefits

Bankruptcy

Federal Criminal Law

Foreign Travel

Indian Child Welfare Act of 1978

Federal Income Tax

Full Faith and Credit

HIPAA

Social Security

Servicemembers Civil Relief Act

Code of Federal Regulations

★★★

TITLE 1*

THE MARRIAGE RELATIONSHIP

As amended through the 82nd Legislature, Regular and First Called Sessions (2011)

Subtitle A. Marriage.

Subtitle B. Property Rights and Liabilities.

Subtitle C. Dissolution of Marriage.

★★★

* History: Note that statutory language newly enacted by the 82nd Legislature in 2011 is displayed in **bold face type** and repealed language in [~~strike through~~] throughout this 2011 edition. The legislative history for each statutory amendment or change is provided.

For a complete amendment history of the Texas Family Code, *see* accompanying CD–ROM.

SUBTITLE A. MARRIAGE

★★★

CHAPTER 1. GENERAL PROVISIONS

SUBCHAPTER A. DEFINITIONS

SUBCHAPTER B. PUBLIC POLICY

SUBCHAPTER A. DEFINITIONS

§ 1.001. Applicability of Definitions

(a) The definitions in this subchapter apply to this title.

(b) Except as provided by this subchapter, the definitions in Chapter 101 apply to terms used in this title.

(c) If, in another part of this title, a term defined by this subchapter has a meaning different from the meaning provided by this subchapter, the meaning of that other provision prevails.

§ 1.002. Court

"Court" means the district court, juvenile court having the jurisdiction of a district court, or other court expressly given jurisdiction of a suit under this title.

§ 1.003. Suit for Dissolution of Marriage

"Suit for dissolution of a marriage" includes a suit for divorce or annulment or to declare a marriage void.

SUBCHAPTER B. PUBLIC POLICY

Introductory Comment

Sections 1.101–.103 declare that a marriage is valid unless made void by Chapter 6 *[Suit for Dissolution of Marriage]*. This reflects a long standing rule in American law. More importantly, when there are two or more marriages alleged, the most recent marriage is presumed valid unless the person challenging validity proves the continued existence of a prior marriage.

CLE/Other Legal Publication

Future of marriage. [This Symposium contains seven articles reviewing the history and possible future of marriage as known today]. 41 FAM. L. Q. 413 (2007) (ABA Summer 2007)

Leading Cases

Rogers v. Office of Personnel Management, 87 F.3d 471 (Fed. Cir. 1996) (first wife's unreasonable delay [35 years] in challenging her husband's purported marriage to second wife is barred by laches)

Davis v. Davis, 521 S.W.2d 603 (Tex. 1975) (landmark case affirming presumption that last marriage is presumed valid)

Texas Employers' Ins. Ass'n v. Elder, 282 S.W.2d 371 (Tex. 1955) (common law marriage upheld in absence of evidence upholding earlier common law marriage)

Cardwell v. Cardwell, 195 S.W.3d 856 (Tex. App.—Dallas 2006, no pet.) (no putative marriage without good faith belief in single status)

Bailey-Mason v. Mason, 122 S.W.3d 894 (Tex. App.—Dallas 2003, pet. denied) (although docket sheet says "divorce granted," no judgment ever presented or signed; undissolved first marriage renders subsequent marriage void)

---

§ 1.101. Every Marriage Presumed Valid

In order to promote the public health and welfare and to provide the necessary records, this code specifies detailed rules to be followed in establishing the marriage relationship. However, in order to provide stability for those entering into the marriage relationship in good faith and to provide for an orderly determination of parentage and security for the children of the relationship, it is the policy of this state to preserve and uphold each marriage against claims of invalidity unless a strong reason exists for holding the marriage void or voidable. Therefore, every marriage entered into in this state is presumed to be valid unless expressly made void by Chapter 6 or unless expressly made voidable by Chapter 6 and annulled as provided by that chapter.

§ 1.102. Most Recent Marriage Presumed Valid

When two or more marriages of a person to different spouses are alleged, the most recent marriage is presumed to be valid as against each marriage that precedes the most recent marriage until one who asserts the validity of a prior marriage proves the validity of the prior marriage.

§ 1.103. Persons Married Elsewhere

The law of this state applies to persons married elsewhere who are domiciled in this state.

§ 1.104. Capacity of Spouse

Except as expressly provided by statute or by the constitution, a person, regardless of age, who has been married in accordance with the law of this state has the capacity and power of an adult, including the capacity to contract.

§ 1.105. Joinder in Civil Suits

(a) A spouse may sue and be sued without the joinder of the other spouse.

(b) When claims or liabilities are joint and several, the spouses may be joined under the rules relating to joinder of parties generally.

Comment

Sections 1.104 and 1.105 make clear that a person, without joinder of his or her spouse, has the full power to act independently of the other spouse, including the right to contract. Historically, a married woman could not sue or be sued without joinder of her husband, but now, either spouse may sue or be sued individually. This freedom, however, does not give a spouse the right to sell jointly managed or titled property, § 3.102, or the homestead, § 5.001 et seq., without joinder of the other spouse.

Leading Cases

Cooper v. Texas Gulf Industries, Inc., 513 S.W.2d 200 (Tex. 1974) (a suit naming only the husband is not binding on the wife; doctrine of virtual representation repudiated)

Few v. Charter Oak Fire Insurance Co., 463 S.W.2d 424 (Tex. 1971) (joinder of spouse not required in lawsuit)

---

§ 1.106. Criminal Conversation Not Authorized

A right of action by one spouse against a third party for criminal conversation is not authorized in this state.

§ 1.107. Alienation of Affection Not Authorized

A right of action by one spouse against a third party for alienation of affection is not authorized in this state.

Comment

Abolition of the torts of criminal conversation and alienation of affection is consistent with the law of the vast majority of American jurisdictions.

CLE/Other Legal Publications

Other causes of action. John F. "Bo" Nichols, 2011 Adv. Fam. L.

Legal ramifications of emotional abuse. Shelly Moore, 2010 Adv. Fam. L.

Personal injury lawsuits in intimate relationships. Jeana L. Lungwitz & Leslie M. Stewart, 2008 U.T. Fam. L. Front Lines

Intentional infliction claims when affections have been alienated. Eric Beal, State Bar Section Report: Family Law Vol. 2008-2

Leading Cases

Helena Laboratories Corp. v. Snyder, 886 S.W.2d 767 (Tex. 1994) (no independent cause of action exists in Texas for negligent interference with the familial relationship)

Smith v. Smith, 126 S.W.3d 660 (Tex. App.—Houston [14th Dist.] 2004, no pet.) (constitutional for legislature to abolish torts of criminal conversation and alienation of affection)

---

§ 1.108. Promise or Agreement Must be in Writing

A promise or agreement made on consideration of marriage or nonmarital conjugal cohabitation is not enforceable unless the promise or agreement or a memorandum of the promise or agreement is in writing and signed by the person obligated by the promise or agreement.

Comment

During the 1997 recodification of Title 1, this section was moved from the Business & Commerce Code, where undoubtedly it was often overlooked.

CLE/Other Legal Publications

Cohabitation and domestic partnership agreements. Katherine A. Kinser, 2010 ADV. FAM. L.

Collaborative law in non-divorce context. Jack Harold Emmott, Julie H. Quaid & Jennifer Tull, 2010 COLLABORATIVE LAW

Litigating family law outside the Family Code: dividing the assets of unmarried parties. Sallee S. Smyth, 2009 ADV. FAM. L.

Cohabitation contracts. Angeline Lindley Bain, 2009 U.T. FAM. L. FRONT LINES

21st century issues dealing with nontraditional relationships: dividing property between unmarried persons. Luke Gunnstaks, 2007 ADV. FAM. L.

21st century issues dealing with nontraditional relationships and seeking relief in nontraditional ways. Heather L. King, 2006 ADV. FAM. L.

Leading Cases

Braddock v. Braddock, 64 S.W.3d 581 (Tex. App.—Texarkana 2001, no pet.) (divorced couple resumed cohabitation but did not remarry, creating a confidential relationship which was sufficient for the court to impose a constructive trust when a dispute arose over property purchased during the cohabitation)

Littleton v. Prange, 9 S.W.3d 223 (Tex. App.—San Antonio 1999, pet. denied), *cert. denied,* 121 S.Ct. 174 (2000) (transsexual born male cannot become legal spouse of male; marriage limited to man and woman)

O'Farrill v. Gonzalez, 974 S.W.2d 237 (Tex. App.—San Antonio 1998, pet. denied) (court enforces written contract between unmarried parents for monthly support and oral agreement to pay mortgage)

Zaremba v. Cliburn, 949 S.W.2d 822 (Tex. App.—Fort Worth 1997, writ denied) (no same-sex palimony without written agreement)

CHAPTER 2. THE MARRIAGE RELATIONSHIP

SUBCHAPTER A. APPLICATION FOR MARRIAGE LICENSE

SUBCHAPTER B. UNDERAGE APPLICANTS

SUBCHAPTER C. CEREMONY AND RETURN OF LICENSE

SUBCHAPTER D. VALIDITY OF MARRIAGE

SUBCHAPTER E. MARRIAGE WITHOUT FORMALITIES

SUBCHAPTER F. RIGHTS AND DUTIES OF SPOUSES

SUBCHAPTER A. APPLICATION FOR MARRIAGE LICENSE

Comment

This subchapter, as originally enacted in 1969, referred to "persons desiring to enter into a ceremonial marriage." Because it was believed such language could be read to imply authorization of marriage of persons of the same sex, it was amended in 1973 to make clear that only persons of the opposite sex can marry. Obviously the proponents of the amendment were well ahead of their time to anticipate that same sex marriages would someday become a matter of public controversy. In 1996, in response to debate over the validity of such marriages, the U.S. Congress enacted the Defense of Marriage Act (a.k.a. DOMA), 28 U.S.C.A. § 1738C, *infra*. In 2003, Texas joined almost 40 other states to enact our own version of DOMA, § 6.204. Recognition of Same Sex Marriage or Civil Union, *infra*.

On Nov. 8, 2005, Texas voters overwhelmingly passed H.J.R. 6 (76% to 24%), a constitutional amendment providing that "marriage in this state consists of the union of one man and one woman." The amendment also forbids creation or recognition of "any legal status identical or similar to marriage." Tex. Const. art. I, § 32, *infra*.

In 2005, the Texas Legislature received reports that a polygamist cult had moved to West Texas, and that children were being married off at an early age, sometimes to close family members. In response, new restrictions were enacted on those who someone may marry. The prohibition on marriage of first cousins and step-relatives is new to Texas law. According to the National Conference of State Legislatures, 31 states (now including Texas) prohibit or restrict marriage of first cousins, while 19 states allow the practice. The prohibition on marriage to a stepchild or stepparent, including a former stepchild or stepparent, reflects a policy to protect traditional family relationships, even if there is no genetic relationship. Proof of identity and age may now be established by any one of a list of different types of documents beyond the mere birth certificate.

Further, the age of parental consent for marriage of a child was raised from 14 to 16. Consistent with quite a bit of past practice, the amendments to this subchapter regulate the prohibited marriages through the otherwise ministerial function of the county clerk to issue marriage licenses.

In April 2008, attention to the polygamists resurfaced in a historic manner. Initially, Children's Protective Services took physical possession of more than 450 children, but the temporary managing conservatorship granted CPS was overturned by way of writ of mandamus. *In re* Texas Dept. of Family and Protective Services, 255 S.W.3d 613 (Tex. 2008, orig proceeding). Numerous criminal cases regarding the actions of the polygamists' leaders remain pending as this publication goes to press, and thus, the final chapter on this action is yet to be written.

Cross References

TX FCA Family § 2.401. Proof of informal marriage, *infra*.

TX FCA Family § 6.102. Annulment of Marriage of Person under Age 18, *infra*; TX FCA Family § 6.205. Marriage to Minor, *infra*; TX FCA Family § 6.206. Marriage to Stepchild or Stepparent, *infra*.

TX FCA Penal § 25.01. Bigamy, *infra*; TX FCA Penal § 25.02. Prohibited Sexual Conduct, *infra*.

CLE/Other Legal Publications

Modern family: headlines in same-sex cases. Amy C. Wright, 2011 U.T. Fam. L. Front Lines

Litigating family law outside the Family Code: dividing the assets of unmarried parties. Sallee S. Smyth, 2009 Adv. Fam. L.

Common law and same sex marriages, adult adoptions, maternity tests, and other unusual topics. Sam M. "Trey" Yates, III, 2009 So. Tex. Fam. L. Conf.

21st century issues dealing with nontraditional relationships: dividing property between unmarried persons. Luke Gunnstaks, 2007 Adv. Fam. L.

21st century issues dealing with nontraditional relationships and seeking relief in nontraditional ways. Heather L. King, 2006 Adv. Fam. L.

Leading Cases

In re Marriage of J.B. and H.B., 326 S.W.3d 654 (Tex. App. —Dallas 2010, pet. granted) (trial court has no subject matter jurisdiction to hear divorce of same sex individuals; statute prohibiting recognition of same sex marriage not unconstitutional)

Littleton v. Prange, 9 S.W.3d 223 (Tex. App.—San Antonio 1999, pet. denied), cert. denied, 121 S.Ct. 174 (2000) (transsexual born male cannot be spouse of male; marriage limited to man and woman)

---

§ 2.001. Marriage License

(a) A man and a woman desiring to enter into a ceremonial marriage must obtain a marriage license from the county clerk of any county of this state.

(b) A license may not be issued for the marriage of persons of the same sex.

§ 2.002. Application for License

Except as provided by Section 2.006, each person applying for a license must:

(1) appear before the county clerk;

(2) submit the person's proof of identity and age as provided by Section 2.005(b);

(3) provide the information applicable to that person for which spaces are provided in the application for a marriage license;

(4) mark the appropriate boxes provided in the application; and

(5) take the oath printed on the application and sign the application before the county clerk.

§ 2.003. Application for License by Minor

In addition to the other requirements provided by this chapter, a person under 18 years of age applying for a license must provide to the county clerk:

(1) documents establishing, as provided by Section 2.102, parental consent for the person to the marriage;

(2) documents establishing that a prior marriage of the person has been dissolved; or

(3) a court order granted under Section 2.103 authorizing the marriage of the person.

§ 2.004. Application Form

(a) The county clerk shall furnish the application form as prescribed by the bureau of vital statistics.

(b) The application form must contain:

(1) a heading entitled "Application for Marriage License, __________ County, Texas";

(2) spaces for each applicant's full name, including the woman's maiden surname, address, social security number, if any, date of birth, and place of birth, including city, county, and state;

(3) a space for indicating the document tendered by each applicant as proof of identity and age;

(4) spaces for indicating whether each applicant has been divorced within the last 30 days;

(5) printed boxes for each applicant to check "true" or "false" in response to the following statement: "I am not presently married and the other applicant is not presently married.";

(6) printed boxes for each applicant to check "true" or "false" in response to the following statement: "The other applicant is not related to me as:

(A) an ancestor or descendant, by blood or adoption;

(B) a brother or sister, of the whole or half blood or by adoption;

(C) a parent's brother or sister, of the whole or half blood or by adoption;

(D) a son or daughter of a brother or sister, of the whole or half blood or by adoption;

(E) a current or former stepchild or stepparent; or

(F) a son or daughter of a parent's brother or sister, of the whole or half blood or by adoption.";

(7) printed boxes for each applicant to check "true" or "false" in response to the following statement: "I am not presently delinquent in the payment of court-ordered child support.";

(8) a printed oath reading: "I SOLEMNLY SWEAR (OR AFFIRM) THAT THE INFORMATION I HAVE GIVEN IN THIS APPLICATION IS CORRECT.";

(9) spaces immediately below the printed oath for the applicants' signatures;

(10) a certificate of the county clerk that:

(A) each applicant made the oath and the date and place that it was made; or

(B) an applicant did not appear personally but the prerequisites for the license have been fulfilled as provided by this chapter;

(11) spaces for indicating the date of the marriage and the county in which the marriage is performed; and

(12) a space for the address to which the applicants desire the completed license to be mailed.

(c) An applicant commits an offense if the applicant knowingly provides false information under Subsection (b)(1), (2), (3), or (4). An offense under this subsection is a Class C misdemeanor.

(d) An applicant commits an offense if the applicant knowingly provides false information under Subsection (b)(5) or (6). An offense under this subsection is a Class A misdemeanor.

§ 2.005. Proof of Identity and Age

(a) The county clerk shall require proof of the identity and age of each applicant.

(b) The proof must be established by:

(1) a driver's license or identification card issued by this state, another state, or a Canadian province that is current or has expired not more than two years preceding the date the identification is submitted to the county clerk in connection with an application for a license;

(2) a United States passport;

(3) a current passport issued by a foreign country or a consular document issued by a state or national government;

(4) an unexpired Certificate of United States Citizenship, Certificate of Naturalization, United States Citizen Identification Card, Permanent Resident Card, Temporary Resident Card, Employment Authorization Card, or other document issued by the federal Department of Homeland Security or the United States Department of State including an identification photograph;

(5) an unexpired military identification card for active duty, reserve, or retired personnel with an identification photograph;

(6) an original or certified copy of a birth certificate issued by a bureau of vital statistics for a state or a foreign government;

(7) an original or certified copy of a Consular Report of Birth Abroad or Certificate of Birth Abroad issued by the United States Department of State;

(8) an original or certified copy of a court order relating to the applicant's name change or sex change;

(9) school records from a secondary school or institution of higher education;

(10) an insurance policy continuously valid for the two years preceding the date of the application for a license;

(11) a motor vehicle certificate of title;

(12) military records, including documentation of release or discharge from active duty or a draft record;

(13) an unexpired military dependent identification card;

(14) an original or certified copy of the applicant's marriage license or divorce decree;

(15) a voter registration certificate;

(16) a pilot's license issued by the Federal Aviation Administration or another authorized agency of the United States;

(17) a license to carry a concealed handgun under Subchapter H, Chapter 411, Government Code;

(18) a temporary driving permit or a temporary identification card issued by the Department of Public Safety; or

(19) an offender identification card issued by the Texas Department of Criminal Justice.

(c) A person commits an offense if the person knowingly provides false, fraudulent, or otherwise inaccurate proof of an applicant's identity or age under this section. An offense under this subsection is a Class A misdemeanor.

§ 2.006. Absent Applicant

(a) If an applicant is unable to appear personally before the county clerk to apply for a marriage license, any adult person or the other applicant may apply on behalf of the absent applicant.

(b) The person applying on behalf of an absent applicant shall provide to the clerk:

(1) notwithstanding Section 132.001, Civil Practice and Remedies Code, the notarized affidavit of the absent applicant as provided by this subchapter;

(2) proof of the identity and age of the absent applicant under Section 2.005(b); and

(3) if required because the absent applicant is a person under 18 years of age, documents establishing that a prior marriage has been dissolved, a court order authorizing the marriage of the absent, underage applicant, or documents establishing consent by a parent or a person who has legal authority to consent to the marriage, including:

(A) proof of identity of the parent or person with legal authority to consent to the marriage under Section 2.005(b); and

(B) proof that the parent or person has the legal authority to consent to the marriage for the applicant under rules adopted under Section 2.102(j).

(c) Notwithstanding Subsection (a), the clerk may not issue a marriage license for which both applicants are absent unless the person applying on behalf of each absent applicant provides to the clerk an affidavit of the applicant declaring that the applicant is:

(1) on active duty as a member of the armed forces of the United States or the state military forces; or

(2) confined in a correctional facility, as defined by Section 1.07, Penal Code.

§ 2.007. Affidavit of Absent Applicant

The affidavit of an absent applicant must include:

(1) the absent applicant's full name, including the maiden surname of a female applicant, address, date of birth, place of birth, including city, county, and state, citizenship, and social security number, if any;

(2) a declaration that the absent applicant has not been divorced within the last 30 days;

(3) a declaration that the absent applicant is:

(A) not presently married; or

(B) married to the other applicant and they wish to marry again;

(4) a declaration that the other applicant is not presently married and is not related to the absent applicant as:

(A) an ancestor or descendant, by blood or adoption;

(B) a brother or sister, of the whole or half blood or by adoption;

(C) a parent's brother or sister, of the whole or half blood or by adoption;

(D) a son or daughter of a brother or sister, of the whole or half blood or by adoption;

(E) a current or former stepchild or stepparent; or

(F) a son or daughter of a parent's brother or sister, of the whole or half blood or by adoption;

(5) a declaration that the absent applicant desires to marry and the name, age, and address of the person to whom the absent applicant desires to be married;

(6) the approximate date on which the marriage is to occur;

(7) the reason the absent applicant is unable to appear personally before the county clerk for the issuance of the license; and

(8) if the absent applicant will be unable to attend the ceremony, the appointment of any adult, other than the other applicant, to act as proxy for the purpose of participating in the ceremony.

Comment

Sections 2.006 and 2.007, along with § 2.203(b), authorize proxy marriage, largely to accommodate members of the armed services.

§ 2.008. Execution of Application by Clerk

(a) The county clerk shall:

(1) determine that all necessary information, other than the date of the marriage ceremony, the county in which the ceremony is conducted, and the name of the person who performs the ceremony, is recorded on the application and that all necessary documents are submitted;

(2) administer the oath to each applicant appearing before the clerk;

(3) have each applicant appearing before the clerk sign the application in the clerk's presence; and

(4) execute the clerk's certificate on the application.

(b) A person appearing before the clerk on behalf of an absent applicant is not required to take the oath on behalf of the absent applicant.

§ 2.009. Issuance of License

(a) Except as provided by Subsections (b) and (d), the county clerk may not issue a license if either applicant:

(1) fails to provide the information required by this subchapter;

(2) fails to submit proof of age and identity;

(3) is under 16 years of age and has not been granted a court order as provided by Section 2.103;

(4) is 16 years of age or older but under 18 years of age and has not presented at least one of the following:

(A) parental consent as provided by Section 2.102;

(B) documents establishing that a prior marriage of the applicant has been dissolved; or

(C) a court order as provided by Section 2.103;

(5) checks "false" in response to a statement in the application, except as provided by Subsection (b) or (d), or fails to make a required declaration in an affidavit required of an absent applicant; or

(6) indicates that the applicant has been divorced within the last 30 days, unless:

(A) the applicants were divorced from each other; or

(B) the prohibition against remarriage is waived as provided by Section 6.802.

(b) If an applicant checks "false" in response to the statement "I am not presently married and the other applicant is not presently married," the county clerk shall inquire as to whether the applicant is presently married to the other applicant. If the applicant states that the applicant is currently married to the other applicant, the county clerk shall record that statement on the license before the administration of the oath. The county clerk may not refuse to issue a license on the ground that the applicants are already married to each other.

(c) On the proper execution of the application, the clerk shall:

(1) prepare the license;

(2) enter on the license the names of the licensees, the date that the license is issued, and, if applicable, the name of the person appointed to act as proxy for an absent applicant, if any;

(3) record the time at which the license was issued;

(4) distribute to each applicant printed materials about acquired immune deficiency syndrome (AIDS) and human immunodeficiency virus (HIV) and note on the license that the distribution was made; and

(5) distribute to each applicant a premarital education handbook provided by the attorney general under Section 2.014.

(d) The county clerk may not refuse to issue a license to an applicant on the ground that the applicant checked "false" in response to the statement "I am not presently delinquent in the payment of court-ordered child support."

Comment

The clerk must time stamp the license at the time of issuance to facilitate enforcing the 72-hour waiting period required by § 2.204. Further, the county clerk is directed to enforce the minimum age of 16 for marriage of a minor with parental consent, and for judicial consent for a minor under 16 by refusing to issue a license absent the steps described. The most important tool for the clerk to enforce the statute is the duty to require proof of identity by checking I.D.'s of applicants for the marriage license and by obtaining the prescribed form from a consenting parent. The 30 day waiting period for remarriage from date of divorce applies to any divorce, regardless of whether or not from a Texas court.

§ 2.010. AIDS Information

Materials providing information about acquired immune deficiency syndrome (AIDS) and human immunodeficiency virus (HIV) shall be prepared and provided to the clerk by the Texas Department of Health and shall be designed to inform the applicants about:

(1) the incidence and mode of transmission of AIDS and HIV;

(2) the local availability of medical procedures, including voluntary testing, designed to show or help show whether a person has AIDS or HIV infection, antibodies to HIV, or infection with any other probable causative agent of AIDS; and

(3) available and appropriate counseling services regarding AIDS and HIV infection.

§ 2.011. Repealed.

§ 2.012. Violation by County Clerk; Penalty

A county clerk or deputy county clerk who violates or fails to comply with this subchapter commits an offense. An offense under this section is a misdemeanor punishable by a fine of not less than $200 and not more than $500.

§ 2.013. Premarital Education Courses

(a) Each person applying for a marriage license is encouraged to attend a premarital education course of at least eight hours during the year preceding the date of the application for the license.

(b) A premarital education course must include instruction in:

(1) conflict management;

(2) communication skills; and

(3) the key components of a successful marriage.

(c) A course under this section should be offered by instructors trained in a skills-based and research-based marriage preparation curricula. The following individuals and organizations may provide courses:

(1) marriage educators;

(2) clergy or their designees;

(3) licensed mental health professionals;

(4) faith-based organizations; and

(5) community-based organizations.

(d) The curricula of a premarital education course must meet the requirements of this section and provide the skills-based and research-based curricula of:

(1) the United States Department of Health and Human Services healthy marriage initiative;

(2) the National Healthy Marriage Resource Center;

(3) criteria developed by the Health and Human Services Commission; or

(4) other similar resources.

(e) The Health and Human Services Commission shall maintain an Internet website on which individuals and organizations described by Subsection (c) may electronically register with the commission to indicate the skills-based and research-based curriculum in which the registrant is trained.

(f) A person who provides a premarital education course shall provide a signed and dated completion certificate to each individual who completes the course. The certificate must include the name of the course, the name of the course provider, and the completion date.

§ 2.014. Family Trust Fund

(a) The family trust fund is created as a trust fund with the state comptroller and shall be administered by the attorney general for the beneficiaries of the fund.

(b) Money in the trust fund is derived from depositing $3 of each marriage license fee as authorized under Section 118.018(c), Local Government Code, and may be used only for:

(1) the development and distribution of a premarital education handbook;

(2) grants to institutions of higher education having academic departments that are capable of research on marriage and divorce that will assist in determining programs, courses, and policies to help strengthen families and assist children whose parents are divorcing;

(3) support for counties to create or administer free or low-cost premarital education courses;

(4) programs intended to reduce the amount of delinquent child support; and

(5) other programs the attorney general determines will assist families in this state.

(c) The premarital education handbook under Subsection (b)(1) shall be distributed to each applicant for a marriage license as provided by Section 2.009(c)(5) and shall contain information on:

(1) conflict management;

(2) communication skills;

(3) children and parenting responsibilities; and

(4) financial responsibilities.

(d) The attorney general shall appoint an advisory committee to assist in the development of the premarital education handbook. The advisory committee shall consist of nine members, including at least three members who are eligible under Section 2.013(d) to provide a premarital education course. A member of the advisory committee is not entitled to reimbursement of the member's expenses.

SUBCHAPTER B. UNDERAGE APPLICANTS

Introductory Comment

This subchapter establishes the basic rule that the minimum age of marriage without parental or judicial consent is 18 years. A previously married underage applicant may remarry without parental consent, thereby recognizing that the first marriage emancipated the minor under § 1.104, *supra*.

In 2005 the Texas Legislature received reports that a polygamist cult in West Texas had some parents regularly consenting to marriage of their 14 and 15 year old children. In response, the legislature raised the age for parental consent from 14 to 16. Thus, while anyone under 16 can only get married with judicial approval, anyone between the ages of 16 to 18 must have either judicial approval or file parental consent with the county clerk on prescribed forms. Once over the age of 18, no approval or consent is required. Aside from the polygamy concerns, the average age for first-time marriage in the United States continues to climb steadily. According to the U.S. Bureau of the Census, the average age for first-time marriages in 2002 was 26.9 years for males and 25.3 years for females—a far cry from the 16-year-olds contemplated by these statutes.

If authorization by a court for marriage of a child under 18 is sought, parents or managing conservators must be served with process. Pregnancy is the usual, and as a practical matter probably the only, reason to justify court approval of an underage marriage over the objection of the parents. Approval of underage marriage is left entirely to the court's discretion, to be exercised on a "best interest" basis.

Cross References

TX FCA FAMILY § 2.004. Application Form, *supra*; TX FCA FAMILY § 2.005. Proof of Identity and Age, *supra*; TX FCA FAMILY § 2.009. Issuance of License, *supra*; TX FCA FAMILY § 6.102. Annulment of Marriage of Person under Age 18, *infra*; TX FCA FAMILY § 6.205. Marriage to Minor, *infra*; TX FCA PENAL § 25.02. Prohibited Sexual Conduct, *infra*.

---

§ 2.101. General Age Requirement

Except as otherwise provided by this subchapter or on a showing that a prior marriage has been dissolved, a county clerk may not issue a marriage license if either applicant is under 18 years of age.

§ 2.102. Parental Consent for Underage Applicant

(a) If an applicant is 16 years of age or older but under 18 years of age, the county clerk shall issue the license if parental consent is given as provided by this section.

(b) Parental consent must be evidenced by a written declaration on a form supplied by the county clerk in which the person consents to the marriage and swears that the person is a parent (if there is no person who has the court-ordered right to consent to marriage for the applicant) or a person who has the court-ordered right to consent to marriage for the applicant (whether an individual, authorized agency, or court).

(c) Except as otherwise provided by this section, consent must be acknowledged before a county clerk.

(d) If the person giving parental consent resides in another state, the consent may be acknowledged before an officer authorized to issue marriage licenses in that state.

(e) If the person giving parental consent is unable because of illness or incapacity to comply with the provisions of Subsection (c) or (d), the consent may be acknowledged before any officer authorized to take acknowledgments. A consent under this subsection must be accompanied by a physician's affidavit stating that the person giving parental consent is unable to comply because of illness or incapacity.

(f) Parental consent must be given at the time the application for the marriage license is made or not earlier than the 30th day preceding the date the application is made.

(g) A person commits an offense if the person knowingly provides parental consent for an underage applicant under this section and the person is not a parent or a person who has the court-ordered right to consent to marriage for the applicant. An offense under this subsection is a Class A misdemeanor.

(h) A parent or a person who has the court-ordered right to consent to marriage for the applicant commits an offense if the parent or other person knowingly provides parental consent under this section for an applicant who is younger than 16 years of age or who is presently married to a person other than the person the applicant desires to marry. An offense under this subsection is a felony of the third degree.

(i) A parent or person who has the legal authority to consent to marriage for an underage applicant who gives consent under this section shall provide:

(1) proof of the parent's or person's identity under Section 2.005(b); and

(2) proof that the parent or person has the legal authority to consent to marriage for the applicant under rules adopted under Subsection (j).

(j) The executive commissioner of the Health and Human Services Commission shall adopt rules detailing acceptable proof of the legal authority to consent to the marriage of an underage applicant. In adopting rules, the executive commissioner shall ensure that the rules:

(1) adequately protect against fraud; and

(2) do not create an undue burden on any class of person legally entitled to consent to the marriage of an underage applicant.

§ 2.103. Court Order for Underage Applicant

(a) A minor may petition the court in the minor's own name for an order granting permission to marry. In a suit under this section, the trial judge may advance the suit if the best interest of the applicant would be served by an early hearing.

(b) The petition must be filed in the county where a parent resides if a court has not awarded another person the right to consent to marriage for the minor. If a court has awarded another person the right to consent to marriage for the minor, the petition must be filed in the county where that person resides. If no parent or person who has the court-ordered right to consent to marriage for the minor resides in this state, the petition must be filed in the county where the minor lives.

(c) The petition must include:

(1) a statement of the reasons the minor desires to marry;

(2) a statement of whether each parent is living or is dead;

(3) the name and residence address of each living parent; and

(4) a statement of whether a court has awarded to a person other than a parent of the minor the right to consent to marriage for the minor.

(d) Process shall be served as in other civil cases on each living parent of the minor or on a person who has the court-ordered right to consent to marriage for the minor, as applicable. Citation may be given by publication as in other civil cases, except that notice shall be published one time only.

(e) The court shall appoint an amicus attorney or an attorney ad litem to represent the minor in the proceeding. The court shall specify a fee to be paid by the minor for the services of the amicus attorney or attorney ad litem. The fee shall be collected in the same manner as other costs of the proceeding.

(f) If after a hearing the court, sitting without a jury, believes marriage to be in the best interest of the minor, the court, by order, shall grant the minor permission to marry.

SUBCHAPTER C. CEREMONY AND RETURN OF LICENSE

Comment

A ceremonial marriage in Texas requires the filing of a license and a ceremony conducted by a person authorized to conduct such a ceremony. A marriage license is valid for 30 days. However, because of the 72–hour waiting period required by § 2.204, there is only a 27–day "window" for the marriage ceremony to take place before the license expires. The window to seek an annulment of a marriage performed during the 72 hour waiting period is almost as narrow, i.e., 30 days after the ceremony, *see* § 6.110, *infra*. In the event a ceremony is conducted after the license expires, section 2.207 allows for a penalty to be assessed against the person who conducted the ceremony but this has almost certainly not happened since the enactment of the Family Code and predictably never will.

The 72 hour waiting period after obtaining a license ostensibly was enacted to prevent couples from marrying in haste without time for proper reflection. The truth is that suburban justices of the peace lobbied for the change because courthouse J.P.'s were taking the lion's share of the lucrative business of performing marriages. Requiring couples to wait 72 hours makes it unlikely that they will return downtown to get married. However, the statute permits a "waiver" of the waiting period. Presumably a "waiver" is less difficult to obtain than securing an "order" to the same effect. As a theoretical incentive to encourage couples to obtain premarital counseling, the 72 hour waiting period is waived for those who complete a course meeting the requirements of section 2.013, *supra*.

Exactly who may conduct a marriage ceremony has been the subject of much legislative maneuvering. Just about the only judicial officers left off of the list are former judges (not retired) and unelected judges (e.g., associate judges). Discrimination in conducting the ceremony based on race, religion, or national origin is prohibited by section 2.205. However, notably missing from the anti-discrimination list is discrimination based on sex. In 2003, the Legislature confirmed that the omission was not accidental by enacting § 6.204. Recognition of Same Sex Marriage or Civil Union, *infra*.

---

§ 2.201. Expiration of License

If a marriage ceremony has not been conducted before the 31st day after the date the license is issued, the marriage license expires.

§ 2.202. Persons Authorized to Conduct Ceremony

(a) The following persons are authorized to conduct a marriage ceremony:

(1) a licensed or ordained Christian minister or priest;

(2) a Jewish rabbi;

(3) a person who is an officer of a religious organization and who is authorized by the organization to conduct a marriage ceremony; and

(4) a justice of the supreme court, judge of the court of criminal appeals, justice of the courts of appeals, judge of the district, county, and probate courts, judge of the county courts at law, judge of the courts of domestic relations, judge of the juvenile courts, retired justice or judge of those courts, justice of the peace, retired justice of the peace, judge of a municipal court, or judge or magistrate of a federal court of this state.

(b) For the purposes of this section, a retired judge or justice is a former judge or justice who is vested in the Judicial Retirement System of Texas Plan One or the Judicial Retirement System of Texas Plan Two or who has an aggregate of at least 12 years of service as judge or justice of any type listed in Subsection (a)(4).

(c) Except as provided by Subsection (d), a person commits an offense if the person knowingly conducts a marriage ceremony without authorization under this section. An offense under this subsection is a Class A misdemeanor.

(d) A person commits an offense if the person knowingly conducts a marriage ceremony of a minor whose marriage is prohibited by law or of a person who by marrying commits an offense under Section 25.01, Penal Code. An offense under this subsection is a felony of the third degree.

§ 2.203. Ceremony

(a) On receiving an unexpired marriage license, an authorized person may conduct the marriage ceremony as provided by this subchapter.

(b) A person unable to appear for the ceremony may assent to marriage by the appearance of a proxy appointed in the affidavit authorized by Subchapter A.

§ 2.204. 72-Hour Waiting Period; Exceptions

(a) Except as provided by this section, a marriage ceremony may not take place during the 72-hour period immediately following the issuance of the marriage license.

(b) The 72–hour waiting period after issuance of a marriage license does not apply to an applicant who:

(1) is a member of the armed forces of the United States and on active duty;

(2) is not a member of the armed forces of the United States but performs work for the United States Department of Defense as a department employee or under a contract with the department;

(3) obtains a written waiver under Subsection (c); or

(4) completes a premarital education course described by Section 2.013, and who provides to the county clerk a premarital education course completion certificate indicating completion of the premarital education course not more than one year before the date the marriage license application is filed with the clerk.

(c) An applicant may request a judge of a court with jurisdiction in family law cases, a justice of the supreme court, a judge of the court of criminal appeals, a county judge, or a judge of a court of appeals for a written waiver permitting the marriage ceremony to take place during the 72-hour period immediately following the issuance of the marriage license. If the judge finds that there is good cause for the marriage to take place during the period, the judge shall sign the waiver. Notwithstanding any other provision of law, a judge under this section has the authority to sign a waiver under this section.

§ 2.205. Discrimination in Conducting Marriage Prohibited

(a) A person authorized to conduct a marriage ceremony by this subchapter is prohibited from discriminating on the basis of race, religion, or national origin against an applicant who is otherwise competent to be married.

(b) On a finding by the State Commission on Judicial Conduct that a person has intentionally violated Subsection (a), the commission may recommend to the supreme court that the person be removed from office.

§ 2.206. Return of License; Penalty

(a) The person who conducts a marriage ceremony shall record on the license the date on which and the county in which the ceremony is performed and the person's name, subscribe the license, and return the license to the county clerk who issued it not later than the 30th day after the date the ceremony is conducted.

(b) A person who fails to comply with this section commits an offense. An offense under this section is a misdemeanor punishable by a fine of not less than $200 and not more than $500.

§ 2.207. Marriage Conducted After License Expired; Penalty

(a) A person who is to conduct a marriage ceremony shall determine whether the license has expired from the county clerk's endorsement on the license.

(b) A person who conducts a marriage ceremony after the marriage license has expired commits an offense. An offense under this section is a misdemeanor punishable by a fine of not less than $200 and not more than $500.

§ 2.208. Recording and Delivery of License

(a) The county clerk shall record a returned marriage license and mail the license to the address indicated on the application.

(b) On the application form the county clerk shall record:

(1) the date of the marriage ceremony;

(2) the county in which the ceremony was conducted; and

(3) the name of the person who conducted the ceremony.

§ 2.209. Duplicate License

(a) On request, the county clerk shall issue a certified copy of a recorded marriage license.

(b) If a marriage license issued by a county clerk is lost, destroyed, or rendered useless, the clerk shall issue a duplicate license.

(c) If one or both parties to a marriage license discover an error on the recorded marriage license, both parties to the marriage shall execute a notarized affidavit stating the error. The county clerk shall file and record the affidavit as an amendment to the marriage license, and the affidavit is considered part of the marriage license. The clerk shall include a copy of the affidavit with any future certified copy of the marriage license issued by the clerk.

(d) The executive commissioner of the Health and Human Services Commission by rule shall prescribe the form of the affidavit under Subsection (c).

SUBCHAPTER D. VALIDITY OF MARRIAGE

Introductory Comment

Texas law supports the validity of marriage. Buttressing the presumption that every marriage is valid, even very serious defects identified in obtaining the marriage license do not affect the validity of the marriage. Additionally, a lack of authority to marry the couple does not affect the validity of the marriage if at least one party acted in good faith.

---

§ 2.301. Fraud, Mistake, or Illegality in Obtaining License

Except as otherwise provided by this chapter, the validity of a marriage is not affected by any fraud, mistake, or illegality that occurred in obtaining the marriage license.

§ 2.302. Ceremony Conducted by Unauthorized Person

The validity of a marriage is not affected by the lack of authority of the person conducting the marriage ceremony if:

(1) there was a reasonable appearance of authority by that person;

(2) at least one party to the marriage participated in the ceremony in good faith and that party treats the marriage as valid; and

(3) neither party to the marriage:

(A) is a minor whose marriage is prohibited by law; or

(B) by marrying commits an offense under Section 25.01, Penal Code.

SUBCHAPTER E. MARRIAGE WITHOUT FORMALITIES

Introductory Comment

Texas recognizes two means of establishing a common law marriage, either by

(1) execution of a declaration under § 2.402; or

(2) a "three-prong test," requiring evidence showing:

(i) an "agreement" to be married;

(ii) "cohabitation" in this state; and,

(iii) "holding out" to others that the parties are married.

Although the caption of the subchapter calls it one thing and the statutes call it another, everyone else calls the relationship created by these statutes a "common law marriage." Until 1989, "cohabitation" and "holding out" constituted a basis for inferring an agreement—in reality basically creating a two prong test. In 1995, the statutes were amended to provide an evidentiary presumption of no marriage if a suit for proof of marriage was not filed within two years of the parties having "separated and ceased living together." Persons under the age of 18 may not enter into an informal marriage. Additionally, in an effort to prevent polygamy within the state, a party may not be in an informal marriage if the person is married to someone else.

The same proof of identity and age needed to obtain a marriage license are required to obtain a declaration of informal marriage.

CLE/Other Legal Publications

Common law and same sex marriages, adult adoptions, maternity tests, and other unusual topics. Sam M. "Trey" Yates, III, 2009 So. Tex. Fam. L. Conf.

Leading Cases

Texas Supreme Court

Russell v. Russell, 865 S.W.2d 929 (Tex. 1993) (proof of informal marriage may be established by direct or circumstantial evidence)

Mossler v. Shields, 818 S.W.2d 752 (Tex. 1991) (prior dismissal of suit with prejudice precludes later claim of common law marriage)

Estate of Claveria v. Claveria, 615 S.W.2d 164 (Tex. 1981) (effort to challenge a second marriage by claiming a prior undissolved common law marriage rejected)

Collora v. Navarro, 574 S.W.2d 65 (Tex. 1978) (upholding a directed verdict finding a common law marriage based on uncorroborated testimony of a surviving spouse)

Courts of Appeals

Agreement

Joplin v. Borusheski, 244 S.W.3d 607 (Tex. App.—Dallas 2008, no pet.) (alleged common law husband filed for divorce more than two years after parties separated—presumption of no agreement to be married not rebutted)

Canady v. Russell, 138 S.W.3d 412 (Tex. App.—Tyler 2004, pet. denied) (prison inmates of opposite sex separated by geography can not form common law marriage by intent alone; must meet all 3 requirements)

Cohabitation (living together)

Lewis v. Anderson, 173 S.W.3d 556 (Tex. App.—Dallas 2005, pet. denied) (couple divorced, then lived together and adopted two children as "H & W"—man's claim of no common law marriage rejected)

Ball v. Smith, 150 S.W.3d 889 (Tex. App.—Dallas 2004, no pet.) (no evidence of either informal marriage or economic partnership)

No Marriage

In re Hughes, 2009 WL 1491866 (Tex. App.—Amarillo 2009, no pet.)(court improperly conducted "final trial" on issue of common law marriage at hearing of temporary orders)

Smith v. Deneve, 285 S.W.3d 904 (Tex. App.—Dallas 2009, no pet.) (evidence supported finding of no common law marriage but property divided under alternative theories, including resulting trusts)

Phillips v. Dow Chemical Company, 186 S.W.3d 121 (Tex. App.—Houston [1st Dist.] 2005, no pet.) (alleged common law marriage invalidated by undissolved prior marriage)

Mills v. Mest, 94 S.W.3d 72 (Tex. App.—Houston [14th Dist.] 2002, no pet.) (cohabitation for over a decade does nothing to prove common law marriage in absence of proof of agreement and holding out)

Reynolds v. Reynolds, 86 S.W.3d 272 (Tex. App.—Austin 2002, no pet.) (no justiciable issue for declaratory judgment on whether Virginia couple have Texas common law marriage)

Lee v. Lee, 44 S.W.3d 151 (Tex. App.—Houston [1st Dist.] 2001, pet. denied) (appellate court found no common law marriage—on remand that is law of case)

Eris v. Phares, 39 S.W.3d 708 (Tex. App.—Houston [1st Dist.] 2001, pet. denied) (insufficient evidence on holding out common law marriage by the woman; although the man represented marital status to others, she never held herself out as married)

Marriage

La Paz v. La Paz, 2009 WL 1238530 (Tex. App.—Corpus Christi 2009, no pet.) (evidence supporting finding of marriage without formalities and finding that properties acquired before ceremonial marriage were community property)

Cardwell v. Cardwell, 195 S.W.3d 856 (Tex. App.—Dallas 2006, no pet.) (common law marriage came into existence at the termination of wife's prior marriage)

Narvaez v. Maldonado, 127 S.W.3d 313 (Tex. App.—Austin 2004, no pet.) (putative husband not entitled to bill of review after default judgment divorce of common law marriage)

Wilson ex rel. C.M.W. v. Estate of Williams, 99 S.W.3d 640 (Tex. App.—Waco 2003, no pet.) (mother #2 proved common law marriage, thereby obtaining heirship for herself and child presumed to be his child)

Ganesan v. Vallabhaneni, 96 S.W.3d 345 (Tex. App.—Austin 2002, no pet.) (jury had sufficient instructions and evidence to support its finding of common law marriage)

Amayé v. Oravetz, 57 S.W.3d 581 (Tex. App.—Houston [14th Dist.] 2001, pet. denied) (woman claiming common law marriage in suit filed more than two years after couple separated bore burden of rebutting presumption of no marriage)

Osteen v. Osteen, 38 S.W.3d 809 (Tex. App.—Houston [14th Dist.] 2001, no pet.) (default divorce defective; claimed "wife" presented no evidence of common law marriage)

Cross References

TX FCA Const. art. 1, § 32 (no caption; defines marriage as "union of one man and one woman"; forbids creation or recognition of same-sex marriages and "any legal status identical or similar"), *infra*.

TX FCA Family § 2.001. Marriage License, *supra*; TX FCA Family § 6.204. Recognition of Same-Sex Marriage or Civil Union, *infra*.

Defense of Marriage Act, TX FCA 28 USCA § 1738C, *infra*.

---

§ 2.401. Proof of Informal Marriage

(a) In a judicial, administrative, or other proceeding, the marriage of a man and woman may be proved by evidence that:

(1) a declaration of their marriage has been signed as provided by this subchapter; or

(2) the man and woman agreed to be married and after the agreement they lived together in this state as husband and wife and there represented to others that they were married.

(b) If a proceeding in which a marriage is to be proved as provided by Subsection (a)(2) is not commenced before the second anniversary of the date on which the parties separated and ceased living together, it is rebuttably presumed that the parties did not enter into an agreement to be married.

(c) A person under 18 years of age may not:

(1) be a party to an informal marriage; or

(2) execute a declaration of informal marriage under Section 2.402.

(d) A person may not be a party to an informal marriage or execute a declaration of an informal marriage if the person is presently married to a person who is not the other party to the informal marriage or declaration of an informal marriage, as applicable.

§ 2.402. Declaration and Registration of Informal Marriage

(a) A declaration of informal marriage must be signed on a form prescribed by the bureau of vital statistics and provided by the county clerk. Each party to the declaration shall provide the information required in the form.

(b) The declaration form must contain:

(1) a heading entitled "Declaration and Registration of Informal Marriage, __________ County, Texas";

(2) spaces for each party's full name, including the woman's maiden surname, address, date of birth, place of birth, including city, county, and state, and social security number, if any;

(3) a space for indicating the type of document tendered by each party as proof of age and identity;

(4) printed boxes for each party to check "true" or "false" in response to the following statement: "The other party is not related to me as:

(A) an ancestor or descendant, by blood or adoption;

(B) a brother or sister, of the whole or half blood or by adoption;

(C) a parent's brother or sister, of the whole or half blood or by adoption;

(D) a son or daughter of a brother or sister, of the whole or half blood or by adoption;

(E) a current or former stepchild or stepparent; or

(F) a son or daughter of a parent's brother or sister, of the whole or half blood or by adoption.";

(5) a printed declaration and oath reading: "I SOLEMNLY SWEAR (OR AFFIRM) THAT WE, THE UNDERSIGNED, ARE MARRIED TO EACH OTHER BY VIRTUE OF THE FOLLOWING FACTS: ON OR ABOUT (DATE) WE AGREED TO BE MARRIED, AND AFTER THAT DATE WE LIVED TOGETHER AS HUSBAND AND WIFE AND IN THIS STATE WE REPRESENTED TO OTHERS THAT WE WERE MARRIED. SINCE THE DATE OF MARRIAGE TO THE OTHER PARTY I HAVE NOT BEEN MARRIED TO ANY OTHER PERSON. THIS DECLARATION IS TRUE AND THE INFORMATION IN IT WHICH I HAVE GIVEN IS CORRECT.";

(6) spaces immediately below the printed declaration and oath for the parties' signatures; and

(7) a certificate of the county clerk that the parties made the declaration and oath and the place and date it was made.

§ 2.403. Proof of Identity and Age; Offense

(a) The county clerk shall require proof of the identity and age of each party to the declaration of informal marriage to be established by a document listed in Section 2.005(b).

(b) A person commits an offense if the person knowingly provides false, fraudulent, or otherwise inaccurate proof of the person's identity or age under this section. An offense under this subsection is a Class A misdemeanor.

§ 2.404. Recording of Certificate or Declaration of Informal Marriage

(a) The county clerk shall:

(1) determine that all necessary information is recorded on the declaration of informal marriage form and that all necessary documents are submitted to the clerk;

(2) administer the oath to each party to the declaration;

(3) have each party sign the declaration in the clerk's presence; and

(4) execute the clerk's certificate to the declaration.

(a–1) On the proper execution of the declaration, the clerk may:

(1) prepare a certificate of informal marriage;

(2) enter on the certificate the names of the persons declaring their informal marriage and the date the certificate or declaration is issued; and

(3) record the time at which the certificate or declaration is issued.

(b) The county clerk may not certify the declaration or issue or record the certificate of informal marriage or declaration if:

(1) either party fails to supply any information or provide any document required by this subchapter;

(2) either party is under 18 years of age; or

(3) either party checks "false" in response to the statement of relationship to the other party.

(c) On execution of the declaration, the county clerk shall record the declaration or certificate of informal marriage, deliver the original of the declaration to the parties, deliver the original of the certificate of informal marriage to the parties, if a certificate was prepared, and send a copy of the declaration of informal marriage to the bureau of vital statistics.

(d) An executed declaration or a certificate of informal marriage recorded as provided in this section is prima facie evidence of the marriage of the parties.

(e) At the time the parties sign the declaration, the clerk shall distribute to each party printed materials about acquired immune deficiency syndrome (AIDS) and human immunodeficiency virus (HIV). The clerk shall note on the declaration that the distribution was made. The materials shall be prepared and provided to the clerk by the Texas Department of Health and shall be designed to inform the parties about:

(1) the incidence and mode of transmission of AIDS and HIV;

(2) the local availability of medical procedures, including voluntary testing, designed to show or help show whether a person has AIDS or HIV infection, antibodies to HIV, or infection with any other probable causative agent of AIDS; and

(3) available and appropriate counseling services regarding AIDS and HIV infection.

§ 2.405. Violation by County Clerk; Penalty

A county clerk or deputy county clerk who violates this subchapter commits an offense. An offense under this section is a misdemeanor punishable by a fine of not less than $200 and not more than $500.

SUBCHAPTER F. RIGHTS AND DUTIES OF SPOUSES

§ 2.501. Duty to Support

(a) Each spouse has the duty to support the other spouse.

(b) A spouse who fails to discharge the duty of support is liable to any person who provides necessaries to the spouse to whom support is owed.

Comment

This section states the basic rule that spouses have a mutual duty to support each other. The liability of a spouse to a third party who furnished necessaries to a spouse codifies Texas case law.

Despite the publicity often given to this provision, it seems to be a dead-letter in today's society not highly reported.

Leading Cases

Case v. Case, 28 S.W.3d 154 (Tex. App.—Texarkana 2000, no pet.) (no right to reimbursement for separate property spent on community living expenses due to duty of spouses to support the family)

Gabel v. Blackburn Operating Corp., 442 S.W.2d 818 (Tex. Civ. App.—Amarillo 1969, no writ) (husband liable to department store for purchases of necessities by wife)

SUBTITLE B. PROPERTY RIGHTS AND LIABILITIES

★★★

CHAPTER 3. MARITAL PROPERTY RIGHTS AND LIABILITIES

SUBCHAPTER A. GENERAL RULES FOR SEPARATE AND COMMUNITY PROPERTY

SUBCHAPTER B. MANAGEMENT, CONTROL, AND DISPOSITION OF MARITAL PROPERTY

SUBCHAPTER C. MARITAL PROPERTY LIABILITIES

SUBCHAPTER D. MANAGEMENT, CONTROL, AND DISPOSITION OF MARITAL PROPERTY UNDER UNUSUAL CIRCUMSTANCES

SUBCHAPTER E. CLAIMS FOR REIMBURSEMENT

SUBCHAPTER A. GENERAL RULES FOR SEPARATE AND COMMUNITY PROPERTY

Introductory Comment

Texas has operated under a community property system since 1840 along with the presumption that all property owned by one or both spouses at anytime during the marriage is community property. Simply stated, property owned before marriage and property acquired during the marriage by gift, devise or descent is a spouse's separate property. Separate property gives the owner exclusive rights of management, is not subject to divestiture at time of divorce, and is solely under the testamentary power of the owner.

In 1913, the Legislature initiated a series of laws which ultimately culminated in 1967 into the current system of divided management and control of community property. Essentially, each spouse is free to control, manage and dispose of that community property the spouse would control if single. Absent fraudulent conduct, a spouse is free to spend his or her income, sell or exchange property, and give away property as that spouse sees fit. There may be property that requires joinder of the spouse, such as an account with a financial institution requiring the signature of both parties.

The Matrimonial Property Act of 1967 also gave women for the first time equality of management in their solely managed community property and an equal voice in the management of jointly controlled community property. A significant change instituted by the Act provided that any recovery from personal injury claims remains separate property. This change abolished the community property defense by which the negligence of one spouse would be imputed to the other.

Section 3.001 merely rephrases (in fewer words) Tex. Const. art. XVI, § 15, *infra*, which establishes the iron rule for separate property. Section 3.002 provides that if property does not fit within the definition of separate property that property is characterized as community property. The constitutional provision and the statutory restatements, coupled with the presumption stated in § 3.003 that all property on hand at the time of dissolution of the marriage by death, divorce, or annulment is community property, form the fundamentals of the Texas marital property regime. Clear and convincing evidence is required to overcome the community property presumption.

During the 150 years under the community property system, Texas courts have engrafted a number of rules with which a practitioner must be familiar in order to fathom the complexities of the community property system, to wit:

1. ***Commingling:*** The separate assets of a spouse have been so hopelessly mixed or combined with community assets that they can no longer be traced.

2. ***Inception of title:*** The character of property is determined at the earliest moment to which the claimant can claim title. With regard to real estate, this is generally the signing of the purchase contract, not necessarily the date of the deed.

3. ***Increases:*** The natural increase or decrease in the value of a separate asset. This fluctuation does not affect character.

4. ***Jury:*** Texas, with its unique jury system in family law cases, allows the jury to determine the character and value of property. However, the judge determines the division of the marital estate; *see* annotations to § 6.703 and §§ 7.001–7.004, *infra*.

5. ***Mutation:*** An asset of a specific character, whether separate or community, retains that character even after undergoing a change in form and when it exists in the form of another asset. For example, a certificate of deposit owned by a spouse before marriage may be used to purchase an automobile or real estate during marriage. The resulting asset is separate property.

6. ***Non-marital property:*** A potpourri of items, including professional goodwill, certain governmental benefits (usually arising from physical disability), college education, and the specific assets of an organized business entity in which the spouse has an ownership interest.

7. ***Property of mixed character:*** An asset is not necessarily entirely community property or entirely separate property. Section 3.006 recognizes that, because the source of funds used to purchase an asset may come from different marital estates, the resulting asset may be owned in differing percentage interests by the different contributing marital estates. A typical example is where one spouse uses separate funds as the down payment on the purchase of a residence, but the general credit of the spouses (*i.e.*, community) is used to secure the balance of the purchase price. An asset acquired in this fashion has mixed character, both separate and community.

8. ***Reimbursement:*** Expenditure of the funds from one estate used to benefit another estate gives rise to a claim for equitable reimbursement. The most typical example is the spending of community funds to discharge the mortgage on separately owned real estate. This gives rise to a claim for reimbursement. Reimbursement claims may also be made where community time, toil and effort or community funds are used to enhance a spouses' separate estate.

9. ***Retirement benefits:*** Retirement benefits are among the most difficult assets to allocate between separate property and community claims. Determining the separate claim for employment before marriage and its proper allocation for service during marriage can give rise to a number of complexities. Case law is extensive on the subject; the rules are discussed at length in the annotations to §§ 3.007, 7.003, *infra*.

10. ***Tracing:*** the documentary evidence necessary to show that an existing asset can be traced back to an asset in another form which was of a particular character—usually separate property. If property of a specified character has been sold, a variety of methods to trace the funds into another asset through the process of mutation have been developed, including:

(a) **Community Out First Method:** If funds from different estates are deposited into a bank account, the first funds withdrawn are presumed to be community property.

(b) **Clearinghouse/Identical Sum Inference Method:** There is a pattern of identifiable deposits and withdrawals of separate funds to and from an account.

(c) **Minimum Sum Balance Method:** The lowest subsequent amount in an account originally containing only separate funds.

(d) **Pro Rata Method:** Apportions ownership of an asset purchased with mixed funds in the ratio of the amount of separate and community funds in an account.

11. ***Transfers between spouses:*** Texas has developed an extensive body of case law dealing with transfers of property between spouses and the doctrine of significant recitals. These rules are quite numerous and are discussed in more detail in the articles cited below. Section 3.005 provides that gifts between spouses are presumed to include any income and property that may arise from the gifted property.

12. ***Trust distributions:*** Depending on the terms of the trust instrument, distributions from a separate property trust may be community or separate.

CLE/Other Legal Publications

Characterization and Tracing

Case law update. Michael C. Shulman & Luisa P. Marrero, 2011 Adv. Fam. L.

Characterization and tracing: Workshop. Kelly Ausley-Flores, Moderator, 2011 Adv. Fam. L.

Property case law update. Georganna L. Simpson, 2011 Marriage Dissolution

Characterization and tracing. Wendy S. Burgower, 2011 Marriage Dissolution

Characterization of property: in-depth discussion, including business interests, trusts and retirement plans. Kathryn J. Murphy, 2011 U.T. Fam. L. Front Lines

Tracing holes without records. William M. Reppeto, 2011 U.T. Fam. L. Front Lines

Property caselaw update. Ann C. McClure, 2010 Adv. Fam. L.

Proving separate property. Chris Nickelson, 2010 Adv. Fam. L.

Troubling issues of characterization, valuation and division. Richard R. Orsinger, 2010 Adv. Fam. L.

Characterization and tracing. Patrice L. Ferguson & Cynthia Nguyen, 2010 Marriage Dissolution

Economic Contribution and Reimbursement

See annotations to chapter 3, subchapter E, *infra*.

Miscellaneous Issues

Understanding business valuations. Autumn Vivienne Kraus, 2011 Adv. Fam. L.

Defending and winning breach of fiduciary claims by summary judgment. Jim Loveless, 2011 Adv. Fam. L.

Fiduciary litigation. John F. Nichols, Sr., Katie Pearson Klein & Brian L. Webb, 2011 Adv. Fam. L.

Dealing with business entities (joinder). Warren Cole, Stephen Michael Orsinger & Cheryl L. Wilson, 2011 Adv. Fam. L.

Unwrapping and understanding future financial benefits. J. Lindsey Short, Jr., 2011 Adv. Fam. L.

Valuation of property, Workshop. Robert C. Sullivan, Jr., Moderator, 2011 Adv. Fam. L.

Breach of fiduciary duty and other causes of action. Charla H. Bradshaw & H.E. Mendez, 2011 Marriage Dissolution

Dealing with damages/recovery as property. John F. Nichols, Sr., 2011 Marriage Dissolution

Businesses and divorce. Jack W. Marr, 2011 Marriage Dissolution

Early withdrawal and retirement benefits. Cheryl L. Wilson, 2011 Marriage Dissolution

How to interpret financial statements, income tax returns and similar documents. Susan Fae McLerran, 2011 Marriage Dissolution

Business entities. Adam J. Morris, 2011 So. Tex. Fam. L.

Valuation: cross-examine of valuation expert. Sherri A. Evans, 2011 U.T. Fam. L. Front Lines

Fiduciary duties: conflicts and overlaps. John F. Nichols, Sr., 2010 Adv. Fam. L.

Stock options, deferred compensation plans and other executive benefits. Christy Adamcik Gammill, 2010 Fam. L. Boot Camp

Business entities from a family law perspective. E. Michelle Bohreer & Sherri A. Evans, 2010 Fam. L. Front Lines

Buy/sell agreements. Kyle W. Sanders, 2010 Adv. Fam. L. Drafting

Creative wealth planning with grantor trusts, family limited partnerships, and family limited liability companies. Robert G. Alexander & Dallas E. Klemmer, 2 Est. Plan. & Community Prop. L.J. 307 (2010)

Trust characterization issues after Sharma. Adam J. Morris, 2010 So. Tex. Fam. L. Conf.

See Accompanying CD–ROM for Additional CLE/Other Legal Publications

---

Leading Cases

Characterization—Community Property

Texas Supreme Court

Pearson v. Fillingim, 332 S.W.3d 361 (Tex. 2011)(community property presumption applied when husband did not appear in trial at divorce)

Douglas v. Delp, 987 S.W.2d 879 (Tex. 1999) (spouse's earning capacity and credit reputation are sole management community property)

Lewis v. Lewis, 944 S.W.2d 630 (Tex. 1997) (worker's compensation benefits for loss of earning capacity are characterized as community)

Broussard v. Tian, 156 Tex. 371, 295 S.W.2d 405 (1956) (payment of community debt with separate property funds does not alter character)

Courts of Appeals

Vardilos v. Vardilos, 219 S.W.3d 920 (Tex. App.—Dallas 2007, no pet.) (wife's testimony traced account to inheritance)

Brock v. Brock, 192 S.W.3d 895 (Tex. App.—Dallas 2006, no pet.) (good evidence of separate property rebuts community property presumption)

Pace v. Pace, 160 S.W.3d 706 (Tex. App.—Dallas 2005, pet. denied) (separate character of real property and financial assets may be proven by testimony of owning spouse)

Characterization—Inception of Title

Welder v. Lambert, 44 S.W. 281 (Tex. 1898) (origin of title determines character of property, not acquisition of final title)

Calder v. Calder, 2010 WL 3370766 (Tex. App.— Austin 2010, no pet.) (wife met burden of proof that Chihuahua was her separate property when funds came from her premarital account)

Characterization—Mixed Title

Gleich v. Bongio, 99 S.W.2d 881 (Tex. 1937) (ratio of ownership of property is in proportion to the consideration supplied by the separate and community estates)

Prague v. Prague, 190 S.W.3d 31 (Tex. App.—Dallas 2005, no pet.) (award of 100% of mixed character TRS retirement to teacher in divorce affirmed under trial court discretion)

Characterization—Separate Property Generally

Tarver v. Tarver, 394 S.W.2d 780 (Tex. 1965) (burden of proof on party asserting separate property claim)

Norris v. Vaughan, 260 S.W.2d 676 (Tex. 1953) (royalty payments for oil and gas production held to be separate property)

Arnold v. Leonard, 273 S.W. 799 (Tex. 1925) (TEX. CONST. defines separate property, cannot be altered by statute)

Graves v. Tomlinson, 329 S.W.3d 128 (Tex. App.—Houston [14th Dist.] 2010, pet. filed) (mischaracterization of farm as husband's separate property was significant enough to warrant remand)

Sharma v. Routh, 302 S.W.3d 355 (Tex. App.—Houston 2009, no pet.) (income distributions to a married beneficiary from an irrevocable trust are only community property if the spouse has a "present possessory interest" in the trust corpus)

LeGrand-Brock v. Brock, 246 S.W.3d 318 (Tex. App.—Beaumont 2008, pet. denied) (corporation dissolution yields mutation of separate property stock into separate property cash)

In re Lewis, 223 S.W.3d 756 (Tex. App.—Texarkana 2007, orig. proceeding) (divorce court lacks power to order sale of separate property)

Characterization—Separate Property by Gift, Devise, or Descent

Wells v. Wells, 251 S.W.3d 834 (Tex. App.—Eastland 2008, no pet.) (mother credibly testified the father conveyed farming equipment to their daughter as gift of separate property)

In re Marriage of Royal, 107 S.W.3d 846 (Tex. App.—Amarillo 2003, no pet.) (testimony of donor grandparents regarding gift to husband rebutted by contrary evidence of forgiven loan as gift to couple)

Economic Contribution/Reimbursement

Heggen v. Pemelton, 836 S.W.2d 145 (Tex. 1992) (lien on homestead for reimbursement claim restricted to purchase money, taxes, and mutually agreed upon home improvement)

Penick v. Penick, 783 S.W.2d 194 (Tex. 1988) (reimbursement for debts, taxes, interest or insurance is measured by amount paid less any benefit received)

Anderson v. Gilliland, 684 S.W.2d 673 (Tex. 1985) (reimbursement for improvements to real estate is enhancement in value less any benefit received)

Jensen v. Jensen, 665 S.W.2d 107 (Tex. 1984) (reimbursement for community time, toil and effort allowed less any benefits received)

Vallone v. Vallone, 644 S.W.2d 455 (Tex. 1982) (party seeking reimbursement has burden of proof)

Norton v. Norton, 2010 WL 2816212 (Tex. App.—Amarillo 2010, no pet.) (economic contribution calculation made by court of appeals to reform trial court award)

In re Marriage of Cigainero, 305 S.W.3d 798 (Tex. App.—Texarkana 2010, no pet.) (economic contribution claim supported by evidence where rental income on separate property was used to pay down debt and make improvements; offsets not to be considered in EC claims)

Baker v. Baker, 2009 WL 3382242 (Tex. App.—San Antonio 2009, no pet.) (husband's reimbursement claim for improvements failed where he did not establish the source of alleged separate property funds or the value of the property before and after the alleged improvements made)

Knight v. Knight, 301 S.W.3d 723 (Tex. App.—Houston 2009, no pet.) (trial court's refusal to grant reimbursement abuse of discretion in light of evidence that community funds used to pay husband's separate property judgments)

Hernandez v. Hernandez, 2009 WL 1547746 (Tex. App.—San Antonio 2009, no pet.) (denial of reimbursement proper where husband failed to offer evidence of net benefit to W's separate estate and of the offsetting benefit to the community).

Phillips v. Phillips, 296 S.W.3d 656 (Tex. App.—El Paso 2009, pet. denied) (reimbursement as an equitable remedy may be considered in offsetting claims against husband for constructive fraud)

Gifts Between Spouses

Rosensky v. Rosensky, 2011 WL 743164 (Tex. App.—Houston [1st Dist.] 2011, no pet.) (finding of no gift to wife affirmed; husband allowed to testify as to lack of donative intent despite "gift letter")

Harrison v. Harrison, 321 S.W.3d 899 (Tex. App.—Houston [14th Dist.] 2010, no pet.) (property purchased with husband's separate property but placed in name of husband and wife presumed gift of interest to wife)

Magness v. Magness, 241 S.W.3d 910 (Tex. App.—Dallas 2007, pet. denied) (granting property deed to spouse creates presumption of gift)

Long v. Long, 234 S.W.3d 34 (Tex. App.—El Paso 2007, pet. denied); Morris v. Morris, 12 S.W.3d 877 (Tex. App.—Texarkana 2000, no pet.) (taking title to husband's separate realty in names of both spouses makes gift to wife of one half interest)

Raymond v. Raymond, 190 S.W.3d 77 (Tex. App.—Houston [1st Dist.] 2005, no pet.) (husband's conveyance by deed of one half of separate property becomes wife's separate property)

Morris v. Morris, 12 S.W.3d 877 (Tex. App.—Texarkana 2000, no pet.) (taking title to husband's separate realty in names of both spouses makes gift to wife of one half interest)

Tracing

Estate of Hanau v. Hanau, 730 S.W.2d 663 (Tex. 1987) (clearinghouse method: identifiable sums of separate funds deposited, identifiable withdrawals made that clearly identify character of transaction)

Sibley v. Sibley, 286 S.W.2d 658 (Tex. 1955), Welder v. Welder, 794 S.W.2d 420 (Tex. App.—Corpus Christi 1990, no writ) ("community out first"; withdrawals from mixed fund presumed to be community, withdrawals presumed separate only when community funds exhausted)

Henslee v. Henslee, 2010 WL 2982928 (Tex. App.—Tyler 2010, no pet.) (husband failed to trace what portion of disability settlement were for separate property; part of payments intended to replace earnings lost while married are community property)

Osorno v. Osorno, 76 S.W.3d 509 (Tex. App.—Houston [14th Dist.] 2002, no pet.) (husband's testimony regarding financial accounts not enough to trace his separate property claim even given premarital agreement)

See Accompanying CD–ROM for Cases Linked to Westlaw and Additional Leading Cases

Cross Reference

TX FCA CONST., art. 16, § 15. Separate and Community Property of Husband and Wife, *infra*.

§ 3.001. Separate Property

A spouse's separate property consists of:

(1) the property owned or claimed by the spouse before marriage;

(2) the property acquired by the spouse during marriage by gift, devise, or descent; and

(3) the recovery for personal injuries sustained by the spouse during marriage, except any recovery for loss of earning capacity during marriage.

§ 3.002. Community Property

Community property consists of the property, other than separate property, acquired by either spouse during marriage.

§ 3.003. Presumption of Community Property

(a) Property possessed by either spouse during or on dissolution of marriage is presumed to be community property.

(b) The degree of proof necessary to establish that property is separate property is clear and convincing evidence.

§ 3.004. Recordation of Separate Property

(a) A subscribed and acknowledged schedule of a spouse's separate property may be recorded in the deed records of the county in which the parties, or one of them, reside and in the county or counties in which the real property is located.

(b) A schedule of a spouse's separate real property is not constructive notice to a good faith purchaser for value or a creditor without actual notice unless the instrument is acknowledged and recorded in the deed records of the county in which the real property is located.

Cross Reference

TEX. PROP. CODE ANN. § 112.001. Instruments Concerning Property.

§ 3.005. Gifts Between Spouses

If one spouse makes a gift of property to the other spouse, the gift is presumed to include all the income and property that may arise from that property.

§ 3.006. Proportional Ownership of Property by Marital Estates

If the community estate of the spouses and the separate estate of a spouse have an ownership interest in property, the respective ownership interests of the marital estates are determined by the rule of inception of title.

§ 3.007. Property Interest in Certain Employee Benefits

Retirement Plans

(a), (b) [Repealed by Acts 2009, 81st Leg., ch. 768, § 11(1).]

(c) The separate property interest of a spouse in a defined contribution retirement plan may be traced using the tracing and characterization principles that apply to a nonretirement asset.

(d) A spouse who is a participant in an employer-provided stock option plan or an employer-provided restricted stock plan has a separate property interest in the options or restricted stock granted to the spouse under the plan as follows:

(1) if the option or stock was granted to the spouse before marriage but required continued employment during marriage before the grant could be exercised or the restriction removed, the spouse's separate property interest is equal to the fraction of the option or restricted stock in which:

(A) the numerator is the sum of:

(i) the period from the date the option or stock was granted until the date of marriage; and

(ii) if the option or stock also required continued employment following the date of dissolution of the marriage before the grant could be exercised or the restriction removed, the period from the date of dissolution of the marriage until the date the grant could be exercised or the restriction removed; and

(B) the denominator is the period from the date the option or stock was granted until the date the grant could be exercised or the restriction removed; and

(2) if the option or stock was granted to the spouse during the marriage but required continued employment following the date of dissolution of the marriage before the grant could be exercised or the restriction removed, the spouse's separate property interest is equal to the fraction of the option or restricted stock in which:

(A) the numerator is the period from the date of dissolution of the marriage until the date the grant could be exercised or the restriction removed; and

(B) the denominator is the period from the date the option or stock was granted until the date the grant could be exercised or the restriction removed.

(e) The computation described by Subsection (d) applies to each component of the benefit requiring varying periods of employment before the grant could be exercised or the restriction removed.

Comment

In 2009, the Texas Legislature repealed subsections (a) and (b) dealing with defined benefit retirement plans. The subsections contained a mathematical error and the Family Law Council urged a return to having case law resolve the allocation of the separate and community property portions. Defined benefit plans are shrinking in significance as employers opt for defined contribution plans. However, federal, state and local government plans remain mostly as defined benefit plans. Subsection (f) dealing with recalculation of property rights in stock options and restricted stock was repealed because of the difficulty having both a final judgment that resolved all property rights and the calculation of the time allocation post-divorce.

Subsection (c) allows for internal tracing within defined contribution plans. Given the overwhelming preference for such retirement plans, often self directed by the employee, it is only logical that internal tracing be allowed. This subsection is a legislative overturning of the "opening balance" theory cases holding that the separate property interest is the account balance on the day of marriage and the community interest is everything else. *See, e.g. Pelzig v. Berkebile, 931 S.W.3d 398 (Tex. App.—Corpus Christi 1996, no writ); Hetteberg v. Hetteberg*, 933 S.W.2d 522 (Tex. App.—Houston [1st Dist.] 1994, no writ). This does not mean that internal tracing will always be easy as often the funds are in mutual funds or similar investments making it more difficult to differentiate between the market appreciation of assets and growth from dividends and interest.

Subsections (d) and (e) address the characterization of stock options and restricted stock. The 1990s witnessed high interest in stock options for employees and the use of restricted stock plans for employees appears to be gaining popularity. These subsections are a legislative overturning of the inception of title rule for such benefits and an adoption of the rule of proportionality based on the service performed by each marital estate. *See, e.g., Charriere v. Charriere*, 7 S.W.2d 217 (Tex. App.—Dallas 1999, no pet.). The allocation looks at options and restricted stock granted before marriage, as well as options and restricted stock granted during marriage but requiring service after divorce. Because the benefits typically have varying lengths of time for maturity, the rule of proportionality will apply to each component.

CLE/Other Legal Publication

Unwrapping and understanding future financial benefits. J. Lindsey Short, Jr., 2011 Adv. Fam. L.

Early withdrawal and retirement benefits. Cheryl L. Wilson, 2011 Marriage Dissolution

Characterization of property in-depth discussion, including business interests, trusts and retirement plans. Kathryn J. Murphy, 2011 U.T. Fam. L. Front Lines

QDRO'S and retirement benefits. Charla Bradshaw Conner, 2010 Adv. Fam. L. Drafting

Stock options, deferred compensation plans and other executive benefits. Christy Adamcik Gammill, 2010 Fam. L. Boot Camp

Defined benefit and contribution plans. Mike Gregory, 2010 Marriage Dissolution

Exploring employment plans and benefits, and drafting QDRO's. (Panel), 2009 Adv. Fam. L.

Unique compensation—what is it and who owns it? Katherine Anne Kinser, 2009 U.T. Fam. L. Front Lines

QDROS and retirement benefits: changes and beyond. William C. Clifton, 2008 Adv. Fam. L. Drafting

Exploring employment plans and benefits. Randall B. Wilhite, 2008 New Frontiers

---

See Accompanying CD–ROM for Additional CLE/Other Legal Publications

---

Leading Cases

See annotations to § 7.003, *infra*.

A Proceeds Remain the same

§ 3.008. Property Interest in Certain Insurance Proceeds

(a) Insurance proceeds paid or payable that arise from a casualty loss to property during marriage are characterized in the same manner as the property to which the claim is attributable.

(b) If a person becomes disabled or is injured, any disability insurance payment or workers' compensation payment is community property to the extent it is intended to replace earnings lost while the disabled or injured person is married. To the extent that any insurance payment or workers' compensation payment is intended to replace earnings while the disabled or injured person is not married, the recovery is the separate property of the disabled or injured spouse.

Replacement income during marriage

Comment

This section clarifies the characterization of insurance proceeds in certain instances. The "replacement" theory is adopted, rejecting the "payment of premiums" and "inception of title" theories.

Under Subsection (a), if a separate property residence is destroyed, the proceeds from the loss are also separate property, even if the community estate paid the insurance premiums. Likewise, if a community automobile is stolen, the proceeds are community property, notwithstanding a spouse having expended separate funds to pay the insurance premiums.

In Subsection (b), disability and workers' compensation benefits are accorded the same treatment as property casualty losses. Thus, if an employee suffers an injury or disability before or during marriage, the payments are characterized in the same manner as the income being replaced. The replacement theory aligns Texas law with the majority rule in American jurisprudence. *See* Leopold, *"Loss of Earning Capacity" Benefits in the Community Jurisdiction–How do you figure?*, 30 St. Mary's L.J. 367 (1999). The subsection is a legislative overturning of older Texas cases such as, *Lewis v. Lewis*, 944 S.W.2d 630 (Tex. 1997) (worker's compensation) and *Simmons v. Simmons*, 568 S.W.2d 169 (Tex. Civ. App.—Dallas 1978, writ dism'd) (disability insurance).

SUBCHAPTER B. MANAGEMENT, CONTROL, AND DISPOSITION OF MARITAL PROPERTY

Introductory Comment

From 1840 to 1913, the husband managed the separate estates of both spouses. From 1913 to 1967, there was a gradual expansion to ratify a woman's right to manage her own separate estate. Since 1967, both spouses have had equal rights to manage their own separate estates, with one major exception: joinder of both spouses is necessary to convey the family homestead, even if it is the separate property of one spouse. For annotations regarding characterization of property, *see* §§ 3.001–.002, *supra*; for annotations regarding management and liability of property, *see* §§ 3.201–.202, *infra*.

Section 3.102 outlines the Texas system provides for divided management and control of community property. Each spouse is entitled to control that portion of the community property as "if single"; those assets consist of that spouse's earnings, revenues from separate property, recoveries for personal injuries, and the increase and mutations of the first three elements. Solely managed community property that is "mixed or combined" with solely managed community property of the other spouse becomes subject to "joint management" unless the parties otherwise agree. 3.102(c) provides that all other community property will be subject to joint management unless the parties otherwise agree. Courts have struggled to determine whether property is "mixed or combined" and subject to "joint" control.

CLE/Other Legal Publications

Defending and winning breach of fiduciary claims by summary judgment. Jim Loveless, 2011 Adv. Fam. L.

Fiduciary litigation. John F. Nichols, Sr., Katie Pearson Klein & Brian L. Webb, 2011 Adv. Fam. L.

Breach of fiduciary duty and other causes of action. Charla H. Bradshaw & H.E. Mendez, 2011 Marriage Dissolution

Fiduciary duties: conflicts and overlaps. John F. Nichols, Sr., 2010 Adv. Fam. L.

A Purse of Her Own: The Case Against Joint Bank Accounts. Lisa R. Mahle, 16 Tex. J. Women & L. 45 (2006)

Leading Cases

Vallone v. Vallone, 644 S.W.2d 455 (Tex. 1982) (discharge of debts by one spouse through bankruptcy does not relieve other spouse of liability to the extent of community property set aside to that spouse in divorce)

Stewart Title Co. v. Huddleston, 608 S.W.2d 611 (Tex. 1980) (wife not personally liable for husband's judgment debt, creditor did not pursue former community property held by her)

Cockerham v. Cockerham, 527 S.W.2d 162 (Tex. 1975) (most often cited as "community debt" case, but actually involves joint action of both spouses)

Cooper v. Texas Gulf Industries, Inc., 513 S.W.2d 200 (Tex. 1974) (suit against a spouse does not bind other spouse under discredited doctrine of virtual representation)

Viera v. Viera, 331 S.W.3d 195 (Tex. App.—El Paso 2011, no pet.) (wife failed to overcome community debt presumption for debt in husband's name)

Montemayor v. Ortiz, 208 S.W.3d 627 (Tex. App.—Corpus Christi 2006, rev. denied) (when wife's business was started with separate property gift and community property contributions were from her sole-managed community property, wife's special community property is not liable for husband's contractual debt)

---

§ 3.101. Managing Separate Property

Each spouse has the sole management, control, and disposition of that spouse's separate property.

§ 3.102. Managing Community Property

(a) During marriage, each spouse has the sole management, control, and disposition of the community property that the spouse would have owned if single, including:

(1) personal earnings;

(2) revenue from separate property;

(3) recoveries for personal injuries; and

(4) the increase and mutations of, and the revenue from, all property subject to the spouse's sole management, control, and disposition.

(b) If community property subject to the sole management, control, and disposition of one spouse is mixed or combined with community property subject to the sole management, control, and disposition of the other spouse, then the mixed or combined community property is subject to the joint management, control, and disposition of the spouses, unless the spouses provide otherwise by power of attorney in writing or other agreement.

(c) Except as provided by Subsection (a), community property is subject to the joint management, control, and disposition of the spouses unless the spouses provide otherwise by power of attorney in writing or other agreement.

§ 3.103. Managing Earnings of Minor

Except as provided by Section 264.0111, during the marriage of the parents of an unemancipated minor for whom a managing conservator has not been appointed, the earnings of the minor are subject to the joint management, control, and disposition of the parents of the minor, unless otherwise provided by agreement of the parents or by judicial order.

Comment

This section provides for parental control of a child's earnings, which probably does not reflect reality in the typical family. No doubt most children with jobs manage to exert control over their earnings. No cases have cited this section in more than 25 years.

The cross-reference to TX FCA Family § 264.0111, *infra*, refers to the section that eliminates ownership and managerial rights of parents to the accumulated earnings of a child who has been returned home after earning money and establishing a bank account while in state custody. Residential treatment centers commonly encourage such children to earn and manage their own money to improve self-esteem and responsibility.

Cross Reference

TEX. PROB. CODE ANN. § 901. Contracts in Arts, Entertainment, Advertisement and Sports.

---

§ 3.104. Protection of Third Persons

(a) During marriage, property is presumed to be subject to the sole management, control, and disposition of a spouse if it is held in that spouse's name, as shown by muniment, contract, deposit of funds, or other evidence of ownership, or if it is in that spouse's possession and is not subject to such evidence of ownership.

(b) A third person dealing with a spouse is entitled to rely, as against the other spouse or anyone claiming from that spouse, on that spouse's authority to deal with the property if:

(1) the property is presumed to be subject to the sole management, control, and disposition of the spouse; and

(2) the person dealing with the spouse:

(A) is not a party to a fraud on the other spouse or another person; and

(B) does not have actual or constructive notice of the spouse's lack of authority.

Comment

This section protects innocent third parties dealing with one spouse in a business transaction, absent fraud or notice of the spouse's lack of authority to deal with the property in question. Millions of transactions occur every day involving Texas community property being bought, sold or transferred by one spouse. The cashing of checks, the use of credit cards, and the purchase of consumer goods ranging from groceries to automobiles are most often done by just one spouse. Whether one spouse can sell his or her interest in jointly titled property without joinder of the spouse has not been definitively resolved.

SUBCHAPTER C. MARITAL PROPERTY LIABILITIES

Introductory Comment

"Community liability" or "community debt" remains an ambiguous and amorphous notion. Since the Matrimonial Property Act of 1967, it has been the intent of Texas law to mandate that one spouse is not personally liable for the debts of the other spouse, except when the other spouse was acting as an agent for the first spouse or incurring a debt for necessaries. The concept of personal liability of a spouse must be distinguished from the liability imposed on property, both community and separate, which may be subject to execution depending upon the type of obligation. The marriage relationship alone does not create a basis for personal liability. Section 3.201, regarding personal liability of the spouses, is specifically intended to clarify the misleading and confusing discussion in Cockerham v. Cockerham, 527 S.W.2d 162 (Tex. 1975) which actually held that both spouses were personally liable for the debts created by a business primarily, but not exclusively, managed by one of them.

As with the Texas system of divided management of community property, a complementary system exists for divided liability of community property. Section 3.202 provides that, essentially, each spouse's solely managed community property is liable for that spouse's own obligations, but it is not liable for the other spouse's non tortious liabilities (almost always meaning contractual liabilities). All community property is liable for tortious conduct of either spouse.

Finally, section 3.203, or the "marshalling statute," permits the court to establish a rank order of liability to satisfy any judgment against a spouse.

CLE/Other Legal Publication

See annotations to § 7.002 Bankruptcy, *infra*.

Tuition or Neiman's: stretching overextended budgets and solutions for the negative balance sheet. Practical suggestions for economic issues, e.g., underwater real estate, inflated credit card debt and lack of liquidity, and in bankruptcy. Wendy S. Burgower, 2011 U.T. Fam. L. Front Lines

Divorce Your Credit. Mark L. Aschermann, 2011 So. Tex. Fam. L.

Division of debt. Kyle W. Sanders, 2009 U.T. Fam. L. Front Lines

Dividing debts: subprime divorce. Kyle Sanders, 2009 Marriage Dissolution

Helping your client deal with debt in divorce. Michelle May O'Neill, 2008 U.T. Fam. L. Front Lines

See Accompanying CD–ROM for Additional CLE/Other Legal Publications

Leading Cases

Carlton v. Estate of Estes, 664 S.W.2d 322 (Tex. 1983) (jointly managed community property subject to other spouse's individually incurred debt)

Stewart Title Co. v. Huddleston, 608 S.W.2d 611 (Tex. 1980) (wife not joined in creditors' action against ex-husband, property awarded to her in divorce may be subject to debts incurred during marriage)

Cockerham v. Cockerham, 527 S.W.2d 162 (Tex. 1975) (personal liability of husband for wife's operation of business founded upon doctrine of "implied assent")

Wilkinson v. Stevison, 514 S.W.2d 895 (Tex. 1974) (marital status alone does not impose liability or imputed negligence)

Viera v. Viera, 331 S.W.3d 195 (Tex. App.—El Paso 2011, no pet.) (wife failed to overcome community debt presumption for debt in husband's name)

Montemayor v. Ortiz, 208 S.W.3d 627 (Tex. App.—Corpus Christi 2006, rev. denied) (when wife's business started with separate property gift and any community property contributions were her sole management community, wife and her separate property and sole management community is not liable for husband's contractual debt)

§ 3.201. Spousal Liability

(a) A person is personally liable for the acts of the person's spouse only if:

(1) the spouse acts as an agent for the person; or

(2) the spouse incurs a debt for necessaries as provided by Subchapter F, Chapter 2.

(b) Except as provided by this subchapter, community property is not subject to a liability that arises from an act of a spouse.

(c) A spouse does not act as an agent for the other spouse solely because of the marriage relationship.

§ 3.202. Rules of Marital Property Liability

(a) A spouse's separate property is not subject to liabilities of the other spouse unless both spouses are liable by other rules of law.

(b) Unless both spouses are personally liable as provided by this subchapter, the community property subject to a spouse's sole management, control, and disposition is not subject to:

(1) any liabilities that the other spouse incurred before marriage; or

(2) any nontortious liabilities that the other spouse incurs during marriage.

(c) The community property subject to a spouse's sole or joint management, control, and disposition is subject to the liabilities incurred by the spouse before or during marriage.

(d) All community property is subject to tortious liability of either spouse incurred during marriage.

(e) For purposes of this section, all retirement allowances, annuities, accumulated contributions, optional benefits, and money in the various public retirement system accounts of this state that are community property subject to the participating spouse's sole management, control, and disposition are not subject to any claim for payment of a criminal restitution judgment entered against the nonparticipant spouse except to the extent of the nonparticipant spouse's interest as determined in a qualified domestic relations order under Chapter 804, Government Code.

§ 3.203. Order in Which Property is Subject to Execution

(a) A judge may determine, as deemed just and equitable, the order in which particular separate or community property is subject to execution and sale to satisfy a judgment, if the property subject to liability for a judgment includes any combination of:

(1) a spouse's separate property;

(2) community property subject to a spouse's sole management, control, and disposition;

(3) community property subject to the other spouse's sole management, control, and disposition; and

(4) community property subject to the spouses' joint management, control, and disposition.

(b) In determining the order in which particular property is subject to execution and sale, the judge shall consider the facts surrounding the transaction or occurrence on which the suit is based.

SUBCHAPTER D. MANAGEMENT, CONTROL, AND DISPOSITION OF MARITAL PROPERTY UNDER UNUSUAL CIRCUMSTANCES

Introductory Comment

The sections in this subchapter deal with seldom-encountered situations in which an unimpaired spouse, not otherwise authorized to manage certain community property, may manage property if the other spouse has become unable to do so for one or more of the specified reasons. In each circumstance, the spouse may petition the court for control and management of the property. If a spouse is judicially declared to be incapacitated, the management of a community estate is governed by Tex. Probate Code §§ 883–884A, Incapacitated Spouse and Community Property. Amendments in 2001 deleted all references to incapacitated spouses in the Family Code, leaving the provisions in the Guardianship chapter of the Probate Code as the sole source of rules governing the management of community property in such fact situations.

---

§ 3.301. Missing, Abandoned, or Separated Spouse

(a) A spouse may file a sworn petition stating the facts that make it desirable for the petitioning spouse to manage, control, and dispose of community property described or defined in the petition that would otherwise be subject to the sole or joint management, control, and disposition of the other spouse if:

(1) the other spouse has disappeared and that spouse's location remains unknown to the petitioning spouse, unless the spouse is reported to be a prisoner of war or missing on public service;

(2) the other spouse has permanently abandoned the petitioning spouse; or

(3) the spouses are permanently separated.

(b) The petition may be filed in a court in the county in which the petitioner resided at the time the separation began, or the abandonment or disappearance occurred, not earlier than the 60th day after the date of the occurrence of the event. If both spouses are nonresidents of this state at the time the petition is filed, the petition may be filed in a court in a county in which any part of the described or defined community property is located.

§ 3.302. Spouse Missing on Public Service

(a) If a spouse is reported by an executive department of the United States to be a prisoner of war or missing on the public service of the United States, the spouse of the prisoner of war or missing person may file a sworn petition stating the facts that make it desirable for the petitioner to manage, control, and dispose of the community property described or defined in the petition that would otherwise be subject to the sole or joint management, control, and disposition of the imprisoned or missing spouse.

(b) The petition may be filed in a court in the county in which the petitioner resided at the time the report was made not earlier than six months after the date of the notice that a spouse is reported to be a prisoner of war or missing on public service. If both spouses were nonresidents of this state at the time the report was made, the petition shall be filed in a court in a county in which any part of the described or defined property is located.

§ 3.303. Appointment of Attorney

(a) Except as provided by Subsection (b), the court may appoint an attorney in a suit filed under this subchapter for the respondent.

(b) The court shall appoint an attorney in a suit filed under this subchapter for a respondent reported to be a prisoner of war or missing on public service.

(c) The court shall allow a reasonable fee for an appointed attorney's services as a part of the costs of the suit.

§ 3.304. Notice of Hearing; Citation

(a) Notice of the hearing, accompanied by a copy of the petition, shall be issued and served on the attorney representing the respondent, if an attorney has been appointed.

(b) If an attorney has not been appointed for the respondent, citation shall be issued and served on the respondent as in other civil cases.

§ 3.305. Citation by Publication

(a) If the residence of the respondent, other than a respondent reported to be a prisoner of war or missing on public service, is unknown, citation shall be published in a newspaper of general circulation published in the county in which the petition was filed. If that county has no newspaper of general circulation, citation shall be published in a newspaper of general circulation in an adjacent county or in the nearest county in which a newspaper of general circulation is published.

(b) The notice shall be published once a week for two consecutive weeks before the hearing, but the first notice may not be published after the 20th day before the date set for the hearing.

§ 3.306. Court Order for Management, Control, and Disposition of Community Property

(a) After hearing the evidence in a suit under this subchapter, the court, on terms the court considers just and equitable, shall render an order describing or defining the community property at issue that will be subject to the management, control, and disposition of each spouse during marriage.

(b) The court may:

(1) impose any condition and restriction the court deems necessary to protect the rights of the respondent;

(2) require a bond conditioned on the faithful administration of the property; and

(3) require payment to the registry of the court of all or a portion of the proceeds of the sale of the property, to be disbursed in accordance with the court's further directions.

§ 3.307. Continuing Jurisdiction of Court; Vacating Original Order

(a) The court has continuing jurisdiction over the court's order rendered under this subchapter.

(b) On the motion of either spouse, the court shall amend or vacate the original order after notice and hearing if:

(1) the spouse who disappeared reappears;

(2) the abandonment or permanent separation ends; or

(3) the spouse who was reported to be a prisoner of war or missing on public service returns.

§ 3.308. Recording Order to Affect Real Property

An order authorized by this subchapter affecting real property is not constructive notice to a good faith purchaser for value or to a creditor without actual notice unless the order is recorded in the deed records of the county in which the real property is located.

§ 3.309. Remedies Cumulative

The remedies provided in this subchapter are cumulative of other rights, powers, and remedies afforded spouses by law.

SUBCHAPTER E. CLAIMS FOR REIMBURSEMENT

Introductory Comment

The 2009 amendments were the most significant changes to Texas marital property law in the past ten years. Amendments to the Family Code in 1999 and 2001 ushered in the concept of economic contribution which attempted to address complications in applying the common law claims of reimbursement, as well as the perceived injustices in the then prevailing rules of its application. For example, if the community estate paid off the mortgage on a separate property residence, the claim for reimbursement would usually fail due to the separate estate's claims of offset for use and enjoyment of the property. *Hernandez v. Hernandez*, 703 S.W. 2d 250 (Tex. App.—Corpus Christi 1985, no writ). However, the bench and bar found application of the economic contribution rules to be complicated and expensive. There was continued confusion as to when to apply economic contribution principles and when to apply equitable reimbursement. Ultimately, the Family Law Council voted to seek repeal of the economic contribution statutes and return to equitable reimbursement as the measure to compensate the contributing estate when expending funds for a benefitted estate. It is to be hoped that the new provisions will bring clarity to this area of the law. The offset rule in *Hernandez, supra* is expressly rejected (§ 3.402 (c)) and the holding in *Anderson v. Gilliland*, 684 S.W.2d 673 (Tex.1985) regarding the measure of reimbursement as to improvements on real estate is codified in § 3.402 (d).

CLE/Other Legal Publications

Reimbursement. Joan F. Jenkins, 2011 Adv. Fam. L.

The new reimbursement statute: the return of common law? Brian L. Webb, 2010 Adv. Fam. L.

Equitable relief/reimbursement. Jonathan J. Bates, 2010 Marriage Dissolution

Reimbursement. Thomas P. Goranson, 2010 Fam. L. Front Lines

Economic contribution is gone: *What happens next*? A. Craig Haston, 2010 So. Tex. Fam. L. Conf.

Reimbursement revisited: The current status of the law and how to effectively make your claim; claims you can make against separate property companies, Jenson claims, alter ego, reverse piercing, representing the spouse who doesn't run the business. (Panel), 2009 Adv. Fam. L.

Economic contribution and reimbursement: where we are and where we are going. Jonathan J. Bates, 2009 U.T. Fam. L. Front Lines

Reimbursement and economic contribution. Warren Cole, 2008 Marriage Dissolution

Economic contribution for the lay person. Andrea Gerber, 2008 So. Tex. Fam. L. Conf.

See Accompanying CD-ROM for Additional CLE/Other Legal Publications

---

Leading Cases

Norton v. Norton, 2010 WL 2816212 (Tex. App.—Amarillo 2010, no pet.) (economic contribution calculation made by court of appeals to reform trial court award)

Bigelow v. Stephens, 286 S.W.3d 619 (Tex. App.—Beaumont 2009, no pet.)(§ 3.408(b) is a non-exhaustive list of potential reimbursement claims but does not limit the court's authority to find other bases for equitable reimbursement)

Rogers v. Foxworth, 214 S.W.3d 196 (Tex. App.—Tyler 2007, no pet.) (contributions of CP to WSP home require proof of increased equity to support economic contribution claim)

Raymond v. Raymond, 190 S.W.3d 77 (Tex. App.—Houston [1st Dist.] 2005, no pet.) (failure to plead economic contribution or prove reimbursement due precludes those claims)

Moroch v. Collins, 174 S.W.3d 849 (Tex. App.—Dallas 2005, pet. denied) (wife's separate property economic contribution exceeded FMV of community home—so she was awarded entire interest in valuable realty)

Garcia v. Garcia, 170 S.W.3d 644 (Tex. App.—El Paso 2005, no pet.) (trial court's award of both common law reimbursement and economic contribution supported by evidence)

---

§ 3.401. Definitions

In this subchapter:

(1) to (3) [Repealed by Acts 2009, 81st Leg., ch. 768, § 11(2).]

(4) "Marital estate" means one of three estates:

(A) the community property owned by the spouses together and referred to as the community marital estate;

(B) the separate property owned individually by the husband and referred to as a separate marital estate; or

(C) the separate property owned individually by the wife, also referred to as a separate marital estate.

(5) "Spouse" means a husband, who is a man, or a wife, who is a woman. A member of a civil union or similar relationship entered into in another state between persons of the same sex is not a spouse.

§ 3.402. Claim for Reimbursement; Offsets

(a) For purposes of this subchapter, a claim for reimbursement includes:

(1) payment by one marital estate of the unsecured liabilities of another marital estate;

(2) inadequate compensation for the time, toil, talent, and effort of a spouse by a business entity under the control and direction of that spouse;

(3) the reduction of the principal amount of a debt secured by a lien on property owned before marriage, to the extent the debt existed at the time of marriage;

(4) the reduction of the principal amount of a debt secured by a lien on property received by a spouse by gift, devise, or descent during a marriage, to the extent the debt existed at the time the property was received;

(5) the reduction of the principal amount of that part of a debt, including a home equity loan:

(A) incurred during a marriage;

(B) secured by a lien on property; and

(C) incurred for the acquisition of, or for capital improvements to, property;

(6) the reduction of the principal amount of that part of a debt:

(A) incurred during a marriage;

(B) secured by a lien on property owned by a spouse;

(C) for which the creditor agreed to look for repayment solely to the separate marital estate of the spouse on whose property the lien attached; and

(D) incurred for the acquisition of, or for capital improvements to, property;

(7) the refinancing of the principal amount described by Subdivisions (3)–(6), to the extent the refinancing reduces that principal amount in a manner described by the applicable subdivision;

(8) capital improvements to property other than by incurring debt; and

(9) the reduction by the community property estate of an unsecured debt incurred by the separate estate of one of the spouses.

(b) The court shall resolve a claim for reimbursement by using equitable principles, including the principle that claims for reimbursement may be offset against each other if the court determines it to be appropriate.

(c) Benefits for the use and enjoyment of property may be offset against a claim for reimbursement for expenditures to benefit a marital estate, except that the separate estate of a spouse may not claim an offset for use and enjoyment of a primary or secondary residence owned wholly or partly by the separate estate against contributions made by the community estate to the separate estate.

(d) Reimbursement for funds expended by a marital estate for improvements to another marital estate shall be measured by the enhancement in value to the benefited marital estate.

(e) The party seeking an offset to a claim for reimbursement has the burden of proof with respect to the offset.

§ 3.403. Repealed.

§ 3.404. Application of Inception of Title Rule; Ownership Interest Not Created

(a) This subchapter does not affect the rule of inception of title under which the character of property is determined at the time the right to own or claim the property arises.

(b) A claim for reimbursement under this subchapter does not create an ownership interest in property, but does create a claim against the property of the benefited estate by the contributing estate. The claim matures on dissolution of the marriage or the death of either spouse.

§ 3.405. Management Rights

This subchapter does not affect the right to manage, control, or dispose of marital property as provided by this chapter.

§ 3.406. Equitable Lien

(a) On dissolution of a marriage, the court may impose an equitable lien on the property of a benefited marital estate to secure a claim for reimbursement against that property by a contributing marital estate.

(b) On the death of a spouse, a court may, on application for a claim for reimbursement brought by the surviving spouse, the personal representative of the estate of the deceased spouse, or any other person interested in the estate, as defined by Section 3, Texas Probate Code, impose an equitable lien on the property of a benefited marital estate to secure a claim for reimbursement against that property by a contributing marital estate.

(c) Repealed by Acts 2009, 81st Leg., ch. 768, § 11(4).

§ 3.407. Repealed.

§ 3.408. Repealed.

§ 3.409. Nonreimbursable Claims

The court may not recognize a marital estate's claim for reimbursement for:

(1) the payment of child support, alimony, or spousal maintenance;
(2) the living expenses of a spouse or child of a spouse;
(3) contributions of property of a nominal value;
(4) the payment of a liability of a nominal amount; or
(5) a student loan owed by a spouse.

§ 3.410. Effect of Marital Property Agreements

A premarital or marital property agreement, whether executed before, on, or after September 1, 2009, that satisfies the requirements of Chapter 4 is effective to waive, release, assign, or partition a claim for economic contribution, reimbursement, or both, under this subchapter to the same extent the agreement would have been effective to waive, release, assign, or partition a claim for economic contribution, reimbursement, or both under the law as it existed immediately before September 1, 2009, unless the agreement provides otherwise.

CHAPTER 4. PREMARITAL AND MARITAL PROPERTY AGREEMENTS

SUBCHAPTER A. UNIFORM PREMARITAL AGREEMENT ACT

SUBCHAPTER B. MARITAL PROPERTY AGREEMENT

SUBCHAPTER C. AGREEMENT TO CONVERT SEPARATE PROPERTY TO COMMUNITY PROPERTY

SUBCHAPTER A. UNIFORM PREMARITAL AGREEMENT ACT

Introductory Comment

This subchapter adopts the Uniform Premarital Agreement Act promulgated by the National Conference of Commissioners on Uniform State Laws. The Act is in effect in twenty-three (23) jurisdictions as of the date of publication, to wit: Arizona, Arkansas, California, Connecticut, Delaware, District of Columbia, Florida, Idaho, Indiana, Kansas, Maine, Montana, Nebraska, Nevada, New Mexico, North Carolina, North Dakota, Oregon, Rhode Island, South Dakota, Texas, Utah and Virginia. The Official Commentary for the Uniform Act can be found on the accompanying CD.

www.nccusl.org/LegislativeFactSheet.aspx?title=Premarital Agreement Act

CLE/Other Legal Publications

Pre and post nuptials. Barbara D. Nunneley, 2011 ADV. FAM. L.

Pre and post-marital agreements. Katherine A. Kinser, 2011 MARRIAGE DISSOLUTION

Pre and post-nuptial agreements. Diana S. Friedman, 2010 ADV. FAM. L. DRAFTING

I don't want my fiancé or spouse to have my property. Alvin L. Zimmerman & Gary J. Zimmerman, 2010 SO. TEX. FAM. L. CONF.

Family law contracts: pre and post marital agreements; divorce decrees; AIDs; Application of transactional contract and related law; enforcement, breach, and contractual defenses. (Panel), 2009 ADV. FAM. L.

Pre-marital and post-marital agreements. Diana S. Friedman, 2009 MARRIAGE DISSOLUTION

Post-nuptial agreements and other partition and exchange agreements. Linda A. Hinds, Harry L. Tindall, & Nicole Wood, 2009 SO. TEX. FAM. LAW. CONF.

Pre and post nuptial agreements. Diana S. Friedman, 2008 ADV. FAM. L. DRAFTING

Premarital agreements and public policy concerns. Rebecca Tillery, 2008-2 (Summer) FAM. L. SECT. REP .

***See* Accompanying CD–ROM for Additional CLE/Other Legal Publications**

Leading Cases

Federal Courts

Manning v. Hayes, 212 F.3d 866 (5th Cir. 2000) (Tex.), *cert. denied*, 121 S.Ct. 1401 (2001) (employer provided life insurance benefits can not be waived by spouse in a premarital agreement)

Calmes v. United States, 926 F.Supp. 582 (N.D. Tex. 1996) (premarital agreement found not to be executed with intent to defraud I.R.S.)

Texas Supreme Court

Fanning v. Fanning, 847 S.W.2d 225 (Tex. 1993) (prenuptial agreement effective on passage of 1980 constitutional amendment—duress and unconscionability separate issues)

Beck v. Beck, 814 S.W.2d 745 (Tex. 1991), cert. denied, 117 L.Ed.2d 494, 112 S.Ct. 1266 (1992) (pre-1980 agreement impliedly validated by passage of constitutional amendment), *cert. denied*, 112 S.Ct. 1266 (1992)

Williams v. Williams, 569 S.W.2d 867 (Tex. 1978) (homestead rights may be waived in a premarital agreement)

Courts of Appeals

Jurek v. Couch- Jurek, 296 S.W.3d 864 (Tex. App.—El Paso 2009, no pet.) (where original or copy of signed premarital agreement could not be found, wife allowed to use extrinsic evidence to establish contents of the agreement, including a copy of her sister's agreement which mirrored hers)

Williams v. Williams, 246 S.W.3d 207 (Tex. App.—Houston [14th Dist.] 2007, no pet.) (clear language of premarital agreement does not include salary or wages—therefore they are community property)

Bufkin v. Bufkin, 259 S.W.3d 343 (Tex. App.—Dallas 2008, rev. denied) (evidence of fault properly excluded where parties had agreed to a specific division of the community estate in premarital agreement)

***See* Accompanying CD–ROM for Cases Linked to Westlaw and Additional Leading Cases**

Cross References

TX FCA CONST., art. 16, § 15. Separate and Community Property of Husband and Wife, *infra*.

TX FCA FAMILY § 1.108. Promise or Agreement Must Be in Writing, *supra*.

TEX. PROB. CODE ANN. § 59A. Contracts Concerning Succession, *infra*.

---

§ 4.001. Definitions

In this subchapter:

(1) "Premarital agreement" means an agreement between prospective spouses made in contemplation of marriage and to be effective on marriage.

(2) "Property" means an interest, present or future, legal or equitable, vested or contingent, in real or personal property, including income and earnings.

§ 4.002. Formalities

A premarital agreement must be in writing and signed by both parties. The agreement is enforceable without consideration.

Comment

Requiring the premarital agreement to be in writing and signed by the parties conforms to Tex. Const. art. 16, § 15 mandating a "written instrument." Note that consideration is explicitly *not required* in order for a premarital contract to be valid and enforceable.

§ 4.003. Content

(a) The parties to a premarital agreement may contract with respect to:

(1) the rights and obligations of each of the parties in any of the property of either or both of them whenever and wherever acquired or located;

(2) the right to buy, sell, use, transfer, exchange, abandon, lease, consume, expend, assign, create a security interest in, mortgage, encumber, dispose of, or otherwise manage and control property;

(3) the disposition of property on separation, marital dissolution, death, or the occurrence or nonoccurrence of any other event;

(4) the modification or elimination of spousal support;

(5) the making of a will, trust, or other arrangement to carry out the provisions of the agreement;

(6) the ownership rights in and disposition of the death benefit from a life insurance policy;

(7) the choice of law governing the construction of the agreement; and

(8) any other matter, including their personal rights and obligations, not in violation of public policy or a statute imposing a criminal penalty.

(b) The right of a child to support may not be adversely affected by a premarital agreement.

Comment

Subject to limits of public policy and criminal laws, this section allows parties to a premarital agreement the broadest possible freedom to arrange their marital property rights as they desire. The most important limitation is that child support may not be "adversely affected" by the premarital agreement.

§ 4.004. Effect of Marriage

A premarital agreement becomes effective on marriage.

Comment

A premarital agreement is not effective until marriage. An agreement not conditioned on marriage would need to comply with § 1.108, *supra,* which requires an agreement arising out of "nonmarital conjugal cohabitation" be in writing and signed by the party charged with the obligation.

§ 4.005. Amendment or Revocation

After marriage, a premarital agreement may be amended or revoked only by a written agreement signed by the parties. The amended agreement or the revocation is enforceable without consideration.

Comment

Tales abound of spouses "tearing up" the premarital agreement or "burning it" in the fireplace. Beware of such practices; this section requires that revocation must be in writing and signed by the parties. Moreover, attorneys who draft such an agreement typically retain a duplicate original.

§ 4.006. Enforcement

(a) A premarital agreement is not enforceable if the party against whom enforcement is requested proves that:

(1) the party did not sign the agreement voluntarily; or

(2) the agreement was unconscionable when it was signed and, before signing the agreement, that party:

(A) was not provided a fair and reasonable disclosure of the property or financial obligations of the other party;

(B) did not voluntarily and expressly waive, in writing, any right to disclosure of the property or financial obligations of the other party beyond the disclosure provided; and

(C) did not have, or reasonably could not have had, adequate knowledge of the property or financial obligations of the other party.

(b) An issue of unconscionability of a premarital agreement shall be decided by the court as a matter of law.

(c) The remedies and defenses in this section are the exclusive remedies or defenses, including common law remedies or defenses.

Comment

The burden of proof is placed on the party challenging the premarital agreement. Unless the agreement was involuntarily signed (usually very difficult to establish), the opponent must show the premarital agreement was unconscionable at the time of signing and that there was improper disclosure of the identity and extent of the other spouse's property. Unconscionability standing alone is not enough.

Subsection (c) overrules those cases suggesting other defenses to premarital agreements than those provided in the statutory text. *Fanning v. Fanning*, 847 S.W.2d 225 (Tex. 1993) speculated that duress and unconscionability were separate issues, and *Daniel v. Daniel*, 779 S.W.2d 110 (Tex. App.—Houston [1st Dist.] 1989, no writ) averred as how "common law defenses" were available in suits to enforce marital agreements.

§ 4.007. Enforcement: Void Marriage

If a marriage is determined to be void, an agreement that would otherwise have been a premarital agreement is enforceable only to the extent necessary to avoid an inequitable result.

Comment

This section is consistent with long-standing Texas law for putative spouses.

§ 4.008. Limitation of Actions

A statute of limitations applicable to an action asserting a claim for relief under a premarital agreement is tolled during the marriage of the parties to the agreement. However, equitable defenses limiting the time for enforcement, including laches and estoppel, are available to either party.

Comment

In order to avoid the potentially disruptive effect of compelling litigation between the spouses in order to escape the running of an applicable statute of limitations, this section tolls any applicable statute during the marriage of the parties.

---

§ 4.009. Application and Construction

This subchapter shall be applied and construed to effect its general purpose to make uniform the law with respect to the subject of this subchapter among states enacting these provisions.

§ 4.010. Short Title

This subchapter may be cited as the Uniform Premarital Agreement Act.

SUBCHAPTER B. MARITAL PROPERTY AGREEMENT

Introductory Comment

Until 1948, Texas residents had no method of changing the character of community property into separate property. By constitutional amendment that year, spouses were permitted to partition or exchange community property and thus convert community property into separate property. The original motivation was to lessen the impact of federal estate taxes (no longer a problem), but after 40 years this method of marital property planning is thoroughly engrafted in Texas jurisprudence.

In 1980, a constitutional amendment allowed Texas domiciliaries to agree that income from separate property would be separate property. This provision is now common in premarital agreements and postmarital agreements.

In 1999, Texas voters dropped the other shoe. By an overwhelming majority, conversion of separate property into community property was authorized by constitutional amendment; *see* §§ 4.201-.206, *infra*.

CLE/Other Legal Publication

See annotations to Subchapter A. Uniform Premarital Agreement Act, *supra*.

Leading Cases

Federal Case

In re Hinsley, 201 F.3d 638 (5th Cir. Tex. 2000) (partition agreement found to be invalid transfer of property as an attempt to impair rights of creditors)

Courts of Appeals

Izzo v. Izzo, 2010 WL 1930179 (Tex. App.—Austin 2010, pet. denied) (post-marital agreement set aside based upon husband's breach of fiduciary obligation to wife which led to agreement being unconscionable)

Moroch v. Collins, 174 S.W.3d 849 (Tex. App.—Dallas 2005, pet. denied) (postmarital partition of all assets into separate property except home of spouses did not affect economic contribution claim regarding that realty)

Sheshunoff v. Sheshunoff, 172 S.W.3d 686 (Tex. App.—Austin 2005, pet. denied) (husband "voluntarily signed" post-nuptial agreement to his great disadvantage)

In re Marriage of Smith, 115 S.W.3d 126 (Tex. App.—Texarkana 2003, pet. denied) (residuary clause in agreement covered pension; 1982 divorce suit never finalized, property division governed by "separation and partition agreement")

Nesmith v. Berger, 64 S.W.3d 110 (Tex. App.—Austin 2001, pet. denied) (couple's post-marital agreement maintained separate estates of both spouses; cash buy-out of wife's separate property share in jointly owned home was appropriate partition between co-tenants)

Byrnes v. Byrnes, 19 S.W.3d 556 (Tex. App.—Fort Worth 2000, no pet.) (agreement incident to divorce not considered a partition agreement unless specifically stated to be the same)

Cross References

TX FCA Const., Art. 16, § 15. Separate and Community Property of Husband and Wife, *infra*.
Tex. Prop. Code Ann. § 12.001. Instruments Concerning Property.

---

§ 4.101. Definition

In this subchapter, "property" has the meaning assigned by Section 4.001.

§ 4.102. Partition or Exchange of Community Property

At any time, the spouses may partition or exchange between themselves all or part of their community property, then existing or to be acquired, as the spouses may desire. Property or a property interest transferred to a spouse by a partition or exchange agreement becomes that spouse's separate property. The partition or exchange of property may also provide that future earnings and income arising from the transferred property shall be the separate property of the owning spouse.

Comment

An amendment in 2003 attempted to clarify an ambiguity by providing that partitioned community property included the future income from that property. Although that result is permitted by Tex. Const. art. XVI, § 15, it is not compelled, *i.e.*, "spouses also may from time to time, by written instrument, agree between themselves that the income . . . from all or part of the separate property then owned or which thereafter might be acquired by only one of them, shall be the separate property of that spouse . . . ." Several commentators argued that an automatic conversion of income from SP to CP is unconstitutional because "income from separate is community." Thus, in 2005, the statute was amended to allow for the agreement to reflect that a partition of may specifically state that the income and earnings of the transferred property are SP.

Therefore, agreements executed between September 1, 2003 and August 31, 2005 by statute implicitly include a partition of income from the transferred property, even if no specific partition was indicated. Agreements after September 1, 2005 must expressly address an intention to partition the income as well as the asset. Whether the question of the constitutionality of the 2003 amendment will ever be answered is wholly speculative.

Cross Reference

TX FCA Const., Art. 16, § 15. Separate and Community Property of Husband and Wife, *infra*.

---

§ 4.103. Agreement Between Spouses Concerning Income or Property From Separate Property

At any time, the spouses may agree that the income or property arising from the separate property that is then owned by one of them, or that may thereafter be acquired, shall be the separate property of the owner.

§ 4.104. Formalities

A partition or exchange agreement under Section 4.102 or an agreement under Section 4.103 must be in writing and signed by both parties. Either agreement is enforceable without consideration.

Comment

Marital agreements must be in writing and signed by the parties. This requirement is consistent with the mandate of Tex. Const., art. XVI, § 15 for a "written instrument." Additionally, as in the context of a premarital agreement, the lack of consideration does not affect enforcement.

§ 4.105. Enforcement

(a) A partition or exchange agreement is not enforceable if the party against whom enforcement is requested proves that:

(1) the party did not sign the agreement voluntarily; or

(2) the agreement was unconscionable when it was signed and, before execution of the agreement, that party:

(A) was not provided a fair and reasonable disclosure of the property or financial obligations of the other party;

(B) did not voluntarily and expressly waive, in writing, any right to disclosure of the property or financial obligations of the other party beyond the disclosure provided; and

(C) did not have, or reasonably could not have had, adequate knowledge of the property or financial obligations of the other party.

(b) An issue of unconscionability of a partition or exchange agreement shall be decided by the court as a matter of law.

(c) The remedies and defenses in this section are the exclusive remedies or defenses, including common law remedies or defenses.

Comment

The same standard of enforcement exists for a postmarital agreement as for a premarital agreement, § 4.006. See *Comment, supra*.

§ 4.106. Rights of Creditors and Recordation Under Partition or Exchange Agreement

(a) A provision of a partition or exchange agreement made under this subchapter is void with respect to the rights of a preexisting creditor whose rights are intended to be defrauded by it.

(b) A partition or exchange agreement made under this subchapter may be recorded in the deed records of the county in which a party resides and in the county in which the real property affected is located. An agreement made under this subchapter is constructive notice to a good faith purchaser for value or a creditor without actual notice only if the instrument is acknowledged and recorded in the county in which the real property is located.

Comment

Recordation of marital agreements is permitted, but not required, as a means of notice to third parties. In reality, very few agreements are recorded because of the privacy concerns of the parties.

SUBCHAPTER C. AGREEMENT TO CONVERT SEPARATE PROPERTY TO COMMUNITY PROPERTY

Introductory Comment

On January 1, 2000, voters approved a Texas Constitutional amendment authorizing the conversion of separate property to community property. This subchapter provides the legislative framework for such conversions, allowing spouses to add separate property into the community estate.

Any conversion of separate property into community property must be in writing and signed voluntarily by both spouses. Additionally, only existing property may be converted; spouses cannot, for example, agree that all future gifts and inheritances will be community property once received. Signing spouses must receive a fair and reasonable disclosure of the legal effect of the agreement, and while this disclosure may not be waived, the statute provides a suggested disclosure statement, which, if conspicuously included in the agreement, establishes a rebuttable presumption that the proper disclosure was made.

---

§ 4.201. Definition

In this subchapter, "property" has the meaning assigned by Section 4.001.

§ 4.202. Agreement to Convert to Community Property

At any time, spouses may agree that all or part of the separate property owned by either or both spouses is converted to community property.

§ 4.203. Formalities of Agreement

(a) An agreement to convert separate property to community property:

(1) must be in writing and:

(A) be signed by the spouses;

(B) identify the property being converted; and

(C) specify that the property is being converted to the spouses' community property; and

(2) is enforceable without consideration.

(b) The mere transfer of a spouse's separate property to the name of the other spouse or to the name of both spouses is not sufficient to convert the property to community property under this subchapter.

§ 4.204. Management of Converted Property

Except as specified in the agreement to convert the property and as provided by Subchapter B, Chapter 3, and other law, property converted to community property under this subchapter is subject to:

(1) the sole management, control, and disposition of the spouse in whose name the property is held;

(2) the sole management, control, and disposition of the spouse who transferred the property if the property is not subject to evidence of ownership;

(3) the joint management, control, and disposition of the spouses if the property is held in the name of both spouses; or

(4) the joint management, control, and disposition of the spouses if the property is not subject to evidence of ownership and was owned by both spouses before the property was converted to community property.

§ 4.205. Enforcement

(a) An agreement to convert property to community property under this subchapter is not enforceable if the spouse against whom enforcement is sought proves that the spouse did not:

(1) execute the agreement voluntarily; or

(2) receive a fair and reasonable disclosure of the legal effect of converting the property to community property.

(b) An agreement that contains the following statement, or substantially similar words, prominently displayed in bold-faced type, capital letters, or underlined, is rebuttably presumed to provide a fair and reasonable disclosure of the legal effect of converting property to community property:

"THIS INSTRUMENT CHANGES SEPARATE PROPERTY TO COMMUNITY PROPERTY. THIS MAY HAVE ADVERSE CONSEQUENCES DURING MARRIAGE AND ON TERMINATION OF THE MARRIAGE BY DEATH OR DIVORCE. FOR EXAMPLE:

"EXPOSURE TO CREDITORS. IF YOU SIGN THIS AGREEMENT, ALL OR PART OF THE SEPARATE PROPERTY BEING CONVERTED TO COMMUNITY PROPERTY MAY BECOME SUBJECT TO THE LIABILITIES OF YOUR SPOUSE. IF YOU DO NOT SIGN THIS AGREEMENT, YOUR SEPARATE PROPERTY IS GENERALLY NOT SUBJECT TO THE LIABILITIES OF YOUR SPOUSE UNLESS YOU ARE PERSONALLY LIABLE UNDER ANOTHER RULE OF LAW.

"LOSS OF MANAGEMENT RIGHTS. IF YOU SIGN THIS AGREEMENT, ALL OR PART OF THE SEPARATE PROPERTY BEING CONVERTED TO COMMUNITY PROPERTY MAY BECOME SUBJECT TO EITHER THE JOINT MANAGEMENT, CONTROL, AND DISPOSITION OF YOU AND YOUR SPOUSE OR THE SOLE MANAGEMENT, CONTROL, AND DISPOSITION OF YOUR SPOUSE ALONE. IN THAT EVENT, YOU WILL LOSE YOUR MANAGEMENT RIGHTS OVER THE PROPERTY. IF YOU DO NOT SIGN THIS AGREEMENT, YOU WILL GENERALLY RETAIN THOSE RIGHTS."

"LOSS OF PROPERTY OWNERSHIP. IF YOU SIGN THIS AGREEMENT AND YOUR MARRIAGE IS SUBSEQUENTLY TERMINATED BY THE DEATH OF EITHER SPOUSE OR BY DIVORCE, ALL OR PART OF THE SEPARATE PROPERTY BEING CONVERTED TO COMMUNITY PROPERTY MAY BECOME THE SOLE PROPERTY OF YOUR SPOUSE OR YOUR SPOUSE'S HEIRS. IF YOU DO NOT SIGN THIS AGREEMENT, YOU GENERALLY CANNOT BE DEPRIVED OF OWNERSHIP OF YOUR SEPARATE PROPERTY ON TERMINATION OF YOUR MARRIAGE, WHETHER BY DEATH OR DIVORCE."

(c) If a proceeding regarding enforcement of an agreement under this subchapter occurs after the death of the spouse against whom enforcement is sought, the proof required by Subsection (a) may be made by an heir of the spouse or the personal representative of the estate of that spouse.

§ 4.206. Rights of Creditors; Recording

(a) A conversion of separate property to community property does not affect the rights of a preexisting creditor of the spouse whose separate property is being converted.

(b) A conversion of separate property to community property may be recorded in the deed records of the county in which a spouse resides and of the county in which any real property is located.

(c) A conversion of real property from separate property to community property is constructive notice to a good faith purchaser for value or a creditor without actual notice only if the agreement to convert the property is acknowledged and recorded in the deed records of the county in which the real property is located.

CHAPTER 5. HOMESTEAD RIGHTS

SUBCHAPTER A. SALE OF HOMESTEAD; GENERAL RULE

SUBCHAPTER B. SALE OF HOMESTEAD UNDER UNUSUAL CIRCUMSTANCES

Introductory Comment

Until 1980, the sanctity of the homestead exemption was an eternal verity in Texas. Since then, there have been multiple amendments to TEX. CONST. art. XVI, §§ 50–51, *infra*. But the statutory formulations contained in this chapter have remained basically unchanged since the enactment of Title 1 of the Family Code in 1969. In 1997, after many years of discussion the Texas Constitution was amended to permit home equity loans and reverse mortgages on the homestead of an individual or family, see Tex. Const. Art. XVI, § 50, infra. Obviously this has been a very difficult concept to draft correctly. Every two years the legislature has gone back to the drawing board for further amendments to the constitution, the last being in 2005.

CLE/Other Legal Publication

Saying goodbye to Texas's homestead protection: one step toward economic efficiency with the Bankruptcy Abuse Prevention and Consumer Protection Act of 2005. Anthony C. Coveny, 44 HOUST. L. REV. 433 (2007)

Leading Cases

U.S. Supreme Court

Farrey v. Sanderfoot, 500 U.S. 291, 114 L.Ed.2d 337, 111 S.Ct. 1825 (1991) (ex-wife's judicial lien on homestead awarded to ex-husband on divorce not discharged by his bankruptcy)

Texas Supreme Court

Benchmark Bank v. Crowder, 919 S.W.2d 657 (Tex. 1996) (bank loan made to pay off tax lien, bank subrogated to IRS lien against homestead—wife entitled to compensation for loss of homestead)

Heggen v. Pemelton, 836 S.W.2d 145 (Tex. 1992) (equitable lien may be imposed on separate property homestead only to secure right of reimbursement for community improvements, not to insure just and right division of community property)

Laster v. First Huntsville Properties Co., 826 S.W.2d 125 (Tex. 1991) (ex-spouse could validly convey his interest in family homestead to third party—ex-wife lost homestead protection when child turned 18 by terms of decree)

Caulley v. Caulley, 806 S.W.2d 795 (Tex. 1991) (once homestead rights are shown to exist, they are presumed to continue, and anyone asserting abandonment has burden of proof)

Courts of Appeals

Borbon & Peniche v. Rodriguez, 2010 WL 2723167 (Tex. App.— Houston [1st Dist.] 2010, no pet.) (wife's challenge to lien against homestead as a result of divorce should have been by appeal or bill of review, not motion to clarify)

In re Garza, 153 S.W.3d 97 (Tex. App.—San Antonio 2004, no pet.) (divorce court's post-decree contingent award to husband of appellate attorney's fees impermissibly encumbers the exempt proceeds of wife's interest in homestead equity)

Lot 39, Section C, Northern Hills v. State, 85 S.W.3d 429 (Tex. App.—Eastland 2002, pet. denied) (homestead exemption inapplicable to forfeiture for criminal conduct on premises)

Duran v. Henderson, 71 S.W.3d 833 (Tex. App.—Texarkana 2002, pet. denied) (debtor, adult daughter and her son are "family" for purposes of homestead exemption)

Montague v. National Loan Investors, 70 S.W.3d 242 (Tex. App.—San Antonio 2002, pet. denied) (wife and husband's estate can claim ranch pledged as security as homestead—jury finding of no estoppel based on disclaimer to obtain loan prevails)

Skelton v. Washington Mut. Bank, F.A., 61 S.W.3d 56 (Tex. App.—Amarillo 2001, no pet.) (only husband signed vendor's lien for community homestead—after his death bank may foreclose notwithstanding absence of wife's signature on lien documents)

Cross References

TX FCA Const. Art. 16, § 50. Homestead; Protection from Forced Sale; Mortgages, Trust Deeds, and Liens, *infra*; TX FCA Const. Art. 16, § 51. Amount of Homestead; Uses, *infra*.

TX FCA Tex. Prop. Code ch. 41, Interests in Land, *infra*.

SUBCHAPTER A. SALE OF HOMESTEAD; GENERAL RULE

§ 5.001. Sale, Conveyance, or Encumbrance of Homestead

Whether the homestead is the separate property of either spouse or community property, neither spouse may sell, convey, or encumber the homestead without the joinder of the other spouse except as provided in this chapter or by other rules of law.

Comment

In 1997, after many years of discussion the Texas Constitution was amended to permit home equity loans and reverse mortgages on the homestead of an individual or family, see Tex. Const. Art. XVI, § 50, *infra*. Obviously this has been a very difficult concept to draft correctly. Every two years the legislature has gone back to the drawing board for further amendments to the constitution, the last being in 2005.

CLE/Other Legal Publication

Saying goodbye to Texas's homestead protection: one step toward economic efficiency with the Bankruptcy Abuse Prevention and Consumer Protection Act of 2005. Anthony C. Coveny, 44 Houst. L. Rev. 433 (2007).

Leading Cases

U.S. Supreme Court

Farrey v. Sanderfoot, 500 U.S. 291, 114 L.Ed.2d 337, 111 S.Ct. 1825 (1991) (ex-wife's judicial lien on homestead awarded to ex-husband on divorce not discharged by his bankruptcy)

Texas Supreme Court

Benchmark Bank v. Crowder, 919 S.W.2d 657 (Tex. 1996) (bank loan made to pay off tax lien, bank subrogated to IRS lien against homestead—wife entitled to compensation for loss of homestead)

Heggen v. Pemelton, 836 S.W.2d 145 (Tex. 1992) (equitable lien may be imposed on separate property homestead only to secure right of reimbursement for community improvements, not to insure just and right division of community property)

Laster v. First Huntsville Properties Co., 826 S.W.2d 125 (Tex. 1991) (ex-spouse could validly convey his interest in family homestead to third party—ex-wife lost homestead protection when child turned 18 by terms of decree)

Caulley v. Caulley, 806 S.W.2d 795 (Tex. 1991) (once homestead rights are shown to exist, they are presumed to continue, and anyone asserting abandonment has burden of proof)

Courts of Appeals

In re Garza, 153 S.W.3d 97 (Tex. App.—San Antonio 2004, no pet.) (divorce court's post-decree contingent award to husband of appellate attorney's fees impermissibly encumbers the exempt proceeds of wife's interest in homestead equity)

Lot 39, Section C, Northern Hills v. State, 85 S.W.3d 429 (Tex. App.—Eastland 2002, pet. denied) (homestead exemption inapplicable to forfeiture for criminal conduct on premises)

Duran v. Henderson, 71 S.W.3d 833 (Tex. App.—Texarkana 2002, pet. denied) (debtor, adult daughter and her son are "family" for purposes of homestead exemption)

Montague v. National Loan Investors, 70 S.W.3d 242 (Tex. App.—San Antonio 2002, pet. denied) (wife (and husband's estate) can claim ranch pledged as security as homestead—jury finding of no estoppel based on disclaimer to obtain loan prevails)

Skelton v. Washington Mut. Bank, F.A., 61 S.W.3d 56 (Tex. App.—Amarillo 2001, no pet.) (only husband signed vendor's lien for community homestead—after his death bank may foreclose notwithstanding absence of wife's signature on lien documents)

Cross References

TX FCA Const. Art. 16, § 50. Homestead; Protection from Forced Sale; Mortgages, Trust Deeds, and Liens, *infra*; TX FCA Const. Art. 16, § 51. Amount of Homestead; Uses, *infra*.

Tex. Prop. Code. ch. 41, *infra*.

§ 5.002. Sale of Separate Homestead After Spouse Judicially Declared Incapacitated

If the homestead is the separate property of a spouse and the other spouse has been judicially declared incapacitated by a court exercising original jurisdiction over guardianship and other matters under Chapter XIII, Texas Probate Code, the owner may sell, convey, or encumber the homestead without the joinder of the other spouse.

Comment

If a spouse has been declared incompetent by a court decree, the other spouse is authorized to act alone to deal with the homestead. Probably an implicit fiduciary duty to act fairly with regard to the interest of the incompetent spouse is presumed, but it is not explicitly stated.

§ 5.003. Sale of Community Homestead After Spouse Judicially Declared Incapacitated

If the homestead is the community property of the spouses and one spouse has been judicially declared incapacitated by a court exercising original jurisdiction over guardianship and other matters under Chapter XIII, Texas Probate Code, the competent spouse may sell, convey, or encumber the homestead without the joinder of the other spouse.

SUBCHAPTER B. SALE OF HOMESTEAD UNDER UNUSUAL CIRCUMSTANCES

Introductory Comment

The sections in this subchapter deal with unusual situations in which a spouse: (1) is incompetent; (2) has disappeared; (3) has abandoned the homestead; or (4) is missing on public service. These sections prescribe procedures for the sale of the homestead which vary depending on whether the property is separate or community. No cases have cited these sections since enactment in 1970.

---

§ 5.101. Sale of Separate Homestead Under Unusual Circumstances

If the homestead is the separate property of a spouse, that spouse may file a sworn petition that gives a description of the property, states the facts that make it desirable for the spouse to sell, convey, or encumber the homestead without the joinder of the other spouse, and alleges that the other spouse:

(1) has disappeared and that the location of the spouse remains unknown to the petitioning spouse;

(2) has permanently abandoned the homestead and the petitioning spouse;

(3) has permanently abandoned the homestead and the spouses are permanently separated; or

(4) has been reported by an executive department of the United States to be a prisoner of war or missing on public service of the United States.

§ 5.102. Sale of Community Homestead Under Unusual Circumstances

If the homestead is the community property of the spouses, one spouse may file a sworn petition that gives a description of the property, states the facts that make it desirable for the petitioning spouse to sell, convey, or encumber the homestead without the joinder of the other spouse, and alleges that the other spouse:

(1) has disappeared and that the location of the spouse remains unknown to the petitioning spouse;

(2) has permanently abandoned the homestead and the petitioning spouse;

(3) has permanently abandoned the homestead and the spouses are permanently separated; or

(4) has been reported by an executive department of the United States to be a prisoner of war or missing on public service of the United States.

§ 5.103. Time for Filing Petition

The petitioning spouse may file the petition in a court of the county in which any portion of the property is located not earlier than the 60th day after the date of the occurrence of an event described by Sections 5.101(1)–(3) and 5.102(1)–(3) or not less than six months after the date the other spouse has been reported to be a prisoner of war or missing on public service.

§ 5.104. Appointment of Attorney

(a) Except as provided by Subsection (b), the court may appoint an attorney in a suit filed under this subchapter for the respondent.

(b) The court shall appoint an attorney in a suit filed under this subchapter for a respondent reported to be a prisoner of war or missing on public service.

(c) The court shall allow a reasonable fee for the appointed attorney's services as a part of the costs of the suit.

§ 5.105. Citation; Notice of Hearing

Citation and notice of hearing for a suit filed as provided by this subchapter shall be issued and served in the manner provided in Subchapter D, Chapter 3.

§ 5.106. Court Order

(a) After notice and hearing, the court shall render an order the court deems just and equitable with respect to the sale, conveyance, or encumbrance of a separate property homestead.

(b) After hearing the evidence, the court, on terms the court deems just and equitable, shall render an order describing or defining the community property at issue that will be subject to the management, control, and disposition of each spouse during marriage.

(c) The court may:

(1) impose any conditions and restrictions the court deems necessary to protect the rights of the respondent;

(2) require a bond conditioned on the faithful administration of the property; and

(3) require payment to the registry of the court of all or a portion of the proceeds of the sale of the property to be disbursed in accordance with the court's further directions.

§ 5.107. Renumbered as V.T.C.A., Family Code § 5.003 by Acts 2001, 77th Leg., ch. 217, § 29, eff. Sept. 1, 2001

§ 5.108. Remedies and Powers Cumulative

The remedies and the powers of a spouse provided by this subchapter are cumulative of the other rights, powers, and remedies afforded the spouses by law.

SUBTITLE C. DISSOLUTION OF MARRIAGE

★★★

CHAPTER 6. SUIT FOR DISSOLUTION OF MARRIAGE

SUBCHAPTER A. GROUNDS FOR DIVORCE AND DEFENSES

SUBCHAPTER B. GROUNDS FOR ANNULMENT

SUBCHAPTER C. DECLARING A MARRIAGE VOID

SUBCHAPTER D. JURISDICTION, VENUE, AND RESIDENCE QUALIFICATIONS

SUBCHAPTER E. FILING SUIT

SUBCHAPTER F. TEMPORARY ORDERS

SUBCHAPTER G. ALTERNATIVE DISPUTE RESOLUTION

SUBCHAPTER H. TRIAL AND APPEAL

SUBCHAPTER I. REMARRIAGE

SUBCHAPTER A. GROUNDS FOR DIVORCE AND DEFENSES

Introductory Comment

The concept of no-fault divorce was introduced to Texas on January 1, 1970, with the introduction of insupportability as a grounds for divorce. This rather quickly became the basis for granting nearly all of the divorces in Texas. In the legislature, no fault divorce has elicited criticism from some social conservatives who have advocated for its repeal when there are children of the marriage. Legislation to this effect has been introduced in every session since 1997 but has yet to be enacted.

Fault grounds continue to exist in the Texas statutes. Cruelty and adultery are the most commonly asserted, most often as an alternative to insupportability and generally to serve as a basis for justifying an unequal division of property or strategically to assist in a dispute over the conservatorship of a child.

Leading Cases

Waite v. Waite, 150 S.W.3d 797 (Tex. App.—Houston [14th Dist.] 2004, pet. denied) (court's exercise of jurisdiction over divorce case did not violate husband's rights under First Amendment even though husband claims marriage was a purely ecclesiastical union); *see also* Waite v. Waite, 64 S.W.3d 217 (Tex. App.—Houston [14th Dist.] 2001, pet. denied) (no fault divorce held constitutional on several grounds)

---

§ 6.001. Insupportability

On the petition of either party to a marriage, the court may grant a divorce without regard to fault if the marriage has become insupportable because of discord or conflict of personalities that destroys the legitimate ends of the marital relationship and prevents any reasonable expectation of reconciliation.

§ 6.002. Cruelty

The court may grant a divorce in favor of one spouse if the other spouse is guilty of cruel treatment toward the complaining spouse of a nature that renders further living together insupportable.

§ 6.003. Adultery

The court may grant a divorce in favor of one spouse if the other spouse has committed adultery.

§ 6.004. Conviction of Felony

(a) The court may grant a divorce in favor of one spouse if during the marriage the other spouse:

(1) has been convicted of a felony;

(2) has been imprisoned for at least one year in the Texas Department of Criminal Justice, a federal penitentiary, or the penitentiary of another state; and

(3) has not been pardoned.

(b) The court may not grant a divorce under this section against a spouse who was convicted on the testimony of the other spouse.

§ 6.005. Abandonment

The court may grant a divorce in favor of one spouse if the other spouse:

(1) left the complaining spouse with the intention of abandonment; and

(2) remained away for at least one year.

§ 6.006. Living Apart

The court may grant a divorce in favor of either spouse if the spouses have lived apart without cohabitation for at least three years.

§ 6.007. Confinement in Mental Hospital

The court may grant a divorce in favor of one spouse if at the time the suit is filed:

(1) the other spouse has been confined in a state mental hospital or private mental hospital, as defined in Section 571.003, Health and Safety Code, in this state or another state for at least three years; and

(2) it appears that the hospitalized spouse's mental disorder is of such a degree and nature that adjustment is unlikely or that, if adjustment occurs, a relapse is probable.

Leading Case

Saldarriaga v. Saldarriaga, 121 S.W.3d 493 (Tex. App.—Austin 2003, no pet.) (allegedly incompetent spouse entitled to guardian in Probate Court, not just next friend in divorce court)

§ 6.008. Defenses

(a) The defenses to a suit for divorce of recrimination and adultery are abolished.

(b) Condonation is a defense to a suit for divorce only if the court finds that there is a reasonable expectation of reconciliation.

Comment

This section has little relevance in the 21st century. Recrimination and condonation as defenses to a suit for divorce were vestiges of family law as it existed before the official implementation of "no fault" divorce on January 1, 1970, the effective date of Title 1, Tex. Fam. Code Ann. The defense of adultery precluded one party from alleging adultery against his or her spouse if that party was also guilty of adultery.

SUBCHAPTER B. GROUNDS FOR ANNULMENT

Introductory Comment

Sections 6.102–.104 provide very limited standing for an aggrieved parent to seek an annulment of the marriage of his or her underage child. Sections 6.105–.109 all relate to alleged defects in the voluntary consent to the marriage, including intoxication, impotence, fraud, duress, or force, mental incapacity, and a concealed divorce. Each expires when the ability to consent is restored. Fraud likely remains the most common ground used for an annulment, with the alleged fraud being a part of the inducement for marriage in the first place. Section 6.110 provides for a short window to annul a marriage based upon not waiting the requisite 72-hours after receiving a marriage license and section 6.111 applies common sense to end the possibility of annulment on the death of a spouse.

Leading Cases

Villarreal v. Villarreal, 2010 WL 2854250 (Tex. App.—Beaumont 2010, no pet.) (when established that wife married husband for Green card, annulment granted based upon fraud in the inducement and property transfers to wife set aside)

Leax v. Leax, 305 S.W.3d 22 (Tex. App.—Houston 2009, pet. denied) (annulment granted on basis of fraud when wife failed to disclose eight prior marriages)

Shahani v. Said, 2009 WL 1693066 (Tex. App.—Corpus Christi 2009, pet. filed) (personal jurisdiction over non-resident Respondent not required to terminate marriage by annulment but is required to divide property)

§ 6.101. Repealed.

§ 6.102. Annulment of Marriage of Person Under Age 18

(a) The court may grant an annulment of a marriage of a person 16 years of age or older but under 18 years of age that occurred without parental consent or without a court order as provided by Subchapters B and E, Chapter 2.

(b) A petition for annulment under this section may be filed by:

(1) a next friend for the benefit of the underage party;

(2) a parent; or

(3) the judicially designated managing conservator or guardian of the person of the underage party, whether an individual, authorized agency, or court.

(c) A suit filed under this subsection by a next friend is barred unless it is filed within 90 days after the date of the marriage.

Cross References

TX FCA Family § 2.004. Application Form, *supra*; TX FCA Family § 2.005. Proof of Identity and Age, *supra*; TX FCA Family § 2.009. Issuance of License, *supra*; TX FCA Family § 2.102. Parental Consent for Underage Applicant, *supra*; TX FCA Family § 2.103. Court Order for Underage Applicant, *supra*; TX FCA Family § 6.205. Marriage to Minor, *infra*; TX FCA Family § 6.206. Marriage to Stepchild or Stepparent, *infra*; TX FCA Penal § 25.01. Bigamy, *infra*; TX FCA Penal § 25.02. Prohibited Sexual Conduct, *infra*.

§ 6.103. Underage Annulment Barred by Adulthood

A suit to annul a marriage may not be filed under Section 6.102 by a parent, managing conservator, or guardian of a person after the 18th birthday of the person.

§ 6.104. Discretionary Annulment of Underage Marriage

(a) An annulment under Section 6.102 of a marriage may be granted at the discretion of the court sitting without a jury.

(b) In exercising its discretion, the court shall consider the pertinent facts concerning the welfare of the parties to the marriage, including whether the female is pregnant.

§ 6.105. Under Influence of Alcohol or Narcotics

The court may grant an annulment of a marriage to a party to the marriage if:

(1) at the time of the marriage the petitioner was under the influence of alcoholic beverages or narcotics and as a result did not have the capacity to consent to the marriage; and

(2) the petitioner has not voluntarily cohabited with the other party to the marriage since the effects of the alcoholic beverages or narcotics ended.

§ 6.106. Impotency

The court may grant an annulment of a marriage to a party to the marriage if:

(1) either party, for physical or mental reasons, was permanently impotent at the time of the marriage;

(2) the petitioner did not know of the impotency at the time of the marriage; and

(3) the petitioner has not voluntarily cohabited with the other party since learning of the impotency.

§ 6.107. Fraud, Duress, or Force

The court may grant an annulment of a marriage to a party to the marriage if:

(1) the other party used fraud, duress, or force to induce the petitioner to enter into the marriage; and

(2) the petitioner has not voluntarily cohabited with the other party since learning of the fraud or since being released from the duress or force.

§ 6.108. Mental Incapacity

(a) The court may grant an annulment of a marriage to a party to the marriage on the suit of the party or the party's guardian or next friend, if the court finds it to be in the party's best interest to be represented by a guardian or next friend, if:

(1) at the time of the marriage the petitioner did not have the mental capacity to consent to marriage or to understand the nature of the marriage ceremony because of a mental disease or defect; and

(2) since the marriage ceremony, the petitioner has not voluntarily cohabited with the other party during a period when the petitioner possessed the mental capacity to recognize the marriage relationship.

(b) The court may grant an annulment of a marriage to a party to the marriage if:

(1) at the time of the marriage the other party did not have the mental capacity to consent to marriage or to understand the nature of the marriage ceremony because of a mental disease or defect;

(2) at the time of the marriage the petitioner neither knew nor reasonably should have known of the mental disease or defect; and

(3) since the date the petitioner discovered or reasonably should have discovered the mental disease or defect, the petitioner has not voluntarily cohabited with the other party.

§ 6.109. Concealed Divorce

(a) The court may grant an annulment of a marriage to a party to the marriage if:

(1) the other party was divorced from a third party within the 30-day period preceding the date of the marriage ceremony;

(2) at the time of the marriage ceremony the petitioner did not know, and a reasonably prudent person would not have known, of the divorce; and

(3) since the petitioner discovered or a reasonably prudent person would have discovered the fact of the divorce, the petitioner has not voluntarily cohabited with the other party.

(b) A suit may not be brought under this section after the first anniversary of the date of the marriage.

§ 6.110. Marriage Less Than 72 Hours After Issuance of License

(a) The court may grant an annulment of a marriage to a party to the marriage if the marriage ceremony took place in violation of Section 2.204 during the 72-hour period immediately following the issuance of the marriage license.

(b) A suit may not be brought under this section after the 30th day after the date of the marriage.

§ 6.111. Death of Party to Voidable Marriage

Except as provided by Section 47A, Texas Probate Code, a marriage subject to annulment may not be challenged in a proceeding instituted after the death of either party to the marriage.

SUBCHAPTER C. DECLARING A MARRIAGE VOID

§ 6.201. Consanguinity

A marriage is void if one party to the marriage is related to the other as:

(1) an ancestor or descendant, by blood or adoption;

(2) a brother or sister, of the whole or half blood or by adoption;

(3) a parent's brother or sister, of the whole or half blood or by adoption; or

(4) a son or daughter of a brother or sister, of the whole or half blood or by adoption.

Comment

Based on reports that a polygamist cult had moved to Texas and that children were being married off at an early age, sometimes to close family members, in 2005 the Texas Legislature enacted new restrictions on who someone may marry. The prohibition on marriage of first cousins is new to Texas law. According to the National Conference of State Legislatures, 31 states (now including Texas) prohibit or restrict marriage of first cousins, while 19 states allow the practice. The prohibition on marriage to a stepchild or stepparent, including a former stepparent or stepchild, reflects a policy to protect traditional family relationships, even if there is no genetic relationship. Apparently an oversight, this section does not list a marriage of first cousins as prohibited by consanguinity; this is inconsistent with the 2005 marriage restrictions found in Chapter 2 of this Code. The prohibition of marriages between step-relatives is undoubtedly based on a similar rationale. *See comment* to § 6.101, *supra*.

Cross References

TX FCA Family § 2.004. Application Form, *supra*; TX FCA Family § 2.005. Proof of Identity and Age, *supra*; TX FCA Family § 2.009. Issuance of License, *supra*; TX FCA Penal § 25.01. Bigamy, *supra*; TX FCA Penal § 25.02. Prohibited Sexual Conduct, *infra*.

---

§ 6.202. Marriage During Existence of Prior Marriage

(a) A marriage is void if entered into when either party has an existing marriage to another person that has not been dissolved by legal action or terminated by the death of the other spouse.

(b) The later marriage that is void under this section becomes valid when the prior marriage is dissolved if, after the date of the dissolution, the parties have lived together as husband and wife and represented themselves to others as being married.

Leading Case

Cardwell v. Cardwell, 195 S.W.3d 856 (Tex. App.—Dallas 2006, no pet.) (no putative marriage without good faith belief in single status)

Cross Reference

TX FCA Penal § 25.01. Bigamy, *infra*.

---

§ 6.203. Certain Void Marriages Validated

Except for a marriage that would have been void under Section 6.201, a marriage that was entered into before January 1, 1970, in violation of the prohibitions of Article 496, Penal Code of Texas, 1925, is validated from the date the marriage commenced if the parties continued until January 1, 1970, to live together as husband and wife and to represent themselves to others as being married.

§ 6.204. Recognition of Same–Sex Marriage or Civil Union

(a) In this section, "civil union" means any relationship status other than marriage that:

(1) is intended as an alternative to marriage or applies primarily to cohabitating persons; and

(2) grants to the parties of the relationship legal protections, benefits, or responsibilities granted to the spouses of a marriage.

(b) A marriage between persons of the same sex or a civil union is contrary to the public policy of this state and is void in this state.

(c) The state or an agency or political subdivision of the state may not give effect to a:

(1) public act, record, or judicial proceeding that creates, recognizes, or validates a marriage between persons of the same sex or a civil union in this state or in any other jurisdiction; or

(2) right or claim to any legal protection, benefit, or responsibility asserted as a result of a marriage between persons of the same sex or a civil union in this state or in any other jurisdiction.

Editors' Note: *S.B. 7, 78th Legis., Reg. Sess. (2003) amended Subchapter C by adding Section 6.204, and contains the following uncodified provision:*

The legislature finds that through the designation of guardians, the appointment of agents, and the use of private contracts persons may adequately and properly appoint guardians and arrange rights relating to hospital visitation, property, and the entitlement to proceeds of life insurance policies without the existence of any legally recognized familial relationship between the persons.

Comment

With the enactment of this section, Texas joins approximately 40 other states that forbid recognition of same-sex marriages or civil unions in accordance with the Defense of Marriage Act, 28 U.S.C.A. § 1738c, *infra.*

On Nov. 8, 2005, Texas voters overwhelmingly passed H.J.R. 6 (76% to 24%), a constitutional amendment providing that "marriage in this state consists of the union of one man and one woman." The amendment also forbids creation or recognition of "any legal status identical or similar to marriage." Tex. Const. art. I, § 32 [no caption], *infra.*

CLE/Other Legal Publications

Modern family: headlines in same-sex cases. Amy C. Wright, 2011 U.T. Fam. L. Front Lines

Litigating family law outside the Family Code: dividing the assets of unmarried parties. Sallee S. Smyth, 2009 Adv. Fam. L.

21st century issues dealing with nontraditional relationships: dividing property between unmarried persons. Luke Gunnstaks, 2007 Adv. Fam. L.

21st century issues dealing with nontraditional relationships and seeking relief in nontraditional ways. Heather L. King, 2006 Adv. Fam. L.

See Accompanying CD–ROM for Additional CLE/Other Legal Publications

---

Leading Case

In re Marriage of J.B. and H.B., 326 S.W.3d 654 (Tex. App.—Dallas August 31, 2010, pet. granted) (trial court has no subject matter jurisdiction to hear divorce of same sex individuals; statute prohibiting recognition of same sex marriage not unconstitutional)

Cross Reference

TX FCA Family § 2.001, Marriage License, *supra*; TX FCA Family § 2.401, Proof of Informal Marriage, *supra*.

Defense of Marriage Act, TX FCA 28 USCA § 1738C, *infra*.

§ 6.205. Marriage to Minor

A marriage is void if either party to the marriage is younger than 16 years of age, unless a court order has been obtained under Section 2.103.

Comment to §§ 6.205 and 6.206

Based on reports that a polygamist cult had moved to Texas and that children were being married off at an early age, sometimes to close family members, the Legislature enacted new restrictions on who someone may marry and raised the age of parental consent for marriage from 14 to 16.

The apparently absolute prohibition of marriages under 16 is inconsistent with both §§ 2.103 and 6.101, which create an exception to the absolute ban if a court order authorizes a marriage of a child under 16. Since the applicable rule of statutory construction is the specific controls the general, the exception would prevail if the issue ever arises in a case, which seems very improbable.

Cross References

TX FCA Family § 2.004. Application Form, *supra*; TX FCA Family § 2.005. Proof of Identity and Age, *supra*; TX FCA Family § 2.009. Issuance of License, *supra*; TX FCA Family § 2.102. Parental Consent for Underage Applicant, *supra*; TX FCA Family § 2.103. Court Order for Underage Applicant, *supra*.

TX FCA Penal § 25.01. Bigamy, *infra*; TX FCA Penal § 25.02. Prohibited Sexual Conduct, *infra*.

§ 6.206. Marriage to Stepchild or Stepparent

A marriage is void if a party is a current or former stepchild or stepparent of the other party.

SUBCHAPTER D. JURISDICTION, VENUE, AND RESIDENCE QUALIFICATIONS

Introductory Comment

In order to maintain an action for divorce, all states, including Texas, have traditionally imposed durational state domiciliary and county residency requirements; six months and one year are most typical. However, historically some states have enacted very short durational residency requirements designed to encourage interstate forum shopping by litigants, e.g., six weeks in Nevada. To counter the image of being a "divorce mill," most states have clearly constitutional laws regarding durational residency. *Sosna v. Iowa,* 419 U.S. 394 (1975). The county durational residency requirement is appropriate because of the size of Texas.

Section 6.302 provides that a nonresident petitioner may bring suit in a respondent's county of residence if the respondent has been domiciled in Texas for six months without regard to how long the respondent has lived in the county. Time a Texan serves outside of the state for military service or other service of the United States or this state, whether their own or their spouses, is considered residence in this state and of their county of residence. Similarly, those in Texas because of service in the armed forces, whether their own or their spouses, may maintain a suit of divorce in Texas if the required domiciliary and residence are met. See §§ 6.303, 6.304, *supra*.

In some divorce suits involving two Texans, the petitioner has a choice of venue if the parties have separated; the action may be filed in the county of residence of either party so long as the durational county residency of 90 days is met.

A Texas court may grant a divorce to a Texas resident even if there is no personal jurisdiction over a non-resident spouse. This "status adjudication" terminates the marriage only and may not provide wholly adequate relief for the Texas spouse, however in the absence of personal jurisdiction over the other spouse. Section 6.305 provides for "long-arm" jurisdiction over the nonresident spouse as long as the parties had lived in Texas as their last marital residence within the last two years, or as long as there is any other basis under the state and federal constitution for exercising jurisdiction. Without this personal jurisdiction, the Texas divorce court is not authorized to render any orders that would require such jurisdiction, including payments of spousal maintenance, attorneys fees, or division of marital property.

CLE/Other Legal Publications

Venue, standing and jurisdiction. Stephen J. Naylor, 2011 MARRIAGE DISSOLUTION

Jurisdiction and standing. Angela Pence England & Harry L. Tindall, 2011 SO. TEX. FAM. L.

Jurisdiction and venue. JoAl Cannon Sheridan, 2010 ADV. FAM. L. DRAFTING

When is a residence really a residence? Jonathan J. Bates, 2010 ADV. FAM. L.

Cases involving foreign nationals. Larry H. Schwartz, 2010 ADV. FAM. L.

Follow the yellow brick road: jurisdiction and venue issues. JoAl Cannon Sheridan, 2010 MARRIAGE DISSOLUTION

Jurisdiction and venue. Brad M. LaMorgese, 2009 MARRIAGE DISSOLUTION

Competing jurisdictions. Jim Loveless, 2008 ADV. FAM. L.

County Courts at Law: What are the limits of their jurisdiction over divorces? John H. Chase, 2008-1 FAM. L. SECT. RPT.

***See* Accompanying CD–ROM for Additional CLE/Other Legal Publications**

Leading U.S. Supreme Court Cases

Burnham v. Superior Court of California, 495 U.S. 604, 109 L.Ed.2d 631, 110 S.Ct. 2105 (1990) (in personam jurisdiction obtained by service of citation in forum state on transient respondent)

Vanderbilt v. Vanderbilt, 354 U.S. 416, 1 L.Ed.2d 1456, 77 S.Ct. 1360 (1957) (Nevada court has jurisdiction to grant divorce but did not have jurisdiction to extinguish wife's right to support from her husband as provided by New York law)

Estin v. Estin, 334 U.S. 541, 92 L.Ed. 1561, 68 S.Ct. 1213 (1948) (service by publication sufficient to satisfy procedural due process for granting of divorce only)

Williams v. North Carolina, 325 U.S. 226, 89 L.Ed. 1577, 65 S.Ct. 1092 (1945) (North Carolina court not required to recognize Nevada divorce where Nevada lacked jurisdiction)

Williams v. North Carolina, 317 U.S. 287, 87 L.Ed. 279, 63 S.Ct. 207 (1942) (domicile of a spouse is a sufficient basis for divorce jurisdiction)

Leading Texas Cases

Alfonso v. Skadden, 251 S.W.3d 52 (Tex. 2008) (no time limitation for collateral attack based on lack of subject matter jurisdiction)

Dawson–Austin v. Austin, 968 S.W.2d 319 (Tex. 1998) (nonresident wife made valid special appearance—no minimum contacts, so no jurisdiction to divide marital estate)

Mitchim v. Mitchim, 518 S.W.2d 362 (Tex. 1975) (Arizona assertion of long-arm jurisdiction over Texas resident entitled to Full Faith and Credit)

Griffith v. Griffith, ___ S.W.3d ___, 2011 WL 17382 (Tex. App.—San Antonio 2011, no pet.) (husband had significant contacts with Texas to justify personal jurisdiction for divorce as he had lived there, purchased property there, borrowed money there, and had assisted wife on her ranch there)

Lai v. Wah, 2009 WL 2152565 (Tex. App.—Dallas 2009, no pet.) (no abuse of discretion by court in dismissing divorce suit after finding that neither party met the residency requirements)

Church v. Quick, 2009 WL 2013799 (Tex. App.—Houston 2009, no pet.) (terms of default decree that went beyond granting the divorce were impermissible in light of trial court's finding that it did not have personal jurisdiction over non-resident wife)

Shahani v. Said, 2009 WL 1693066 (Tex. App.—Corpus Christi 2009, pet. filed) (personal jurisdiction over non-resident Respondent not required to terminate marriage by annulment but is required to divide property)

Stallworth v. Stallworth, 201 S.W.3d 338 (Tex. App.—Dallas 2006, no pet.) (citation served on nonresident wife/mother provides Texas with divorce jurisdiction)

Seung Ok Lee v. Ki Pong Na, 198 S.W.3d 492 (Tex. App.—Dallas 2006, no pet.) (whether Korean nationals are married properly presented to Texas court—*forum non conveniens* not proven)

McAlister v. McAlister, 75 S.W.3d 481 (Tex. App.—San Antonio 2002, pet. denied) (first-filed divorce by wife in her dual residence county has dominant jurisdiction over husband's later suit)

***See* Accompanying CD–ROM for Cases Linked to Westlaw and Additional Leading Cases**

Cross References

TX FCA FAMILY § 102.011, Acquiring Jurisdiction Over Nonresident, *infra*; TX FCA FAMILY § 102.012, Exercising Partial Jurisdiction, *infra*; ch. 152, subch. C. Jurisdiction, *infra*, TX FCA FAMILY §§ 152.201 *et seq.* [Uniform Child Custody Jurisdiction and Enforcement Act], *infra*; ch. 159, subch. C. Jurisdiction, *infra*, TX FCA FAMILY §§ 159.201 *et seq.* [Uniform Interstate Family Support Act], *infra*; TX FCA FAMILY § 160.604, Personal Jurisdiction [Uniform Parentage Act], *infra*.

---

§ 6.301. General Residency Rule for Divorce Suit

6 mos State
3 mos County

A suit for divorce may not be maintained in this state unless at the time the suit is filed either the petitioner or the respondent has been:

(1) a domiciliary of this state for the preceding six-month period; and

(2) a resident of the county in which the suit is filed for the preceding 90-day period.

§ 6.302. Suit for Divorce by Nonresident Spouse

If one spouse has been a domiciliary of this state for at least the last six months, a spouse domiciled in another state or nation may file a suit for divorce in the county in which the domiciliary spouse resides at the time the petition is filed.

§ 6.303. Absence on Public Service

Time spent by a Texas domiciliary outside this state or outside the county of residence of the domiciliary while in the service of the armed forces or other service of the United States or of this state**, or while accompanying the domiciliary's spouse in the spouse's service of the armed forces or other service of the United States or of this state,** is considered residence in this state and in that county.

Amended by Acts 2011, 82nd Leg., ch. 436 (S.B. 1159), § 1, eff. June 17, 2011.

Cross Reference

Servicemembers Civil Relief Act of 2004, 50 App. U.S.C. 501 *et seq.*, *infra*.

---

§ 6.304. Armed Forces Personnel Not Previously Residents

A person not previously a resident of this state who is serving in the armed forces of the United States and has been stationed at one or more military installations in this state for at least the last six months and at a military installation in a county of this state for at least the last 90 days**, or who is accompanying the person's spouse during the spouse's military service in those locations and for those periods,** is considered to be a Texas domiciliary and a resident of that county for those periods for the purpose of filing suit for dissolution of a marriage.

Amended by Acts 2011, 82nd Leg., ch. 436 (S.B. 1159), § 1, eff. June 17, 2011.

CLE/Other Legal Publications

Special problems for military families. Hon. David D. Farr, 2011 Adv. Fam. L.

Military issues. Hon. David D. Farr, 2010 Adv. Fam. L. Drafting

Primer: the military. James N. Higdon, 2010 Fam. L. Front Lines

Drafting issues for military families and spouses. James N. Higdon, 2008 Adv. Fam. L. Drafting

Military retirement & military divorce—things the practitioner should be aware of. James N. Higdon, 2008 Adv. Fam. L.

Military issues. Hon. David D. Farr, 2008 So. Tex. Fam. L. Conf.

When parents go to war. James N. Higdon, 2007 Adv. Fam. L.

***See* Accompanying CD–ROM for Additional CLE/Other Legal Publications**

Cross Reference

Servicemembers Civil Relief Act of 2004, 50 App. U.S.C. 501 *et seq.*, *infra*.

§ 6.305. Acquiring Jurisdiction Over Nonresident Respondent

(a) If the petitioner in a suit for dissolution of a marriage is a resident or a domiciliary of this state at the time the suit for dissolution is filed, the court may exercise personal jurisdiction over the respondent or over the respondent's personal representative although the respondent is not a resident of this state if:

(1) this state is the last marital residence of the petitioner and the respondent and the suit is filed before the second anniversary of the date on which marital residence ended; or

(2) there is any basis consistent with the constitutions of this state and the United States for the exercise of the personal jurisdiction.

(b) A court acquiring jurisdiction under this section also acquires jurisdiction over the respondent in a suit affecting the parent-child relationship.

§ 6.306. Jurisdiction to Annul Marriage

(a) A suit for annulment of a marriage may be maintained in this state only if the parties were married in this state or if either party is domiciled in this state.

(b) A suit for annulment is a suit in rem, affecting the status of the parties to the marriage.

Comment

A suit for an annulment or an action to declare a marriage void, § 6.307, *infra*, is declared to be an in rem proceeding dissolving the marriage without further elaboration. The statute states that suit may be maintained in Texas only if the marriage took place in this state or if one of the parties is domiciled in this state. Importantly, there are no prescribed periods of durational residency or a requirement of domicile such as those established in § 6.301 for maintaining a divorce. Rather obviously, the statute has a potential for unconstitutional application if literally applied under certain fact circumstances. For example, suppose that an out-of-state couple marries while on vacation on South Padre Island and returns forthwith to their home state where they reside for a number of years.

If one of the spouses returns to Texas for an annulment, it seems rather clear that a decree of annulment granted by a Texas court will exceed the bounds of constitutional due process. This conclusion is purely speculative; apparently no one has attempted this particular course of action—at least no one with a reported case.

There is a common misconception that once a marriage is annulled, it is considered to have never existed. Texas law clearly holds to the contrary. Property acquired and children born during an annulled marriage receive the same treatment as if the marriage is dissolved by divorce.

§ 6.307. Jurisdiction to Declare Marriage Void

(a) Either party to a marriage made void by this chapter may sue to have the marriage declared void, or the court may declare the marriage void in a collateral proceeding.

(b) The court may declare a marriage void only if:

(1) the purported marriage was contracted in this state; or

(2) either party is domiciled in this state.

(c) A suit to have a marriage declared void is a suit in rem, affecting the status of the parties to the purported marriage.

Comment

A void marriage can be attacked in a collateral proceeding. Such a procedure is not permitted for an attack on a voidable marriage, which may be dissolved by annulment (or divorce).

§ 6.308. Exercising Partial Jurisdiction

(a) A court in which a suit for dissolution of a marriage is filed may exercise its jurisdiction over those portions of the suit for which it has authority.

(b) The court's authority to resolve the issues in controversy between the parties may be restricted because the court lacks:

(1) the required personal jurisdiction over a nonresident party in a suit for dissolution of the marriage;

(2) the required jurisdiction under Chapter 152; or

(3) the required jurisdiction under Chapter 159.

SUBCHAPTER E. FILING SUIT

§ 6.401. Caption

(a) Pleadings in a suit for divorce or annulment shall be styled "In the Matter of the Marriage of ________ and ________."

(b) Pleadings in a suit to declare a marriage void shall be styled "A Suit To Declare Void the Marriage of ________ and ________."

§ 6.402. Pleadings

(a) A petition in a suit for dissolution of a marriage is sufficient without the necessity of specifying the underlying evidentiary facts if the petition alleges the grounds relied on substantially in the language of the statute.

(b) Allegations of grounds for relief, matters of defense, or facts relied on for a temporary order that are stated in short and plain terms are not subject to special exceptions because of form or sufficiency.

(c) The court shall strike an allegation of evidentiary fact from the pleadings on the motion of a party or on the court's own motion.

Comment

This section was designed to purge divorce pleadings of detailed, often inflammatory allegations of marital misbehavior commonplace in earlier times. Before enactment of the Family Code, Texas practitioners were quite vivid in their pleadings when describing the allegations of marital misconduct against the opposing party. The statute does not deal with ancillary litigation, such as issues of alter ego, wasting of marital assets, or third-party claims.

---

§ 6.403. Answer

monday following 20 days at 10Am

The respondent in a suit for dissolution of a marriage is not required to answer on oath or affirmation.

Comment

As in other civil cases, a respondent in a divorce case must file a written answer to the petition for divorce or face the consequences of a default judgment. In a default judgment proceeding, the petitioner must still put on evidence sufficient for the court to grant a divorce and for other appropriate relief, such as the division of property and orders regarding conservatorship of any children of the marriage. The degree of proof necessarily depends upon the particular case and the practice of the local court, but rather obviously a sworn statement of "insupportability" is universally sufficient to prove a no fault ground.

Leading Cases

Zavala v. Schexnayder, 2009 WL 4695681 (Tex. App.—San Antonio 2009, no pet.) (no verified return of service made it defective and thus, husband not entitled to default divorce)

Hale v. Hale, 2009 WL 3030750 (Tex. App.—San Antonio 2009, no pet.) (bill of review not proper as collateral attack on default judgment entered after motion for new trial orally granted but never signed)

Watson v. Watson, 286 S.W.3d 519 (Tex. App.—Fort Worth 2009, no pet.)(sufficient evidence of property and values needed to support division of property by default judgment)

Schmieding v. Lavender, 2009 WL 1425158 (Tex. App.—Fort Worth 2009, no pet.) (incarcerated husband had right to participate in divorce trial either by affidavit, deposition, telephone or other means if requested)

Barry v. Barry, 193 S.W.3d 72 (Tex. App.—Houston [1st Dist.] 2006, no pet.) (default judgment reversed because prove-up lacked sufficient testimony to sustain property division)

---

§ 6.4035. Waiver of Service

(a) A party to a suit for the dissolution of a marriage may waive the issuance or service of process after the suit is filed by filing with the clerk of the court in which the suit is filed the waiver of the party acknowledging receipt of a copy of the filed petition.

(b) The waiver must contain the mailing address of the party who executed the waiver.

(c) The waiver must be sworn but may not be sworn before an attorney in the suit.

(d) The Texas Rules of Civil Procedure do not apply to a waiver executed under this section.

Leading Case

Smith v. Smith, 241 S.W.3d 904 (Tex. App.—Beaumont 2007, no pet.) (waiver of service of one amended petition once does not cover another amended petition)

---

§ 6.404. Information Regarding Protective Orders

At any time while a suit for dissolution of a marriage is pending, if the court believes, on the basis of any information received by the court, that a party to the suit or a member of the party's family or household may be a victim of family violence, the court shall inform that party of the party's right to apply for a protective order under Title 4.

§ 6.405. Protective Order

(a) The petition in a suit for dissolution of a marriage must state whether a protective order under Title 4 is in effect or if an application for a protective order is pending with regard to the parties to the suit.

(b) The petitioner shall attach to the petition a copy of each protective order issued under Title 4 in which one of the parties to the suit was the applicant and the other party was the respondent without regard to the date of the order. If a copy of the protective order is not available at the time of filing, the petition must state that a copy of the order will be filed with the court before any hearing.

CLE/Other Legal Publications

See annotations to Chapter 71, *infra*.

---

§ 6.406. Mandatory Joinder of Suit Affecting Parent-Child Relationship

(a) The petition in a suit for dissolution of a marriage shall state whether there are children born or adopted of the marriage who are under 18 years of age or who are otherwise entitled to support as provided by Chapter 154.

(b) If the parties are parents of a child, as defined by Section 101.003, and the child is not under the continuing jurisdiction of another court as provided by Chapter 155, the suit for dissolution of a marriage must include a suit affecting the parent-child relationship under Title 5.

Leading Case

Diaz v. Diaz, 126 S.W.3d 406 (Tex. App.—Corpus Christi 2004, no pet.) (default divorce void for failure to include SAPCR in pleading; merely mentioning children in petition not enough)

---

§ 6.407. Transfer of Suit Affecting Parent-Child Relationship to Divorce Court

(a) If a suit affecting the parent-child relationship is pending at the time the suit for dissolution of a marriage is filed, the suit affecting the parent-child relationship shall be transferred as provided by Section 103.002 to the court in which the suit for dissolution is filed.

(b) If the parties are parents of a child, as defined by Section 101.003, and the child is under the continuing jurisdiction of another court under Chapter 155, either party to the suit for dissolution of a marriage may move that court for transfer of the suit affecting the parent-child relationship to the court having jurisdiction of the suit for dissolution. The court with continuing jurisdiction shall transfer the proceeding as provided by Chapter 155. On the transfer of the proceedings, the court with jurisdiction of the suit for dissolution of a marriage shall consolidate the two causes of action.

(c) After transfer of a suit affecting the parent-child relationship as provided in Chapter 155, the court with jurisdiction of the suit for dissolution of a marriage has jurisdiction to render an order in the suit affecting the parent-child relationship as provided by Title 5.

Comment

The TEXAS FAMILY CODE authorizes distinct actions under Title 1 (*The Marriage Relationship*), Title 4 (*Protective Orders and Family Violence*), and Title 5 (*Parent and Child*), which may be joined in one suit. Indeed, if a child born to the wife during the marriage is under 18 at the time a suit for dissolution of marriage is filed, a SAPCR must be joined in the lawsuit. Texas lawyers and judges have long become accustomed to this conceptual arrangement of Texas family law—but sometimes forget that two separate causes of action are actually involved. This section provides the critical bridge between Title 1 and Title 5 actions.

Leading Case

Neal v. Avey, 853 S.W.2d 707 (Tex. App.—Houston [14th Dist.] 1993, writ denied) (filing divorce mandates transfer of termination action)

---

§ 6.408. Service of Citation

Citation on the filing of an original petition in a suit for dissolution of a marriage shall be issued and served as in other civil cases. Citation may also be served on any other person who has or who may assert an interest in the suit for dissolution of the marriage.

CLE/Other Legal Publications

When is a residence really a residence? Jonathan J. Bates, 2010 Adv. Fam. L.

When Ron runs: service of citation on a non-resident. Amy Ann Geistweidt, 2005 Adv. Fam. L.

Leading Cases

In re Marriage of Seals, 83 S.W.3d 870 (Tex. App.—Texarkana 2002, no pet.) (DWOP of inmate's divorce petition for "failure to appear" reversed)

McAlister v. McAlister, 75 S.W.3d 481 (Tex. App.—San Antonio 2002, pet. denied) (wife's attorney did not unreasonably delay procuring citation such that she was stopped from asserting dominant jurisdiction)

---

§ 6.409. Citation by Publication

(a) Citation in a suit for dissolution of a marriage may be by publication as in other civil cases, except that notice shall be published one time only.

(b) The notice shall be sufficient if given in substantially the following form:

To (name of person to be served with citation), and to all whom it may concern (if the name of any person to be served with citation is unknown), Respondent(s),

"STATE OF TEXAS

"You have been sued. You may employ an attorney. If you or your attorney do not file a written answer with the clerk who issued this citation by 10 a.m. on the Monday next following the expiration of 20 days after you were served this citation and petition, a default judgment may be taken against you. The petition of ________, Petitioner, was filed in the Court of ________ County, Texas, on the _____ day of ________, against ________, Respondent(s), numbered _____, and entitled 'In the Matter of Marriage of ________ and ________. The suit requests ________ (statement of relief sought).'

"The Court has authority in this suit to enter any judgment or decree dissolving the marriage and providing for the division of property that will be binding on you.

"Issued and given under my hand and seal of said Court at ________, Texas, this the _____ day of ________, _____.

"________________________

Clerk of the ________ Court of

________ County, Texas

By ______, Deputy."

(c) The form authorized in this section and the form authorized by Section 102.010 may be combined in appropriate situations.

(d) If the citation is for a suit in which a parent-child relationship does not exist, service by publication may be completed by posting the citation at the courthouse door for seven days in the county in which the suit is filed.

(e) If the petitioner or the petitioner's attorney of record makes an oath that no child presently under 18 years of age was born or adopted by the spouses and that no appreciable amount of property was accumulated by the spouses during the marriage, the court may dispense with the appointment of an attorney ad litem. In a case in which citation was by publication, a statement of the evidence, approved and signed by the judge, shall be filed with the papers of the suit as a part of the record.

Comment

This section prescribes the contents of citation by publication in a suit to dissolve a marriage. The statute authorizes a procedure dramatically different from that prescribed for other civil lawsuits. The notice need appear only once in a legal newspaper, not four times, and the time for the respondent to answer is shorter (the usual time after regular personal service of citation). If there are no children, the citation may be posted in the courthouse for seven days. The court, under limited circumstances, may waive the appointment of an attorney ad litem.

Leading Case

In re A.Y., 16 S.W.3d 387 (Tex. App.—El Paso 2000, no pet.) (rejection of argument that publication should be in county of last known residence of respondent rather than county in which suit is pending)

Cross References

TX FCA Family § 102.010. Service of Citation by Publication, *infra*.

Tex. R. Civ. P. 109, Citation by Publication; Tex. R. Civ. P. 114, Citation by Publication—Requisites; Tex. R. Civ. P. 116, Service of Citation by Publication; Tex. R. Civ. P. 117, Return of Citation by Publication.

§ 6.410. Report to Accompany Petition

At the time a petition for divorce or annulment of a marriage is filed, the petitioner shall also file a completed report that may be used by the district clerk, at the time the petition is granted, to comply with Section 194.002, Health and Safety Code.

§ 6.411. Confidentiality of Pleadings

(a) This section applies only in a county with a population of 3.4 million or more.

(b) Except as otherwise provided by law, all pleadings and other documents filed with the court in a suit for dissolution of a marriage are confidential, are excepted from required public disclosure under Chapter 552, Government Code, and may not be released to a person who is not a party to the suit until after the date of service of citation or the 31st day after the date of filing the suit, whichever date is sooner.

Comment

In an effort to regulate solicitation of business by family law attorneys in Harris County, the legislature recognized a need to prevent notification about the filing of a lawsuit to a respondent in the context of divorce, SAPCR, or a protective order prior to service of citation. In these types of cases there is the potential of violence or destruction of assets before a restraining order can be served. On the other hand, arguably solicitation of legal representation in family law cases is protected under the U.S. Constitution. Therefore, the legislature created confidentiality requirements in an attempt to balance the competing interests of safety and free speech.

For Harris County only, there is a statutorily mandated delay of public disclosure of the filing of this type of litigation. If the Houston practice of this particular version of legal advertising spreads to other counties, it seems likely that the application of the statute solely to Harris County may be expanded.

SUBCHAPTER F. TEMPORARY ORDERS

Introductory Comment

The authorization of temporary orders attempts to balance the rights of the parties with respect to temporary restraining orders, temporary injunctions, and other orders. A trial court may not issue a temporary restraining order that excludes a spouse from the family home, prohibits reasonable and necessary spending of funds for living expenses, or forbids reasonable and necessary conduct of a party's usual business. At the hearing for the temporary injunction after both parties have been given notice and opportunity to be heard, the court may enter more extensive orders, including temporary injunctions, orders for support of a spouse, and interim attorney's fees, as well as for temporary exclusive use of marital property.

The court may also render a protective order under Title 4 of the Texas Family Code in conjunction with a divorce proceeding. However, such an order must be in a separate document so that it is not confused with the other temporary orders in a divorce case.

CLE/Other Legal Publications

Trying the temporary orders hearing. Michael E. Jarrett, 2011 Marriage Dissolution

Temporary hearings and/or time/trial limits. Stewart Gagnon, 2010 Ultimate Trial Notebook

Temporary orders. Shannon Taylor Moore, 2010 Fam. L. Boot Camp

Temporary orders: what you can get and how to get it. Thomas L. Ausley & John T. Eck, 2010 Marriage Dissolution Boot Camp

Temporary orders on the fly. Maisie Barringer, 2010 So. Tex. Fam. L. Conf.

Temporary orders. Gary L. Nickelson, 2009 Fam. L. Boot Camp

Effective presentation: what good lawyers forget and presenting your case on temporary and final. Sara C. Springer & Gabe Thomas Vick, III, 2009 Adv. Fam. L.

Property issues at temporary order hearings. Robert Bruce McFarling, Joseph H. Amberson III & Alma R. Benavides, 2009 Marriage Dissolution

Temporary hearings at break-neck speed. John F. (Bo) Nichols, Jr. & Barbara D. Nunneley, 2008 U.T. Fam. L. Front Lines

Trying and defending the contempt case—details, details, details. Kristy D. Piazza, 2008 Adv. Fam. L. Boot Camp

What to do when you need emergency relief. Rhonda F. Hunter, 2008 Adv. Fam. L.

Preparation for temporary order(s) hearings—what do you do for the last 100 days/hours/minutes, burdensome limitations. Jonathan J. Bates, 2008 Marriage Dissolution

---

See Accompanying CD–ROM for Additional CLE/Other Legal Publications

---

Leading Cases

Texas Supreme Court

Ex parte Hall, 854 S.W.2d 656 (Tex. 1993) (temporary support order requires evidence, cannot be based on premarital agreement)

Walker v. Towslee, 677 S.W.2d 502 (Tex. 1984) (interim fees cannot be granted as part of motion for new trial)

Courts of Appeals

Conner v. Guemez, ___ S.W.3d ___, 2010 WL 4812991 (Tex. App.—Fort Worth 2010, no pet.) (order must be signed before receiver's tasks performed; receiver is arm of the court, not a trustee)

In re Marriage of Hallman, 2010 WL 619290 (Tex. App.—Texarkana, pet. denied) (enforcement of Rule 11 for temporary support enforced by court as contract in final property division of the parties)

In re Marriage of Hughes, 2009 WL 1491866 (Tex. App.—Amarillo 2009, no pet.) (court improperly conducted "final trial" on issue of common law marriage at hearing of temporary orders)

In re R.E.D., 278 S.W.3d 850 (Tex. App.—Houston [1st Dist.] 2009, orig. proceeding) (husband considered a trustee who can be held in contempt for willfully refusing to obey temporary order of court requiring funds to be paid to registry of court)

In re Ashton, 266 S.W.3d 602 (Tex. App.—Dallas 2008, no pet.) (since trust was not a party to the divorce suit, husband trustee cannot be ordered to pay support or fees from trust)

In re B.M., 228 S.W.3d 462 (Tex. App.—Dallas 2007, no pet.) (trial court may not render final order if only temporary orders sought)

---

§ 6.501. Temporary Restraining Order

(a) After the filing of a suit for dissolution of a marriage, on the motion of a party or on the court's own motion, the court may grant a temporary restraining order without notice to the adverse party for the preservation of the property and for the protection of the parties as necessary, including an order prohibiting one or both parties from:

(1) intentionally communicating by telephone or in writing with the other party by use of vulgar, profane, obscene, or indecent language or in a coarse or offensive manner, with intent to annoy or alarm the other;

(2) threatening the other, by telephone or in writing, to take unlawful action against any person, intending by this action to annoy or alarm the other;

(3) placing a telephone call, anonymously, at an unreasonable hour, in an offensive and repetitious manner, or without a legitimate purpose of communication with the intent to annoy or alarm the other;

(4) intentionally, knowingly, or recklessly causing bodily injury to the other or to a child of either party;

(5) threatening the other or a child of either party with imminent bodily injury;

(6) intentionally, knowingly, or recklessly destroying, removing, concealing, encumbering, transferring, or otherwise harming or reducing the value of the property of the parties or either party with intent to obstruct the authority of the court to order a division of the estate of the parties in a manner that the court deems just and right, having due regard for the rights of each party and any children of the marriage;

(7) intentionally falsifying a writing or record relating to the property of either party;

(8) intentionally misrepresenting or refusing to disclose to the other party or to the court, on proper request, the existence, amount, or location of any property of the parties or either party;

(9) intentionally or knowingly damaging or destroying the tangible property of the parties or either party; or

(10) intentionally or knowingly tampering with the tangible property of the parties or either party and causing pecuniary loss or substantial inconvenience to the other.

(b) A temporary restraining order under this subchapter may not include a provision:

(1) the subject of which is a requirement, appointment, award, or other order listed in Section 64.104, Civil Practice and Remedies Code; or

(2) that:

(A) excludes a spouse from occupancy of the residence where that spouse is living except as provided in a protective order made in accordance with Title 4;

(B) prohibits a party from spending funds for reasonable and necessary living expenses; or

(C) prohibits a party from engaging in acts reasonable and necessary to conduct that party's usual business and occupation.

§ 6.502. Temporary Injunction and Other Temporary Orders

(a) While a suit for dissolution of a marriage is pending and on the motion of a party or on the court's own motion after notice and hearing, the court may render an appropriate order, including the granting of a temporary injunction for the preservation of the property and protection of the parties as deemed necessary and equitable and including an order directed to one or both parties:

(1) requiring a sworn inventory and appraisement of the real and personal property owned or claimed by the parties and specifying the form, manner, and substance of the inventory and appraisal and list of debts and liabilities;

(2) requiring payments to be made for the support of either spouse;

(3) requiring the production of books, papers, documents, and tangible things by a party;

(4) ordering payment of reasonable attorney's fees and expenses;

(5) appointing a receiver for the preservation and protection of the property of the parties;

(6) awarding one spouse exclusive occupancy of the residence during the pendency of the case;

(7) prohibiting the parties, or either party, from spending funds beyond an amount the court determines to be for reasonable and necessary living expenses;

(8) awarding one spouse exclusive control of a party's usual business or occupation; or

(9) prohibiting an act described by Section 6.501(a).

(b) Not later than the 30th day after the date a receiver is appointed under Subsection (a)(5), the receiver shall give notice of the appointment to each lienholder of any property under the receiver's control.

§ 6.503. Affidavit, Verified Pleading, and Bond Not Required

(a) A temporary restraining order or temporary injunction under this subchapter:

(1) may be granted without an affidavit or a verified pleading stating specific facts showing that immediate and irreparable injury, loss, or damage will result before notice can be served and a hearing can be held; and

(2) need not:

(A) define the injury or state why it is irreparable;

(B) state why the order was granted without notice; or

(C) include an order setting the suit for trial on the merits with respect to the ultimate relief sought.

(b) In a suit for dissolution of a marriage, the court may dispense with the issuance of a bond between the spouses in connection with temporary orders for the protection of the parties and their property.

§ 6.504. Protective Orders

On the motion of a party to a suit for dissolution of a marriage, the court may render a protective order as provided by Subtitle B, Title 4.

Cross References

TX FCA Family Title 4, Protective Orders and Family Violence, TX FCA Family § 71.001 *et seq.*, *infra.*

TX FCA Penal § 25.07, Violation of Protective Order or Magistrate's Order, *infra*; TX FCA Penal § 42.07, Harassment, *infra*; TX FCA Penal § 42.072, Stalking, *infra*.

---

§ 6.505. Counseling

(a) While a divorce suit is pending, the court may direct the parties to counsel with a person named by the court.

(b) The person named by the court to counsel the parties shall submit a written report to the court and to the parties before the final hearing. In the report, the counselor shall give only an opinion as to whether there exists a reasonable expectation of reconciliation of the parties and, if so, whether further counseling would be beneficial. The sole purpose of the report is to aid the court in determining whether the suit for divorce should be continued pending further counseling.

(c) A copy of the report shall be furnished to each party.

(d) If the court believes that there is a reasonable expectation of the parties' reconciliation, the court may by written order continue the proceedings and direct the parties to a person named by the court for further counseling for a period fixed by the court not to exceed 60 days, subject to any terms, conditions, and limitations the court considers desirable. In ordering counseling, the court shall consider the circumstances of the parties, including the needs of the parties' family and the availability of counseling services. At the expiration of the period specified by the court, the counselor to whom the parties were directed shall report to the court whether the parties have complied with the court's order. Thereafter, the court shall proceed as in a divorce suit generally.

(e) If the court orders counseling under this section and the parties to the marriage are the parents of a child under 18 years of age born or adopted during the marriage, the counseling shall include counseling on issues that confront children who are the subject of a suit affecting the parent-child relationship.

Leading Cases

Baxla v. Baxla, 522 S.W.2d 736 (Tex. Civ. App.—Dallas 1975), *appeal after remand*, 623 S.W.2d 462 (Tex. App.—Waco 1981, writ dism'd w.o.j.) (if there is hesitancy about divorce, court may refer parties to marriage counseling)

Philp v. Philp, 516 S.W.2d 294 (Tex. Civ. App.—Waco 1974, no writ) (there is no abuse of court's discretion in not ordering parties to counseling)

---

§ 6.506. Contempt

The violation of a temporary restraining order, temporary injunction, or other temporary order issued under this subchapter is punishable as contempt.

Comment

Most of the caselaw relating to contempt has been developed in SAPCRs rather than in the divorce cause of action. The due process restrictions on incarceration are identical, however. This subject is annotated extensively in Chapter 157 *[Enforcement]*, *infra*.

---

§ 6.507. Interlocutory Appeal

An order under this subchapter, except an order appointing a receiver, is not subject to interlocutory appeal.

CLE/Other Legal Publications

Appellate practice from every angle. Georganna L. Simpson, Lawrence M. Doss, Chris Nickelson & Jimmy Vaught, 2010 Adv. Fam. L.

Appellate purgatory: actions you can take during appeal and after remand. Jimmy Vaught, 2010 Adv. Fam. L.

Appellate and Post-Trial Motions. Georganna L. Simpson, 2010 Adv. Fam. L. Drafting

The nuts and bolts of the appellate process: appeals, limited appeals, restricted appeals, interlocutory appeals, and mandamus. Pamela E. George, 2005 Marriage Dissolution

---

SUBCHAPTER G. ALTERNATIVE DISPUTE RESOLUTION

Introductory Comment

No innovation of recent years has had a greater impact on the practice of family law than the advent of "court-ordered ADR." In fact, in many of the largest Texas counties a case will not be tried until the parties have attempted ADR. In most courts handling family law matters, mediation is virtually mandatory in order to have a day in court. Notwithstanding the initial grumbling in courthouse halls, the docket congestion of many counties has been significantly reduced, largely thanks to this process.

As dockets continue to be congested, the use of arbitration in family law is also growing in popularity. Additionally, the use of collaborative law as a means to avoid the litigation process all together continues to see rapid growth in Texas.

Very similar ADR rules, although not quite identical, are in force in both Title 1 and Title 5 litigation.

CLE/Other Legal Publications

General ADR and Negotiation

Rule 11s, MSA's and arbitrations. Wendy S. Burgower, 2011 ADV. FAM. L.

Alternative dispute resolution in family law cases. Randall B. Wilhite, 2011 ADV. FAM. L.

Negotiation and mediation: There was never a pancake so thin that it didn't have two sides. Coye Conner & Mike Gregory, 2011 ADV. FAM. L.

Other non-adversarial approaches to family law cases. Donald R. Royall, Harry L. Tindall & Norma L. Trusch, 2011 ADV. FAM. L.

The ADR playing field today. Joan F. Jenkins, 2011 MARRIAGE DISSOLUTION

The art of negotiation. Gary L. Nickelson, 2010 ADV. FAM. L.

Agreements between counsel and parties: Rule 11, stipulations, MSA's and informal settlement agreements. Charla Bradshaw Conner & Rothwell B. Pool, 2010 ADV. FAM. L.

Alternate dispute resolution. Thomas L. Ausley, 2010 FAM. L. BOOT CAMP

Negotiation techniques for getting the case settled. Larry H. Schwartz, 2010 MARRIAGE DISSOLUTION

Finalizing the deal: Rule 11 and the importance of getting orders timely signed. Chris Nickelson & Gary L. Nickelson, 2010 MARRIAGE DISSOLUTION

Negotiation. Mark R. Otis, 2010 COLLABORATIVE LAW

Negotiation ethics. Christopher K. Wrampelmeier, 2010 FAM. L. FRONT LINES

Alternative dispute resolution methods. Hons. Conrad L. Moran, Brenda G. Mullinix, & Leta S. Parks, 2010 SO. TEX. FAM. L. CONF.

Mediation

Defending or Attacking a Mediated Settlement Agreement. Brian L. Webb, 2011 MARRIAGE DISSOLUTION

Preparing for mediation. Barbara K. Runge, 2011 SO. TEX. FAM. L.

Mediation and ADR. Steve A. Bavousett, 2010 ADV. FAM. L. DRAFTING

Effective mediation. Christopher K. Wrampelmeier, 2010 MARRIAGE DISSOL. BOOT CAMP

Preparing for mediation. Jane A. Joseph, 2010 SO. TEX. FAM. L. CONF.

Productive mediation: preparation, participation, the role of mediator, attorney, and client; closing the deal and crafting the MSA. (Panel), 2009 ADV. FAM. L.

Mediation. Michael B. Paddock & Coye Conner, Jr., 2009 ADV. FAM. L. BOOT CAMP

Creative mediation techniques. Solomon J. Casseb, III & Coye Conner, Jr & Charles E. Hardy & Randall B. Wilhite, 2008 ADV. FAM. L.

Maximizing results at mediation. Randall B. Wilhite, 2008 MARRIAGE DISSOLUTION

The ethics of ADR negotiation and settlement. Frances Ann Harris, 2008 MARRIAGE DISSOLUTION

Rules judges have to follow: "tiptoe through the rulebook" ethical considerations of mediators, arbitrators and judges. B. Frank Pennypacker III, 2008 MARRIAGE DISSOLUTION

Arbitration

Arbitration: does it have a place in family law? Joan F. Jenkins, 2010 ADV. FAM. L.

Alternatives to trial. Barbara K. Runge, 2010 SO. TEX. FAM. L. CONF.

Collaborative Law

See 2011 COLLABORATIVE LAW INSTITUTE (various articles)

Do I have to drink the kool-aid: maintaining a litigation and collaborative practice.

Who are our collaborative clients?—The Texas profile from the IACP research project. Gay G. Cox, 2010 ADV. FAM. L.

Informed consent—fallout from the ABA ethics opinion on collaborative law. Janice L. Green, 2010 ADV. FAM. L.

Case autopsy—an informative dissection of a challenging collaboration. Cristi Trusler, Mary Ann Osborne, Lisa M. Walker & Melissa Williams, 2010 ADV. FAM. L.

Building a collaborative community—the old and new challenges. Kristen A. Algert, Sally H. Emerson & Steven G. Palmer, 2010 ADV. FAM. L.

See 2010 COLLABORATIVE LAW INSTITUTE (various articles)

See 2010 COLLABORATIVE LAW PROCESS (various articles)

Collaborative law. Harry L. Tindall, 2010 SO. TEX. FAM. L. CONF.

Collaborative law and negotiation workshop. Various speakers, 2009 ADV. FAM. L.

Process issues: dealing with potholes, fallen trees, and icy roads along the road map to resolution. Jody L. Johnson, 2009 ADV. FAM. L.

In 2008, SBOT CLE sponsored a single issue conference, COLLABORATIVE L. SPRING CONFERENCE, which provided 18 articles over 2 1/2 days.

ADR drafting issues: collaborative law, mediation and arbitration. Joan F. Jenkins, 2008 ADV. FAM. L. DRAFTING

Workshop: Issues for the advancing collaborative law practice. 2008 ADV. FAM. L.

See Accompanying CD-ROM for Additional CLE/Other Legal Publications

---

Leading Cases

Arbitration

Nafta Traders, Inc. v. Quinn, 339 S.W.3d 84 (Tex. 2011) (parties may agree to allow for an appeal of arbitrator's award)

In re Provine, 312 S.W.3d 824 (Tex. App.—Houston 2009, no pet.) (wife's post-divorce enforcement issues fell within mediated settlement agreement's arbitration clause that stated the mediator would arbitrate any disputes regarding the drafting, interpretation, and/or enforcement of the MSA)

Goetz v. Goetz, 130 S.W.3d 359 (Tex. App.—Houston [14th Dist.] 2004, pet. denied) (court may appoint arbitrator when agreement does not specify method for appointment)

Jabri v. Qaddura, 108 S.W.3d 404 (Tex. App.—Fort Worth 2003, no pet.) (parties agreed to resolve marital disputes by religious arbitration; trial court erred in not compelling them to do so)

Koch v. Koch, 27 S.W.3d 93 (Tex. App.—San Antonio 2000, no pet.) (provision to arbitrate disputes over prenuptial agreement binding on divorce court)

Mediation

Roth v. Roth, ___ S.W.3d ___, 2010 WL 5541701 (Tex. App.—Corpus Christi 2010, no pet.) (additional terms regarding taxes included in the decree but not in the parties' settlement agreement held improper)

Green v. Green, ___ S.W.3d ___, 2011 WL 2119742 (Tex. App.—Beaumont, no pet.) (trial court set aside MSA affirmed based upon husband's misrepresentations of value and existence of assets)

Milner v. Milner, ___ S.W.3d ___, 2010 WL 2243558 (Tex. App.—Fort Worth 2010, pet. filed) (mediated settlement agreement should have been set aside based upon "no meeting of the minds" with regards to its terms)

In re Provine, 312 S.W.3d 824 (Tex. App.—Houston 2009, no pet.) (wife's post-divorce enforcement issues fell within the mediated settlement agreement's arbitration clause that stated the mediator would arbitrate any disputes regarding the drafting, interpretation, and/or enforcement of the MSA)

Loehr v. Loehr, 2009 WL 2645025 (Tex. App.—Corpus Christi 2009, no pet.) (wife offered no evidence of fraudulent inducement to set aside mediated settlement agreement and section 6.602 does not include a contractual defense of mistake)

In re Green, 2009 WL 2616258 (Tex. App.—Beaumont 2009, mandamus denied) (once court granted new trial, must consider whether or not wife's allegations of wrongdoing with regards to the mediated settlement agreement invalidate the agreement)

Wright v. Wright, 280 S.W.3d 901 (Tex. App.—Eastland 2009, no pet.) (wife's immaterial breach of mediated settlement agreement did not provide husband right to rescind)

Spiegel v. KLRU Endowment Fund, 228 S.W.3d 237 (Tex. App.—Austin 2007, pet. denied) (MSA enforceable even after wife's death before rendition of divorce)

In re K.A.R., 171 S.W.3d 705 (Tex. App.—Houston [14th Dist.] 2005, no pet.) (significant sanctions against attorney for not showing up at ordered mediation upheld)

In re T.M.G.R., 164 S.W.3d 851 (Tex. App.—Beaumont 2005, no pet.) (without copy of "original" mediated settlement agreement, no way to tell if signed document varies from agreement of parties)

See Accompanying CD–ROM for Cases Linked to Westlaw and Additional Leading Cases

Collaborative Law

In re Mabray, ___ S.W.3d ___, 2010 WL 3448198 (Tex. App.—Houston [1st Dist.] 2010, pet. filed) (cooperative law agreement, although not a collaborative law agreement, does not violate public policy as providing for an alternative to litigation, namely arbitration)

Pribyl v. Pribyl, 307 S.W.3d 882 (Tex. App.—Austin 2010, no pet.) (wife's cause of action for breach of the collaborative law contract which required full disclosure was improper collateral attack on judgment)

Cross Reference

TX FCA Civ Prac & Rem § 154.001*et seq., infra.*

§ 6.601. Arbitration Procedures

(a) On written agreement of the parties, the court may refer a suit for dissolution of a marriage to arbitration. The agreement must state whether the arbitration is binding or nonbinding.

(b) If the parties agree to binding arbitration, the court shall render an order reflecting the arbitrator's award.

§ 6.6015. Determination of Validity and Enforceability of Contract Containing Agreement to Arbitrate

(a) If a party to a suit for dissolution of a marriage opposes an application to compel arbitration or makes an application to stay arbitration and asserts that the contract

containing the agreement to arbitrate is not valid or enforceable, notwithstanding any provision of the contract to the contrary, the court shall try the issue promptly and may order arbitration only if the court determines that the contract containing the agreement to arbitrate is valid and enforceable against the party seeking to avoid arbitration.

(b) A determination under this section that a contract is valid and enforceable does not affect the court's authority to stay arbitration or refuse to compel arbitration on any other ground provided by law.

(c) This section does not apply to:

(1) a court order;

(2) a mediated settlement agreement described by Section 6.602;

(3) a collaborative law agreement described by Section 6.603;

(4) a written settlement agreement reached at an informal settlement conference described by Section 6.604; or

(5) any other agreement between the parties that is approved by a court.

Enacted by Acts 2011, 82nd Leg., ch. 1088 (S.B. 1216), § 1, eff. June 17, 2011.

Comment

Subsection (a) of this new statute requires a court to promptly determine the validity and enforceability of a contract containing an agreement to arbitrate notwithstanding the arbitration agreement. It further mandates that a court may compel arbitration only if the contract is valid and enforceable. However, subsection (b) clarifies that a finding of validity and enforceability of a contract does not abrogate a courts ability to either stay arbitration or refuse to compel arbitration on another ground of law.

This new section of the Texas Family Code is a departure from the general standard for challenging a contract containing an arbitration agreement under the Texas Civil Practice and Remedies Code. Chapter 171 of the Civil Practice and Remedies Code provides that a court may determine the validity of an agreement to arbitrate; however, it does not provide for a court to determine the validity or enforceability of the contract that contains such an agreement in its entirety. Tex. Civ. Prac. & Rem. Code ch. 171. Reflecting the lack of such provisions, the Texas Supreme Court has ruled that when a challenge is to the entirety of a contract containing an arbitration agreement as well as to the agreement itself, the challenge must be taken to arbitration, not court. *In re* Labatt Food Service, L.P., 279 S.W.3d 640 (Tex. 2009).

Of note, the bill analysis of this statute reflects the underlying concern that parties may be forced into an agreement to arbitrate as a part of a larger contract. The example given was that of a party having a gun held to his or her head while signing a contract containing an arbitration agreement or clause. The analysis likewise expresses concern that a party forced to enter an agreement for arbitration as the part of a larger contract would have difficulty obtaining a fair outcome in arbitration. However, provisions requiring arbitration in divorce decrees and other settlement documents or court orders are not subject to this court review.

§ 6.602. Mediation Procedures

(a) On the written agreement of the parties or on the court's own motion, the court may refer a suit for dissolution of a marriage to mediation.

(b) A mediated settlement agreement is binding on the parties if the agreement:

(1) provides, in a prominently displayed statement that is in boldfaced type or capital letters or underlined, that the agreement is not subject to revocation;

(2) is signed by each party to the agreement; and

(3) is signed by the party's attorney, if any, who is present at the time the agreement is signed.

(c) If a mediated settlement agreement meets the requirements of this section, a party is entitled to judgment on the mediated settlement agreement notwithstanding Rule 11, Texas Rules of Civil Procedure, or another rule of law.

(d) A party may at any time prior to the final mediation order file a written objection to the referral of a suit for dissolution of a marriage to mediation on the basis of family violence having been committed against the objecting party by the other party. After an objection is filed, the suit may not be referred to mediation unless, on the request of the other party, a hearing is held and the court finds that a preponderance of the evidence does not support the objection. If the suit is referred to mediation, the court shall order appropriate measures be taken to ensure the physical and emotional safety of the party who filed the objection. The order shall provide that the parties not be required to have face-to-face contact and that the parties be placed in separate rooms during mediation.

§ 6.603. ~~Collaborative Law~~

~~(a) On a written agreement of the parties and their attorneys, a dissolution of marriage proceeding may be conducted under collaborative law procedures.~~

~~(b) Collaborative law is a procedure in which the parties and their counsel agree in writing to use their best efforts and make a good faith attempt to resolve their dissolution of marriage dispute on an agreed basis without resorting to judicial intervention except to have the court approve the settlement agreement, make the legal pronouncements, and sign the orders required by law to effectuate the agreement of the parties as the court determines appropriate. The parties' counsel may not serve as litigation counsel except to ask the court to approve the settlement agreement.~~

~~(c) A collaborative law agreement must include provisions for:~~

~~(1) full and candid exchange of information between the parties and their attorneys as necessary to make a proper evaluation of the case;~~

~~(2) suspending court intervention in the dispute while the parties are using collaborative law procedures;~~

~~(3) hiring experts, as jointly agreed, to be used in the procedure;~~

~~(4) withdrawal of all counsel involved in the collaborative law procedure if the collaborative law procedure does not result in settlement of the dispute; and~~

~~(5) other provisions as agreed to by the parties consistent with a good faith effort to collaboratively settle the matter.~~

~~(d) Notwithstanding Rule 11, Texas Rules of Civil Procedure, or another rule or law, a party is entitled to judgment on a collaborative law settlement agreement if the agreement:~~

~~(1) provides, in a prominently displayed statement that is boldfaced, capitalized, or underlined, that the agreement is not subject to revocation; and~~

~~(2) is signed by each party to the agreement and the attorney of each party.~~

~~(e) Subject to Subsection (g), a court that is notified 30 days before trial that the parties are using collaborative law procedures to attempt to settle a dispute may not, until a party notifies the court that the collaborative law procedures did not result in a settlement:~~

~~(1) set a hearing or trial in the case;~~

~~(2) impose discovery deadlines;~~

~~(3) require compliance with scheduling orders; or~~

~~(4) dismiss the case.~~

~~(f) The parties shall notify the court if the collaborative law procedures result in a settlement. If they do not, the parties shall file:~~

~~(1) a status report with the court not later than the 180th day after the date of the written agreement to use the procedures; and~~

~~(2) a status report on or before the first anniversary of the date of the written agreement to use the procedures, accompanied by a motion for continuance that the court shall grant if the status report indicates the desire of the parties to continue to use collaborative law procedures.~~

~~(g) If the collaborative law procedures do not result in a settlement on or before the second anniversary of the date that the suit was filed, the court may:~~

~~(1) set the suit for trial on the regular docket; or~~

~~(2) dismiss the suit without prejudice.~~

~~(h) The provisions for confidentiality of alternative dispute resolution procedures as provided in Chapter 154, Civil Practice and Remedies Code, apply equally to collaborative law procedures under this section.~~

Repealed by Acts 2011, 82nd Leg., ch. 1048 (H.B. 3833), § 2, eff. Sept. 1, 2011

Comment

Title 1A of the Texas Family Code is added in 2011 adopting the Uniform Collaborative Law Act in Texas. Now all of the provisions for collaborative law are contained in its own title.

§ 6.604. Informal Settlement Conference

(a) The parties to a suit for dissolution of a marriage may agree to one or more informal settlement conferences and may agree that the settlement conferences may be conducted with or without the presence of the parties' attorneys, if any.

(b) A written settlement agreement reached at an informal settlement conference is binding on the parties if the agreement:

(1) provides, in a prominently displayed statement that is in boldfaced type or in capital letters or underlined, that the agreement is not subject to revocation;

(2) is signed by each party to the agreement; and

(3) is signed by the party's attorney, if any, who is present at the time the agreement is signed.

(c) If a written settlement agreement meets the requirements of Subsection (b), a party is entitled to judgment on the settlement agreement notwithstanding Rule 11, Texas Rules of Civil Procedure, or another rule of law.

(d) If the court finds that the terms of the written informal settlement agreement are just and right, those terms are binding on the court. If the court approves the agreement, the court may set forth the agreement in full or incorporate the agreement by reference in the final decree.

(e) If the court finds that the terms of the written informal settlement agreement are not just and right, the court may request the parties to submit a revised agreement or set the case for a contested hearing.

Comment

An agreement incident to divorce reached in accordance with § 7.006, *infra*, may be withdrawn or revised at any time before rendition of judgment by the trial court. *See Lee v. Lee*, 158 S.W.3d 612 (Tex. App.—Fort Worth 2005, no pet.). However, this section provides for the enforcement of an informal settlement agreement reached between parties, as long as the agreement bears the same formalities required of an enforceable mediated settlement agreement, *see* § 6.603, *supra*.

SUBCHAPTER H. TRIAL AND APPEAL

Introductory Comment

Although some might argue that family law is merely a subset of general civil litigation, the CLE publications listed below contradict such an assertion. Indeed existence of separate subchapters in this chapter establishing special rules for venue, jurisdiction, trial and appeal also indicate otherwise.

CLE/Other Legal Publications

Appeals

Trying a case with appeal in mind. Chris Nickelson, 2011 ADV. FAM. L.

Appellate CYA. Chris Nickelson, 2011 MARRIAGE DISSOLUTION

Appellate practice from every angle. Georganna L. Simpson, Lawrence M. Doss, Chris Nickelson, Jimmy Vaught, 2010 ADV. FAM. L.

Purgatory: actions you can take during appeal and after remand. Jimmy Vaught, 2010 ADV. FAM. L.

Appellate and post-trial motions. Georganna L. Simpson, 2010 ADV. FAM. L. DRAFTING

Post-trial motions: what really happens after both sides rest. Angela Pence England, 2010 SO. TEX. TRIAL TIPS & TECHNIQUES

Appellate issues for the family law practitioner. Lucy Forbes and Chad Forbes, 2010 SO. TEX. TRIAL TIPS & TECHNIQUES

Preserving the record from every angle: the art of preserving the record throughout your case, not just during trial. Georganna L. Simpson & Hon. Linda B. Thomas, 2009 ADV. FAM. L.

Post-Trial and Appellate Deadlines. Hon. Ann C. McClure, 2009 ADV. FAM. L. BOOT CAMP

Mandamus and more: are pre-trial appellate rulings a new free-for-all or just the same-old-same-old? Richard L. Flowers & Michelle May O'Neil, 2009 U.T. FAM. L. FRONT LINES

Discovery

Discovery on a shoestring. Adam Joel Morris, 2011 ADV. FAM. L.

Drafting discovery requests. Brian L. Webb, 2011 ADV. FAM. L.

Discovery traps. Kristal C. Cordova Thomson, 2011 ADV. FAM. L.

Social media electronic discovery procedures and ethical challenges. Craig D. Ball, Scott A. Beauchamp, Michael Long & Harold C. Zuflacht, 2011 ADV. FAM. L.

Discovery. Rhonda F. Hunter, 2011 MARRIAGE DISSOLUTION

Discovery: from economical to expensive: traditional requests and electronic and high-tech evidence. JoAl Cannon Sheridan, 2011 U.T. FAM. L. FRONT LINES

Obtaining and enforcing discovery from third parties. Randall B. Wilhite, 2010 ADV. FAM. L.

Interstate and foreign discovery. John F. 'Bo' Nichols, Jr., 2010 ADV. FAM. L.

Spoliation of evidence: how to discover it and address it. Rhonda F. Hunter, 2010 ADV. FAM. L.

Computer forensics in family law cases. Reginald A. Hirsch, 2010 ADV. FAM. L.

Discovery. William M. Reppeto, III, 2010 ADV. FAM. L. BOOT CAMP

Electronic discovery. Kristal M. Cordova, 2010 MARRIAGE DISSOLUTION

Electronic evidence and discovery. Reginald A. Hirsh, Kyle W. Sanders & Amy C. Allen, 2010 SO. TEX. TRIAL TIPS & TECHNIQUES

Discovery and drafting in the computer age. Joseph Indelicato Jr., 2010 ADV. FAM. L. DRAFTING

Using discovery and selecting documents to use at trial. Randall B. Wilhite, 2010 ULTIMATE TRIAL NOTEBOOK

Evidence

Technology evidentiary protocols and avoiding danger. Stephen Michael Orsinger, 2011 ADV. FAM. L.

Evidence. Heather L. King, 2011 ADV. FAM. L.

Hearsay. Joseph Indelicato, Jr., 2011 ADV. FAM. L.

Social networking/social media. Sherri A. Evans, 2011 ADV. FAM. L.

Modern Evidentiary Issues. Heather L. King, 2011 MARRIAGE DISSOLUTION

Social networking evidence: various uses, discredibility, and evidentiary issues. John G. Browning, 2011 U.T. FAM. L. FRONT LINES

Predicates and other evidentiary issues. Joseph D. Terry & L. Lee Thweat, 2011 SO. TEX. FAM. L.

Evidence: in or out? Scott A. Beauchamp, Heather L. King & Lynn Kamin, 2010 ADV. FAM. L.

Spoliation of evidence: how to discover it and address it. Rhonda F. Hunter, 2010 ADV. FAM. L.

Electronic evidence: how to avoid getting shocked. Reginald A. Hirsch, Rick Robertson, & Cindy V. Tinsdale, 2009, 2010 ULTIMATE TRIAL NOTEBOOK

Electronic evidence. Joseph Indelicato, Jr., 2010 MARRIAGE DISSOLUTION

Social networking evidence (Facebook, Twitter, etc.) and the ethical landmines: how to get it and how to get it in. Alyson Gregory Richter, 2010 MARRIAGE DISSOLUTION

Electronic evidence. John F. Nichols & John F. (Bo) Nichols, Jr., 2010 FAM. L. FRONT LINES

Electronic evidence and discovery. Reginald A. Hirsh, Kyle W. Sanders & Amy C. Allen, 2010 SO. TEX. TRIAL TIPS & TECHNIQUES

Predicates and objections: getting it in and keeping it out. Warren Cole & Cali V. Schwarz, 2010 SO. TEX. TRIAL TIPS & TECHNIQUES

Expert Witnesses/Testimony

Valuation: cross-examine of valuation expert. Sherri A. Evans, 2011 U.T. FAM. L. FRONT LINES

Cross-examination of experts. James E. Monnig, 2010 ULTIMATE TRIAL NOTEBOOK

Expert witnesses: pitfalls and warnings. Sherri A. Evans, 2010 ADV. FAM. L.

Effective uses of financial advisors in family law cases. Christy Adamcik Gammill & Christopher Martin Lake, 2010 ADV. FAM. L.

Preparing your expert for cross examination. Richard L. Flowers, Jr., 2010 FAM. L. FRONT LINES.

Witness preparation. Joseph Indelicato, Jr., 2010 SO. TEX. TRIAL TIPS & TECHNIQUES

Due diligence of the valuation expert. Haran D. Levy, 2009 ADV. FAM. L.

Jury

See annotations to § 6.703, *infra*.

Summary Judgment and Disposition without Trial

Defending and winning breach of fiduciary claims by summary judgment. Jim Loveless, 2011 ADV. FAM. L.

Just saying "no" is not enough: affirmative defenses, motions for summary judgment and other pleadings. Christopher K. Wrampelmeier, 2011 U.T. FAM. L. FRONT LINES

Summary judgments. Chris Nickelson, 2010 ADV. FAM. L. DRAFTING

Narrowing the issues: motions in limine/stipulations/agreements/summary judgments. Kristal M. Cordova, 2009, 2010 ULTIMATE TRIAL NOTEBOOK

Alternatives to trial. Barbara K. Runge, 2010 SO. TEX. FAM. L. CONF.

Winning your case before you go to trial: summary judgments, declaratory judgments, and other methods of resolving issues before trial. Michelle May O'Neil & Hon. William W. Harris, 2009 ADV. FAM. L.

Shortening the dance: the effective use of summary judgments in family law cases. Karl E. Hays, 2009 U.T. FAM. L. FRONT LINES

Eliminating the issues: summary judgments and special exceptions. William M. Reppeto III, 2008 ADV. FAM. L. DRAFTING

Trial Techniques

Playing nice with others–getting along with opposing counsel, judges, and court staff. Thomas H. Watkins, 2011 ADV. FAM. L.

Client relations. Rick Robertson, 2011 ADV. FAM. L.

Effective and efficient case presentation. Stewart W. Gagnon, 2011, 2010 ADV. FAM. L.

Tools of effective advocacy: designing and delivering a winning agreement. Richard R. Orsinger, 2011 ADV. FAM. L.

30 hot technology tips in 30 minutes. Reginald A. Hirsch & Rick Robertson, 2011 ADV. FAM. L.

Maximizing paralegal skills during trial and assisting during preparation. Judy C. Cottrell, Sarah J. Whyte & Kim Splawn, 2010 ULTIMATE TRIAL NOTEBOOK

Witness preparation and assessment. Joseph Indelicato, Jr. & Lisa Stewart, 2010 ULTIMATE TRIAL NOTEBOOK

Effective use of prior testimony. Heather L. King, 2010 ULTIMATE TRIAL NOTEBOOK

What to do the first two hours before you call your first witness. Victor H. Negron, Jr., 2010 ULTIMATE TRIAL NOTEBOOK

The ultimate judge's notebook. Charla Bradshaw Conner, 2010 ULTIMATE TRIAL NOTEBOOK

Demonstrative aids: cheap and easy exhibits. Lydia Dews, 2010 ULTIMATE TRIAL NOTEBOOK

Fine-tuning your case for court. Roy L. Moore & John F. "Bo" Nichols, Jr., 2011 SO. TEX. FAM. L.

I didn't go to law school to check boxes and fill in the blanks: creative advocacy. Jim Loveless, 2010 ADV. FAM. L.

The art of persuasive speaking. Mike McCurley, 2010 ADV. FAM. L.

Representing the unsophisticated client with assets. G. Thomas Vick, Jr., 2010 ADV. FAM. L.

Trying the property case on a shoestring. Christopher K. Wrampelmeier, 2010 ADV. FAM. L.

Final trial. Mike Gregory, 2010 FAM. L. BOOT CAMP

Managing clients' expectations at trial. G. Thomas Vick, Jr., 2010 MARRIAGE DISSOL. BOOT CAMP

Theming your case; and using electronic media to make your trial presentation. Wendy S. Burgower & Lynn Kamin, 2010 FAM. L. FRONT LINES

Impacts at trial: saving your trial from mistakes. Chris Nickelson, 2010 FAM. L. FRONT LINES

Witness preparation. Joseph Indelicato, Jr., 2010 SO. TEX. TRIAL TIPS & TECHNIQUES

See Accompanying CD–ROM for Additional CLE/Other Legal Publications

---

Leading Cases

Daubert v. Merrill Dow Pharmaceuticals, Inc., 113 S.Ct. 2786 (1993) (landmark case excluding "junk science")

In re Kuntz, 124 S.W.3d 179 (Tex. 2003) (ex-husband had access to documents sought in discovery at work but did not have physical possession, therefore, not required to produce)

Gammill v. Jack Williams Chevrolet, Inc., 972 S.W.2d 713 (Tex. 1998) (*Daubert* standards apply to all experts, not just novel scientific techniques)

E.I. Dupont de Nemours and Co., Inc. v. Robinson, 923 S.W.2d 549 (Tex. 1995) (landmark Texas case excluding "junk science")

Young v. Young, 2009 WL 1507021 (Tex. App.—Fort Worth 2009, no pet.) (AJ's ruling that if wife didn't comply with orders regarding production of documents, etc., was sufficient advance notice of possible death penalty sanctions)

Von Hohn v. Von Hohn, 260 S.W.3d 631 (Tex. App.—Tyler 2008, no pet.) (business evaluator survived *Daubert* challenge based on his prior experience in valuing law firm partnership interests and reliance on evidence regarding case values)

Allen v. Mancini, 170 S.W.3d 167 (Tex. App.—Eastland 2005, pet. denied) (illegal wire tap evidence admissible on civil side of the docket)

Ham v. Ham, 59 S.W.3d 326 (Tex. App.—Texarkana 2001, no pet.) (whether fraud procured wife's signature on divorce decree question of material fact precluding summary judgment)

Daugherty v. Daugherty, 42 S.W.3d 331 (Tex. App.—Texarkana 2001, no pet.) (prisoner deprived of right to participate in divorce to present evidence on property issues)

§ 6.701. Failure to Answer

In a suit for divorce, the petition may not be taken as confessed if the respondent does not file an answer.

Comment

As in other civil cases, a respondent in a divorce case must file a written answer to the petition for divorce or face the consequences of a default judgment. Individuals unfamiliar with the process might be surprised to learn that a large number of divorces are granted by default. In any event, the petitioner must put on evidence sufficient for the court to grant a divorce and other appropriate relief, such as the division of property and orders regarding conservatorship of children of the marriage. The degree of proof necessary depends upon the particular case and the practice of the local court. No doubt due to the no-fault aspect of Texas divorce practice, summary testimony of "insupportability" is universally sufficient to prove grounds for divorce.

Leading Cases

Texas Supreme Court

Matthis v. Lockwood, 156 S.W.3d 743 (Tex. 2005) (counsel's testimony that notice of final hearing mailed not sufficient to sustain default judgment without further evidence)

Courts of Appeals

Tucker v. Tucker, ___ S.W.3d ___, 2010 WL 4705588 (Tex. App.—Dallas 2010, no pet.) (default property division and award of damages for assault reversed due to lack of evidence presented by wife)

Hollis v. Hollis, ___ S.W.3d ___, 2010 WL 3440330 (Tex. App.—Tyler 2010, no pet.) (default divorce division reversed where husband failed to provide testimony of values of property divided)

Barry v. Barry, 193 S.W.3d 72 (Tex. App.—Houston [1st Dist.] 2006, no pet.) (default judgment reversed because prove-up lacked sufficient testimony to sustain property division)

In re Marriage of Runberg, 159 S.W.3d 194 (Tex. App.—Amarillo 2005, no pet.) (husband appeared and announced ready at temporary hearing—default divorce set aside)

O'Neal v. O'Neal, 69 S.W.3d 347 (Tex. App.—Eastland 2002, no pet.) (husband's conclusory testimony in default divorce is no evidence regarding just and right division)

---

§ 6.702. Waiting Period

60 day wait - Day 61 - Divorced - Granted

(a) Except as provided by Subsection (c), the court may not grant a divorce before the 60th day after the date the suit was filed. A decree rendered in violation of this subsection is not subject to collateral attack.

(b) A waiting period is not required before a court may grant an annulment or declare a marriage void other than as required in civil cases generally.

(c) A waiting period is not required under Subsection (a) before a court may grant a divorce in a suit in which the court finds that:

(1) the respondent has been finally convicted of or received deferred adjudication for an offense involving family violence as defined by Section 71.004 against the petitioner or a member of the petitioner's household; or

(2) the petitioner has an active protective order under Title 4 or an active magistrate's order for emergency protection under Article 17.292, Code of Criminal Procedure, based on a finding of family violence, against the respondent because of family violence committed during the marriage.

Comment

The 60–day waiting period required before a divorce may be granted is based on the rationale that parties ought not rush into divorce when there might still be a genuine prospect for reconciliation. Whether this comports with modern-day realities of marriage and divorce is debated by some, but the fact remains that a significant percentage of divorce suits are filed and not finalized by way of nonsuit or dismissal for want of prosecution. However, the 60-day waiting period may be waived by the court in cases involving family violence.

Leading Case

Whiteman v. Whiteman, 682 S.W.2d 357 (Tex. App.—Dallas 1984, no writ) (divorce granted 38 days after filing an amended petition held to be reversible error)

§ 6.703. Jury

In a suit for dissolution of a marriage, either party may demand a jury trial unless the action is a suit to annul an underage marriage under Section 6.102.

Comment

Texas has always accorded divorce litigants the right to a trial by jury. This is almost unique in American jurisprudence, but is a time-tested Texas institution widely supported by the practicing bar. However, even their strongest advocates must admit that jury trials are more talked-about than practiced. For example, for the fiscal year ending August 31, 2005, the Office of Court Administration produced some rather startling statistics. Texas district courts granted 89,642 divorces. Of these, there were 150 jury verdicts and 43 directed verdicts. In sum, 0.2% of all district court divorces tried to a final judgment in fiscal 2005 involved a jury trial. Interestingly, a very different ratio was produced in those county courts at-law having divorce jurisdiction, to wit: 203 jury verdicts out of 9,572 final divorce decrees, or 2.1% of the total. Thus, county courts at law had thirteen times the rate of jury verdicts in divorces than in district courts, and yet resolving the dispute by jury still constitutes a relatively small fraction of the cases. Nonetheless, threat of a jury trial remains a favorite tactical weapon in the litigator's bag of persuasive arguments. Although the Texas Constitution grants the right to trial by jury in civil cases, that right is conditioned by the fact that the legislature may prescribe the circumstances of its exercise in certain cases, *e.g.*, adoption.

CLE/Other Legal Publications

Sharpening your jury skills. Wendy S. Burgower, 2010 Adv. Fam. L.
Jury charge: beyond the boilerplate. Sandra D. Hachem & Kevin Carter Hart, 2010 Adv. Fam. L.
The art of persuasive speaking. Mike McCurley, 2010 Adv. Fam. L.
Jury issues. H.E. Mendez, 2010 Adv. Fam. L. Drafting
Organizing and using the trial notebook. Wendy S. Burgower, 2010 Ultimate Trial Notebook
Jury selection in the 21st century. Marty D. Carden, 2010 Ultimate Trial Notebook
Family law jury trial workshop. (Panel), 2009 Adv. Fam. L.
Jury selection in the age of Twitter. Kevin Karlson, 2009 U.T. Fam. L. Front Lines

Leading Cases

Texas Supreme Court

Texas Dept. of Human Services v. E.B., 802 S.W.2d 647 (Tex. 1990) (broad form submission explained in termination of parental rights case)

Courts of Appeals

In re Marriage of Stein, 190 S.W.3d 73 (Tex. App.—Amarillo 2005, no pet.) (appellant has right to jury demand after decision of bench trial reversed and remanded)

Crittenden v. Crittenden, 52 S.W.3d 768 (Tex. App.—San Antonio 2001, pet. denied) (presumptively valid jury demand denied on showing it is only attempt to delay divorce)

Cross References

Tex. Const., art. 1, § 15, Right of Trial by Jury; Tex. Const., art. 5, § 10, Trial by Jury.

§ 6.704. Testimony of Husband or Wife

(a) In a suit for dissolution of a marriage, the husband and wife are competent witnesses for and against each other. A spouse may not be compelled to testify as to a matter that will incriminate the spouse.

(b) If the husband or wife testifies, the court or jury trying the case shall determine the credibility of the witness and the weight to be given the witness's testimony.

Comment

This section codifies long-standing Texas case law that husband and wife are competent to testify against each other in civil matters, but may not be required to testify about matters that may tend to incriminate the person so testifying.

---

§ 6.705. Testimony by Marriage Counselor

(a) The report by the person named by the court to counsel the parties to a suit for divorce may not be admitted as evidence in the suit.

(b) The person named by the court to counsel the parties is not competent to testify in any suit involving the parties or their children.

(c) The files, records, and other work products of the counselor are privileged and confidential for all purposes and may not be admitted as evidence in any suit involving the parties or their children.

§ 6.706. Change of Name

(a) In a decree of divorce or annulment, the court shall change the name of a party specifically requesting the change to a name previously used by the party unless the court states in the decree a reason for denying the change of name.

(b) The court may not deny a change of name solely to keep the last name of family members the same.

(c) A change of name does not release a person from liability incurred by the person under a previous name or defeat a right the person held under a previous name.

(d) A person whose name is changed under this section may apply for a change of name certificate from the clerk of the court as provided by Section 45.106.

Comment

Texas has long allowed a party (read almost exclusively "the wife") to change his or her name at the time of divorce. This statute is not restricted to a woman desiring to return to her maiden name, but is restricted to a name "previously used." In 1995, reports reached the legislature that some courts were still denying women name changes if the order would result in the mother and her child having different last names. Although it took appellate litigation, it is now clear that a woman must be accorded the right to choose her surname without regard to the gender bias of some trial judges.

Leading Cases

Fly v. Fly, 590 S.W.2d 179 (Tex. Civ. App.—Corpus Christi 1979, no writ) (trial court erred in changing wife's name without her consent)

Lindsey v. Lindsey, 564 S.W.2d 143 (Tex. Civ. App.—Austin 1978, no writ) (court acted properly in granting the wife a change of name over objection of husband)

Cross Reference

TX FCA FAMILY § 45.001 *et seq.*, Change of Name, *infra*.

---

§ 6.707. Transfers and Debts Pending Decree

(a) A transfer of real or personal community property or a debt incurred by a spouse while a suit for divorce or annulment is pending that subjects the other spouse or the community property to liability is void with respect to the other spouse if the transfer was made or the debt incurred with the intent to injure the rights of the other spouse.

(b) A transfer or debt is not void if the person dealing with the transferor or debtor spouse did not have notice of the intent to injure the rights of the other spouse.

(c) The spouse seeking to void a transfer or debt incurred while a suit for divorce or annulment is pending has the burden of proving that the person dealing with the transferor or debtor spouse had notice of the intent to injure the rights of the spouse seeking to void the transaction.

Comment

This section provides limited protection to the innocent spouse if during the pendency of a divorce a culpable spouse attempts to transfer property or incur debt for the purpose of injuring the property rights of the innocent spouse. A transfer of the economic interest in the property or the incurring of a debt is void if a third party had notice of the spouse's intent to injure the innocent spouse. Without such notice, however, the transfer is valid; the burden of proof rests with the complaining spouse. While this section seeks to serve an important social purpose, its application to ordinary consumer debt is problematic. With respect to insider transactions, such as those between family members or with business associates, the burden of proof may not be as onerous as in most other scenarios involving the concept.

Leading Case

Chu v. Hong, 249 S.W.3d 441 (Tex. 2008) (no conspiracy found between husband, his attorney, and buyers of donut shop where husband sold parties' interest during divorce)

Cross Reference

Tex. Bus. & Com. Code Ann. § 24.001 *et seq.*, Uniform Fraudulent Transfer Act.

§ 6.708. Costs

(a) In a suit for dissolution of a marriage, the court as it considers reasonable may award costs to a party. Costs may not be adjudged against a party against whom a divorce is granted for confinement in a mental hospital under Section 6.007.

(b) The expenses of counseling may be taxed as costs against either or both parties.

Comment

This section refers to fees and expenses collected by the clerk of the court, court reporters, and other related charges typically included in a costs bill. Costs ordinarily do not include attorney's fees, *see* annotations to §§ 7.001–.002, *infra*.

§ 6.709. Temporary Orders During Appeal

(a) Not later than the 30th day after the date an appeal is perfected, on the motion of a party or on the court's own motion, after notice and hearing, the trial court may render a temporary order necessary for the preservation of the property and for the protection of the parties during the appeal, including an order to:

(1) require the support of either spouse;

(2) require the payment of reasonable attorney's fees and expenses;

(3) appoint a receiver for the preservation and protection of the property of the parties; or

(4) award one spouse exclusive occupancy of the parties' residence pending the appeal.

(b) The trial court retains jurisdiction to enforce a temporary order under this section unless the appellate court, on a proper showing, supersedes the trial court's order.

CLE/Other Legal Publications

Trying a case with appeal in mind. Chris Nickelson, 2011 ADV. FAM. L

Appellate CYA. Chris Nickelson, 2011 MARRIAGE DISSOLUTION

Appellate and post-trial motions. Georganna L. Simpson, 2010 ADV. FAM. L. DRAFTING

Appellate practice from every angle. Georganna L. Simpson, Lawrence M. Doss, Chris Nickelson, Jimmy Vaught, 2010 ADV. FAM. L

Purgatory: actions you can take during appeal and after remand. Jimmy Vaught, 2010 ADV. FAM. L.

Post-trial motions: what really happens after both sides rest. Angela Pence England, 2010 SO. TEX. TRIAL TIPS & TECHNIQUES

Appellate issues for the family law practitioner. Lucy Forbes & Chad Forbes, 2010 SO. TEX. TRIAL TIPS & TECHNIQUES

Leading Cases

Texas Supreme Court

In re Gabbai, 968 S.W.2d 929 (Tex. 1998) (trial court lacks jurisdiction to enforce by contempt an order of appellate court)

Courts of Appeals

Sheikh v. Sheikh, 248 S.W.3d 381 (Tex. App.—Houston [1st Dist.] 2007, orig. proceeding) (post-divorce turnover-and-receivership order may not enforce property division pending appeal)

In re Fischer–Stoker, 174 S.W.3d 268 (Tex. App.—Houston [1st Dist.] 2005, pet. denied) (appeal blocks trial court's authority to enforce terms of property division in divorce decree by contempt while appeal pending)

In re Boyd, 34 S.W.3d 708 (Tex. App.—Fort Worth 2000, no pet.) (temporary orders to preserve litigant's property rights on appeal of divorce decree must be timely or they are void)

§ 6.710. Notice ~~Copy~~ of Final Decree

The clerk of the court shall mail a **notice of the signing** ~~copy~~ of the final decree of dissolution of a marriage to the party who waived service of process under Section 6.4035 ~~by mailing the copy of the decree to the party~~ at the mailing address contained in the waiver or ~~to~~ the office of the party's attorney of record. **The notice must state that a copy of the decree is available at the office of the clerk of the court and include the physical address of that office.**

Amended by Acts 2011, 82nd Leg., ch. 529 (H.B. 2422), § 1, eff. June 17, 2011.

Comment

This section requires that the court send notice that the decree has been signed and that a copy is available at the clerk's office to any party who waived service of process.

§ 6.711. Findings of Fact and Conclusions of Law

(a) In a suit for dissolution of a marriage in which the court has rendered a judgment dividing the estate of the parties, on request by a party, the court shall state in writing its findings of fact and conclusions of law concerning:

(1) the characterization of each party's assets, liabilities, claims, and offsets on which disputed evidence has been presented; and

(2) the value or amount of the community estate's assets, liabilities, claims, and offsets on which disputed evidence has been presented.

(b) A request for findings of fact and conclusions of law under this section must conform to the Texas Rules of Civil Procedure.

CLE/Other Legal Publications

Think before you write: preparing findings of fact and conclusions of law. Maryellen Whitlock Hicks, 2007 ADV. FAM. L.

Think before you write: preparing findings of fact and conclusions of law. Hon. Eva Guzman & Nina K. Reilly, 2006 ADV. FAM. L.

SUBCHAPTER I. REMARRIAGE

Introductory Comment

The prohibition on remarriage for 30 days prescribed by § 6.801 is akin to the 60-day waiting period for divorce prescribed in § 6.702—an attempt by the legislature to stop an impulsive remarriage. This section has no application to divorced parties wishing to remarry each other.

Section 6.802 provides the court may waive the restriction on remarriage for good cause. Neither § 6.801 or this section have out of state application. It is common knowledge that a recently divorced party may immediately drive to a neighboring state for a quick marriage following a Texas divorce.

Leading Case

Galbraith v. Galbraith, 619 S.W.2d 238 (Tex. Civ. App.—Texarkana 1981, no writ) (remarriage within 30 days does not render a marriage voidable where parties continue to cohabit thereafter)

---

§ 6.801. Remarriage 31 days after Divorce Decreed

(a) Except as otherwise provided by this subchapter, neither party to a divorce may marry a third party before the 31st day after the date the divorce is decreed.

(b) The former spouses may marry each other at any time.

§ 6.802. Waiver of Prohibition Against Remarriage

For good cause shown the court may waive the prohibition against remarriage provided by this subchapter as to either or both spouses if a record of the proceedings is made and preserved or if findings of fact and conclusions of law are filed by the court.

CHAPTER 7. AWARD OF MARITAL PROPERTY

Introductory Comment

Sections 7.001 and 7.002 are the most important sections in Title 1. The origins of these statutes date from 1841; the mandate consistently has been for the courts to divide the property in a manner that the judge deems "just and right," not "50/50" or "equally" as many people seem to think. The Supreme Court of Texas has held that these sections apply only to community property and that they do not authorize the divesting or division of a spouse's separate property.

While the statutory mandate to divide the property in a "just and right" manner may seem simple, its application is fraught with complexity. The valuation of the marital assets, factors to be considered in making a just and right division of the property, and the technique for dividing the marital assets can be very complicated. Issues regarding disposition of the homestead, division of retirement benefits, as well as payment of attorney's fees, further compound the problems. Decrees of divorce, often exceeding 50 to 75 pages, are necessary in order to properly divide and dispose of property.

Always looming in the background is the specter that a spouse may abscond with property, waste assets, fail to disclose important assets, or in the event of an undesired ruling, seek protection of the United States Bankruptcy Court. Finally, an aggrieved spouse may appeal the case seeking a reversal of the division of property and seek a new trial for a re-division of the assets.

Texas lawyers and judges appeared to be quite content with our system of community property for the years between 1988 and 1998. Until the 1999 legislative session, the Texas Legislature enacted relatively few amendments to the Texas Family Code affecting the substantive rules of marital property rights and liabilities. That year and the following sessions in 2001 and 2003 saw the apparent equilibrium in this quiet corner of family law came to an end, and the great social forces of the 1960s through the 1980s which wrought so much change in the remainder of the Family Code reappeared in connection with "conversion of separate property to community," *see* §§ 4.201–.206, and reimbursement and economic contribution, §§ 3.401–.410 and § 7.007.

Section 7.002(b) provides for the same treatment of out of state property, regardless of whether it is claimed to be separate or community. Logically, because property acquired in another jurisdiction that would have been community property if acquired in Texas is treated in the same manner as community, property acquired in another jurisdiction that would have been separate property if acquired in Texas requires identical treatment.

Section 7.002(c) allows spouses to partition earnings and wages in the year of separation or any other year. This provides statutory approval to the practice of divorcing spouses filing separate tax returns and reporting their individual earnings at the end of the year of divorce, thus avoiding the need to suffer the complication of reporting one half of each other's income up to the day of divorce.

CLE/Other Legal Publications

Alimony

See annotations to § 8.001 *et seq.*, *infra.*

Appeals

See annotations to subch. H, ch. 6, *supra.*

Attorney's Fees

Attorney's fees (getting paid for what you do). Charles E. Hardy, 2011 Adv. Fam. L.

Attorney's fees agreements. Kathryn J. Murphy, 2011 Adv. Fam. L.

Attorney fees. Jonathan J. Bates, 2009, 2010 Ultimate Trial Notebook

Attorney fees: asking for them, getting them, and collecting them. Charles M. Wilson, III, 2009 Adv. Fam. L.

Show me the money—your financial relationship with your client. Charles E. Hardy, 2008 Adv. Fam. L.

Attorney's Fees—ways and means. Charles E. Hardy, 2007 Marriage Dissolution

Bankruptcy

Bankruptcy issues. Joseph A. Friedman, 2011 Adv. Fam. L.

Tuition or Neiman's: stretching overextended budgets and solutions for the negative balance sheet. Practical suggestions for economic issues, e.g., underwater real estate, inflated credit card debt and lack of liquidity, and in bankruptcy. Wendy S. Burgower, 2011 U.T. Fam. L. Front Lines

Divorce your credit. Mark L. Aschermann, 2011 So. Tex. Fam. L.

Marital property liabilities: dispelling the myth of community debt. Tom Featherston & Allison Dickson, 73 Tex. B.J. 16 (Jan. 2010)

Financial crisis: selected issues in bankruptcy. Joseph A. Friedman, 2010 Adv. Fam. L.

Bankruptcy and family law. Leta S. Parks, 2010 Fam. L. Front Lines

The intersection of family law and bankruptcy law. Hon. Jeff Bohm & John "Bo" Nichols, Jr., 2010 So. Tex. Fam. L. Conf.

Family law isn't just the Family Code: understanding how other codes apply to Family and Bankruptcy Code. Debra H. Lehrmann & Joseph Friedman, 2009 Adv. Fam. L.

Dividing debts: subprime divorce. Kyle Sanders, 2009 Marriage Dissolution

Division of debt. Kyle W. Sanders, 2009 U.T. Fam. L. Front Lines

Characterization, Reimbursement, and Tracing

See annotations to §§ 3.001–.002, *supra*.

Dividing Community Property

Troubling issues of characterization, valuation, and division. Richard R. Orsinger, 2010 Adv. Fam. L.

Representing the unsophisticated client with assets. G. Thomas Vick, Jr., 2010 Adv. Fam. L.

Property division in a depressed economy. Warren Cole, 2010 Adv. Fam. L.

Trying the property case on a shoestring. Christopher K. Wrampelmeier, 2010 Adv. Fam. L.

Property division and enforcement in the real world. Cheryl L. Wilson, 2010 Marriage Dissolution

Securing the deal. Jack W. Marr, 2010 Marriage Dissolution

Inventories/proposed division. Richard L. Flowers, Jr., 2010 Marriage Dissol. Boot Camp

Property division workshop: getting a disproportionate division; what is "fair and equitable"; creative property division; finding the money. (Panel), 2009 Adv. Fam. L.

Analyzing your property case: a prequel to characterization, valuation, and division of the marital estate. Charles E. Hardy, 2009 Adv. Fam. L.

Disproportionate division. Warren Cole, 2009 U.T. Fam. L. Front Lines

Dividing debts: subprime divorce. Kyle Sanders, 2009 Marriage Dissolution

Disproportionate divisions. Charles E. Hardy, 2009 Marriage Dissolution

Drafting Techniques

Creative drafting. Bret A. Bosker & Kate H. McConnico, 2011 So. Tex. Fam. L.

Alternative drafting orders and decrees to those found in the Family Law Practice Manual. Jimmy Vaught. 2010 Adv. Fam. L. Drafting

New forms in the few Family Law Practice Manual (3rd Ed.). Christopher K. Wrampelmeier, 2010 ADV. FAM. L. DRAFTING

Getting IT: dotting the I's and crossing the t's on requesting relief. Hon. Judy L. Warne and Janet McCullar Vavra, 2010 ULTIMATE TRIAL NOTEBOOK

Drafting decrees and closing documents. Rachel Hooland Moore, 2010 ADV. FAM. L.

Drafting and entering orders. Kyle W. Sanders, 2009, 2010 ULTIMATE TRIAL NOTEBOOK

Drafting decrees and closing documents. Diana S. Friedman, 2009 ADV. FAM. L. BOOT CAMP

The law of interpreting contracts: how to draft contracts to avoid or win litigation. Richard R. Orsinger, 2008 ADV. FAM. L.

Economic Contribution

See annotations to §§ 3.401–.410, *supra*.

Marital Property Liabilities

See annotations to § 3.202, *supra*.

Pension Plans

See annotations to § 7.003, *infra*.

Property Subject to Division

Dealing with business entities. Warren Cole, Stephen M. Orsinger, & Cheryl Wilson, 2011 ADV. FAM. L.

Unwrapping and understanding future financial benefits. J. Lindsey Short, 2011 ADV. FAM. L.

Real estate, oil & gas, and estate planning. Thomas P. Goranson, Moderator, 2011 ADV. FAM. L.

Dealing with Damages/Recovery as Property. John F. Nichols, Sr., 2011 MARRIAGE DISSOLUTION

Business entities. Adam J. Morris, 2011 SO. TEX. FAM. L.

Buy/Sell agreements. Kyle W. Sanders, 2010 ADV. FAM. L. DRAFTING

Business entities from a family law perspective. E Michelle Bohreer and Sherri A. Evans, 2010 U.T. FAM. LAW FRONT LINES

Dr. Strangelove: Frozen Eggs and Sperm. Charles R. Hodges, 2010 ADV. FAM. L.

Stock options, deferred compensation plans and other executive benefits. Christy Adamcik Gammill, 2010 FAM. L. BOOT CAMP

Defined benefit and contribution plans. Mike Gregory, 2010 MARRIAGE DISSOLUTION

Trust characterization issues after Sharma. Adam J. Morris, 2010 SO. TEX. FAM. L. CONF.

Reimbursement

See annotations to §§ 3.001–.002, *supra*.

Retirement Benefits

See annotations to § 7.003, *infra* .

Taxation Issues

How to interpret financial statements, income tax returns, and similar documents. Susan Fae McLerran, 2011 MARRIAGE DISSOLUTION

Family law and tax: 25 questions, 17 answers. (Panel), 2009 ADV. FAM. L.

Dealing with complex business entities on divorce (financial, accounting, tax, valuation, characterization, and related topics). Patrice L. Ferguson, 2008 NEW FRONTIERS

Tax issues in divorce. Melvyn B. Frumkes, 2008 ADV. FAM. L.

Divorce calculations and how to present them to the trier of fact. Haran Levy, 2007 U.T. FAM. L. FRONT LINES

Torts

Other causes of action. John F. "Bo" Nichols, 2011 ADV. FAM. L.

Dealing with damages/recovery as property. John F. Nichols, Sr., 2011 MARRIAGE DISSOLUTION

The Impact of Domestic Violence on a Divorce. Hon. Doug Warne, Scott A. Beauchamp, & Judith G. Wells, 2011 Marriage Dissolution

Legal ramifications of emotional abuse. Shelly Moore, 2010 Adv. Fam. L.

Torts in divorce. Kate H. McConnico, 2010 So. Tex. Fam. L. Conf.

The latest causes of action in family law. Charla Bradshaw Conner, 2009 Adv. Fam. L.

Personal injury lawsuits in intimate relationships. Jeana L. Lungwitz & Leslie M. Stewart, 2008 U.T. Fam. L. Front Lines

Economic and physical torts: proving waste and fraud for a disproportionate division. Bruce D. Bain, 2008 Marriage Dissolution

Trial Techniques

See annotations to ch. 6, Subchapter H. Trial and Appeal, *supra*.

Valuation

Valuation of Property: Panel discussion. Robert C. Sullivan, Jr., Moderator, 2011 Adv. Fam. L.

Understanding business valuations. Autumn V. Kraus, 2011 Adv. Fam. L.

Troubling issues of characterization, valuation and division. Richard R. Orsinger, 2010 Adv. Fam. L.

Valuation: approaches, assets, and authority. R. Scott Downing, 2010 Adv. Fam. L.

Analyzing your property case: a prequel to characterization, valuation, and division of the marital estate. Charles E. Hardy, 2009 Adv. Fam. L.

Valuation: the impact of buy/sell agreements. Becky A. Beaver, Rachel Bacarri, & Susannah Stinson, 2009 Adv. Fam. L.

Due diligence for the business evaluation. Haran Levy, 2009 Adv. Fam. L.

Current valuation challenges. (Panel), 2009 Adv. Fam. L.

Protecting your characterization and valuation claims: avoiding waiver or admission in inventories, discovery responses, and testimony. Barbara D. Nunneley, 2009 Adv. Fam. L.

Valuation. Sherri A. Evans, 2009 Marriage Dissolution

See Accompanying CD–ROM for Additional CLE/Other Legal Publications

Leading Cases

Alimony

See annotations to Chapter 8, *infra*.

Attorney's Fees

Brown v. Fullenweider, 52 S.W.3d 169 (Tex. 2001) (attorney's fees not subject to post divorce clarification and enforcement provisions)

Carle v. Carle, 149 Tex. 469, 234 S.W.2d 1002 (1950) (attorney's fees are a factor in making a just and right division)

Coleman v. Coleman, ___ S.W.3d ___, 2010 WL 5187612 (Tex. App.—Houston [1st Dist.] 2010, no pet.) (husband waived right to complain about failure to make a prior demand for attorneys fees by not bringing it up at trial court)

Smith v. Deneve, 285 S.W.3d 904 (Tex. App.—Dallas 2009, no pet (even though no common law marriage found, attorneys fees allowed since underlying suit brought was a suit for divorce).

Aland v. Martin, 271 S.W.3d 424 (Tex. App.—Dallas 2008, no pet.) (evidence insufficient to find that attorney intended to injury husband by not lifting attorney lien on marital residence as security for payment of fees)

Brockie v. Webb, 244 S.W.3d 905 (Tex. App.—Dallas 2008, no pet.) (unpaid fees recovered—attorney's fees can be recoverable for defending against malpractice counterclaim, but need sufficient evidence reasonable and necessary)

Bankruptcy

U.S. Supreme Court

Farrey v. Sanderfoot, 500 U.S. 291, 114 L.Ed.2d 337, 111 S.Ct. 1825 (1991) (ex-wife's judicial lien on homestead awarded to ex-husband on divorce not discharged by his bankruptcy)

Federal Courts

In re Davidson, 947 F.2d 1294 (5th Cir. 1991) (quasi-estoppel precludes discharge of alimony obligations)

In re Badgett, 647 F.2d 550 (5th Cir. 1981); *In re* Nunnally, 506 F.2d 1024 (5th Cir. 1975) (Texas-style contractual alimony not dischargeable)

In re Finch 130 B.R. 753 (S.D. Tex. 1991) (judicial lien imposed for "just and right" division not dischargeable in bankruptcy)

Texas Supreme Court

Douglas v. Delp, 987 S.W.2d 879 (Tex. 1999) (malpractice suit as an asset of the community swept into husband's bankruptcy)

Courts of Appeals

Dickinson v. Dickinson, 324 S.W.3d 653, (Tex. App.—Fort Worth 2010, no pet.) (no violation of bankruptcy stay when decree included only "recommendations to the bankruptcy court)

Cleaver v. Cleaver, 140 S.W.3d 771 (Tex. App.—Tyler 2004, no pet.) (failure to list pending claim of potential community property in bankruptcy estops assertion of claim)

Characterization, Reimbursement, and Tracing

See annotations to §§ 3.001–3.002, *supra*.

Dividing Community Property

U.S. Supreme Court

Boggs v. Boggs, 520 U.S. 833, 117 S.Ct. 1754, 138 L.Ed.2d 49 (1997) (ERISA preempts LA community property law—first wife's attempt to leave "her share" of husband's retirement plan to her heirs ineffective; second wife takes as surviving spouse)

Texas Supreme Court

Keen v. Weaver, 121 S.W.3d 721 (Tex. 2003) (retirement plans preempted by ERISA governed by federal common law—divorce decree sufficient to waive nonemployee's interest in ex-spouse' retirement plans)

Schlueter v. Schlueter, 975 S.W.2d 584 (Tex. 1998) (fraud on the community factor for division but not separate tort)

Dawson–Austin v. Austin, 968 S.W.2d 319 (Tex. 1998) (Texas divorce law governs separate property acquired in Minnesota because Texas has most significant relationship to the action)

Wilde v. Murchie, 949 S.W.2d 331 (Tex. 1997) (words of divestiture not required to convey interest in homestead)

Tenery v. Tenery, 932 S.W.2d 29 (Tex. 1996) (failure of trial court to file findings of fact and conclusions of law not reversible error)

Cameron v. Cameron, 641 S.W.2d 210 (Tex. 1982) (court may not divest spouse of separate personalty)

Murff v. Murff, 615 S.W.2d 696 (Tex. 1981) (list of factors court may consider in making division, including earning disparity)

Eggemeyer v. Eggemeyer, 554 S.W.2d 137 (Tex. 1977) (court may not divest spouse of his or her separate realty)

McKnight v. McKnight, 543 S.W.2d 863 (Tex. 1976) (appellate court can reverse trial court's division, but cannot divide property itself)

Nail v. Nail, 486 S.W.2d 761 (Tex. 1972) (professional goodwill not to be valued in dividing marital estate)

Courts of Appeals

Macias v. Macias, 2010 WL 2697139 (Tex. App.—Corpus Christi 2010, pet. denied) (award to wife of 40% of husband's military benefits in decree not limited to community property portion)

Sanchez v. Sanchez, 2010 WL 3249905 (Tex. App.—2010, no pet.) (wife not entitled to bill of review on property division after learning that value of business she received was less due to transfer of assets within company by husband prior to the divorce)

Pribyl v. Pribyl, 307 S.W.3d 882 (Tex. App.—Austin 2010, no pet.) (decree awarded husband any and all benefits from his employment which included the stock options he failed to disclose)

Jurek v. Couch- Jurek, 296 S.W.3d 864 (Tex. App.—El Paso 2009, no pet.) (husband failed to establish how mischaracterizations of rent houses as wife separate property caused harm in the division of property)

Bhatti v. Bhatti, 2009 WL 2545057 (Tex. App.—Corpus Christi 2009, no pet.) (court's adoption of special masters rulings on property division affirmed over wife's objection for failure to request trial de novo)

See also annotations to Characterization, Reimbursement, and Tracing, Subchapter A, Chapter 3, *supra*.

Quasi-Community Property

Estate of Hanau v. Hanau, 730 S.W.2d 663 (Tex. 1987) (quasi-community property inapplicable in probate proceedings)

Cameron v. Cameron, 641 S.W.2d 210 (Tex. 1982) (common law application of statutory rule for quasi-community property before statute effective)

Zorilla v. Wahid, 83 S.W.3d 247 (Tex. App.—Corpus Christi 2002, no pet.) (children's "educational fund" quasi-community property subject to 60–40 split)

Reimbursement

See also annotations to Characterization, Reimbursement, and Tracing, §§ 3.001–.002, *supra*.

Heggen v. Pemelton, 836 S.W.2d 145 (Tex. 1992) (equitable lien may be imposed on separate property homestead only to secure right of reimbursement for community improvements, not to insure just and right division of community property)

Penick v. Penick, 783 S.W.2d 194 (Tex. 1988) (enhancement of separate estate offset by benefit to community estate)

Anderson v. Gilliland, 684 S.W.2d 673 (Tex. 1985) (reimbursement measured by enhancement)

Jensen v. Jensen, 665 S.W.2d 107 (Tex. 1984) (community time, toil, and effort contributed towards value of separate estate)

Separate Property

Calder v. Calder, ___ S.W.3d ___, 2010 WL 3370766 (Tex. App.—Austin 2010, no pet.) (wife met burden of proof that Chihuahua was her separate property when funds came from her premarital account)

Langston v. Langston, 82 S.W.3d 686 (Tex. App.—Eastland 2002, no pet.) (husband's separate property home cannot be awarded to wife even though community claim for economic contribution may impose lien on property)

Osorno v. Osorno, 76 S.W.3d 509 (Tex. App.—Houston [14th Dist.] 2002, no pet.) (husband's testimony regarding financial accounts not enough to trace his separate property claim, even with premarital agreement)

McClary v. Thompson, 65 S.W.3d 829 (Tex. App.—Fort Worth 2002, pet. denied) (parties' premarital agreement identified the separate property existing at the time of the marriage but did not provide a basis to assert that future additions to a defined retirement benefit would be the husband's separate property)

Taxation Issues

United States v. Mitchell, 403 U.S. 190, 29 L.Ed.2d 406, 91 S.Ct. 1763 (1971) (state law controls whether income is separate or community for tax purposes)

Roth v. Roth, ___ S.W.3d ___, 2010 WL 5541701 (Tex. App.—Corpus Christi 2010, no pet.) (additional terms regarding taxes included in the decree but not in the parties' settlement agreement impermissible)

Durden v. McClure, 281 S.W.3d 137 (Tex. App.—San Antonio 2008, no pet.) (consent judgment in which mother relinquished rights to tax exemption for dependents upheld as valid agreement in accordance with Tax Code)

Torts

Texas Supreme Court

Chu v. Hong, 249 S.W.3d 441 (Tex. 2008) (third-party is not liable for tort of fraud on community—issue is for division of property)

Vickery v. Vickery, 999 S.W.2d 342 (Tex. 1999) (*Schlueter* still the law, notwithstanding unpublished opinion complicating the picture)

Schlueter v. Schlueter, 975 S.W.2d 584 (Tex. 1998) (fraud on the community factor for division but not separate tort)

Twyman v. Twyman, 855 S.W.2d 619 (Tex. 1993) (Texas recognizes tort of intentional infliction of emotional distress, which may be joined in divorce if "double-counting" eliminated)

Bounds v. Caudle, 560 S.W.2d 925 (Tex. 1977) (no spousal immunity for intentional tort)

Courts of Appeals

Chek Investments, LLC, KEH Properties, LTD and Red Hot Plantation, LLC v. LR, 260 S.W.3d 704 (Tex. App.—Dallas 2008, no pet.) (no interlocutory appeal for denial of special appearance filed by third party entities operated by husband)

Solares v. Solares, 232 S.W.3d 873 (Tex. App.—Dallas 2007, no pet.) (divorce court lacks jurisdiction over wife's independent fraud and conversion claims) (fiduciary duty between spouses ends at divorce)

Ginsburg v. Chernoff/Silver & Associates, Inc., 137 S.W.3d 231 (Tex. App.—Houston [1st Dist.] 2004, no pet.) (divorce agreement and decree eliminated spouses' claims against third parties because it equitably divided the spouse's estate, taking into consideration all claims and counterclaims between them)

Valuation

Graves v. Tomlinson, 329 S.W.3d 128 (Tex. App.–Houston [14th Dist.] 2010, pet. filed) (mischaracterization was significant enough to warrant remand; wife's issues with valuation methodology could not be brought for first time on appeal, should have been addressed at trial court)

Green v. Green, ___ S.W.3d ___, 2011 WL 2119742 (Tex. App.—Beaumont, no pet.) (trial court setting aside of MSA affirmed based upon husband's misrepresentations of value and existence of assets)

Sanchez v. Sanchez, ___ S.W.3d ___, 2010 WL 3249905 (Tex. App.—2010, no pet.) (wife not entitled to bill of review on property division after learning that value of business she received was less due to transfer of assets within company by husband prior to the divorce)

Mandell v. Mandell, ___ S.W.3d ___, 2010 WL 1006406 (Tex. App.—Fort Worth 2010, no pet.) (when valuing shares of closely held company with restriction that shares must first be offered to the corporation or other shareholders at value in shareholder agreement, fair market value is zero and parties may show actual value of the property interest to the owner)

Von Hohn v. Von Hohn, 260 S.W.3d 631 (Tex. App.—Tyler 2008, no pet.) (partnership agreement not determinative as to value of husband's interest in firm and other evidence can be considered, but to future earnings)

Morris v. Morris, 12 S.W.3d 877 (Tex. App.—Texarkana 2000, no pet.) (valuation of items of property acquired when it is component of cash award controlling issue)

Roberts v. Roberts, 999 S.W.2d 424 (Tex. App.—El Paso 1999, no pet.) (valuation of assets required in order for appellate court to determine whether trial court abused its discretion)

Pelzig v. Berkebile, 931 S.W.2d 398 (Tex. App.—Corpus Christi 1996, no writ) (court has discretion in choosing value assigned to property)

See Accompanying CD–ROM for Cases Linked to Westlaw and Additional Leading Cases

Cross References

TEX. CIV. PRAC. & REM. CODE § 31.001, Passage of Title; TEX. CIV. PRAC. & REM. CODE, § 64.001 *et seq.*, Receivership.

§ 7.001. General Rule of Property Division

In a decree of divorce or annulment, the court shall order a division of the estate of the parties in a manner that the court deems just and right, having due regard for the rights of each party and any children of the marriage.

§ 7.002. Division and Disposition of Certain Property Under Special Circumstances

(a) In addition to the division of the estate of the parties required by Section 7.001, in a decree of divorce or annulment the court shall order a division of the following real and personal property, wherever situated, in a manner that the court deems just and right, having due regard for the rights of each party and any children of the marriage:

(1) property that was acquired by either spouse while domiciled in another state and that would have been community property if the spouse who acquired the property had been domiciled in this state at the time of the acquisition; or

(2) property that was acquired by either spouse in exchange for real or personal property and that would have been community property if the spouse who acquired the property so exchanged had been domiciled in this state at the time of its acquisition.

(b) In a decree of divorce or annulment, the court shall award to a spouse the following real and personal property, wherever situated, as the separate property of the spouse:

(1) property that was acquired by the spouse while domiciled in another state and that would have been the spouse's separate property if the spouse had been domiciled in this state at the time of acquisition; or

(2) property that was acquired by the spouse in exchange for real or personal property and that would have been the spouse's separate property if the spouse had been domiciled in this state at the time of acquisition.

(c) In a decree of divorce or annulment, the court shall confirm the following as the separate property of a spouse if partitioned or exchanged by written agreement of the spouses:

(1) income and earnings from the spouses' property, wages, salaries, and other forms of compensation received on or after January 1 of the year in which the suit for dissolution of marriage was filed; or

(2) income and earnings from the spouses' property, wages, salaries, and other forms of compensation received in another year during which the spouses were married for any part of the year.

§ 7.003. Disposition of Retirement and Employment Benefits and Other Plans

In a decree of divorce or annulment, the court shall determine the rights of both spouses in a pension, retirement plan, annuity, individual retirement account, employee stock option plan, stock option, or other form of savings, bonus, profit-sharing, or other employer plan or financial plan of an employee or a participant, regardless of whether the person is self-employed, in the nature of compensation or savings.

CLE/Other Legal Publications

Unwrapping and understanding future financial benefits. J. Lindsey Short, Jr., 2011 Adv. Fam. L.

Early withdrawal and retirement benefits. Cheryl L. Wilson, 2011 Marriage Dissolution

Characterization of property in-depth discussion, including business interests, trusts and retirement plans. Kathryn J. Murphy, 2011 U.T. Fam. L. Front Lines

QDRO'S and retirement benefits. Charla Bradshaw Conner, 2010 Adv. Fam. L. Drafting

Primer: the military. James N. Higdon, 2010 Fam. L. Front Lines

Military retirement benefits. James N. Higdon, 2010 Marriage Dissolution

Defined benefit and contribution plans. Mike Gregory, 2010 Marriage Dissolution

Division of Military Retired Pay. John E. Kirchner, 43 Fam. L.Q. 367 (2009)

Exploring employment plans and benefits, and drafting QDRO's. (Panel), 2009 Adv. Fam. L.

Unique compensation—what is it and who owns it? Katherine Anne Kinser, 2009 U.T. Fam. L. Front Lines

---

See Accompanying CD–ROM for Additional CLE/Other Legal Publications

---

Leading Cases

Formula for Division

Texas Supreme Court

Grier v. Grier, 731 S.W.2d 931 (Tex. 1987) (division of community interest in military retirement pay based on the rank held by service member on day of divorce)

Berry v. Berry, 647 S.W.2d 945 (Tex. 1983) (defined benefit retirement payments to be apportioned based on community's interest at time of divorce)

Taggart v. Taggart, 552 S.W.2d 422 (Tex. 1977) (community interest in retirement benefit is the fraction of number of months married divided by the number of months employed)

Courts of Appeals

Howell v. Howell, 2009 WL 2025266 (Tex. App.—Texarkana 2009, no pet.) (mem. op.) (specific values of 401k award in decree were merely demonstrative and did not indicate a lump sum award; wife's award in QDRO were clearly subject to post-divorce gains and losses on the account)

Baker v. Donovan, 199 S.W.3d 577 (Tex. App.—Houston [1st Dist.] 2006, rev. denied) (wife awarded 50% of military retirement as of date of divorce—years later receipt of VA benefits as substitute does not affect res judicata affect)

Prague v. Prague, 190 S.W.3d 31 (Tex. App.—Dallas 2005, no pet.) (wife's TRS retirement partially her separate property; *Taggart*, not *Berry* controls disproportionate division when retirement "in pay" status)

Loria v. Loria, 189 S.W.3d 797 (Tex. App.—Houston [1st Dist.] 2006, no pet.) (restriction in QDRO and divorce decree on military member's right to substitute disability pay for retirement impermissible interference with federal law)

Enforcement

Texas Supreme Court

Reiss v. Reiss, 118 S.W.3d 439 (Tex. 2003) (division of retirement benefits enforced as res judicata—error in applying law not appealed cannot be collaterally corrected)

Shanks v. Treadway, 110 S.W.3d 444 (Tex. 2003) (1981 prospective division of retirement benefits enforced as decreed—remedy for division contrary to current law was not appealed, so ex-wife takes 25% of 1998 retirement benefits)

Keen v. Weaver, 121 S.W.3d 721 (Tex. 2003) (ex-wife's interest in ERISA plan enforceable under federal common law)

Courts of Appeals

In re Marriage of Jones, 154 S.W.3d 225 (Tex. App.—Texarkana 2005, no pet.) (division of retirement benefits clarified by subsequent QDRO)

Charriere v. Charriere, 7 S.W.3d 217 (Tex. App.—Dallas 1999, no pet.) (stock options received during marriage but not exercised are community property—whether continued employment as requirement doesn't affect character)

Governmental/Military Benefits

U.S. Supreme Court/Federal Courts

Mansell v. Mansell, 490 U.S. 581, 104 L.Ed.2d 675, 109 S.Ct. 2023 (1989) (VA disability benefits are not divisible community property)

Kunin v. Feofanov, 69 F.3d 59 (5th Cir. 1995) (termination of nonemployee spouse's interest in public pension plan upheld—Tex. Gov't Code doesn't violate state constitution)

Texas Supreme Court

Hagen v. Hagen, 282 S.W.3d 899 (Tex. 2009) (for purposes of divorce decree, "military retirement pay" did not include VA disability benefits)

Holmes v. Kent, 221 S.W.3d 622 (Tex. 2007) (statutory requirements for revocation of TRS benefits must be followed—no exceptions) (pre-decree designation of spouse as beneficiary stands when divorced teacher dies)

Havlen v. McDougall, 22 S.W.3d 343 (Tex. 2000) (pre–1981 divorce decree silent about partition of military retirement, USFSPA amendments prohibit post-divorce partition)

Veterans Administration v. Kee, 706 S.W.2d 101 (Tex. 1986) (VA disability benefits not subject to garnishment)

Courts of Appeals

Macias v. Macias, ___ S.W.3d ___, 2010 WL 2697139, (Tex. App.—Corpus Christi 2010, pet. denied) (award to wife of 40% of husband's military benefits in decree not limited to community property portion)

Gillin v. Gillin, 307 S.W.3d 395 (Tex. App.—San Antonio 2009, no pet.) (trial court's inclusion of language that prohibited husband from electing military disability benefits instead of retirement pay post-divorce preempted by federal law which allows for such an election)

Sharp v. Sharp, 314 S.W.3d 22 (Tex. App.—San Antonio 2009, no pet.)(wife's award of 50% of husband's disposable retired or retainer pay did not include his Combat Related Special Compensation benefit, even though receipt of CBSC benefits reduces the retirement pay benefit he was eligible to receive)

Zamarripa v. Zamarripa, 2009 WL 1875580 (Tex. App.—Houston 2009, pet. denied) (mem. op.) (even when husband and wife both acknowledged that husband had contributed years of service to pension before marriage, affirmed as community property where both spouses listed pension as community and husband failed to corroborate his pre-marriage contributions)

Thomas v. Piorkowski, 286 S.W.3d 662 (Tex. App.—Corpus Christi 2009, no pet.) (award of portion of US Armed Forces "disposable retirement pay" to wife expressly excludes temporary disability benefits husband was receiving)

Stavinoha v. Stavinoha, 126 S.W.3d 604 (Tex. App.—Houston 14th Dist. 2004, no pet.) (police officer's deferred retirement benefits community property under *Taggert*)

Undivided Retirement Benefits Subject To Partition

Buys v. Buys, 924 S.W.2d 369 (Tex. 1996) (residuary clause unambiguously awarded retirement benefits to nonemployee spouse although benefits not expressly mentioned)

Koepke v. Koepke, 732 S.W.2d 299 (Tex. 1987) (partition mandated of undivided retirement benefits that were not expressly awarded in divorce decree)

Allison v. Allison, 700 S.W.2d 914 (Tex. 1985) and Constance v. Constance, 544 S.W.2d 659 (Tex. 1976) (express award of retirement benefits bars subsequent partition)

Berry v. Berry, 647 S.W.2d 945 (Tex. 1983) (defined benefit retirement payments to be apportioned based on the community's interest at time of divorce)

Taggart v. Taggart, 552 S.W.2d 422 (Tex. 1977) *and* Cearley v. Cearley, 544 S.W.2d 661 (Tex. 1976) (spouse has community property interest in nonvested, nonmatured retirement benefits not divided on divorce)

***See* Accompanying CD–ROM for Cases Linked to Westlaw and Additional Leading Cases**

Cross References

TX FCA Family § 9.001 *et seq.*, Post–Decree Proceedings, *infra*; TX FCA Family § 9.302, Pre–Decree Designation of Ex–Spouse as Beneficiary in Retirement Benefits and Other Financial Plans, *infra.*

TX FCA Govt § 804.001 *et seq.*, Domestic Relations Orders and Spousal Consent, *infra.*

Civil Service Retirement Benefits. 5 U.S.C.A. §§ 2105, 8331 *et seq.*

Uniformed Services Former Spouses Protection Act, 10 U.S.C.A. § 1072 *et seq.*, 10 U.S.C.A. § 1408 *et seq.*

Retirement Equity Act. 26 U.S.C.A. §§ 401, 402, 414.

Employee Retirement Income Security Act of 1974. 29 U.S.C.A. § 1055 *et seq.*

§ 7.004. Disposition of Rights in Insurance

In a decree of divorce or annulment, the court shall specifically divide or award the rights of each spouse in an insurance policy.

Comment

Specifically directing the trial court to divide insurance that is a community asset is a truism and redundant. But, while true, historically such a reminder has proven to be crucially necessary. Although this set of community assets has generated far fewer cases and CLE materials, unless reminded many a lawyer and trial court have failed to allocate insurance in the division of community property.

CLE/Legal Publications

Dealing with damages/recovery as property. John F. Nichols, Sr., 2011 Marriage Dissolution

Destroyed Community Property, Damaged Persons, and Insurers' Duty to Indemnify Innocent Spouses and Other Co-Insured Fiduciaries: An Attempt to Harmonize Conflicting Federal and State Courts' Declaratory Judgments. Willy E. Rice, 2 Est. Plan. & Community Prop. L.J. 63 (2009)

Leading Cases

Egelhoff v. Egelhoff, 532 U.S. 141, 121 S.Ct. 1322 (2001) (ERISA preempts state statute voiding pre-divorce designation of spouse as beneficiary of employee's life insurance and pension)

Barnett v. Barnett, 67 S.W.3d 107 (Tex. 2001), *reversing pet. granted in part,* 985 S.W.2d 520 (federal ERISA preempts Texas Family Code regarding life insurance obtained through employment)

Hawkins v. Hawkins, ___ S.W.3d ___, 2010 WL 5514344 (Tex. App.—Houston [14th Dist.] 2010, no pet.) (insurance proceeds for claim regarding house not awarded in decree, only interest in house was)

J.C. Penney Life Ins. Co. v. Heinrich, 32 S.W.3d 280 (Tex. App.—San Antonio 2000, pet. denied) (widow wins when separated widow and cohabitant—putative common law wife—battle for man's life insurance proceeds)

Cross References

TX FCA Family § 9.001 *et seq.*, Post-Decree Proceedings, *infra*; TX FCA Family § 9.301, Pre-Decree Designation of Ex-Spouse as Beneficiary of Life Insurance, *infra*.

---

§ 7.005. Insurance Coverage Not Specifically Awarded

(a) If in a decree of divorce or annulment the court does not specifically award all of the rights of the spouses in an insurance policy other than life insurance in effect at the time the decree is rendered, the policy remains in effect until the policy expires according to the policy's own terms.

(b) The proceeds of a valid claim under the policy are payable as follows:

(1) if the interest in the property insured was awarded solely to one former spouse by the decree, to that former spouse;

(2) if an interest in the property insured was awarded to each former spouse, to those former spouses in proportion to the interests awarded; or

(3) if the insurance coverage is directly related to the person of one of the former spouses, to that former spouse.

(c) The failure of either former spouse to change the endorsement on the policy to reflect the distribution of proceeds established by this section does not relieve the insurer of liability to pay the proceeds or any other obligation on the policy.

(d) This section does not affect the right of a former spouse to assert an ownership interest in an undivided life insurance policy, as provided by Subchapter D, Chapter 9.

Leading Case

Brandon v. Travelers Insurance Co., 18 F.3d 1321 (5th Cir. 1994) (Texas statute requiring redesignation of ex-spouse as beneficiary on life insurance policy preempted by ERISA), *cert. denied,* 115 S.Ct. 732 (1995)

Cross Reference

TX FCA Family § 9.001 *et seq.*, Post–Decree Proceedings, *infra*; TX FCA Family § 9.201, Procedure for Division of Certain Property Not Divided on Divorce or Annulment, *et seq., infra.*

Tex. Prob. Code Ann. § 69. Voidness Arising from Divorce.

---

§ 7.006. Agreement Incident to Divorce or Annulment

(a) To promote amicable settlement of disputes in a suit for divorce or annulment, the spouses may enter into a written agreement concerning the division of the property and the liabilities of the spouses and maintenance of either spouse. The agreement may be revised or repudiated before rendition of the divorce or annulment unless the agreement is binding under another rule of law.

(b) If the court finds that the terms of the written agreement in a divorce or annulment are just and right, those terms are binding on the court. If the court approves the agreement, the court may set forth the agreement in full or incorporate the agreement by reference in the final decree.

(c) If the court finds that the terms of the written agreement in a divorce or annulment are not just and right, the court may request the spouses to submit a revised agreement or may set the case for a contested hearing.

Comment

This section attempts to reflect the reality of Texas family law practice wherein ordinarily parties enter into settlement agreements. Whether these agreements are incorporated into the final decree of divorce varies widely around Texas. Some lawyers prefer to embody all terms of the settlement in the agreement and file a very short decree of divorce that merely refers to the agreement, which most often is not filed of record. Other lawyers prefer a single document, the final decree of divorce, which embodies the agreement as evidenced by signing. The decree may or may not itself be a contract. A settlement that also constitutes a contract may contain additional provisions that ordinarily could not be included in a decree, *e.g.,* contractual remedies, fixing of venue, and college education for the children.

Undoubtedly, by far the most significant impact on day-to-day practice involving agreements incident to divorce (AID, a.k.a. property settlement agreements, PSA) are the statutory rules applicable to mediated agreements and those resulting from collaborative law, *see* §§ 6.602–.603, and annotations, *supra*. Settlement agreements reached through those procedures are binding on the court because "a party is entitled to judgment" on such agreements.

CLE/Other Legal Publications

Securing agreements and judgments. Larry L. Martin, 2011 ADV. FAM. L.

The Road to Settlement: Rule 11 Agreements, Informal Settlement Agreements and Mediated Settlement Agreements. Jimmy Vaught, 2011 MARRIAGE DISSOLUTION

Agreements between counsel and parties: Rule 11, stipulations, MSA's and informal settlement agreements. Charla Bradshaw Conner & Rothwell B. Pool, 2010 ADV. FAM. L.

Finalizing the deal: Rule 11 and the importance of getting orders timely signed. Chris Nickelson & Gary L. Nickelson, 2010 MARRIAGE DISSOLUTION

Leading Cases

Texas Supreme Court

Chisholm v. Chisholm, 209 S.W.3d 96 (Tex. 2006) (wife's statements in open court demonstrated a lack of consent to agreed judgment at time of rendition—moreover, judgment did not literally conform to purported agreement)

Buys v. Buys, 924 S.W.2d 369 (Tex. 1996) (ex-wife owns military retirement benefits covered by property settlement residuary clause incorporated into divorce decree)

Padilla v. LaFrance, 907 S.W.2d 454 (Tex. 1995) (series of letters between the parties constitutes Rule 11 Settlement Agreement, enforceable by the court as a binding contract)

Courts of Appeals

Roth v. Roth, ___ S.W.3d ___, 2010 WL 5541701 (Tex. App.—Corpus Christi 2010, no pet.) (additional terms regarding taxes included in the decree but not in the parties' settlement agreement impermissible)

Snider v. Snider, ___ S.W.3d ___, 2010 WL 3687031 (Tex. App.—El Paso 2010, no pet.) (when wife questioned division of retirement benefits in Rule 11 agreement for property division, court could not insert its own division)

Schwartz v. Schwartz, 247 S.W.3d 804 (Tex. App.—Dallas 2008, no pet.) (contract law applies to AID after incorporated by reference in divorce degree)

Cook v. Cook, 243 S.W.3d 800 (Tex. App.—Fort Worth 2007, no pet.) (trial court approval of AID not rendition of judgment; revocation of consent is effective until judge announces decision)

Henderson v. Chambers, 208 S.W.3d 546 (Tex. App.—Austin 2006, no pet.) (divorce settlement agreement voids all subsequent claims of intrinsic fraud tried in the prior lawsuit)

***See* Accompanying CD–ROM for Cases Linked to Westlaw and Additional Leading Cases**

Cross References

TX FCA CIV PRAC & REM § 154.001, *et seq.*, Alternative Dispute Resolution Procedures, *infra*.

TX FCA FAMILY § 6.604, Informed Settlement Conference, *supra*; TX FCA FAMILY § 153.007, Agreement Concerning Conservatorship, *infra*; TX FCA FAMILY § 153.0071, Alternative Dispute Resolution Procedures, *infra*; TX FCA FAMILY § 154.124, Agreement Concerning Support, *infra*.

§ 7.007. Disposition of Claim for Reimbursement

In a decree of divorce or annulment, the court shall determine the rights of both spouses in a claim for reimbursement as provided by Subchapter E, Chapter 3, and shall apply equitable principles to:

(1) determine whether to recognize the claim after taking into account all the relative circumstances of the spouses; and

(2) order a division of the claim for reimbursement, if appropriate, in a manner that the court considers just and right, having due regard for the rights of each party and any children of the marriage.

Leading Case

Langston v. Langston, 82 S.W.3d 686 (Tex. App.—Eastland 2002, no pet.) (husband's separate property home cannot be awarded to wife even though community claim for economic contribution may impose lien on property)

§ 7.008. Consideration of Taxes

In ordering the division of the estate of the parties to a suit for dissolution of a marriage, the court may consider:

(1) whether a specific asset will be subject to taxation; and

(2) if the asset will be subject to taxation, when the tax will be required to be paid.

Comment

This section represents a legislative rejection of those appellate decisions holding that taxes may not be considered in the division of a marital estate. Obviously, tax free cash in a checking account is quite different from untaxed funds in a 401(k) retirement account. Calculation of the taxes to be paid in the future and the discount to be used requires some thought and calculation, but this is preferable to the complete prohibition of such consideration. In reality, recognition of taxes as an important factor in reaching an agreement has been the rule of practice for able lawyers. If the case is to be decided by the court rather than by the parties, taxes are no less an important financial fact of life.

CLE/Other Legal Publications

See annotations, Introductory Comment, Chapter 7, *supra*.

§ 7.009. Fraud on the Community; Division and Disposition of Reconstituted Estate

(a) In this section, "reconstituted estate" means the total value of the community estate that would exist if an actual or constructive fraud on the community had not occurred.

(b) If the trier of fact determines that a spouse has committed actual or constructive fraud on the community, the court shall:

(1) calculate the value by which the community estate was depleted as a result of the fraud on the community and calculate the amount of the reconstituted estate; and

(2) divide the value of the reconstituted estate between the parties in a manner the court deems just and right.

(c) In making a just and right division of the reconstituted estate under Section 7.001, the court may grant any legal or equitable relief necessary to accomplish a just and right division, including:

(1) awarding to the wronged spouse an appropriate share of the community estate remaining after the actual or constructive fraud on the community;

(2) awarding a money judgment in favor of the wronged spouse against the spouse who committed the actual or constructive fraud on the community; or

(3) awarding to the wronged spouse both a money judgment and an appropriate share of the community estate.

Enacted by Acts 2011, 82nd Leg., ch. 487 (H.B. 908), § 1, eff. Sept. 1, 2011.

Comment

With the passage of this section, the Texas Legislature has codified and further clarified the Texas Supreme Court decision in *Schlueter v. Schlueter* setting forth statutory remedies for actual or constructive fraud on the community estate. 975 S.W.2d 584 (Tex. 1998). This statute requires the court to reconstitute the community estate by valuing the depletion of the community estate and adding that back in to the actual, existing value of the estate. Once the court has determined the reconstituted community estate, the court is given much discretion in rendering a just and right division of the reconstituted value, which may include the award of a share of the remaining estate to the injured spouse or a money judgment or both. While this section provides clarification of the law, it does not represent a departure from existing case law. Importantly, the statute still does not provide for an award of exemplary damages to the wronged spouse.

CHAPTER 8. MAINTENANCE

SUBCHAPTER G. MODIFICATION, REDUCTION, OR TERMINATION OF WITHHOLDING

Introductory Comment

This chapter authorizing post-divorce alimony in Texas clearly marked a significant change in Texas family law, albeit somewhat more symbolic than practical. For many years Texas was the only state without any form of post-divorce court-ordered alimony. The passage of this law in 1995 resulted from the wave of "welfare reform" sweeping the country. Spousal maintenance was enacted, at least in part, allegedly as a measure to prevent an economically displaced spouse from going on welfare. On the other hand, the significant post-divorce income splitting advantages provided by the federal Internal Revenue Code were recognized considerably earlier, *see* 26 U.S.C.A. § 71, *infra*. Almost thirty years before the dawn of statutory spousal maintenance, the usefulness of contractual alimony was sanctioned, *Francis v. Francis*, 412 S.W.2d 29 (Tex. 1967).

As originally drafted, the spousal maintenance statutes attempted to eliminate the legendary abuses surrounding Hollywood-style alimony by requiring a marriage of ten years or more and limiting the amount and duration of the support to no more than the less of $2,500.00 or 20% of the payor's income, whichever is less for no more than 3 years. Exceptions were included as to qualifications in certain cases of family violence and in duration in cases involving a disabled spouse or child of the marriage.

2011 legislation, however, expands the qualifications to eliminate a 10 year marriage requirement in the event a spouse suffers an incapacitating mental or physical disability or is the custodian of a child of the marriage of any age who requires substantial care and personal supervision because of a disability. It also extends the ability of the court to order spousal maintenance for up to 10 years depending on the length of the marriage unless because of a disability of the spouse or child, in which case it may still be ordered for as long as the disability continues. The amount of support is also increased to the lesser of $5,000.00 or 20 percent of the obligor's average monthly gross income. An obligor who over pays the court ordered support may seek repayment and attorneys fees to recover the overpayment amounts.

In the wake of a constitutional amendment, the provisions authorizing wage-withholding orders for the collection of spousal maintenance were enacted in 1999 and later further clarified.

CLE/Other Legal Publications

Spousal maintenance. Charla Bradshaw, 2011 Adv. Fam. L.

Spousal maintenance. Linda B. Thomas, 2011 Marriage Dissolution

Making the case for spousal maintenance. Linda B. Thomas, 2010 Adv. Fam. L.

Spousal maintenance and alimony. Sally H. Emerson & Hon. Don R. Emerson, 2009 Adv. Fam. L.

Alimony and spousal support. A. Craig Haston, 2009 So. Tex. Fam. L. Conf.

A guide to spousal support and property division claims under the Bankruptcy Abuse Prevention and Consumer Protection Act of 2005. Janet Leach Richards, 41 Fam. L.Q. 227 (2007)

Alimony. A. Craig Haston, 2008 So. Tex. Fam. L. Conf.

***See* Accompanying CD–ROM for Additional CLE/Other Legal Publications**

Leading Cases

Spousal maintenance

Federal Court

In re Davidson, 947 F.2d 1294 (5th Cir. 1991) (Tex.) (parties' conduct precludes claim that contractual alimony not agreed upon)

Texas Supreme Court

In re Green, 221 S.W.3d 645 (Tex. 2007) (contractual alimony not subject to enforcement by contempt—distinguished from statutory spousal maintenance)

In re Sheshtawy, 154 S.W.3d 114 (Tex. 2004) (reversal of spousal maintenance award precludes contempt except for period trial court order was in effect)

Courts of Appeals

Ammann v. Ammann, ___ S.W.3d ___, 2010 WL 4260955 (Tex. App.—Austin 2010, no pet.) (although called "chapter 8" maintenance in decree, could not be anything but contractual support because lasted longer than three years)

Diaz v. Diaz, ___ S.W.3d ___, 2011 WL 2465455 (Tex. App.—San Antonio 2011, no pet.) (award of maintenance affirmed; wife was seeking employment and property received subject to debt which made it insufficient to meet her living expenses)

In re Marriage of Hallman, 2010 WL 619290 (Tex. App.—Texarkana, pet. denied) (support of spousal maintenance in the amount of $1000 per month for 36 months affirmed)

Petra v. Petra, 2010 WL 374388 (Tex. App.—San Antonio 2010, no pet.) (award of maintenance an abuse of discretion where no evidence to establish that wife's living expenses per month were reasonable or that the value of the property she received was not sufficient to provide for her support)

Nesbitt v. Nesbitt, 2009 WL 1896074 (Tex. App.—Austin 2009, no pet.) (court's termination/reduction of wife's spousal maintenance payments as punishment for wife's contempt in property division not a proper remedy)

Blair v. Blair, 2009 WL 1270268 (Tex. App.—Houston 2009, no pet.) (correction of reference to spousal maintenance in decree where parties had agreed only to contractual alimony was proper nunc pro tunc)

Chavez v. McNeely, 287 S.W.3d 840 (Tex. App.—Houston 2009, no pet.) (provisions for future support of former spouse too ambiguous to be enforceable as either order of the court or contract)

Brooks v. Brooks, 257 S.W.3d 418 (Tex. App.—Fort Worth 2008, rev. denied) (wife's testimony sufficient to support order for indefinite spousal maintenance, even without expert testimony)

Contractual Alimony

In re Green, 221 S.W.3d 645 (Tex. 2007) (contractual alimony not subject to enforcement by contempt—distinguished from statutory spousal maintenance)

Francis v. Francis, 412 S.W.2d 29 (Tex. 1967) (pre statute seminal case; agreed payment of contractual alimony enforceable by law of contracts, not by law of judgments)

Kee v. Kee, 307 S.W.3d 812 (Tex. App.—Dallas 2010, no pet.) (when post-divorce support payments last longer than the statute allows or are for more than the statute allows, they are contractual alimony, not spousal maintenance; no wage withholding for contractual alimony)

***See* Accompanying CD–ROM for Additional Leading Cases**

SUBCHAPTER A. GENERAL PROVISIONS

§ 8.001. Definitions

In this chapter:

(1) "Maintenance" means an award in a suit for dissolution of a marriage of periodic payments from the future income of one spouse for the support of the other spouse.

(2) "Notice of application for a writ of withholding" means the document delivered to an obligor and filed with the court as required by this chapter for the nonjudicial determination of arrears and initiation of withholding for spousal maintenance.

(3) "Obligee" means a person entitled to receive payments under the terms of an order for spousal maintenance.

(4) "Obligor" means a person required to make periodic payments under the terms of an order for spousal maintenance.

(5) "Writ of withholding" means the document issued by the clerk of a court and delivered to an employer, directing that earnings be withheld for payment of spousal maintenance as provided by this chapter.

SUBCHAPTER B. COURT–ORDERED MAINTENANCE

§ 8.051. Eligibility for Maintenance; Court Order*

In a suit for dissolution of a marriage or in a proceeding for maintenance in a court with personal jurisdiction over both former spouses following the dissolution of their marriage by a court that lacked personal jurisdiction over an absent spouse, the court may order maintenance for either spouse only if **the spouse seeking maintenance will lack sufficient property, including the spouse's separate property, on dissolution of the marriage to provide for the spouse's minimum reasonable needs and:**

(1) the spouse from whom maintenance is requested was convicted of or received deferred adjudication for a criminal offense that also constitutes an act of family violence, as defined by Section 71.004, committed during the marriage against the other spouse or the other spouse's child and the offense occurred:

(A) within two years before the date on which a suit for dissolution of the marriage is filed; or

(B) while the suit is pending; or

(2) the spouse seeking maintenance:

(A) is unable to earn sufficient income to provide for the spouse's minimum reasonable needs because of an incapacitating physical or mental disability;

(B) has been married to the other spouse for 10 years or longer and lacks the ability to earn sufficient income to provide for the spouse's minimum reasonable needs; or

(C) ~~: (1) the spouse from whom maintenance is requested was convicted of or received deferred adjudication for a criminal offense that also constitutes an act of family violence under Title 4 and the offense occurred: (A) within two years before the date on which a suit for dissolution of the marriage is filed; or (B) while the suit is pending; or (2) the duration of the marriage was 10 years or longer, the spouse seeking maintenance lacks sufficient property, including property distributed to the spouse under this code, to provide for the~~

~~spouse's minimum reasonable needs, as limited by Section 8.054, and the spouse seeking maintenance: (A) is unable to support himself or herself through appropriate employment because of an incapacitating physical or mental disability; (B)~~is the custodian of a child of the marriage of any age who requires substantial care and personal supervision because **of** a physical or mental disability **that prevents the spouse from earning sufficient income to provide for the spouse's minimum reasonable needs** ~~makes it necessary, taking into consideration the needs of the child, that the spouse not be employed outside the home; or (C) clearly lacks earning ability in the labor market adequate to provide support for the spouse's minimum reasonable needs, as limited by Section 8.054~~.

Amended by Acts 2011, 82nd Leg., ch. 486 (H.B. 901), § 1, eff. Sept. 1, 2011.

* Editor's Note: Because of the extensive changes to these sections, a "clean" version of the enacted statute is shown to assist the reader.

§ 8.051. Eligibility for Maintenance; Court Order

In a suit for dissolution of a marriage or in a proceeding for maintenance in a court with personal jurisdiction over both former spouses following the dissolution of their marriage by a court that lacked personal jurisdiction over an absent spouse, the court may order maintenance for either spouse only if the spouse seeking maintenance will lack sufficient property, including the spouse's separate property, on dissolution of the marriage to provide for the spouse's minimum reasonable needs and:

(1) the spouse from whom maintenance is requested was convicted of or received deferred adjudication for a criminal offense that also constitutes an act of family violence, as defined by Section 71.004, committed during the marriage against the other spouse or the other spouse's child and the offense occurred:

(A) within two years before the date on which a suit for dissolution of the marriage is filed; or

(B) while the suit is pending; or

(2) the spouse seeking maintenance:

(A) is unable to earn sufficient income to provide for the spouse's minimum reasonable needs because of an incapacitating physical or mental disability;

(B) has been married to the other spouse for 10 years or longer and lacks the ability to earn sufficient income to provide for the spouse's minimum reasonable needs; or

(C) is the custodian of a child of the marriage of any age who requires substantial care and personal supervision because of a physical or mental disability that prevents the spouse from earning sufficient income to provide for the spouse's minimum reasonable needs.

Amended by Acts 2011, 82nd Leg., ch. 486 (H.B. 901), § 1, eff. Sept. 1, 2011.

§ 8.052. Factors in Determining Maintenance*

A court that determines that a spouse is eligible to receive maintenance under this chapter shall determine the nature, amount, duration, and manner of periodic payments by considering all relevant factors, including:

(1) **each**~~the financial resources of the spouse seeking maintenance, including the community and separate property and liabilities apportioned to that spouse in the dissolution proceeding, and that~~ spouse's ability to **provide for that** ~~meet the~~ spouse's **minimum reasonable** needs independently**, considering that spouse's financial resources on dissolution of the marriage**;

(2) the education and employment skills of the spouses, the time necessary to acquire sufficient education or training to enable the spouse seeking maintenance to **earn sufficient income, and** ~~find appropriate employment,~~ the availability **and feasibility** of that education or training~~, and the feasibility of that education or training~~;

(3) the duration of the marriage;

(4) the age, employment history, earning ability, and physical and emotional condition of the spouse seeking maintenance;

(5) the **effect on each spouse's** ability **to provide for that spouse's minimum reasonable needs while providing** ~~of the spouse from whom maintenance is requested to meet that spouse's personal needs and to provide~~ periodic child support payments **or maintenance**, if applicable~~, while meeting the personal needs of the spouse seeking maintenance~~;

(6) acts by either spouse resulting in excessive or abnormal expenditures or destruction, concealment, or fraudulent disposition of community property, joint tenancy, or other property held in common;

(7) ~~the comparative financial resources of the spouses, including medical, retirement, insurance, or other benefits, and the separate property of each spouse; (8)~~the contribution by one spouse to the education, training, or increased earning power of the other spouse;

(8)~~(9)~~ the property brought to the marriage by either spouse;

(9)~~(10)~~ the contribution of a spouse as homemaker;

(10)~~(11)~~ marital misconduct**, including adultery and cruel treatment, by either spouse during the marriage** ~~of the spouse seeking maintenance~~; and

(11) any history or pattern of family violence, as defined by Section 71.004 ~~(12) the efforts of the spouse seeking maintenance to pursue available employment counseling as provided by Chapter 304, Labor Code~~.

Amended by Acts 2011, 82nd Leg., ch.486 (H.B. 901), § 1, eff. Sept. 1, 2011.

* Editor's Note: Because of the extensive changes to these sections, a "clean" version of the enacted statute is shown to assist the reader.

§ 8.052. Factors in Determining Maintenance

A court that determines that a spouse is eligible to receive maintenance under this chapter shall determine the nature, amount, duration, and manner of periodic payments by considering all relevant factors, including:

(1) each spouse's ability to provide for that spouse's minimum reasonable needs independently, considering that spouse's financial resources on dissolution of the marriage;

(2) the education and employment skills of the spouses, the time necessary to acquire sufficient education or training to enable the spouse seeking maintenance to earn sufficient income, and the availability and feasibility of that education or training;

(3) the duration of the marriage;

(4) the age, employment history, earning ability, and physical and emotional condition of the spouse seeking maintenance;

(5) the effect on each spouse's ability to provide for that spouse's minimum reasonable needs while providing periodic child support payments or maintenance, if applicable;

(6) acts by either spouse resulting in excessive or abnormal expenditures or destruction, concealment, or fraudulent disposition of community property, joint tenancy, or other property held in common;

(7) the contribution by one spouse to the education, training, or increased earning power of the other spouse;

(8) the property brought to the marriage by either spouse;

(9) the contribution of a spouse as homemaker;

(10) marital misconduct, including adultery and cruel treatment, by either spouse during the marriage; and

(11) any history or pattern of family violence, as defined by Section 71.004.

Amended by Acts 2011, 82nd Leg., ch.486 (H.B. 901), § 1, eff. Sept. 1, 2011.

§ 8.053. Presumption*

(a) **It**~~Except as provided by Subsection (b), it~~ is **a rebuttable presumption** ~~presumed~~ that maintenance under Section **8.051(2)(B)** ~~8.051(2)~~ is not warranted unless the spouse seeking maintenance has exercised diligence in:

(1) **earning sufficient income to provide for the spouse's minimum reasonable needs** ~~seeking suitable employment~~; or

(2) developing the necessary skills to **provide for the spouse's minimum reasonable needs** ~~become self-supporting~~ during a period of separation and during the time the suit for dissolution of the marriage is pending.

~~(b) This section does not apply to a spouse who is not able to satisfy the presumption in Subsection (a) because the spouse:~~

~~(1) has an incapacitating physical or mental disability; or~~

~~(2) is the custodian of a child of the marriage of any age who requires substantial care and personal supervision because a physical or mental disability makes it necessary, taking into consideration the needs of the child, that the spouse not be employed outside the home.~~

Amended by Acts 2011, 82nd Leg., ch. 486 (H.B. 901), §§ 2, 9(1), eff. Sept. 1, 2011.

* Editor's Note: Because of the extensive changes to these sections, a "clean" version of the enacted statute is shown to assist the reader.

§ 8.053. Presumption

(a) It is a rebuttable presumption that maintenance under Section 8.051(2)(B) is not warranted unless the spouse seeking maintenance has exercised diligence in:

(1) earning sufficient income to provide for the spouse's minimum reasonable needs; or

(2) developing the necessary skills to provide for the spouse's minimum reasonable needs during a period of separation and during the time the suit for dissolution of the marriage is pending.

Amended by Acts 2011, 82nd Leg., ch. 486 (H.B. 901), §§ 2, 9(1), eff. Sept. 1, 2011.

§ 8.054. Duration of Maintenance Order*

(a) Except as provided by Subsection (b), a court:

(1) may not order maintenance that remains in effect for more than:

(A) five ~~three~~ years after the date of the order**, if:**

(i) the spouses were married to each other for less than 10 years and the eligibility of the spouse for whom maintenance is ordered is established under Section 8.051(1); or

(ii) the spouses were married to each other for at least 10 years but not more than 20 years;

(B) seven years after the date of the order, if the spouses were married to each other for at least 20 years but not more than 30 years; or

(C) 10 years after the date of the order, if the spouses were married to each other for 30 years or more; and

(2) shall limit the duration of a maintenance order to the shortest reasonable period that allows the spouse seeking maintenance to **earn sufficient income to provide for** ~~meet~~ the spouse's minimum reasonable needs ~~by obtaining appropriate employment or developing an appropriate skill~~, unless the ability of the spouse to provide for the spouse's minimum reasonable needs ~~through employment~~ is substantially or totally diminished because of:

(A) physical or mental disability **of the spouse seeking maintenance**;

(B) duties as the custodian of an infant or young child **of the marriage**; or

(C) another compelling impediment to **earning sufficient income to provide for the spouse's minimum reasonable needs** ~~gainful employment~~.

(b) **The** ~~If a spouse seeking maintenance is unable to support himself or herself through appropriate employment because the spouse has an incapacitating physical or mental disability or because the spouse is the custodian of a child of the marriage of any age who has a physical or mental disability, the~~ court may order maintenance **for a spouse to whom Section 8.051(2)(A) or (C) applies** for as long as **the spouse continues to satisfy the eligibility criteria prescribed by the applicable provision** ~~the disability continues. The court may order periodic review of its order, on the request of either party or on its own motion, to determine whether the disability continues to render the spouse unable to support himself or herself through appropriate employment. The continuation of spousal maintenance under these circumstances is subject to a motion to modify as provided by Section 8.057.~~

(c) On the request of either party or on the court's own motion, the court may order the periodic review of its order for maintenance under Subsection (b).

(d) The continuation of maintenance ordered under Subsection (b) is subject to a motion to modify as provided by Section 8.057.

Amended by Acts 2011, 82nd Leg., ch. 486 (H.B. 901), § 3, eff. Sept. 1, 2011.

* Editor's Note: Because of the extensive changes to these sections, a "clean" version of the enacted statute is shown to assist the reader.

§ 8.054. Duration of Maintenance Order

(a) Except as provided by Subsection (b), a court:

(1) may not order maintenance that remains in effect for more than:

(A) five years after the date of the order, if:

(i) the spouses were married to each other for less than 10 years and the eligibility of the spouse for whom maintenance is ordered is established under Section 8.051(1); or

(ii) the spouses were married to each other for at least 10 years but not more than 20 years;

(B) seven years after the date of the order, if the spouses were married to each other for at least 20 years but not more than 30 years; or

(C) 10 years after the date of the order, if the spouses were married to each other for 30 years or more; and

(2) shall limit the duration of a maintenance order to the shortest reasonable period that allows the spouse seeking maintenance to earn sufficient income to provide for the spouse's minimum reasonable needs, unless the ability of the spouse to provide for the spouse's minimum reasonable needs is substantially or totally diminished because of:

(A) physical or mental disability of the spouse seeking maintenance;

(B) duties as the custodian of an infant or young child of the marriage; or

(C) another compelling impediment to earning sufficient income to provide for the spouse's minimum reasonable needs.

(b) The court may order maintenance for a spouse to whom Section 8.051(2)(A) or (C) applies for as long as the spouse continues to satisfy the eligibility criteria prescribed by the applicable provision.

(c) On the request of either party or on the court's own motion, the court may order the periodic review of its order for maintenance under Subsection (b).

(d) The continuation of maintenance ordered under Subsection (b) is subject to a motion to modify as provided by Section 8.057.

Amended by Acts 2011, 82nd Leg., ch. 486 (H.B. 901), § 3, eff. Sept. 1, 2011.

§ 8.055. Amount of Maintenance

(a) A court may not order maintenance that requires an obligor to pay monthly more than the lesser of:

(1) **$5,000** ~~$2,500~~; or

(2) 20 percent of the spouse's average monthly gross income.

(a–1) For purposes of this chapter, gross income:

(1) includes:

(A) 100 percent of all wage and salary income and other compensation for personal services (including commissions, overtime pay, tips, and bonuses);

(B) interest, dividends, and royalty income;

(C) self-employment income;

(D) net rental income (defined as rent after deducting operating expenses and mortgage payments, but not including noncash items such as depreciation); and

(E) all other income actually being received, including severance pay, retirement benefits, pensions, trust income, annuities, capital gains, unemployment benefits, interest income from notes regardless of the source, gifts and prizes, maintenance, and alimony; and

(2) does not include:

(A) return of principal or capital;

(B) accounts receivable;

(C) benefits paid in accordance with federal public assistance programs;

(D) benefits paid in accordance with the Temporary Assistance for Needy Families program;

(E) payments for foster care of a child;

(F) Department of Veterans Affairs service-connected disability compensation;

(G) supplemental security income (SSI), social security benefits, and disability benefits; or

(H) workers' compensation benefits.

~~(b) The court shall set the amount that an obligor is required to pay in a maintenance order to provide for the minimum reasonable needs of the obligee, considering employment or property received in the dissolution of the marriage or otherwise owned by the obligee that contributes to the minimum reasonable needs of the obligee.~~

~~(c) Department of Veterans Affairs service-connected disability compensation, social security benefits and disability benefits, and workers' compensation benefits are excluded from maintenance.~~

~~(d) For purposes of this chapter, "gross income" means resources as defined in Sections 154.062(b) and (c), disregarding any deductions listed in Section 154.062(d) and disregarding those benefits excluded under Subsection (c) of this section.~~

Amended by Acts 2011, 82nd Leg., ch. 486 (H.B. 901), §§ 4, 9(2), eff. Sept. 1, 2011.

§ 8.056. Termination

(a) The obligation to pay future maintenance terminates on the death of either party or on the remarriage of the obligee.

(b) After a hearing, the court shall **order the termination of** ~~terminate~~ the maintenance **obligation** ~~order~~ if **the court finds that** the obligee cohabits with another person **with whom the obligee has a dating or romantic relationship** in a permanent place of abode on a continuing~~, conjugal~~ basis.

(c) Termination of the maintenance obligation does not terminate the obligation to pay any maintenance that accrued before the date of termination, whether as a result of death or remarriage under Subsection (a) or a court order under Subsection (b).

Amended by Acts 2011, 82nd Leg., ch. 486 (H.B. 901), § 5, eff. Sept. 1, 2011.

§ 8.057. Modification of Maintenance Order

(a) The amount of maintenance specified in a court order or the portion of a decree that provides for the support of a former spouse may be reduced by the filing of a motion in the court that originally rendered the order. A party affected by the order or the portion of the decree to be modified may file the motion.

(b) Notice of a motion to modify maintenance and the response, if any, are governed by the Texas Rules of Civil Procedure applicable to the filing of an original lawsuit. Notice must be given by service of citation, and a response must be in the form of an answer due on or before 10 a.m. of the first Monday after 20 days after the date of service. A court shall set a hearing on the motion in the manner provided by Rule 245, Texas Rules of Civil Procedure.

(c) After a hearing, the court may modify an original or modified order or portion of a decree providing for maintenance on a proper showing of a material and substantial change in circumstances, **including circumstances reflected in the factors specified in Section 8.052, relating to** ~~of~~ either party **or to a child of the marriage described by Section 8.051(2)(C), if applicable**. The court shall apply the modification only to payment accruing after the filing of the motion to modify.

(d) A loss of employment or circumstances that render a former spouse unable to **provide for the spouse's minimum reasonable needs** ~~support himself or herself through appropriate employment~~ by reason of incapacitating physical or mental disability that occur after the divorce or annulment are not grounds for the institution of spousal maintenance for the benefit of the former spouse.

Amended by Acts 2011, 82nd Leg., ch. 486 (H.B. 901), § 6, eff. Sept. 1, 2011.

§ 8.058. Maintenance Arrearages

A spousal maintenance payment not timely made constitutes an arrearage.

§ 8.059. Enforcement of Maintenance Order

(a) The court may enforce by contempt **against the obligor** the court's maintenance order or an agreement for the payment of maintenance **under the terms of this chapter** voluntarily entered into between the parties and approved by the court. **The court may not enforce by contempt any provision of an agreed order for maintenance for any period of maintenance beyond the period of maintenance the court could have ordered under this chapter.**

(b) On the suit to enforce by an obligee, the court may render judgment against a defaulting party for the amount of arrearages after notice by service of citation, answer, if any, and a hearing finding that the defaulting party has failed or refused to **comply with** ~~carry out~~ the terms of the order. The judgment may be enforced by any means available for the enforcement of judgment for debts.

(c) It is an affirmative defense to an allegation of contempt of court or the violation of a condition of probation requiring payment of court-ordered maintenance that the obligor:

(1) lacked the ability to provide maintenance in the amount ordered;

(2) lacked property that could be sold, mortgaged, or otherwise pledged to raise the funds needed;

(3) attempted unsuccessfully to borrow the needed funds; and

(4) did not know of a source from which the money could have been borrowed or otherwise legally obtained.

(d) The issue of the existence of an affirmative defense does not arise **until pleaded. An** ~~unless evidence is admitted supporting the defense. If the issue of the existence of an affirmative defense arises, an~~ obligor must prove the affirmative defense by a preponderance of the evidence.

~~(e) A court may enforce an order for spousal maintenance under this chapter by ordering garnishment of the obligor's wages or by any other means available under this section.~~

Amended by Acts 2011, 82nd Leg., ch. 486 (H.B. 901), §§ 7, 9(3), eff. Sept. 1, 2011.

§ 8.0591. Overpayment

(a) If an obligor is not in arrears on the obligor's maintenance obligation and the obligor's maintenance obligation has terminated, the obligee must return to the obligor any maintenance payment made by the obligor that exceeds the amount of maintenance ordered or approved by the court, regardless of whether the payment was made before, on, or after the date the maintenance obligation terminated.

(b) An obligor may file a suit to recover overpaid maintenance under Subsection (a). If the court finds that the obligee failed to return overpaid maintenance under Subsection (a), the court shall order the obligee to pay the obligor's attorney's fees and all court costs in addition to the amount of the overpaid maintenance. For good cause shown, the court may waive the requirement that the obligee pay attorney's fees and court costs if the court states in its order the reasons supporting that finding.

Enacted by Acts 2011, 82nd Leg., ch. 486 (H.B. 901), § 8, eff. Sept. 1, 2011.

§ 8.060. Putative Spouse

In a suit to declare a marriage void, a putative spouse who did not have knowledge of an existing impediment to a valid marriage may be awarded maintenance if otherwise qualified to receive maintenance under this chapter.

§ 8.061. Unmarried Cohabitants

An order for maintenance is not authorized between unmarried cohabitants under any circumstances.

SUBCHAPTER C. INCOME WITHHOLDING

Introductory Comment

This subchapter, along with subchapters D, E, and F, set forth the procedures for payment of spousal maintenance through income withholding. Based largely on the procedures for child support, these provisions closely resemble those found in Chapter 158 [*Withholding from Earnings for Child Support*]. Texas voters approved the amendment in 1999 to allow for the garnishment of wages to enforce spousal maintenance. However, there was no statutory guidance regarding the procedure to accomplish this goal. Furthermore, there was confusion as to whether or not income withholding could be ordered only in the event of enforcement for non-payment.

Effective September 2001, any court ordered spousal maintenance payments, along with certain contractual payments, may be subject to income withholding. However, current child support obligations take precedence over spousal maintenance withholding.

§ 8.101. Income Withholding; General Rule

(a) In a proceeding in which periodic payments of spousal maintenance are ordered, modified, or enforced, the court may order that income be withheld from the disposable earnings of the obligor as provided by this chapter.

(b) This subchapter does not apply to contractual alimony or spousal maintenance, regardless of whether the alimony or maintenance is taxable, unless:

(1) the contract specifically permits income withholding; or

(2) the alimony or maintenance payments are not timely made under the terms of the contract.

(c) An order or writ of withholding for spousal maintenance may be combined with an order or writ of withholding for child support only if the obligee has been appointed managing conservator of the child for whom the child support is owed and is the conservator with whom the child primarily resides.

(d) An order or writ of withholding that combines withholding for spousal maintenance and child support must:

(1) require that the withheld amounts be paid to the appropriate place of payment under Section 154.004;

(2) be in the form prescribed by the Title IV-D agency under Section 158.106;

(3) clearly indicate the amounts withheld that are to be applied to current spousal maintenance and to any maintenance arrearages; and

(4) subject to the maximum withholding allowed under Section 8.106, order that withheld income be applied in the following order of priority:

(A) current child support;

(B) current spousal maintenance;

(C) child support arrearages; and

(D) spousal maintenance arrearages.

(e) Garnishment for the purposes of spousal maintenance does not apply to unemployment insurance benefit payments.

§ 8.102. Withholding for Arrearages in Addition to Current Spousal Maintenance

(a) The court may order that, in addition to income withheld for current spousal maintenance, income be withheld from the disposable earnings of the obligor to be applied toward the liquidation of any arrearages.

(b) The additional amount withheld to be applied toward arrearages must be whichever of the following amounts will discharge the arrearages in the least amount of time:

(1) an amount sufficient to discharge the arrearages in not more than two years; or

(2) 20 percent of the amount withheld for current maintenance.

§ 8.103. Withholding for Arrearages When Current Maintenance is Not Due

A court may order income withholding to be applied toward arrearages in an amount sufficient to discharge those arrearages in not more than two years if current spousal maintenance is no longer owed.

§ 8.104. Withholding to Satisfy Judgment for Arrearages

The court, in rendering a cumulative judgment for arrearages, may order that a reasonable amount of income be withheld from the disposable earnings of the obligor to be applied toward the satisfaction of the judgment.

§ 8.105. Priority of Withholding

An order or writ of withholding under this chapter has priority over any garnishment, attachment, execution, or other order affecting disposable earnings, except for an order or writ of withholding for child support under Chapter 158.

§ 8.106. Maximum Amount Withheld From Earnings

An order or writ of withholding must direct that an obligor's employer withhold from the obligor's disposable earnings the lesser of:

(1) the amount specified in the order or writ; or

(2) an amount that, when added to the amount of income being withheld by the employer for child support, is equal to 50 percent of the obligor's disposable earnings.

§ 8.107. Order or Writ Binding on Employer Doing Business in This State

An order or writ of withholding issued under this chapter and delivered to an employer doing business in this state is binding on the employer without regard to whether the obligor resides or works outside this state.

§ 8.108. Voluntary Writ of Withholding by Obligor

(a) An obligor may file with the clerk of the court a notarized or acknowledged request signed by the obligor and the obligee for the issuance and delivery to the obligor's employer of a writ of withholding. The obligor may file the request under this section regardless of whether a writ or order has been served on any party or whether the obligor owes arrearages.

(b) On receipt of a request under this section, the clerk shall issue and deliver a writ of withholding in the manner provided by this subchapter.

(c) An employer who receives a writ of withholding issued under this section may request a hearing in the same manner and according to the same terms provided by Section 8.205.

(d) An obligor whose employer receives a writ of withholding issued under this section may request a hearing in the manner provided by Section 8.258.

(e) An obligee may contest a writ of income withholding issued under this section by requesting, not later than the 180th day after the date on which the obligee discovers that the writ was issued, a hearing to be conducted in the manner provided by Section 8.258 for a hearing on a motion to stay.

(f) A writ of withholding under this section may not reduce the total amount of spousal maintenance, including arrearages, owed by the obligor.

SUBCHAPTER D. PROCEDURE

§ 8.151. Time Limit

The court may issue an order or writ for withholding under this chapter at any time before all spousal maintenance and arrearages are paid.

§ 8.152. Contents of Order of Withholding

(a) An order of withholding must state:

(1) the style, cause number, and court having jurisdiction to enforce the order;

(2) the name, address, and, if available, the social security number of the obligor;

(3) the amount and duration of the spousal maintenance payments, including the amount and duration of withholding for arrearages, if any; and

(4) the name, address, and, if available, the social security number of the obligee.

(b) The order for withholding must require the obligor to notify the court promptly of any material change affecting the order, including a change of employer.

(c) On request by an obligee, the court may exclude from an order of withholding the obligee's address and social security number if the obligee or a member of the obligee's family or household is a victim of family violence and is the subject of a protective order to which the obligor is also subject. On granting a request under this subsection, the court shall order the clerk to:

(1) strike the address and social security number required by Subsection (a) from the order or writ of withholding; and

(2) maintain a confidential record of the obligee's address and social security number to be used only by the court.

§ 8.153. Request for Issuance of Order or Writ of Withholding

An obligor or obligee may file with the clerk of the court a request for issuance of an order or writ of withholding.

§ 8.154. Issuance and Delivery of Order or Writ of Withholding

(a) On receipt of a request for issuance of an order or writ of withholding, the clerk of the court shall deliver a certified copy of the order or writ to the obligor's current employer or to any subsequent employer of the obligor. The clerk shall attach a copy of Subchapter E to the order or writ.

(b) Not later than the fourth working day after the date the order is signed or the request is filed, whichever is later, the clerk shall issue and deliver the certified copy of the order or writ by:

(1) certified or registered mail, return receipt requested, to the employer; or

(2) service of citation to:

(A) the person authorized to receive service of process for the employer in civil cases generally; or

(B) a person designated by the employer by written notice to the clerk to receive orders or notices of income withholding.

SUBCHAPTER E. RIGHTS AND DUTIES OF EMPLOYER

§ 8.201. Order or Writ Binding on Employer

(a) An employer required to withhold income from earnings under this chapter is not entitled to notice of the proceedings before the order of withholding is rendered or writ of withholding is issued.

(b) An order or writ of withholding is binding on an employer regardless of whether the employer is specifically named in the order or writ.

§ 8.202. Effective Date and Duration of Income Withholding

An employer shall begin to withhold income in accordance with an order or writ of withholding not later than the first pay period after the date the order or writ was delivered to the employer. The employer shall continue to withhold income as required by the order or writ as long as the obligor is employed by the employer.

§ 8.203. Remitting Withheld Payments

(a) The employer shall remit to the person or office named in the order or writ of withholding the amount of income withheld from an obligor on each pay date. The remittance must include the date on which the income withholding occurred.

(b) The employer shall include with each remittance:

(1) the cause number of the suit under which income withholding is required;

(2) the payor's name; and

(3) the payee's name, unless the remittance is made by electronic funds transfer.

§ 8.204. Employer May Deduct Fee From Earnings

An employer may deduct an administrative fee of not more than $5 each month from the obligor's disposable earnings in addition to the amount withheld as spousal maintenance.

§ 8.205. Hearing Requested by Employer

(a) Not later than the 20th day after the date an order or writ of withholding is delivered to an employer, the employer may file with the court a motion for a hearing on the applicability of the order or writ to the employer.

(b) The hearing under this section must be held on or before the 15th day after the date the motion is made.

(c) An order or writ of withholding is binding and the employer shall continue to withhold income and remit the amount withheld pending further order of the court.

§ 8.206. Liability and Obligation of Employer for Payments

(a) An employer who complies with an order or writ of withholding under this chapter is not liable to the obligor for the amount of income withheld and remitted as required by the order or writ.

(b) An employer who receives, but does not comply with, an order or writ of withholding is liable to:

(1) the obligee for any amount of spousal maintenance not paid in compliance with the order or writ;

(2) the obligor for any amount withheld from the obligor's disposable earnings, but not remitted to the obligee; and

(3) the obligee or obligor for reasonable attorney's fees and court costs incurred in recovering an amount described by Subdivision (1) or (2).

(c) An employer shall comply with an order of withholding for spousal maintenance or alimony issued in another state that appears regular on its face in the same manner as an order issued by a tribunal of this state. The employer shall notify the employee of the order and comply with the order in the manner provided by Subchapter F, Chapter 159, with respect to an order of withholding for child support issued by another state. The employer may contest the order of withholding in the manner provided by that subchapter with respect to an order of withholding for child support issued by another state.

§ 8.207. Employer Receiving Multiple Orders or Writs

(a) An employer who receives more than one order or writ of withholding to withhold income from the same obligor shall withhold the combined amounts due under each order or writ unless the combined amounts due exceed the maximum total amount of allowed income withholding under Section 8.106.

(b) If the combined amounts to be withheld under multiple orders or writs for the same obligor exceed the maximum total amount of allowed income withholding under Section 8.106, the employer shall pay, until that maximum is reached, in the following order of priority:

(1) an equal amount toward current child support owed by the obligor in each order or writ until the employer has complied fully with each current child support obligation;

(2) an equal amount toward current maintenance owed by the obligor in each order or writ until the employer has complied fully with each current maintenance obligation;

(3) an equal amount toward child support arrearages owed by the obligor in each order or writ until the employer has complied fully with each order or writ for child support arrearages; and

(4) an equal amount toward maintenance arrearages owed by the obligor in each order or writ until the employer has complied fully with each order or writ for spousal maintenance arrearages.

§ 8.208. Employer's Liability for Discriminatory Hiring or Discharge

(a) An employer may not use an order or writ of withholding as grounds in whole or part for the termination of employment of, or for any other disciplinary action against, an employee.

(b) An employer may not refuse to hire an employee because of an order or writ of withholding.

(c) An employer who intentionally discharges an employee in violation of this section is liable to that employee for current wages, other employment benefits, and reasonable attorney's fees and court costs incurred in enforcing the employee's rights.

(d) In addition to liability imposed under Subsection (c), the court shall order with respect to an employee whose employment was suspended or terminated in violation of this section appropriate injunctive relief, including reinstatement of:

(1) the employee's position with the employer; and

(2) fringe benefits or seniority lost as a result of the suspension or termination.

(e) An employee may bring an action to enforce the employee's rights under this section.

§ 8.209. Penalty for Noncompliance

(a) In addition to the civil remedies provided by this subchapter or any other remedy provided by law, an employer who knowingly violates this chapter by failing to withhold income for spousal maintenance or to remit withheld income in accordance with an order or writ of withholding issued under this chapter commits an offense.

(b) An offense under this section is punishable by a fine not to exceed $200 for each violation.

§ 8.210. Notice of Termination of Employment and of New Employment

(a) An obligor who terminates employment with an employer who has been withholding income and the obligor's employer shall each notify the court and the obligee of:

(1) the termination of employment not later than the seventh day after the date of termination;

(2) the obligor's last known address; and

(3) the name and address of the obligor's new employer, if known.

(b) The obligor shall inform a subsequent employer of the order or writ of withholding after obtaining employment.

SUBCHAPTER F. WRIT OF WITHHOLDING ISSUED BY CLERK

§ 8.251. Notice of Application for Writ of Withholding; Filing

(a) An obligor or obligee may file a notice of application for a writ of withholding if income withholding was not ordered at the time spousal maintenance was ordered.

(b) The obligor or obligee may file the notice of application for a writ of withholding in the court that ordered the spousal maintenance under Subchapter B.

§ 8.252. Contents of Notice of Application for Writ of Withholding

The notice of application for a writ of withholding must be verified and:

(1) state the amount of monthly maintenance due, including the amount of arrearages or anticipated arrearages, and the amount of disposable earnings to be withheld under a writ of withholding;

(2) state that the withholding applies to each current or subsequent employer or period of employment;

(3) state that the obligor's employer will be notified to begin the withholding if the obligor does not contest the withholding on or before the 10th day after the date the obligor receives the notice;

(4) describe the procedures for contesting the issuance and delivery of a writ of withholding;

(5) state that the obligor will be provided an opportunity for a hearing not later than the 30th day after the date of receipt of the notice of contest if the obligor contests the withholding;

(6) state that the sole ground for successfully contesting the issuance of a writ of withholding is a dispute concerning the identity of the obligor or the existence or amount of the arrearages;

(7) describe the actions that may be taken if the obligor contests the notice of application for a writ of withholding, including the procedures for suspending issuance of a writ of withholding; and

(8) include with the notice a suggested form for the motion to stay issuance and delivery of the writ of withholding that the obligor may file with the clerk of the appropriate court.

§ 8.253. Interstate Request for Withholding

(a) The registration of a foreign order that provides for spousal maintenance or alimony as provided in Chapter 159 is sufficient for filing a notice of application for a writ of withholding.

(b) The notice must be filed with the clerk of the court having venue as provided in Chapter 159.

(c) The notice of application for a writ of withholding may be delivered to the obligor at the same time that an order is filed for registration under Chapter 159.

§ 8.254. Additional Arrearages

If the notice of application for a writ of withholding states that the obligor has failed to pay more than one spousal maintenance payment according to the terms of the spousal maintenance order, the writ of withholding may include withholding for arrearages that accrue between the filing of the notice and the date of the hearing or the issuance of the writ.

§ 8.255. Delivery of Notice of Application for Writ of Withholding; Time of Delivery

(a) The party who files a notice of application for a writ of withholding shall deliver the notice to the obligor by:

(1) first-class or certified mail, return receipt requested, addressed to the obligor's last known address or place of employment; or

(2) service of citation as in civil cases generally.

(b) If the notice is delivered by mail, the party who filed the notice shall file with the court a certificate stating the name, address, and date the party mailed the notice.

(c) The notice is considered to have been received by the obligor:

(1) on the date of receipt, if the notice was mailed by certified mail;

(2) on the 10th day after the date the notice was mailed, if the notice was mailed by first-class mail; or

(3) on the date of service, if the notice was delivered by service of citation.

§ 8.256. Motion to Stay Issuance of Writ of Withholding

(a) The obligor may stay issuance of a writ of withholding by filing a motion to stay with the clerk of the court not later than the 10th day after the date the notice of application for a writ of withholding was received.

(b) The grounds for filing a motion to stay issuance are limited to a dispute concerning the identity of the obligor or the existence or the amount of the arrearages.

(c) The obligor shall verify that the statements of fact in the motion to stay issuance of the writ are correct.

§ 8.257. Effect of Filing Motion to Stay

If the obligor files a motion to stay as provided by Section 8.256, the clerk of the court may not deliver the writ of withholding to the obligor's employer before a hearing is held.

§ 8.258. Hearing on Motion to Stay

(a) If the obligor files a motion to stay as provided by Section 8.256, the court shall set a hearing on the motion and the clerk of the court shall notify the obligor and obligee of the date, time, and place of the hearing.

(b) The court shall hold a hearing on the motion to stay not later than the 30th day after the date the motion was filed unless the obligor and obligee agree and waive the right to have the motion heard within 30 days.

(c) After the hearing, the court shall:

(1) render an order for income withholding that includes a determination of any amount of arrearages; or

(2) grant the motion to stay.

§ 8.259. Special Exceptions

(a) A defect in a notice of application for a writ of withholding is waived unless the respondent specially excepts in writing and cites with particularity the alleged defect, obscurity, or other ambiguity in the notice.

(b) A special exception under this section must be heard by the court before hearing the motion to stay issuance.

(c) If the court sustains an exception, the court shall provide the party filing the notice an opportunity to refile and shall continue the hearing to a specified date without requiring additional service.

§ 8.260. Writ of Withholding After Arrearages Are Paid

(a) The court may not refuse to order withholding solely on the basis that the obligor paid the arrearages after the obligor received the notice of application for a writ of withholding.

(b) The court shall order that a reasonable amount of income be withheld and applied toward the liquidation of arrearages, even though a judgment confirming arrearages was rendered against the obligor.

§ 8.261. Request for Issuance and Delivery of Writ of Withholding

(a) If a notice of application for a writ of withholding is delivered and the obligor does not file a motion to stay within the time provided by Section 8.256, the party who filed the notice shall file with the clerk of the court a request for issuance of the writ of withholding stating the amount of current spousal maintenance, the amount of arrearages, and the amount to be withheld from the obligor's income.

(b) The party who filed the notice may not file a request for issuance before the 11th day after the date the obligor received the notice of application for a writ of withholding.

§ 8.262. Issuance and Delivery of Writ of Withholding

The clerk of the court shall, on the filing of a request for issuance of a writ of withholding, issue and deliver the writ as provided by Subchapter D not later than the second working day after the date the request is filed. The clerk shall charge a fee in the amount of $15 for issuing the writ of withholding.

§ 8.263. Contents of Writ of Withholding

A writ of withholding must direct that an obligor's employer or a subsequent employer withhold from the obligor's disposable earnings an amount for current spousal maintenance and arrearages consistent with this chapter.

§ 8.264. Extension of Repayment Schedule by Party; Unreasonable Hardship

A party who files a notice of application for a writ of withholding and who determines that the schedule for repaying arrearages would cause unreasonable hardship to the obligor or the obligor's family may extend the payment period in the writ.

§ 8.265. Remittance of Amount to be Withheld

The obligor's employer shall remit the amount withheld to the person or office named in the writ on each pay date and shall include with the remittance the date on which the withholding occurred.

§ 8.266. Failure to Receive Notice of Application for Writ of Withholding

(a) Not later than the 30th day after the date of the first pay period after the date the obligor's employer receives a writ of withholding, the obligor may file an affidavit with the court stating that:

(1) the obligor did not timely file a motion to stay because the obligor did not receive the notice of application for a writ of withholding; and

(2) grounds exist for a motion to stay.

(b) The obligor may:

(1) file with the affidavit a motion to withdraw the writ of withholding; and

(2) request a hearing on the applicability of the writ.

(c) Income withholding may not be interrupted until after the hearing at which the court renders an order denying or modifying withholding.

§ 8.267. Issuance and Delivery of Writ of Withholding to Subsequent Employer

(a) After the clerk of the court issues a writ of withholding, a party authorized to file a notice of application for a writ of withholding under this subchapter may deliver a copy of the writ to a subsequent employer of the obligor by certified mail.

(b) Except as provided by an order under Section 8.152, the writ of withholding must include the name, address, and signature of the party and clearly indicate that the writ is being issued to a subsequent employer.

(c) The party shall file:

(1) a copy of the writ of withholding with the clerk not later than the third working day after the date of delivery of the writ to the subsequent employer; and

(2) the postal return receipt from the delivery to the subsequent employer not later than the third working day after the date the party receives the receipt.

(d) The party shall pay the clerk a fee in the amount of $15 for filing the copy of the writ.

SUBCHAPTER G. MODIFICATION, REDUCTION, OR TERMINATION OF WITHHOLDING

§ 8.301. Agreement by Parties Regarding Amount or Duration of Withholding

(a) An obligor and obligee may agree to reduce or terminate income withholding for spousal maintenance on the occurrence of any contingency stated in the order.

(b) The obligor and obligee may file a notarized or acknowledged request with the clerk of the court under Section 8.108 for a revised writ of withholding or notice of termination of withholding.

(c) The clerk shall issue and deliver to the obligor's employer a writ of withholding that reflects the agreed revision or a notice of termination of withholding.

(d) An agreement by the parties under this section does not modify the terms of an order for spousal maintenance.

§ 8.302. Modifications to or Termination of Withholding in Voluntary Withholding Cases

(a) If an obligor initiates voluntary withholding under Section 8.108, the obligee may file with the clerk of the court a notarized request signed by the obligor and the obligee for the issuance and delivery to the obligor of:

(1) a modified writ of withholding that reduces the amount of withholding; or

(2) a notice of termination of withholding.

(b) On receipt of a request under this section, the clerk shall issue and deliver a modified writ of withholding or notice of termination in the manner provided by Section 8.301.

(c) The clerk may charge a fee in the amount of $15 for issuing and delivering the modified writ of withholding or notice of termination.

(d) An obligee may contest a modified writ of withholding or notice of termination issued under this section by requesting a hearing in the manner provided by Section 8.258 not later than the 180th day after the date the obligee discovers that the writ or notice was issued.

§ 8.303. Termination of Withholding in Mandatory Withholding Cases

(a) An obligor for whom withholding for maintenance owed or withholding for maintenance and child support owed is mandatory may file a motion to terminate withholding. On a showing by the obligor that the obligor has complied fully with the terms of the maintenance or child support order, as applicable, the court shall render an order for the issuance and delivery to the obligor of a notice of termination of withholding.

(b) The clerk shall issue and deliver the notice of termination ordered under this section to the obligor.

(c) The clerk may charge a fee in the amount of $15 for issuing and delivering the notice.

§ 8.304. Delivery of Order of Reduction or Termination of Withholding

Any person may deliver to the obligor's employer a certified copy of an order that reduces the amount of spousal maintenance to be withheld or terminates the withholding.

§ 8.305. Liability of Employers

The provisions of this chapter regarding the liability of employers for withholding apply to an order that reduces or terminates withholding.

CHAPTER 9. POST-DECREE PROCEEDINGS

SUBCHAPTER A. SUIT TO ENFORCE DECREE

SUBCHAPTER B. POST-DECREE QUALIFIED DOMESTIC RELATIONS ORDER

SUBCHAPTER C. POST-DECREE DIVISION OF PROPERTY

SUBCHAPTER D. DISPOSITION OF UNDIVIDED BENEFICIAL INTEREST

SUBCHAPTER A. SUIT TO ENFORCE DECREE

Introductory Comment

TEX. FAM. CODE ANN. §§ 7.001-.007, *supra*, authorizing a division of the marital estate do not automatically result in the property awarded to a spouse being delivered promptly and intact. This subchapter was enacted to grant a trial court wide-ranging enforcement powers to carry out the terms of its decree. Although trial court is not authorized to modify its decree, it is authorized to issue clarifying and enforcing orders. This subchapter does not apply to property previously undivided; that is covered by TEX. FAM. CODE ANN. § 9.201 *et seq.*

However, as a counterpart to § 9.001, section 9.007 prohibits the trial court from attempting to substantively redivide the property of the parties. The duty of the trial court is simply to enforce its original order; it may only issue implementing orders to enforce or clarify its earlier ruling. As the cases cited below indicate, this mandate is somewhat easier to state categorically than to execute in practice (a.k.a., easier said than done).

CLE/Other Legal Publications

Securing agreements and judgments. Larry L. Martin, 2011 ADV. FAM. L.

Enforcement: how to make it stick or get it unstuck. Michelle May O'Neil, 2011 MARRIAGE DISSOLUTION

Contempt and enforcement. David D. Farr, 2011 SO. TEX. FAM. L.

Enforcing the property division. Mike Gregory, 2010 ADV. FAM. L.

Enforcement. Brenda Hull Thompson, 2010 FAM. L. BOOT CAMP

Property division and enforcement in the real world. Cheryl L. Wilson, 2010 MARRIAGE DISSOLUTION

Getting what you bargained for. Warren Cole, 2010 FAM. L. FRONT LINES

Enforcement: nuts and bolts. Hon. Roy L. Moore, 2010 SO. TEX. FAM. L. CONF.

Enforcement of property division. Rhonda F. Hunter, 2009 ADV. FAM. L.

Enforcement. Warren Cole, 2009 ADV. FAM. L. BOOT CAMP

See Accompanying CD–ROM for Additional CLE/Other Legal Publications

---

Leading Cases

U.S. Supreme Court

Farrey v. Sanderfoot, 500 U.S. 291, 114 L.Ed.2d 337, 111 S.Ct. 1825 (1991) (lien on homestead awarded ex-wife by divorce not discharged in ex-husband's bankruptcy)

Federal Court

In re Finch, 130 B.R. 753 (S.D. Tex. 1991) (ex-wife's equitable lien on homestead awarded to ex-husband survives his bankruptcy)

Texas Supreme Court

Gold v. Gold, 145 S.W.3d 212 (Tex. 2004) (ex-wife's suit for fraudulent violation of Agreement Incident to Divorce erroneously dismissed without proper notice—bill of review acceptable method of attack)

Brown v. Fullenweider, 52 S.W.3d 169 (Tex. 2001) (attorney's fees not subject to post divorce clarification and enforcement provisions)

Schwartz v. Jefferson, 520 S.W.2d 881 (Tex. 1975) (court could properly enter orders to enforce its decree)

Courts of Appeals

Snodgrass v. Snodgrass, 332 S.W.3d 653 (Tex. App.—Houston [14th Dist.] 2010, no pet.) (orig. proceeding) (award of residence to husband upon wife's failure to refinance was improper modification of provisions of decree)

Henderson v. Henderson, ___ S.W.3d ___, 2010 WL 4924955 (Tex. App.—Fort Worth 2010, no pet.) (closing documents wife was ordered to sign by court effectively improperly modified the division)

Watson v. Heaton, ___ S.W.3d ___, 2010 WL 5132565 (Tex. App.—Houston [14th Dist.] 2010, no pet.) (wife's right to "repossess" residence if husband didn't pay mortgage found to be right to foreclose on property, not take physical possession)

Hawkins v. Hawkins, ___ S.W.3d ___, 2010 WL 5514344 (Tex. App.—Houston [14th Dist.] 2010, no pet.) (although requiring husband to sign deed of property to wife did not modify decree, compelling him to sign insurance assignment did, since the insurance proceeds were not divided in the divorce decree)

Kazerani v. Chong, ___ S.W.3d ___, 2010 WL 5541702 (Tex. App.—Corpus Christi 2010, no pet.) (award of fees in enforcement proceeding, combined with multiple other claims, found permissible under section 9.014)

DeAcetis v. Whitley, 2010 WL 1077904 (Tex. App.—Houston [14th Dist.] 2010, pet. denied) (husband's complaint about residence owned by corporation owned by sons being awarded to wife could not be brought at wife's post-divorce enforcement action; should have been brought during divorce proceeding)

Treuil v. Treuil, 311 S.W.3d 114 (Tex. App.—Beaumont 2010, no pet.) (wife's suit to enforce award of retirement benefits from husband barred when she failed to file until 5 years after learning of his taking of a lump sum distribution)

Thomas v. Thomas, ___ S.W.3d ___, 2010 WL 1230516 (Tex. App.—El Paso 2010, no pet.) (post-divorce enforcement can not order turnover of car awarded to wife to husband simply because she failed to make payments; nor could husband get a money judgment for payments he had not made)

***See* Accompanying CD–ROM for Cases Linked to Westlaw and Additional Leading Cases**

§ 9.001. Enforcement of Decree

(a) A party affected by a decree of divorce or annulment providing for a division of property as provided by Chapter 7 may request enforcement of that decree by filing a suit to enforce as provided by this chapter in the court that rendered the decree.

(b) Except as otherwise provided in this chapter, a suit to enforce shall be governed by the Texas Rules of Civil Procedure applicable to the filing of an original lawsuit.

(c) A party whose rights, duties, powers, or liabilities may be affected by the suit to enforce is entitled to receive notice by citation and shall be commanded to appear by filing a written answer. Thereafter, the proceedings shall be as in civil cases generally.

§ 9.002. Continuing Authority to Enforce Decree

The court that rendered the decree of divorce or annulment retains the power to enforce the property division as provided by Chapter 7.

§ 9.003. Filing Deadlines

(a) A suit to enforce the division of tangible personal property in existence at the time of the decree of divorce or annulment must be filed before the second anniversary of the date the decree was signed or becomes final after appeal, whichever date is later, or the suit is barred.

(b) A suit to enforce the division of future property not in existence at the time of the original decree must be filed before the second anniversary of the date the right to the property matures or accrues or the decree becomes final, whichever date is later, or the suit is barred.

§ 9.004. Applicability to Undivided Property

The procedures and limitations of this subchapter do not apply to existing property not divided on divorce, which are governed by Subchapter C and by the rules applicable to civil cases generally.

§ 9.005. No Jury

A party may not demand a jury trial if the procedures to enforce a decree of divorce or annulment provided by this subchapter are invoked.

§ 9.006. Enforcement of Division of Property

(a) Except as provided by this subchapter and by the Texas Rules of Civil Procedure, the court may render further orders to enforce the division of property made in the decree of divorce or annulment to assist in the implementation of or to clarify the prior order.

(b) The court may specify more precisely the manner of effecting the property division previously made if the substantive division of property is not altered or changed.

(c) An order of enforcement does not alter or affect the finality of the decree of divorce or annulment being enforced.

§ 9.007. Limitation on Power of Court to Enforce

(a) A court may not amend, modify, alter, or change the division of property made or approved in the decree of divorce or annulment. An order to enforce the division is limited to an order to assist in the implementation of or to clarify the prior order and may not alter or change the substantive division of property.

(b) An order under this section that amends, modifies, alters, or changes the actual, substantive division of property made or approved in a final decree of divorce or annulment is beyond the power of the divorce court and is unenforceable.

(c) The power of the court to render further orders to assist in the implementation of or to clarify the property division is abated while an appellate proceeding is pending.

§ 9.008. Clarification Order

(a) On the request of a party or on the court's own motion, the court may render a clarifying order before a motion for contempt is made or heard, in conjunction with a motion for contempt or on denial of a motion for contempt.

(b) On a finding by the court that the original form of the division of property is not specific enough to be enforceable by contempt, the court may render a clarifying order setting forth specific terms to enforce compliance with the original division of property.

(c) The court may not give retroactive effect to a clarifying order.

(d) The court shall provide a reasonable time for compliance before enforcing a clarifying order by contempt or in another manner.

Comment

This section provides the trial court with an important enforcement tool to secure compliance with its orders. Subsection (a) authorizes the court to issue its own clarifying order in conjunction with a contempt motion. A court determining that its order might be unenforceable by that ultimate remedy may issue a clarifying order to make its order truly effective.

Leading Cases

Pearson v. Fillingim, 332 S.W.3d 361 (Tex. 2011) (court improperly allowed husband to prove his separate property interest in proceeding to clarify; community property presumption applied when husband did not appear in trial at divorce)

Murray v. Murray, 276 S.W.3d 138 (Tex. App.—Fort Worth 2008, pet. dismissed) (trial court properly clarified divorce decree too ambiguous to be enforced)

Karigan v. Karigan, 239 S.W.3d 436 (Tex. App.—Dallas 2007, no pet.) (family home awarded to wife—equitable lien granted to husband to secure money judgment was clarifying order)

Appleton v. Appleton, 76 S.W.3d 78 (Tex. App.—Houston [14th Dist.] 2002, no pet.) (post-divorce attack on unambiguous award of community property elicits Rule 13 sanctions for attorney's fees)

Bishop v. Bishop, 74 S.W.3d 877 (Tex. App.—San Antonio 2002, no pet.) (divorce awarded wife the home and husband the mortgage—her rental of house doesn't create ambiguity in decree)

Lundy v. Lundy, 973 S.W.2d 687 (Tex. App.—Tyler 1998, pet. denied) (alleged clarifying order in fact was impermissible substantive change of unambiguous child support order)

§ 9.009. Delivery of Property

To enforce the division of property made in a decree of divorce or annulment, the court may make an order to deliver the specific existing property awarded, without regard to whether the property is of especial value, including an award of an existing sum of money or its equivalent.

Comment

Before 1983 Texas appellate courts had held that a trial court could not order a party to deliver any specific item of property unless it was "of especial value." This section reverses those cases and specifically authorizes the court to require delivery of property that may not be of especial value, such as stock certificates, certificates of deposit, ordinary automobiles, and the like.

§ 9.010. Reduction to Money Judgment

(a) If a party fails to comply with a decree of divorce or annulment and delivery of property awarded in the decree is no longer an adequate remedy, the court may render a money judgment for the damages caused by that failure to comply.

(b) If a party did not receive payments of money as awarded in the decree of divorce or annulment, the court may render judgment against a defaulting party for the amount of unpaid payments to which the party is entitled.

(c) The remedy of a reduction to money judgment is in addition to the other remedies provided by law.

(d) A money judgment rendered under this section may be enforced by any means available for the enforcement of judgment for debt.

Comment

If all else fails and the property is not (or cannot be) delivered as ordered, the court is authorized to render a money judgment against a recalcitrant party.

Cross References

TEX. CIV. PRAC. & REM. CODE ANN. § 31.002, Collection of Judgment Through Court Proceeding; TEX. CIV. PRAC. & REM. CODE ANN. § 31.0025, Authority of Court To Order Turnover of Wages.

§ 9.011. Right to Future Property

(a) The court may, by any remedy provided by this chapter, enforce an award of the right to receive installment payments or a lump-sum payment due on the maturation of an existing vested or nonvested right to be paid in the future.

(b) The subsequent actual receipt by the non-owning party of property awarded to the owner in a decree of divorce or annulment creates a fiduciary obligation in favor of the owner and imposes a constructive trust on the property for the benefit of the owner.

Comment

This section is designed primarily for the division of pension and annuity benefits. Its passage predated the enactment of the federal Retirement Equity Act, which authorizes direct payment from pension trusts and annuities. See ERISA, 29 U.S.C.A. § 1055, *et seq.*

Leading Case

Zeolla v. Zeolla, 15 S.W.3d 239 (Tex. App.—Houston [14th Dist.] 2000, pet. denied) (original decree had latent ambiguity when husband retired early—cured by proportional adjustment to reflect early retirement plus payback of benefits already received within trial court's power)

---

§ 9.012. Contempt

(a) The court may enforce by contempt an order requiring delivery of specific property or an award of a right to future property.

(b) The court may not enforce by contempt an award in a decree of divorce or annulment of a sum of money payable in a lump sum or in future installment payments in the nature of debt, except for:

(1) a sum of money in existence at the time the decree was rendered; or

(2) a matured right to future payments as provided by Section 9.011.

(c) This subchapter does not detract from or limit the general power of a court to enforce an order of the court by appropriate means.

Comment

This section makes clear that an order of the court to deliver specific property is enforceable by contempt.

---

§ 9.013. Costs

The court may award costs in a proceeding to enforce a property division under this subchapter as in other civil cases.

§ 9.014. Attorney's Fees

The court may award reasonable attorney's fees in a proceeding under this subchapter. The court may order the attorney's fees to be paid directly to the attorney, who may enforce the order for fees in the attorney's own name by any means available for the enforcement of a judgment for debt.

Comment

Before passage of this section there was no provision for the recovery of attorney's fees against an uncooperative party after a divorce. Thwarting the order of the court elicited no punitive consequences, even when a party was found to be the wrongdoer. This section now makes clear that the award of attorney's fees is appropriate in such a fact situation.

CLE/Other Legal Publications

See annotations to §§ 7.001–.002, *supra*.

Leading Cases

Kazerani v. Chong, ___ S.W.3d ___, 2010 WL 5541702 (Tex. App.—Corpus Christi 2010, no pet.) (award of fees in enforcement proceeding, combined with multiple other claims, found permissible under section 9.014)

Mullins v. Mullins, 785 S.W.2d 5 (Tex. App.—Fort Worth 1990, no writ) ($3,500 awarded as attorney's fees for enforcement of court order)

McEntire v. McEntire, 706 S.W.2d 347 (Tex. App.—San Antonio 1986, writ dism'd w.o.j.) (attorney's fees awarded to enforce and clarify agreed decree of divorce)

SUBCHAPTER B. POST-DECREE QUALIFIED DOMESTIC RELATIONS ORDER

Introductory Comment

This subchapter authorizes a court to issue a new, corrective and amended domestic relations order for direct payment of retirement benefits. Somewhat akin to the concept of continuing, exclusive jurisdiction in Title 5 cases, the court that first attempts to divide retirement benefits retains continuing jurisdiction to render a new order to provide direct payment of retirement benefits. This remedial statute is to be liberally construed to effect its purpose.

CLE/Other Legal Publications

See annotations to § 7.003, *supra*.

Leading Cases

In re Marriage of Jones, 154 S.W.3d 225 (Tex. App.—Texarkana 2005, no pet.) (division of retirement benefits clarified by subsequent QDRO)

Harvey v. Harvey, 905 S.W.2d 760 (Tex. App.—Austin 1995, no writ) (survivor benefits awarded to ex-spouse in clarifying order)

---

§ 9.101. Jurisdiction for Qualified Domestic Relations Order

(a) Notwithstanding any other provision of this chapter, the court that rendered a final decree of divorce or annulment or another final order dividing property under this title retains continuing, exclusive jurisdiction to render an enforceable qualified domestic relations order or similar order permitting payment of pension, retirement plan, or other employee benefits divisible under the law of this state or of the United States to an alternate payee or other lawful payee.

(b) Unless prohibited by federal law, a suit seeking a qualified domestic relations order or similar order under this section applies to a previously divided pension, retirement plan, or other employee benefit divisible under the law of this state or of the United States, whether the plan or benefit is private, state, or federal.

§ 9.102. Procedure

(a) A party to a decree of divorce or annulment may petition the court for a qualified domestic relations order or similar order.

(b) Except as otherwise provided by this code, a petition under this subchapter is governed by the Texas Rules of Civil Procedure that apply to the filing of an original lawsuit.

(c) Each party whose rights may be affected by the petition is entitled to receive notice by citation and shall be commanded to appear by filing a written answer.

(d) The proceedings shall be conducted in the same manner as civil cases generally.

§ 9.103. Prior Failure to Render Qualified Domestic Relations Order

A party may petition a court to render a qualified domestic relations order or similar order if the court that rendered a final decree of divorce or annulment or another final order dividing property under this chapter did not provide a qualified domestic relations order or similar order permitting payment of benefits to an alternate payee or other lawful payee.

§ 9.104. Defective Prior Domestic Relations Order

If a plan administrator or other person acting in an equivalent capacity determines that a domestic relations order does not satisfy the requirements of a qualified domestic relations order or similar order, the court retains continuing, exclusive jurisdiction over the parties and their property to the extent necessary to render a qualified domestic relations order.

§ 9.1045. Amendment of Qualified Domestic Relations Order

(a) A court that renders a qualified domestic relations order retains continuing, exclusive jurisdiction to amend the order to correct the order or clarify the terms of the order to effectuate the division of property ordered by the court.

(b) An amended domestic relations order under this section must be submitted to the plan administrator or other person acting in an equivalent capacity to determine whether the amended order satisfies the requirements of a qualified domestic relations order. Section 9.104 applies to a domestic relations order amended under this section.

§ 9.105. Liberal Construction

The court shall liberally construe this subchapter to effect payment of retirement benefits that were divided by a previous decree that failed to contain a qualified domestic relations order or similar order or that contained an order that failed to meet the requirements of a qualified domestic relations order or similar order.

§ 9.106. Attorney's Fees

In a proceeding under this subchapter, the court may award reasonable attorney's fees incurred by a party to a divorce or annulment against the other party to the divorce or annulment. The court may order the attorney's fees to be paid directly to the attorney, who may enforce the order for fees in the attorney's own name by any means available for the enforcement of a judgment for debt.

Comment

Before passage of this section there was no provision for the recovery of attorney's fees in obtaining a qualified domestic relations order. This section now makes clear that the award of attorney's fees is appropriate in such a fact situation.

SUBCHAPTER C. POST-DECREE DIVISION OF PROPERTY

§ 9.201. Procedure for Division of Certain Property Not Divided on Divorce or Annulment

(a) Either former spouse may file a suit as provided by this subchapter to divide property not divided or awarded to a spouse in a final decree of divorce or annulment.

(b) Except as otherwise provided by this subchapter, the suit is governed by the Texas Rules of Civil Procedure applicable to the filing of an original lawsuit.

Leading Cases

Texas Supreme Court

Wilde v. Murchie, 949 S.W.2d 331 (Tex. 1997) (surrounding circumstances of divorce and post-divorce actions compel conclusion marital home awarded to ex-husband)

Courts of Appeals

Preston v. Burmeister, 52 S.W.3d 386 (Tex. App.—Fort Worth 2001, no pet.) (error for a Texas court to award retirement benefits not addressed in a 1979 Florida divorce; issue of marital property not divided on divorce is for Florida law to determine)

Mayes v. Stewart, 11 S.W.2d 440 (Tex. App.—Houston [14th Dist.] 1999, pet. denied) (ex-wife proves lottery winnings were community property for division)

McPherren v. McPherren, 967 S.W.2d 485 (Tex. App.—El Paso 1998, no pet.) (partition suit fails because "Mother Hubbard" clause awarded benefits)

Ballesteros v. Jones, 985 S.W.2d 485 (Tex. App.—San Antonio 1998, no writ) (evidence supports jury's finding of lawyer's negligence in not discovering assets held in husband's name)

Burgess v. Easley, 893 S.W.2d 87 (Tex. App.—Dallas 1995, no writ) (divorced parties became "co-tenants or joint owners" of overlooked community property which is subject to division when discovered)

---

§ 9.202. Limitations

(a) A suit under this subchapter must be filed before the second anniversary of the date a former spouse unequivocally repudiates the existence of the ownership interest of the other former spouse and communicates that repudiation to the other former spouse.

(b) The two-year limitations period is tolled for the period that a court of this state does not have jurisdiction over the former spouses or over the property.

Leading Cases

Sagester v. Waltrip, 970 S.W.2d 767 (Tex. App.—Austin 1998, pet. denied) (general denial and failure to pay did not constitute "unequivocal repudiation")

Phillips v. Phillips, 951 S.W.2d 955 (Tex. App.—Waco 1997, writ denied) (material issue of fact regarding post-divorce partition of undivided community property subject to limitations—Property Code § 21.001 may provide additional remedy)

---

§ 9.203. Division of Undivided Assets When Prior Court Had Jurisdiction

(a) If a court of this state failed to dispose of property subject to division in a final decree of divorce or annulment even though the court had jurisdiction over the spouses or over the property, the court shall divide the property in a manner that the court deems just and right, having due regard for the rights of each party and any children of the marriage.

(b) If a final decree of divorce or annulment rendered by a court in another state failed to dispose of property subject to division under the law of that state even though the court had jurisdiction to do so, a court of this state shall apply the law of the other state regarding undivided property as required by Section 1, Article IV, United States Constitution (the full faith and credit clause), and enabling federal statutes.

Leading Cases

Forgason v. Forgason, 911 S.W.2d 893 (Tex. App.—Amarillo 1995, writ denied) (first wife's just and right share of undivided retirement benefits was to take nothing)

Walton v. Lee, 888 S.W.2d 604 (Tex. App.—Beaumont 1994, writ denied) (trial court allowed to divide previously undivided retirement benefits in partition suit)

---

§ 9.204. Division of Undivided Assets When Prior Court Lacked Jurisdiction

(a) If a court of this state failed to dispose of property subject to division in a final decree of divorce or annulment because the court lacked jurisdiction over a spouse or the property, and if that court subsequently acquires the requisite jurisdiction, that court may divide the property in a manner that the court deems just and right, having due regard for the rights of each party and any children of the marriage.

(b) If a final decree of divorce or annulment rendered by a court in another state failed to dispose of property subject to division under the law of that state because the court lacked jurisdiction over a spouse or the property, and if a court of this state subsequently acquires the requisite jurisdiction over the former spouses or over the property, the court in this state may divide the property in a manner that the court deems just and right, having due regard for the rights of each party and any children of the marriage.

§ 9.205. Attorney's Fees

In a proceeding to divide property previously undivided in a decree of divorce or annulment as provided by this subchapter, the court may award reasonable attorney's fees. The court may order the attorney's fees to be paid directly to the attorney, who may enforce the order in the attorney's own name by any means available for the enforcement of a judgment for debt.

CLE/Other Legal Publications

See annotations to §§ 7.001–.002, *supra.*

SUBCHAPTER D. DISPOSITION OF UNDIVIDED BENEFICIAL INTEREST

§ 9.301. Pre-Decree Designation of Ex-Spouse as Beneficiary of Life Insurance

(a) If a decree of divorce or annulment is rendered after an insured has designated the insured's spouse as a beneficiary under a life insurance policy in force at the time of rendition, a provision in the policy in favor of the insured's former spouse is not effective unless:

(1) the decree designates the insured's former spouse as the beneficiary;

(2) the insured redesignates the former spouse as the beneficiary after rendition of the decree; or

(3) the former spouse is designated to receive the proceeds in trust for, on behalf of, or for the benefit of a child or a dependent of either former spouse.

(b) If a designation is not effective under Subsection (a), the proceeds of the policy are payable to the named alternative beneficiary or, if there is not a named alternative beneficiary, to the estate of the insured.

(c) An insurer who pays the proceeds of a life insurance policy issued by the insurer to the beneficiary under a designation that is not effective under Subsection (a) is liable for payment of the proceeds to the person or estate provided by Subsection (b) only if:

(1) before payment of the proceeds to the designated beneficiary, the insurer receives written notice at the home office of the insurer from an interested person that the designation is not effective under Subsection (a); and

(2) the insurer has not interpleaded the proceeds into the registry of a court of competent jurisdiction in accordance with the Texas Rules of Civil Procedure.

Comment

This section attempted to correct an anomaly in Texas law regarding disposition of certain property rights in insurance policies. For example, formerly if a party was awarded an interest in a life insurance policy but did not change the designation of the ex-spouse as the beneficiary following the parties' divorce, the policy benefits would be paid to the ex-spouse on death of the insured. This was inconsistent with the Texas Probate Code rule that a beneficial designation of an ex-spouse in a will was voided by an intervening divorce. Except in rare cases, the former rule would result in an unintended disposition of benefits from a life insurance policy (a non-probate asset).

This section also deals with other forms of insurance to provide that the insurance protection is awarded to the party receiving the property unless the court otherwise expressly provides.

Unfortunately, the attempt at reform was only partially successful. The federal ERISA preempts state law governing insurance plans directly related to the employment of the insured. As the cases cited below demonstrate, the exact extent of preemption is a work in progress. Fortunately, a very substantial portion of insurance is not derived from employment, *e.g.*, perhaps most life insurance and virtually all automobile and homeowners policies. In those instances the federal intervention into regulation of family law is inapplicable. Moreover, questions remain unanswered, such as whether a life insurance policy derived from employment may be awarded to the nonemployee spouse in the division of community property on divorce.

Of course, the employee ex-spouse may redesignate the former spouse as the beneficiary of life insurance following divorce, or the court may require the party to name the former spouse as a beneficiary or as trustee of the proceeds. The latter is often ordered to protect the interest of the children in their continued support.

CLE/Other Legal Publications

See annotations, § 7.004, *supra*.

Leading Cases

U.S. Supreme Court

Egelhoff v. Egelhoff, 532 U.S. 141, 121 S.Ct. 1322 (2001) (ERISA preempts state statute voiding pre-divorce designation of spouse as beneficiary of employee's life insurance and pension)

Federal Courts

Clift v. Clift, 210 F.3d 268 (5th Cir. 2000) (Tex.) (award to husband of "any and all insurance policies insuring the life of Husband" sufficient to prevent wife from collecting proceeds under policy; language is valid waiver under ERISA)

Brandon v. Travelers Insurance Co., 18 F.3d 1321 (5th Cir. 1994)(Tex.) (although Texas statute requiring redesignation of ex-spouse as beneficiary on life insurance policy preempted by ERISA, divorce decree language was bona fide waiver of former wife's rights to proceeds), *cert. denied,* 115 S.Ct. 732 (1995)

Texas Supreme Court

Barnett v. Barnett, 67 S.W.3d 107 (Tex. 2001) (federal ERISA preempts Texas Family Code regarding beneficiary designation of life insurance obtained through employment; employee has absolute right to designate the beneficiary, notwithstanding fact that life insurance policy is community property)

Cross Reference

TEX. PROB. CODE ANN. § 69. Voidness Arising from Divorce.

---

§ 9.302. Pre-Decree Designation of Ex-Spouse as Beneficiary in Retirement Benefits and Other Financial Plans

(a) If a decree of divorce or annulment is rendered after a spouse, acting in the capacity of a participant, annuitant, or account holder, has designated the other spouse as a beneficiary under an individual retirement account, employee stock option plan, stock option, or other form of savings, bonus, profit-sharing, or other employer plan or financial plan of an employee or a participant in force at the time of rendition, the designating provision in the plan in favor of the other former spouse is not effective unless:

(1) the decree designates the other former spouse as the beneficiary;

(2) the designating former spouse redesignates the other former spouse as the beneficiary after rendition of the decree; or

(3) the other former spouse is designated to receive the proceeds or benefits in trust for, on behalf of, or for the benefit of a child or dependent of either former spouse.

(b) If a designation is not effective under Subsection (a), the benefits or proceeds are payable to the named alternative beneficiary or, if there is not a named alternative beneficiary, to the designating former spouse.

(c) A business entity, employer, pension trust, insurer, financial institution, or other person obligated to pay retirement benefits or proceeds of a financial plan covered by this section who pays the benefits or proceeds to the beneficiary under a designation of the other former spouse that is not effective under Subsection (a) is liable for payment of the benefits or proceeds to the person provided by Subsection (b) only if:

(1) before payment of the benefits or proceeds to the designated beneficiary, the payor receives written notice at the home office or principal office of the payor from an interested person that the designation of the beneficiary or fiduciary is not effective under Subsection (a); and

(2) the payor has not interpleaded the benefits or proceeds into the registry of a court of competent jurisdiction in accordance with the Texas Rules of Civil Procedure.

(d) This section does not affect the right of a former spouse to assert an ownership interest in an undivided pension, retirement, annuity, or other financial plan described by this section as provided by this subchapter.

(e) This section does not apply to the disposition of a beneficial interest in a retirement benefit or other financial plan of a public retirement system as defined by Section 802.001, Government Code.

Comment

This companion measure to the preceding section was an attempt to deal with the disposition of the beneficial interest in retirement benefits after a divorce. A non-employee ex-spouse could make claims on the retirement benefits of a deceased ex-spouse if the deceased had not taken action following their divorce to change the designation of the non-employee ex-spouse as a beneficiary of the retirement plan. Unfortunately, the attempt at reform was only partially successful and, to a large extent, the anomaly persists. The federal ERISA preempts state law governing retirement plans directly related to employment. No doubt the vast majority of retirement plans are directly derived from employment, so perhaps only some individual retirement plans (IRA's) are not subject to ERISA coverage. Fortunately, every competent Texas lawyer is fully aware of the necessity to award separate ownership interests in retirement plans to the spouses on divorce. With that knowledge should come legal advice to arrange the beneficial interest to conform to the client's intent.

Of course, the employee ex-spouse may redesignate the former spouse as the beneficiary of retirement benefits following divorce, or the court may require the party to name the former spouse as a beneficiary.

CLE/Other Legal Publications

See annotations to § 7.003, *supra*.

Leading Cases

U.S. Supreme Court

Egelhoff v. Egelhoff, 532 U.S. 141, 121 S.Ct. 1322 (2001) (ERISA preempts state statute voiding pre-divorce designation of spouse as beneficiary of employee's life insurance and pension)

Keen v. Weaver, 121 S.W.3d 721 (Tex. 2003) (ex-wife's interest in ERISA plan enforceable under federal common law)

Reiss v. Reiss, 118 S.W.3d 439 (Tex. 2003) (division of retirement benefits enforced as res judicata—error in applying law not appealed cannot be collaterally corrected)

Cross References

TX FCA GOVT § 804.001 *et seq.*, Domestic Relations Orders and Spousal Consent, *infra*.

Civil Service Retirement Benefits. 5 U.S.C.A. §§ 2105, 8331 *et seq.*

Uniformed Services Former Spouses Protection Act, 10 U.S.C.A. § 1072 *et seq.*, 10 U.S.C.A. § 1408 *et seq.*

Retirement Equity Act. 26 U.S.C.A. §§ 401, 402, 414.

Employee Retirement Income Security Act of 1974. 29 U.S.C.A. § 1055 *et seq.*

TITLE 1-A
COLLABORATIVE FAMILY LAW

Enacted by the 82nd Texas Legislature, Regular Session (2011)

Authors' Note: Title 1-A: Collaborative Family Law contains guest commentary contributed by:

Kristen Algert, President, Collaborative Law Institute of Texas

Thomas L. Ausley, Chair, Family Law Section, State Bar of Texas

Gay G. Cox, Former Board Member, Intl Academy of Collaborative Professionals

Kevin Fuller, Immediate Past President, Collaborative Law Institute of Texas

Norma Levine Trusch, Chair, Collaborative Law Section, State Bar of Texas

---

Enacted by Acts 2011, 82nd Leg., ch. 1048 (H.B. 3833), § 1, eff. Sept. 1, 2011. Title 1–A "applies only to a collaborative family law participation agreement signed on or after" that date, and an agreement signed before that date is governed by the law in effect at the time the agreement was signed.

Historical Background

The history of collaborative law began in 1990, when a creative Minnesota family lawyer, Stuart G. Webb, decided to create a new form of alternative dispute resolution that he dubbed "collaborative law." After receiving encouragement from a friend who was a Justice on the Minnesota Supreme Court, Webb was able to persuade several Minneapolis family attorneys to join him in this new process. These lawyers found collaborative law to be very successful and popular with their clients.

For several years the approach gained adherents in several states and a few Canadian provinces. In 1999, John McShane and Larry Hance, Dallas family law attorneys, heard about collaborative law and shortly thereafter, brought a training program to Texas in January 2000.

The enthusiasm for the collaborative law process among the Texas attendees was instantaneous and led to the passage in 2001 of Texas Family Code Sections 6.603 and 153.0072, sanctioning the use of collaborative law in family law matters–the first such statutes to be passed anywhere in the world.

With the formation of the Collaborative Law Institute of Texas, Inc., and the hosting in Galveston of the annual meeting of the International Academy of Collaborative Professionals (IACP) in 2003, the movement took on even greater momentum. In 2007, the National Conference of Commissioners for Uniform State Laws (now the Uniform Law Commission) formed a drafting committee for a Uniform Collaborative Law Act (UCLA). The committee was headed by Texas Uniform Law Commissioners Peter Munson of Sherman and Harry L. Tindall of Houston. Norma Levine Trusch, Houston, represented the IACP and Lawrence R. Maxwell, Jr., Dallas, represented the ABA Section of Dispute Resolution. The UCLA was approved and promulgated as a uniform act by the Uniform Law Commission in July, 2009.

In May, 2011, the 82nd Texas Legislature passed House Bill 3833, the Uniform Collaborative Family Law Act, which was assigned to the new Title 1-A of the Texas Family Code, effective September 1, 2011. Texas joins Utah and Nevada as the third state to enact the uniform act.

Historical Background

Commissioner's Comment with modifications by Guest Commentators[1]

The overall goal of the Collaborative Family Law Act (also known as the Uniform Collaborative Law Act) is to encourage the continued development and growth of collaborative law as a voluntary dispute resolution option.

The Collaborative Family Law Act aims to standardize the most important features of collaborative law participation agreements, both to protect consumers and to facilitate party entry into a collaborative law process. It mandates essential elements of a process of disclosure and discussion between prospective collaborative lawyers and prospective parties to better insure that parties who sign participation agreements do so with informed consent. It requires collaborative lawyers to make reasonable inquiries regarding any history of family violence and to discuss reasonable steps to address concerns regarding family violence with any prospective client with such a history. The act also mandates the inclusion of collaborative law's key features—especially the disqualification provision and voluntary disclosure of information provision—as provisions of written participation agreements that seek the benefits of the rights and obligations of the act.

Finally, the act creates an evidentiary privilege for collaborative law communications to facilitate candid discussions during the collaborative law process.

Specifically, the Collaborative Family Law Act:

- applies only to collaborative family law participation agreements that meet the requirements of the act, thus seeking to insure that parties do not inadvertently enter into a collaborative law process. *Sections 15.052 and 15.101.*
- establishes minimum requirements for collaborative law participation agreements, written agreements that state the parties' intention to resolve their matter through a collaborative law process under the act, a description of the matter submitted to a collaborative law process, and a designation of collaborative lawyers. *Section 15.101(a).*
- emphasizes that party participation in collaborative law is voluntary by prohibiting tribunals from ordering a party into a collaborative law process over that party's objection. *Section 15.102(b).*
- specifies when and how a collaborative law process begins and is concluded. *Section 15.102.*
- creates a stay of proceedings when parties sign a participation agreement to attempt to resolve a matter related to a proceeding pending before a tribunal while allowing the tribunal to ask for periodic status reports. *Section 15.103.*
- makes an exception to the stay of proceedings for emergency orders to protect health, safety, welfare or interests of a party, a family member or a dependent. *Section 15.104.*
- authorizes tribunals to enforce settlements arising out of a collaborative law process. *Section 15.105.*
- codifies the disqualification requirement for collaborative lawyers when a collaborative law process concludes. *Section 15.106.*
- defines the scope of the disqualification requirement to include both the collaborative matter and a matter "related to the collaborative matter" and those involving the "same parties, transaction or occurrence, nucleus of operative fact, dispute, claim, or issue as the collaborative matter." *Sections 15.106(b) and 15.052(12).*

---

[1] This commentary and the section by section Comments have been adapted and abridged from the Uniform Law Commission's Official Commentary by the Authors and Guest Commentators. For the complete version of the Official Commentary, see www.uniformlaws.org.

• extends the disqualification requirement beyond the individual collaborative lawyer to lawyers in a law firm with which the collaborative lawyer is associated (imputed disqualification). *Section 15.106(c).*

• relaxes imputed disqualification if the firm represents low-income parties for no fee, the parties agree to the exception in advance in their collaborative law participation agreement, and the original collaborative lawyer is screened from further participation in the matter or related matters. *Section 15.107.*

• creates a similar exception for collaborative lawyers for government agencies. *Section 15.108.*

• requires parties to voluntarily disclose relevant information during the collaborative law process without formal discovery requests and update information previously disclosed that has materially changed. The parties may also agree on the scope of disclosure required during a collaborative law process if that scope is not inconsistent with other law. *Section 15.109.*

• acknowledges that standards of professional responsibility and child abuse reporting for lawyers and other professionals are not changed by their participation in a collaborative law process. *Section 15.110.*

• requires that lawyers disclose and discuss the material risks and benefits of a collaborative law process as compared to other dispute resolution processes such as litigation, mediation, and arbitration to help insure parties enter into collaborative law participation agreements with informed consent. *Section 15.111(2).*

• creates an obligation on collaborative lawyers to screen clients for family violence (defined as in Chapter 71, Family Code) and, if present, requires that the client request a beginning or continuation of the process and the lawyer's determination of what steps could be taken to address those concerns. *Section 15.112.*

• authorizes parties to reach an agreement on the scope of confidentiality of their collaborative law communications. *Section 15.113.*

• creates an evidentiary privilege for collaborative law communications which are sought to be introduced into evidence before a tribunal. *Section 15.114.*

• provides for the possibility of waiver of and limited exceptions to the evidentiary privilege based on important countervailing public policies (such as the protection of bodily integrity, crime prevention, child abuse, fraud, duress, dishonesty). *Section 15.115.*

• authorizes tribunal discretion to enforce agreements that result from a collaborative law process, the disqualification requirement and the evidentiary privilege provisions of the act, despite the lawyers' mistakes in required disclosures before collaborative law participation agreements are executed and in the written participation agreements themselves. *Section 15.116.*

The Balance Between Regulation and Party Autonomy

The Collaborative Family Law Act supports a trend that emphasizes client autonomy and greater reliance on governance of lawyer-client relationship by contract. The act's philosophy is to set a standard minimum floor for collaborative law participation agreements to inform and protect prospective parties and make a collaborative law process easier to administer. Beyond minimum requirements, however, the act leaves the collaborative law process to agreement between parties and collaborative lawyers.

The act's regulatory philosophy encourages parties and their collaborative lawyers to design a collaborative law process through contract that best satisfies their needs and economic circumstances. Parties can add additional provisions to their agreements as long as they are not inconsistent with the core features of collaborative law.

Professional Responsibility Obligations of Lawyers

Ethics opinions by various bar associations—including one from the American Bar Association—have concluded that collaborative lawyers are bound by the same rules of ethics as other lawyers and that the practice of collaborative law is consistent with those rules. *See* "Informed Consent to Participation in Collaborative Law," *infra*. To avoid any possible confusion, section 15.110 of the

Collaborative Family Law Act explicitly states the act does not change the professional responsibility obligations of collaborative lawyers.

Legal Representation Mandatory in Collaborative Law

Under the act, parties can sign a collaborative law participation agreement only if they engage a collaborative lawyer. Collaborative law is not an option for the self-represented.

Collaborative law is, however, a private, contractual agreement between parties to attempt to resolve disputes out of court. Parties are required to agree to waive their right to self-representation as a condition for participating in collaborative law and getting its benefits, but they must do so with informed consent and be aware of the risks and benefits of their decision.

Collaborative Law in Pending Cases

The purpose of the act is to provide parties an additional option for resolving a matter without judicial intervention. That purpose is furthered even if parties choose collaborative law after a case is commenced in court.

Notice to the tribunal that a collaborative law participation agreement has been signed stays further proceedings, except for status reports. *See* Section 15.103 (c).

The stay is lifted when the collaborative law process concludes. Section 15.103 (e). Section 15.104 also explicitly creates an exception to the stay of proceedings for "emergency orders to protect the health, safety, welfare, or interest of a party" or family or household member.

The Scope of the Disqualification Requirement

The disqualification requirement for collaborative lawyers after collaborative law concludes is a fundamental defining characteristic of collaborative law. Section 15.106 extends the requirement to not only the collaborative matter but also to matters "related to a collaborative matter." In addition, the act prohibits lawyers affiliated with a collaborative lawyer from continuing representation of a party (imputed disqualification), thus reducing further the chances of circumventing the disqualification requirement.

"Related to the collaborative matter," in turn, is defined in section 15.052 (12) as "involving the same parties, transaction or occurrence, nucleus of operative fact, dispute, claim, or issue as the collaborative matter." The policy behind these definitions is to prevent the collaborative lawyer from representing a party in court, for example, in an enforcement or modification action resulting from a divorce judgment if the divorce itself was the subject of a completed collaborative law process between the same parties. Involvement in an enforcement or modification involving the same parties via the collaborative law process would not be prohibited.

Section 15.106 (b) adapts the rule of "imputed disqualification" by extending the disqualification requirement to lawyers in a law firm with which the collaborative lawyer is associated in addition to the lawyer him or herself. The policy behind the imputed disqualification requirement is to prevent the collaborative lawyer from indirectly profiting from the continued representation by an affiliated lawyer when the original collaborative lawyer agreed to assume the economic burden of the disqualification requirement. Under section 15.106 (b), a litigator in a law firm with which the collaborative lawyer is associated could not, for example, represent the same party in litigation related to the matter if collaborative law concludes.

Exceptions to Imputed Disqualification

Section 15.107 modifies the imputed disqualification rule for lawyers in law firms with which the collaborative lawyer is associated which represents a very low-income client without fee. The goal of this section is to allow the legal aid office, law firm, law school clinic, or the private firm doing pro bono work to continue to represent the party in the matter if collaborative law concludes. Section 15.107 only applies to parties with "an annual income that qualifies the party for free legal representation under the criteria established by the law firm for free legal representation." Section 15.107 (1).

Section 15.108 creates an exception to imputed disqualification similar to that in section 15.107 for lawyers in a law firm with which a collaborative lawyer is associated which represents government parties. The act's definition of "law firm" includes "the legal department of a government or government subdivision, agency, or instrumentality." Section 15.052 (6).

The conditions for the continued representation are advance consent of all parties to the continued representation and the screening of the individual collaborative lawyer from further participation in it and related matters. Section 15.108 (c).

Voluntary Disclosure of Information in Collaborative Law

The obligation of voluntary disclosure imposed by Section 15.109 on parties to a collaborative law process reflects a trend in civil litigation to encourage voluntary disclosure without formal discovery requests early in a matter in the hope of encouraging careful assessment and settlement.

It is important to remember that a party can unilaterally terminate collaborative law at any time and for any reason, including failure of another party to produce requested information. *See* Sections 15.102 (b), (f). Thus, if a party wishes to abandon collaborative law in favor of litigation for failure in voluntary disclosure, the party is free to do so and to engage in any court sanctioned discovery that might be available. Parties to a collaborative law process are thus no different than parties who participate in litigation or other dispute resolution processes in having to make cost-benefit assessments with the aid of their counsel about whether they have enough information from the informal process of disclosure to settle at any particular time or need or want more.

Informed Consent to Participation in Collaborative Law

The bar ethics committee's opinions that find collaborative law practice consistent with the lawyer's professional responsibility standards emphasize the importance of parties entering into collaborative law with informed consent.

Section 15.111 thus places a duty on a potential collaborative lawyer to actively facilitate client informed consent to participate in collaborative law. The American Bar Association Model Rules of Professional Conduct define informed consent as "the agreement by a person to a proposed course of conduct after the lawyer has communicated adequate information and explanation about the material risks of and reasonably available alternatives to the proposed course of conduct." Model Rules of Prof'l Conduct R. 1.0(e) (2009).

Family Violence

Family violence is recognized as a factor making the collaborative law process potentially more difficult and thus more costly, more likely to conclude without a settlement agreement, and more likely to expose a party to risks associated with dispute resolution processes not directly overseen by a court. Hence, section 15.112 places a duty on a potential collaborative lawyer to make a reasonable inquiry regarding whether a prospective party to a collaborative law participation agreement has a history of family violence with another prospective party. If for any reason the lawyer believes that a prospective party or a party who has signed a collaborative law participation agreement has a history of family violence with another prospective party or party to the agreement, the lawyer has a duty not to begin or continue the collaborative family law process, unless 1) the prospective party or party requests beginning or continuing the process; and 2) the lawyer determines with the prospective party or party what, if any, reasonable steps could be taken to address the concerns regarding family violence. It is possible the determination will be made that the party wishes to proceed in the process with no special precautions, but such a decision will be an informed one after a discussion of available safeguards which could have been taken. These steps could include designing a process that would not include face-to-face meetings, requiring meetings to be held in a secure environment, and requiring the involvement of a collaboratively trained mental health professional with expertise in the area of family violence.

Collaborative Law Communications and Evidentiary Privilege

A major contribution of the Collaborative Family Law Act is to create a privilege for collaborative law communications in legal proceedings, where it would otherwise either not be available or not be available in a uniform way across the states. The Collaborative Family Law Act's privilege for communications made in the collaborative law process is similar to the privilege provided to communications during mediation under Section 154.073, Civil Practice and Remedies Act.

The evidentiary privilege in the act applies to an array of communications not limited to those produced in a formal collaborative joint meeting, such as communications in preparation for the meeting and those in which the meeting is de-briefed. In addition, the privilege allows parties to block not only their own testimony from future disclosure, but also communications by any other participant in the collaborative law process such as jointly retained experts and collaborative professionals. To encourage open and honest communication and to encourage non-parties such as mental health professionals and financial experts to participate in the collaborative law process, the act allows them to block their own communications from being introduced into evidence. The act protects the communications made by and to the collaborative lawyers as non-party participants from disclosure as well.

The act also explicitly lists the exceptions to the evidentiary privilege it creates. As with the privilege for mediation communications, the privilege for collaborative law communications has limits and exceptions codified in section 15.115, primarily to give appropriate weight to other valid justice system values, such as the protections of bodily integrity, to prosecute and protect against serious crime, and fraud.

CLE/Other Legal Publications

See COLLABORATIVE LAW INSTITUTE, February 2011 (various articles)

See COLLABORATIVE LAW PROCESS, February 2011 (various articles)

Do I have to drink the Kool-Aid: Maintaining a litigation and collaborative practice. John P. Friday and Amy L. Lambert, 2011 ADV. FAM. L.

Inheriting the failed collaborative case. Keith D. Maples, 2011 ADV. FAM. L.

Succeeding collaboratively in a soft economy. Curtis W. Harrison, II, 2011 ADV. FAM. L.

Solutions for the complex case. Suzanne G. Blake and Latrelle B. Joy, 2011 ADV. FAM. L.

Who are our collaborative clients?—The Texas profile from the IACP research project. Gay G. Cox, 2010 ADV. FAM. L.

Informed consent—fallout from the ABA ethics opinion on collaborative law. Janice L. Green, 2010 ADV. FAM. L.

Case autopsy—an informative dissection of a challenging collaboration. Cristi Trusler, Mary Ann Osborne, Lisa M. Walker & Melissa Williams, 2010 ADV. FAM. L.

Building a collaborative community—the old and new challenges. Kristen A. Algert, Sally H. Emerson & Steven G. Palmer, 2010 ADV. FAM. L.

Collaborative law. Harry L. Tindall, 2010 SO. TEX. FAM. L. CONF.

Collaborative law and negotiation. (Workshop). 2009 ADV. FAM. L.

Process issues: dealing with potholes, fallen trees, and icy roads along the road map to resolution. Jody L. Johnson, 2009 ADV. FAM. L.

Leading Cases

In re Mabray, ___ S.W.3d ___, 2010 WL 344 8198 (Tex. App.—Houston [1st. Dist.] Aug. 31, 2010, pet. filed) (distinguishing between cooperative and collaborative law agreements)

Pribyl v. Pribyl, 307 S.W.3d 882 (Tex. App.—Austin 2010, no pet.) (wife's cause of action for breach of the collaborative law contract which required full disclosure was improper collateral attack on judgment).

CHAPTER 15. COLLABORATIVE FAMILY LAW ACT [new]

SUBCHAPTER A. APPLICATION AND CONSTRUCTION

SUBCHAPTER B. GENERAL PROVISIONS

SUBCHAPTER C. COLLABORATIVE FAMILY LAW PROCESS

SUBCHAPTER A. APPLICATION AND CONSTRUCTION

§ 15.001. Policy

It is the policy of this state to encourage the peaceable resolution of disputes, with special consideration given to disputes involving the parent-child relationship, including disputes involving the conservatorship of, possession of or access to, and support of a child, and the early settlement of pending litigation through voluntary settlement procedures.

Added by Acts 2011, 82nd Leg., ch. 1048 (H.B. 3833), § 1, eff. Sept. 1, 2011.

Comment

A similar public policy statement is contained in Section 154.002, Civil Practice and Remedies Code.

---

§ 15.002. Conflicts Between Provisions

If a provision of this chapter conflicts with another provision of this code or another statute or rule of this state and the conflict cannot be reconciled, this chapter prevails.

Added by Acts 2011, 82nd Leg., ch. 1048 (H.B. 3833), § 1, eff. Sept. 1, 2011.

Comment

Similar provisions are contained in other uniform acts in the Family Code. See Section 152.002, Uniform Child Custody Jurisdiction and Enforcement Act; Section 159.001, Uniform Interstate Family Support Act; and Section 160.002, Uniform Parentage Act.

---

§ 15.003. Uniformity of Application and Construction

In applying and construing this chapter, consideration must be given to the need to promote uniformity of the law with respect to its subject matter among states that enact a collaborative law process Act for family law matters.

Added by Acts 2011, 82nd Leg., ch. 1048 (H.B. 3833), § 1, eff. Sept. 1, 2011.

Comment

Similar provisions are contained in other uniform acts in the Family Code. See Section 152.001, Uniform Child Custody Jurisdiction and Enforcement Act; Section 159.901, Uniform Interstate Family Support Act; and Section 160.001 Uniform Parentage Act.

---

§ 15.004. Relation to Electronic Signatures in Global and National Commerce Act

This chapter modifies, limits, and supersedes the federal Electronic Signatures in Global and National Commerce Act (15 U.S.C. Section 7001 et seq.) but does not modify, limit, or supersede Section 101(c) of that Act (15 U.S.C. Section 7001(c)), or authorize electronic delivery of any of the notices described in Section 103(b) of that Act (15 U.S.C. Section 7003(b)).

Added by Acts 2011, 82nd Leg., ch. 1048 (H.B. 3833), § 1, eff. Sept. 1, 2011.

SUBCHAPTER B. GENERAL PROVISIONS

§ 15.051. Short Title

This chapter may be cited as the Collaborative Family Law Act.

Added by Acts 2011, 82nd Leg., ch. 1048 (H.B. 3833), § 1, eff. Sept. 1, 2011.

Comment

Derived from Section 1, Official Version of the Uniform Collaborative Law Act.

---

§ 15.052. Definitions

In this chapter:

(1) "Collaborative family law communication" means a statement made by a party or nonparty participant, whether oral or in a record, or verbal or nonverbal, that:

(A) is made to conduct, participate in, continue, or reconvene a collaborative family law process; and

(B) occurs after the parties sign a collaborative family law participation agreement and before the collaborative family law process is concluded.

(2) "Collaborative family law participation agreement" means an agreement by persons to participate in a collaborative family law process.

(3) "Collaborative family law matter" means a dispute, transaction, claim, problem, or issue for resolution that arises under Title 1 or 5 and that is described in a collaborative family law participation agreement. The term includes a dispute, claim, or issue in a proceeding.

(4) "Collaborative family law process" means a procedure intended to resolve a collaborative family law matter without intervention by a tribunal in which parties:

(A) sign a collaborative family law participation agreement; and

(B) are represented by collaborative family law lawyers.

(5) "Collaborative lawyer" means a lawyer who represents a party in a collaborative family law process.

(6) "Law firm" means:

(A) lawyers who practice law together in a partnership, professional corporation, sole proprietorship, limited liability company, or association; and

(B) lawyers employed in a legal services organization or in the legal department of a corporation or other organization or of a government or governmental subdivision, agency, or instrumentality.

(7) "Nonparty participant" means a person, including a collaborative lawyer, other than a party, who participates in a collaborative family law process.

(8) "Party" means a person who signs a collaborative family law participation agreement and whose consent is necessary to resolve a collaborative family law matter.

(9) "Proceeding" means a judicial, administrative, arbitral, or other adjudicative process before a tribunal, including related prehearing and posthearing motions, conferences, and discovery.

(10) "Prospective party" means a person who discusses with a prospective collaborative lawyer the possibility of signing a collaborative family law participation agreement.

(11) "Record" means information that is inscribed on a tangible medium or that is stored in an electronic or other medium and is retrievable in perceivable form.

(12) "Related to a collaborative family law matter" means a matter involving the same parties, transaction or occurrence, nucleus of operative fact, dispute, claim, or issue as the collaborative family law matter.

(13) "Sign" means, with present intent to authenticate or adopt a record, to:

(A) execute or adopt a tangible symbol; or

(B) attach to or logically associate with the record an electronic symbol, sound, or process.

(14) "Tribunal" means a court, arbitrator, administrative agency, or other body acting in an adjudicative capacity that, after presentation of evidence or legal argument, has jurisdiction to render a decision affecting a party's interests in a matter.

Added by Acts 2011, 82nd Leg., ch. 1048 (H.B. 3833), § 1, eff. Sept. 1, 2011.

Comment

"Collaborative Family Law Matter." The definition of "collaborative family law matter" is limited to a dispute, transaction, claim, problem or issue for resolution or in a proceeding that arises under Title 1 or 5 of the Family Code.

"Law Firm." This definition of "law firm" is adapted from the definition of the term in the American Bar Association's Model Rules of Professional Conduct Rule 1.0-(c). MODEL RULES OF PROF'L CONDUCT R. 1.18(a) (2009). It includes lawyers representing governmental entities whether employed by the government or by a private law firm. It is included to help define the scope of the imputed disqualification requirement of Section 15.106.

"Nonparty participant." The definition of nonparty participants as adopted in Texas is expanded beyond the Official Version of the Uniform Collaborative Law Act, to include the collaborative lawyers, as well as other persons who participate in the collaborative family law process. This was done to embrace the concept of the broad process privilege that protects the communications of all participants.

"Party." The definition of "party" is central to determining who has rights and obligations under the act. Fortunately, parties to a collaborative law process are relatively easy to identify—they are signatories to a collaborative law participation agreement and they engage designated collaborative lawyers.

"Person." "Person" was a term defined in the Official Version of the Uniform Collaborative Law Act, but is not defined in the Texas Act. The Texas Act's limitation to family law matters means that the common meaning of the word as used throughout the Family Code is not expanded.

"Proceeding and Tribunal." The definitions of "proceeding" and "tribunal" in Texas, in contrast to the Official Version of the Uniform Collaborative Law Act, do not include a legislative hearing or similar process or a legislative body conducting such a hearing or process, because the statute is limited to family law matters.

"Prospective Party." The definition of "prospective party" is drawn from the ABA Model Rules of Professional Conduct Rule 1.18(a) which defines a lawyer's duty to a prospective client. MODEL RULES OF PROF'L CONDUCT R. 1.18(a) (2009). The rules use the term "party" rather than "client" to clarify that it does not change the standards of professional responsibility applicable to lawyers. The collaborative lawyer's obligations to prospective parties are described in Sections 15.111 and 15.112.

"Related to a collaborative matter." Under Section 15.106, a collaborative lawyer and lawyers in a law firm with which the collaborative law is associated are disqualified from representing parties in court in a matter "related to a collaborative matter" when a collaborative law process concludes. The definition of "related to a collaborative matter" thus determines the scope of the disqualification provision.

"Tribunal." The definition of "tribunal" is adapted from Rule 1.0(m) of the ABA Model Rules of Professional Conduct. MODEL RULES OF PROF'L CONDUCT R. 1.0(m) (2009). It is included to insure the provisions of these rules are applicable in judicial and other forums such as arbitration and is consistent with the broad definition of "proceeding" in subsection (10).

§ 15.053. Applicability

This chapter applies only to a matter arising under Title 1 or 5.

Added by Acts 2011, 82nd Leg., ch. 1048 (H.B. 3833), § 1, eff. Sept. 1, 2011.

Comment

This is an option in the Official Version of the Uniform Collaborative Law Act. See Uniform Act, Section 2, Definition 3, Alternative A (to have the act apply only to family law cases).

SUBCHAPTER C. COLLABORATIVE FAMILY LAW PROCESS

§ 15.101. Requirements for Collaborative Family Law Participation Agreement

(a) A collaborative family law participation agreement must:

(1) be in a record;

(2) be signed by the parties;

(3) state the parties' intent to resolve a collaborative family law matter through a collaborative family law process under this chapter;

(4) describe the nature and scope of the collaborative family law matter;

(5) identify the collaborative lawyer who represents each party in the collaborative family law process; and

(6) contain a statement by each collaborative lawyer confirming the lawyer's representation of a party in the collaborative family law process.

(b) A collaborative family law participation agreement must include provisions for:

(1) suspending tribunal intervention in the collaborative family law matter while the parties are using the collaborative family law process; and

(2) unless otherwise agreed in writing, jointly engaging any professionals, experts, or advisors serving in a neutral capacity.

(c) Parties may agree to include in a collaborative family law participation agreement additional provisions not inconsistent with this chapter.

Added by Acts 2011, 82nd Leg., ch. 1048 (H.B. 3833), § 1, eff. Sept. 1, 2011.

Comment

Subsection (a) sets minimum conditions for the validity of collaborative law participation agreements. They are designed to insure that a written record evidences the parties' agreement and intent to participate in a collaborative law process under the rules. They were formulated to require collaborative law participation agreements to be fundamentally fair, but simple and thus to make collaborative law more accessible to potential parties.

To qualify as a collaborative law participation agreement, the parties must explicitly state their intention to proceed "under this chapter." The participation agreement must specifically reference this chapter to make its provisions such as the evidentiary privilege for collaborative law communications applicable. This requirement is designed to help insure that parties make a deliberate decision to "opt into" a collaborative law process rather than participate by inadvertence. It is also designed to differentiate a collaborative law process under this chapter from other types of cooperative or collaborative behavior or dispute resolution involving parties and lawyers.

Parties are, however, free to supplement the required provisions under this chapter with additional terms that meet their particular needs and circumstances that are not inconsistent with the fundamental nature of the collaborative law process. For example, they may define the scope of voluntary disclosure under section 15.109. They may provide for broader protection for the confidentiality of collaborative law communications than the privilege against disclosure in legal proceedings provided in section 15.113, *infra*. They may provide, as do many models of collaborative law practice, for the engagement of jointly retained neutral experts to participate in collaborative law and prohibit parties from retaining their own experts. They may provide that experts retained for the purpose of consulting with parties during the collaborative law process may testify at trial if the collaborative law process concludes. They may provide that if the collaborative law process terminates, litigation may not be instituted for a short, set period of time, a common provision in collaborative law participation agreements.

A change in practice in Texas is heralded by the requirement that the agreement "contain a statement confirming the lawyer's representation of a party in the collaborative family law process." Lawyers will no longer be signatories to the participation agreement itself. The signature lines will be separated from the clients' signatures similar to how a lawyer's signature appears on a decree "approving as to form only," but not as to substance.

Subsection (b) requires provisions in the participation agreement suspending tribunal intervention while the collaborative law process is ongoing and, except when otherwise agreed, the joint engagement of any professionals, experts or advisors serving in a neutral capacity. This subsection was derived from the repealed Sections 6.603 and 153.0072.

Derived from Section 4, Official Version of the Uniform Collaborative Law Act.

§ 15.102. Beginning and Concluding Collaborative Family Law Process

(a) A collaborative family law process begins when the parties sign a collaborative family law participation agreement.

(b) A tribunal may not order a party to participate in a collaborative family law process over that party's objection.

(c) A collaborative family law process is concluded by:

(1) resolution of a collaborative family law matter as evidenced by a signed record;

(2) resolution of a part of a collaborative family law matter, evidenced by a signed record, in which the parties agree that the remaining parts of the matter will not be resolved in the process; or

(3) termination of the process under Subsection (d).

(d) A collaborative family law process terminates:

(1) when a party gives notice to other parties in a record that the process is ended;

(2) when a party:

(A) begins a proceeding related to a collaborative family law matter without the agreement of all parties; or

(B) in a pending proceeding related to the matter:

(i) without the agreement of all parties, initiates a pleading, motion, or request for a conference with the tribunal;

(ii) initiates an order to show cause or requests that the proceeding be put on the tribunal's active calendar; or

(iii) takes similar action requiring notice to be sent to the parties; or

(3) except as otherwise provided by Subsection (g), when a party discharges a collaborative lawyer or a collaborative lawyer withdraws from further representation of a party.

(e) A party's collaborative lawyer shall give prompt notice in a record to all other parties of the collaborative lawyer's discharge or withdrawal.

(f) A party may terminate a collaborative family law process with or without cause.

(g) Notwithstanding the discharge or withdrawal of a collaborative lawyer, a collaborative family law process continues if, not later than the 30th day after the date the notice of the collaborative lawyer's discharge or withdrawal required by Subsection (e) is sent to the parties:

(1) the unrepresented party engages a successor collaborative lawyer; and

(2) in a signed record:

(A) the parties consent to continue the process by reaffirming the collaborative family law participation agreement;

(B) the agreement is amended to identify the successor collaborative lawyer; and

(C) the successor collaborative lawyer confirms the lawyer's representation of a party in the collaborative process.

(h) A collaborative family law process does not conclude if, with the consent of the parties to a signed record resolving all or part of the collaborative matter, a party requests a tribunal to approve a resolution of the collaborative family law matter or any part of that matter as evidenced by a signed record.

(i) A collaborative family law participation agreement may provide additional methods of concluding a collaborative family law process.

Added by Acts 2011, 82nd Leg., ch. 1048 (H.B. 3833), § 1, eff. Sept. 1, 2011.

Comment

Section 15.104 protects a party's right to terminate participation in a collaborative law process at any time, with or without reason or cause for any or for no reason. Subsection (b) emphasizes the voluntary nature of participation in a collaborative law process by prohibiting tribunals from ordering a person to participate in a collaborative law process over that person's objection.

This section is also designed to make it as administratively easy for parties and tribunals as possible to determine when a collaborative law process begins and ends. To the extent feasible, it links those events to signed records communicated between the parties and collaborative lawyers or events that are documented in the record of a tribunal. Establishing the beginning and end of a collaborative law process is particularly important for application of the evidentiary privilege for collaborative law communications recognized by section 15.114 which applies only to communications in that period, unless the parties agree in accordance with section 15.113 (3) that communications occurring before the beginning of the process are confidential. Such an agreement may be included in the signed participation agreement.

Subsections (d) (2) (B) (i) and (ii) differ from the Official Version of the Uniform Collaborative Law Act, in that the Texas Act permits the parties in a pending proceeding by agreement to initiate a pleading (such as the filing of a counter-petition), motion (such as an agreed motion), or request for a conference with a tribunal (such as a conference to pre-determine whether agreed terms will be approved). Placing a case on the court's trial docket, setting an adversarial hearing, or any other unilateral act to involve the court will result in a termination of the process.

Derived from Section 5, Official Version of the Uniform Collaborative Law Act.

§ 15.103. Proceedings Pending Before Tribunal; Status Report

(a) The parties to a proceeding pending before a tribunal may sign a collaborative family law participation agreement to seek to resolve a collaborative family law matter related to the proceeding. The parties shall file promptly with the tribunal a notice of the agreement after the agreement is signed. Subject to Subsection (c) and Sections 15.104 and 15.105, the filing operates as a stay of the proceeding.

(b) A tribunal that is notified, not later than the 30th day before the date of a proceeding, that the parties are using the collaborative family law process to attempt to settle a collaborative family law matter may not, until a party notifies the tribunal that the collaborative family law process did not result in a settlement:

(1) set a proceeding or a hearing in the collaborative family law matter;

(2) impose discovery deadlines;

(3) require compliance with scheduling orders; or

(4) dismiss the proceeding.

(c) The parties shall notify the tribunal in a pending proceeding if the collaborative family law process results in a settlement. If the collaborative family law process does not result in a settlement, the parties shall file a status report:

(1) not later than the 180th day after the date the collaborative family law participation agreement was signed or, if the proceeding was filed by agreement after the collaborative family law participation agreement was signed, not later than the 180th day after the date the proceeding was filed; and

(2) on or before the first anniversary of the date the collaborative family law participation agreement was signed or, if the proceeding was filed by agreement after the collaborative family law participation agreement was signed, on or before the first anniversary of the date the proceeding was filed, accompanied by a motion for continuance.

(d) The tribunal shall grant a motion for continuance filed under Subsection (c) (2) if the status report indicates that the parties desire to continue to use the collaborative family law process.

(e) If the collaborative family law process does not result in a settlement on or before the second anniversary of the date the proceeding was filed, the tribunal may:

(1) set the proceeding for trial on the regular docket; or

(2) dismiss the proceeding without prejudice.

(f) Each party shall file promptly with the tribunal notice in a record when a collaborative family law process concludes. The stay of the proceeding under Subsec-

tion (a) is lifted when the notice is filed. The notice may not specify any reason for termination of the process.

(g) A tribunal in which a proceeding is stayed under Subsection (a) may require the parties and collaborative lawyers to provide a status report on the collaborative family law process and the proceeding. A status report:

(1) may include only information on whether the process is ongoing or concluded; and

(2) may not include a report, assessment, evaluation, recommendation, finding, or other communication regarding a collaborative family law process or collaborative family law matter.

(h) A tribunal may not consider a communication made in violation of Subsection (g).

(i) A tribunal shall provide parties notice and an opportunity to be heard before dismissing a proceeding based on delay or failure to prosecute in which a notice of collaborative family law process is filed.

Added by Acts 2011, 82nd Leg., ch. 1048 (H.B. 3833), § 1, eff. Sept. 1, 2011.

Comment

Derived from Section 6, Official Version of the Uniform Collaborative Law Act.

Subsections (b), (c), (d) and (e) are derived from the repealed Family Code Sections 6.603 and 153.0072 and are unique to Texas. The stay in Texas is automatic and mandatory; it does not operate as a mere application for a stay. What is and is not to be included in a status report and how it is to be used are now defined in accordance with the Official Version of the Uniform Collaborative Law Act.

---

§ 15.104. Emergency Order

During a collaborative family law process, a tribunal may issue an emergency order to protect the health, safety, welfare, or interest of a party or a family, as defined by Section 71.003. If the emergency order is granted without the agreement of all parties, the granting of the order terminates the collaborative process.

Added by Acts 2011, 82nd Leg., ch. 1048 (H.B. 3833), § 1, eff. Sept. 1, 2011.

Comment

Under this section tribunals are authorized to issue emergency orders despite the execution of a collaborative law participation agreement or a stay of proceedings under Section 15.103 (a). A collaborative lawyer is also authorized to seek or defend an application for an emergency order despite the termination of the collaborative law process under the time limited terms and conditions of Section 15.106 (d) (2).

This section addresses the safety needs of victims of family violence in collaborative law. It is based on the concern that a party in a collaborative law process may be a victim of violence or a dependent of a party such as a child may be threatened with abuse or abduction while a collaborative law process is ongoing. A party should not be left without access to a tribunal during such an emergency.

The reach of this section is also not limited to emergencies involving threats to physical safety. The term "interest" encompasses financial interest or reputational interest as well.

The Texas version of the Uniform Collaborative Law Act clarifies that the granting of an emergency order without the agreement of all parties triggers the termination of the process, and once the emergency protection is obtained the collaborative lawyers must withdraw.

Derived from Section 7, Official Version of the Uniform Collaborative Law Act.

§ 15.105. Effect of Written Settlement Agreement

(a) A settlement agreement under this chapter is enforceable in the same manner as a written settlement agreement under Section 154.071, Civil Practice and Remedies Code.

(b) Notwithstanding Rule 11, Texas Rules of Civil Procedure, or another rule or law, a party is entitled to judgment on a collaborative family law settlement agreement if the agreement:

(1) provides, in a prominently displayed statement that is in boldfaced type, capitalized, or underlined, that the agreement is not subject to revocation; and

(2) is signed by each party to the agreement and the collaborative lawyer of each party.

Added by Acts 2011, 82nd Leg., ch. 1048 (H.B. 3833), § 1, eff. Sept. 1, 2011.

Comment

This section is derived from now repealed Family Code Sections 6.603 and 153.0072. The drafters of the Texas act wanted to preserve existing law as to enforceability of settlement agreements. This section is a departure from the Official draft, Section 8.

§ 15.106. Disqualification of Collaborative Lawyer and Lawyers in Associated Law Firm; Exception

(a) In this section, "family" has the meaning assigned by Section 71.003.

(b) Except as provided by Subsection (d), a collaborative lawyer is disqualified from appearing before a tribunal to represent a party in a proceeding related to the collaborative family law matter regardless of whether the collaborative lawyer is representing the party for a fee.

(c) Except as provided by Subsection (d) and Sections 15.107 and 15.108, a lawyer in a law firm with which the collaborative lawyer is associated is disqualified from appearing before a tribunal to represent a party in a proceeding related to the collaborative family law matter if the collaborative lawyer is disqualified from doing so under Subsection (b).

(d) A collaborative lawyer or a lawyer in a law firm with which the collaborative lawyer is associated may represent a party:

(1) to request a tribunal to approve an agreement resulting from the collaborative family law process; or

(2) to seek or defend an emergency order to protect the health, safety, welfare, or interest of a party or a family if a successor lawyer is not immediately available to represent that party.

(e) The exception prescribed by Subsection (d) does not apply after the party is represented by a successor lawyer or reasonable measures are taken to protect the health, safety, welfare, or interest of that party or family.

Added by Acts 2011, 82nd Leg., ch. 1048 (H.B. 3833), § 1, eff. Sept. 1, 2011.

Comment

The disqualification requirement for collaborative lawyers after collaborative law concludes is a fundamental defining characteristic of collaborative law. This rule extends the disqualification provision to "matters related to the collaborative matter" in addition to the matter described in the collaborative law participation agreement. See *supra*. It also extends the disqualification provision to lawyers in a law firm with which the collaborative lawyer is associated in addition to the collaborative lawyer him or herself, so called "imputed disqualification." Appropriate exceptions to the disqualification requirement are made for representation to seek emergency orders for a limited time (see Section 15.104) and to allow collaborative lawyers to present agreements to a tribunal for approval (Section 15.102 (h)).

Derived from Section 9, Official Version of the Uniform Collaborative Law Act.

---

§ 15.107. Exception From Disqualification for Representation of Low–Income Parties

After a collaborative family law process concludes, another lawyer in a law firm with which a collaborative lawyer disqualified under Section 15.106(b) is associated may represent a party without a fee in the collaborative family law matter or a matter related to the collaborative family law matter if:

(1) the party has an annual income that qualifies the party for free legal representation under the criteria established by the law firm for free legal representation;

(2) the collaborative family law participation agreement authorizes that representation; and

(3) the collaborative lawyer is isolated from any participation in the collaborative family law matter or a matter related to the collaborative family law matter through procedures within the law firm that are reasonably calculated to isolate the collaborative lawyer from such participation.

Added by Acts 2011, 82nd Leg., ch. 1048 (H.B. 3833), § 1, eff. Sept. 1, 2011.

Comment

Derived from Section 10, Official Version of the Uniform Collaborative Law Act.

---

§ 15.108. Governmental Entity as Party

(a) In this section, "governmental entity" has the meaning assigned by Section 101.014.

(b) The disqualification prescribed by Section 15.106(b) applies to a collaborative lawyer representing a party that is a governmental entity.

(c) After a collaborative family law process concludes, another lawyer in a law firm with which the collaborative lawyer is associated may represent a governmental entity in the collaborative family law matter or a matter related to the collaborative family law matter if:

(1) the collaborative family law participation agreement authorizes that representation; and

(2) the collaborative lawyer is isolated from any participation in the collaborative family law matter or a matter related to the collaborative family law matter through procedures within the law firm that are reasonably calculated to isolate the collaborative lawyer from such participation.

Added by Acts 2011, 82nd Leg., ch. 1048 (H.B. 3833), § 1, eff. Sept. 1, 2011.

Comment

Derived from Section 11, Official Version of the Uniform Collaborative Law Act.

---

§ 15.109. Disclosure of Information

(a) Except as provided by law other than this chapter, during the collaborative family law process, on the request of another party, a party shall make timely, full,

candid, and informal disclosure of information related to the collaborative matter without formal discovery. A party shall update promptly any previously disclosed information that has materially changed.

(b) The parties may define the scope of the disclosure under Subsection (a) during the collaborative family law process.

Added by Acts 2011, 82nd Leg., ch. 1048 (H.B. 3833), § 1, eff. Sept. 1, 2011.

Comment

Derived from Section 12, Official Version of the Uniform Collaborative Law Act.

§ 15.110. Standards of Professional Responsibility and Mandatory Reporting Not Affected

This chapter does not affect:

(1) the professional responsibility obligations and standards applicable to a lawyer or other licensed professional; or

(2) the obligation of a person under other law to report abuse or neglect, abandonment, or exploitation of a child or adult.

Added by Acts 2011, 82nd Leg., ch. 1048 (H.B. 3833), § 1, eff. Sept. 1, 2011.

Comment

Derived from Section 13, Official Version of the Uniform Collaborative Law Act.

§ 15.111. Informed Consent

Before a prospective party signs a collaborative family law participation agreement, a prospective collaborative lawyer must:

(1) assess with the prospective party factors the lawyer reasonably believes relate to whether a collaborative family law process is appropriate for the prospective party's matter;

(2) provide the prospective party with information that the lawyer reasonably believes is sufficient for the prospective party to make an informed decision about the material benefits and risks of a collaborative family law process as compared to the material benefits and risks of other reasonably available alternatives for resolving the proposed collaborative matter, including litigation, mediation, arbitration, or expert evaluation; and

(3) advise the prospective party that:

(A) after signing an agreement, if a party initiates a proceeding or seeks tribunal intervention in a pending proceeding related to the collaborative family law matter, the collaborative family law process terminates;

(B) participation in a collaborative family law process is voluntary and any party has the right to terminate unilaterally a collaborative family law process with or without cause; and

(C) the collaborative lawyer and any lawyer in a law firm with which the collaborative lawyer is associated may not appear before a tribunal to represent a party in a proceeding related to the collaborative family law matter, except as authorized by Section 15.106(d), 15.107, or 15.108(c).

Added by Acts 2011, 82nd Leg., ch. 1048 (H.B. 3833), § 1, eff. Sept. 1, 2011.

Comment

Derived from Section 14, Official Version of the Uniform Collaborative Law Act.

§ 15.112. Family Violence

(a) In this section:

(1) "Dating relationship" has the meaning assigned by Section 71.0021(b).

(2) "Family violence" has the meaning assigned by Section 71.004.

(3) "Household" has the meaning assigned by Section 71.005.

(4) "Member of a household" has the meaning assigned by Section 71.006.

(b) Before a prospective party signs a collaborative family law participation agreement in a collaborative family law matter in which another prospective party is a member of the prospective party's family or household or with whom the prospective party has or has had a dating relationship, a prospective collaborative lawyer must make reasonable inquiry regarding whether the prospective party has a history of family violence with the other prospective party.

(c) If a collaborative lawyer reasonably believes that the party the lawyer represents, or the prospective party with whom the collaborative lawyer consults, as applicable, has a history of family violence with another party or prospective party, the lawyer may not begin or continue a collaborative family law process unless:

(1) the party or prospective party requests beginning or continuing a process; and

(2) the collaborative lawyer or prospective collaborative lawyer determines with the party or prospective party what, if any, reasonable steps could be taken to address the concerns regarding family violence.

Added by Acts 2011, 82nd Leg., ch. 1048 (H.B. 3833), § 1, eff. Sept. 1, 2011.

Comment

The Texas version of the Uniform Collaborative Law Act references the existing statutes pertaining to family violence. It does not adopt the more expansive language included in the Official Version of the Uniform Collaborative Law Act—"a history of a coercive or violent relationship." These terms were not defined in the Official Version. There was no intention in adopting the Texas Collaborative Family Law Act to expand the definitions or application of Texas law pertaining to family violence. Many collaborative family law practitioners recognized that most divorces, however handled, involve elements of perceived coercion. The Official Version envisioned a continuous assessment by the collaborative lawyers concerning whether such a history was present. No other lawyers are required to continuously assess whether coercion or violence is occurring, and some would argue lawyers do not have the skills to do this. The Official Version required that in order to begin or continue a collaborative process, the lawyer must form a reasonable belief that the safety of the party could be adequately protected for the duration of the process. Lawyers are not equipped to predict future violence, much less future coercion by third parties. Lawyers cannot warrant a client's safety in any process.

The approach taken in the Texas version of the Uniform Collaborative Law Act is to place a duty on the collaborative lawyer to make a reasonable inquiry regarding whether a prospective party to a collaborative law participation agreement has a history of family violence with another prospective party. If for any reason the lawyer believes that a prospective party or a party who has signed a collaborative law participation agreement has a history of family violence with another prospective party or party to the agreement, the lawyer has a duty not to begin or continue the collaborative family law process, unless 1) the prospective party or party requests beginning or continuing the process; and 2) the lawyer determines with the prospective party or party what, if any, reasonable steps could be taken to address the concerns regarding family violence. It is possible the determination will be made that the party wishes to proceed in the process with no special precautions, but such a decision will be an informed one after a discussion of available safeguards which could have been taken. These steps could include designing a process that would not include face-to-face meetings, requiring meetings to be held in a secure environment, and requiring the involvement of a collaboratively trained mental health professional with expertise in the area of family violence.

Derived, with changes, from Section 15, Official Version of the Uniform Collaborative Law Act.

§ 15.113. Confidentiality of Collaborative Family Law Communication

(a) A collaborative family law communication is confidential to the extent agreed to by the parties in a signed record or as provided by law other than this chapter.

(b) If the parties agree in a signed record, the conduct and demeanor of the parties and nonparty participants, including their collaborative lawyers, are confidential.

(c) If the parties agree in a signed record, communications related to the collaborative family law matter occurring before the signing of the collaborative family law participation agreement are confidential.

Added by Acts 2011, 82nd Leg., ch. 1048 (H.B. 3833), § 1, eff. Sept. 1, 2011.

Comment

Subsections (b) and (c) are unique to Texas. Subsection (b) applies the confidentiality provided in Civil Practice and Remedies Code, Section 154.053(c) concerning the conduct and demeanor of parties and counsel to the collaborative law process. It does not go as far in that it does not prohibit the conduct and demeanor from ever being disclosed to anyone, but under Subsection (a) the parties could agree to such a prohibition and place a permanent "gag" on the parties from ever speaking of this to third parties.

Subsection (c) protects the long-standing practice of collaborative lawyers communicating with each other prior to the signing of the participation agreement to prepare for the commencement of the collaborative process. It allows the participation agreement to cloak retroactively those communications with confidentiality without the risk that the lawyers or other collaborative professionals would be called to testify about the pre-collaboration communications in the event the process terminated.

Derived, with changes, from Section 16, Official Version of the Uniform Collaborative Law Act.

§ 15.114. Privilege Against Disclosure of Collaborative Family Law Communication

(a) Except as provided by Section 15.115, a collaborative family law communication, whether made before or after the institution of a proceeding, is privileged and not subject to disclosure and may not be used as evidence against a party or nonparty participant in a proceeding.

(b) Any record of a collaborative family law communication is privileged, and neither the parties nor the nonparty participants may be required to testify in a proceeding related to or arising out of the collaborative family law matter or be subject to a process requiring disclosure of privileged information or data related to the collaborative matter.

(c) An oral communication or written material used in or made a part of a collaborative family law process is admissible or discoverable if it is admissible or discoverable independent of the collaborative family law process.

(d) If this section conflicts with other legal requirements for disclosure of communications, records, or materials, the issue of privilege may be presented to the tribunal having jurisdiction of the proceeding to determine, in camera, whether the facts, circumstances, and context of the communications or materials sought to be disclosed warrant a protective order of the tribunal or whether the communications or materials

are subject to disclosure. The presentation of the issue of privilege under this subsection does not constitute a termination of the collaborative family law process under Section 15.102(d)(2)(B).

(e) A party or nonparty participant may disclose privileged collaborative family law communications to a party's successor counsel, subject to the terms of confidentiality in the collaborative family law participation agreement. Collaborative family law communications disclosed under this subsection remain privileged.

(f) A person who makes a disclosure or representation about a collaborative family law communication that prejudices the rights of a party or nonparty participant in a proceeding may not assert a privilege under this section. The restriction provided by this subsection applies only to the extent necessary for the person prejudiced to respond to the disclosure or representation.

Added by Acts 2011, 82nd Leg., ch. 1048 (H.B. 3833), § 1, eff. Sept. 1, 2011.

Comment

Subsection (a) derives in part from Section 17 of the Official Version of the Uniform Collaborative Law Act in that it defines collaborative family law communications as privileged, and not merely confidential. The remaining language in subsection (a) is derived from Civil Practice and Remedies Code, Section 154.073(a). Subsection (b) is derived from Civil Practice and Remedies Code, Section 154.073(b). Subsection (c) is derived from Civil Practice and Remedies Code, Section 154.073(c). Subsection (d) is derived from Civil Practice and Remedies Code, Section 154.073(e). The in camera inspection required in Subsection (d) does not adopt the denial of privilege in Section 19 (c) of the Official Version, which allowed the need for the evidence to outweigh the interest in protecting confidentiality in criminal proceedings or in proceedings seeking reformation of a contract or to avoid liability on the contract. Other than in proceedings involving abuse and neglect (see Section 15.115 below), there are no special types of proceedings that warrant relaxation of the privilege. Subsection (f) was derived from the Section 18, Official Version of the Uniform Collaborative Law Act.

The privilege in the Texas Act is treated as a privilege of the process itself and not a party's to assert or not. This is similar to the confidentiality afforded any communication relating to the subject matter of any civil or criminal dispute made by a participant in an alternative dispute resolution procedure. Civil Practice and Remedies Code, Section 154.073(a). The repealed sections 6.603(h) and 153.0072(h), Family Code, applied the provisions for confidentiality of alternative dispute resolution procedures as provided in Chapter 154, Civil Practice and Remedies Code to collaborative law. The intent of the Texas version of the Uniform Collaborative Law Act is to preserve these provisions and strengthen them by affording the collaborative law communications with the status of being privileged communications. Subsection (e) provides that the communications remain privileged when revealed to a party's successor counsel, the disclosure to whom is permitted unless prohibited by the terms of confidentiality in the collaborative law participation agreement. This allows for the smooth transition of a client's matter to successor collaborative or litigation counsel.

Derived, with changes, from Section 17, Official Version of the Uniform Collaborative Law Act.

§ 15.115. Limits of Privilege

(a) The privilege prescribed by Section 15.114 does not apply to a collaborative family law communication that is:

(1) in an agreement resulting from the collaborative family law process, evidenced in a record signed by all parties to the agreement;

(2) subject to an express waiver of the privilege in a record or orally during a proceeding if the waiver is made by all parties and nonparty participants;

(3) available to the public under Chapter 552, Government Code, or made during a session of a collaborative family law process that is open, or is required by law to be open, to the public;

(4) a threat or statement of a plan to inflict bodily injury or commit a crime of violence;

(5) a disclosure of a plan to commit or attempt to commit a crime, or conceal an ongoing crime or ongoing criminal activity;

(6) a disclosure in a report of:

(A) suspected abuse or neglect of a child to an appropriate agency under Subchapter B, Chapter 261, or in a proceeding regarding the abuse or neglect of a child, except that evidence may be excluded in the case of communications between an attorney and client under Subchapter C, Chapter 261; or

(B) abuse, neglect, or exploitation of an elderly or disabled person to an appropriate agency under Subchapter B, Chapter 48, Human Resources Code; or

(7) sought or offered to prove or disprove:

(A) a claim or complaint of professional misconduct or malpractice arising from or related to a collaborative family law process;

(B) an allegation that the settlement agreement was procured by fraud, duress, coercion, or other dishonest means or that terms of the settlement agreement are illegal;

(C) the necessity and reasonableness of attorney's fees and related expenses incurred during a collaborative family law process or to challenge or defend the enforceability of the collaborative family law settlement agreement; or

(D) a claim against a third person who did not participate in the collaborative family law process.

(b) If a collaborative family law communication is subject to an exception under Subsection (a), only the part of the communication necessary for the application of the exception may be disclosed or admitted.

(c) The disclosure or admission of evidence excepted from the privilege under Subsection (a) does not make the evidence or any other collaborative family law communication discoverable or admissible for any other purpose.

Added by Acts 2011, 82nd Leg., ch. 1048 (H.B. 3833), § 1, eff. Sept. 1, 2011.

Comment

Subsection (a) (2) differs from the Sections 18 (a) and 19(f) of the Official Version of the Uniform Collaborative Law Act in that in Texas there must be an agreement of all parties and all nonparty participants for there to be an effective waiver of the privilege, and not only by the parties and the nonparty participant about whose communication testimony is sought. This means that in Texas, the parties, the lawyers and any other nonparty participants must all waive the privilege for evidence of collaborative law communications to be used in a proceeding. The privilege does not belong to the parties alone or to the parties joined by a nonparty participant allowing them to circumvent the privilege afforded the process itself without concurrence of the other participants.

Subsection (a) (5) excepts as non-privileged a disclosure of a plan to commit a crime, not merely a communication used in the plan to commit the crime. Texas does not shield plans to commit future crimes. Disclosures of past crimes are not excepted from privileged communication, but disclosure may be required under other rules of law, such as Section 38.171, Failure to Report Felony, Texas Penal Code, that requires the report of an observed offense in which serious bodily injury or death may have resulted or 18 U.S.C. Section 4, which makes it a crime punishable by a fine or imprisonment for up to three years if anyone "having knowledge of the actual commission of a felony cognizable by a court of the United States, conceals and does not as soon as possible make known the same to some judge or other person in civil or military authority under the United States."

Subsection (a) (6) differs from the Section 19 (b) (2) in that the loss of privilege pertains only to reports of suspected abuse or neglect of a child either to an appropriate agency or in a proceeding regarding the abuse or neglect. Section 261.101 (c), Family Code, states that "the requirement to report [suspected abuse or neglect] applies without exception to an individual whose personal communications may otherwise be privileged, including an attorney ... [and] mental health professional." The contents of such reports will be admissible and excepted from the collaborative law communications privilege, except that Section 261.201, Family Code, will require certain matters in a report to remain confidential, such as the "identity of the person who made the report." Section 261.202, provides that "in a proceeding regarding the abuse or neglect of a child, evidence may not be excluded on the ground of privileged communication except in the case of communications between an attorney and client." The Collaborative Family Law Act preserves this attorney-client communications privilege. The mirror provision for the exception for adult abuse or neglect does not reference the attorney client communications privilege, since the Human Resources Code does not expressly provide for retention of this privilege.

Disclosures about what might arguably support a claim of abuse or neglect that are part of the collaborative law communications, but not contained in the reports of the abuse or neglect, remain inadmissible whether or not the Texas Department of Family and Protective Services is a party or otherwise participates in the process. There is no blanket loss of the privilege simply because "the communication is sought or offered to prove or disprove abuse, neglect, abandonment, or exploitation of a child or an adult" as set out in the Official Version of the Uniform Collaborative Law Act. Inquiring in discovery or in a hearing about the communication in an effort to seek to prove or disprove abuse or neglect was viewed in Texas as overbroad, because in a child custody proceeding many of the communications concerning the children or the development of the parenting plan could be proffered as evidence supporting an unreported claim of emotional abuse or some type of neglect of a child. This could chill the candid exchange of information about the children in a collaborative process for fear that communications would be used in evidence against a parent.

Subsection 7 codifies common case law exceptions in Texas to the confidentiality of communications in dispute resolution processes, such as when evidence is offered to prove or disprove a claim of malpractice; that the settlement agreement was procured by fraud or other dishonest means or its terms were illegal; attorneys' fees; a challenge to the enforceability of the settlement agreement; or a claim against a third party who was not a participant to the collaborative law process.

Derived, with changes, from Sections 18 and 19, Official Version of the Uniform Collaborative Law Act.

---

§ 15.116. Authority of Tribunal in Case of Noncompliance

(a) Notwithstanding that an agreement fails to meet the requirements of Section 15.101 or that a lawyer has failed to comply with Section 15.111 or 15.112, a tribunal may find that the parties intended to enter into a collaborative family law participation agreement if the parties:

(1) signed a record indicating an intent to enter into a collaborative family law participation agreement; and

(2) reasonably believed the parties were participating in a collaborative family law process.

(b) If a tribunal makes the findings specified in Subsection (a) and determines that the interests of justice require the following action, the tribunal may:

(1) enforce an agreement evidenced by a record resulting from the process in which the parties participated;

(2) apply the disqualification provisions of Sections 15.106, 15.107, and 15.108; and

(3) apply the collaborative family law privilege under Section 15.114.

Added by Acts 2011, 82nd Leg., ch. 1048 (H.B. 3833), § 1, eff. Sept. 1, 2011.

Comment

The rules protect persons from inadvertently or inappropriately entering into collaborative law participation agreements by establishing protections that cannot be waived by the parties. Section

15.101 sets forth minimum standards for a collaborative law participation agreement. Section 15.111 sets forth requirements for a lawyer's facilitating informed party consent to participate in collaborative law. Section 15.112 requires a lawyer to inquire into a history of family violence and consider with the client what reasonable steps, if any, could be taken to address the concerns. This subsection allows the court to cure a non-compliant participation agreement or the failure of the lawyer to fulfill the duty to facilitate informed consent, by affording the clients the benefits and protections of the process, so long as the parties agreed in writing to enter a collaborative law process and reasonably believed they were participating in such a process.

Derived from Section 20, Official Version of the Uniform Collaborative Law Act.

TITLE 2
CHILD IN RELATION TO THE FAMILY

As amended through the 82nd Legislature, Regular and First Called Sessions (2011)

Subtitle A. Limitations of Minority.

Subtitle B. Parental Liability.

Subtitle C. Change of Name.

★★★

SUBTITLE A. LIMITATIONS OF MINORITY

Chapter

★★★

CHAPTER 31. REMOVAL OF DISABILITIES OF MINORITY

Introductory Comment

Lowering the age of majority from 21 to 18 in 1973 largely eliminated the utility of this chapter. On rare occasions, a 17-year-old, or even a 16-year-old, may be sufficiently independent and self-supporting to be eligible for the limited removal of disabilities permitted by this chapter. Although the general rule is that the minor will then have the power and capacity of an adult, a wide variety of specific constitutional and statutory restrictions based on age will remain in place, *e.g.*, no voting, no drinking, etc.

Cross References

TEX. EDUC. CODE ANN. § 21.032. Compulsory Attendance.

TX FCA FAMILY § 1.104, Capacity of Spouses, *supra*; TX FCA FAMILY § 101.001 *et seq.*, Definitions, *infra*.

TX FCA CIV PRAC & REM § 129.001*et seq.*, Age of Minority, *infra*.

TEX. R. CIV. P. Rule 44. May Appear by Next Friend; TEX. R. CIV. P. Rule 173.1 *et seq.*, Guardian Ad Litem.

§ 31.001. Requirements

(a) A minor may petition to have the disabilities of minority removed for limited or general purposes if the minor is:

(1) a resident of this state;

(2) 17 years of age, or at least 16 years of age and living separate and apart from the minor's parents, managing conservator, or guardian; and

(3) self-supporting and managing the minor's own financial affairs.

(b) A minor may file suit under this chapter in the minor's own name. The minor need not be represented by next friend.

§ 31.002. Requisites of Petition; Verification

(a) The petition for removal of disabilities of minority must state:

(1) the name, age, and place of residence of the petitioner;

(2) the name and place of residence of each living parent;

(3) the name and place of residence of the guardian of the person and the guardian of the estate, if any;

(4) the name and place of residence of the managing conservator, if any;

(5) the reasons why removal would be in the best interest of the minor; and

(6) the purposes for which removal is requested.

(b) A parent of the petitioner must verify the petition, except that if a managing conservator or guardian of the person has been appointed, the petition must be verified by that person. If the person who is to verify the petition is unavailable or that person's whereabouts are unknown, the amicus attorney or attorney ad litem shall verify the petition.

§ 31.003. Venue

The petitioner shall file the petition in the county in which the petitioner resides.

§ 31.004. Representation of Petitioner

The court shall appoint an amicus attorney or attorney ad litem to represent the interest of the petitioner at the hearing.

§ 31.005. Order

The court by order, or the Texas Supreme Court by rule or order, may remove the disabilities of minority of a minor, including any restriction imposed by Chapter 32, if the court or the Texas Supreme Court finds the removal to be in the best interest of the petitioner. The order or rule must state the limited or general purposes for which disabilities are removed.

§ 31.006. Effect of General Removal

Except for specific constitutional and statutory age requirements, a minor whose disabilities are removed for general purposes has the capacity of an adult, including the capacity to contract. Except as provided by federal law, all educational rights accorded to the parent of a student, including the right to make education decisions under Section 151.003(a)(10), transfer to the minor whose disabilities are removed for general purposes.

§ 31.007. Registration of Order of Another State or Nation

(a) A nonresident minor who has had the disabilities of minority removed in the state of the minor's residence may file a certified copy of the order removing disabilities in the deed records of any county in this state.

(b) When a certified copy of the order of a court of another state or nation is filed, the minor has the capacity of an adult, except as provided by Section 31.006 and by the terms of the order.

CHAPTER 32. CONSENT TO TREATMENT OF CHILD BY NON–PARENT OR CHILD

SUBCHAPTER A. CONSENT TO MEDICAL, DENTAL, PSYCHOLOGICAL, AND SURGICAL TREATMENT

SUBCHAPTER B. IMMUNIZATION

SUBCHAPTER C. MISCELLANEOUS PROVISIONS

SUBCHAPTER A. CONSENT TO MEDICAL, DENTAL, PSYCHOLOGICAL, AND SURGICAL TREATMENT

Introductory Comment

If the person ordinarily empowered to consent to medical treatment of a child is unavailable, this chapter provides for backup consent in an emergency.

Leading Cases

Miller ex rel. Miller v. HCA, Inc., 118 S.W.3d 758 (Tex. 2003) (exigent circumstances create exception to parental consent to treatment of child)

Little v. Little, 576 S.W.2d 493 (Tex. Civ. App.—San Antonio 1979, no writ) (general rule is that a minor cannot consent to medical or surgical treatment)

Cross Reference

TEX. HUM. RES. CODE ANN. § 42.001 *et seq.*, Child Care Facilities.

---

§ 32.001. Consent by Non-Parent

(a) The following persons may consent to medical, dental, psychological, and surgical treatment of a child when the person having the right to consent as otherwise provided by law cannot be contacted and that person has not given actual notice to the contrary:

(1) a grandparent of the child;

(2) an adult brother or sister of the child;

(3) an adult aunt or uncle of the child;

(4) an educational institution in which the child is enrolled that has received written authorization to consent from a person having the right to consent;

(5) an adult who has actual care, control, and possession of the child and has written authorization to consent from a person having the right to consent;

(6) a court having jurisdiction over a suit affecting the parent-child relationship of which the child is the subject;

(7) an adult responsible for the actual care, control, and possession of a child under the jurisdiction of a juvenile court or committed by a juvenile court to the care of an agency of the state or county; or

(8) a peace officer who has lawfully taken custody of a minor, if the peace officer has reasonable grounds to believe the minor is in need of immediate medical treatment.

(b) Except as otherwise provided by this subsection, the Texas Youth Commission may consent to the medical, dental, psychological, and surgical treatment of a child committed to the Texas Youth Commission under Title 3 when the person having the right to consent has been contacted and that person has not given actual notice to the contrary. Consent for medical, dental, psychological, and surgical treatment of a child for whom the Department of Family and Protective Services has been appointed managing conservator and who is committed to the Texas Youth Commission is governed by Sections 266.004, 266.009, and 266.010.

(c) This section does not apply to consent for the immunization of a child.

(d) A person who consents to the medical treatment of a minor under Subsection (a)(7) or (8) is immune from liability for damages resulting from the examination or treatment of the minor, except to the extent of the person's own acts of negligence. A physician or dentist licensed to practice in this state, or a hospital or medical facility at which a minor is treated is immune from liability for damages resulting from the examination or treatment of a minor under this section, except to the extent of the person's own acts of negligence.

§ 32.002. Consent Form

(a) Consent to medical treatment under this subchapter must be in writing, signed by the person giving consent, and given to the doctor, hospital, or other medical facility that administers the treatment.

(b) The consent must include:

(1) the name of the child;

(2) the name of one or both parents, if known, and the name of any managing conservator or guardian of the child;

(3) the name of the person giving consent and the person's relationship to the child;

(4) a statement of the nature of the medical treatment to be given; and

(5) the date the treatment is to begin.

§ 32.003. Consent to Treatment by Child

(a) A child may consent to medical, dental, psychological, and surgical treatment for the child by a licensed physician or dentist if the child:

(1) is on active duty with the armed services of the United States of America;

(2) is:

(A) 16 years of age or older and resides separate and apart from the child's parents, managing conservator, or guardian, with or without the consent of the parents, managing conservator, or guardian and regardless of the duration of the residence; and

(B) managing the child's own financial affairs, regardless of the source of the income;

(3) consents to the diagnosis and treatment of an infectious, contagious, or communicable disease that is required by law or a rule to be reported by the licensed physician or dentist to a local health officer or the Texas Department of Health, including all diseases within the scope of Section 81.041, Health and Safety Code;

(4) is unmarried and pregnant and consents to hospital, medical, or surgical treatment, other than abortion, related to the pregnancy;

(5) consents to examination and treatment for drug or chemical addiction, drug or chemical dependency, or any other condition directly related to drug or chemical use;

(6) is unmarried, is the parent of a child, and has actual custody of his or her child and consents to medical, dental, psychological, or surgical treatment for the child; or

(7) is serving a term of confinement in a facility operated by or under contract with the Texas Department of Criminal Justice, unless the treatment would constitute a prohibited practice under Section 164.052(a)(19), Occupations Code.

(b) Consent by a child to medical, dental, psychological, and surgical treatment under this section is not subject to disaffirmance because of minority.

(c) Consent of the parents, managing conservator, or guardian of a child is not necessary in order to authorize hospital, medical, surgical, or dental care under this section.

(d) A licensed physician, dentist, or psychologist may, with or without the consent of a child who is a patient, advise the parents, managing conservator, or guardian of the child of the treatment given to or needed by the child.

(e) A physician, dentist, psychologist, hospital, or medical facility is not liable for the examination and treatment of a child under this section except for the provider's or the facility's own acts of negligence.

(f) A physician, dentist, psychologist, hospital, or medical facility may rely on the written statement of the child containing the grounds on which the child has capacity to consent to the child's medical treatment.

§ 32.004. Consent to Counseling

(a) A child may consent to counseling for:

(1) suicide prevention;

(2) chemical addiction or dependency; or

(3) sexual, physical, or emotional abuse.

(b) A licensed or certified physician, psychologist, counselor, or social worker having reasonable grounds to believe that a child has been sexually, physically, or emotionally abused, is contemplating suicide, or is suffering from a chemical or drug addiction or dependency may:

(1) counsel the child without the consent of the child's parents or, if applicable, managing conservator or guardian;

(2) with or without the consent of the child who is a client, advise the child's parents or, if applicable, managing conservator or guardian of the treatment given to or needed by the child; and

(3) rely on the written statement of the child containing the grounds on which the child has capacity to consent to the child's own treatment under this section.

(c) Unless consent is obtained as otherwise allowed by law, a physician, psychologist, counselor, or social worker may not counsel a child if consent is prohibited by a court order.

(d) A physician, psychologist, counselor, or social worker counseling a child under this section is not liable for damages except for damages resulting from the person's negligence or wilful misconduct.

(e) A parent, or, if applicable, managing conservator or guardian, who has not consented to counseling treatment of the child is not obligated to compensate a physician, psychologist, counselor, or social worker for counseling services rendered under this section.

§ 32.005. Examination Without Consent of Abuse or Neglect of Child

(a) Except as provided by Subsection (c), a physician, dentist, or psychologist having reasonable grounds to believe that a child's physical or mental condition has been adversely affected by abuse or neglect may examine the child without the consent of the child, the child's parents, or other person authorized to consent to treatment under this subchapter.

(b) An examination under this section may include X-rays, blood tests, photographs, and penetration of tissue necessary to accomplish those tests.

(c) Unless consent is obtained as otherwise allowed by law, a physician, dentist, or psychologist may not examine a child:

(1) 16 years of age or older who refuses to consent; or

(2) for whom consent is prohibited by a court order.

(d) A physician, dentist, or psychologist examining a child under this section is not liable for damages except for damages resulting from the physician's or dentist's negligence.

SUBCHAPTER B. IMMUNIZATION

§ 32.101. Who May Consent to Immunization of Child

(a) In addition to persons authorized to consent to immunization under Chapter 151 and Chapter 153, the following persons may consent to the immunization of a child:

(1) a guardian of the child; and

(2) a person authorized under the law of another state or a court order to consent for the child.

(b) If the persons listed in Subsection (a) are not available and the authority to consent is not denied under Subsection (c), consent to the immunization of a child may be given by:

(1) a grandparent of the child;

(2) an adult brother or sister of the child;

(3) an adult aunt or uncle of the child;

(4) a stepparent of the child;

(5) an educational institution in which the child is enrolled that has written authorization to consent for the child from a parent, managing conservator, guardian, or other person who under the law of another state or a court order may consent for the child;

(6) another adult who has actual care, control, and possession of the child and has written authorization to consent for the child from a parent, managing conservator, guardian, or other person who, under the law of another state or a court order, may consent for the child;

(7) a court having jurisdiction of a suit affecting the parent-child relationship of which the minor is the subject;

(8) an adult having actual care, control, and possession of the child under an order of a juvenile court or by commitment by a juvenile court to the care of an agency of the state or county; or

(9) an adult having actual care, control, and possession of the child as the child's primary caregiver.

(c) A person otherwise authorized to consent under Subsection (a) may not consent for the child if the person has actual knowledge that a parent, managing conservator, guardian of the child, or other person who under the law of another state or a court order may consent for the child:

(1) has expressly refused to give consent to the immunization;

(2) has been told not to consent for the child; or

(3) has withdrawn a prior written authorization for the person to consent.

(d) The Texas Youth Commission may consent to the immunization of a child committed to it if a parent, managing conservator, or guardian of the minor or other person who, under the law of another state or court order, may consent for the minor has been contacted and:

(1) refuses to consent; and

(2) does not expressly deny to the Texas Youth Commission the authority to consent for the child.

(e) A person who consents under this section shall provide the health care provider with sufficient and accurate health history and other information about the minor for whom the consent is given and, if necessary, sufficient and accurate health history and information about the minor's family to enable the person who may consent to the minor's immunization and the health care provider to determine adequately the risks and benefits inherent in the proposed immunization and to determine whether immunization is advisable.

(f) Consent to immunization must meet the requirements of Section 32.002(a).

§ 32.102. Informed Consent to Immunization

(a) A person authorized to consent to the immunization of a child has the responsibility to ensure that the consent, if given, is an informed consent. The person authorized to consent is not required to be present when the immunization of the child is requested if a consent form that meets the requirements of Section 32.002 has been given to the health care provider.

(b) The responsibility of a health care provider to provide information to a person consenting to immunization is the same as the provider's responsibility to a parent.

(c) As part of the information given in the counseling for informed consent, the health care provider shall provide information to inform the person authorized to consent to immunization of the procedures available under the National Childhood Vaccine Injury Act of 1986 (42 U.S.C. Section 300aa–1 et seq.) to seek possible recovery for unreimbursed expenses for certain injuries arising out of the administration of certain vaccines.

§ 32.103. Limited Liability for Immunization

(a) In the absence of wilful misconduct or gross negligence, a health care provider who accepts the health history and other information given by a person who is delegated the authority to consent to the immunization of a child during the informed consent counseling is not liable for an adverse reaction to an immunization or for other injuries to the child resulting from factual errors in the health history or information given by the person to the health care provider.

(b) A person consenting to immunization of a child, a physician, nurse, or other health care provider, or a public health clinic, hospital, or other medical facility is not liable for damages arising from an immunization administered to a child authorized under this subchapter except for injuries resulting from the person's or facility's own acts of negligence.

SUBCHAPTER C. MISCELLANEOUS PROVISIONS

§ 32.201. Emergency Shelter or Care for Minors

(a) An emergency shelter facility may provide shelter and care to a minor and the minor's child or children, if any.

(b) An emergency shelter facility may provide shelter or care only during an emergency constituting an immediate danger to the physical health or safety of the minor or the minor's child or children.

(c) Shelter or care provided under this section may not be provided after the 15th day after the date the shelter or care is commenced unless:

(1) the facility receives consent to continue services from the minor in accordance with Section 32.202; or

(2) the minor has qualified for financial assistance under Chapter 31, Human Resources Code, and is on the waiting list for housing assistance.

§ 32.202. Consent to Emergency Shelter or Care by Minor

(a) A minor may consent to emergency shelter or care to be provided to the minor or the minor's child or children, if any, under Section 32.201(c) if the minor is:

(1) 16 years of age or older and:

(A) resides separate and apart from the minor's parent, managing conservator, or guardian, regardless of whether the parent, managing conservator, or guardian consents to the residence and regardless of the duration of the residence; and

(B) manages the minor's own financial affairs, regardless of the source of income; or

(2) unmarried and is pregnant or is the parent of a child.

(b) Consent by a minor to emergency shelter or care under this section is not subject to disaffirmance because of minority.

(c) An emergency shelter facility may, with or without the consent of the minor's parent, managing conservator, or guardian, provide emergency shelter or care to the minor or the minor's child or children under Section 32.201(c).

(d) An emergency shelter facility is not liable for providing emergency shelter or care to the minor or the minor's child or children if the minor consents as provided by this section, except that the facility is liable for the facility's own acts of negligence.

(e) An emergency shelter facility may rely on the minor's written statement containing the grounds on which the minor has capacity to consent to emergency shelter or care.

(f) To the extent of any conflict between this section and Section 32.003, Section 32.003 prevails.

CHAPTER 33. NOTICE OF ABORTION

Introductory Comment

Chapter 33 was the first legislation to be enacted in Texas affecting reproductive rights since the landmark decision of *Roe v. Wade*, 410 U.S. 113 (1973). Approximately 35 other states have similar parental involvement laws. In 2003, Texas legislation was passed entitled "Woman's Right To Know Act" imposing a 24 hour waiting period before an abortion may be performed.

Requiring parental notification or judicial approval before a minor can have an abortion has been addressed in a number of cases. In *Bellotti v. Baird (Bellotti II)*, 443 U.S. 622 (1979), the Supreme Court held that a judicial bypass for a parental consent must satisfy four criteria: the court hearing the young woman's request must authorize the abortion if she possesses the maturity to make her decision, regardless of her best interest; her abortion must be permitted if it is in her best interest, regardless of her maturity; the court proceedings must be confidential; and, the proceedings must be expedient. In *Ohio v. Akron Center for Reproductive Health (Akron II)*, 497 U.S. 502 (1990), the Court upheld Ohio's one-parent notification law, which included judicial bypass. In *Hodgson v. Minnesota,* 497 U.S. 417 (1990), the Court upheld only the section of that state's two-parent notification law that provided for judicial bypass. Lastly, in *Lambert v. Wicklund,* 520 U.S. 292 (1997), the Court upheld Montana's one-parent notification statute, including a judicial bypass in which the court must decide whether parental notification, rather than the abortion itself, is or is not in the minor's best interest. However the Supreme Court specifically declined to decide whether parental notification statutes must include some sort of judicial bypass to be constitutional. It is safe to predict that further litigation on this subject will cause additional decisions to be forthcoming in the years ahead.

In a related action, in 2005 the legislature enacted S.B. 419, which makes the following amendment to Texas Occupations Code § 164.052:

> (a) A physician or an applicant for a license to practice medicine commits a prohibited practice if that person:
>
> (19) performs an abortion on an unemancipated minor without the written consent of the child's parent, managing conservator, or legal guardian or without a court order, as provided by Section 33.003 or 33.004, Family Code, authorizing the minor to consent to the abortion, unless the physician concludes that on the basis of the physician's good faith clinical judgment, a condition exists that complicates the medical condition of the pregnant minor and necessitates the immediate abortion of her pregnancy to avert her death or to avoid a serious risk of substantial impairment of a major bodily function and that there is insufficient time to obtain the consent of the child's parent, managing conservator, or legal guardian.
>
> (c) The board shall adopt the forms necessary for physicians to obtain the consent required for an abortion to be performed on an unemancipated minor under Subsection (a). The form executed to obtain consent or any other required documentation must be retained by

the physician until the later of the fifth anniversary of the date of the minor's majority or the seventh anniversary of the date the physician received or created the documentation for the record.

The Board of Medical Examiners may take disciplinary action against a medical doctor who engages in a "prohibited practice." *Id.* at § 164.051.

CLE/Other Legal Publications

Parental notification. Sherri L. Cothrun, 2002 Adv. Fam. L.

Parental Notification Act Chapter 33, Texas Family Code: representing Jane Doe. Sherri L. Cothrun, 2001 Adv. Fam. L. Drafting

Leading Cases

In re Jane Doe 11, 92 S.W.3d 511 (Tex. 2002) (district court's failure to follow statute again results in minor's application for judicial bypass of parental notification of minor's abortion to be deemed granted)

In re Jane Doe 10, 78 S.W.3d 338 (Tex. 2002) (trial court's failure to issue findings of fact and conclusions of law on asserted ground of potential physical or emotional abuse required Supreme Court to deem application granted)

In re Jane Doe 4 (II), 19 S.W.3d 337 (Tex. 2000), *In re* Doe 4 (I) 19 S.W.3d 322 (Tex. 2000); *In re* Jane Doe 3, 19 S.W.3d 300 (Tex. 2000) (minor failed to prove she is mature and sufficiently well informed to have an abortion without notifying her parents)

In re Jane Doe, 19 S.W.3d 249 (Tex. 2000); *In re* Jane Doe (II) 19 S.W.3d 346 (Tex. 2000); *In re* Jane Doe 2, 19 S.W.3d 278 (Tex. 2000) (clarification of the "mature and sufficiently well informed" and "best interest" requirements)

Cross Reference

Tex. Health and Safety Code Ann. § 171.001 *et seq.*, Woman's Right To Know Act.

---

§ 33.001. Definitions

In this chapter:

(1) "Abortion" means the use of any means to terminate the pregnancy of a female known by the attending physician to be pregnant, with the intention that the termination of the pregnancy by those means will with reasonable likelihood cause the death of the fetus. This definition, as applied in this chapter, applies only to an unemancipated minor known by the attending physician to be pregnant and may not be construed to limit a minor's access to contraceptives.

(2) "Fetus" means an individual human organism from fertilization until birth.

(3) "Guardian" means a court-appointed guardian of the person of the minor.

(4) "Physician" means an individual licensed to practice medicine in this state.

(5) "Unemancipated minor" includes a minor who:

(A) is unmarried; and

(B) has not had the disabilities of minority removed under Chapter 31.

§ 33.002. Parental Notice

(a) A physician may not perform an abortion on a pregnant unemancipated minor unless:

(1) the physician performing the abortion gives at least 48 hours actual notice, in person or by telephone, of the physician's intent to perform the abortion to:

(A) a parent of the minor, if the minor has no managing conservator or guardian; or

(B) a court-appointed managing conservator or guardian;

(2) the judge of a court having probate jurisdiction, the judge of a county court at law, the judge of a district court, including a family district court, or a court of appellate jurisdiction issues an order authorizing the minor to consent to the abortion as provided by Section 33.003 or 33.004;

(3) a probate court, county court at law, district court, including a family district court, or court of appeals, by its inaction, constructively authorizes the minor to consent to the abortion as provided by Section 33.003 or 33.004; or

(4) the physician performing the abortion:

(A) concludes that on the basis of the physician's good faith clinical judgment, a condition exists that complicates the medical condition of the pregnant minor and necessitates the immediate abortion of her pregnancy to avert her death or to avoid a serious risk of substantial and irreversible impairment of a major bodily function; and

(B) certifies in writing to the Texas Department of Health and in the patient's medical record the medical indications supporting the physician's judgment that the circumstances described by Paragraph (A) exist.

(b) If a person to whom notice may be given under Subsection (a)(1) cannot be notified after a reasonable effort, a physician may perform an abortion if the physician gives 48 hours constructive notice, by certified mail, restricted delivery, sent to the last known address, to the person to whom notice may be given under Subsection (a)(1). The period under this subsection begins when the notice is mailed. If the person required to be notified is not notified within the 48-hour period, the abortion may proceed even if the notice by mail is not received.

(c) The requirement that 48 hours actual notice be provided under this section may be waived by an affidavit of:

(1) a parent of the minor, if the minor has no managing conservator or guardian; or

(2) a court-appointed managing conservator or guardian.

(d) A physician may execute for inclusion in the minor's medical record an affidavit stating that, according to the best information and belief of the physician, notice or constructive notice has been provided as required by this section. Execution of an affidavit under this subsection creates a presumption that the requirements of this section have been satisfied.

(e) The Texas Department of Health shall prepare a form to be used for making the certification required by Subsection (a)(4).

(f) A certification required by Subsection (a)(4) is confidential and privileged and is not subject to disclosure under Chapter 552, Government Code, or to discovery, subpoena, or other legal process. Personal or identifying information about the minor, including her name, address, or social security number, may not be included in a certification under Subsection (a)(4). The physician must keep the medical records on the minor in compliance with the rules adopted by the Texas State Board of Medical Examiners under Section 153.003, Occupations Code.

(g) A physician who intentionally performs an abortion on a pregnant unemancipated minor in violation of this section commits an offense. An offense under this subsection is punishable by a fine not to exceed $10,000. In this subsection, "intentionally" has the meaning assigned by Section 6.03(a), Penal Code.

(h) It is a defense to prosecution under this section that the minor falsely represented her age or identity to the physician to be at least 18 years of age by displaying an apparently valid governmental record of identification such that a reasonable person under similar circumstances would have relied on the representation. The defense does not apply if the physician is shown to have had independent knowledge of the minor's actual age or identity or failed to use due diligence in determining the minor's age or identity. In this subsection, "defense" has the meaning and application assigned by Section 2.03, Penal Code.

(i) In relation to the trial of an offense under this section in which the conduct charged involves a conclusion made by the physician under Subsection (a)(4), the defendant may seek a hearing before the Texas State Board of Medical Examiners on whether the physician's conduct was necessary to avert the death of the minor or to avoid a serious risk of substantial and irreversible impairment of a major bodily function. The findings of the Texas State Board of Medical

Examiners under this subsection are admissible on that issue in the trial of the defendant. Notwithstanding any other reason for a continuance provided under the Code of Criminal Procedure or other law, on motion of the defendant, the court shall delay the beginning of the trial for not more than 30 days to permit a hearing under this subsection to take place.

§ 33.003. Judicial Approval

(a) A pregnant minor who wishes to have an abortion without notification to one of her parents, her managing conservator, or her guardian may file an application for a court order authorizing the minor to consent to the performance of an abortion without notification to either of her parents or a managing conservator or guardian.

(b) The application may be filed in any county court at law, court having probate jurisdiction, or district court, including a family district court, in this state.

(c) The application must be made under oath and include:

(1) a statement that the minor is pregnant;

(2) a statement that the minor is unmarried, is under 18 years of age, and has not had her disabilities removed under Chapter 31;

(3) a statement that the minor wishes to have an abortion without the notification of either of her parents or a managing conservator or guardian; and

(4) a statement as to whether the minor has retained an attorney and, if she has retained an attorney, the name, address, and telephone number of her attorney.

(d) The clerk of the court shall deliver a courtesy copy of the application made under this section to the judge who is to hear the application.

(e) The court shall appoint a guardian ad litem for the minor. If the minor has not retained an attorney, the court shall appoint an attorney to represent the minor. If the guardian ad litem is an attorney admitted to the practice of law in this state, the court may appoint the guardian ad litem to serve as the minor's attorney.

(f) The court may appoint to serve as guardian ad litem:

(1) a person who may consent to treatment for the minor under Sections 32.001(a)(1)–(3);

(2) a psychiatrist or an individual licensed or certified as a psychologist under Chapter 501, Occupations Code;

(3) an appropriate employee of the Department of **Family and** Protective ~~and Regulatory~~ Services;

(4) a member of the clergy; or

(5) another appropriate person selected by the court.

(g) The court shall fix a time for a hearing on an application filed under Subsection (a) and shall keep a record of all testimony and other oral proceedings in the action. The court shall enter judgment on the application immediately after the hearing is concluded.

(h) The court shall rule on an application submitted under this section and shall issue written findings of fact and conclusions of law not later than 5 p.m. on the second business day after the date the application is filed with the court. On request by the minor, the court shall grant an extension of the period specified by this subsection. If a request for an extension is made, the court shall rule on an application and shall issue written findings of fact and conclusions of law not later than 5 p.m. on the second business day after the date the minor states she is ready to proceed to hearing. If the court fails to rule on the application and issue written findings of fact and conclusions of law within the period specified by this subsection, the application is deemed to be granted and the physician may perform the abortion as if the court had issued an order authorizing the minor to consent to the performance of the abortion without notification under Section 33.002. Proceedings under this section shall be given precedence over other pending matters to the extent necessary to assure that the court reaches a decision promptly.

(i) The court shall determine by a preponderance of the evidence whether the minor is mature and sufficiently well informed to make the decision to have an abortion performed without notification to either of her parents or a managing conservator or guardian, whether notification would not be in the best interest of the minor, or whether notification may lead to physical, sexual, or emotional abuse of the minor. If the court finds that the minor is mature and sufficiently well informed, that notification would not be in the minor's best interest, or that notification may lead to physical, sexual, or emotional abuse of the minor, the court shall enter an order authorizing the minor to consent to the performance of the abortion without notification to either of her parents or a managing conservator or guardian and shall execute the required forms.

(j) If the court finds that the minor does not meet the requirements of Subsection (i), the court may not authorize the minor to consent to an abortion without the notification authorized under Section 33.002(a)(1).

(k) The court may not notify a parent, managing conservator, or guardian that the minor is pregnant or that the minor wants to have an abortion. The court proceedings shall be conducted in a manner that protects the anonymity of the minor. The application and all other court documents pertaining to the proceedings are confidential and privileged and are not subject to disclosure under Chapter 552, Government Code, or to discovery, subpoena, or other legal process. The minor may file the application using a pseudonym or using only her initials.

(*l*) An order of the court issued under this section is confidential and privileged and is not subject to disclosure under Chapter 552, Government Code, or discovery, subpoena, or other legal process. The order may not be released to any person but the pregnant minor, the pregnant minor's guardian ad litem, the pregnant minor's attorney, another person designated to receive the order by the minor, or a governmental agency or attorney in a criminal or administrative action seeking to assert or protect the interest of the minor. The supreme court may adopt rules to permit confidential docketing of an application under this section.

(m) The clerk of the supreme court shall prescribe the application form to be used by the minor filing an application under this section.

(n) A filing fee is not required of and court costs may not be assessed against a minor filing an application under this section.

Amended by Acts 2011, 82nd Leg., ch. 110 (H.B. 841), § 1, eff. May 21, 2011.

§ 33.004. Appeal

(a) A minor whose application under Section 33.003 is denied may appeal to the court of appeals having jurisdiction over civil matters in the county in which the application was filed. On receipt of a notice of appeal, the clerk of the court that denied the application shall deliver a copy of the notice of appeal and record on appeal to the clerk of the court of appeals. On receipt of the notice and record, the clerk of the court of appeals shall place the appeal on the docket of the court.

(b) The court of appeals shall rule on an appeal under this section not later than 5 p.m. on the second business day after the date the notice of appeal is filed with the court that denied the application. On request by the minor, the court shall grant an extension of the period specified by this subsection. If a request for an extension is made, the court shall rule on the appeal not later than 5 p.m. on the second business day after the date the minor states she is ready to proceed. If the court of appeals fails to rule on the appeal within the period specified by this subsection, the appeal is deemed to be granted and the physician may perform the abortion as if the court had issued an order authorizing the minor to consent to the performance of the abortion without notification under Section 33.002. Proceedings under this section shall be given precedence over other pending matters to the extent necessary to assure that the court reaches a decision promptly.

(c) A ruling of the court of appeals issued under this section is confidential and privileged and is not subject to disclosure under Chapter 552, Government Code, or discovery, subpoena, or other legal process. The ruling may not be released to any person but the pregnant minor, the pregnant minor's guardian ad litem, the pregnant minor's attorney, another person designated to receive the ruling by the minor, or a governmental agency or attorney in a criminal or administrative action seeking to assert or protect the interest of the minor. The supreme court may adopt rules to permit confidential docketing of an appeal under this section.

(d) The clerk of the supreme court shall prescribe the notice of appeal form to be used by the minor appealing a judgment under this section.

(e) A filing fee is not required of and court costs may not be assessed against a minor filing an appeal under this section.

(f) An expedited confidential appeal shall be available to any pregnant minor to whom a court of appeals denies an order authorizing the minor to consent to the performance of an abortion without notification to either of her parents or a managing conservator or guardian.

Leading Case

In re Jane Doe 11, 92 S.W.3d 511 (Tex. 2002) (order not appealable because district court failed to deny minor's application—thereby abortion deemed granted)

---

§ 33.005. Affidavit of Physician

(a) A physician may execute for inclusion in the minor's medical record an affidavit stating that, after reasonable inquiry, it is the belief of the physician that:

(1) the minor has made an application or filed a notice of an appeal with a court under this chapter;

(2) the deadline for court action imposed by this chapter has passed; and

(3) the physician has been notified that the court has not denied the application or appeal.

(b) A physician who in good faith has executed an affidavit under Subsection (a) may rely on the affidavit and may perform the abortion as if the court had issued an order granting the application or appeal.

§ 33.006. Guardian ad Litem Immunity

A guardian ad litem appointed under this chapter and acting in the course and scope of the appointment is not liable for damages arising from an act or omission of the guardian ad litem committed in good faith. The immunity granted by this section does not apply if the conduct of the guardian ad litem is committed in a manner described by Sections 107.003(b)(1)–(4).

§ 33.007. Costs Paid by State

(a) A court acting under Section 33.003 or 33.004 may issue an order requiring the state to pay:

(1) the cost of any attorney ad litem and any guardian ad litem appointed for the minor;

(2) notwithstanding Sections 33.003(n) and 33.004(e), the costs of court associated with the application or appeal; and

(3) any court reporter's fees incurred.

(b) An order issued under Subsection (a) must be directed to the comptroller, who shall pay the amount ordered from funds appropriated to the Texas Department of Health.

§ 33.008. Physician's Duty to Report Abuse of a Minor; Investigation and Assistance

(a) A physician who has reason to believe that a minor has been or may be physically or sexually abused by a person responsible for the minor's care, custody, or welfare, as that term is defined by Section 261.001, shall immediately report the suspected abuse to the Department of **Family and** Protective ~~and Regulatory~~ Services and shall refer the minor to the department for services or intervention that may be in the best interest of the minor.

(b) The Department of **Family and** Protective ~~and Regulatory~~ Services shall investigate suspected abuse reported under this section and, if appropriate, shall assist the minor in making an application with a court under Section 33.003.

Amended by Acts 2011, 82nd Leg., ch. 110 (H.B. 841), § 2, eff. May 21, 2011.

§ 33.009. Other Reports of Sexual Abuse of a Minor

A court or the guardian ad litem or attorney ad litem for the minor shall report conduct reasonably believed to violate Section 21.02, 22.011, 22.021, or 25.02, Penal Code, based on information obtained during a confidential court proceeding held under this chapter to:

(1) any local or state law enforcement agency;

(2) the Department of Family and Protective Services, if the alleged conduct involves a person responsible for the care, custody, or welfare of the child;

(3) the state agency that operates, licenses, certifies, or registers the facility in which the alleged conduct occurred, if the alleged conduct occurred in a facility operated, licensed, certified, or registered by a state agency; or

(4) an appropriate agency designated by the court.

§ 33.010. Confidentiality

Notwithstanding any other law, information obtained by the Department of Family and Protective Services or another entity under Section 33.008 or 33.009 is confidential except to the extent necessary to prove a violation of Section 21.02, 22. 011, 22.021, or 25.02, Penal Code.

§ 33.011. Information Relating to Judicial Bypass

The Texas Department of Health shall produce and distribute informational materials that explain the rights of a minor under this chapter. The materials must explain the procedures established by Sections 33.003 and 33.004 and must be made available in English and in Spanish. The material provided by the department shall also provide information relating to alternatives to abortion and health risks associated with abortion.

CHAPTER 34. AUTHORIZATION AGREEMENT FOR NONPARENT RELATIVE

Introductory Comment

Chapter 34 allows for a parent to provide specific authorization to a grandparent, adult sibling, or adult aunt or uncle of a child to provide medical, educational, and other parental consents in a parent's absence.

CLE/Leading Legal Publication

Yours, mine, ours?—why the Texas legislature should simplify caretaker consent capabilities for minor children and the implications of the addition of Chapter 34 to the Texas Family Code. John W. Ellis, 42 Tex. Tech L. Rev. 987 (2010)

New Chapter 34: authorization agreements for nonparent relatives. Judy L. Warne, 2010 Marriage Dissolution

---

§ 34.001. Applicability

This chapter applies only to**:**

(1) an authorization agreement between a parent of a child and a person who is the child's:

(A) ~~(1)~~grandparent;

(B) ~~(2)~~adult sibling; or

(C) ~~(3)~~adult aunt or uncle**; and**

(2) an authorization agreement between a parent of a child and the person with whom the child is placed under a parental child safety placement agreement.

Amended by Acts 2011, 82nd Leg., ch. 484 (H.B. 848), § 1, eff. Sept. 1, 2011.

§ 34.0015. Definition

In this chapter, "parent" has the meaning assigned by Section 101.024.

Added by Acts 2011, 82nd Leg., ch. 897 (S.B. 482), § 1, eff. Sept. 1, 2011.

§ 34.002. Authorization Agreement

(a) A parent or both parents of a child may enter into an authorization agreement with a relative of the child listed in Section 34.001 to authorize the relative to perform the following acts in regard to the child:

(1) to authorize medical, dental, psychological, or surgical treatment and immunization of the child, including executing any consents or authorizations for the release of information as required by law relating to the treatment or immunization;

(2) to obtain and maintain health insurance coverage for the child and automobile insurance coverage for the child, if appropriate;

(3) to enroll the child in a day-care program or preschool or in a public or private primary or secondary school;

(4) to authorize the child to participate in age-appropriate extracurricular, civic, social, or recreational activities, including athletic activities;

(5) to authorize the child to obtain a learner's permit, driver's license, or state-issued identification card;

(6) to authorize employment of the child; and

(7) to apply for and receive public benefits on behalf of the child.

(b) To the extent of any conflict or inconsistency between this chapter and any other law relating to the eligibility requirements other than parental consent to obtain a service under Subsection (a), the other law controls.

(c) An authorization agreement under this chapter does not confer on a relative of the child listed in Section 34.001 **or a relative or other person with whom the child is placed under a child safety placement agreement** the right to authorize the performance of an abortion on the child or the administration of emergency contraception to the child.

(d) Only one authorization agreement may be in effect for a child at any time. An authorization agreement is void if it is executed while a prior authorization agreement remains in effect.

Amended by Acts 2011, 82nd Leg., ch. 484 (H.B. 848), § 2, eff. Sept. 1, 2011; Acts 2011, 82nd Leg., ch. 897 (S.B. 482), § 2, eff. Sept. 1, 2011.

§ 34.0021. Authorization Agreement by Parent in Child Protective Services Case

A parent may enter into an authorization agreement with a relative or other person with whom a child is placed under a parental child safety placement agreement approved by the Department of Family and Protective Services to allow the person to perform the acts described by Section 34.002(a) with regard to the child:

(1) during an investigation of abuse or neglect; or

(2) while the department is providing services to the parent.

Added by Acts 2011, 82nd Leg., ch. 484 (H.B. 848), § 3, eff. Sept. 1, 2011.

§ 34.003. Contents of Authorization Agreement

(a) The authorization agreement must contain:

(1) the following information from the relative of the child to whom the parent is giving authorization:

(A) the name and signature of the relative;

(B) the relative's relationship to the child; and

(C) the relative's current physical address and telephone number or the best way to contact the relative;

(2) the following information from the parent:

(A) the name and signature of the parent; and

(B) the parent's current address and telephone number or the best way to contact the parent;

(3) the information in Subdivision (2) with respect to the other parent, if applicable;

(4) a statement that the relative has been given authorization to perform the functions listed in Section 34.002(a) as a result of a voluntary action of the parent and that the relative has voluntarily assumed the responsibility of performing those functions;

(5) statements that neither the parent nor the relative has knowledge that a parent, guardian, custodian, licensed child-placing agency, or other authorized agency asserts any claim or authority inconsistent with the authorization agreement under this chapter with regard to actual physical possession or care, custody, or control of the child;

(6) statements that:

(A) to the best of the parent's and relative's knowledge:

(i) there is no court order or pending suit affecting the parent-child relationship concerning the child;

(ii) there is no pending litigation in any court concerning:

(a) custody, possession, or placement of the child; or

(b) access to or visitation with the child; and

(iii) the court does not have continuing jurisdiction concerning the child; or

(B) the court with continuing jurisdiction concerning the child has given written approval for the execution of the authorization agreement accompanied by the following information:

(i) the county in which the court is located;

(ii) the number of the court; and

(iii) the cause number in which the order was issued or the litigation is pending;

(7) **a statement that to the best of the parent's and relative's knowledge there is no current, valid authorization agreement regarding the child;**

(8) a statement that the authorization is made in conformance with this chapter;

(9)~~(8)~~ a statement that the parent and the relative understand that each party to the authorization agreement is required by law to immediately provide to each other party information regarding any change in the party's address or contact information;

(10)~~(9)~~ a statement by the parent that establishes the circumstances under which the authorization agreement expires, including that the authorization agreement:

(A) is valid until revoked;

(B) continues in effect after the death or during any incapacity of the parent; or

(C) expires on a date stated in the authorization agreement; and

(11)~~(10)~~ space for the signature and seal of a notary public.

(b) The authorization agreement must contain the following warnings and disclosures:

(1) that the authorization agreement is an important legal document;

(2) that the parent and the relative must read all of the warnings and disclosures before signing the authorization agreement;

(3) that the persons signing the authorization agreement are not required to consult an attorney but are advised to do so;

(4) that the parent's rights as a parent may be adversely affected by placing or leaving the parent's child with another person;

(5) that the authorization agreement does not confer on the relative the rights of a managing or possessory conservator or legal guardian;

(6) that a parent who is a party to the authorization agreement may terminate the authorization agreement and resume custody, possession, care, and control of the child on demand and that at any time the parent may request the return of the child;

(7) that failure by the relative to return the child to the parent immediately on request may have criminal and civil consequences;

(8) that, under other applicable law, the relative may be liable for certain expenses relating to the child in the relative's care but that the parent still retains the parental obligation to support the child;

(9) that, in certain circumstances, the authorization agreement may not be entered into without written permission of the court;

(10) that the authorization agreement may be terminated by certain court orders affecting the child;

(11) **that the authorization agreement does not supersede, invalidate, or terminate any prior authorization agreement regarding the child;**

(12) that the authorization agreement is void if a prior authorization agreement regarding the child is in effect and has not expired or been terminated;

(13) that, **except as provided by Section 34.005(a–1),** the authorization agreement is void unless:

(A) the parties mail a copy of the authorization agreement **by certified mail, return receipt requested, or international registered mail, return receipt requested, as applicable,** to a parent who was not a party to the authorization agreement, if the parent is living and the parent's parental rights have not been terminated, not later than the 10th day after the date the authorization agreement is signed; and

(B) if the parties do not receive a response from the parent who is not a party to the authorization agreement before the 20th day after the date the copy of the authorization agreement is mailed under Paragraph (A), the parties mail a second copy of the authorization agreement by first class mail or international first class mail, as applicable, to the parent not later than the 45th day after the date the authorization agreement is signed; and

(14)~~(12)~~ that the authorization agreement does not confer on a relative of the child the right to authorize the performance of an abortion on the child or the administration of emergency contraception to the child.

Amended by Acts 2011, 82nd Leg., ch. 897 (S.B. 482), § 3, eff. Sept. 1, 2011.

§ 34.004. Execution of Authorization Agreement

(a) The authorization agreement must be signed and sworn to before a notary public by the parent and the relative.

(b) A parent may not execute an authorization agreement without a written order by the appropriate court if:

(1) there is a court order or pending suit affecting the parent-child relationship concerning the child;

(2) there is pending litigation in any court concerning:

(A) custody, possession, or placement of the child; or

(B) access to or visitation with the child; or

(3) the court has continuing, exclusive jurisdiction over the child.

(c) An authorization agreement obtained in violation of Subsection (b) is void.

§ 34.005. Duties of Parties to Authorization Agreement

(a) If both parents did not sign the authorization agreement, the parties shall mail a copy of the executed authorization agreement **by certified mail, return receipt requested, or international registered mail, return receipt requested, as applicable,** to the parent who was not a party to the authorization agreement at the parent's last known address not later than the 10th day after the date the authorization agreement is executed if that parent is living and that parent's parental rights have not been terminated. **If the parties do not receive a response from the parent who is not a party to the authorization agreement before the 20th day after the date the copy of the authorization agreement is mailed, the parties shall mail a second copy of the executed authorization agreement by first class mail or international first class mail, as applicable, to the parent at the same address not later than**

the 45th day after the date the authorization agreement is executed. An authorization agreement is void if the parties fail to comply with this subsection.

(a–1) Subsection (a) does not apply to an authorization agreement if the parent who was not a party to the authorization agreement:

(1) does not have court-ordered possession of or access to the child who is the subject of the authorization agreement; and

(2) has previously committed an act of family violence, as defined by Section 71.004, or assault against the parent who is a party to the authorization agreement, the child who is the subject of the authorization agreement, or another child of the parent who is a party to the authorization agreement, as documented by one or more of the following:

(A) the issuance of a protective order against the parent who was not a party to the authorization agreement as provided under Chapter 85 or under a similar law of another state; or

(B) the conviction of the parent who was not a party to the authorization agreement of an offense under Title 5, Penal Code, or of another criminal offense in this state or in another state an element of which involves a violent act or prohibited sexual conduct.

(b) A party to the authorization agreement shall immediately inform each other party of any change in the party's address or contact information. If a party fails to comply with this subsection, the authorization agreement is voidable by the other party.

Amended by Acts 2011, 82nd Leg., ch. 897 (S.B. 482), § 4, eff. Sept. 1, 2011.

§ 34.006. Authorization Voidable

An authorization agreement is voidable by a party if the other party knowingly:

(1) obtained the authorization agreement by fraud, duress, or misrepresentation; or

(2) made a false statement on the authorization agreement.

§ 34.007. Effect of Authorization Agreement

(a) A person who is not a party to the authorization agreement who relies in good faith on an authorization agreement under this chapter, without actual knowledge that the authorization agreement is void, revoked, or invalid, is not subject to civil or criminal liability to any person, and is not subject to professional disciplinary action, for that reliance if the agreement is completed as required by this chapter.

(b) The authorization agreement does not affect the rights of the child's parent or legal guardian regarding the care, custody, and control of the child, and does not mean that the relative has legal custody of the child.

(c) An authorization agreement executed under this chapter does not confer or affect standing or a right of intervention in any proceeding under Title 5.

§ 34.008. Termination of Authorization Agreement

(a) Except as provided by Subsection (b), an authorization agreement under this chapter terminates if, after the execution of the authorization agreement, a court enters an order:

(1) affecting the parent-child relationship;

(2) concerning custody, possession, or placement of the child;

(3) concerning access to or visitation with the child; or

(4) regarding the appointment of a guardian for the child under Section 676, Texas Probate Code.

(b) An authorization agreement may continue after a court order described by Subsection (a) is entered if the court entering the order gives written permission.

(c) An authorization agreement under this chapter terminates on written revocation by a party to the authorization agreement if the party:

(1) gives each party written notice of the revocation;

(2) files the written revocation with the clerk of the county in which:

(A) the child resides;

(B) the child resided at the time the authorization agreement was executed; or

(C) the relative resides; and

(3) files the written revocation with the clerk of each court:

(A) that has continuing, exclusive jurisdiction over the child;

(B) in which there is a court order or pending suit affecting the parent-child relationship concerning the child;

(C) in which there is pending litigation concerning:

(i) custody, possession, or placement of the child; or

(ii) access to or visitation with the child; or

(D) that has entered an order regarding the appointment of a guardian for the child under Section 676, Texas Probate Code.

(d) If an authorization agreement executed under this chapter does not state when the authorization agreement expires, the authorization agreement is valid until revoked.

(e) If both parents have signed the authorization agreement, either parent may revoke the authorization agreement without the other parent's consent.

(f) Execution of a subsequent authorization agreement does not by itself supersede, invalidate, or terminate a prior authorization agreement.

Amended by Acts 2011, 82nd Leg., ch. 897 (S.B. 482), § 5, eff. Sept. 1, 2011.

§ 34.009. Penalty

(a) A person commits an offense if the person knowingly:

(1) presents a document that is not a valid authorization agreement as a valid authorization agreement under this chapter;

(2) makes a false statement on an authorization agreement; or

(3) obtains an authorization agreement by fraud, duress, or misrepresentation.

(b) An offense under this section is a Class B misdemeanor.

SUBTITLE B. PARENTAL LIABILITY

★★★

CHAPTER 41. LIABILITY OF PARENTS FOR CONDUCT OF CHILD

Introductory Comment

The liability of a parent for a child's tortious conduct that injures property is more theoretical than real. While a parent can be held liable for up to $25,000 in damages for negligent or malicious acts of the child, very few instances of a court actually holding parents liable have been reported. Undoubtedly the relatively low limit on recoverable damages severely limits the availability of legal representation, whether by hourly employment or contingent fee.

CLE/Other Legal Publications

Increasing the price of parenthood: when should parents be held civilly liable for the torts of their children? Andrew C. Gratz, 39 HOUSTON L. REV. 169 (2002)

Paying for the sins of another in Texas for the torts of children. David F. Johnson, 8 TEX. WESLEYAN L. REV. 359 (2002)

Leading Case

In re D.M. 191 S.W.3d 381 (Tex. App.—Austin 2006, pet. denied) (to escape per se liability, parents of delinquent must prove "good faith efforts" to prevent tortious conduct)

Cross References

TX FCA FAMILY § 54.041, Orders Affecting Parents and Others, *infra*; TX FCA FAMILY § 151.003, Rights and Duties of Parent, *infra*; TX FCA FAMILY § 153.001 *et seq.*, Conservatorship, Possession and Access, *infra*.

---

§ 41.001. Liability

A parent or other person who has the duty of control and reasonable discipline of a child is liable for any property damage proximately caused by:

(1) the negligent conduct of the child if the conduct is reasonably attributable to the negligent failure of the parent or other person to exercise that duty; or

(2) the wilful and malicious conduct of a child who is at least 10 years of age but under 18 years of age.

§ 41.002. Limit of Damages

Recovery for damage caused by wilful and malicious conduct is limited to actual damages, not to exceed $25,000 per occurrence, plus court costs and reasonable attorney's fees.

§ 41.0025. Liability for Property Damage to an Inn or Hotel

(a) Notwithstanding Section 41.002, recovery of damages by an inn or hotel for wilful and malicious conduct is limited to actual damages, not to exceed $25,000 per occurrence, plus court costs and reasonable attorney's fees.

(b) In this section "occurrence" means one incident on a single day in one hotel room. The term does not include incidents in separate rooms or incidents that occur on different days.

Comment

Reports of prom night bashes that got out of hand led to this legislative response. This section was strongly supported by the hotel industry.

§ 41.003. Venue

A suit as provided by this chapter may be filed in the county in which the conduct of the child occurred or in the county in which the defendant resides.

CHAPTER 42. CIVIL LIABILITY FOR INTERFERENCE WITH POSSESSORY INTEREST IN CHILD

Introductory Comment

This chapter is intended to be a "comprehensive attack on parental kidnapping," but it has been little used to date. Although a broad range of individuals who assist a child-snatching parent may be held liable for their actions, obviously a statute permitting money damages will have a significant deterrent effect only on middle class and wealthy parents. Deterrence to encourage poor folks from engaging in the prohibited conduct will have to come from the Penal Code, *see* Cross References below.

CLE/Other Legal Publication

Symposium. Increasing the price of parenthood: when should parents be held civilly liable for the torts of their children? Andrew C. Gratz, 39 HOUSTON L. REV. 169 (2002)

Leading Cases

Lozano v. Lozano, 52 S.W.3d 141 (Tex. 2001) (mother has cause of action against father's siblings who assisted him in snatching and concealing child)

Ex parte Rhodes, 974 S.W.2d 735 (Tex. Crim. App. 1998) (prior criminal contempt conviction bars prosecution for interference with child custody based on double jeopardy)

Weirich v. Weirich, 833 S.W.2d 942 (Tex. 1992) (whether grandmother entitled to notice of suit filed under provisions of earlier version of this chapter depends on whether she aided and assisted the father's interference with child custody)

Silcott v. Oglesby, 721 S.W.2d 290 (Tex. 1986) (Texas recognized the common law tort of child abduction before enactment of *[now Chapter 42]*)

Rodriguez v. Rodriguez, 2010 WL 816186 (Tex. App.—San Antonio 2010, pet. denied) (husband's filing of interference with child custody suit based on temporary orders in one county did not allow wife to file counter-suit for divorce when a previously filed suit for divorce was already pending in another county)

Eberle v. Adams, 73 S.W.3d 322 (Tex. App.—Houston [1st Dist.] 2001, pet. denied) (jury verdict of almost $1.4 million affirmed against father's ex-parents-in-law and mother's boyfriend—only uncle and aunt escape liability)

A.H. Belo Corp. v. Corcoran, 52 S.W.3d 375 (Tex. App.—Houston [1st Dist.] 2001, pet. denied) (TV interview did not interfere with possessory interests of father; no duty owed to father to reveal location of child)

Smith v. Smith, 720 S.W.2d 586 (Tex. App.—Houston [1st Dist.] 1986, no writ) (actual costs and expenses include prospective damages; future damages and attorney's fees tried by consent, so pleadings not necessary)

Cross References

TX FCA Penal § 25.03, Interference with Child Custody, *infra*; TX FCA Penal § 25.031, Agreement To Abduct from Custody, *infra*; TX FCA Penal § 25.04, Enticing a Child, *infra*.

---

§ 42.001. Definitions

In this chapter:

(1) "Order" means a temporary or final order of a court of this state or another state or nation.

(2) "Possessory right" means a court-ordered right of possession of or access to a child, including conservatorship, custody, and visitation.

§ 42.002. Liability for Interference with Possessory Right

(a) A person who takes or retains possession of a child or who conceals the whereabouts of a child in violation of a possessory right of another person may be liable for damages to that person.

(b) A possessory right is violated by the taking, retention, or concealment of a child at a time when another person is entitled to possession of or access to the child.

§ 42.003. Aiding or Assisting Interference with Possessory Right

(a) A person who aids or assists in conduct for which a cause of action is authorized by this chapter is jointly and severally liable for damages.

(b) A person who was not a party to the suit in which an order was rendered providing for a possessory right is not liable unless the person at the time of the violation:

(1) had actual notice of the existence and contents of the order; or

(2) had reasonable cause to believe that the child was the subject of an order and that the person's actions were likely to violate the order.

§ 42.004. Repealed.

§ 42.005. Venue

A suit may be filed in a county in which:

(1) the plaintiff resides;

(2) the defendant resides;

(3) a suit affecting the parent-child relationship as provided by Chapter 102 may be brought, concerning the child who is the subject of the court order; or

(4) a court has continuing, exclusive jurisdiction as provided by Chapter 155.

§ 42.006. Damages

(a) Damages may include:

(1) the actual costs and expenses incurred, including attorney's fees, in:

(A) locating a child who is the subject of the order;

(B) recovering possession of the child if the petitioner is entitled to possession; and

(C) enforcing the order and prosecuting the suit; and

(2) mental suffering and anguish incurred by the plaintiff because of a violation of the order.

(b) A person liable for damages who acted with malice or with an intent to cause harm to the plaintiff may be liable for exemplary damages.

§ 42.007. Affirmative Defense

The defendant may plead as an affirmative defense that the defendant acted in violation of the order with the express consent of the plaintiff.

§ 42.008. Remedies Not Affected

This chapter does not affect any other civil or criminal remedy available to any person, including the child, for interference with a possessory right, nor does it affect the power of a parent to represent the interest of a child in a suit filed on behalf of the child.

§ 42.009. Frivolous Suit

A person sued for damages as provided by this chapter is entitled to recover attorney's fees and court costs if:

(1) the claim for damages is dismissed or judgment is awarded to the defendant; and

(2) the court or jury finds that the claim for damages is frivolous, unreasonable, or without foundation.

SUBTITLE C. CHANGE OF NAME

★★★

CHAPTER 45. CHANGE OF NAME

SUBCHAPTER A. CHANGE OF NAME OF CHILD

SUBCHAPTER B. CHANGE OF NAME OF ADULT

SUBCHAPTER A. CHANGE OF NAME OF CHILD

Introductory Comment

Most often this chapter is used to change the name of a minor to conform the child's "legal name" to the name by which the child is known. Occasionally, however, litigation has resulted when one parent sought to change the name of a child allegedly in derogation of the rights of the other parent or of the child.

Leading Cases

In re Mayol, 137 S.W.3d 103 (Tex. App.—Houston [1st Dist.] 2004, no pet.) (trial court's refusal to change adult's name based on inadequate evidence of identity and public interest within discretion)

In re M.C.F., 121 S.W.3d 891 (Tex. App.—Fort Worth 2003, no pet.) (trial court abused discretion by ordering child's name changed to surname of putative father—not in child's best interest)

In re Guthrie, 45 S.W.3d 719 (Tex. App.—Dallas 2001, pet. denied) (Texas ERA mandates parents of child-without-presumed-father have equal right to choose surname—best interests test yields surname of biological father here)

In re C.B.M., 14 S.W.3d 855 (Tex. App.—Beaumont 2000, no pet.) (no abuse of discretion in refusing to change child's name to father's after paternity established)

---

§ 45.001. Who May File; Venue

A parent, managing conservator, or guardian of a child may file a petition requesting a change of name of the child in the county where the child resides.

§ 45.002. Requirements of Petition

(a) A petition to change the name of a child must be verified and include:

(1) the present name and place of residence of the child;

(2) the reason a change of name is requested;

(3) the full name requested for the child;

(4) whether the child is subject to the continuing exclusive jurisdiction of a court under Chapter 155; and

(5) whether the child is subject to the registration requirements of Chapter 62, Code of Criminal Procedure.

(b) If the child is 10 years of age or older, the child's written consent to the change of name must be attached to the petition.

§ 45.003. Citation

(a) The following persons are entitled to citation in a suit under this subchapter:

(1) a parent of the child whose parental rights have not been terminated;

(2) any managing conservator of the child; and

(3) any guardian of the child.

(b) Citation must be issued and served in the same manner as under Chapter 102.

§ 45.004. Order

(a) The court may order the name of a child changed if:

(1) the change is in the best interest of the child; and

(2) for a child subject to the registration requirements of Chapter 62, Code of Criminal Procedure:

(A) the change is in the interest of the public; and

(B) the person petitioning on behalf of the child provides the court with proof that the child has notified the appropriate local law enforcement authority of the proposed name change.

(b) If the child is subject to the continuing jurisdiction of a court under Chapter 155, the court shall send a copy of the order to the central record file as provided in Chapter 108.

(c) In this section, "local law enforcement authority" has the meaning assigned by Article 62.001, Code of Criminal Procedure.

§ 45.005. Liabilities and Rights Unaffected

A change of name does not:

(1) release a child from any liability incurred in the child's previous name; or

(2) defeat any right the child had in the child's previous name.

SUBCHAPTER B. CHANGE OF NAME OF ADULT

Introductory Comment

Women now routinely choose to resume a maiden name or a prior married name on divorce. This chapter provides that a name change may also be accomplished in an independent action by either an adult man or woman.

Cross Reference

TX FCA Family § 6.706. Change of Name, *supra*.

§ 45.101. Who May File; Venue

An adult may file a petition requesting a change of name in the county of the adult's place of residence.

§ 45.102. Requirements of Petition

(a) A petition to change the name of an adult must be verified and include:

(1) the present name and place of residence of the petitioner;

(2) the full name requested for the petitioner;

(3) the reason the change in name is requested;

(4) whether the petitioner has been the subject of a final felony conviction;

(5) whether the petitioner is subject to the registration requirements of Chapter 62, Code of Criminal Procedure; and

(6) a legible and complete set of the petitioner's fingerprints on a fingerprint card format acceptable to the Department of Public Safety and the Federal Bureau of Investigation.

(b) The petition must include each of the following or a reasonable explanation why the required information is not included:

(1) the petitioner's:

(A) full name;

(B) sex;

(C) race;

(D) date of birth;

(E) driver's license number for any driver's license issued in the 10 years preceding the date of the petition;

(F) social security number; and

(G) assigned FBI number, state identification number, if known, or any other reference number in a criminal history record system that identifies the petitioner;

(2) any offense above the grade of Class C misdemeanor for which the petitioner has been charged; and

(3) the case number and the court if a warrant was issued or a charging instrument was filed or presented for an offense listed in Subsection (b)(2).

§ 45.103. Order

(a) The court shall order a change of name under this subchapter for a person other than a person with a final felony conviction or a person subject to the registration requirements of Chapter 62, Code of Criminal Procedure, if the change is in the interest or to the benefit of the petitioner and in the interest of the public.

(b) A court may order a change of name under this subchapter for a person with a final felony conviction if, in addition to the requirements of Subsection (a), the person has:

(1) received a certificate of discharge by the Texas Department of Criminal Justice or completed a period of community supervision or juvenile probation ordered by a court and not less than two years have passed from the date of the receipt of discharge or completion of community supervision or juvenile probation; or

(2) been pardoned.

(c) A court may order a change of name under this subchapter for a person subject to the registration requirements of Chapter 62, Code of Criminal Procedure, if, in addition to the requirements of Subsection (a), the person provides the court with proof that the person has notified the appropriate local law enforcement authority of the proposed name change. In this subsection, "local law enforcement authority" has the meaning assigned by Article 62.001, Code of Criminal Procedure.

§ 45.104. Liabilities and Rights Unaffected

A change of name under this subchapter does not release a person from liability incurred in that person's previous name or defeat any right the person had in the person's previous name.

§ 45.105. Change of Name in Divorce Suit

(a) On the final disposition of a suit for divorce, for annulment, or to declare a marriage void, the court shall enter a decree changing the name of a party specially praying for the change to a prior used name unless the court states in the decree a reason for denying the change of name. The court may not deny a change of name solely to keep last names of family members the same.

(b) A person whose name is changed under this section may apply for a change of name certificate from the clerk of the court as provided by Section 45.106.

§ 45.106. Change of Name Certificate

(a) A person whose name is changed under Section 6.706 or 45.105 may apply to the clerk of the court ordering the name change for a change of name certificate.

(b) A certificate under this section is a one-page document that includes:

(1) the name of the person before the change of name was ordered;

(2) the name to which the person's name was changed by the court;

(3) the date on which the name change was made;

(4) the person's social security number and driver's license number, if any;

(5) the name of the court in which the name change was ordered; and

(6) the signature of the clerk of the court that issued the certificate.

(c) An applicant for a certificate under this section shall pay a $10 fee to the clerk of the court for issuance of the certificate.

(d) A certificate under this section constitutes proof of the change of name of the person named in the certificate.

TITLE 3
JUVENILE JUSTICE CODE

As amended through the 82nd Legislature, Regular and First Called Sessions (2011)

Title 3 Annotated by
STEPHANIE STEVENS
Clinical Professor
St. Mary's University of San Antonio School of Law

Chapter

Introductory Comment

Title 3, consisting of Chapters 51 through 61, is the Juvenile Justice Code for Texas. It deals with adolescent misconduct in the form of delinquent conduct and conduct indicating a need for supervision and prescribes the procedural framework for responding to that misconduct. Other aspects of children and the law, such as child abuse and neglect, child support, paternity and adoption, appear in Title 5 of the Family Code.

Chapter 51 states most of the general principles that guide the juvenile justice system. Chapters 52 through 56 are procedural, each dealing with a different segment of the process. Chapter 57 deals with rights of victims of juvenile offenses. Chapter 58 creates a state-wide juvenile justice information system. Chapter 59 creates a system of progressive sanctions guidelines for the juvenile system. Chapter 60 is the Uniform Interstate Compact on Juveniles. Chapter 61 deals with the rights and responsibilities of the parents of children in the juvenile justice process.

CLE/Other Legal Publications

The State Bar of Texas Family Law Section Report provided commentaries on amendments to Title 3 following the 1977, 1979, 1981, 1983 and 1985 legislative sessions: Vols. 77–2 (June 1977); 79–2 (June 1979); 81–2 (Summer 1981); 83–2 (Summer 1983); 85–2 (Special Legis. 1985).

Thereafter, commentaries on amendments to Title 3 following the 1987, 1989, 1991, 1993, 1995, 1997, 1999, 2001, 2003, 2005, 2007, and 2009 legislative sessions appeared in the State Bar of Texas Juvenile Law Section Report: Vols. 1–3 (Sept. 1987); 3–3 (Sept. 1989); 5–3 (Sept. 1991); 7–3 (Sept. 1993), 9–3 (Special Legis. 1995), 11–3 (Special Legis. 1997), 13–3 (Special Legis. 1999), 15–3 (Special Legis. 2001), 17–3 (Special Legis. 2003), 19–3 (Special Legis. 2005), 21–3 (Special Legis. 2007), and 23-3 (Special Legis. 2009).

There are two treatises on Texas Juvenile Law:

R. Dawson, *Texas Juvenile Law (Texas Juvenile Probation Commission*, 7th Ed. 2008), 7th Edition Supplement (2010)

T. Morgan and H. Gaither, *Juvenile Law and Practice, 3rd* (Vols. 29 & 29A, TEXAS PRACTICE SERIES 2010)

Cross References

TEX. HUM. RES. CODE ANN. § 61.001 *et seq.*, Texas Youth Commission; TEX. HUM. RES. CODE ANN. § 141.001 *et seq.*, Texas Juvenile Probation Commission; TEX. HUM. RES. CODE ANN. § 142.001 *et seq.*, Juvenile Probation Departments; TEX. HUM. RES. CODE ANN. § 152.001 *et seq.*, Juvenile Boards.

TEX. GOV'T CODE ANN. § 54.001 *et seq.*, Juvenile Law Referees and Family Law Masters.

★★★

CHAPTER 51. GENERAL PROVISIONS

Introductory Comment

Chapter 51 states the general principles of law that govern the juvenile justice system. Chapters 52 through 61 deal with specific procedural steps or functions of the juvenile system.

---

§ 51.01. Purpose and Interpretation

This title shall be construed to effectuate the following public purposes:

(1) to provide for the protection of the public and public safety;

(2) consistent with the protection of the public and public safety:

(A) to promote the concept of punishment for criminal acts;

(B) to remove, where appropriate, the taint of criminality from children committing certain unlawful acts; and

(C) to provide treatment, training, and rehabilitation that emphasizes the accountability and responsibility of both the parent and the child for the child's conduct;

(3) to provide for the care, the protection, and the wholesome moral, mental, and physical development of children coming within its provisions;

(4) to protect the welfare of the community and to control the commission of unlawful acts by children;

(5) to achieve the foregoing purposes in a family environment whenever possible, separating the child from the child's parents only when necessary for the child's welfare or in the interest of public safety and when a child is removed from the child's family, to give the child the care that should be provided by parents; and

(6) to provide a simple judicial procedure through which the provisions of this title are executed and enforced and in which the parties are assured a fair hearing and their constitutional and other legal rights recognized and enforced.

§ 51.02. Definitions

In this title:

(1) "Aggravated controlled substance felony" means an offense under Subchapter D, Chapter 481, Health and Safety Code, that is punishable by:

(A) a minimum term of confinement that is longer than the minimum term of confinement for a felony of the first degree; or

(B) a maximum fine that is greater than the maximum fine for a felony of the first degree.

(2) "Child" means a person who is:

(A) ten years of age or older and under 17 years of age; or

(B) seventeen years of age or older and under 18 years of age who is alleged or found to have engaged in delinquent conduct or conduct indicating a need for supervision as a result of acts committed before becoming 17 years of age.

(3) "Custodian" means the adult with whom the child resides.

(4) "Guardian" means the person who, under court order, is the guardian of the person of the child or the public or private agency with whom the child has been placed by a court.

(5) "Judge" or "juvenile court judge" means the judge of a juvenile court.

(6) "Juvenile court" means a court designated under Section 51.04 of this code to exercise jurisdiction over proceedings under this title.

(7) "Law-enforcement officer" means a peace officer as defined by Article 2.12, Code of Criminal Procedure.

(8) "Nonoffender" means a child who:

(A) is subject to jurisdiction of a court under abuse, dependency, or neglect statutes under Title 5 for reasons other than legally prohibited conduct of the child; or

(B) has been taken into custody and is being held solely for deportation out of the United States.

(8–a) "Nonsecure correctional facility" means a facility, other than a secure correctional facility, that accepts only juveniles who are on probation and that is operated by or under contract with a governmental unit, as defined by Section 101.001, Civil Practice and Remedies Code.

(9) "Parent" means the mother or the father of a child, but does not include a parent whose parental rights have been terminated.

(10) "Party" means the state, a child who is the subject of proceedings under this subtitle, or the child's parent, spouse, guardian, or guardian ad litem.

(11) "Prosecuting attorney" means the county attorney, district attorney, or other attorney who regularly serves in a prosecutory capacity in a juvenile court.

(12) "Referral to juvenile court" means the referral of a child or a child's case to the office or official, including an intake officer or probation officer, designated by the juvenile board to process children within the juvenile justice system.

(13) "Secure correctional facility" means any public or private residential facility, including an alcohol or other drug treatment facility, that:

(A) includes construction fixtures designed to physically restrict the movements and activities of juveniles or other individuals held in lawful custody in the facility; and

(B) is used for the placement of any juvenile who has been adjudicated as having committed an offense, any nonoffender, or any other individual convicted of a criminal offense.

(14) "Secure detention facility" means any public or private residential facility that:

(A) includes construction fixtures designed to physically restrict the movements and activities of juveniles or other individuals held in lawful custody in the facility; and

(B) is used for the temporary placement of any juvenile who is accused of having committed an offense, any nonoffender, or any other individual accused of having committed a criminal offense.

(15) "Status offender" means a child who is accused, adjudicated, or convicted for conduct that would not, under state law, be a crime if committed by an adult, including:

(A) truancy under Section 51.03(b)(2);

(B) running away from home under Section 51.03(b)(3);

(C) a fineable only offense under Section 51.03(b)(1) transferred to the juvenile court under Section 51.08(b), but only if the conduct constituting the offense would not have been criminal if engaged in by an adult;

(D) failure to attend school under Section 25.094, Education Code;

(E) a violation of standards of student conduct as described by Section 51.03(b)(5);

(F) a violation of a juvenile curfew ordinance or order;

(G) a violation of a provision of the Alcoholic Beverage Code applicable to minors only; or

(H) a violation of any other fineable only offense under Section 8.07(a)(4) or (5), Penal Code, but only if the conduct constituting the offense would not have been criminal if engaged in by an adult.

(16) "Traffic offense" means:

(A) a violation of a penal statute cognizable under Chapter 729, Transportation Code, except for conduct for which the person convicted may be sentenced to imprisonment or confinement in jail; or

(B) a violation of a motor vehicle traffic ordinance of an incorporated city or town in this state.

(17) "Valid court order" means a court order entered under Section 54.04 concerning a child adjudicated to have engaged in conduct indicating a need for supervision as a status offender.

Comment

The most important definition is that of "child." The conduct must have been engaged in when the person was at least 10 years of age but under 17 years of age for the juvenile court to have jurisdiction. The juvenile court has jurisdiction over a 17 year old for an offense committed before his or her 17th birthday.

The "aggravated controlled substance felony" defined by Subsection (1) is included as a covered offense in the determinate sentence provisions. *See* § 53.045.

The definition of "referral to juvenile court" in Subsection (12) is used to define when the right to send a juvenile record to the state-wide system is triggered in Chapter 58.

The definitions of "nonoffender" in Subsection (8), "secure correctional facility" in Subsection (13), "secure detention facility" in Subsection (14), "status offender" in Subsection (15) and "valid court order" in Subsection (17) are all related to various provisions dealing with conforming Texas law to federal requirements respecting the detention of status offenders and nonoffenders in any facilities and the detention of juvenile offenders in adult facilities. *See* §§ 51.12, 52.027, 52.028, 54.011, 54.022, and 54.04.

The definition of traffic offense in Subsection (16) has been changed to exclude any offense that carries a punishment of incarceration, even if it's classified as a traffic offense in the Texas Transportation Code.

Sec. (8-a) defines a correctional facility that accepts only juveniles on probation.

Leading Cases

Adair v. Kupper, Judge, 890 S.W.2d 216 (Tex. App.—Amarillo 1994, leave denied) (parents have right to participate in proceedings in which state seeks to hold them liable for money)

In re A.S., 875 S.W.2d 402 (Tex. App.—Corpus Christi 1994, no writ) (proof of age jurisdictional); but see *In re* E.D.C., 88 S.W.3d 789 (Tex. App.—El Paso 2002, no writ)

---

§ 51.03. Delinquent Conduct; Conduct Indicating a Need for Supervision

(a) Delinquent conduct is:

(1) conduct, other than a traffic offense, that violates a penal law of this state or of the United States punishable by imprisonment or by confinement in jail;

(2) conduct that violates a lawful order of a court under circumstances that would constitute contempt of that court in:

(A) a justice or municipal court; or

(B) a county court for conduct punishable only by a fine;

(3) conduct that violates Section 49.04, 49.05, 49.06, 49.07, or 49.08, Penal Code; or

(4) conduct that violates Section 106.041, Alcoholic Beverage Code, relating to driving under the influence of alcohol by a minor (third or subsequent offense).

(b) Conduct indicating a need for supervision is:

(1) subject to Subsection (f), conduct, other than a traffic offense, that violates:

(A) the penal laws of this state of the grade of misdemeanor that are punishable by fine only; or

(B) the penal ordinances of any political subdivision of this state;

(2) the absence of a child on 10 or more days or parts of days within a six-month period in the same school year or on three or more days or parts of days within a four-week period from school;

(3) the voluntary absence of a child from the child's home without the consent of the child's parent or guardian for a substantial length of time or without intent to return;

(4) conduct prohibited by city ordinance or by state law involving the inhalation of the fumes or vapors of paint and other protective coatings or glue and other adhesives and the volatile chemicals itemized in Section 485.001, Health and Safety Code;

(5) an act that violates a school district's previously communicated written standards of student conduct for which the child has been expelled under Section 37.007(c), Education Code; ~~or~~

(6) conduct that violates a reasonable and lawful order of a court entered under Section 264.305; **or**

Text of subsec. (b)(7), as added by Acts 2011, 82nd Leg., ch. 1150 (H.B. 2015), § 1

(7) notwithstanding Subsection (a)(1), conduct described by Section 43. 02(a)(1) or (2), Penal Code.

Text of subsec. (b)(7), as added by Acts 2011, 82nd Leg., ch. 1322 (S.B. 407), § 4

(7) conduct that violates Section 43.261, Penal Code.

(c) Nothing in this title prevents criminal proceedings against a child for perjury.

(d) It is an affirmative defense to an allegation of conduct under Subsection (b)(2) that one or more of the absences required to be proven under that subsection have been excused by a school official or by the court or that one or more of the absences were involuntary, but only if there is an insufficient number of unexcused or voluntary absences remaining to constitute conduct under Subsection (b)(2). The burden is on the respondent to show by a preponderance of the evidence that the absence has been or should be excused or that the absence was involuntary. A decision by the court to excuse an absence for purposes of this subsection does not affect the ability of the school district to determine whether to excuse the absence for another purpose.

(e) For the purposes of Subsection (b)(3), "child" does not include a person who is married, divorced, or widowed.

(e–1) Notwithstanding any other law, for purposes of conduct described by Subsection (b)(2), "child" means a person who is:

(1) 10 years of age or older;

(2) alleged or found to have engaged in the conduct as a result of acts committed before becoming 18 years of age; and

(3) required to attend school under Section 25.085, Education Code.

(f) Except as provided by Subsection (g), conduct described under Subsection (b)(1) does not constitute conduct indicating a need for supervision unless the child has been referred to the juvenile court under Section 51.08(b).

(g) In a county with a population of less than 100,000, conduct described by Subsection (b)(1)(A) that violates Section 25.094, Education Code, is conduct indicating a need for supervision.

Amended by Acts 2011, 82nd Leg., ch. 1098 (S.B. 1489), § 2, eff. Sept. 1, 2011; Acts 2011, 82nd Leg., ch. 1150 (H.B. 2015), § 1, eff. Sept. 1, 2011; Acts 2011, 82nd Leg., ch. 1322 (S.B. 407), § 4, eff. Sept. 1, 2011.

Comment

Two types of juvenile misconduct are defined by this section: delinquent conduct and conduct indicating a need for supervision. The principal difference is that a child adjudicated of delinquent conduct can be placed on probation or, under certain conditions, be committed to the Texas Youth Commission or Texas Juvenile Justice Department, while a child adjudicated for conduct indicating a need for supervision cannot be committed to the TYC or TJJD.

There are four types of delinquent conduct: violation of a felony or jailable misdemeanor statute, contempt of a justice or municipal court, D.W.I. and related offenses, and third offense driving by a minor while under the influence of alcohol.

There are seven types of conduct indicating a need for supervision: fineable only offense that has been transferred to a juvenile court from a municipal or justice court, truancy, running away from home, violation of an inhalant abuse statute or ordinance, an act that violated a school disciplinary code resulting in expulsion, and violation of a court order under the Services to At–Risk Youth program in Chapter 264 of Title 5. In 2011, (7) was added to include engaging in prostitution as conduct indicating a need for supervision. The Texas Supreme court held that a child under 14 cannot be prosecuted for prostitution because children cannot legally consent to sex with an adult. *See In re* B.W., 313 S.W.3d 818 (Tex. 2010).

Subsection (d) and § 25.094 of the Education Code make clear that the affirmative defense of excused or involuntary absences prevent a finding of truancy only when there are insufficient unexcused or voluntary absences remaining to constitute a violation of law.

Section 25.0951(a) of the Education Code clarifies that a school district must file a complaint or referral against a student for failure to attend school under this section within 7 days of the student's 10th unexcused absence. This codifies Attorney General Opinion GA–0417 (2006).

In 2009 public intoxication cases were removed from the jurisdiction of juvenile courts and placed in municipal and justice of the peace courts, which have already been presiding over minors possessing and consuming alcohol cases.

Leading Cases

Qutb v. Strauss, 11 F.3d 488 (5th Cir. 1993) (constitutionality of Dallas juvenile curfew ordinance upheld)

Urbanski v. State, 993 S.W.2d 789 (Tex. App.—Dallas 1999, no pet.) (absence for less than 24 hours still substantial under definition of running away)

Ponce v. State, 985 S.W.2d 594 (Tex. App.—Houston [1st Dist.] 1999, no pet.) (13–year-old may be convicted of aggravated perjury without juvenile court certification)

In re M.E., 982 S.W.2d 528 (Tex. App.—San Antonio 1998, no writ) (marriage does not preclude juvenile court jurisdiction in delinquent conduct cases)

Attorney General Opinions

Tex. Atty. Gen. Op. GA–0574 (2007) (school district may file a new complaint listing some of the same absences from the prior dismissed complaint along with the subsequent 10th unexcused absence)

Tex. Atty. Gen. Op. GA–0417 (2006) (school district must file a complaint against a student within 7 school days of the student's 10 unexcused absence within a 6 month period or the complaint must be dismissed by the trial court)

Tex. Atty. Gen. Op. No. GA–0125 (2003) (unemancipated 17 year old who voluntarily leaves home is not a missing child if parents know of child's whereabouts)

Tex. Atty. Gen. Op. No. GA–0131 (2003) (child referred for contempt of JP court may be detained if criteria warrant but may not be placed in secure post-adjudication facility)

Tex. Atty. Gen. Op. No. JC–0454 (2002) (J.P. cannot order confinement in juvenile detention facility for contempt)

CLE/Other Legal Publications

Cross-over youth in CPS cases and juvenile cases. Dustin Rynders, 2011 Adv. Fam. L.

§ 51.031. Habitual Felony Conduct

(a) Habitual felony conduct is conduct violating a penal law of the grade of felony, other than a state jail felony, if:

(1) the child who engaged in the conduct has at least two previous final adjudications as having engaged in delinquent conduct violating a penal law of the grade of felony;

(2) the second previous final adjudication is for conduct that occurred after the date the first previous adjudication became final; and

(3) all appeals relating to the previous adjudications considered under Subdivisions (1) and (2) have been exhausted.

(b) For purposes of this section, an adjudication is final if the child is placed on probation or committed to the Texas Youth Commission.

(c) An adjudication based on conduct that occurred before January 1, 1996, may not be considered in a disposition made under this section.

Comment

Habitual felony conduct, as defined by this section, is part of the determinate sentence act. It is patterned after § 12.42 of the Texas Penal Code.

§ 51.04. Jurisdiction

(a) This title covers the proceedings in all cases involving the delinquent conduct or conduct indicating a need for supervision engaged in by a person who was a child within the meaning of this title at the time the person engaged in the conduct, and, except as provided by Subsection (h), the juvenile court has exclusive original jurisdiction over proceedings under this title.

(b) In each county, the county's juvenile board shall designate one or more district, criminal district, domestic relations, juvenile, or county courts or county courts at law as the juvenile court, subject to Subsections (c) and (d) of this section.

(c) If the county court is designated as a juvenile court, at least one other court shall be designated as the juvenile court. A county court does not have jurisdiction of a proceeding involving a petition approved by a grand jury under Section 53.045 of this code.

(d) If the judge of a court designated in Subsection (b) or (c) of this section is not an attorney licensed in this state, there shall also be designated an alternate court, the judge of which is an attorney licensed in this state.

(e) A designation made under Subsection (b) or (c) of this section may be changed from time to time by the authorized boards or judges for the convenience of the people and the welfare of children. However, there must be at all times a juvenile court designated for each county. It is the intent of the legislature that in selecting a court to be the juvenile court of each county, the selection shall be made as far as practicable so that the court designated as the juvenile court will be one which is presided over by a judge who has a sympathetic understanding of the problems of child welfare and that changes in the designation of juvenile courts be made only when the best interest of the public requires it.

(f) If the judge of the juvenile court or any alternate judge named under Subsection (b) or (c) is not in the county or is otherwise unavailable, any magistrate may make a determination under Section 53.02(f) or may conduct the detention hearing provided for in Section 54.01.

(g) The juvenile board may appoint a referee to make determinations under Section 53.02(f) or to conduct hearings under this title. The referee shall be an attorney licensed to practice law in this state and shall comply with Section 54.10. Payment of any referee services shall be provided from county funds.

(h) In a county with a population of less than 100,000, the juvenile court has concurrent jurisdiction with the justice and municipal courts over conduct engaged in by a child that violates Section 25.094, Education Code.

Comment

This section gives juvenile courts exclusive, original jurisdiction over proceedings under Title 3. There are no courts in Texas that have been created as juvenile courts. However, any district level or county level court can be designated by the county juvenile board to exercise juvenile jurisdiction. More than one court may and usually is designated to exercise juvenile jurisdiction. A court must be currently designated as a juvenile court to have juvenile jurisdiction. If the constitutional county court is designated to exercise juvenile jurisdiction, the juvenile board must also designate an alternate juvenile court. The constitutional county court does not have jurisdiction over determinate sentence proceedings.

CLE/Other Legal Publication

Texas Family Code Designations—A Primer. Darlene A. Whitten, 8TH ANN. JUVE. L. CONF. (Feb. 1995)

Leading Case

R.X.F. v. State, 921 S.W.2d 888 (Tex. App.—Waco 1996, no writ) (county court at law has jurisdiction under the determinate sentence act)

---

§ 51.041. Jurisdiction After Appeal

(a) The court retains jurisdiction over a person, without regard to the age of the person, for conduct engaged in by the person before becoming 17 years of age if, as a result of an appeal by the person or the state under Chapter 56 or by the person under Article 44.47, Code of Criminal

Procedure, of an order of the court, the order is reversed or modified and the case remanded to the court by the appellate court.

(b) If the respondent is at least 18 years of age when the order of remand from the appellate court is received by the juvenile court, the juvenile court shall proceed as provided by Sections 54.02(*o*)–(r) for the detention of a person at least 18 years of age in discretionary transfer proceedings. Pending retrial of the adjudication or transfer proceeding, the juvenile court may:

(1) order the respondent released from custody;

(2) order the respondent detained in a juvenile detention facility; or

(3) set bond and order the respondent detained in a county adult facility if bond is not made.

Comment

Under this section, the fact that the respondent has turned 18 years of age during the pendency of an appeal does not prevent the juvenile court from continuing with the case following appellate reversal and remand. It thus creates an exception to the rule that the jurisdiction of the juvenile court ends at the person's 18th birthday.

Subsection (b) provides for detention of the now-adult respondent in a juvenile detention facility or the county jail pending re-hearing by the juvenile court.

Subsection (a) reflects the addition of 56.03 which enables the State to appeal in certain determinate sentence act cases from the juvenile court to the court of appeals. The language "by the person" is intended to restrict appeals from certification proceedings to the person who is the subject to the proceedings and to continue the policy to exclude the State from taking such appeals.

Leading Case

In re D.W.R., 990 S.W.2d 446 (Tex. App.—San Antonio 1999, no pet.) (this section makes clear that juvenile court has jurisdiction to decide bond issue for 19 year old who engaged in conduct when he was 16)

---

§ 51.0411. Jurisdiction for Transfer or Release Hearing

The court retains jurisdiction over a person, without regard to the age of the person, who is referred to the court under Section 54.11 for transfer to the Texas Department of Criminal Justice or release under supervision.

Comment

The juvenile court has jurisdiction in a release/transfer hearing under the determinate sentence act even if the subject person is 18 years of age or older at the time of the proceedings.

---

§ 51.0412. Jurisdiction Over Incomplete Proceedings

The court retains jurisdiction over a person, without regard to the age of the person, who is a respondent in an adjudication proceeding, a disposition proceeding, a proceeding to modify disposition, or a motion for transfer of determinate sentence probation to an appropriate district court if:

(1) the petition **or**~~,~~ motion to modify~~, or motion for transfer~~ was filed while the respondent was younger than 18 years of age **or the motion for transfer was filed while the respondent was younger than 19 years of age**;

(2) the proceeding is not complete before the respondent becomes 18 **or 19** years of age**, as applicable**; and

(3) the court enters a finding in the proceeding that the prosecuting attorney exercised due diligence in an attempt to complete the proceeding before the respondent became 18 **or 19** years of age**, as applicable**.

Amended by Acts 2011, 82nd Leg., ch. 438 (S.B. 1208), § 1, eff. Sept. 1, 2011.

Comment

This section abrogates the rule of *In re* N.J.A. 997 S.W.2d 554 (Tex. 1999), in which the Texas Supreme Court held that the juvenile court loses jurisdiction over proceedings when the child becomes 18. This section extends that jurisdiction to enable completion of the proceedings if the adjudication petition or motion or petition to modify was filed before age 18 or 19 and the State proceeds with diligence.

The section also provides juvenile court with jurisdiction in a motion to transfer determinate sentence probation to adult court for a juvenile age 18 or older who has fled the jurisdiction before a transfer hearing could be held, but only if the motion to transfer was timely filed and the prosecutor exercised due diligence to complete the proceeding before the child turned 18 or 19.

2011 Amendments allow for determinate sentence probation to be extended from age 18 to age 19 in order to provide a greater opportunity for rehabilitation.

Leading Case

In re V.A., 140 S.W.3d 858 (Tex. App.—Ft. Worth 2004, no pet.) (court can modify probation even after child turns 18 if petition or motion to modify was filed prior to child's 18th birthday and despite due diligence on the part of the prosecutor the proceedings were not completed before age 18)

---

§ 51.042. Objection to Jurisdiction Because of Age of the Child

(a) A child who objects to the jurisdiction of the court over the child because of the age of the child must raise the objection at the adjudication hearing or discretionary transfer hearing, if any.

(b) A child who does not object as provided by Subsection (a) waives any right to object to the jurisdiction of the court because of the age of the child at a later hearing or on appeal.

Comment

Age of the respondent is an element of the State's proof in a juvenile proceeding. This section provides that the respondent must make an age objection to juvenile proceedings at the adjudication or transfer hearing or he or she waives the right to complain on appeal or habeas that the State has failed to prove age.

Leading Cases

In re T.A.W., 234 S.W.3d 704 (Tex. App.—Houston [14th Dist.], rev. denied) (complaint of jurisdiction waived if no objection is made at adjudication hearing)

In re E.D.C., 88 S.W.3d 789 (Tex. App.—El Paso 2002, no writ) (state is no longer required to prove age as an element as a result of this statutory provision)

Adams v. State, 161 S.W.3d 113 (Tex. App.—Houston [14th Dist.] 2004, pet. ref'd) (appellant waived his right to challenge the district court's jurisdiction when he entered a plea without objecting as required by Tex. Code Crim. Proc. Ann. art. 4.18)

Cross Reference

Tex. Code Crim. Proc. Ann. art 4.18. Requires a written pretrial motion be filed in order to object to the lack of jurisdiction of a criminal district court because of age.

---

§ 51.045. Juries in County Courts at Law

If a provision of this title requires a jury of 12 persons, that provision prevails over any other law that limits the number of members of a jury in a particular county court at law. The state and the defense are entitled to the same number of peremptory challenges allowed in a district court.

Comment

This section applies only to determinate sentence cases filed in a juvenile court presided over by a county court-at-law judge.

§ 51.05. Court Sessions and Facilities

(a) The juvenile court shall be deemed in session at all times. Suitable quarters shall be provided by the commissioners court of each county for the hearing of cases and for the use of the judge, the probation officer, and other employees of the court.

(b) The juvenile court and the juvenile board shall report annually to the commissioners court on the suitability of the quarters and facilities of the juvenile court and may make recommendations for their improvement.

§ 51.06. Venue

(a) A proceeding under this title shall be commenced in

(1) the county in which the alleged delinquent conduct or conduct indicating a need for supervision occurred; or

(2) the county in which the child resides at the time the petition is filed, but only if:

(A) the child was under probation supervision in that county at the time of the commission of the delinquent conduct or conduct indicating a need for supervision;

(B) it cannot be determined in which county the delinquent conduct or conduct indicating a need for supervision occurred; or

(C) the county in which the child resides agrees to accept the case for prosecution, in writing, prior to the case being sent to the county of residence for prosecution.

(b) An application for a writ of habeas corpus brought by or on behalf of a person who has been committed to an institution under the jurisdiction of the Texas Youth Commission and which attacks the validity of the judgment of commitment shall be brought in the county in which the court that entered the judgment of commitment is located.

Comment

Subsection (a) restricts residence venue in order to prevent the "dumping" of juvenile cases into the county of residence from the county in which the offense was committed.

§ 51.07. Transfer to Another County for Disposition

When a child has been found to have engaged in delinquent conduct or conduct indicating a need for supervision under Section 54.03, the juvenile court may transfer the case and transcripts of records and documents to the juvenile court of the county where the child resides for disposition of the case under Section 54.04. Consent by the court of the county where the child resides is not required.

Comment

Subsection (a) deals with the situation in which the offense was committed in one county but the child resides in another. It permits the adjudication hearing to be held in the county where the offense was committed but the disposition hearing to be held in the county in which the child resides. There is no requirement that the child consent to the transfer.

Attorney General Opinion

Tex. Atty. Gen. Op. 95–030 (1995) (consent of receiving court not required for transfer for disposition under § 51.07(a))

§ 51.071. Transfer of Probation Supervision Between Counties: Courtesy Supervision Prohibited

Except as provided by Section 51.075, a juvenile court or juvenile probation department may not engage in the practice of courtesy supervision of a child on probation.

Comment

This section is designed to assist officials in the juvenile justice system with children who are on probation in one county and residing in another county and need adequate supervision and services.

Subsection (b) eliminates the use of courtesy supervision for offenses occurring on or after September 1, 2005.

Subsection (c) defines the sending and receiving counties for transferring probation.

---

§ 51.072. Transfer of Probation Supervision Between Counties: Interim Supervision

(a) In this section:

(1) "Receiving county" means the county to which a child on probation has moved or intends to move.

(2) "Sending county" means the county that:

(A) originally placed the child on probation; or

(B) assumed permanent supervision of the child under an inter-county transfer of probation supervision.

(b) When a child on probation moves or intends to move from one county to another and intends to remain in the receiving county for at least 60 days, the juvenile probation department of the sending county shall request that the juvenile probation department of the receiving county provide interim supervision of the child. If the receiving county and the sending county are member counties within a judicial district served by one juvenile probation department, then a transfer of probation supervision is not required.

(c) The juvenile probation department of the receiving county may refuse the request to provide interim supervision only if:

(1) the residence of the child in the receiving county is in a residential placement facility arranged by the sending county; or

(2) the residence of the child in the receiving county is in a foster care placement arranged by the Department of Family and Protective Services.

(d) The juvenile probation department of the sending county shall initiate the request for interim supervision by electronic communication to the probation officer designated as the inter-county transfer officer for the juvenile probation department of the receiving county or, in the absence of this designation, to the chief juvenile probation officer.

(e) The juvenile probation department of the sending county shall provide the juvenile probation department of the receiving county with the following information in the request for interim supervision initiated under Subsection (d):

(1) the child's name, sex, age, race, and date of birth;

(2) the name, address, date of birth, and social security or driver's license number, and telephone number, if available, of the person with whom the child proposes to reside or is residing in the receiving county;

(3) the offense for which the child is on probation;

(4) the length of the child's probation term;

(5) a brief summary of the child's history of referrals;

(6) a brief statement of any special needs of the child;

(7) the name and telephone number of the child's school in the receiving county, if available; and

(8) the reason for the child moving or intending to move to the receiving county.

(f) Not later than 10 business days after a receiving county has agreed to provide interim supervision of a child, the juvenile probation department of the sending county shall provide the juvenile probation department of the receiving county with a copy of the following documents:

(1) the petition and the adjudication and disposition orders for the child, including the child's thumbprint;

(2) the child's conditions of probation;

(3) the social history report for the child;

(4) any psychological or psychiatric reports concerning the child;

(5) the Department of Public Safety CR 43J form or tracking incident number concerning the child;

(6) any law enforcement incident reports concerning the offense for which the child is on probation;

(7) any sex offender registration information concerning the child;

(8) any juvenile probation department progress reports concerning the child and any other pertinent documentation for the child's probation officer;

(9) case plans concerning the child;

(10) the Texas Juvenile Probation Commission standard assessment tool results for the child;

(11) the computerized referral and case history for the child, including case disposition;

(12) the child's birth certificate;

(13) the child's social security number or social security card, if available;

(14) the name, address, and telephone number of the contact person in the sending county's juvenile probation department;

(15) Title IV–E eligibility screening information for the child, if available;

(16) the address in the sending county for forwarding funds collected to which the sending county is entitled;

(17) any of the child's school or immunization records that the juvenile probation department of the sending county possesses; and

(18) any victim information concerning the case for which the child is on probation.

(f–1) The inter-county transfer officers in the sending and receiving counties shall agree on the official start date for the period of interim supervision, which must begin no later than three business days after the date the documents required under Subsection (f) have been received and accepted by the receiving county.

(g) The juvenile probation department of the receiving county shall supervise the child under the probation conditions imposed by the sending county and provide services similar to those provided to a child placed on probation under the same conditions in the receiving county. On request of the juvenile probation department of the receiving county, the juvenile court of the receiving county may modify the original probation conditions and impose new conditions using the procedures in Section 54.05. The juvenile court of the receiving county may not modify a financial probation condition imposed by the juvenile court of the sending county or the length of the child's probation term. The juvenile court of the receiving county shall designate a cause number for identifying the modification proceedings.

(h) The juvenile court of the sending county may revoke probation for a violation of a condition imposed by the juvenile court of the sending county only if the condition has not been specifically modified or replaced by the juvenile court of the receiving county. The juvenile court of the receiving county may revoke probation for a violation of a condition of probation that the juvenile court of the receiving county has modified or imposed.

(i) If a child is reasonably believed to have violated a condition of probation imposed by the juvenile court of the sending county, the juvenile court of the sending or receiving county may issue a directive to apprehend or detain the child in a certified detention facility, as in other cases of probation violation. In order to respond to a probation violation under this subsection, the juvenile court of the receiving county may:

(1) modify the conditions of probation or extend the probation term; or

(2) require that the juvenile probation department of the sending county resume direct supervision for the child.

(j) On receiving a directive from the juvenile court of the receiving county under Subsection (i)(2), the juvenile probation department of the sending county shall arrange for the prompt transportation of the child back to the sending county at the expense of the sending county. The juvenile probation department in the receiving county shall provide the sending county with supporting written documentation of the incidents of violation of probation on which the request to resume direct supervision is based.

(k) The juvenile probation department of the receiving county is entitled to any probation supervision fees collected from the child or the child's parent while providing interim supervision for the child. During the period of interim supervision, the receiving county shall collect and distribute to the victim monetary restitution payments in the manner specified by the sending county. At the expiration of the period of interim supervision, the receiving county shall collect and distribute directly to the victim any remaining payments.

(*l*) The sending county is financially responsible for any special treatment program or placement that the juvenile court of the sending county requires as a condition of probation if the child's family is financially unable to pay for the program or placement.

(m) Except as provided by Subsection (n), a period of interim supervision may not exceed 180 days. Permanent supervision automatically transfers to the juvenile probation department of the receiving county after the expiration of the period of interim supervision. The juvenile probation department of the receiving county may request permanent supervision from the juvenile probation department of the sending county at any time before the 180–day interim supervision period expires. After signing and entry of an order of transfer of permanent supervision by the sending county juvenile court, the juvenile probation department shall, in accordance with Section 51.073(b), promptly send the permanent supervision order and related documents to the receiving county.

(m–1) If a child on interim supervision moves to another county of residence or is otherwise no longer in the receiving county before the expiration of 180 days, the receiving county shall direct the sending county to resume supervision of the child.

(n) Notwithstanding Subsection (m), the period of interim supervision of a child who is placed on probation under Section 54.04(q) does not expire until the child has satisfactorily completed the greater of either 180 days or one-third of the term of probation, including one-third of the term of any extension of the probation term ordered under Section 54.05. Permanent supervision automatically transfers to the probation department of the receiving county after the expiration of the period of interim supervision under this subsection. If the state elects to initiate transfer proceedings under Section 54.051, the juvenile court of the sending county may order transfer of the permanent supervision before the expiration of the period of interim supervision under this subsection.

(*o*) At least once every 90 days during the period of interim supervision, the juvenile probation department of the receiving county shall provide the juvenile probation department of the sending county with a progress report of supervision concerning the child.

Comment

This section eliminates courtesy supervision and provides specifically for interim supervision and permanent supervision when a child commits delinquent conduct or CINS in one county but resides in another county.

Subsection (b) clarifies that if the receiving and sending county are in the same judicial district which is served by one juvenile probation department, then a transfer of probation is not needed.

The first 180 days that a child on probation resides in a different county fall within the provision for interim supervision. This 180 day interim period may be shortened, but it cannot be lengthened. After

180 days, interim supervision must expire and the probation automatically transfers to the receiving county for permanent supervision.

Subsection (e) requires the sending county juvenile probation department provide additional information on the child.

Subsection (f) increases the time from 5 to 10 business days for the sending county juvenile probation department to provide the required documentation. Additionally, subsection (f–1) was added to require inter-county transfer officers in the sending and receiving counties to agree on an official start date for interim supervision.

Subsections (g) and (h) allow the receiving probation department flexibility to have the juvenile court in the receiving county modify conditions or upon proper petition, revoke probation. Monetary conditions that are set in the sending county cannot, however, be amended or altered by the receiving court.

Subsection (j) requires the receiving county juvenile probation department to provide the sending county with written documentation of probation violation incidents if a request is made to resume direct supervision.

Subsection (k) places the duty on the receiving county to collect and distribute to the victim monetary restitution payments in the manner specified by the sending county.

Subsection (m) provides for the sending county to resume supervision of the child if the child moves to another county before the end of the 180 days.

Subsection (n) clarifies that the period of interim supervision for determinate sentence probation does not expire until the child has satisfactorily completed the greater of either 180 days or one-third of the probation.

CLE/Other Legal Publication

Transfer of probation supervision between counties: information and implementation package for the new statutory system contained in House Bill 1575. Pierre Williams, Nydia Thomas, Lisa Capers, 19 JUVE. L. SECT. RPT. (SEPT. 2005)

---

§ 51.073. Transfer of Probation Supervision Between Counties: Permanent Supervision

(a) In this section:

(1) "Receiving county" means the county to which a child on probation has moved or intends to move.

(2) "Sending county" means the county that:

(A) originally placed the child on probation; or

(B) assumed permanent supervision of the child under an inter-county transfer of probation supervision.

(b) On transfer of permanent supervision of a child under Section 51.072(m) or (n), the juvenile court of the sending county shall order the juvenile probation department of the sending county to provide the juvenile probation department of the receiving county with the order of transfer. On receipt of the order of transfer, the juvenile probation department of the receiving county shall ensure that the order of transfer, the petition, the order of adjudication, the order of disposition, and the conditions of probation are filed with the clerk of the juvenile court of the receiving county.

(c) The juvenile court of the receiving county shall require that the child be brought before the court in order to impose new or different conditions of probation than those originally ordered by the sending county or ordered by the receiving county during the period of interim supervision. The child shall be represented by counsel as provided by Section 51.10.

(d) Once permanent supervision is transferred to the juvenile probation department of the receiving county, the receiving county is fully responsible for selecting and imposing conditions of probation, providing supervision, modifying conditions of probation, and revoking probation. The sending county has no further jurisdiction over the child's case.

(d–1) On the final transfer of a case involving a child who has been adjudicated as having committed an offense for which registration is required under Chapter 62, Code of Criminal Procedure, the receiving county shall have jurisdiction to conduct a hearing under that chapter. This subsection does not prohibit the receiving county juvenile court from considering the written recommendations of the sending county juvenile court.

(e) This section does not affect the sending county's jurisdiction over any new offense committed by the child in the sending county.

Comment

This section provides the conditions for permanent supervision when probation is transferred to a new county. Once interim supervision is complete and the receiving county becomes the place of permanent supervision, the sending county is relieved of all duties and responsibilities toward the child.

A hearing must be conducted to officially transfer the probation permanently and the child is entitled to an attorney at this hearing.

Subsection (c) clarifies that new or different conditions of probation can only be imposed by bringing the child before the receiving county juvenile court.

Subsection (d–1) gives jurisdiction to the receiving county to conduct a sex offender registration hearing on the final transfer of the case if a registration hearing is required under Chapter 62 of the Code of Criminal Procedure.

§ 51.074. Transfer of Probation Supervision Between Counties: Deferred Prosecution

(a) A juvenile court may transfer interim supervision, but not permanent supervision, to the county where a child on deferred prosecution resides.

(b) On an extension of a previous order of deferred prosecution authorized under Section 53.03(j), the child shall remain on interim supervision for an additional period not to exceed 180 days.

(c) On a violation of the conditions of the original deferred prosecution agreement, the receiving county shall forward the case to the sending county for prosecution or other action in the manner provided by Sections 51.072(i) and (j), except that the original conditions of deferred prosecution may not be modified by the receiving county.

Comment

Since the maximum term of supervision for a deferred prosecution is 180 days, this section qualifies transfers of deferred prosecution cases as interim supervision only.

Subsection (b) requires interim supervision to be extended for up to 180 days if the child's deferred adjudication has been extended.

Subsection (c) prohibits the receiving county from modifying the original conditions of deferred prosecution and requires that upon a violation of a condition of the original deferred prosecution, the receiving county must return the case to the sending county.

§ 51.075. Collaborative Supervision Between Adjoining Counties

(a) If a child who is on probation in one county spends substantial time in an adjoining county, including residing, attending school, or working in the adjoining county, the juvenile probation departments of the two counties may enter into a collaborative supervision arrangement regarding the child.

(b) Under a collaborative supervision arrangement, the juvenile probation department of the adjoining county may authorize a probation officer for the county to provide supervision and other services for the child as an agent of the juvenile probation department of the county in which the child was placed on probation. The probation officer providing supervision and other services for the child in the adjoining county shall provide the probation officer supervising the child in the county in which the child was placed on probation with periodic oral, electronic, or written reports concerning the child.

(c) The juvenile court of the county in which the child was placed on probation retains sole authority to modify, amend, extend, or revoke the child's probation.

Comment

The only form of "courtesy supervision" remaining is reserved for situations in which a child lives near county boundaries such that a child may reside in one county, but attend school or work in an adjacent county. The child remains on probation in the county in which the child was originally placed on probation. The adjacent county or counties may, however, informally share in the supervision.

---

§ 51.08. Transfer from Criminal Court

(a) If the defendant in a criminal proceeding is a child who is charged with an offense other than perjury, a traffic offense, a misdemeanor punishable by fine only, or a violation of a penal ordinance of a political subdivision, unless the child has been transferred to criminal court under Section 54.02, the court exercising criminal jurisdiction shall transfer the case to the juvenile court, together with a copy of the accusatory pleading and other papers, documents, and transcripts of testimony relating to the case, and shall order that the child be taken to the place of detention designated by the juvenile court, or shall release the child to the custody of the child's parent, guardian, or custodian, to be brought before the juvenile court at a time designated by that court.

(b) A court in which there is pending a complaint against a child alleging a violation of a misdemeanor offense punishable by fine only other than a traffic offense or a violation of a penal ordinance of a political subdivision other than a traffic offense:

(1) except as provided by Subsection (d), shall waive its original jurisdiction and refer the child to juvenile court if**:**

(A) the complaint pending against the child alleges a violation of a misdemeanor offense under Section 43.261, Penal Code, that is punishable by fine only; or

(B) the child has previously been convicted of:

(i) ~~(A)~~ two or more misdemeanors punishable by fine only other than a traffic offense;

(ii) ~~(B)~~ two or more violations of a penal ordinance of a political subdivision other than a traffic offense; or

(iii) ~~(C)~~ one or more of each of the types of misdemeanors described in **Subparagraph (i) or (ii)** ~~Paragraph (A) or (B)~~; and

(2) may waive its original jurisdiction and refer the child to juvenile court if the child:

(A) has not previously been convicted of a misdemeanor punishable by fine only other than a traffic offense or a violation of a penal ordinance of a political subdivision other than a traffic offense; or

(B) has previously been convicted of fewer than two misdemeanors punishable by fine only other than a traffic offense or two violations of a penal ordinance of a political subdivision other than a traffic offense.

(c) A court in which there is pending a complaint against a child alleging a violation of a misdemeanor offense punishable by fine only other than a traffic offense or a violation of a penal ordinance of a political subdivision other than a traffic offense shall notify the juvenile court of the county in which the court is located of the pending complaint and shall furnish to the juvenile court a copy of the final disposition of any matter for which the court does not waive its original jurisdiction under Subsection (b).

(d) A court that has implemented a juvenile case manager program under Article 45.056, Code of Criminal Procedure, may, but is not required to, waive its original jurisdiction under Subsection **(b)(1)(B)** ~~(b)(1)~~.

(e) A juvenile court may not refuse to accept the transfer of a case brought under Section 25.094, Education Code, for a child described by Subsection (b)(1) if a prosecuting attorney for the court determines under Section 53.012 that the case is legally sufficient under Section 53.01 for adjudication in juvenile court.

Amended by Acts 2011, 82nd Leg., ch. 1322 (S.B. 407), § 16, eff. Sept. 1, 2011.

Comment

Subsection (a) requires a criminal court to transfer a case to juvenile court upon discovery that the defendant is underage. Subsection (b) establishes the system for criminal prosecution of children who are believed to have committed fineable only offenses other than traffic offenses. The criminal court may transfer any such case to juvenile court, but is required to transfer a case if the child has two prior convictions of fineable only offenses. Subsection (c) makes the juvenile court the county-wide depository of records concerning these cases. Subsection (d) creates an exception to the mandatory transfer rule if the justice or municipal court has a juvenile case manager available to aid it in handling cases of persistent juvenile misconduct.

Public intoxication cases are the province of justice of the peace or municipal courts. These cases are required, however, to be transferred to juvenile court when two or more prior convictions of public intoxication have occurred.

Cross References

TEX. CODE CRIM. PROC. ANN. art. 45.051, Suspension of Sentence and Deferral of Final Disposition; TEX. CODE CRIM. PROC. ANN. art. 45.052, Dismissal of Misdemeanor Charge on Completion of Teen Court; TEX. CODE CRIM. PROC. ANN. art. 45.0216, Expunction of Certain Conviction Records of Children; TEX. CODE CRIM. PROC. ANN. art. 45.056, Authority to Employ Juvenile Case Managers.

§ 51.09. Waiver of Rights

Unless a contrary intent clearly appears elsewhere in this title, any right granted to a child by this title or by the constitution or laws of this state or the United States may be waived in proceedings under this title if:

(1) the waiver is made by the child and the attorney for the child;

(2) the child and the attorney waiving the right are informed of and understand the right and the possible consequences of waiving it;

(3) the waiver is voluntary; and

(4) the waiver is made in writing or in court proceedings that are recorded.

Comment

This section sets the requirements for waiver of rights except in the context of custodial interrogation, which is dealt with by § 51.095.

Leading Case

R.X.F. v. State, 921 S.W.2d 888 (Tex. App.—Waco, 1996, no writ) (by taking stand, child waives self-incrimination privilege under § 51.09)

§ 51.095. Admissibility of a Statement of a Child

(a) Notwithstanding Section 51.09, the statement of a child is admissible in evidence in any future proceeding concerning the matter about which the statement was given if:

(1) the statement is made in writing under a circumstance described by Subsection (d) and:

(A) the statement shows that the child has at some time before the making of the statement received from a magistrate a warning that:

(i) the child may remain silent and not make any statement at all and that any statement that the child makes may be used in evidence against the child;

(ii) the child has the right to have an attorney present to advise the child either prior to any questioning or during the questioning;

(iii) if the child is unable to employ an attorney, the child has the right to have an attorney appointed to counsel with the child before or during any interviews with peace officers or attorneys representing the state; and

(iv) the child has the right to terminate the interview at any time;

(B) and:

(i) the statement must be signed in the presence of a magistrate by the child with no law enforcement officer or prosecuting attorney present, except that a magistrate may require a bailiff or a law enforcement officer if a bailiff is not available to be present if the magistrate determines that the presence of the bailiff or law enforcement officer is necessary for the personal safety of the magistrate or other court personnel, provided that the bailiff or law enforcement officer may not carry a weapon in the presence of the child; and

(ii) the magistrate must be fully convinced that the child understands the nature and contents of the statement and that the child is signing the same voluntarily, and if a statement is taken, the magistrate must sign a written statement verifying the foregoing requisites have been met;

(C) the child knowingly, intelligently, and voluntarily waives these rights before and during the making of the statement and signs the statement in the presence of a magistrate; and

(D) the magistrate certifies that the magistrate has examined the child independent of any law enforcement officer or prosecuting attorney, except as required to ensure the personal safety of the magistrate or other court personnel, and has determined that the child understands the nature and contents of the statement and has knowingly, intelligently, and voluntarily waived these rights;

(2) the statement is made orally and the child makes a statement of facts or circumstances that are found to be true and tend to establish the child's guilt, such as the finding of secreted or stolen property, or the instrument with which the child states the offense was committed;

(3) the statement was res gestae of the delinquent conduct or the conduct indicating a need for supervision or of the arrest;

(4) the statement is made:

(A) in open court at the child's adjudication hearing;

(B) before a grand jury considering a petition, under Section 53.045, that the child engaged in delinquent conduct; or

(C) at a preliminary hearing concerning the child held in compliance with this code, other than at a detention hearing under Section 54.01; or

(5) subject to Subsection (f), the statement is made orally under a circumstance described by Subsection (d) and the statement is recorded by an electronic recording device, including a device that records images, and:

(A) before making the statement, the child is given the warning described by Subdivision (1)(A) by a magistrate, the warning is a part of the recording, and the child knowingly, intelligently, and voluntarily waives each right stated in the warning;

(B) the recording device is capable of making an accurate recording, the operator of the device is competent to use the device, the recording is accurate, and the recording has not been altered;

(C) each voice on the recording is identified; and

(D) not later than the 20th day before the date of the proceeding, the attorney representing the child is given a complete and accurate copy of each recording of the child made under this subdivision.

(b) This section and Section 51.09 do not preclude the admission of a statement made by the child if:

(1) the statement does not stem from interrogation of the child under a circumstance described by Subsection (d); or

(2) without regard to whether the statement stems from interrogation of the child under a circumstance described by Subsection (d), the statement is:

(A) voluntary and has a bearing on the credibility of the child as a witness; **or**

(B) recorded by an electronic recording device, including a device that records images, and is obtained:

(i) in another state in compliance with the laws of that state or this state; or

(ii) by a federal law enforcement officer in this state or another state in compliance with the laws of the United States.

(c) An electronic recording of a child's statement made under Subsection (a)(5) **or (b)(2)(B)** shall be preserved until all juvenile or criminal matters relating to any conduct referred to in the statement are final, including the exhaustion of all appeals, or barred from prosecution.

(d) Subsections (a)(1) and (a)(5) apply to the statement of a child made:

(1) while the child is in a detention facility or other place of confinement;

(2) while the child is in the custody of an officer; or

(3) during or after the interrogation of the child by an officer if the child is in the possession of the Department of **Family and** Protective ~~and Regulatory~~ Services and is suspected to have engaged in conduct that violates a penal law of this state.

(e) A juvenile law referee or master may perform the duties imposed on a magistrate under this section without the approval of the juvenile court if the juvenile board of the county in which the statement of the child is made has authorized a referee or master to perform the duties of a magistrate under this section.

(f) A magistrate who provides the warnings required by Subsection (a)(5) for a recorded statement may at the time the warnings are provided request by speaking on the recording that the officer return the child and the recording to the magistrate at the conclusion of the process of questioning. The magistrate may then view the recording with the child or have the child view the recording to enable the magistrate to determine whether the child's statements were given voluntarily. The magistrate's determination of voluntariness shall be reduced to writing and signed and dated by the magistrate. If a magistrate uses the procedure described by this subsection, a child's statement is not admissible unless the magistrate determines that the statement was given voluntarily.

Amended by Acts 2011, 82nd Leg., ch. 110 (H.B. 841), § 3, eff. May 21, 2011; Acts 2011, 82nd Leg., ch. 1158 (H.B. 2337), § 1, eff. Sept. 1, 2011.

Comment

Tape-recorded oral statements are authorized to be admitted into evidence, as they have been for a number of years under Tex. Code Crim. Proc. Ann. art. 38.22. There is one difference in that the warnings must be given by a magistrate in this section but may be given by a peace officer or magistrate under art. 38.22.

A magistrate who is providing the appropriate warnings to a juvenile on a recorded statement may require that the officer return the child to the magistrate after the questioning is complete. The magistrate can then determine from the recorded statement whether the child gave the statement voluntarily. This subsection requires that the magistrate's determination of voluntariness be in writing and signed and dated by the magistrate. The statement will be inadmissible if these procedures are invoked by the magistrate and not followed.

In 2011 this section was amended to broaden the admissibility of statements to include those made in compliance with another state's laws or in compliance with laws of the Federal government.

CLE/Other Legal Publication

What effect will Yarborough v. Alvarado have on Texas law enforcement interrogation of suspect minors? Lydia D. Johnson, 30 T. Marshall L. Rev. 409 (2005)

Leading Cases

Procedure

In re M.A.C., ___ S.W.3d ___, 2011 WL 1519351 (Tex. App.—Eastland, no pet.) (the prohibition against having a weapon in the room only applies to written statements and not recorded ones)

In re D.J.C., 312 S.W.3d 704 (Tex. App.—Houston [1st Dist.] 2009, no pet.) (magistrate failed to warn child that his recorded statement could be used "in evidence" against him (magistrate simply said it could be used against him) and this violated 51.095)

Age

Yarborough v. Alvarado, 124 S.Ct. 2140 (2004) (age and lack of experience with law enforcement not factors in determining whether suspect was in custody during interrogation)

Martinez v. State, 131 S.W.3d 22 (Tex. App.—San Antonio 2003, no pet.)(custody occurs if a reasonable child of the same age would believe his freedom of movement was restrained)

Childs v. State, 21 S.W.3d 631 (Tex. App.—Houston [14th Dist.] 2000, pet. refused) (claim by juvenile that he is 17 waived Family Code interrogation protections)

Invocation of Counsel

Fare v. C., 442 U.S. 707, 61 L.Ed.2d 197, 99 S.Ct. 2560 (1979) (juvenile's request to speak to probation officer not invocation of right to counsel; voluntariness determined by totality of circumstances)

In re R.D., 627 S.W.2d 803 (Tex. App.—Tyler 1982, no writ) (request to speak to mother not invocation of right to counsel)

In re H.V., 252 S.W.3d 319 (Tex. 2008) (when 16 year old requested to call his mother and have her ask for an attorney it was an unambiguous request for counsel)

Out-of-state Statement

Vega v. State, 255 S.W.3d 87 (Tex. App.—Corpus Christi 2007, pet ref'd.)(absence of magistrate does not require suppression of statement when out-of-state authorities made sure child understood her statement and knowingly, intelligently, and voluntarily signed it)

Vega v. State, 84 S.W.3d 613 (Tex. Crim. App. 2002) (statement taken by Illinois authorities not automatically rendered inadmissible even though § 51.095 not followed)

In re T.R.S., 931 S.W.2d 756 (Tex. App.—Waco 1996, no writ) (admissibility of statement given in Oklahoma determined by applying Texas law)

Laird v. State, 933 S.W.2d 707 (Tex. App.—Houston [14th Dist.] 1996, write ref'd) (custodial statement given in Pennsylvania admissible although not given in juvenile processing office)

Fruit of the Poisonous Tree

In re R.J.H., 79 S.W.3d 1 (Tex. 2002) (oral statements given after written statement, which did not comply with § 51.095 and was inadmissible, were not "fruit of the poisonous tree" because written statement only violated statutory rights, not constitutional protections)

Griffin v. State, 765 S.W.2d 422 (Tex. Crim. App. 1989) (written statement as fruit of prior, inadmissible oral statement)

Kendrick v. State, 942 S.W.2d 120 (Tex. App.—Beaumont 1997, no writ) (oral custodial statement leading to tangible evidence admissible in criminal trial)

Custody

Martinez v. State, 337 S.W.3d 446 (Tex. App.—Eastland,2011 no pet.) (the issue of custody equivalent to arrest arises when the requirements of 51.095 are not met)

In re D.J.C., 312 S.W.3d 704 (Tex. App.—Houston [1st Dist.] 2009, no pet.) (excluding child's grandmother from interrogation room, having a magistrate read the warnings, and locking the door to the interview room changed the non-custodial interrogation into a custodial one)

Martinez v. State, 131 S.W.3d 22 (Tex. App.—San Antonio 2003, no pet.) (capital murder statement admissible because juvenile not in custody)

In re D.A.R., 73 S.W.3d 505 (Tex. App.—El Paso 2002, no pet.) (statement excluded because questioning by police officer in school was custodial)

Diaz v. State, 61 S.W.3d 525 (Tex. App.—San Antonio 2001, no pet.) (statement involuntary because magistrate made error in advising as to punishment range for offense)

Rushing v. State, 50 S.W.3d 715 (Tex. App.—Waco 2001, rev. denied) (oral statements made to probation officer in detention admissible because no interrogation)

In re V.P., 55 S.W.3d 25 (Tex. App.—Austin 2001, rev. denied) (questioning by assistant principal about handgun on campus not custodial)

In re L.M., 993 S.W.2d 276 (Tex. App.—Austin 1999, rev. denied) (young child in DFPS custody is in police custody for questioning)

Attorney General Opinion

Tex. Atty. Gen. Op. DM–476 (1998) (school may not block DFPS child abuse interview or insist that school official be present)

---

§ 51.10. Right to Assistance of Attorney; Compensation

(a) A child may be represented by an attorney at every stage of proceedings under this title, including:

(1) the detention hearing required by Section 54.01 of this code;

(2) the hearing to consider transfer to criminal court required by Section 54.02 of this code;

(3) the adjudication hearing required by Section 54.03 of this code;

(4) the disposition hearing required by Section 54.04 of this code;

(5) the hearing to modify disposition required by Section 54.05 of this code;

(6) hearings required by Chapter 55 of this code;

(7) habeas corpus proceedings challenging the legality of detention resulting from action under this title; and

(8) proceedings in a court of civil appeals or the Texas Supreme Court reviewing proceedings under this title.

(b) The child's right to representation by an attorney shall not be waived in:

(1) a hearing to consider transfer to criminal court as required by Section 54.02 of this code;

(2) an adjudication hearing as required by Section 54.03 of this code;

(3) a disposition hearing as required by Section 54.04 of this code;

(4) a hearing prior to commitment to the Texas Youth Commission as a modified disposition in accordance with Section 54.05(f) of this code; or

(5) hearings required by Chapter 55 of this code.

(c) If the child was not represented by an attorney at the detention hearing required by Section 54.01 of this code and a determination was made to detain the child, the child shall immediately be entitled to representation by an attorney. The court shall order the retention of an attorney according to Subsection (d) or appoint an attorney according to Subsection (f).

(d) The court shall order a child's parent or other person responsible for support of the child to employ an attorney to represent the child, if:

(1) the child is not represented by an attorney;

(2) after giving the appropriate parties an opportunity to be heard, the court determines that the parent or other person responsible for support of the child is financially able to employ an attorney to represent the child; and

(3) the child's right to representation by an attorney:

(A) has not been waived under Section 51.09 of this code; or

(B) may not be waived under Subsection (b) of this section.

(e) The court may enforce orders under Subsection (d) by proceedings under Section 54.07 or by appointing counsel and ordering the parent or other person responsible for support of the child to pay a reasonable attorney's fee set by the court. The order may be enforced under Section 54.07.

(f) The court shall appoint an attorney to represent the interest of a child entitled to representation by an attorney, if:

(1) the child is not represented by an attorney;

(2) the court determines that the child's parent or other person responsible for support of the child is financially unable to employ an attorney to represent the child; and

(3) the child's right to representation by an attorney:

(A) has not been waived under Section 51.09 of this code; or

(B) may not be waived under Subsection (b) of this section.

(g) The juvenile court may appoint an attorney in any case in which it deems representation necessary to protect the interests of the child.

(h) Any attorney representing a child in proceedings under this title is entitled to 10 days to prepare for any adjudication or transfer hearing under this title.

(i) Except as provided in Subsection (d) of this section, an attorney appointed under this section to represent the interests of a child shall be paid from the general fund of the county in which the proceedings were instituted according to the schedule in Article 26.05 of the Texas Code of Criminal Procedure, 1965. For this purpose, a bona fide appeal to a court of civil appeals or proceedings on the merits in the Texas Supreme Court are considered the equivalent of a bona fide appeal to the Texas Court of Criminal Appeals.

(j) The juvenile board of a county may make available to the public the list of attorneys eligible for appointment to represent children in proceedings under this title as provided in the plan adopted under Section 51.102. The list of attorneys must indicate the level of case for which each attorney is eligible for appointment under Section 51.102(b)(2).

(k) Subject to Chapter 61, the juvenile court may order the parent or other person responsible for support of the child to reimburse the county for payments the county made to counsel appointed to represent the child under Subsection (f) or (g). The court may:

(1) order payment for each attorney who has represented the child at any hearing, including a detention hearing, discretionary transfer hearing, adjudication hearing, disposition hearing, or modification of disposition hearing;

(2) include amounts paid to or on behalf of the attorney by the county for preparation time and investigative and expert witness costs; and

(3) require full or partial reimbursement to the county.

(*l*) The court may not order payments under Subsection (k) that exceed the financial ability of the parent or other person responsible for support of the child to meet the payment schedule ordered by the court.

Comment

A juvenile has a right to counsel at all stages of Title 3 proceedings. That right cannot be waived in a transfer, adjudication, disposition, probation revocation, or Chapter 55 proceeding. Counsel, appointed or retained, is entitled to 10 days to prepare for an adjudication or transfer hearing.

As a result of the Fair Defense Act, each juvenile board must maintain a list of attorneys eligible for appointment to juvenile cases. Subsection (j) permits the board to make that list available to the public to aid parents and others to choose an attorney to retain for a juvenile case.

Subsections (k) and (*l*) recognize the power of the juvenile court to order parents and others to reimburse the county for its expenditures to and on behalf of appointed counsel. Enforcement of such orders is governed by Chapter 61.

Leading Cases

In re Gault, 387 U.S. 1, 18 L.Ed.2d 527, 87 S.Ct. 1428 (1967) (juvenile has right to counsel under 14th Amendment)

In re James Allen Hall, 286 S.W.3d 925 (Tex. 2009) (this code provision entitles a child to a lawyer for habeas proceeding involving pre-adjudication detention, not post-adjudication detention)

In re I.R., 124 S.W.3d 294 (Tex. App.—El Paso 2003, no pet.) (failure to subpoena alibi witness was ineffective assistance of counsel)

Attorney General Opinion

Tex. Atty. Gen. Op. LO–97–063 (1997) (county must pay fee of appointed counsel even when there is a public defender office in the county)

Cross Reference

Tex. Code Crim. Proc. Ann. art. 26.05. Compensation of Counsel Appointed To Defend.

---

§ 51.101. Appointment of Attorney and Continuation of Representation

(a) If an attorney is appointed at the initial detention hearing and the child is detained, the attorney shall continue to represent the child until the case is terminated, the family retains an attorney, or a new attorney is appointed by the juvenile court. Release of the child from detention does not terminate the attorney's representation.

(b) If there is an initial detention hearing without an attorney and the child is detained, the attorney appointed under Section 51.10(c) shall continue to represent the child until the case is terminated, the family retains an attorney, or a new attorney is appointed by the juvenile court. Release of the child from detention does not terminate the attorney's representation.

(c) The juvenile court shall determine, on the filing of a petition, whether the child's family is indigent if:

(1) the child is released by intake;

(2) the child is released at the initial detention hearing; or

(3) the case was referred to the court without the child in custody.

(d) A juvenile court that makes a finding of indigence under Subsection (c) shall appoint an attorney to represent the child on or before the fifth working day after the date the petition for adjudication or discretionary transfer hearing was served on the child. An attorney appointed under this subsection shall continue to represent the child until the case is terminated, the family retains an attorney, or a new attorney is appointed by the juvenile court.

(e) The juvenile court shall determine whether the child's family is indigent if a motion or petition is filed under Section 54.05 seeking to modify disposition by committing the child to the Texas Youth Commission or placing the child in a secure correctional facility. A court that makes a finding of indigence shall appoint an attorney to represent the child on or before the fifth working day after the date the petition or motion has been filed. An attorney appointed under this subsection shall continue to represent the child until the court rules on the motion or petition, the family retains an attorney, or a new attorney is appointed.

Comment

This section seeks to assure that an appointed attorney is provided early enough in the process to benefit the respondent. In some counties, an attorney appointed for a detention hearing represents the child only for that hearing. If the child is detained, he or she may be without counsel until the

State files a petition. This section provides that if the child is detained, that same attorney becomes the attorney for the merits of the case until the case is terminated or other counsel is provided.

There is an exception for a child who is released by police, intake, or at the initial detention hearings. Because many such children will be handled nonjudicially and without prejudicing their rights, providing counsel for them would be expensive and not particularly productive. Children in such cases must have counsel appointed if their families are indigent when a petition is filed; counties are free to provide counsel in such cases earlier in the process.

§ 51.102. Appointment of Counsel Plan

(a) The juvenile board in each county shall adopt a plan that:

(1) specifies the qualifications necessary for an attorney to be included on an appointment list from which attorneys are appointed to represent children in proceedings under this title; and

(2) establishes the procedures for:

(A) including attorneys on the appointment list and removing attorneys from the list; and

(B) appointing attorneys from the appointment list to individual cases.

(b) A plan adopted under Subsection (a) must:

(1) to the extent practicable, comply with the requirements of Article 26.04, Code of Criminal Procedure, except that:

(A) the income and assets of the child's parent or other person responsible for the child's support must be used in determining whether the child is indigent; and

(B) any alternative plan for appointing counsel is established by the juvenile board in the county; and

(2) recognize the differences in qualifications and experience necessary for appointments to cases in which:

(A) the allegation is:

(i) conduct indicating a need for supervision or delinquent conduct, and commitment to the Texas Youth Commission is not an authorized disposition; or

(ii) delinquent conduct, and commitment to the Texas Youth Commission without a determinate sentence is an authorized disposition; or

(B) determinate sentence proceedings have been initiated or proceedings for discretionary transfer to criminal court have been initiated.

Comment

This section implements the Texas Fair Defense Act by requiring the juvenile board to devise and make public a plan for the qualifications of and appointment of attorneys to represent indigent juveniles.

The Fair Defense Act provides for a state-wide standard setting and monitoring agency in the Office of Court Administration to implement the legislation and for an estimated 12 million dollars per year in state aid to counties to aid in paying for attorneys, investigative expenses and the fees of expert witnesses.

§ 51.11. Guardian Ad Litem

(a) If a child appears before the juvenile court without a parent or guardian, the court shall appoint a guardian ad litem to protect the interests of the child. The juvenile court need not appoint a guardian ad litem if a parent or guardian appears with the child.

(b) In any case in which it appears to the juvenile court that the child's parent or guardian is incapable or unwilling to make decisions in the best interest of the child with respect to proceedings under this title, the court may appoint a guardian ad litem to protect the interests of the child in the proceedings.

(c) An attorney for a child may also be his guardian ad litem. A law-enforcement officer, probation officer, or other employee of the juvenile court may not be appointed guardian ad litem.

Comment

A guardian ad litem must be appointed where there is no parent or guardian in court with the child. The defense attorney may be appointed guardian ad litem.

Leading Cases

Flynn v. State, 707 S.W.2d 87 (Tex. Crim. App. 1986) (error but harmless not to appoint guardian ad litem when respondent's aunt was in court)

In re P.S.G., 942 S.W.2d 227 (Tex. App.—Beaumont 1997, no writ) (refusal to appoint GAL when same person was victim and respondent's mother OK)

---

§ 51.115. Attendance at Hearing: Parent or Other Guardian

(a) Each parent of a child, each managing and possessory conservator of a child, each court-appointed custodian of a child, and a guardian of the person of the child shall attend each hearing affecting the child held under:

(1) Section 54.02 (waiver of jurisdiction and discretionary transfer to criminal court);

(2) Section 54.03 (adjudication hearing);

(3) Section 54.04 (disposition hearing);

(4) Section 54.05 (hearing to modify disposition); and

(5) Section 54.11 (release or transfer hearing).

(b) Subsection (a) does not apply to:

(1) a person for whom, for good cause shown, the court waives attendance;

(2) a person who is not a resident of this state; or

(3) a parent of a child for whom a managing conservator has been appointed and the parent is not a conservator of the child.

(c) A person required under this section to attend a hearing is entitled to reasonable written or oral notice that includes a statement of the place, date, and time of the hearing and that the attendance of the person is required. The notice may be included with or attached to any other notice required by this chapter to be given the person. Separate notice is not required for a disposition hearing that convenes on the adjournment of an adjudication hearing. If a person required under this section fails to attend a hearing, the juvenile court may proceed with the hearing.

(d) A person who is required by Subsection (a) to attend a hearing, who receives the notice of the hearing, and who fails to attend the hearing may be punished by the court for contempt by a fine of not less than $100 and not more than $1,000. In addition to or in lieu of contempt, the court may order the person to receive counseling or to attend an educational course on the duties and responsibilities of parents and skills and techniques in raising children.

Comment

This provision is intended to induce greater parental responsibility in the juvenile process. Parents and others can be ordered to attend juvenile court hearings and fined for contempt of court for failure to attend.

---

§ 51.116. Right to Reemployment

(a) An employer may not terminate the employment of a permanent employee because the employee is required under Section 51.115 to attend a hearing.

(b) An employee whose employment is terminated in violation of this section is entitled to return to the same employment that the employee held when notified of the hearing if the employee, as soon as practical after the hearing, gives the employer actual notice that the employee intends to return.

(c) A person who is injured because of a violation of this section is entitled to reinstatement to the person's former position and to damages, but the damages may not exceed an amount equal to six months' compensation at the rate at which the person was compensated when required to attend the hearing.

(d) The injured person is also entitled to reasonable attorney's fees in an amount approved by the court.

(e) It is a defense to an action brought under this section that the employer's circumstances changed while the employee attended the hearing so that reemployment was impossible or unreasonable. To establish a defense under this subsection, an employer must prove that the termination of employment was because of circumstances other than the employee's attendance at the hearing.

Comment

This section, a companion to § 51.115, is intended to facilitate the attendance of parents and other adults at juvenile court hearings by prohibiting employers from firing an employee for attending a hearing in response to a juvenile court order. This section is modeled on a similar provision to protect jurors from being fired for responding to a jury summons. *See* Tex. Civ. Prac. & Rem. Code § 122.001.

§ 51.12. Place and Conditions of Detention

(a) Except as provided by Subsection (h), a child may be detained only in a:

(1) juvenile processing office in compliance with Section 52.025;

(2) place of nonsecure custody in compliance with Article 45.058, Code of Criminal Procedure;

(3) certified juvenile detention facility that complies with the requirements of Subsection (f);

(4) secure detention facility as provided by Subsection (j); or

(5) county jail or other facility as provided by Subsection (*l*).

(b) The proper authorities in each county shall provide a suitable place of detention for children who are parties to proceedings under this title, but the juvenile board shall control the conditions and terms of detention and detention supervision and shall permit visitation with the child at all reasonable times.

(b–1) A pre-adjudication secure detention facility may be operated only by:

(1) a governmental unit in this state as defined by Section 101.001, Civil Practice and Remedies Code; or

(2) a private entity under a contract with a governmental unit in this state.

(c) In each county, each judge of the juvenile court and a majority of the members of the juvenile board shall personally inspect all public or private juvenile pre-adjudication secure detention facilities that are located in the county at least annually and shall certify in writing to the authorities responsible for operating and giving financial support to the facilities and to the Texas Juvenile Probation Commission that the facilities are suitable or unsuitable for the detention of children. In determining whether a facility is suitable or unsuitable for the detention of children, the juvenile court judges and juvenile board members shall consider:

(1) current monitoring and inspection reports and any noncompliance citation reports issued by the Texas Juvenile Probation Commission, including the report provided under Subsection (c–1), and the status of any required corrective actions;

(2) current governmental inspector certification regarding the facility's compliance with local fire codes;

(3) current building inspector certification regarding the facility's compliance with local building codes;

(4) for the 12-month period preceding the inspection, the total number of allegations of abuse, neglect, or exploitation reported by the facility and a summary of the findings of any investigations of abuse, neglect, or exploitation conducted by the facility, a local law enforcement agency, and the Texas Juvenile Probation Commission;

(5) the availability of health and mental health services provided to facility residents;

(6) the availability of educational services provided to facility residents; and

(7) the overall physical appearance of the facility, including the facility's security, maintenance, cleanliness, and environment.

(c-1) The Texas Juvenile Probation Commission shall annually inspect each public or private juvenile pre-adjudication secure detention facility. The Texas Juvenile Probation Commission shall provide a report to each juvenile court judge presiding in the same county as an inspected facility indicating whether the facility is suitable or unsuitable for the detention of children in accordance with:

(1) the requirements of Subsections (a), (f), and (g); and

(2) minimum professional standards for the detention of children in pre-adjudication secure confinement promulgated by the Texas Juvenile Probation Commission or, at the election of the juvenile board of the county in which the facility is located, the current standards promulgated by the American Correctional Association.

(d) Except as provided by Subsections (j) and (*l*), a child may not be placed in a facility that has not been certified under Subsection (c) as suitable for the detention of children and registered under Subsection (i). Except as provided by Subsections (j) and (*l*), a child detained in a facility that has not been certified under Subsection (c) as suitable for the detention of children or that has not been registered under Subsection (i) shall be entitled to immediate release from custody in that facility.

(e) If there is no certified place of detention in the county in which the petition is filed, the designated place of detention may be in another county.

(f) A child detained in a building that contains a jail, lockup, or other place of secure confinement, including an alcohol or other drug treatment facility, shall be separated by sight and sound from adults detained in the same building. Children and adults are separated by sight and sound only if they are unable to see each other and conversation between them is not possible. The separation must extend to all areas of the facility, including sally ports and passageways, and those areas used for admission, counseling, sleeping, toileting, showering, dining, recreational, educational, or vocational activities, and health care. The separation may be accomplished through architectural design. **A person who has been transferred for prosecution in criminal court under Section 54.02 and is under 17 years of age is considered a child for the purposes of this subsection.**

(g) Except for a child detained in a juvenile processing office, a place of nonsecure custody, a secure detention facility as provided by Subsection (j), or a facility as provided by Subsection (*l*), a child detained in a building that contains a jail or lockup may not have any contact with:

(1) part-time or full-time security staff, including management, who have contact with adults detained in the same building; or

(2) direct-care staff who have contact with adults detained in the same building.

(h) This section does not apply to a person:

(1) **who has been transferred** ~~after transfer~~ to criminal court for prosecution under Section 54.02 **and is at least 17 years of age**; or

(2) who is at least 17 years of age and who has been taken into custody after having:

(A) escaped from a juvenile facility operated by or under contract with the Texas Youth Commission; or

(B) violated a condition of release under supervision of the Texas Youth Commission.

(i) Except for a facility as provided by Subsection (*l*), a governmental unit or private entity that operates or contracts for the operation of a juvenile pre-adjudication secure detention facility under Subsection (b–1) in this state shall:

(1) register the facility annually with the Texas Juvenile Probation Commission; and

(2) adhere to all applicable minimum standards for the facility.

(j) After being taken into custody, a child may be detained in a secure detention facility until the child is released under Section 53.01, 53.012, or 53.02 or until a detention hearing is held under Section 54.01(a), regardless of whether the facility has been certified under Subsection (c), if:

(1) a certified juvenile detention facility is not available in the county in which the child is taken into custody;

(2) the detention facility complies with:

(A) the short-term detention standards adopted by the Texas Juvenile Probation Commission; and

(B) the requirements of Subsection (f); and

(3) the detention facility has been designated by the county juvenile board for the county in which the facility is located.

(k) If a child who is detained under Subsection (j) or (*l*) is not released from detention at the conclusion of the detention hearing for a reason stated in Section 54.01(e), the child may be detained after the hearing only in a certified juvenile detention facility.

(*l*) A child who is taken into custody and required to be detained under Section 53.02(f) may be detained in a county jail or other facility until the child is released under Section 53.02(f) or until a detention hearing is held as required by Section 54.01(p), regardless of whether the facility complies with the requirements of this section, if:

(1) a certified juvenile detention facility or a secure detention facility described by Subsection (j) is not available in the county in which the child is taken into custody or in an adjacent county;

(2) the facility has been designated by the county juvenile board for the county in which the facility is located;

(3) the child is separated by sight and sound from adults detained in the same facility through architectural design or time-phasing;

(4) the child does not have any contact with management or direct-care staff that has contact with adults detained in the same facility on the same work shift;

(5) the county in which the child is taken into custody is not located in a metropolitan statistical area as designated by the United States Bureau of the Census; and

(6) each judge of the juvenile court and a majority of the members of the juvenile board of the county in which the child is taken into custody have personally inspected the facility at least annually and have certified in writing to the Texas Juvenile Probation Commission that the facility complies with the requirements of Subdivisions (3) and (4).

(m) The Texas Juvenile Probation Commission may deny, suspend, or revoke the registration of any facility required to register under Subsection (i) if the facility fails to:

(1) adhere to all applicable minimum standards for the facility; or

(2) timely correct any notice of noncompliance with minimum standards.

Amended by Acts 2011, 82nd Leg., ch. 1087 (S.B. 1209), § 1, eff. Sept. 1, 2011.

Comment

Currently, no juveniles in Texas are detained in jail except for very brief periods awaiting transport elsewhere. Detention occurs in over 60 regional juvenile detention facilities located throughout the state. A child may be detained in an approved facility located outside the county where the offense is believed to have been committed.

Subsection (b–1) authorizes a pre-adjudication secure detention facility operated only under control of a governmental unit of Texas.

Subsection (c) removes the requirement of the juvenile judge and juvenile board members to personally inspect all post-adjudication facilities and only requires annual inspection of all public or private pre-adjudication secure detention facilities located in their county.

Several amendments were passed in 2011 to protect children certified to stand trial as adults. In particular (f) now defines persons under 17 years of age but transferred to criminal court as a child for purposes of this section regarding detention.

Subsection (h) excludes probation violations from the authority to detain in the county jail. Of course, if a 17 year old on juvenile probation violates it by committing a new offense, he or she can be detained in the county jail for the new offense or in the juvenile detention facility for the probation violation.

Subsection (j) permits juveniles taken into custody in a county without a certified juvenile detention facility to be temporarily detained in an adult detention facility that complies with statutory requirements on sight and sound separation, that meets TJPC standards for temporary detention and that has been designated by the local juvenile board. Detention in such a facility is authorized only until the initial detention hearing is conducted. The maximum period of detention in such a facility would therefore be four nights. The purpose of the provision is to reduce travel to and from out-of-county detention facilities.

Subsection (m) authorizes TJPC to deny, suspend or revoke the registration of any facility listed under subsection (i) if it fails to adhere to all applicable standards.

Leading Case

In re M.C., 915 S.W.2d 118 (Tex. App.—San Antonio 1996, no writ) (certification of detention facility by juvenile board requires majority, not unanimous, action by board members)

Attorney General Opinions

Tex. Atty. Gen. Op. DM–439 (1997) (juvenile court's control over detention overrides contract between county and private provider)

Tex. Atty. Gen. Op. DM–38 (1991) (arrested person 18 or older cannot be detained in same compartment of detention facility as juvenile)

---

§ 51.125. Post–Adjudication Correctional Facilities

(a) A post-adjudication secure correctional facility for juvenile offenders may be operated only by:

(1) a governmental unit in this state as defined by Section 101.001, Civil Practice and Remedies Code; or

(2) a private entity under a contract with a governmental unit in this state.

(b) In each county, each judge of the juvenile court and a majority of the members of the juvenile board shall personally inspect all public or private juvenile post-adjudication secure correctional facilities that are not operated by the Texas Youth Commission and that are located in the county at least annually and shall certify in writing to the authorities responsible for operating and giving financial support to the facilities and to the Texas Juvenile Probation Commission that the facility or facilities are suitable or unsuitable for the confinement of children. In determining whether a facility is suitable or unsuitable for the confinement of children, the juvenile court judges and juvenile board members shall consider:

(1) current monitoring and inspection reports and any noncompliance citation reports issued by the Texas Juvenile Probation Commission, including the report provided under Subsection (c), and the status of any required corrective actions; and

(2) the other factors described under Sections 51.12(c)(2)–(7).

(c) The Texas Juvenile Probation Commission shall annually inspect each public or private juvenile post-adjudication secure correctional facility that is not operated by the Texas Youth Commission. The Texas Juvenile Probation Commission shall provide a report to each juvenile court judge presiding in the same county as an inspected facility indicating whether the facility is suitable or unsuitable for the confinement of children in accordance with minimum professional standards for the confinement of children in post-adjudication secure confinement promulgated by the Texas Juvenile Probation Commission or, at the election of the juvenile board of the county in which the facility is located, the current standards promulgated by the American Correctional Association.

(d) A governmental unit or private entity that operates or contracts for the operation of a juvenile post-adjudication secure correctional facility in this state under Subsection (a), except for a facility operated by or under contract with the Texas Youth Commission, shall:

(1) register the facility annually with the Texas Juvenile Probation Commission; and

(2) adhere to all applicable minimum standards for the facility.

(e) The Texas Juvenile Probation Commission may deny, suspend, or revoke the registration of any facility required to register under Subsection (d) if the facility fails to:

(1) adhere to all applicable minimum standards for the facility; or

(2) timely correct any notice of noncompliance with minimum standards.

Comment

This section provides for post-adjudication correctional facilities to be operated only by governmental units in Texas and requires juvenile judges and juvenile board members to personally inspect all facilities in their county annually. Furthermore, TJPC is authorized to act in the event the facility does not adhere to applicable standards.

§ 51.126. Nonsecure Correctional Facilities

(a) A nonsecure correctional facility for juvenile offenders may be operated only by:

(1) a governmental unit, as defined by Section 101.001, Civil Practice and Remedies Code; or

(2) a private entity under a contract with a governmental unit in this state.

(b) In each county, each judge of the juvenile court and a majority of the members of the juvenile board shall personally inspect, at least annually, all nonsecure correctional facilities that are located in the county and shall certify in writing to the authorities responsible for operating and giving financial support to the facilities and to the Texas Juvenile **Justice Department** ~~Probation Commission~~ that the facility or facilities are suitable or unsuitable for the confinement of children. In determining whether a facility is suitable or unsuitable for the confinement of children, the juvenile court judges and juvenile board members shall consider:

(1) current monitoring and inspection reports and any noncompliance citation reports issued by the Texas Juvenile **Justice Department** ~~Probation Commission~~, including the report provided under Subsection (c), and the status of any required corrective actions; and

(2) the other factors described under Sections 51.12(c)(2)–(7).

(c) The Texas Juvenile **Justice Department** ~~Probation Commission~~ shall annually inspect each nonsecure correctional facility. The Texas Juvenile **Justice Department** ~~Probation Commission~~ shall provide a report to each juvenile court judge presiding in the same county as an inspected facility indicating whether the facility is suitable or unsuitable for the confinement of children in accordance with minimum professional standards for the confinement of children in nonsecure confinement promulgated by the Texas Juvenile **Justice Department** ~~Probation Commission~~ or, at the election of the juvenile board of the county in which the facility is located, the current standards promulgated by the American Correctional Association.

(d) A governmental unit or private entity that operates or contracts for the operation of a juvenile nonsecure correctional facility in this state under Subsection (a), except for a facility operated by or under contract with the **Texas Juvenile Justice Department** ~~Texas Youth Commission~~, shall:

(1) register the facility annually with the Texas Juvenile **Justice Department** ~~Probation Commission~~; and

(2) adhere to all applicable minimum standards for the facility.

(e) The Texas Juvenile **Justice Department** ~~Probation Commission~~ may deny, suspend, or revoke the registration of any facility required to register under Subsection (d) if the facility fails to:

(1) adhere to all applicable minimum standards for the facility; or

(2) timely correct any notice of noncompliance with minimum standards.

(f) In this section, "Texas Juvenile Justice Department" means the Texas Juvenile Probation Commission. This subsection expires December 1, 2011.

Amended by Acts 2011, 82nd Leg., ch. 85 (S.B. 653), § 2.001, eff. Sept. 1, 2011.

Comment

Nonsecure facilities for juvenile offenders are to be operated only by a governmental unit. The facility must be annually inspected and, if not under the control of TYC or TJJD, then it must register with TJPC or TJJD. This is a continuation of the juvenile justice reform started in 2007.

§ 51.13. Effect of Adjudication or Disposition

(a) Except as provided by **Subsections (d) and (e)** ~~Subsection (d)~~, an order of adjudication or disposition in a proceeding under this title is not a conviction of crime. Except as provided by Chapter 841, Health and Safety Code, an order of adjudication or disposition does not impose any civil disability ordinarily resulting from a conviction or operate to disqualify the child in any civil service application or appointment.

(b) The adjudication or disposition of a child or evidence adduced in a hearing under this title may be used only in subsequent:

(1) proceedings under this title in which the child is a party;

(2) sentencing proceedings in criminal court against the child to the extent permitted by the Texas Code of Criminal Procedure, 1965; or

(3) civil commitment proceedings under Chapter 841, Health and Safety Code.

(c) A child may not be committed or transferred to a penal institution or other facility used primarily for the execution of sentences of persons convicted of crime, except:

(1) for temporary detention in a jail or lockup pending juvenile court hearing or disposition under conditions meeting the requirements of Section 51.12 ~~of this code~~;

(2) after transfer for prosecution in criminal court under Section 54.02**, unless the juvenile court orders the detention of the child in a certified juvenile detention facility under Section 54.02(h)** ~~of this code~~; or

(3) after transfer from the Texas **Juvenile Justice Department** ~~Youth Commission~~ under Section **245.151(c)** ~~61.084~~, Human Resources Code.

(d) An adjudication under Section 54.03 that a child engaged in conduct that occurred on or after January 1, 1996, and that constitutes a felony offense resulting in commitment to the Texas Youth Commission under Section 54.04(d)(2), (d)(3), or (m) or 54.05(f) is a final felony conviction only for the purposes of Sections 12.42(a), (b), (c)(1), and (e), Penal Code.

(e) A finding that a child engaged in conduct indicating a need for supervision as described by Section 51.03(b)(7) is a conviction only for the purposes of Sections 43.261(c) and (d), Penal Code.

Amended by Acts 2011, 82nd Leg., ch. 85 (S.B. 653), § 3.004, eff. Sept. 1, 2011; Acts 2011, 82nd Leg., ch. 1087 (S.B. 1209), § 2, eff. Sept. 1, 2011; Acts 2011, 82nd Leg., ch. 1322 (S.B. 407), § 17, eff. Sept. 1, 2011.

Comment

This section establishes that an adjudication in juvenile court is not a criminal conviction and imposes none of the legal disabilities of a criminal conviction. It also establishes the basic confidentiality rule for evidence and rulings of the juvenile court.

In 2011 subsection (c)(2) was amended to allow judges to order a child who has been certified for trial in criminal court to be detained in a certified juvenile detention facility in order to protect the child from the harsh conditions of adult jail.

Subsection (d) provides that a felony adjudication with a TYC or TJJD commitment constitutes a prior felony conviction under TEX. PENAL CODE ANN. § 12.42 should the respondent later be charged with a felony as an adult in criminal court. Only enhancement of punishment, not habitual offender treatment, is affected by this provision. A prior juvenile adjudication does not count as a felony conviction for mandatory life imprisonment upon second conviction of a sex crime under Section 12.42.

The legislature established a system of super intensive post-incarceration supervision for certain released inmates classified as "sexual predators." To be eligible for intensive supervision, a person must have two criminal convictions or juvenile adjudications for a sexually violent offense. To qualify, a juvenile adjudication for a sexually violent offense must have been under the determinate sentence act and must have led to a TYC or TJJD commitment. If after the first conviction or adjudication, the person commits a new sexually violent offense, is convicted for it and receives a prison sentence to TDCJ, he or she becomes eligible for consideration as a sexually violent predator upon release. The offenses that qualify as sexually violent offenses are indecency with a child by contact, sexual assault, aggravated sexual assault, aggravated kidnapping for a sexual purpose, burglary for a sexual purpose, or an attempt, conspiracy or solicitation to commit any of those offenses. Therefore, an adjudication for one of those offenses under the determinate sentence act resulting in a TYC or TJJD commitment can be the first step toward sexual predator status.

CLE/Other Legal Publication

That isn't fair judge: The costs of using prior juvenile delinquency adjudications in criminal court sentencing. Ellen Marrus, 40 HOUS. L. REV. 1323 (2004)

Leading Cases

Davis v. Alaska, 415 U.S. 308, 39 L.Ed.2d 347, 94 S.Ct. 1105 (1974) (defendant may cross-examine witness for bias and show he is on juvenile probation)

Irby v. State, 377 S.W.3d 138 (Tex. Crim. App. 2010) (neither Davis nor the confrontation clause require courts to permit the use of a prior juvenile record, in a non-Title 3 proceeding, for general impeachment of credibility.

Thompson v. State, 267 S.W.3d 514 (Tex. App.—Austin, 2008 pet. ref'd.) (prior juvenile felony adjudication does not prevent applying for probation in adult criminal court, but can be used to enhance adult sentence)

Ex parte Rodney Keith Cash, 178 S.W.3d 816 (Tex. Crim. App. 2005) (a juvenile felony adjudication is not a final felony conviction with respect to eligibility for probation in criminal district court)

Goodman v. State, 701 S.W.2d 850 (Tex. Crim. App. 1985) (juvenile adjudication admissible before jury in penalty phase of capital case)

Love v. State, 533 S.W.2d 6 (Tex. Crim. App. 1976) (may cross-examine character witness about juvenile record with "have you heard" questions)

Garner v. State, 957 S.W.2d 112 (Tex. App.—Amarillo 1997, no writ) (juvenile court packet admissible at penalty when limited to adjudications)

Zepeda v. State, 797 S.W.2d 258 (Tex. App.—Corpus Christi 1990, pet. ref'd) (juvenile proceedings may be used as deposition if witness becomes unavailable)

Cross References

TEX. R. EVID. 609(d). Juvenile Adjudication Not Admissible to Impeach in Civil or Criminal Proceedings.

TEX. CODE CRIM. PROC. ANN. art. 37.07. Admissibility of Juvenile Felony and Jailable Misdemeanor Adjudications in the Penalty Phase of Criminal Proceedings.

§ 51.14. Repealed by Acts 1995, 74th Leg., ch. 262, § 100(a), eff. Jan. 1, 1996

§ 51.15. Repealed by Acts 1995, 74th Leg., ch. 262, § 100(a), eff. Jan. 1, 1996

§ 51.151. Polygraph Examination

If a child is taken into custody under Section 52.01 of this code, a person may not administer a polygraph examination to the child without the consent of the child's attorney or the juvenile court unless the child is transferred to criminal court for prosecution under Section 54.02 of this code.

Leading Case

Romero v. State, 493 S.W.2d 206 (Tex. Crim. App. 1973) (polygraph results not admissible in criminal proceedings)

Attorney General Opinion

Tex. Atty. Gen. Op. JM–1141 (1990) (§ 51.151 does not apply to child witnesses not in custody under Title 3)

---

§ 51.16. Repealed by Acts 1995, 74th Leg., ch. 262, § 100(a), eff. Jan. 1, 1996; Acts 1997, 75th Leg., ch. 165, § 10.05(b), eff. Sept. 1, 1997

§ 51.17. Procedure and Evidence

(a) Except as provided by Section 56.01(b–1) and except for the burden of proof to be borne by the state in adjudicating a child to be delinquent or in need of supervision under Section 54.03(f) or otherwise when in conflict with a provision of this title, the Texas Rules of Civil Procedure govern proceedings under this title.

(b) Discovery in a proceeding under this title is governed by the Code of Criminal Procedure and by case decisions in criminal cases.

(c) Except as otherwise provided by this title, the Texas Rules of Evidence apply to criminal cases and Articles 33.03 and 37.07 and Chapter 38, Code of Criminal Procedure, apply in a judicial proceeding under this title.

(d) When on the motion for appointment of an interpreter by a party or on the motion of the juvenile court, in any proceeding under this title, the court determines that the child, the child's parent or guardian, or a witness does not understand and speak English, an interpreter must be sworn to interpret for the person as provided by Article 38.30, Code of Criminal Procedure.

(e) In any proceeding under this title, if a party notifies the court that the child, the child's parent or guardian, or a witness is deaf, the court shall appoint a qualified interpreter to interpret the proceedings in any language, including sign language, that the deaf person can understand, as provided by Article 38.31, Code of Criminal Procedure.

(f) Any requirement under this title that a document contain a person's signature, including the signature of a judge or a clerk of the court, is satisfied if the document contains the signature of the person as captured on an electronic device or as a digital signature. Article 2.26, Code of Criminal Procedure, applies in a proceeding held under this title.

(g) Articles 21.07, 26.07, 26.08, 26.09, and 26.10, Code of Criminal Procedure, relating to the name of an adult defendant in a criminal case, apply to a child in a proceeding held under this title.

(h) Articles 57.01 and 57.02, Code of Criminal Procedure, relating to the use of a pseudonym by a victim in a criminal case, apply in a proceeding held under this title.

(i) Except as provided by Section 56.03(f), the state is not required to pay any cost or fee otherwise imposed for court proceedings in either the trial or appellate courts.

Comment

Discovery rules are criminal, not civil. Thus, the primary sources of discovery law in juvenile cases are chapter 38 of the TEX. CODE CRIM. PROC. ANN. and the caselaw dealing with the prosecutor's obligations under due process of law to disclose exculpatory and mitigatory material to the defense, rather than the Rules of Civil Procedure.

If there is a difference between civil and criminal rules under the TEXAS RULES OF EVIDENCE, the criminal version controls. Articles 33.03 (relating to the presence of the defendant) and 37.07 (relating to verdicts in criminal cases) of the Code of Criminal Procedure apply to juvenile proceedings. Importantly, this section allows for the admission of extraneous acts.

With these exceptions, the Rules of Civil Procedure govern procedure in the absence of a specific provision in the Family Code.

Subsections (d) and (e) require the appointment of language interpreters and interpreters for the deaf under the same circumstances as in criminal cases. Subsection (f) permits digital signatures to be employed to the same extent they can be used in criminal cases.

Subsection (g) allows prosecutors to allege either name if a child is known by more than one name. Further, if a child's name is incorrect, the child or his lawyer can provide the correct name to the court and it will be noted on the petition.

Subsection (h) allows for victims of offenses listed under Chapter 62 of the Code of Criminal Procedure (offenses that require sex offender registration) may use a pseudonym in the manner allowed in criminal cases.

Subsection (i) limits the court costs to be paid by the state to only those provided for in section 56.03(f).

The legislature clarified that with regards to a motion for new trial, the criminal rule, T.R.A.P. 21 applies.

§ 51.18. Election Between Juvenile Court and Alternate Juvenile Court

(a) This section applies only to a child who has a right to a trial before a juvenile court the judge of which is not an attorney licensed in this state.

(b) On any matter that may lead to an order appealable under Section 56.01 of this code, a child may be tried before either the juvenile court or the alternate juvenile court.

(c) The child may elect to be tried before the alternate juvenile court only if the child files a written notice with that court not later than 10 days before the date of the trial. After the notice is filed, the child may be tried only in the alternate juvenile court. If the child does not file a notice as provided by this subsection, the child may be tried only in the juvenile court.

(d) If the child is tried before the juvenile court, the child is not entitled to a trial de novo before the alternate juvenile court.

(e) The child may appeal any order of the juvenile court or alternate juvenile court only as provided by Section 56.01 of this code.

§ 51.19. Limitation Periods

(a) The limitation periods and the procedures for applying the limitation periods under Chapter 12, Code of Criminal Procedure, and other statutory law apply to proceedings under this title.

(b) For purposes of computing a limitation period, a petition filed in juvenile court for a transfer or an adjudication hearing is equivalent to an indictment or information and is treated as presented when the petition is filed in the proper court.

(c) The limitation period is two years for an offense or conduct that is not given a specific limitation period under Chapter 12, Code of Criminal Procedure, or other statutory law.

Comment

This section specifies that criminal statutes of limitation, as provided by Chapter 12 of the TEX. CODE CRIM. PROC. ANN. or elsewhere in connection with the statutory definition of the offense, apply to juvenile proceedings despite their legal character as civil proceedings. The residuary limitations period is 2 years.

---

§ 51.20. Physical or Mental Examination

(a) At any stage of the proceedings under this title, the juvenile court may order a child who is referred to the juvenile court or who is alleged by a petition or found to have engaged in delinquent conduct or conduct indicating a need for supervision to be examined by a disinterested expert, including a physician, psychiatrist, or psychologist, qualified by education and clinical training in mental health or mental retardation and experienced in forensic evaluation, to determine whether the child has a mental illness as defined by Section 571.003, Health and Safety Code, or is a person with mental retardation as defined by Section 591.003, Health and Safety Code. If the examination is to include a determination of the child's fitness to proceed, an expert may be appointed to conduct the examination only if the expert is qualified under Subchapter B, Chapter 46B, Code of Criminal Procedure, to examine a defendant in a criminal case, and the examination and the report resulting from an examination under this subsection must comply with the requirements under Subchapter B, Chapter 46B, Code of Criminal Procedure, for the examination and resulting report of a defendant in a criminal case.

(b) If, after conducting an examination of a child ordered under Subsection (a) and reviewing any other relevant information, there is reason to believe that the child has a mental illness or mental retardation, the probation department shall refer the child to the local mental health or mental retardation authority for evaluation and services, unless the prosecuting attorney has filed a petition under Section 53.04.

(c) If, while a child is under deferred prosecution supervision or court-ordered probation, a qualified professional determines that the child has a mental illness or mental retardation and the child is not currently receiving treatment services for the mental illness or mental retardation, the probation department shall refer the child to the local mental health or mental retardation authority for evaluation and services.

(d) A probation department shall report each referral of a child to a local mental health or mental retardation authority made under Subsection (b) or (c) to the Texas Juvenile Probation Commission in a format specified by the commission.

(e) At any stage of the proceedings under this title, the juvenile court may order a child who has been referred to the juvenile court or who is alleged by the petition or found to have engaged in delinquent conduct or conduct indicating a need for supervision to be subjected to a physical examination by a licensed physician.

Comment

This section authorizes a judge to order an appropriate physical or mental examination of any child who is in the juvenile system. The section is placed here because it is of general applicability and is not limited to Chapter 55 proceedings. Thus, for example, this section would authorize a judge to require a physical examination prior to a child being admitted to a boot camp. Subsection (a) also makes it clear that the authority to order an examination is not dependent upon whether a petition has been filed.

Subsection (a) establishes standards for mental health or retardation examiners and for fitness to stand trial examinations.

Subsection (b) addresses the situation in which a child referred to the juvenile court may be mentally ill or retarded. It places on the probation department the responsibility to refer such a child for services if the case is in a pre-petition status. This provision furthers the overall Family Code policy to facilitate treatment for mental illness or mental retardation of children in the juvenile justice system.

Subsection (e) makes explicit the authority of the juvenile court to order physical examinations as well as mental examinations.

§ 51.21. Mental Health Screening and Referral

(a) A probation department that administers the mental health screening instrument or clinical assessment required by Section **221.003** ~~141.042(e)~~, Human Resources Code, shall refer the child to the local mental health authority for assessment and evaluation if:

(1) the child's scores on the screening instrument or clinical assessment indicate a need for further mental health assessment and evaluation; and

(2) the department and child do not have access to an internal, contract, or private mental health professional.

(b) A probation department shall report each referral of a child to a local mental health authority made under Subsection (a) to the Texas Juvenile Probation Commission in a format specified by the commission.

Amended by Acts 2011, 82nd Leg., ch. 85 (S.B. 653), § 3.005, eff. Sept. 1, 2011.

CHAPTER 52. PROCEEDINGS BEFORE AND INCLUDING REFERRAL TO JUVENILE COURT

Introductory Comment

Chapter 52 deals with police work with juveniles, including the circumstances under which police may take juveniles into custody and what may be done with juveniles taken into custody.

§ 52.01. Taking into Custody; Issuance of Warning Notice

(a) A child may be taken into custody:

(1) pursuant to an order of the juvenile court under the provisions of this subtitle;

(2) pursuant to the laws of arrest;

(3) by a law-enforcement officer, including a school district peace officer commissioned under Section 37.081, Education Code, if there is probable cause to believe that the child has engaged in:

(A) conduct that violates a penal law of this state or a penal ordinance of any political subdivision of this state;

(B) delinquent conduct or conduct indicating a need for supervision; or

(C) conduct that violates a condition of probation imposed by the juvenile court;

(4) by a probation officer if there is probable cause to believe that the child has violated a condition of probation imposed by the juvenile court;

(5) pursuant to a directive to apprehend issued as provided by Section 52.015; or

(6) by a probation officer if there is probable cause to believe that the child has violated a condition of release imposed by the juvenile court or referee under Section 54.01.

(b) The taking of a child into custody is not an arrest except for the purpose of determining the validity of taking him into custody or the validity of a search under the laws and constitution of this state or of the United States.

(c) A law-enforcement officer authorized to take a child into custody under Subdivisions (2) and (3) of Subsection (a) of this section may issue a warning notice to the child in lieu of taking the child into custody if:

(1) guidelines for warning disposition have been issued by the law-enforcement agency in which the officer works;

(2) the guidelines have been approved by the juvenile board of the county in which the disposition is made;

(3) the disposition is authorized by the guidelines;

(4) the warning notice identifies the child and describes the child's alleged conduct;

(5) a copy of the warning notice is sent to the child's parent, guardian, or custodian as soon as practicable after disposition; and

(6) a copy of the warning notice is filed with the law-enforcement agency and the office or official designated by the juvenile board.

(d) A warning notice filed with the office or official designated by the juvenile board may be used as the basis of further action if necessary.

(e) A law-enforcement officer who has probable cause to believe that a child is in violation of the compulsory school attendance law under Section 25.085, Education Code, may take the child into custody for the purpose of returning the child to the school campus of the child to ensure the child's compliance with compulsory school attendance requirements.

Comment

Subsection (a) permits a juvenile to be taken into custody under seven circumstances: (1) when the juvenile court has endorsed a custody order on the summons that accompanies a juvenile petition; (2) pursuant to the laws of arrest for adults; (3) if there is probable cause to believe the child engaged in delinquent conduct or conduct indicating a need for supervision; (4) by a probation officer if there is probable cause to believe that probation has been violated; (5) by a probation officer if there is probable cause to believe a child violated a condition of release from detention; (6) pursuant to a juvenile court's directive to apprehend (juvenile arrest warrant); or (7) a law enforcement officer may take a child into custody without a warrant for a violation of judicial probation.

Subsections (c) and (d) permit law enforcement officers to issue warning notices (like traffic citations) in lieu of taking the child into custody.

Leading Cases

Cornealius v. State, 900 S.W.2d 731 (Tex. Crim. App. 1995) (juvenile arrest without warrant valid under Family Code; warrant not required for arrest on front porch)

Coronado v. State, 835 S.W.2d 636 (Tex. Crim. App. 1992) (school search unconstitutional)

Lanes v. State, 767 S.W.2d 789 (Tex. Crim. App. 1989) (juvenile arrest requires probable cause)

Vasquez v. State, 739 S.W.2d 37 (Tex. Crim. App. 1987), *reh'g denied*, 816 S.W.2d 750 (Tex. Crim. App. 1991) (arrest of juvenile governed by Family Code, not Code of Criminal Procedure)

Russell v. State, 74 S.W.3d 887 (Tex. App.—Waco 2002, pet. ref'd) (search of pocket of baggy trousers worn on school campus lawful without probable cause or a warrant)

In re D.G., 96 S.W.3d 465 (Tex. App.—Austin 2002, no pet.) (talking to juvenile was voluntary encounter, not stop, and search that uncovered crack was consensual)

In re J.D., 68 S.W.3d 775 (Tex. App.—San Antonio 2001, rev. denied) (warrantless search of juvenile's home justified as an emergency)

Wilcher v. State, 876 S.W.2d 466 (Tex. App.—El Paso 1994, no writ) (school search based on weapon report valid)

Attorney General Opinions

Tex. Atty. Gen. Op. DM–294 (1994) (scope of school notification requirements)

Tex. Atty. Gen. Op. LO–94–058 (1994) (authority to arrest for truancy)

Cross References

Tex. Code Crim. Proc. Ann. Art. 2.12. Law governing who is a peace officer.

Tex. Code Crim. Proc. Ann. art. 14.01 *et seq.* and Tex. Code Crim. Proc. Ann. art. 18.16, Laws governing arrests of adults.

Tex. Educ. Code § 37.081. School district peace officers.

§ 52.015. Directive to Apprehend

(a) On the request of a law-enforcement or probation officer, a juvenile court may issue a directive to apprehend a child if the court finds there is probable cause to take the child into custody under the provisions of this title.

(b) On the issuance of a directive to apprehend, any law-enforcement or probation officer shall take the child into custody.

(c) An order under this section is not subject to appeal.

§ 52.0151. Bench Warrant; Attachment of Witness in Custody

(a) If a witness is in a placement in the custody of the Texas Youth Commission, a juvenile secure detention facility, or a juvenile secure correctional facility, the court may issue a bench warrant or direct that an attachment issue to require a peace officer or probation officer to secure custody of the person at the placement and produce the person in court. Once the person is no longer needed as a witness, the court shall order the peace officer or probation officer to return the person to the placement from which the person was released.

(b) The court may order that the person who is the witness be detained in a certified juvenile detention facility if the person is younger than 17 years of age. If the person is at least 17 years of age, the court may order that the person be detained without bond in an appropriate county facility for the detention of adults accused of criminal offenses.

Comment

This provision allows for juveniles who are in the custody of the Texas Youth Commission or Texas Juvenile Justice Department to be transported by law enforcement to various courts in order to appear as a witness in a civil or criminal proceeding.

---

§ 52.02. Release or Delivery to Court

(a) Except as provided by Subsection (c), a person taking a child into custody, without unnecessary delay and without first taking the child to any place other than a juvenile processing office designated under Section 52.025, shall do one of the following:

(1) release the child to a parent, guardian, custodian of the child, or other responsible adult upon that person's promise to bring the child before the juvenile court as requested by the court;

(2) bring the child before the office or official designated by the juvenile board if there is probable cause to believe that the child engaged in delinquent conduct, conduct indicating a need for supervision, or conduct that violates a condition of probation imposed by the juvenile court;

(3) bring the child to a detention facility designated by the juvenile board;

(4) bring the child to a secure detention facility as provided by Section 51.12(j);

(5) bring the child to a medical facility if the child is believed to suffer from a serious physical condition or illness that requires prompt treatment;

(6) dispose of the case under Section 52.03; or

(7) if school is in session and the child is a student, bring the child to the school campus to which the child is assigned if the principal, the principal's designee, or a peace officer assigned to the campus agrees to assume responsibility for the child for the remainder of the school day.

(b) A person taking a child into custody shall promptly give notice of the person's action and a statement of the reason for taking the child into custody, to:

(1) the child's parent, guardian, or custodian; and

(2) the office or official designated by the juvenile board.

(c) A person who takes a child into custody and who has reasonable grounds to believe that the child has been operating a motor vehicle in a public place while having any detectable amount of alcohol in the child's system may, before complying with Subsection (a):

(1) take the child to a place to obtain a specimen of the child's breath or blood as provided by Chapter 724, Transportation Code; and

(2) perform intoxilyzer processing and videotaping of the child in an adult processing office of a law enforcement agency.

(d) Notwithstanding Section 51.09(a), a child taken into custody as provided by Subsection (c) may submit to the taking of a breath specimen or refuse to submit to the taking of a breath specimen without the concurrence of an attorney, but only if the request made of the child to give the specimen and the child's response to that request is videotaped. A videotape made under this subsection must be maintained until the disposition of any proceeding against the child relating to the arrest is final and be made available to an attorney representing the child during that period.

Comment

Subsection (a) requires a law enforcement officer who has taken a child into custody immediately to dispose of the case in one of six different ways: (1) take the child to the juvenile processing office designated by the juvenile board, (2) release the child to a parent or other responsible adult, (3) bring the child to the office or official designated by the juvenile board, (4) bring the child to the designated detention facility, (5) bring the child to a medical facility for treatment of physical condition or illness, or (6) dispose of the case without referral to the juvenile court as authorized by § 52.03.

Subsection (a) authorizes a peace officer to bring a juvenile in custody back to the school campus if the school officials agree to assume responsibility for the child for the remainder of the day. This amendment prevents children from having to go to detention for a minor offense when the parent or guardian cannot be located to take the child.

Subsection (b) requires notice to the child's parent and to the office designated by the juvenile board that the child has been taken into custody.

Subsections (c) and (d) authorize bringing a child who has been taken into custody for driving under the influence of alcohol to an adult processing facility but only for the purpose of taking a blood sample, administering an intoxilyzer test or being videotaped. The child is permitted to waive or assert his or her rights regarding taking an intoxilyzer without the concurrence of an attorney, but the offering of the intoxilyzer and the child's response must be videotaped.

Leading Cases

Causal connection

Martinez v. State, 337 S.W.3d 446 (Tex. App.—Eastland 2011, no pet.) (failure to notify father without further connection to the statement of child will not warrant suppression of the statement)

Pham v. State, 175 S.W.3d 767 (Tex. Crim. App. 2005) (juvenile has the initial burden to produce evidence of a causal connection between the statutory violation and any confession, state may attempt to disprove connection or demonstrate attenuation of the taint)

Comer v. State, 776 S.W.2d 191 (Tex. Crim. App. 1989) (taking child to Justice of the Peace, who had not been designated, made confession inadmissible; consent of juvenile court to interrogation required)

Unnecessary delay

Martinez v. State, 337 S.W.3d 446 (Tex. App.—Eastland 2011, no pet.) (unnecessary delay is not violated because child is not promptly taken to the judge if the child is taken to one of the designated juvenile places, such as a JPO)

Contreras v. State, 67 S.W.3d 181 (Tex. Crim. App. 2001) (50 minute delay to secure murder scene not unnecessary)

Roquemore v. State, 60 S.W.3d 862 (Tex. Crim. App. 2001) (detour to recover stolen property on way to processing office violates Family Code)

Parental notification

Vann v. State, 93 S.W.3d 1182 (Tex. App.—Houston [14th Dist.] 2002, pet. ref'd) (notification to child's adult cousin with whom he sometimes resided was proper as a custodian under the meaning of the code)

In re J.A.B., 281 S.W.3d 62 (Tex. App.—El Paso 2008, no pet.)(forty minute delay in notifying mother not unreasonable in light of time required to process in juvenile system)

Vann v. State, 93 S.W.3d 182 (Tex. App.—Houston [14th Dist.] 2002, pet. ref'd) (arrest notice can be given to adult cousin as custodian; two and one-half hour delay OK)

Hampton v. State, 86 S.W.3d 603 (Tex. Crim. App. 2002) (requiring parental notice of reason for taking into custody doesn't require notice of interrogation purpose)

State v. Simpson, 105 S.W.3d 238 (Tex. App.—Tyler, 2003, no pet.) (delay in notifying parents of arrest invalidated confession under causal connection rule of *Gonzales*)

Ray v. State, 176 S.W.3d 544 (Tex. App.—Houston [1st Dist.] 2004, pet. ref'd) (parental notification eight and one-half hours after taking into custody prompt when prior efforts failed)

In re E.M.R., 55 S.W.3d 712 (Tex. App.—Corpus Christi 2001, no pet.) (parental notification requirement doesn't apply to juvenile questioned when not in custody)

Marsh v. State, 140 S.W.3d 901 (Tex. App.—Houston [14th Dist.] 2004, pet. ref'd) (parental notification requirement still satisfied even when parents given wrong address where juvenile is detained)

---

§ 52.025. Designation of Juvenile Processing Office

(a) The juvenile board may designate an office or a room, which may be located in a police facility or sheriff's offices, as the juvenile processing office for the temporary detention of a child taken into custody under Section 52.01. The office may not be a cell or holding facility used for detentions other than detentions under this section. The juvenile board by written order may prescribe the conditions of the designation and limit the activities that may occur in the office during the temporary detention.

(b) A child may be detained in a juvenile processing office only for:

(1) the return of the child to the custody of a person under Section 52.02(a)(1);

(2) the completion of essential forms and records required by the juvenile court or this title;

(3) the photographing and fingerprinting of the child if otherwise authorized at the time of temporary detention by this title;

(4) the issuance of warnings to the child as required or permitted by this title; or

(5) the receipt of a statement by the child under Section 51.095(a)(1), (2), (3), or (5).

(c) A child may not be left unattended in a juvenile processing office and is entitled to be accompanied by the child's parent, guardian, or other custodian or by the child's attorney.

(d) A child may not be detained in a juvenile processing office for longer than six hours.

Comment

A statement of a child taken in a juvenile processing office designated by a juvenile board will not be excluded from evidence because of a § 52.02 violation. The child can be detained in such an office only for a maximum period of six hours, reflecting federal limitations on the time a juvenile can be detained in a secure adult detention facility.

Leading Cases

Cortez v. State, 240 S.W.3d 372 (Tex. App.—Austin 2007, no pet.)(No reasonable expectation of privacy existed in phone conversation made to mother while in JPO)

In re U.G., 128 S.W.3d 797 (Tex. App.—Corpus Christi 2004, pet. ref'd) (statute violated when juvenile was not taken to JPO; confession admission was harmless error)

Anthony v. State, 954 S.W.2d 132 (Tex. App.—San Antonio 1997, no writ) (order designating entire police station not specific enough to be valid)

Wilson v. State, 948 S.W.2d 21 (Tex. App.—Eastland 1997, pet. ref'd) (permission of probation department for interrogation in processing office not required)

In re R.R., 931 S.W.2d 11 (Tex. App.—Corpus Christi 1996, no writ) (confession excluded because police did not use juvenile processing office)

Attorney General Opinion

Tex. Atty. Gen. Op. LO–93–38 (1993) (juvenile court may designate multiple juvenile processing offices in a county)

§ 52.026. Responsibility for Transporting Juvenile Offenders

(a) It shall be the duty of the law enforcement officer who has taken a child into custody to transport the child to the appropriate detention facility or to the school campus to which the child is assigned as provided by Section 52.02(a)(7) if the child is not released to the parent, guardian, or custodian of the child.

(b) If the juvenile detention facility is located outside the county in which the child is taken into custody, it shall be the duty of the law enforcement officer who has taken the child into custody or, if authorized by the commissioners court of the county, the sheriff of that county to transport the child to the appropriate juvenile detention facility unless the child is:

(1) detained in a secure detention facility under Section 51.12(j); or

(2) released to the parent, guardian, or custodian of the child.

(c) On adoption of an order by the juvenile board and approval of the juvenile board's order by record vote of the commissioners court, it shall be the duty of the sheriff of the county in which the child is taken into custody to transport the child to and from all scheduled juvenile court proceedings and appearances and other activities ordered by the juvenile court.

Comment

This section places responsibility for transporting juveniles primarily in the hands of law-enforcement officers. It abrogates Tex. Atty. Gen. Op. DM–87 (1992) that opined law enforcement could not be required to provide such transportation service to the juvenile court. Subsection (b) places primary responsibility on the law enforcement officer who took the child into custody to transport the child to an out-of-county juvenile detention facility.

Attorney General Opinion

Tex. Atty. Gen. Op. LO–94–065 (1994) (sheriff is required to transport juveniles only upon juvenile court order and commissioner's court approval)

§ 52.027. Repealed.

§ 52.028. Repealed.

§ 52.03. Disposition Without Referral to Court

(a) A law-enforcement officer authorized by this title to take a child into custody may dispose of the case of a child taken into custody without referral to juvenile court, if:

(1) guidelines for such disposition have been adopted by the juvenile board of the county in which the disposition is made as required by Section 52.032;

(2) the disposition is authorized by the guidelines; and

(3) the officer makes a written report of the officer's disposition to the law-enforcement agency, identifying the child and specifying the grounds for believing that the taking into custody was authorized.

(b) No disposition authorized by this section may involve:

(1) keeping the child in law-enforcement custody; or

(2) requiring periodic reporting of the child to a law-enforcement officer, law-enforcement agency, or other agency.

(c) A disposition authorized by this section may involve:

(1) referral of the child to an agency other than the juvenile court;

(2) a brief conference with the child and his parent, guardian, or custodian; or

(3) referral of the child and the child's parent, guardian, or custodian for services under Section 264.302.

(d) Statistics indicating the number and kind of dispositions made by a law-enforcement agency under the authority of this section shall be reported at least annually to the office or official designated by the juvenile board, as ordered by the board.

Comment

About one-quarter of all juveniles taken into custody by police are not referred to the juvenile courts. These cases, usually very minor in seriousness, are disposed of under this section or the next.

Cross Reference

TX FCA FAMILY § 264.302. Early Youth Intervention Services of Texas Department of Protective and Regulatory Services, *infra*.

---

§ 52.031. First Offender Program

(a) A juvenile board may establish a first offender program under this section for the referral and disposition of children taken into custody for:

(1) conduct indicating a need for supervision; or

(2) delinquent conduct other than conduct that constitutes:

(A) a felony of the first, second, or third degree, an aggravated controlled substance felony, or a capital felony; or

(B) a state jail felony or misdemeanor involving violence to a person or the use or possession of a firearm, illegal knife, or club, as those terms are defined by Section 46.01, Penal Code, or a prohibited weapon, as described by Section 46.05, Penal Code.

(b) Each juvenile board in the county in which a first offender program is established shall designate one or more law enforcement officers and agencies, which may be law enforcement agencies, to process a child under the first offender program.

(c) The disposition of a child under the first offender program may not take place until guidelines for the disposition have been adopted by the juvenile board of the county in which the disposition is made as required by Section 52.032.

(d) A law enforcement officer taking a child into custody may refer the child to the law enforcement officer or agency designated under Subsection (b) for disposition under the first offender program and not refer the child to juvenile court only if:

(1) the child has not previously been adjudicated as having engaged in delinquent conduct;

(2) the referral complies with guidelines for disposition under Subsection (c); and

(3) the officer reports in writing the referral to the agency, identifying the child and specifying the grounds for taking the child into custody.

(e) A child referred for disposition under the first offender program may not be detained in law enforcement custody.

(f) The parent, guardian, or other custodian of the child must receive notice that the child has been referred for disposition under the first offender program. The notice must:

(1) state the grounds for taking the child into custody;

(2) identify the law enforcement officer or agency to which the child was referred;

(3) briefly describe the nature of the program; and

(4) state that the child's failure to complete the program will result in the child being referred to the juvenile court.

(g) The child and the parent, guardian, or other custodian of the child must consent to participation by the child in the first offender program.

(h) Disposition under a first offender program may include:

(1) voluntary restitution by the child or the parent, guardian, or other custodian of the child to the victim of the conduct of the child;

(2) voluntary community service restitution by the child;

(3) educational, vocational training, counseling, or other rehabilitative services; and

(4) periodic reporting by the child to the law enforcement officer or agency to which the child has been referred.

(i) The case of a child who successfully completes the first offender program is closed and may not be referred to juvenile court, unless the child is taken into custody under circumstances described by Subsection (j)(3).

(j) The case of a child referred for disposition under the first offender program shall be referred to juvenile court if:

(1) the child fails to complete the program;

(2) the child or the parent, guardian, or other custodian of the child terminates the child's participation in the program before the child completes it; or

(3) the child completes the program but is taken into custody under Section 52.01 before the 90th day after the date the child completes the program for conduct other than the conduct for which the child was referred to the first offender program.

(k) A statement made by a child to a person giving advice or supervision or participating in the first offender program may not be used against the child in any proceeding under this title or any criminal proceeding.

(*l*) The law enforcement agency must report to the juvenile board in December of each year the following:

(1) the last known address of the child, including the census tract;

(2) the gender and ethnicity of the child referred to the program; and

(3) the offense committed by the child.

Comment

The first offender program described by this section is a particular version of the more general program authorized by § 52.03.

§ 52.032. Informal Disposition Guidelines

The juvenile board of each county, in cooperation with each law enforcement agency in the county, shall adopt guidelines for the disposition of a child under Section 52.03 or 52.031. The guidelines adopted under this section shall not be considered mandatory.

Comment

This section requires juvenile boards to promulgate non-binding guidelines for informal disposition or first offender programs. The purpose of the section is to encourage more law enforcement agencies to use such programs.

§ 52.04. Referral to Juvenile Court; Notice to Parents

(a) The following shall accompany referral of a child or a child's case to the office or official designated by the juvenile board or be provided as quickly as possible after referral:

(1) all information in the possession of the person or agency making the referral pertaining to the identity of the child and the child's address, the name and address of the child's parent, guardian, or custodian, the names and addresses of any witnesses, and the child's present whereabouts;

(2) a complete statement of the circumstances of the alleged delinquent conduct or conduct indicating a need for supervision;

(3) when applicable, a complete statement of the circumstances of taking the child into custody; and

(4) when referral is by an officer of a law-enforcement agency, a complete statement of all prior contacts with the child by officers of that law-enforcement agency.

(b) The office or official designated by the juvenile board may refer the case to a law-enforcement agency for the purpose of conducting an investigation to obtain necessary information.

(c) If the office of the prosecuting attorney is designated by the juvenile court to conduct the preliminary investigation under Section 53.01, the referring entity shall first transfer the child's case to the juvenile probation department for statistical reporting purposes only. On the creation of a statistical record or file for the case, the probation department shall within three business days forward the case to the prosecuting attorney for review under Section 53.01.

(d) On referral of the case of a child who has not been taken into custody to the office or official designated by the juvenile board, the office or official designated by the juvenile board shall promptly give notice of the referral and a statement of the reason for the referral to the child's parent, guardian, or custodian.

Comment

Subsection (a) specifies the information that must accompany the referral of a case to the juvenile court. Subsection (b) permits court intake to return a case to law enforcement for further investigation, which may include interrogation of the juvenile under specified procedures.

Subsection (c) requires that all referrals be made to the juvenile probation department for statistics-gathering purposes even if the prosecutor exercises the intake function in the county.

Subsection (d) requires that intake notify parents when a child has been referred to the court without being in custody.

§ 52.041. Referral of Child to Juvenile Court After Expulsion

(a) A school district that expels a child shall refer the child to juvenile court in the county in which the child resides.

(b) The board of the school district or a person designated by the board shall deliver a copy of the order expelling the student and any other information required by Section 52.04 on or before the second working day after the date of the expulsion hearing to the authorized officer of the juvenile court.

(c) Within five working days of receipt of an expulsion notice under this section by the office or official designated by the juvenile board, a preliminary investigation and determination shall be conducted as required by Section 53.01.

(d) The office or official designated by the juvenile board shall within two working days notify the school district that expelled the child if:

(1) a determination was made under Section 53.01 that the person referred to juvenile court was not a child within the meaning of this title;

(2) a determination was made that no probable cause existed to believe the child engaged in delinquent conduct or conduct indicating a need for supervision;

(3) no deferred prosecution or formal court proceedings have been or will be initiated involving the child;

(4) the court or jury finds that the child did not engage in delinquent conduct or conduct indicating a need for supervision and the case has been dismissed with prejudice; or

(5) the child was adjudicated but no disposition was or will be ordered by the court.

(e) In any county where a juvenile justice alternative education program is operated, no student shall be expelled without written notification by the board of the school district or its designated agent to the juvenile board's designated representative. The notification shall be made not later than two business days following the board's determination that the student is to be expelled. Failure to timely notify the designated representative of the juvenile board shall result in the child's duty to continue attending the school district's educational program, which shall be provided to that child until such time as the notification to the juvenile board's designated representative is properly made.

Comment

This section enacts the principle that each child expelled from school must be referred to the juvenile court to determine whether juvenile court action is needed. Education Code § 37.010 contains a similar provision.

Subsection (c) requires the juvenile court to complete its investigation of the case within five working days of receiving the referral and expulsion notice. Subsection (d) requires the juvenile court to notify the school district within two working days if the case on which the expulsion was based terminated without an adjudication and disposition. Subsection (e) provides that in a county with a juvenile justice alternative education program an expulsion is not legally effective until the juvenile system is notified of the expulsion.

CHAPTER 53. PROCEEDINGS PRIOR TO JUDICIAL PROCEEDINGS

Introductory Comment

Chapter 53 deals with that phase of the juvenile system beginning with referral to the court and ending with judicial proceedings. The scope of the determinate sentence act is in this chapter, as are the requirements of the petition and summons.

---

§ 53.01. Preliminary Investigation and Determinations; Notice to Parents

(a) On referral of a person believed to be a child or on referral of the person's case to the office or official designated by the juvenile board, the intake officer, probation officer, or other person authorized by the board shall conduct a preliminary investigation to determine whether:

(1) the person referred to juvenile court is a child within the meaning of this title; and

(2) there is probable cause to believe the person:

(A) engaged in delinquent conduct or conduct indicating a need for supervision; or

(B) is a nonoffender who has been taken into custody and is being held solely for deportation out of the United States.

(b) If it is determined that the person is not a child or there is no probable cause, the person shall immediately be released.

(c) When custody of a child is given to the office or official designated by the juvenile board, the intake officer, probation officer, or other person authorized by the board shall promptly give notice of the whereabouts of the child and a statement of the reason the child was taken into custody to the child's parent, guardian, or custodian unless the notice given under Section 52.02(b) provided fair notice of the child's present whereabouts.

(d) Unless the juvenile board approves a written procedure proposed by the office of prosecuting attorney and chief juvenile probation officer which provides otherwise, if it is determined that the person is a child and, regardless of a finding of probable cause, or a lack thereof, there is an allegation that the child engaged in delinquent conduct of the grade of felony, or conduct constituting a misdemeanor offense involving violence to a person or the use or possession of a firearm, illegal knife, or club, as those terms are defined by Section 46.01, Penal Code, or prohibited weapon, as described by Section 46.05, Penal Code, the case shall be promptly forwarded to the office of the prosecuting attorney, accompanied by:

(1) all documents that accompanied the current referral; and

(2) a summary of all prior referrals of the child to the juvenile court, juvenile probation department, or a detention facility.

(e) If a juvenile board adopts an alternative referral plan under Subsection (d), the board shall register the plan with the Texas Juvenile Probation Commission.

(f) A juvenile board may not adopt an alternate referral plan that does not require the forwarding of a child's case to the prosecuting attorney as provided by Subsection (d) if probable cause exists to believe that the child engaged in delinquent conduct that violates Section 19.03, Penal Code (capital murder), or Section 19.02, Penal Code (murder).

Comment

This is the "gatekeeping" requirement. A case referred to the juvenile court must be subjected to an intake inquiry. There, the intake worker must determine that the person referred is a child as defined in Title 3 and that there is probable cause to believe he or she committed delinquent conduct or conduct indicating a need for supervision. Unless these findings are made, the child must be immediately released from custody and all proceedings terminated.

Unless a local agreement provides otherwise, if the referral is for a felony, an offense involving violence, or a weapon offense, the case must be referred with proper documentation to the prosecutor for a decision whether to file a petition or to handle the matter nonjudicially. Referral to the prosecutor is required even if the intake officer has made a finding of no probable case. Cases that fall outside the scope of mandatory prosecutorial referral may continue to be handled nonjudicially by intake.

Subsection (a) is intended to make unlawful the confinement of alien juveniles for the sole purpose of facilitating their deportation. It should be read in conjunction with Section 54.011(f).

---

§ 53.012. Review by Prosecutor

(a) The prosecuting attorney shall promptly review the circumstances and allegations of a referral made under Section 53.01 for legal sufficiency and the desirability of prosecution and may file a petition without regard to whether probable cause was found under Section 53.01.

(b) If the prosecuting attorney does not file a petition requesting the adjudication of the child referred to the prosecuting attorney, the prosecuting attorney shall:

(1) terminate all proceedings, if the reason is for lack of probable cause; or

(2) return the referral to the juvenile probation department for further proceedings.

(c) The juvenile probation department shall promptly refer a child who has been returned to the department under Subsection (b)(2) and who fails or refuses to participate in a program of the department to the prosecuting attorney for review of the child's case and determination of whether to file a petition.

Comment

The decision whether to file a petition rests exclusively with the prosecutor. If the prosecutor declines prosecution, the case is to be returned to probation for nonjudicial handling, unless the reason for declining to prosecute is lack of probable cause as determined by the prosecutor.

---

§ 53.013. Progressive Sanctions Program

Each juvenile board may adopt a progressive sanctions program using the model for progressive sanctions in Chapter 59.

Comment

Chapter 59 establishes a set of progressive guidelines for the disposition of juvenile cases. Departure from the guidelines is permitted upon documentation as to the reason for the deviation.

Local authorities are relieved from the burdens of filing a deviation report because normal case documentation provides state officials with access to the same information. See Chapter 59 for more of this set of amendments.

---

§ 53.02. Release from Detention

(a) If a child is brought before the court or delivered to a detention facility as authorized by Sections 51.12(a)(3) and (4), the intake or other authorized officer of the court shall immediately make an investigation and shall release the child unless it appears that his detention is warranted under Subsection (b). The release may be conditioned upon requirements reasonably necessary to insure the child's appearance at later proceedings, but the conditions of the release must be in writing and filed with the office or official designated by the court and a copy furnished to the child.

(b) A child taken into custody may be detained prior to hearing on the petition only if:

(1) the child is likely to abscond or be removed from the jurisdiction of the court;

(2) suitable supervision, care, or protection for the child is not being provided by a parent, guardian, custodian, or other person;

(3) the child has no parent, guardian, custodian, or other person able to return the child to the court when required;

(4) the child may be dangerous to himself or herself or the child may threaten the safety of the public if released;

(5) the child has previously been found to be a delinquent child or has previously been convicted of a penal offense punishable by a term in jail or prison and is likely to commit an offense if released; or

(6) the child's detention is required under Subsection (f).

(c) If the child is not released, a request for detention hearing shall be made and promptly presented to the court, and an informal detention hearing as provided in Section 54.01 of this code shall be held promptly, but not later than the time required by Section 54.01 of this code.

(d) A release of a child to an adult under Subsection (a) must be conditioned on the agreement of the adult to be subject to the jurisdiction of the juvenile court and to an order of contempt by the court if the adult, after notification, is unable to produce the child at later proceedings.

(e) Unless otherwise agreed in the memorandum of understanding under Section 37.011, Education Code, in a county with a population greater than 125,000, if a child being released under this section is expelled under Section 37.007, Education Code, the release shall be conditioned on the child's attending a juvenile justice alternative education program pending a deferred prosecution or formal court disposition of the child's case.

(f) A child who is alleged to have engaged in delinquent conduct and to have used, possessed, or exhibited a firearm, as defined by Section 46.01, Penal Code, in the commission of the offense shall be detained until the child is released at the direction of the judge of the juvenile court, a substitute judge authorized by Section 51.04(f), or a referee appointed under Section 51.04(g), including an oral direction by telephone, or until a detention hearing is held as required by Section 54.01.

Comment

This section authorizes intake workers to release a child from detention without the necessity of a detention hearing. The release must be conditioned on an adult agreeing to be responsible for producing the child in court when required upon pain of contempt.

Subsection (e) requires that a release from detention be accompanied by an order requiring a child to attend the JJAEP pending court hearing in a county of more than 125,000 people.

Subsection (f) requires detention for a firearms offense in a secure juvenile detention facility, or a secure adult facility under § 51.12, until the initial detention hearing or until released by order of a judge, referee, or magistrate. Offenses covered include all offenses committed with a firearm as well as illegal carrying or possessing a firearm.

§ 53.03. Deferred Prosecution

(a) Subject to Subsections (e) and (g), if the preliminary investigation required by Section 53.01 of this code results in a determination that further proceedings in the case are authorized, the probation officer or other designated officer of the court, subject to the direction of the juvenile court, may advise the parties for a reasonable period of time not to exceed six months concerning deferred prosecution and rehabilitation of a child if:

(1) deferred prosecution would be in the interest of the public and the child;

(2) the child and his parent, guardian, or custodian consent with knowledge that consent is not obligatory; and

(3) the child and his parent, guardian, or custodian are informed that they may terminate the deferred prosecution at any point and petition the court for a court hearing in the case.

(b) Except as otherwise permitted by this title, the child may not be detained during or as a result of the deferred prosecution process.

(c) An incriminating statement made by a participant to the person giving advice and in the discussions or conferences incident thereto may not be used against the declarant in any court hearing.

(d) The juvenile board may adopt a fee schedule for deferred prosecution services and rules for the waiver of a fee for financial hardship in accordance with guidelines that the Texas Juvenile Probation Commission shall provide. The maximum fee is $15 a month. If the board adopts a schedule and rules for waiver, the probation officer or other designated officer of the court shall collect the fee authorized by the schedule from the parent, guardian, or custodian of a child for whom a deferred prosecution is authorized under this section or waive the fee in accordance with the rules adopted by the board. The officer shall deposit the fees received under this section in the county treasury to the credit of a special fund that may be used only for juvenile probation or community-based juvenile corrections services or facilities in which a juvenile may be required to live while under court supervision. If the board does not adopt a schedule and rules for waiver, a fee for deferred prosecution services may not be imposed.

(e) A prosecuting attorney may defer prosecution for any child. A probation officer or other designated officer of the court:

(1) may not defer prosecution for a child for a case that is required to be forwarded to the prosecuting attorney under Section 53.01(d); and

(2) may defer prosecution for a child who has previously been adjudicated for conduct that constitutes a felony only if the prosecuting attorney consents in writing.

(f) The probation officer or other officer designated by the court supervising a program of deferred prosecution for a child under this section shall report to the juvenile court any violation by the child of the program.

(g) Prosecution may not be deferred for a child alleged to have engaged in conduct that:

(1) is an offense under Section 49.04, 49.05, 49.06, 49.07, or 49.08, Penal Code; or

(2) is a third or subsequent offense under Section 106.04 or 106.041, Alcoholic Beverage Code.

(h) If the child is alleged to have engaged in delinquent conduct or conduct indicating a need for supervision that violates Section 28.08, Penal Code, deferred prosecution under this section may include:

(1) voluntary attendance in a class with instruction in self-responsibility and empathy for a victim of an offense conducted by a local juvenile probation department, if the class is available; and

(2) voluntary restoration of the property damaged by the child by removing or painting over any markings made by the child, if the owner of the property consents to the restoration.

(i) The court may defer prosecution for a child at any time:

(1) for an adjudication that is to be decided by a jury trial, before the jury is sworn;

(2) for an adjudication before the court, before the first witness is sworn; or

(3) for an uncontested adjudication, before the child pleads to the petition or agrees to a stipulation of evidence.

(j) The court may add the period of deferred prosecution under Subsection (i) to a previous order of deferred prosecution, except that the court may not place the child on deferred prosecution for a combined period longer than one year.

(k) In deciding whether to grant deferred prosecution under Subsection (i), the court may consider professional representations by the parties concerning the nature of the case and the background of the respondent. The representations made under this subsection by the child or counsel for the child are not admissible against the child at trial should the court reject the application for deferred prosecution.

Comment

This section authorizes use of a 6–month period of voluntary (informal) probation, thereby permitting many cases to be disposed of without a formal court petition, hearing and disposition.

Subject to Subsection (i), consent of the prosecutor is required to employ this disposition in any case within the scope of mandatory prosecutorial referral under § 53.01(d). Prosecutorial consent is also required for use of this disposition in any case when the juvenile has a prior felony adjudication.

Subsection (g) prohibits deferred prosecution for DWI and related offenses, third-offense consumption of alcohol by a minor, or third-offense driving by minor under the influence of alcohol.

Subsections (i) and (j) permit the juvenile court to place a child on deferred prosecution without consent of or over objection of the prosecutor. Under (j), this may be done even if the child has already experienced deferred prosecution for that same offense. The court, like probation and the prosecutor, is subject to the prohibition of (g) not to grant deferred prosecution for one of the enumerated alcohol-related offenses.

Subsection (k) permits the parties, including the judge, to discuss the nature and circumstances of the offense when deciding whether to grant deferred prosecution. The information cannot be used at trial should the deferred prosecution be denied.

Cross References

Alcoholic Beverage Code Section 106.04, Consumption of Alcohol by Minor Alcoholic Beverage Code Section 106.041 Driving or Operating Under Influence by of Alcohol By Minor (deferred prosecution is considered a conviction under these sections)

Education Code Section 25.0341, Transfer of Students Involved in Sexual Assault and Education Code Section 37.006, Removal of Children for Certain Conduct, and Education Code Sections 37.006, 37.0081 and 37.011 Removal of Children and Expulsion and Juvenile Justice Alternative Education (children on deferred prosecution for felonies may be subject to these sections)

Attorney General Opinion

Tex. Atty. Gen. Op. LO–98–069 (1998) (deferred prosecution not violated by offense committed after it has expired)

---

§ 53.035. Grand Jury Referral

(a) The prosecuting attorney may, before filing a petition under Section 53.04, refer an offense to a grand jury in the county in which the offense is alleged to have been committed.

(b) The grand jury has the same jurisdiction and powers to investigate the facts and circumstances concerning an offense referred to the grand jury under this section as it has to investigate other criminal activity.

(c) If the grand jury votes to take no action on an offense referred to the grand jury under this section, the prosecuting attorney may not file a petition under Section 53.04 concerning the offense unless the same or a successor grand jury approves the filing of the petition.

(d) If the grand jury votes for approval of the prosecution of an offense referred to the grand jury under this section, the prosecuting attorney may file a petition under Section 53.04.

(e) The approval of the prosecution of an offense by a grand jury under this section does not constitute approval of a petition by a grand jury for purposes of Section 53.045.

Comment

This section authorizes a prosecutor to refer any juvenile case for a grand jury "advisory opinion" as to whether prosecution should occur. This is the same power the prosecutor has to refer sensitive adult cases to the grand jury. Approval by the grand jury is not an indictment, but merely authorizes the prosecutor who has elected this procedure to file a juvenile court petition. This procedure is entirely separate from the determinate sentence act grand jury function under § 53.045.

---

§ 53.04. Court Petition; Answer

(a) If the preliminary investigation, required by Section 53.01 of this code results in a determination that further proceedings are authorized and warranted, a petition for an adjudication or transfer hearing of a child alleged to have engaged in delinquent conduct or conduct indicating a need for supervision may be made as promptly as practicable by a prosecuting attorney who has knowledge of the facts alleged or is informed and believes that they are true.

(b) The proceedings shall be styled "In the matter of ______________."

(c) The petition may be on information and belief.

(d) The petition must state:

(1) with reasonable particularity the time, place, and manner of the acts alleged and the penal law or standard of conduct allegedly violated by the acts;

(2) the name, age, and residence address, if known, of the child who is the subject of the petition;

(3) the names and residence addresses, if known, of the parent, guardian, or custodian of the child and of the child's spouse, if any;

(4) if the child's parent, guardian, or custodian does not reside or cannot be found in the state, or if their places of residence are unknown, the name and residence address of any known adult relative residing in the county or, if there is none, the name and residence address of the known adult relative residing nearest to the location of the court; and

(5) if the child is alleged to have engaged in habitual felony conduct, the previous adjudications in which the child was found to have engaged in conduct violating penal laws of the grade of felony.

(e) An oral or written answer to the petition may be made at or before the commencement of the hearing. If there is no answer, a general denial of the alleged conduct is assumed.

Comment

The requirements of the juvenile petition are specified in this section. The meat of the section is Subsection (d)(1) requiring the petition to state "with reasonable particularity the time, place, and manner of the acts alleged."

When habitual felony conduct is charged to invoke determinate sentence proceedings, the State is required to allege in the petition the prior felony adjudications upon which it intends to rely.

Leading Cases

In re T.L.K., 316 S.W.3d 701 (Tex. App.—Fort Worth, no pet.) (state's petition which failed to state the "place" where the delinquent conduct allegedly occurred was fatally defective)

In re D.L., 160 S.W.3d 155 (Tex. App.—Tyler 2005, no pet.) (consolidation of charges proper under civil standards and severance of charges is pursuant to civil procedure, not penal code)

In re S.D.W., 811 S.W.2d 739 (Tex. App.—Houston [1st Dist.] 1991, no writ) (law of parties need not be plead)

In re H.R.A., 790 S.W.2d 102 (Tex. App.—Beaumont 1990, no writ) (Penal Code section violation need not be pleaded)

T.R.S. v. State, 663 S.W.2d 920 (Tex. App.—Fort Worth 1984, no writ) (criminal procedure property description requirements do not apply to juvenile petitions)

In re A.N., 683 S.W.2d 118 (Tex. App.—San Antonio 1984, no writ) (burglary petition should have alleged address)

In re M.H., 662 S.W.2d 764 (Tex. App.—Corpus Christi 1983, no writ) (specific prayer for restitution not required)

In re W.H.C., 580 S.W.2d 606 (Tex. Civ. App.—Amarillo 1979, no writ) (all elements of offense must be plead)

In re H.S., 564 S.W.2d 446 (Tex. Civ. App.—Amarillo 1978, no writ) (petition must allege county in which acts occurred)

§ 53.045. Violent or Habitual Offenders

(a) Except as provided by Subsection (e), the prosecuting attorney may refer the petition to the grand jury of the county in which the court in which the petition is filed presides if the petition alleges that the child engaged in delinquent conduct that constitutes habitual felony conduct as described by Section 51.031 or that included the violation of any of the following provisions:

(1) Section 19.02, Penal Code (murder);

(2) Section 19.03, Penal Code (capital murder);

(3) Section 19.04, Penal Code (manslaughter);

(4) Section 20.04, Penal Code (aggravated kidnapping);

(5) Section 22.011, Penal Code (sexual assault) or Section 22.021, Penal Code (aggravated sexual assault);

(6) Section 22.02, Penal Code (aggravated assault);

(7) Section 29.03, Penal Code (aggravated robbery);

(8) Section 22.04, Penal Code (injury to a child, elderly individual, or disabled individual), if the offense is punishable as a felony, other than a state jail felony;

(9) Section 22.05(b), Penal Code (felony deadly conduct involving discharging a firearm);

(10) Subchapter D, Chapter 481, Health and Safety Code, if the conduct constitutes a felony of the first degree or an aggravated controlled substance felony (certain offenses involving controlled substances);

(11) Section 15.03, Penal Code (criminal solicitation);

(12) Section 21.11(a)(1), Penal Code (indecency with a child);

(13) Section 15.031, Penal Code (criminal solicitation of a minor);

(14) Section 15.01, Penal Code (criminal attempt), if the offense attempted was an offense under Section 19.02, Penal Code (murder), or Section 19.03, Penal Code (capital murder), or an offense listed by Section 3g(a)(1), Article 42.12, Code of Criminal Procedure;

(15) Section 28.02, Penal Code (arson), if bodily injury or death is suffered by any person by reason of the commission of the conduct;

(16) Section 49.08, Penal Code (intoxication manslaughter); or

(17) Section 15.02, Penal Code (criminal conspiracy), if the offense made the subject of the criminal conspiracy includes a violation of any of the provisions referenced in Subdivisions (1) through (16).

(b) A grand jury may approve a petition submitted to it under this section by a vote of nine members of the grand jury in the same manner that the grand jury votes on the presentment of an indictment.

(c) The grand jury has all the powers to investigate the facts and circumstances relating to a petition submitted under this section as it has to investigate other criminal activity but may not issue an indictment unless the child is transferred to a criminal court as provided by Section 54.02 of this code.

(d) If the grand jury approves of the petition, the fact of approval shall be certified to the juvenile court, and the certification shall be entered in the record of the case. For the purpose of the transfer of a child to the Texas Department of Criminal Justice as provided by Section

245.151(c)~~61.084(c)~~, Human Resources Code, a juvenile court petition approved by a grand jury under this section is an indictment presented by the grand jury.

(e) The prosecuting attorney may not refer a petition that alleges the child engaged in conduct that violated Section 22.011(a)(2), Penal Code, or Sections 22.021(a)(1)(B) and (2)(B), Penal Code, unless the child is more than three years older than the victim of the conduct.

Amended by Acts 2011, 82nd Leg., ch. 85 (S.B. 653), § 3.006, eff. Sept. 1, 2011.

Comment

This section defines the scope of the Texas determinate sentence act for juveniles. Under it, a juvenile court judge or jury can sentence a respondent adjudicated to have committed one of the covered felonies to probation or a sentence of incarceration. Criminal conspiracy to commit any of the existing offenses listed also falls under the determinate sentence act.

Initially, the sentence is served in the TYC or TJJD. The TYC or TJJD can administratively parole a juvenile without a court hearing who has served a statutory minimum length of stay-10 years for capital murder, 3 years for a first degree felony, 2 years for a second degree felony and 1 year for a third degree felony. If the juvenile is paroled by TYC before he or she becomes 19, he or she remains on TYC parole until age 19.

TYC can petition the juvenile court for parole before the statutory minimum length of stay has been served. It can also petition the juvenile court to transfer any determinate sentenced youth 16 or older to the institutional division of TDCJ. A youth who violates TYC or TJJD parole must be revoked before the TYC can petition the juvenile court to transfer him or her to the institutional division.

Leading Cases

In re J.B.L., 318 S.W.3d 544 (Tex. App.—Beaumont 2010 rev. denied)(53.045 does not violate Apprendi because the jury determines the maximum punishment allowed under the charging instrument)

Blays v. State, 319 S.W.3d 857 (Tex. App.—San Antonio 2010, no pet.) (decision to refer petition to grand jury is the state's option)

In re J.G., 195 S.W.3d 161 (Tex. App.—San Antonio 2006, no pet.) (no requirement to recertify by grand jury an amended petition when a lesser offense is waived)

In re G.A.T., 16 S.W.3d 818 (Tex. App.—Houston [14th Dist.] 2000, pet. denied) (failure to serve amended petition approved by grand jury on juvenile not jurisdictional defect)

In re S.J., 977 S.W.2d 147 (Tex. App.—San Antonio 1998, no writ) (mistakes in grand jury approval certification not fatal)

In re A.R.A., 898 S.W.2d 14 (Tex. App.—Austin 1995, no writ) (juvenile and lawyer have capacity to waive grand jury approval if § 51.09 complied with)

In re A.G.G., 860 S.W.2d 160 (Tex. App.—Dallas 1993, no writ) (State's waiver of right to proceed under DSA precludes determinate sentence)

In re S.D.W., 811 S.W.2d 739 (Tex. App.—Houston [1st Dist.] 1991, no writ) (written grand jury certificate of approval required; amendments in petition; lesser included offenses)

In re S.C., 790 S.W.2d 766 (Tex. App.—Austin 1990, writ denied) (prohibition on involuntary servitude not violated; adult parole rules apply after transfer to prison)

In re J.T.H., 779 S.W.2d 954 (Tex. App.—Austin 1989, no writ) (right to grand jury indictment not violated; statute not vague; no equal protection violation)

In re R.L.H., 771 S.W.2d 697 (Tex. App.—Austin 1989, writ denied) (act does not violate equal protection of the laws; no violation of right to grand jury indictment)

Cross References

TX FCA Family § 54.04, Disposition Hearing, *infra*; TX FCA Family § 54.11, Release or Transfer Hearing, *infra*.

Tex. Hum. Res. Code Ann. § 244.014, Referral for Transfer; Tex. Hum. Res. Code Ann. § 245.051, Minimum lengths of stay; Tex. Hum. Res. Code Ann. § 245.151, Parole and Administrative Transfer.

TEX. GOV'T CODE ANN. § 499.053, Transfers from Texas Youth Commission; TEX. GOV'T CODE ANN. § 508.156, Determinate Sentence Parole.

§ 53.05. Time Set for Hearing

(a) After the petition has been filed, the juvenile court shall set a time for the hearing.

(b) The time set for the hearing shall not be later than 10 working days after the day the petition was filed if:

(1) the child is in detention; or

(2) the child will be taken into custody under Section 53.06(d) of this code.

Leading Cases

In re J.W.G., 988 S.W.2d 318 (Tex. App.—Houston [1st Dist.] 1999, no pet.) (one year delay not a denial of speedy trial)

In re S.D.W., 811 S.W.2d 739 (Tex. App.—Houston [1st Dist.] 1991, no writ) (Texas Supreme Court's guidelines for prompt disposition are not binding on juvenile court)

Melendez v. State, 873 S.W.2d 723 (Tex. App.—San Antonio 1994, no pet.) (failure to hold hearing within 10 days doesn't invalidate court's decision)

§ 53.06. Summons

(a) The juvenile court shall direct issuance of a summons to:

(1) the child named in the petition;

(2) the child's parent, guardian, or custodian;

(3) the child's guardian ad litem; and

(4) any other person who appears to the court to be a proper or necessary party to the proceeding.

(b) The summons must require the persons served to appear before the court at the time set to answer the allegations of the petition. A copy of the petition must accompany the summons.

(c) The court may endorse on the summons an order directing the person having the physical custody or control of the child to bring the child to the hearing. A person who violates an order entered under this subsection may be proceeded against under Section 53.08 or 54.07 of this code.

(d) If it appears from an affidavit filed or from sworn testimony before the court that immediate detention of the child is warranted under Section 53.02(b) of this code, the court may endorse on the summons an order that a law-enforcement officer shall serve the summons and shall immediately take the child into custody and bring him before the court.

(e) A party, other than the child, may waive service of summons by written stipulation or by voluntary appearance at the hearing.

Comment

Service of summons may be waived by voluntary appearance by any person except the juvenile respondent. Personal service on the juvenile respondent is required to give the juvenile court jurisdiction over the case.

Leading Cases

In re C.J.F., 183 S.W.3d 841 (Tex. App.—Houston [1st Dist] 2005 rev. denied) (service of subsequent amended petitions is not required for court to maintain jurisdiction)

Carlson v. State, 151 S.W.3d 643 (Tex. App.—Eastland 2004, no pet.) (when parental summons was not effective, juvenile court lacked jurisdiction to transfer child to district court)

In re M.D.R., 113 S.W.3d 552 (Tex. App.—Texarkana 2003, no pet.) (no affirmative showing in the record of service of a copy of the petition to juvenile means no jurisdiction obtained by court)

Alaniz v. State, 2 S.W.3d 451 (Tex. App.—San Antonio 1999, no pet.) (failure to serve juvenile requires reversal; service on juvenile's attorney not sufficient)

In re P.C., 858 S.W.2d 6 (Tex. App.—Houston [1st Dist.] 1993, no writ) (directing service of summons on only one parent sufficient)

In re K.P.S., 840 S.W.2d 706 (Tex. App.—Corpus Christi 1992, no writ) (oral notice of hearing date by judge in court sufficient notice)

Carner v. State, 592 S.W.2d 618 (Tex. Crim. App. 1980) (juvenile court may proceed with hearing in absence of parent who was summoned)

Grayless v. State, 567 S.W.2d 216 (Tex. Crim. App. 1978) (failure to serve transfer motion on respondent deprives criminal court of jurisdiction)

In re W.L.C., 562 S.W.2d 454 (Tex. 1978) (burden on State to show that respondent was personally served)

---

§ 53.07. Service of Summons

(a) If a person to be served with a summons is in this state and can be found, the summons shall be served upon him personally at least two days before the day of the adjudication hearing. If he is in this state and cannot be found, but his address is known or can with reasonable diligence be ascertained, the summons may be served on him by mailing a copy by registered or certified mail, return receipt requested, at least five days before the day of the hearing. If he is outside this state but he can be found or his address is known, or his whereabouts or address can with reasonable diligence be ascertained, service of the summons may be made either by delivering a copy to him personally or mailing a copy to him by registered or certified mail, return receipt requested, at least five days before the day of the hearing.

(b) The juvenile court has jurisdiction of the case if after reasonable effort a person other than the child cannot be found nor his post-office address ascertained, whether he is in or outside this state.

(c) Service of the summons may be made by any suitable person under the direction of the court.

(d) The court may authorize payment from the general funds of the county of the costs of service and of necessary travel expenses incurred by persons summoned or otherwise required to appear at the hearing.

(e) Witnesses may be subpoenaed in accordance with the Texas Code of Criminal Procedure, 1965.

Leading Cases

In re D.W.L., 828 S.W.2d 520 (Tex. App.—Houston [14th Dist.] 1992, no writ) (State used reasonable effort to serve parents)

In re D.B.C, 695 S.W.2d 248 (Tex. App.—Austin 1985, no writ) (court order authorizing probation officer to serve summons not required)

P.G. v. State, 616 S.W.2d 635 (Tex. Civ. App.—San Antonio 1981, writ ref'd n.r.e.) (juvenile probation officer may serve summons)

Attorney General Opinion

Op. Tex. Att'y Gen. No. GA-0017 (2003) (juvenile court may order child or parent to reimburse county for cost of service of summons if child is adjudicated)

---

§ 53.08. Writ of Attachment

(a) The juvenile court may issue a writ of attachment for a person who violates an order entered under Section 53.06(c).

(b) A writ of attachment issued under this section is executed in the same manner as in a criminal proceeding as provided by Chapter 24, Code of Criminal Procedure.

Comment

If the juvenile court has required a person served to bring the respondent to the court and that person fails to do so, this section authorizes the issuance of an attachment to take the adult into custody and bring him or her before the court. Previously, the sole remedy was contempt of court proceedings under § 54.07.

CHAPTER 54. JUDICIAL PROCEEDINGS

Introductory Comment

Chapter 54 deals with six different kinds of judicial hearings: detention; discretionary transfer (certification); adjudication, disposition; modification of disposition hearings; and release/transfer hearings under the determinate sentence act.

§ 54.01. Detention Hearing

(a) Except as provided by Subsection (p), if the child is not released under Section 53.02, a detention hearing without a jury shall be held promptly, but not later than the second working day after the child is taken into custody; provided, however, that when a child is detained on a Friday or Saturday, then such detention hearing shall be held on the first working day after the child is taken into custody.

(b) Reasonable notice of the detention hearing, either oral or written, shall be given, stating the time, place, and purpose of the hearing. Notice shall be given to the child and, if they can be found, to his parents, guardian, or custodian. Prior to the commencement of the hearing, the court shall inform the parties of the child's right to counsel and to appointed counsel if they are indigent and of the child's right to remain silent with respect to any allegations of delinquent conduct, conduct indicating a need for supervision, or conduct that violates an order of probation imposed by a juvenile court.

(c) At the detention hearing, the court may consider written reports from probation officers, professional court employees, or professional consultants in addition to the testimony of witnesses. Prior to the detention hearing, the court shall provide the attorney for the child with access to all written matter to be considered by the court in making the detention decision. The court may order counsel not to reveal items to the child or his parent, guardian, or guardian ad litem if such disclosure would materially harm the treatment and rehabilitation of the child or would substantially decrease the likelihood of receiving information from the same or similar sources in the future.

(d) A detention hearing may be held without the presence of the child's parents if the court has been unable to locate them. If no parent or guardian is present, the court shall appoint counsel or a guardian ad litem for the child.

(e) At the conclusion of the hearing, the court shall order the child released from detention unless it finds that:

(1) he is likely to abscond or be removed from the jurisdiction of the court;

(2) suitable supervision, care, or protection for him is not being provided by a parent, guardian, custodian, or other person;

(3) he has no parent, guardian, custodian, or other person able to return him to the court when required;

(4) he may be dangerous to himself or may threaten the safety of the public if released; or

(5) he has previously been found to be a delinquent child or has previously been convicted of a penal offense punishable by a term in jail or prison and is likely to commit an offense if released.

(f) Unless otherwise agreed in the memorandum of understanding under Section 37.011, Education Code, a release may be conditioned on requirements reasonably necessary to insure the child's appearance at later proceedings, but the conditions of the release must be in writing and a copy furnished to the child. In a county with a population greater than 125,000, if a child being released under this section is expelled under Section 37.007, Education Code, the release shall be conditioned on the child's attending a juvenile justice alternative education program pending a deferred prosecution or formal court disposition of the child's case.

(g) No statement made by the child at the detention hearing shall be admissible against the child at any other hearing.

(h) A detention order extends to the conclusion of the disposition hearing, if there is one, but in no event for more than 10 working days. Further detention orders may be made following subsequent detention hearings. The initial detention hearing may not be waived but subsequent detention hearings may be waived in accordance with the requirements of Section 51.09. Each subsequent detention order shall extend for no more than 10 working days, except that in a county that does not have a certified juvenile detention facility, as described by Section 51.12(a)(3), each subsequent detention order shall extend for no more than 15 working days.

(i) A child in custody may be detained for as long as 10 days without the hearing described in Subsection (a) of this section if:

(1) a written request for shelter in detention facilities pending arrangement of transportation to his place of residence in another state or country or another county of this state is voluntarily executed by the child not later than the next working day after he was taken into custody;

(2) the request for shelter contains:

(A) a statement by the child that he voluntarily agrees to submit himself to custody and detention for a period of not longer than 10 days without a detention hearing;

(B) an allegation by the person detaining the child that the child has left his place of residence in another state or country or another county of this state, that he is in need of shelter, and that an effort is being made to arrange transportation to his place of residence; and

(C) a statement by the person detaining the child that he has advised the child of his right to demand a detention hearing under Subsection (a) of this section; and

(3) the request is signed by the juvenile court judge to evidence his knowledge of the fact that the child is being held in detention.

(j) The request for shelter may be revoked by the child at any time, and on such revocation, if further detention is necessary, a detention hearing shall be held not later than the next working day in accordance with Subsections (a) through (g) of this section.

(k) Notwithstanding anything in this title to the contrary, the child may sign a request for shelter without the concurrence of an adult specified in Section 51.09 of this code.

(*l*) The juvenile board may appoint a referee to conduct the detention hearing. The referee shall be an attorney licensed to practice law in this state. Such payment or additional payment as may be warranted for referee services shall be provided from county funds. Before commencing the detention hearing, the referee shall inform the parties who have appeared that they are entitled to have the hearing before the juvenile court judge or a substitute judge authorized by Section 51.04(f). If a party objects to the referee conducting the detention hearing, an authorized judge shall conduct the hearing within 24 hours. At the conclusion of the hearing, the referee shall transmit written findings and recommendations to the juvenile court judge or substitute judge. The juvenile court judge or substitute judge shall adopt, modify, or reject the referee's recommendations not later than the next working day after the day that the judge receives the recommendations. Failure to act within that time results in release of the child by operation of law. A recommendation that the child be released operates to secure the child's immediate release, subject to the power of the juvenile court judge or substitute judge to reject or modify that recommendation. The effect of an order detaining a child shall be computed from the time of the hearing before the referee.

(m) The detention hearing required in this section may be held in the county of the designated place of detention where the child is being held even though the designated place of detention is outside the county of residence of the child or the county in which the alleged delinquent conduct, conduct indicating a need for supervision, or probation violation occurred.

(n) An attorney appointed by the court under Section 51.10(c) because a determination was made under this section to detain a child who was not represented by an attorney may request on behalf of the child and is entitled to a de novo detention hearing under this section. The attorney must make the request not later than the 10th working day after the date the attorney is appointed. The hearing must take place not later than the second working day after the date the attorney filed a formal request with the court for a hearing.

(*o*) The court or referee shall find whether there is probable cause to believe that a child taken into custody without an arrest warrant or a directive to apprehend has engaged in delinquent conduct, conduct indicating a need for supervision, or conduct that violates an order of probation imposed by a juvenile court. The court or referee must make the finding within 48 hours, including weekends and holidays, of the time the child was taken into custody. The court or referee may make the finding on any reasonably reliable information without regard to admissibility of that information under the Texas Rules of Evidence. A finding of probable cause is required to detain a child after the 48th hour after the time the child was taken into custody. If a court or referee finds probable cause, additional findings of probable cause are not required in the same cause to authorize further detention.

(p) If a child is detained in a county jail or other facility as provided by Section 51.12(*l*) and the child is not released under Section 53.02(f), a detention hearing without a jury shall be held promptly, but not later than the 24th hour, excluding weekends and holidays, after the time the child is taken into custody.

(q) If a child has not been released under Section 53.02 or this section and a petition has not been filed under Section 53.04 or 54.05 concerning the child, the court shall order the child released from detention not later than:

(1) the 30th working day after the date the initial detention hearing is held, if the child is alleged to have engaged in conduct constituting a capital felony, an aggravated controlled substance felony, or a felony of the first degree; or

(2) the 15th working day after the date the initial detention hearing is held, if the child is alleged to have engaged in conduct constituting an offense other than an offense listed in Subdivision (1) or conduct that violates an order of probation imposed by a juvenile court.

(q–1) The juvenile board may impose an earlier deadline than the specified deadlines for filing petitions under Subsection (q) and may specify the consequences of not filing a petition by the deadline the juvenile board has established. The juvenile board may authorize but not require the juvenile court to release a respondent from detention for failure of the prosecutor to file a petition by the juvenile board's deadline.

(r) On the conditional release of a child from detention by judicial order under Subsection (f), the court, referee, or detention magistrate may order that the child's parent, guardian, or custodian present in court at the detention hearing engage in acts or omissions specified by the court, referee, or detention magistrate that will assist the child in complying with the conditions of release. The order must be in writing and a copy furnished to the parent, guardian, or custodian. An order entered under this subsection may be enforced as provided by Chapter 61.

Comment

If a child is not released from detention administratively, a detention hearing before a judge, referee or master must be conducted within the second working day after the child was taken into custody. The hearing may be informal and the child may be, but need not be, represented by counsel. This section requires release from detention unless one or more of five specified grounds justifying detention is found to exist.

The section codifies the constitutional requirement of a judicial determination of probable cause within 48 hours of the juvenile being taken into custody.

Subsection (q) requires the filing of a petition within 30 or 15 working days, depending upon the offense, after the initial detention hearing if the child is detained. The remedy for violation of this requirement is release of the child from detention, not dismissal of the case. Subsection (q–1) allows a local juvenile board to impose shorter filing deadlines. This can be done to avoid problems with overcrowding in local detention facilities. Nonetheless, the board cannot force the juvenile court to release a child if the shorter deadline is not met.

Subsections (b), (*o*), and (q) make it clear that a child being detained for violation of probation is entitled to detention hearings on the same basis as a child being held on new charges.

Subsection (r) authorizes the court or referee to place a parent of a released child under an order of cooperation that can be enforced by contempt proceedings under new Chapter 61.

CLE/Other Legal Publication

Get my baby out of jail: a quick guide to juvenile detention hearings. Daniel Peugh, 69 Tex. B.J. 348 (2006)

Leading Cases

County of Riverside v. McLaughlin, 500 U.S. 44, 114 L.Ed.2d 49, 111 S.Ct. 1661 (1991) ("prompt" under *Gerstein v. Pugh* means within 48 hours)

Schall v. Martin, 467 U.S. 253, 81 L.Ed.2d 207, 104 S.Ct. 2403 (1984) (preventive detention of juveniles constitutional under some circumstances)

Gerstein v. Pugh, 420 U.S. 103, 43 L.Ed.2d 54, 95 S.Ct. 854 (1975) (4th Amendment requires prompt judicial finding of probable cause to detain arrestee)

Moss v. Weaver, 525 F.2d 1258 (5th Cir. 1976) (*Gerstein v. Pugh* applies to juvenile proceedings)

Ex parte D.W.C., 1 S.W.3d 896 (Tex. App.—Beaumont 1999, no pet.) (juvenile has no constitutional right to bail)

D.B. v. State, 556 S.W.2d 845 (Tex. Civ. App.—Houston [14th Dist.] 1977, no writ) (failure to hold detention hearing does not invalidate adjudication)

In re G.T.H., 541 S.W.2d 527 (Tex. Civ. App.—Eastland 1976, no writ) (holding child in uncertified detention facility requires immediate release on habeas)

Attorney General Opinion

Tex. Atty. Gen. Op. DM–411 (1996) (hearing-impaired party to juvenile detention hearing entitled to interpreter, but custodian is not)

---

§ 54.011. Detention Hearings for Status Offenders and Nonoffenders; Penalty

(a) The detention hearing for a status offender or nonoffender who has not been released administratively under Section 53.02 shall be held before the 24th hour after the time the child arrived at a detention facility, excluding hours of a weekend or a holiday. Except as otherwise provided by this section, the judge or referee conducting the detention hearing shall release the status offender or nonoffender from secure detention.

(b) The judge or referee may order a child in detention accused of the violation of a valid court order as defined by Section 51.02 detained not longer than 72 hours after the time the detention order was entered, excluding weekends and holidays, if:

(1) the judge or referee finds at the detention hearing that there is probable cause to believe the child violated the valid court order; and

(2) the detention of the child is justified under Section 54.01(e)(1), (2), or (3).

(c) Except as provided by Subsection (d), a detention order entered under Subsection (b) may be extended for one additional 72-hour period, excluding weekends and holidays, only on a finding of good cause by the juvenile court.

(d) A detention order for a child under this section may be extended on the demand of the child's attorney only to allow the time that is necessary to comply with the requirements of Section 51.10(h), entitling the attorney to 10 days to prepare for an adjudication hearing.

(e) A status offender may be detained for a necessary period, not to exceed five days, to enable the child's return to the child's home in another state under Chapter 60.

(f) Except as provided by Subsection (a), a nonoffender, including a person who has been taken into custody and is being held solely for deportation out of the United States, may not be detained for any period of time in a secure detention facility or secure correctional facility, regardless of whether the facility is publicly or privately operated. A nonoffender who is detained in violation of this subsection is entitled to immediate release from the facility and may bring a civil action for compensation for the illegal detention against any person responsible for the detention. A person commits an offense if the person knowingly detains or assists in detaining a nonoffender in a secure detention facility or secure correctional facility in violation of this subsection. An offense under this subsection is a Class B misdemeanor.

Comment

This section enacts federal restrictions on the detention of status offenders into Texas law. *See* § 51.02(15) for the definition of status offender. A status offender can be kept in a secure detention facility for a maximum of 24 hours, not counting weekend and holiday hours, unless he or she is charged with violation of a valid court order from a previous case.

Subsection (f) makes confinement of an alien juvenile for the purpose of deportation illegal after 24 hours. A civil lawsuit and criminal prosecution for a B misdemeanor are authorized by this section.

§ 54.012. Interactive Video Recording of Detention Hearing

(a) A detention hearing under Section 54.01 may be held using interactive video equipment if:

(1) the child and the child's attorney agree to the video hearing; and

(2) the parties to the proceeding have the opportunity to cross-examine witnesses.

(b) A detention hearing may not be held using video equipment unless the video equipment for the hearing provides for a two-way communication of image and sound among the child, the court, and other parties at the hearing.

(c) A recording of the communications shall be made. The recording shall be preserved until the earlier of:

(1) the 91st day after the date on which the recording is made if the child is alleged to have engaged in conduct constituting a misdemeanor;

(2) the 120th day after the date on which the recording is made if the child is alleged to have engaged in conduct constituting a felony; or

(3) the date on which the adjudication hearing ends.

(d) An attorney for the child may obtain a copy of the recording on payment of the reasonable costs of reproducing the copy.

Comment

This section authorizes detention hearings, even initial detention hearings, to be conducted by two-way television, much like criminal court arraignments are conducted in some cities.

§ 54.02. Waiver of Jurisdiction and Discretionary Transfer to Criminal Court

(a) The juvenile court may waive its exclusive original jurisdiction and transfer a child to the appropriate district court or criminal district court for criminal proceedings if:

(1) the child is alleged to have violated a penal law of the grade of felony;

(2) the child was:

(A) 14 years of age or older at the time he is alleged to have committed the offense, if the offense is a capital felony, an aggravated controlled substance felony, or a felony of the first degree, and no adjudication hearing has been conducted concerning that offense; or

(B) 15 years of age or older at the time the child is alleged to have committed the offense, if the offense is a felony of the second or third degree or a state jail felony, and no adjudication hearing has been conducted concerning that offense; and

(3) after a full investigation and a hearing, the juvenile court determines that there is probable cause to believe that the child before the court committed the offense alleged and that because of the seriousness of the offense alleged or the background of the child the welfare of the community requires criminal proceedings.

(b) The petition and notice requirements of Sections 53.04, 53.05, 53.06, and 53.07 of this code must be satisfied, and the summons must state that the hearing is for the purpose of considering discretionary transfer to criminal court.

(c) The juvenile court shall conduct a hearing without a jury to consider transfer of the child for criminal proceedings.

(d) Prior to the hearing, the juvenile court shall order and obtain a complete diagnostic study, social evaluation, and full investigation of the child, his circumstances, and the circumstances of the alleged offense.

(e) At the transfer hearing the court may consider written reports from probation officers, professional court employees, or professional consultants in addition to the testimony of witnesses.

At least five days prior to the transfer hearing, the court shall provide the attorney for the child and the prosecuting attorney with access to all written matter to be considered by the court in making the transfer decision. The court may order counsel not to reveal items to the child or the child's parent, guardian, or guardian ad litem if such disclosure would materially harm the treatment and rehabilitation of the child or would substantially decrease the likelihood of receiving information from the same or similar sources in the future.

(f) In making the determination required by Subsection (a) of this section, the court shall consider, among other matters:

(1) whether the alleged offense was against person or property, with greater weight in favor of transfer given to offenses against the person;

(2) the sophistication and maturity of the child;

(3) the record and previous history of the child; and

(4) the prospects of adequate protection of the public and the likelihood of the rehabilitation of the child by use of procedures, services, and facilities currently available to the juvenile court.

(g) If the petition alleges multiple offenses that constitute more than one criminal transaction, the juvenile court shall either retain or transfer all offenses relating to a single transaction. **Except as provided by Subsection (g-1), a** ~~A~~ child is not subject to criminal prosecution at any time for any offense arising out of a criminal transaction for which the juvenile court retains jurisdiction.

(g-1) A child may be subject to criminal prosecution for an offense committed under Chapter 19 or Section 49.08, Penal Code, if:

(1) the offense arises out of a criminal transaction for which the juvenile court retained jurisdiction over other offenses relating to the criminal transaction; and

(2) on or before the date the juvenile court retained jurisdiction, one or more of the elements of the offense under Chapter 19 or Section 49.08, Penal Code, had not occurred.

(h) If the juvenile court waives jurisdiction, it shall state specifically in the order its reasons for waiver and certify its action, including the written order and findings of the court, and shall transfer the person to the appropriate court for criminal proceedings and cause the results of the diagnostic study of the person ordered under Subsection (d), including psychological information, to be transferred to the appropriate criminal prosecutor. On transfer of the person for criminal proceedings, the person shall be dealt with as an adult and in accordance with the Code of Criminal Procedure, **except that if detention in a certified juvenile detention facility is authorized under Section 152.0015, Human Resources Code, the juvenile court may order the person to be detained in the facility pending trial or until the criminal court enters an order under Article 4.19, Code of Criminal Procedure**. **A** ~~The~~ transfer of custody **made under this subsection** is an arrest.

(i) A waiver under this section is a waiver of jurisdiction over the child and the criminal court may not remand the child to the jurisdiction of the juvenile court.

(j) The juvenile court may waive its exclusive original jurisdiction and transfer a person to the appropriate district court or criminal district court for criminal proceedings if:

(1) the person is 18 years of age or older;

(2) the person was:

(A) 10 years of age or older and under 17 years of age at the time the person is alleged to have committed a capital felony or an offense under Section 19.02, Penal Code;

(B) 14 years of age or older and under 17 years of age at the time the person is alleged to have committed an aggravated controlled substance felony or a felony of the first degree other than an offense under Section 19.02, Penal Code; or

(C) 15 years of age or older and under 17 years of age at the time the person is alleged to have committed a felony of the second or third degree or a state jail felony;

(3) no adjudication concerning the alleged offense has been made or no adjudication hearing concerning the offense has been conducted;

(4) the juvenile court finds from a preponderance of the evidence that:

(A) for a reason beyond the control of the state it was not practicable to proceed in juvenile court before the 18th birthday of the person; or

(B) after due diligence of the state it was not practicable to proceed in juvenile court before the 18th birthday of the person because:

(i) the state did not have probable cause to proceed in juvenile court and new evidence has been found since the 18th birthday of the person;

(ii) the person could not be found; or

(iii) a previous transfer order was reversed by an appellate court or set aside by a district court; and

(5) the juvenile court determines that there is probable cause to believe that the child before the court committed the offense alleged.

(k) The petition and notice requirements of Sections 53.04, 53.05, 53.06, and 53.07 of this code must be satisfied, and the summons must state that the hearing is for the purpose of considering waiver of jurisdiction under Subsection (j) of this section.

(*l*) The juvenile court shall conduct a hearing without a jury to consider waiver of jurisdiction under Subsection (j) of this section.

(m) Notwithstanding any other provision of this section, the juvenile court shall waive its exclusive original jurisdiction and transfer a child to the appropriate district court or criminal court for criminal proceedings if:

(1) the child has previously been transferred to a district court or criminal district court for criminal proceedings under this section, unless:

(A) the child was not indicted in the matter transferred by the grand jury;

(B) the child was found not guilty in the matter transferred;

(C) the matter transferred was dismissed with prejudice; or

(D) the child was convicted in the matter transferred, the conviction was reversed on appeal, and the appeal is final; and

(2) the child is alleged to have violated a penal law of the grade of felony.

(n) A mandatory transfer under Subsection (m) may be made without conducting the study required in discretionary transfer proceedings by Subsection (d). The requirements of Subsection (b) that the summons state that the purpose of the hearing is to consider discretionary transfer to criminal court does not apply to a transfer proceeding under Subsection (m). In a proceeding under Subsection (m), it is sufficient that the summons provide fair notice that the purpose of the hearing is to consider mandatory transfer to criminal court.

(*o*) If a respondent is taken into custody for possible discretionary transfer proceedings under Subsection (j), the juvenile court shall hold a detention hearing in the same manner as provided by Section 54.01, except that the court shall order the respondent released unless it finds that the respondent:

(1) is likely to abscond or be removed from the jurisdiction of the court;

(2) may be dangerous to himself or herself or may threaten the safety of the public if released; or

(3) has previously been found to be a delinquent child or has previously been convicted of a penal offense punishable by a term of jail or prison and is likely to commit an offense if released.

(p) If the juvenile court does not order a respondent released under Subsection (*o*), the court shall, pending the conclusion of the discretionary transfer hearing, order that the respondent be detained in:

(1) a certified juvenile detention facility as provided by Subsection (q); or

(2) an appropriate county facility for the detention of adults accused of criminal offenses.

(q) The detention of a respondent in a certified juvenile detention facility must comply with the detention requirements under this title, except that, to the extent practicable, the person shall be kept separate from children detained in the same facility.

(r) If the juvenile court orders a respondent detained in a county facility under Subsection (p), the county sheriff shall take custody of the respondent under the juvenile court's order. The juvenile court shall set or deny bond for the respondent as required by the Code of Criminal Procedure and other law applicable to the pretrial detention of adults accused of criminal offenses.

Amended by Acts 2011, 82nd Leg., ch. 1087 (S.B. 1209), § 4, eff. Sept. 1, 2011; Acts 2011, 82nd Leg., ch. 1103 (S.B. 1617), § 1, eff. Sept. 1, 2011.

Cross References

Tex. Penal Code Section 12.31 holds that an individual transferred to criminal court under this section for a capital felony cannot receive the sentence of life without parole, but rather is sentenced to life with a possibility of parole in 40 calendar years. This law, however, is not retroactive to certified children who committed murder before September 1, 2009. Meadoux v. State, 307 S.W.3d 401 (Tex. App.—San Antonio 2009, pet. granted). Additionally, the Supreme Court has also held that a juvenile cannot be sentenced to life without parole for a non-homicide crime. Graham v. Florida, 560 U.S., 130 S.Ct. 2011 (2010).

Comment

A juvenile court in its discretion may waive its exclusive jurisdiction and transfer a child to criminal court for prosecution as an adult if certain conditions exist. The certification hearing is without a jury and the mandatory investigative/diagnostic report is admissible in evidence. The court is directed to consider four factors in making the transfer decision, but need not make any particular factual findings on any of the factors.

Juvenile certifications have increased in the last few years. This is possibly a result of lowering the maximum age to 19 that TYC or TJJD can keep children incarcerated. Thus, to make the process as fair as possible, all attorneys must have access to all written material to be considered at least five days prior to the hearing.

Subsections (m) and (n) establish that once a juvenile is certified, he is certified for subsequent felonies committed before age 17. A hearing in juvenile court is required to establish the predicate facts for mandatory certification in this circumstance.

Subsection (h) requires that the criminal court prosecutor be provided with a copy of the diagnostic study when a child is transferred to criminal court. This subsection was amended in 2011 to allow for a child certified to stand trial as an adult to be detained in a certified juvenile detention facility while waiting for trial. This change was made to alleviate concerns for children being incarcerated in adult facilities.

The post–18 year old certification provision in Subsection (j) encompasses any circumstance beyond the control of the state which precluded proceeding before the respondent became 18 and reversals of previous certification orders by a district court or on appeal.

Subsection (j) permits certification of a person who is 18 who is alleged to have committed murder or capital murder between the ages of 10 and 14 if the State could not have proceeded earlier. Such cases are now likely to arise as a result of solving cold cases through DNA testing.

Subsections (*o*) through (r) give the juvenile court judge discretion to detain a person 18 or older being held for a certification hearing either in the juvenile detention facility or in the county jail. A detention hearing must be held using detention criteria, excluding those applicable only to children. If the juvenile court orders the person detained in a county jail, the juvenile court must set or deny bail as provided by law for adults.

CLE/Other Legal Publication

Certification: An Overview. Helen Jackson, 47-Dec HouLaw 14 (2009)

Leading Cases

Constitutional Issues

Breed v. Jones, 421 U.S. 519, 95 S.Ct. 1779, 44 L.Ed.2d 346 (1975) (double jeopardy requirements in transfer proceedings)

Kent v. United States, 383 U.S. 541, 16 L.Ed.2d 84, 86 S.Ct. 1045 (1966) (due process requirements in transfer proceedings)

In re S.J.M, 922 S.W.2d 241 (Tex. App.—Houston [14th Dist.] 1996, no writ) (no constitutional right to confrontation of witnesses at transfer hearing)

State v. Lopez, 196 S.W.3d 872 (Tex. App.—Dallas 2006, pet. ref'd), *cert. denied* 127 S.Ct. 1380 (2007) (statute allowing transfer hearing without jury does not violate principle of *Apprendi v. New Jersey*)

Procedural Issues

State v. Rhinehart, 333 S.W.3d 154 (Tex. Crim. App. 2011) (the state cannot complain on appeal for the first time that the criminal district court was without jurisdiction to grant a motion to quash based on lack of due diligence to proceed with the case before the child's 18th birthday)

Faisst v. State, 98 S.W.3d 226 (Tex. Crim. App. 2003) (certified juvenile may challenge juvenile court transfer after open plea in criminal court)

In re M.A.V., 40 S.W.3d 581 (Tex. App.—San Antonio 2001, no pet.) (visiting judge should have recused himself on respondent's demand)

Ex parte Gomez, 15 S.W.3d 103 (Tex. Crim. App. 2000) (juvenile entitled to good conduct credit on criminal sentence for time in juvenile detention before certification)

In re R.A.G., 866 S.W.2d 199 (Tex. 1993) (probable cause for each offense transferred required to be shown at certification hearing)

In re Joseph, 864 S.W.2d 737 (Tex. App.—Houston [1st Dist.] 1993, no writ) (failure to transfer uncharged offense does not preclude transfer of charged offense)

L.M.C. v. State, 861 S.W.2d 541 (Tex. App.—Houston [14th Dist.] 1993, no writ) (confession and autopsy report admissible without regard to rules of evidence)

Turner v. State, 796 S.W.2d 492 (Tex. App.—Dallas 1990, no writ) (State may nonsuit unproved charges to permit transfer of all remaining charges)

Hardesty v. State, 659 S.W.2d 823 (Tex. Crim. App. 1983) (requirement that summons state purpose of hearing can be satisfied by summons' reference to petition)

In re I.B., 619 S.W.2d 584 (Tex. Civ. App.—Amarillo 1981, no writ) (full investigation does not require field investigation that resolves conflicting stories)

Ex parte Allen, 618 S.W.2d 357 (Tex. Crim. App. 1981) (respondent can be prosecuted only for conduct for which juvenile court ordered transfer)

R.S. v. State, 575 S.W.2d 641 (Tex. Civ. App.—Austin 1978, no writ) (court's refusal to disclose written material to defense attorney reversible error)

Diagnostic Study

In re B.T., 323 S.W.3d 158 (Tex. 2010) (juvenile court must not conduct the transfer hearing until the diagnostic study is complete)

McKaine v. State, 170 S.W.3d 285 (Tex. App.—Corpus Christi 2005, no pet.)(use of diagnostic study is admissible despite being hearsay because strict rules of evidence are not applied in transfer proceedings)

Simpson v. State, 181 S.W.3d 743 (Tex. App.—Tyler 2005, pet. ref'd) (if diagnostic study is used for incriminating evidence then Fifth Amendment protections apply)

Cantu v. State, 999 S.W.2d 721 (Tex. App.—Austin 1999 pet. ref'd) (when only used for certification hearing, examination for diagnostic study is not custodial interrogation)

R.E.M. v. State, 541 S.W.2d 841 (Tex. Civ. App.—San Antonio 1976, writ ref'd n.r.e.) (failure to do a complete study not fatal when respondent refused to cooperate)

R.E.M. v. State, 532 S.W.2d 645 (Tex. Civ. App.—San Antonio 1975, no writ) (requirement of diagnostic study is mandatory)

Cross References

Tex. Code Crim. Proc. Ann. art. 4.19 Transfer of a Child. (This section allows the criminal court judge to order a child to be detained in another facility)

Tex. Hum. Res. Code Ann. § 152.007 Pretrial Detention Policy for Certain Juveniles

---

§ 54.021. County, Justice, or Municipal Court: Truancy

(a) The juvenile court may waive its exclusive original jurisdiction and transfer a child to the constitutional county court, if the county has a population of **1.75** ~~two~~ million or more, or to an appropriate justice or municipal court, with the permission of the county, justice, or municipal court, for disposition in the manner provided by Subsection (b) if the child **is 12 years of age or older and** is alleged to have engaged in conduct described in Section 51.03(b)(2). A waiver of jurisdiction under this subsection may be for an individual case or for all cases in which a child is alleged to have engaged in conduct described in Section 51.03(b)(2). The waiver of a juvenile court's exclusive original jurisdiction for all cases in which a child is alleged to have engaged in conduct described in Section 51.03(b)(2) is effective for a period of one year.

(b) A county, justice, or municipal court may exercise jurisdiction over a person alleged to have engaged in conduct indicating a need for supervision by engaging in conduct described in Section 51.03(b)(2) in a case where:

(1) **the person is 12 years of age or older;**

(2) the juvenile court has waived its original jurisdiction under this section; and

(3)~~(2)~~ a complaint is filed by the appropriate authority in the county, justice, or municipal court charging an offense under Section 25. 094, Education Code.

(c) A proceeding in a county, justice, or municipal court on a complaint charging an offense under Section 25.094, Education Code, is governed by Chapter 45, Code of Criminal Procedure.

(d) Notwithstanding any other law, the costs assessed in a case filed in or transferred to a constitutional county court for an offense under Section 25.093 or 25.094, Education Code, must be the same as the costs assessed for a case filed in a justice court for an offense under Section 25. 093 or 25.094, Education Code.

(e) The proceedings before a constitutional county court related to an offense under Section 25.093 or 25.094, Education Code, may be recorded in any manner provided by Section 30.00010, Government Code, for recording proceedings in a municipal court of record.

Amended by Acts 2011, 82nd Leg., ch. 148 (H.B. 734), § 3, eff. Sept. 1, 2011; Acts 2011, 82nd Leg., ch. 1098 (S.B. 1489), § 3, eff. Sept. 1, 2011.

Comment

This section authorizes the juvenile court judge to transfer a conduct indicating a need for supervision case based on truancy, if the child is 12 or older, to a justice or municipal court or constitutional county court (if the county has a population of 1.75 million or more) for adjudication and disposition proceedings. Consent of the receiving court is required for waiver. Further, waiver can be for only one truancy case or of all cases by all juveniles and this is authorized for one year.

When a juvenile court sends a truancy case to a justice or municipal court or constitutional county court, that court may exercise jurisdiction over the case as Failure to Attend School under the Education Code, not as an agent of the juvenile court, which was the case under prior law.

Old subsections (c) through (h) were repealed, revised, and re-enacted as article 45.054 of the Code of Criminal Procedure.

Leading Case

In re B.A.M., 980 S.W.2d 788 (Tex. App.—San Antonio 1998, pet. denied) (juvenile has no right to appointed counsel when charged in justice court with failure to attend school)

Attorney General Opinions

Tex. Atty. Gen. Op. JC–0110 (1999) (JP or MC may compel custodian to attend court in truancy or failure to attend school case)

Tex. Atty. Gen. Op. LO–94–058 (1994) (community service as punishment; duty of schools to readmit)

Tex. Atty. Gen. Op. DM–200 (1993) (hearing not required before transfer to J.P.; juvenile entitled to counsel in J.P. court)

Cross References

TEX. EDUC. CODE ANN. § 7.111. High School Equivalency Examinations.

TEX. EDUC. CODE ANN. § 25.093 Parent Contributing to Nonattendance

TEX. EDUC. CODE ANN. § 25.094 Failure to Attend School

TEX. CODE CRIM. PROC. ANN. art. 45.056 Juvenile Case Managers (This provision was amended in 2011 to require juvenile case managers to give priority to truancy cases)

---

§ 54.022. Repealed by Acts 2001, 77th Leg., ch. 1514, § 19(b), eff. Sept. 1, 2001.

§ 54.023. Repealed by Acts 2003, 78th Leg., ch. 283, § 61(1), eff. Sept. 1, 2003.

§ 54.03. Adjudication Hearing

(a) A child may be found to have engaged in delinquent conduct or conduct indicating a need for supervision only after an adjudication hearing conducted in accordance with the provisions of this section.

(b) At the beginning of the adjudication hearing, the juvenile court judge shall explain to the child and his parent, guardian, or guardian ad litem:

(1) the allegations made against the child;

(2) the nature and possible consequences of the proceedings, including the law relating to the admissibility of the record of a juvenile court adjudication in a criminal proceeding;

(3) the child's privilege against self-incrimination;

(4) the child's right to trial and to confrontation of witnesses;

(5) the child's right to representation by an attorney if he is not already represented; and

(6) the child's right to trial by jury.

(c) Trial shall be by jury unless jury is waived in accordance with Section 51.09. If the hearing is on a petition that has been approved by the grand jury under Section 53.045, the jury must consist of 12 persons and be selected in accordance with the requirements in criminal cases. If the hearing is on a petition that alleges conduct that violates a penal law of this state of the grade of misdemeanor, the jury must consist of the number of persons required by Article 33.01(b), Code of Criminal Procedure. Jury verdicts under this title must be unanimous.

(d) Except as provided by Section 54.031, only material, relevant, and competent evidence in accordance with the Texas Rules of Evidence applicable to criminal cases and Chapter 38, Code of Criminal Procedure, may be considered in the adjudication hearing. Except in a detention or discretionary transfer hearing, a social history report or social service file shall not be viewed by the court before the adjudication decision and shall not be viewed by the jury at any time.

(e) A child alleged to have engaged in delinquent conduct or conduct indicating a need for supervision need not be a witness against nor otherwise incriminate himself. An extrajudicial statement which was obtained without fulfilling the requirements of this title or of the constitution of this state or the United States, may not be used in an adjudication hearing. A statement made by the child out of court is insufficient to support a finding of delinquent conduct or conduct indicating a need for supervision unless it is corroborated in whole or in part by other evidence. An adjudication of delinquent conduct or conduct indicating a need for supervision cannot be had upon the testimony of an accomplice unless corroborated by other evidence tending to connect the child with the alleged delinquent conduct or conduct indicating a need for supervision; and the corroboration is not sufficient if it merely shows the commission of the alleged conduct. Evidence illegally seized or obtained is inadmissible in an adjudication hearing.

(f) At the conclusion of the adjudication hearing, the court or jury shall find whether or not the child has engaged in delinquent conduct or conduct indicating a need for supervision. The finding must be based on competent evidence admitted at the hearing. The child shall be presumed to be innocent of the charges against the child and no finding that a child has engaged in delinquent conduct or conduct indicating a need for supervision may be returned unless the state has proved such beyond a reasonable doubt. In all jury cases the jury will be instructed that the burden is on the state to prove that a child has engaged in delinquent conduct or is in need of supervision beyond a reasonable doubt. A child may be adjudicated as having engaged in conduct constituting a lesser included offense as provided by Articles 37.08 and 37.09, Code of Criminal Procedure.

(g) If the court or jury finds that the child did not engage in delinquent conduct or conduct indicating a need for supervision, the court shall dismiss the case with prejudice.

(h) If the finding is that the child did engage in delinquent conduct or conduct indicating a need for supervision, the court or jury shall state which of the allegations in the petition were found to be established by the evidence. The court shall also set a date and time for the disposition hearing.

(i) In order to preserve for appellate or collateral review the failure of the court to provide the child the explanation required by Subsection (b), the attorney for the child must comply with Rule 33.1, Texas Rules of Appellate Procedure, before testimony begins or, if the adjudication is uncontested, before the child pleads to the petition or agrees to a stipulation of evidence.

(j) When the state and the child agree to the disposition of the case, in whole or in part, the prosecuting attorney shall inform the court of the agreement between the state and the child. The court shall inform the child that the court is not required to accept the agreement. The court may delay a decision on whether to accept the agreement until after reviewing a report filed under Section 54.04(b). If the court decides not to accept the agreement, the court shall inform the child of the court's decision and give the child an opportunity to withdraw the plea or stipulation of evidence. If the court rejects the agreement, no document, testimony, or other evidence placed before the court that relates to the rejected agreement may be considered by the court in a subsequent hearing in the case. A statement made by the child before the court's rejection of the agreement to a person writing a report to be filed under Section 54.04(b) may not be admitted into evidence in a subsequent hearing in the case. If the court accepts the agreement, the court shall make a disposition in accordance with the terms of the agreement between the state and the child.

Comment

This section specifies the procedures to be used in adjudication hearings. The hearing must be separate from the disposition hearing. The child has a right to a trial by jury. The State must prove the allegations of its petition beyond a reasonable doubt. Illegally-seized evidence or an unlawfully-obtained confession is inadmissible. The testimony of an accomplice must be corroborated.

The Rules of Evidence applicable in criminal cases control in adjudication proceedings.

Subsection (c) requires that misdemeanor juvenile adjudication hearings be governed by the Code of Criminal Procedure article 33.01, which provides for 6 jurors in most misdemeanor cases.

Subsection (i) requires a contemporaneous trial objection to preserve a failure to admonish claim for appellate or collateral review. Subsection (j), provides safeguards for the juvenile in plea bargaining by requiring that if the juvenile court judge refuses to honor the agreement, he or she must give the juvenile the opportunity to withdraw the plea.

Subsection (f) makes clear that a court or jury may adjudicate for any lesser included offense raised by the evidence, even if the original charge was brought under the determinate sentence act.

Subsection (c) provides that jury selection in determinate sentence trials is governed by the Code of Criminal Procedure. Among other matters, that means that each party is entitled to 10 strikes, not six.

Leading Cases

Constitutional protections

In re Gault, 387 U.S. 1, 18 L.Ed.2d 527, 87 S.Ct. 1428 (1967) (due process requires notice, counsel, confrontation and privilege against self-incrimination in adjudication hearing)

In re Winship, 397 U.S. 358, 25 L.Ed.2d 368, 90 S.Ct. 1068 (1970) (due process requires State to prove charges beyond a reasonable doubt in juvenile adjudication proceedings)

McKeiver v. Pennsylvania, 403 U.S. 528, 29 L.Ed.2d 647, 91 S.Ct. 1976 (1971) (due process does not require right to jury trial in adjudication hearing)

Breed v. Jones, 421 U.S. 519, 95 S.Ct. 1779, 44 L.Ed.2d 346 (1975) (children given constitutional protection against double jeopardy)

In re C.J.F., 183 S.W.3d 841 (Tex. App.—Houston [1st Dist.] 2005, no pet.) (jeopardy attaches in a juvenile proceeding when jury has been empaneled and sworn)

Jury issues

Edmonson v. Leesville Concrete Co., 500 U.S. 614, 114 L.Ed.2d 660, 111 S.Ct. 2077 (1991) (*Batson* applies to strikes by private parties in civil litigation)

Powers v. Ohio, 499 U.S. 400, 113 L.Ed.2d 411, 111 S.Ct. 1364 (1991) (defendant and person struck from panel need not be of same race)

Batson v. Kentucky, 476 U.S. 79, 90 L.Ed.2d 69, 106 S.Ct. 1712 (1986) (State's use of peremptory strikes to eliminate racial group from jury violates equal protection)

In re S.G., 304 S.W.3d 518 (Tex. App.—Waco 2009, no pet.)(trial court erred in conducting bench trial without affirmative waiver of jury)

C.E.J. v. State, 788 S.W.2d 849 (Tex. App.—Dallas 1990, writ denied) (State's striking panel members on account of race violated equal protection in juvenile case)

In re C.D.F., 852 S.W.2d 281 (Tex. App.—Dallas 1993, no writ) (jury waiver requires concurrence of attorney on record)

V.C.H. v. State, 630 S.W.2d 787 (Tex. App.—Houston [1st Dist.] 1982, no writ) (jury waiver requires assent by child as well as attorney)

Admonishments

In re C.D.H., 273 S.W.3d 421 (Tex. App.—Texarkana 2008, no pet.)(error complaining of failure to sentence in accordance with mistaken admonition was not objected to and not preserved), but see, *In re* T.W.C., 285 S.W.3d 218 (Tex. App.—Houston [1st Dist.] 2008, no pet.)(held that while omitted or incomplete admonitions require objections, erroneous admonishments do not)

In re M.D.T., 153 S.W.3d 285 (Tex. App.—El Paso 2004, no pet.)(54.03(i) requires objection to failure to admonish to preserve error)

In re J.W., 57 S.W.3d 446 (Tex. App.—Houston [14th Dist.] 2001, no pet.) (admonition as to adult record erroneous, but harmless)

In re D.I.B., 988 S.W.2d 753 (Tex. 1999) (defect in probation eligibility admonition harmful error)

In re E.J.G.P., 5 S.W.3d 868 (Tex. App.—El Paso 1999, no pet.) (no duty to admonish as to immigration consequences of a juvenile adjudication)

In re K.L.C., 990 S.W.2d 242 (Tex. 1999) (prosecutor reading petition does not relieve trial court of duty to explain allegations, but error is harmless)

In re B.G.M., 929 S.W.2d 604 (Tex. App.—Texarkana 1996, no writ) (court not required to admonish as to sex offender registration requirements)

W.J.M.A. v. State, 602 S.W.2d 397 (Tex. Civ. App.—Beaumont 1980, no writ) (admonitions must be directed at child, not attorney)

A.E.M. v. State, 552 S.W.2d 952 (Tex. Civ. App.—San Antonio 1977, no writ) (court required to admonish regarding lesser included offenses)

In re D.L.K., 690 S.W.2d 654 (Tex. App.—Eastland 1985, no writ) (not required to admonish on every possible lesser included offense)

Jury Instructions

In re F.L.R., 293 S.W.3d 278 (Tex. App.—Waco 2009, no pet.)(dictating desired instruction does not preserve request under Tex.R. Civ. P. 278, which requires written request)

Other Adjudication Hearing Issues

In re J.R.R., 696 S.W.2d 382 (Tex. 1985) (failure to corroborate accomplice requires acquittal of respondent)

In re M.P., 126 S.W.3d 228 (Tex. App.—San Antonio 2003, no pet.) (error not to require unanimous verdict on at least one of four theories of aggravated sexual assault alleged)

In re D.D., 101 S.W.3d 695 (Tex. App.—Austin 2003, no pet.) (no jurisdiction to adjudicate for an offense not alleged in the petition or included in what was alleged)

In re M.A.V., 40 S.W.3d 581 (Tex. App.—San Antonio 2001, no pet.) (visiting judge should have recused himself on respondent's demand)

In re C.T.C., 2 S.W.3d 407 (Tex. App.—San Antonio 1999, no pet.) (OK to proceed with trial when juvenile fled after jury selected)

In re C.P., 998 S.W.2d 703 (Tex. App.—Waco 1999, no pet.) (error harmless, not to sever two counts of unauthorized use of motor vehicle)

In re C.L., 930 S.W.2d 935 (Tex. App.—Houston [14th Dist.] 1996, no writ) (error for prosecutor to argue that jury should find delinquent conduct to remove juvenile from abusive home)

In re A.G.G., 860 S.W.2d 160 (Tex. App.—Dallas 1993, no writ) (failure to appoint guardian ad litem reversible error)

In re N.S.D., 555 S.W.2d 807 (Tex. Civ. App.—El Paso 1977, no writ) (adjudication hearing cannot be waived)

Plea Bargains

In re M.C.S, Jr., 327 S.W.3d 802 (Tex. App.—Fort Worth 2010, no pet.) (a juvenile's stipulation is valid without orally reaffirming the state's recitation of the stipulation during the adjudication hearing)

In re M.D.G., 180 S.W.3d 747 (Tex. App.—Eastland 2005, no pet.)(Court abused discretion by not allowing child to withdraw stipulations when court refused to follow plea bargain)

Attorney General Opinions

Tex. Atty. Gen. Op. JC–0242 (2000) (state has no right to jury trial in juvenile proceedings)

Tex. Atty. Gen. Op. JC–0103 (1999) (juvenile court lacks jurisdiction over truancy by 17 year old)

Cross Reference

TEX. CODE CRIM. PROC. ANN. art. 33.01(b). A misdemeanor offense tried in district court shall have a jury consisting of six qualified jurors.

---

§ 54.031. Hearsay Statement of Certain Abuse Victims

(a) This section applies to a hearing under this title in which a child is alleged to be a delinquent child on the basis of a violation of any of the following provisions of the Penal Code, if a child 12 years of age or younger or a person with a disability is the alleged victim of the violation:

(1) Chapter 21 (Sexual Offenses) or 22 (Assaultive Offenses);

(2) Section 25.02 (Prohibited Sexual Conduct); ~~or~~

(3) Section 43.25 (Sexual Performance by a Child);

(4) Section 20A.02(a)(7) or (8) (Trafficking of Persons); or

(5) Section 43.05(a)(2) (Compelling Prostitution).

(b) This section applies only to statements that describe the alleged violation that:

(1) were made by the child or person with a disability who is the alleged victim of the violation; and

(2) were made to the first person, 18 years of age or older, to whom the child or person with a disability made a statement about the violation.

(c) A statement that meets the requirements of Subsection (b) is not inadmissible because of the hearsay rule if:

(1) on or before the 14th day before the date the hearing begins, the party intending to offer the statement:

(A) notifies each other party of its intention to do so;

(B) provides each other party with the name of the witness through whom it intends to offer the statement; and

(C) provides each other party with a written summary of the statement;

(2) the juvenile court finds, in a hearing conducted outside the presence of the jury, that the statement is reliable based on the time, content, and circumstances of the statement; and

(3) the child or person with a disability who is the alleged victim testifies or is available to testify at the hearing in court or in any other manner provided by law.

(d) In this section, "person with a disability" means a person 13 years of age or older who because of age or physical or mental disease, disability, or injury is substantially unable to protect the person's self from harm or to provide food, shelter, or medical care for the person's self.

Amended by Acts 2011, 82nd Leg., ch. 1 (S.B. 24), § 4.01, eff. Sept. 1, 2011.

Comment

This section, patterned after TEX. CODE CRIM. PROC. ANN. art. 38.072, authorizes under limited circumstances "outcry" statements of a child to be admitted into evidence against a claim of hearsay.

Outcry statements from someone over the age of 12 if they have a disability are admissible. This was added in response to the concern over individuals with intellectual or developmental disabilities being victims of abuse

2011 legislation added the offenses of trafficking and compelling prostitution.

Leading Cases

In re M.A.C., ___ S.W.3d ___, 2011 WL 1519351 (Tex. App.—Eastland 2011, no pet.) ("when a child discloses a general allusion of abuse to an adult, rather than a clear description of the event, that adult is not the proper outcry witness")

In re Z.L.B., 102 S.W.3d 120 (Tex. 2003) (respondent must prove outcry witness was not the first told about the sexual offense)

In re J.G., 195 S.W.3d 161 (Tex. App.—San Antonio 2006, no pet.) (juvenile outcry statute should be interpreted as the parallel rule in the Code of Criminal Procedure)

In re J.S., 35 S.W.3d 287 (Tex. App.—Ft. Worth 2001, no pet.) (service of notice to present evidence of outcry of sexual abuse on juvenile's guardian was acceptable when juvenile was not represented by attorney at time)

§ 54.032. Deferral of Adjudication and Dismissal of Certain Cases on Completion of Teen Court Program

(a) A juvenile court may defer adjudication proceedings under Section 54.03 for not more than 180 days if the child:

(1) is alleged to have engaged in conduct indicating a need for supervision that violated a penal law of this state of the grade of misdemeanor that is punishable by fine only or a penal ordinance of a political subdivision of this state;

(2) waives, under Section 51.09, the privilege against self-incrimination and testifies under oath that the allegations are true;

(3) presents to the court an oral or written request to attend a teen court program; and

(4) has not successfully completed a teen court program in the two years preceding the date that the alleged conduct occurred.

(b) The teen court program must be approved by the court.

(c) A child for whom adjudication proceedings are deferred under Subsection (a) shall complete the teen court program not later than the 90th day after the date the teen court hearing to determine punishment is held or the last day of the deferral period, whichever date is earlier. The court shall dismiss the case with prejudice at the time the child presents satisfactory evidence that the child has successfully completed the teen court program.

(d) A case dismissed under this section may not be part of the child's records for any purpose.

(e) The court may require a child who requests a teen court program to pay a fee not to exceed $10 that is set by the court to cover the costs of administering this section. The court shall deposit the fee in the county treasury of the county in which the court is located. A child who requests a teen court program and does not complete the program is not entitled to a refund of the fee.

(f) A court may transfer a case in which proceedings have been deferred as provided by this section to a court in another county if the court to which the case is transferred consents. A case may not be transferred unless it is within the jurisdiction of the court to which it is transferred.

(g) In addition to the fee authorized by Subsection (e), the court may require a child who requests a teen court program to pay a $10 fee to cover the cost to the teen court for performing its duties under this section. The court shall pay the fee to the teen court program, and the teen court program must account to the court for the receipt and disbursal of the fee. A child who pays a fee under this subsection is not entitled to a refund of the fee, regardless of whether the child successfully completes the teen court program.

(h) Notwithstanding Subsection (e) or (g), a juvenile court that is located in the Texas–Louisiana border region, as defined by Section 2056.002, Government Code, may charge a fee of $20 under those subsections.

Cross Reference

TEX. CODE CRIM. PROC. ANN. art. 45.052. Dismissal of Misdemeanor Charge on Completion of Teen Court Program.

§ 54.0325. Deferral of Adjudication and Dismissal of Certain Cases on Completion of Teen Dating Violence Court Program

(a) In this section:

(1) "Dating violence" has the meaning assigned by Section 71.0021.

(2) "Family violence" has the meaning assigned by Section 71.004.

(3) "Teen dating violence court program" means a program that includes:

(A) a 12–week program designed to educate children who engage in dating violence and encourage them to refrain from engaging in that conduct;

(B) a dedicated teen victim advocate who assists teen victims by offering referrals to additional services, providing counseling and safety planning, and explaining the juvenile justice system;

(C) a court-employed resource coordinator to monitor children's compliance with the 12–week program;

(D) one judge who presides over all of the cases in the jurisdiction that qualify for the program; and

(E) an attorney in the district attorney's office or the county attorney's office who is assigned to the program.

(b) On the recommendation of the prosecuting attorney, the juvenile court may defer adjudication proceedings under Section 54.03 for not more than 180 days if the child is a first offender who is alleged to have engaged in conduct:

(1) that violated a penal law of this state of the grade of misdemeanor; and

(2) involving dating violence.

(c) For the purposes of Subsection (b), a first offender is a child who has not previously been referred to juvenile court for allegedly engaging in conduct constituting dating violence, family violence, or an assault.

(d) Before implementation, the teen dating violence court program must be approved by:

(1) the court; and

(2) the commissioners court of the county.

(e) A child for whom adjudication proceedings are deferred under Subsection (b) shall:

(1) complete the teen dating violence court program not later than the last day of the deferral period; and

(2) appear in court once a month for monitoring purposes.

(f) The court shall dismiss the case with prejudice at the time the child presents satisfactory evidence that the child has successfully completed the teen dating violence court program.

(g) The court may require a child who participates in a teen dating violence court program to pay a fee not to exceed $10 that is set by the court to cover the costs of administering this section. The court shall deposit the fee in the county treasury of the county in which the court is located.

(h) In addition to the fee authorized by Subsection (g), the court may require a child who participates in a teen dating violence court program to pay a fee of $10 to cover the cost to the teen dating violence court program for performing its duties under this section. The court shall pay the fee to the teen dating violence court program, and the teen dating violence court program must account to the court for the receipt and disbursal of the fee.

(i) The court shall track the number of children ordered to participate in the teen dating violence court program, the percentage of victims meeting with the teen victim advocate, and the compliance rate of the children ordered to participate in the program.

Added by Acts 2011, 82nd Leg., ch. 1299 (H.B. 2496), § 1, eff. Sept. 1, 2011.

Comment

In order to reach the underlying issues causing teen dating violence, the legislature in 2011 created a teen dating violence court program. A first offender at the misdemeanor level may receive deferred prosecution and attend the program.

§ 54.033. Sexually Transmitted Disease, AIDS, and HIV Testing

(a) A child found at the conclusion of an adjudication hearing under Section 54.03 of this code to have engaged in delinquent conduct that included a violation of Sections 21.11(a)(1), 22.011, or 22.021, Penal Code, shall undergo a medical procedure or test at the direction of the juvenile court designed to show or help show whether the child has a sexually transmitted disease, acquired immune deficiency syndrome (AIDS), human immunodeficiency virus (HIV) infection, antibodies to HIV, or infection with any other probable causative agent of AIDS. The court may direct the child to undergo the procedure or test on the court's own motion or on the request of the victim of the delinquent conduct.

(b) If the child or another person who has the power to consent to medical treatment for the child refuses to submit voluntarily or consent to the procedure or test, the court shall require the child to submit to the procedure or test.

(c) The person performing the procedure or test shall make the test results available to the local health authority. The local health authority shall be required to notify the victim of the delinquent conduct and the person found to have engaged in the delinquent conduct of the test result.

(d) The state may not use the fact that a medical procedure or test was performed on a child under this section or use the results of the procedure or test in any proceeding arising out of the delinquent conduct.

(e) Testing under this section shall be conducted in accordance with written infectious disease control protocols adopted by the Texas Board of Health that clearly establish procedural guidelines that provide criteria for testing and that respect the rights of the child and the victim of the delinquent conduct.

(f) Nothing in this section allows a court to release a test result to anyone other than a person specifically authorized under this section. Section 81.103(d), Health and Safety Code, may not be construed to allow the disclosure of test results under this section except as provided by this section.

Comment

This section is similar to Article 21.31 of the TEX. CODE CRIM. PROC. ANN. in that it authorizes a court to order tests for HIV of a respondent adjudicated for sexual assault, aggravated sexual assault or indecency with a child.

Cross Reference

TEX. HEALTH & SAFETY CODE ANN. § 81.103. Confidentiality; Criminal Penalty.

---

§ 54.034. Limited Right to Appeal: Warning

Before the court may accept a child's plea or stipulation of evidence in a proceeding held under this title, the court shall inform the child that if the court accepts the plea or stipulation and the court makes a disposition in accordance with the agreement between the state and the child regarding the disposition of the case, the child may not appeal an order of the court entered under Section 54.03, 54.04, or 54.05, unless:

(1) the court gives the child permission to appeal; or

(2) the appeal is based on a matter raised by written motion filed before the proceeding in which the child entered the plea or agreed to the stipulation of evidence.

Comment

This provision requires the court to warn the child about the restrictions on appeal in a plea-bargained case that are imposed by § 56.01(n).

---

§ 54.04. Disposition Hearing

(a) The disposition hearing shall be separate, distinct, and subsequent to the adjudication hearing. There is no right to a jury at the disposition hearing unless the child is in jeopardy of a determinate sentence under Subsection (d)(3) or (m), in which case, the child is entitled to a jury of 12 persons to determine the sentence, but only if the child so elects in writing before the commencement of the voir dire examination of the jury panel. If a finding of delinquent conduct is returned, the child may, with the consent of the attorney for the state, change the child's election of one who assesses the disposition.

(b) At the disposition hearing, the juvenile court, notwithstanding the Texas Rules of Evidence or Chapter 37, Code of Criminal Procedure, may consider written reports from probation officers, professional court employees, or professional consultants in addition to the testimony of witnesses. Prior to the disposition hearing, the court shall provide the attorney for the child with access to all written matter to be considered in disposition. The court may order counsel not to reveal items to the child or the child's parent, guardian, or guardian ad litem if such disclosure would materially harm the treatment and rehabilitation of the child or would substantially decrease the likelihood of receiving information from the same or similar sources in the future.

(c) No disposition may be made under this section unless the child is in need of rehabilitation or the protection of the public or the child requires that disposition be made. If the court or jury does not so find, the court shall dismiss the child and enter a final judgment without any disposition. No disposition placing the child on probation outside the child's home may be made under this section unless the court or jury finds that the child, in the child's home, cannot be provided the quality of care and level of support and supervision that the child needs to meet the conditions of the probation.

(d) If the court or jury makes the finding specified in Subsection (c) allowing the court to make a disposition in the case:

(1) the court or jury may, in addition to any order required or authorized under Section 54.041 or 54.042, place the child on probation on such reasonable and lawful terms as the court may determine:

(A) in the child's own home or in the custody of a relative or other fit person; or

(B) subject to the finding under Subsection (c) on the placement of the child outside the child's home, in:

(i) a suitable foster home;

(ii) a suitable public or private residential treatment facility licensed by a state governmental entity or exempted from licensure by state law, except a facility operated by the Texas Youth Commission; or

(iii) a suitable public or private post-adjudication secure correctional facility that meets the requirements of Section 51.125, except a facility operated by the Texas Youth Commission;

(2) if the court or jury found at the conclusion of the adjudication hearing that the child engaged in delinquent conduct that violates a penal law of this state or the United States of the grade of felony and if the petition was not approved by the grand jury under Section 53.045, the court may commit the child to the Texas Youth Commission without a determinate sentence;

(3) if the court or jury found at the conclusion of the adjudication hearing that the child engaged in delinquent conduct that included a violation of a penal law listed in Section 53.045(a) and if the petition was approved by the grand jury under Section 53.045, the court or jury may sentence the child to commitment in the Texas Youth Commission with a possible transfer to the Texas Department of Criminal Justice for a term of:

(A) not more than 40 years if the conduct constitutes:

(i) a capital felony;

(ii) a felony of the first degree; or

(iii) an aggravated controlled substance felony;

(B) not more than 20 years if the conduct constitutes a felony of the second degree; or

(C) not more than 10 years if the conduct constitutes a felony of the third degree;

(4) the court may assign the child an appropriate sanction level and sanctions as provided by the assignment guidelines in Section 59.003; or

(5) if applicable, the court or jury may make a disposition under Subsection (m).

(e) The Texas Youth Commission shall accept a person properly committed to it by a juvenile court even though the person may be 17 years of age or older at the time of commitment.

(f) The court shall state specifically in the order its reasons for the disposition and shall furnish a copy of the order to the child. If the child is placed on probation, the terms of probation shall be written in the order.

(g) If the court orders a disposition under Subsection (d)(3) or (m) and there is an affirmative finding that the defendant used or exhibited a deadly weapon during the commission of the conduct or during immediate flight from commission of the conduct, the court shall enter the finding in the order. If there is an affirmative finding that the deadly weapon was a firearm, the court shall enter that finding in the order.

(h) At the conclusion of the dispositional hearing, the court shall inform the child of:

(1) the child's right to appeal, as required by Section 56.01; and

(2) the procedures for the sealing of the child's records under Section 58.003.

(i) If the court places the child on probation outside the child's home or commits the child to the Texas Youth Commission, the court:

(1) shall include in its order its determination that:

(A) it is in the child's best interests to be placed outside the child's home;

(B) reasonable efforts were made to prevent or eliminate the need for the child's removal from the home and to make it possible for the child to return to the child's home; and

(C) the child, in the child's home, cannot be provided the quality of care and level of support and supervision that the child needs to meet the conditions of probation; and

(2) may approve an administrative body to conduct permanency hearings pursuant to 42 U.S.C. Section 675 if required during the placement or commitment of the child.

(j) If the court or jury found that the child engaged in delinquent conduct that included a violation of a penal law of the grade of felony or jailable misdemeanor, the court:

(1) shall require that the child's thumbprint be affixed or attached to the order; and

(2) may require that a photograph of the child be attached to the order.

(k) Except as provided by Subsection (m), the period to which a court or jury may sentence a person to commitment to the Texas Youth Commission with a transfer to the Texas Department of Criminal Justice under Subsection (d)(3) applies without regard to whether the person has previously been adjudicated as having engaged in delinquent conduct.

(*l*) Except as provided by Subsection (q), a court or jury may place a child on probation under Subsection (d)(1) for any period, except that probation may not continue on or after the child's 18th birthday. Except as provided by Subsection (q), the court may, before the period of probation ends, extend the probation for any period, except that the probation may not extend to or after the child's 18th birthday.

(m) The court or jury may sentence a child adjudicated for habitual felony conduct as described by Section 51.031 to a term prescribed by Subsection (d)(3) and applicable to the conduct adjudicated in the pending case if:

(1) a petition was filed and approved by a grand jury under Section 53.045 alleging that the child engaged in habitual felony conduct; and

(2) the court or jury finds beyond a reasonable doubt that the allegation described by Subdivision (1) in the grand jury petition is true.

(n) A court may order a disposition of secure confinement of a status offender adjudicated for violating a valid court order only if:

(1) before the order is issued, the child received the full due process rights guaranteed by the Constitution of the United States or the Texas Constitution; and

(2) the juvenile probation department in a report authorized by Subsection (b):

(A) reviewed the behavior of the child and the circumstances under which the child was brought before the court;

(B) determined the reasons for the behavior that caused the child to be brought before the court; and

(C) determined that all dispositions, including treatment, other than placement in a secure detention facility or secure correctional facility, have been exhausted or are clearly inappropriate.

(*o*) In a disposition under this title:

(1) a status offender may not, under any circumstances, be committed to the Texas Youth Commission for engaging in conduct that would not, under state or local law, be a crime if committed by an adult;

(2) a status offender may not, under any circumstances other than as provided under Subsection (n), be placed in a post-adjudication secure correctional facility; and

(3) a child adjudicated for contempt of a county, justice, or municipal court order may not, under any circumstances, be placed in a post-adjudication secure correctional facility or committed to the Texas Youth Commission for that conduct.

(p) Except as provided by Subsection (*l*), a court that places a child on probation under Subsection (d)(1) for conduct described by Section 54.0405(b) and punishable as a felony shall specify a minimum probation period of two years.

(q) If a court or jury sentences a child to commitment in the Texas Youth Commission under Subsection (d)(3) for a term of not more than 10 years, the court or jury may place the child on probation under Subsection (d)(1) as an alternative to making the disposition under Subsection (d)(3). The court shall prescribe the period of probation ordered under this subsection for a term of not more than 10 years. The court may, before the sentence of probation expires, extend the probationary period under Section 54.05, except that the sentence of probation and any extension may not exceed 10 years. The court may, before the child's **19th** ~~18th~~ birthday, discharge the child from the sentence of probation. If a sentence of probation ordered under this subsection and any extension of probation ordered under Section 54.05 will continue after the child's **19th** ~~18th~~ birthday, the court shall discharge the child from the sentence of probation on the child's **19th** ~~18th~~ birthday unless the court transfers the child to an appropriate district court under Section 54.051.

(r) If the judge orders a disposition under this section and there is an affirmative finding that the victim or intended victim was younger than 17 years of age at the time of the conduct, the judge shall enter the finding in the order.

(s), (t) Repealed by Acts 2007, 80th Leg., ch. 263, § 64(1).

(u) For the purposes of disposition under Subsection (d)(2), delinquent conduct that violates a penal law of this state of the grade of felony does not include conduct that violates a lawful order of a county, municipal, justice, or juvenile court under circumstances that would constitute contempt of that court.

(v) If the judge orders a disposition under this section for delinquent conduct based on a violation of an offense, on the motion of the attorney representing the state the judge shall make an affirmative finding of fact and enter the affirmative finding in the papers in the case if the judge determines that, regardless of whether the conduct at issue is the subject of the prosecution or part of the same criminal episode as the conduct that is the subject of the prosecution, a victim in the trial:

(1) is or has been a victim of a severe form of trafficking in persons, as defined by 22 U.S.C. Section 7102(8); or

(2) has suffered substantial physical or mental abuse as a result of having been a victim of criminal activity described by 8 U.S.C. Section 1101(a)(15)(U)(iii).

(w) That part of the papers in the case containing an affirmative finding under Subsection (v):

(1) must include specific information identifying the victim, as available;

(2) may not include information identifying the victim's location; and

(3) is confidential, unless written consent for the release of the affirmative finding is obtained from the victim or, if the victim is younger than 18 years of age, the victim's parent or guardian.

(x) A child may be detained in an appropriate detention facility following disposition of the child's case under Subsection (d) or (m) pending:

(1) transportation of the child to the ordered placement; and

(2) the provision of medical or other health care services for the child that may be advisable before transportation, including health care services for children in the late term of pregnancy.

(y) A juvenile court conducting a hearing under this section involving a child for whom the Department of Family and Protective Services has been appointed managing conservator may communicate with the court having continuing jurisdiction over the child before the disposition hearing. The juvenile court may allow the parties to the suit affecting the parent-child relationship in which the Department of Family and Protective Services is a party to participate in the communication under this subsection.

Amended by Acts 2011, 82nd Leg., ch. 438 (S.B. 1208), § 2, eff. Sept. 1, 2011.

Comment

This section establishes the procedures for the disposition hearing.

In 2011 the Texas Youth Commission and Texas Juvenile Probation Commission were abolished and a new agency was created known as the Texas Juvenile Justice Department.

Except in a determinate sentence case, there is no right to a jury at the disposition hearing. The child must elect in writing before voir dire if the child wants a jury to decide sentencing in a determinate case. The election may by changed after the adjudication hearing is complete, but only with consent from the prosecutor. A social history report is admissible in evidence with prior disclosure to the parties. A child adjudicated for conduct indicating a need for supervision may not be committed to the TYC or TJJD and there are restrictions on the commitment of a child adjudicated of a misdemeanor. A child can also be placed in the post-adjudication secure correctional facility described in section 51.125. A child adjudicated under the determinate sentence act may be given probation for up to 10 years or a sentence of up to 40 years for a capital or first degree felony, 20 years for a second degree felony and 10 years for a third degree felony.

The court or jury must find that the child is in need of rehabilitation or that the protection of the public requires disposition or else dismiss the case.

The legislature has prohibited the placement of a status offender in a secure correctional facility except as authorized by (n). It also prohibited the placement of a child adjudicated for contempt of a justice or municipal court in a secure facility or commitment to the TYC or TJJD.

Subsection (q) authorizes up to 10 years probation in a determinate sentence act case. Probation is granted by the judge or jury as the case may be, but the length of the probation term is set by the court. Provisions under § 54.051 permit transfer of supervision to criminal court at age 18 or 19. This change is intended to make probation a more realistic possibility in some determinate sentence act cases. Furthermore, in 2011, (q) was amended to extend determinate sentencing probation jurisdiction in juvenile court to age 19.

A commitment to TYC or TJJD for misdemeanant conduct is prohibited.

Subsection (y) allows the juvenile court hearing the disposition phase to communicate with the parties involved if the juvenile has the Department of Family and Protective Services appointed as managing conservator. This is so that all state agencies dealing with the child can coordinate meeting the needs of the child.

Leading Cases

In re E.F.Z.R., 250 S.W.3d 173 (Tex. App.—El Paso 2008, no pet.) (no finding of threat to public safety required for TYC commitment)

In re M.P., 220 S.W.3d 99 (Tex. App.—Waco 2007, rev. denied) (juvenile has no Sixth Amendment right of confrontation, nor under the Texas Constitution, in the disposition phase)

In re E.G., 212 S.W.3d 536 (Tex. App.—Austin 2006, no pet.) (an order modifying a juvenile disposition is not subject to the requirements of § 54.04(n)).

In re C.J.H., 79 S.W.3d 698 (Tex. App.—Fort Worth 2002, no pet.) (TYC commitment OK when placements rejected respondent because of his sexual orientation)

In re A.N., 54 S.W.3d 487 (Tex. App.—Fort Worth 2001, rev. denied) (child must have 2 misdemeanor adjudications besides current adjudication before the child can be sentenced to TYC)

In re J.S.S., 20 S.W.3d 837 (Tex. App.—El Paso 2000, rev. denied) (privilege against self-incrimination applies to interview for social history report)

In re M.A.C., 999 S.W.2d 442 (Tex. App.—El Paso, 1999, no pet.) (no equal protection violation to commit Mexican national to TYC because of probation limitations)

In re J.S., 993 S.W.2d 370 (Tex. App.—San Antonio 1999, no pet.) (abuse of discretion in TYC commitment for sexual assault)

In re K.L.C., 972 S.W.2d 203 (Tex. App.—Beaumont 1998, no pet.) (factual insufficiency to support efforts to keep child at home requires commitment reversal)

In re A.F., 895 S.W.2d 481 (Tex. App.—Austin 1995, no writ) (social history report need not comply with rules of evidence; deadly weapon finding requires proof respondent personally used weapon)

K.K.B. v. State, 609 S.W.2d 824 (Tex. Civ. App.—Texarkana 1980, no writ) (court did not unlawfully delegate to foster parents power to fix conditions)

In re D.H, 556 S.W.2d 628 (Tex. Civ. App.—Waco 1977, writ ref'd n.r.e.) (court cannot order DHS to pay for treatment of DHS child in residential facility)

Attorney General Opinions

Tex. Atty. Gen. Op. ORD–645 (1996) (sex offender registration records are public)

Tex. Atty. Gen. Op. LO–93–95 (1993) (dress and hair probation conditions may violate juvenile's free expression rights)

§ 54.0401. Community–Based Programs

(a) This section applies only to a county that has a population of at least 335,000.

(b) A juvenile court of a county to which this section applies may require a child who is found to have engaged in delinquent conduct that violates a penal law of the grade of misdemeanor and for whom the requirements of Subsection (c) are met to participate in a community-based program administered by the county's juvenile board.

(c) A juvenile court of a county to which this section applies may make a disposition under Subsection (b) for delinquent conduct that violates a penal law of the grade of misdemeanor:

(1) if:

(A) the child has been adjudicated as having engaged in delinquent conduct violating a penal law of the grade of misdemeanor on at least two previous occasions;

(B) of the previous adjudications, the conduct that was the basis for one of the adjudications occurred after the date of another previous adjudication; and

(C) the conduct that is the basis of the current adjudication occurred after the date of at least two previous adjudications; or

(2) if:

(A) the child has been adjudicated as having engaged in delinquent conduct violating a penal law of the grade of felony on at least one previous occasion; and

(B) the conduct that is the basis of the current adjudication occurred after the date of that previous adjudication.

(d) The Texas Juvenile Probation Commission shall establish guidelines for the implementation of community-based programs described by this section. The juvenile board of each county to which this section applies shall implement a community-based program that complies with those guidelines.

(e) The Texas Juvenile Probation Commission shall provide grants to selected juvenile boards to assist with the implementation of a system of community-based programs under this section.

(f) Expired.

Comment

In counties with a population of at least 335,000, the juvenile board may establish community based programs for children who previously were eligible for TYC commitment for misdemeanant conduct under section 54.04 subsections (s) or (t) which were repealed in 2007.

---

§ 54.0402. Dispositional Order for Failure to Attend School

A dispositional order regarding conduct under Section 51.03(b)(2) is effective for the period specified by the court in the order but may not extend beyond the 180th day after the date of the order or beyond the end of the school year in which the order was entered, whichever period is longer.

Added by Acts 2011, 82nd Leg., ch. 1098 (S.B. 1489), § 4, eff. Sept. 1, 2011.

§ 54.0404. Electronic Transmission of Certain Visual Material Depicting Minor: Educational Programs

(a) If a child is found to have engaged in conduct indicating a need for supervision described by Section 51. 03(b)(7), the juvenile court may enter an order requiring the child to attend and successfully complete an educational program described by Section 37.218, Education Code, or another equivalent educational program.

(b) A juvenile court that enters an order under Subsection (a) shall require the child or the child's parent or other person responsible for the child's support to pay the cost of attending an educational program under Subsection (a) if the court determines that the child, parent, or other person is financially able to make payment.

Added by Acts 2011, 82nd Leg., ch. 1322 (S.B. 407), § 18, eff. Sept. 1, 2011.

§ 54.0405. Child Placed on Probation for Conduct Constituting Sexual Offense

(a) If a court or jury makes a disposition under Section 54.04 in which a child described by Subsection (b) is placed on probation, the court:

(1) may require as a condition of probation that the child:

(A) attend psychological counseling sessions for sex offenders as provided by Subsection (e); and

(B) submit to a polygraph examination as provided by Subsection (f) for purposes of evaluating the child's treatment progress; and

(2) shall require as a condition of probation that the child:

(A) register under Chapter 62, Code of Criminal Procedure; and

(B) submit a blood sample or other specimen to the Department of Public Safety under Subchapter G, Chapter 411, Government Code, for the purpose of creating a DNA record of the child, unless the child has already submitted the required specimen under other state law.

(b) This section applies to a child placed on probation for conduct constituting an offense for which the child is required to register as a sex offender under Chapter 62, Code of Criminal Procedure.

(c) Psychological counseling required as a condition of probation under Subsection (a) must be with an individual or organization that:

(1) provides sex offender treatment or counseling;

(2) is specified by the local juvenile probation department supervising the child; and

(3) meets minimum standards of counseling established by the local juvenile probation department.

(d) A polygraph examination required as a condition of probation under Subsection (a) must be administered by an individual who is:

(1) specified by the local juvenile probation department supervising the child; and

(2) licensed as a polygraph examiner under Chapter 1703, Occupations Code.

(e) A local juvenile probation department that specifies a sex offender treatment provider under Subsection (c) to provide counseling to a child shall:

(1) establish with the cooperation of the treatment provider the date, time, and place of the first counseling session between the child and the treatment provider;

(2) notify the child and the treatment provider, not later than the 21st day after the date the order making the disposition placing the child on probation under Section 54.04 becomes final, of the date, time, and place of the first counseling session between the child and the treatment provider; and

(3) require the treatment provider to notify the department immediately if the child fails to attend any scheduled counseling session.

(f) A local juvenile probation department that specifies a polygraph examiner under Subsection (d) to administer a polygraph examination to a child shall arrange for a polygraph examination to be administered to the child:

(1) not later than the 60th day after the date the child attends the first counseling session established under Subsection (e); and

(2) after the initial polygraph examination, as required by Subdivision (1), on the request of the treatment provider specified under Subsection (c).

(g) A court that requires as a condition of probation that a child attend psychological counseling under Subsection (a) may order the parent or guardian of the child to:

(1) attend four sessions of instruction with an individual or organization specified by the court relating to:

(A) sexual offenses;

(B) family communication skills;

(C) sex offender treatment;

(D) victims' rights;

(E) parental supervision; and

(F) appropriate sexual behavior; and

(2) during the period the child attends psychological counseling, participate in monthly treatment groups conducted by the child's treatment provider relating to the child's psychological counseling.

(h) A court that orders a parent or guardian of a child to attend instructional sessions and participate in treatment groups under Subsection (g) shall require:

(1) the individual or organization specified by the court under Subsection (g) to notify the court immediately if the parent or guardian fails to attend any scheduled instructional session; and

(2) the child's treatment provider specified under Subsection (c) to notify the court immediately if the parent or guardian fails to attend a session in which the parent or guardian is required to participate in a scheduled treatment group.

(i) A court that requires as a condition of probation that a child attend psychological counseling under Subsection (a) may, before the date the probation period ends, extend the probation for any additional period necessary to complete the required counseling as determined by the treatment provider, except that the probation may not be extended to a date after the date of the child's 18th birthday**, or 19th birthday if the child is placed on determinate sentence probation under Section 54.04(q)**.

Amended by Acts 2011, 82nd Leg., ch. 438 (S.B. 1208), § 3, eff. Sept. 1, 2011.

Comment

This section prescribes a particular form of sex offender treatment involving counseling and regular polygraph examinations and authorizes, but does not require, that the juvenile court make participation in that therapy a condition of probation. The entire section applies only to cases involving the commission of sex offenses against children under the age of 17. Similar provisions authorize making participation in counseling/polygraphing a condition of TYC parole. See TEX. HUM. RES. CODE ANN. § 245.053.

2011 Amendments allow a juvenile court to extend probation in these cases, if they are determinate sentence cases, to age 19 to allow completion of psychological counseling.

Leading Case

In re D.L.C., 124 S.W.3d 354 (Tex. App.—Fort Worth 2003, no pet.) (requirement of DNA sample is constitutional and applies to probationers with excused registration)

Attorney General Opinions

Tex. Atty. Gen. Op. JC–0070 (1999) (probationer has 5th but not 6th Amendment rights in sex treatment program)

Tex. Atty. Gen. Op. DM–458 (1997) (registered sex offender treatment provider must report all information, even if dated or incomplete, regarding child abuse)

Cross References

TEX. GOV'T CODE § 411.148. Mandatory DNA records to be maintained.

TEX. CODE CRIM. PROC. ANN. art 62.001 *et seq.*, Sex Offender Registration Program.

42 U.S.C. § 16901 Sex Offender Registration and Notification Act (SORNA)

---

§ 54.0406. Child Placed on Probation for Conduct Involving a Handgun

(a) If a court or jury places a child on probation under Section 54.04(d) for conduct that violates a penal law that includes as an element of the offense the possession, carrying, using, or exhibiting of a handgun, as defined by Section 46.01, Penal Code, and if at the adjudication hearing the court or jury affirmatively finds that the child personally possessed, carried, used, or exhibited the handgun, the court shall require as a condition of probation that the child, not later than the 30th day after the date the court places the child on probation, notify the juvenile probation officer who is supervising the child of the manner in which the child acquired the handgun, including the date and place of and any person involved in the acquisition.

(b) On receipt of information described by Subsection (a), a juvenile probation officer shall promptly notify the appropriate local law enforcement agency of the information.

(c) Information provided by a child to a juvenile probation officer as required by Subsection (a) and any other information derived from that information may not be used as evidence against the child in any juvenile or criminal proceeding.

Comment

This section requires a child placed on probation for an offense involving a handgun to inform his or her probation officer of how he or she acquired the handgun. Subsection (c) insures that anything said by the child in conformity to the requirements of this section cannot be used against the child in later judicial proceedings.

---

§ 54.0407. Cruelty to Animals: Counseling Required

If a child is found to have engaged in delinquent conduct constituting an offense under Section 42.09 or 42.092, Penal Code, the juvenile court shall order the child to participate in psychological counseling for a period to be determined by the court.

§ 54.0408. Referral of Child Exiting Probation to Mental Health or Mental Retardation Authority

A juvenile probation officer shall refer a child who has been determined to have a mental illness or mental retardation to an appropriate local mental health or mental retardation authority at least three months before the child is to complete the child's juvenile probation term unless the child is currently receiving treatment from the local mental health or mental retardation authority of the county in which the child resides.

§ 54.0409. DNA Sample Required on Certain Felony Adjudications

(a) This section applies only to conduct constituting the commission of a felony:

(1) that is listed in Section 3g(a)(1), Article 42.12, Code of Criminal Procedure; or

(2) for which it is shown that a deadly weapon, as defined by Section 1.07, Penal Code, was used or exhibited during the commission of the conduct or during immediate flight from the commission of the conduct.

(b) If a court or jury makes a disposition under Section 54.04 in which a child is adjudicated as having engaged in conduct constituting the commission of a felony to which this section applies and the child is placed on probation, the court shall require as a condition of probation that the child provide a DNA sample under Subchapter G, Chapter 411, Government Code, for the purpose of creating a DNA record of the child, unless the child has already submitted the required sample under other state law.

Comment

Children adjudicated delinquent and sentenced to TYC are required to submit a DNA sample. This section now requires children on probation for certain felony offenses to submit a DNA specimen.

§ 54.041. Orders Affecting Parents and Others

(a) When a child has been found to have engaged in delinquent conduct or conduct indicating a need for supervision and the juvenile court has made a finding that the child is in need of rehabilitation or that the protection of the public or the child requires that disposition be made, the juvenile court, on notice by any reasonable method to all persons affected, may:

(1) order any person found by the juvenile court to have, by a wilful act or omission, contributed to, caused, or encouraged the child's delinquent conduct or conduct indicating a need for supervision to do any act that the juvenile court determines to be reasonable and necessary for the welfare of the child or to refrain from doing any act that the juvenile court determines to be injurious to the welfare of the child;

(2) enjoin all contact between the child and a person who is found to be a contributing cause of the child's delinquent conduct or conduct indicating a need for supervision;

(3) after notice and a hearing of all persons affected order any person living in the same household with the child to participate in social or psychological counseling to assist in the rehabilitation of the child and to strengthen the child's family environment; or

(4) after notice and a hearing of all persons affected order the child's parent or other person responsible for the child's support to pay all or part of the reasonable costs of treatment programs in which the child is required to participate during the period of probation if the court finds the child's parent or person responsible for the child's support is able to pay the costs.

(b) If a child is found to have engaged in delinquent conduct or conduct indicating a need for supervision arising from the commission of an offense in which property damage or loss or personal injury occurred, the juvenile court, on notice to all persons affected and on hearing, may order the child or a parent to make full or partial restitution to the victim of the offense. The program of restitution must promote the rehabilitation of the child, be appropriate to the age and physical, emotional, and mental abilities of the child, and not conflict with the child's schooling. When practicable and subject to court supervision, the court may approve a restitution program based on a settlement between the child and the victim of the offense. An order under this subsection may provide for periodic payments by the child or a parent of the child for the period specified in the order but except as provided by Subsection (h), that period may not extend past the date of the 18th birthday of the child or past the date the child is no longer enrolled in an accredited secondary school in a program leading toward a high school diploma, whichever date is later.

(c) Restitution under this section is cumulative of any other remedy allowed by law and may be used in addition to other remedies; except that a victim of an offense is not entitled to receive more than actual damages under a juvenile court order.

(d) A person subject to an order proposed under Subsection (a) of this section is entitled to a hearing on the order before the order is entered by the court.

(e) An order made under this section may be enforced as provided by Section 54.07 of this code.

(f) If a child is found to have engaged in conduct indicating a need for supervision described under Section 51.03(b)(2) or (g), the court may order the child's parents or guardians to attend a program described by Section 25.093(f), Education Code, if a program is available.

(g) On a finding by the court that a child's parents or guardians have made a reasonable good faith effort to prevent the child from engaging in delinquent conduct or engaging in conduct indicating a need for supervision and that, despite the parents' or guardians' efforts, the child continues to engage in such conduct, the court shall waive any requirement for restitution that may be imposed on a parent under this section.

(h) If the juvenile court places the child on probation in a determinate sentence proceeding initiated under Section 53.045 and transfers supervision on the child's **19th** ~~18th~~ birthday to a district court for placement on community supervision, the district court shall require the payment of any unpaid restitution as a condition of the community supervision. The liability of the child's parent for restitution may not be extended by transfer to a district court for supervision.

Amended by Acts 2011, 82nd Leg., ch. 438 (S.B. 1208), § 4, eff. Sept. 1, 2011.

Comment

This section authorizes and limits the orders that may be placed by the juvenile court on the parents or other persons associated with a juvenile who has been adjudicated under Title 3.

The addition of (h) authorizes extension of the child's but not a parent's obligations to make restitution beyond age 19 when the child is placed on determinate sentence probation and the probation is transferred to criminal district court.

Subsection (a)(4) authorizes a parental order to pay for treatment of the child while on probation.

Leading Cases

In re D.K., 247 S.W.3d 802 (Tex. App.—Dallas 2008, no pet.)(child's claim that restitution amount was illegal because it would interfere with school was rejected because father and brothers required to pay also)

In re D.M., 191 S.W.3d 381 (Tex. App.—Austin 2006, rev. denied) (54.041 does not violate due process nor open-courts provision of Texas Constitution)

In re C.T., 43 S.W.3d 600 (Tex. App.—Corpus Christi 2001, no pet.) (restitution may be ordered for vehicle damage from accident when adjudication is for leaving the scene)

In re M.S., 985 S.W.2d 278 (Tex. App.—Corpus Christi 1999, no pet.) (child and parent can be ordered to make restitution to victim's insurance company)

In re D.S., 921 S.W.2d 860 (Tex. App.—San Antonio 1996, no writ) (cannot order restitution in criminal trespass case because loss not caused by offense)

In re J.R., 907 S.W.2d 107 (Tex. App.—Austin 1995, no writ) (restitution—no requirement that State show that medical bills were reasonable charges)

Cross References

TX FCA FAMILY §§ 41.001, 41.002, Parental Liability, *supra*.

§ 54.0411. Juvenile Probation Diversion Fund

(a) If a disposition hearing is held under Section 54.04 of this code, the juvenile court, after giving the child, parent, or other person responsible for the child's support a reasonable opportunity to be heard, shall order the child, parent, or other person, if financially able to do so, to pay a fee as costs of court of $20.

(b) Orders for the payment of fees under this section may be enforced as provided by Section 54.07 of this code.

(c) An officer collecting costs under this section shall keep separate records of the funds collected as costs under this section and shall deposit the funds in the county treasury.

(d) Each officer collecting court costs under this section shall file the reports required under Article 103.005, Code of Criminal Procedure. If no funds due as costs under this section have been collected in any quarter, the report required for each quarter shall be filed in the regular manner, and the report must state that no funds due under this section were collected.

(e) The custodian of the county treasury may deposit the funds collected under this section in interest-bearing accounts. The custodian shall keep records of the amount of funds on deposit collected under this section and not later than the last day of the month following each calendar quarter shall send to the comptroller of public accounts the funds collected under this section during the preceding quarter. A county may retain 10 percent of the funds as a service fee and may retain the interest accrued on the funds if the custodian of a county treasury keeps records of the amount of funds on deposit collected under this section and remits the funds to the comptroller within the period prescribed under this subsection.

(f) Funds collected are subject to audit by the comptroller and funds expended are subject to audit by the State Auditor.

(g) The comptroller shall deposit the funds in a special fund to be known as the juvenile probation diversion fund.

(h) The legislature shall determine and appropriate the necessary amount from the juvenile probation diversion fund to the Texas Juvenile Probation Commission for the purchase of services the commission considers necessary for the diversion of any juvenile who is at risk of commitment to the Texas Youth Commission. The Texas Juvenile Probation Commission shall develop guidelines for the use of the fund. The commission may not purchase the services if a person responsible for the child's support or a local juvenile probation department is financially able to provide the services.

§ 54.042. License Suspension

(a) A juvenile court, in a disposition hearing under Section 54.04, shall:

(1) order the Department of Public Safety to suspend a child's driver's license or permit, or if the child does not have a license or permit, to deny the issuance of a license or permit to the child if the court finds that the child has engaged in conduct that:

(A) violates a law of this state enumerated in Section 521.342(a), Transportation Code; or

(B) violates a penal law of this state or the United States, an element or elements of which involve a severe form of trafficking in persons, as defined by 22 U.S.C. Section 7102; or

(2) notify the Department of Public Safety of the adjudication, if the court finds that the child has engaged in conduct that violates a law of this state enumerated in Section 521.372(a), Transportation Code.

(b) A juvenile court, in a disposition hearing under Section 54.04, may order the Department of Public Safety to suspend a child's driver's license or permit or, if the child does not have a license or permit, to deny the issuance of a license or permit to the child, if the court finds that the child has engaged in conduct that violates Section 28.08, Penal Code.

(c) The order under Subsection (a)(1) shall specify a period of suspension or denial of 365 days.

(d) The order under Subsection (b) shall specify a period of suspension or denial:

(1) not to exceed 365 days; or

(2) of 365 days if the court finds the child has been previously adjudicated as having engaged in conduct violating Section 28.08, Penal Code.

(e) A child whose driver's license or permit has been suspended or denied pursuant to this section may, if the child is otherwise eligible for, and fulfills the requirements for issuance of, a provisional driver's license or permit under Chapter 521, Transportation Code, apply for and receive an occupational license in accordance with the provisions of Subchapter L of that chapter.

(f) A juvenile court, in a disposition hearing under Section 54.04, may order the Department of Public Safety to suspend a child's driver's license or permit or, if the child does not have a license or permit, to deny the issuance of a license or permit to the child for a period not to exceed 12 months if the court finds that the child has engaged in conduct in need of supervision or delinquent conduct other than the conduct described by Subsection (a).

(g) A juvenile court that places a child on probation under Section 54.04 may require as a reasonable condition of the probation that if the child violates the probation, the court may order the Department of Public Safety to suspend the child's driver's license or permit or, if the child does not have a license or permit, to deny the issuance of a license or permit to the child for a period not to exceed 12 months. The court may make this order if a child that is on probation under this condition violates the probation. A suspension under this subsection is cumulative of any other suspension under this section.

(h) If a child is adjudicated for conduct that violates Section 49.04, 49.07, or 49.08, Penal Code, and if any conduct on which that adjudication is based is a ground for a driver's license suspension under Chapter 524 or 724, Transportation Code, each of the suspensions shall be imposed. The court imposing a driver's license suspension under this section shall credit a period of suspension imposed under Chapter 524 or 724, Transportation Code, toward the period of suspension required under this section, except that if the child was previously adjudicated for conduct that violates Section 49.04, 49.07, or 49.08, Penal Code, credit may not be given.

Comment

The juvenile court is required to order the suspension of the driver's license of a juvenile who has been adjudicated for DWI or a controlled substance violation. The juvenile court may order the suspension of the juvenile's driving license for any other offense or as part of the revocation of probation.

Subsection (b) authorizes, but does not require, a juvenile court to order suspension or denial of driver's license upon adjudication of the offense of graffiti writing. Subsection (f) deals with the relationship of a license suspension for DWI and administrative license suspension.

Subsections (c) and (d) conform the duration of suspensions for children to those authorized by other laws in cases of adults.

Leading Cases

In re R.S.J., 999 S.W.2d 871 (Tex. App.—Tyler 1999, no pet.) (misdemeanor POM does not authorize license denial until age 19; automatic provisions apply)

In re C.E.M., 981 S.W.2d 771 (Tex. App.—Houston [1st Dist.] 1998, no pet.) (no authority to suspend driver's license until age 19 for felony controlled substance violation)

Cross References

TEX. TRANSP. CODE ANN. § 521.241 *et seq.*, subchapter L, Occupational Driver's License; TEX. TRANSP. CODE ANN. § 521.342, Suspension of License for Person Under 21; TEX. TRANSP. CODE ANN. § 521.372, Automatic Suspension of License on Conviction of Certain Felony Drug Violations.

§ 54.043. Monitoring School Attendance

If the court places a child on probation under Section 54.04(d) and requires as a condition of probation that the child attend school, the probation officer charged with supervising the child shall monitor the child's school attendance and report to the court if the child is voluntarily absent from school.

§ 54.044. Community Service

(a) If the court places a child on probation under Section 54.04(d), the court shall require as a condition of probation that the child work a specified number of hours at a community service project approved by the court and designated by the juvenile probation department as provided by Subsection (e), unless the court determines and enters a finding on the order placing the child on probation that:

(1) the child is physically or mentally incapable of participating in the project;

(2) participating in the project will be a hardship on the child or the family of the child; or

(3) the child has shown good cause that community service should not be required.

(b) The court may also order under this section that the child's parent perform community service with the child.

(c) The court shall order that the child and the child's parent perform a total of not more than 500 hours of community service under this section.

(d) A municipality or county that establishes a program to assist children and their parents in rendering community service under this section may purchase insurance policies protecting the municipality or county against claims brought by a person other than the child or the child's parent for a cause of action that arises from an act of the child or parent while rendering community service. The municipality or county is not liable under this section to the extent that damages are recoverable under a contract of insurance or under a plan of self-insurance authorized by statute. The liability of the municipality or county for a cause of action that arises from an action of the child or the child's parent while rendering community service may not exceed $100,000 to a single person and $300,000 for a single occurrence in the case of personal injury or death, and $10,000 for a single occurrence of property damage. Liability may not extend to punitive or exemplary damages. This subsection does not waive a defense, immunity, or jurisdictional bar available to the municipality or county or its officers or employees, nor shall this section be construed to waive, repeal, or modify any provision of Chapter 101, Civil Practice and Remedies Code.

(e) For the purposes of this section, a court may submit to the juvenile probation department a list of organizations or projects approved by the court for community service. The juvenile probation department may:

(1) designate an organization or project for community service only from the list submitted by the court; and

(2) reassign or transfer a child to a different organization or project on the list submitted by the court under this subsection without court approval.

(f) A person subject to an order proposed under Subsection (a) or (b) is entitled to a hearing on the order before the order is entered by the court.

(g) On a finding by the court that a child's parents or guardians have made a reasonable good faith effort to prevent the child from engaging in delinquent conduct or engaging in conduct indicating a need for supervision and that, despite the parents' or guardians' efforts, the child continues to engage in such conduct, the court shall waive any requirement for community service that may be imposed on a parent under this section.

(h) An order made under this section may be enforced as provided by Section 54.07.

(i) In a disposition hearing under Section 54.04 in which the court finds that a child engaged in conduct violating Section 521.453, Transportation Code, the court, in addition to any other order authorized under this title and if the court is located in a municipality or county that has established a community service program, may order the child to perform eight hours of community service as a condition of probation under Section 54.04(d) unless the child is shown to have previously engaged in conduct violating Section 521.453, Transportation Code, in which case the court may order the child to perform 12 hours of community service.

Comment

This section makes community service a mandatory condition of all juvenile probation orders. It also authorizes the juvenile court to order parents to perform community service with the child.

Subsection (i) authorizes but does not require community service of 8 hours for first offense and 12 hours for subsequent offense of possessing a fictitious driver's license or certificate.

§ 54.045. Admission of Unadjudicated Conduct

(a) During a disposition hearing under Section 54.04, a child may:

(1) admit having engaged in delinquent conduct or conduct indicating a need for supervision for which the child has not been adjudicated; and

(2) request the court to take the admitted conduct into account in the disposition of the child.

(b) If the prosecuting attorney agrees in writing, the court may take the admitted conduct into account in the disposition of the child.

(c) A court may take into account admitted conduct over which exclusive venue lies in another county only if the court obtains the written permission of the prosecuting attorney for that county.

(d) A child may not be adjudicated by any court for having engaged in conduct taken into account under this section, except that, if the conduct taken into account included conduct over which exclusive venue lies in another county and the written permission of the prosecuting attorney of that county was not obtained, the child may be adjudicated for that conduct, but the child's admission under this section may not be used against the child in the adjudication.

Comment

This section tracks Tex. Pen. Code Ann. § 12.45.

§ 54.046. Conditions of Probation for Damaging Property With Graffiti

(a) If a juvenile court places on probation under Section 54.04(d) a child adjudicated as having engaged in conduct in violation of Section 28.08, Penal Code, in addition to other conditions of probation, the court:

(1) shall order the child to:

(A) reimburse the owner of the property for the cost of restoring the property; or

(B) with consent of the owner of the property, restore the property by removing or painting over any markings made by the child on the property; and

(2) if the child made markings on public property, a street sign, or an official traffic-control device in violation of Section 28.08, Penal Code, shall order the child to:

(A) make to the political subdivision that owns the public property or erected the street sign or official traffic-control device restitution in an amount equal to the lesser of the cost to the political subdivision of replacing or restoring the public property, street sign, or official traffic-control device; or

(B) with the consent of the political subdivision, restore the public property, street sign, or official traffic-control device by removing or painting over any markings made by the child on the property, sign, or device.

(a–1) For purposes of Subsection (a), "official traffic-control device" has the meaning assigned by Section 541.304, Transportation Code.

(b) In addition to a condition imposed under Subsection (a), the court may require the child as a condition of probation to attend a class with instruction in self-responsibility and empathy for a victim of an offense conducted by a local juvenile probation department.

(c) If a juvenile court orders a child to make restitution under Subsection (a) and the child, child's parent, or other person responsible for the child's support is financially unable to make the restitution, the court may order the child to perform a specific number of hours of community service, in addition to the hours required under Subsection (d), to satisfy the restitution.

(d) If a juvenile court places on probation under Section 54.04(d) a child adjudicated as having engaged in conduct in violation of Section 28.08, Penal Code, in addition to other conditions of probation, the court shall order the child to perform:

(1) at least 15 hours of community service if the amount of pecuniary loss resulting from the conduct is $50 or more but less than $500; or

(2) at least 30 hours of community service if the amount of pecuniary loss resulting from the conduct is $500 or more.

(e) The juvenile court shall direct a child ordered to make restitution under this section to deliver the amount or property due as restitution to a juvenile probation department for transfer to the owner. The juvenile probation department shall notify the juvenile court when the child has delivered the full amount of restitution ordered.

Comment

A separate offense of graffiti exists in § 28.08 of the Penal Code. This section requires the juvenile court to order restorative measures as conditions of probation for that offense and authorizes minimum community service hours.

§ 54.0461. Payment of Juvenile Delinquency Prevention Fees

(a) If a child is adjudicated as having engaged in delinquent conduct that violates Section 28.08, Penal Code, the juvenile court shall order the child, parent, or other person responsible for the child's support to pay to the court a $50 juvenile delinquency prevention fee as a cost of court.

(b) The court shall deposit fees received under this section to the credit of the county juvenile delinquency prevention fund provided for under Article 102.0171, Code of Criminal Procedure.

(c) If the court finds that a child, parent, or other person responsible for the child's support is unable to pay the juvenile delinquency prevention fee required under Subsection (a), the court shall enter into the child's case records a statement of that finding. The court may waive a fee under this section only if the court makes the finding under this subsection.

§ 54.0462. Payment of Fees for Offenses Requiring DNA Testing

(a) If a child is adjudicated as having engaged in delinquent conduct that constitutes the commission of a felony and the provision of a DNA sample is required under Section 54.0409 or other law, the juvenile court shall order the child, parent, or other person responsible for the child's support to pay to the court as a cost of court:

(1) a $50 fee if the disposition of the case includes a commitment to a facility operated by or under contract with the Texas Youth Commission; and

(2) a $34 fee if the disposition of the case does not include a commitment described by Subdivision (1) and the child is required to submit a DNA sample under Section 54.0409 or other law.

(b) The clerk of the court shall transfer to the comptroller any funds received under this section. The comptroller shall credit the funds to the Department of Public Safety to help defray the cost of any analyses performed on DNA samples provided by children with respect to whom a court cost is collected under this section.

(c) If the court finds that a child, parent, or other person responsible for the child's support is unable to pay the fee required under Subsection (a), the court shall enter into the child's case records a statement of that finding. The court may waive a fee under this section only if the court makes the finding under this subsection.

§ 54.047. Alcohol Related Offense

If the court or jury finds at an adjudication hearing for a child that the child engaged in conduct indicating a need for supervision or delinquent conduct that violates the alcohol-related offenses in Section 106.02, 106.025, 106.04, 106.05, or 106.07, Alcoholic Beverage Code, or Section 49.02, Penal Code, the court shall, subject to a finding under Section 54.04(c), order, in addition to any other order authorized by this title, that, in the manner provided by Section 106.071(d), Alcoholic Beverage Code:

(1) the child perform community service; and

(2) the child's driver's license or permit be suspended or that the child be denied issuance of a driver's license or permit.

Comment

By reference to § 106.071(d), Alcoholic Beverage Code, this section requires the court to impose 8 to 12 hours of community service for the first offense and 20 to 40 hours for subsequent offenses and requires the court to order driver's license suspension for 30 days for a first offender, 60 days for a second-time offender and 180 for a third time offender.

---

§ 54.048. Restitution

(a) A juvenile court, in a disposition hearing under Section 54.04, may order restitution to be made by the child and the child's parents.

(b) This section applies without regard to whether the petition in the case contains a plea for restitution.

§ 54.0481. Restitution for Damaging Property With Graffiti

(a) A juvenile court, in a disposition hearing under Section 54.04 regarding a child who has been adjudicated to have engaged in delinquent conduct that violates Section 28.08, Penal Code:

(1) may order the child or a parent or other person responsible for the child's support to make restitution by:

(A) reimbursing the owner of the property for the cost of restoring the property; or

(B) with the consent of the owner of the property, personally restoring the property by removing or painting over any markings the child made; and

(2) if the child made markings on public property, a street sign, or an official traffic-control device in violation of Section 28.08, Penal Code, may order the child or a parent or other person responsible for the child's support to:

(A) make to the political subdivision that owns the public property or erected the street sign or official traffic-control device restitution in an amount equal to the lesser of the cost to the political subdivision of replacing or restoring the public property, street sign, or official traffic-control device; or

(B) with the consent of the political subdivision, restore the public property, street sign, or official traffic-control device by removing or painting over any markings made by the child on the property, sign, or device.

(b) If a juvenile court orders a child to make restitution under Subsection (a) and the child, child's parent, or other person responsible for the child's support is financially unable to make the restitution, the court may order the child to perform a specific number of hours of community service to satisfy the restitution.

(c) For purposes of Subsection (a), "official traffic-control device" has the meaning assigned by Section 541.304, Transportation Code.

Comment

This section requires the probation department to immediately place payments to victims in interest bearing accounts and notify the victims by certified mail. The section further defines procedures for unclaimed victim payments.

§ 54.0482. Treatment of Restitution Payments

(a) A juvenile probation department that receives a payment to a victim as the result of a juvenile court order for restitution shall immediately:

(1) deposit the payment in an interest-bearing account in the county treasury; and

(2) notify the victim by certified mail, sent to the last known address of the victim, that a payment has been received.

(b) The juvenile probation department shall promptly remit the payment to a victim who has been notified under Subsection (a) and makes a claim for payment.

(c) On or before the fifth anniversary of the date the juvenile probation department receives a payment for a victim that is not claimed by the victim, the department shall make and document a good faith effort to locate and notify the victim that an unclaimed payment exists, including:

(1) confirming, if possible, the victim's most recent address with the Department of Public Safety; and

(2) making at least one additional certified mailing to the victim.

(d) A juvenile probation department satisfies the good faith requirement under Subsection (c) by sending by certified mail to the victim, during the period the child is required by the juvenile court order to make payments to the victim, a notice that the victim is entitled to an unclaimed payment.

(e) If a victim claims a payment on or before the fifth anniversary of the date on which the juvenile probation department mailed a notice to the victim under Subsection (a), the juvenile probation department shall pay the victim the amount of the original payment, less any interest earned while holding the payment.

(f) If a victim does not claim a payment on or before the fifth anniversary of the date on which the juvenile probation department mailed a notice to the victim under Subsection (a), the department:

(1) has no liability to the victim or anyone else in relation to the payment; and

(2) shall transfer the payment from the interest-bearing account to a special fund of the county treasury, the unclaimed juvenile restitution fund.

(g) The county may spend money in the unclaimed juvenile restitution fund only for the same purposes for which the county may spend juvenile state aid.

§ 54.049. Conditions of Probation for Desecrating a Cemetery or Abusing a Corpse

(a) If a juvenile court places on probation under Section 54.04(d) a child adjudicated to have engaged in conduct in violation of Section 28.03(f), Penal Code, involving damage or destruction inflicted on a place of human burial or under Section 42.08, Penal Code, in addition to other conditions of probation, the court shall order the child to make restitution to a cemetery organization operating a cemetery affected by the conduct in an amount equal to the cost to the cemetery of repairing any damage caused by the conduct.

(b) If a juvenile court orders a child to make restitution under Subsection (a) and the child is financially unable to make the restitution, the court may order:

(1) the child to perform a specific number of hours of community service to satisfy the restitution; or

(2) a parent or other person responsible for the child's support to make the restitution in the amount described by Subsection (a).

(c) In this section, "cemetery" and "cemetery organization" have the meanings assigned by Section 711.001, Health and Safety Code.

Comment

This provision allows for a juvenile court to order restitution to a cemetery organization or to have the child perform community service hours or to order the parents or persons responsible for the child to pay restitution.

§ 54.0491. Gang–Related Conduct

(a) In this section:

(1) "Criminal street gang" has the meaning assigned by Section 71.01, Penal Code.

(2) "Gang-related conduct" means conduct that violates a penal law of the grade of Class B misdemeanor or higher and in which a child engages with the intent to:

(A) further the criminal activities of a criminal street gang of which the child is a member;

(B) gain membership in a criminal street gang; or

(C) avoid detection as a member of a criminal street gang.

(b) A juvenile court, in a disposition hearing under Section 54.04 regarding a child who has been adjudicated to have engaged in delinquent conduct that is also gang-related conduct, shall order the child to participate in a criminal street gang intervention program that is appropriate for the child based on the child's level of involvement in the criminal activities of a criminal street gang. The intervention program:

(1) must include at least 12 hours of instruction; and

(2) may include voluntary tattoo removal.

(c) If a child required to attend a criminal street gang intervention program is committed to the Texas Youth Commission as a result of the gang-related conduct, the child must complete the intervention program before being discharged from the custody of or released under supervision by the commission.

Cross References

Tex. Penal Code section 71.01

Comment

Juveniles adjudicated delinquent of gang related conduct shall be required to participate in gang intervention programs whether the child is placed on probation or in TYC or TJJD.

§ 54.05. Hearing to Modify Disposition

(a) **Except as provided by Subsection (a–1), any**~~Any~~ disposition, except a commitment to the Texas Youth Commission, may be modified by the juvenile court as provided in this section until:

(1) the child reaches**:**

(A) the child's ~~his~~ 18th birthday; or

(B) the child's 19th birthday, if the child was placed on determinate sentence probation under Section 54.04(q); or

(2) the child is earlier discharged by the court or operation of law.

(a–1) A disposition regarding conduct under Section 51.03(b)(2) may be modified by the juvenile court as provided by this section until the expiration of the period described by Section 54.0402.

Text of subsec. (b), as amended by Acts 2011, 81st Leg., ch. 483 (S.B. 1208), § 5

(b) Except for a commitment to the Texas Youth Commission **or a placement on determinate sentence probation under Section 54.04(q)**, all dispositions automatically terminate when the child reaches **the child's** ~~his~~ 18th birthday.

Text of subsec. (b), as amended by Acts 2011, 81st Leg., ch. 1098 (S.B. 1489), § 5

(b) Except for a commitment to the Texas Youth Commission **or a disposition under Section 54.0402**, all dispositions automatically terminate when the child reaches his 18th birthday.

(c) There is no right to a jury at a hearing to modify disposition.

(d) A hearing to modify disposition shall be held on the petition of the child and his parent, guardian, guardian ad litem, or attorney, or on the petition of the state, a probation officer, or the court itself. Reasonable notice of a hearing to modify disposition shall be given to all parties.

(e) After the hearing on the merits or facts, the court may consider written reports from probation officers, professional court employees, or professional consultants in addition to the testimony of other witnesses. Prior to the hearing to modify disposition, the court shall provide the attorney for the child with access to all written matter to be considered by the court in deciding whether to modify disposition. The court may order counsel not to reveal items to the child or his parent, guardian, or guardian ad litem if such disclosure would materially harm the treatment and rehabilitation of the child or would substantially decrease the likelihood of receiving information from the same or similar sources in the future.

(f) Except as provided by Subsection (j), a disposition based on a finding that the child engaged in delinquent conduct that violates a penal law of this state or the United States of the grade of felony may be modified so as to commit the child to the Texas Youth Commission if the court after a hearing to modify disposition finds by a preponderance of the evidence that the child violated a reasonable and lawful order of the court. A disposition based on a finding that the child engaged in habitual felony conduct as described by Section 51.031 or in delinquent conduct that included a violation of a penal law listed in Section 53.045(a) may be modified to commit the child to the Texas Youth Commission with a possible transfer to the Texas Department of Criminal Justice for a definite term prescribed by Section 54.04(d)(3) if the original petition was approved by the grand jury under Section 53.045 and if after a hearing to modify the disposition the court finds that the child violated a reasonable and lawful order of the court.

(g) Except as provided by Subsection (j), a disposition based solely on a finding that the child engaged in conduct indicating a need for supervision may not be modified to commit the child to the Texas Youth Commission. A new finding in compliance with Section 54.03 must be made that the child engaged in delinquent conduct that meets the requirements for commitment under Section 54.04.

(h) A hearing shall be held prior to placement in a post-adjudication secure correctional facility for a period longer than 30 days or commitment to the Texas Youth Commission as a modified disposition. In other disposition modifications, the child and the child's parent, guardian, guardian ad litem, or attorney may waive hearing in accordance with Section 51.09.

(i) The court shall specifically state in the order its reasons for modifying the disposition and shall furnish a copy of the order to the child.

(j) If, after conducting a hearing to modify disposition without a jury, the court finds by a preponderance of the evidence that a child violated a reasonable and lawful condition of probation ordered under Section 54.04(q), the court may modify the disposition to commit the child to the Texas Youth Commission under Section 54.04(d)(3) for a term that does not exceed the original sentence assessed by the court or jury.

(k) Repealed by Acts 2007, 80th Leg., ch. 263, § 64(2).

(*l*) The court may extend a period of probation under this section at any time during the period of probation or, if a motion for revocation or modification of probation is filed before the period of supervision ends, before the first anniversary of the date on which the period of probation expires.

(m) If the court places the child on probation outside the child's home or commits the child to the Texas Youth Commission, the court:

(1) shall include in the court's order a determination that:

(A) it is in the child's best interests to be placed outside the child's home;

(B) reasonable efforts were made to prevent or eliminate the need for the child's removal from the child's home and to make it possible for the child to return home; and

(C) the child, in the child's home, cannot be provided the quality of care and level of support and supervision that the child needs to meet the conditions of probation; and

(2) may approve an administrative body to conduct a permanency hearing pursuant to 42 U.S.C. Section 675 if required during the placement or commitment of the child.

Amended by Acts 2011, 82nd Leg., ch. 438 (S.B. 1208), § 5, eff. Sept. 1, 2011; Acts 2011, 82nd Leg., ch. 1098 (S.B. 1489), § 5, eff. Sept. 1, 2011.

Comment

This section specifies the procedures for a wide range of modifications of dispositional orders, from early termination of probation through its revocation and commitment to the TYC or TJJD.

2011 amendments extend modification of disposition in determinate sentence probation cases to age 19.

Subsection (j) authorizes the revocation of determinate sentence act probation and the imposition of any sentence up to the sentence that was originally assessed by the judge or jury. Because determinate sentence act probation now has a ceiling of 10 years upon revocation, the right to a jury at the revocation hearing has been eliminated.

A modification of probation to commitment to TYC or TJJD based on an original adjudication of a misdemeanor is prohibited.

Subsection (h) requires that a modification hearing be held for a modification that results in a term of longer than 30 days in a local secure correctional facility, just as in the case of commitment to the TYC. Waiver of the hearing is not permitted.

Subsection (*l*) permits the court to extend the probation term at any time up to one year after it expired. It is modeled on a provision in the Code of Criminal Procedure applicable to criminal cases.

Subsection (m) requires the same findings necessary under § 54.04 prior to removing a child from home be made when modifying a disposition and ordering a child's removal from home. This amendment came in response to the Texas Supreme Court decision *In re* J.P., 136 S.W.3d 629 (Tex. 2004).

Leading Cases

In re J.M., 287 S.W.3d 481 (Tex. App.—Texarkana 2009, no pet.)(54.05i requires supplemental findings in addition to a mere recitation of the statutory language)

In re A.D., 287 S.W.3d 356 (Tex. App.—Texarkana 2009, pet. denied)(new disposition hearing required where no evidence was presented to show reasonable efforts were made to avoid removing child from home)

In re A.G., 292 S.W.3d 755 (Tex. App.—Eastland 2009, no pet.)(although child was arrested for new offense, no showing of alternative placement efforts was made)

In re E.G., 212 S.W.3d 536 (Tex. App.—Austin 2006, no pet.) (an order modifying a juvenile disposition is not subject to the requirements of § 54.04(n)).

In re J.M., 133 S.W.3d 721 (Tex. App.—Corpus Christi 2003, no pet.) (juvenile may raise affirmative defense of inability to pay restitution)

In re E.D., 127 S.W.3d 860 (Tex. App.—Austin 2004, no pet.) (probation report authorized court to place runaway in secure confinement)

In re B.J., 100 S.W.3d 448 (Tex. App.—Texarkana 2003, no pet.) (non-association violation requires proof juvenile knew of other's probation status)

In re J.L.D., 74 S.W.3d 166 (Tex. App.—Texarkana 2002, no pet.) (violates due process to revoke probation for same offense for which the probation term had earlier been extended)

In re D.S.S., 72 S.W.3d 725 (Tex. App.—Waco 2002, no pet.) (written matter disclosure requirement applies only to penalty phase of modification hearing)

In re M.A.W., 55 S.W.3d 101 (Tex. App.—Amarillo 2001, no pet.) (for 30 days court has plenary power to change probation term previously set by it)

In re J.A.D., 31 S.W.3d 668 (Tex. App.—Waco 2000, no pet.) (cannot revoke probation based on motion filed after probation expired)

In re S.H., 846 S.W.2d 103 (Tex. App.—Corpus Christi 1992, no writ) (no right to jury trial at modification hearing)

In re M.L.S., 590 S.W.2d 626 (Tex. Civ. App.—San Antonio 1979, no writ) (10 days' notice of revocation required)

In re S.C., 556 S.W.2d 119 (Tex. Civ. App.—Waco 1977, no writ) (no requirement of 10 days notice of revocation hearing)

In re R.A.B., 525 S.W.2d 892 (Tex. Civ. App.—Corpus Christi 1975, no writ) (illegally seized evidence inadmissible in probation revocation hearing)

In re E.B., 525 S.W.2d 543 (Tex. Civ. App.—Amarillo 1975, writ ref'd n.r.e.) (Chapter 55 applies to modification proceedings)

In re D.E.P., 512 S.W.2d 789 (Tex. Civ. App.—Houston [14th Dist.] 1974, no writ) (probation condition violated must have been a reasonable one)

---

§ 54.051. Transfer of Determinate Sentence Probation to Appropriate District Court

(a) On motion of the state concerning a child who is placed on probation under Section 54.04(q) for a period, including any extension ordered under Section 54.05, that will continue after the child's **19th** ~~18th~~ birthday, the juvenile court shall hold a hearing to determine whether to transfer the child to an appropriate district court or discharge the child from the sentence of probation.

(b) The hearing must be conducted before the child's **19th** ~~18th~~ birthday and in the same manner as a hearing to modify disposition under Section 54.05.

(c) If, after a hearing, the court determines to discharge the child, the court shall specify a date on or before the child's **19th** ~~18th~~ birthday to discharge the child from the sentence of probation.

(d) If, after a hearing, the court determines to transfer the child, the court shall transfer the child to an appropriate district court on the child's **19th** ~~18th~~ birthday.

(e) A district court that exercises jurisdiction over a child transferred under Subsection (d) shall place the child on community supervision under Article 42.12, Code of Criminal Procedure, for the remainder of the child's probationary period and under conditions consistent with those ordered by the juvenile court.

(e–1) The restrictions on a judge placing a defendant on community supervision imposed by Section 3g, Article 42.12, Code of Criminal Procedure, do not apply to a case transferred from the juvenile court. The minimum period of community supervision imposed by Section 3(b), Article 42.12, Code of Criminal Procedure, does not apply to a case transferred from the juvenile court.

(e–2) If a child who is placed on community supervision under this section violates a condition of that supervision or if the child violated a condition of probation ordered under Section 54.04(q) and that probation violation was not discovered by the state before the child's **19th** ~~18th~~ birthday, the district court shall dispose of the violation of community supervision or probation, as appropriate, in the same manner as if the court had originally exercised jurisdiction over the case.

If the judge revokes community supervision, the judge may reduce the prison sentence to any length without regard to the minimum term imposed by Section 23(a), Article 42.12, Code of Criminal Procedure.

(e–3) The time that a child serves on probation ordered under Section 54.04(q) is the same as time served on community supervision ordered under this section for purposes of determining the child's eligibility for early discharge from community supervision under Section 20, Article 42.12, Code of Criminal Procedure.

(f) The juvenile court may transfer a child to an appropriate district court as provided by this section without a showing that the child violated a condition of probation ordered under Section 54.04(q).

(g) If the juvenile court places the child on probation for an offense for which registration as a sex offender is required by Chapter 62, Code of Criminal Procedure, and defers the registration requirement until completion of treatment for the sex offense under Subchapter H, Chapter 62, Code of Criminal Procedure, the authority under that article to reexamine the need for registration on completion of treatment is transferred to the court to which probation is transferred.

(h) If the juvenile court places the child on probation for an offense for which registration as a sex offender is required by Chapter 62, Code of Criminal Procedure, and the child registers, the authority of the court to excuse further compliance with the registration requirement under Subchapter H, Chapter 62, Code of Criminal Procedure, is transferred to the court to which probation is transferred.

(i) If the juvenile court exercises jurisdiction over a person who is 18 years of age or older under Section 51.041 or 51.0412, the court or jury may, if the person is otherwise eligible, place the person on probation under Section 54.04(q). The juvenile court shall set the conditions of probation and immediately transfer supervision of the person to the appropriate court exercising criminal jurisdiction under Subsection (e).

Amended by Acts 2011, 82nd Leg., ch. 438 (S.B. 1208), § 6, eff. Sept. 1, 2011.

Comment

This section deals with the mechanics of administering the ten year determinate sentence act probation provision of § 54.04(q). If the juvenile court has imposed a probation term that extends beyond the child's 19 birthday, a hearing must be held before that date. to determine whether to transfer the probation or to terminate it. If the child is transferred, he or she is placed on adult community supervision on substantially the same terms as were provided for juvenile probation. A revocation after transfer or discovered after transfer is handled in the criminal courts; a pre-age 19 revocation is handled in the juvenile court.

Subsection (e–1) states that when a juvenile court transfers probation to criminal court, the criminal court is not prohibited by so-called 3g offense restrictions (aggravated offenses or deadly weapon findings) from placing the child on adult probation. It also makes it clear that minimum probation terms of adult law—2 years for second or third degree felony and 5 years for a first degree felony—do not apply. Subsection (e–2) relieves the criminal court judge of the minimum prison sentence restrictions upon revocation—2 years for a second or third degree felony and 5 years for a first degree felony.

Subsection (g) makes it clear that the authority to re-examine the need for sex offender registration in cases of registration deferral is transferred to the criminal court if probation supervision is transferred to criminal court. Under (h), authority to grant de-registration of a registered juvenile probationer is transferred to criminal court if probation supervision is transferred.

Subsection (i) permits a juvenile court to place a person 18 or older properly adjudicated under the determinate sentence act on probation and immediately transfer supervision to adult court. This means that a child does not lose probation eligibility just because disposition of his or her case is delayed until after the 18th birthday.

Leading Case

Krupa v. State, 286 S.W.3d 74 (Tex. App.—Waco 2009, no pet.)(once a juvenile case has been transferred to adult court, that court can extend the term of probation)

In re J.H., 176 S.W.3d 677 (Tex. App.—Dallas 2005, no pet.) (an order transferring determinate sentence probation to criminal district court is not appealable)

§ 54.052. Credit for Time Spent in Detention Facility for Child With Determinate Sentence

(a) This section applies only to a child who is committed to the Texas Youth Commission under a determinate sentence under Section 54.04(d)(3) or (m) or Section 54.05(f).

(b) The judge of the court in which a child is adjudicated shall give the child credit on the child's sentence for the time spent by the child, in connection with the conduct for which the child was adjudicated, in a secure detention facility before the child's transfer to a Texas Youth Commission facility.

(c) If a child appeals the child's adjudication and is retained in a secure detention facility pending the appeal, the judge of the court in which the child was adjudicated shall give the child credit on the child's sentence for the time spent by the child in a secure detention facility pending disposition of the child's appeal. The court shall endorse on both the commitment and the mandate from the appellate court all credit given the child under this subsection.

(d) The Texas Youth Commission shall grant any credit under this section in computing the child's eligibility for parole and discharge.

Comment

This section requires the trial judge to give credit toward a determinate sentence for time spent in a secure detention facility while waiting transfer to TYC or TJJD or while an appeal is pending.

§ 54.06. Judgments for Support

(a) At any stage of the proceeding, when a child has been placed outside the child's home, the juvenile court, after giving the parent or other person responsible for the child's support a reasonable opportunity to be heard, shall order the parent or other person to pay in a manner directed by the court a reasonable sum for the support in whole or in part of the child or the court shall waive the payment by order. The court shall order that the payment for support be made to the local juvenile probation department to be used only for residential care and other support for the child unless the child has been committed to the Texas Youth Commission, in which case the court shall order that the payment be made to the Texas Youth Commission for deposit in a special account in the general revenue fund that may be appropriated only for the care of children committed to the commission.

(b) At any stage of the proceeding, when a child has been placed outside the child's home and the parent of the child is obligated to pay support for the child under a court order under Title 5, the juvenile court shall order that the person entitled to receive the support assign the person's right to support for the child placed outside the child's home to the local juvenile probation department to be used for residential care and other support for the child unless the child has been committed to the Texas Youth Commission, in which event the court shall order that the assignment be made to the Texas Youth Commission.

(c) A court may enforce an order for support under this section by ordering garnishment of the wages of the person ordered to pay support or by any other means available to enforce a child support order under Title 5.

(d) Repealed by Acts 2003, 78th Leg., ch. 283, § 61(1).

(e) The court shall apply the child support guidelines under Subchapter C, Chapter 154, in an order requiring the payment of child support under this section. The court shall also require in an order to pay child support under this section that health insurance be provided for the child. Subchapter D, Chapter 154, applies to an order requiring health insurance for a child under this section.

(f) An order under this section prevails over any previous child support order issued with regard to the child to the extent of any conflict between the orders.

Comment

Subsection (d) was repealed in 2003 by HB 2319, Section 61(1) because Section 54.07, to which it refers, was modified to speak only to court orders other than child support. Subsection (c) accesses all Title 5 remedies for child support orders entered under this section.

---

§ 54.061. Payment of Probation Fees

(a) If a child is placed on probation under Section 54.04(d)(1) of this code, the juvenile court, after giving the child, parent, or other person responsible for the child's support a reasonable opportunity to be heard, shall order the child, parent, or other person, if financially able to do so, to pay to the court a fee of not more than $15 a month during the period that the child continues on probation.

(b) Orders for the payment of fees under this section may be enforced as provided by Section 54.07 of this code.

(c) The court shall deposit the fees received under this section in the county treasury to the credit of a special fund that may be used only for juvenile probation or community-based juvenile corrections services or facilities in which a juvenile may be required to live while under court supervision.

(d) If the court finds that a child, parent, or other person responsible for the child's support is financially unable to pay the probation fee required under Subsection (a), the court shall enter into the records of the child's case a statement of that finding. The court may waive a fee under this section only if the court makes the finding under this subsection.

§ 54.07. Enforcement of Order

(a) Except as provided by Subsection (b) or a juvenile court child support order, any order of the juvenile court may be enforced as provided by Chapter 61.

(b) A violation of any of the following orders of the juvenile court may not be enforced by contempt of court proceedings against the child:

(1) an order setting conditions of probation;

(2) an order setting conditions of deferred prosecution; and

(3) an order setting conditions of release from detention.

(c) This section and Chapter 61 do not preclude a juvenile court from summarily finding a child or other person in direct contempt of the juvenile court for conduct occurring in the presence of the judge of the court. Direct contempt of the juvenile court by a child is punishable by a maximum of 10 days' confinement in a secure juvenile detention facility or by a maximum of 40 hours of community service, or both. The juvenile court may not impose a fine on a child for direct contempt.

(d) This section and Chapter 61 do not preclude a juvenile court in an appropriate case from using a civil or coercive contempt proceeding to enforce an order.

Comment

This section conforms to the enactment of Chapter 61 dealing with parental rights and responsibilities. Subsection (a) excepts child support orders from Title 3 enforcement of parental orders because 54.06 accesses the full range of Title 5 enforcement remedies for such orders. Subsection (b) prohibits using contempt of court proceedings to enforce violations of probation, deferred prosecution or conditional release from detention, since specific remedies for such violations are provided elsewhere. Subsection (c) saves direct contempt from the procedural complexities of Chapter 61 and restricts the penalties that may be imposed for direct contempt by juveniles. Subsection (d) saves civil or coercive contempt—confinement until the subject complies with a court order—from the requirements of Chapter 61.

§ 54.08. Public Access to Court Hearings

(a) Except as provided by this section, the court shall open hearings under this title to the public unless the court, for good cause shown, determines that the public should be excluded.

(b) The court may not prohibit a person who is a victim of the conduct of a child, or the person's family, from personally attending a hearing under this title relating to the conduct by the child unless the victim or member of the victim's family is to testify in the hearing or any subsequent hearing relating to the conduct and the court determines that the victim's or family member's testimony would be materially affected if the victim or member of the victim's family hears other testimony at trial.

(c) If a child is under the age of 14 at the time of the hearing, the court shall close the hearing to the public unless the court finds that the interests of the child or the interests of the public would be better served by opening the hearing to the public.

(d) In this section, "family" has the meaning assigned by Section 71.003.

Comment

Subsection (b) expands the victim's right to attend a juvenile hearing to include members of the victim's family. Subsection (c) provides that if the respondent is under the age of 14 at the time of the hearing, the hearing is presumed to be closed, but may be opened by the judge upon a finding that the interests of the child or the public would be better served by an open hearing. If the child is 14 years of age or older, the hearing is presumptively open but the court can for good cause shown close the hearing.

§ 54.09. Recording of Proceedings

All judicial proceedings under this chapter except detention hearings shall be recorded by stenographic notes or by electronic, mechanical, or other appropriate means. Upon request of any party, a detention hearing shall be recorded.

Leading Cases

In re S.P., 9 S.W.3d 304 (Tex. App.—San Antonio 1999, no writ) (failure to record bench conferences did not require reversal when no showing made of harm on appellate argument)

In re S.J., 940 S.W.2d 332 (Tex. App.—San Antonio 1997, no writ) (juvenile waived under § 51.09 right to have proceedings recorded)

S.S. v. State, 879 S.W.2d 395 (Tex. App.—Eastland 1994, no writ) (failure to record jury argument reversible error)

§ 54.10. Hearings Before Referee

Text of section effective until Jan. 1, 2012, if H.B. 79 of the First Called Session of the 82nd Legislature becomes law. At time of publication, Texas Governor Rick Perry had yet to take action on this bill, which was enrolled and sent to the governor on June 29, 2011.

(a) Except as provided by Subsection (e), a hearing under Section 54.03, 54.04, or 54.05, including a jury trial, a hearing under Chapter 55, including a jury trial, or a hearing under the Interstate Compact for Juveniles (Chapter 60) may be held by a referee appointed in accordance with Section 51.04(g) or a master appointed under Chapter 54, Government Code, provided:

(1) the parties have been informed by the referee or master that they are entitled to have the hearing before the juvenile court judge; and

(2) after each party is given an opportunity to object, no party objects to holding the hearing before the referee or master.

(b) The determination under Section 53.02(f) whether to release a child may be made by a referee appointed in accordance with Section 51.04(g) if:

(1) the child has been informed by the referee that the child is entitled to have the determination made by the juvenile court judge or a substitute judge authorized by Section 51.04(f); or

(2) the child and the attorney for the child have in accordance with Section 51.09 waived the right to have the determination made by the juvenile court judge or a substitute judge.

(c) If a child objects to a referee making the determination under Section 53.02(f), the juvenile court judge or a substitute judge authorized by Section 51.04(f) shall make the determination.

(d) At the conclusion of the hearing or immediately after making the determination, the referee shall transmit written findings and recommendations to the juvenile court judge. The juvenile court judge shall adopt, modify, or reject the referee's recommendations not later than the next working day after the day that the judge receives the recommendations. Failure to act within that time results in release of the child by operation of law and a recommendation that the child be released operates to secure the child's immediate release subject to the power of the juvenile court judge to modify or reject that recommendation.

(e) The hearings provided by Sections 54.03, 54.04, and 54.05 may not be held before a referee if the grand jury has approved of the petition and the child is subject to a determinate sentence.

Added by Acts 1975, 64th Leg., p. 2157, ch. 693, § 19, eff. Sept. 1, 1975. Amended by Acts 1979, 66th Leg., p. 1830, ch. 743, § 2, eff. Aug. 27, 1979; Acts 1987, 70th Leg., ch. 385, § 12, eff. Sept. 1, 1987; Acts 1991, 72nd Leg., ch. 74, § 1, eff. Sept. 1, 1991; Acts 1997, 75th Leg., ch. 1086, § 13, eff. Sept. 1, 1997; Acts 1999, 76th Leg., ch. 232, § 5, eff. Sept. 1, 1999; Acts 1999, 76th Leg., ch. 1477, § 13, eff. Sept. 1, 1999; Acts 2005, 79th Leg., ch. 1007, § 2.03, eff. Aug. 26, 2008.

§ 54.10. Hearings Before Referee

Text of section effective Jan. 1, 2012, if H.B. 79 of the First Called Session of the 82nd Legislature becomes law. At time of publication, Texas Governor Rick Perry had yet to take action on this bill, which was enrolled and sent to the governor on June 29, 2011.

(a) Except as provided by Subsection (e), a hearing under Section 54.03, 54.04, or 54.05, including a jury trial, a hearing under Chapter 55, including a jury trial, or a hearing under the Interstate Compact for Juveniles (Chapter 60) may be held by a referee appointed in accordance with Section 51.04(g) or **an associate judge** ~~a master~~ appointed under Chapter **54A** ~~54~~, Government Code, provided:

(1) the parties have been informed by the referee or **associate judge** ~~master~~ that they are entitled to have the hearing before the juvenile court judge; and

(2) after each party is given an opportunity to object, no party objects to holding the hearing before the referee or **associate judge** ~~master~~.

(b) The determination under Section 53.02(f) whether to release a child may be made by a referee appointed in accordance with Section 51.04(g) if:

(1) the child has been informed by the referee that the child is entitled to have the determination made by the juvenile court judge or a substitute judge authorized by Section 51.04(f); or

(2) the child and the attorney for the child have in accordance with Section 51.09 waived the right to have the determination made by the juvenile court judge or a substitute judge.

(c) If a child objects to a referee making the determination under Section 53.02(f), the juvenile court judge or a substitute judge authorized by Section 51.04(f) shall make the determination.

(d) At the conclusion of the hearing or immediately after making the determination, the referee shall transmit written findings and recommendations to the juvenile court judge. The juvenile court judge shall adopt, modify, or reject the referee's recommendations not later than the next working day after the day that the judge receives the recommendations. Failure to act within that time results in release of the child by operation of law and a recommendation that the child be released operates to secure the child's immediate release subject to the power of the juvenile court judge to modify or reject that recommendation.

(e) The hearings provided by Sections 54.03, 54.04, and 54.05 may not be held before a referee if the grand jury has approved of the petition and the child is subject to a determinate sentence.

Amended by Acts 2011, 82nd Leg., 1st C.S. (H.B. 79), § 6.08, eff. Jan. 1, 2012.

Comment

An associate judge may conduct a detention hearing, an adjudication hearing, a disposition hearing or a modification of disposition hearing. He or she may not conduct a transfer (certification) hearing but may conduct a chapter 55 (mental illness or retardation) hearing and may conduct a jury trial if otherwise authorized to conduct that type of hearing. An associate judge may not conduct an adjudication, disposition or modification hearing under the determinate sentence act.

Leading Cases

Swisher v. Brady, 438 U.S. 204, 57 L.Ed.2d 705, 98 S.Ct. 2699 (1978) (double jeopardy not violated by judge's overruling referee's recommendation that respondent be acquitted)

In re D.L.M., 982 S.W.2d 146 (Tex. App.—Houston [1st Dist.] 1998, no pet.) (juvenile law "masters" must also comply with this section)

§ 54.11. Release or Transfer Hearing

(a) On receipt of a referral under Section **244.014(a)** ~~61.079(a)~~, Human Resources Code, for the transfer to the Texas Department of Criminal Justice of a person committed to the Texas **Juvenile Justice Department** ~~Youth Commission~~under Section 54.04(d)(3), 54.04(m), or 54.05(f), or on receipt of a request by the **Texas Juvenile Justice Department** ~~commission~~under Section **245.051(d)** ~~61.081(g)~~, Human Resources Code, for approval of the release under supervision of a person committed to the **Texas Juvenile Justice Department** ~~commission~~under Section 54.04(d)(3), 54.04(m), or 54.05(f), the court shall set a time and place for a hearing on the release of the person.

(b) The court shall notify the following of the time and place of the hearing:

(1) the person to be transferred or released under supervision;

(2) the parents of the person;

(3) any legal custodian of the person, including the Texas Youth Commission;

(4) the office of the prosecuting attorney that represented the state in the juvenile delinquency proceedings;

(5) the victim of the offense that was included in the delinquent conduct that was a ground for the disposition, or a member of the victim's family; and

(6) any other person who has filed a written request with the court to be notified of a release hearing with respect to the person to be transferred or released under supervision.

(c) Except for the person to be transferred or released under supervision and the prosecuting attorney, the failure to notify a person listed in Subsection (b) of this section does not affect the validity of a hearing conducted or determination made under this section if the record in the case reflects that the whereabouts of the persons who did not receive notice were unknown to the court and a reasonable effort was made by the court to locate those persons.

(d) At a hearing under this section the court may consider written reports from probation officers, professional court employees, professional consultants, or employees of the Texas Youth

Commission, in addition to the testimony of witnesses. At least one day before the hearing, the court shall provide the attorney for the person to be transferred or released under supervision with access to all written matter to be considered by the court.

(e) At the hearing, the person to be transferred or released under supervision is entitled to an attorney, to examine all witnesses against him, to present evidence and oral argument, and to previous examination of all reports on and evaluations and examinations of or relating to him that may be used in the hearing.

(f) A hearing under this section is open to the public unless the person to be transferred or released under supervision waives a public hearing with the consent of his attorney and the court.

(g) A hearing under this section must be recorded by a court reporter or by audio or video tape recording, and the record of the hearing must be retained by the court for at least two years after the date of the final determination on the transfer or release of the person by the court.

(h) The hearing on a person who is referred for transfer under Section **244.014(a)** ~~61.079(a)~~, Human Resources Code, shall be held not later than the 60th day after the date the court receives the referral.

(i) On conclusion of the hearing on a person who is referred for transfer under Section **244.014(a)** ~~61.079(a)~~, Human Resources Code, the court may order:

(1) the return of the person to the Texas **Juvenile Justice Department** ~~Youth Commission~~; or

(2) the transfer of the person to the custody of the Texas Department of Criminal Justice for the completion of the person's sentence.

(j) On conclusion of the hearing on a person who is referred for release under supervision under Section **245.051(c)** ~~61.081(f)~~, Human Resources Code, the court may order the return of the person to the Texas **Juvenile Justice Department** ~~Youth Commission~~:

(1) with approval for the release of the person under supervision; or

(2) without approval for the release of the person under supervision.

(k) In making a determination under this section, the court may consider the experiences and character of the person before and after commitment to the youth commission, the nature of the penal offense that the person was found to have committed and the manner in which the offense was committed, the abilities of the person to contribute to society, the protection of the victim of the offense or any member of the victim's family, the recommendations of the youth commission and prosecuting attorney, the best interests of the person, and any other factor relevant to the issue to be decided.

(*l*) Pending the conclusion of a transfer hearing, the juvenile court shall order that the person who is referred for transfer be detained in a certified juvenile detention facility as provided by Subsection (m). If the person is at least 17 years of age, the juvenile court may order that the person be detained without bond in an appropriate county facility for the detention of adults accused of criminal offenses.

(m) The detention of a person in a certified juvenile detention facility must comply with the detention requirements under this title, except that, to the extent practicable, the person must be kept separate from children detained in the same facility.

(n) If the juvenile court orders that a person who is referred for transfer be detained in a county facility under Subsection (*l*), the county sheriff shall take custody of the person under the juvenile court's order.

Amended by Acts 2011, 82nd Leg., ch. 85 (S.B. 653), § 3.007, eff. Sept. 1, 2011.

Comment

A hearing is required only upon discretionary request of the TYC or TJJD to release a youth before the statutory minimum length of stay has been served to transfer a youth 16 years or older to TDCJ.

Subsections (*l*) through (n) authorize a juvenile court, pending a transfer/release hearing, to confine a person 17 or older in a certified juvenile detention facility or without bond in the county jail.

Leading Cases

In re J.B.L., 318 S.W.3d 544 (Tex. App.—Beaumont, rev. denied) (transfer procedure of 54.11 does not violate *Apprendi* as child is never exposed to greater punishment than jury verdict)

In re J.J., 276 S.W.3d 171 (Tex. App.—Austin 2008, rev. denied) (although Human Resource Code section 61.048 was amended to require transfer before age 19, 54.11 was not amended and 61.079 and 61.084 do not apply retrospectively to persons adjudicated delinquent prior to 2007). See also, *In re* T.L.S., II, 294 S.W.3d 397 (Tex. App.—Tyler 2009, no pet.)

In re F.D., 245 S.W.3d 110 (Tex. App.—Dallas [5th Dist.] 2008, no pet.)(juvenile has no right of confrontation at transfer hearing because it is dispositional rather than adjudicative)

In re F.M., 238 S.W.3d 837 (Tex. App.—El Paso 2007, rev. denied) (trial court has no authority to reduce term of years at determinate sentencing transfer hearing)

In re D.L., 198 S.W.3d 228 (Tex. App.—San Antonio 2006, rev. denied) (right of confrontation not violated by admission of TYC report)

In re C.D.T., III, 98 S.W.3d 280 (Tex. App.—Houston [1st Dist.] 2003, rev. denied) (OK for TYC to give judge letters from juvenile; gatekeeper finding not required for experts)

In re J.L.S., 47 S.W.3d 128 (Tex. App.—Waco 2001, no pet.) (notice in court of time and place of hearing to consider transfer to TDCJ complies with statute)

In re R.D.B., 20 S.W.3d 255 (Tex. App.—Texarkana 2000, no pet.) (ineffective assistance of counsel in failure to seek appointment of mental health expert for transfer hearing)

In re B.D., 16 S.W.3d 77 (Tex. App.—Houston [1st Dist.] 2000, pet. denied) (Chapter 55 does not apply to release/transfer hearing when respondent is 18 or older)

In re M.R., 5 S.W.3d 879 (Tex. App.—San Antonio 1999, no pet.) (failure to grant continuance in hearing denied confrontation right)

In re R.G., 994 S.W.2d 309 (Tex. App.—Houston [1st Dist.] 1999, no pet.) (no discretion abuse in transfer contrary to expert recommendation)

In re J.M.O., 980 S.W.2d 811 (Tex. App.—San Antonio 1998, pet. denied) (confrontation right not violated by hearsay testimony at hearing)

In re J.E.H., 972 S.W.2d 928 (Tex. App.—Beaumont 1998, no writ) (error not to appoint mental health expert for child at hearing)

In re T.C.K., 877 S.W.2d 43 (Tex. App.—Beaumont 1994, no writ) (hearsay testimony of TYC employee admissible at hearing)

CHAPTER 55. PROCEEDINGS CONCERNING CHILDREN WITH MENTAL ILLNESS OR MENTAL RETARDATION

SUBCHAPTER A. GENERAL PROVISIONS

SUBCHAPTER B. CHILD WITH MENTAL ILLNESS

SUBCHAPTER C. CHILD UNFIT TO PROCEED AS A RESULT OF MENTAL ILLNESS OR MENTAL RETARDATION

SUBCHAPTER D. LACK OF RESPONSIBILITY FOR CONDUCT AS A RESULT OF MENTAL ILLNESS OR MENTAL RETARDATION

§ 55.61. Referral for Commitment Proceedings for Mental Retardation.

Introductory Comment

Chapter 55 deals with children who are before the juvenile court for delinquent conduct or conduct indicating a need for supervision and who are believed to be suffering from some form of mental illness or mental retardation.

Specifically, this chapter deals with three different situations. (1) The child who is before the juvenile court and is believed to be mentally ill is covered by Subchapter B. (2) The child who is believed to be unfit (incompetent) to proceed because of mental illness or mental retardation is covered by Subchapter C. (3) The child who is believed to be not responsible for his conduct because of mental illness or mental retardation is covered by Subchapter D.

SUBCHAPTER A. GENERAL PROVISIONS

§ 55.01. Meaning of "Having a Mental Illness"

For purposes of this chapter, a child who is described as having a mental illness means a child who suffers from mental illness as defined by Section 571.003, Health and Safety Code.

Comment

Section 571.003(14) of the Health and Safety Code defines mental illness as "an illness, disease, or condition, other than epilepsy, senility, alcoholism, or mental deficiency, that: (A) substantially impairs a person's thought, perception of reality, emotional process, or judgment; or (B) grossly impairs behavior as demonstrated by recent disturbed behavior."

The provision authorizing the juvenile court to order a physical or mental examination is § 51.20.

Leading Cases

S.D.J. v. State, 879 S.W.2d 370 (Tex. App.—Eastland 1994, writ denied) (insufficient evidence to require hearing on motion suggesting mental illness)

In re M.D.B., 757 S.W.2d 415 (Tex. App.—Houston [14th Dist.] 1988, no writ) (child committed under § 55.02 [now Subchapter B] can be placed in any TDMHMR facility)

T.P.S. v. State, 590 S.W.2d 946 (Tex. Civ. App.—Dallas 1979, writ ref'd n.r.e.) (§ 55.02 [now Subchapter B] is applicable in transfer proceedings)

R.K.A. v. State, 553 S.W.2d 781 (Tex. Civ. App.—Fort Worth 1977, no writ) (§ 55.02 [now Subchapter B] is not applicable in transfer proceedings)

---

§ 55.02. Mental Health and Mental Retardation Jurisdiction

For the purpose of initiating proceedings to order mental health or mental retardation services for a child or for commitment of a child as provided by this chapter, the juvenile court has jurisdiction of proceedings under Subtitle C or D, Title 7, Health and Safety Code.

Comment

Tex. Health & Safety Code Ann. Subtitle C deals with persons with mental illness and Subtitle D with persons with mental retardation.

---

§ 55.03. Standards of Care

(a) Except as provided by this chapter, a child for whom inpatient mental health services is ordered by a court under this chapter shall be cared for as provided by Subtitle C, Title 7, Health and Safety Code.

(b) Except as provided by this chapter, a child who is committed by a court to a residential care facility for mental retardation shall be cared for as provided by Subtitle D, Title 7, Health and Safety Code.

§ 55.04. Renumbered as V.T.C.A., Family Code §§ 55.31, 55.32 by Acts 1999, 76th Leg., ch. 1477, § 14, eff. Sept. 1, 1999

§ 55.05. Renumbered as V.T.C.A., Family Code § 55.51 by Acts 1999, 76th Leg., ch. 1477, § 14, eff. Sept. 1, 1999

SUBCHAPTER B. CHILD WITH MENTAL ILLNESS

Introductory Comment

Subchapter B deals with children who are believed to be mentally ill but who are not necessarily also unfit to proceed because of mental illness or not responsible for their conduct because of mental illness.

§ 55.11. Mental Illness Determination; Examination

(a) On a motion by a party, the juvenile court shall determine whether probable cause exists to believe that a child who is alleged by petition or found to have engaged in delinquent conduct or conduct indicating a need for supervision has a mental illness. In making its determination, the court may:

(1) consider the motion, supporting documents, professional statements of counsel, and witness testimony; and

(2) make its own observation of the child.

(b) If the court determines that probable cause exists to believe that the child has a mental illness, the court shall temporarily stay the juvenile court proceedings and immediately order the child to be examined under Section 51.20. The information obtained from the examination must include expert opinion as to whether the child has a mental illness and whether the child meets the commitment criteria under Subtitle C, Title 7, Health and Safety Code. If ordered by the court, the information must also include expert opinion as to whether the child is unfit to proceed with the juvenile court proceedings.

(c) After considering all relevant information, including information obtained from an examination under Section 51.20, the court shall:

(1) if the court determines that evidence exists to support a finding that the child has a mental illness and that the child meets the commitment criteria under Subtitle C, Title 7, Health and Safety Code, proceed under Section 55.12; or

(2) if the court determines that evidence does not exist to support a finding that the child has a mental illness or that the child meets the commitment criteria under Subtitle C, Title 7, Health and Safety Code, dissolve the stay and continue the juvenile court proceedings.

Comment

If the juvenile court from any source has probable cause to believe that a child before it may be mentally ill, it is required to stay juvenile proceedings temporarily and to order an appropriate examination. If from that examination, the court determines there is evidence to support a finding that the child is mentally ill and committable, it proceeds under the next section; otherwise, it dissolves the stay and proceeds with the juvenile case.

Leading Case

In re E.M.R., 55 S.W.3d 712 (Tex. App.—Corpus Christi 2001, no writ) (trial court has power to conduct a hearing sua sponte, but does not have duty to do so)

---

§ 55.12. Initiation of Commitment Proceedings

If, after considering all relevant information, the juvenile court determines that evidence exists to support a finding that a child has a mental illness and that the child meets the commitment criteria under Subtitle C, Title 7, Health and Safety Code, the court shall:

(1) initiate proceedings as provided by Section 55.13 to order temporary or extended mental health services, as provided in Subchapter C, Chapter 574, Health and Safety Code; or

(2) refer the child's case as provided by Section 55.14 to the appropriate court for the initiation of proceedings in that court for commitment of the child under Subchapter C, Chapter 574, Health and Safety Code.

Comment

If there is evidence to support a finding the child is mentally ill and committable, the juvenile court has an option: it may conduct commitment proceedings itself or it may refer the case to the appropriate court (ordinarily the county court) to conduct commitment proceedings. The referral option is new and is intended to relieve juvenile courts that are not comfortable with conducting commitment proceedings (because they are called upon to do so infrequently) or with the responsibility for doing so.

---

§ 55.13. Commitment Proceedings in Juvenile Court

(a) If the juvenile court initiates proceedings for temporary or extended mental health services under Section 55.12(1), the prosecuting attorney or the attorney for the child may file with the juvenile court an application for court-ordered mental health services under Section 574.001, Health and Safety Code. The juvenile court shall:

(1) set a date for a hearing and provide notice as required by Sections 574.005 and 574.006, Health and Safety Code; and

(2) conduct the hearing in accordance with Subchapter C, Chapter 574, Health and Safety Code.

(b) The burden of proof at the hearing is on the party who filed the application.

(c) The juvenile court shall appoint the number of physicians necessary to examine the child and to complete the certificates of medical examination for mental illness required under Section 574.009, Health and Safety Code.

(d) After conducting a hearing on an application under this section, the juvenile court shall:

(1) if the criteria under Section 574.034, Health and Safety Code, are satisfied, order temporary mental health services for the child; or

(2) if the criteria under Section 574.035, Health and Safety Code, are satisfied, order extended mental health services for the child.

Comment

At this stage, juvenile proceedings are stayed pending outcome of the commitment proceedings. This section spells out the procedures when the juvenile court elects to conduct the commitment proceedings itself. The prosecutor or the juvenile's attorney has discretion to file an application for commitment or not. Juvenile proceedings cannot be resumed until the commitment issue is resolved by application and hearing. The burden of proof at the commitment hearing is upon the party who filed the application.

The juvenile court decides the case according to the commitment criteria for temporary or extended mental health services that are in the Health and Safety Code.

---

§ 55.14. Referral for Commitment Proceedings

(a) If the juvenile court refers the child's case to the appropriate court for the initiation of commitment proceedings under Section 55.12(2), the juvenile court shall:

(1) send all papers relating to the child's mental illness to the clerk of the court to which the case is referred;

(2) send to the office of the appropriate county attorney or, if a county attorney is not available, to the office of the appropriate district attorney, copies of all papers sent to the clerk of the court under Subdivision (1); and

(3) if the child is in detention:

(A) order the child released from detention to the child's home or another appropriate place;

(B) order the child detained in an appropriate place other than a juvenile detention facility; or

(C) if an appropriate place to release or detain the child as described by Paragraph (A) or (B) is not available, order the child to remain in the juvenile detention facility subject to further detention orders of the court.

(b) The papers sent to the clerk of a court under Subsection (a)(1) constitute an application for mental health services under Section 574.001, Health and Safety Code.

Comment

If the juvenile court elects the referral option, the papers are sent to the appropriate court and prosecuting authority. If the child is in detention, he or she may be released or detained in the juvenile detention facility pending outcome of the commitment proceedings. If detained, the requirements of § 54.01 respecting the duration of detention orders and subsequent detention hearings must be met.

---

§ 55.15. Standards of Care; Expiration of Court Order for Mental Health Services

If the juvenile court or a court to which the child's case is referred under Section 55.12(2) orders mental health services for the child, the child shall be cared for, treated, and released in conformity to Subtitle C, Title 7, Health and Safety Code, except:

(1) a court order for mental health services for a child automatically expires on the 120th day after the date the child becomes 18 years of age; and

(2) the administrator of a mental health facility shall notify, in writing, by certified mail, return receipt requested, the juvenile court that ordered mental health services or the juvenile court that referred the case to a court that ordered the mental health services of the intent to discharge the child at least 10 days prior to discharge.

Comment

Unlike commitments of adults, a commitment of a child from a juvenile court or juvenile court referral automatically expires 120 days after the child's 18th birthday. Under some circumstances, § 55.19 provides for transfer of such cases to criminal court on the child's 18th birthday. If the care provider intends to discharge the child, it is required to give certified mail notice to the juvenile court in order to permit the court to resume custody of the child for possible further proceedings in juvenile court.

---

§ 55.16. Order for Mental Health Services; Stay of Proceedings

(a) If the court to which the child's case is referred under Section 55.12(2) orders temporary or extended inpatient mental health services for the child, the court shall immediately notify in writing the referring juvenile court of the court's order for mental health services.

(b) If the juvenile court orders temporary or extended inpatient mental health services for the child or if the juvenile court receives notice under Subsection (a) from the court to which the child's case is referred, the proceedings under this title then pending in juvenile court shall be stayed.

Comment

If the child is committed, juvenile proceedings must be stayed for the duration of the commitment.

§ 55.17. Mental Health Services Not Ordered; Dissolution of Stay

(a) If the court to which a child's case is referred under Section 55.12(2) does not order temporary or extended inpatient mental health services for the child, the court shall immediately notify in writing the referring juvenile court of the court's decision.

(b) If the juvenile court does not order temporary or extended inpatient mental health services for the child or if the juvenile court receives notice under Subsection (a) from the court to which the child's case is referred, the juvenile court shall dissolve the stay and continue the juvenile court proceedings.

Comment

If the child is not committed following a hearing, the stay of juvenile proceedings must be dissolved so the proceedings can be resumed.

§ 55.18. Discharge From Mental Health Facility Before Reaching 18 Years of Age.

If the child is discharged from the mental health facility before reaching 18 years of age, the juvenile court may:

(1) dismiss the juvenile court proceedings with prejudice; or

(2) continue with proceedings under this title as though no order of mental health services had been made.

Comment

If the child is discharged before age 18, the juvenile court has discretion, in the interest of justice, either to dismiss the juvenile proceedings or permit them to continue.

§ 55.19. Transfer to Criminal Court on 18th Birthday

(a) The juvenile court shall transfer all pending proceedings from the juvenile court to a criminal court on the 18th birthday of a child for whom the juvenile court or a court to which the child's case is referred under Section 55.12(2) has ordered inpatient mental health services if:

(1) the child is not discharged or furloughed from the inpatient mental health facility before reaching 18 years of age; and

(2) the child is alleged to have engaged in delinquent conduct that included a violation of a penal law listed in Section 53.045 and no adjudication concerning the alleged conduct has been made.

(b) The juvenile court shall send notification of the transfer of a child under Subsection (a) to the inpatient mental health facility. The criminal court shall, within 90 days of the transfer, institute proceedings under Chapter 46B, Code of Criminal Procedure. If those or any subsequent proceedings result in a determination that the defendant is competent to stand trial, the defendant may not receive a punishment for the delinquent conduct described by Subsection (a)(2) that results in confinement for a period longer than the maximum period of confinement the defendant could have received if the defendant had been adjudicated for the delinquent conduct while still a child and within the jurisdiction of the juvenile court.

Comment

This section mandates the transfer to the criminal justice system of a child charged with a determinate sentence offense who is confined under a juvenile court mental health commitment when the child becomes 18 years of age. The criminal court is to conduct a competency examination and proceed appropriately with the case depending upon the results of the examination.

SUBCHAPTER C. CHILD UNFIT TO PROCEED AS A RESULT OF MENTAL ILLNESS OR MENTAL RETARDATION

Introductory Comment

Section 55.03, dealing with children with mental retardation, is repealed. The criteria and procedures for proceedings involving mental retardation are distributed in this and the next subchapter.

This subchapter deals with children who are or may be unfit to proceed in juvenile court because of either mental illness or mental retardation.

Leading Cases

In re E.M.R., 55 S.W.3d 712 (Tex. App.—Corpus Christi 2001, no pet.) (juvenile court has no duty to order fitness hearing without motion for hearing)

Pratt v. State, 907 S.W.2d 38 (Tex. App.—Dallas 1995, error denied) (burden of proof beyond a reasonable doubt on juvenile who files application for mental retardation commitment)

§ 55.31. Unfitness to Proceed Determination; Examination

(a) A child alleged by petition or found to have engaged in delinquent conduct or conduct indicating a need for supervision who as a result of mental illness or mental retardation lacks capacity to understand the proceedings in juvenile court or to assist in the child's own defense is unfit to proceed and shall not be subjected to discretionary transfer to criminal court, adjudication, disposition, or modification of disposition as long as such incapacity endures.

(b) On a motion by a party, the juvenile court shall determine whether probable cause exists to believe that a child who is alleged by petition or who is found to have engaged in delinquent conduct or conduct indicating a need for supervision is unfit to proceed as a result of mental illness or mental retardation. In making its determination, the court may:

(1) consider the motion, supporting documents, professional statements of counsel, and witness testimony; and

(2) make its own observation of the child.

(c) If the court determines that probable cause exists to believe that the child is unfit to proceed, the court shall temporarily stay the juvenile court proceedings and immediately order the child to be examined under Section 51.20. The information obtained from the examination must include expert opinion as to whether the child is unfit to proceed as a result of mental illness or mental retardation.

(d) After considering all relevant information, including information obtained from an examination under Section 51.20, the court shall:

(1) if the court determines that evidence exists to support a finding that the child is unfit to proceed, proceed under Section 55.32; or

(2) if the court determines that evidence does not exist to support a finding that the child is unfit to proceed, dissolve the stay and continue the juvenile court proceedings.

Comment

Due process of law prohibits placing a person on trial who because of mental illness or retardation cannot comprehend the nature of the proceedings or assist in his or her own defense. This section defines the fitness standard and specifies the procedures to initiate a fitness inquiry.

This section is on a parallel with § 55.11 dealing with initiating an inquiry into whether a child before the juvenile court is mentally ill.

Leading Cases

Dusky v. United States, 362 U.S. 402, 4 L.Ed.2d 824, 80 S.Ct. 788 (1960) (constitutional requirement for competency to stand trial)

In re J.K.N., 115 S.W.3d 166 (Tex. App.—Fort Worth 2003, no pet.) (fitness inquiry not required without motion from party)

M.A.V. v. Webb County Court at Law, 842 S.W.2d 739 (Tex. App.—San Antonio 1992, writ denied) (jury trial required upon request)

In re K.A.H., 700 S.W.2d 782 (Tex. App.—Fort Worth 1985, no writ) (raising the issue of fitness to proceed)

V.C.H. v. State, 630 S.W.2d 787 (Tex. App.—Houston [1st Dist.] 1982, no writ) (jury waiver for fitness to proceed hearing must be by both child and attorney)

In re V.C.H., 605 S.W.2d 643 (Tex. Civ. App.—Houston [1st Dist.] 1980, no writ) (fitness to proceed must be tried in a separate proceeding from adjudication)

---

§ 55.32. Hearing on Issue of Fitness to Proceed

(a) If the juvenile court determines that evidence exists to support a finding that a child is unfit to proceed as a result of mental illness or mental retardation, the court shall set the case for a hearing on that issue.

(b) The issue of whether the child is unfit to proceed as a result of mental illness or mental retardation shall be determined at a hearing separate from any other hearing.

(c) The court shall determine the issue of whether the child is unfit to proceed unless the child or the attorney for the child demands a jury before the 10th day before the date of the hearing.

(d) Unfitness to proceed as a result of mental illness or mental retardation must be proved by a preponderance of the evidence.

(e) If the court or jury determines that the child is fit to proceed, the juvenile court shall continue with proceedings under this title as though no question of fitness to proceed had been raised.

(f) If the court or jury determines that the child is unfit to proceed as a result of mental illness or mental retardation, the court shall:

(1) stay the juvenile court proceedings for as long as that incapacity endures; and

(2) proceed under Section 55.33.

(g) The fact that the child is unfit to proceed as a result of mental illness or mental retardation does not preclude any legal objection to the juvenile court proceedings which is susceptible of fair determination prior to the adjudication hearing and without the personal participation of the child.

Comment

A fitness hearing is required if there is evidence to support a finding of unfitness to proceed. The hearing is to be before the judge, unless the defense demands a jury. If the child is found to be unfit to proceed, juvenile proceedings are stayed pending the outcome of commitment proceedings.

---

§ 55.33. Proceedings Following Finding of Unfitness to Proceed

(a) If the juvenile court or jury determines under Section 55.32 that a child is unfit to proceed with the juvenile court proceedings for delinquent conduct, the court shall:

(1) if the unfitness to proceed is a result of mental illness or mental retardation:

(A) provided that the child meets the commitment criteria under Subtitle C or D, Title 7, Health and Safety Code, order the child placed with the Texas Department of Mental Health and Mental Retardation for a period of not more than 90 days, which order may not specify a shorter period, for placement in a facility designated by the department; or

(B) on application by the child's parent, guardian, or guardian ad litem, order the child placed in a private psychiatric inpatient facility for a period of not more than 90 days, which order may not specify a shorter period, but only if the placement is agreed to in writing by the administrator of the facility; or

(2) if the unfitness to proceed is a result of mental illness and the court determines that the child may be adequately treated in an alternative setting, order the child to receive treatment for mental illness on an outpatient basis for a period of not more than 90 days, which order may not specify a shorter period.

(b) If the court orders a child placed in a private psychiatric inpatient facility under Subsection (a)(1)(B), the state or a political subdivision of the state may be ordered to pay any costs associated with the child's placement, subject to an express appropriation of funds for the purpose.

Comment

If there is a finding that the juvenile is unfit to proceed, the court has three alternatives: order a placement with MHMR for 90 days, order a placement in a private facility for 90 days, or if the cause is mental illness, order outpatient evaluation for 90 days. The court must find that the child meets commitment criteria to order MHMR placement, but that finding is based on the evidence already heard by the court and does not require a separate commitment hearing since the purpose of the placement is to obtain an evaluation to be used in a later commitment hearing. Under Subsection (b), the court can order the government to pay for placement in a private psychiatric inpatient facility only if there are funds expressly made available for that purpose.

§ 55.34. Transportation to and From Facility

(a) If the court issues a placement order under Section 55.33(a)(1), the court shall order the probation department or sheriff's department to transport the child to the designated facility.

(b) On receipt of a report from a facility to which a child has been transported under Subsection (a), the court shall order the probation department or sheriff's department to transport the child from the facility to the court. If the child is not transported to the court before the 11th day after the date of the court's order, an authorized representative of the facility shall transport the child from the facility to the court.

(c) The county in which the juvenile court is located shall reimburse the facility for the costs incurred in transporting the child to the juvenile court as required by Subsection (b).

Comment

The court is responsible for ordering transportation to and from the placement facility. If the court does not have the child transported back to the county upon notice of discharge, MHMR may do so and the county is responsible for the transportation cost.

§ 55.35. Information Required to be Sent to Facility; Report to Court

(a) If the juvenile court issues a placement order under Section 55.33(a), the court shall order the probation department to send copies of any information in the possession of the department and relevant to the issue of the child's mental illness or mental retardation to the public or private facility or outpatient center, as appropriate.

(b) Not later than the 75th day after the date the court issues a placement order under Section 55.33(a), the public or private facility or outpatient center, as appropriate, shall submit to the court a report that:

(1) describes the treatment of the child provided by the facility or center; and

(2) states the opinion of the director of the facility or center as to whether the child is fit or unfit to proceed.

(c) The court shall provide a copy of the report submitted under Subsection (b) to the prosecuting attorney and the attorney for the child.

Comment

The juvenile court must order all relevant information, including information in the possession of the probation department, to be sent to the evaluation facility. Not later than 75 days after placement, the facility is required to report to the court on the mental condition of the child.

§ 55.36. Report That Child is Fit to Proceed; Hearing on Objection

(a) If a report submitted under Section 55.35(b) states that a child is fit to proceed, the juvenile court shall find that the child is fit to proceed unless the child's attorney objects in writing or in open court not later than the second day after the date the attorney receives a copy of the report under Section 55.35(c).

(b) On objection by the child's attorney under Subsection (a), the juvenile court shall promptly hold a hearing to determine whether the child is fit to proceed, except that the hearing may be held after the date that the placement order issued under Section 55.33(a) expires. At the hearing, the court shall determine the issue of the fitness of the child to proceed unless the child or the child's attorney demands in writing a jury before the 10th day before the date of the hearing.

(c) If, after a hearing, the court or jury finds that the child is fit to proceed, the court shall dissolve the stay and continue the juvenile court proceedings as though a question of fitness to proceed had not been raised.

(d) If, after a hearing, the court or jury finds that the child is unfit to proceed, the court shall proceed under Section 55.37.

Comment

The 90 day evaluation placement gives MHMR the opportunity, in the case of mental illness, to stabilize the child on medication in order to make the child fit to proceed. If the report states the child is fit to proceed, the court may dissolve the stay and proceed with juvenile proceedings unless the defense objects, in which event a hearing, which may be with a jury, must be held on the question of fitness to proceed.

§ 55.37. Report That Child is Unfit to Proceed as a Result of Mental Illness; Initiation of Commitment Proceedings

If a report submitted under Section 55.35(b) states that a child is unfit to proceed as a result of mental illness and that the child meets the commitment criteria for civil commitment under Subtitle C, Title 7, Health and Safety Code, the director of the public or private facility or outpatient center, as appropriate, shall submit to the court two certificates of medical examination for mental illness. On receipt of the certificates, the court shall:

(1) initiate proceedings as provided by Section 55.38 in the juvenile court for commitment of the child under Subtitle C, Title 7, Health and Safety Code; or

(2) refer the child's case as provided by Section 55.39 to the appropriate court for the initiation of proceedings in that court for commitment of the child under Subtitle C, Title 7, Health and Safety Code.

Comment

If the report states the child is unfit to proceed because of mental illness, the juvenile court must either initiate commitment proceedings or refer those proceedings to the appropriate court. The two medical certificates are required by the Health and Safety Code to initiate mental health commitment proceedings.

---

§ 55.38. Commitment Proceedings in Juvenile Court for Mental Illness

(a) If the juvenile court initiates commitment proceedings under Section 55.37(1), the prosecuting attorney may file with the juvenile court an application for court-ordered mental health services under Section 574.001, Health and Safety Code. The juvenile court shall:

(1) set a date for a hearing and provide notice as required by Sections 574.005 and 574.006, Health and Safety Code; and

(2) conduct the hearing in accordance with Subchapter C, Chapter 574, Health and Safety Code.

(b) After conducting a hearing under Subsection (a)(2), the juvenile court shall:

(1) if the criteria under Section 574.034, Health and Safety Code, are satisfied, order temporary mental health services; or

(2) if the criteria under Section 574.035, Health and Safety Code, are satisfied, order extended mental health services.

Comment

If the juvenile court elects to initiate commitment proceedings, the prosecutor must file the application, if one is to be filed. After hearing, the juvenile court orders temporary or extended mental health services based upon the evidence and the commitment criteria.

---

§ 55.39. Referral for Commitment Proceedings for Mental Illness

(a) If the juvenile court refers the child's case to an appropriate court for the initiation of commitment proceedings under Section 55.37(2), the juvenile court shall:

(1) send all papers relating to the child's unfitness to proceed, including the verdict and judgment of the juvenile court finding the child unfit to proceed, to the clerk of the court to which the case is referred;

(2) send to the office of the appropriate county attorney or, if a county attorney is not available, to the office of the appropriate district attorney, copies of all papers sent to the clerk of the court under Subdivision (1); and

(3) if the child is in detention:

(A) order the child released from detention to the child's home or another appropriate place;

(B) order the child detained in an appropriate place other than a juvenile detention facility; or

(C) if an appropriate place to release or detain the child as described by Paragraph (A) or (B) is not available, order the child to remain in the juvenile detention facility subject to further detention orders of the court.

(b) The papers sent to a court under Subsection (a)(1) constitute an application for mental health services under Section 574.001, Health and Safety Code.

Comment

If the juvenile court elects to refer commitment proceedings to the county court, the papers go to that court and to the appropriate prosecutor's office. If the child is in detention, the court may release the child or detain the child under detention orders as specified in § 54.01.

---

§ 55.40. Report That Child is Unfit to Proceed as a Result of Mental Retardation

If a report submitted under Section 55.35(b) states that a child is unfit to proceed as a result of mental retardation and that the child meets the commitment criteria for civil commitment under Subtitle D, Title 7, Health and Safety Code, the director of the residential care facility shall submit to the court an affidavit stating the conclusions reached as a result of the diagnosis. On receipt of the affidavit, the court shall:

(1) initiate proceedings as provided by Section 55.41 in the juvenile court for commitment of the child under Subtitle D, Title 7, Health and Safety Code; or

(2) refer the child's case as provided by Section 55.42 to the appropriate court for the initiation of proceedings in that court for commitment of the child under Subtitle D, Title 7, Health and Safety Code.

Comment

If the evaluative report states the child is unfit to proceed because of mental retardation, the juvenile court must either initiate commitment proceedings or refer those proceedings to the appropriate county court.

---

§ 55.41. Commitment Proceedings in Juvenile Court for Mental Retardation

(a) If the juvenile court initiates commitment proceedings under Section 55.40(1), the prosecuting attorney may file with the juvenile court an application for placement under Section 593.041, Health and Safety Code. The juvenile court shall:

(1) set a date for a hearing and provide notice as required by Sections 593.047 and 593.048, Health and Safety Code; and

(2) conduct the hearing in accordance with Sections 593.049–593.056, Health and Safety Code.

(b) After conducting a hearing under Subsection (a)(2), the juvenile court may order commitment of the child to a residential care facility if the commitment criteria under Section 593.052, Health and Safety Code, are satisfied.

(c) On receipt of the court's order, the Texas Department of Mental Health and Mental Retardation or the appropriate community center shall admit the child to a residential care facility.

Comment

If the juvenile court elects to conduct the proceedings, the prosecutor must file the application if one is to be filed. If after hearing it is shown that the commitment criteria of the Health and Safety Code are met, the court commits the child to a residential care facility.

Subsection (c) requires MHMR or a community center to accept a child committed under this section.

---

§ 55.42. Referral for Commitment Proceedings for Mental Retardation

(a) If the juvenile court refers the child's case to an appropriate court for the initiation of commitment proceedings under Section 55.40(2), the juvenile court shall:

(1) send all papers relating to the child's mental retardation to the clerk of the court to which the case is referred;

(2) send to the office of the appropriate county attorney or, if a county attorney is not available, to the office of the appropriate district attorney, copies of all papers sent to the clerk of the court under Subdivision (1); and

(3) if the child is in detention:

(A) order the child released from detention to the child's home or another appropriate place;

(B) order the child detained in an appropriate place other than a juvenile detention facility; or

(C) if an appropriate place to release or detain the child as described by Paragraph (A) or (B) is not available, order the child to remain in the juvenile detention facility subject to further detention orders of the court.

(b) The papers sent to a court under Subsection (a)(1) constitute an application for placement under Section 593.041, Health and Safety Code.

Comment

If the juvenile court elects to refer mental retardation commitment proceedings to the county court, the juvenile court sends the papers to the appropriate court and prosecutor's office. The matter of detention is dealt with in the same manner as for mental health proceedings under § 55.39.

§ 55.43. Restoration Hearing

(a) The prosecuting attorney may file with the juvenile court a motion for a restoration hearing concerning a child if:

(1) the child is found unfit to proceed as a result of mental illness or mental retardation; and

(2) the child:

(A) is not:

(i) ordered by a court to receive inpatient mental health services;

(ii) committed by a court to a residential care facility; or

(iii) ordered by a court to receive treatment on an outpatient basis; or

(B) is discharged or currently on furlough from a mental health facility or outpatient center before the child reaches 18 years of age.

(b) At the restoration hearing, the court shall determine the issue of whether the child is fit to proceed.

(c) The restoration hearing shall be conducted without a jury.

(d) The issue of fitness to proceed must be proved by a preponderance of the evidence.

(e) If, after a hearing, the court finds that the child is fit to proceed, the court shall continue the juvenile court proceedings.

(f) If, after a hearing, the court finds that the child is unfit to proceed, the court shall dismiss the motion for restoration.

Comment

This section gives the State the right to demand a restoration hearing if the child was found unfit to proceed but was not committed for treatment or was discharged from treatment or on furlough from treatment before becoming 18. If after a hearing without a jury the court finds the child is fit to proceed, then juvenile proceedings can resume.

§ 55.44. Transfer to Criminal Court on 18th Birthday of Child

(a) The juvenile court shall transfer all pending proceedings from the juvenile court to a criminal court on the 18th birthday of a child for whom the juvenile court or a court to which the child's case is referred has ordered inpatient mental health services or residential care for persons with mental retardation if:

(1) the child is not discharged or currently on furlough from the facility before reaching 18 years of age; and

(2) the child is alleged to have engaged in delinquent conduct that included a violation of a penal law listed in Section 53.045 and no adjudication concerning the alleged conduct has been made.

(b) The juvenile court shall send notification of the transfer of a child under Subsection (a) to the facility. The criminal court shall, before the 91st day after the date of the transfer, institute proceedings under Chapter 46B, Code of Criminal Procedure. If those or any subsequent proceedings result in a determination that the defendant is competent to stand trial, the defendant may not receive a punishment for the delinquent conduct described by Subsection (a)(2) that results in confinement for a period longer than the maximum period of confinement the defendant could have received if the defendant had been adjudicated for the delinquent conduct while still a child and within the jurisdiction of the juvenile court.

Comment

This section is parallel to § 55.19. It requires transfer of the juvenile case to criminal court if the child is charged with a determinate sentence offense and is still committed for treatment at age 18.

§ 55.45. Standards of Care; Notice of Release or Furlough

(a) If the juvenile court or a court to which the child's case is referred under Section 55.37(2) orders mental health services for the child, the child shall be cared for, treated, and released in accordance with Subtitle C, Title 7, Health and Safety Code, except that the administrator of a mental health facility shall notify, in writing, by certified mail, return receipt requested, the juvenile court that ordered mental health services or that referred the case to a court that ordered mental health services of the intent to discharge the child on or before the 10th day before the date of discharge.

(b) If the juvenile court or a court to which the child's case is referred under Section 55.40(2) orders the commitment of the child to a residential care facility, the child shall be cared for, treated, and released in accordance with Subtitle D, Title 7, Health and Safety Code, except that the administrator of the residential care facility shall notify, in writing, by certified mail, return receipt requested, the juvenile court that ordered commitment of the child or that referred the case to a court that ordered commitment of the child of the intent to discharge or furlough the child on or before the 20th day before the date of discharge or furlough.

(c) If the referred child, as described in Subsection (b), is alleged to have committed an offense listed in Section 3g, Article 42.12, Code of Criminal Procedure, the administrator of the residential care facility shall apply, in writing, by certified mail, return receipt requested, to the juvenile court that ordered commitment of the child or that referred the case to a court that ordered commitment of the child and show good cause for any release of the child from the facility for more than 48 hours. Notice of this request must be provided to the prosecuting attorney responsible for the case. The prosecuting attorney, the juvenile, or the administrator may apply for a hearing on this application. If no one applies for a hearing, the trial court shall resolve the application on the written submission. The rules of evidence do not apply to this hearing. An appeal of the trial court's ruling on the application is not allowed. The release of a child described in this subsection without the express approval of the trial court is punishable by contempt.

Comment

Any juvenile in a residential care facility who is charged with an offense listed under article 42.12, Section 3g of the Code of Criminal Procedure cannot be released from that facility for more than 48 hours without first notifying the juvenile court. A prosecutor may request a hearing on the matter. If no hearing is requested, the trial court may resolve it.

SUBCHAPTER D. LACK OF RESPONSIBILITY FOR CONDUCT AS A RESULT OF MENTAL ILLNESS OR MENTAL RETARDATION

Introductory Comment

Subchapter D deals with non-responsibility for conduct as a result of mental illness or mental retardation, what in criminal law is called legal insanity.

---

§ 55.51. Lack of Responsibility for Conduct Determination; Examination

(a) A child alleged by petition to have engaged in delinquent conduct or conduct indicating a need for supervision is not responsible for the conduct if at the time of the conduct, as a result of mental illness or mental retardation, the child lacks substantial capacity either to appreciate the wrongfulness of the child's conduct or to conform the child's conduct to the requirements of law.

(b) On a motion by a party in which it is alleged that a child may not be responsible as a result of mental illness or mental retardation for the child's conduct, the court shall order the child to be examined under Section 51.20. The information obtained from the examinations must include expert opinion as to whether the child is not responsible for the child's conduct as a result of mental illness or mental retardation.

(c) The issue of whether the child is not responsible for the child's conduct as a result of mental illness or mental retardation shall be tried to the court or jury in the adjudication hearing.

(d) Lack of responsibility for conduct as a result of mental illness or mental retardation must be proved by a preponderance of the evidence.

(e) In its findings or verdict the court or jury must state whether the child is not responsible for the child's conduct as a result of mental illness or mental retardation.

(f) If the court or jury finds the child is not responsible for the child's conduct as a result of mental illness or mental retardation, the court shall proceed under Section 55.52.

(g) A child found to be not responsible for the child's conduct as a result of mental illness or mental retardation shall not be subject to proceedings under this title with respect to such conduct, other than proceedings under Section 55.52.

Comment

This section is the same in substance as the prior law. If a question of lack of responsibility is raised, an examination must be ordered. The question of lack of responsibility is litigated before the judge or jury in the adjudication hearing with any other adjudication issues that may be present.

Leading Cases

In re A.W.B., ___ S.W.3d ___, 2010 WL 364250 (Tex. App.—Amarillo 2010, no pet.) (trial court not required to hold separate hearing to determine if child is responsible for his conduct)

W.D.A. v. State, 835 S.W.2d 227 (Tex. App.—Waco 1992, no writ) (Family Code, not Penal Code, definition of legal insanity controls)

T.P.S. v. State, 620 S.W.2d 728 (Tex. Civ. App.—Dallas 1981, no writ) (§ 55.05 does not apply to transfer proceedings)

In re A.N.M., 542 S.W.2d 916 (Tex. Civ. App.—Dallas 1976, no writ) (raising issue of insanity)

In re E.B., 525 S.W.2d 543 (Tex. Civ. App.—Amarillo 1975, writ ref'd n.r.e.) (insanity defense applies at probation revocation proceedings)

---

§ 55.52. Proceedings Following Finding of Lack of Responsibility for Conduct

(a) If the court or jury finds that a child is not responsible for the child's conduct under Section 55.51, the court shall:

(1) if the lack of responsibility is a result of mental illness or mental retardation:

(A) provided that the child meets the commitment criteria under Subtitle C or D, Title 7, Health and Safety Code, order the child placed with the Texas Department of Mental Health and Mental Retardation for a period of not more than 90 days, which order may not specify a shorter period, for placement in a facility designated by the department; or

(B) on application by the child's parent, guardian, or guardian ad litem, order the child placed in a private psychiatric inpatient facility for a period of not more than 90 days, which order may not specify a shorter period, but only if the placement is agreed to in writing by the administrator of the facility; or

(2) if the child's lack of responsibility is a result of mental illness and the court determines that the child may be adequately treated in an alternative setting, order the child to receive treatment on an outpatient basis for a period of not more than 90 days, which order may not specify a shorter period.

(b) If the court orders a child placed in a private psychiatric inpatient facility under Subsection (a)(1)(B), the state or a political subdivision of the state may be ordered to pay any costs associated with the child's placement, subject to an express appropriation of funds for the purpose.

Comment

If the child is found not responsible because of mental illness or mental retardation, a 90 day evaluative placement must be ordered. The requirement that the child must meet the commitment criteria of the Health and Safety Code is met by a finding by the court based on the evidence already before it; a commitment hearing is not required since the purpose of the 90 day placement is to obtain expert assistance in determining whether the child is committable under those same criteria.

§ 55.53. Transportation to and From Facility

(a) If the court issues a placement order under Section 55.52(a)(1), the court shall order the probation department or sheriff's department to transport the child to the designated facility.

(b) On receipt of a report from a facility to which a child has been transported under Subsection (a), the court shall order the probation department or sheriff's department to transport the child from the facility to the court. If the child is not transported to the court before the 11th day after the date of the court's order, an authorized representative of the facility shall transport the child from the facility to the court.

(c) The county in which the juvenile court is located shall reimburse the facility for the costs incurred in transporting the child to the juvenile court as required by Subsection (b).

Comment

This section deals with transportation when the child has been found unfit to proceed.

§ 55.54. Information Required to be Sent to Facility; Report to Court

(a) If the juvenile court issues a placement order under Section 55.52(a), the court shall order the probation department to send copies of any information in the possession of the department and relevant to the issue of the child's mental illness or mental retardation to the public or private facility or outpatient center, as appropriate.

(b) Not later than the 75th day after the date the court issues a placement order under Section 55.52(a), the public or private facility or outpatient center, as appropriate, shall submit to the court a report that:

(1) describes the treatment of the child provided by the facility or center; and

(2) states the opinion of the director of the facility or center as to whether the child is mentally ill or mentally retarded.

(c) The court shall send a copy of the report submitted under Subsection (b) to the prosecuting attorney and the attorney for the child.

Comment

This section parallels § 55.35, dealing with a child found unfit to proceed.

§ 55.55. Report That Child is Not Mentally Ill or Mentally Retarded; Hearing on Objection

(a) If a report submitted under Section 55.54(b) states that a child does not have a mental illness or mental retardation, the juvenile court shall discharge the child unless:

(1) an adjudication hearing was conducted concerning conduct that included a violation of a penal law listed in Section 53.045(a) and a petition was approved by a grand jury under Section 53.045; and

(2) the prosecuting attorney objects in writing not later than the second day after the date the attorney receives a copy of the report under Section 55.54(c).

(b) On objection by the prosecuting attorney under Subsection (a), the juvenile court shall hold a hearing without a jury to determine whether the child has a mental illness or mental retardation and whether the child meets the commitment criteria for civil commitment under Subtitle C or D, Title 7, Health and Safety Code.

(c) At the hearing, the burden is on the state to prove by clear and convincing evidence that the child has a mental illness or mental retardation and that the child meets the commitment criteria for civil commitment under Subtitle C or D, Title 7, Health and Safety Code.

(d) If, after a hearing, the court finds that the child does not have a mental illness or mental retardation and that the child does not meet the commitment criteria under Subtitle C or D, Title 7, Health and Safety Code, the court shall discharge the child.

(e) If, after a hearing, the court finds that the child has a mental illness or mental retardation and that the child meets the commitment criteria under Subtitle C or D, Title 7, Health and Safety Code, the court shall issue an appropriate commitment order.

Comment

If the report states the child is not mentally ill or mentally retarded, the court is required to discharge the child unless in a determinate sentence case the State objects. In that event, a hearing is held in which the State is given the opportunity to prove by clear and convincing evidence that the child is mentally ill or mentally retarded. The juvenile court is empowered to commit the child contrary to the evaluation of MHMR if that burden is carried by the State at the hearing.

§ 55.56. Report That Child Has Mental Illness; Initiation of Commitment Proceedings

If a report submitted under Section 55.54(b) states that a child has a mental illness and that the child meets the commitment criteria for civil commitment under Subtitle C, Title 7, Health and Safety Code, the director of the public or private facility or outpatient center, as appropriate, shall submit to the court two certificates of medical examination for mental illness. On receipt of the certificates, the court shall:

(1) initiate proceedings as provided by Section 55.57 in the juvenile court for commitment of the child under Subtitle C, Title 7, Health and Safety Code; or

(2) refer the child's case as provided by Section 55.58 to the appropriate court for the initiation of proceedings in that court for commitment of the child under Subtitle C, Title 7, Health and Safety Code.

Comment

If the report states the child is mentally ill, then the juvenile court either initiates commitment proceedings or refers those proceedings to the appropriate county court.

---

§ 55.57. Commitment Proceedings in Juvenile Court for Mental Illness

(a) If the juvenile court initiates commitment proceedings under Section 55.56(1), the prosecuting attorney may file with the juvenile court an application for court-ordered mental health services under Section 574.001, Health and Safety Code. The juvenile court shall:

(1) set a date for a hearing and provide notice as required by Sections 574.005 and 574.006, Health and Safety Code; and

(2) conduct the hearing in accordance with Subchapter C, Chapter 574, Health and Safety Code.

(b) After conducting a hearing under Subsection (a)(2), the juvenile court shall:

(1) if the criteria under Section 574.034, Health and Safety Code, are satisfied, order temporary mental health services; or

(2) if the criteria under Section 574.035, Health and Safety Code, are satisfied, order extended mental health services.

Comment

If the juvenile court elects to conduct commitment proceedings itself, the application must be filed by the prosecutor, if one is to be filed. Appropriate commitment orders are to be entered depending upon the evidence at the hearing.

---

§ 55.58. Referral for Commitment Proceedings for Mental Illness

(a) If the juvenile court refers the child's case to an appropriate court for the initiation of commitment proceedings under Section 55.56(2), the juvenile court shall:

(1) send all papers relating to the child's mental illness, including the verdict and judgment of the juvenile court finding that the child was not responsible for the child's conduct, to the clerk of the court to which the case is referred;

(2) send to the office of the appropriate county attorney or, if a county attorney is not available, to the office of the district attorney, copies of all papers sent to the clerk of the court under Subdivision (1); and

(3) if the child is in detention:

(A) order the child released from detention to the child's home or another appropriate place;

(B) order the child detained in an appropriate place other than a juvenile detention facility; or

(C) if an appropriate place to release or detain the child as described by Paragraph (A) or (B) is not available, order the child to remain in the juvenile detention facility subject to further detention orders of the court.

(b) The papers sent to a court under Subsection (a)(1) constitute an application for mental health services under Section 574.001, Health and Safety Code.

Comment

This section parallels § 55.39, dealing with unfitness to proceed. It sets out the procedures when the juvenile court elects to refer commitment proceedings to the county court.

---

§ 55.59. Report That Child Has Mental Retardation; Initiation of Commitment Proceedings

If a report submitted under Section 55.54(b) states that a child has mental retardation and that the child meets the commitment criteria for civil commitment under Subtitle D, Title 7, Health and Safety Code, the director of the residential care facility shall submit to the court an affidavit stating the conclusions reached as a result of the diagnosis. On receipt of an affidavit, the juvenile court shall:

(1) initiate proceedings in the juvenile court as provided by Section 55.60 for commitment of the child under Subtitle D, Title 7, Health and Safety Code; or

(2) refer the child's case to the appropriate court as provided by Section 55.61 for the initiation of proceedings in that court for commitment of the child under Subtitle D, Title 7, Health and Safety Code.

Comment

This section is parallel to § 55.40, dealing with unfitness to proceed. If the report states the child is mentally retarded, the juvenile court must either initiate commitment proceedings or refer them to the appropriate county court.

§ 55.60. Commitment Proceedings in Juvenile Court for Mental Retardation

(a) If the juvenile court initiates commitment proceedings under Section 55.59(1), the prosecuting attorney may file with the juvenile court an application for placement under Section 593.041, Health and Safety Code. The juvenile court shall:

(1) set a date for a hearing and provide notice as required by Sections 593.047 and 593.048, Health and Safety Code; and

(2) conduct the hearing in accordance with Sections 593.049–593.056, Health and Safety Code.

(b) After conducting a hearing under Subsection (a)(2), the juvenile court may order commitment of the child to a residential care facility only if the commitment criteria under Section 593.052, Health and Safety Code, are satisfied.

(c) On receipt of the court's order, the Texas Department of Mental Health and Mental Retardation or the appropriate community center shall admit the child to a residential care facility.

Comment

This section parallels § 55.41, dealing with unfitness to proceed. It sets out the procedures when the juvenile court elects to conduct commitment proceedings for mental retardation itself.

Subsection (c) requires MHMR or a community center to admit a child committed by a juvenile court under this section.

§ 55.61. Referral for Commitment Proceedings for Mental Retardation

(a) If the juvenile court refers the child's case to an appropriate court for the initiation of commitment proceedings under Section 55.59(2), the juvenile court shall:

(1) send all papers relating to the child's mental retardation to the clerk of the court to which the case is referred;

(2) send to the office of the appropriate county attorney or, if a county attorney is not available, to the office of the appropriate district attorney, copies of all papers sent to the clerk of the court under Subdivision (1); and

(3) if the child is in detention:

(A) order the child released from detention to the child's home or another appropriate place;

(B) order the child detained in an appropriate place other than a juvenile detention facility; or

(C) if an appropriate place to release or detain the child as described by Paragraph (A) or (B) is not available, order the child to remain in the juvenile detention facility subject to further detention orders of the court.

(b) The papers sent to a court under Subsection (a)(1) constitute an application for placement under Section 593.041, Health and Safety Code.

Comment

This section parallels § 55.42, dealing with unfitness to proceed. It sets out the procedures when the juvenile court elects to refer mental retardation commitment proceedings to the county court.

CHAPTER 56. APPEAL

Introductory Comment

This chapter deals with the child's rights of appeal and with providing the appellate court with a record of the trial proceedings. It also grants the State a limited right of appeal from certain rulings in determinate sentence proceedings.

§ 56.01. Right to Appeal

(a) Except as provided by Subsection (b–1), an appeal from an order of a juvenile court is to a court of appeals and the case may be carried to the Texas Supreme Court by writ of error or upon certificate, as in civil cases generally.

(b) The requirements governing an appeal are as in civil cases generally. When an appeal is sought by filing a notice of appeal, security for costs of appeal, or an affidavit of inability to pay the costs of appeal, and the filing is made in a timely fashion after the date the disposition order is signed, the appeal must include the juvenile court adjudication and all rulings contributing to that adjudication. An appeal of the adjudication may be sought notwithstanding that the adjudication order was signed more than 30 days before the date the notice of appeal, security for costs of appeal, or affidavit of inability to pay the costs of appeal was filed.

(b–1) A motion for new trial seeking to vacate an adjudication is:

(1) timely if the motion is filed not later than the 30th day after the date on which the disposition order is signed; and

(2) governed by Rule 21, Texas Rules of Appellate Procedure.

(c) An appeal may be taken:

(1) except as provided by Subsection (n), by or on behalf of a child from an order entered under:

(A) Section 54.03 with regard to delinquent conduct or conduct indicating a need for supervision;

(B) Section 54.04 disposing of the case;

(C) Section 54.05 respecting modification of a previous juvenile court disposition; or

(D) Chapter 55 by a juvenile court committing a child to a facility for the mentally ill or mentally retarded; or

(2) by a person from an order entered under Section 54.11(i)(2) transferring the person to the custody of the Texas Department of Criminal Justice.

(d) A child has the right to:

(1) appeal, as provided by this subchapter;

(2) representation by counsel on appeal; and

(3) appointment of an attorney for the appeal if an attorney cannot be obtained because of indigency.

(e) On entering an order that is appealable under this section, the court shall advise the child and the child's parent, guardian, or guardian ad litem of the child's rights listed under Subsection (d) of this section.

(f) If the child and his parent, guardian, or guardian ad litem express a desire to appeal, the attorney who represented the child before the juvenile court shall file a notice of appeal with the juvenile court and inform the court whether that attorney will handle the appeal. Counsel shall be appointed under the standards provided in Section 51.10 of this code unless the right to appeal is waived in accordance with Section 51.09 of this code.

(g) An appeal does not suspend the order of the juvenile court, nor does it release the child from the custody of that court or of the person, institution, or agency to whose care the child is committed, unless the juvenile court so orders. However, the appellate court may provide for a personal bond.

(h) If the order appealed from takes custody of the child from his parent, guardian, or custodian, the appeal has precedence over all other cases.

(i) The appellate court may affirm, reverse, or modify the judgment or order, including an order of disposition or modified disposition, from which appeal was taken. It may reverse or modify an order of disposition or modified order of disposition while affirming the juvenile court adjudication that the child engaged in delinquent conduct or conduct indicating a need for supervision. It may remand an order that it reverses or modifies for further proceedings by the juvenile court.

(j) Neither the child nor his family shall be identified in an appellate opinion rendered in an appeal or habeas corpus proceedings related to juvenile court proceedings under this title. The appellate opinion shall be styled, "In the matter of ....," identifying the child by his initials only.

(k) The appellate court shall dismiss an appeal on the state's motion, supported by affidavit showing that the appellant has escaped from custody pending the appeal and, to the affiant's knowledge, has not voluntarily returned to the state's custody on or before the 10th day after the date of the escape. The court may not dismiss an appeal, or if the appeal has been dismissed, shall reinstate the appeal, on the filing of an affidavit of an officer or other credible person showing that the appellant voluntarily returned to custody on or before the 10th day after the date of the escape.

(*l*) The court may order the child, the child's parent, or other person responsible for support of the child to pay the child's costs of appeal, including the costs of representation by an attorney, unless the court determines the person to be ordered to pay the costs is indigent.

(m) For purposes of determining indigency of the child under this section, the court shall consider the assets and income of the child, the child's parent, and any other person responsible for the support of the child.

(n) A child who enters a plea or agrees to a stipulation of evidence in a proceeding held under this title may not appeal an order of the juvenile court entered under Section 54.03, 54.04, or 54.05 if the court makes a disposition in accordance with the agreement between the state and the child regarding the disposition of the case, unless:

(1) the court gives the child permission to appeal; or

(2) the appeal is based on a matter raised by written motion filed before the proceeding in which the child entered the plea or agreed to the stipulation of evidence.

(*o*) This section does not limit a child's right to obtain a writ of habeas corpus.

Comment

Except as provided by § 56.03, only the child or the child's representative may appeal from the juvenile court to the Court of Appeals. The appeal is governed by civil, not criminal, rules. The child is entitled to be represented by counsel, including appointed counsel if his or her family is indigent. The juvenile court must inform the child of his or her right to appeal at all appropriate stages of the proceedings.

It is no longer possible to appeal directly from the entry of a certification order. The issues that formerly could be raised in such a direct appeal can now be raised but only in an appeal from a criminal conviction as provided by art. 44.47 of the Code of Criminal Procedure.

The provision concerning dismissing an appeal when the juvenile escapes from custody tracks the language in Rule 42.4 of the Rules of Appellate Procedure.

Subsection (b) provides that timely initiating an appeal following a disposition decision is also an appeal of adjudication issues even if no separate notice of appeal is filed for adjudication and even if the disposition decision occurred more than 30 days after the adjudication decision.

This section requires a motion for new trial be filed by the 30th day after the disposition order was signed and notes that Rule 21 of the Texas Rules of Appellate Procedure, which is the criminal rule, apply. This means that a motion for new trial is no longer required to preserve error for jury argument or factual sufficiency complaints.

Subsection (c) reflects the option given juvenile courts to conduct commitment proceedings themselves or refer them to county courts. If referral is elected, appeal rights are determined by the Health and Safety Code.

The addition of Subsection (n) restricts the right of appeal when the child received a plea-bargained disposition to those cases in which the juvenile court grants permission or in which issues are raised by written pretrial motion, such as a motion to suppress evidence. This is similar to the adult provision in the Texas Rules of Appellate Procedure, but with the difference that, unlike under criminal practice, in juvenile practice it is not necessary to state the basis of appeal in the notice of appeal.

Subsection (*o*) states the obvious principle that in creating a right of appeal this section does not restrict the constitutional right of the juvenile to petition for release on habeas corpus.

Leading Cases

Habeas

In re James Allen Hall, 286 S.W.3d 925 (Tex. 2009)(Juvenile Justice Code does not provide mandatory right to assistance of counsel to an adult pursuing a post-adjudication habeas corpus claim involving commitment as a juvenile)

Ex parte Valle, 104 S.W.3d 888 (Tex. Crim. App. 2003) (constitutional habeas, not CCP 11.07, is appropriate to challenge confinement in TDCJ under determinate sentence act); *but see In re* Altschul, 207 S.W.3d 427 (Tex. App.—Waco 2006, no pet.) (juvenile can file writ when alleging collateral consequences, such as void juvenile adjudications being used to enhance a federal sentence)

M.B. v. State, 905 S.W.2d 344 (Tex. App.—El Paso 1995, no writ) (juvenile may not challenge adjudication by habeas while direct appeal is still pending)

Notice of Appeal

In re J.S., 35 S.W.3d 287 (Tex. App.—Ft. Worth 2001, no pet.) (even though juvenile's probation was transferred to his county of residence, notice of appeal properly filed in court where proceedings occurred)

In re C.F., 897 S.W.2d 464 (Tex. App.—El Paso 1995, no writ) (good faith filing of notice of appeal sufficient to perfect appeal)

In re G.C.F., 42 S.W.3d 194 (Tex. App.—Fort Worth 2001, no pet.) (notice of appeal must be filed not later than 30 days following disposition)

Modifying Judgments

In re I.A.G., 297 S.W.3d 505 (Tex. App.—Beaumont 2009, no pet.)(56.01(i) allows appellate court to correct, modify or reform a judgment to make the record correct)

Anders Brief

In re D.A.S., 973 S.W.2d 296 (Tex. 1998) (Anders frivolous appeal procedures apply to juvenile cases)

In re J.A.H., 986 S.W.2d 39 (Tex. App.—Waco 1998, no pet.) (*Anders* brief must be served on parent or guardian as well as child)

Standing

In re D.D.H., 143 S.W.3d 906 (Tex. App.—Beaumont 2004, no pet.) (child has no standing to appeal restitution order assessed to parents)

In re A.E.E., 89 S.W.3d 250 (Tex. App.—Texarkana 2002, no pet.) (juvenile's father lacks standing to appeal a plea bargained disposition)

Mootness

In re R.M., Jr., 234 S.W.3d 103 (Tex. App.—El Paso 2007, no pet.) (appeal from order modifying probation dismissed as moot when probation was terminated before appeal resolved); *but see* Carrillo v. State, 480 S.W.2d 612 (Tex. 1972) (appeal of original adjudication of delinquency not moot even though probation was completed before appeal)

Appeal Bonds

In re D.W.R., 990 S.W.2d 446 (Tex. App.—San Antonio 1999, no pet.) (court of appeals sets conditions for appeal bond)

In re J.V., 944 S.W.2d 15 (Tex. App.—El Paso 1997, no writ) (court of appeals details factors in discretionary denial of personal bond on appeal)

Appealable Orders

In re R.J.M., 211 S.W.3d 393 (Tex. App.—San Antonio 2006, rev. denied) (juvenile not statutorily authorized to appeal denial of counsel to assist in filing post-adjudication motion for forensic DNA testing)

Rodriguez v. State, 191 S.W.3d 909 (Tex. App.—Dallas 2006, no pet.) (can only appeal order certifying child to stand trial as adult in conjunction with appeal from conviction or order of deferred adjudication in criminal court)

Faisst v. State, 98 S.W.3d 226 (Tex. Crim. App. 2003) (juvenile can still appeal a defect in transfer proceeding even with a guilty plea as it amounts to a jurisdictional claim)

In re J.H., 176 S.W.3d 677 (Tex. App.—Dallas 2005, no pet.) (child may not appeal order transferring determinate sentence probation to criminal district court)

Right to Counsel

In re A.G., 195 S.W.3d 886 (Tex. App.—Waco 2006, no pet.) (retained counsel allowed to withdraw from appeal once trial court determines indigency of child)

Standard of Review

In re M.P., 126 S.W.3d 228 (Tex. App.—San Antonio 2003, no pet.) (civil harm analysis used for jury instruction error)

In re J.D.P., 85 S.W.3d 420 (Tex. App.—Ft. Worth 2001, no pet.) (criminal standard of evidence sufficiency review applied)

In re T.K.E., 5 S.W.3d 782 (Tex. App.—San Antonio 1999, no pet.) (civil standard for reviewing legal sufficiency at disposition phase)

In re D.V., 955 S.W.2d 379 (Tex. App.—San Antonio 1997, no writ) (civil harmless error rule used in indeterminate commitment cases; criminal used in determinate sentence cases)

In re D.Z., 869 S.W.2d 561 (Tex. App.—Corpus Christi 1993, writ denied) (criminal harmless error standard applies in appeal of determinate sentence act case)

Cross References

TX FCA FAMILY § 61.004. Parent or other eligible person against whom a final juvenile court order has been entered may appeal, *infra*.

TEX. R. CIVIL PROC. 324. Complaints that require as a prerequisite to appeal a motion for new trial.

TEX. R. APP. PROC. 25.1. Requirements for Notice of Appeal.

§ 56.02. Transcript on Appeal

(a) An attorney retained to represent a child on appeal who desires to have included in the record on appeal a transcription of notes of the reporter has the responsibility of obtaining and paying for the transcription and furnishing it to the clerk in duplicate in time for inclusion in the record.

(b) The juvenile court shall order the reporter to furnish a transcription without charge to the attorney if the court finds, after hearing or on an affidavit filed by the child's parent or other person responsible for support of the child that the parent or other responsible person is unable to pay or to give security therefor.

(c) On certificate of the court that a transcription has been provided without charge, payment therefor shall be made from the general funds of the county in which the proceedings appealed from occurred.

(d) The court reporter shall report any portion of the proceedings requested by either party or directed by the court and shall report the proceedings in question and answer form unless a narrative transcript is requested.

Comment

This section deals with responsibility for providing the appellate court with a record of the trial proceedings, including payment for the record when the child's family is indigent.

Leading Cases

In re K.C.A., 36 S.W.3d 501 (Tex. 2000) (an indigence finding can be predicated on either a hearing or an affidavit of the child's parents)

B.J.M. v. State, 997 S.W.2d 626 (Tex. App.—Dallas 1999, no pet.) (failure of court to enter written order sustaining indigency contest results in free transcript)

§ 56.03. Appeal by State in Cases of Violent or Habitual Offender

(a) In this section, "prosecuting attorney" means the county attorney, district attorney, or criminal district attorney who has the primary responsibility of presenting cases in the juvenile court. The term does not include an assistant prosecuting attorney.

(b) The state is entitled to appeal an order of a court in a juvenile case in which the grand jury has approved of the petition under Section 53.045 if the order:

(1) dismisses a petition or any portion of a petition;

(2) arrests or modifies a judgment;

(3) grants a new trial;

(4) sustains a claim of former jeopardy; or

(5) grants a motion to suppress evidence, a confession, or an admission and if:

(A) jeopardy has not attached in the case;

(B) the prosecuting attorney certifies to the trial court that the appeal is not taken for the purpose of delay; and

(C) the evidence, confession, or admission is of substantial importance in the case.

(c) The prosecuting attorney may not bring an appeal under Subsection (b) later than the 15th day after the date on which the order or ruling to be appealed is entered by the court.

(d) The state is entitled to a stay in the proceedings pending the disposition of an appeal under Subsection (b).

(e) The court of appeals shall give preference in its docket to an appeal filed under Subsection (b).

(f) The state shall pay all costs of appeal under Subsection (b), other than the cost of attorney's fees for the respondent.

(g) If the respondent is represented by appointed counsel, the counsel shall continue to represent the respondent as appointed counsel on the appeal. If the respondent is not represented by appointed counsel, the respondent may seek the appointment of counsel to represent the respondent on appeal. The juvenile court shall determine whether the parent or other person responsible for support of the child is financially able to obtain an attorney to represent the respondent on appeal. If the court determines that the parent or other person is financially unable to obtain counsel for the appeal, the court shall appoint counsel to represent the respondent on appeal.

(h) If the state appeals under this section and the respondent is not detained, the court shall permit the respondent to remain at large subject only to the condition that the respondent appear in court for further proceedings when required by the court. If the respondent is detained, on the state's filing of notice of appeal under this section, the respondent is entitled to immediate release from detention on the allegation that is the subject of the appeal. The court shall permit the respondent to remain at large regarding that allegation subject only to the condition that the respondent appear in court for further proceedings when required by the court.

(i) The Texas Rules of Appellate Procedure apply to a petition by the state to the supreme court for review of a decision of a court of appeals in a juvenile case.

Comment

This section is modeled after Code of Criminal Procedure article 44.01. It permits the State to appeal in determinate sentence proceedings under circumstances in which conducting further proceedings following appellate reversal is not precluded by double jeopardy.

Leading Case

In re H.V., 252 S.W.3d 319 (Tex. 2008)(Supreme Court has jurisdiction to hear state's appeal of trial court's granting of Motion to Suppress because Government Code § 22.225(c) allows for jurisdiction when a conflict from courts of appeals exists.)

CHAPTER 57. RIGHTS OF VICTIMS

Introductory Comment

This chapter deals with victims of juvenile offenses and defines their rights in the juvenile process.

CLE/Other Legal Publication

Voices for change: the victim movement in Texas. Raven Kazen, 69 TEX. B.J. 248 (2006).

---

§ 57.001. Definitions

In this chapter:

(1) "Close relative of a deceased victim" means a person who was the spouse of a deceased victim at the time of the victim's death or who is a parent or adult brother, sister, or child of the deceased victim.

(2) "Guardian of a victim" means a person who is the legal guardian of the victim, whether or not the legal relationship between the guardian and victim exists because of the age of the victim or the physical or mental incompetency of the victim.

(3) "Victim" means a person who as the result of the delinquent conduct of a child suffers a pecuniary loss or personal injury or harm.

Comment

This chapter includes property offenses committed by juveniles. And this chapter defines victim broadly to include anyone injured in any fashion by delinquent conduct.

---

§ 57.002. Victim's Rights

(a) A victim, guardian of a victim, or close relative of a deceased victim is entitled to the following rights within the juvenile justice system:

(1) the right to receive from law enforcement agencies adequate protection from harm and threats of harm arising from cooperation with prosecution efforts;

(2) the right to have the court or person appointed by the court take the safety of the victim or the victim's family into consideration as an element in determining whether the child should be detained before the child's conduct is adjudicated;

(3) the right, if requested, to be informed of relevant court proceedings, including appellate proceedings, and to be informed in a timely manner if those court proceedings have been canceled or rescheduled;

(4) the right to be informed, when requested, by the court or a person appointed by the court concerning the procedures in the juvenile justice system, including general procedures relating to:

(A) the preliminary investigation and deferred prosecution of a case; and

(B) the appeal of the case;

(5) the right to provide pertinent information to a juvenile court conducting a disposition hearing concerning the impact of the offense on the victim and the victim's family by testimony, written statement, or any other manner before the court renders its disposition;

(6) the right to receive information regarding compensation to victims as provided by Subchapter B, Chapter 56, Code of Criminal Procedure, including information related to the costs that may be compensated under that subchapter and the amount of compensation, eligibility for compensation, and procedures for application for compensation under that subchapter, the payment of medical expenses under Section 56.06, Code of Criminal Procedure, for a victim of a sexual assault, and when requested, to referral to available social service agencies that may offer additional assistance;

(7) the right to be informed, upon request, of procedures for release under supervision or transfer of the person to the custody of the Texas Department of Criminal Justice for parole, to participate in the release or transfer for parole process, to be notified, if requested, of the person's release, escape, or transfer for parole proceedings concerning the person, to provide to the Texas Youth Commission for inclusion in the person's file information to be considered by the commission before the release under supervision or transfer for parole of the person, and to be notified, if requested, of the person's release or transfer for parole;

(8) the right to be provided with a waiting area, separate or secure from other witnesses, including the child alleged to have committed the conduct and relatives of the child, before testifying in any proceeding concerning the child, or, if a separate waiting area is not available, other safeguards should be taken to minimize the victim's contact with the child and the child's relatives and witnesses, before and during court proceedings;

(9) the right to prompt return of any property of the victim that is held by a law enforcement agency or the attorney for the state as evidence when the property is no longer required for that purpose;

(10) the right to have the attorney for the state notify the employer of the victim, if requested, of the necessity of the victim's cooperation and testimony in a proceeding that may necessitate the absence of the victim from work for good cause;

(11) the right to be present at all public court proceedings related to the conduct of the child as provided by Section 54.08, subject to that section; and

(12) any other right appropriate to the victim that a victim of criminal conduct has under Article 56.02, Code of Criminal Procedure.

(b) In notifying a victim of the release or escape of a person, the Texas Youth Commission shall use the same procedure established for the notification of the release or escape of an adult offender under Article 56.11, Code of Criminal Procedure.

§ 57.003. Duties of Juvenile Board and Victim Assistance Coordinator

(a) The juvenile board shall ensure to the extent practicable that a victim, guardian of a victim, or close relative of a deceased victim is afforded the rights granted by Section 57.002 and, on request, an explanation of those rights.

(b) The juvenile board may designate a person to serve as victim assistance coordinator in the juvenile board's jurisdiction for victims of juvenile offenders.

(c) The victim assistance coordinator shall ensure that a victim, or close relative of a deceased victim, is afforded the rights granted victims, guardians, and relatives by Section 57.002 and, on request, an explanation of those rights. The victim assistance coordinator shall work closely with appropriate law enforcement agencies, prosecuting attorneys, the Texas Juvenile Probation Commission, and the Texas Youth Commission in carrying out that duty.

(d) The victim assistance coordinator shall ensure that at a minimum, a victim, guardian of a victim, or close relative of a deceased victim receives:

(1) a written notice of the rights outlined in Section 57.002;

(2) an application for compensation under the Crime Victims' Compensation Act (Subchapter B, Chapter 56, Code of Criminal Procedure); and

(3) a victim impact statement with information explaining the possible use and consideration of the victim impact statement at detention, adjudication, and release proceedings involving the juvenile.

(e) The victim assistance coordinator shall, on request, offer to assist a person receiving a form under Subsection (d) to complete the form.

(f) The victim assistance coordinator shall send a copy of the victim impact statement to the court conducting a disposition hearing involving the juvenile.

(g) The juvenile board, with the approval of the commissioners court of the county, may approve a program in which the victim assistance coordinator may offer not more than 10 hours of posttrial psychological counseling for a person who serves as a juror or an alternate juror in an adjudication hearing involving graphic evidence or testimony and who requests the posttrial psychological counseling not later than the 180th day after the date on which the jury in the adjudication hearing is dismissed. The victim assistance coordinator may provide the counseling using a provider that assists local juvenile justice agencies in providing similar services to victims.

Comment

This section allows jurors to receive post-trial psychiatric counseling if the adjudication hearing involved graphic evidence or testimony.

§ 57.0031. Notification of Rights of Victims of Juveniles

At the initial contact or at the earliest possible time after the initial contact between the victim of a reported crime and the juvenile probation office having the responsibility for the disposition of the juvenile, the office shall provide the victim a written notice:

(1) containing information about the availability of emergency and medical services, if applicable;

(2) stating that the victim has the right to receive information regarding compensation to victims of crime as provided by the Crime Victims' Compensation Act (Subchapter B, Chapter 56, Code of Criminal Procedure), including information about:

(A) the costs that may be compensated and the amount of compensation, eligibility for compensation, and procedures for application for compensation;

(B) the payment for a medical examination for a victim of a sexual assault; and

(C) referral to available social service agencies that may offer additional assistance;

(3) stating the name, address, and phone number of the victim assistance coordinator for victims of juveniles;

(4) containing the following statement: "You may call the crime victim assistance coordinator for the status of the case and information about victims' rights.";

(5) stating the rights of victims of crime under Section 57.002;

(6) summarizing each procedural stage in the processing of a juvenile case, including preliminary investigation, detention, informal adjustment of a case, disposition hearings, release proceedings, restitution, and appeals;

(7) suggesting steps the victim may take if the victim is subjected to threats or intimidation;

(8) stating the case number and assigned court for the case; and

(9) stating that the victim has the right to file a victim impact statement and to have it considered in juvenile proceedings.

§ 57.004. Notification

A court, a person appointed by the court, or the Texas Youth Commission is responsible for notifying a victim, guardian of a victim, or close relative of a deceased victim of a proceeding under this chapter only if the victim, guardian of a victim, or close relative of a deceased victim requests the notification in writing and provides a current address to which the notification is to be sent.

§ 57.005. Liability

The Texas Youth Commission, a juvenile board, a court, a person appointed by a court, an attorney for the state, a peace officer, or a law enforcement agency is not liable for a failure or inability to provide a right listed under Section 57.002 of this code.

§ 57.006. Appeal

The failure or inability of any person to provide a right or service listed under Section 57.002 of this code may not be used by a child as a ground for appeal or for a post conviction writ of habeas corpus.

§ 57.007. Standing

A victim, guardian of a victim, or close relative of a victim does not have standing to participate as a party in a juvenile proceeding or to contest the disposition of any case.

§ 57.008. Court Order for Protection From Juveniles

(a) A court may issue an order for protection from juveniles directed against a child to protect a victim of the child's conduct who, because of the victim's participation in the juvenile justice system, risks further harm by the child.

(b) In the order, the court may prohibit the child from doing specified acts or require the child to do specified acts necessary or appropriate to prevent or reduce the likelihood of further harm to the victim by the child.

CHAPTER 58. RECORDS; JUVENILE JUSTICE INFORMATION SYSTEM

SUBCHAPTER A. RECORDS

SUBCHAPTER B. JUVENILE JUSTICE INFORMATION SYSTEM

SUBCHAPTER C. AUTOMATIC RESTRICTION OF ACCESS TO RECORDS

SUBCHAPTER D. LOCAL JUVENILE JUSTICE INFORMATION SYSTEM

SUBCHAPTER D–1. REPORTS ON COUNTY INTERNET WEBSITES

SUBCHAPTER E. STATEWIDE JUVENILE INFORMATION AND CASE MANAGEMENT SYSTEM

Introductory Comment

Chapter 58 is a comprehensive regulation of juvenile records. It creates a state-wide computerized juvenile records system operated by the DPS as part of the adult system created by Chapter 60 of the TEX. CODE CRIM. PROC. ANN.

Subchapter A deals with local records and with sealing of records. Subchapter B deals with the state-wide system. Subchapter C deals with a new method of automatic restriction of access to records and Subchapter D deals with local juvenile justice information systems.

CLE/Other Legal Publication

Juvenile Records as Adult Punishment Evidence—"I Will Follow You." Catherine Greene Burnett, 13TH ANN. JUVE. L. CONF. (Feb. 2000)

Attorney General Opinion

Tex. Atty. Gen. Op. ORD–655 (1997) (housing authority can obtain juvenile records from DPS)

SUBCHAPTER A. RECORDS

§ 58.001. Collection of Records of Children

(a) Law enforcement officers and other juvenile justice personnel shall collect information described by Section 58.104 as a part of the juvenile justice information system created under Subchapter B.

(b) The information is available as provided by Subchapter B.

(c) A law enforcement agency shall forward information, including fingerprints, relating to a child who has been taken into custody under Section 52.01 by the agency to the Department of Public Safety for inclusion in the juvenile justice information system created under Subchapter B, but only if the child is referred to juvenile court on or before the 10th day after the date the child is taken into custody under Section 52.01. If the child is not referred to juvenile court within that time, the law enforcement agency shall destroy all information, including photographs and fingerprints, relating to the child unless the child is placed in a first offender program under Section 52.031 or on informal disposition under Section 52.03. The law enforcement agency may not forward any information to the Department of Public Safety relating to the child while the child is in a first offender program under Section 52.031, or during the 90 days following successful completion of the program or while the child is on informal disposition under Section 52.03. Except as provided by Subsection (f), after the date the child completes an informal disposition under Section 52.03 or after the 90th day after the date the child successfully completes a first offender program under Section 52.031, the law enforcement agency shall destroy all information, including photographs and fingerprints, relating to the child.

(d) If information relating to a child is contained in a document that also contains information relating to an adult and a law enforcement agency is required to destroy all information relating to the child under this section, the agency shall alter the document so that the information relating to the child is destroyed and the information relating to the adult is preserved.

(e) The deletion of a computer entry constitutes destruction of the information contained in the entry.

(f) A law enforcement agency may maintain information relating to a child after the 90th day after the date the child successfully completes a first offender program under Section 52.031 only to determine the child's eligibility to participate in a first offender program.

Comment

A law enforcement agency may photograph and fingerprint any child taken into custody for a criminal offense of the grade of B misdemeanor or higher under § 58.002, *infra*. However, it may send those documents and other information to the state-wide system only if it makes a referral to the juvenile court system within 10 days of arrest. If it chooses not to make a referral, the records must be destroyed, unless the child is placed on informal disposition or in a first offender program.

Subsection (c) prohibits law enforcement from sending juvenile records to DPS for ninety days after successful completion of a first offender program and, subject to (f), requires records destruction at that time. Subsection (d) makes it clear that when law enforcement is required to destroy juvenile records, it can do so by eliminating any reference to the identity of the juvenile and need not also destroy those parts of the record that are needed for successful prosecution of a criminal case. Subsection (e) states that deletion of a computer entry is destruction of that record even though the record could possibly be reconstructed by a computer expert. Subsection (f) permits law enforcement to keep a record beyond the 90 day destruction deadline for the sole purpose of determining future ineligibility for a first offender program.

Law enforcement agencies are required to submit information to the DPS relating to any child it takes into custody if a referral to the juvenile court is made within 10 days. This requirement applies only to children taken into full custody, not just temporarily detained in a public place.

Attorney General Opinion

Tex. Atty. Gen. Op. DM–435 (1997) (obligation under § 58.001 to destroy law enforcement information explained)

§ 58.002. Photographs and Fingerprints of Children

(a) Except as provided by Chapter 63, Code of Criminal Procedure, a child may not be photographed or fingerprinted without the consent of the juvenile court unless the child is taken into custody or referred to the juvenile court for conduct that constitutes a felony or a misdemeanor punishable by confinement in jail.

(b) On or before December 31 of each year, the head of each municipal or county law enforcement agency located in a county shall certify to the juvenile board for that county that the photographs and fingerprints required to be destroyed under Section 58.001 have been destroyed. The juvenile board shall conduct or cause to be conducted an audit of the records of the law enforcement agency to verify the destruction of the photographs and fingerprints and the law enforcement agency shall make its records available for this purpose. If the audit shows that the certification provided by the head of the law enforcement agency is false, that person is subject to prosecution for perjury under Chapter 37, Penal Code.

(c) This section does not prohibit a law enforcement officer from photographing or fingerprinting a child who is not in custody if the child's parent or guardian voluntarily consents in writing to the photographing or fingerprinting of the child.

(d) This section does not apply to fingerprints that are required or authorized to be submitted or obtained for an application for a driver's license or personal identification card.

(e) This section does not prohibit a law enforcement officer from fingerprinting or photographing a child as provided by Section 58.0021.

Comment

Only children arrested for B misdemeanors or above may be fingerprinted and photographed without the consent of the juvenile court. The juvenile board has the duty to determine by audit of law enforcement records that those records that should be destroyed are destroyed.

Subsection (a) is intended to authorize juvenile intake and probation officials to fingerprint and photograph children who are referred to the juvenile court without being taken into custody.

Subsection (c) provides that a law enforcement officer may fingerprint or photograph a child not in custody but only with written parental consent.

Leading Cases

Hayes v. Florida, 470 U.S. 811, 84 L.Ed.2d 705, 105 S.Ct. 1643 (1985) (taking fingerprints from arrestee without consent requires probable cause)

Lanes v. State, 767 S.W.2d 789 (Tex. Crim. App. 1989) (probable cause as well as juvenile court's consent required to take fingerprints from arrestee)

In re Franklin, 699 S.W.2d 689 (Tex. App.—Texarkana 1985, no writ) (failure to send juvenile photograph to court does not preclude in-court identification)

---

§ 58.0021. Fingerprints or Photographs for Comparison in Investigation

(a) A law enforcement officer may take temporary custody of a child to take the child's fingerprints if:

(1) the officer has probable cause to believe that the child has engaged in delinquent conduct;

(2) the officer has investigated that conduct and has found other fingerprints during the investigation; and

(3) the officer has probable cause to believe that the child's fingerprints will match the other fingerprints.

(b) A law enforcement officer may take temporary custody of a child to take the child's photograph if:

(1) the officer has probable cause to believe that the child has engaged in delinquent conduct; and

(2) the officer has probable cause to believe that the child's photograph will be of material assistance in the investigation of that conduct.

(c) Temporary custody for the purpose described by Subsection (a) or (b):

(1) is not a taking into custody under Section 52.01; and

(2) may not be reported to the juvenile justice information system under Subchapter B.

(d) If a law enforcement officer does not take the child into custody under Section 52.01, the child shall be released from temporary custody authorized under this section as soon as the fingerprints or photographs are obtained.

(e) A law enforcement officer who under this section obtains fingerprints or photographs from a child shall:

(1) immediately destroy them if they do not lead to a positive comparison or identification; and

(2) make a reasonable effort to notify the child's parent, guardian, or custodian of the action taken.

(f) A law enforcement officer may under this section obtain fingerprints or photographs from a child at:

(1) a juvenile processing office; or

(2) a location that affords reasonable privacy to the child.

Comment

Under prior law, if a law enforcement officer had probable cause and wished to fingerprint or photograph a child to confirm or dispel suspicion, the officer, absent consent by the juvenile, was required to take the juvenile into custody to enable fingerprinting and photographing as part of the booking process. That action creates statewide and nationwide records of the event. This section affords a less intrusive alternative when the officer has probable cause. It enables the information to be obtained without creating a record.

§ 58.0022. Fingerprints or Photographs to Identify Runaways

A law enforcement officer who takes a child into custody with probable cause to believe that the child has engaged in conduct indicating a need for supervision as described by Section 51.03(b)(3) and who after reasonable effort is unable to determine the identity of the child, may fingerprint or photograph the child to establish the child's identity. On determination of the child's identity or that the child cannot be identified by the fingerprints or photographs, the law enforcement officer shall immediately destroy all copies of the fingerprint records or photographs of the child.

Comment

This section permits an officer who has taken a runaway into custody to fingerprint and photograph the person if necessary to identify the person.

§ 58.003. Sealing of Records

(a) Except as provided by Subsections (b) and (c), on the application of a person who has been found to have engaged in delinquent conduct or conduct indicating a need for supervision, or a person taken into custody to determine whether the person engaged in delinquent conduct or conduct indicating a need for supervision, on the juvenile court's own motion the court shall order the sealing of the records in the case if the court finds that:

(1) two years have elapsed since final discharge of the person or since the last official action in the person's case if there was no adjudication; and

(2) since the time specified in Subdivision (1), the person has not been convicted of a felony or a misdemeanor involving moral turpitude or found to have engaged in delinquent conduct or conduct indicating a need for supervision and no proceeding is pending seeking conviction or adjudication.

(b) A court may not order the sealing of the records of a person who has received a determinate sentence for engaging in delinquent conduct that violated a penal law listed in Section 53.045 or engaging in habitual felony conduct as described by Section 51.031.

(c) Subject to Subsection (b), a court may order the sealing of records concerning a person adjudicated as having engaged in delinquent conduct that violated a penal law of the grade of felony only if:

(1) the person is **19** ~~21~~ years of age or older;

(2) the person was not transferred by a juvenile court under Section 54.02 to a criminal court for prosecution;

(3) the records have not been used as evidence in the punishment phase of a criminal proceeding under Section 3(a), Article 37.07, Code of Criminal Procedure; and

(4) the person has not been convicted of a penal law of the grade of felony after becoming age 17.

(c–1) Notwithstanding Subsections (a) and (c) and subject to Subsection (b), a juvenile court may order the sealing of records concerning a child adjudicated as having engaged in delinquent conduct or conduct indicating a need for supervision that violated a penal law of the grade of misdemeanor or felony if the child successfully completed a drug court program under Chapter 469, Health and Safety Code. The court may:

(1) order the sealing of the records immediately and without a hearing; or

(2) hold a hearing to determine whether to seal the records.

(c–2) If the court orders the sealing of a child's records under Subsection (c–1), a prosecuting attorney or juvenile probation department may maintain until the child's 17th birthday a separate record of the child's name and date of birth and the date the child successfully completed the drug court program. The prosecuting attorney or juvenile probation department, as applicable, shall send the record to the court as soon as practicable after the child's 17th birthday to be added to the child's other sealed records.

Text of subsec. (c–3), as added by Acts 2011, 82nd Leg., ch. 1150 (H.B. 2015), § 2

(c–3) Notwithstanding Subsections (a) and (c) and subject to Subsection (b), a juvenile court, on the court's own motion and without a hearing, shall order the sealing of records concerning a child found to have engaged in conduct indicating a need for supervision described by Section 51.03(b)(7) or taken into custody to determine whether the child engaged in conduct indicating a need for supervision described by Section 51.03(b)(7). This subsection applies only to records related to conduct indicating a need for supervision described by Section 51.03(b)(7).

Text of subsec. (c–3), as added by Acts 2011, 82nd Leg., ch. 1322 (S.B. 407), § 19

(c–3) Notwithstanding Subsections (a) and (c) and subject to Subsection (b), a juvenile court may order the sealing of records concerning a child found to have engaged in conduct indicating a need for supervision that violates Section 43.261, Penal Code, or taken into custody to determine whether the child engaged in conduct indicating a need for supervision that violates Section 43.261, Penal Code, if the child attends and successfully completes an educational program described by Section 37.218, Education Code, or another equivalent educational program. The court may:

(1) order the sealing of the records immediately and without a hearing; or

(2) hold a hearing to determine whether to seal the records.

Text of subsec. (c–4), as added by Acts 2011, 82nd Leg., ch. 1150 (H.B. 2015), § 2

(c–4) A prosecuting attorney or juvenile probation department may maintain until a child's 17th birthday a separate record of the child's name and date of birth and the date on which the child's records are sealed, if the child's records are sealed under Subsection (c–3). The prosecuting attorney or juvenile probation department, as applicable, shall send the record to the court as soon as practicable after the child's 17th birthday to be added to the child's other sealed records.

Text of subsec. (c–4), as added by Acts 2011, 82nd Leg., ch. 1322 (S.B. 407), § 19

(c–4) A prosecuting attorney or juvenile probation department may maintain until a child's 17th birthday a separate record of the child's name and date of birth and the date on which the child successfully completed the educational program, if the child's records are sealed under Subsection (c–3). The prosecuting attorney or juvenile probation department, as applicable, shall send the record to the court as soon as practicable after the child's 17th birthday to be added to the child's other sealed records.

Text of subsec. (d), as amended by Acts 2011, 82nd Leg., ch. 1150 (H.B. 2015), § 2

(d) The court may grant **to a child** the relief authorized in Subsection (a)**,** ~~or~~ (c–1)**, or (c–3)** at any time after final discharge of the **child** ~~person~~ or after the last official action in the case if there was no adjudication, subject**, if applicable,** to Subsection (e). If the child is referred to the juvenile court for conduct constituting any offense and at the adjudication hearing the child is found to be not guilty of each offense alleged, the court shall immediately and without any additional hearing order the sealing of all files and records relating to the case.

Text of subsec. (d), as amended by Acts 2011, 82nd Leg., ch. 1322 (S.B. 407), § 19

(d) The court may grant the relief authorized in Subsection (a)**,** ~~or~~ (c–1)**, or (c–3)** at any time after final discharge of the person or after the last official action in the case if there was no adjudication, subject**, if applicable,** to Subsection (e). If the child is referred to the juvenile court for conduct constituting any offense and at the adjudication hearing the child is found to be not guilty of each offense alleged, the court shall immediately and without any additional hearing order the sealing of all files and records relating to the case.

(e) The court shall hold a hearing before sealing a person's records under Subsection (a) or (c) unless the applicant waives the right to a hearing in writing and the court and the prosecuting attorney for the juvenile court consent. Reasonable notice of the hearing shall be given to:

(1) the person who made the application or who is the subject of the records named in the motion;

(2) the prosecuting attorney for the juvenile court;

(3) the authority granting the discharge if the final discharge was from an institution or from parole;

(4) the public or private agency or institution having custody of records named in the application or motion; and

(5) the law enforcement agency having custody of files or records named in the application or motion.

(f) A copy of the sealing order shall be sent to each agency or official named in the order.

(g) On entry of the order:

(1) all law enforcement, prosecuting attorney, clerk of court, and juvenile court records ordered sealed shall be sent before the 61st day after the date the order is received to the court issuing the order;

(2) all records of a public or private agency or institution ordered sealed shall be sent before the 61st day after the date the order is received to the court issuing the order;

(3) all index references to the records ordered sealed shall be deleted before the 61st day after the date the order is received, and verification of the deletion shall be sent before the 61st day after the date of the deletion to the court issuing the order;

(4) the juvenile court, clerk of court, prosecuting attorney, public or private agency or institution, and law enforcement officers and agencies shall properly reply that no record exists with respect to the person on inquiry in any matter; and

(5) the adjudication shall be vacated and the proceeding dismissed and treated for all purposes other than a subsequent capital prosecution, including the purpose of showing a prior finding of delinquent conduct, as if it had never occurred.

(g–1) Any records collected or maintained by the Texas Juvenile **Justice Department**,~~Probation Commission~~ including statistical data submitted under Section **221.007**~~141.044~~, Human Resources Code, are not subject to a sealing order issued under this section.

(h) Inspection of the sealed records may be permitted by an order of the juvenile court on the petition of the person who is the subject of the records and only by those persons named in the order.

(i) On the final discharge of a child or on the last official action in the case if there is no adjudication, the child shall be given a written explanation of the child's rights under this section and a copy of the provisions of this section.

(j) A person whose records have been sealed under this section is not required in any proceeding or in any application for employment, information, or licensing to state that the person has been the subject of a proceeding under this title and any statement that the person has never been found to be a delinquent child shall never be held against the person in any criminal or civil proceeding.

(k) A prosecuting attorney may, on application to the juvenile court, reopen at any time the files and records of a person adjudicated as having engaged in delinquent conduct that violated a penal law of the grade of felony sealed by the court under this section for the purposes of Sections 12.42(a)–(c) and (e), Penal Code.

(*l*) On the motion of a person in whose name records are kept or on the court's own motion, the court may order the destruction of records that have been sealed under this section if:

(1) the records relate to conduct that did not violate a penal law of the grade of felony or a misdemeanor punishable by confinement in jail;

(2) five years have elapsed since the person's 16th birthday; and

(3) the person has not been convicted of a felony.

(m) On request of the Department of Public Safety, a juvenile court shall reopen and allow the department to inspect the files and records of the juvenile court relating to an applicant for a license to carry a concealed handgun under Subchapter H, Chapter 411, Government Code.

(n) A record created or maintained under Chapter 62, Code of Criminal Procedure, may not be sealed under this section if the person who is the subject of the record has a continuing obligation to register under that chapter.

(*o*) An agency or official named in the order that cannot seal the records because the information required in the order under Subsection (p) is incorrect or insufficient shall notify the court issuing the order before the 61st day after the date the agency or official receives the order. The court shall notify the person who made the application or who is the subject of the records named in the motion, or the attorney for that person, before the 61st day after the date the court receives the notice that the agency or official cannot seal the records because there is incorrect or insufficient information in the order.

(p) A person who is eligible to seal records may file an application for the sealing of records in a juvenile court of the county in which the proceedings occurred. The application and sealing order entered on the application must include the following information or an explanation for why one or more of the following is not included:

(1) the applicant's:

(A) full name;

(B) sex;

(C) race or ethnicity;

(D) date of birth;

(E) driver's license or identification card number; and

(F) social security number;

(2) the offense charged against the applicant or for which the applicant was referred to the juvenile justice system;

(3) the date on which and the county where the offense was alleged to have been committed; and

(4) if a petition was filed in the juvenile court, the cause number assigned to the petition and the court and county in which the petition was filed.

Amended by Acts 2011, 82nd Leg., ch. 85 (S.B. 653), § 3.008, eff. Sept. 1, 2011; Acts 2011, 82nd Leg., ch. 731 (H.B. 961), § 3, eff. June 17, 2011; Acts 2011, 82nd Leg., ch. 1150 (H.B. 2015), § 2, eff. Sept. 1, 2011; Acts 2011, 82nd Leg., ch. 1322 (S.B. 407), § 19, eff. Sept. 1, 2011.

Comment

This section establishes five different categories relating to the sealing of a juvenile's records: (1) If the juvenile has received a determinate sentence, the records can never be sealed; (2) If the juvenile has been adjudicated for any other felony, the sealing applicant must wait until he becomes 19 years of age; (3) The right to seal any non-felony adjudication records arises two years after the juvenile exits the system; (4) The juvenile court has discretion to order sealing for non-felony adjudication records anytime after the juvenile exits the system; (5) Finally, if the juvenile is found not guilty of all offenses, no matter what the charges, the records must immediately be ordered sealed by the juvenile court.

Subsections (c–1) and (c–2) allow for an immediate sealing of records if a child successfully completes a drug court program. This provides an incentive for juveniles to seek and complete treatment. It also allows a record to be sealed before the age of 21 and at a time when juveniles are attempting to gain employment, apply for college or join the military. The prosecutor or juvenile probation department may maintain a record of the child's name, date of birth, and date of completion of the drug program. Those agencies must, however, seal this as well on the child's 17th birthday.

In 2011 subsection (c–3) and (c–4) were added to allow a juvenile court on its own motion to order the sealing of records in a CINS case involving a child engaging in prostitution.

Subsection (m) prohibits the sealing of sex offender registration records so long as there is a continuing duty to register. All other juvenile records can be sealed as provided by this section. Sex offender registration records can be sealed once the juvenile no longer has an obligation to register.

Subsection (g) requires that agencies holding records comply with a sealing order within 60 days of receiving the order. If the order is insufficient, the agency under Subsection (*o*) must report that back to the court within 60 days.

Further, subsection (g) allows the Texas Juvenile Probation Commission (TJPC) or TJJD to maintain all juvenile justice records for statistical purposes.

Attorney General Opinion

Tex. Atty. Gen. Op. DM–9 (1991) (unless record sealed, juvenile must report adjudication on employment application)

CLE/Other Legal Publication

Sealing A Juvenile Record: Why and How To Do It. Jeanice Dawes, 47 Dec. HouLaw 22 (Dec. 2009)

---

§ 58.004. Repealed by Acts 1997, 75th Leg., ch. 1086, § 49(a), eff. Sept. 1, 1997

§ 58.005. Confidentiality of Records

(a) Records and files concerning a child, including personally identifiable information, and information obtained for the purpose of diagnosis, examination, evaluation, or treatment or for making a referral for treatment of a child by a public or private agency or institution providing supervision of a child by arrangement of the juvenile court or having custody of the child under order of the juvenile court may be disclosed only to:

(1) the professional staff or consultants of the agency or institution;

(2) the judge, probation officers, and professional staff or consultants of the juvenile court;

(3) an attorney for the child;

(4) a governmental agency if the disclosure is required or authorized by law;

(5) a person or entity to whom the child is referred for treatment or services if the agency or institution disclosing the information has entered into a written confidentiality agreement with the person or entity regarding the protection of the disclosed information;

(6) the Texas Department of Criminal Justice and the Texas Juvenile Probation Commission for the purpose of maintaining statistical records of recidivism and for diagnosis and classification; or

(7) with leave of the juvenile court, any other person, agency, or institution having a legitimate interest in the proceeding or in the work of the court.

(b) This section does not apply to information collected under Section 58. 104 or under Subchapter D–1.

Comment

This section is restricted to treatment and social information and other personally-identifiable information. It covers information in the possession of local probation departments, the TYC, public and private placement facilities, court consultants and treatment personnel. The reference to § 58.104 is to information that is sent to the Juvenile Justice Information System.

Attorney General Opinion

Tex. Atty. Gen. Op. DM–334 (1995) (victim of juvenile's offense may have legitimate interest in juvenile court records)

---

§ 58.0051. Interagency Sharing of Educational Records

(a) **In this section:**

(1) "Educational records" means records in the possession of a primary or secondary educational institution that contain information relating to a student, including information relating to the student's:

(A) identity;

(B) special needs;

(C) educational accommodations;

(D) assessment or diagnostic test results;

(E) attendance records;

(F) disciplinary records;

(G) medical records; and

(H) psychological diagnoses.

(2) "Juvenile service provider" means a governmental entity that provides juvenile justice or prevention, medical, educational, or other support services to a juvenile. The term includes:

(A) a state or local juvenile justice agency as defined by Section 58.101;

(B) health and human services agencies, as defined by Section 531.001, Government Code, and the Health and Human Services Commission;

(C) the Department of Public Safety;

(D) the Texas Education Agency;

(E) an independent school district;

(F) a juvenile justice alternative education program;

(G) a charter school;

(H) a local mental health or mental retardation authority;

(I) a court with jurisdiction over juveniles;

(J) a district attorney's office;

(K) a county attorney's office; and

(L) a children's advocacy center established under Section 264.402.

(3)"Student" means a person who:

(A) is registered or in attendance at a primary or secondary educational institution; and

(B) is younger than 18 years of age.

(b) At the request of a juvenile service provider, an independent school district or a charter school shall disclose to the juvenile service provider confidential information contained in the student's educational records if the student has been:

(1) taken into custody under Section 52.01; or

(2) referred to a juvenile court for allegedly engaging in delinquent conduct or conduct indicating a need for supervision.

(c) An independent school district or charter school that discloses confidential information to a juvenile service provider under Subsection (b) may not destroy a record of the disclosed information before the seventh anniversary of the date the information is disclosed.

(d) An independent school district or charter school shall comply with a request under Subsection (b) regardless of whether other state law makes that information confidential.

(e) ~~Within each county, a district school superintendent and the juvenile probation department may enter into a written interagency agreement to share information about juvenile offenders. The agreement must specify the conditions under which summary criminal history information is to be made available to appropriate school personnel and the conditions under which school records are to be made available to appropriate juvenile justice agencies. (b) Information disclosed under this section by a school district must relate to the juvenile system's ability to serve, before adjudication, the student whose records are being released. (c)~~ A juvenile **service provider that** ~~justice agency official who~~ receives **confidential** ~~educational~~ information under this section shall:

(1) certify in writing that the **juvenile service provider** ~~institution or individual~~ receiving the **confidential** ~~personally identifiable~~ information has agreed not to disclose it to a third party, other than another juvenile **service provider; and**

(2) use the confidential information only to:

(A) verify the identity of a student involved in the juvenile justice system; and

(B) provide delinquency prevention or treatment services to the student ~~justice agency~~.

(f) A juvenile service provider may establish an internal protocol for sharing information with other juvenile service providers as necessary to efficiently and promptly disclose and accept the information. The protocol may specify the types of information that may be shared under this section without violating federal law, including any federal funding requirements. A juvenile service provider may enter into a memorandum of understanding with another juvenile service provider to share information according to the juvenile service provider's protocols. A juvenile service provider shall comply with this section regardless of whether the juvenile service provider establishes an internal protocol or enters into a memorandum of understanding under this subsection unless compliance with this section violates federal law.

(g) This section does not affect the confidential status of the information being shared. The information may be released to a third party only as directed by a court order or as otherwise authorized by law. Personally identifiable information disclosed to a juvenile service provider under this section is not subject to disclosure to a third party under Chapter 552, Government Code.

(h)~~(d)~~ A juvenile **service provider that requests information under this section shall pay a fee to the disclosing juvenile service provider in the same amounts charged for the provision of public information under Subchapter F, Chapter 552, Government Code, unless:**

(1) a memorandum of understanding between the requesting provider and the disclosing provider:

(A) prohibits the payment of a fee;

(B) provides for the waiver of a fee; or

(C) provides an alternate method of assessing a fee;

(2) the disclosing provider waives the payment of the fee; or

(3) disclosure of the information is required by law other than this subchapter ~~justice agency that receives educational information under this section shall destroy all information when the child is no longer under the jurisdiction of a juvenile court. (e) The Texas Juvenile Probation Commission may, in conformity with Section 58.0072 of this code and Section 37.084, Education Code, enter into an interagency agreement to share educational information for research, audit, and analytical purposes with the: (1) Texas Education Agency; (2) Texas Youth Commission; and (3) Texas Department of Criminal Justice~~.

Amended by Acts 2011, 82nd Leg., ch. 653 (S.B. 1106), § 2, eff. June 17, 2011.

Comment

In 2011 the legislature changed this section to specifically apply to the sharing of educational records. Juvenile justice providers are entitled to a student's otherwise confidential educational records if that child has been taken into custody or referred to a juvenile court. The information is strictly to be used to verify the identity of a student and/or to provide delinquency prevention or treatment services.

---

§ 58.0052. Interagency Sharing of Noneducational Records

(a) In this section:

(1) "Juvenile service provider" has the meaning assigned by Section 58.0051.

(2) "Multi-system youth" means a person who:

(A) is younger than 19 years of age; and

(B) has received services from two or more juvenile service providers.

(3) "Personal health information" means personally identifiable information regarding a multi-system youth's physical or mental health or the provision of or payment for health care services, including case management services, to a multi-system youth. The term does not include clinical psychological notes or substance abuse treatment information.

(b) At the request of a juvenile service provider, another juvenile service provider shall disclose to that provider a multi-system youth's personal health information or a history of governmental services provided to the multi-system youth, including:

(1) identity;

(2) medical records;

(3) assessment results;

(4) special needs;

(5) program placements; and

(6) psychological diagnoses.

(c) A juvenile service provider may disclose personally identifiable information under this section only for the purposes of:

(1) identifying a multi-system youth;

(2) coordinating and monitoring care for a multi-system youth; and

(3) improving the quality of juvenile services provided to a multi-system youth.

(d) To the extent that this section conflicts with another law of this state with respect to confidential information held by a governmental agency, this section controls.

(e) A juvenile service provider may establish an internal protocol for sharing information with other juvenile service providers as necessary to efficiently and promptly disclose and accept the information. The protocol may specify the types of information that may be shared under this section without violating federal law, including any

federal funding requirements. A juvenile service provider may enter into a memorandum of understanding with another juvenile service provider to share information according to the juvenile service provider's protocols. A juvenile service provider shall comply with this section regardless of whether the juvenile service provider establishes an internal protocol or enters into a memorandum of understanding under this subsection unless compliance with this section violates federal law.

(f) This section does not affect the confidential status of the information being shared. The information may be released to a third party only as directed by a court order or as otherwise authorized by law. Personally identifiable information disclosed to a juvenile service provider under this section is not subject to disclosure to a third party under Chapter 552, Government Code.

(g) This section does not affect the authority of a governmental agency to disclose to a third party for research purposes information that is not personally identifiable as provided by the governmental agency's protocol.

(h) A juvenile service provider that requests information under this section shall pay a fee to the disclosing juvenile service provider in the same amounts charged for the provision of public information under Subchapter F, Chapter 552, Government Code, unless:

(1) a memorandum of understanding between the requesting provider and the disclosing provider:

(A) prohibits the payment of a fee;

(B) provides for the waiver of a fee; or

(C) provides an alternate method of assessing a fee;

(2) the disclosing provider waives the payment of the fee; or

(3) disclosure of the information is required by law other than this subchapter.

Added by Acts 2011, 82nd Leg., ch. 653 (S.B. 1106), § 2, eff. June 17, 2011.

Comment

This section, added in 2011, allows one juvenile service provider to disclose to another a child's health information or history of governmental services provided, strictly for the purposes of identity of a child, coordinating care, and/or improving the quality of services.

---

§ 58.006. Destruction of Certain Records

The court shall order the destruction of the records relating to the conduct for which a child is taken into custody, including records contained in the juvenile justice information system, if:

(1) a determination that no probable cause exists to believe the child engaged in the conduct is made under Section 53.01 and the case is not referred to a prosecutor for review under Section 53.012; or

(2) a determination that no probable cause exists to believe the child engaged in the conduct is made by a prosecutor under Section 53.012.

Comment

This section requires the automatic destruction, not just sealing, of records when a determination of no probable cause is made by intake or by the prosecutor.

---

§ 58.007. Physical Records or Files

(a) This section applies only to the inspection and maintenance of a physical record or file concerning a child and the storage of information, by electronic means or otherwise, concerning the child from which a physical record or file could be generated and does not affect the collection, dissemination, or maintenance of information as provided by Subchapter B. This section does not apply to a record or file relating to a child that is:

(1) required or authorized to be maintained under the laws regulating the operation of motor vehicles in this state;

(2) maintained by a municipal or justice court; or

(3) subject to disclosure under Chapter 62, Code of Criminal Procedure.

(b) Except as provided by Article 15.27, Code of Criminal Procedure, the records and files of a juvenile court, a clerk of court, a juvenile probation department, or a prosecuting attorney relating to a child who is a party to a proceeding under this title are open to inspection only by:

(1) the judge, probation officers, and professional staff or consultants of the juvenile court;

(2) a juvenile justice agency as that term is defined by Section 58.101;

(3) an attorney for a party to the proceeding;

(4) a public or private agency or institution providing supervision of the child by arrangement of the juvenile court, or having custody of the child under juvenile court order; or

(5) with leave of the juvenile court, any other person, agency, or institution having a legitimate interest in the proceeding or in the work of the court.

(c) Except as provided by Subsection (d), law enforcement records and files concerning a child and information stored, by electronic means or otherwise, concerning the child from which a record or file could be generated may not be disclosed to the public and shall be:

(1) if maintained on paper or microfilm, kept separate from adult files and records;

(2) if maintained electronically in the same computer system as records or files relating to adults, be accessible under controls that are separate and distinct from controls to access electronic data concerning adults; and

(3) maintained on a local basis only and not sent to a central state or federal depository, except as provided by Subchapters B, D, and E.

(d) The law enforcement files and records of a person who is transferred from the Texas Youth Commission to the Texas Department of Criminal Justice may be transferred to a central state or federal depository for adult records on or after the date of transfer.

(e) Law enforcement records and files concerning a child may be inspected or copied by a juvenile justice agency as that term is defined by Section 58.101, a criminal justice agency as that term is defined by Section 411.082, Government Code, the child, and the child's parent or guardian.

(f) If a child has been reported missing by a parent, guardian, or conservator of that child, information about the child may be forwarded to and disseminated by the Texas Crime Information Center and the National Crime Information Center.

(g) For the purpose of offering a record as evidence in the punishment phase of a criminal proceeding, a prosecuting attorney may obtain the record of a defendant's adjudication that is admissible under Section 3(a), Article 37.07, Code of Criminal Procedure, by submitting a request for the record to the juvenile court that made the adjudication. If a court receives a request from a prosecuting attorney under this subsection, the court shall, if the court possesses the requested record of adjudication, certify and provide the prosecuting attorney with a copy of the record.

(h) The juvenile court may disseminate to the public the following information relating to a child who is the subject of a directive to apprehend or a warrant of arrest and who cannot be located for the purpose of apprehension:

(1) the child's name, including other names by which the child is known;

(2) the child's physical description, including sex, weight, height, race, ethnicity, eye color, hair color, scars, marks, and tattoos;

(3) a photograph of the child; and

(4) a description of the conduct the child is alleged to have committed, including the level and degree of the alleged offense.

(i) In addition to the authority to release information under Subsection (b)(5), a juvenile probation department may release information contained in its records without leave of the juvenile court pursuant to guidelines adopted by the juvenile board.

(j) Before a child or a child's parent or guardian may inspect or copy a record or file concerning the child under Subsection (e), the custodian of the record or file shall redact:

(1) any personally identifiable information about a juvenile suspect, offender, victim, or witness who is not the child; and

(2) any information that is excepted from required disclosure under Chapter 552, Government Code, or other law.

Comment

This section deals with physical records other than the information contained in the statewide Juvenile Justice Information System. Examples would be offense or incident reports, a witness statement, and laboratory reports. Those records must be maintained on a local basis and are subject to confidentiality restrictions similar to those that apply to treatment records.

Subsection (a) restates the rule that municipal or justice court records of criminal cases involving juveniles are not subject to the confidentiality requirements of this section. Subsection (c) is intended to abrogate Open Records Decision 644 (1996) that the Family Code does not make law enforcement physical records of juvenile cases confidential. Subsections (a) and (c) specify confidentiality rules for electronic data maintained locally. Subsection (a)(3) provides that sex offender registration information is not subject to the confidentiality provisions of this section. Subsection (h) permits public disclosure by a juvenile court of information that may be helpful to apprehend a child who is the subject of an arrest warrant or directive to apprehend and who cannot be located by law enforcement.

Subsection (e) was amended and subsection (j) added in 2007 to allow parents and the juvenile himself to inspect the records. Thus, parents can be aware of the child's conduct. Additionally, juveniles are now able to access this information as needed for college or employment applications.

Subsection (i), permits juvenile probation departments to release information under juvenile board guidelines without having to obtain juvenile court permission in every case.

Leading Case

In re W.R.M., 534 S.W.2d 178 (Tex. Civ. App.—Eastland 1976, no writ) (§ 51.14 does not grant discovery rights to respondent)

Attorney General Opinion

Tex. Atty. Gen. Op. DM–334 (1995) (victim has legitimate interest in juvenile records to authorize disclosure, which is in discretion of juvenile court)

---

§ 58.0071. Destruction of Certain Physical Records and Files

(a) In this section:

(1) "Juvenile case" means:

(A) a referral for conduct indicating a need for supervision or delinquent conduct; or

(B) if a petition was filed, all charges made in the petition.

(2) "Physical records and files" include entries in a computer file or information on microfilm, microfiche, or any other electronic storage media.

(b) The custodian of physical records and files in a juvenile case may destroy the records and files if the custodian duplicates the information in the records and files in a computer file or information on microfilm, microfiche, or any other electronic storage media.

(c) The following persons may authorize, subject to Subsections (d) and (e) and any other restriction the person may impose, the destruction of the physical records and files relating to a closed juvenile case:

(1) a juvenile board in relation to the records and files in the possession of the juvenile probation department;

(2) the head of a law enforcement agency in relation to the records and files in the possession of the agency; and

(3) a prosecuting attorney in relation to the records and files in the possession of the prosecuting attorney's office.

(d) The physical records and files of a juvenile case may only be destroyed if the child who is the respondent in the case:

(1) is at least 18 years of age and:

(A) the most serious allegation adjudicated was conduct indicating a need for supervision;

(B) the most serious allegation was conduct indicating a need for supervision and there was not an adjudication; or

(C) the referral or information did not relate to conduct indicating a need for supervision or delinquent conduct and the juvenile court or the court's staff did not take action on the referral or information for that reason;

(2) is at least 21 years of age and:

(A) the most serious allegation adjudicated was delinquent conduct that violated a penal law of the grade of misdemeanor; or

(B) the most serious allegation was delinquent conduct that violated a penal law of the grade of misdemeanor or felony and there was not an adjudication; or

(3) is at least 31 years of age and the most serious allegation adjudicated was delinquent conduct that violated a penal law of the grade of felony.

(e) If a record or file contains information relating to more than one juvenile case, information relating to each case may only be destroyed if:

(1) the destruction of the information is authorized under this section; and

(2) the information can be separated from information that is not authorized to be destroyed under this section.

(f) This section does not affect the destruction of physical records and files authorized by the Texas State Library Records Retention Schedule.

Comment

This is a "spring cleaning" provision that enables juvenile justice agencies to clean out old, unnecessary files that are expensive to maintain. Destruction of clerk of court files is not authorized unless they are duplicated and put into electronic form. This section is not a sealing provision, but is intended to benefit those records custodians who wish to take advantage of it.

---

§ 58.00711. Records Relating to Children Convicted of Fine–Only Misdemeanors

Except as provided by Article 45.0217(b), Code of Criminal Procedure, all records and files and information stored by electronic means or otherwise, from which a record or file could be generated, relating to a child who is convicted of and has satisfied the judgment for a fine-only misdemeanor offense other than a traffic offense are confidential and may not be disclosed to the public.

Added by Acts 2011, 82nd Leg., ch. 731 (H.B. 961), § 4, eff. June 17, 2011.

Comment

This provision, added in 2011, makes confidential all records for a child who is convicted of and has satisfied the judgment on a Class C misdemeanor other than a traffic offense.

§ 58.0072. Dissemination of Juvenile Justice Information

(a) Except as provided by this section, juvenile justice information collected and maintained by the Texas Juvenile Probation Commission for statistical and research purposes is confidential information for the use of the commission and may not be disseminated by the commission.

(b) Juvenile justice information consists of information of the type described by Section 58.104, including statistical data in any form or medium collected, maintained, or submitted to the Texas Juvenile **Justice Department** ~~Probation Commission~~ under Section **221.007** ~~141.044~~, Human Resources Code.

(c) The Texas Juvenile Probation Commission may grant the following entities access to juvenile justice information for research and statistical purposes or for any other purpose approved by the commission:

(1) criminal justice agencies as defined by Section 411.082, Government Code;

(2) the Texas Education Agency, as authorized under Section 37.084, Education Code;

(3) any agency under the authority of the Health and Human Services Commission; or

(4) a public or private university.

(d) The Texas Juvenile Probation Commission may grant the following entities access to juvenile justice information only for a purpose beneficial to and approved by the commission to:

(1) a person working on a research or statistical project that:

(A) is funded in whole or in part by state or federal funds; and

(B) meets the requirements of and is approved by the commission; or

(2) a governmental entity that has a specific agreement with the commission, if the agreement:

(A) specifically authorizes access to information;

(B) limits the use of information to the purposes for which the information is given;

(C) ensures the security and confidentiality of the information; and

(D) provides for sanctions if a requirement imposed under Paragraph (A), (B), or (C) is violated.

(e) The Texas Juvenile Probation Commission shall grant access to juvenile justice information for legislative purposes under Section 552.008, Government Code.

(f) The Texas Juvenile Probation Commission may not release juvenile justice information in identifiable form, except for information released under Subsection (c)(1), (2), or (3) or under the terms of an agreement entered into under Subsection (d)(2). For purposes of this subsection, identifiable information means information that contains a juvenile offender's name or other personal identifiers or that can, by virtue of sample size or other factors, be reasonably interpreted as referring to a particular juvenile offender.

(g) The Texas Juvenile Probation Commission is not required to release or disclose juvenile justice information to any person not identified under this section.

Amended by Acts 2011, 82nd Leg., ch. 85 (S.B. 653), § 3.009, eff. Sept. 1, 2011.

Comment

This section allows the Texas Juvenile Probation Commission or TJJD to disseminate certain information with specified agencies.

SUBCHAPTER B. JUVENILE JUSTICE INFORMATION SYSTEM

Introductory Comment

This subchapter establishes a state-wide computerized database for juvenile justice information, which is maintained by the Texas Department of Public Safety as part of its adult records system. The information is subject to the Automatic Fingerprint Identification System, which permits computer-matching of latent fingerprints with those in the database, as in the case of adults.

Information relating to juvenile arrests, prosecutions, adjudications and dispositions are sent to the DPS.

This information is subject to sealing of the records in accordance with § 58.003.

Unlike records of adult cases in the DPS system, juvenile case records are not public but may be accessed only by criminal justice agencies and other agencies identified by statute.

---

§ 58.101. Definitions

In this subchapter:

(1) "Criminal justice agency" has the meaning assigned by Section 411.082, Government Code.

(2) "Department" means the Department of Public Safety of the State of Texas.

(3) "Disposition" means an action that results in the termination, transfer of jurisdiction, or indeterminate suspension of the prosecution of a juvenile offender.

(4) "Incident number" means a unique number assigned to a child during a specific custodial or detention period or for a specific referral to the office or official designated by the juvenile board, if the juvenile offender was not taken into custody before the referral.

(5) "Juvenile justice agency" means an agency that has custody or control over juvenile offenders.

(6) "Juvenile offender" means a child who has been assigned an incident number.

(7) "State identification number" means a unique number assigned by the department to a child in the juvenile justice information system.

(8) "Uniform incident fingerprint card" means a multiple-part form containing a unique incident number with space for information relating to the conduct for which a child has been taken into custody, detained, or referred, the child's fingerprints, and other relevant information.

§ 58.102. Juvenile Justice Information System

(a) The department is responsible for recording data and maintaining a database for a computerized juvenile justice information system that serves:

(1) as the record creation point for the juvenile justice information system maintained by the state; and

(2) as the control terminal for entry of records, in accordance with federal law, rule, and policy, into the federal records system maintained by the Federal Bureau of Investigation.

(b) The department shall develop and maintain the system with the cooperation and advice of the:

(1) Texas Youth Commission;

(2) Texas Juvenile Probation Commission;

(3) Criminal Justice Policy Council; and

(4) juvenile courts and clerks of juvenile courts.

(c) The department may not collect or retain information relating to a juvenile if this chapter prohibits or restricts the collection or retention of the information.

(d) The database must contain the information required by this subchapter.

(e) The department shall designate the offense codes and has the sole responsibility for designating the state identification number for each juvenile whose name appears in the juvenile justice system.

§ 58.103. Purpose of System

The purpose of the juvenile justice information system is to:

(1) provide agencies and personnel within the juvenile justice system accurate information relating to children who come into contact with the juvenile justice system of this state;

(2) provide, where allowed by law, adult criminal justice agencies accurate and easily accessible information relating to children who come into contact with the juvenile justice system;

(3) provide an efficient conversion, where appropriate, of juvenile records to adult criminal records;

(4) improve the quality of data used to conduct impact analyses of proposed legislative changes in the juvenile justice system; and

(5) improve the ability of interested parties to analyze the functioning of the juvenile justice system.

§ 58.104. Types of Information Collected

(a) Subject to Subsection (f), the juvenile justice information system shall consist of information relating to delinquent conduct committed by a juvenile offender that, if the conduct had been committed by an adult, would constitute a criminal offense other than an offense punishable by a fine only, including information relating to:

(1) the juvenile offender;

(2) the intake or referral of the juvenile offender into the juvenile justice system;

(3) the detention of the juvenile offender;

(4) the prosecution of the juvenile offender;

(5) the disposition of the juvenile offender's case, including the name and description of any program to which the juvenile offender is referred; and

(6) the probation or commitment of the juvenile offender.

(b) To the extent possible and subject to Subsection (a), the department shall include in the juvenile justice information system the following information for each juvenile offender taken into custody, detained, or referred under this title for delinquent conduct:

(1) the juvenile offender's name, including other names by which the juvenile offender is known;

(2) the juvenile offender's date and place of birth;

(3) the juvenile offender's physical description, including sex, weight, height, race, ethnicity, eye color, hair color, scars, marks, and tattoos;

(4) the juvenile offender's state identification number, and other identifying information, as determined by the department;

(5) the juvenile offender's fingerprints;

(6) the juvenile offender's last known residential address, including the census tract number designation for the address;

(7) the name and identifying number of the agency that took into custody or detained the juvenile offender;

(8) the date of detention or custody;

(9) the conduct for which the juvenile offender was taken into custody, detained, or referred, including level and degree of the alleged offense;

(10) the name and identifying number of the juvenile intake agency or juvenile probation office;

(11) each disposition by the juvenile intake agency or juvenile probation office;

(12) the date of disposition by the juvenile intake agency or juvenile probation office;

(13) the name and identifying number of the prosecutor's office;

(14) each disposition by the prosecutor;

(15) the date of disposition by the prosecutor;

(16) the name and identifying number of the court;

(17) each disposition by the court, including information concerning custody of a juvenile offender by a juvenile justice agency or probation;

(18) the date of disposition by the court;

(19) any commitment or release under supervision by the Texas Youth Commission;

(20) the date of any commitment or release under supervision by the Texas Youth Commission; and

(21) a description of each appellate proceeding.

(c) The department may designate codes relating to the information described by Subsection (b).

(d) The department shall designate a state identification number for each juvenile offender.

(e) This subchapter does not apply to a disposition that represents an administrative status notice of an agency described by Section 58.102(b).

(f) Records maintained by the department in the depository are subject to being sealed under Section 58.003.

Comment

Under Subsection (a) only Class B misdemeanors and above are part of the Juvenile Justice Information System. Class C cases and status offender cases, such as truancy and running away, are not part of the system.

Subsection (f) no longer requires DPS to notify local juvenile courts when it certifies a juvenile record is eligible for sealing.

---

§ 58.105. Duties of Juvenile Board

Each juvenile board shall provide for:

(1) the compilation and maintenance of records and information needed for reporting information to the department under this subchapter;

(2) the transmittal to the department, in the manner provided by the department, of all records and information required by the department under this subchapter; and

(3) access by the department to inspect records and information to determine the completeness and accuracy of information reported.

§ 58.106. Confidentiality

(a) Except as otherwise provided by this section, information contained in the juvenile justice information system is confidential information for the use of the department and may not be disseminated by the department except:

(1) with the permission of the juvenile offender, to military personnel of this state or the United States;

(2) to a person or entity to which the department may grant access to adult criminal history records as provided by Section 411.083, Government Code;

(3) to a juvenile justice agency;

(4) to the Texas Youth Commission and the Texas Juvenile Probation Commission for analytical purposes; ~~and~~

(5) to the office of independent ombudsman of the Texas Youth Commission; **and**

(6) to a county, justice, or municipal court exercising jurisdiction over a juvenile under Section 54.021.

(a–1) Information disseminated under Subsection (a) remains confidential after dissemination and may be disclosed by the recipient only as provided by this title.

(b) Subsection (a) does not apply to a document maintained by a juvenile justice agency that is the source of information collected by the department.

(c) The department may, if necessary to protect the welfare of the community, disseminate to the public the following information relating to a juvenile who has escaped from the custody of the Texas Youth Commission or from another secure detention or correctional facility:

(1) the juvenile's name, including other names by which the juvenile is known;

(2) the juvenile's physical description, including sex, weight, height, race, ethnicity, eye color, hair color, scars, marks, and tattoos;

(3) a photograph of the juvenile; and

(4) a description of the conduct for which the juvenile was committed to the Texas Youth Commission or detained in the secure detention or correctional facility, including the level and degree of the alleged offense.

(d) The department may, if necessary to protect the welfare of the community, disseminate to the public the information listed under Subsection (c) relating to a juvenile offender when notified by a law enforcement agency of this state that the law enforcement agency has been issued a directive to apprehend the offender or an arrest warrant for the offender or that the law enforcement agency is otherwise authorized to arrest the offender and that the offender is suspected of having:

(1) committed a felony offense under the following provisions of the Penal Code:

(A) Title 5;

(B) Section 29.02; or

(C) Section 29.03; and

(2) fled from arrest or apprehension for commission of the offense.

Amended by Acts 2011, 82nd Leg., ch. 186 (S.B. 1241), § 1, eff. Sept. 1, 2011; Acts 2011, 82nd Leg., ch. 653 (S.B. 1106), § 3, eff. June 17, 2011; Acts 2011, 82nd Leg., ch. 1098 (S.B. 1489), § 11, eff. Sept. 1, 2011.

Comment

The information in the Juvenile Justice Information System is not open to public inspection. It is available only to juvenile justice, criminal justice or certain other agencies and organizations authorized by statute. As to most of those agencies, the information will be available by computer search, as in the case of information in the criminal history system. Numerous public and private organizations are given access to information under Chapter 411 of the Government Code. Virtually all occupational licensing agencies have such access. Examples are the Board of Law Examiners and the Central Education Agency.

2011 Amendments allow magistrates, justice and municipal courts that exercise jurisdiction in truancy cases to have access to this information.

§ 58.107. Compatibility of Data

Data supplied to the juvenile justice information system must be compatible with the system and must contain both incident numbers and state identification numbers.

§ 58.108. Duties of Agencies and Courts

(a) A juvenile justice agency and a clerk of a juvenile court shall:

(1) compile and maintain records needed for reporting data required by the department;

(2) transmit to the department in the manner provided by the department data required by the department;

(3) give the department or its accredited agents access to the agency or court for the purpose of inspection to determine the completeness and accuracy of data reported; and

(4) cooperate with the department to enable the department to perform its duties under this chapter.

(b) A juvenile justice agency and clerk of a court shall retain documents described by this section.

§ 58.109. Uniform Incident Fingerprint Card

(a) The department may provide for the use of a uniform incident fingerprint card in the maintenance of the juvenile justice information system.

(b) The department shall design, print, and distribute to each law enforcement agency and juvenile intake agency uniform incident fingerprint cards.

(c) The incident cards must:

(1) be serially numbered with an incident number in a manner that allows each incident of referral of a juvenile offender who is the subject of the incident fingerprint card to be readily ascertained; and

(2) be multiple-part forms that can be transmitted with the juvenile offender through the juvenile justice process and that allow each agency to report required data to the department.

(d) Subject to available telecommunications capacity, the department shall develop the capability to receive by electronic means from a law enforcement agency the information on the uniform incident fingerprint card. The information must be in a form that is compatible to the form required of data supplied to the juvenile justice information system.

§ 58.110. Reporting

(a) The department by rule shall develop reporting procedures that ensure that the juvenile offender processing data is reported from the time a juvenile offender is initially taken into custody, detained, or referred until the time a juvenile offender is released from the jurisdiction of the juvenile justice system.

(b) The law enforcement agency or the juvenile intake agency that initiates the entry of the juvenile offender into the juvenile justice information system for a specific incident shall prepare a uniform incident fingerprint card and initiate the reporting process for each incident reportable under this subchapter.

(c) The clerk of the court exercising jurisdiction over a juvenile offender's case shall report the disposition of the case to the department. A clerk of the court who violates this subsection commits an offense. An offense under this subsection is a Class C misdemeanor.

(d) In each county, the reporting agencies may make alternative arrangements for reporting the required information, including combined reporting or electronic reporting, if the alternative reporting is approved by the juvenile board and the department.

(e) Except as otherwise required by applicable state laws or regulations, information required by this chapter to be reported to the department shall be reported promptly. The information shall be reported not later than the 30th day after the date the information is received by the agency responsible for reporting the information, except that a juvenile offender's custody or detention without previous custody shall be reported to the department not later than the seventh day after the date of the custody or detention.

(f) Subject to available telecommunications capacity, the department shall develop the capability to receive by electronic means the information required under this section to be reported to the department. The information must be in a form that is compatible to the form required of data to be reported under this section.

Comment

The central idea of this section is that as a case is initiated and passes through the juvenile justice system, the agency responsible for the case adds information to the system as to the status of the case, resulting in a complete step-by-step record of the case.

Subsection (e) deletes the requirement to report to DPS juvenile referrals without a custody event within 7 days.

---

§ 58.111. Local Data Advisory Boards

The commissioners court of each county may create a local data advisory board to perform the same duties relating to the juvenile justice information system as the duties performed by a local data advisory board in relation to the criminal history record system under Article 60.09, Code of Criminal Procedure.

§ 58.112. Report to Legislature

Not later than August 15 of each year, the Texas Juvenile Probation Commission shall submit to the lieutenant governor, the speaker of the house of representatives, and the governor a report that contains the following statistical information relating to children referred to a juvenile court during the preceding year:

(1) the ages, races, and counties of residence of the children transferred to a district court or criminal district court for criminal proceedings; and

(2) the ages, races, and counties of residence of the children committed to the Texas Youth Commission, placed on probation, or discharged without any disposition.

§ 58.113. Warrants

The department shall maintain in a computerized database that is accessible by the same entities that may access the juvenile justice information system information relating to a warrant of arrest, as that term is defined by Article 15.01, Code of Criminal Procedure, or a directive to apprehend under Section 52.015 for any child, without regard to whether the child has been taken into custody.

Comment

Warrants are kept in a separate database from criminal history information. This section allows warrant information on juveniles to be maintained by DPS in that database and restricts access to those agencies that may access criminal history information.

SUBCHAPTER C. AUTOMATIC RESTRICTION OF ACCESS TO RECORDS

Introductory Comment

This subchapter introduces a new concept to Texas juvenile law: automatic restriction of access to records. When a record is placed on restricted access, it is not destroyed, nor is it sealed. It remains in place but access is thereafter restricted to criminal justice agencies for a criminal justice purpose. For collateral purposes—employers, the military, occupational licensing agencies, educational institutions—the record ceases to exist and the subject is authorized to deny the occurrence of the events that gave rise to the creation of the record. This restriction occurs automatically by action of the DPS and local juvenile justice agencies; unlike sealing, it does not require the juvenile's family to employ an attorney to draft, file and present a petition to the juvenile court. Therefore, unlike sealing, restriction of access should be available regardless of the economic status of the subject or the subject's family.

---

§ 58.201. Definition

In this subchapter, "department" means the Department of Public Safety of the State of Texas.

§ 58.202. Exempted Records

The following records are exempt from this subchapter:

(1) sex offender registration records maintained by the department or a local law enforcement agency under Chapter 62, Code of Criminal Procedure; and

(2) records relating to a criminal combination or criminal street gang maintained by the department or a local law enforcement agency under Chapter 61, Code of Criminal Procedure.

§ 58.203. Certification

(a) The department shall certify to the juvenile probation department to which a referral was made that resulted in information being submitted to the juvenile justice information system that the records relating to a person's juvenile case are subject to automatic restriction of access if:

(1) the person is at least **17** ~~21~~ years of age;

(2) the juvenile case did not include violent or habitual felony conduct resulting in proceedings in the juvenile court under Section 53.045; **and**

(3) the juvenile case was not certified for trial in criminal court under Section 54.02~~; and (4) the department has not received a report in its criminal history system that the person was granted deferred adjudication for or convicted of a felony or a misdemeanor punishable by confinement in jail for an offense committed after the person became 17 years of age~~.

(b) If the department's records relate to a juvenile court with multicounty jurisdiction, the department shall issue the certification described by Subsection (a) to each juvenile probation department that serves the court. On receipt of the certification, each juvenile probation department shall determine whether it received the referral and, if it received the referral, take the restrictive action notification required by law.

(c) The department may issue the certification described by Subsection (a) by electronic means, including by electronic mail.

Amended by Acts 2011, 82nd Leg., ch. 731 (H.B. 961), § 5, eff. June 17, 2011.

Comment

To be eligible for restricted access, the subject must be 17, must not have been adjudicated under the determinate sentence act or have been certified to criminal court.

DPS is required to send notice directly to the probation department, thus streamlining the process.

§ 58.204. Restricted Access on Certification

(a) On certification of records in a case under Section 58.203, the department, except as provided by Subsection (b):

(1) may not disclose the existence of the records or any information from the records in response to an inquiry from:

(A) a law enforcement agency;

(B) a criminal or juvenile justice agency;

(C) a governmental or other agency given access to information under Chapter 411, Government Code; or

(D) any other person, agency, organization, or entity; and

(2) shall respond to a request for information about the records by stating that the records do not exist.

(b) On certification of records in a case under Section 58.203, the department may permit access to the information in the juvenile justice information system relating to the case of an individual only:

(1) by a criminal justice agency for a criminal justice purpose, as those terms are defined by Section 411.082, Government Code; or

(2) for research purposes, by the Texas Juvenile Probation Commission, the Texas Youth Commission, or the Criminal Justice Policy Council.

Comment

Once access to a record is restricted, it can thereafter be accessed only by a criminal justice agency for a criminal justice purpose. Under the Government Code definition, criminal justice purpose includes employment screening for employment by a criminal justice agency.

§ 58.205. Request to the Federal Bureau of Investigation on Certification

On certification of records in a case under Section 58.203, the department shall request the Federal Bureau of Investigation to:

(1) place the information in its files on restricted status, with access only by a criminal justice agency for a criminal justice purpose, as those terms are defined by Section 411.082, Government Code; or

(2) if the action described in Subdivision (1) is not feasible, delete all information in its database concerning the case.

Comment

Since nobody is certain how the FBI will regard restricted access, the alternatives are to first request the FBI to honor the restrictions and, failing that, to request that it delete the record totally, which the FBI says it will do upon DPS request. Upon implementation of restricted access in March 2003, the FBI informed DPS that it cannot impose restricted access on the records, so will delete them, when time and resources permit.

§ 58.206. Effect of Certification in Relation to the Protected Person

(a) On certification of records in a case under Section 58.203:

(1) the person who is the subject of the records is not required to state in any proceeding, except as otherwise authorized by law in a criminal proceeding in which the person is testifying as a defendant, or in any application for employment, licensing, or other public or private benefit that the person has been a respondent in a case under this title and may not be punished, by perjury prosecution or otherwise, for denying:

(A) the existence of the records; or

(B) the person's participation in a juvenile proceeding related to the records; and

(2) information from the records may not be admitted against the person who is the subject of the records in a civil or criminal proceeding except a proceeding in which a juvenile adjudication was admitted under:

(A) Section 12.42, Penal Code;

(B) Article 37.07, Code of Criminal Procedure; or

(C) as otherwise authorized by criminal procedural law.

(b) A person who is the subject of records certified under this subchapter may not waive the restricted status of the records or the consequences of the restricted status.

§ 58.207. Juvenile Court Orders on Certification

(a) On certification of records in a case under Section 58.203, the juvenile court shall order:

(1) that the following records relating to the case may be accessed only as provided by Section 58.204(b):

(A) if the respondent was committed to the Texas Youth Commission, records maintained by the commission;

(B) records maintained by the juvenile probation department;

(C) records maintained by the clerk of the court;

(D) records maintained by the prosecutor's office; and

(E) records maintained by a law enforcement agency; and

(2) the juvenile probation department to make a reasonable effort to notify the person who is the subject of records for which access has been restricted of the action restricting access and the legal significance of the action for the person, but only if the person has requested the notification in writing and has provided the juvenile probation department with a current address.

(b) On receipt of an order under Subsection (a)(1), the agency maintaining the records:

(1) may allow access only as provided by Section 58.204(b); and

(2) shall respond to a request for information about the records by stating that the records do not exist.

Comment

The requirement that probation notify all agencies that provided care or custody of the child was eliminated as unduly burdensome.

---

§ 58.208. Information to Child on Discharge

On the final discharge of a child from the juvenile system or on the last official action in the case, if there is no adjudication, the appropriate juvenile justice official shall provide to the child:

(1) a written explanation of how automatic restricted access under this subchapter works;

(2) a copy of this subchapter; and

(3) a statement that if the child wishes to receive notification of an action restricting access to the child's records under Section 58.207(a), the child must before the child's **17th** ~~21st~~ birthday provide the juvenile probation department with a current address where the child can receive notification.

Amended by Acts 2011, 82nd Leg., ch. 731 (H.B. 961), § 6, eff. June 17, 2011.

Comment

The probation department is now only required to notify persons if they have provided an address before their 17th birthday.

---

§ 58.209. Information to Child by Probation Officer or Texas Youth Commission

(a) When a child is placed on probation for an offense that may be eligible for automatic restricted access at age **17** ~~21~~ or when a child is received by the Texas Youth Commission on an indeterminate commitment, a probation officer or an official at the Texas Youth Commission reception center, as soon as practicable, shall explain the substance of the following information to the child:

(1) if the child was adjudicated as having committed delinquent conduct for a felony or jailable misdemeanor, that the child probably has a juvenile record with the department and the Federal Bureau of Investigation;

(2) that the child's juvenile record is a permanent record that is not destroyed or erased unless the record is eligible for sealing and the child or the child's family hires a lawyer and files a petition in court to have the record sealed;

(3) that the child's juvenile record, other than treatment records made confidential by law, can be accessed by police, sheriff's officers, prosecutors, probation officers, correctional officers, and other criminal and juvenile justice officials in this state and elsewhere;

(4) that the child's juvenile record, other than treatment records made confidential by law, can be accessed by employers, educational institutions, licensing agencies, and other organizations when the child applies for employment or educational programs;

(5) if the child's juvenile record is placed on restricted access when the child becomes **17** ~~21~~ years of age, that access will be denied to employers, educational institutions, and others except for criminal justice agencies; **and**

(6) ~~that to have the child's juvenile record placed on restricted access at age 21, the child must not: (A) commit a felony or jailable misdemeanor; and (B) receive deferred adjudication for or be convicted in adult court of a felony or jailable misdemeanor; and (7)~~that restricted access does not require any action by the child or the child's family, including the filing of a petition or hiring of a lawyer, but occurs automatically at age **17** ~~21 if the child does not commit a criminal offense in the future~~.

(b) The probation officer or Texas Youth Commission official shall:

(1) give the child a written copy of the explanation provided; and

(2) communicate the same information to at least one of the child's parents or, if none can be found, to the child's guardian or custodian.

(c) The Texas Juvenile Probation Commission and the Texas Youth Commission shall adopt rules to implement this section and to facilitate the effective explanation of the information required to be communicated by this section.

Amended by Acts 2011, 82nd Leg., ch. 731 (H.B. 961), § 7, eff. June 17, 2011.

§ 58.210. Sealing or Destruction of Records Not Affected

(a) This subchapter does not prevent or restrict the sealing or destruction of juvenile records as authorized by law.

(b) Restricted access provided under this subchapter is in addition to sealing or destruction of juvenile records.

(c) A person who is the subject of records certified under this subchapter is entitled to access to the records for the purpose of preparing and presenting a motion to seal or destroy the records.

§ 58.211. Rescinding Restricted Access

(a) If the department has notified a juvenile probation department that a record has been placed on restricted access and the department later receives information in the department's criminal history system that the subject of the records has been convicted of or placed on deferred adjudication for a felony or a misdemeanor punishable by confinement in jail for an offense committed after the person reached the age of 17, the person's juvenile records are no longer subject to restricted access. The department shall notify the appropriate local juvenile probation departments in the manner described by Section 58.203 that the person's records are no longer subject to restricted access.

(b) On receipt of the notification described by Subsection (a), the juvenile probation department shall notify the agencies that maintain the person's juvenile records under Section 58.207(b) that the person's records are no longer subject to restricted access.

Comment

This section requires DPS to notify local juvenile probation departments when records are no longer restricted.

SUBCHAPTER D. LOCAL JUVENILE JUSTICE INFORMATION SYSTEM

Introductory Comment

This subchapter sets out in detail how a computerized juvenile records system that is being constructed in Dallas County is intended to operate. It was enacted to present a model of an integrated local juvenile justice information system for other counties to copy. The model is only a model; it is not mandatory. No county is required to have such a system and if it chooses to have a local juvenile justice information system, it is not required to follow the Dallas model.

The system seeks to integrate information about juveniles from the police, schools, justice and municipal courts, prosecutor's office, juvenile court and probation departments in the county, while protecting confidentiality of such information and restricting access on a need to know basis.

---

§ 58.301. Definitions

In this subchapter:

(1) "County juvenile board" means a juvenile board created under Chapter 152, Human Resources Code.

(2) "Governmental placement facility" means a juvenile residential placement facility operated by a unit of government.

(3) "Governmental service provider" means a juvenile justice service provider operated by a unit of government.

(4) "Local juvenile justice information system" means a county or multicounty computerized database of information concerning children, with data entry and access by the partner agencies that are members of the system.

(5) "Partner agency" means a governmental service provider or governmental placement facility that is authorized by this subchapter to be a member of a local juvenile justice information system or that has applied to be a member of a local juvenile justice information system and has been approved by the county juvenile board or regional juvenile board committee as a member of the system.

(6) "Regional juvenile board committee" means a committee that is composed of two members from each county juvenile board in a region that comprises a multicounty local juvenile information system.

§ 58.302. Purposes of System

The purposes of a local juvenile justice information system are to:

(1) provide accurate information at the county or regional level relating to children who come into contact with the juvenile justice system;

(2) assist in the development and delivery of services to children in the juvenile justice system;

(3) assist in the development and delivery of services to children:

(A) who school officials have reasonable cause to believe have committed an offense for which a report is required under Section 37.015, Education Code; or

(B) who have been expelled, the expulsion of which school officials are required to report under Section 52.041;

(4) provide for an efficient transmission of juvenile records from justice and municipal courts to county juvenile probation departments and the juvenile court and from county juvenile probation departments and juvenile court to the state juvenile justice information system created by Subchapter B;

(5) provide efficient computerized case management resources to juvenile courts, prosecutors, court clerks, county juvenile probation departments, and partner agencies authorized by this subchapter;

(6) provide a directory of services available to children to the partner agencies to facilitate the delivery of services to children;

(7) provide an efficient means for municipal and justice courts to report filing of charges, adjudications, and dispositions of juveniles to the juvenile court as required by Section 51.08; and

(8) provide a method for agencies to fulfill their duties under Section 58.108, including the electronic transmission of information required to be sent to the Department of Public Safety by Section 58.110(f).

§ 58.303. Local Juvenile Justice Information System

(a) Juvenile justice agencies in a county or region of this state may jointly create and maintain a local juvenile justice information system to aid in processing the cases of children under this code, to facilitate the delivery of services to children in the juvenile justice system, and to aid in the early identification of at-risk and delinquent children.

(b) A local juvenile justice information system may contain the following components:

(1) case management resources for juvenile courts, court clerks, prosecuting attorneys, and county juvenile probation departments;

(2) reporting systems to fulfill statutory requirements for reporting in the juvenile justice system;

(3) service provider directories and indexes of agencies providing services to children;

(4) victim-witness notices required under Chapter 57;

(5) electronic filing of complaints or petitions, court orders, and other documents filed with the court, including documents containing electronic signatures;

(6) electronic offense and intake processing;

(7) case docket management and calendaring;

(8) communications by email or other electronic communications between partner agencies;

(9) reporting of charges filed, adjudications and dispositions of juveniles by municipal and justice courts and the juvenile court, and transfers of cases to the juvenile court as authorized or required by Section 51.08;

(10) reporting to schools under Article 15.27, Code of Criminal Procedure, by law enforcement agencies, prosecuting attorneys, and juvenile courts;

(11) records of adjudications and dispositions, including probation conditions ordered by the juvenile court; and

(12) warrant management and confirmation capabilities.

(c) Blank.

(d) Membership in a local juvenile justice information system is determined by this subchapter. Membership in a regional juvenile justice information system is determined by the regional juvenile board committee from among partner agencies that have applied for membership.

§ 58.304. Types of Information Contained in a Local Juvenile Information System

(a) Subject to Subsection (d), a local juvenile justice information system must consist of:

(1) information relating to all referrals to the juvenile court of any type, including referrals for conduct indicating a need for supervision and delinquent conduct; and

(2) information relating to:

(A) the juvenile;

(B) the intake or referral of the juvenile into the juvenile justice system for any offense or conduct;

(C) the detention of the juvenile;

(D) the prosecution of the juvenile;

(E) the disposition of the juvenile's case, including the name and description of any program to which the juvenile is referred; and

(F) the probation, placement, or commitment of the juvenile.

(b) To the extent possible and subject to Subsections (a) and (d), the local juvenile justice information system may include the following information for each juvenile taken into custody, detained, or referred under this title:

(1) the juvenile's name, including other names by which the juvenile is known;

(2) the juvenile's date and place of birth;

(3) the juvenile's physical description, including sex, weight, height, race, ethnicity, eye color, hair color, scars, marks, and tattoos;

(4) the juvenile's state identification number and other identifying information;

(5) the juvenile's fingerprints and photograph;

(6) the juvenile's last known residential address, including the census tract number designation for the address;

(7) the name, address, and phone number of the juvenile's parent, guardian, or custodian;

(8) the name and identifying number of the agency that took into custody or detained the juvenile;

(9) each date of custody or detention;

(10) a detailed description of the conduct for which the juvenile was taken into custody, detained, or referred, including the level and degree of the alleged offense;

(11) the name and identifying number of the juvenile intake agency or juvenile probation office;

(12) each disposition by the juvenile intake agency or juvenile probation office;

(13) the date of disposition by the juvenile intake agency or juvenile probation office;

(14) the name and identifying number of the prosecutor's office;

(15) each disposition by the prosecutor;

(16) the date of disposition by the prosecutor;

(17) the name and identifying number of the court;

(18) each disposition by the court, including information concerning custody of a juvenile by a juvenile justice agency or county juvenile probation department;

(19) the date of disposition by the court;

(20) any commitment or release under supervision by the Texas Youth Commission, including the date of the commitment or release;

(21) information concerning each appellate proceeding; and

(22) electronic copies of all documents filed with the court.

(c) If the Department of Public Safety assigns a state identification number for the juvenile, the identification number shall be entered in the local juvenile information system.

(d) Information obtained for the purpose of diagnosis, examination, evaluation, or treatment or for making a referral for treatment of a child by a public or private agency or institution providing supervision of a child by arrangement of the juvenile court or having custody of the child under order of the juvenile court may not be collected under Subsection (a) or (b).

§ 58.305. Partner Agencies

(a) A local juvenile justice information system shall to the extent possible include the following partner agencies within that county:

(1) the juvenile court and court clerk;

(2) justice of the peace and municipal courts;

(3) the county juvenile probation department;

(4) the prosecuting attorneys who prosecute juvenile cases in juvenile court, municipal court, or justice court;

(5) law enforcement agencies;

(6) each public school district in the county;

(7) governmental service providers approved by the county juvenile board; and

(8) governmental placement facilities approved by the county juvenile board.

(b) A local juvenile justice information system for a multicounty region shall to the extent possible include the partner agencies listed in Subsections (a)(1)–(6) for each county in the region and the following partner agencies from within the multicounty region that have applied for membership in the system and have been approved by the regional juvenile board committee:

(1) governmental service providers; and

(2) governmental placement facilities.

Comment

In order to provide more flexibility to counties wanting to construct local juvenile justice information systems, §§ 58.301, 58.303, and 58.305 contain the discretionary language of "may".

§ 58.306. Access to Information; Levels

(a) This section describes the level of access to information to which each partner agency in a local juvenile justice information system is entitled.

(b) Information is at Access Level 1 if the information relates to a child:

(1) who:

(A) a school official has reasonable grounds to believe has committed an offense for which a report is required under Section 37.015, Education Code; or

(B) has been expelled, the expulsion of which is required to be reported under Section 52.041; and

(2) who has not been charged with a fineable only offense, a status offense, or delinquent conduct.

(c) Information is at Access Level 2 if the information relates to a child who:

(1) is alleged in a justice or municipal court to have committed a fineable only offense, municipal ordinance violation, or status offense; and

(2) has not been charged with delinquent conduct or conduct indicating a need for supervision.

(d) Information is at Access Level 3 if the information relates to a child who is alleged to have engaged in delinquent conduct or conduct indicating a need for supervision.

(e) Level 1 Access is by public school districts in the county or region served by the local juvenile justice information system.

(f) Level 2 Access is by:

(1) justice of the peace courts that process juvenile cases; and

(2) municipal courts that process juvenile cases.

(g) Level 3 Access is by:

(1) the juvenile court and court clerk;

(2) the prosecuting attorney;

(3) the county juvenile probation department;

(4) law enforcement agencies;

(5) governmental service providers that are partner agencies; and

(6) governmental placement facilities that are partner agencies.

(h) Access for Level 1 agencies is only to information at Level 1. Access for Level 2 agencies is only to information at Levels 1 and 2. Access for Level 3 agencies is to information at Levels 1, 2, and 3.

§ 58.307. Confidentiality of Information

(a) Information that is part of a local juvenile justice information system is not public information and may not be released to the public, except as authorized by law.

(b) Information that is part of a local juvenile justice information system is for the professional use of the partner agencies that are members of the system and may be used only by authorized employees of those agencies to discharge duties of those agencies.

(c) Information from a local juvenile justice information system may not be disclosed to persons, agencies, or organizations that are not members of the system except to the extent disclosure is authorized or mandated by this title.

(d) Information in a local juvenile justice information system is subject to destruction, sealing, or restricted access as provided by this title.

(e) Information in a local juvenile justice information system, including electronic signature systems, shall be protected from unauthorized access by a system of access security and any access to information in a local juvenile information system performed by browser software shall be at the level of at least 128–bit encryption. A juvenile board or a regional juvenile board committee shall require all partner agencies to maintain security and restrict access in accordance with the requirements of this title.

SUBCHAPTER D–1. REPORTS ON COUNTY INTERNET WEBSITES

Introductory Comment

This subchapter requires the juvenile judge in counties with a population of 600,000 or more to post reports on the internet describing children committed to TYC.

---

§ 58.351. Applicability

This subchapter applies only to a county with a population of 600,000 or more.

§ 58.352. Information Posted on County Website

(a) A juvenile court judge in a county to which this subchapter applies shall post a report on the Internet website of the county in which the court is located. The report must include:

(1) the total number of children committed by the judge to a correctional facility operated by the Texas Youth Commission; and

(2) for each child committed to a facility described by Subdivision (1):

(A) a general description of the offense committed by the child or the conduct of the child that led to the child's commitment to the facility;

(B) the year the child was committed to the facility; and

(C) the age range, race, and gender of the child.

(b) Not later than the 10th day following the first day of each quarter, a juvenile court judge shall update the information posted on a county Internet website under Subsection (a).

§ 58.353. Confidentiality

A record posted on a county Internet website under this subchapter may not include any information that personally identifies a child.

SUBCHAPTER E. STATEWIDE JUVENILE INFORMATION AND CASE MANAGEMENT SYSTEM

Introductory Comment

This subchapter authorizes TJPC to create and maintain a statewide data system to aid in the processing of juvenile cases, to aid in identifying at-risk children; and to allow sharing of information on juvenile offenders between criminal and juvenile justice agencies.

§ 58.401. Definitions

In this subchapter:

(1) "Commission" means the Texas Juvenile Probation Commission.

(2) "Criminal justice agency" has the meaning assigned by Section 411.082, Government Code.

(3) "Juvenile justice agency" means an agency that has custody or control over juvenile offenders.

(4) "Partner agencies" means those agencies described in Section 58.305 as well as private service providers to the juvenile justice system.

(5) "System" means an automated statewide juvenile information and case management system.

§ 58.402. Purposes of System

The purposes of the system are to:

(1) provide accurate information at the statewide level relating to children who come into contact with the juvenile justice system;

(2) facilitate communication and information sharing between authorized entities in criminal and juvenile justice agencies and partner agencies regarding effective and efficient identification of and service delivery to juvenile offenders; and

(3) provide comprehensive juvenile justice information and case management abilities that will meet the common data collection, reporting, and management needs of juvenile probation departments in this state and provide the flexibility to accommodate individualized requirements.

§ 58.403. Juvenile Information System

(a) Through the adoption of an interlocal contract under Chapter 791, Government Code, with one or more counties, the commission may participate in and assist counties in the creation, operation, and maintenance of a system that is intended for statewide use to:

(1) aid in processing the cases of children under this title;

(2) facilitate the delivery of services to children in the juvenile justice system;

(3) aid in the early identification of at-risk and delinquent children; and

(4) facilitate cross-jurisdictional sharing of information related to juvenile offenders between authorized criminal and juvenile justice agencies and partner agencies.

(b) The commission may use funds appropriated for the implementation of this section to pay costs incurred under an interlocal contract described by Subsection (a), including license fees, maintenance and operations costs, administrative costs, and any other costs specified in the interlocal contract.

(c) The commission may provide training services to counties on the use and operation of a system created, operated, or maintained by one or more counties under Subsection (a).

(d) Subchapter L, Chapter 2054, Government Code, does not apply to the statewide juvenile information and case management system created under this subchapter.

Amended by Acts 2011, 82nd Leg., ch. 85 (S.B. 653), § 2.002, eff. Sept. 1, 2011.

Comment

In 2009 this section was amended to authorize expansion of the juvenile justice case management system to track the complete history of juvenile offenders across Texas.

§ 58.404. Information Collected by Commission

The commission may collect and maintain all information related to juvenile offenders and all offenses committed by a juvenile offender, including all information collected and maintained under Subchapters B and D.

§ 58.405. Authority Cumulative

The authority granted by this subchapter is cumulative of all other authority granted by this chapter to a county, the commission, or a juvenile justice agency and nothing in this subchapter limits the authority of a county, the commission, or a juvenile justice agency under this chapter to create an information system or to share information related to a juvenile.

CHAPTER 59. PROGRESSIVE SANCTIONS MODEL

---

§ 59.001. Purposes

The purposes of the progressive sanctions model are to:

(1) ensure that juvenile offenders face uniform and consistent consequences and punishments that correspond to the seriousness of each offender's current offense, prior delinquent history, special treatment or training needs, and effectiveness of prior interventions;

(2) balance public protection and rehabilitation while holding juvenile offenders accountable;

(3) permit flexibility in the decisions made in relation to the juvenile offender to the extent allowed by law;

(4) consider the juvenile offender's circumstances;

(5) recognize that departure of a disposition from this model is not necessarily undesirable and in some cases is highly desirable; and

(6) improve juvenile justice planning and resource allocation by ensuring uniform and consistent reporting of disposition decisions at all levels.

Comment

Chapter 59 was re-evaluated by the legislature in 2003. The legislature came to realize that departures from the progressive sanctions model were more often desirable than undesirable and should not be treated as dispositional failures.

CLE/Other Legal Publication

Tough on crime or soft on justice: an argument for the mandatory application of the Texas Juvenile Justice Code's progressive sanctions guidelines. Clifford MacKenzie, 10 TEX. WESLEYAN L. REV. 501 (2004)

---

§ 59.002. Sanction Level Assignment by Probation Department

(a) The probation department may assign a sanction level of one to a child referred to the probation department under Section 53.012.

(b) The probation department may assign a sanction level of two to a child for whom deferred prosecution is authorized under Section 53.03.

Comment

Of the seven sanction levels, a juvenile probation department may make assignment without court order only to levels one and two.

---

§ 59.003. Sanction Level Assignment Model

(a) Subject to Subsection (e), after a child's first commission of delinquent conduct or conduct indicating a need for supervision, the probation department or prosecuting attorney may, or the juvenile court may, in a disposition hearing under Section 54.04 or a modification hearing under Section 54.05, assign a child one of the following sanction levels according to the child's conduct:

(1) for conduct indicating a need for supervision, other than conduct described in Section 51.03(b)(4) or (5) or a Class A or B misdemeanor, the sanction level is one;

(2) for conduct indicating a need for supervision under Section 51.03(b)(4) or (5) or a Class A or B misdemeanor, other than a misdemeanor involving the use or possession of a firearm, or for delinquent conduct under Section 51.03(a)(2), the sanction level is two;

(3) for a misdemeanor involving the use or possession of a firearm or for a state jail felony or a felony of the third degree, the sanction level is three;

(4) for a felony of the second degree, the sanction level is four;

(5) for a felony of the first degree, other than a felony involving the use of a deadly weapon or causing serious bodily injury, the sanction level is five;

(6) for a felony of the first degree involving the use of a deadly weapon or causing serious bodily injury, for an aggravated controlled substance felony, or for a capital felony, the sanction level is six; or

(7) for a felony of the first degree involving the use of a deadly weapon or causing serious bodily injury, for an aggravated controlled substance felony, or for a capital felony, if the petition has been approved by a grand jury under Section 53.045, or if a petition to transfer the child to criminal court has been filed under Section 54.02, the sanction level is seven.

(b) Subject to Subsection (e), if the child subsequently is found to have engaged in delinquent conduct in an adjudication hearing under Section 54.03 or a hearing to modify a disposition under Section 54.05 on two separate occasions and each involves a violation of a penal law of a classification that is less than the classification of the child's previous conduct, the juvenile court may assign the child a sanction level that is one level higher than the previously assigned sanction level, unless the child's previously assigned sanction level is six.

(c) Subject to Subsection (e), if the child's subsequent commission of delinquent conduct or conduct indicating a need for supervision involves a violation of a penal law of a classification that is the same as or greater than the classification of the child's previous conduct, the juvenile court may assign the child a sanction level authorized by law that is one level higher than the previously assigned sanction level.

(d) Subject to Subsection (e), if the child's previously assigned sanction level is four or five and the child's subsequent commission of delinquent conduct is of the grade of felony, the juvenile court may assign the child a sanction level that is one level higher than the previously assigned sanction level.

(e) The probation department may, in accordance with Section 54.05, request the extension of a period of probation specified under sanction levels one through five if the circumstances of the child warrant the extension.

(f) Before the court assigns the child a sanction level that involves the revocation of the child's probation and the commitment of the child to the Texas Youth Commission, the court shall hold a hearing to modify the disposition as required by Section 54.05.

Comment

Each offense is assigned to one of the seven sanction levels. That sanction level is the presumptive disposition for that offense. However, it is not mandatory that the sanction level disposition match the assignment guidelines. It is required that departures must be documented.

The disposition of juvenile cases must conform to the dispositional authorizations in the Family Code. Because the entire progressive sanctions program is discretionary with respect to each case, if there is a conflict between the progressive sanctions guidelines and the dispositional authorization elsewhere in the Family Code, the dispositional authorization must control.

Subsection (a) elevates inhalant abuse to a sanction level two to reflect the seriousness of the offense.

---

§ 59.004. Sanction Level One

(a) For a child at sanction level one, the juvenile court or probation department may:

(1) require counseling for the child regarding the child's conduct;

(2) inform the child of the progressive sanctions that may be imposed on the child if the child continues to engage in delinquent conduct or conduct indicating a need for supervision;

(3) inform the child's parents or guardians of the parents' or guardians' responsibility to impose reasonable restrictions on the child to prevent the conduct from recurring;

(4) provide information or other assistance to the child or the child's parents or guardians in securing needed social services;

(5) require the child or the child's parents or guardians to participate in a program for services under Section 264.302, if a program under Section 264.302 is available to the child or the child's parents or guardians;

(6) refer the child to a community-based citizen intervention program approved by the juvenile court; ~~and~~

(7) release the child to the child's parents or guardians**; and**

(8) require the child to attend and successfully complete an educational program described by Section 37.218, Education Code, or another equivalent educational program.

(b) The probation department shall discharge the child from the custody of the probation department after the provisions of this section are met.

Amended by Acts 2011, 82nd Leg., ch. 1322 (S.B. 407), § 20, eff. Sept. 1, 2011.

Comment

Sanction level one is customarily called supervisory caution.

The reference to § 264.302 (in Title 5 of the Family Code) is a reference to the Early Youth Intervention Services program operated by the Texas Department of Regulatory and Protective Services for youth as young as seven years of age.

---

§ 59.005. Sanction Level Two

(a) For a child at sanction level two, the juvenile court, the prosecuting attorney, or the probation department may, as provided by Section 53.03:

(1) place the child on deferred prosecution for not less than three months or more than six months;

(2) require the child to make restitution to the victim of the child's conduct or perform community service restitution appropriate to the nature and degree of harm caused and according to the child's ability;

(3) require the child's parents or guardians to identify restrictions the parents or guardians will impose on the child's activities and requirements the parents or guardians will set for the child's behavior;

(4) provide the information required under Sections 59.004(a)(2) and (4);

(5) require the child or the child's parents or guardians to participate in a program for services under Section 264.302, if a program under Section 264.302 is available to the child or the child's parents or guardians;

(6) refer the child to a community-based citizen intervention program approved by the juvenile court; and

(7) if appropriate, impose additional conditions of probation.

(b) The juvenile court or the probation department shall discharge the child from the custody of the probation department on the date the provisions of this section are met or on the child's 18th birthday, whichever is earlier.

Comment

Sanction level two describes what is called Deferred Prosecution. It is a period of pre-adjudication probation that may extend for up to six months in length.

---

§ 59.006. Sanction Level Three

(a) For a child at sanction level three, the juvenile court may:

(1) place the child on probation for not less than six months;

(2) require the child to make restitution to the victim of the child's conduct or perform community service restitution appropriate to the nature and degree of harm caused and according to the child's ability;

(3) impose specific restrictions on the child's activities and requirements for the child's behavior as conditions of probation;

(4) require a probation officer to closely monitor the child's activities and behavior;

(5) require the child or the child's parents or guardians to participate in programs or services designated by the court or probation officer; and

(6) if appropriate, impose additional conditions of probation.

(b) The juvenile court shall discharge the child from the custody of the probation department on the date the provisions of this section are met or on the child's 18th birthday, whichever is earlier.

Comment

This sanction level describes judicial probation.

---

§ 59.007. Sanction Level Four

(a) For a child at sanction level four, the juvenile court may:

(1) require the child to participate as a condition of probation for not less than three months or more than 12 months in an intensive services probation program that emphasizes frequent contact and reporting with a probation officer, discipline, intensive supervision services, social responsibility, and productive work;

(2) after release from the program described by Subdivision (1), continue the child on probation supervision;

(3) require the child to make restitution to the victim of the child's conduct or perform community service restitution appropriate to the nature and degree of harm caused and according to the child's ability;

(4) impose highly structured restrictions on the child's activities and requirements for behavior of the child as conditions of probation;

(5) require a probation officer to closely monitor the child;

(6) require the child or the child's parents or guardians to participate in programs or services designed to address their particular needs and circumstances; and

(7) if appropriate, impose additional sanctions.

(b) The juvenile court shall discharge the child from the custody of the probation department on the date the provisions of this section are met or on the child's 18th birthday, whichever is earlier.

Comment

Sanction level four can be viewed as intensive probation supervision for a period of at least 3 months, to be followed by normal supervision. The program need not follow the boot camp model.

§ 59.008. Sanction Level Five

(a) For a child at sanction level five, the juvenile court may:

(1) as a condition of probation, place the child for not less than six months or more than 12 months in a post-adjudication secure correctional facility;

(2) after release from the program described by Subdivision (1), continue the child on probation supervision;

(3) require the child to make restitution to the victim of the child's conduct or perform community service restitution appropriate to the nature and degree of harm caused and according to the child's ability;

(4) impose highly structured restrictions on the child's activities and requirements for behavior of the child as conditions of probation;

(5) require a probation officer to closely monitor the child;

(6) require the child or the child's parents or guardians to participate in programs or services designed to address their particular needs and circumstances; and

(7) if appropriate, impose additional sanctions.

(b) The juvenile court shall discharge the child from the custody of the probation department on the date the provisions of this section are met or on the child's 18th birthday, whichever is earlier.

Comment

Sanction level five is probation with secure residential placement outside the home.

§ 59.009. Sanction Level Six

(a) For a child at sanction level six, the juvenile court may commit the child to the custody of the Texas Youth Commission. The commission may:

(1) require the child to participate in a highly structured residential program that emphasizes discipline, accountability, fitness, training, and productive work for not less than nine months or more than 24 months unless the commission extends the period and the reason for an extension is documented;

(2) require the child to make restitution to the victim of the child's conduct or perform community service restitution appropriate to the nature and degree of the harm caused and according to the child's ability, if there is a victim of the child's conduct;

(3) require the child and the child's parents or guardians to participate in programs and services for their particular needs and circumstances; and

(4) if appropriate, impose additional sanctions.

(b) On release of the child under supervision, the Texas Youth Commission parole programs may:

(1) impose highly structured restrictions on the child's activities and requirements for behavior of the child as conditions of release under supervision;

(2) require a parole officer to closely monitor the child for not less than six months; and

(3) if appropriate, impose any other conditions of supervision.

(c) The Texas Youth Commission may discharge the child from the commission's custody on the date the provisions of this section are met or on the child's 19th birthday, whichever is earlier.

Comment

Sanction level six is indeterminate commitment to the TYC, authorizing that agency to maintain custody of the youth until age 21.

§ 59.010. Sanction Level Seven

(a) For a child at sanction level seven, the juvenile court may certify and transfer the child under Section 54.02 or sentence the child to commitment to the Texas Youth Commission under Section 54.04(d)(3), 54.04(m), or 54.05(f). The commission may:

(1) require the child to participate in a highly structured residential program that emphasizes discipline, accountability, fitness, training, and productive work for not less than 12 months or more than 10 years unless the commission extends the period and the reason for the extension is documented;

(2) require the child to make restitution to the victim of the child's conduct or perform community service restitution appropriate to the nature and degree of harm caused and according to the child's ability, if there is a victim of the child's conduct;

(3) require the child and the child's parents or guardians to participate in programs and services for their particular needs and circumstances; and

(4) impose any other appropriate sanction.

(b) On release of the child under supervision, the Texas Youth Commission parole programs may:

(1) impose highly structured restrictions on the child's activities and requirements for behavior of the child as conditions of release under supervision;

(2) require a parole officer to monitor the child closely for not less than 12 months; and

(3) impose any other appropriate condition of supervision.

Comment

Sanction level seven is determinate sentencing and certification to criminal court. Obviously, how long the TYC keeps the juvenile depends on the sentence given by the judge or jury, not the guidelines in this sanction level description.

§ 59.011. Duty of Juvenile Board

A juvenile board shall require the juvenile probation department to report progressive sanction data electronically to the Texas Juvenile Probation Commission in the format and time frames specified by the commission.

§ 59.012. Reports by Criminal Justice Policy Council

(a) The Criminal Justice Policy Council shall analyze trends related to juvenile referrals and the impact of reforms on recidivism rates using standard scientific sampling or appropriate scientific methodologies to represent statewide patterns. The council shall compile other policy studies as determined by the executive director of the council or as requested by the governor, lieutenant governor, or speaker of the house of representatives to assist in policy development.

(b) The Criminal Justice Policy Council shall report its findings and related recommendations to improve juvenile justice policies to the governor and the members of the legislature on or before January 15 of each odd-numbered year.

(c) The Criminal Justice Policy Council may incorporate its findings and recommendations under this section into its report required under Section 413.013, Government Code.

Comment

One of the purposes of creating sanction level guidelines was to gather data on the dispositions employed by the juvenile justice system using a uniform terminology. Nevertheless, it is a mistake to focus on departures from guidelines at the expense of other features of juvenile justice decision-making. This section directs the Criminal Justice Policy Council to study all juvenile justice reforms, not just departures from guidelines, in its evaluative reports on juvenile justice.

§ 59.013. Liability

The Texas Youth Commission, a juvenile board, a court, a person appointed by a court, an attorney for the state, a peace officer, or a law enforcement agency is not liable for a failure or inability to provide a service listed under Sections 59.004–59.010.

§ 59.014. Appeal

A child may not bring an appeal or a postconviction writ of habeas corpus based on:

(1) the failure or inability of any person to provide a service listed under Sections 59.004–59.010;

(2) the failure of a court or of any person to make a sanction level assignment as provided in Section 59.002 or 59.003;

(3) a departure from the sanction level assignment model provided by this chapter; or

(4) the failure of a juvenile court or probation department to report a departure from the model.

Comment

Failure to report a departure from the guidelines is not grounds for appeal. Subsection (3) in the second provision makes it abundantly clear that a deviation from the guidelines is not grounds for appeal.

Leading Case

In re A.G., 292 S.W.3d 755 (Tex. App.–Eastland 2009, no pet.) (child may not bring an appeal for a departure from the guidelines)

§ 59.015. Waiver of Sanctions on Parents or Guardians

On a finding by the juvenile court or probation department that a child's parents or guardians have made a reasonable good faith effort to prevent the child from engaging in delinquent conduct or engaging in conduct indicating a need for supervision and that, despite the parents' or guardians' efforts, the child continues to engage in such conduct, the court or probation department shall waive any sanction that may be imposed on the parents or guardians at any sanction level.

CHAPTER 60. UNIFORM INTERSTATE COMPACT ON JUVENILES

Introductory Comment

This chapter consists of the Uniform Interstate Compact on Juveniles and supplementary enactments. The Interstate Compact deals with many of the same issues as the Uniform Criminal Extradition Act in article 51.13 of the Code of Criminal Procedure

In 1965, the legislature enacted what is now Chapter 60, which required the Texas Governor to enter into the Interstate Compact with other American states. All fifty states and the District of Columbia have now joined the Compact.

The 2005 amendment expands the findings and purposes of the compact. Section 60.010 was added to enact the Interstate Compact and to create the Interstate Commission for Juveniles. The Commission shall be a joint agency of all the compacting states. The Commission shall meet at least once a year and promulgate rules to effectuate the compact. The rules will be binding on the compacting states.

---

§ 60.001. Definitions

In this chapter:

(1) "Commission" means the Interstate Commission for Juveniles.

(2) "Compact" means the Interstate Compact for Juveniles.

(3) "Compact administrator" has the meaning assigned by Article II of the compact.

§§ 60.002 to 60.004. Repealed by Acts 2005, 79th Leg., ch. 1007, § 3.02, eff. Aug. 26, 2008

§ 60.005. Juvenile Compact Administrator

Under the compact, the governor may designate an officer as the compact administrator. The administrator, acting jointly with like officers of other party states, shall adopt regulations to carry out more effectively the terms of the compact. The compact administrator serves at the pleasure of the governor. The compact administrator shall cooperate with all departments, agencies, and officers of and in the government of this state and its subdivisions in facilitating the proper administration of the compact or of a supplementary agreement entered into by this state.

§ 60.006. Supplementary Agreements

A compact administrator may make supplementary agreements with appropriate officials of other states pursuant to the compact. If a supplementary agreement requires or contemplates the use of an institution or facility of this state or requires or contemplates the provision of a service of this state, the supplementary agreement has no force or effect until approved by the head of the department or agency under whose jurisdiction the institution is operated, or whose department or agency is charged with performing the service.

§ 60.007. Financial Arrangements

The compact administrator may make or arrange for the payments necessary to discharge the financial obligations imposed upon this state by the compact or by a supplementary agreement made under the compact, subject to legislative appropriations.

§ 60.008. Enforcement

The courts, departments, agencies, and officers of this state and its subdivisions shall enforce this compact and shall do all things appropriate to effectuate its purposes and intent which are within their respective jurisdictions.

§ 60.009. Additional Procedures Not Precluded

In addition to any procedures developed under the compact for the return of a runaway juvenile, the particular states, the juvenile, or his parents, the courts, or other legal custodian involved may agree upon and adopt any plan or procedure legally authorized under the laws of this state and the other respective party states for the return of the runaway juvenile.

Leading Case

In re: The State of Texas, Relator, 97 S.W.3d 746 (Tex. App.—El Paso 2003, no pet.) (Texas judge under duty to honor Arizona request for return of a runaway)

---

§ 60.010. Interstate Compact for Juveniles

ARTICLE I

PURPOSE

The compacting states to this Interstate Compact recognize that each state is responsible for the proper supervision or return of juveniles, delinquents, and status offenders who are on probation or parole and who have absconded, escaped, or run away from supervision and control and in so doing have endangered their own safety and the safety of others. The compacting states also recognize that each state is responsible for the safe return of juveniles who have run away from home and in doing so have left their state of residence. The compacting states also recognize that congress, by enacting the Crime Control Act, 4 U.S.C. Section 112 (1965), has authorized and encouraged compacts for cooperative efforts and mutual assistance in the prevention of crime.

It is the purpose of this compact, through means of joint and cooperative action among the compacting states to: (A) ensure that the juveniles who are moved under this compact to another state for probation or parole supervision and services are governed in the receiving state by the same standards that apply to juveniles receiving such supervision and services in the receiving state; (B) ensure that the public safety interests of the citizens, including the victims of juvenile offenders, in both the sending and receiving states are adequately protected and balanced with the juvenile's and the juvenile's family's best interests and welfare when an interstate movement is under consideration; (C) return juveniles who have run away, absconded, or escaped from supervision or control or have been accused of an offense to the state requesting their return through a fair and prompt judicial review process that ensures that the requisition is in order and that the transport is properly supervised; (D) make provisions for contracts between member states for the cooperative institutionalization in public facilities in member states for delinquent youth needing special services; (E) provide for the effective tracking of juveniles who move interstate under the compact's provisions; (F) equitably allocate the costs, benefits, and obligations of the compacting states; (G) establish procedures to manage the movement between states of juvenile offenders released to the community under the jurisdiction of courts, juvenile departments, or any other criminal or juvenile justice agency which has jurisdiction over juvenile offenders, ensuring that a receiving state accepts supervision of a juvenile when the juvenile's parent or other person having legal custody resides or is undertaking residence there; (H) ensure immediate notice to jurisdictions where defined offenders are authorized to travel or to relocate across state lines; (I) establish a system of uniform data collection on information pertaining to juveniles who move interstate under this compact that prevents public disclosure of identity and individual treatment information but allows access by authorized juvenile justice and criminal justice officials and regular reporting of compact activities to heads of state executive, judicial, and legislative branches and juvenile and criminal justice administrators; (J) monitor compliance with rules governing interstate movement of juveniles and initiate interventions to address and correct noncompliance; (K) coordinate training and education regarding the regulation of interstate movement of juveniles for officials involved in such activity; and (L) coordinate the implementation and operation of the compact with the Interstate Compact for the Placement of Children, the Interstate Compact for Adult Offender Supervision and other compacts affecting juveniles particularly in those cases where concurrent or overlapping supervision issues arise. It is the policy of the compacting states that the activities conducted by the Interstate Commission created herein are the formation of public policies and therefore are public business. Furthermore, the compacting states shall cooperate and observe their individual and collective duties and responsibilities for the prompt return and acceptance of juveniles subject to the provisions of this compact. The provisions of this compact shall be reasonably and liberally construed to accomplish the purposes and policies of the compact.

ARTICLE II
DEFINITIONS

As used in this compact, unless the context clearly requires a different construction:

A. "Bylaws" means those bylaws established by the Interstate Commission for its governance or for directing or controlling the Interstate Commission's actions or conduct.

B. "Compact administrator" means the individual in each compacting state appointed pursuant to the terms of this compact responsible for the administration and management of the state's supervision and transfer of juveniles subject to the terms of this compact and to the rules adopted by the Interstate Commission under this compact.

C. "Compacting state" means any state which has enacted the enabling legislation for this compact.

D. "Commissioner" means the voting representative of each compacting state appointed pursuant to Article III of this compact.

E. "Court" means any court having jurisdiction over delinquent, neglected, or dependent children.

F. "Deputy compact administrator" means the individual, if any, in each compacting state appointed to act on behalf of a compact administrator pursuant to the terms of this compact, responsible for the administration and management of the state's supervision and transfer of juveniles subject to the terms of this compact and to the rules adopted by the Interstate Commission under this compact.

G. "Interstate Commission" means the Interstate Commission for Juveniles created by Article III of this compact.

H. "Juvenile" means any person defined as a juvenile in any member state or by the rules of the Interstate Commission, including:

(1) Accused Delinquent—a person charged with an offense that, if committed by an adult, would be a criminal offense;

(2) Adjudicated Delinquent—a person found to have committed an offense that, if committed by an adult, would be a criminal offense;

(3) Accused Status Offender—a person charged with an offense that would not be a criminal offense if committed by an adult;

(4) Adjudicated Status Offender—a person found to have committed an offense that would not be a criminal offense if committed by an adult; and

(5) Nonoffender—a person in need of supervision who has not been accused or adjudicated a status offender or delinquent.

I. "Noncompacting state" means any state which has not enacted the enabling legislation for this compact.

J. "Probation or parole" means any kind of supervision or conditional release of juveniles authorized under the laws of the compacting states.

K. "Rule" means a written statement by the Interstate Commission promulgated pursuant to Article VI of this compact that is of general applicability, implements, interprets, or prescribes a policy or provision of the compact, or an organizational, procedural, or practice requirement of the Interstate Commission, and has the force and effect of statutory law in a compacting state, and includes the amendment, repeal, or suspension of an existing rule.

L. "State" means a state of the United States, the District of Columbia (or its designee), the Commonwealth of Puerto Rico, the U.S. Virgin Islands, Guam, American Samoa, and the Northern Marianas Islands.

ARTICLE III

INTERSTATE COMMISSION FOR JUVENILES

A. The compacting states hereby create the Interstate Commission for Juveniles. The Interstate Commission shall be a body corporate and joint agency of the compacting states. The commission shall have all the responsibilities, powers, and duties set forth herein, and such additional powers as may be conferred upon it by subsequent action of the respective legislatures of the compacting states in accordance with the terms of this compact.

B. The Interstate Commission shall consist of commissioners appointed by the appropriate appointing authority in each state pursuant to the rules and requirements of each compacting state. The commissioner shall be the compact administrator, deputy compact administrator, or designee from that state who shall serve on the Interstate Commission in such capacity under or pursuant to the applicable law of the compacting state.

C. In addition to the commissioners who are the voting representatives of each state, the Interstate Commission shall include individuals who are not commissioners, but who are members of interested organizations. Such noncommissioner members must include a member of the national organizations of governors, legislators, state chief justices, attorneys general, Interstate Compact for Adult Offender Supervision, Interstate Compact for the Placement of Children, juvenile justice and juvenile corrections officials, and crime victims. All noncommissioner members of the Interstate Commission shall be ex officio (nonvoting) members. The Interstate Commission may provide in its bylaws for such additional ex officio (nonvoting) members, including members of other national organizations, in such numbers as shall be determined by the commission.

D. Each compacting state represented at any meeting of the Interstate Commission is entitled to one vote. A majority of the compacting states shall constitute a quorum for the transaction of business, unless a larger quorum is required by the bylaws of the Interstate Commission.

E. The Interstate Commission shall meet at least once each calendar year. The chairperson may call additional meetings and, upon the request of a simple majority of the compacting states, shall call additional meetings. Public notice shall be given of all meetings and meetings shall be open to the public.

F. The Interstate Commission shall establish an executive committee, which shall include commission officers, members, and others as determined by the bylaws. The executive committee shall have the power to act on behalf of the Interstate Commission during periods when the Interstate Commission is not in session, with the exception of rulemaking or amendment to the compact. The executive committee shall oversee the day-to-day activities of the administration of the compact managed by an executive director and Interstate Commission staff; administers enforcement and compliance with the provisions of the compact, its bylaws and rules, and performs such other duties as directed by the Interstate Commission or set forth in the bylaws.

G. Each member of the Interstate Commission shall have the right and power to cast a vote to which that compacting state is entitled and to participate in the business and affairs of the Interstate Commission. A member shall vote in person and shall not delegate a vote to another compacting state. However, a commissioner shall appoint another authorized representative, in the absence of the commissioner from that state, to cast a vote on behalf of the compacting state at a specified meeting. The bylaws may provide for members' participation in meetings by telephone or other means of telecommunication or electronic communication.

H. The Interstate Commission's bylaws shall establish conditions and procedures under which the Interstate Commission shall make its information and official records available to the public for inspection or copying. The Interstate Commission may exempt from disclosure any information or official records to the extent they would adversely affect personal privacy rights or proprietary interests.

I. Public notice shall be given of all meetings and all meetings shall be open to the public, except as set forth in the rules or as otherwise provided in the compact. The Interstate Commission and any of its committees may close a meeting to the public when it determines by two-thirds vote that an open meeting would be likely to:

1. Relate solely to the Interstate Commission's internal personnel practices and procedures;

2. Disclose matters specifically exempted from disclosure by statute;

3. Disclose trade secrets or commercial or financial information which is privileged or confidential;

4. Involve accusing any person of a crime or formally censuring any person;

5. Disclose information of a personal nature where disclosure would constitute a clearly unwarranted invasion of personal privacy;

6. Disclose investigative records compiled for law enforcement purposes;

7. Disclose information contained in or related to examination, operating or condition reports prepared by, or on behalf of or for the use of, the Interstate Commission with respect to a regulated person or entity for the purpose of regulation or supervision of such person or entity;

8. Disclose information, the premature disclosure of which would significantly endanger the stability of a regulated person or entity; or

9. Specifically relate to the Interstate Commission's issuance of a subpoena, or its participation in a civil action or other legal proceeding.

J. For every meeting closed pursuant to this provision, the Interstate Commission's legal counsel shall publicly certify that, in the legal counsel's opinion, the meeting may be closed to the public, and shall reference each relevant exemptive provision. The Interstate Commission shall keep minutes which shall fully and clearly describe all matters discussed in any meeting and shall provide a full and accurate summary of any actions taken, and the reasons therefore, including a description of each of the views expressed on any item and the record of any roll call vote (reflected in the vote of each member on the question). All documents considered in connection with any action shall be identified in such minutes.

K. The Interstate Commission shall collect standardized data concerning the interstate movement of juveniles as directed through its rules which shall specify the data to be collected, the means of collection and data exchange, and reporting requirements. Such methods of data collection, exchange, and reporting shall insofar as is reasonably possible conform to up-to-date technology and coordinate the Interstate Commission's information functions with the appropriate repository of records.

The commission shall have the following powers and duties:

ARTICLE IV

POWERS AND DUTIES OF THE INTERSTATE COMMISSION

1. To provide for dispute resolution among compacting states.

2. To promulgate rules to effect the purposes and obligations as enumerated in this compact, which shall have the force and effect of statutory law and shall be binding in the compacting states to the extent and in the manner provided in this compact.

3. To oversee, supervise, and coordinate the interstate movement of juveniles subject to the terms of this compact and any bylaws adopted and rules promulgated by the Interstate Commission.

4. To enforce compliance with the compact provisions, the rules promulgated by the Interstate Commission, and the bylaws, using all necessary and proper means, including but not limited to the use of judicial process.

5. To establish and maintain offices which shall be located within one or more of the compacting states.

6. To purchase and maintain insurance and bonds.

7. To borrow, accept, hire, or contract for services of personnel.

8. To establish and appoint committees and hire staff which it deems necessary for the carrying out of its functions including, but not limited to, an executive committee as required by Article III of this compact, which shall have the power to act on behalf of the Interstate Commission in carrying out its powers and duties hereunder.

9. To elect or appoint officers, attorneys, employees, agents, or consultants, and to fix their compensation, define their duties, and determine their qualifications, and to establish the Interstate Commission's personnel policies and programs relating to, inter alia, conflicts of interest, rates of compensation, and qualifications of personnel.

10. To accept any and all donations and grants of money, equipment, supplies, materials, and services, and to receive, utilize, and dispose of same.

11. To lease, purchase, accept contributions or donations of, or otherwise to own, hold, improve, or use any property, whether real, personal, or mixed.

12. To sell, convey, mortgage, pledge, lease, exchange, abandon, or otherwise dispose of any property, whether real, personal, or mixed.

13. To establish a budget and make expenditures and levy dues as provided in Article VIII of this compact.

14. To sue and be sued.

15. To adopt a seal and bylaws governing the management and operation of the Interstate Commission.

16. To perform such functions as may be necessary or appropriate to achieve the purposes of this compact.

17. To report annually to the legislatures, governors, and judiciary of the compacting states concerning the activities of the Interstate Commission during the preceding year. Such reports shall also include any recommendations that may have been adopted by the Interstate Commission.

18. To coordinate education, training, and public awareness regarding the interstate movement of juveniles for officials involved in such activity.

19. To establish uniform standards of the reporting, collecting, and exchanging of data.

20. The Interstate Commission shall maintain its corporate books and records in accordance with the bylaws.

ARTICLE V

ORGANIZATION AND OPERATION OF THE INTERSTATE COMMISSION

Sec. A. Bylaws

1. The Interstate Commission shall, by a majority of the members present and voting, within 12 months of the first Interstate Commission meeting, adopt bylaws to govern its conduct as may be necessary or appropriate to carry out the purposes of the compact, including, but not limited to:

a. Establishing the fiscal year of the Interstate Commission;

b. Establishing an executive committee and such other committees as may be necessary;

c. Providing for the establishment of committees governing any general or specific delegation of any authority or function of the Interstate Commission;

d. Providing reasonable procedures for calling and conducting meetings of the Interstate Commission and ensuring reasonable notice of each such meeting;

e. Establishing the titles and responsibilities of the officers of the Interstate Commission;

f. Providing a mechanism for concluding the operations of the Interstate Commission and the return of any surplus funds that may exist upon the termination of the compact after the payment or reserving of all of its debts and obligations;

g. Providing start-up rules for initial administration of the compact; and

h. Establishing standards and procedures for compliance and technical assistance in carrying out the compact.

Sec. B. Officers and Staff

1. The Interstate Commission shall, by a majority of the members, elect annually from among its members a chairperson and a vice chairperson, each of whom shall have such authority and duties as may be specified in the bylaws. The chairperson or, in the chairperson's absence or disability, the vice chairperson shall preside at all meetings of the Interstate Commission. The officers so elected shall serve without compensation or remuneration from the Interstate Commission, provided that, subject to the availability of budgeted funds, the officers shall be reimbursed for any ordinary and necessary costs and expenses incurred by them in the performance of their duties and responsibilities as officers of the Interstate Commission.

2. The Interstate Commission shall, through its executive committee, appoint or retain an executive director for such period, upon such terms and conditions, and for such compensation as the Interstate Commission may deem appropriate. The executive director shall serve as secretary to the Interstate Commission, but shall not be a member and shall hire and supervise such other staff as may be authorized by the Interstate Commission.

Sec. C. Qualified Immunity, Defense, and Indemnification

1. The Interstate Commission's executive director and employees shall be immune from suit and liability, either personally or in their official capacity, for any claim for damage to or loss of property or personal injury or other civil liability caused or arising out of or relating to any actual or alleged act, error, or omission that occurred, or that such person had a reasonable basis for believing occurred, within the scope of Interstate Commission employment, duties, or responsibilities, provided that any such person shall not be protected from suit or liability for any damage, loss, injury, or liability caused by the intentional or wilful and wanton misconduct of any such person.

2. The liability of any commissioner, or the employee or agent of a commissioner, acting within the scope of such person's employment or duties for acts, errors, or omissions occurring within such person's state may not exceed the limits of liability set forth under the constitution and laws of that state for state officials, employees, and agents. Nothing in this subsection shall be construed to protect any such person from suit or liability for any damage, loss, injury, or liability caused by the intentional or wilful and wanton misconduct of any such person.

3. The Interstate Commission shall defend the executive director or the employees or representatives of the Interstate Commission and, subject to the approval of the attorney general of the state represented by any commissioner of a compacting state, shall defend such commissioner or the commissioner's representatives or employees in any civil action seeking to impose liability arising out of any actual or alleged act, error, or omission that occurred within the scope of Interstate Commission employment, duties, or responsibilities, or that the defendant had a reasonable basis for believing occurred within the scope of Interstate Commission employment, duties, or responsibilities, provided that the actual or alleged act, error, or omission did not result from intentional or wilful and wanton misconduct on the part of such person.

4. The Interstate Commission shall indemnify and hold the commissioner of a compacting state, or the commissioner's representatives or employees, or the Interstate Commission's representatives or employees, harmless in the amount of any settlement or judgment obtained against such persons arising out of any actual or alleged act, error, or omission that occurred within the scope of Interstate Commission employment, duties, or responsibilities, or that such persons had a reasonable basis for believing occurred within the scope of Interstate Commission employment, duties, or responsibilities, provided that the actual or alleged act, error, or omission did not result from intentional or wilful and wanton misconduct on the part of such persons.

ARTICLE VI
RULEMAKING FUNCTIONS OF THE INTERSTATE COMMISSION

A. The Interstate Commission shall promulgate and publish rules in order to effectively and efficiently achieve the purposes of the compact.

B. Rulemaking shall occur pursuant to the criteria set forth in this article and the bylaws and rules adopted pursuant thereto. Such rulemaking shall substantially conform to the principles of the "Model State Administrative Procedures Act," 1981 Act, Uniform Laws Annotated, Vol. 15, p.1 (2000), or such other administrative procedures act, as the Interstate Commission deems appropriate consistent with due process requirements under the United States Constitution as now or hereafter interpreted by the United States Supreme Court. All rules and amendments shall become binding as of the date specified, as published with the final version of the rule as approved by the Interstate Commission.

C. When promulgating a rule, the Interstate Commission shall, at a minimum:

1. Publish the proposed rule's entire text stating the reason or reasons for that proposed rule;

2. Allow and invite persons to submit written data, facts, opinions, and arguments, which information shall be added to the record and be made publicly available;

3. Provide an opportunity for an informal hearing, if petitioned by 10 or more persons; and

4. Promulgate a final rule and its effective date, if appropriate, based on input from state or local officials, or interested parties.

D. Allow, not later than 60 days after a rule is promulgated, any interested person to file a petition in the United States District Court for the District of Columbia or in the federal district court where the Interstate Commission's principal office is located for judicial review of the rule. If the court finds that the Interstate Commission's action is not supported by substantial evidence in the rulemaking record, the court shall hold the rule unlawful and set it aside. For purposes of this subsection, evidence is substantial if it would be considered substantial evidence under the Model State Administrative Procedures Act.

E. If a majority of the legislatures of the compacting states rejects a rule, those states may, by enactment of a statute or resolution in the same manner used to adopt the compact, cause that such rule shall have no further force and effect in any compacting state.

F. The existing rules governing the operation of the Interstate Compact on Juveniles superceded by this Act shall be null and void 12 months after the first meeting of the Interstate Commission created under this compact.

G. Upon determination by the Interstate Commission that an emergency exists, the Interstate Commission may promulgate an emergency rule which shall become effective immediately upon adoption, provided that the usual rulemaking procedures provided hereunder shall be retroactively applied to said rule as soon as reasonably possible, but no later than 90 days after the effective date of the emergency rule.

ARTICLE VII
OVERSIGHT, ENFORCEMENT, AND DISPUTE RESOLUTION BY THE INTERSTATE COMMISSION

Sec. A. Oversight

1. The Interstate Commission shall oversee the administration and operations of the interstate movement of juveniles subject to this compact in the compacting states and shall monitor such activities being administered in noncompacting states which may significantly affect compacting states.

2. The courts and executive agencies in each compacting state shall enforce this compact and shall take all actions necessary and appropriate to effectuate the compact's purposes and intent. The provisions of this compact and the rules promulgated hereunder shall be received by all the judges, public officers, commissions, and departments of the state government as evidence of the authorized statute and administrative rules. All courts shall take judicial notice of the compact and the rules. In any judicial or administrative proceeding in a compacting state pertaining to the subject matter of this compact which may affect the powers, responsibilities, or actions of the Interstate Commission, the Interstate Commission shall be entitled to receive all service of process in any such proceeding, and shall have standing to intervene in the proceeding for all purposes.

Sec. B. Dispute Resolution

1. The compacting states shall report to the Interstate Commission on all issues and activities necessary for the administration of the compact as well as issues and activities pertaining to compliance with the provisions of the compact and its bylaws and rules.

2. The Interstate Commission shall attempt, upon the request of a compacting state, to resolve any disputes or other issues which are subject to the compact and which may arise among compacting states and between compacting and noncompacting states. The Interstate Commission shall promulgate a rule providing for both mediation and binding dispute resolution for disputes among the compacting states.

3. The Interstate Commission, in the reasonable exercise of its discretion, shall enforce the provisions and rules of this compact using any or all means set forth in Article X of this compact.

ARTICLE VIII

FINANCE

A. The Interstate Commission shall pay or provide for the payment of the reasonable expenses of its establishment, organization, and ongoing activities.

B. The Interstate Commission shall levy on and collect an annual assessment from each compacting state to cover the cost of the internal operations and activities of the Interstate Commission and its staff which must be in a total amount sufficient to cover the Interstate Commission's annual budget as approved each year. The aggregate annual assessment amount shall be allocated based upon a formula to be determined by the Interstate Commission, taking into consideration the population of each compacting state and the volume of interstate movement of juveniles in each compacting state. The Interstate Commission shall promulgate a rule binding upon all compacting states that governs said assessment.

C. The Interstate Commission shall not incur any obligations of any kind prior to securing the funds adequate to meet the same, nor shall the Interstate Commission pledge the credit of any of the compacting states, except by and with the authority of the compacting state.

D. The Interstate Commission shall keep accurate accounts of all receipts and disbursements. The receipts and disbursements of the Interstate Commission shall be subject to the audit and accounting procedures established under its bylaws. However, all receipts and disbursements of funds handled by the Interstate Commission shall be audited yearly by a certified or licensed public accountant and the report of the audit shall be included in and become part of the annual report of the Interstate Commission.

ARTICLE IX

COMPACTING STATES, EFFECTIVE DATE, AND AMENDMENT

A. Any state, as defined in Article II of this compact, is eligible to become a compacting state.

B. The compact shall become effective and binding upon legislative enactment of the compact into law by no less than 35 of the states. The initial effective date shall be the later of July 1, 2004, or upon enactment into law by the 35th jurisdiction. Thereafter, the compact shall become effective and binding, as to any other compacting state, upon enactment of the compact into law by that state. The governors of noncompacting states or their designees shall be invited to participate in Interstate Commission activities on a nonvoting basis prior to adoption of the compact by all states.

C. The Interstate Commission may propose amendments to the compact for enactment by the compacting states. No amendment shall become effective and binding upon the Interstate Commission and the compacting states unless and until it is enacted into law by unanimous consent of the compacting states.

ARTICLE X

WITHDRAWAL, DEFAULT, TERMINATION, AND JUDICIAL ENFORCEMENT

Sec. A. Withdrawal

1. Once effective, the compact shall continue in force and remain binding upon each and every compacting state, provided that a compacting state may withdraw from the compact by specifically repealing the statute which enacted the compact into law.

2. The effective date of withdrawal is the effective date of the repeal.

3. The withdrawing state shall immediately notify the chairperson of the Interstate Commission in writing upon the introduction of legislation repealing this compact in the withdrawing state. The Interstate Commission shall notify the other compacting states of the withdrawing state's intent to withdraw within 60 days of its receipt thereof.

4. The withdrawing state is responsible for all assessments, obligations, and liabilities incurred through the effective date of withdrawal, including any obligations, the performance of which extend beyond the effective date of withdrawal.

5. Reinstatement following withdrawal of any compacting state shall occur upon the withdrawing state reenacting the compact or upon such later date as determined by the Interstate Commission.

Sec. B. Technical Assistance, Fines, Suspension, Termination, and Default

1. If the Interstate Commission determines that any compacting state has at any time defaulted in the performance of any of its obligations or responsibilities under this compact, or the bylaws or duly promulgated rules, the Interstate Commission may impose any or all of the following penalties:

a. Remedial training and technical assistance as directed by the Interstate Commission;

b. Alternative dispute resolution;

c. Fines, fees, and costs in such amounts as are deemed to be reasonable as fixed by the Interstate Commission; and

d. Suspension or termination of membership in the compact, which shall be imposed only after all other reasonable means of securing compliance under the bylaws and rules have been exhausted and the Interstate Commission has determined that the offending state is in default. Immediate notice of suspension shall be given by the Interstate Commission to the governor, the chief justice or the chief judicial officer of the state, and the majority and minority leaders of the defaulting state's legislature. The grounds for default include, but are not limited to, failure of a compacting state to perform such obligations or responsibilities imposed upon it by this compact, the bylaws or duly promulgated rules, and any other grounds designated in commission bylaws and rules. The Interstate Commission shall immediately notify the defaulting state in writing of the penalty imposed by the Interstate Commission and of the default pending a cure of the default. The Interstate Commission shall stipulate the conditions and the time period within which the defaulting state must cure its default. If the defaulting state fails to cure the default within the time period specified by the Interstate Commission, the defaulting state shall be terminated from the compact upon an affirmative vote of a majority of the compacting states and all rights, privileges, and benefits conferred by this compact shall be terminated from the effective date of termination.

2. Within 60 days of the effective date of termination of a defaulting state, the Interstate Commission shall notify the governor, the chief justice or chief judicial officer of the state, and the majority and minority leaders of the defaulting state's legislature of such termination.

3. The defaulting state is responsible for all assessments, obligations, and liabilities incurred through the effective date of termination including any obligations, the performance of which extends beyond the effective date of termination.

4. The Interstate Commission shall not bear any costs relating to the defaulting state unless otherwise mutually agreed upon in writing between the Interstate Commission and the defaulting state.

5. Reinstatement following termination of any compacting state requires both a reenactment of the compact by the defaulting state and the approval of the Interstate Commission pursuant to the rules.

Sec. C. Judicial Enforcement

The Interstate Commission may, by majority vote of the members, initiate legal action in the United States District Court for the District of Columbia or, at the discretion of the Interstate Commission, in the federal district where the Interstate Commission has its offices, to enforce compliance with the provisions of the compact, its duly promulgated rules and bylaws, against any compacting state in default. In the event judicial enforcement is necessary the prevailing party shall be awarded all costs of such litigation including reasonable attorney's fees.

Sec. D. Dissolution of Compact

1. The compact dissolves effective upon the date of the withdrawal or default of the compacting state, which reduces membership in the compact to one compacting state.

2. Upon the dissolution of this compact, the compact becomes null and void and shall be of no further force or effect, and the business and affairs of the Interstate Commission shall be concluded and any surplus funds shall be distributed in accordance with the bylaws.

ARTICLE XI

SEVERABILITY AND CONSTRUCTION

A. The provisions of this compact shall be severable, and if any phrase, clause, sentence, or provision is deemed unenforceable, the remaining provisions of the compact shall be enforceable.

B. The provisions of this compact shall be liberally construed to effectuate its purposes.

ARTICLE XII

BINDING EFFECT OF COMPACT AND OTHER LAWS

Sec. A. Other Laws

1. Nothing herein prevents the enforcement of any other law of a compacting state that is not inconsistent with this compact.

2. All compacting states' laws other than state constitutions and other interstate compacts conflicting with this compact are superseded to the extent of the conflict.

Sec. B. Binding Effect of the Compact

1. All lawful actions of the Interstate Commission, including all rules and bylaws promulgated by the Interstate Commission, are binding upon the compacting states.

2. All agreements between the Interstate Commission and the compacting states are binding in accordance with their terms.

3. Upon the request of a party to a conflict over meaning or interpretation of Interstate Commission actions, and upon a majority vote of the compacting states, the Interstate Commission may issue advisory opinions regarding such meaning or interpretation.

4. In the event any provision of this compact exceeds the constitutional limits imposed on the legislature of any compacting state, the obligations, duties, powers, or jurisdiction sought to

be conferred by such provision upon the Interstate Commission shall be ineffective and such obligations, duties, powers, or jurisdiction shall remain in the compacting state and shall be exercised by the agency thereof to which such obligations, duties, powers, or jurisdiction are delegated by law in effect at the time this compact becomes effective.

§ 60.011. Effect of Texas Laws

If the laws of this state conflict with the compact, the compact controls, except that in the event of a conflict between the compact and the Texas Constitution, as determined by the courts of this state, the Texas Constitution controls.

§ 60.012. Liabilities for Certain Commission Agents

The compact administrator and each member, officer, executive director, employee, or agent of the commission acting within the scope of the person's employment or duties is, for the purpose of acts or omissions occurring within this state, entitled to the same protections under Chapter 104, Civil Practice and Remedies Code, as an employee, a member of the governing board, or any other officer of a state agency, institution, or department.

CHAPTER 61. RIGHTS AND RESPONSIBILITIES OF PARENTS AND OTHER ELIGIBLE PERSONS

SUBCHAPTER A. ENTRY OF ORDERS AGAINST PARENTS AND OTHER ELIGIBLE PERSONS

SUBCHAPTER B. ENFORCEMENT OF ORDER AGAINST PARENT OR OTHER ELIGIBLE PERSON

SUBCHAPTER C. RIGHTS OF PARENTS

Introductory Comment

Chapter 61 attempts to bring the strengths and resources of parents to the juvenile justice system to assist the child in making life-altering efforts at change. Subchapter A deals with entering juvenile court orders requiring parents to take actions or refrain from taking actions to benefit their child. Subchapter B deals with the judicial process by which those orders are enforced. Subchapter C deals with parental rights to know about their child's case and to participate in its handling.

CLE/Other Legal Publication

Parental rights and responsibilities. Nydia D. Thomas, 20th ANN. JUVE. L. CONF. (Feb. 2007).

SUBCHAPTER A. ENTRY OF ORDERS AGAINST PARENTS AND OTHER ELIGIBLE PERSONS

§ 61.001. Definitions

In this chapter:

(1) "Juvenile court order" means an order by a juvenile court in a proceeding to which this chapter applies requiring a parent or other eligible person to act or refrain from acting.

(2) "Other eligible person" means the respondent's guardian, the respondent's custodian, or any other person described in a provision under this title authorizing the court order.

Comment

This chapter is directed primarily at parents, but also includes other persons who under Title 3 substantive provisions are eligible to have the juvenile court order them to take or refrain from action.

§ 61.002. Applicability

(a) Except as provided by Subsection (b), this chapter applies to a proceeding to enter a juvenile court order:

(1) for payment of probation fees under Section 54.061;

(2) for restitution under Sections 54.041(b) and 54.048;

(3) for payment of graffiti eradication fees under Section 54.0461;

(4) for community service under Section 54.044(b);

(5) for payment of costs of court under Section 54.0411 or other provisions of law;

(6) requiring the person to refrain from doing any act injurious to the welfare of the child under Section 54.041(a)(1);

(7) enjoining contact between the person and the child who is the subject of a proceeding under Section 54.041(a)(2);

(8) ordering a person living in the same household with the child to participate in counseling under Section 54.041(a)(3);

(9) requiring a parent or guardian of a child found to be truant to participate in an available program addressing truancy under Section 54.041(f);

(10) requiring a parent or other eligible person to pay reasonable attorney's fees for representing the child under Section 51.10(e);

(11) requiring the parent or other eligible person to reimburse the county for payments the county has made to an attorney appointed to represent the child under Section 51.10(j);

(12) requiring payment of deferred prosecution supervision fees under Section 53.03(d);

(13) requiring a parent or other eligible person to attend a court hearing under Section 51.115;

(14) requiring a parent or other eligible person to act or refrain from acting to aid the child in complying with conditions of release from detention under Section 54.01(r);

(15) requiring a parent or other eligible person to act or refrain from acting under any law imposing an obligation of action or omission on a parent or other eligible person because of the parent's or person's relation to the child who is the subject of a proceeding under this title; ~~or~~

(16) for payment of fees under Section 54.0462**; or**

(17) for payment of the cost of attending an educational program under Section 54.0404.

(b) This subchapter does not apply to the entry and enforcement of a child support order under Section 54.06.

Amended by Acts 2011, 82nd Leg., ch. 1322 (S.B. 407), § 21, eff. Sept. 1, 2011.

Comment

Subsection (a) lists each instance in Title 3 in which a juvenile court is authorized to enter an order against a parent or other eligible adult. Subsection (a)(15) is an open-ended clause intended to catch any provisions omitted from the list or that may be enacted by later legislatures. It is important to note that a Chapter 61 order can be imposed only if a substantive basis elsewhere in Title 3 can be found authorizing the order. Subsection (b) excludes child support orders because their enforcement is dealt with by the comprehensive tools available to the court under Title 5.

§ 61.003. Entry of Juvenile Court Order Against Parent or Other Eligible Person

(a) To comply with the requirements of due process of law, the juvenile court shall:

(1) provide sufficient notice in writing or orally in a recorded court hearing of a proposed juvenile court order; and

(2) provide a sufficient opportunity for the parent or other eligible person to be heard regarding the proposed order.

(b) A juvenile court order must be in writing and a copy promptly furnished to the parent or other eligible person.

(c) The juvenile court may require the parent or other eligible person to provide suitable identification to be included in the court's file. Suitable identification includes fingerprints, a driver's license number, a social security number, or similar indicia of identity.

Comment

Subsection (a) sets out the basics of procedural due process—adequate notice and sufficient opportunity to be heard. Subchapter B makes it a defense to enforcement efforts that due process was not afforded when the order was entered. Subsection (c) requires documentation of identification to facilitate any enforcement efforts that may later become necessary.

§ 61.0031. Transfer of Order Affecting Parent or Other Eligible Person to County of Child's Residence

(a) This section applies only when:

(1) a juvenile court has placed a parent or other eligible person under a court order under this chapter;

(2) the child who was the subject of the juvenile court proceedings in which the order was entered:

(A) resides in a county other than the county in which the order was entered;

(B) has moved to a county other than the county in which the order was entered and intends to remain in that county for at least 60 days; or

(C) intends to move to a county other than the county in which the order was entered and to remain in that county for at least 60 days; and

(3) the parent or other eligible person resides or will reside in the same county as the county in which the child now resides or to which the child has moved or intends to move.

(b) A juvenile court that enters an order described by Subsection (a)(1) may transfer the order to the juvenile court of the county in which the parent now resides or to which the parent has moved or intends to move.

(c) The juvenile court shall provide the parent or other eligible person written notice of the transfer. The notification must identify the court to which the order has been transferred.

(d) The juvenile court to which the order has been transferred shall require the parent or other eligible person to appear before the court to notify the person of the existence and terms of the order. Failure to do so renders the order unenforceable.

(e) If the notice required by Subsection (d) is provided, the juvenile court to which the order has been transferred may modify, extend, or enforce the order as though the court originally entered the order.

Comment

To coincide with §§ 51.071 through 51.074, which were added in 2005, this section was also added to transfer any court orders against parents or guardians to the new court.

§ 61.004. Appeal

(a) The parent or other eligible person against whom a final juvenile court order has been entered may appeal as provided by law from judgments entered in civil cases.

(b) The movant may appeal from a judgment denying requested relief regarding a juvenile court order as provided by law from judgments entered in civil cases.

(c) The pendency of an appeal initiated under this section does not abate or otherwise affect the proceedings in juvenile court involving the child.

Comment

Both the parent and the state may appeal an order or denial of order as in other civil cases. Subsection (c) makes it clear that the appeal is between the parent and the state and does not affect the handling of the child's case.

SUBCHAPTER B. ENFORCEMENT OF ORDER AGAINST PARENT OR OTHER ELIGIBLE PERSON

§ 61.051. Motion for Enforcement

(a) A party initiates enforcement of a juvenile court order by filing a written motion. In ordinary and concise language, the motion must:

(1) identify the provision of the order allegedly violated and sought to be enforced;

(2) state specifically and factually the manner of the person's alleged noncompliance;

(3) state the relief requested; and

(4) contain the signature of the party filing the motion.

(b) The movant must allege in the same motion for enforcement each violation by the person of the juvenile court orders described by Section 61. 002(a) that the movant had a reasonable basis for believing the person was violating when the motion was filed.

(c) The juvenile court retains jurisdiction to enter a contempt order if the motion for enforcement is filed not later than six months after the child's 18th birthday.

Comment

Subsection (a) sets out the requirements of the written motion for enforcement. Subsection (b) mandates joinder of all claims the party filing the motion has a reasonable basis for believing exist; the person filing the motion for enforcement cannot hold back claims for later proceedings. Subsection (c) permits a motion for enforcement to be filed up to six months after the child becomes 18 since some violations will not be discovered until after the child is discharged from the system at age 18.

---

§ 61.052. Notice and Appearance

(a) On the filing of a motion for enforcement, the court shall by written notice set the date, time, and place of the hearing and order the person against whom enforcement is sought to appear and respond to the motion.

(b) The notice must be given by personal service or by certified mail, return receipt requested, on or before the 10th day before the date of the hearing on the motion. The notice must include a copy of the motion for enforcement. Personal service must comply with the Code of Criminal Procedure.

(c) If a person moves to strike or specially excepts to the motion for enforcement, the court shall rule on the exception or motion to strike before the court hears evidence on the motion for enforcement. If an exception is sustained, the court shall give the movant an opportunity to replead and continue the hearing to a designated date and time without the requirement of additional service.

(d) If a person who has been personally served with notice to appear at the hearing does not appear, the juvenile court may not hold the person in contempt, but may issue a capias for the arrest of the person. The court shall set and enforce bond as provided by Subchapter C, Chapter 157. If a person served by certified mail, return receipt requested, with notice to appear at the hearing does not appear, the juvenile court may require immediate personal service of notice.

Comment

Subsection (b) permits either personal or certified mail service of the motion for enforcement and notice of hearing. Subsection (d) permits a capias to be issued when a person personally served fails to appear, but requires personal service if the non-appearing person was only originally served by certified mail.

§ 61.053. Attorney for the Person

(a) In a proceeding on a motion for enforcement where incarceration is a possible punishment against a person who is not represented by an attorney, the court shall inform the person of the right to be represented by an attorney and, if the person is indigent, of the right to the appointment of an attorney.

(b) If the person claims indigency and requests the appointment of an attorney, the juvenile court may require the person to file an affidavit of indigency. The court may hear evidence to determine the issue of indigency.

(c) The court shall appoint an attorney to represent the person if the court determines that the person is indigent.

(d) The court shall allow an appointed or retained attorney at least 10 days after the date of the attorney's appointment or retention to respond to the movant's pleadings and to prepare for the hearing. The attorney may waive the preparation time or agree to a shorter period for preparation.

Comment

Subsection (a) was amended in the Senate to add the words "where incarceration is a possible punishment." Since under Section 61.057(a) incarceration is always a possible punishment, the Senate language added nothing to the subsection. Subsections (b) and (c) codify federal constitutional mandates by requiring the court to appoint counsel for an indigent parent to represent that person in enforcement proceedings.

§ 61.054. Compensation of Appointed Attorney

(a) An attorney appointed to represent an indigent person is entitled to a reasonable fee for services to be paid from the general fund of the county according to the schedule for compensation adopted by the county juvenile board. The attorney must meet the qualifications required of attorneys for appointment to Class B misdemeanor cases in juvenile court.

(b) For purposes of compensation, a proceeding in the supreme court is the equivalent of a proceeding in the court of criminal appeals.

(c) The juvenile court may order the parent or other eligible person for whom it has appointed counsel to reimburse the county for the fees the county pays to appointed counsel.

Comment

Subsection (a) requires that an attorney appointed to represent a parent must meet the qualifications for handing Class B misdemeanor juvenile cases. That qualification was chosen since it most closely approximates the punishment authorized for contempt of court.

§ 61.055. Conduct of Enforcement Hearing

(a) The juvenile court shall require that the enforcement hearing be recorded as provided by Section 54.09.

(b) The movant must prove beyond a reasonable doubt that the person against whom enforcement is sought engaged in conduct constituting contempt of a reasonable and lawful court order as alleged in the motion for enforcement.

(c) The person against whom enforcement is sought has a privilege not to be called as a witness or otherwise to incriminate himself or herself.

(d) The juvenile court shall conduct the enforcement hearing without a jury.

(e) The juvenile court shall include in its judgment findings as to each violation alleged in the motion for enforcement and the punishment, if any, to be imposed.

(f) If the person against whom enforcement is sought was not represented by counsel during any previous court proceeding involving a motion for enforcement, the person may through counsel raise any defense or affirmative defense to the proceeding that could have been lodged in the previous court proceeding but was not because the person was not represented by counsel.

(g) It is an affirmative defense to enforcement of a juvenile court order that the juvenile court did not provide the parent or other eligible person with due process of law in the proceeding in which the court entered the order.

Comment

Subsection (f) makes available to the parent in enforcement proceedings any defense that could have been presented in previous court proceedings but was not because the parent was unrepresented. Subsection (g) makes failure to provide due process as provided in § 61.003(a) an affirmative defense to enforcement proceedings.

---

§ 61.056. Affirmative Defense of Inability to Pay

(a) In an enforcement hearing in which the motion for enforcement alleges that the person against whom enforcement is sought failed to pay restitution, court costs, supervision fees, or any other payment ordered by the court, it is an affirmative defense that the person was financially unable to pay.

(b) The burden of proof to establish the affirmative defense of inability to pay is on the person asserting it.

(c) In order to prevail on the affirmative defense of inability to pay, the person asserting it must show that the person could not have reasonably paid the court-ordered obligation after the person discharged the person's other important financial obligations, including payments for housing, food, utilities, necessary clothing, education, and preexisting debts.

Comment

This section makes inability to make court-ordered payments an affirmative defense to enforcement proceedings. It is modeled on article 42.12, Sec. 21(c) of the Code of Criminal Procedure. Subsection (c) defines inability to pay in terms of whether the defendant could have paid the court-ordered money in light of the defendant's legal duties to pay pre-existing obligations.

---

§ 61.057. Punishment for Contempt

(a) On a finding of contempt, the juvenile court may commit the person to the county jail for a term not to exceed six months or may impose a fine in an amount not to exceed $500, or both.

(b) The court may impose only a single jail sentence not to exceed six months or a single fine not to exceed $500, or both, during an enforcement proceeding, without regard to whether the court has entered multiple findings of contempt.

(c) On a finding of contempt in an enforcement proceeding, the juvenile court may, instead of issuing a commitment to jail, enter an order requiring the person's future conduct to comply with the court's previous orders.

(d) Violation of an order entered under Subsection (c) may be the basis of a new enforcement proceeding.

(e) The juvenile court may assign a juvenile probation officer to assist a person in complying with a court order issued under Subsection (c).

(f) A juvenile court may reduce a term of incarceration or reduce payment of all or part of a fine at any time before the sentence is fully served or the fine fully paid.

(g) A juvenile court may reduce the burden of complying with a court order issued under Subsection (c) at any time before the order is fully satisfied, but may not increase the burden except following a new finding of contempt in a new enforcement proceeding.

Comment

Subsection (a) makes contempt punishable to the same extent of contempt of court under the Government Code for any other order of a district or county level court. Subsection (b) restricts the court to one finding of contempt per enforcement proceeding and prohibits the imposition of multiple sentences. Section 61.051(b) required the state to join all reasonably knowable violations in a single enforcement proceeding. Instead of imposing a fine and/or incarceration, the court is authorized by Subsection (c) to enter a further court order as a sanction for contempt, a violation of which may later become the basis of fresh enforcement proceedings. Under Subsection (e) the court may assign a juvenile probation officer to assist the defendant in complying with a newly-entered court order. Subsection (f) permits the court to reduce a term of incarceration or remit a fine before it has been fully served or paid.

SUBCHAPTER C. RIGHTS OF PARENTS

§ 61.101. Definition

In this subchapter, "parent" includes the guardian or custodian of a child.

§ 61.102. Right to be Informed of Proceeding

(a) The parent of a child referred to a juvenile court is entitled as soon as practicable after the referral to be informed by staff designated by the juvenile board, based on the information accompanying the referral to the juvenile court, of:

(1) the date and time of the offense;

(2) the date and time the child was taken into custody;

(3) the name of the offense and its penal category;

(4) the type of weapon, if any, that was used;

(5) the type of property taken or damaged and the extent of damage, if any;

(6) the physical injuries, if any, to the victim of the offense;

(7) whether there is reason to believe that the offense was gang-related;

(8) whether there is reason to believe that the offense was related to consumption of alcohol or use of an illegal controlled substance;

(9) if the child was taken into custody with adults or other juveniles, the names of those persons;

(10) the aspects of the juvenile court process that apply to the child;

(11) if the child is in detention, the visitation policy of the detention facility that applies to the child;

(12) the child's right to be represented by an attorney and the local standards and procedures for determining whether the parent qualifies for appointment of counsel to represent the child; and

(13) the methods by which the parent can assist the child with the legal process.

(b) If the child was released on field release citation, or from the law enforcement station by the police, by intake, or by the judge or associate judge at the initial detention hearing, the information required by Subsection (a) may be communicated to the parent in person, by telephone, or in writing.

(c) If the child is not released before or at the initial detention hearing, the information required by Subsection (a) shall be communicated in person to the parent unless that is not feasible, in which event it may be communicated by telephone or in writing.

(d) Information disclosed to a parent under Subsection (a) is not admissible in a judicial proceeding under this title as substantive evidence or as evidence to impeach the testimony of a witness for the state.

Comment

This section gives the parent the right to be informed of certain facts about the arrest of his or her child. Those facts that a parent would reasonably be expected to want to know are included, but not included is a general narrative of the offense as it would appear in an offense report. Duty to inform the parent is placed on probation staff. All of the information can be obtained from the law enforcement incident report that accompanied the referral. Subsection (d) provides that this information disclosed to the parent is for the benefit of the parent and may not be admitted in proceedings in juvenile court involving the child.

§ 61.103. Right of Access to Child

(a) The parent of a child taken into custody for delinquent conduct, conduct indicating a need for supervision, or conduct that violates a condition of probation imposed by the juvenile court has the right to communicate in person privately with the child for reasonable periods of time while the child is in:

(1) a juvenile processing office;

(2) a secure detention facility;

(3) a secure correctional facility;

(4) a court-ordered placement facility; or

(5) the custody of the Texas Youth Commission.

(b) The time, place, and conditions of the private, in-person communication may be regulated to prevent disruption of scheduled activities and to maintain the safety and security of the facility.

Comment

This section gives parents a right of access to their children at all times, subject to reasonable regulation by the custodian.

§ 61.104. Parental Written Statement

(a) When a petition for adjudication, a motion or petition to modify disposition, or a motion or petition for discretionary transfer to criminal court is served on a parent of the child, the parent must be provided with a form prescribed by the Texas Juvenile Probation Commission on which the parent can make a written statement about the needs of the child or family or any other matter relevant to disposition of the case.

(b) The parent shall return the statement to the juvenile probation department, which shall transmit the statement to the court along with the discretionary transfer report authorized by

Section 54.02(e), the disposition report authorized by Section 54.04(b), or the modification of disposition report authorized by Section 54.05(e), as applicable. The statement shall be disclosed to the parties as appropriate and may be considered by the court at the disposition, modification, or discretionary transfer hearing.

Comment

This section creates the opportunity for a parent to communicate relevant dispositional information to the juvenile court as part of the social history report. It is modeled on victim's impact statement procedures used in both criminal and juvenile cases.

§ 61.105. Parental Oral Statement

(a) After all the evidence has been received but before the arguments of counsel at a hearing for discretionary transfer to criminal court, a disposition hearing without a jury, or a modification of disposition hearing, the court shall give a parent who is present in court a reasonable opportunity to address the court about the needs or strengths of the child or family or any other matter relevant to disposition of the case.

(b) The parent may not be required to make the statement under oath and may not be subject to cross-examination, but the court may seek clarification or expansion of the statement from the person giving the statement.

(c) The court may consider and act on the statement as the court considers appropriate.

Comment

This section gives the parent the right to make an unsworn oral statement to the juvenile court regarding disposition of his or her child's case and for the court to give such a statement whatever weight it believes appropriate. To encourage parents to provide such an oral statement, cross-examination by either state or child's attorney is prohibited. The court may ask clarifying questions only.

§ 61.106. Appeal or Collateral Challenge

The failure or inability of a person to perform an act or to provide a right or service listed under this subchapter may not be used by the child or any party as a ground for:

(1) appeal;

(2) an application for a post-adjudication writ of habeas corpus; or

(3) exclusion of evidence against the child in any proceeding or forum.

Comment

The rights provided by this subchapter belong to the parent, not the child. This section precludes using failure to provide parental rights as a defense in the trial, appeal or collateral attack in the child's case. A similar provision appears in the victim's rights chapter, for similar reasons. See § 57.006.

§ 61.107. Liability

The Texas Youth Commission, a juvenile board, a court, a person appointed by the court, an employee of a juvenile probation department, an attorney for the state, a peace officer, or a law enforcement agency is not liable for a failure or inability to provide a right listed in this chapter.

Comment

This provision protects public officials from civil liability for failure to provide a right defined by this subchapter. A similar provision appears in the victim's rights chapter. See § 57.005.

TITLE 4

PROTECTIVE ORDERS AND FAMILY VIOLENCE

As amended through the 82nd Legislature, Regular and First Called Sessions (2011)

★★★

Editors' Note: Title 4 contains guest commentary throughout by Jeana L. Lungwitz, Clinical Professor, Domestic Violence Clinic, University of Texas School of Law, and Bree Buchanan, former Public Policy Director, Texas Council on Family Violence.

Introductory Comment

"Protection of the Family," as Title 4 was originally named, had a somewhat later start than the rest of the Family Code. Thanks to the efforts of attorneys from Gulf Coast Legal Aid (Houston), that omission was cured in 1979. Further, one of the very most effective public advocacy organizations, Texas Council on Family Violence (TCFV), has moved the cause along quite smartly. A complete recodification in 1997 provided the current organization of the title.

In 2011 the 82nd Legislature enacted several amendments to Title 4, ranging from allowing provisions regarding the possession of pets to be set out in the orders to expanding the duration of protective orders in certain circumstances. In addition to these legislative changes, the courts spent the last year interpreting some of the existing statutory provisions. These changes and interpretations are set out below.

Prevalence of Family Violence. Family violence is a well documented epidemic in Texas and the nation as a whole. Approximately 1.3 million women and 835,000 men are physically assaulted by an intimate partner annually in the United States. (http://www.nij.gov/nij/topics/crime/intimate-partner-violence/extent.htm-Site last visited June 8, 2011).

Health related costs alone exceed $5.8 billion each year. Victims lose a total of nearly eight million days of paid work (the equivalent of 32,000 full time jobs) each year as a result of the violence. Costs of Intimate Partner Violence, Center for Disease Control, 2003. Recent studies also reveal that domestic violence is experienced by young women at disproportionate rates. Specifically, women between 16 and 24 are nearly three times more vulnerable to intimate partner violence than women in other age groups. Intimate Partner Violence and Age of Victim, Bureau of Justice Statistics, October 2001.

Intimate partner homicide occurs in Texas at one of the highest rates in the country. Surveillance for Homicide Among Intimate Partners, Center for Disease Control, October 2001. In 2009 Texans reported 196,713 incidents of family violence to law enforcement, and 111 women were killed by their intimate partners. http://www.tcfv.org/resources/abuse-in-texas—Site last visited June 8, 2011). While these numbers may seem staggering, studies show that only approximately 50% of all family violence incidents are actually reported to the police. Intimate Partner Violence, Bureau of Justice Statistics, May 2000. Of those reports received in 2007, the age group with the highest number of victims was the 20 to 24 year old bracket. 2007 Crime in Texas, Texas Department of Public Safety. In 2009, 79,367 adult victims and their children were served by family violence programs across the state. http://www.tcfv.org/wp-content/uploads/2007/10/tcfv_stats20091.pdf—Site last visited June 8, 2011)

History of Protective Orders in Texas. Since 1979, protective orders have existed as the primary civil legal remedy for victims of family violence in Texas. As society's tolerance for family violence has decreased over the past two decades, the protections afforded under this title have consistently increased. In 1989 the definition of "family violence" was amended to include threats of violence, in addition to violent acts. Two years later, mutual protective orders were prohibited. In 1995, the magistrate's order of emergency protection was added to Tex. Code Crim. Proc. art. 17.292. Further, a centralized protective order registry was established as part of the Texas Crime Information Center (TCIC), which is linked with the National Crime Information Center (NCIC), the federal counterpart at the FBI.

As originally passed, the protective order statute allowed for only one year protective orders. Later, the legislature doubled the maximum duration to two years. In 2011 a significant change was made to the statute, allowing courts to issue orders that will be effective for longer than two years in two different situations: 1) cases where, due to continuing violence or violations of previous protective orders, the applicant re-applies for a protective order; or 2) where the first-time applicant suffered serious bodily injury at the hands of the respondent. In 2003 the entry of a Title 4–style protective order for victims of sexual assault was authorized. See Tex. Code Crim. Proc. ch. 7A. In 2011, this provision was expanded to include stalking victims as well.

Effectiveness of Protective Orders. Many believe that a victim will be safe once separated from the abuser. To the contrary, statistics have shown the risk of violent assault increases whenever a victim takes action that challenges the abuser's control (making plans to separate, filing for divorce, calling the police). WILSON AND DALY, SPOUSAL HOMICIDE RISK AND ESTRANGEMENT: VIOLENCE AND VICTIMS, 1993. Over half of the murders of women by an intimate partner in Texas in 1998 occurred after separation or while she was attempting to leave, GRIM TALLY, TEXAS COUNCIL ON FAMILY VIOLENCE, 1998.

Protective orders can be an effective method for intervening in the often escalating violence that occurs at separation, particularly when orders are crafted with specificity and the relief granted addresses the particular needs of the applicant (including orders regarding children and property). A 2002 study concluded that a victim is 80% less likely to be re victimized after being granted a protective order. CIVIL PROTECTIVE ORDERS AND RISK OF SUBSEQUENT POLICE-REPORTED VIOLENCE, 288 J. AMER. MED. ASSN. 589.

The power of protective orders lies in their quasi criminal nature. For first time offenders a violation of one of the provisions of TEX. FAM. CODE § 85.022(b) is a Class A misdemeanor, punishable by confinement up to one year and/or a fine up to $4,000. TEX. PENAL CODE ANN. § 25.07. The penalty is enhanced for repeat offenders. TEX. PENAL CODE ANN. § 25.07(g). Peace officers are required to arrest a person whom the officer has probable cause to believe has violated a protective order. TEX. CODE CRIM. PROC. art. 14.03.

In April 2005, the Supreme Court of Texas and the Texas Equal Access to Justice Commission unveiled a pro se protective order packet. Further, the Supreme Court of Texas approved forms for the documents necessary to obtain an protective order. A copy may be downloaded at www.texaslawhelp.org. For information regarding local family violence services, contact the National Domestic Violence Hotline at 1–800–799–7233.

Online Resources: Domestic and Sexual Violence

National Center for Victims of Crime *http://www.ncvc.org*

National Domestic Violence Hotline *http://www.ndvh.org*

National Sexual Violence Resource Center *http://www.nsvrc.org*

Texas Association Against Sexual Assault *http://www.taasa.org*

Texas Council on Family Violence *http://www.tcfv.org*

U.S. Department of Justice Office on Violence Against Women *http://www.ojp.usdoj.gov/ovc*

Violence Against Women Online *http://www.vaw.umn.edu*

Texas Advocacy Project *http://www.texasadvocacyproject.org*

Texas Law Help *http://www.texaslawhelp.org*

CLE/Other Legal Publications

Protective orders. Sally H. Emerson, 2011 ADV. FAM. L.

The impact of domestic violence on a divorce. Doug Warne, Scott A. Beauchamp & Judith G. Wells, 2011 MARRIAGE DISSOLUTION

Protective orders: the nuts and bolts. Lynn Bradshaw-Hull, 2011 SO. TEX. FAM. L.

Protective orders: who needs them and how to get them. Carlos Guillermo Salinas, 2011 U.T. FAM. L. FRONT LINES

Domestic violence and protective orders. Judy L. Warne, 2010 ADV. FAM. L. DRAFTING

Family violence protective orders: collateral consequences—civil and criminal Frederick S. Adams, Jr., 2010 ADV. FAM. L.

The military report card concerning domestic violence and sexual assault, including compliance with the Lautenberg Amendment. Kathlene J. Somerville, 43 FAM. L.Q. 349 (2009)

The impact of domestic violence on the child: understanding the impact of domestic violence on the child as it effects development of the legal case. Jeana Lungwitz, 2009 ADV. FAM. L.

Report from the Wingspread Conference on Domestic Violence. Nancy Ver Steegh, 2009 ADV. FAM. L.

Drafting an enforceable protective order. Aubrey Meachum Connatser & Ashley W. McDowell, 2009 ADV. FAM. L.

Where family law and criminal law collide: electronic eavesdropping, family violence, and child abuse. Kathryn L. Pruitt & Robert N. Udashen, 2009 U.T. PARENT-CHILD REL.

The littlest victims: how domestic violence impacts your SAPCR. Angela Pence England, 2008 U.T. FAM. L. FRONT LINES

See Accompanying CD-ROM for Additional CLE/Other Legal Publications

Leading Cases

U.S. v. Morrison, 529 U.S. 598, 120 S.Ct. 1740, 146 L.Ed.2d 658 (2000) (VAWA's federal civil remedy for victims of gender-motivated violence, 42 U.S.C.A. § 13981, exceeds Congress' constitutional authority)

Villarreal v. State, 286 S.W.3d 321 (Tex. Crim. App. 2009) (order explicitly prohibited defendant from committing further "family violence" against his girlfriend or her family, and any reasonable person would have understood that this prohibition included "dating violence" against his girlfriend)

Pena v. Pena, 8 S.W.3d 639 (Tex. 1999) (appellate court statement that provocation might be relevant in determining existence of "pattern of abuse" disapproved)

Wilkerson v. Wilkerson, 321 S.W.3d 110 (Tex. App.— Houston [1st Dist.] 2010, pet. denied) (actual physical harm is not necessary for a finding of family violence; threats that included discharging a gun was plenty to prove family violence occurred)

Bedinghaus v. Adams, 2009 WL 279388 (Tex. App.—Corpus Christi, 2009, no pet.) (not released for publication) (threats to harm without actual physical violence meet the definition of "family violence" for the purpose of obtaining a protective order)

Gonzalez v. Galvan, 2009 WL 1089472 (Tex. App.—Corpus Christi, 2009, no pet.)(not released for publication) (affirming trial court's ruling that evidence did not support a finding that family violence was likely to occur in the future despite the court's observation that the parties should "Get away from one another and knock it off before one of you ends up in prison because that's where this is going")

In re Meiwes, 2008 WL 4107978 (Tex .App.—Amarillo, no pet.) (not released for publication) (cannot complain about service on appeal when you appear for a hearing and say nothing about the absence of a show cause order or the improper execution of process; portions of a decree that are void can be severed from those which are valid; one is not entitled to a jury trial in a contempt hearing for violation of a protective order)

In re Skero, 253 S.W.3d 884 (Tex. App.—Beaumont 2008, no pet.) (attorneys fees awarded in protective order proceeding enforceable by contempt)

Clements v. Haskovec, 251 S.W.3d 79 (Tex. App.—Corpus Christi 2008, no pet.) (pattern of past violence enough to show likelihood of future violence; expired protective order is subject to review due to "collateral consequence" exception to the mootness doctrine)

Cross References

TEX. CIV. PRAC. & REM. CODE ch. 85. Liability for Stalking

TX FCA CRIM.PROC. Art. 5.01 *et seq.*, Family Violence Prevention, *infra*; TX FCA CRIM. PROC. art. 17.292, Magistrate's Order for Emergency Protection, *infra*; TEX. CODE CRIM. PROC. art. 42.141 *et seq.*, Battering Intervention and Prevention Program, *infra*; TEX. CODE CRIM. PROC. art, 7A.01 *et seq.*; Protective Order for Victim of Sexual Assault and Stalking, *infra*; TEX. CODE CRIM. PROC. art. 56.01 *et seq.*, Rights of Crime Victims, *infra*; TEX. CODE CRIM. PROC. art. 56.31 *et seq.*, Crime Victim Compensation, *infra*; TEX. CODE CRIM. PROC. art. 57B.01 *et seq.*, Confidentiality of Identifying Information of Family Violence Victims, *infra*.

TX FCA FAMILY § 6.404, Information Regarding Protective Orders, *supra*; TX FCA FAMILY §§ 6.501 to 6.502, Temporary Orders, *supra*; TX FCA FAMILY § 6.504, Protective Orders, *supra*; TX FCA

FAMILY § 42.001 et seq., Interference with Possessory Interest in Child, *supra*; TX FCA FAMIL §§ 105.001, 105.0011, Information Regarding Protective Orders and Temporary Orders, *infra*; TX FCA FAMILY § 153.004, History of Domestic Violence, *infra*; TX FCA FAMILY § 153.010, Order for Family Counseling, *infra*; TX FCA FAMILY § 153.131, Presumption that Parent To Be Appointed Managing Conservator, *infra*; TX FCA FAMILY §§ 153.501 to 153.503, Prevention of International Parental Child Abduction, *infra*; TX FCA FAMILY § 159.312, Nondisclosure of Information in Exceptional Circumstances, *infra*; § 233.015, Issuance of Child Support Review Order, *infra*; TX FCA FAMILY § 262.102, Emergency Order Authorizing Possession of Child, *infra*; TX FCA FAMILY § 262.201, Full Adversary Hearing, *infra*.

TEX. HEALTH & SAFETY CODE ANN. § 672.001, Adult Fatality Review & Investigations.

TX FCA PENAL § 22.01, Assault, *infra*; TX FCA PENAL § 22.07, Terroristic Threat, *infra*; TX FCA PENAL § 25.03, Interference with Child Custody, *infra*; TX FCA PENAL § 25.07, Violation of Protective Order and Magistrate's Order, *infra*; TX FCA PENAL § 42.062, Interference with Emergency Telephone Call, *infra*; TX FCA PENAL § 42.07, Harassment, *infra*; TX FCA PENAL § 42.072, Stalking, *infra*.

TX FCA PROPERTY § 92.016, Right to Vacate and Avoid Liability Following Family Violence, *infra*.

VIOLENCE AGAINST WOMEN ACT, 18 U.S.C.A. § 2265 et seq.; 42 U.S.C.A. § 13931, et seq. (see, also TX FCA 18 USCA §2265, *infra*).

E A. GENERAL PROVISIONS

PTER 71. DEFINITIONS

---

§ 71.001. Applicability of Definitions

(a) Definitions in this chapter apply to this title.

(b) If, in another part of this title, a term defined by this chapter has a meaning different from the meaning provided by this chapter, the meaning of that other provision prevails.

(c) Except as provided by this chapter, the definitions in Chapter 101 apply to terms used in this title.

§ 71.002. Court

"Court" means the district court, court of domestic relations, juvenile court having the jurisdiction of a district court, statutory county court, constitutional county court, or other court expressly given jurisdiction under this title.

§ 71.0021. Dating Violence

(a) "Dating violence" means an act**, other than a defensive measure to protect oneself,** by an **actor** ~~individual~~ that:

(1) is **committed** against **a victim:**

(A) ~~another individual~~ with whom **the actor** ~~that person~~ has or has had a dating relationship**; or**

(B) because of the victim's marriage to or dating relationship with an individual with whom the actor is or has been in a dating relationship or marriage; and

(2) ~~that~~ is intended to result in physical harm, bodily injury, assault, or sexual assault or that is a threat that reasonably places the **victim** ~~individual~~ in fear of imminent physical harm, bodily injury, assault, or sexual assault~~, but does not include defensive measures to protect oneself~~.

(b) For purposes of this title, "dating relationship" means a relationship between individuals who have or have had a continuing relationship of a romantic or intimate nature. The existence of such a relationship shall be determined based on consideration of:

(1) the length of the relationship;

(2) the nature of the relationship; and

(3) the frequency and type of interaction between the persons involved in the relationship.

(c) A casual acquaintanceship or ordinary fraternization in a business or social context does not constitute a "dating relationship" under Subsection (b).

Amended by Acts 2011, 82nd Leg., ch. 872 (S.B. 116), § 2, eff. June 17, 2011.

Comment

In 2001, the legislature extended the relief afforded under this title to victims who have a "continuing relationship of a romantic or intimate nature" with an abusive individual. The definition of "dating relationship" mirrors the federal definition found in the Violence Against Women Act of 2000 (42 U.S.C.A. 3796).

Before 2001 victims of family violence perpetrated by intimate partners violence who had never been married, lived together, or had a child together were ineligible to apply for a protective order. This, notwithstanding that the dynamics of violence in their relationships usually were similar or identical to those who were otherwise eligible to apply. Ironically, research has found that young adults ages 16 to 24 experience the highest rate of intimate partner violence. Yet this was the age group least likely to meet the eligibility criteria. *Intimate Partner Violence*, Bureau of Justice Statistics, May 2000.

In 2005 the legislature clarified that repeated acts of "dating violence," as well as those involving a deadly weapon, are subject to the same penalty enhancements as for acts of "family violence." *See* Tex. Pen. Code §§ 22.01–.02. At that same time the legislature authorized a peace officer to make a warrantless arrest of a person who the officer believes has committed an act of "dating violence." *See* Tex. Code Crim. Proc. art. 14.03.

§ 71.003. Family

"Family" includes individuals related by consanguinity or affinity, as determined under Sections 573.022 and 573.024, Government Code, individuals who are former spouses of each other, individuals who are the parents of the same child, without regard to marriage, and a foster child and foster parent, without regard to whether those individuals reside together.

Comment

The definition of "family" is very broad in order to maximize protection and to minimize domestic violence.

§ 71.004. Family Violence

"Family violence" means:

(1) an act by a member of a family or household against another member of the family or household that is intended to result in physical harm, bodily injury, assault, or sexual assault or that is a threat that reasonably places the member in fear of imminent physical harm, bodily injury, assault, or sexual assault, but does not include defensive measures to protect oneself;

(2) abuse, as that term is defined by Sections 261.001(1)(C), (E), and (G), by a member of a family or household toward a child of the family or household; or

(3) dating violence, as that term is defined by Section 71.0021.

Comment

The inclusion of "dating violence" in the definition of family violence, ensures that dating violence protective orders are subject to the same procedures and penalties as all other family violence protective orders. Because magistrate's orders for emergency protection are authorized "after arrest for an offense involving family violence," victims of dating violence are also eligible for these 61 to 91 day protective orders. *See* Tex. Code Crim. Proc. art. 17.292.

Leading Cases

Wilkerson v. Wilkerson, 321 S.W.3d 110 (Tex. App.—Houston 2010, reh. overruled) (actual physical harm is not necessary for a finding of family violence; threats that included discharging a gun was plenty to prove family violence occurred)

In re Wean, 2010 WL 3431708 (Tex. App.—Austin 2010) (for corporal punishment to constitute family violence there must be some evidence that the punishment transcends reasonable parental discretion looking at the severity of injury, type of instrument used, and mental or emotional state of person applying corporal punishment)

§ 71.005. Household

"Household" means a unit composed of persons living together in the same dwelling, without regard to whether they are related to each other.

§ 71.006. Member of a Household

"Member of a household" includes a person who previously lived in a household.

§ 71.007. Prosecuting Attorney

"Prosecuting attorney" means the attorney, determined as provided in this title, who represents the state in a district or statutory county court in the county in which venue of the application for a protective order is proper.

SUBTITLE B. PROTECTIVE ORDERS

Introductory Comment

The structure of Title 4 is quite different from the rest of the Family Code. First, in Chapter 71 the focus is basically on a single subject—domestic violence. Second, in Chapters 81-88 the focus is on one method to deal with that issue, a protective order, out of a range of possible responses, including the criminal law. Underlying this approach is the principle that in many instances problems of domestic violence may be solved by court intervention on the civil side of the docket. Experience has demonstrated that this principle is correct—with the clear understanding that not all cases will result in the hoped for outcome, i.e., compliance with the order. Finally, Chapters 91-92 encourage the general public to assist in the system by reporting instances of domestic violence to law enforcement.

CLE/Other Legal Publications

Protective orders. Sally H. Emerson, 2011 Adv. Fam. L.

The impact of domestic violence on a divorce. Doug Warne, Scott A. Beauchamp & Judith G. Wells, 2011 Marriage Dissolution

Protective orders: the nuts and bolts. Lynn Bradshaw-Hull, 2011 So. Tex. Fam. L.

Protective orders: who needs them and how to get them. Carlos Guillermo Salinas, 2011 U.T. Fam. L. Front Lines

Domestic violence and protective orders. Judy L. Warne, 2010 Adv. Fam. L. Drafting

Family violence protective orders: collateral consequences—civil and criminal. Frederick S. Adams, Jr., 2010 Adv. Fam. L.

Drafting an enforceable protective order. Aubrey Meachum Connatser & Ashley W. McDowell, 2009 Adv. Fam. L.

Presenting a domestic violence case to the court. Jeana L. Lungwitz, 2007 U.T. Fam. L. Front Lines

Leading Cases

Villarreal v. State, 286 S.W.3d 321 (Tex. Crim. App. 2009) (order explicitly prohibited defendant from committing further "family violence" against his girlfriend or her family, and any reasonable person would have understood that this prohibition included "dating violence" against his girlfriend)

Pena v. Pena, 8 S.W.3d 639 (Tex. 1999) (appellate court statement that provocation might be relevant in determining existence of "pattern of abuse" disapproved)

nghaus v. Adams, No. 2 08 096 CV, 2009 WL 279388 (Tex. App.—Corpus Christi, 2009, no et.) (not released for publication) (threats to harm without actual physical violence meet the efinition of "family violence" for the purpose of obtaining a protective order)

nzalez v. Galvan, No. 13 08 488 CV, 2009 WL 1089472 (Tex. App.—Corpus Christi, 2009, no pet.)(not released for publication) (affirming trial court's ruling that evidence did not support a finding that family violence was likely to occur in the future despite the court's observation that the parties should "Get away from one another and knock it off before one of you ends up in prison because that's where this is going")

In re Meiwes, 2008 WL 4107978 (Tex. App.—Amarillo 2008, no pet.) (cannot complain about service on appeal when you appear for a hearing and say nothing about the absence of a show cause order or the improper execution of process; portions of a decree that are void can be severed from those which are valid; one is not entitled to a jury trial in a contempt hearing for violation of a protective order)

In re Skero, 253 S.W.3d 884 (Tex. App.—Beaumont 2008, no pet.) (attorneys fees awarded in protective order proceeding enforceable by contempt)

Clements v. Haskovec, 251 S.W.3d 79 (Tex. App.—Corpus Christi 2008, no pet.) (pattern of past violence enough to show likelihood of future violence; expired protective order is subject to review due to "collateral consequence" exception to the mootness doctrine)

***See* Accompanying CD–ROM for Additional Leading Cases.**

★★★

CHAPTER 81. GENERAL PROVISIONS

§ 81.001. Entitlement to Protective Order.
§ 81.002. No Fee for Applicant.
§ 81.003. Fees and Costs Paid by Party Found to Have Committed Family Violence.
§ 81.004. Contempt for Nonpayment of Fee.
§ 81.005. Attorney's Fees. **[amended]**
§ 81.006. Payment of Attorney's Fees. **[amended]**
§ 81.007. Prosecuting Attorney.
§ 81.0075. Representation by Prosecuting Attorney in Certain Subsequent Actions. **[amended]**
§ 81.008. Relief Cumulative.
§ 81.009. Appeal.
§ 81.010. Court Enforcement. [new]

§ 81.001. Entitlement to Protective Order

A court shall render a protective order as provided by Section 85.001(b) if the court finds that family violence has occurred and is likely to occur in the future.

Comment

The Code of Criminal Procedure provides for an application for a protective order by victims of sexual assault and stalking without regard to the relationship between the applicant and the alleged offender. *See* Tex. Code Crim. Proc. ch. 7A, *infra.*

Leading Cases

Clements v. Haskovec, 251 S.W.3d 79 (Tex. App.—Corpus Christi 2008, no pet.) (pattern of past violence enough to show likelihood of future violence; expired protective order is subject to review due to "collateral consequence" exception to the mootness doctrine)

Schaban-Maurer v. Maurer-Schaban, 238 S.W.3d 815 (Tex. App.—Fort Worth 2007, no pet.) (pattern of past violence supports finding that family violence is likely to occur again in the future)

---

§ 81.002. No Fee for Applicant

An applicant for a protective order or an attorney representing an applicant may not be assessed a fee, cost, charge, or expense by a district or county clerk of the court or a sheriff, constable, or other public official or employee in connection with the filing, serving, or entering of a protective order or for any other service described by this subsection, including:

(1) a fee to dismiss, modify, or withdraw a protective order;

(2) a fee for certifying copies;

(3) a fee for comparing copies to originals;

(4) a court reporter fee;

(5) a judicial fund fee;

(6) a fee for any other service related to a protective order; or

(7) a fee to transfer a protective order.

Comment

The Texas Legislature has made a series of attempts to make protective orders available to all in need of emergency protection. First, filing fees and court costs were set at a nominal amount. Even then, some people could not afford them. Later, the *Texas Family Code* was amended to specify that affidavits of inability to pay costs could be filed with protective orders. Even after that some counties were charging "administrative costs" and other add-ons, making protective orders unavailable to some victims. This section makes it clear that an applicant (or lawyer for an applicant) cannot be charged any fees by the county.

---

§ 81.003. Fees and Costs Paid by Party Found to Have Committed Family Violence

(a) Except on a showing of good cause or of the indigence of a party found to have committed family violence, the court shall require in a protective order that the party against whom the order is rendered pay the $16 protective order fee, the standard fees charged by the clerk of the court in a general civil proceeding for the cost of serving the order, the costs of court, and all other fees, charges, or expenses incurred in connection with the protective order.

(b) The court may order a party against whom an agreed protective order is rendered under Section 85.005 to pay the fees required in Subsection (a).

§ 81.004. Contempt for Nonpayment of Fee

(a) A party who is ordered to pay fees and costs and who does not pay before the date specified by the order may be punished for contempt of court as provided by Section 21.002, Government Code.

(b) If a date is not specified by the court under Subsection (a), payment of costs is required before the 60th day after the date the order was rendered.

§ 81.005. Attorney's Fees

(a) The court may assess reasonable attorney's fees against the party found to have committed family violence or a party against whom an agreed protective order is rendered under Section

85.005 as compensation for the services of a private or prosecuting attorney or an attorney employed by the Department of **Family and** Protective ~~and Regulatory~~ Services.

(b) In setting the amount of attorney's fees, the court shall consider the income and ability to pay of the person against whom the fee is assessed.

Amended by Acts 2011, 82nd Leg., ch. 110 (H.B. 841), § 4, eff. May 21, 2011.

Leading Cases

In re A.W.R., a Child, ___ S.W.3d ___, 2010 WL 3272304 (Tex. App.—Waco 2010, no pet.) (Respondent's claims that 81.005 and 81.006 violate due process and equal protection are denied. Court cannot say that Respondent is treated disparately when Applicant represented by State's attorney.)

In re Skero, 253 S.W.3d 884 (Tex. App.—Beaumont 2008, no pet.) (attorneys fees awarded in protective order proceeding enforceable by contempt)

In re S.S., 217 S.W.3d 685 (Tex. App.—Eastland 2007, no pet.) (ex-wife awarded attorney's fees after ex-husband's unsuccessful appeal of protective order)

§ 81.006. Payment of Attorney's Fees

The amount of fees collected under this chapter as compensation for the fees:

(1) of a private attorney shall be paid to the private attorney who may enforce the order for fees in the attorney's own name;

(2) of a prosecuting attorney shall be paid to the credit of the county fund from which the salaries of the employees of the prosecuting attorney are paid or supplemented; and

(3) of an attorney employed by the Department of **Family and** Protective ~~and Regulatory~~ Services shall be deposited in the general revenue fund to the credit of the Department of **Family and** Protective ~~and Regulatory~~ Services.

Amended by Acts 2011, 82nd Leg., ch. 110 (H.B. 841), § 5, eff. May 21, 2011.

Leading Case

In re A.W.R., a Child, 2010 WL 3272304 (Tex. App.—Waco 2010) (Court cannot say that Respondent is treated disparately when Applicant represented by state's attorney)

§ 81.007. Prosecuting Attorney

(a) The county attorney or the criminal district attorney is the prosecuting attorney responsible for filing applications under this subtitle unless the district attorney assumes the responsibility by giving notice of that assumption to the county attorney.

(b) The prosecuting attorney responsible for filing an application under this subtitle shall provide notice of that responsibility to all law enforcement agencies in the jurisdiction of the prosecuting attorney.

(c) The prosecuting attorney shall comply with Article 5.06, Code of Criminal Procedure, in filing an application under this subtitle.

Comment

Despite this section of the code, there are still counties in Texas where there is no prosecutor who files protective orders on behalf of their constituents. In some counties where prosecutors are filing protective orders, they have office policies unrelated to the statutory requirements that limit those who would otherwise be eligible for protective orders.

§ 81.0075. Representation by Prosecuting Attorney in Certain Subsequent Actions

A prosecuting attorney who represents a party in a proceeding under this subtitle is not precluded from representing the Department of **Family and** Protective ~~and Regulatory~~ Services in a subsequent action involving the party.

Amended by Acts 2011, 82nd Leg., ch. 110 (H.B. 841), § 6, eff. May 21, 2011.

§ 81.008. Relief Cumulative

Except as provided by this subtitle, the relief and remedies provided by this subtitle are cumulative of other relief and remedies provided by law.

§ 81.009. Appeal

(a) Except as provided by Subsections (b) and (c), a protective order rendered under this subtitle may be appealed.

(b) A protective order rendered against a party in a suit for dissolution of a marriage may not be appealed until the time the final decree of dissolution of the marriage becomes a final, appealable order.

(c) A protective order rendered against a party in a suit affecting the parent-child relationship may not be appealed until the time an order providing for support of the child or possession of or access to the child becomes a final, appealable order.

Comment

For several years the question of whether protective orders are final and subject to appellate review was a subject of debate. Seemingly the debate was resolved in 2005 when the general trend among appellate court decisions was codified. Nonappealable temporary protective orders entered in conjunction with ongoing litigation in a custody or divorce proceeding are to be distinguished from appealable orders rendered as final in that context and those requested in a stand-alone suit filed under Title 4.

From 1982 through March, 2005, at least 28 appellate court decisions were published on the issue of whether a protective order was appealable. The nuanced answer, distinguishing between a Title 4 protective order and a Title 5 protective order, was long overdue. Obtaining a Title 4 order is the essence of the litigation—a right to appeal the final act of the trial court seems the only logical consequence. Orders which are deemed interlocutory under Title 5 should not be appealable until the divorce or SAPCR decree is final. Orders rendered at the conclusion of this specialized litigation, when continued in effect, are appropriately appealable.

Leading Case

Keck v. Loftin, 329 S.W.3d 658 (Tex. App.—Houston [14th Dist.] 2010) (despite the fact that a SAPCR was pending, protective order is final appealable order since the P.O. and SAPCR were filed in different courts with different cause numbers)

Thompson v. Thompson, 2008 WL 4793648 (Tex. App.—Tyler, 2008) (appeals of protective orders will not be entertained while a divorce is pending—must wait until the divorce is final)

---

§ 81.010. Court Enforcement

(a) A court of this state with jurisdiction of proceedings arising under this title may enforce a protective order rendered by another court in the same manner that the court that rendered the order could enforce the order, regardless of whether the order is transferred under Subchapter D, Chapter 85.

(b) A court's authority under this section includes the authority to enforce a protective order through contempt.

(c) A motion for enforcement of a protective order rendered under this title may be filed in:

(1) any court in the county in which the order was rendered with jurisdiction of proceedings arising under this title;

(2) a county in which the movant or respondent resides; or

(3) a county in which an alleged violation of the order occurs.

Added by Acts 2011, 82nd Leg., ch. 632 (S.B. 819), § 1, eff. Sept. 1, 2011.

Comments

This section clarifies where actions for the enforcement of protective orders may be brought—particularly in those situations where the enforcement is brought in a court other than the one that issued the order.

CHAPTER 82. APPLYING FOR PROTECTIVE ORDER

SUBCHAPTER A. APPLICATION FOR PROTECTIVE ORDER

SUBCHAPTER B. PLEADINGS BY RESPONDENT

SUBCHAPTER C. NOTICE OF APPLICATION FOR PROTECTIVE ORDER

SUBCHAPTER A. APPLICATION FOR PROTECTIVE ORDER

§ 82.001. Application

A proceeding under this subtitle is begun by filing "An Application for a Protective Order" with the clerk of the court.

§ 82.002. Who May File Application

(a) With regard to family violence under Section 71.004(1) or (2), an adult member of the family or household may file an application for a protective order to protect the applicant or any other member of the applicant's family or household

(b) With regard to family violence under Section 71.004(3), an application for a protective order to protect the applicant may be filed by:

(1) a ~~an adult~~ member of the dating relationship**, regardless of whether the member is an adult or a child; or**

(2) an adult member of the marriage, if the victim is or was married as described by Section 71.0021(a)(1)(B).

(c) Any adult may apply for a protective order to protect a child from family violence.

(d) In addition, an application may be filed for the protection of any person alleged to be a victim of family violence by:

(1) a prosecuting attorney; or

(2) the Department of **Family and** Protective ~~and Regulatory~~ Services.

(e) The person alleged to be the victim of family violence in an application filed under Subsection (c) or (d) is considered to be the applicant for a protective order under this subtitle.

Amended by Acts 2011, 82nd Leg., ch. 110 (H.B. 841), § 7, eff. May 21, 2011; Acts 2011, 82nd Leg., ch. 632 (S.B. 819), § 2, eff. Sept. 1, 2011; Acts 2011, 82nd Leg., ch. 872 (S.B. 116), § 3, eff. June 14, 2011.

Comment

Until 2011, a minor child would have to find an adult to file an application for a protective order on their behalf. However, with new legislation children in dating relationships may file for a protective order on their own behalf. It is still true, however, that any adult may apply for a protective order for the benefit of a child, including a child who is a victim of dating violence.

Leading Cases

Wilkerson v. Wilkerson, 321 S.W.3d 110 (Tex. App.—Houston 2010, reh. overruled) ("member of the family or household" includes stepparent's relationship to stepchild even after the marriage ends, so long as parent and stepparent have a living child together)

B.C. v. Rhodes, 116 S.W.3d 878 (Tex. App.—Austin 2003, no pet.) (because "dating violence" is expressly defined as a type of "family violence," any adult may apply for a protective order to protect a child from dating violence)

§ 82.003. Venue

An application may be filed in:

(1) the county in which the applicant resides; or

(2) the county in which the respondent resides.

Comment

The ability of the applicant to file in his or her own county of residence is a significant departure from TEX. PRAC. & REM. CODE ANN. § 15.002, but certainly not without precedent in the Texas Family Code.

Leading Case

Magill v. Sheffield, 612 S.W.2d 677 (Tex. Civ. App.—Dallas 1981, no writ) (venue for protective order governed by Title 4; continuing jurisdiction of SAPCR court not relevant)

§ 82.004. Contents of Application

An application must state:

(1) the name and county of residence of each applicant;

(2) the name and county of residence of each individual alleged to have committed family violence;

(3) the relationships between the applicants and the individual alleged to have committed family violence; and

(4) a request for one or more protective orders.

§ 82.005. Application Filed During Suit for Dissolution of Marriage or Suit Affecting Parent-Child Relationship

A person who wishes to apply for a protective order with respect to the person's spouse and who is a party to a suit for the dissolution of a marriage or a suit affecting the parent-child relationship that is pending in a court must file the application as required by Subchapter D, Chapter 85.

§ 82.006. Application Filed After Dissolution of Marriage

If an applicant for a protective order is a former spouse of the individual alleged to have committed family violence, the application must include:

(1) a copy of the decree dissolving the marriage; or

(2) a statement that the decree is unavailable to the applicant and that a copy of the decree will be filed with the court before the hearing on the application.

§ 82.007. Application Filed for Child Subject to Continuing Jurisdiction

An application that requests a protective order for a child who is subject to the continuing exclusive jurisdiction of a court under Title 5 or alleges that a child who is subject to the continuing exclusive jurisdiction of a court under Title 5 has committed family violence must include:

(1) a copy of each court order affecting the conservatorship, support, and possession of or access to the child; or

(2) a statement that the orders affecting the child are unavailable to the applicant and that a copy of the orders will be filed with the court before the hearing on the application.

§ 82.008. Application Filed After Expiration of Former Protective Order

(a) An application for a protective order that is filed after a previously rendered protective order has expired must include:

(1) a copy of the expired protective order attached to the application or, if a copy of the expired protective order is unavailable, a statement that the order is unavailable to the applicant and that a copy of the order will be filed with the court before the hearing on the application;

(2) a description of either:

(A) the violation of the expired protective order, if the application alleges that the respondent violated the expired protective order by committing an act prohibited by that order before the order expired; or

(B) the threatened harm that reasonably places the applicant in fear of imminent physical harm, bodily injury, assault, or sexual assault; and

(3) if a violation of the expired order is alleged, a statement that the violation of the expired order has not been grounds for any other order protecting the applicant that has been issued or requested under this subtitle.

(b) The procedural requirements for an original application for a protective order apply to a protective order requested under this section.

§ 82.0085. Application Filed Before Expiration of Previously Rendered Protective Order

(a) If an application for a protective order alleges that an unexpired protective order applicable to the respondent is due to expire not later than the 30th day after the date the application was filed, the application for the subsequent protective order must include:

(1) a copy of the previously rendered protective order attached to the application or, if a copy of the previously rendered protective order is unavailable, a statement that the order is unavailable to the applicant and that a copy of the order will be filed with the court before the hearing on the application; and

(2) a description of the threatened harm that reasonably places the applicant in fear of imminent physical harm, bodily injury, assault, or sexual assault.

(b) The procedural requirements for an original application for a protective order apply to a protective order requested under this section.

§ 82.009. Application for Temporary ex Parte Order

(a) An application that requests the issuance of a temporary ex parte order under Chapter 83 must:

(1) contain a detailed description of the facts and circumstances concerning the alleged family violence and the need for the immediate protective order; and

(2) be signed by each applicant under an oath that the facts and circumstances contained in the application are true to the best knowledge and belief of each applicant.

(b) For purposes of this section, a statement signed under oath by a child is valid if the statement otherwise complies with this chapter.

Amended by Acts 2011, 82nd Leg., ch. 632 (S.B. 819), § 3, eff. Sept. 1, 2011.

Comment

It is clear that minors may sign the affidavit required for ex parte relief.

---

§ 82.010. Confidentiality of Application

(a) This section applies only in a county with a population of 3.4 million or more.

(b) Except as otherwise provided by law, an application for a protective order is confidential, is excepted from required public disclosure under Chapter 552, Government Code, and may not be released to a person who is not a respondent to the application until after the date of service of notice of the application or the date of the hearing on the application, whichever date is sooner.

(c) Except as otherwise provided by law, an application requesting the issuance of a temporary ex parte order under Chapter 83 is confidential, is excepted from required public disclosure under Chapter 552, Government Code, and may not be released to a person who is not a respondent to the application until after the date that the court or law enforcement informs the respondent of the court's order.

Comment

For some time family law attorneys in Harris County have complained about a local practice that arguably created an unreasonable risk of harm for applicants for protective orders, to wit; notification of a respondent regarding the filing of an application for protective order before the respondent was served notice of the application as a method of solicitation for legal services by an enterprising attorney. Particularly in the protective order context, such early notification of the respondent might facilitate additional domestic violence.

For Harris County only, a delay in full public disclosure at the time of filing is statutorily mandated for three types of suits: divorce, SAPCRs, and protective order applications. If the Houston practice of early notice of filed family law litigation spreads to other counties, the limitation of the statute to Harris County may be expanded to apply statewide.

SUBCHAPTER B. PLEADINGS BY RESPONDENT

§ 82.021. Answer

A respondent to an application for a protective order who is served with notice of an application for a protective order may file an answer at any time before the hearing. A respondent is not required to file an answer to the application.

§ 82.022. Request by Respondent for Protective Order

To apply for a protective order, a respondent to an application for a protective order must file a separate application.

Comment

In some cases, respondents claim that the applicant has committed family violence against them. This section of the code requires that the respondent file a written application for a protective order instead of arriving at the hearing and orally requesting a protective order. This requirement gives the applicant proper notice that a protective order is being sought against her or him.

Leading Case

State for Protection of Cockerham v. Cockerham, 218 S.W.3d 298 (Tex. App.—Texarkana 2007, no pet.) (court cannot issue a protective order for a person who has not filed an application, expired protective order is subject to review due to the collateral consequences exception to mootness doctrine)

SUBCHAPTER C. NOTICE OF APPLICATION FOR PROTECTIVE ORDER

§ 82.041. Contents of Notice of Application

(a) A notice of an application for a protective order must:

(1) be styled "The State of Texas";

(2) be signed by the clerk of the court under the court's seal;

(3) contain the name and location of the court;

(4) show the date the application was filed;

(5) show the date notice of the application for a protective order was issued;

(6) show the date, time, and place of the hearing;

(7) show the file number;

(8) show the name of each applicant and each person alleged to have committed family violence;

(9) be directed to each person alleged to have committed family violence;

(10) show the name and address of the attorney for the applicant or the mailing address of the applicant, if the applicant is not represented by an attorney; and

(11) contain the address of the clerk of the court.

(b) The notice of an application for a protective order must state: "An application for a protective order has been filed in the court stated in this notice alleging that you have committed family violence. You may employ an attorney to defend you against this allegation. You or your attorney may, but are not required to, file a written answer to the application. Any answer must be filed before the hearing on the application. If you receive this notice within 48 hours before the time set for the hearing, you may request the court to reschedule the hearing not later than 14 days after the date set for the hearing. If you do not attend the hearing, a default judgment may be taken and a protective order may be issued against you."

§ 82.042. Issuance of Notice of Application

(a) On the filing of an application, the clerk of the court shall issue a notice of an application for a protective order and deliver the notice as directed by the applicant.

(b) On request by the applicant, the clerk of the court shall issue a separate or additional notice of an application for a protective order.

§ 82.043. Service of Notice of Application

(a) Each respondent to an application for a protective order is entitled to service of notice of an application for a protective order.

(b) An applicant for a protective order shall furnish the clerk with a sufficient number of copies of the application for service on each respondent.

(c) Notice of an application for a protective order must be served in the same manner as citation under the Texas Rules of Civil Procedure, except that service by publication is not authorized.

(d) Service of notice of an application for a protective order is not required before the issuance of a temporary ex parte order under Chapter 83.

(e) The requirements of service of notice under this subchapter do not apply if the application is filed as a motion in a suit for dissolution of a marriage. Notice for the motion is given in the same manner as any other motion in a suit for dissolution of a marriage.

Comment

Because the protective order has the unusual quality of being criminally enforceable, service by publication, typically allowable in a civil case, is not an acceptable form of service in a protective order case.

CHAPTER 83. TEMPORARY EX PARTE ORDERS

---

§ 83.001. Requirements for Temporary ex Parte Order

(a) If the court finds from the information contained in an application for a protective order that there is a clear and present danger of family violence, the court, without further notice to the individual alleged to have committed family violence and without a hearing, may enter a temporary ex parte order for the protection of the applicant or any other member of the family or household of the applicant.

(b) In a temporary ex parte order, the court may direct a respondent to do or refrain from doing specified acts.

§ 83.002. Duration of Order; Extension

(a) A temporary ex parte order is valid for the period specified in the order, not to exceed 20 days.

(b) On the request of an applicant or on the court's own motion, a temporary ex parte order may be extended for additional 20-day periods.

Comment

Temporary ex parte protective orders historically have been enforced through contempt proceedings as opposed to arrest, due to the lack of due process on the respondent who typically is not present when the order is rendered. However, effective November 6, 2007, the Texas Constitution was amended to specifically provide that, along with magistrate's emergency protective orders and regular protective orders, a respondent who has violated a temporary ex parte order after having been served with the order may be arrested. Further, the respondent "may be taken into custody and, pending trial or other court proceedings, denied release on bail if following a hearing a judge or magistrate in this state determines by a preponderance of the evidence that the person violated the order or engaged in the conduct constituting the offense." TEX. CONST. ART. 1, § 11C.

Leading Case

Amir-Sharif v. Hawkins, 246 S.W.3d 267 (Tex. App.—Dallas 2007, rev. dismissed w.o.j.) (repeated extensions of ex parte order was allowed where respondent being evaluated for competency to stand trial)

---

§ 83.003. Bond Not Required

The court, at the court's discretion, may dispense with the necessity of a bond for a temporary ex parte order.

§ 83.004. Motion to Vacate

Any individual affected by a temporary ex parte order may file a motion at any time to vacate the order. On the filing of the motion to vacate, the court shall set a date for hearing the motion as soon as possible.

10/30

§ 83.005. Conflicting Orders

During the time the order is valid, a temporary ex parte order prevails over any other court order made under Title 5 to the extent of any conflict between the orders.

Comment

In 2003, the legislature addressed the confusion caused by the entry of a temporary ex parte order under Title 4 after the entry of a magistrate's order of emergency protection under TEX. CRIM. PROC. CODE. art. 17.292. That statute provides that the terms and conditions imposed by the magistrate's order prevail unless the court issuing the subsequent temporary ex parte order is informed of the existence of the magistrate's order, and makes a finding that the court is superseding the magistrate's order. The terms of a final protective order rendered after a magistrate's order of emergency protection always prevail over the magistrate's order.

---

§ 83.006. Exclusion of Party From Residence

(a) Subject to the limitations of Section 85.021(2), a person may only be excluded from the occupancy of the person's residence by a temporary ex parte order under this chapter if the applicant:

(1) files a sworn affidavit that provides a detailed description of the facts and circumstances requiring the exclusion of the person from the residence; and

(2) appears in person to testify at a temporary ex parte hearing to justify the issuance of the order without notice.

(b) Before the court may render a temporary ex parte order excluding a person from the person's residence, the court must find from the required affidavit and testimony that:

(1) the applicant requesting the excluding order either resides on the premises or has resided there within 30 days before the date the application was filed;

(2) the person to be excluded has within the 30 days before the date the application was filed committed family violence against a member of the household; and

(3) there is a clear and present danger that the person to be excluded is likely to commit family violence against a member of the household.

(c) The court may recess the hearing on a temporary ex parte order to contact the respondent by telephone and provide the respondent the opportunity to be present when the court resumes the hearing. Without regard to whether the respondent is able to be present at the hearing, the court shall resume the hearing before the end of the working day.

Amended by Acts 2011, 82nd Leg., ch. 632 (S.B. 819), § 4, eff. Sept. 1, 2011.

§ 83.007. ~~Recess of Hearing to Contact Respondent~~

~~The court may recess the hearing on a temporary ex parte order to contact the respondent by telephone and provide the respondent the opportunity to be present when the court resumes the hearing. Without regard to whether the respondent is able to be present at the hearing, the court shall resume the hearing before the end of the working day.~~

Repealed by Acts 2011, 82nd Leg., ch. 632 (S.B. 819), § 6(1), eff. Sept. 1, 2011.

CHAPTER 84. HEARING

---

§ 84.001. Time Set for Hearing

(a) On the filing of an application for a protective order, the court shall set a date and time for the hearing unless a later date is requested by the applicant. Except as provided by Section 84.002, the court may not set a date later than the 14th day after the date the application is filed.

(b) The court may not delay a hearing on an application in order to consolidate it with a hearing on a subsequently filed application.

Comment

As a defensive measure, respondents in protective order cases sometimes counter-file protective order applications and request that the hearing be delayed in order to have the two cases heard together. This section of the code prevents this strategic maneuver.

Leading Case

In re Barbee, 2010 WL 3341518 (Tex. App.—Tyler 2010, no pet.) (mandamus not available where appellant/respondent failed to provide any authority for his premise that failure to set a P.O. hearing within fourteen days results in the court losing jurisdiction.)

---

§ 84.002. Extended Time for Hearing in District Court In Certain Counties

(a) On the request of the prosecuting attorney in a county with a population of more than **two** ~~1.5~~ million or in a county in a judicial district that is composed of more than one county, the district court shall set the hearing on a date and time not later than 20 days after the date the application is filed or 20 days after the date a request is made to reschedule a hearing under Section 84.003.

(b) The district court shall grant the request of the prosecuting attorney for an extended time in which to hold a hearing on a protective order either on a case-by-case basis or for all cases filed under this subtitle.

Amended by Acts 2011, 82nd Leg., ch. 1163 (H.B. 2702), § 17, eff. Sept. 1, 2011.

§ 84.003. Hearing Rescheduled for Failure of Service

(a) If a hearing set under this chapter is not held because of the failure of a respondent to receive service of notice of an application for a protective order, the applicant may request the court to reschedule the hearing.

(b) Except as provided by Section 84.002, the date for a rescheduled hearing shall be not later than 14 days after the date the request is made.

§ 84.004. Hearing Rescheduled for Insufficient Notice

(a) If a respondent receives service of notice of an application for a protective order within 48 hours before the time set for the hearing, on request by the respondent, the court shall reschedule the hearing for a date not later than 14 days after the date set for the hearing.

(b) The respondent is not entitled to additional service for a hearing rescheduled under this section.

§ 84.005. Legislative Continuance

If a proceeding for which a legislative continuance is sought under Section 30.003, Civil Practice and Remedies Code, includes an application for a protective order, the continuance is discretionary with the court.

§ 84.006. Hearsay Statement of Child Victim of Family Violence

In a hearing on an application for a protective order, a statement made by a child 12 years of age or younger that describes alleged family violence against the child is admissible as evidence in the same manner that a child's statement regarding alleged abuse against the child is admissible under Section 104.006 in a suit affecting the parent-child relationship.

Added by Acts 2011, 82nd Leg., ch. 59 (H.B. 905), § 1, eff. Sept. 1, 2011.

Comment

In 2011 the Texas Legislature added this section to clarify that certain hearsay statements of children are admissible in a P.O. proceeding just as they are in a SAPCR proceeding.

CHAPTER 85. ISSUANCE OF PROTECTIVE ORDER

SUBCHAPTER A. FINDINGS AND ORDERS

SUBCHAPTER B. CONTENTS OF PROTECTIVE ORDER

SUBCHAPTER C. DELIVERY OF PROTECTIVE ORDER

SUBCHAPTER D. RELATIONSHIP BETWEEN PROTECTIVE ORDER AND SUIT FOR DISSOLUTION OF MARRIAGE AND SUIT AFFECTING PARENT-CHILD RELATIONSHIP

Comment

In 1999, the legislature significantly enhanced the effectiveness of protective orders by extending their duration from a maximum of one year to two years. In 2011, the legislature gave courts permission to use their discretion to determine the length of protective orders under circumstances where the violence caused serious injury or where previous protective orders were violated causing the applicant to re-apply for a protective order on more than one occasion. This amendment will potentially allow for permanent protective orders in the most serious cases, shifting the burden of lifting the protective order to the bad actor instead of requiring the victim to go back to court every two years to get a new protective order.

Leading Cases

Mercer v. State, 2008 WL 2930290 (Tex. App.—Corpus Christi 2008, no pet.)(not released for publication)(questions about applicant's supposed probation violations were not relevant in a family violence protective order hearing, and thus the trial court did not abuse its discretion in halting the cross-examination)

In re Compton, 117 S.W.3d 548 (Tex. App.—Texarkana 2003, no pet.) (transfer protective order action to court in which divorce or custody suit is pending discretionary; statutory scheme recognizes two actions might proceed simultaneously); accord Bilyeu v. Bilyeu, 86 S.W.3d 278 (Tex. App.—Austin 2002, no pet.)

In re Marriage of Edwards, 79 S.W.3d 88 (Tex. App.—Texarkana 2002, no. pet.) (protective order against husband issued in conjunction with divorce must be in separate document)

Sisk v. State, 74 S.W.3d 893 (Tex. App.—Fort Worth 2002, no pet.) (defendant more than once intentionally followed alleged victim knowing she would regard his conduct as threatening bodily injury)

Ex parte Pool, 71 S.W.3d 462 (Tex. App.—Tyler 2002, no pet.) (defendant pled guilty to violation of a protective order to escape burglary charge stemming from the same incident—not double jeopardy)

Williams v. Williams, 19 S.W.3d 544 (Tex. App.—Fort Worth 2000, pet. denied) (denial of in-court request for a jury trial at time of hearing not abuse of discretion—husband not entitled to jury determination of whether family violence occurred or likely to occur in future); *accord* Teel v. Shifflett, 309 S.W.3d 597 (Tex. App.—Houston [14 Dist.] 2010)

Poteet v. State, 957 S.W.2d 165 (Tex. App.—Fort Worth 1997, no writ) (respondent who appeared at hearing on protective order cannot collaterally attack its validity by alleging failure of service)

SUBCHAPTER A. FINDINGS AND ORDERS

§ 85.001. Required Findings and Orders

(a) At the close of a hearing on an application for a protective order, the court shall find whether:

(1) family violence has occurred; and

(2) family violence is likely to occur in the future.

(b) If the court finds that family violence has occurred and that family violence is likely to occur in the future, the court:

(1) shall render a protective order as provided by Section 85.022 applying only to a person found to have committed family violence; and

(2) may render a protective order as provided by Section 85.021 applying to both parties that is in the best interest of the person protected by the order or member of the family or household of the person protected by the order.

(c) A protective order that requires the first applicant to do or refrain from doing an act under Section 85.022 shall include a finding that the first applicant has committed family violence and is likely to commit family violence in the future.

(d) If the court renders a protective order for a period of more than two years, the court must include in the order a finding described by Section 85.025(a-1).

Amended by Acts 2011, 82nd Leg., ch. 627 (S.B. 789), § 1, eff. Sept. 1, 2011.

Comment

Historically, judges would often enter mutual protective orders against both parties without a written pleading from the respondent. In addition, applicants would sometimes agree to mutual protective orders to avoid acrimonious hearings, then find themselves haunted by the protective order against them in future divorce and custody proceedings. Additionally, law enforcement officers called out on protective order violations where the protective order was mutual faced the dilemma of who to arrest. Often, the police would arrest both or neither of the parties.

This section corresponds with the provisions of the federal Violence Against Women Act (18 U.S.C. 2265(c)) and § 88.003(g) of this code that discourage the entry of mutual protective orders unless both parties have filed written pleadings and can prove the elements for a protective order.

Leading Cases

In re I.E.W., 2010 WL 3418276 (Tex. App.—Corpus Christi 2010, no pet.) (not released for publication) (A valid P.O.—even an agreed one—requires findings that family violence occurred and is likely to occur again in the future.)

In re Wean, 2010 WL 3431708 (Tex. App.–Austin 2010, no pet.) (for corporal punishment to constitute family violence there must be some evidence that the punishment transcends reasonable parental discretion looking at the severity of injury, type of instrument used, and mental or emotional state of person applying corporal punishment)

Teel v. Shifflett, 309 S.W.3d 597 (Tex. App.—Houston [14 Dist.] 2010, no pet.) (evidence of past abusive behavior permits an inference that violence likely to occur in the future)

Bruhl v. Roberts, 2009 WL 2461295 (Tex. App.—Beaumont, 2009, no pet.) (not released for publication)(multiple instances of past violence, threats to kill, as well as a particularly vicious attack in which appellant attempted to strangle appellee and shot at her with a pistol was more than a scintilla of evidence to support the trial court's finding of a likelihood of future violence)

Gonzalez v. Galvan, 2009 WL 1089472 (Tex. App.—Corpus Christi, 2009, no pet.)(not released for publication) (trial court's ruling that evidence did not support a finding that family violence was likely to occur in the future despite the court's observation that the parties should "Get away from one another and knock it off before one of you ends up in prison because that's where this is going")

In re Epperson, 213 S.W.3d 541 (Tex. App.—Texarkana 2006, no pet.) (threats by former live in boyfriend sufficient to warrant protective order; past violent behavior is indicator of a likelihood to commit future violence)

§ 85.002. Exception for Violation of Expired Protective Order

If the court finds that a respondent violated a protective order by committing an act prohibited by the order as provided by Section 85.022, that the order was in effect at the time of the violation, and that the order has expired after the date that the violation occurred, the court, without the necessity of making the findings described by Section 85.001(a), shall render a protective order as provided by Section 85.022 applying only to the respondent and may render a protective order as provided by Section 85.021.

Leading Case

Sharpe v. McDole, 2010 WL 2010849, (Tex. App.—Austin 2010, no pet. hist.) (the only finding necessary on the application for a second protective order based on the violation of a first protective order is whether the Respondent violated the first protective order; Applicant's violations of the protective order, if any, are irrelevant)

§ 85.003. Separate Protective Orders Required

(a) A court that renders separate protective orders that apply to both parties and require both parties to do or refrain from doing acts under Section 85.022 shall render two distinct and separate protective orders in two separate documents that reflect the appropriate conditions for each party.

(b) A court that renders protective orders that apply to both parties and require both parties to do or refrain from doing acts under Section 85.022 shall render the protective orders in two separate documents. The court shall provide one of the documents to the applicant and the other document to the respondent.

(c) A court may not render one protective order under Section 85.022 that applies to both parties.

10/30/12

Leading Case

Moreno v. Moore, 897 S.W.2d 439 (Tex. App.—Corpus Christi 1995, no writ) (mutual protective order void; requirements of the source statute prior to the 1997 recodification not complied with)

---

§ 85.004. Protective Order in Suit for Dissolution of Marriage

A protective order in a suit for dissolution of a marriage must be in a separate document entitled "PROTECTIVE ORDER."

§ 85.005. Agreed Order

(a) To facilitate settlement, the parties to a proceeding may agree in writing to the terms of a protective order as provided by Section 85.021. An agreement under this subsection is subject to the approval of the court.

(b) To facilitate settlement, a respondent may agree in writing to the terms of a protective order as provided by Section 85.022, subject to the approval of the court. The court may not approve an agreement that requires the applicant to do or refrain from doing an act under Section 85.022. The agreed order is enforceable civilly or criminally.

(c) If the court approves an agreement between the parties, the court shall render an agreed protective order that is in the best interest of the applicant, the family or household, or a member of the family or household.

(d) An agreed protective order is not enforceable as a contract.

(e) An agreed protective order expires on the date the court order expires.

Comment

An agreed protective order is enforceable in the same manner as a protective order granted subsequent to an evidentiary hearing. Why there ever was a question on this point is unclear. After all, agreed orders in family law litigation are the rule, not the exception.

Leading Case

U.S. v. Spruill, 292 F.3d 207 (5th Cir. Tex. 2002) ("agreed" protective order issued without hearing failed to satisfy criminal statute's "after a hearing" requirement)

---

§ 85.006. Default Order

(a) A court may render a protective order that is binding on a respondent who does not attend a hearing if the respondent received service of the application and notice of the hearing.

(b) If the court reschedules the hearing under Chapter 84, a protective order may be rendered if the respondent does not attend the rescheduled hearing.

Leading Case

Amir-Sharif v. Hawkins, 246 S.W.3d 267 (Tex. App.—Dallas 2007) (failure to appear at a protective order hearing after proper notice does not deprive respondent of his right to confront his accuser)

excludes Address/Phone if you move

§ 85.007. Confidentiality of Certain Information

(a) On request by a person protected by an order or member of the family or household of a person protected by an order, the court may exclude from a protective order the address and telephone number of:

(1) a person protected by the order, in which case the order shall state the county in which the person resides;

10/30/12

(2) the place of employment or business of a person protected by the order; or

(3) the child-care facility or school a child protected by the order attends or in which the child resides.

(b) On granting a request for confidentiality under this section, the court shall order the clerk to:

(1) strike the information described by Subsection (a) from the public records of the court; and

(2) maintain a confidential record of the information for use only by the court.

§ 85.008. Repealed.

§ 85.009. Order Valid Until Superseded

A protective order rendered under this chapter is valid and enforceable pending further action by the court that rendered the order until the order is properly superseded by another court with jurisdiction over the order.

SUBCHAPTER B. CONTENTS OF PROTECTIVE ORDER

§ 85.021. Requirements of Order Applying to Any Party

In a protective order, the court may:

(1) prohibit a party from:

(A) removing a child who is a member of the family or household from:

(i) the possession of a person named in the order; or

(ii) the jurisdiction of the court; ~~or~~

(B) transferring, encumbering, or otherwise disposing of property, other than in the ordinary course of business, that is mutually owned or leased by the parties; **or**

(C) removing a pet, companion animal, or assistance animal, as defined by Section 121.002, Human Resources Code, from the possession of a person named in the order;

(2) grant exclusive possession of a residence to a party and, if appropriate, direct one or more parties to vacate the residence if the residence:

(A) is jointly owned or leased by the party receiving exclusive possession and a party being denied possession;

(B) is owned or leased by the party retaining possession; or

(C) is owned or leased by the party being denied possession and that party has an obligation to support the party or a child of the party granted possession of the residence;

(3) provide for the possession of and access to a child of a party if the person receiving possession of or access to the child is a parent of the child;

(4) require the payment of support for a party or for a child of a party if the person required to make the payment has an obligation to support the other party or the child; or

(5) award to a party the use and possession of specified property that is community property or jointly owned or leased property.

Amended by Acts 2011, 82nd Leg., ch. 136 (S.B. 279), § 1, eff. Sept. 1, 2011.

Comment

Similar to the connection between intimate partner violence and child abuse, there is also a link between family violence and abuse of animals. Recognizing this association, in 2011 the Texas legislature amended this section to add a prohibition against removing animals from the possession of a person named in the order.

In addition to safety, two big issues that cause people to stay in abusive relationships are finances and their children. This section of civilly enforceable provisions available in a protective order can be essential to helping applicants escape the abuse.

---

§ 85.022. Requirements of Order Applying to Person Who Committed Family Violence

(a) In a protective order, the court may order the person found to have committed family violence to perform acts specified by the court that the court determines are necessary or appropriate to prevent or reduce the likelihood of family violence and may order that person to:

(1) complete a battering intervention and prevention program accredited under Article 42.141, Code of Criminal Procedure;

(2) beginning on September 1, 2008, if the referral option under Subdivision (1) is not available, complete a program or counsel with a provider that has begun the accreditation process described by Subsection (a–1); or

(3) if the referral option under Subdivision (1) or, beginning on September 1, 2008, the referral option under Subdivision (2) is not available, counsel with a social worker, family service agency, physician, psychologist, licensed therapist, or licensed professional counselor who has completed family violence intervention training that the community justice assistance division of the Texas Department of Criminal Justice has approved, after consultation with the licensing authorities described by Chapters 152, 501, 502, 503, and 505, Occupations Code, and experts in the field of family violence.

(a–1) Beginning on September 1, 2009, a program or provider serving as a referral option for the courts under Subsection (a)(1) or (2) must be accredited under Section 4A, Article 42.141, Code of Criminal Procedure, as conforming to program guidelines under that article.

(b) In a protective order, the court may prohibit the person found to have committed family violence from:

(1) committing family violence;

(2) communicating:

(A) directly with a person protected by an order or a member of the family or household of a person protected by an order, in a threatening or harassing manner;

(B) a threat through any person to a person protected by an order or a member of the family or household of a person protected by an order; and

(C) if the court finds good cause, in any manner with a person protected by an order or a member of the family or household of a person protected by an order, except through the party's attorney or a person appointed by the court;

(3) going to or near the residence or place of employment or business of a person protected by an order or a member of the family or household of a person protected by an order;

(4) going to or near the residence, child-care facility, or school a child protected under the order normally attends or in which the child normally resides;

(5) engaging in conduct directed specifically toward a person who is a person protected by an order or a member of the family or household of a person protected by an order, including following the person, that is reasonably likely to harass, annoy, alarm, abuse, torment, or embarrass the person; ~~and~~

(6) possessing a firearm, unless the person is a peace officer, as defined by Section 1.07, Penal Code, actively engaged in employment as a sworn, full-time paid employee of a state agency or political subdivision; **and**

(7) harming, threatening, or interfering with the care, custody, or control of a pet, companion animal, or assistance animal, as defined by Section 121.002, Human Resources Code, that is possessed by a person protected by an order or by a member of the family or household of a person protected by an order.

(c) In an order under Subsection (b)(3) or (4), the court shall specifically describe each prohibited location and the minimum distances from the location, if any, that the party must maintain. This subsection does not apply to an order in which Section 85.007 applies.

(d) In a protective order, the court shall suspend a license to carry a concealed handgun issued under Subchapter H, Chapter 411, Government Code, that is held by a person found to have committed family violence.

(e) In this section, "firearm" has the meaning assigned by Section 46.01, Penal Code.

Amended by Acts 2011, 82nd Leg., ch. 136 (S.B. 279), § 2, eff. Sept. 1, 2011.

Comment

Subsection (b)(6) authorizes the court to prohibit a person from possessing a firearm for the duration of a protective order. This subsection conforms to the Penal Code regarding an offense for possession of a firearm by an individual while subject to an active protective order, or for possession of a firearm for five years following conviction for a family violence assault. TEX. PENAL CODE ANN. § 46.04. This legislation was enacted to give local law enforcement agencies authority to take action against weapons declared illegal by federal law (albeit rarely enforced in that context), *see* 18 U.S.C.A. §922(g)(8), (9). The "official use exemption" for on-duty peace officers mirrors language in the corresponding federal statute. 18 U.S.C.A. §922(a).

The 81st Texas Legislature amended this chapter to require, rather than permit, the court to suspend a license to carry a concealed handgun for someone who is the subject of a Protective Order. This amendment aligns state law to the existing federal law prohibiting those who are subject to protective orders from possessing a firearm. 18 U.S.C.A. §922(g).

In 2011, protection available was extended to prohibit a respondent from using pets or service animals to further abuse, harm, or threaten the applicant. One thing is certain; respondents are creative in their efforts engage in bad conduct, and the legislature has been responsive to requests to counter that creativity.

§ 85.023. Effect on Property Rights

A protective order or an agreement approved by the court under this subtitle does not affect the title to real property.

§ 85.024. Enforcement of Counseling Requirement

(a) A person found to have engaged in family violence who is ordered to attend a program or counseling under Section 85.022(a)(1), (2), or (3) shall file with the court an affidavit before the 60th day after the date the order was rendered stating either that the person has begun the program or counseling or that a program or counseling is not available within a reasonable distance from the person's residence. A person who files an affidavit that the person has begun the program or counseling shall file with the court before the date the protective order expires a statement that the person completed the program or counseling not later than the 30th day before the expiration date of the protective order or the 30th day before the first anniversary of the date the protective order was issued, whichever date is earlier. An affidavit under this subsection must be accompanied by a letter, notice, or certificate from the program or counselor that verifies the person's completion of the program or counseling. A person who fails to comply with this subsection may be punished for contempt of court under Section 21.002, Government Code.

(b) A protective order under Section 85.022 must specifically advise the person subject to the order of the requirement of this section and the possible punishment if the person fails to comply with the requirement.

10/30/12 2 years most orders - If doesn't state goes to 2nd Anniversary of date of order

§ 85.025. Duration of Protective Order

(a) Except as **otherwise** provided by **this section** ~~Subsection (b) or (c)~~, an order under this subtitle is effective:

(1) for the period stated in the order, not to exceed two years; or

(2) if a period is not stated in the order, until the second anniversary of the date the order was issued.

(a–1) The court may render a protective order sufficient to protect the applicant and members of the applicant's family or household that is effective for a period that exceeds two years if the court finds that the person who is the subject of the protective order:

(1) caused serious bodily injury to the applicant or a member of the applicant's family or household; or

(2) was the subject of two or more previous protective orders rendered:

(A) to protect the person on whose behalf the current protective order is sought; and

(B) after a finding by the court that the subject of the protective order:

(i) has committed family violence; and

(ii) is likely to commit family violence in the future.

(b) A person who is the subject of a protective order may file a motion not earlier than the first anniversary of the date on which the order was rendered requesting that the court review the protective order and determine whether there is a continuing need for the order. **A person who is the subject of a protective order under Subsection (a–1) that is effective for a period that exceeds two years may file a subsequent motion requesting that the court review the protective order and determine whether there is a continuing need for the order not earlier than the first anniversary of the date on which the court rendered an order on a previous motion by the person under this subsection.** After a hearing on the motion, if the court **does not make a finding that**~~finds~~ there is **no** ~~a~~continuing need for the protective order, the protective order remains in effect until the date the order expires under this section. **Evidence of the movant's compliance with the protective order does not by itself support a finding by the court that there is no continuing need for the protective order.** If the court finds there is no continuing need for the protective order, the court shall order that the protective order expires on a date set by the court.

(c) If a person who is the subject of a protective order is confined or imprisoned on the date the protective order would expire under Subsection (a) **or (a–1)**, the period for which the order is effective is extended, and the order expires on the first anniversary of the date the person is released from confinement or imprisonment.

Amended by Acts 2011, 82nd Leg., ch. 627 (S.B. 789), § 2, eff. Sept. 1, 2011.

Comment

One of the most far reaching amendments to this title in 2011 allows the court to enter a Protective Order of any duration in limited circumstances.

Leading Cases

In re I.E.W., 2010 WL 197270 (Tex. App.—Corpus Christi, 2010) (burden is on person requesting modification of protective order to establish that there was no "continuing need" for the order)

B.C. v. Rhodes, 116 S.W.3d 878 (Tex. App.—Austin 2003, no pet.) (protective orders generally in effect for the period stated, not to exceed two years or until modified by issuing court)

---

§ 85.026. Warning on Protective Order

(a) Each protective order issued under this subtitle, including a temporary ex parte order, must contain the following prominently displayed statements in boldfaced type, capital letters, or underlined:

"A PERSON WHO VIOLATES THIS ORDER MAY BE PUNISHED FOR CONTEMPT OF COURT BY A FINE OF AS MUCH AS $500 OR BY CONFINEMENT IN JAIL FOR AS LONG AS SIX MONTHS, OR BOTH."

"NO PERSON, INCLUDING A PERSON WHO IS PROTECTED BY THIS ORDER, MAY GIVE PERMISSION TO ANYONE TO IGNORE OR VIOLATE ANY PROVISION OF THIS ORDER. DURING THE TIME IN WHICH THIS ORDER IS VALID, EVERY PROVISION OF THIS ORDER IS IN FULL FORCE AND EFFECT UNLESS A COURT CHANGES THE ORDER."

"IT IS UNLAWFUL FOR ANY PERSON, OTHER THAN A PEACE OFFICER, AS DEFINED BY SECTION 1.07, PENAL CODE, ACTIVELY ENGAGED IN EMPLOYMENT AS A SWORN, FULL-TIME PAID EMPLOYEE OF A STATE AGENCY OR POLITICAL SUBDIVISION, WHO IS SUBJECT TO A PROTECTIVE ORDER TO POSSESS A FIREARM OR AMMUNITION."

"A VIOLATION OF THIS ORDER BY COMMISSION OF AN ACT PROHIBITED BY THE ORDER MAY BE PUNISHABLE BY A FINE OF AS MUCH AS $4,000 OR BY CONFINEMENT IN JAIL FOR AS LONG AS ONE YEAR, OR BOTH. AN ACT THAT RESULTS IN FAMILY VIOLENCE MAY BE PROSECUTED AS A SEPARATE MISDEMEANOR OR FELONY OFFENSE. IF THE ACT IS PROSECUTED AS A SEPARATE FELONY OFFENSE, IT IS PUNISHABLE BY CONFINEMENT IN PRISON FOR AT LEAST TWO YEARS."

~~(b) Each protective order issued under this subtitle, except for a temporary ex parte order, must contain the following prominently displayed statement in boldfaced type, capital letters, or underlined:~~

~~"A VIOLATION OF THIS ORDER BY COMMISSION OF AN ACT PROHIBITED BY THE ORDER MAY BE PUNISHABLE BY A FINE OF AS MUCH AS $4,000 OR BY CONFINEMENT IN JAIL FOR AS LONG AS ONE YEAR, OR BOTH. AN ACT THAT RESULTS IN FAMILY VIOLENCE MAY BE PROSECUTED AS A SEPARATE MISDEMEANOR OR FELONY OFFENSE. IF THE ACT IS PROSECUTED AS A SEPARATE FELONY OFFENSE, IT IS PUNISHABLE BY CONFINEMENT IN PRISON FOR AT LEAST TWO YEARS."~~

(c) Each protective order issued under this subtitle, including a temporary ex parte order, must contain the following prominently displayed statement in boldfaced type, capital letters, or underlined:

"NO PERSON, INCLUDING A PERSON WHO IS PROTECTED BY THIS ORDER, MAY GIVE PERMISSION TO ANYONE TO IGNORE OR VIOLATE ANY PROVISION OF THIS ORDER. DURING THE TIME IN WHICH THIS ORDER IS VALID, EVERY PROVISION OF THIS ORDER IS IN FULL FORCE AND EFFECT UNLESS A COURT CHANGES THE ORDER."

Amended by Acts 2011, 82nd Leg., ch. 632 (S.B. 819), §§ 5, 6(2), eff. Sept. 1, 2011.

SUBCHAPTER C. DELIVERY OF PROTECTIVE ORDER

§ 85.041. Delivery to Respondent

(a) A protective order rendered under this subtitle shall be:

(1) delivered to the respondent as provided by Rule 21a, Texas Rules of Civil Procedure;

(2) served in the same manner as a writ of injunction; or

(3) served in open court at the close of the hearing as provided by this section.

(b) The court shall serve an order in open court to a respondent who is present at the hearing by giving to the respondent a copy of the order, reduced to writing and signed by the judge or master. A certified copy of the signed order shall be given to the applicant at the time the order is given to the respondent. If the applicant is not in court at the conclusion of the hearing, the clerk of the court shall mail a certified copy of the order to the applicant not later than the third business day after the date the hearing is concluded.

(c) If the order has not been reduced to writing, the court shall give notice orally to a respondent who is present at the hearing of the part of the order that contains prohibitions under

Section 85.022 or any other part of the order that contains provisions necessary to prevent further family violence. The clerk of the court shall mail a copy of the order to the respondent and a certified copy of the order to the applicant not later than the third business day after the date the hearing is concluded.

(d) If the respondent is not present at the hearing and the order has been reduced to writing at the conclusion of the hearing, the clerk of the court shall immediately provide a certified copy of the order to the applicant and mail a copy of the order to the respondent not later than the third business day after the date the hearing is concluded.

§ 85.042. Delivery of Order to Other Persons

(a) The clerk of the court issuing an original or modified protective order under this subtitle shall send a copy of the order, along with the information provided by the applicant or the applicant's attorney that is required under Section 411.042(b)(6), Government Code, to the chief of police of the municipality in which the person protected by the order resides, if the person resides in a municipality, or to the appropriate constable and the sheriff of the county in which the person resides, if the person does not reside in a municipality.

(a–1) This subsection applies only if the respondent, at the time of issuance of an original or modified protective order under this subtitle, is a member of the state military forces or is serving in the armed forces of the United States in an active-duty status. In addition to complying with Subsection (a), the clerk of the court shall also provide a copy of the protective order and the information described by that subsection to the staff judge advocate at Joint Force Headquarters or the provost marshal of the military installation to which the respondent is assigned with the intent that the commanding officer will be notified, as applicable.

(b) If a protective order made under this chapter prohibits a respondent from going to or near a child-care facility or school, the clerk of the court shall send a copy of the order to the child-care facility or school.

(c) The clerk of a court that vacates an original or modified protective order under this subtitle shall notify **each individual or entity** ~~the chief of police or constable and sheriff~~ who received a copy of the original or modified order **from the clerk under this section** that the order is vacated.

(d) The applicant or the applicant's attorney shall provide to the clerk of the court:

(1) the name and address of each law enforcement agency, child-care facility, ~~and~~ school**, and other individual or entity** to which the clerk is required to mail a copy of the order under this section; and

(2) any other information required under Section 411.042(b)(6), Government Code.

(e) The clerk of the court issuing an original or modified protective order under Section 85.022 that suspends a license to carry a concealed handgun shall send a copy of the order to the appropriate division of the Department of Public Safety at its Austin headquarters. On receipt of the order suspending the license, the department shall:

(1) record the suspension of the license in the records of the department;

(2) report the suspension to local law enforcement agencies, as appropriate; and

(3) demand surrender of the suspended license from the license holder.

Amended by Acts 2011, 82nd Leg., ch. 327 (H.B. 2624), § 1, eff. Sept. 1, 2011.

Comment

In addition to the existing provisions requiring the clerk of the court to provide a copy of the protective order to schools and law enforcement, in 2011 this section was amended to require delivery of a copy of the order to the staff judge advocate at Joint Force Headquarters or the provost marshal of the military installation to which the respondent is assigned, if the respondent is a member of the military. The bill amending this section also amended Tex. Code of Crim. Proc. Articles 5.05 and 42.0182 to require notification of military officials if a suspect or defendant in a family violence case is a member of the military.

SUBCHAPTER D. RELATIONSHIP BETWEEN PROTECTIVE ORDER AND SUIT FOR DISSOLUTION OF MARRIAGE AND SUIT AFFECTING PARENT-CHILD RELATIONSHIP

Introductory Comment

This subchapter attempts to harmonize two conflicting policies: first, the need of a victim of family violence to have convenient access to court; and second, deciding which court order should prevail in the event of conflicting orders. As enacted, the protective order prevails even when there is a pending suit for dissolution of marriage or a SAPCR. The subchapter, however, does provide for a method to transfer protective orders back to the original court under § 85.064. The tension between these two conflicting legal policies will doubtless continue.

Leading Case

In re M.R., 975 S.W.2d 51 (Tex. App.—San Antonio 1998, pet. denied) (trial court mandated to consider evidence of domestic violence in making conservatorship decision)

---

§ 85.061. Dismissal of Application Prohibited; Subsequently Filed Suit for Dissolution of Marriage or Suit Affecting Parent-Child Relationship

If an application for a protective order is pending, a court may not dismiss the application or delay a hearing on the application on the grounds that a suit for dissolution of marriage or suit affecting the parent-child relationship is filed after the date the application was filed.

Comment

As a defensive measure respondents in protective order cases sometimes respond by filing divorce suits and request that the protective order hearing be delayed in order to have the two cases heard together. This section of the code prevents this strategic maneuver.

---

§ 85.062. Application Filed While Suit for Dissolution of Marriage or Suit Affecting Parent-Child Relationship Pending

(a) If a suit for dissolution of a marriage or suit affecting the parent-child relationship is pending, a party to the suit may apply for a protective order against another party to the suit by filing an application:

(1) in the court in which the suit is pending; or

(2) in a court in the county in which the applicant resides if the applicant resides outside the jurisdiction of the court in which the suit is pending.

(b) An applicant subject to this section shall inform the clerk of the court that renders a protective order that a suit for dissolution of a marriage or a suit affecting the parent-child relationship is pending in which the applicant is party.

(c) If a final protective order is rendered by a court other than the court in which a suit for dissolution of a marriage or a suit affecting the parent-child relationship is pending, the clerk of the court that rendered the protective order shall:

(1) inform the clerk of the court in which the suit is pending that a final protective order has been rendered; and

(2) forward a copy of the final protective order to the court in which the suit is pending.

(d) A protective order rendered by a court in which an application is filed under Subsection (a)(2) is subject to transfer under Section 85.064.

§ 85.063. Application Filed After Final Order Rendered in Suit for Dissolution of Marriage or Suit Affecting Parent-Child Relationship

(a) If a final order has been rendered in a suit for dissolution of marriage or suit affecting the parent-child relationship, an application for a protective order by a party to the suit against another party to the suit filed after the date the final order was rendered, and that is:

(1) filed in the county in which the final order was rendered, shall be filed in the court that rendered the final order; and

(2) filed in another county, shall be filed in a court having jurisdiction to render a protective order under this subtitle.

(b) A protective order rendered by a court in which an application is filed under Subsection (a)(2) is subject to transfer under Section 85.064.

Leading Case

Cooke v. Cooke, 65 S.W.3d 785 (Tex. App.—Dallas 2001, no pet.) (statutory requirements for filing protective order application in court that rendered divorce decree)

---

§ 85.064. Transfer of Protective Order

(a) If a protective order was rendered before the filing of a suit for dissolution of marriage or suit affecting the parent-child relationship or while the suit is pending as provided by Section 85.062, the court that rendered the order may, on the motion of a party or on the court's own motion, transfer the protective order to the court having jurisdiction of the suit if the court makes the finding prescribed by Subsection (c).

(b) If a protective order that affects a party's right to possession of or access to a child is rendered after the date a final order was rendered in a suit affecting the parent-child relationship, on the motion of a party or on the court's own motion, the court may transfer the protective order to the court of continuing, exclusive jurisdiction if the court makes the finding prescribed by Subsection (c).

(c) A court may transfer a protective order under this section if the court finds that the transfer is:

(1) in the interest of justice; or

(2) for the safety or convenience of a party or a witness.

(d) The transfer of a protective order under this section shall be conducted according to the procedures provided by Section 155.207.

(e) Except as provided by Section 81.002, the fees or costs associated with the transfer of a protective order shall be paid by the movant.

§ 85.065. Effect of Transfer

~~(a) A protective order transferred under Section 85.064 has the same effect as if the order remained in the court that rendered the order. The protective order may be enforced by the court that receives the order in the same manner as if the court originally rendered the order.~~

~~(b) A protective order that is transferred is enforceable by contempt or by any other means by which the court that rendered the order could enforce the order. The court that receives the protective order may punish a violation of the order regardless of whether the violation occurred before or after the date of the transfer.~~

(c) A protective order that is transferred is subject to modification by the court that receives the order to the same extent modification is permitted under Chapter 87 by a court that rendered the order.

Amended by Acts 2011, 82nd Leg., ch. 632 (S.B. 819), § 6(3), eff. Sept. 1, 2011.

CHAPTER 86. LAW ENFORCEMENT DUTIES RELATING TO PROTECTIVE ORDERS

---

§ 86.001. Adoption of Procedures by Law Enforcement Agency

(a) To ensure that law enforcement officers responding to calls are aware of the existence and terms of protective orders issued under this subtitle, each law enforcement agency shall establish procedures in the agency to provide adequate information or access to information for law enforcement officers of the names of each person protected by an order issued under this subtitle and of each person against whom protective orders are directed.

(b) A law enforcement agency may enter a protective order in the agency's computer records of outstanding warrants as notice that the order has been issued and is currently in effect. On receipt of notification by a clerk of court that the court has vacated or dismissed an order, the law enforcement agency shall remove the order from the agency's computer record of outstanding warrants.

§ 86.0011. Duty to Enter Information Into Statewide Law Enforcement Information System

On receipt of an original or modified protective order from the clerk of the issuing court, a law enforcement agency shall immediately, but not later than the 10th day after the date the order is received, enter the information required by Section 411.042(b)(6), Government Code, into the statewide law enforcement information system maintained by the Department of Public Safety.

Comment

In 1995 the legislature directed the Department of Public Safety to establish a centralized protective order database that would promote statewide and national enforcement of protective orders granted by Texas courts. The registry of protective orders is maintained as part of the Texas Crime Information Center (TCIC), and is linked with the FBI National Crime Information Center (NCIC). The law enforcement agency with jurisdiction over the protected person is charged with the duty of registering the order with TCIC. *See* § 85.042(a), *supra*.

Because the original statute did not provide a timeframe for registration, many orders were not entered until weeks or even months after receipt. Thus, in 2001 the legislature sought to remedy this situation by describing with specificity the duty of a law enforcement agency in this stand alone section, requiring entry "immediately, but not later than the 10th day" after the order is received.

---

§ 86.002. Duty to Provide Information to Firearms Dealers

(a) On receipt of a request for a law enforcement information system record check of a prospective transferee by a licensed firearms dealer under the Brady Handgun Violence Prevention Act, 18 U.S.C. Section 922, the chief law enforcement officer shall determine whether the Department of Public Safety has in the department's law enforcement information system a record indicating the existence of an active protective order directed to the prospective transferee.

(b) If the department's law enforcement information system indicates the existence of an active protective order directed to the prospective transferee, the chief law enforcement officer shall immediately advise the dealer that the transfer is prohibited.

§ 86.003. Court Order for Law Enforcement Assistance Under Temporary Order

On request by an applicant obtaining a temporary ex parte protective order that excludes the respondent from the respondent's residence, the court granting the temporary order shall render a written order to the sheriff, constable, or chief of police to provide a law enforcement officer from the department of the chief of police, constable, or sheriff to:

(1) accompany the applicant to the residence covered by the order;

(2) inform the respondent that the court has ordered that the respondent be excluded from the residence;

(3) protect the applicant while the applicant takes possession of the residence; and

(4) protect the applicant if the respondent refuses to vacate the residence while the applicant takes possession of the applicant's necessary personal property.

§ 86.004. Court Order for Law Enforcement Assistance Under Final Order

On request by an applicant obtaining a final protective order that excludes the respondent from the respondent's residence, the court granting the final order shall render a written order to the sheriff, constable, or chief of police to provide a law enforcement officer from the department of the chief of police, constable, or sheriff to:

(1) accompany the applicant to the residence covered by the order;

(2) inform the respondent that the court has ordered that the respondent be excluded from the residence;

(3) protect the applicant while the applicant takes possession of the residence and the respondent takes possession of the respondent's necessary personal property; and

(4) if the respondent refuses to vacate the residence:

(A) remove the respondent from the residence; and

(B) arrest the respondent for violating the court order.

§ 86.005. Protective Order From Another Jurisdiction

To ensure that law enforcement officers responding to calls are aware of the existence and terms of a protective order from another jurisdiction, each law enforcement agency shall establish procedures in the agency to provide adequate information or access to information for law enforcement officers regarding the name of each person protected by an order rendered in another jurisdiction and of each person against whom the protective order is directed.

CHAPTER 87. MODIFICATION OF PROTECTIVE ORDERS

Leading Cases

B.C. v. Rhodes, 116 S.W.3d 878 (Tex. App.—Austin 2003, no pet.) (trial court's jurisdiction during first year of protective order limited to modification)

Bilyeu v. Bilyeu, 86 S.W.3d 278 (Tex. App.—Austin 2002, no pet.) (transferred protective order subject to modification by court receiving order to same extent as original issuing court)

---

§ 87.001. Modification of Protective Order

On the motion of any party, the court, after notice and hearing, may modify an existing protective order to:

(1) exclude any item included in the order; or

(2) include any item that could have been included in the order.

§ 87.002. Modification May Not Extend Duration of Order

A protective order may not be modified to extend the period of the order's validity beyond the second anniversary of the date the original order was rendered or beyond the date the order expires under Section **85.025(a–1) or (c)**~~85. 025(c)~~, whichever date occurs later.

Amended by Acts 2011, 82nd Leg., ch. 627 (S.B. 789), § 3, eff. Sept. 1, 2011.

§ 87.003. Notification of Motion to Modify

Notice of a motion to modify a protective order is sufficient if delivery of the motion is attempted on the respondent at the respondent's last known address by registered or certified mail as provided by Rule 21a, Texas Rules of Civil Procedure.

§ 87.004. Change of Address or Telephone Number

(a) If a protective order contains the address or telephone number of a person protected by the order, of the place of employment or business of the person, or of the child-care facility or school of a child protected by the order and that information is not confidential under Section 85.007, the person protected by the order may file a notification of change of address or telephone number with the court that rendered the order to modify the information contained in the order.

(b) The clerk of the court shall attach the notification of change to the protective order and shall deliver a copy of the notification to the respondent by registered or certified mail as provided by Rule 21a, Texas Rules of Civil Procedure.

(c) The filing of a notification of change of address or telephone number and the attachment of the notification to a protective order does not affect the validity of the order.

CHAPTER 88. UNIFORM INTERSTATE ENFORCEMENT OF PROTECTIVE ORDERS ACT

Editors' Introductory Comment

The Violence Against Women Act, 18 U.S.C.A. § 2265 *et seq.*; 42 U.S.C.A. § 13931, *et seq.*, requires that states give full faith and credit to protective orders from other states. Because ordinarily full faith and credit is granted only to "final" orders, a number of states, including Texas, had held that protective orders were "temporary orders" not entitled to such respect. *See Normand v. Fox*, 940 S.W.2d 401 (Tex. App.—Waco 1997, no pet.). In 2000 the National Conference of Commissioners on Uniform State Laws promulgated a new uniform act and urged enactment by all states to facilitate nationwide uniform treatment of protective orders across state lines. The Texas Legislature responded favorably to this recommendation in 2001.

To date, 19 states have adopted the Act: Alabama; California; Delaware; District of Columbia; Idaho; Indiana; Kansas; Mississippi; Montana; Nebraska; North Dakota; Oklahoma; Rhode Island; South Carolina; South Dakota; Texas; U.S. Virgin Islands; Utah; and West Virginia. To keep up-to-date with the list of enacting jurisdictions, *see www.nccusl.org.* The uniform act has been cited by Texas appellate courts on only six occasions, none of which actually involved a protective order issued by a court of another state.

CLE/Leading Publications

Border crossings; understanding the civil, criminal, and immigration implications for battered women fleeing across state lines with their children. Catherine F. Klein, Leslye E. Orloff & Hema Sarangapani, 39 FAM. L.Q. 109 (2005)

Uniform Interstate Enforcement of Domestic–Violence Protection Orders Act (with prefatory note and comments). Andrew Spiropoulos, 35 FAM. L. Q. 205 (2001)

COMMISSIONERS' OFFICIAL PREFATORY NOTE TO THE UNIFORM INTERSTATE ENFORCEMENT OF DOMESTIC–VIOLENCE PROTECTION ORDERS ACT

I. Introduction

The Uniform Interstate Enforcement of Domestic–Violence Protection Orders Act ("the Act") provides a uniform mechanism for the interstate enforcement of domestic-violence protective orders. The need for such a mechanism is founded on the widespread understanding that states have not consistently or effectively enforced domestic-violence protective orders issued by other states. The Act, therefore, has two main purposes. First, it defines the meaning of interstate enforcement in the context of the enforcement of domestic-violence protective orders. Second, it establishes uniform procedures for the effective interstate enforcement of domestic-violence protective orders.

Many states, recognizing the severity of the problems regarding the interstate enforcement of domestic-violence protective orders, have enacted legislation requiring their courts to enforce the domestic-violence protective orders of other states. Many of these statutes, however, while mandating enforcement, are either silent or ambiguous regarding several important questions that must be answered in order to establish an effective system for the interstate enforcement of these orders. The Congress of the United States, as well, has enacted legislation requiring interstate enforcement of domestic-violence protective orders, but this legislation is also silent or ambiguous regarding these important questions.

First, many of the existing statutes do not sufficiently explain the core requirements of interstate enforcement of protective orders. For example, many of the state statutes, and the federal legislation, require courts and law enforcement officers to enforce the orders of other states as if they were the protective orders of the enforcing state. This provision, however, does not answer the question of whether state courts and officers are required to enforce provisions of foreign protective orders that would not be authorized by the law of the enforcing state. This question, and others, must be answered if there is to be effective uniform enforcement of protective orders. Second, many of the existing statutes do not specify the procedures state courts and officers must follow in enforcing foreign protective orders. For example, many of the statutes are silent on whether individuals seeking the enforcement of a protective order must register or file the order with the enforcing state before action can be taken on their behalf. This Act resolves the issues left unanswered in existing legislation and provides a uniform scheme for enforcement of these orders.

II. The Requirements of Interstate Enforcement

The Act first defines what it means to accord interstate enforcement to domestic-violence protective orders. These orders must be enforced if the issuing tribunals had jurisdiction over both the parties and the matter under the law of the issuing state and if the individuals against whom the order is enforced were given reasonable notice and had an opportunity to be heard consistent with the right to due process. If the order was obtained ex parte, this notice and opportunity to be heard must be provided within a reasonable time.

The Act makes it clear that all the terms of the orders of the issuing states must be enforced, including terms that provide relief that the courts of the enforcing state would lack power to provide. The Act also provides that all protective orders that both recognize the standing of the protected individual to seek enforcement of the order and satisfy the criteria of validity established by the Act must be enforced. In addition, provisions of protective orders governing custody and visitation matters are enforceable under this Act. Terms that concern support are not. The terms of mutual protective orders which favor of a respondent are also not enforceable if they were not issued in response to a written pleading filed by the respondent and if the issuing tribunal did not make specific findings in favor of the respondent.

Editors' Note: *The Texas enactment allows for enforcement of support.*

III. Enforcement Procedures

The Act also provides uniform procedures for the interstate enforcement of domestic-violence protective orders. The Act envisions that the enforcement of foreign protective orders will require law enforcement officers of enforcing states to rely on probable cause judgments that a valid order exists and has been violated. The Act, however, provides that if a protected individual can provide direct proof of the existence of a facially valid order, by, for example, presenting a paper copy or through an electronic registry, probable cause is conclusively established. If no such proof is forthcoming, the Act provides that if officers, relying on the totality of the circumstances, determine that there is probable cause to believe that a valid protective order exists and has been violated, the order will be enforced. The individual against whom the order is enforced will have sufficient opportunity to demonstrate that the order is invalid when the case is brought before the enforcing tribunal. Law enforcement officers, as well as other government agents, will be encouraged to rely on probable cause judgments by the Act's inclusion of an immunity provision, protecting agents of the government acting in good faith.

The Act does not require individuals seeking the enforcement of a protective order to register or file the order with the enforcing state. The Act does, however, include an optional registration process. This process permits individuals to register a protective order by presenting a copy of the order to a responsible state agency or any state officer or agency. The copy presented must be certified by the issuing state. The purpose of these procedures is to make it as easy as possible for the protected individual to register the protective order and thus facilitate its enforcement.

Editors' Note: *Texas has traditionally used the term "protective order," not "protection order" as is used in federal law and in this uniform act. The drafters decided to retain the term "protective order" except in the title of the Act. The editors have taken the liberty of making a similar change in the official commentary for ease of reading. The Texas enactment departs from the uniform version in a few sections; the commentary has been edited to reflect those changes. The full act, with unedited commentary, is found at the National Conference of Commissioners on Uniform State Laws' website: www.nccusl.org., and 9 IB U.L.A. 133 (2005).*

§ 88.001. Short Title

This chapter may be cited as the Uniform Interstate Enforcement of Domestic Violence Protection Orders Act.

§ 88.002. Definitions

In this chapter:

(1) "Foreign protective order" means a protective order issued by a tribunal of another state.

(2) "Issuing state" means the state in which a tribunal issues a protective order.

(3) "Mutual foreign protective order" means a foreign protective order that includes provisions issued in favor of both the protected individual seeking enforcement of the order and the respondent.

(4) "Protected individual" means an individual protected by a protective order.

(5) "Protective order" means an injunction or other order, issued by a tribunal under the domestic violence or family violence laws or another law of the issuing state, to prevent an individual from engaging in violent or threatening acts against, harassing, contacting or communicating with, or being in physical proximity to another individual.

(6) "Respondent" means the individual against whom enforcement of a protective order is sought.

(7) "State" means a state of the United States, the District of Columbia, the Commonwealth of Puerto Rico, the United States Virgin Islands, or a territory or insular possession subject to the jurisdiction of the United States. The term includes a military tribunal of the United States, an Indian tribe or band, and an Alaskan native village that has jurisdiction to issue protective orders.

(8) "Tribunal" means a court, agency, or other entity authorized by law to issue or modify a protective order.

Commissioners' Comment to Section 88.002

The term "protective order" includes those orders issued under the domestic-violence, family-violence laws or other law of the issuing state. The scope of enforceable protective orders is limited by the provisions of Section 88.003(d). In addition, the term "protective order" includes an order modifying a previous order. Thus, a modified order, is enforceable, under the Act, in the same manner as a newly issued order. The terms "protected individual" and "respondent" refer to the relief sought by the parties in the action brought in the enforcing state. The Act recognizes that neither the protected individual nor the respondent may have been a named party in the action brought in the issuing state; the Act applies to individuals meeting the definition of protected individual or respondent whether they were named in the caption or the body of the protective order. The Act also recognizes that the parties may have been called by different terms, *e.g.* plaintiff, defendant, petitioner, in the issuing state.

The term "mutual protective orders" refers to protective orders in which an issuing state includes provisions protecting both parties. Enforcement of these foreign protective orders is governed by Section 88.003(g).

The Violence Against Women Act, 18 U.S.C.A. Sec. 2265, requires that states accord full faith and credit to tribal protective orders. Like state orders, tribal orders must satisfy the criteria for validity, as defined in Section 88.003(e), in order to qualify for interstate enforcement across state or tribal lines.

The Act uses the term "tribunal", rather than "court", in order to accommodate states that rely upon administrative or other entities to issue or modify protective orders.

---

§ 88.003. Judicial Enforcement of Order

(a) A tribunal of this state shall enforce the terms of a foreign protective order, including a term that provides relief that a tribunal of this state would not have power to provide but for this section. The tribunal shall enforce the order regardless of whether the order was obtained by independent action or in another proceeding, if the order is an order issued in response to a complaint, petition, or motion filed by or on behalf of an individual seeking protection. In a proceeding to enforce a foreign protective order, the tribunal shall follow the procedures of this state for the enforcement of protective orders.

(b) A tribunal of this state shall enforce the provisions of the foreign protective order that govern the possession of and access to a child if the provisions were issued in accordance with the jurisdictional requirements governing the issuance of possession and access orders in the issuing state.

(c) A tribunal of this state may enforce a provision of the foreign protective order relating to child support if the order was issued in accordance with the jurisdictional requirements of Chapter 159 and the federal Full Faith and Credit for Child Support Orders Act, 28 U.S.C. Section 1738B, as amended.

(d) A foreign protective order is valid if the order:

(1) names the protected individual and the respondent;

(2) is currently in effect;

(3) was rendered by a tribunal that had jurisdiction over the parties and the subject matter under the law of the issuing state; and

(4) was rendered after the respondent was given reasonable notice and an opportunity to be heard consistent with the right to due process, either:

(A) before the tribunal issued the order; or

(B) in the case of an ex parte order, within a reasonable time after the order was rendered.

(e) A protected individual seeking enforcement of a foreign protective order establishes a prima facie case for its validity by presenting an order that is valid on its face.

(f) It is an affirmative defense in an action seeking enforcement of a foreign protective order that the order does not meet the requirements for a valid order under Subsection (d).

(g) A tribunal of this state may enforce the provisions of a mutual foreign protective order that favor a respondent only if:

(1) the respondent filed a written pleading seeking a protective order from the tribunal of the issuing state; and

(2) the tribunal of the issuing state made specific findings in favor of the respondent.

Commissioners' Comment to Section 88.003

Subsection (a) implements the core purpose of the Act. Effective interstate enforcement of protective orders is founded on the principle that enforcing states must enforce all the substantive terms of a foreign protective order, including terms that provide relief that a tribunal of the enforcing state would lack power to provide, but for this Act. This provision means that the tribunals of enforcing states must enforce the specific terms of a foreign protective order even if their state law would not allow the relief in question. For example, if the law of the issuing state provides that a court may issue a protective order including terms that concern the possession of property, *e.g.*, an order giving the protected individual possession of the family automobile, but the law of the enforcing state does not authorize such substantive relief, the tribunal of the enforcing state must enforce the order in its entirety. To give another example, if the law of the issuing state allows protective orders to remain effective for a longer period than is allowed by the enforcing state, the tribunal of the enforcing state should enforce the order for the time specified in the order of the issuing state. In a proceeding to enforce the substantive terms of the foreign protective order, however, the court of the enforcing state shall follow its own procedures.

Subsection (a) provides that any person authorized by the law of the enforcing state to seek enforcement of a protective order may seek enforcement of valid foreign protective order in the enforcing state. This provision recognizes that states frequently authorize public agencies and officers, such as a local prosecutor, to bring enforcement actions on behalf of a protected individual. The Act, however, in recognizing the importance of these agencies and officers, should not be interpreted to mean that states, and their agencies and officers, are required to bring these actions when possible. This subsection further provides that only protective orders that were issued in response to a complaint, petition, or motion filed by or on behalf of an individual seeking protection can be enforced under this Act; orders issued sua sponte are not enforceable under this Act.

Subsections (b) and (c) further define the scope of enforceable protective orders under the Act. Subsection (b) provides that the provisions of protective orders that govern custody and visitation rights must be enforced. Enforcement of these provisions is essential because, first, the award of custody is often essential for the protection of children from potential violence, and, second, because the protected individual will not seek a safe distance from a threatening individual if custody of a child is jeopardized. These provisions may only be enforced, however, if they were issued in accordance with the jurisdictional requirements for the issuance of all custody and visitation orders, contained, depending on the state, either in the Uniform Child Custody Jurisdiction Act or the Uniform Child Custody Jurisdiction and Enforcement Act, and the federal Parental Kidnapping Prevention Act. This Act, however, does not provide for the enforcement of orders governing custody and visitation rights that are not included in a protective order.

Under Subsection (c) support orders are enforceable if issued consistent with the jurisdictional standards of Uniform Interstate Family Support Act and federal law.

Subsection (d) requires that, to be valid for the purpose of enforcement under this Act, a foreign protective order must be "currently in effect." This provision includes orders that have been modified; the modified order is the one currently in effect. While the Act requires that a foreign protective order, to be valid, identify the protected individual and respondent, merely technical errors, such as an incorrect spelling of a name, should not preclude enforcement of the order. The question of the validity of an order is a question of law for the court of the enforcing state. Once an order is adjudged valid, the proceeding shall be governed by the established procedures of the enforcing state.

The respondent's constitutional right to due process is protected by the opportunity to raise defenses in the enforcement proceeding, as provided in Subsection (f). If, for example, the respondent was not provided with reasonable notice and opportunity to be heard by the tribunal of the state issuing the protective order, the enforcing tribunal may not enforce the order. Thus, the interstate enforcement of a valid foreign protective order, even without a prior hearing, does not deprive the respondent of any rights to due process because the respondent was provided with reasonable notice and opportunity to be heard when the order was issued.

The enforcement mechanisms established by the Act do not require the presentation by the protected individual of an authenticated copy of the foreign protective order. While states, as required by the Constitution and federal statutes that articulate authentication requirements, including 28 U.S.C.A. Sec. 1738, must accord properly authenticated foreign judgments full faith and credit enforcement, they may choose to enforce foreign orders they would not be required to enforce under the provisions of the Constitution or other federal law. By adopting this Act, states have chosen to give that extra measure of full faith and credit to foreign protective orders.

In addition, in recent years, particularly with regard to the enforcement of domestic relations orders, the federal government has employed the power granted to it by Article IV, Sec. 1 of the Constitution of the United States to prescribe the manner in which states give full faith and credit to the acts, records, and proceedings of other states to require states to enforce foreign orders in circumstances in which states have traditionally been reluctant to render such enforcement. For example, the federal Parental Kidnapping Prevention Act, 28 U.S.C.A. Sec. 1738A, requires greater interstate enforcement of child custody orders and the federal Personal Responsibility and Work Opportunity Reconciliation Act, 110 Stat. 2105 (1996), requires that states, in order to facilitate the enforcement of support orders, adopt the provisions of the Uniform Interstate Family Support Act. The Violence Against Women Act extends the principle of these laws to the subject of the interstate enforcement of domestic-violence protective orders.

Subsection (g), adapted from the federal Violence Against Women Act, 18 U.S.C.A. Sec. 2265(c), addresses the enforcement of mutual foreign protective orders, which contain provisions protecting both the protected individual and the respondent. Provisions of a mutual foreign protective order issued in favor of the respondent will not be enforced without proof that the respondent filed a written pleading seeking a protective order. If a respondent can prove that he or she made a specific request for relief and that the issuing tribunal made specific findings that the respondent was entitled to the requested relief, the protective orders will be enforced against the protected individual.

In order to facilitate the interstate enforcement of foreign protective orders, states should strongly consider requiring tribunals that issue protective orders to state clearly that these orders are entitled to interstate enforcement under both federal and state law. Such enforcement would also be greatly facilitated if issuing states provided each protected individual with a certified copy of the protective order. In addition, states should consider adopting a standard certification or confirmation form stating the protective order issued by their tribunals satisfies the criteria of validity articulated in Subsection (d), thus qualifying the protective order for interstate enforcement. Use of the following certification form is recommended.

(Name),	)	**IN THE COURT OF**
Plaintiff	)	**(County/Judicial District)**
	)	**(State/Territory)**
vs.	)	**CIVIL ACTION–LAW**
	)	**PROTECTIVE/RESTRAINING**
(Name),	)	**ORDER**
Defendant	)	**Docket No.___________, 200___**

Certification of Protective/Restraining Order

It is hereby certified that the attached is a true and correct copy of the order entered in the above-captioned action on ______(date) and that the original of the attached order was duly executed by the judicial authority whose signature appears thereon. The order expires on ______ (date).

The order is: [ ] a civil protective/restraining order

OR [ ] a criminal protective/restraining order, that recognizes the standing of the plaintiff to seek enforcement of the order

It is further certified that:

(a) the issuing court determined that it had jurisdiction over the parties and the subject matter under the laws of ________________________ (state or Indian tribe).

(b) the defendant was given reasonable notice and had opportunity to be heard before this order was issued; or if the order was issued ex parte, the defendant was given notice and had opportunity to be heard after the order was issued, consistent with the rights of the defendant to due process.

(c) the order was otherwise issued in accordance with the requirements of the Uniform Interstate Enforcement of Domestic–Violence Protection Orders Act, and the Violence Against Women Act, 18 U.S.C. § 2265.

For custody and visitation orders:

The order was issued in accordance with the requirements of the Uniform Child Custody Jurisdiction Act or the Uniform Child Custody Jurisdiction and Enforcement Act of this state/territory and is consistent with the provisions of the Parental Kidnapping Prevention Act. 28 U.S.C. § 1738A.

The attached order shall be presumed to be valid and enforceable in this and other jurisdictions.

Signature of Clerk of Court or other authorized official:__________________________

Judicial District:__________________________

Address:__________________________ Phone:__________________________

Fax:__________________________ Date:__________________________

Seal:

§ 88.004. Nonjudicial Enforcement of Order

(a) A law enforcement officer of this state, on determining that there is probable cause to believe that a valid foreign protective order exists and that the order has been violated, shall enforce the foreign protective order as if it were an order of a tribunal of this state. A law enforcement officer has probable cause to believe that a foreign protective order exists if the protected individual presents a foreign protective order that identifies both the protected individual and the respondent and on its face, is currently in effect.

(b) For the purposes of this section, a foreign protective order may be inscribed on a tangible medium or may be stored in an electronic or other medium if it is retrievable in a perceivable form. Presentation of a certified copy of a protective order is not required for enforcement.

(c) If a protected individual does not present a foreign protective order, a law enforcement officer may determine that there is probable cause to believe that a valid foreign protective order exists by relying on any relevant information.

(d) A law enforcement officer of this state who determines that an otherwise valid foreign protective order cannot be enforced because the respondent has not been notified or served with the order shall inform the respondent of the order and make a reasonable effort to serve the order on the respondent. After informing the respondent and attempting to serve the order, the officer shall allow the respondent a reasonable opportunity to comply with the order before enforcing the order.

(e) The registration or filing of an order in this state is not required for the enforcement of a valid foreign protective order under this chapter.

Commissioners' Comment to Section 88.004

The enforcement procedures in Subsections (a) and (b) rely on the sound exercise of the judgment of law enforcement officers to determine whether there exists probable cause to believe that a valid foreign protective order exists and has been violated. These procedures anticipate that there will be many instances in which the protected individual does not have, or cannot, under the circumstances, produce a paper copy of the foreign protective order. Subsections (a) and (b) establish a per se rule for determining probable cause of the existence of an order. If the protected individual presents, whether by providing a paper copy (which need not be certified) of a protective order or through an electronic medium, such as access to a state registry of orders, proof of a facially valid order, the order should be enforced. In determining whether there is proof of a facially valid order, a law enforcement officer, where possible, may, and, indeed, should, search, using an electronic or other medium, a state or federal registry of orders.

Subsection (c) concerns the circumstance in which the protected individual cannot present direct proof of the protective order. In this situation, law enforcement officers are expected to obtain information from all available sources, including interviewing the parties and contacting other law enforcement agencies, to determine whether there is a valid protective order in effect. If the officer finds, after considering the totality of the circumstances, that there is probable cause to believe that a valid foreign protective order exists and has been violated, he or she should enforce the order. This probable cause determination must meet the constitutional standards for determining probable cause. If it is later determined that no such order was in place or the order was otherwise unenforceable, law enforcement agencies, officers, or other state officials will be protected by the immunity provision of Section 88.006 for actions taken in good faith.

Subsection (d) provides that if a law enforcement officer discovers in the course of a probable cause investigation that the respondent has not been notified of the issuance of or served with an otherwise valid foreign protective order, the officer must then inform the respondent of the terms and conditions of the protective order and make a reasonable effort to serve the order upon the respondent. The respondent must be allowed a reasonable opportunity to comply with the order before the order is enforced.

Subsection (e) makes clear that, if a state either adopts its own process for the registration or filing of foreign protective orders or adopts the process provided in Section 5, the state shall not require the registration or filing of a foreign protective order for enforcement.

---

§ 88.005. Registration of Order

(a) An individual may register a foreign protective order in this state. To register a foreign protective order, an individual shall:

(1) present a certified copy of the order to a sheriff, constable, or chief of police responsible for the registration of orders in the local computer records and in the statewide law enforcement system maintained by the Texas Department of Public Safety; or

(2) present a certified copy of the order to the Department of Public Safety and request that the order be registered in the statewide law enforcement system maintained by the Department of Public Safety.

(b) On receipt of a foreign protective order, the agency responsible for the registration of protective orders shall register the order in accordance with this section and furnish to the individual registering the order a certified copy of the registered order.

(c) The agency responsible for the registration of protective orders shall register a foreign protective order on presentation of a copy of a protective order that has been certified by the issuing state. A registered foreign protective order that is inaccurate or not currently in effect shall be corrected or removed from the registry in accordance with the law of this state.

(d) An individual registering a foreign protective order shall file an affidavit made by the protected individual that, to the best of the protected individual's knowledge, the order is in effect.

(e) A foreign protective order registered under this section may be entered in any existing state or federal registry of protective orders, in accordance with state or federal law.

(f) A fee may not be charged for the registration of a foreign protective order.

Commissioners' Comment to Section 88.005

While a protected individual is not required to register a valid foreign protective order in order for it to be enforced, it is highly desirable that states provide an optional registration process. A registration system supplies law enforcement officers and agencies more accurate information, more quickly, about both the existence and status of foreign protective orders and their terms and conditions. An enforcing state may facilitate the collection and dissemination of this information either by establishing a central registry or by providing a process by which information regarding registered orders is distributed to law enforcement officers and agencies across the state.

While the management of state registries is purely governed by state law, in implementing a registration system, however, enforcing states should strongly consider keeping these protective orders under seal. The purpose of more effectively protecting victims of domestic violence will be undermined if respondents can use the process of registration to locate the very people who are trying to escape from them. In addition, the federal Violence Against Women Act, prohibits states that provide for the registration or filing of orders from, without the permission of the individual registering or filing the order, notifying other states of the registration or filing of the order.

Subsection (a) provides that any person, including a potential respondent, may register foreign protective orders. This reason behind this provision is to ensure that all parties have the opportunity to provide relevant information to the state. Orders, for example, may be modified with custody arrangements. Subsection (a) also requires that a person seeking to register a foreign protective order must present a certified copy of that order. The copy must be a writing on paper, thus exempting this requirement from the provisions of the Uniform Electronic Transactions Act.

Subsection (c) provides that if the state has registered orders that are no longer in effect or are inaccurate, these orders must be removed from the registry or, in the case of error, corrected. The precise method of how state and federal registries manage their registries, including the deletion of inaccurate information, is governed by each government's law regarding the management of records.

If an order is registered under this Section, the individual who registered the order is expected to inform the enforcing state of any modifications to the registered protective order.

§ 88.006. Immunity

A state or local governmental agency, law enforcement officer, prosecuting attorney, clerk of court, or any state or local governmental official acting in an official capacity is immune from civil and criminal liability for an act or omission arising from the registration or enforcement of a foreign protective order or the detention or arrest of a person alleged to have violated a foreign protective order if the act or omission was done in good faith in an effort to comply with this chapter.

Commissioners' Comment to Section 88.006

This immunity provision includes States, state and local governmental agencies, and all state and local government officials acting in their official capacity in order to prevent those seeking the imposition of criminal and civil liability for acts or omissions done in good faith in an effort to comply with the provisions of this Act from circumventing this immunity provision. The necessity for a generous immunity provision for the enforcement of foreign protection orders does not preclude state and local governments from using personnel and other internal sanctions in order to prevent and punish actions that, in the absence of this immunity provision, would have rendered the government agencies, officers, or officials civilly or criminally liable.

§ 88.007. Other Remedies

A protected individual who pursues a remedy under this chapter is not precluded from pursuing other legal or equitable remedies against the respondent.

Commissioners' Comment to Section 88.007

This section clarifies that the protective orders enforced under the Act are not the only means of protection available to victims of domestic violence. Other legal remedies, such as tort actions and criminal prosecution, are left undisturbed by this Act.

§ 88.008. Uniformity of Application and Construction

In applying and construing this chapter, consideration shall be given to the need to promote uniformity of the law with respect to its subject matter among the states that enact the Uniform Interstate Enforcement of Domestic Violence Protection Orders Act.

Editors' Note: The official text of the Uniform Act contains "Section 9. Severability Clause," which was not enacted by the Texas Legislature. The omitted provision is designed to take into account the possibility that the related provision in the federal Violence Against Women Act might be declared unconstitutional.

SUBTITLE C. REPORTING FAMILY VIOLENCE

Chapter

★★★

CHAPTER 91. REPORTING FAMILY VIOLENCE

§ 91.001. Definitions

In this subtitle:

(1) "Family violence" has the meaning assigned by Section 71.004.

(2) "Medical professional" means a licensed doctor, nurse, physician assistant, or emergency medical technician.

§ 91.002. Reporting by Witnesses Encouraged

A person who witnesses family violence is encouraged to report the family violence to a local law enforcement agency.

§ 91.003. Information Provided by Medical Professionals

A medical professional who treats a person for injuries that the medical professional has reason to believe were caused by family violence shall:

(1) immediately provide the person with information regarding the nearest family violence shelter center;

(2) document in the person's medical file:

(A) the fact that the person has received the information provided under Subdivision (1); and

(B) the reasons for the medical professional's belief that the person's injuries were caused by family violence; and

(3) give the person a written notice in substantially the following form, completed with the required information, in both English and Spanish:

"It is a crime for any person to cause you any physical injury or harm even if that person is a member or former member of your family or household.

"NOTICE TO ADULT VICTIMS OF FAMILY VIOLENCE

"You may report family violence to a law enforcement officer by calling the following telephone numbers: ____________________.

"If you, your child, or any other household resident has been injured or if you feel you are going to be in danger after a law enforcement officer investigating family violence leaves your residence or at a later time, you have the right to:

"Ask the local prosecutor to file a criminal complaint against the person committing family violence; and

"Apply to a court for an order to protect you. You may want to consult with a legal aid office, a prosecuting attorney, or a private attorney. A court can enter an order that:

"(1) prohibits the abuser from committing further acts of violence;

"(2) prohibits the abuser from threatening, harassing, or contacting you at home;

"(3) directs the abuser to leave your household; and

"(4) establishes temporary custody of the children or any property.

"A VIOLATION OF CERTAIN PROVISIONS OF COURT-ORDERED PROTECTION MAY BE A FELONY.

"CALL THE FOLLOWING VIOLENCE SHELTERS OR SOCIAL ORGANIZATIONS IF YOU NEED PROTECTION: ______________________________."

Comment

Despite widespread confusion, this section only mandates that medical professionals provide patients whom they believe to have been victims of family violence with information regarding the local shelter and document their injuries. Medical professionals are not required to report family violence injuries to law enforcement, unless the victim is a child (Tex. Fam. Code Ann. § 261.101), elderly or disabled person (Tex. Hum. Res. Code Ann. § 48.051(d)) or the injury involves a gunshot wound (Tex. Health & Safety Code Ann. § 161.041).

§ 91.004. Application of Subtitle

This subtitle does not affect a duty to report child abuse under Chapter 261.

CHAPTER 92. IMMUNITY

§ 92.001. Immunity

(a) Except as provided by Subsection (b), a person who reports family violence under Section 91.002 or provides information under Section 91.003 is immune from civil liability that might otherwise be incurred or imposed.

(b) A person who reports the person's own conduct or who otherwise reports family violence in bad faith is not protected from liability under this section.

TITLE 5

THE PARENT–CHILD RELATIONSHIP AND THE SUIT AFFECTING THE PARENT–CHILD RELATIONSHIP

As amended through the 82nd Legislature, Regular and First Called Sessions (2011)

Subtitle A. General Provisions

Chapter

Subtitle B. Suits Affecting the Parent–Child Relationship

Subtitle C. Judicial Resources and Services

Subtitle D. Administrative Services

Subtitle E. Protection of the Child

★★★

SUBTITLE A. GENERAL PROVISIONS

Introductory Comment to Subtitle A

Subtitle A contains eleven short chapters that establish general provisions intended to govern all of the wide variety of suits affecting the parent-child relationship (commonly known as SAPCR's). Unless otherwise specified, the general provisions apply whether the action is between parents for conservatorship and support, between parents and relatives for conservatorship or visitation, and perhaps for support, for termination and adoption, or between the state and the parents for any of these aspects of the relief available in a SAPCR. On occasion this creates a certain awkwardness because the issues involved in such different types of litigation vary considerably, especially given the constitutional dimensions of the parent-child relationship when the state intervenes in the family.

★★★

CHAPTER 101. DEFINITIONS

Introductory Comment

The 1995 recodification of the Family Code that created Title 5 took the innovative step of listing definitions in alphabetical order in this separate chapter. This allowed insertions of new definitions in their proper place for ease of use. In 1995 there were 35 definitions, and as of September 1, 2009, there are 48 in this section. That doesn't come near telling the full story. Note that the first definition, § 101.001, warns that this chapter is not exclusive. Other definitions appear elsewhere in Title 5, most commonly in the uniform acts: Chapter 152, Uniform Child Custody Jurisdiction Enforcement Act, contains an additional 17 definitions; Chapter 159, Uniform Interstate Family Support Act, supplies 24 more; and, Chapter 160, Uniform Parentage Act, chips in another 17. There are also other definitions scattered throughout, and cross-references are made to definitions in other codes from time to time. Be alert to the fact that if a specific definition is supplied in an individual statute, the construction of the word is bound to that statutory description.

§ 101.001. Applicability of Definitions

(a) Definitions in this subchapter apply to this title.

(b) If, in another part of this title, a term defined by this chapter has a meaning different from the meaning provided by this chapter, the meaning of that other provision prevails.

§ 101.0010. Acknowledged Father

"Acknowledged father" means a man who has established a father-child relationship under Chapter 160.

§ 101.0011. Administrative Writ of Withholding

"Administrative writ of withholding" means the document issued by the Title IV–D agency or domestic relations office and delivered to an employer directing that earnings be withheld for payment of child support as provided by Chapter 158.

§ 101.0015. Alleged Father

(a) "Alleged father" means a man who alleges himself to be, or is alleged to be, the genetic father or a possible genetic father of a child, but whose paternity has not been determined.

(b) The term does not include:

(1) a presumed father;

(2) a man whose parental rights have been terminated or declared to not exist; or

(3) a male donor.

§ 101.0017. Amicus Attorney

"Amicus attorney" has the meaning assigned by Section 107.001.

§ 101.0018. Attorney Ad Litem

"Attorney ad litem" has the meaning assigned by Section 107.001.

§ 101.002. Authorized Agency

"Authorized agency" means a public social agency authorized to care for children, including the ~~Texas~~ Department of **Family and** Protective ~~and Regulatory~~ Services.

Amended by Acts 2011, 82nd Leg., ch. 110 (H.B. 841), § 8, eff. May 21, 2011.

§ 101.0021. Bureau of Vital Statistics

"Bureau of vital statistics" means the bureau of vital statistics of the Texas Department of Health.

§ 101.003. Child or Minor; Adult

(a) "Child" or "minor" means a person under 18 years of age who is not and has not been married or who has not had the disabilities of minority removed for general purposes.

(b) In the context of child support, "child" includes a person over 18 years of age for whom a person may be obligated to pay child support.

(c) "Adult" means a person who is not a child.

§ 101.004. Child Support Agency

"Child support agency" means:

(1) the Title IV–D agency;

(2) a county or district attorney or any other county officer or county agency that executes a cooperative agreement with the Title IV–D agency to provide child support services under Part D of Title IV of the federal Social Security Act (42 U.S.C. Section 651 et seq.) and Chapter 231; or

(3) a domestic relations office.

§ 101.005. Child Support Review Officer

"Child support review officer" means an individual designated and trained by a child support agency to conduct reviews under this title.

§ 101.006. Child Support Services

"Child support services" means administrative or court actions to:

(1) establish paternity;

(2) establish, modify, or enforce child support or medical support obligations;

(3) locate absent parents; or

(4) cooperate with other states in these actions and any other action authorized or required under Part D of Title IV of the federal Social Security Act (42 U.S.C. Section 651 et seq.) or Chapter 231.

§ 101.007. Clear and Convincing Evidence

"Clear and convincing evidence" means the measure or degree of proof that will produce in the mind of the trier of fact a firm belief or conviction as to the truth of the allegations sought to be established.

§ 101.008. Court

"Court" means the district court, juvenile court having the same jurisdiction as a district court, or other court expressly given jurisdiction of a suit affecting the parent-child relationship.

§ 101.009. Danger to Physical Health or Safety of Child

"Danger to the physical health or safety of a child" includes exposure of the child to loss or injury that jeopardizes the physical health or safety of the child without regard to whether there has been an actual prior injury to the child.

§ 101.010. Disposable Earnings

"Disposable earnings" means the part of the earnings of an individual remaining after the deduction from those earnings of any amount required by law to be withheld, union dues, nondiscretionary retirement contributions, and medical, hospitalization, and disability insurance coverage for the obligor and the obligor's children.

§ 101.011. Earnings

"Earnings" means a payment to or due an individual, regardless of source and how denominated. The term includes a periodic or lump-sum payment for:

(1) wages, salary, compensation received as an independent contractor, overtime pay, severance pay, commission, bonus, and interest income;

(2) payments made under a pension, an annuity, workers' compensation, and a disability or retirement program; and

(3) unemployment benefits.

§ 101.012. Employer

"Employer" means a person, corporation, partnership, workers' compensation insurance carrier, governmental entity, the United States, or any other entity that pays or owes earnings to an individual. The term includes, for the purposes of enrolling dependents in a group health insurance plan, a union, trade association, or other similar organization.

§ 101.0125. Family Violence

"Family violence" has the meaning assigned by Section 71.004.

§ 101.013. Filed

"Filed" means officially filed with the clerk of the court.

§ 101.014. Governmental Entity

"Governmental entity" means the state, a political subdivision of the state, or an agency of the state.

§ 101.0145. Guardian Ad Litem

"Guardian ad litem" has the meaning assigned by Section 107.001.

§ 101.015. Health Insurance

"Health insurance" means insurance coverage that provides basic health care services, including usual physician services, office visits, hospitalization, and laboratory, X-ray, and emergency services, that may be provided through a health maintenance organization or other private or public organization, other than medical assistance under Chapter 32, Human Resources Code.

§ 101.016. Joint Managing Conservatorship

"Joint managing conservatorship" means the sharing of the rights and duties of a parent by two parties, ordinarily the parents, even if the exclusive right to make certain decisions may be awarded to one party.

§ 101.0161. Judicial Writ of Withholding

"Judicial writ of withholding" means the document issued by the clerk of a court and delivered to an employer directing that earnings be withheld for payment of child support as provided by Chapter 158.

§ 101.017. Licensed Child Placing Agency

"Licensed child placing agency" means a person, private association, or corporation approved by the Department of **Family and** Protective ~~and Regulatory~~ Services to place children for adoption through a license, certification, or other means.

Amended by Acts 2011, 82nd Leg., ch. 110 (H.B. 841), § 9, eff. May 21, 2011.

§ 101.018. Local Registry

"Local registry" means a county agency or public entity operated under the authority of a district clerk, county government, juvenile board, juvenile probation office, domestic relations office, or other county agency or public entity that serves a county or a court that has jurisdiction under this title and that:

(1) receives child support payments;

(2) maintains records of child support payments;

(3) distributes child support payments as required by law; and

(4) maintains custody of official child support payment records.

§ 101.019. Managing Conservatorship

"Managing conservatorship" means the relationship between a child and a managing conservator appointed by court order.

§ 101.020. Medical Support

"Medical support" means periodic payments or a lump-sum payment made under an order to cover medical expenses, including health insurance coverage, incurred for the benefit of a child.

§ 101.0201. Notice of Application for Judicial Writ of Withholding

"Notice of application for judicial writ of withholding" means the document delivered to an obligor and filed with the court as required by Chapter 158 for the nonjudicial determination of arrears and initiation of withholding.

§ 101.021. Obligee

"Obligee" means a person or entity entitled to receive payments of child support, including an agency of this state or of another jurisdiction to which a person has assigned the person's right to support.

§ 101.022. Obligor

"Obligor" means a person required to make payments under the terms of a support order for a child.

§ 101.023. Order

"Order" means a final order unless identified as a temporary order or the context clearly requires a different meaning. The term includes a decree and a judgment.

§ 101.024. Parent

(a) "Parent" means the mother, a man presumed to be the father, a man legally determined to be the father, a man who has been adjudicated to be the father by a court of competent jurisdiction, a man who has acknowledged his paternity under applicable law, or an adoptive mother or father. Except as provided by Subsection (b), the term does not include a parent as to whom the parent-child relationship has been terminated.

(b) For purposes of establishing, determining the terms of, modifying, or enforcing an order, a reference in this title to a parent includes a person ordered to pay child support under Section 154.001(a–1) or to provide medical support for a child.

§ 101.025. Parent-Child Relationship

"Parent-child relationship" means the legal relationship between a child and the child's parents as provided by Chapter 160. The term includes the mother and child relationship and the father and child relationship.

§ 101.0255. Record

"Record" means information that is:

(1) inscribed on a tangible medium or stored in an electronic or other medium; and

(2) retrievable in a perceivable form.

§ 101.026. Render

"Render" means the pronouncement by a judge of the court's ruling on a matter. The pronouncement may be made orally in the presence of the court reporter or in writing, including on the court's docket sheet or by a separate written instrument.

§ 101.027. Parent Locator Service

"Parent locator service" means the service established under 42 U.S.C. Section 653.

§ 101.028. School

"School" means a primary or secondary school in which a child is enrolled or, if the child is not enrolled in a primary or secondary school, the public school district in which the child primarily resides.

§ 101.029. Standard Possession Order

"Standard possession order" means an order that provides a parent with rights of possession of a child in accordance with the terms and conditions of Subchapter F, Chapter 153.

§ 101.030. State

"State" means a state of the United States, the District of Columbia, the Commonwealth of Puerto Rico, or a territory or insular possession subject to the jurisdiction of the United States. The term includes an Indian tribe and a foreign jurisdiction that has established procedures for rendition and enforcement of an order that are substantially similar to the procedures of this title.

§ 101.0301. State Case Registry

"State case registry" means the registry established and operated by the Title IV-D agency under 42 U.S.C. Section 654a that has responsibility for maintaining records with respect to child support orders in all Title IV-D cases and in all other cases in which a support order is rendered or modified under this title on or after October 1, 1998.

§ 101.0302. State Disbursement Unit

"State disbursement unit" means the unit established and operated by the Title IV–D agency under 42 U.S.C. Section 654b that has responsibility for receiving, distributing, maintaining, and furnishing child support payments and records on or after October 1, 1999.

§ 101.031. Suit

"Suit" means a suit affecting the parent-child relationship.

§ 101.032. Suit Affecting the Parent-Child Relationship

(a) "Suit affecting the parent-child relationship" means a suit filed as provided by this title in which the appointment of a managing conservator or a possessory conservator, access to or support of a child, or establishment or termination of the parent-child relationship is requested.

(b) The following are not suits affecting the parent-child relationship:

(1) a habeas corpus proceeding under Chapter 157;

(2) a proceeding filed under Chapter 159 to determine parentage or to establish, enforce, or modify child support, whether this state is acting as the initiating or responding state; and

(3) a proceeding under Title 2.

§ 101.033. Title IV–D Agency

"Title IV–D agency" means the state agency designated under Chapter 231 to provide services under Part D of Title IV of the federal Social Security Act (42 U.S.C. Section 651 et seq.).

§ 101.034. Title IV-D Case

"Title IV-D case" means an action in which services are provided by the Title IV-D agency under Part D, Title IV, of the federal Social Security Act (42 U.S.C. Section 651 et seq.), relating to the location of an absent parent, determination of parentage, or establishment, modification, or enforcement of a child support or medical support obligation.

§ 101.035. Tribunal

"Tribunal" means a court, administrative agency, or quasi-judicial entity of a state authorized to establish, enforce, or modify support orders or to determine parentage.

CHAPTER 102. FILING SUIT

§ 102.001. Suit Authorized; Scope of Suit

(a) A suit may be filed as provided in this title.

(b) One or more matters covered by this title may be determined in the suit. The court, on its own motion, may require the parties to replead in order that any issue affecting the parent-child relationship may be determined in the suit.

§ 102.002. Commencement of Suit

An original suit begins by the filing of a petition as provided by this chapter.

§ 102.003. General Standing to File Suit

(a) An original suit may be filed at any time by:

(1) a parent of the child;

(2) the child through a representative authorized by the court;

(3) a custodian or person having the right of visitation with or access to the child appointed by an order of a court of another state or country;

(4) a guardian of the person or of the estate of the child;

(5) a governmental entity;

(6) an authorized agency;

(7) a licensed child placing agency;

(8) a man alleging himself to be the father of a child filing in accordance with Chapter 160, subject to the limitations of that chapter, but not otherwise;

(9) a person, other than a foster parent, who has had actual care, control, and possession of the child for at least six months ending not more than 90 days preceding the date of the filing of the petition;

(10) a person designated as the managing conservator in a revoked or unrevoked affidavit of relinquishment under Chapter 161 or to whom consent to adoption has been given in writing under Chapter 162;

(11) a person with whom the child and the child's guardian, managing conservator, or parent have resided for at least six months ending not more than 90 days preceding the date of the filing of the petition if the child's guardian, managing conservator, or parent is deceased at the time of the filing of the petition;

(12) a person who is the foster parent of a child placed by the Department of **Family and** Protective ~~and Regulatory~~ Services in the person's home for at least 12 months ending not more than 90 days preceding the date of the filing of the petition;

(13) a person who is a relative of the child within the third degree by consanguinity, as determined by Chapter 573, Government Code, if the child's parents are deceased at the time of the filing of the petition; or

(14) a person who has been named as a prospective adoptive parent of a child by a pregnant woman or the parent of the child, in a verified written statement to confer standing executed under Section 102.0035, regardless of whether the child has been born.

(b) In computing the time necessary for standing under Subsections (a)(9), (11), and (12), the court may not require that the time be continuous and uninterrupted but shall consider the child's principal residence during the relevant time preceding the date of commencement of the suit.

(c) Notwithstanding the time requirements of Subsection (a)(12), a person who is the foster parent of a child may file a suit to adopt a child for whom the person is providing foster care at any time after the person has been approved to adopt the child. The standing to file suit under this subsection applies only to the adoption of a child who is eligible to be adopted.

Amended by Acts 2011, 82nd Leg., ch. 110 (H.B. 841), § 10, eff. May 21, 2011.

Comment

As originally enacted in 1973, the standing to sue provision was extremely short, allowing "any person with an interest in the child" to bring a SAPCR. Hard as it is to believe, this formulation was more restrictive than the prior statute, at least in an alleged abuse or neglect situation which had granted "any adult" the authority to bring a suit. Unfortunately, the then-new code provision was sometimes tightly construed with regard to exactly who "had an interest" in the child. Some decisions had the effect of unduly restricting access to the courts, at least in the retrospective judgment of the legislature. As a result, over time the legislature has defined a wide variety of specific fact situations for which standing to sue is granted. Considerably more predictability is brought to the subject, with the result that there has been a marked fall off in litigation over questions of standing.

For years, controversy has raged over the standing of foster parents to seek an independent remedy apart from that sought by DFPS when a child has lived in the foster parents' home for a considerable period of time. That time period has changed from 18 months in 1997 to the current 12 months, and it is clear that the legislature has limited application of the Subsection (a)(9) "actual care, control and possession of the child" grounds for standing to a person "other than a foster parent"; foster parents have their own provision.

Subsection (a)(13) adds an extremely narrow provision applicable only if the child's parents are deceased at the time of the filing of the petition. In that case, a person "within the third degree by consanguinity" has standing. Third degree of consanguinity of an individual includes parents, grandparents, and great-grandparents, paternal and maternal uncles and aunts, siblings, and nephews and nieces of the parent.

Subsection (14) provides that a pregnant woman or a parent of a child may confer standing to a prospective adoptive parent. Section 102.0035 provides specific details that must be contained in a statement to confer standing on a prospective adoptive parent.

Subsection (c) adds yet another more particularized standing provision that applies to a narrow range of foster parents who have been approved to adopt a child eligible for adoption.

CLE/Other Legal Publications

Jurisdiction/standing. Christopher K. Wrampelmeier, 2011 ADV. FAM. L.
Standing: where do I begin? Janet McCullar Vavra, 2011 U.T. ADVANCED PARENT-CHILD RELATIONSHIPS
Jurisdiction and standing. Angela Pence England & Harry L. Tindall, 2011 SO. TEX. FAM. L.
Venue/jurisdiction: where to file a SAPCR. Harry L. Tindall, 2011 U.T. PARENT-CHILD RELATIONSHIPS: BASICS

Venue, standing and jurisdiction. Stephen J. Naylor, 2011 MARRIAGE DISSOLUTION

International and domestic jurisdiction issues: UIFSA, UCCJEA, UCAPA, PKPA, FFCCSOA, ICARA. Karl E. Hays & Janet McCullar Vavra, 2011 UT FAM. L. FRONT LINES

Follow the yellow brick road: jurisdiction and venue issues. JoAl Cannon Sheridan, 2010 MARRIAGE DISSOLUTION

***See* Accompanying CD-ROM for Additional CLE/Other Legal Publications.**

Leading Cases

Jones v. Fowler, 969 S.W.2d 429 (Tex. 1998) (omission of "immediately" before "proceeding" in recodification of statute was not a substantive change in law)

In re J.W.T., 872 S.W.2d 189 (Tex. 1994) (under described factual circumstances, biological father has Tex. Const. right to establish his paternity over objections of mother and her husband)

In re M.K.S.-V., 301 S.W. 3d 460 (Tex. App.—Dallas 2009, no pet.)(visitation per agreement gave former lesbian partner standing to seek conservatorship—but not adoption)

In re Roxsane R., 249 S.W.3d 764 (Tex. App.—Fort Worth 2008, orig. proceeding) (nonsuit of TDFPS suit requires dismissal of foster parent's plea in intervention because they had no other affirmative pleadings on file)

In re M.J.G., 248 S.W.3d 753 (Tex. App.—Fort Worth 2008, no pet.) (grandparents lacked standing to file a motion for new trial)

In re J.P., 196 S.W.3d 434 (Tex. App.—Dallas 2006, no pet.) (termination of father's parentage rights removes paternal aunt's standing as well)

In re C.M.C., 192 S.W.3d 866 (Tex. App.—Texarkana 2006, no pet.) (out of state grandparents denied standing to seek adoption after termination of parental rights when paternal aunt children)

In re Sullivan, 157 S.W.3d 911 (Tex. App.—Houston [14th Dist.] 2005, orig. proceeding) (man who donated sperm had standing to adjudicate parentage)

§ 102.0035. Statement to Confer Standing

(a) A pregnant woman or a parent of a child may execute a statement to confer standing to a prospective adoptive parent as provided by this section to assert standing under Section 102.003(a)(14). A statement to confer standing under this section may not be executed in a suit brought by a governmental entity under Chapter 262 or 263.

(b) A statement to confer standing must contain:

(1) the signature, name, age, and address of the person named as a prospective adoptive parent;

(2) the signature, name, age, and address of the pregnant woman or of the parent of the child who is consenting to the filing of a petition for adoption or to terminate the parent-child relationship as described by Subsection (a);

(3) the birth date of the child or the anticipated birth date if the child has not been born; and

(4) the name of the county in which the suit will be filed.

(c) The statement to confer standing must be attached to the petition in a suit affecting the parent-child relationship. The statement may not be used for any purpose other than to confer standing in a proceeding for adoption or to terminate the parent-child relationship.

(d) A statement to confer standing may be signed at any time during the pregnancy of the mother of the unborn child whose parental rights are to be terminated.

(e) A statement to confer standing is not required in a suit brought by a person who has standing to file a suit affecting the parent-child relationship under Sections 102.003(a)(1)–(13) or any other law under which the person has standing to file a suit.

(f) A person who executes a statement to confer standing may revoke the statement at any time before the person executes an affidavit for voluntary relinquishment of parental rights. The revocation of the statement must be in writing and must be sent by certified mail, return receipt requested, to the prospective adoptive parent.

(g) On filing with the court proof of the delivery of the revocation of a statement to confer standing under Subsection (f), the court shall dismiss any suit affecting the parent-child relationship filed by the prospective adoptive parent named in the statement.

§ 102.004. Standing for Grandparent or Other Person

(a) In addition to the general standing to file suit provided by Section 102.003, a grandparent, or another relative of the child related within the third degree by consanguinity, may file an original suit requesting managing conservatorship if there is satisfactory proof to the court that:

(1) the order requested is necessary because the child's present circumstances would significantly impair the child's physical health or emotional development; or

(2) both parents, the surviving parent, or the managing conservator or custodian either filed the petition or consented to the suit.

(b) An original suit requesting possessory conservatorship may not be filed by a grandparent or other person. However, the court may grant a grandparent or other person deemed by the court to have had substantial past contact with the child leave to intervene in a pending suit filed by a person authorized to do so under this subchapter if there is satisfactory proof to the court that appointment of a parent as a sole managing conservator or both parents as joint managing conservators would significantly impair the child's physical health or emotional development.

(c) Possession of or access to a child by a grandparent is governed by the standards established by Chapter 153.

Comment

Grandparents have long had standing to request managing conservatorship in cases in which a child's environment was physically or emotionally dangerous. In 2007, that same standing was given to any relative of the child related within the third degree of consanguinity, thereby allowing such suits to be brought by great-grandparents, siblings, and blood aunts and uncles.

Leading Cases

In re M.J.G., 248 S.W.3d 753 (Tex. App.—Fort Worth 2008, no pet.) (grandparents lacked standing to file a motion for new trial)

In re J.P., 196 S.W.3d 434 (Tex. App.—Dallas 2006, no pet.) (termination of father's parentage rights removes paternal aunt's standing as well)

In re C.M.C., 192 S.W.3d 866 (Tex. App.—Texarkana 2006, no pet.) (out-of-state grandparents denied standing to seek adoption after termination of parental rights)

§ 102.0045. Standing for Sibling

(a) The sibling of a child may file an original suit requesting access to the child as provided by Section 153.551 if the sibling is at least 18 years of age.

(b) Access to a child by a sibling of the child is governed by the standards established by Section 153.551.

§ 102.005. Standing to Request Termination and Adoption

An original suit requesting only an adoption or for termination of the parent-child relationship joined with a petition for adoption may be filed by:

(1) a stepparent of the child;

(2) an adult who, as the result of a placement for adoption, has had actual possession and control of the child at any time during the 30–day period preceding the filing of the petition;

(3) an adult who has had actual possession and control of the child for not less than two months during the three-month period preceding the filing of the petition;

(4) an adult who has adopted, or is the foster parent of and has petitioned to adopt, a sibling of the child; or

(5) another adult whom the court determines to have had substantial past contact with the child sufficient to warrant standing to do so.

§ 102.006. Limitations on Standing

(a) Except as provided by Subsections (b) and (c), if the parent-child relationship between the child and every living parent of the child has been terminated, an original suit may not be filed by:

(1) a former parent whose parent-child relationship with the child has been terminated by court order;

(2) the father of the child; or

(3) a family member or relative by blood, adoption, or marriage of either a former parent whose parent-child relationship has been terminated or of the father of the child.

(b) The limitations on filing suit imposed by this section do not apply to a person who:

(1) has a continuing right to possession of or access to the child under an existing court order; or

(2) has the consent of the child's managing conservator, guardian, or legal custodian to bring the suit.

(c) The limitations on filing suit imposed by this section do not apply to an adult sibling of the child, a grandparent of the child, an aunt who is a sister of a parent of the child, or an uncle who is a brother of a parent of the child if the adult sibling, grandparent, aunt, or uncle files an original suit or a suit for modification requesting managing conservatorship of the child not later than the 90th day after the date the parent-child relationship between the child and the parent is terminated in a suit filed by the Department of Family and Protective Services requesting the termination of the parent-child relationship.

§ 102.007. Standing of Title IV–D Agency

In providing services authorized by Chapter 231, the Title IV–D agency or a political subdivision contracting with the attorney general to provide Title IV–D services under this title may file a child support action authorized under this title, including a suit for modification or a motion for enforcement.

§ 102.008. Contents of Petition

(a) The petition and all other documents in a proceeding filed under this title, except a suit for adoption of an adult, shall be entitled "In the interest of ________, a child." In a suit in which adoption of a child is requested, the style shall be "In the interest of a child."

(b) The petition must include:

(1) a statement that the court in which the petition is filed has continuing, exclusive jurisdiction or that no court has continuing jurisdiction of the suit;

(2) the name and date of birth of the child, except that if adoption of a child is requested, the name of the child may be omitted;

(3) the full name of the petitioner and the petitioner's relationship to the child or the fact that no relationship exists;

(4) the names of the parents, except in a suit in which adoption is requested;

(5) the name of the managing conservator, if any, or the child's custodian, if any, appointed by order of a court of another state or country;

(6) the names of the guardians of the person and estate of the child, if any;

(7) the names of possessory conservators or other persons, if any, having possession of or access to the child under an order of the court;

(8) the name of an alleged father of the child or a statement that the identity of the father of the child is unknown;

(9) a full description and statement of value of all property owned or possessed by the child;

(10) a statement describing what action the court is requested to take concerning the child and the statutory grounds on which the request is made; and

(11) any other information required by this title.

Comment

Prior to September 1, 2001, certain identification information was required in an application for a protective order, the registration for enforcement of a support order, and a petition in a SAPCR. *See* §§ 82.004 and 159.602. In some counties, a few attorneys searched the public records in order to notify respondents of the existence of proceedings under the Family Code before service could be effected. The Family Law Council expressed concern that some of the information required, especially the petitioner's address, could provide a method for an abusive spouse to locate the abused spouse. In response, the 2001 amendment to this section (and the others cited above) removes the requirement that certain information be included in the specified applications and petitions in order to protect the location of a party until the court can make a determination of whether that location should be revealed. The information deleted from the filed documents includes the address requirement for an application for a protective order and registration for enforcement of a support order, and the sex, age, place of birth, and place of residence of a child in a SAPCR petition.

Cross Reference

TX FCA FAMILY § 6.406, Mandatory Joinder of SAPCR, *supra*; TX FCA FAMILY § 6.407, *supra*, SAPCR To Be Transferred to Divorce Court, *supra*.

§ 102.0085. Repealed.

§ 102.0086. Confidentiality of Pleadings

(a) This section applies only in a county with a population of 3.4 million or more.

(b) Except as otherwise provided by law, all pleadings and other documents filed with the court in a suit affecting the parent-child relationship are confidential, are excepted from required public disclosure under Chapter 552, Government Code, and may not be released to a person who is not a party to the suit until after the date of service of citation or the 31st day after the date of filing the suit, whichever date is sooner.

Comment

This is the latest installment in the struggle to regulate solicitation of business by family law attorneys in Harris County. The legislature previously noted and attempted to prevent notification of respondents in a divorce, SAPCR, or protective order context prior to service of citation. Particularly in the protective order context, notification of an application for a protective order was thought to have a potential for facilitating additional domestic violence. Notwithstanding this argument, the federal Fifth Circuit has ruled that solicitation of business and family law cases is legal under the U.S. Constitution. Confidentiality requirements in this new section are deemed by the legislature not to be inconsistent with that decision. For Harris County only there is a delay in full public disclosure at the time of filing for three types of suits: divorce, SAPCRs, and protective order applications. If the Houston practice spreads to other counties, it seems likely that the limitation of the statute to Harris County may be altered.

§ 102.009. Service of Citation

(a) Except as provided by Subsection (b), the following are entitled to service of citation on the filing of a petition in an original suit:

(1) a managing conservator;

(2) a possessory conservator;

(3) a person having possession of or access to the child under an order;

(4) a person required by law or by order to provide for the support of the child;

(5) a guardian of the person of the child;

(6) a guardian of the estate of the child;

(7) each parent as to whom the parent-child relationship has not been terminated or process has not been waived under Chapter 161;

(8) an alleged father, unless there is attached to the petition an affidavit of waiver of interest in a child executed by the alleged father as provided by Chapter 161 or unless the petitioner has complied with the provisions of Section 161.002(b)(2), (3), or (4);

(9) a man who has filed a notice of intent to claim paternity as provided by Chapter 160;

(10) the Department of Family and Protective Services, if the petition requests that the department be appointed as managing conservator of the child;

(11) the Title IV–D agency, if the petition requests the termination of the parent-child relationship and support rights have been assigned to the Title IV–D agency under Chapter 231;

(12) a prospective adoptive parent to whom standing has been conferred under Section 102.0035; and

(13) a person designated as the managing conservator in a revoked or unrevoked affidavit of relinquishment under Chapter 161 or to whom consent to adoption has been given in writing under Chapter 162.

(b) Citation may be served on any other person who has or who may assert an interest in the child.

(c) Citation on the filing of an original petition in a suit shall be issued and served as in other civil cases.

(d) If the petition requests the establishment, termination, modification, or enforcement of a support right assigned to the Title IV–D agency under Chapter 231 or the rescission of a voluntary acknowledgment of paternity under Chapter 160, notice shall be given to the Title IV–D agency in a manner provided by Rule 21a, Texas Rules of Civil Procedure.

(e) In a proceeding under Chapter 233, the requirements imposed by Subsections (a) and (c) do not apply to the extent of any conflict between those requirements and the provisions in Chapter 233.

Leading Cases

Matthis v. Lockwood, 156 S.W.3d 743 (Tex. 2005) (counsel's testimony that notice of final hearing mailed not enough to sustain default judgment without further evidence)

In re K.B.A., 145 S.W.3d 685 (Tex. App.—Fort Worth 2004, no pet.) (failure to give notice voids termination order)

Griggs v. Latham, 98 S.W.3d 382 (Tex. App.—Corpus Christi 2003, pet. denied) (father JMC necessary party in maternal grandparent's access suit; nonsuiting him and continuing to seek access reversible error)

§ 102.010. Service of Citation by Publication

(a) Citation may be served by publication as in other civil cases to persons entitled to service of citation who cannot be notified by personal service or registered or certified mail and to persons whose names are unknown.

(b) Citation by publication shall be published one time. If the name of a person entitled to service of citation is unknown, the notice to be published shall be addressed to "All Whom It May Concern." One or more causes to be heard on a certain day may be included in one notice and hearings may be continued from time to time without further notice.

(c) Citation by publication shall be sufficient if given in substantially the following form:

To (names of persons to be served with citation) and to all whom it may concern (if the name of any person to be served with citation is unknown), Respondent(s),

"STATE OF TEXAS

"You have been sued. You may employ an attorney. If you or your attorney do (does) not file a written answer with the clerk who issued this citation by 10 a.m. on the Monday next following the expiration of 20 days after you were served this citation and petition, a default judgment may be taken against you. The petition of __________, Petitioner, was filed in the Court of __________ County, Texas, on the ___ day of _______, ____, against ________, Respondent(s), numbered ____, and entitled 'In the interest of ________, a child (or children).' The suit requests (statement of relief requested, e.g., 'terminate the parent-child relationship'). The date and place of birth of the child (children) who is (are) the subject of the suit: __________.

"The court has authority in this suit to render an order in the child's (children's) interest that will be binding on you, including the termination of the parent-child relationship, the determination of paternity, and the appointment of a conservator with authority to consent to the child's (children's) adoption.

"Issued and given under my hand and seal of the Court at _______, Texas, this the ___ day of ______, ____.

"________________________
Clerk of the District Court of
__________ County, Texas.
By ______, Deputy."

(d) In any suit in which service of citation is by publication, a statement of the evidence of service, approved and signed by the court, must be filed with the papers of the suit as a part of the record.

(e) In a suit filed under Chapter 161 or 262 in which the last name of the respondent is unknown, the court may order substituted service of citation by publication, including publication by posting the citation at the courthouse door for a specified time, if the court finds and states in its order that the method of substituted service is as likely as citation by publication in a newspaper in the manner described by Subsection (b) to give the respondent actual notice of the suit. If the court orders that citation by publication shall be completed by posting the citation at the courthouse door for a specified time, service must be completed on, and the answer date is computed from, the expiration date of the posting period. If the court orders another method of substituted service of citation by publication, service shall be completed as directed by the court.

Comment

Generally, in civil cases a court may order citation by publication through posting notice at the courthouse door, provided the court finds this method will give respondent actual notice of the proceeding. Heretofore, there has been some question as to whether this method of service is applicable in a SAPCR. Henceforth, posting at the courthouse door is an acceptable method of citation by publication if the court deems it to be appropriate.

Leading Case

Rider v. Farris, 718 S.W.2d 883 (Tex. App.—Beaumont 1986, writ dism'd w.o.j.) (inadequate citation by publication)

§ 102.011. Acquiring Jurisdiction over Nonresident

(a) The court may exercise status or subject matter jurisdiction over the suit as provided by Chapter 152.

(b) The court may also exercise personal jurisdiction over a person on whom service of citation is required or over the person's personal representative, although the person is not a resident or domiciliary of this state, if:

(1) the person is personally served with citation in this state;

(2) the person submits to the jurisdiction of this state by consent, by entering a general appearance, or by filing a responsive document having the effect of waiving any contest to personal jurisdiction;

(3) the child resides in this state as a result of the acts or directives of the person;

(4) the person resided with the child in this state;

(5) the person resided in this state and provided prenatal expenses or support for the child;

(6) the person engaged in sexual intercourse in this state and the child may have been conceived by that act of intercourse;

(7) the person, as provided by Chapter 160:

(A) registered with the paternity registry maintained by the bureau of vital statistics; or

(B) signed an acknowledgment of paternity of a child born in this state; or

(8) there is any basis consistent with the constitutions of this state and the United States for the exercise of the personal jurisdiction.

Comment

Following the enactment of the UCCJA in 1983, coupled with the federal enactment of the PKPA in 1980, and culminating in the enactment of the UCCJEA in 1999, any possible argument that personal jurisdiction is required to adjudicate managing conservatorship or custody has been definitively repudiated and replaced with the concept that a determination of conservatorship or visitation is a "status adjudication." Thus, conservatorship issues may be decided by a court with SAPCR jurisdiction even if there is no personal jurisdiction over an absent parent. If the court has jurisdiction over the custody status, a valid assertion of long arm personal jurisdiction over an absent respondent will enable a Texas court to settle all issues in a SAPCR, including child support.

CLE/Other Legal Publications

UCCJEA/UIFSA. Harry L. Tindall, 2011 U.T. ADVANCED PARENT-CHILD RELATIONSHIPS

Ding! You are now free to move about the country: UCCJEA and UIFSA. JoAl Cannon Sheridan, 2011 ADV. FAM. L.

International and domestic jurisdiction issues: UIFSA, UCCJEA, UCAPA, PKPA, FFCCSOA, ICARA. Karl E. Hays & Janet McCullar Vavra, 2011 U.T. FAM. L. FRONT LINES

Jurisdiction/standing. Christopher K. Wrampelmeier, 2011 ADV. FAM. L.

Standing: where do I begin? Janet McCullar Vavra, 2011 U.T. ADVANCED PARENT-CHILD RELATIONSHIPS

Jurisdiction and standing. Angela Pence England & Harry L. Tindall, 2011 SO. TEX. FAM. L.

Uniform Child Custody Jurisdiction and Enforcement Act (with Prefatory Notes and Comment). Robert G. Spector, 32 FAM. L.Q. 301 (1998)

Leading Cases

Burnham v. Superior Court of California, 495 U.S. 604, 109 L.Ed.2d 631, 110 S.Ct. 2105 (1990) (in personam jurisdiction obtained by service of citation in forum state on transient respondent)

Kulko v. Superior Court of California, 436 U.S. 84, 56 L.Ed.2d 132, 98 S.Ct. 1690 (1978) (application of California long-arm statute did not conform to constitutional requirements)

May v. Anderson, 345 U.S. 528, 97 L.Ed. 1221, 73 S.Ct. 840 (1953) (leading pre-UCCJA case on custody jurisdiction)

In re Forlenza, 140 S.W.3d 373 (Tex. 2004) (UCCJEA jurisdiction continues in Texas when resident-parent's contacts with out-of-state children remain significant)

In re Burk, 252 S.W.3d 736 (Tex. App.—Houston [14th Dist.] 2008, mand. denied) (Texas is home state of child less than 6 months old when child is absent from state but a parent continues to live in Texas)

In re A.B., 207 S.W.3d 434 (Tex. App.—Dallas 2006, no pet.) (old default judgment for child support based on service by publication is enough to establish personal jurisdiction over nonresident obligor)

In re Brown, 203 S.W.3d 888 (Tex. App.—Fort Worth 2006, no pet.) (Missouri, not Texas, was home state of older child and infant had significant connections with Missouri as well)

In re G.L.A., 195 S.W.3d 787 (Tex. App.—Beaumont 2006, rev. denied) (UIFSA enforcement of Maryland child support required of Texas trial court because obligor submitted to personal jurisdiction)

Ruffier v. Ruffier, 190 S.W.3d 884 (Tex. App.—El Paso 2006, no pet.) (when Belarus, not Texas, is home state, Texas has no jurisdiction to decide custody)

In re J.S., 175 S.W.3d 526 (Tex. App.—Texarkana 2005, no pet.) (under UCCJEA, Georgia as home state has custody jurisdiction; personal jurisdiction of both parents in Texas irrelevant)

Dickerson v. Doyle, 170 S.W.3d 713 (Tex. App.—El Paso 2005, no pet.) (Texas court appropriately declined jurisdiction over parentage suit where Alabama was more convenient forum)

In re M.G.M., 163 S.W.3d 191 (Tex. App.—Beaumont 2005, no pet.) (temporary protective order proper under UCCJEA even if Texas not home state; valid until home state acts)

Cross Reference

Parental Kidnapping Prevention Act (PKPA) TX FCA 28 USCA § 1738A, *infra*.

---

§ 102.012. Exercising Partial Jurisdiction

(a) A court in which a suit is filed may exercise its jurisdiction over those portions of the suit for which it has authority.

(b) The court's authority to resolve all issues in controversy between the parties may be restricted because the court lacks:

(1) the required personal jurisdiction over a nonresident party;

(2) the required jurisdiction under Chapter 152; or

(3) the required jurisdiction under Chapter 159.

(c) If a provision of Chapter 152 or Chapter 159 expressly conflicts with another provision of this title and the conflict cannot be reconciled, the provision of Chapter 152 or Chapter 159 prevails.

(d) In exercising jurisdiction, the court shall seek to harmonize the provisions of this code, the federal Parental Kidnapping Prevention Act (28 U.S.C. Section 1738A), and the federal Full Faith and Credit for Child Support Order Act (28 U.S.C. Section 1738B).

§ 102.013. Docketing Requirements

(a) In a suit for modification or a motion for enforcement, the clerk shall file the petition or motion and all related papers under the same docket number as the prior proceeding without additional letters, digits, or special designations.

(b) If a suit requests the adoption of a child, the clerk shall file the suit and all other papers relating to the suit in a new file having a new docket number.

(c) In a suit to determine parentage under this title in which the court has rendered an order relating to an earlier born child of the same parents, the clerk shall file the suit and all other papers relating to the suit under the same docket number as the prior parentage action. For all other purposes, including the assessment of fees and other costs, the suit is a separate suit.

CHAPTER 103. VENUE AND TRANSFER OF ORIGINAL PROCEEDINGS

Introductory Comment

The basic venue rule for an original SAPCR is to file where the child resides. The numerous exceptions to the general rule have not resulted in much reported litigation. Further, SAPCR venue applies only in a case in which a divorce suit is not pending, because divorce venue controls if there is conflict between divorce venue and SAPCR venue, § 6.407, § 103.002. Even in the event that an action for divorce is filed later than the SAPCR, the SAPCR court is required to transfer the action to the divorce county. However, there is a special exception to the rule of divorce venue dominance in instances in which DFPS files a SAPCR alleging abuse or neglect. *See* § 6.407 and § 262.203.

CLE/Other Legal Publications

Venue/jurisdiction: where to file a SAPCR. Harry L. Tindall, 2011 U.T. Parent-Child Relationships: Basics

Venue, standing and jurisdiction. Stephen J. Naylor, 2011 Marriage Dissolution

Jurisdiction and venue. Brad M. LaMorgese, 2009 Marriage Dissolution

Leading Cases

In re Ferguson, 172 S.W.3d 122 (Tex. App.—Beaumont 2005, orig. proceeding) (mandatory transfer of SAPCR to county of child's residence does not recognize "dual residence" concept)

Chalu v. Shamala, 125 S.W.3d 737 (Tex. App.—Houston [1st Dist.] 2003, no pet.) (no interlocutory appeal from transfer orders)

Cross References

TX FCA Family § 155.001 *et seq.*, Continuing, Exclusive Jurisdiction: Transfer, *infra*; TX FCA Family § 155.201 *et seq.*, subch. C, *infra*. Transfer of Continuing, Exclusive Jurisdiction, *infra*.

11/5/12

§ 103.001. Venue for Original Suit

(a) Except as otherwise provided by this title, an original suit shall be filed in the county where the child resides, unless:

(1) another court has continuing exclusive jurisdiction under Chapter 155; or

(2) venue is fixed in a suit for dissolution of a marriage under Subchapter D, Chapter 6.

(b) A suit in which adoption is requested may be filed in the county where the child resides or in the county where the petitioners reside.

(c) A child resides in the county where the child's parents reside or the child's parent resides, if only one parent is living, except that:

(1) if a guardian of the person has been appointed by order of a county or probate court and a managing conservator has not been appointed, the child resides in the county where the guardian of the person resides;

(2) if the parents of the child do not reside in the same county and if a managing conservator, custodian, or guardian of the person has not been appointed, the child resides in the county where the parent having actual care, control, and possession of the child resides;

(3) if the child is in the care and control of an adult other than a parent and a managing conservator, custodian, or guardian of the person has not been appointed, the child resides where the adult having actual care, control, and possession of the child resides;

(4) if the child is in the actual care, control, and possession of an adult other than a parent and the whereabouts of the parent and the guardian of the person is unknown, the child resides where the adult having actual possession, care, and control of the child resides;

(5) if the person whose residence would otherwise determine venue has left the child in the care and control of the adult, the child resides where that adult resides;

(6) if a guardian or custodian of the child has been appointed by order of a court of another state or country, the child resides in the county where the guardian or custodian resides if that person resides in this state; or

(7) if it appears that the child is not under the actual care, control, and possession of an adult, the child resides where the child is found.

end

§ 103.002. Transfer of Original Proceedings Within State

(a) If venue of a suit is improper in the court in which an original suit is filed and no other court has continuing, exclusive jurisdiction of the suit, on the timely motion of a party other than the petitioner, the court shall transfer the proceeding to the county where venue is proper.

(b) On a showing that a suit for dissolution of the marriage of the child's parents has been filed in another court, a court in which a suit is pending shall transfer the proceedings to the court where the dissolution of the marriage is pending.

(c) The procedures in Chapter 155 apply to a transfer of:

(1) an original suit under this section; or

(2) a suit for modification or a motion for enforcement under this title.

§ 103.003. Transfer of Original Suit Within State when Party or Child Resides Outside State

(a) A court of this state in which an original suit is filed or in which a suit for child support is filed under Chapter 159 shall transfer the suit to the county of residence of the party who is a resident of this state if all other parties and children affected by the proceedings reside outside this state.

(b) If one or more of the parties affected by the suit reside outside this state and if more than one party or one or more children affected by the proceeding reside in this state in different counties, the court shall transfer the suit according to the following priorities:

(1) to the court of continuing, exclusive jurisdiction, if any;

(2) to the county of residence of the child, if applicable, provided that:

(A) there is no court of continuing, exclusive jurisdiction; or

(B) the court of continuing, exclusive jurisdiction finds that neither a party nor a child affected by the proceeding resides in the county of the court of continuing jurisdiction; or

(3) if Subdivisions (1) and (2) are inapplicable, to the county most appropriate to serve the convenience of the resident parties, the witnesses, and the interest of justice.

(c) If a transfer of an original suit or suit for child support under Chapter 159 is sought under this section, Chapter 155 applies to the procedures for transfer of the suit.

CHAPTER 104. EVIDENCE

Introductory Comment

Several distinctive procedures that apply to the testimony of a child in a SAPCR are established by this chapter. The first is designed to facilitate the testimony of a child given at trial, either by remote live broadcast or by prerecorded tape. The second deals with a wholly unrelated matter, *i.e.*, the videotape pretrial recording of the "first outcry" of an allegedly abused or neglected child. If the methodology described is followed carefully, the resulting videotape may be introduced into evidence at trial as yet another exception to the hearsay rule. Third, procedures are detailed for remote broadcast of a child's testimony at trial. Finally, provisions are made for a variety of other methods to put the child's statements in the record, including expert testimony given via video conference.

CLE/Other Legal Publications

Child evidentiary issues and child testimony in CPS cases. Hon. J. Andrew Hathcock, 2009 ADV. FAM. L.

Special evidentiary issues relating to children. Judy L. Warne, 2009 U.T. PARENT-CHILD REL.

Giving the kids a voice in the courtroom. Wendy S. Burgower, 2008 ADV. FAM. L.

Leading Cases

Kumho Tire Company, Ltd. v. Carmichael, 526 U.S. 137, 119 S.Ct. 1167 (1999) (*Daubert* factors apply to scientific testimony not just to "scientific" testimony)

In re Kuntz, 124 S.W.3d 179 (Tex. 2003) (defining what is required regarding discovery or documents in person's "possession, custody, or control")

Thompson v. Davis, 901 S.W.2d 939 (Tex. 1995) (court abused discretion by extending discovery sanction in child support action to custody case)

Richardson v. Green, 677 S.W.2d 497 (Tex. 1984) (termination reversed, videotape of child replete with leading questions by caseworker)

In re E.A.K., 192 S.W.3d 133 (Tex. App.—Houston [14th Dist.] 2006, pet. denied) (inadmissible evidence of father sexually abusing stepdaughter causes reversal and second trial)

Allen v. Mancini, 170 S.W.3d 167 (Tex. App.—Eastland 2005, pet. denied) (illegal wiretap evidence admissible on civil side of the docket)

In re S.E.W., 168 S.W.3d 875 (Tex. App.—Dallas 2005, no pet.) (even in CPS case "expert" must be qualified to testify)

In re S.P., 168 S.W.3d 197 (Tex. App.—Dallas 2005, no pet.) (admissibility of minor child's videotaped statement)

In re K.L.R., 162 S.W.3d 291 (Tex. App.—Tyler 2005, no pet.) (expert testimony in soft science must be reliable under standards applicable to the subject matter of testimony)

---

§ 104.001. Rules of Evidence

Except as otherwise provided, the Texas Rules of Evidence apply as in other civil cases.

§ 104.002. Prerecorded Statement of Child

If a child 12 years of age or younger is alleged in a suit under this title to have been abused, the recording of an oral statement of the child recorded prior to the proceeding is admissible into evidence if:

(1) no attorney for a party was present when the statement was made;

(2) the recording is both visual and aural and is recorded on film or videotape or by other electronic means;

(3) the recording equipment was capable of making an accurate recording, the operator was competent, and the recording is accurate and has not been altered;

(4) the statement was not made in response to questioning calculated to lead the child to make a particular statement;

(5) each voice on the recording is identified;

(6) the person conducting the interview of the child in the recording is present at the proceeding and available to testify or be cross-examined by either party; and

(7) each party is afforded an opportunity to view the recording before it is offered into evidence.

§ 104.003. Prerecorded Videotaped Testimony of Child

(a) The court may, on the motion of a party to the proceeding, order that the testimony of the child be taken outside the courtroom and be recorded for showing in the courtroom before the court, the finder of fact, and the parties to the proceeding.

(b) Only an attorney for each party, an attorney ad litem for the child or other person whose presence would contribute to the welfare and well-being of the child, and persons necessary to operate the equipment may be present in the room with the child during the child's testimony.

(c) Only the attorneys for the parties may question the child.

(d) The persons operating the equipment shall be placed in a manner that prevents the child from seeing or hearing them.

(e) The court shall ensure that:

(1) the recording is both visual and aural and is recorded on film or videotape or by other electronic means;

(2) the recording equipment was capable of making an accurate recording, the operator was competent, and the recording is accurate and is not altered;

(3) each voice on the recording is identified; and

(4) each party to the proceeding is afforded an opportunity to view the recording before it is shown in the courtroom.

§ 104.004. Remote Televised Broadcast of Testimony of Child

(a) If in a suit a child 12 years of age or younger is alleged to have been abused, the court may, on the motion of a party to the proceeding, order that the testimony of the child be taken in a room other than the courtroom and be televised by closed-circuit equipment in the courtroom to be viewed by the court and the parties.

(b) The procedures that apply to prerecorded videotaped testimony of a child apply to the remote broadcast of testimony of a child.

Leading Cases

Maryland v. Craig, 497 U.S. 836, 111 L.Ed.2d 666, 110 S.Ct. 3157 (1990) (closed circuit TV testimony by child victim of criminal sexual abuse does not violate confrontation clause)

In re S.P., 168 S.W.3d 197 (Tex. App.—Dallas 2005, no pet.) (minor child's videotaped statement held to be inadmissible)

§ 104.005. Substitution for In-Court Testimony of Child

(a) If the testimony of a child is taken as provided by this chapter, the child may not be compelled to testify in court during the proceeding.

(b) The court may allow the testimony of a child of any age to be taken in any manner provided by this chapter if the child, because of a medical condition, is incapable of testifying in open court.

Comment

The special rules for testimony of a child 12 or younger are extended to older children if the court finds that a child is incapable of testifying in open court. The literal language seems to limit this exception to a medical condition, and not to a psychological or emotional condition. This, of course, leads to the option of "medical treatment" by a psychiatrist, thereby opening the door for the argument that psychiatric difficulties are a medical condition.

---

§ 104.006. Hearsay Statement of Child Abuse Victim

In a suit affecting the parent-child relationship, a statement made by a child 12 years of age or younger that describes alleged abuse against the child, without regard to whether the statement is otherwise inadmissible as hearsay, is admissible as evidence if, in a hearing conducted outside the presence of the jury, the court finds that the time, content, and circumstances of the statement provide sufficient indications of the statement's reliability and:

(1) the child testifies or is available to testify at the proceeding in court or in any other manner provided for by law; or

(2) the court determines that the use of the statement in lieu of the child's testimony is necessary to protect the welfare of the child.

Comment

Prosecutors representing DFPS, or other litigants alleging child abuse, may find this section extremely useful. Third parties may testify as to hearsay statements by a child about abuse. Several requirements are imposed. Either the child must be available to testify, or actually does testify. More importantly, the court may determine that the introduction of the statement is an appropriate substitute for the child's testimony if necessary to protect the child's welfare. Of course, the court must also find the statement to be reliable. A young child whose memory is of the short term variety thus may have the original outcry reproduced in court by a substitute witness.

Leading Cases

In re S.P., 168 S.W.3d 197 (Tex. App.—Dallas 2005, no pet.) (minor child's videotaped statement held inadmissible)

In re P.E.W., 105 S.W.3d 771 (Tex. App.—Amarillo 2003, no pet.) (child's abuse statements deemed reliable)

---

§ 104.007. Video Testimony of Certain Professionals

(a) In this section, "professional" has the meaning assigned by Section 261.101(b).

(b) In a proceeding brought by the Department of Protective and Regulatory Services concerning a child who is alleged in a suit to have been abused or neglected, the court may order, with the agreement of the state's counsel and the defendant's counsel, that the testimony of a professional be taken outside the courtroom by videoconference.

(c) In ordering testimony to be taken as provided by Subsection (b), the court shall ensure that the videoconference testimony allows:

(1) the parties and attorneys involved in the proceeding to be able to see and hear the professional as the professional testifies; and

(2) the professional to be able to see and hear the parties and attorneys examining the professional while the professional is testifying.

(d) If the court permits the testimony of a professional by videoconference as provided by this section to be admitted during the proceeding, the professional may not be compelled to be physically present in court during the same proceeding to provide the same testimony unless ordered by the court.

Comment

Over the years, the courts have become accustomed to the relatively rare situation in which a child is permitted to testify either by pre-recorded videotape or by remote live televised broadcast. The extension of this privilege to professionals to accept video conference testimony regarding alleged abuse or neglect of a child is obviously based on a quite different philosophy. That is, the child's testimony through video means is to protect the child, while this extension will be necessary only for the convenience of the professional and perhaps the attorneys.

CHAPTER 105. SETTINGS, HEARINGS, AND ORDERS

§ 105.001. Temporary Orders Before Final Order

(a) In a suit, the court may make a temporary order, including the modification of a prior temporary order, for the safety and welfare of the child, including an order:

(1) for the temporary conservatorship of the child;

(2) for the temporary support of the child;

(3) restraining a party from disturbing the peace of the child or another party;

(4) prohibiting a person from removing the child beyond a geographical area identified by the court; or

(5) for payment of reasonable attorney's fees and expenses.

(b) Except as provided by Subsection (c), temporary restraining orders and temporary injunctions under this section shall be granted without the necessity of an affidavit or verified pleading stating specific facts showing that immediate and irreparable injury, loss, or damage will result before notice can be served and a hearing can be held. Except as provided by Subsection (h), an order may not be rendered under Subsection (a)(1), (2), or (5) except after notice and a hearing. A temporary restraining order or temporary injunction granted under this section need not:

(1) define the injury or state why it is irreparable;

(2) state why the order was granted without notice; or

(3) include an order setting the cause for trial on the merits with respect to the ultimate relief requested.

(c) Except on a verified pleading or an affidavit in accordance with the Texas Rules of Civil Procedure, an order may not be rendered:

(1) attaching the body of the child;

(2) taking the child into the possession of the court or of a person designated by the court; or

(3) excluding a parent from possession of or access to a child.

(d) In a suit, the court may dispense with the necessity of a bond in connection with temporary orders on behalf of the child.

(e) Temporary orders rendered under this section are not subject to interlocutory appeal.

(f) The violation of a temporary restraining order, temporary injunction, or other temporary order rendered under this section is punishable by contempt and the order is subject to and enforceable under Chapter 157.

(g) The rebuttable presumptions established in favor of the application of the guidelines for a child support order and for the standard possession order under Chapters 153 and 154 apply to temporary orders. The presumptions do not limit the authority of the court to render other temporary orders.

(h) An order under Subsection (a)(1) may be rendered without notice and an adversary hearing if the order is an emergency order sought by a governmental entity under Chapter 262.

Comment

A trial court has great discretion in rendering temporary orders, particularly because those orders are nonappealable. Temporary orders for custody and child support may be entered only after a hearing, although the status quo may be maintained by an *ex parte* court order pending a hearing. The legislature has decided that an *ex parte* order awarding use of the family home may be rendered in situations involving domestic violence. The broad power of a trial court permits modification of temporary orders at any time. The test for rendition of a new temporary order in a SAPCR is identical to that for the original order, *i.e.*, "for the safety and welfare of the child."

Chapter 262 provides that a court has the power to enter a temporary order when the DPRS seeks an emergency order to authorize a rescue of an allegedly abused or neglected child or to approve a prior rescue of a child from an emergency situation. Subsection (h) recognizes that authority and declares the temporary order statute is consistent with such emergency orders.

CLE/Other Legal Publications

Trying the temporary orders hearing. Michael E. Jarrett, 2011 Marriage Dissolution

Temporary orders: what you can get and how to get it. Thomas L. Ausley & John T. Eck, 2010 Marriage Dissol. Boot Camp

Temporary orders on the fly. Maisie Barringer, 2010 So. Tex. Fam. L. Conf.

Temporary hearings and/or time/trial limits. Stewart Gagnon, 2009 Ultimate Trial Notebook.

See Accompanying CD–ROM for Additional CLE/Other Legal Publications.

Leading Cases

Baltimore City Dept. Social Services v. Bouknight, 493 U.S. 549, 110 S.Ct. 900, 107 L.Ed.2d 992 (1990) (mother may be ordered to produce suspected abused child; contempt upheld, 5th amendment does not apply)

In re Coppock, 277 S.W.3d 417 (Tex. 2009) (ex-wife can't be held in contempt for "course or offensive language" absent command language in divorce decree)

In re Texas Dept. of Family and Protective Services, 255 S.W.3d 613 (Tex. 2008, orig. proceeding) (grant of emergency custody to TDFPS not warranted before fully litigating whether FLDS parents should have retained custody)

Grigsby v. Coker, 904 S.W.2d 619 (Tex. 1995) ("gag order" only valid in civil proceeding under strict conditions not present in this case)

Ex parte Slavin, 412 S.W.2d 43 (Tex. 1967) (specificity required for contempt enforcement)

Cross References

TX FCA Family §§ 6.501 to 6.502, *supra*, Temporary Orders; TX FCA Family § 6.504, Protective Orders., *supra*.

Tex. R. Civ. P. 171, Master in Chancery; Tex. R. Civ. P. 680, Temporary Restraining Order.

§ 105.0011. Information Regarding Protective Orders

At any time while a suit is pending, if the court believes, on the basis of any information received by the court, that a party to the suit or a member of the party's family or household may be a victim of family violence, the court shall inform that party of the party's right to apply for a protective order under Title 4.

CLE/Other Legal Publications

Protective orders. Sally H. Emerson, 2011 Adv. Fam. L.

Protective orders: who needs them and how to get them. Carlos Guillermo Salinas, 2011 U.T. FAM. L. FRONT LINES

Protective orders: the nuts and bolts. Lynn Bradshaw-Hull, 2011 SO. TEX. FAM. L.

Domestic violence and protective orders. Judy L. Warne, 2010 ADV. FAM. L. DRAFTING

§ 105.002. Jury

(a) Except as provided by Subsection (b), a party may demand a jury trial.

(b) A party may not demand a jury trial in:

(1) a suit in which adoption is sought, including a trial on the issue of denial or revocation of consent to the adoption by the managing conservator; or

(2) a suit to adjudicate parentage under Chapter 160.

(c) In a jury trial:

(1) a party is entitled to a verdict by the jury and the court may not contravene a jury verdict on the issues of:

(A) the appointment of a sole managing conservator;

(B) the appointment of joint managing conservators;

(C) the appointment of a possessory conservator;

(D) the determination of which joint managing conservator has the exclusive right to designate the primary residence of the child;

(E) the determination of whether to impose a restriction on the geographic area in which a joint managing conservator may designate the child's primary residence; and

(F) if a restriction described by Paragraph (E) is imposed, the determination of the geographic area within which the joint managing conservator must designate the child's primary residence; and

(2) the court may not submit to the jury questions on the issues of:

(A) support under Chapter 154 or Chapter 159;

(B) a specific term or condition of possession of or access to the child; or

(C) any right or duty of a conservator, other than the determination of which joint managing conservator has the exclusive right to designate the primary residence of the child under Subdivision (1)(D).

(d) Repealed by Acts 2003, 78th Leg., ch. 1036, § 22.

Comment

Lawyers in other states regard Texas with a mixture of wonderment, awe and distaste because of our wide ranging availability of jury trials in SAPCRs. Texas lawyers not only are accustomed to the practice, but swear by it. In truth, jury trials are more talked and written about than actually conducted because of the time and cost involved.

There are limits to jury trials in SAPCR's; the prohibition of a jury in an adoption case long-predates the Family Code. In 1999, the legislature conformed to the demands of the U.S. Congress prohibiting a jury trial in a parentage action. The 1996 Welfare Reform Act, commonly known as PRWORA, tied the federal child support subsidy to such a prohibition. 42 U.S.C.A. § 666(a)(5)(I).

For over 25 years the rule has been that when a trial court disagrees with a jury verdict on custody, the court cannot enter a judgment N.O.V. Rather, the court's power is limited to ordering a new trial.

The restriction prohibiting rendition of a judgment that contravenes the jury's determination of custody was potentially undercut by the enactment of a presumptive award of joint managing conservatorship. Award of a JMC "ordinarily should involve the designation of a primary residence for the child." A real question arose regarding whether the designation of the primary residence was to be left to the discretion of the trial court on the principle that the terms of the JMC were to be decided by the court. In the opinion of many, including the Family Law Council, such a statutory construction would virtually eliminate the utility of a custody jury trial. A 1997 amendment attempted to settle this issue by declaring that the primary residence of the child is for the jury to decide, which decision of the jury may not be contravened by the trial court. The issue probably is best viewed as a recognition that the ultimate issue is no longer "which party should be sole MC?" Rather, it is "which JMC should determine the child's principal residence?" From that perspective, the amendment continues broad form submission and does not herald a return to special issues practice.

Notwithstanding the revised language of 1997, the balance between the determination of a jury for the fundamental issues of custody and the details left to the court as terms of conservatorship remained in an uneasy balance. This was exemplified by the extended litigation and final resolution of the case of *Lenz v. Lenz*, 79 S.W.3d 10 (Tex. 2002), which held that the trial court had improperly contravened the jury's verdict when it ruled that the mother's right to establish the primary residence of the child could be restricted by the court to Bexar County. The operative language was:

> [A]lthough the trial court ordered modification 'pursuant to the jury's verdict,' it imposed its own primary residence restriction. By doing this, the trial court rejected the jury's verdict giving [the mother] the exclusive right to decide her sons' primary residence and granted their alternative remedy [the father] sought in his motion, which was to restrict the children's primary residence to Bexar County. In this way, the trial court implicitly disposed of the motion for judgment notwithstanding the verdict. ... [The mother] is correct that the statute's plain language means that she was entitled to a jury verdict in this case, and the trial court was not authorized to contravene that verdict by imposing an additional geographical restriction. *Id*. at 13, 20.

In 2003 the legislature again sought to settle the issue and resolve the balance in favor of the jury. If the issue is relocation, the issue is primary residence, and not just title of joint managing conservator, but rather the primary conservator versus the JMC who in other states would be called the noncustodial parent. The legislature has come down on the side of a jury verdict on this issue. Other issues, such as child support and other terms of conservatorship, are left for the judge to decide.

CLE/Other Legal Publications

Jury issues. H.E. Mendez, 2010 Adv. Fam. L. Drafting

Jury selection in the 21st Century. Marty D. Carden, 2010 Ultimate Trial Notebook

Jury charge: beyond the boilerplate. Sandra D. Hachem & Kevin Carter Hart, 2010 Adv. Fam. L.

Unique issues in a jury trial. J. Lindsey Short & Charles M. Wilson III, 2008 Adv. Fam. L.

Use of technology in trial. Bruce L. Beverly, 2008 UT Fam. L. Front Lines

---

See Accompanying CD-ROM for Additional CLE/Other Legal Publications.

Leading Cases

J.E.B. v. T.B., 511 U.S. 127, 128 L.Ed.2d 89, 114 S.Ct. 1419 (1994) (U.S. Const. prohibits discrimination in jury selection on basis of sex)

Ex parte Sproull, 815 S.W.2d 250 (Tex. 1991) (alleged contemnor has right to jury trial, contempt yields sentence longer than six months)

Texas Dept. of Human Services v. E.B., 802 S.W.2d 647 (Tex. 1990) (controlling question in termination of parental rights case; PJC–5 approved)

Martin v. Martin, 776 S.W.2d 572 (Tex. 1989) (no absolute right to jury when issue is terms and conditions of conservatorship; answers would not bind court)

In re A.S., 241 S.W.3d 661 (Tex. App.—Texarkana 2007, no pet.) (jury demand survived sanctions and striking of pleadings)

Harris v. Texas Dept. of Family and Protective Services, 228 S.W.3d 819 (Tex. App.—Austin 2007, no pet.) (jury verdict may not be disregarded if there is any evidence to support the findings)

Cross References

Tex. Const. art. 1, § 15, Right of Trial by Jury; Tex. Const. art. 5, § 10, Trial by Jury.

---

§ 105.003. Procedure for Contested Hearing

(a) Except as otherwise provided by this title, proceedings shall be as in civil cases generally.

(b) On the agreement of all parties to the suit, the court may limit attendance at the hearing to only those persons who have a direct interest in the suit or in the work of the court.

(c) A record shall be made as in civil cases generally unless waived by the parties with the consent of the court.

(d) When information contained in a report, study, or examination is before the court, the person making the report, study, or examination is subject to both direct examination and cross-examination as in civil cases generally.

(e) The hearing may be adjourned from time to time.

Comment

Although this section states that rules of evidence and procedure are to be applied as in other civil cases, the trial of a SAPCR is likely to be technically less scrupulous because of the overriding interests of the child. Indeed, authority abounds for the proposition that "the paramount concern is the best interest of the children and the technical rules of pleading and practice are not of controlling importance." Barrow v. Durham, 574 S.W.2d 857 (Tex. Civ. App.—Corpus Christi 1978), affirmed, 600 S.W.2d 756 (Tex. 1980).

---

§ 105.004. Preferential Setting

After a hearing, the court may:

(1) grant a motion filed by a party or by the amicus attorney or attorney ad litem for the child for a preferential setting for a trial on the merits; and

(2) give precedence to that hearing over other civil cases if the court finds that the delay created by ordinary scheduling practices will unreasonably affect the best interest of the child.

§ 105.005. Findings

Except as otherwise provided by this title, the court's findings shall be based on a preponderance of the evidence.

Comment

Although issues in a SAPCR are always serious, an enhanced burden of proof is accorded explicit recognition in the statute only when the state seeks to terminate parental rights. *See*, §§ 161.001, et. seq. But, because the parental preference is based on constitutional considerations. *See*, § 153.131, the state's burden when litigating against parents very well may be enhanced despite the fact that the statute nominally provides that a preponderance of the evidence is all that is ordinarily required in a SAPCR.

Leading Case

Lewelling v. Lewelling, 796 S.W.2d 164 (Tex. 1990) (parental preference creates very strong presumption)

---

§ 105.006. Contents of Final Order

(a) A final order, other than in a proceeding under Chapter 161 or 162, must contain:

(1) the social security number and driver's license number of each party to the suit, including the child, except that the child's social security number or driver's license number is not required if the child has not been assigned a social security number or driver's license number; and

(2) each party's current residence address, mailing address, home telephone number, name of employer, address of employment, and work telephone number, except as provided by Subsection (c).

(b) Except as provided by Subsection (c), the court shall order each party to inform each other party, the court that rendered the order, and the state case registry under Chapter 234 of an intended change in any of the information required by this section as long as any person, as a result of the order, is under an obligation to pay child support or is entitled to possession of or access to a child. The court shall order that notice of the intended change be given at the earlier of:

(1) the 60th day before the date the party intends to make the change; or

(2) the fifth day after the date that the party knew of the change, if the party did not know or could not have known of the change in sufficient time to comply with Subdivision (1).

(c) If a court finds after notice and hearing that requiring a party to provide the information required by this section to another party is likely to cause the child or a conservator harassment, abuse, serious harm, or injury, the court may:

(1) order the information not to be disclosed to another party; or

(2) render any other order the court considers necessary.

(d) An order in a suit that orders child support or possession of or access to a child must contain the following prominently displayed statement in boldfaced type, capital letters, or underlined:

"FAILURE TO OBEY A COURT ORDER FOR CHILD SUPPORT OR FOR POSSESSION OF OR ACCESS TO A CHILD MAY RESULT IN FURTHER LITIGATION TO ENFORCE THE ORDER, INCLUDING CONTEMPT OF COURT. A FINDING OF CONTEMPT MAY BE PUNISHED BY CONFINEMENT IN JAIL FOR UP TO SIX MONTHS, A FINE OF UP TO $500 FOR EACH VIOLATION, AND A MONEY JUDGMENT FOR PAYMENT OF ATTORNEY'S FEES AND COURT COSTS."

"FAILURE OF A PARTY TO MAKE A CHILD SUPPORT PAYMENT TO THE PLACE AND IN THE MANNER REQUIRED BY A COURT ORDER MAY RESULT IN THE PARTY NOT RECEIVING CREDIT FOR MAKING THE PAYMENT."

"FAILURE OF A PARTY TO PAY CHILD SUPPORT DOES NOT JUSTIFY DENYING THAT PARTY COURT-ORDERED POSSESSION OF OR ACCESS TO A CHILD. REFUSAL BY A PARTY TO ALLOW POSSESSION OF OR ACCESS TO A CHILD DOES NOT JUSTIFY FAILURE TO PAY COURT-ORDERED CHILD SUPPORT TO THAT PARTY."

(e) Except as provided by Subsection (c), an order in a suit that orders child support or possession of or access to a child must also contain the following prominently displayed statement in boldfaced type, capital letters, or underlined:

"EACH PERSON WHO IS A PARTY TO THIS ORDER IS ORDERED TO NOTIFY EACH OTHER PARTY, THE COURT, AND THE STATE CASE REGISTRY OF ANY CHANGE IN THE PARTY'S CURRENT RESIDENCE ADDRESS, MAILING ADDRESS, HOME TELEPHONE NUMBER, NAME OF EMPLOYER, ADDRESS OF EMPLOYMENT, DRIVER'S LICENSE NUMBER, AND WORK TELEPHONE NUMBER. THE PARTY IS ORDERED TO GIVE NOTICE OF AN INTENDED CHANGE IN ANY OF THE REQUIRED INFORMATION TO EACH OTHER PARTY, THE COURT, AND THE STATE CASE REGISTRY ON OR BEFORE THE 60TH DAY BEFORE THE INTENDED CHANGE. IF THE PARTY DOES NOT KNOW OR COULD NOT HAVE KNOWN OF THE CHANGE IN SUFFICIENT TIME TO PROVIDE 60-DAY NOTICE, THE PARTY IS ORDERED TO GIVE NOTICE OF THE CHANGE ON OR BEFORE THE FIFTH DAY AFTER THE DATE THAT THE PARTY KNOWS OF THE CHANGE."

"THE DUTY TO FURNISH THIS INFORMATION TO EACH OTHER PARTY, THE COURT, AND THE STATE CASE REGISTRY CONTINUES AS LONG AS ANY PERSON, BY VIRTUE OF THIS ORDER, IS UNDER AN OBLIGATION TO PAY CHILD SUPPORT OR ENTITLED TO POSSESSION OF OR ACCESS TO A CHILD."

"FAILURE BY A PARTY TO OBEY THE ORDER OF THIS COURT TO PROVIDE EACH OTHER PARTY, THE COURT, AND THE STATE CASE REGISTRY WITH THE CHANGE IN THE REQUIRED INFORMATION MAY RESULT IN FURTHER LITIGATION TO ENFORCE THE ORDER, INCLUDING CONTEMPT OF COURT. A FINDING OF CONTEMPT MAY BE PUNISHED BY CONFINEMENT IN JAIL FOR UP TO SIX MONTHS, A FINE OF UP TO $500 FOR EACH VIOLATION, AND A MONEY JUDGMENT FOR PAYMENT OF ATTORNEY'S FEES AND COURT COSTS."

(e–1) An order in a suit that provides for the possession of or access to a child must contain the following prominently displayed statement in boldfaced type, in capital letters, or underlined:

"NOTICE TO ANY PEACE OFFICER OF THE STATE OF TEXAS: YOU MAY USE REASONABLE EFFORTS TO ENFORCE THE TERMS OF CHILD CUSTODY SPECIFIED IN THIS ORDER. A PEACE OFFICER WHO RELIES ON THE TERMS OF A COURT ORDER AND THE OFFICER'S AGENCY ARE ENTITLED TO THE APPLICABLE IMMUNITY AGAINST ANY CLAIM, CIVIL OR OTHERWISE, REGARDING THE OFFICER'S GOOD FAITH ACTS PERFORMED IN THE SCOPE OF THE OFFICER'S DUTIES IN ENFORCING THE TERMS OF THE ORDER THAT RELATE TO CHILD CUSTODY. ANY PERSON WHO KNOWINGLY PRESENTS FOR ENFORCEMENT AN ORDER THAT IS INVALID OR NO LONGER IN EFFECT COMMITS AN OFFENSE THAT MAY BE PUNISHABLE BY CONFINEMENT IN JAIL FOR AS LONG AS TWO YEARS AND A FINE OF AS MUCH AS $10,000."

(f) Except for an action in which contempt is sought, in any subsequent child support enforcement action, the court may, on a showing that diligent effort has been made to determine the location of a party, consider due process requirements for notice and service of process to be met with respect to that party on delivery of written notice to the most recent residential or employer address filed by that party with the court and the state case registry.

(g) The Title IV–D agency shall promulgate and provide forms for a party to use in reporting to the court and the state case registry under Chapter 234 the information required under this section.

(h) The court may include in a final order in a suit in which a party to the suit makes an allegation of child abuse or neglect a finding on whether the party who made the allegation knew that the allegation was false. This finding shall not constitute collateral estoppel for any criminal proceeding. The court may impose on a party found to have made a false allegation of child abuse or neglect any civil sanction permitted under law, including attorney's fees, costs of experts, and any other costs.

Comment

As complexity in SAPCR litigation has grown, so has the length of this section detailing what must be contained in a final order. Yet, this is but a pale reflection of the extraordinary length of SAPCR decrees currently in vogue. The advent of statutory support guidelines and, more importantly, statutory visitation guidelines, significantly increased the length of the documentation thought to be necessary to regulate the behavior of the parties after a final SAPCR decree.

Subsection (e–1) gives Texas peace officers reasonable authority and responsibility to enforce terms of child custody orders in good faith. Exactly what "reasonable efforts to enforce" may ultimately be decided by court decisions at a later time. If the statute actually assists in keeping the peace and facilitates visitation, it will have fulfilled its purpose.

§ 105.007. Compliance With Order Requiring Notice of Change of Required Information

(a) A party shall comply with the order by giving written notice to each other party of an intended change in the party's current residence address, mailing address, home telephone number, name of employer, address of employment, and work telephone number.

(b) The party must give written notice by registered or certified mail of an intended change in the required information to each other party on or before the 60th day before the change is made. If the party does not know or could not have known of the change in sufficient time to provide 60-day notice, the party shall provide the written notice of the change on or before the fifth day after the date that the party knew of the change.

(c) The court may waive the notice required by this section on motion by a party if it finds that the giving of notice of a change of the required information would be likely to expose the child or the party to harassment, abuse, serious harm, or injury.

Comment

If possession of a child is to have meaning, the physical location of the child must be known. This section requires parties to keep each other informed of the child's current address. However, the mandate for conservators to notify each other of a pending move does not include a penalty for its violation.

---

§ 105.008. Record of Support Order for State Case Registry

(a) The clerk of the court shall provide the state case registry with a record of a court order for child support. The record of an order shall include information provided by the parties on a form developed by the Title IV–D agency. The form shall be completed by the petitioner and submitted to the clerk at the time the order is filed for record.

(b) To the extent federal funds are available, the Title IV-D agency shall reimburse the clerk of the court for the costs incurred in providing the record of support order required under this section.

§ 105.009. Parent Education and Family Stabilization Course

(a) In a suit affecting the parent-child relationship, including an action to modify an order in a suit affecting the parent-child relationship providing for possession of or access to a child, the court may order the parties to the suit to attend a parent education and family stabilization course if the court determines that the order is in the best interest of the child.

(b) The parties to the suit may not be required to attend the course together. The court, on its own motion or the motion of either party, may prohibit the parties from taking the course together if there is a history of family violence in the marriage.

(c) A course under this section must be at least four hours, but not more than 12 hours, in length and be designed to educate and assist parents with regard to the consequences of divorce on parents and children. The course must include information on the following issues:

(1) the emotional effects of divorce on parents;

(2) the emotional and behavioral reactions to divorce by young children and adolescents;

(3) parenting issues relating to the concerns and needs of children at different development stages;

(4) stress indicators in young children and adolescents;

(5) conflict management;

(6) family stabilization through development of a coparenting relationship;

(7) the financial responsibilities of parenting;

(8) family violence, spousal abuse, and child abuse and neglect; and

(9) the availability of community services and resources.

(d) A course may not be designed to provide individual mental health therapy or individual legal advice.

(e) A course satisfies the requirements of this section if it is offered by:

(1) a mental health professional who has at least a master's degree with a background in family therapy or parent education; or

(2) a religious practitioner who performs counseling consistent with the laws of this state or another person designated as a program counselor by a church or religious institution if the litigant so chooses.

(f) Information obtained in a course or a statement made by a participant to a suit during a course may not be considered in the adjudication of the suit or in any subsequent legal proceeding. Any report that results from participation in the course may not become a record in the suit unless the parties stipulate to the record in writing.

(g) The court may take appropriate action with regard to a party who fails to attend or complete a course ordered by the court under this section, including holding the party in contempt of court, striking pleadings, or invoking any sanction provided by Rule 215, Texas Rules of Civil Procedure. The failure or refusal by a party to attend or complete a course required by this section may not delay the court from rendering a judgment in a suit affecting the parent-child relationship.

(h) The course required under this section may be completed by:

(1) personal instruction;

(2) videotape instruction;

(3) instruction through an electronic medium; or

(4) a combination of those methods.

(i) On completion of the course, the course provider shall issue a certificate of completion to each participant. The certificate must state:

(1) the name of the participant;

(2) the name of the course provider;

(3) the date the course was completed; and

(4) whether the course was provided by:

(A) personal instruction;

(B) videotape instruction;

(C) instruction through an electronic medium; or

(D) a combination of those methods.

(j) The county clerk in each county may establish a registry of course providers in the county and a list of locations at which courses are provided. The clerk shall include information in the registry identifying courses that are offered on a sliding fee scale or without charge.

(k) The court may not order the parties to a suit to attend a course under this section if the parties cannot afford to take the course. If the parties cannot afford to take a course, the court may direct the parties to a course that is offered on a sliding fee scale or without charge, if a course of that type is available. A party to a suit may not be required to pay more than $100 to attend a course ordered under this section.

(*l*) A person who has attended a course under this section may not be required to attend the course more than twice before the fifth anniversary of the date the person completes the course for the first time.

Text of subsec. (m) as added by Acts 2005, 79th Leg., ch. 916, § 6

(m) A course under this section must be available in both English and Spanish.

Text of subsec. (m) as added by Acts 2005, 79th Leg., ch. 1171, § 3

(m) A course under this section in a suit filed in a county with a population of more than two million that is adjacent to a county with a population of more than one million must be available in both English and Spanish.

CHAPTER 106. COSTS AND ATTORNEY'S FEES

CLE/Other Legal Publications

Attorney fees: asking for them, getting them, and collecting them. Charles M. Wilson, III, Addison, 2009 ADV. FAM. L.

Advanced collection methods. Stephen J. Naylor, 2008 ADV. FAM. L.

Show me the money—your financial relationship with your client. Charles E. Hardy, 2008 ADV. FAM. L.

Cross References

TX FCA FAMILY § 6.708, Costs, *supra*; TX FCA FAMILY §§ 9.013 to 9.014. Costs, Attorney's Fees, *supra*.

TEX. CIV. PRAC. & REM. CODE ANN. § 38.001 *et seq.*, Attorney's Fee.

§ 106.001. Costs

The court may award costs in a suit or motion under this title and in a habeas corpus proceeding.

§ 106.002. Attorney's Fees and Expenses

(a) In a suit under this title, the court may render judgment for reasonable attorney's fees and expenses and order the judgment and postjudgment interest to be paid directly to an attorney.

(b) A judgment for attorney's fees and expenses may be enforced in the attorney's name by any means available for the enforcement of a judgment for debt.

CHAPTER 107. SPECIAL APPOINTMENTS AND SOCIAL STUDIES

SUBCHAPTER A. COURT–ORDERED REPRESENTATION IN SUITS AFFECTING THE PARENT–CHILD RELATIONSHIP

SUBCHAPTER B. APPOINTMENTS IN CERTAIN SUITS

SUBCHAPTER C. APPOINTMENT OF VOLUNTEER ADVOCATES

SUBCHAPTER D. SOCIAL STUDY

Introductory Comment

Since the original enactment of the Texas Family Code in 1973, courts have had discretionary authority to appoint a guardian ad litem [GAL] in any suit affecting the parent child relationship

[SAPCR]. Following a federal court decision in 1978 holding the then Texas law unconstitutional, Texas courts have been required to appoint an attorney ad litem [AAL] "to represent the interests of a child" in a suit filed by the agency now known as the Department of Family and Protective Services [formerly DPW, DHR, DPRS], a.k.a. on the local level as Children's Protective Services [CPS]. This rule applies whether the state is seeking conservatorship or termination of parental rights based on alleged child abuse or neglect. Further, since 1997 the court must also appoint a GAL as well as an AAL for an allegedly abused or neglected child. This was the result of mandates in the federal Adoption Assistance Act. An attorney may be appointed to serve both roles [AAL/GAL], or an attorney may be appointed to serve as AAL and a volunteer advocate (a.k.a., CASA) may be appointed as the GAL.

During much of the time before the revisions of this chapter in 2003 and 2005, lawyers were required to intuit their duties from study of the very few cases and the disciplinary rules. Many lawyers found their appointed role mystifying. A major source of the confusion stemmed from the debate about whether a court appointed attorney for a child should advocate according to the child's directions or whether the lawyer should advocate the child's "best interests." Prior to 1984, attorneys appointed to represent children in family law cases generally believed that they should be best interest directed. The passage of the Child Abuse Prevention and Treatment Act (CAPTA) in 1974 seemed to codify this widely held view by requiring states to appoint a "guardian ad litem" in order to receive federal funding, 42 U.S.C. § 5101 et seq.

By 1984, however, a paradigm shift began to appear in the legal literature written by attorneys and law professors with experience in representing allegedly abused or neglected children in CPS cases. The authors almost universally argued that the function of an attorney, based upon ethical mandates, is to pursue legal objectives chosen by the child—if the child is capable of formulating such directives. Thus, the tone was set for a divisive debate, often pitting advocates dealing with CPS cases against those familiar with private custody cases.

By 1995 the Texas Legislature began to respond to complaints about the performance of the child's appointed legal representatives in abuse and neglect cases heard on the civil side of the docket. Major reform occurred in 1997 when, at the urging of the state office of CASA, the legislature sought to clarify the responsibilities of AALs and GALs for children, focusing on CPS cases. The roles and duties of the ad litems were spelled out in detail, volunteer advocates (CASAs) were authorized to serve as GALs, and the distinctions between the roles of GALs and AALs were clarified. On a parallel track, in an attempt to improve and clarify the role of legal representatives of children, in 1996 the American Bar Association adopted Standards of Practice for Attorneys Representing Children in Abuse and Neglect Cases, 29 Fam. L. Q. 375 (1995). The ABA Standards are readily available at *www.abanet.org/child*. Seizing this good idea, in 1997 the legislature required AALs to "become familiar with" the ABA standards. After more than a decade of drafting, the ABA Family Law Section promulgated comparable guidelines for private custody cases, approved by the ABA in August, 2003. In 2005, the Texas Legislature added these to the list of what an appointed attorney should become familiar with.

CLE/Other Legal Publications

Amicus/ad litems. Kevin R. Fuller, 2011 Adv. Fam. L.

Amicus/ad litem issues. Linda Anne Thompson, 2011 U.T. Advanced Parent-Child Relationships

Being an effective amicus/ad litem/guardian ad litem. Jolyn C. Wilkins, 2010 U.T. Parent-Child Relationships

Foster children and their attorneys ad litem: resources for children in care. Carole Hurley, 2010 Adv. Fam. L.

Permanency and eligibility: financial benefits in the child welfare system. Audrey Celeste Carmical, 2010 Adv. Fam. L.

Child evidentiary issues and child testimony in CPS cases. Hon. J. Andrew Hathcock, 2009 Adv. Fam. L.

Ethical issues for the appointed attorney when representing children. Charles G. Childress, 2009 Adv. Fam. L.

Children and youth in court: statutory and ethical duties and responsibilities of the appointed attorney. Hon. Karin Bonicoro, 2009 ADV. FAM. L.

COURT-APPOINTED LEGAL REPRESENTATION OF CHILDREN IN FAMILY LAW CASES. Debra H. Lehrmann (LexisNexis 2006)

Leading Cases

Lassiter v. Department of Social Services, 452 U.S. 18, 68 L.Ed.2d 640, 101 S.Ct. 2153 (1981) (due process does not require appointment of ad litem for indigent parent in termination case—but a state statutory right to such appointment is the majority rule)

In re Scheller, 325 S.W.3d 640 (Tex. 2010) (trial court abused discretion as grandfather failed to prove father not acting in children's best interest when he disputed temporary telephone access and bi-monthly weekends; parent's *Troxel* rights upheld, but only on 2d mandamus petition) (appointment of psychologist as GAL didn't violate *Troxel* rule)

In re K.M.M., 326 S.W.3d 714 (Tex. App.—Amarillo 2010, no pet.) (presumed father in private termination case protested failure to appoint AAL or amicus attorney for child; seldom can a court find one party adequately represents a child's interest or that party's interests are not adverse)

Zeifman v. Nowlin, 322 S.W.3d 804 (Tex. App.—Austin 2010, no pet.) (amicus attorney has statutory immunity for father's fraud and gross negligence suit; duties owed to child, not to parent) (groundless claim elicits $40,000 in sanctions)

In re Collins, 242 S.W.3d 837 (Tex. App.—Houston [14th Dist.] 2007, no pet.) (appointment of amicus attorney as next friend as opposed to father was error)

Phillips v. Dallas County Child Services, 197 S.W.3d 862 (Tex. App.—Dallas 2006, rev. denied) (answer by court appointed attorney ad litem representing patient in mental hospital constitutes general appearance justifying default judgment)

In re C.D.S., 172 S.W.3d 179 (Tex. App.—Fort Worth 2005, no pet.) (failure to appoint an attorney ad litem for indigent mother in termination case)

In re D.M.C., 168 S.W.3d 319 (Tex. App.—Texarkana 2005, no pet.) (guardian ad litem not required to conduct investigation into best interests of child)

In re R.C.S., 167 S.W.3d 145 (Tex. App.—Dallas 2005, pet. denied) (guardian ad litem's agreement with mother's position on three motions does not mean alignment with party; ad litem entitled to independent jury strikes)

SUBCHAPTER A. COURT–ORDERED REPRESENTATION IN SUITS AFFECTING THE PARENT–CHILD RELATIONSHIP

§ 107.001. Definitions

In this chapter:

(1) "Amicus attorney" means an attorney appointed by the court in a suit, other than a suit filed by a governmental entity, whose role is to provide legal services necessary to assist the court in protecting a child's best interests rather than to provide legal services to the child.

(2) "Attorney ad litem" means an attorney who provides legal services to a person, including a child, and who owes to the person the duties of undivided loyalty, confidentiality, and competent representation.

(3) "Developmentally appropriate" means structured to account for a child's age, level of education, cultural background, and degree of language acquisition.

(4) "Dual role" means the role of an attorney who is appointed under Section 107.0125 to act as both guardian ad litem and attorney ad litem for a child in a suit filed by a governmental entity.

(5) "Guardian ad litem" means a person appointed to represent the best interests of a child. The term includes:

(A) a volunteer advocate appointed under Subchapter C;

(B) a professional, other than an attorney, who holds a relevant professional license and whose training relates to the determination of a child's best interests;

(C) an adult having the competence, training, and expertise determined by the court to be sufficient to represent the best interests of the child; or

(D) an attorney ad litem appointed to serve in the dual role.

Comment

"Amicus attorney" is a new role for attorneys appointed in private custody cases. Note that this appointment may not be made in a suit filed by a governmental entity, a.k.a. a CPS case involving alleged abuse or neglect.

The definitions of "attorney ad litem," "developmentally appropriate," and "dual role," confirm the understanding of those terms prior to the enactment of this thoroughly revised chapter.

A restricted definition is provided for "guardian ad litem" [GAL], who may be a qualified nonlawyer, either a volunteer advocate or another trained professional, a layperson who the court deems to be the equivalent of the foregoing, or an attorney who serves in a dual role in CPS cases as provided in § 107.0125. Further, an individual who happens to be an attorney may serve as a volunteer CASA, so long as no "lawyering" is performed in that role.

---

§ 107.002. Powers and Duties of Guardian ad Litem for Child

(a) A guardian ad litem appointed for a child under this chapter is not a party to the suit but may:

(1) conduct an investigation to the extent that the guardian ad litem considers necessary to determine the best interests of the child; and

(2) obtain and review copies of the child's relevant medical, psychological, and school records as provided by Section 107.006.

(b) A guardian ad litem appointed for the child under this chapter shall:

(1) within a reasonable time after the appointment, interview:

(A) the child in a developmentally appropriate manner, if the child is four years of age or older;

(B) each person who has significant knowledge of the child's history and condition, including any foster parent of the child; and

(C) the parties to the suit;

(2) seek to elicit in a developmentally appropriate manner the child's expressed objectives;

(3) consider the child's expressed objectives without being bound by those objectives;

(4) encourage settlement and the use of alternative forms of dispute resolution; and

(5) perform any specific task directed by the court.

(c) A guardian ad litem appointed for the child under this chapter is entitled to:

(1) receive a copy of each pleading or other paper filed with the court in the case in which the guardian ad litem is appointed;

(2) receive notice of each hearing in the case;

(3) participate in case staffings by an authorized agency concerning the child;

(4) attend all legal proceedings in the case but may not call or question a witness or otherwise provide legal services unless the guardian ad litem is a licensed attorney who has been appointed in the dual role;

(5) review and sign, or decline to sign, an agreed order affecting the child; and

(6) explain the basis for the guardian ad litem's opposition to the agreed order if the guardian ad litem does not agree to the terms of a proposed order.

(d) The court may compel the guardian ad litem to attend a trial or hearing and to testify as necessary for the proper disposition of the suit.

(e) Unless the guardian ad litem is an attorney who has been appointed in the dual role and subject to the Texas Rules of Evidence, the court shall ensure in a hearing or in a trial on the merits that a guardian ad litem has an opportunity to testify regarding, and is permitted to submit a report regarding, the guardian ad litem's recommendations relating to:

(1) the best interests of the child; and

(2) the bases for the guardian ad litem's recommendations.

(f) In a nonjury trial, a party may call the guardian ad litem as a witness for the purpose of cross-examination regarding the guardian's report without the guardian ad litem being listed as a witness by a party. If the guardian ad litem is not called as a witness, the court shall permit the guardian ad litem to testify in the narrative.

(g) In a contested case, the guardian ad litem shall provide copies of the guardian ad litem's report, if any, to the attorneys for the parties as directed by the court, but not later than the earlier of:

(1) the date required by the scheduling order; or

(2) the 10th day before the date of the commencement of the trial.

(h) Disclosure to the jury of the contents of a guardian ad litem's report to the court is subject to the Texas Rules of Evidence.

Comment

Effective September 1, 2003, the GAL is reserved for non-lawyers, other professionals, CASA volunteers, or other laypersons appointed by the court to speak for the best interests of a child. Courts are no longer permitted to appoint attorneys with the sole title of GAL with the expectation that the attorney will serve a role as a lawyer in the case and as a guardian ad litem for the child.

The phrase "objective of representation" clarifies that the GAL has no duty "of representation" to the child, but rather the GAL is to make recommendations based on his or her determination of best interest of the child. The fact that a CASA is a "special advocate" for the child does not create a right or duty of representation in the legal sense.

The appointing judge decides who is qualified to serve as a GAL. A volunteer advocate CASA who is converted into a GAL by appointment faces additional responsibilities to serve as a substitute decision-maker for the child in the SAPCR. This section specifically states that a GAL is "not a party to the suit," and therefore is not entitled to service of citation, § 102.009. Nonetheless, the GAL is authorized to act on the behalf of the real party in interest, *i.e.,* the child who is the subject of the suit.

Leading Case

In re Scheller, 325 S.W.3d 640 (Tex. 2010) (trial court may appoint the same person to serve as expert psychologist and GAL; role of the psychologist consistent with role of GAL, both give court best interests recommendations)

---

§ 107.003. Powers and Duties of Attorney ad Litem for Child and Amicus Attorney

An attorney ad litem appointed to represent a child or an amicus attorney appointed to assist the court:

(1) shall:

(A) subject to Rules 4.02, 4.03, and 4.04, Texas Disciplinary Rules of Professional Conduct, and within a reasonable time after the appointment, interview:

(i) the child in a developmentally appropriate manner, if the child is four years of age or older;

(ii) each person who has significant knowledge of the child's history and condition, including any foster parent of the child; and

(iii) the parties to the suit;

(B) seek to elicit in a developmentally appropriate manner the child's expressed objectives of representation;

(C) consider the impact on the child in formulating the attorney's presentation of the child's expressed objectives of representation to the court;

(D) investigate the facts of the case to the extent the attorney considers appropriate;

(E) obtain and review copies of relevant records relating to the child as provided by Section 107.006;

(F) participate in the conduct of the litigation to the same extent as an attorney for a party;

(G) take any action consistent with the child's interests that the attorney considers necessary to expedite the proceedings;

(H) encourage settlement and the use of alternative forms of dispute resolution; and

(I) review and sign, or decline to sign, a proposed or agreed order affecting the child;

(2) must be trained in child advocacy or have experience determined by the court to be equivalent to that training; and

(3) is entitled to:

(A) request clarification from the court if the role of the attorney is ambiguous;

(B) request a hearing or trial on the merits;

(C) consent or refuse to consent to an interview of the child by another attorney;

(D) receive a copy of each pleading or other paper filed with the court;

(E) receive notice of each hearing in the suit;

(F) participate in any case staffing concerning the child conducted by an authorized agency; and

(G) attend all legal proceedings in the suit.

Comment

A child enmeshed in the CPS system has a statutory right to be represented by an attorney ad litem, § 107.012, while appointment of an attorney as either an AAL or amicus attorney in other civil litigation is strictly left to the discretion of the court. This section deals with the powers and duties of both an AAL and an amicus attorney by stating the expectations that a court will have for the legal services to be performed. The legislative determinations made in years past that lawyers needed instructions in how to conduct their business in cases in which they have received court appointments has not diminished. Originally the legislature passed the major provisions regulating attorney conduct (formerly § 107.014) in response to complaints about the poor quality of AAL representation of allegedly abused and neglected children when the state, via DFPS, intervened in a family. These complaints included the fact that some lawyers never saw or talked to their child clients, even if they were teenagers. This testimony to the legislature alleged that the quality of representation varied significantly, not only from county to county, but from lawyer to lawyer. Because the child client has no choice of legal representation, the legislature found it desirable to guarantee a minimum level of that representation. Note that this section applies equally to attorneys in CPS cases and private custody cases, notwithstanding the fact that the complaints voiced to the legislature related only to CPS cases. Just to ensure that lawyers get the point, the legislature continues to remind attorneys that they must comply with the disciplinary rules (as if there ever is a time when that is not the case).

Over the years the legislature continued to tighten attorney discretion, changing "may" to "shall" with regard to crucial duties. Thus, the attorney is required to investigate (but only to the extent that the attorney determines is appropriate), and to perform other duties, such as obtaining the relevant records of the child and interviewing people who know facts about the child's situation. This includes a specification that the attorney interview a child's foster parents. Most challenging is the requirement to "interview the parties to the suit." When counsel for the child's parents won't consent to the interview, however, the requirement might appear to mandate formal discovery to comply with the statute without violating the prohibition against communicating with represented parties in the Disciplinary Rules. *See* Art. 10 § 9 Texas Disciplinary Rule of Professional Conduct 4.02. In fact, alternative means are usually found, including meeting parents in the courthouse under various circumstances.

This section identifies the actions necessary for a GAL to undertake. The duties of the GAL under Subsections (a) (c) parallel many of the activities and duties of the AAL or amicus attorney in §§ 107.003–.005. But, Subsection (c)(4) states that the GAL may not call or question a witness or otherwise provide legal services, thereby disqualifying an attorney from performing any lawyer like activities in the case. Although GALs are not parties, some of the rights and duties described resemble the rights of a party, e.g. receiving copies of pleadings and notice of hearings. Other named rights do not go that far. For example, although a GAL is entitled to review an agreed order affecting the child and sign or refuse to sign the agreement, the statute does not authorize the GAL to veto an agreement of the actual parties to the litigation

The right of a GAL to testify is confirmed under Subsection (e). More than that, Subsections (d) and (f) make it clear that the testimony of a GAL may be compelled. That action is forbidden in the case of a lawyer, who may not be a witness and an attorney in the same proceeding. Subsection (e) now makes very clear that the GAL has both the opportunity to testify and to submit a report to the court (in a bench trial). Some persons were reading the "or" as forcing the GAL to a choice between the two, which was neither intended nor the proper construction of the language (if "and" had been used, some might construe that the GAL "must do both"). The court is to ensure the GAL's rights, but the "opportunity" may be waived, subject to the GAL being compelled to attend and testify under Subsection (d).

§ 107.004. Additional Duties of Attorney Ad Litem for Child

(a) Except as otherwise provided by this chapter, the attorney ad litem appointed for a child shall, in a developmentally appropriate manner:

(1) advise the child;

(2) represent the child's expressed objectives of representation and follow the child's expressed objectives of representation during the course of litigation if the attorney ad litem determines that the child is competent to understand the nature of an attorney-client relationship and has formed that relationship with the attorney ad litem; and

(3) as appropriate, considering the nature of the appointment, become familiar with the American Bar Association's standards of practice for attorneys who represent children in abuse and neglect cases, the suggested amendments to those standards adopted by the National Association of Counsel for Children, and the American Bar Association's standards of practice for attorneys who represent children in custody cases.

(b) An attorney ad litem appointed for a child in a proceeding under Chapter 262 or 263 shall complete at least three hours of continuing legal education relating to child advocacy as described by Subsection (c) as soon as practicable after the attorney ad litem's appointment. An attorney ad litem is not required to comply with this subsection if the court finds that the attorney ad litem has experience equivalent to the required education.

(c) The continuing legal education required by Subsection (b) must:

(1) be low-cost and available to persons throughout this state, including on the Internet provided through the State Bar of Texas; and

(2) focus on the duties of an attorney ad litem in, and the procedures of and best practices for, a proceeding under Chapter 262 or 263.

(d) Except as provided by Subsection (e), an attorney ad litem appointed for a child in a proceeding under Chapter 262 or 263 shall:

(1) meet before each court hearing with:

(A) ~~(1)~~ the child, if the child is at least four years of age; or

(B) ~~(2)~~ the individual with whom the child ordinarily resides, including the child's parent, conservator, guardian, caretaker, or custodian, if the child is younger than four years of age; **and**

(2) if the child or individual is not present at the court hearing, file a written statement with the court indicating that the attorney ad litem complied with Subdivision (1).

(d–1) A meeting required by Subsection (d) must take place:

(1) a sufficient time before the hearing to allow the attorney ad litem to prepare for the hearing in accordance with the child's expressed objectives of representation; and

(2) in a private setting that allows for confidential communications between the attorney ad litem and the child or individual with whom the child ordinarily resides, as applicable.

(e) An attorney ad litem appointed for a child in a proceeding under Chapter 262 or 263 is not required to comply with Subsection (d) before a hearing if the court finds at that hearing that the attorney ad litem has shown good cause why the attorney ad litem's compliance with that subsection is not feasible or in the best interest of the child. Additionally, a court may, on a showing of good cause, authorize an attorney ad litem to comply with Subsection (d) by conferring with the child or other individual, as appropriate, by telephone or video conference.

Amended by Acts 2011, 82nd Leg., ch. 572 (H.B. 3311), § 1, eff. Sept. 1, 2011; Acts 2011, 82nd Leg., ch. 573 (H.B. 3314), § 1, eff. Sept. 1, 2011.

Comment

This section and the next make distinctions between lawyering required of an AAL and the lawyering expected from an amicus attorney. The major difference is that the AAL has a client. Subsection (a)(2) provides that an appointed lawyer "shall follow the child's expressed objectives of representation if the AAL determines that the child is competent" to provide such direction. This language was derived from the National Association of Counsel for Children (NACC) Revised ABA Abuse and Neglect Standards. In the event the AAL determines that the child lacks that competence, reference is to be made to § 107.008 (substituted judgment). Thus, whether a child client can actually direct the activities of the AAL is to be decided on a case by case basis. As will be discussed infra, the amicus attorney does not have a client but rather functions as an independent counsel to elicit all appropriate evidence regarding best interest of the child.

Subsection (a)(3) refers the AAL to the ABA standards of practice for attorneys who represent children in abuse and neglect cases, 29 Fam. L.Q. 375 (1995), also available at www.abanet.org/child. At their core, these standards tell lawyers to be lawyers, giving a child client the "same duties of undivided loyalty, confidentiality, and competent representation . . . as is due an adult client." See Art. 10, §9 Texas Disciplinary Rules of Professional Conduct 4.02. The standards mandate that lawyers advise and guide their clients, eliciting "the child's preferences in a developmentally appropriate manner," representing "the child's expressed preferences," and following "the child's direction throughout the course of litigation." When a child cannot or will not express preferences, the lawyer may determine the child's legal interests and advocate that position. Lawyers are also referred to the ABA Standards as amended and adopted by the NACC in 1999. These standards recognize that children "are not simply small adults and it would be inappropriate to treat them as such. All of the components of representation of adults are not readily transferable to the representation of children. Perhaps the next legislative step will be to require strict sanctions against lawyers who do not comply with the statutory directives. The irony of losing money for misconduct on an already markedly underpaid appointment may make professional duties harder to ignore.

Subsections (b) and (c) are designed to ensure that an attorney ad litem appointed for the child will have at least a minimal amount of additional CLE to prepare for the legal representation of children.

Complaints about the fact that attorneys ad litem consistently do not interview their child-clients in CPS cases have been voiced to the legislature since at least 1995 when the first statute was enacted on the subject. Subsections (d) and (e) have repeatedly attempted to require professional responsibilities through statutory management of the AAL's manner of practicing law. Continuing complaints about AAL's, "they don't see their clients," has elicited repeated, specific directives to do so. The requirement that the AAL and the client "shall meet before each court hearing" if the client is over four years old perhaps went a bit too far in some circumstances, *e.g.*, the child resides a considerable distance from the courthouse, sometimes hundreds, and even thousands, of miles away is a distant state, or perhaps even in another country. Such meetings may be by telephone if appropriate.

Once again (actually twice again) the same theme has been heard from the Capitol building. Two separate bills, one amending subsection (d) and the other adding a new (d–1) were enacted in 2011 to emphasize the importance of attorney-client personal contact, deemed especially crucial when a child is involved. Perhaps the next step will be to authorize fines on lawyers who do not comply with the statutes. The irony of losing money from an already markedly underpaid appointment will be hard to ignore.

§ 107.0045. Discipline of Attorney Ad Litem

An attorney ad litem who fails to perform the duties required by Sections 107.003 and 107.004 is subject to disciplinary action under Subchapter E, Chapter 81, Government Code.

Comment

This section reminds the attorney that failure to faithfully carry out professional responsibilities can have adverse professional consequences.

§ 107.005. Additional Duties of Amicus Attorney

(a) Subject to any specific limitation in the order of appointment, an amicus attorney shall advocate the best interests of the child after reviewing the facts and circumstances of the case. Notwithstanding Subsection (b), in determining the best interests of the child, an amicus attorney is not bound by the child's expressed objectives of representation.

(b) An amicus attorney shall, in a developmentally appropriate manner:

(1) with the consent of the child, ensure that the child's expressed objectives of representation are made known to the court;

(2) explain the role of the amicus attorney to the child;

(3) inform the child that the amicus attorney may use information that the child provides in providing assistance to the court; and

(4) become familiar with the American Bar Association's standards of practice for attorneys who represent children in custody cases.

(c) An amicus attorney may not disclose confidential communications between the amicus attorney and the child unless the amicus attorney determines that disclosure is necessary to assist the court regarding the best interests of the child.

Comment

The confusion surrounding the duties of a court-appointed lawyer for a child has left many judges unclear about their ability to appoint a lawyer to ensure that sufficient evidence is presented to the court to enable it to render a decision that is in the child's best interest. This is particularly problematic in custody cases, where there is no guardian ad litem to act as a safety net. This section clarifies that in a custody case the court has the authority to appoint a lawyer to advocate for the best interests of the child, without the attorney being bound by the child's objectives of representation.

The new role, denominated as "amicus attorney," at least in part is a codification of the way that many experienced attorneys appointed in the ambiguous role of GAL have conducted their representation of children in custody disputes. The attorney is to advocate for the best interest of the child, taking into account a wide variety of information, including the views of the child. However, it is clear that the child does not direct the activities of the amicus attorney, nor does the child have an attorney-client relationship with the amicus attorney. Subsection (b)(7) indicates that the amicus attorney may use information that the child provides, even if the child has not authorized the disclosure of that information, or even has requested nondisclosure.

Subsection (b)(3) directs the amicus attorney to explain his role to the child, which, assuming that honesty is the hallmark, must include the fact that there is no assurance of confidential communications. Subsection (b)(4) directs the amicus attorney to become familiar with the ABA Standards of Practice for Custody Cases (2003); the original ABA standards for abuse and neglect cases are not mentioned because a court may not appoint an amicus attorney to those cases.

Subsection (c) indicates something of a conflicted position, but leaves it entirely to the discretion of the amicus attorney whether to reveal information that otherwise would be a "confidential communication" if an attorney client relationship existed. Now Section 107.007 provides other protections for the relationship between the amicus attorney and the child.

---

§ 107.006. Access to Child and Information Relating to Child

(a) **In** ~~Except as provided by Subsection (c), in~~ conjunction with an appointment under this chapter, other than an appointment of an attorney ad litem for an adult or a parent, the court shall issue an order authorizing the attorney ad litem, guardian ad litem for the child, or amicus attorney to have immediate access to the child and any information relating to the child.

(b) Without requiring a further order or release, the custodian of any relevant records relating to the child, including records regarding social services, law enforcement records, school records, records of a probate or court proceeding, and records of a trust or account for which the child is a beneficiary, shall provide access to a person authorized to access the records under Subsection (a).

(c) **Without requiring a further order or release, the custodian of a** ~~A~~ medical, mental health, or drug or alcohol treatment record of a child that is privileged or confidential under other law **shall release the record** ~~may be released~~ to a person **authorized to access the record** ~~appointed~~ under Subsection (a)**, except that a child's drug or alcohol treatment record that is confidential under 42 U.S.C. Section 290dd–2 may only be released as provided under applicable federal regulations** ~~only in accordance with the other law~~.

(d) The disclosure of a confidential record under this section does not affect the confidentiality of the record, and the person provided access to the record may not disclose the record further except as provided by court order or other law.

(e) Notwithstanding the provisions of this section, the requirements of Section 159.008, Occupations Code, apply.

(f) Records obtained under this section shall be destroyed on termination of the appointment.

Amended by Acts 2011, 82nd Leg., ch. 206 (H.B. 2488), § 1, eff. May 30, 2011.

Comment

The GAL, AAL, and amicus attorney basically have the same right to access to information about the child by court order. Each has an obligation to review pertinent medical and mental health records of the child in order to fulfill their respective duties of representation. The 2011 amendments deal with the concern that existing law did not clearly address whether medical and mental health providers are prohibited by federal law from providing these records to such child advocates, who can experience significant delays in receiving the records or may not receive them at all. Appointees under this chapter need to be aware of the restrictions on the access to the medical mental health or other personal records established by federal HIPAA (Health Insurance Portability and Accountability

Act of 1996). *See*, 45 C.F.R. 164.102 (2002). The 2011 amendments seek to address the issues by requiring, rather than permitting, certain medical and mental health providers to release these records to the court-appointed representatives in proceedings relating to a SAPCR.

Subsection (a) requires the court, in conjunction with an appointment under this chapter other than an appointment of an attorney ad litem for an adult or a parent, to issue an order authorizing the attorney ad litem, guardian ad litem for the child, or amicus attorney to have immediate access to the child and to any information relating to the child.

Without requiring a further order or release, subsection (c) requires the custodian of a medical, mental health, or drug or alcohol treatment record of a child that is privileged or confidential under other law to release the record to a person authorized to access the record under Subsection (a), except that a child's drug or alcohol treatment record that is confidential under 42 U.S.C. Section 290dd-2 may only be released as provided under applicable federal regulations.

Subsection (d) provides that the disclosure of a confidential record under this section does not affect the confidentiality of the record, and prohibits the person provided access to the record from disclosing the record further except as provided by court order or other law.

CLE/Other Legal Publications

HIPAA and other releases. Bridget Danielle Burke & Gabe Thomas Vick III, 2011 Adv. Fam. L.

§ 107.007. Attorney Work Product and Testimony

(a) An attorney ad litem, an attorney serving in the dual role, or an amicus attorney may not:

(1) be compelled to produce attorney work product developed during the appointment as an attorney;

(2) be required to disclose the source of any information;

(3) submit a report into evidence; or

(4) testify in court except as authorized by Rule 3.08, Texas Disciplinary Rules of Professional Conduct.

(b) Subsection (a) does not apply to the duty of an attorney to report child abuse or neglect under Section 261.101.

Comment

An attorney ad litem, an attorney serving in the AAL/GAL dual role, and the amicus attorney are all protected by the work product and testimonial privileges. The lawyer's work product is confidential and not subject to discovery. Moreover, a lawyer serving in any of these roles may not submit a report to the court, or be compelled to testify. Of course, the lawyer may testify in the narrow fashion authorized by the disciplinary rules, e.g., on the matter of attorney fees. These attorney-client protections are particularly relevant to an amicus attorney, who by definition does not exactly have a client.

Subsection (b) clarifies that an attorney who is required to report child abuse or neglect under § 261.101 is not exempt from that duty after being appointed in either a CPS case or a private custody case.

§ 107.008. Substituted Judgment of Attorney for Child

(a) An attorney ad litem appointed to represent a child or an attorney appointed in the dual role may determine that the child cannot meaningfully formulate the child's objectives of representation in a case because the child:

(1) lacks sufficient maturity to understand and form an attorney-client relationship with the attorney;

(2) despite appropriate legal counseling, continues to express objectives of representation that would be seriously injurious to the child; or

(3) for any other reason is incapable of making reasonable judgments and engaging in meaningful communication.

(b) An attorney ad litem or an attorney appointed in the dual role who determines that the child cannot meaningfully formulate the child's expressed objectives of representation may present to the court a position that the attorney determines will serve the best interests of the child.

(c) If a guardian ad litem has been appointed for the child in a suit filed by a governmental entity requesting termination of the parent-child relationship or appointment of the entity as conservator of the child, an attorney ad litem who determines that the child cannot meaningfully formulate the child's expressed objectives of representation:

(1) shall consult with the guardian ad litem and, without being bound by the guardian ad litem's opinion or recommendation, ensure that the guardian ad litem's opinion and basis for any recommendation regarding the best interests of the child are presented to the court; and

(2) may present to the court a position that the attorney determines will serve the best interests of the child.

Comment

This section addresses a fact situation that is far more discussed than is actually encountered in practice by attorneys representing abused or neglected children (AAL or AAL/GAL). In point of fact, an actual abused or neglected child virtually never directs an AAL's activities in a manner that would seriously endanger the child's physical or emotional health. The issue does not arise for an amicus attorney because that attorney does not have a child client. But when an AAL or an AAL/GAL does have a client who may be capable of forming an attorney client relationship with the attorney, that client may rely on the confidentiality privilege in attempting to direct the attorney to advocate a position that would be "seriously injurious" to the child client. This section, based substantially on the NACC amended ABA Standards, seeks to balance the obligation of a lawyer to represent a child client with the obligation of the AAL to insure that serious injury to the child does not result from the legal representation. This is an expansion of the lawyer's traditional duty to take protective action for an incompetent client.

The ABA Standards and the NACC Revised Standards recognize that when a child cannot meaningfully participate in the formulation of a legal position (either because the child is preverbal, very young or for some other reason is incapable of judgment and meaningful communication), the AAL, or AAL/GAL must provide substituted judgment in order to serve the child's interests. The AAL must apply objective criteria, rather than rely on life experience or instinct. Criteria to reach a decision include a full and efficient investigation, review of all the options, and consideration of the available evidence. The net result is that if there is a disagreement with regard to the best interest of the child all positions will be presented to the court.

§ 107.009. Immunity

(a) A guardian ad litem, an attorney ad litem, or an amicus attorney appointed under this chapter is not liable for civil damages arising from an action taken, a recommendation made, or an opinion given in the capacity of guardian ad litem, attorney ad litem, or amicus attorney.

(b) Subsection (a) does not apply to an action taken, a recommendation made, or an opinion given:

(1) with conscious indifference or reckless disregard to the safety of another;

(2) in bad faith or with malice; or

(3) that is grossly negligent or wilfully wrongful.

Comment

Fear of liability has reportedly frightened off some potential volunteer advocates, and probably more than a few lawyers. This section extends the immunity formerly provided only for the GAL to the AAL and amicus attorney as well. This is consistent with the spirit of Delcourt v. Silverman, 919 S.W.2d 777 (Tex. App.—Houston [14th Dist.] 1996, no writ), although the immunity language in the statute goes beyond the facts and language of the Delcourt decision. This expanded immunity for ad litems of any stripe may seem excessive to some, especially the AAL who does have a client, sometimes even a sentient one. However, since it is only opinions and recommendations that are immunized, the section is not a general license to fall asleep at trial or otherwise commit malpractice. There is good justification to immunize an amicus attorney who, after all, is appointed by the court to represent the best interests of the child and to provide legal services to that end rather than to the end of representing a client.

Leading Case

Zeifman v. Nowlin, 322 S.W.3d 804 (Tex. App.—Austin 2010, no pet.) (amicus attorney has statutory immunity for father's fraud and gross negligence suit; duties owed to child, not to parent) (groundless claim elicits $40,000 in sanctions)

---

§ 107.010. Discretionary Appointment of Attorney ad Litem for Incapacitated Person

The court may appoint an attorney to serve as an attorney ad litem for a person entitled to service of citation in a suit if the court finds that the person is incapacitated. The attorney ad litem shall follow the person's expressed objectives of representation and, if appropriate, refer the proceeding to the proper court for guardianship proceedings.

Comment

This section provides for an appointment in a fact situation in which an adult is incapacitated and needs legal representation. The attorney ad litem appointed in that context is encouraged to seek guardianship proceedings if the attorney deems that to be appropriate.

SUBCHAPTER B. APPOINTMENTS IN CERTAIN SUITS

PART 1. APPOINTMENTS IN SUITS BY GOVERNMENTAL ENTITY

§ 107.011. Mandatory Appointment of Guardian ad Litem

(a) Except as otherwise provided by this subchapter, in a suit filed by a governmental entity seeking termination of the parent-child relationship or the appointment of a conservator for a child, the court shall appoint a guardian ad litem to represent the best interests of the child immediately after the filing of the petition but before the full adversary hearing.

(b) The guardian ad litem appointed for a child under this section may be:

(1) a charitable organization composed of volunteer advocates or an individual volunteer advocate appointed under Subchapter C;

(2) an adult having the competence, training, and expertise determined by the court to be sufficient to represent the best interests of the child; or

(3) an attorney appointed in the dual role.

(c) The court may not appoint a guardian ad litem in a suit filed by a governmental entity if an attorney is appointed in the dual role unless the court appoints another person to serve as guardian ad litem for the child and restricts the role of the attorney to acting as an attorney ad litem for the child.

(d) The court may appoint an attorney to serve as guardian ad litem for a child without appointing the attorney to serve in the dual role only if the attorney is specifically appointed to serve only in the role of guardian ad litem. An attorney appointed solely as a guardian ad litem:

(1) may take only those actions that may be taken by a nonattorney guardian ad litem; and

(2) may not:

(A) perform legal services in the case; or

(B) take any action that is restricted to a licensed attorney, including engaging in discovery other than as a witness, making opening and closing statements, or examining witnesses.

§ 107.012. Mandatory Appointment of Attorney ad Litem for Child

In a suit filed by a governmental entity requesting termination of the parent-child relationship or to be named conservator of a child, the court shall appoint an attorney ad litem to represent the interests of the child immediately after the filing, but before the full adversary hearing, to ensure adequate representation of the child.

Comment

The required appointment of an attorney ad litem for a child subject of a CPS suit is the only provision in this chapter that has remained constant.

§ 107.0125. Appointment of Attorney in Dual Role

(a) In order to comply with the mandatory appointment of a guardian ad litem under Section 107.011 and the mandatory appointment of an attorney ad litem under Section 107.012, the court may appoint an attorney to serve in the dual role.

(b) If the court appoints an attorney to serve in the dual role under this section, the court may at any time during the pendency of the suit appoint another person to serve as guardian ad litem for the child and restrict the attorney to acting as an attorney ad litem for the child.

(c) An attorney appointed to serve in the dual role may request the court to appoint another person to serve as guardian ad litem for the child. If the court grants the attorney's request, the attorney shall serve only as the attorney ad litem for the child.

(d) Unless the court appoints another person as guardian ad litem in a suit filed by a governmental entity, an appointment of an attorney to serve as an attorney ad litem in a suit filed by a governmental entity is an appointment to serve in the dual role regardless of the terminology used in the appointing order.

Comment

A child in a CPS case is entitled to appointment of both an AAL and a GAL. For reasons of efficiency and protection of the public fisc, in many counties it is common practice to appoint a lawyer in the dual role of AAL/GAL. A lawyer so appointed hypothetically may face ethical dilemmas inherent in the dual role. See, commentary to § 107.008, *supra*. Even more troublesome is the fact that in some counties the common practice has been to appoint a lawyer with the title of "GAL," and to ignore the fact that Texas law requires that the child in a CPS case be appointed both a guardian ad litem and an attorney ad litem. The lawyer appointed as "GAL" is expected to provide legal representation to the child in the CPS case in both roles.

Subsection (b) provides the court with full discretion to place a lawyer serving in a dual role with a nonlawyer GAL, and further, a lawyer in the dual role may request to be relieved of the GAL role. Formerly, this was a specific directive if the lawyer found that the two roles were in conflict. The requirement to continue as AAL was, and is, mandated by the fact that the lawyer assuredly could come to that conclusion from a dispute over the child's decision about best interest which is based, at least in part, on information obtained in the role of attorney for the child.

Subsection (d) anticipates that lawyers may no longer be appointed solely as "guardian ad litem" in CPS cases. Because news of a change in the law historically has traveled slowly, lawyers are instructed that such an appointment is as AAL/GAL by operation of law. In fact, the law has required an AAL be appointed for the child since 1979 (yes, 30 years have passed since the terminology was supposed to have changed). The legislature makes it clear that when an attorney appointed in a

CPS case is expected to provide legal services, the appointment is as an AAL/GAL unless another individual has been appointed GAL.

Texas Disciplinary Rule of Professional Conduct 1.02(g) requires an attorney to "take reasonable action to secure the appointment of a guardian or other legal representative for, or seek other protective orders with respect to, a client whenever the lawyer reasonably believes that the client lacks legal competence and that such action should be taken to protect the client." This required protective action may be in the form of using substituted judgment in certain conflict situations, as set out in § 107.008, *supra*.

§ 107.013. Mandatory Appointment of Attorney ad Litem for Parent

(a) In a suit filed by a governmental entity in which termination of the parent-child relationship is requested, the court shall appoint an attorney ad litem to represent the interests of:

(1) an indigent parent of the child who responds in opposition to the termination;

(2) a parent served by citation by publication;

(3) an alleged father who failed to register with the registry under Chapter 160 and whose identity or location is unknown; and

(4) an alleged father who registered with the paternity registry under Chapter 160, but the petitioner's attempt to personally serve citation at the address provided to the registry and at any other address for the alleged father known by the petitioner has been unsuccessful.

(b) If both parents of the child are entitled to the appointment of an attorney ad litem under this section and the court finds that the interests of the parents are not in conflict, the court may appoint an attorney ad litem to represent the interests of both parents.

(c) In a suit filed by a governmental entity requesting temporary managing conservatorship of a child, the court shall appoint an attorney ad litem to represent the interests of an indigent parent of the child who responds in opposition to the suit.

(d) A parent who claims indigence under Subsection (a) must file an affidavit of indigence in accordance with Rule 145(b) of the Texas Rules of Civil Procedure before the court can conduct a hearing to determine the parent's indigence under this section.

(e) A parent who the court has determined is indigent for purposes of this section is presumed to remain indigent for the duration of the suit and any subsequent appeal unless the court, after reconsideration on the motion of the parent, the attorney ad litem for the parent, or the attorney representing the governmental entity, determines that the parent is no longer indigent due to a material and substantial change in the parent's financial circumstances.

Amended by Acts 2011, 82nd Leg., ch. 75 (H.B. 906), § 1, eff. Sept. 1, 2011.

Comment

The appointment of an attorney for an indigent parent in a CPS case is not constitutionally mandated but has been statutorily mandated in Texas since 1979. The new restriction regarding the fact that the suit must be filed by a governmental entity is tied directly to the succeeding section dealing with attorney's fees. There is no statutory or constitutional requirement for appointment of counsel in a private termination case.

Leading Cases

In re M.S., 115 S.W.3d 534 (Tex. 2003) (attorney's failure to preserve factual sufficiency issue for appeal constitutes ineffective assistance of counsel)

Valencia v. Texas Dept. of Family and Protective Serv., ___ S.W.3d ___, 2010 WL 1240988 (Tex. App.—Houston [1st Dist.] 2010, no pet.) (father received no meaningful assistance of counsel; prejudice to his defense presumed)

See Chapters 161 and 263, *infra,* and Accompanying CD–ROM for Cases Linked to Westlaw and Additional Leading Cases

---

§ 107.0131. Powers and Duties of Attorney Ad Litem for Parent

(a) An attorney ad litem appointed under Section 107.013 to represent the interests of a parent:

(1) shall:

(A) subject to Rules 4.02, 4.03, and 4.04, Texas Disciplinary Rules of Professional Conduct, and within a reasonable time after the appointment, interview:

(i) the parent, unless the parent's location is unknown;

(ii) each person who has significant knowledge of the case;and

(iii) the parties to the suit;

(B) investigate the facts of the case;

(C) to ensure competent representation at hearings, mediations, pretrial matters, and the trial on the merits:

(i) obtain and review copies of all court files in the suit during the attorney ad litem's course of representation; and

(ii) when necessary, conduct formal discovery under the Texas Rules of Civil Procedure or the discovery control plan;

(D) take any action consistent with the parent's interests that the attorney ad litem considers necessary to expedite the proceedings;

(E) encourage settlement and the use of alternative forms of dispute resolution;

(F) review and sign, or decline to sign, a proposed or agreed order affecting the parent;

(G) meet before each court hearing with the parent, unless the court:

(i) finds at that hearing that the attorney ad litem has shown good cause why the attorney ad litem's compliance is not feasible; or

(ii) on a showing of good cause, authorizes the attorney ad litem to comply by conferring with the parent, as appropriate, by telephone or video conference;

(H) become familiar with the American Bar Association's standards of practice for attorneys who represent parents in abuse and neglect cases;

(I) complete at least three hours of continuing legal education relating to child protection law as described by Subsection (b) as soon as practicable after the attorney ad litem is appointed, unless the court finds that the attorney ad litem has experience equivalent to that education; and

(J) abide by the parent's objectives of representation;

(2) must be trained in child protection law or have experience determined by the court to be equivalent to that training; and

(3) is entitled to:

(A) request clarification from the court if the role of the attorney ad litem is ambiguous;

(B) request a hearing or trial on the merits;

(C) consent or refuse to consent to an interview of the parent by another attorney;

(D) receive a copy of each pleading or other paper filed with the court;

(E) receive notice of each hearing in the suit;

(F) participate in any case staffing conducted by the Department of Family and Protective Services in which the parent is invited to participate, including, as

appropriate, a case staffing to develop a family plan of service, a family group conference, a permanency conference, a mediation, a case staffing to plan for the discharge and return of the child to the parent, and any other case staffing that the department determines would be appropriate for the parent to attend, but excluding any internal department staffing or staffing between the department and the department's legal representative; and

(G) attend all legal proceedings in the suit.

(b) The continuing legal education required by Subsection (a)(1)(I) must:

(1) be low-cost and available to persons throughout this state, including on the Internet provided through the State Bar of Texas; and

(2) focus on the duties of an attorney ad litem in, and the procedures of and best practices for, a proceeding under Chapter 262 or 263.

Added by Acts 2011, 82nd Leg., ch. 647 (S.B. 1026), § 1, eff. Sept. 1, 2011.

Comment

A recent study conducted by the Permanent Judicial Commission for Children, Youth and Families to assess attorney appointments in child protective services (CPS) cases indicated that, although the existing statutes specify the powers, duties, and training requirements of attorneys ad litem for children, the statutes do not adequately address these requirements for attorneys representing parents. Interested parties contended the issues very often are not adequately addressed, in large part because attorneys who are appointed to represent parents in CPS cases may not have sufficient training or experience in child-protection law to undertake these cases. Thus, in some instances the attorney is not able to provide fair, quality representation. Moreover, effective legal representation can hasten a family's reunification or, when reunification is not a viable option, a child's placement in a permanent home.

The three new sections addressing this problem address these issues by specifying the powers and duties of an attorney ad litem representing a parent, or an alleged father, in certain SAPCR's, including continuing education requirements, and making such an attorney ad litem subject to disciplinary action if the attorney fails to perform required duties. The duties to a parent are modeled on, and closely track those required of an attorney ad litem appointed to represent a child in a CPS case. Indeed, the only significant difference is that under appropriate circumstances an attorney ad litem may substitute judgment to overrule the directives of the client. *See* §107.008.

To ensure competent representation at hearings, mediations, pretrial matters, and the trial on the merits, the attorney ad litem is required to obtain and review copies of all court files during the course of representation and, when necessary, conduct formal discovery under the Tex. R. Civ. P. or the discovery control plan. In the original formulation of the legislation the "when necessary" exception was also applicable with regard to the review of all court files.

---

§ 107.0132. Powers and Duties of Attorney Ad Litem for Alleged Father

(a) An attorney ad litem appointed under Section 107.013 to represent the interests of an alleged father shall:

(1) conduct an investigation regarding the petitioner's due diligence in locating the alleged father, including by verifying that the petitioner has obtained a certificate of the results of a search of the paternity registry under Chapter 160;

(2) interview any party or other person who has significant knowledge of the case who may have information relating to the identity or location of the alleged father; and

(3) conduct an independent investigation to identify or locate the alleged father, as applicable.

(b) If the attorney ad litem identifies and locates the alleged father, the attorney ad litem shall:

(1) provide to each party and the court the alleged father's name and address and any other locating information; and

(2) if appropriate, request the court's approval for the attorney ad litem to assist the alleged father in establishing paternity.

(c) If the alleged father is adjudicated to be a parent of the child and is determined by the court to be indigent, the court may appoint the attorney ad litem to continue to represent the father's interests as a parent under Section 107.013(a)(1) or (c).

(d) If the attorney ad litem is unable to identify or locate the alleged father, the attorney ad litem shall submit to the court a written summary of the attorney ad litem's efforts to identify or locate the alleged father with a statement that the attorney ad litem was unable to identify or locate the alleged father.

Added by Acts 2011, 82nd Leg., ch. 647 (S.B. 1026), § 1, eff. Sept. 1, 2011.

Comment

Representation by an ad litem attorney of an alleged father very often presents a different set of professional problems, given the fact that the parentage of the client is uncertain. An attorney ad litem in this circumstance must conduct an investigation regarding the department's due diligence in locating the alleged father, including obtaining a certificate of the results of a search of the paternity registry under the Uniform Parentage Act; interview any party or other person who has significant knowledge of the case who may have information relating to the identity or location of the alleged father; and conduct an independent investigation to identify or locate the alleged father, as applicable. If the attorney ad litem identifies and locates the alleged father, the ad litem must provide to each party and the court the client's name and address and any other locating information and, if appropriate, request the court's approval for the attorney ad litem to assist the alleged father in establishing paternity. The court may appoint the attorney ad litem to continue to represent the father's interests as a parent if he is adjudicated to be a parent of the child and is determined by the court to be indigent. An ad litem unable to identify or locate the alleged father must submit a written summary of the efforts that failed in the task.

§ 107.0133. Discipline of Attorney Ad Litem for Parent or Alleged Father

An attorney ad litem appointed for a parent or an alleged father who fails to perform the duties required by Section 107.0131 or 107.0132, as applicable, is subject to disciplinary action under Subchapter E, Chapter 81, Government Code.

Added by Acts 2011, 82nd Leg., ch. 647 (S.B. 1026), § 1, eff. Sept. 1, 2011.

§ 107.015. Attorney Fees

(a) An attorney appointed under this chapter to serve as an attorney ad litem for a child, an attorney in the dual role, or an attorney ad litem for a parent is entitled to reasonable fees and expenses in the amount set by the court to be paid by the parents of the child unless the parents are indigent.

(b) If the court determines that one or more of the parties are able to defray the fees and expenses of an attorney ad litem or guardian ad litem for the child as determined by the reasonable and customary fees for similar services in the county of jurisdiction, the fees and expenses may be ordered paid by one or more of those parties, or the court may order one or more of those parties, prior to final hearing, to pay the sums into the registry of the court or into an account authorized by the court for the use and benefit of the payee on order of the court. The sums may be taxed as costs to be assessed against one or more of the parties.

(c) If indigency of the parents is shown, an attorney ad litem appointed to represent a child or parent in a suit filed by a governmental entity shall be paid from the general funds of the county according to the fee schedule that applies to an attorney appointed to represent a child in a suit under Title 3 as provided by Chapter 51. The court may not award attorney ad litem fees under this chapter against the state, a state agency, or a political subdivision of the state except as provided by this subsection.

(d) A person appointed as a guardian ad litem or attorney ad litem shall complete and submit to the court a voucher or claim for payment that lists the fees charged and hours worked by the guardian ad litem or attorney ad litem. Information submitted under this section is subject to disclosure under Chapter 552, Government Code.

Comment

Fees paid to attorneys ad litem in CPS cases have been a controversial subject only to those who serve in that capacity. Notably, the fees are some of the lowest paid in the legal profession.

Subsections (b) and (c) codify the rule that parents are to pay the legal fees if able; if not, the county pays. The state doesn't pay, even though DFPS, a state agency, has filed the SAPCR for conservatorship or termination that resulted in the AAL's appointment.

---

§ 107.016. Continued Representation; Duration of Appointment

In a suit filed by a governmental entity in which termination of the parent-child relationship or appointment of the entity as conservator of the child is requested**:**

(1) ~~,~~ an order appointing the Department of **Family and** Protective ~~and Regulatory~~ Services as the child's managing conservator may provide for the continuation of the appointment of the guardian ad litem or attorney ad litem for the child for any period set by the court**; and**

(2) an attorney appointed under this subchapter to serve as an attorney ad litem for a parent or an alleged father continues to serve in that capacity until the earliest of:

(A) the date the suit affecting the parent-child relationship is dismissed;

(B) the date all appeals in relation to any final order terminating parental rights are exhausted or waived; or

(C) the date the attorney is relieved of the attorney's duties or replaced by another attorney after a finding of good cause is rendered by the court on the record.

Amended by Acts 2011, 82nd Leg., ch. 75 (H.B. 906), § 2, eff. Sept. 1, 2011.

Comment

At the discretion of the court, the appointment of an attorney ad litem may be continued until the child ages out of the system at 18. Between the time DFPS is named permanent managing conservator and that birthday, the main effort is social work; usually very little lawyering is needed.

---

§ 107.0161. Ad Litem Appointments for Child Committed to Texas Youth Commission

If an order appointing the Department of Family and Protective Services as managing conservator of a child does not continue the appointment of the child's guardian ad litem or attorney ad litem and the child is committed to the Texas Youth Commission or released under supervision by the Texas Youth Commission, the court may appoint a guardian ad litem or attorney ad litem for the child.

§ 107.017. Appointment of Amicus Attorney Prohibited

The court may not appoint a person to serve as an amicus attorney in a suit filed by a governmental entity under this chapter.

Comment

The appointment of an amicus attorney in a CPS case is explicitly forbidden.

PART 2. APPOINTMENTS IN SUITS OTHER THAN SUITS BY GOVERNMENTAL ENTITY

Comment

Subchapter B, Part 2, is directed at private custody cases. As such, it is intended to codify what is described in the Editors' Note to this chapter as "best practices."

---

§ 107.021. Discretionary Appointments

(a) In a suit in which the best interests of a child are at issue, other than a suit filed by a governmental entity requesting termination of the parent-child relationship or appointment of the entity as conservator of the child, the court may appoint one of the following:

(1) an amicus attorney;

(2) an attorney ad litem; or

(3) a guardian ad litem.

(a–1) In a suit requesting termination of the parent-child relationship that is not filed by a governmental entity, the court shall, unless the court finds that the interests of the child will be represented adequately by a party to the suit whose interests are not in conflict with the child's interests, appoint one of the following:

(1) an amicus attorney; or

(2) an attorney ad litem.

(b) In determining whether to make an appointment under this section, the court:

(1) shall:

(A) give due consideration to the ability of the parties to pay reasonable fees to the appointee; and

(B) balance the child's interests against the cost to the parties that would result from an appointment by taking into consideration the cost of available alternatives for resolving issues without making an appointment;

(2) may make an appointment only if the court finds that the appointment is necessary to ensure the determination of the best interests of the child, unless the appointment is otherwise required by this code; and

(3) may not require a person appointed under this section to serve without reasonable compensation for the services rendered by the person.

Comment

Subsection (a) makes it clear that in private custody cases, the court will appoint only one person to represent the child or assist the court. This means either a lawyer serving in the role of amicus attorney or ad litem attorney, or a layperson serving as GAL. In many counties, the option of appointing a nonlawyer as a guardian ad litem is not practical. First, § 107.022(2) prohibits the court from appointing a volunteer advocate (CASA volunteer) from serving as a guardian ad litem in a custody case unless the training of the volunteer is designed for participation in suits other than those filed by a governmental entity. Such training generally is not available in the state. Moreover, psychologists or private social workers to serve as GAL may not be available.

In sum, the court has the option in a private custody case of designating a court appointed lawyer as either an amicus attorney or an attorney ad litem. There is an implicit presumption that multiple children in a family will not require multiple appointed attorneys. Indeed, given the fact that the amicus attorney is seeking best interest for children without being their lawyer, it is difficult to conceive a situation in which multiple legal appointments would be appropriate. On the other hand, it is at least theoretically possible that an attorney ad litem appointed in a custody case might decide that two or more children in a custody dispute have such irreconcilable differences that their legal representation by one attorney ad litem is ethically precluded.

Subsection (a)(1) is written in mandatory language, but the "unless clause" makes the appointment purely discretionary in virtually all cases. That is, the determination of parental rights by the other parent or by relatives most commonly will be in step parent adoptions. In those circumstances, the obvious finding is that the interest of the child will be represented by the petitioner. If not, an attorney should be appointed.

Subsection (b) gives guidance to the court for appointments in private custody disputes. The involved legislators specifically indicated through comments and actions that such appointments can, and probably sometimes are, being abused by courts. Part of that abuse is the fact that appointments in private custody cases often go unpaid, or are paid at far less than at market rate. Secondly, such appointments are sometimes inimical to the functioning of the adversary system. The section directs the court to take into account the financial impact of the appointment, and also to restrict appointments to situations in which the "appointment is necessary to insure the determination of best interests of the child." The application of that test, of course, is left to the discretion of the court.

Leading Cases

In re Scheller, 325 S.W.3d 640 (Tex. 2010) (trial court abused discretion as grandfather failed to prove father not acting in children's best interest when he disputed temporary telephone access and bi-monthly weekends; parent's *Troxel* rights upheld, but only on 2d mandamus petition) (appointment of psychologist as GAL didn't violate *Troxel* rule)

In re K.M.M., 326 S.W.3d 714 (Tex. App.—Amarillo 2010, no pet.) (presumed father in private termination case protested failure to appoint AAL. or amicus attorney for child; seldom can a court find one party adequately represents a child's interest or that party's interests are not adverse)

---

§ 107.022. Certain Prohibited Appointments

In a suit other than a suit filed by a governmental entity requesting termination of the parent-child relationship or appointment of the entity as conservator of the child, the court may not appoint:

(1) an attorney to serve in the dual role; or

(2) a volunteer advocate to serve as guardian ad litem for a child unless the training of the volunteer advocate is designed for participation in suits other than suits filed by a governmental entity requesting termination of the parent-child relationship or appointment of the entity as conservator of the child.

Comment

This section places two important restrictions on an appointment in a private custody case. First, the lawyer will either be an AAL or an amicus attorney; there is no dual role. Secondly, CASA volunteers are not to be appointed in private custody cases because their training is not designed for participation in suits other than those filed by CPS. In the event that there is a voluntary advocate program that trains its volunteers to participate in private custody cases, those members are eligible for appointment as a GAL. Reportedly, the only such program was in the Houston area, and it has been discontinued.

The prohibition against the court appointing a CASA in a non CPS case is made even stronger by identifying the fact that CASA training does not qualify for private custody suits.

---

§ 107.023. Fees in Suits Other Than Suits by Governmental Entity

(a) In a suit other than a suit filed by a governmental entity requesting termination of the parent-child relationship or appointment of the entity as conservator of the child, in addition to the attorney's fees that may be awarded under Chapter 106, the following persons are entitled to reasonable fees and expenses in an amount set by the court and ordered to be paid by one or more parties to the suit:

(1) an attorney appointed as an amicus attorney or as an attorney ad litem for the child; and

(2) a professional who holds a relevant professional license and who is appointed as guardian ad litem for the child, other than a volunteer advocate.

(b) The court shall:

(1) determine the fees and expenses of an amicus attorney, an attorney ad litem, or a guardian ad litem by reference to the reasonable and customary fees for similar services in the county of jurisdiction;

(2) order a reasonable cost deposit to be made at the time the court makes the appointment; and

(3) before the final hearing, order an additional amount to be paid to the credit of a trust account for the use and benefit of the amicus attorney, attorney ad litem, or guardian ad litem.

(c) A court may not award costs, fees, or expenses to an amicus attorney, attorney ad litem, or guardian ad litem against the state, a state agency, or a political subdivision of the state under this part.

(d) The court may determine that fees awarded under this subchapter to an amicus attorney, an attorney ad litem for the child, or a guardian ad litem for the child are necessaries for the benefit of the child.

Comment

This section attempts to resolve issues regarding payment of professional fees, whether to an attorney or to another individual with a relevant professional license, *e.g.,* a GAL with a MSW or a doctorate in psychology or child development. This section makes it clear that a lawyer appointed as either an amicus attorney or an attorney ad litem is entitled to a reasonable fee.

Payment to attorneys appointed in private custody suits or professionals who serve as GAL's in suits has always been a problem to collect. Subsection (b) attempts to assist in that collection by declaring the fees are awarded as necessaries. Collection of necessaries includes a wide variety of enforcement devices; enforcement by contempt does not happen to be one of them, although the turnover statute may be applicable. To help further ensure that payments are made in a timely fashion, Subsection (b) directs that reasonable payments be made, plus reasonable cost deposits and partial payments, as the case develops.

Subsection (c) immunizes governmental entities from attorney's fees in private custody matters.

SUBCHAPTER C. APPOINTMENT OF VOLUNTEER ADVOCATES

§ 107.031. Volunteer Advocates

(a) In a suit filed by a governmental entity requesting termination of the parent-child relationship or appointment of the entity as conservator of the child, the court may appoint a charitable organization composed of volunteer advocates whose charter mandates the provision of services to allegedly abused and neglected children or an individual who has received the court's approved training regarding abused and neglected children and who has been certified by the court to appear at court hearings as a guardian ad litem for the child or as a volunteer advocate for the child.

(b) In a suit other than a suit filed by a governmental entity requesting termination of the parent-child relationship or appointment of the entity as conservator of the child, the court may appoint a charitable organization composed of volunteer advocates whose training provides for the provision of services in private custody disputes or a person who has received the court's approved training regarding the subject matter of the suit and who has been certified by the court to appear at court hearings as a guardian ad litem for the child or as a volunteer advocate for the child. A person appointed under this subsection is not entitled to fees under Section 107.023.

(c) A court-certified volunteer advocate appointed under this section may be assigned to act as a surrogate parent for the child, as provided by 20 U.S.C. Section 1415(b), if:

(1) the child is in the conservatorship of the Department of Family and Protective Services;

(2) the volunteer advocate is serving as guardian ad litem for the child; and

(3) a foster parent of the child is not acting as the child's parent under Section 29.015, Education Code.

Comment

Since the early 1990's, volunteer advocacy programs authorized by this subchapter have proliferated throughout Texas. Usually known as CASAs (Court–Appointed Special Advocates), private individuals have been appointed as volunteer advocates for children in child protection litigation. Official recognition of the vital role played by CASAs came in 1997 when, via amendments to § 107.001, the legislature authorized the court to appoint a volunteer advocate as the guardian ad litem for the child. This brought Texas into compliance with federal funding requirements, P.L. 104–235, 42 U.S.C. § 5106A (b)(2)(ix) (1997). Appointing CASA as GAL transforms the volunteer advocate appointed into a substitute decision maker on behalf of the child in CPS litigation.

Subsection (a) provides that the appointment may be to the CASA organization itself and does not necessarily require the appointment of an identified single individual.

Subsection (b) opens the way for non-CASA organizations to provide volunteer advocates in private custody disputes if that is the choice of the entity.

SUBCHAPTER D. SOCIAL STUDY

Introductory Comment

Although a social study is not "evidence," it may have a significant impact on judicial decision making. A peculiar aspect of the statute is that DFPS sought and received a statutory exemption from making social studies except in cases in which the agency is a party-litigant. How the agency can be both a party and a neutral fact-finder is left to the imagination (but this has been the case for decades).

The provisions regarding social studies provide guidance and uniformity in the practice. "Social study" and "social study evaluator" are provided definitions for the first time, and statutory minimum qualifications for those completing social studies in counties with populations of over 500,000 are outlined. Finally, exactly what is expected to be done in conjunction with a social study and included within the social study report are statutorily defined.

CLE/Other Legal Publications

Custody workshop: examining the examiner: qualifications, reliability, and relevance; making effective use of the expert's report. (Panel), 2009 Adv. Fam. L.

Custody workshop: mental health experts: conflicting roles within the mental health expert appointment: evaluator, therapist, or consulting expert? What to do when the boundaries become blurred? (Panel), 2009 Adv. Fam. L.

Mental health experts: mini-workshop on the MMPI-2. (Panel), 2009 Adv. Fam. L.

Preparing your client for the social, psychological or home study. Beth M. Maultsby, 2008 UT Fam. L. Front Lines

Making the most of social studies and psychological evaluations. Diana S. Friedman, Scott A. Beauchamp, Barry S. Coakley & Christy Bradshaw Schmidt, 2008 UT Fam. L. Front Lines

How to respond to a horrible social study (social study from A-Z) attaching psychological evaluations. Stephen Thorne & Peter A. Sakai, 2008 MARRIAGE DISSOLUTION

The world of court appointees: amicus attorneys, attorney ad litems, guardian ad litems, and social studies. Reginald A. Hirsch & Joseph Indelicato, Jr., 2007 UT DEFINITIVE SAPCR

Social studies vs. psychological evaluations: what you can ask an expert and what you can't—risks of dealing with social studies. Marilea Whatley Lewis, 2007 ADV. FAM. L.

How to effectively cross-examine a psychologist or social study. Jonathan Gould & Lynn Kamin, 2007 U.T. FAM. L. FRONT LINES

Experts for kids. Matthew Riek, 2007 MARRIAGE DISSOLUTION

Leading Cases

Green v. Remling, 608 S.W.2d 905 (Tex. 1980) (court properly considered social study; failure to call social worker as witness not reversible error)

Chacon v. Chacon, 978 S.W.2d 633 (Tex. App.—El Paso 1998, no pet.) (written observations submitted by CASA as "court report" do not constitute a social study)

Bingham v. Bingham, 811 S.W.2d 678 (Tex. App.—Fort Worth 1991, no writ) (social study admissible as a governmental report)

Rossen v. Rossen, 792 S.W.2d 277 (Tex. App.—Houston [1st Dist.] 1990, no writ) (social study is generally inadmissible hearsay; author of report testified about procedure used in making report and her conclusions)

---

§ 107.0501. Definitions

In this subchapter:

(1) "Social study" means an evaluative process through which information and recommendations regarding adoption of a child, conservatorship of a child, or possession of or access to a child may be made to a court, the parties, and the parties' attorneys. The term does not include services provided in accordance with the Interstate Compact on the Placement of Children adopted under Subchapter B, Chapter 162, or an evaluation conducted in accordance with Section 262.114 by an employee of or contractor with the Department of Family and Protective Services.

(2) "Social study evaluator" means an individual who conducts a social study under this subchapter.

§ 107.051. Order for Social Study

(a) The court may order the preparation of a social study into the circumstances and condition of:

(1) a child who is the subject of a suit or a party to a suit; and

(2) the home of any person requesting conservatorship of, possession of, or access to a child.

(b) The social study may be made by a private entity, a person appointed by the court, a domestic relations office, or a state agency, including the Department of Family and Protective Services if the department is a party to the suit.

(c) In a suit in which adoption is requested or conservatorship of, possession of, or access to a child is an issue and in which a social study has been ordered and the Department of Family and Protective Services is not a party, the court shall appoint a private agency, another person, or a domestic relations office to conduct the social study.

(d) Except as provided by Section 107.0511(b), each individual who conducts a social study must be qualified under Section 107.0511.

Comment

The local Children's Protective Services (CPS) involvement with social studies continues to be one of the strangest sections in the Family Code. Despite the fact that CPS is a party to a lawsuit espousing its own legal position, it is permissible for the department to be ordered to prepare a social study in that suit. However, if CPS is not a party, and thereby neutral on the subject by definition, the court is forbidden to appoint CPS to conduct a social study—a unusual bizarre system from a due process perspective.

---

§ 107.0511. Social Study Evaluator: Minimum Qualifications

(a) In this section:

(1) "Full-time experience" means a period during which an individual works at least 30 hours per week.

(2) "Human services field of study" means a field of study designed to prepare an individual in the disciplined application of counseling, family therapy, psychology, or social work values, principles, and methods.

(b) The minimum qualifications prescribed by this section do not apply to an individual conducting a social study:

(1) in connection with a suit pending before a court located in a county with a population of less than 500,000;

(2) in connection with an adoption governed by rules adopted under Section 107.0519(a);

(3) as an employee or other authorized representative of a licensed child-placing agency; or

(4) as an employee or other authorized representative of the Department of Family and Protective Services.

(c) The executive commissioner of the Health and Human Services Commission shall adopt rules prescribing the minimum qualifications that an individual described by Subsection (b)(3) or (4) must possess in order to conduct a social study under this subchapter.

(d) To be qualified to conduct a social study under this subchapter, an individual must:

(1) have a bachelor's degree from an accredited college or university in a human services field of study and a license to practice in this state as a social worker, professional counselor, marriage and family therapist, or psychologist and:

(A) have two years of full-time experience or equivalent part-time experience under professional supervision during which the individual performed functions involving the evaluation of physical, intellectual, social, and psychological functioning and needs and the potential of the social and physical environment, both present and prospective, to meet those needs; and

(B) have participated in the performance of at least 10 court-ordered social studies under the supervision of an individual qualified under this section;

(2) meet the requirements of Subdivision (1)(A) and be practicing under the direct supervision of an individual qualified under this section in order to complete at least 10 court-ordered social studies under supervision; or

(3) be employed by a domestic relations office, provided that the individual conducts social studies relating only to families ordered by a court to participate in social studies conducted by the office.

(e) If an individual meeting the requirements of this section is not available in the county served by the court, the court may authorize an individual determined by the court to be otherwise qualified to conduct the social study.

(f) In addition to the qualifications prescribed by this section, an individual must complete at least eight hours of family violence dynamics training provided by a family violence service provider to be qualified to conduct a social study under this subchapter.

(g) The minimum qualifications prescribed by this section do not apply to an individual who, before September 1, 2007:

(1) lived in a county that has a population of 500,000 or more and is adjacent to two or more counties each of which has a population of 50,000 or more;

(2) received a four-year degree from an accredited institution of higher education;

(3) worked as a child protective services investigator for the Department of Family and Protective Services for at least four years;

(4) worked as a community supervision and corrections department officer; and

(5) conducted at least 100 social studies in the previous five years.

(h) A person described by Subsection (g) who performs a social study must:

(1) complete at least eight hours of family violence dynamics training provided by a family violence service provider; and

(2) participate annually in at least 15 hours of continuing education for child custody evaluators that meets the Model Standards of Practice for Child Custody Evaluation adopted by the Association of Family and Conciliation Courts as those standards existed May 1, 2009, or a later version of those standards if adopted by rule of the executive commissioner of the Health and Human Services Commission.

(i) Subsections (g) and (h) and this subsection expire September 1, 2017.

§ 107.0512. Social Study Evaluator: Conflicts of Interest and Bias

(a) A social study evaluator who has a conflict of interest with any party in a disputed suit or who may be biased on the basis of previous knowledge, other than knowledge obtained in a court-ordered evaluation, shall:

(1) decline to conduct a social study for the suit; or

(2) disclose any issue or concern to the court before accepting the appointment or assignment.

(b) A social study evaluator who has previously conducted a social study for a suit may conduct all subsequent evaluations in the suit unless the court finds that the evaluator is biased.

(c) This section does not prohibit a court from appointing an employee of the Department of Family and Protective Services to conduct a social study in a suit in which adoption is requested or possession of or access to a child is an issue and in which the department is a party or has an interest.

§ 107.0513. General Provisions Applicable to Conduct of Social Study and Preparation of Report

(a) Unless otherwise directed by a court or prescribed by a provision of this title, a social study evaluator's actions in conducting a social study shall be in conformance with the professional standard of care applicable to the evaluator's licensure and any administrative rules, ethical standards, or guidelines adopted by the state agency that licenses the evaluator.

(b) In addition to the requirements prescribed by this subchapter, a court may impose requirements or adopt local rules applicable to a social study or a social study evaluator.

(c) A social study evaluator shall follow evidence-based practice methods and make use of current best evidence in making assessments and recommendations.

(d) A social study evaluator shall disclose to each attorney of record any communication regarding a substantive issue between the evaluator and an attorney of record representing a party in a disputed suit. This subsection does not apply to a communication between a social study evaluator and an attorney ad litem or amicus attorney.

(e) To the extent possible, a social study evaluator shall verify each statement of fact pertinent to a social study and shall note the sources of verification and information in the report.

(f) A social study evaluator shall state the basis for the evaluator's conclusions or recommendations in the report. A social study evaluator who has evaluated only one side of a disputed case shall refrain from making a recommendation regarding conservatorship of a child or possession of or access to a child, but may state whether the party evaluated appears to be suitable for conservatorship.

(g) Each social study subject to this subchapter must be conducted in compliance with this subchapter, regardless of whether the study is conducted:

(1) by a single social study evaluator or multiple evaluators working separately or together; or

(2) within a county served by the court with continuing jurisdiction or at a geographically distant location.

(h) A social study report must include the name, license number, and basis for qualification under Section 107.0511 of each social study evaluator who conducted any portion of the social study.

§ 107.0514. Elements of Social Study

(a) The basic elements of a social study under this subchapter consist of:

(1) a personal interview of each party to the suit;

(2) an interview, conducted in a developmentally appropriate manner, of each child at issue in the suit who is at least four years of age;

(3) observation of each child at issue in the suit, regardless of the age of the child;

(4) the obtaining of information from relevant collateral sources;

(5) evaluation of the home environment of each party seeking conservatorship of a child at issue in the suit or possession of or access to the child, unless the condition of the home environment is identified as not being in dispute in the court order requiring the social study;

(6) for each individual residing in a residence subject to the social study, consideration of any criminal history information and any contact with the Department of Family and Protective Services or a law enforcement agency regarding abuse or neglect; and

(7) assessment of the relationship between each child at issue in the suit and each party seeking possession of or access to the child.

(b) The additional elements of a social study under this subchapter consist of:

(1) balanced interviews and observation of each child at issue in the suit so that a child who is interviewed or observed while in the care of one party to the suit is also interviewed or observed while in the care of each other party to the suit;

(2) an interview of each individual residing in a residence subject to the social study; and

(3) evaluation of the home environment of each party seeking conservatorship of a child at issue in the suit or possession of or access to the child, regardless of whether the home environment is in dispute.

(c) A social study evaluator may not offer an opinion regarding conservatorship of a child at issue in a suit or possession of or access to the child unless each basic element of a social study under Subsection (a) has been completed. A social study evaluator shall identify in the report any additional element of a social study under Subsection (b) that was not completed and shall explain the reasons that the element was not completed.

§ 107.0515. Reports of Certain Placements for Adoption

A social study evaluator shall report to the Department of Family and Protective Services any adoptive placement that appears to have been made by someone other than a licensed child-placing agency or the child's parents or managing conservator.

§ 107.0519. Pre–Adoptive Social Study

(a) This section does not apply to a study prepared by a licensed child-placing agency or the Department of Family and Protective Services. The procedures required in relation to a study prepared by a licensed child-placing agency or the Department of Family and Protective Services are governed by rules adopted by the executive commissioner of the Health and Human Services Commission, including rules adopted under Chapter 42, Human Resources Code.

(b) A pre-adoptive social study shall be conducted as provided by this section to evaluate each party in a proceeding described by Subsection (c) who requests termination of the parent-child relationship or an adoption.

(c) The social study under this section shall be filed in any suit for:

(1) termination of the parent-child relationship in which a person other than a parent may be appointed managing conservator of a child; or

(2) an adoption.

(d) The social study under this section must be filed with the court before the court may sign the final order for termination of the parent-child relationship.

(e) The costs of a social study in a suit for adoption under this section shall be paid by the prospective adoptive parent.

(f) Unless otherwise agreed to by the court, the social study under this section must comply with the minimum requirements for the study under rules adopted by the executive commissioner of the Health and Human Services Commission.

(g) In a suit filed after the child begins residence in the prospective adoptive home, the pre-adoptive social study under this section and the post-placement adoptive social study under Section 107.052 may be combined in a single report. Under this subsection, the pre-adoptive social study will be completed after the child is placed in the home.

§ 107.052. Post–Placement Adoptive Social Study And Report

(a) In a proceeding in which a pre-adoptive social study is required by Section 107.0519 for an adoption, a post-placement adoptive social study must be conducted and a report filed with the court before the court may render a final order in the adoption.

(b) Unless otherwise agreed to by the court, the post-placement adoptive social study must comply with the minimum requirements for the study under rules adopted by the executive commissioner of the Health and Human Services Commission.

Comment

When a licensed child placing agency or adoptive parent files a suit for adoption, the court is required by statute to order a home screening prior to placement of the child and a follow-up social study, relabeled "post placement adoptive report." In some cases of private adoptions, judges have ordered a home screening but not a social study. To ensure the best interest of the child, both a home screening and the post placement report are fundamental. To that end, there was a thorough reworking of this system, basically adding two new provisions and further modifications to establish pre adoptive home screenings and post placement adoptive reports in adoption cases in an effort to study the home environment of the adoptive parents

A pre adoptive home screening must be conducted to evaluate each party who requests termination of the parent child relationship or an adoption. Except for a suit brought by a licensed child placing agency or the Department of Family and Protective Services (DFPS), prescribed suits include any such suit in which a person other than a parent is authorized to be appointed managing conservator of a child. The screening is to be paid for by the prospective adoptive parent, and, unless otherwise agreed to by the court, must comply with the rules promulgated by the Board of DFPS.

Former provisions relating to the standards for conducting a social study, an adoptive home screening, and the time for an adoption hearing have been repealed. The details are left to compliance with the requirements set forth by the rules of the DFPS Board. The documentation must be filed with the court before it may render a final order in the adoption. In a step-parent adoption, the screening and the report may be combined. A social study may be made by a private entity, a person appointed by the court, or a state agency, including the department if the department is a party to the suit.

Finally, the court is required to grant a motion for a preferential setting for a final hearing on certain merits and to give precedence to that hearing over other civil cases under prescribed conditions. The final order in a termination of the parent-child relationship or adoption proceeding is not required to contain certain information regarding each party in the suit.

§ 107.053. Prospective Adoptive Parents to Receive Copy

In all adoptions a copy of the report shall be made available to the prospective adoptive parents prior to a final order of adoption.

§ 107.054. Report Filed With Court

The agency or person making the social study shall file with the court on a date set by the court a report containing its findings and conclusions. The report shall be made a part of the record of the suit.

§ 107.055. Introduction of Report at Trial

(a) Disclosure to the jury of the contents of a report to the court of a social study is subject to the rules of evidence.

(b) In a contested case, the agency or person making the social study shall furnish copies of the report to the attorneys for the parties before the earlier of:

(1) the seventh day after the date the social study is completed; or

(2) the fifth day before the date of commencement of the trial.

(c) The court may compel the attendance of witnesses necessary for the proper disposition of the suit, including a representative of the agency making the social study, who may be compelled to testify.

§ 107.056. Preparation Fee

If the court orders a social study to be conducted, the court shall award the agency or other person a reasonable fee for the preparation of the study that shall be imposed in the form of a money judgment and paid directly to the agency or other person. The person or agency may enforce the judgment for the fee by any means available under law for civil judgments.

CHAPTER 108. CENTRAL RECORD FILE; VITAL STATISTICS

Introductory Comment

Since 1995, the Bureau of Vital Statistics (BVS) has maintained the central record file that identifies courts of continuing, exclusive jurisdiction in SAPCR cases. This central record file is not related to CANRIS, the computerized records of reports of alleged child abuse and neglect, which is maintained by the Department of Family and Protective Services (DFPS). *See* § 261.002, *infra*.

---

§ 108.001. Transmittal of Records of Suit by Clerk

(a) Except as provided by this chapter, the clerk of the court shall transmit to the bureau of vital statistics a certified record of the order rendered in a suit, together with the name and all prior names, birth date, and place of birth of the child on a form provided by the bureau. The form shall be completed by the petitioner and submitted to the clerk at the time the order is filed for record.

(b) The bureau of vital statistics shall maintain these records in a central file according to the name, birth date, and place of birth of the child, the court that rendered the order, and the docket number of the suit.

(c) Except as otherwise provided by law, the records required under this section to be maintained by the bureau of vital statistics are confidential.

(d) In a Title IV–D case, the Title IV–D agency may transmit the record and information specified by Subsection (a) to the bureau of vital statistics, with a copy to the clerk of the court on request by the clerk. The record and information are not required to be certified if transmitted by the Title IV–D agency under this subsection.

§ 108.002. Dissolution of Marriage Records Maintained by Clerk

A clerk may not transmit to the central record file the pleadings, papers, studies, and records relating to a suit for divorce or annulment or to declare a marriage void.

§ 108.003. Transmittal of Information Regarding Adoption

(a) The clerk of a court that renders a decree of adoption shall, not later than the 10th day of the first month after the month in which the adoption is rendered, transmit to the central registry of the bureau of vital statistics certified report of adoption that includes:

(1) the name of the adopted child after adoption as shown in the adoption order;

(2) the birth date of the adopted child;

(3) the docket number of the adoption suit;

(4) the identity of the court rendering the adoption;

(5) the date of the adoption order;

(6) the name and address of each parent, guardian, managing conservator, or other person whose consent to adoption was required or waived under Chapter 162, or whose parental rights were terminated in the adoption suit;

(7) the identity of the licensed child placing agency, if any, through which the adopted child was placed for adoption; and

(8) the identity, address, and telephone number of the registry through which the adopted child may register as an adoptee.

(b) Except as otherwise provided by law, for good cause shown, or on an order of the court that granted the adoption or terminated the proceedings under Section 155.001, the records concerning a child maintained by the district clerk after rendition of a decree of adoption, the records of a child-placing agency that has ceased operations, and the records required under this section to be maintained by the bureau of vital statistics are confidential, and no person is entitled to access to or information from these records.

(c) If the bureau of vital statistics determines that a report filed with the bureau under this section requires correction, the bureau shall mail the report directly to an attorney of record with respect to the adoption. The attorney shall return the corrected report to the bureau. If there is no attorney of record, the bureau shall mail the report to the clerk of the court for correction.

§ 108.004. Transmittal of Files on Loss of Jurisdiction

On the loss of jurisdiction of a court under Chapter 155, 159, or 262, the clerk of the court shall transmit to the central registry of the bureau of vital statistics a certified record, on a form provided by the bureau, stating that jurisdiction has been lost, the reason for the loss of jurisdiction, and the name and all previous names, date of birth, and place of birth of the child.

§ 108.005. Adoption Records Received by Bureau of Vital Statistics

(a) When the bureau of vital statistics receives a record from the district clerk showing that continuing, exclusive jurisdiction of a child has been lost due to the adoption of the child, the bureau shall close the records concerning that child.

(b) An inquiry concerning a child who has been adopted shall be handled as though the child had not previously been the subject of a suit affecting the parent-child relationship.

§ 108.006. Fees

(a) The bureau of vital statistics may charge a reasonable fee to cover the cost of determining and sending information concerning the identity of the court with continuing, exclusive jurisdiction.

(b) On the filing of a suit requesting the adoption of a child, the clerk of the court shall collect an additional fee of $15.

(c) The clerk shall send the fees collected under Subsection (b) to the bureau of vital statistics for deposit in a special fund in the state treasury from which the legislature may appropriate money only to operate and maintain the central file and central registry of the bureau.

(d) The receipts from the fees charged under Subsection (a) shall be deposited in a financial institution as determined by the director of the bureau of vital statistics and withdrawn as necessary for the sole purpose of operating and maintaining the central record file.

§ 108.007. Microfilm

(a) The bureau of vital statistics may use microfilm or other suitable means for maintaining the central record file.

(b) A certified reproduction of a document maintained by the bureau of vital statistics is admissible in evidence as the original document.

§ 108.008. Filing Information After Determination of Paternity

(a) On a determination of paternity, the petitioner shall provide the clerk of the court in which the order was rendered the information necessary to prepare the report of determination of paternity. The clerk shall:

(1) prepare the report on a form provided by the Bureau of Vital Statistics; and

(2) complete the report immediately after the order becomes final.

(b) On completion of the report, the clerk of the court shall forward to the state registrar a report for each order that became final in that court.

§ 108.009. Birth Certificate

(a) The state registrar shall substitute a new birth certificate for the original based on the order in accordance with laws or rules that permit the correction or substitution of a birth certificate for an adopted child or a child whose parents marry each other subsequent to the birth of the child.

(b) The new certificate may not show that the father and child relationship was established after the child's birth but may show the child's actual place and date of birth.

§ 108.110. Release of Information by Bureau of Vital Statistics

(a) The bureau of vital statistics shall provide to the Department of Protective and Regulatory Services:

(1) adoption information as necessary for the department to comply with federal law or regulations regarding the compilation or reporting of adoption information to federal officials; and

(2) other information as necessary for the department to administer its duties.

(b) The bureau may release otherwise confidential information from the bureau's central record files to another governmental entity that has a specific need for the information and maintains appropriate safeguards to prevent further dissemination of the information.

Cross Reference

TEX. HEALTH & SAFETY CODE ANN. § 192.001 *et seq.*, Birth Records.

CHAPTER 109. APPEALS

Introductory Comment

The life of a child who is the subject of a SAPCR is often significantly affected by the appellate process. To mitigate the negative effect, the legislature has directed that expedited appeals occur if an adoption would be delayed.

CLE/Other Legal Publications

Preserving your case for appeal. Eva Guzman & Nina Reilly Indelicato, 2008 Adv. Fam. L.

Think before your write: preparing findings of fact and conclusions of law. Maryellen Whitlock Hicks, 2007 Adv. Fam. L.

Leading Cases

In re M.S., 115 S.W.3d 534 (Tex. 2003) (attorney's failure to preserve factual sufficiency issue for appeal constitutes ineffective assistance of counsel)

Stubbs v. Stubbs, 685 S.W.2d 643 (Tex. 1985) (signing of waiver is not participation in trial precluding writ of error)

§ 109.001. Temporary Orders During Pendency of Appeal

(a) Not later than the 30th day after the date an appeal is perfected, on the motion of any party or on the court's own motion and after notice and hearing, the court may make any order necessary to preserve and protect the safety and welfare of the child during the pendency of the appeal as the court may deem necessary and equitable. In addition to other matters, an order may:

(1) appoint temporary conservators for the child and provide for possession of the child;

(2) require the temporary support of the child by a party;

(3) restrain a party from molesting or disturbing the peace of the child or another party;

(4) prohibit a person from removing the child beyond a geographical area identified by the court;

(5) require payment of reasonable attorney's fees and expenses; or

(6) suspend the operation of the order or judgment that is being appealed.

(b) A court retains jurisdiction to enforce its orders rendered under this section unless the appellate court, on a proper showing, supersedes the court's order.

(c) A temporary order rendered under this section is not subject to interlocutory appeal.

(d) The court may not suspend under Subsection (a)(6) the operation of an order or judgment terminating the parent-child relationship in a suit brought by the state or a political subdivision of the state permitted by law to bring the suit.

Comment

Trial and appellate courts are authorized to suspend the operation of a judgment in any case involving the parent-child relationship. Because there was no express limitation, these provisions appeared to authorize the suspension of such a judgment even in a suit brought by DFPS in an abuse or neglect case. Although there were several protections and procedures under pre–2001 law for the child's placement during the pendency of a suit to terminate parental rights, there were no express procedures in place in the event of a suspension of a judgment. Thus, the appeals process could conceivably last longer than the time period involved in the pendency of a suit for termination at trial. As a result, a final judgment suspended by a trial court could leave the parties in limbo without the protections afforded them before the appeal.

To resolve this issue, Subsection (d) prohibits a trial or an appellate court from suspending a judgment that terminates the parent-child relationship in a suit brought by the state or an authorized political subdivision of the state. An appeal in a DFPS suit in which termination of the parent-child relationship is at issue must accelerated by the appellate courts in accordance with the procedures for an accelerated appeal under TEX. R. APP. P.

---

§ 109.002. Appeal

(a) An appeal from a final order rendered in a suit, when allowed under this section or under other provisions of law, shall be as in civil cases generally **under the Texas Rules of Appellate Procedure**. An appeal in a suit in which termination of the parent-child relationship is in issue shall be given precedence over other civil cases and shall be accelerated by the appellate courts. The procedures for an accelerated appeal under the Texas Rules of Appellate Procedure apply to an appeal in which the termination of the parent-child relationship is in issue.

(b) An appeal may be taken by any party to a suit from a final order rendered under this title.

(c) An appeal from a final order, with or without a supersedeas bond, does not suspend the order unless suspension is ordered by the court rendering the order. The appellate court, on a proper showing, may permit the order to be suspended, unless the order provides for the termination of the parent-child relationship in a suit brought by the state or a political subdivision of the state permitted by law to bring the suit.

(d) On the motion of the parties or on the court's own motion, the appellate court in its opinion may identify the parties by fictitious names or by their initials only.

Amended by Acts 2011, 82nd Leg., ch. 75 (H.B. 906), § 3, eff. Sept. 1, 2011.

Comment

Delay in legal procedures related to the disposition of a case involving the termination of parental rights virtually by definition is not in the best interest of the children of this state. In an accelerated appeal, briefs and the notice of appeal must be filed within 20 days, instead of 30 days, of the last action. The clerk and the reporter must file the record of the appeal within 10 days after the notice, rather than taking up to 120 days to file. If so requested, the appellate court is authorized to hear the appeal on original papers forwarded by the trial court, or on sworn and uncontroverted copies of the papers.

---

§ 109.003. Payment for Statement of Facts

(a) If the party requesting a statement of facts in an appeal of a suit has filed an affidavit stating the party's inability to pay costs as provided by Rule 20, Texas Rules of Appellate Procedure, and the affidavit is approved by the trial court, the trial court may order the county in which the trial was held to pay the costs of preparing the statement of facts.

(b) Nothing in this section shall be construed to permit an official court reporter to be paid more than once for the preparation of the statement of facts.

CHAPTER 110. COURT FEES

§ 110.001. General Rule

Except as provided by this chapter, fees in a matter covered by this title shall be as in civil cases generally.

§ 110.002. Filing Fees and Deposits

(a) The clerk of the court may collect a filing fee of $15 in a suit for filing:

(1) a suit or motion for modification;

(2) a motion for enforcement;

(3) a notice of application for judicial writ of withholding;

(4) a motion to transfer;

(5) a petition for license suspension;

(6) a motion to revoke a stay of license suspension; or

(7) a motion for contempt.

(b) No other filing fee may be collected or required for an action described in this section.

(c) The clerk may collect a deposit as in other cases, in the amount set by the clerk for payment of expected costs and other expenses arising in the proceeding.

Comment

The statute sets a relatively modest fee for filing a motion to modify or to enforce. The Texas Attorney General, as the IV–D agency, is required to pay a filing fee for various motions to enforce. This provision is intended to assist counties in meeting expenses and generate additional federal funding for child support enforcement.

§ 110.003. No Separate or Additional Filing Fee

The clerk of the court may not require:

(1) a separate filing fee in a suit joined with a suit for dissolution of marriage under Title 1; or

(2) an additional filing fee if more than one form of relief is requested in a suit.

§ 110.004. Fee for Issuing and Delivering Withholding Order or Writ

The clerk of the court may charge a reasonable fee, not to exceed $15, for each order or writ of income withholding issued by the clerk and delivered to an employer.

§ 110.005. Transfer Fee

(a) The fee for filing a transferred case is $45 payable to the clerk of the court to which the case is transferred. No portion of this fee may be sent to the state.

(b) A party may not be assessed any other fee, cost, charge, or expense by the clerk of the court or other public official in connection with filing of the transferred case.

(c) The fee limitation in this section does not affect a fee payable to the court transferring the case.

§ 110.006. Domestic Relations Office Operations Fees and Child Support Service Fees

(a) If an administering entity of a domestic relations office adopts an initial operations fee under Section 203.005(a)(1), the clerk of the court shall:

(1) collect the operations fee at the time the original suit, motion for modification, or motion for enforcement, as applicable, is filed; and

(2) send the fee to the domestic relations office.

(b) If an administering entity of a domestic relations office adopts an initial child support service fee under Section 203.005(a)(2), the clerk of the court shall:

(1) collect the child support service fee at the time the original suit is filed; and

(2) send the fee to the domestic relations office.

(c) The fees described by Subsections (a) and (b) are not filing fees for purposes of Section 110.002 or 110.003.

CHAPTER 111. GUIDELINES FOR POSSESSION AND CHILD SUPPORT

Introductory Comment

The caption of the chapter is somewhat misleading; this chapter merely provides general provisions for the promulgation and review of the child support and visitation guidelines, which are found in Chapters 153 and 154. For more than a decade the Texas Supreme Court was charged with appointing a committee to assist the legislature in formulating and reviewing guidelines. Since 1999 that duty has been performed by legislative committees.

§ 111.001. Review of Guidelines

(a) Prior to each regular legislative session, the standing committees of each house of the legislature having jurisdiction over family law issues shall review and, if necessary, recommend revisions to the guidelines for possession of and access to a child under Chapter 153 ~~and for support of a child under Chapter 154~~. The committee shall report the results of the review and shall include any recommended revisions in the committee's report to the legislature.

(b) **At least once every four years** ~~Not later than December 1 of each even-numbered year~~, the Title IV–D agency shall **review the child support guidelines under Chapter 154 as required by 42 U.S.C. Section 667(a) and report the results of the review and any recommendations for any changes to the guidelines and their manner of application** ~~submit a report~~ to the standing committees of each house of the legislature having jurisdiction over family law issues ~~for use by the committee in conducting the review required by Subsection (a). The report must contain:~~

~~(1) economic data obtained from the United States Department of Agriculture on the cost of raising children;~~

~~(2) an analysis of case data on the application of and deviations from the child support guidelines; and~~

~~(3) a summary of any federal legislation enacted since the date of the last review~~.

Amended by Acts 2011, 82nd Leg., ch. 8 (S.B. 716), § 1, eff. Sept. 1, 2011.

Comment

Federal law (42 U.S.C. 667) requires each state to establish child support guidelines and to review those guidelines at least once every four years as a condition for having its Title IV-D child support "State plan" approved. Disapproval of the Title IV-D State plan could result in the loss to the state of federal funding for both its child support enforcement program and its public assistance programs.

In Texas, responsibility for the periodic review of the guidelines fell initially (1985 to 1999) to an advisory committee appointed by the Texas Supreme Court. In 1999, the Texas Legislature assigned that task to the committees of the legislature having oversight responsibility for family law issues. In 2011, however, the legislature determined that, to ensure compliance with federal requirements, the Title IV-D agency should have direct responsibility for undertaking a comprehensive, periodic review of the guidelines, submitting to the appropriate committees of the legislature findings and recommendations (in the form of legislative proposals) for any changes to the guidelines and their application. A non-statutory provision of the legislation authorizing this change required the Title IV-D agency to submit its first report, with findings and recommendations, by not later than January 1, 2013. *(A.G.K. & H.P.S.)*

§ 111.002. Guidelines Supersede Court Rules

(a) The guidelines in this title supersede local court rules and rules of the supreme court that conflict with the guidelines.

(b) Notwithstanding other law, the guidelines may not be repealed or modified by a rule adopted by the supreme court.

§ 111.003. Posting Guidelines

A copy of the guidelines for possession of and access to a child under Chapter 153 and a copy of the guidelines for the support of a child under Chapter 154 shall be prominently displayed at or near the entrance to the courtroom of every court having jurisdiction of a suit.

SUBTITLE B. SUITS AFFECTING THE PARENT–CHILD RELATIONSHIP

Chapter

★★★

CHAPTER 151. RIGHTS AND DUTIES IN PARENT-CHILD RELATIONSHIP

Introductory Comment

Originally, this chapter was intended to define the parent-child relationship, which included the presumption of paternity, the elimination of the concept of illegitimacy, and baby-steps towards the brave new world of science through recognition of the only method of assisted reproduction known to the world in 1973 when the Family Code was first enacted, so-called "artificial insemination." Several years later, oocyte and embryo donation were statutorily recognized as advancements in the medical possibilities of that process.

The enactment of the Uniform Parentage Act in 2001 involved moving all of the provisions related to parentage to Chapter 160, *infra*. The net effect is that this chapter contains virtually no substantive law. Specifically, the laundry list of parental rights in this chapter is hortatory only. But, the substantive rights of parents flow from this litany, as the remaining chapters in Title 5 amply demonstrate.

CLE/Other Legal Publications

Constitutional rights of children. Barbara J. Elias-Perciful, 2010 ADV. FAM. L.

Deconstructing rights, powers, and duties: what do they really mean? Angela G. Pence England, 2009 U.T. PARENT-CHILD REL.

Children's rights in court. Ronda G. Hurley, 2009 U.T. PARENT-CHILD REL.

CHAPTER 152. UNIFORM CHILD CUSTODY JURISDICTION AND ENFORCEMENT ACT

SUBCHAPTER A. APPLICATION AND CONSTRUCTION

SUBCHAPTER B. GENERAL PROVISIONS

SUBCHAPTER C. JURISDICTION

SUBCHAPTER D. ENFORCEMENT

Introductory Comment

Effective September 1, 1999, Texas adopted the Uniform Child Custody Jurisdiction and Enforcement Act (1997) [UCCJEA], replacing the previous Uniform Child Custody Jurisdiction Act (1968)

[UCCJA]. This version of the uniform act was adopted by the National Conference of Commissioners on Uniform State Law in 1997 and recommended for approval by all states by the American Bar Association in 1998. As the 2011 edition of this book goes to print, 51 jurisdictions have adopted the UCCJEA. The only jurisdictions (of the 53 defined as states) that have not enacted it are Puerto Rico and Massachusetts. Vermont is a 2011 convert, and the act has been introduced in Massachusetts (once again) according to the NCCUSL/ULC website.

CLE/Other Legal Publications

Ding! You are now free to move about the country: UCCJEA and UIFSA. JoAl Cannon Sheridan, 2011 Adv. Fam. L.

International and domestic jurisdiction issues: UIFSA, UCCJEA, UCAPA, PKPA, FFCCSOA, ICARA. Karl E. Hays & Janet McCullar Vavra, 2011 U.T. Fam. L. Front Lines

UCCJEA/UIFSA. Harry L. Tindall, 2011 U.T. Adv. Parent-Child Relationships

Follow the yellow brick road: jurisdiction and venue issues. JoAl Cannon Sheridan, 2010 Marriage Dissolution

Practice tips for handling UCCJEA cases. Janet McCullar Vavra, 2010 Marriage Dissolution

Caution! Acronyms ahead: traveling on the interstate case highway. Karen L. Marvel & John Christopher Nickelson, 2010 U.T. Parent-Child Relationships

UCCJEA and UIFSA—can they be modified. Angela Pence England, 2009 So. Tex. Fam. L. Conf.

Jurisdiction, standing, venue, and more: special appearances, UCCJEA, 3rd party standing, Hague. JoAl Cannon Sheridan, 2009 Adv. Fam. L.

Parenting across state lines. Brian L. Webb, 2009 U.T. Parent-Child Rel.

Uniform Child Custody Jurisdiction and Enforcement Act (with Prefatory Notes and Comment). Robert G. Spector, 32 Fam. L.Q. 301 (1998)

See Accompanying CD–ROM for Additional CLE/Other Legal Publications.

Leading Cases

Abbott v. Abbott, ___ U.S. ___, 130 S.Ct. 1983 (2010) (ne exeat order grants right of custody to both parents and is enforceable under Hague Abduction Convention)

Alfonso v. Skadden, 251 S.W.3d 52 (Tex. 2008) (subject-matter jurisdiction under UCCJEA cannot be waived, and can be raised at any time)

Powell v. Stover, 165 S.W.3d 322 (Tex. 2005) (child lived with both parents in Tennessee as home state and mother's alleged intent to return to Texas irrelevant in UCCJEA application)

In re Forlenza, 140 S.W.3d 373 (Tex. 2004) (UCCJEA jurisdiction continues in Texas when resident-parent's contacts with out-of-state children remain significant)

In re K.M.P., 323 S.W. 3d 601 (Tex. App.—Austin 2010, no pet.) (if child has another home state Texas court lacks subject matter jurisdiction to decide custody)

In re Kamstra, 2010 WL 708857 (Tex. App.—Tyler 2010, no pet.) (neither Hague Abduction Convention nor UCCJEA § 152.204 provide emergency jurisdiction for custody determination)

In re Lester, 254 S.W.3d 663 (Tex. App.—Beaumont 2008, orig. proceeding) (modification of a divorce decree from a different state is not considered an original proceeding in Texas)

Hart v. Kozik, 242 S.W.3d 102 (Tex. App.—Eastland 2007, no pet.) (inconvenient forum does not require a best interest finding)

In re A.B., 207 S.W.3d 434 (Tex. App.—Dallas 2006, no pet.) (old default judgment for child support based on service by publication is enough to establish personal jurisdiction over non-resident obligor)

In re Brown, 203 S.W.3d 888 (Tex. App.—Fort Worth 2006, no pet.) (Missouri, not Texas was home state of older child and infant had significant connections with Missouri as well)

In re G.L.A., 195 S.W.3d 787 (Tex. App.—Beaumont 2006, rev. denied) (UIFSA enforcement of Maryland child support required of Texas trial court because obligor submitted to personal jurisdiction)

***See* Accompanying CD–ROM for Cases Linked to Westlaw and Additional Leading Cases.**

COMMISSIONERS' OFFICIAL PREFATORY NOTE TO UCCJEA

This Act, the Uniform Child Custody Jurisdiction and Enforcement Act (UCCJEA), revisits the problem of the interstate child almost thirty years after the Conference promulgated the Uniform Child Custody Jurisdiction Act (UCCJA). The UCCJEA accomplishes two major purposes.

First, it revises the law on child custody jurisdiction in light of federal enactments and almost thirty years of inconsistent case law. Article 2 of this Act provides clearer standards for which states can exercise original jurisdiction over a child custody determination. It also, for the first time, enunciates a standard of continuing jurisdiction and clarifies modification jurisdiction. Other aspects of the article harmonize the law on simultaneous proceedings, clean hands, and forum non conveniens.

Second, this Act provides in Article 3 for a remedial process to enforce interstate child custody and visitation determinations. In doing so, it brings a uniform procedure to the law of interstate enforcement that is currently producing inconsistent results. In many respects, this Act accomplishes for custody and visitation determinations the same uniformity that has occurred in interstate child support with the promulgation of the Uniform Interstate Family Support Act (UIFSA).

Revision of Uniform Child Custody Jurisdiction Act

The UCCJA was adopted as law in all 50 states, the District of Columbia, and the Virgin Islands. A number of adoptions, however, significantly departed from the original text. In addition, almost thirty years of litigation since the promulgation of the UCCJA produced substantial inconsistency in interpretation by state courts. As a result, the goals of the UCCJA were rendered unobtainable in many cases.

In 1980, the federal government enacted the Parental Kidnapping Prevention Act (PKPA), 28 U.S.C. § 1738A, to address the interstate custody jurisdictional problems that continued to exist after the adoption of the UCCJA. The PKPA mandates that state authorities give full faith and credit to other states' custody determinations, so long as those determinations were made in conformity with the provisions of the PKPA. The PKPA provisions regarding bases for jurisdiction, restrictions on modifications, preclusion of simultaneous proceedings, and notice requirements are similar to those in the UCCJA. There are, however, some significant differences. For example, the PKPA authorizes continuing exclusive jurisdiction in the original decree state so long as one parent or the child remains there and that state has continuing jurisdiction under its own law. The UCCJA did not directly address this issue. To further complicate the process, the PKPA partially incorporates state UCCJA law in its language. The relationship between these two statutes became "technical enough to delight a medieval property lawyer." Homer H. Clark, *Domestic Relations* § 12.5 at 494 (2d ed. 1988).

As documented in an extensive study by the American Bar Association's Center on Children and the Law, *Obstacles to the Recovery and Return of Parentally Abducted Children* (1993) (*Obstacles Study*), inconsistency of interpretation of the UCCJA and the technicalities of applying the PKPA, resulted in a loss of uniformity among the states. The Obstacles Study suggested a number of amendments which would eliminate the inconsistent state interpretations and harmonize the UCCJA with the PKPA.

The revisions of the jurisdictional aspects of the UCCJA eliminate the inconsistent state interpretations and can be summarized as follows:

1. Home state priority. The PKPA prioritizes "home state" jurisdiction by requiring that full faith and credit cannot be given to a child custody determination by a state that exercises initial jurisdiction as a "significant connection state" when there is a "home state." Initial custody determinations based on "significant connections" are not entitled to PKPA enforcement unless there is no home state. The UCCJA, however, specifically authorizes four independent bases of jurisdiction without prioritization. Under the UCCJA, a significant connection custody determination may have to be enforced even it if it would be denied enforcement under the PKPA. The UCCJEA prioritizes home state jurisdiction in Section 201.

2. Clarification of emergency jurisdiction. There are several problems with the current emergency jurisdiction provision of the UCCJA § 3(a)(3). First, the language of the UCCJA does not specify that emergency jurisdiction may be exercised only to protect the child on a temporary basis until the court with appropriate jurisdiction issues a permanent order. Some courts have interpreted the UCCJA language to so provide. Other courts, however, have held that there is no time limit on a custody determination based on emergency jurisdiction. Simultaneous proceedings and conflicting custody orders have resulted from these different interpretations.

Second, the emergency jurisdiction provisions predated the widespread enactment of state domestic violence statutes. Those statutes are often invoked to keep one parent away from the other parent and the children when there is a threat of violence. Whether these situations are sufficient to invoke the emergency jurisdiction provision of the UCCJA has been the subject of some confusion since the emergency jurisdiction provision does not specifically refer to violence directed against the parent of the child or against a sibling of the child.

The UCCJEA contains a separate section on emergency jurisdiction at Section 204 which addresses these issues.

3. Exclusive continuing jurisdiction for the state that entered the decree. The failure of the UCCJA to clearly enunciate that the decree-granting state retains exclusive continuing jurisdiction to modify a decree has resulted in two major problems. First, different interpretations of the UCCJA on continuing jurisdiction have produced conflicting custody decrees. States also have different interpretations as to how long continuing jurisdiction lasts. Some courts have held that modification jurisdiction continues until the last contestant leaves the state, regardless of how many years the child has lived outside the state or how tenuous the child's connections to the state have become. Other courts have held that continuing modification jurisdiction ends as soon as the child has established a new home state, regardless of how significant the child's connections to the decree state remain. Still other states distinguish between custody orders and visitation orders. This divergence of views leads to simultaneous proceedings and conflicting custody orders.

The second problem arises when it is necessary to determine whether the state with continuing jurisdiction has relinquished it. There should be a clear basis to determine when that court has relinquished jurisdiction. The UCCJA provided no guidance on this issue. The ambiguity regarding whether a court has declined jurisdiction can result in one court improperly exercising jurisdiction because it erroneously believes that the other court has declined jurisdiction. This caused simultaneous proceedings and conflicting custody orders. In addition, some courts have declined jurisdiction after only informal contact between courts with no opportunity for the parties to be heard. This raised significant due process concerns. The UCCJEA addresses these issues in Section 110, 202, and 206.

4. Specification of what custody proceedings are covered. The definition of custody proceeding in the UCCJA is ambiguous. States have rendered conflicting decisions regarding certain types of proceedings. There is no general agreement on whether the UCCJA applies to neglect, abuse, dependency, wardship, guardianship, termination of parental rights, and protection from domestic violence proceedings. The UCCJEA includes a sweeping definition that, with the exception of adoption, includes virtually all cases that can involve custody of or visitation with a child as a "custody determination."

5. Role of "Best Interests." The jurisdictional scheme of the UCCJA was designed to promote the best interests of the children whose custody was at issue by discouraging parental abduction and providing that, in general, the state with the closest connections to, and the most evidence regarding a child should decide that child's custody. The "best interest" language in the jurisdictional sections of the UCCJA was not intended to be an invitation to address the merits of the custody dispute in the jurisdictional determination or to otherwise provide that "best interests" considerations should override jurisdictional determinations or provide an additional jurisdictional basis.

The UCCJEA eliminates the term "best interests" in order to clearly distinguish between the jurisdictional standards and the substantive standards relating to custody and visitation of children.

6. Other Changes. This draft also makes a number of additional amendments to the UCCJA. Many of these changes were made to harmonize the provisions of this Act with those of the Uniform Interstate Family Support Act. One of the policy bases underlying this Act is to make uniform the law of interstate family proceedings to the extent possible, given the very different jurisdictional foundations. It simplifies the life of the family law practitioner when the same or similar provisions are found in both Acts.

Enforcement Provisions

One of the major purposes of the revision of the UCCJA was to provide a remedy for interstate visitation and custody cases. As with child support, state borders have become one of the biggest obstacles to enforcement of custody and visitation orders. If either parent leave the state where the custody determination was made, the other parent faces considerable difficulty in enforcing the visitation and custody provisions of the decree. Locating the child, making service of process, and preventing adverse modification in a new forum all present problems.

There is currently no uniform method of enforcing custody and visitation orders validly entered in another state. As documented by the *Obstacles Study*, despite the fact that both the UCCJA and the PKPA direct the enforcement of visitation and custody orders entered in accordance with mandated jurisdictional prerequisites and due process, neither act provides enforcement procedures or remedies.

As the *Obstacles Study* pointed out, the lack of specificity in enforcement procedures has resulted in the law of enforcement evolving differently in different jurisdictions. In one state, it might be common practice to file a Motion to Enforce or a Motion to Grant Full Faith and Credit to initiate an enforcement proceeding. In another state, a Writ of Habeas Corpus or a Citation for Contempt might be commonly used. In some states, Mandamus and Prohibition also may be utilized. All of these enforcement procedures differ from jurisdiction to jurisdiction. While many states tend to limit considerations in enforcement proceedings to whether the court which issued the decree had jurisdiction to make the custody determination, others broaden the considerations to scrutiny of whether enforcement would be in the best interests of the child.

Lack of uniformity complicates the enforcement process in several ways: (1) It increases the costs of the enforcement action in part because the services of more than one lawyer may be required—one in the original forum and one in the state where enforcement is sought; (2) It decreases the certainty of outcome; (3) It can turn enforcement into a long and drawn out procedure. A parent opposed to the provisions of a visitation determination may be able to delay implementation for many months, possibly even years, thereby frustrating not only the other parent, but also the process that led to the issuance of the original court order.

The provisions of Article 3 provide several remedies for the enforcement of a custody determination. First, there is a simple procedure for registering a custody determination in another state. This will allow a party to know in advance whether that state will recognize the party's custody determination. This is extremely important in estimating the risk of the child's non-return when the child is sent on visitation. The provision should prove to be very useful in international custody cases.

Second, the Act provides a swift remedy along the lines of habeas corpus. Time is extremely important in visitation and custody cases. If visitation rights cannot be enforced quickly, they often cannot be enforced at all. This is particularly true if there is a limited time within which visitation can be exercised such as may be the case when one parent has been granted visitation during the winter or spring holiday period. Without speedy consideration and resolution of the enforcement of such visitation rights, the ability to visit may be lost entirely. Similarly, a custodial parent must be able to obtain prompt enforcement when the noncustodial parent visitation extension will infringe on the school year. A swift enforcement mechanism is desirable for violations of both custody and visitation provisions.

The scope of the enforcing court's inquiry is limited to the issue of whether the decree court had jurisdiction and complied with due process in rendering the original custody decree. No further inquiry is necessary because neither Article 2 nor the PKPA allows an enforcing court to modify a custody determination.

Third, the enforcing court will be able to utilize an extraordinary remedy. If the enforcing court is concerned that the parent, who has physical custody of the child, will flee or harm the child, a warrant to take physical possession of the child is available.

Finally, there is a role for public authorities, such as prosecutors, in the enforcement process. Their involvement will encourage the parties to abide by the terms of the custody determination. If the parties know that public authorities and law enforcement officers are available to help in securing compliance with custody determinations, the parties may be deterred from interfering with the exercise of rights established by court order.

The involvement of public authorities will also prove more effective in remedying violations of custody determinations. Most parties do not have the resources to enforce a custody determination in another jurisdiction. The availability of the public authorities as an enforcement agency will help ensure that this remedy can be made available regardless of income level. In addition, the public authorities may have resources to draw on that are available to the average litigant.

This Act does not authorize the public authorities to be involved in the action leading up to the making of the custody determination, except when requested by the court, when there is a violation of the Hague Convention on the Civil Aspects of International Child Abduction, or when the person holding the child has violated a criminal statute. The Act does not mandate that public authorities be involved in all cases. Not all states, or local authorities, have the funds necessary for an effective custody and visitation enforcement program.

SUBCHAPTER A. APPLICATION AND CONSTRUCTION

§ 152.001. Application and Construction

This chapter shall be applied and construed to promote the uniformity of the law among the states that enact it.

§ 152.002. Conflicts Between Provisions

If a provision of this chapter conflicts with a provision of this title or another statute or rule of this state and the conflict cannot be reconciled, this chapter prevails.

Comment

This section is not found in the uniform version of the UCCJEA, but was added by the legislature to make certain that the terms of this chapter prevail over any inconsistency that may exist elsewhere in the Family Code.

SUBCHAPTER B. GENERAL PROVISIONS

§ 152.101. Short Title

This chapter may be cited as the Uniform Child Custody Jurisdiction and Enforcement Act.

Commissioners' Comment

Section 1 of the UCCJA was a statement of the purposes of the Act. Although extensively cited by courts, it was eliminated because Uniform Acts no longer contain such a section. Nonetheless, this Act should be interpreted according to its purposes which are to:

(1) Avoid jurisdictional competition and conflict with courts of other states in matters of child custody which have in the past resulted in the shifting of children from state to state with harmful effects on their well-being;

(2) Promote cooperation with the courts of other states to the end that a custody decree is rendered in that state which can best decide the case in the interest of the child;

(3) Discourage the use of the interstate system for continuing controversies over child custody;

(4) Deter abductions of children;

(5) Avoid relitigation of custody decisions of other states in this state; and

(6) Facilitate the enforcement of custody decrees of other states;

§ 152.102. Definitions

In this chapter:

(1) "Abandoned" means left without provision for reasonable and necessary care or supervision.

(2) "Child" means an individual who has not attained 18 years of age.

(3) "Child custody determination" means a judgment, decree, or other order of a court providing for legal custody, physical custody, or visitation with respect to a child. The term includes permanent, temporary, initial, and modification orders. The term does not include an order relating to child support or another monetary obligation of an individual.

(4) "Child custody proceeding" means a proceeding in which legal custody, physical custody, or visitation with respect to a child is an issue. The term includes a proceeding for divorce, separation, neglect, abuse, dependency, guardianship, paternity, termination of parental rights, and protection from domestic violence in which the issue may appear. The term does not include a proceeding involving juvenile delinquency, contractual emancipation, or enforcement under Subchapter D.

(5) "Commencement" means the filing of the first pleading in a proceeding.

(6) "Court" means an entity authorized under the law of a state to establish, enforce, or modify a child custody determination.

(7) "Home state" means the state in which a child lived with a parent or a person acting as a parent for at least six consecutive months immediately before the commencement of a child custody proceeding. In the case of a child less than six months of age, the term means the state in which the child lived from birth with a parent or a person acting as a parent. A period of temporary absence of a parent or a person acting as a parent is part of the period.

(8) "Initial determination" means the first child custody determination concerning a particular child.

(9) "Issuing court" means the court that makes a child custody determination for which enforcement is sought under this chapter.

(10) "Issuing state" means the state in which a child custody determination is made.

(11) "Legal custody" means the managing conservatorship of a child.

(12) "Modification" means a child custody determination that changes, replaces, supersedes, or is otherwise made after a previous determination concerning the same child, whether or not it is made by the court that made the previous determination.

(13) "Person acting as a parent" means a person, other than a parent, who:

(A) has physical custody of the child or has had physical custody for a period of six consecutive months, including any temporary absence, within one year immediately before the commencement of a child custody proceeding; and

(B) has been awarded legal custody by a court or claims a right to legal custody under the law of this state.

(14) "Physical custody" means the physical care and supervision of a child.

(15) "Tribe" means an Indian tribe or band, or Alaskan Native village, that is recognized by federal law or formally acknowledged by a state.

(16) "Visitation" means the possession of or access to a child.

(17) "Warrant" means an order issued by a court authorizing law enforcement officers to take physical custody of a child.

Commissioners' Comment

The UCCJA did not contain a definition of "child." The definition here is taken from the PKPA.

The definition of "child-custody determination" now closely tracks the PKPA definition. It encompasses any judgment, decree or other order which provides for the custody of, or visitation with, a child, regardless of local terminology, including such labels as "managing conservatorship" or "parenting plan."

The definition of "child-custody proceeding" has been expanded from the comparable definition in the UCCJA. These listed proceedings have generally been determined to be the type of proceeding to which the UCCJA and PKPA are applicable. The list of examples removes any controversy about the types of proceedings where a custody determination can occur. Proceedings that affect access to the child are subject to this Act. The inclusion of proceedings related to protection from domestic violence is necessary because in some states domestic violence proceedings may affect custody of and visitation with a child. Juvenile delinquency or proceedings to confer contractual rights are not "custody proceedings" because they do not relate to civil aspects of access to a child. While a determination of paternity is covered under the Uniform Interstate Family Support Act, the custody and visitation aspects of paternity cases are custody proceedings. Cases involving the Hague Convention on the Civil Aspects of International Child Abduction have not been included at this point because custody of the child is not determined in a proceeding under the International Child Abductions Remedies Act. Those proceedings are specially included in the Article 3 enforcement process.

"Commencement" has been included in the definitions as a replacement for the term "pending" found in the UCCJA. Its inclusion simplifies some of the simultaneous proceedings provisions of this Act.

The definition of "home state" has been reworded slightly. No substantive change is intended from the UCCJA.

The term "issuing state" is borrowed from UIFSA. In UIFSA, it refers to the court that issued the support or parentage order. Here, it refers to the state, or the court, which made the custody determination that is sought to be enforced. It is used primarily in Article 3.

The term "person" has been added to ensure that the provisions of this Act apply when the state is the moving party in a custody proceeding or has legal custody of a child. The definition of "person" is the one that is mandated for all Uniform Acts.

The term "person acting as a parent" has been slightly redefined. It has been broadened from the definition in the UCCJA to include a person who has acted as a parent for a significant period of time prior to the filing of the custody proceeding as well as a person who currently has physical custody of the child. In addition, a person acting as a parent must either have legal custody or claim a right to legal custody under the law of this state. The reference to the law of this state means that a court determines the issue of whether someone is a "person acting as a parent" under its own law. This reaffirms the traditional view that a court in a child custody case applies its own substantive law. The court does not have to undertake a choice-of-law analysis to determine whether the individual who is claiming to be a person acting as a parent has standing to seek custody of the child.

The definition of "tribe" is the one mandated for use in Uniform Acts. Should a state choose to apply this Act to tribal adjudications, this definition should be enacted as well as the entirety of Section 104.

The term "contestant" has been omitted from this revision. It was defined in the UCCJA § 2(1) as "a person, including a parent, who claims a right to custody or visitation rights with respect to a child." It seems to have served little purpose over the years, and whatever function it once had has been subsumed by state laws on who has standing to seek custody of or visitation with a child. In addition UCCJA § 2(5), which defined "decree" and "custody decree," has been eliminated as duplicative of the definition of "custody determination."

§ 152.103. Proceedings Governed by Other Law

This chapter does not govern an adoption proceeding or a proceeding pertaining to the authorization of emergency medical care for a child.

Commissioners' Comment

Two proceedings are governed by other acts. Adoption cases are excluded from this Act because adoption is a specialized area which is thoroughly covered by the Uniform Adoption Act (UAA) (1994). Most states either will adopt that Act or will adopt the jurisdictional provisions of that Act. Therefore the jurisdictional provisions governing adoption proceeding are generally found elsewhere.

However, there are likely to be a number of instances where it will be necessary to apply this Act in an adoption proceeding. For example, if a state adopts the UAA, then Section 3 § 101 of the Act specifically refers in places to the Uniform Child Custody Jurisdiction Act which will become a reference to this Act. Second, the UAA requires that if an adoption is denied or set aside, the court is to determine the child's custody. UAA § 3—704. Those custody proceedings would be subject to this Act. *See* Joan Heifetz Hollinger, *The Uniform Adoption Act: Reporter's Ruminations*, 30 FAM. L. Q. 345 (1996).

Children that are the subject of interstate placements for adoption or foster care are governed by the Interstate Compact on the Placement of Children (ICPC). The UAA § 2—107 provides that the provisions of the compact, although not jurisdictional, supply the governing rules for all children who are subject to it. As stated in the Comments to that section: "Once a court exercises jurisdiction, the ICPC helps determine the legality of an interstate placement." For a discussion of the relationship between the UCCJA and the ICPC. *See J.D.S. v. Franks*, 893 P.2d 732 (Ariz. 1995).

Proceedings pertaining to the authorization of emergency medical care for children are outside the scope of this Act since they are not custody determinations. All states have procedures which allow the state to temporarily supersede parental authority for purposes of emergency medical procedures. Those provisions will govern without regard to this Act.

§ 152.104. Application to Indian Tribes

(a) A child custody proceeding that pertains to an Indian child as defined in the Indian Child Welfare Act of 1978 (25 U.S.C. Section 1901 et seq.) is not subject to this chapter to the extent that it is governed by the Indian Child Welfare Act.

(b) A court of this state shall treat a tribe as if it were a state of the United States for the purpose of applying this subchapter and Subchapter C.

(c) A child custody determination made by a tribe under factual circumstances in substantial conformity with the jurisdictional standards of this chapter must be recognized and enforced under Subchapter D.

Commissioners' Comment

This section allows states the discretion to extend the terms of this Act to Indian tribes by removing the brackets. The definition of "tribe" is found at Section 102(16). This Act does not purport to legislate custody jurisdiction for tribal courts. However, a Tribe could adopt this Act as enabling legislation by simply replacing references to "this State" with "this Tribe."

Subsection (a) is not bracketed. If the Indian Child Welfare Act requires that a case be heard in tribal court, then its provisions determine jurisdiction.

§ 152.105. International Application of Chapter

(a) A court of this state shall treat a foreign country as if it were a state of the United States for the purpose of applying this subchapter and Subchapter C.

(b) Except as otherwise provided in Subsection (c), a child custody determination made in a foreign country under factual circumstances in substantial conformity with the jurisdictional standards of this chapter must be recognized and enforced under Subchapter D.

(c) A court of this state need not apply this chapter if the child custody law of a foreign country violates fundamental principles of human rights.

(d) A record of all of the proceedings under this chapter relating to a child custody determination made in a foreign country or to the enforcement of an order for the return of the child made under the Hague Convention on the Civil Aspects of International Child Abduction shall be made by a court reporter or as provided by Section 201.009.

Amended by Acts 2011, 82nd Leg., ch. 92 (S.B. 1490), § 1, eff. Sept. 1, 2011.

Commissioners' Comment

The provisions of this Act have international application to child custody proceedings and determinations of other countries. Another country will be treated as if it were a state of the United States for purposes of applying Articles 1 and 2 of this Act. Custody determinations of other countries will be enforced if the facts of the case indicate that jurisdiction was in substantial compliance with the requirements of this Act.

In this section, the term "child-custody determination" should be interpreted to include proceedings relating to custody or analogous institutions of the other country. *See* generally, Article 3 of The Hague Convention on Jurisdiction, Applicable Law, Recognition, Enforcement and Co-operation in Respect of Parental Responsibility and Measures for the Protection of Children, 35 I.L.M. 1391 (1996).

A court of this state may refuse to apply this Act when the child custody law of the other country violates basic principles relating to the protection of human rights and fundamental freedoms. The same concept is found in Section 20 of the Hague Convention on the Civil Aspects of International Child Abduction (return of the child may be refused if this would not be permitted by the fundamental principles of the requested state relating to the protection of human rights and fundamental freedoms). In applying Subsection (c), the court's scrutiny should be on the child custody law of the foreign country and not on other aspects of the other legal system. This Act takes no position on what laws relating to child custody would violate fundamental freedoms. While the provision is a traditional one in international agreements, it is invoked only in the most egregious cases.

This section is derived from Section 23 of the UCCJA.

§ 152.106. Effect of Child Custody Determination

A child custody determination made by a court of this state that had jurisdiction under this chapter binds all persons who have been served in accordance with the laws of this state or notified in accordance with Section 152.108 or who have submitted to the jurisdiction of the court and who have been given an opportunity to be heard. As to those persons, the determination is conclusive as to all decided issues of law and fact except to the extent the determination is modified.

Commissioners' Comment

No substantive changes have been made to this section which was Section 12 of the UCCJA.

§ 152.107. Priority

If a question of existence or exercise of jurisdiction under this chapter is raised in a child custody proceeding, the question, upon request of a party, must be given priority on the calendar and handled expeditiously.

Commissioners' Comment

No substantive change was made to this section which was Section 24 of the UCCJA. The section is placed toward the beginning of Article 1 to emphasize its importance.

The language change from "case" to "question" is intended to clarify that it is the jurisdictional issue which must be expedited and not the entire custody case. Whether the entire custody case should be given priority is a matter of local law.

---

§ 152.108. Notice to Persons Outside State

(a) Notice required for the exercise of jurisdiction when a person is outside this state may be given in a manner prescribed by the law of this state for service of process or by the law of the state in which the service is made. Notice must be given in a manner reasonably calculated to give actual notice but may be by publication if other means are not effective.

(b) Proof of service may be made in the manner prescribed by the law of this state or by the law of the state in which the service is made.

(c) Notice is not required for the exercise of jurisdiction with respect to a person who submits to the jurisdiction of the court.

Commissioners' Comment

This section authorizes notice and proof of service to be made by any method allowed by either the state which issues the notice or the state where the notice is received. This eliminates the need to specify the type of notice in the Act and therefore the provisions of Section 5 of the UCCJA which specified how notice was to be accomplished were eliminated. The change reflects an approach in this Act to use local law to determine many procedural issues. Thus, service by facsimile is permissible if allowed by local rule in either state. In addition, where special service or notice rules are available for some procedures, in either jurisdiction, they could be utilized under this Act. For example, if a case involves domestic violence and the statute of either state would authorize notice to be served by a peace officer, such service could be used under this Act.

Although Section 105 requires foreign countries to be treated as states for purposes of this Act, attorneys should be cautioned about service and notice in foreign countries. Countries have their own rules on service which must usually be followed. Attorneys should consult the Hague Convention on the Service Abroad of Judicial and Extrajudicial Documents in Civil or Commercial Matters, 20 U.S.T. 36, T.I.A.S. 6638 (1965).

---

§ 152.109. Appearance and Limited Immunity

(a) A party to a child custody proceeding, including a modification proceeding, or a petitioner or respondent in a proceeding to enforce or register a child custody determination, is not subject to personal jurisdiction in this state for another proceeding or purpose solely by reason of having participated, or of having been physically present for the purpose of participating, in the proceeding.

(b) A person who is subject to personal jurisdiction in this state on a basis other than physical presence is not immune from service of process in this state. A party present in this state who is subject to the jurisdiction of another state is not immune from service of process allowed under the laws of that state.

(c) The immunity granted by Subsection (a) does not extend to civil litigation based on acts unrelated to the participation in a proceeding under this chapter committed by an individual while present in this state.

Commissioners' Comment

This section establishes a general principle that participation in a custody proceeding does not, by itself, give the court jurisdiction over any issue for which personal jurisdiction over the individual is required. The term "participate" should be read broadly. For example, if jurisdiction is proper under Article 2, a respondent in an original custody determination, or a party in a modification determination, should be able to request custody without this constituting the seeking of affirmative relief that would waive personal jurisdictional objections. Once jurisdiction is proper under Article 2, a party should not be placed in the dilemma of choosing between seeking custody or protecting a right not to be subject to a monetary judgment by a court with no other relationship to the party.

This section is comparable to the immunity provision of UIFSA § 314. A party who is otherwise not subject to personal jurisdiction can appear in a custody proceeding or an enforcement action without being subject to the general jurisdiction of the state by virtue of the appearance. However, if the petitioner would otherwise be subject to the jurisdiction of the state, appearing in a custody proceeding or filing an enforcement proceeding will not provide immunity. Thus, if the non-custodial parent moves from the state that decided the custody determination, that parent is still subject to the state's jurisdiction for enforcement of child support if the child or an individual obligee continues to reside there. *See* UIFSA § 205. If the non-custodial parent returns to enforce the visitation aspects of the custody determination, the state can utilize any appropriate means to collect the back-due child support. However, the situation is different if both parties move from State A after the determination, with the custodial parent and the child establishing a new home state in State B, and the non-custodial parent moving to State C. The non-custodial parent is not, at this point, subject to the jurisdiction of State B for monetary matters. *See Kulko v. Superior Court*, 436 U.S. 84 (1978). If the non-custodial parent comes into State B to enforce the visitation aspects of the determination, the non-custodial parent is not subject to the jurisdiction of State B for those proceedings and issues requiring personal jurisdiction by filing the enforcement action.

A party also is immune from service of process during the time in the state for an enforcement action except for those claims for which jurisdiction could be based on contacts other than mere physical presence. Thus, when the non-custodial parent comes into State B to enforce the visitation aspects of the decree, State B cannot acquire jurisdiction over the child support aspects of the decree by serving the non-custodial parent in the state. *Cf.* UIFSA § 611 (personally serving the obligor in the state of the residence of the obligee is not by itself a sufficient jurisdictional basis to authorize a modification of child support). However, a party who is in this state and subject to the jurisdiction of another state may be served with process to appear in that state, if allowable under the laws of that state.

As the Comments to UIFSA § 314 note, the immunity provided by this section is limited. It does not provide immunity for civil litigation unrelated to the enforcement action. For example, a party to an enforcement action is not immune from service regarding a claim that involves an automobile accident occurring while the party is in the state.

---

§ 152.110. Communication Between Courts

(a) In this section, "record" means information that is inscribed on a tangible medium or that is stored in an electronic or other medium and is retrievable in perceivable form.

(b) A court of this state may communicate with a court in another state concerning a proceeding arising under this chapter.

(c) The court may allow the parties to participate in the communication. If the parties are not able to participate in the communication, they must be given the opportunity to present facts and legal arguments before a decision on jurisdiction is made.

(d) If proceedings involving the same parties are pending simultaneously in a court of this state and a court of another state, the court of this state shall inform the other court of the simultaneous proceedings. The court of this state shall request that the other court hold the proceeding in that court in abeyance until the court in this state conducts a hearing to determine whether the court has jurisdiction over the proceeding.

(e) Communication between courts on schedules, calendars, court records, and similar matters may occur without informing the parties. A record need not be made of the communication.

(f) Except as otherwise provided in Subsection (e), a record must be made of any communication under this section. The parties must be informed promptly of the communication and granted access to the record.

Commissioners' Comment

This section emphasizes the role of judicial communications. It authorizes a court to communicate concerning any proceeding arising under this Act. This includes communication with foreign tribunals and tribal courts. Communication can occur in many different ways such as by telephonic conference and by on-line or other electronic communication. The Act does not preclude any method of communication and recognizes that there will be increasing use of modern communication techniques.

Communication between courts is required under Sections 204, 206, and 306 and strongly suggested in applying Section 207. Apart from those sections, there may be less need under this Act for courts to communicate concerning jurisdiction due to the prioritization of home state jurisdiction. Communication is authorized, however, whenever the court finds it would be helpful. The court may authorize the parties to participate in the communication. However, the Act does not mandate participation. Communication between courts is often difficult to schedule and participation by the parties may be impractical. Phone calls often have to be made after-hours or whenever the schedules of judges allow.

This section does require that a record be made of the conversation and that the parties have access to that record in order to be informed of the content of the conversation. The only exception to this requirement is when the communication involves relatively inconsequential matters such as scheduling, calendars, and court records. Included within this latter type of communication would be matters of cooperation between courts under Section 112. A record includes notes or transcripts of a court reporter who listened to a conference call between the courts, an electronic recording of a telephone call, a memorandum or an electronic record of the communication between the courts, or a memorandum or an electronic record made by a court after the communication.

The second sentence of Subsection (b) protects the parties against unauthorized ex parte communications. The parties' participation in the communication may amount to a hearing if there is an opportunity to present facts and jurisdictional arguments. However, absent such an opportunity, the participation of the parties should not be considered a substitute for a hearing and the parties must be given an opportunity to fairly and fully present facts and arguments on the jurisdictional issue before a determination is made. This may be done through a hearing or, if appropriate, by affidavit or memorandum. The court is expected to set forth the basis for its jurisdictional decision, including any court-to-court communication which may have been a factor in the decision.

§ 152.111. Taking Testimony in Another State

(a) In addition to other procedures available to a party, a party to a child custody proceeding may offer testimony of witnesses who are located in another state, including testimony of the parties and the child, by deposition or other means allowed in this state for testimony taken in another state. The court on its own motion may order that the testimony of a person be taken in another state and may prescribe the manner in which and the terms upon which the testimony is taken.

(b) A court of this state may permit an individual residing in another state to be deposed or to testify by telephone, audiovisual means, or other electronic means before a designated court or at another location in that state. A court of this state shall cooperate with courts of other states in designating an appropriate location for the deposition or testimony.

(c) Documentary evidence transmitted from another state to a court of this state by technological means that do not produce an original writing may not be excluded from evidence on an objection based on the means of transmission.

Commissioners' Comment

No substantive changes have been made to Subsection (a) which was Section 18 of the UCCJA.

Subsections (b) and (c) merely provide that modern modes of communication are permissible in the taking of testimony and the transmittal of documents. *See* UIFSA § 316.

---

§ 152.112. Cooperation Between Courts; Preservation of Records

(a) A court of this state may request the appropriate court of another state to:

(1) hold an evidentiary hearing;

(2) order a person to produce or give evidence pursuant to procedures of that state;

(3) order that an evaluation be made with respect to the custody of a child involved in a pending proceeding;

(4) forward to the court of this state a certified copy of the transcript of the record of the hearing, the evidence otherwise presented, and any evaluation prepared in compliance with the request; and

(5) order a party to a child custody proceeding or any person having physical custody of the child to appear in the proceeding with or without the child.

(b) Upon request of a court of another state, a court of this state may hold a hearing or enter an order described in Subsection (a).

(c) Travel and other necessary and reasonable expenses incurred under Subsections (a) and (b) may be assessed against the parties according to the law of this state.

(d) A court of this state shall preserve the pleadings, orders, decrees, records of hearings, evaluations, and other pertinent records with respect to a child custody proceeding until the child attains 18 years of age. Upon appropriate request by a court or law enforcement official of another state, the court shall forward a certified copy of those records.

Commissioners' Comment

This section is the heart of judicial cooperation provision of this Act. It provides mechanisms for courts to cooperate with each other in order to decide cases in an efficient manner without causing undue expense to the parties. Courts may request assistance from courts of other states and may assist courts of other states.

The provision on the assessment of costs for travel provided in the UCCJA § 19 has been changed. The UCCJA provided that the costs may be assessed against the parties or the state or county. Assessment of costs against a government entity in a case where the government is not involved is inappropriate and therefore that provision has been removed. In addition, if the state is involved as a party, assessment of costs and expenses against the state must be authorized by other law. It should be noted that the term "expenses" means out-of-pocket costs. Overhead costs should not be assessed as expenses.

No other substantive changes have been made. The term "social study" as used in the UCCJA was replaced with the modern term: "custody evaluation." The Act does not take a position on the admissibility of a custody evaluation that was conducted in another state. It merely authorizes a court to seek assistance of, or render assistance to, a court of another state.

This section combines the text of Sections 19–22 of the UCCJA.

SUBCHAPTER C. JURISDICTION

§ 152.201. Initial Child Custody Jurisdiction

(a) Except as otherwise provided in Section 152.204, a court of this state has jurisdiction to make an initial child custody determination only if:

(1) this state is the home state of the child on the date of the commencement of the proceeding, or was the home state of the child within six months before the commencement of the proceeding and the child is absent from this state but a parent or person acting as a parent continues to live in this state;

(2) a court of another state does not have jurisdiction under Subdivision (1), or a court of the home state of the child has declined to exercise jurisdiction on the ground that this state is the more appropriate forum under Section 152.207 or 152.208, and:

(A) the child and the child's parents, or the child and at least one parent or a person acting as a parent, have a significant connection with this state other than mere physical presence; and

(B) substantial evidence is available in this state concerning the child's care, protection, training, and personal relationships;

(3) all courts having jurisdiction under Subdivision (1) or (2) have declined to exercise jurisdiction on the ground that a court of this state is the more appropriate forum to determine the custody of the child under Section 152.207 or 152.208; or

(4) no court of any other state would have jurisdiction under the criteria specified in Subdivision (1), (2), or (3).

(b) Subsection (a) is the exclusive jurisdictional basis for making a child custody determination by a court of this state.

(c) Physical presence of, or personal jurisdiction over, a party or a child is not necessary or sufficient to make a child custody determination.

Commissioners' Comment

This section provides mandatory jurisdictional rules for the original child custody proceeding. It generally continues the provisions of the UCCJA § 3. However, there have been a number of changes to the jurisdictional bases.

1. Home State Jurisdiction. The jurisdiction of the home state has been prioritized over other jurisdictional bases. Section 3 of the UCCJA provided four independent and concurrent bases of jurisdiction. The PKPA provides that full faith and credit can only be given to an initial custody determination of a "significant connection" State when there is no home state. This Act prioritizes home state jurisdiction in the same manner as the PKPA thereby eliminating any potential conflict between the two acts.

The six-month extended home state provision of Subsection (a)(1) has been modified slightly from the UCCJA. The UCCJA provided that home state jurisdiction continued for six months when the child had been removed by a person seeking the child's custody or for other reasons and a parent or a person acting as a parent continues to reside in the home state. Under this Act, it is no longer necessary to determine why the child has been removed. The only inquiry relates to the status of the person left behind. This change provides a slightly more refined home state standard than the UCCJA or the PKPA, which also requires a determination that the child has been removed "by a contestant or for other reasons." The scope of the PKPA's provision is theoretically narrower than this Act. However, the phrase "or for other reasons" covers most fact situations where the child is not in the home state and, therefore, the difference has no substantive effect.

In another sense, the six-month extended home state jurisdiction provision in this Act is narrower than the comparable provision in the PKPA. The PKPA's definition of extended home state is more expansive because it applies whenever a "contestant" remains in the home state. That class of individuals has been eliminated in this Act. This Act retains the original UCCJA classification of "parent or person acting as parent" to define who must remain for a state to exercise the six-month extended home state jurisdiction. This eliminates the undesirable jurisdictional determinations which would occur as a result of differing state substantive laws on visitation involving grandparents and others. For example, if State A's law provided that grandparents could obtain visitation with a child after the death of one of the parents, then the grandparents, who would be considered "contestants" under the PKPA, could file a proceeding within six months after the remaining parent moved and have the case heard in State A. However, if State A did not provide that grandparents could seek visitation under such circumstances, the grandparents would not be considered "contestants" and State B where the child acquired a new home state would provide the only forum. This Act bases jurisdiction on the parent and child or person acting as a parent and child relationship without regard to grandparents or other potential seekers of custody or visitation. There is no conflict with the broader provision of the PKPA. The PKPA in § (c)(1) authorizes states to narrow the scope of their jurisdiction.

2. Significant connection jurisdiction. This jurisdictional basis has been amended in four particulars from the UCCJA. First, the "best interest" language of the UCCJA has been eliminated. This phrase tended to create confusion between the jurisdictional issue and the substantive custody determination. Since the language was not necessary for the jurisdictional issue, it has been removed.

Second, the UCCJA based jurisdiction on the presence of a significant connection between the child and the child's parents or the child and at least one contestant. This Act requires that the significant connections be between the child, the child's parents or the child and a person acting as a parent.

Third, a significant connection state may assume jurisdiction only when there is no home state or when the home state decides that the significant connection state would be a more appropriate forum under Section 207 or 208. Fourth, the determination of significant connections has been changed to eliminate the language of "present or future care." The jurisdictional determination should be made by determining whether there is sufficient evidence in the state for the court to make an informed custody determination. That evidence might relate to the past as well as to the "present or future."

Emergency jurisdiction has been moved to a separate section. This is to make it clear that the power to protect a child in crisis does not include the power to enter a permanent order for that child except as provided by that section.

Paragraph (a)(3) provides for jurisdiction when all states with jurisdiction under paragraphs (a)(1) and (2) determine that this state is a more appropriate forum. The determination would have to be made by all states with jurisdiction under Subsection (a)(1) and (2). Jurisdiction would not exist under this paragraph because the home state determined it is a more appropriate place to hear the case if there is another state that could exercise significant connection jurisdiction under Subsection (a)(2).

Paragraph (a)(4) retains the concept of jurisdiction by necessity as found in the UCCJA and in the PKPA. This default jurisdiction only occurs if no other state would have jurisdiction under Subsections (a)(1) through (a)(3).

Subsections (b) and (c) clearly state the relationship between jurisdiction under this Act and other forms of jurisdiction. Personal jurisdiction over, or the physical presence of, a parent or the child is neither necessary nor required under this Act. In other words neither minimum contacts nor service within the state is required for the court to have jurisdiction to make a custody determination. Further, the presence of minimum contacts or service within the state does not confer jurisdiction to make a custody determination. Subject to Section 204, satisfaction of the requirements of Subsection (a) is mandatory.

The requirements of this section, plus the notice and hearing provisions of the Act, are all that is necessary to satisfy due process. This Act, like the UCCJA and the PKPA is based on Justice Frankfurter's concurrence in *May v. Anderson*, 345 U.S. 528 (1953). As pointed out by Professor Bodenheimer, the reporter for the UCCJA, no "workable interstate custody law could be built around [Justice] Burton's plurality opinion. . . ." Bridgette Bodenheimer, *The Uniform Child Custody Jurisdiction Act: A Legislative Remedy for Children Caught in the Conflict of Laws*, 22 VAND. L. REV. 1207, 1233 (1969). It should also be noted that since jurisdiction to make a child custody determination is subject matter jurisdiction, an agreement of the parties to confer jurisdiction on a court that would not otherwise have jurisdiction under this Act is ineffective.

§ 152.202. Exclusive Continuing Jurisdiction

(a) Except as otherwise provided in Section 152.204, a court of this state which has made a child custody determination consistent with Section 152.201 or 152.203 has exclusive continuing jurisdiction over the determination until:

(1) a court of this state determines that neither the child, nor the child and one parent, nor the child and a person acting as a parent, have a significant connection with this state and that substantial evidence is no longer available in this state concerning the child's care, protection, training, and personal relationships; or

(2) a court of this state or a court of another state determines that the child, the child's parents, and any person acting as a parent do not presently reside in this state.

(b) A court of this state which has made a child custody determination and does not have exclusive, continuing jurisdiction under this section may modify that determination only if it has jurisdiction to make an initial determination under Section 152.201.

Commissioners' Comment

This is a new section addressing continuing jurisdiction. Continuing jurisdiction was not specifically addressed in the UCCJA. Its absence caused considerable confusion, particularly because the PKPA, § 1738(d), requires other states to give Full Faith and Credit to custody determinations made by the original decree state pursuant to the decree state's continuing jurisdiction so long as that state has jurisdiction under its own law and remains the residence of the child or any contestant.

This section provides the rules of continuing jurisdiction and borrows from UIFSA as well as recent UCCJA case law. The continuing jurisdiction of the original decree state is exclusive. It continues until one of two events occurs:

1. If a parent or a person acting as a parent remains in the original decree state, continuing jurisdiction is lost when neither the child, the child and a parent, nor the child and a person acting as a parent continue to have a significant connection with the original decree state and there is no longer substantial evidence concerning the child's care, protection, training and personal relations in that state. In other words, even if the child has acquired a new home state, the original decree state retains exclusive, continuing jurisdiction, so long as the general requisites of the "substantial connection" jurisdiction provisions of Section 201 are met. If the relationship between the child and the person remaining in the state with exclusive, continuing jurisdiction becomes so attenuated that the court could no longer find significant connections and substantial evidence, jurisdiction would no longer exist.

The use of the phrase "a court of this State" under Subsection (a)(1) makes it clear that the original decree state is the sole determinant of whether jurisdiction continues. A party seeking to modify a custody determination must obtain an order from the original decree state stating that it no longer has jurisdiction.

2. Continuing jurisdiction is lost when the child, the child's parents, and any person acting as a parent no longer reside in the original decree state. The exact language of subparagraph (a)(2) was the subject of considerable debate. Ultimately the Conference settled on the phrase that "a court of this State or a court of another State determines that the child, the child's parents, and any person acting as a parent do not presently reside in this State" to determine when the exclusive, continuing jurisdiction of a state ended. The phrase is meant to be identical in meaning to the language of the PKPA which provides that full faith and credit is to be given to custody determinations made by a state in the exercise of its continuing jurisdiction when that "State remains the residence of.... "The phrase is also the equivalent of the language "continues to reside" which occurs in UIFSA § 205(a)(1) to determine the exclusive, continuing jurisdiction of the state that made a support order. The phrase "remains the residence of" in the PKPA has been the subject of conflicting case law. It is the intention of this Act that paragraph (a)(2) of this section means that the named persons no longer continue to actually live within the state. Thus, unless a modification proceeding has been commenced, when the child, the parents, and all persons acting as parents physically leave the state to live elsewhere, the exclusive, continuing jurisdiction ceases.

The phrase "do not presently reside" is not used in the sense of a technical domicile. The fact that the original determination state still considers one parent a domiciliary does not prevent it from losing exclusive, continuing jurisdiction after the child, the parents, and all persons acting as parents have moved from the state.

If the child, the parents, and all persons acting as parents have all left the state which made the custody determination prior to the commencement of the modification proceeding, considerations of waste of resources dictate that a court in State B, as well as a court in State A, can decide that State A has lost exclusive, continuing jurisdiction.

The continuing jurisdiction provisions of this section are narrower than the comparable provisions of the PKPA. That statute authorizes continuing jurisdiction so long as any "contestant" remains in the original decree state and that state continues to have jurisdiction under its own law. This Act eliminates the contestant classification. The Conference decided that a remaining grandparent or other third party who claims a right to visitation, should not suffice to confer exclusive, continuing jurisdiction on the state that made the original custody determination after the departure of the child, the parents and any person acting as a parent. The significant connection to the original decree state must relate to the child, the child and a parent, or the child and a person acting as a parent. This revision does not present a conflict with the PKPA. The PKPA's reference in § 1738(d) to § 1738(c)(1) recognizes that states may narrow the class of cases that would be subject to exclusive, continuing jurisdiction. However, during the transition from the UCCJA to this Act, some states may continue to base continuing jurisdiction on the continued presence of a contestant, such as a grandparent. The PKPA will require that such decisions be enforced. The problem will disappear as states adopt this Act to replace the UCCJA.

Jurisdiction attaches at the commencement of a proceeding. If State A had jurisdiction under this section at the time a modification proceeding was commenced there, it would not be lost by all parties moving out of the state prior to the conclusion of the proceeding. State B would not have jurisdiction to hear a modification unless State A decided that State B was more appropriate under Section 207.

Exclusive, continuing jurisdiction is not reestablished if, after the child, the parents, and all persons acting as parents leave the state, the non-custodial parent returns. As Subsection (b) provides, once a state has lost exclusive, continuing jurisdiction, it can modify its own determination only if it has jurisdiction under the standards of Section 201. If another state acquires exclusive continuing jurisdiction under this section, then its orders cannot be modified even if this state has once again become the home state of the child.

In accordance with the majority of UCCJA case law, the state with exclusive, continuing jurisdiction may relinquish jurisdiction when it determines that another state would be a more convenient forum under the principles of Section 207.

§ 152.203. Jurisdiction to Modify Determination

Except as otherwise provided in Section 152.204, a court of this state may not modify a child custody determination made by a court of another state unless a court of this state has jurisdiction to make an initial determination under Section 152.201(a)(1) or (2) and:

(1) the court of the other state determines it no longer has exclusive continuing jurisdiction under Section 152.202 or that a court of this state would be a more convenient forum under Section 152.207; or

(2) a court of this state or a court of the other state determines that the child, the child's parents, and any person acting as a parent do not presently reside in the other state.

Commissioners' Comment

This section complements Section 202 and is addressed to the court that is confronted with a proceeding to modify a custody determination of another state. It prohibits a court from modifying a custody determination made consistently with this Act by a court in another state unless a court of that state determines that it no longer has exclusive, continuing jurisdiction under Section 202 or that this state would be a more convenient forum under Section 207. The modification state is not authorized to determine that the original decree state has lost its jurisdiction. The only exception is when the child, the child's parents, and any person acting as a parent do not presently reside in the other state. In other words, a court of the modification state can determine that all parties have moved away from the original state. The court of the modification state must have jurisdiction under the standards of Section 201.

§ 152.204. Temporary Emergency Jurisdiction

(a) A court of this state has temporary emergency jurisdiction if the child is present in this state and the child has been abandoned or it is necessary in an emergency to protect the child because the child, or a sibling or parent of the child, is subjected to or threatened with mistreatment or abuse.

(b) If there is no previous child custody determination that is entitled to be enforced under this chapter and a child custody proceeding has not been commenced in a court of a state having jurisdiction under Sections 152.201 through 152.203, a child custody determination made under this section remains in effect until an order is obtained from a court of a state having jurisdiction under Sections 152.201 through 152.203. If a child custody proceeding has not been or is not commenced in a court of a state having jurisdiction under Sections 152.201 through 152.203, a child custody determination made under this section becomes a final determination, if it so provides and this state becomes the home state of the child.

(c) If there is a previous child custody determination that is entitled to be enforced under this chapter, or a child custody proceeding has been commenced in a court of a state having jurisdiction under Sections 152.201 through 152.203, any order issued by a court of this state under this section must specify in the order a period that the court considers adequate to allow the person seeking an order to obtain an order from the state having jurisdiction under Sections 152.201 through 152.203. The order issued in this state remains in effect until an order is obtained from the other state within the period specified or the period expires.

(d) A court of this state which has been asked to make a child custody determination under this section, upon being informed that a child custody proceeding has been commenced in or a child custody determination has been made by a court of a state having jurisdiction under Sections 152.201 through 152.203, shall immediately communicate with the other court. A court of this state which is exercising jurisdiction pursuant to Sections 152.201 through 152.203, upon being informed that a child custody proceeding has been commenced in or a child custody determination has been made by a court of another state under a statute similar to this section shall immediately communicate with the court of that state to resolve the emergency, protect the safety of the parties and the child, and determine a period for the duration of the temporary order.

Commissioners' Comment

The provisions of this section are an elaboration of what was formerly Section 3(a)(3) of the UCCJA. It remains, as Professor Bodenheimer's comments to that section noted, "an extraordinary jurisdiction reserved for extraordinary circumstances."

This section codifies and clarifies several aspects of what has become common practice in emergency jurisdiction cases under the UCCJA and PKPA. First, a court may take jurisdiction to protect the child even though it can claim neither home state nor significant connection jurisdiction. Second, the duties of states to recognize, enforce and not modify a custody determination of another state do not take precedence over the need to enter a temporary emergency order to protect the child. Third, a custody determination made under the emergency jurisdiction provisions of this section is a temporary order. The purpose of the order is to protect the child until the state that has jurisdiction under Sections 201–203 enters an order.

Under certain circumstances, however, Subsection (b) provides that an emergency custody determination may become a final custody determination. If there is no existing custody determination, and no custody proceeding is filed in a state with jurisdiction under Sections 201–203, an emergency custody determination made under this section becomes a final determination, if it so provides, when the state that issues the order becomes the home state of the child.

Subsection (c) is concerned with the temporary nature of the order when there exists a prior custody order that is entitled to be enforced under this Act or when a subsequent custody proceeding is filed in a state with jurisdiction under Sections 201–203. Subsection (c) allows the temporary order to remain in effect only so long as is necessary for the person who obtained the determination under this section to present a case and obtain an order from the state with jurisdiction under Sections 201–203. That time period must be specified in the order. If there is an existing order by a state with jurisdiction under Sections 201–203, that order need not be reconfirmed. The temporary emergency determination would lapse by its own terms at the end of the specified period or when an order is obtained from the court with jurisdiction under Sections 202–203. The court with appropriate jurisdiction also may decide, under the provisions of 207, that the court that entered the emergency order is in a better position to address the safety of the person who obtained the emergency order, or the child, and decline jurisdiction under Section 207.

Any hearing in the state with jurisdiction under Sections 201–203 on the temporary emergency determination is subject to the provisions of Sections 111 and 112. These sections facilitate the presentation of testimony and evidence taken out of state. If there is a concern that the person obtaining the temporary emergency determination under this section would be in danger upon returning to the state with jurisdiction under Sections 201–203, these provisions should be used.

Subsection (d) requires communication between the court of the state that is exercising jurisdiction under this section and the court of another state that is exercising jurisdiction under Sections 201–203. The pleading rules of Section 209 apply fully to determinations made under this section. Therefore, a person seeking a temporary emergency custody determination is required to inform the court pursuant to Section 209(d) of any proceeding concerning the child that has been commenced elsewhere. The person commencing the custody proceeding under Sections 201–203 is required under Section 209(a) to inform the court about the temporary emergency proceeding. These pleading requirements are to be strictly followed so that the courts are able to resolve the emergency, protect the safety of the parties and the child, and determine a period for the duration of the temporary order.

Relationship to the PKPA. The definition of emergency has been modified to harmonize it with the PKPA. The PKPA's definition of emergency jurisdiction does not use the term "neglect." It defines an emergency as "mistreatment or abuse." Therefore "neglect" has been eliminated as a basis for the assumption of temporary emergency jurisdiction. Neglect is so elastic a concept that it could justify taking emergency jurisdiction in a wide variety of cases. Under the PKPA, if a state exercised temporary emergency jurisdiction based on a finding that the child was neglected without a finding of mistreatment or abuse, the order would not be entitled to federal enforcement in other states.

Relationship to Protective Order Proceedings. The UCCJA and the PKPA were enacted long before the advent of state procedures on the use of protective orders to alleviate problems of domestic violence. Issues of custody and visitation often arise within the context of protective order proceedings since the protective order is often invoked to keep one parent away from the other parent and the children when there is a threat of violence. This Act recognizes that a protective order proceeding will often be the procedural vehicle for invoking jurisdiction by authorizing a court to assume temporary emergency jurisdiction when the child's parent or sibling has been subjected to or threatened with mistreatment or abuse.

In order for a protective order that contains a custody determination to be enforceable in another state it must comply with the provisions of this Act and the PKPA. Although the Violence Against Women's Act (VAWA), 18 U.S.C. § 2265, does provide an independent basis for the granting of full faith and credit to protective orders, it expressly excludes "custody" orders from the definition of "protective order," 22 U.S.C. § 2266.

Many states authorize the issuance of protective orders in an emergency without notice and hearing. This Act does not address the propriety of that procedure. It is left to local law to determine the circumstances under which such an order could be issued, and the type of notice that is required, in a case without an interstate element. However, an order issued after the assumption of temporary emergency jurisdiction is entitled to interstate enforcement and nonmodification under this Act and the PKPA only if there has been notice and a reasonable opportunity to be heard as set out in Section 205. Although VAWA does require that full faith and credit be accorded to ex parte protective orders if notice will be given and there will be a reasonable opportunity to be heard, it does not include a "custody" order within the definition of "protective order."

VAWA does play an important role in determining whether an emergency exists. That Act requires a court to give full faith and credit to a protective order issued in another state if the order is made in accordance with the VAWA. This would include those findings of fact contained in the order. When a court is deciding whether an emergency exists under this section, it may not relitigate the existence of those factual findings.

Leading Case

In re Kamstra, not reported, 2010 WL 708857 (Tex. App.—Tyler 2010, no pet.) (neither this § 152.204 nor Hague Abduction Convention authorize Texas trial court to issue temporary emergency orders regarding dual nationality children taken from nonsignatory country to East Texas by mother)

---

§ 152.205. Notice; Opportunity to be Heard; Joinder

(a) Before a child custody determination is made under this chapter, notice and an opportunity to be heard in accordance with the standards of Section 152.108 must be given to all persons entitled to notice under the law of this state as in child custody proceedings between residents of this state, any parent whose parental rights have not been previously terminated, and any person having physical custody of the child.

(b) This chapter does not govern the enforceability of a child custody determination made without notice or an opportunity to be heard.

(c) The obligation to join a party and the right to intervene as a party in a child custody proceeding under this chapter are governed by the law of this state as in child custody proceedings between residents of this state.

Commissioners' Comment

This section generally continues the notice provisions of the UCCJA. However, it does not attempt to dictate who is entitled to notice. Local rules vary with regard to persons entitled to seek custody of a child. Therefore, this section simply indicates that persons entitled to seek custody should receive notice but leaves the rest of the determination to local law. Parents whose parental rights have not been previously terminated and persons having physical custody of the child are specifically mentioned as persons who must be given notice. The PKPA, § 1738A(e), requires that they be given notice in order for the custody determination to be entitled to full faith and credit under that Act.

State laws also vary with regard to whether a court has the power to issue an enforceable temporary custody order without notice and hearing in a case without any interstate element. Such temporary orders may be enforceable, as against due process objections, for a short period of time if issued as a protective order or a temporary restraining order to protect a child from harm. Whether such orders are enforceable locally is beyond the scope of this Act. Subsection (b) clearly provides that the validity of such orders and the enforceability of such orders is governed by the law which authorizes them and not by this Act. An order is entitled to interstate enforcement and nonmodification under this Act only if there has been notice and an opportunity to be heard. The PKPA, § 1738A(e), also requires that a custody determination is entitled to full faith and credit only if there has been notice and an opportunity to be heard.

Rules requiring joinder of people with an interest in the custody of and visitation with a child also vary widely throughout the country. The UCCJA has a separate section on joinder of parties which has been eliminated. The issue of who is entitled to intervene and who must be joined in a custody proceeding is to be determined by local state law.

A sentence of the UCCJA § 4 which indicated that persons outside the state were to be given notice and an opportunity to be heard in accordance with the provision of that Act has been eliminated as redundant.

---

§ 152.206. Simultaneous Proceedings

(a) Except as otherwise provided in Section 152.204, a court of this state may not exercise its jurisdiction under this subchapter if, at the time of the commencement of the proceeding, a proceeding concerning the custody of the child has been commenced in a court of another state having jurisdiction substantially in conformity with this chapter, unless the proceeding has been terminated or is stayed by the court of the other state because a court of this state is a more convenient forum under Section 152.207.

(b) Except as otherwise provided in Section 152.204, a court of this state, before hearing a child custody proceeding, shall examine the court documents and other information supplied by the parties pursuant to Section 152.209. If the court determines that a child custody proceeding has been commenced in a court in another state having jurisdiction substantially in accordance with this chapter, the court of this state shall stay its proceeding and communicate with the court of the other state. If the court of the state having jurisdiction substantially in accordance with this chapter does not determine that the court of this state is a more appropriate forum, the court of this state shall dismiss the proceeding.

(c) In a proceeding to modify a child custody determination, a court of this state shall determine whether a proceeding to enforce the determination has been commenced in another state. If a proceeding to enforce a child custody determination has been commenced in another state, the court may:

(1) stay the proceeding for modification pending the entry of an order of a court of the other state enforcing, staying, denying, or dismissing the proceeding for enforcement;

(2) enjoin the parties from continuing with the proceeding for enforcement; or

(3) proceed with the modification under conditions it considers appropriate.

Commissioners' Comment

This section represents the remnants of the simultaneous proceedings provision of the UCCJA § 6. The problem of simultaneous proceedings is no longer a significant issue. Most of the problems have been resolved by the prioritization of home state jurisdiction under Section 201; the exclusive, continuing jurisdiction provisions of Section 202; and the prohibitions on modification of Section 203. If there is a home state, there can be no exercise of significant connection jurisdiction in an initial child custody determination and, therefore, no simultaneous proceedings. If there is a state of exclusive, continuing jurisdiction, there cannot be another state with concurrent jurisdiction and, therefore, no simultaneous proceedings. Of course, the home state, as well as the state with exclusive, continuing jurisdiction, could defer to another state under Section 207. However, that decision is left entirely to the home state or the state with exclusive, continuing jurisdiction.

Under this Act, the simultaneous proceedings problem will arise only when there is no home state, no state with exclusive, continuing jurisdiction and more than one significant connection state. For those cases, this section retains the "first in time" rule of the UCCJA. Subsection (b) retains the UCCJA's policy favoring judicial communication. Communication between courts is required when it is determined that a proceeding has been commenced in another state.

Subsection (c) concerns the problem of simultaneous proceedings in the state with modification jurisdiction and enforcement proceedings under Article 3. This section authorizes the court with exclusive, continuing jurisdiction to stay the modification proceeding pending the outcome of the enforcement proceeding, to enjoin the parties from continuing with the enforcement proceeding, or to continue the modification proceeding under such conditions as it determines are appropriate. The court may wish to communicate with the enforcement court. However, communication is not mandatory. Although the enforcement state is required by the PKPA to enforce according to its terms a custody determination made consistently with the PKPA, that duty is subject to the decree being modified by a state with the power to do so under the PKPA. An order to enjoin the parties from enforcing the decree is the equivalent of a temporary modification by a state with the authority to do so. The concomitant provision addressed to the enforcement court is Section 306 of this Act. That section requires the enforcement court to communicate with the modification court in order to determine what action the modification court wishes the enforcement court to take.

The term "pending" that was utilized in the UCCJA section on simultaneous proceeding has been replaced. It has caused considerable confusion in the case law. It has been replaced with the term "commencement of the proceeding" as more accurately reflecting the policy behind this section. The latter term is defined in Section 102(5).

---

§ 152.207. Inconvenient Forum

(a) A court of this state which has jurisdiction under this chapter to make a child custody determination may decline to exercise its jurisdiction at any time if it determines that it is an inconvenient forum under the circumstances and that a court of another state is a more appropriate forum. The issue of inconvenient forum may be raised upon motion of a party, the court's own motion, or request of another court.

(b) Before determining whether it is an inconvenient forum, a court of this state shall consider whether it is appropriate for a court of another state to exercise jurisdiction. For this purpose, the court shall allow the parties to submit information and shall consider all relevant factors, including:

(1) whether domestic violence has occurred and is likely to continue in the future and which state could best protect the parties and the child;

(2) the length of time the child has resided outside this state;

(3) the distance between the court in this state and the court in the state that would assume jurisdiction;

(4) the relative financial circumstances of the parties;

(5) any agreement of the parties as to which state should assume jurisdiction;

(6) the nature and location of the evidence required to resolve the pending litigation, including testimony of the child;

(7) the ability of the court of each state to decide the issue expeditiously and the procedures necessary to present the evidence; and

(8) the familiarity of the court of each state with the facts and issues in the pending litigation.

(c) If a court of this state determines that it is an inconvenient forum and that a court of another state is a more appropriate forum, the court shall stay the proceedings upon condition that a child custody proceeding be promptly commenced in another designated state and may impose any other condition the court considers just and proper.

(d) A court of this state may decline to exercise its jurisdiction under this chapter if a child custody determination is incidental to an action for divorce or another proceeding while still retaining jurisdiction over the divorce or other proceeding.

Commissioners' Comment

This section retains the focus of Section 7 of the UCCJA. It authorizes courts to decide that another state is in a better position to make the custody determination, taking into consideration the relative circumstances of the parties. If so, the court may defer to the other state.

The list of factors that the court may consider has been updated from the UCCJA. The list is not meant to be exclusive. Several provisions require comment. Subparagraph (1) is concerned specifically with domestic violence and other matters affecting the health and safety of the parties. For this purpose, the court should determine whether the parties are located in different states because one party is a victim of domestic violence or child abuse. If domestic violence or child abuse has occurred, this factor authorizes the court to consider which state can best protect the victim from further violence or abuse.

In applying subparagraph (3), courts should realize that distance concerns can be alleviated by applying the communication and cooperation provisions of Sections 111 and 112.

In applying Subsection (7) on expeditious resolution of the controversy, the court could consider the different procedural and evidentiary laws of the two states, as well as the flexibility of the court dockets. It also should consider the ability of a court to arrive at a solution to all the legal issues surrounding the family. If one state has jurisdiction to decide both the custody and support issues, it would be desirable to determine that state to be the most convenient forum. The same is true when children of the same family live in different states. It would be inappropriate to require parents to have custody proceedings in several states when one state could resolve the custody of all the children.

Before determining whether to decline or retain jurisdiction, the court of this state may communicate, in accordance with Section 110, with a court of another state and exchange information pertinent to the assumption of jurisdiction by either court.

There are two departures from Section 7 of the UCCJA. First, the court may not simply dismiss the action. To do so would leave the case in limbo. Rather the court shall stay the case and direct the parties to file in the state that has been found to be the more convenient forum. The court is also authorized to impose any other conditions it considers appropriate. This might include the issuance of temporary custody orders during the time necessary to commence a proceeding in the designated state, dismissing the case if the custody proceeding is not commenced in the other state or resuming jurisdiction if a court of the other state refuses to take the case.

Second, UCCJA, § 7(g) which allowed the court to assess fees and costs if it was a clearly inappropriate court, has been eliminated. If a court has jurisdiction under this Act, it could not be a clearly inappropriate court.

§ 152.208. Jurisdiction Declined by Reason of Conduct

(a) Except as otherwise provided in Section 152.204 or other law of this state, if a court of this state has jurisdiction under this chapter because a person seeking to invoke its jurisdiction has engaged in unjustifiable conduct, the court shall decline to exercise its jurisdiction unless:

(1) the parents and all persons acting as parents have acquiesced in the exercise of jurisdiction;

(2) a court of the state otherwise having jurisdiction under Sections 152.201 through 152.203 determines that this state is a more appropriate forum under Section 152.207; or

(3) no court of any other state would have jurisdiction under the criteria specified in Sections 152.201 through 152.203.

(b) If a court of this state declines to exercise its jurisdiction pursuant to Subsection (a), it may fashion an appropriate remedy to ensure the safety of the child and prevent a repetition of the unjustifiable conduct, including staying the proceeding until a child custody proceeding is commenced in a court having jurisdiction under Sections 152.201 through 152.203.

(c) If a court dismisses a petition or stays a proceeding because it declines to exercise its jurisdiction pursuant to Subsection (a), it shall assess against the party seeking to invoke its jurisdiction necessary and reasonable expenses including costs, communication expenses, attorney's fees, investigative fees, expenses for witnesses, travel expenses, and child care during the course of the proceedings, unless the party from whom fees are sought establishes that the assessment would be clearly inappropriate. The court may not assess fees, costs, or expenses against this state unless authorized by law other than this chapter.

Commissioners' Comment

The "Clean Hands" section of the UCCJA has been truncated in this Act. Since there is no longer a multiplicity of jurisdictions which could take cognizance of a child-custody proceeding, there is less of a concern that one parent will take the child to another jurisdiction in an attempt to find a more favorable forum. Most of the jurisdictional problems generated by abducting parents should be solved by the prioritization of home state in Section 201; the exclusive, continuing jurisdiction provisions of Section 202; and the ban on modification in Section 203. For example, if a parent takes the child from the home state and seeks an original custody determination elsewhere, the stay-at-home parent has six months to file a custody petition under the extended home state jurisdictional provision of Section 201, which will ensure that the case is retained in the home state. If a petitioner for a modification determination takes the child from the state that issued the original custody determination, another state cannot assume jurisdiction as long at the first state exercises exclusive, continuing jurisdiction.

Nonetheless, there are still a number of cases where parents, or their surrogates, act in a reprehensible manner, such as removing, secreting, retaining, or restraining the child. This section ensures that abducting parents will not receive an advantage for their unjustifiable conduct. If the conduct that creates the jurisdiction is unjustified, courts must decline to exercise jurisdiction that is inappropriately invoked by one of the parties. For example, if one parent abducts the child pre-decree and establishes a new home state, that jurisdiction will decline to hear the case. There are exceptions. If the other party has acquiesced in the court's jurisdiction, the court may hear the case. Such acquiescence may occur by filing a pleading submitting to the jurisdiction, or by not filing in the court that would otherwise have jurisdiction under this Act. Similarly, if the court that would have jurisdiction finds that the court of this state is a more appropriate forum, the court may hear the case.

This section applies to those situations where jurisdiction exists because of the unjustified conduct of the person seeking to invoke it. If, for example, a parent in the state with exclusive, continuing jurisdiction under Section 202 has either restrained the child from visiting with the other parent, or has retained the child after visitation, and seeks to modify the decree, this section in inapplicable. The conduct of restraining or retaining the child did not create jurisdiction. Jurisdiction existed under this Act without regard to the parent's conduct. Whether a court should decline to hear the parent's request to modify is a matter of local law.

The focus in this section is on the unjustified conduct of the person who invokes the jurisdiction of the court. A technical illegality or wrong is insufficient to trigger the applicability of this section. This is particularly important in cases involving domestic violence and child abuse. Domestic violence victims should not be charged with unjustifiable conduct for conduct that occurred in the process of fleeing domestic violence, even if their conduct is technically illegal. Thus, if a parent flees with a child to escape domestic violence and in the process violates a joint custody decree, the case should not be automatically dismissed under this section. An inquiry must be made into whether the flight was justified under the circumstances of the case. However, an abusive parent who seizes the child and flees to another state to establish jurisdiction has engaged in unjustifiable conduct and the new state must decline to exercise jurisdiction under this section.

Subsection (b) authorizes the court to fashion an appropriate remedy for the safety of the child and to prevent a repetition of the unjustified conduct. Thus, it would be appropriate for the court to notify the other parent and to provide for foster care for the child until the child is returned to the other parent. The court could also stay the proceeding and require that a custody proceeding be instituted in another state that would have jurisdiction under this Act. It should be noted that the court is not making a forum non conveniens analysis in this section. If the conduct is unjustifiable, it must decline jurisdiction. It may, however, retain jurisdiction until a custody proceeding is commenced in the appropriate tribunal if such retention is necessary to prevent a repetition of the wrongful conduct or to ensure the safety of the child.

The attorney's fee standard for this section is patterned after the International Child Abduction Remedies Act, 42 U.S.C. § 11607(b)(3). The assessed costs and fees are to be paid to the respondent who established that jurisdiction was based on unjustifiable conduct.

---

§ 152.209. Information to be Submitted to Court

(a) Except as provided by Subsection (e) or unless each party resides in this state, in a child custody proceeding, each party, in its first pleading or in an attached affidavit, shall give information, if reasonably ascertainable, under oath as to the child's present address or whereabouts, the places where the child has lived during the last five years, and the names and present addresses of the persons with whom the child has lived during that period. The pleading or affidavit must state whether the party:

(1) has participated, as a party or witness or in any other capacity, in any other proceeding concerning the custody of or visitation with the child and, if so, identify the court, the case number, and the date of the child custody determination, if any;

(2) knows of any proceeding that could affect the current proceeding, including proceedings for enforcement and proceedings relating to domestic violence, protective orders, termination of parental rights, and adoptions and, if so, identify the court, the case number, and the nature of the proceeding; and

(3) knows the names and addresses of any person not a party to the proceeding who has physical custody of the child or claims rights of legal custody or physical custody of, or visitation with, the child and, if so, the names and addresses of those persons.

(b) If the information required by Subsection (a) is not furnished, the court, upon motion of a party or its own motion, may stay the proceeding until the information is furnished.

(c) If the declaration as to any of the items described in Subsections (a)(1) through (3) is in the affirmative, the declarant shall give additional information under oath as required by the court. The court may examine the parties under oath as to details of the information furnished and other matters pertinent to the court's jurisdiction and the disposition of the case.

(d) Each party has a continuing duty to inform the court of any proceeding in this or any other state that could affect the current proceeding.

(e) If a party alleges in an affidavit or a pleading under oath that the health, safety, or liberty of a party or child would be jeopardized by disclosure of identifying information, the information must be sealed and may not be disclosed to the other party or the public unless the court orders the disclosure to be made after a hearing in which the court takes into consideration the health, safety, or liberty of the party or child and determines that the disclosure is in the interest of justice.

Commissioners' Comment

The pleading requirements from Section 9 of the UCCJA are generally carried over into this Act. However, the information is made subject to local law on the protection of names and other identifying information in certain cases. A number of states have enacted laws relating to the protection of victims in domestic violence and child abuse cases which provide for the confidentiality of victims names, addresses, and other information. These procedures must be followed if the child-custody proceeding of the state requires their applicability. See, *e.g.*, California Family Law Code § 3409(a). If a state does not have local law that provides for protecting names and addresses, then Subsection (e) or a similar provision should be adopted. Subsection (e) is based on the National Council of Juvenile and Family Court Judge's, Model Code on Domestic and Family Violence § 304(c). There are other models to choose from, in particular UIFSA § 312.

In Subsection (a)(2), the term "proceedings" should be read broadly to include more than custody proceedings. Thus, if one parent was being criminally prosecuted for child abuse or custodial interference, those proceedings should be disclosed. If the child is subject to the Interstate Compact on the Placement of Children, facts relating to compliance with the Compact should be disclosed in the pleading or affidavit.

Subsection (b) has been added. It authorizes the court to stay the proceeding until the information required in Subsection (a) has been disclosed, although failure to provide the information does not deprive the court of jurisdiction to hear the case. This follows the majority of jurisdictions which held that failure to comply with the pleading requirements of the UCCJA did not deprive the court of jurisdiction to make a custody determination.

---

§ 152.210. Appearance of Parties and Child

(a) In a child custody proceeding in this state, the court may order a party to the proceeding who is in this state to appear before the court in person with or without the child. The court may order any person who is in this state and who has physical custody or control of the child to appear in person with the child.

(b) If a party to a child custody proceeding whose presence is desired by the court is outside this state, the court may order that a notice given pursuant to Section 152.108 include a statement directing the party to appear in person with or without the child and informing the party that failure to appear may result in a decision adverse to the party.

(c) The court may enter any orders necessary to ensure the safety of the child and of any person ordered to appear under this section.

(d) If a party to a child custody proceeding who is outside this state is directed to appear under Subsection (b) or desires to appear personally before the court with or without the child, the court may require another party to pay reasonable and necessary travel and other expenses of the party so appearing and of the child.

Commissioners' Comment

No major changes have been made to this section which was Section 11 of the UCCJA. Language was added to Subsection (a) to authorize the court to require a non-party who has physical custody of the child to produce the child.

Subsection (c) authorizes the court to enter orders providing for the safety of the child and the person ordered to appear with the child. If safety is a major concern, the court, as an alternative to ordering a party to appear with the child, could order and arrange for the party's testimony to be taken in another state under Section 111. This alternative might be important when there are safety concerns regarding requiring victims of domestic violence or child abuse to travel to the jurisdiction where the abuser resides.

SUBCHAPTER D. ENFORCEMENT

§ 152.301. Definitions

In this subchapter:

(1) "Petitioner" means a person who seeks enforcement of an order for return of a child under the Hague Convention on the Civil Aspects of International Child Abduction or enforcement of a child custody determination.

(2) "Respondent" means a person against whom a proceeding has been commenced for enforcement of an order for return of a child under the Hague Convention on the Civil Aspects of International Child Abduction or enforcement of a child custody determination.

Commissioners' Comment

For purposes of this article, "petitioner" and "respondent" are defined. The definitions clarify certain aspects of the notice and hearing sections.

§ 152.302. Enforcement Under Hague Convention

Under this subchapter a court of this state may enforce an order for the return of the child made under the Hague Convention on the Civil Aspects of International Child Abduction as if it were a child custody determination.

Commissioners' Comment

This section applies the enforcement remedies provided by this article to orders requiring the return of a child issued under the authority of the International Child Abduction Remedies Act (ICARA), 42 U.S.C. § 11601 *et seq.*, implementing the Hague Convention on the Civil Aspects of International Child Abduction. Specific mention of ICARA proceedings is necessary because they often occur prior to any formal custody determination. However, the need for a speedy enforcement remedy for an order to return the child is just as necessary.

§ 152.303. Duty to Enforce

(a) A court of this state shall recognize and enforce a child custody determination of a court of another state if the latter court exercised jurisdiction in substantial conformity with this chapter or the determination was made under factual circumstances meeting the jurisdictional standards of this chapter and the determination has not been modified in accordance with this chapter.

(b) A court of this state may utilize any remedy available under other law of this state to enforce a child custody determination made by a court of another state. The remedies provided in this subchapter are cumulative and do not affect the availability of other remedies to enforce a child custody determination.

Commissioners' Comment

This section is based on Section 13 of the UCCJA which contained the basic duty to enforce. The language of the original section has been retained and the duty to enforce is generally the same.

Enforcement of custody determinations of issuing states is also required by federal law in the PKPA, 28 U.S.C. § 1738A(a). The changes made in Article 2 of this Act now make a state's duty to enforce and not modify a child custody determination of another state consistent with the enforcement and nonmodification provisions of the PKPA. Therefore custody determinations made by a state pursuant to the UCCJA that would be enforceable under the PKPA will generally be enforced under this Act. However, if a state custody determination made pursuant to the UCCJA would not be enforceable under the PKPA, it will also not be enforceable under this Act. Thus a custody determination made by a "significant connection" jurisdiction when there is a home state is not enforceable under the PKPA regardless of whether a proceeding was ever commenced in the home state. Even though such a determination would be enforceable under the UCCJA with its four concurrent bases of jurisdiction, it would not be enforceable under this Act. This carries out the policy of the PKPA of strongly discouraging a state from exercising its concurrent "significant connection" jurisdiction under the UCCJA when another state could exercise "home state" jurisdiction.

This section also incorporates the concept of Section 15 of the UCCJA to the effect that a custody determination of another state will be enforced in the same manner as a custody determination made by a court of this state. Whatever remedies are available to enforce a local determination can be utilized to enforce a custody determination of another state. However, it remains a custody determination of the state that issued it. A child-custody determination of another state is not subject to modification unless the state would have jurisdiction to modify the determination under Article 2.

The remedies provided by this article for the enforcement of a custody determination will normally be used. This article does not detract from other remedies available under other local law. There is often a need for a number of remedies to ensure that a child-custody determination is obeyed. If other remedies would easily facilitate enforcement, they are still available. The petitioner, for example, can still cite the respondent for contempt of court or file a tort claim for intentional interference with custodial relations if those remedies are available under local law.

§ 152.304. Temporary Visitation

(a) A court of this state which does not have jurisdiction to modify a child custody determination may issue a temporary order enforcing:

(1) a visitation schedule made by a court of another state; or

(2) the visitation provisions of a child custody determination of another state that does not provide for a specific visitation schedule.

(b) If a court of this state makes an order under Subsection (a)(2), the court shall specify in the order a period that it considers adequate to allow the petitioner to obtain an order from a court having jurisdiction under the criteria specified in Subchapter C. The order remains in effect until an order is obtained from the other court or the period expires.

Commissioners' Comment

This section authorizes a court to issue a temporary order if it is necessary to enforce visitation rights without violating the rules on nonmodification contained in Section 303. Therefore, if there is a visitation schedule provided in the custody determination that was made in accordance with Article 2, a court can issue an order under this section implementing the schedule. An implementing order may include make-up or substitute visitation.

A court may also issue a temporary order providing for visitation if visitation was authorized in the custody determination, but no specific schedule was included in the custody determination. Such an order could include a substitution of a specific visitation schedule for "reasonable and seasonable."

However, a court may not, under Subsection (a)(2) provide for a permanent change in visitation. Therefore, requests for a permanent change in the visitation schedule must be addressed to the court with exclusive, continuing jurisdiction under Section 202 or modification jurisdiction under Section 203. As under Section 204, Subsection (b) of this section requires that the temporary visitation order stay in effect only long enough to allow the person who obtained the order to obtain a permanent modification in the state with appropriate jurisdiction under Article 2.

---

§ 152.305. Registration of Child Custody Determination

(a) A child custody determination issued by a court of another state may be registered in this state, with or without a simultaneous request for enforcement, by sending to the appropriate court in this state:

(1) a letter or other document requesting registration;

(2) two copies, including one certified copy, of the determination sought to be registered and a statement under penalty of perjury that to the best of the knowledge and belief of the person seeking registration the order has not been modified; and

(3) except as otherwise provided in Section 152.209, the name and address of the person seeking registration and any parent or person acting as a parent who has been awarded custody or visitation in the child custody determination sought to be registered.

(b) On receipt of the documents required by Subsection (a), the registering court shall:

(1) cause the determination to be filed as a foreign judgment, together with one copy of any accompanying documents and information, regardless of their form; and

(2) serve notice upon the persons named pursuant to Subsection (a)(3) and provide them with an opportunity to contest the registration in accordance with this section.

(c) The notice required by Subsection (b)(2) must state that:

(1) a registered determination is enforceable as of the date of the registration in the same manner as a determination issued by a court of this state;

(2) a hearing to contest the validity of the registered determination must be requested within 20 days after service of notice; and

(3) failure to contest the registration will result in confirmation of the child custody determination and preclude further contest of that determination with respect to any matter that could have been asserted.

(d) A person seeking to contest the validity of a registered order must request a hearing within 20 days after service of the notice. At that hearing, the court shall confirm the registered order unless the person contesting registration establishes that:

(1) the issuing court did not have jurisdiction under Subchapter C;

(2) the child custody determination sought to be registered has been vacated, stayed, or modified by a court having jurisdiction to do so under Subchapter C; or

(3) the person contesting registration was entitled to notice, but notice was not given in accordance with the standards of Section 152.108, in the proceedings before the court that issued the order for which registration is sought.

(e) If a timely request for a hearing to contest the validity of the registration is not made, the registration is confirmed as a matter of law and the person requesting registration and all persons served must be notified of the confirmation.

(f) Confirmation of a registered order, whether by operation of law or after notice and hearing, precludes further contest of the order with respect to any matter that could have been asserted at the time of registration.

Commissioners' Comment

The remainder of this article provides enforcement mechanisms for interstate child custody determinations.

This section authorizes a simple registration procedure that can be used to predetermine the enforceability of a custody determination. It parallels the process in UIFSA for the registration of child support orders. It should be as much of an aid to pro se litigants as the registration procedure of UIFSA.

A custody determination can be registered without any accompanying request for enforcement. This may be of significant assistance in international cases. For example, the custodial parent under a foreign custody order can receive an advance determination of whether that order would be recognized and enforced before sending the child to the United States for visitation. Article 26 of the 1996 Hague Convention on Jurisdiction, Applicable Law, Recognition and Cooperation in Respect of Parental Responsibility and Measures for the Protection of Children, 35 I.L.M. 1391 (1996), requires those states which accede to the Convention to provide such a procedure.

§ 152.306. Enforcement of Registered Determination

(a) A court of this state may grant any relief normally available under the law of this state to enforce a registered child custody determination made by a court of another state.

(b) A court of this state shall recognize and enforce, but may not modify, except in accordance with Subchapter C, a registered child custody determination of a court of another state.

Commissioners' Comment

A registered child-custody determination can be enforced as if it was a child-custody determination of this state. However, it remains a custody determination of the state that issued it. A registered custody order is not subject to modification unless the state would have jurisdiction to modify the order under Article 2.

§ 152.307. Simultaneous Proceedings

If a proceeding for enforcement under this subchapter is commenced in a court of this state and the court determines that a proceeding to modify the determination is pending in a court of another state having jurisdiction to modify the determination under Subchapter C, the enforcing court shall immediately communicate with the modifying court. The proceeding for enforcement continues unless the enforcing court, after consultation with the modifying court, stays or dismisses the proceeding.

Commissioners' Comment

The pleading rules of Section 308, require the parties to disclose any pending proceedings. Normally, an enforcement proceeding will take precedence over a modification action since the

PKPA requires enforcement of child custody determinations made in accordance with its terms. However, the enforcement court must communicate with the modification court in order to avoid duplicative litigation. The courts might decide that the court with jurisdiction under Article 2 shall continue with the modification action and stay the enforcement proceeding. Or they might decide that the enforcement proceeding shall go forward. The ultimate decision rests with the court having exclusive, continuing jurisdiction under Section 202, or if there is no state with exclusive, continuing jurisdiction, then the decision rests with the state that would have jurisdiction to modify under Section 203. Therefore, if that court determines that the enforcement proceeding should be stayed or dismissed, the enforcement court should stay or dismiss the proceeding. If the enforcement court does not do so, the court with exclusive, continuing jurisdiction under Section 202, or with modification jurisdiction under Section 203, could enjoin the parties from continuing with the enforcement proceeding.

---

§ 152.308. Expedited Enforcement of Child Custody Determination

(a) A petition under this subchapter must be verified. Certified copies of all orders sought to be enforced and of any order confirming registration must be attached to the petition. A copy of a certified copy of an order may be attached instead of the original.

(b) A petition for enforcement of a child custody determination must state:

(1) whether the court that issued the determination identified the jurisdictional basis it relied upon in exercising jurisdiction and, if so, what the basis was;

(2) whether the determination for which enforcement is sought has been vacated, stayed, or modified by a court whose decision must be enforced under this chapter and, if so, identify the court, the case number, and the nature of the proceeding;

(3) whether any proceeding has been commenced that could affect the current proceeding, including proceedings relating to domestic violence, protective orders, termination of parental rights, and adoptions and, if so, identify the court, the case number, and the nature of the proceeding;

(4) the present physical address of the child and the respondent, if known;

(5) whether relief in addition to the immediate physical custody of the child and attorney's fees is sought, including a request for assistance from law enforcement officials and, if so, the relief sought; and

(6) if the child custody determination has been registered and confirmed under Section 152.305, the date and place of registration.

(c) Upon the filing of a petition, the court shall issue an order directing the respondent to appear in person with or without the child at a hearing and may enter any order necessary to ensure the safety of the parties and the child. The hearing must be held on the next judicial day after service of the order unless that date is impossible. In that event, the court shall hold the hearing on the first judicial day possible. The court may extend the date of hearing at the request of the petitioner.

(d) An order issued under Subsection (c) must state the time and place of the hearing and advise the respondent that at the hearing the court will award the petitioner immediate physical custody of the child and order the payment of fees, costs, and expenses under Section 152.312, and may schedule a hearing to determine whether further relief is appropriate, unless the respondent appears and establishes that:

(1) the child custody determination has not been registered and confirmed under Section 152.305 and that:

(A) the issuing court did not have jurisdiction under Subchapter C;

(B) the child custody determination for which enforcement is sought has been vacated, stayed, or modified by a court having jurisdiction to do so under Subchapter C; or

(C) the respondent was entitled to notice, but notice was not given in accordance with the standards of Section 152.108, in the proceedings before the court that issued the order for which enforcement is sought; or

(2) the child custody determination for which enforcement is sought was registered and confirmed under Section 152.305, but has been vacated, stayed, or modified by a court of a state having jurisdiction to do so under Subchapter C.

Commissioners' Comment

This section provides the normal remedy that will be used in interstate cases: the production of the child in a summary, remedial process based on habeas corpus.

The petition is intended to provide the court with as much information as possible. Attaching certified copies of all orders sought to be enforced allows the court to have the necessary information. Most of the information relates to the permissible scope of the court's inquiry. The petitioner has the responsibility to inform the court of all proceedings that would affect the current enforcement action. Specific mention is made of certain proceedings to ensure that they are disclosed. A "procedure relating to domestic violence" includes not only protective order proceedings but also criminal prosecutions for child abuse or domestic violence.

The order requires the respondent to appear at a hearing on the next judicial day. The term "next judicial day" in this section means the next day when a judge is at the courthouse. At the hearing, the court will order the child to be delivered to the petitioner unless the respondent is prepared to assert that the issuing state lacked jurisdiction, that notice was not given in accordance with Section 108, or that the order sought to be enforced has been vacated, modified, or stayed by a court with jurisdiction to do so under Article 2. The court is also to order payment of the fees and expenses set out in Section 312. The court may set another hearing to determine whether additional relief available under this state's law should be granted.

If the order has been registered and confirmed in accordance with Section 304, the only defense to enforcement is that the order has been vacated, stayed or modified since the registration proceeding by a court with jurisdiction to do so under Article 2.

§ 152.309. Service of Petition and Order

Except as otherwise provided in Section 152.311, the petition and order must be served, by any method authorized by the law of this state, upon the respondent and any person who has physical custody of the child.

Commissioners' Comment

In keeping with other sections of this Act, the question of how the petition and order should be served is left to local law.

§ 152.310. Hearing and Order

(a) Unless the court issues a temporary emergency order pursuant to Section 152.204, upon a finding that a petitioner is entitled to immediate physical custody of the child, the court shall order that the petitioner may take immediate physical custody of the child unless the respondent establishes that:

(1) the child custody determination has not been registered and confirmed under Section 152.305 and that:

(A) the issuing court did not have jurisdiction under Subchapter C;

(B) the child custody determination for which enforcement is sought has been vacated, stayed, or modified by a court of a state having jurisdiction to do so under Subchapter C; or

(C) the respondent was entitled to notice, but notice was not given in accordance with the standards of Section 152.108, in the proceedings before the court that issued the order for which enforcement is sought; or

(2) the child custody determination for which enforcement is sought was registered and confirmed under Section 152.305 but has been vacated, stayed, or modified by a court of a state having jurisdiction to do so under Subchapter C.

(b) The court shall award the fees, costs, and expenses authorized under Section 152.312 and may grant additional relief, including a request for the assistance of law enforcement officials, and set a further hearing to determine whether additional relief is appropriate.

(c) If a party called to testify refuses to answer on the ground that the testimony may be self-incriminating, the court may draw an adverse inference from the refusal.

(d) A privilege against disclosure of communications between spouses and a defense of immunity based on the relationship of husband and wife or parent and child may not be invoked in a proceeding under this subchapter.

Commissioners' Comment

The scope of inquiry for the enforcing court is quite limited. Federal law requires the court to enforce the custody determination if the issuing state's decree was rendered in compliance with the PKPA. 28 U.S.C. § 1738A(a). This Act requires enforcement of custody determinations that are made in conformity with Article 2's jurisdictional rules.

The certified copy, or a copy of the certified copy, of the custody determination entitling the petitioner to the child is prima facie evidence of the issuing court's jurisdiction to enter the order. If the order is one that is entitled to be enforced under Article 2 and if it has been violated, the burden shifts to the respondent to show that the custody determination is not entitled to enforcement.

It is a defense to enforcement that another jurisdiction has issued a custody determination that is required to be enforced under Article 2. An example is when one court has based its original custody determination on the UCCJA § 3(a)(2) (significant connections) and another jurisdiction has rendered an original custody determination based on the UCCJA § 3(a)(1) (home state). When this occurs, Article 2 of this Act, as well as the PKPA, mandate that the home state determination be enforced in all other states, including the state that rendered the significant connections determination.

Lack of notice in accordance with Section 108 by a person entitled to notice and opportunity to be heard at the original custody determination is a defense to enforcement of the custody determination. The scope of the defense under this Act is the same as the defense would be under the law of the state that issued the notice. Thus, if the defense of lack of notice would not be available under local law if the respondent purposely hid from the petitioner, took deliberate steps to avoid service of process or elected not to participate in the initial proceedings, the defense would also not be available under this Act.

There are no other defenses to an enforcement action. If the child would be endangered by the enforcement of a custody or visitation order, there may be a basis for the assumption of emergency jurisdiction under Section 204 of this Act. Upon the finding of an emergency, the court issues a temporary order and directs the parties to proceed either in the court that is exercising continuing jurisdiction over the custody proceeding under Section 202, or the court that would have jurisdiction to modify the custody determination under Section 203.

The court shall determine at the hearing whether fees should be awarded under Section 312. If so, it should order them paid. The court may determine if additional relief is appropriate, including requesting law enforcement officers to assist the petitioner in the enforcement of the order. The court may set a hearing to determine whether further relief should be granted.

The remainder of this section is derived from UIFSA § 316 with regard to the privilege of self-incrimination, spousal privileges, and immunities. It is included to keep parallel the procedures for child support and child custody proceedings to the extent possible.

§ 152.311. Warrant to Take Physical Custody of Child

(a) Upon the filing of a petition seeking enforcement of a child custody determination, the petitioner may file a verified application for the issuance of a warrant to take physical custody of the child if the child is imminently likely to suffer serious physical harm or be removed from this state.

(b) If the court, upon the testimony of the petitioner or other witness, finds that the child is imminently likely to suffer serious physical harm or be removed from this state, it may issue a warrant to take physical custody of the child. The petition must be heard on the next judicial day after the warrant is executed unless that date is impossible. In that event, the court shall hold the hearing on the first judicial day possible. The application for the warrant must include the statements required by Section 152.308(b).

(c) A warrant to take physical custody of a child must:

(1) recite the facts upon which a conclusion of imminent serious physical harm or removal from the jurisdiction is based;

(2) direct law enforcement officers to take physical custody of the child immediately; ~~and~~

(3) **state the date for the hearing on the petition; and**

(4) **provide for the safe interim placement of the child pending further order of the court and impose conditions on placement of the child to ensure the appearance of the child and the child's custodian** ~~provide for the placement of the child pending final relief~~.

(c–1) If the petition seeks to enforce a child custody determination made in a foreign country or an order for the return of the child made under the Hague Convention on the Civil Aspects of International Child Abduction, the court may place a child with a parent or family member in accordance with Subsection (c)(4) only if the parent or family member has significant ties to the jurisdiction of the court. If a parent or family member of the child does not have significant ties to the jurisdiction of the court, the court shall provide for the delivery of the child to the Department of Family and Protective Services in the manner provided for the delivery of a missing child by Section 262.007(c).

(d) The respondent must be served with the petition, warrant, and order immediately after the child is taken into physical custody.

(e) A warrant to take physical custody of a child is enforceable throughout this state. If the court finds on the basis of the testimony of the petitioner or other witness that a less intrusive remedy is not effective, it may authorize law enforcement officers to enter private property to take physical custody of the child. If required by exigent circumstances of the case, the court may authorize law enforcement officers to make a forcible entry at any hour.

~~(f) The court may impose conditions upon placement of a child to ensure the appearance of the child and the child's custodian.~~

Amended by Acts 2011, 82nd Leg., ch. 92 (S.B. 1490), §§ 2, 4, eff. Sept. 1, 2011.

Commissioners' Comment

The section provides a remedy for emergency situations where there is a reason to believe that the child will suffer imminent, serious physical harm or be removed from the jurisdiction once the respondent learns that the petitioner has filed an enforcement proceeding. If the court finds such harm exists, it should temporarily waive the notice requirements and issue a warrant to take physical custody of the child. Immediately after the warrant is executed, the respondent is to receive notice of the proceedings.

The term "harm" cannot be totally defined and, as in the issuance of temporary restraining orders, the appropriate issuance of a warrant is left to the circumstances of the case. Those circumstances include cases where the respondent is the subject of a criminal proceeding as well as situations where the respondent is secreting the child in violation of a court order, abusing the child, a flight risk and other circumstances that the court concludes make the issuance of notice a danger to the child. The court must hear the testimony of the petitioner or another witness prior to issuing the warrant. The testimony may be heard in person, via telephone, or by any other means acceptable under local law. The court must state the reasons for the issuance of the warrant. The warrant can be enforced by law enforcement officers wherever the child is found in the state. The warrant may authorize entry upon private property to pick up the child if no less intrusive means are possible. In extraordinary cases, the warrant may authorize law enforcement to make a forcible entry at any hour.

The warrant must provide for the placement of the child pending the determination of the enforcement proceeding. Since the issuance of the warrant would not occur absent a risk of serious harm to the child, placement cannot be with the respondent. Normally, the child would be placed with the petitioner. However, if placement with the petitioner is not indicated, the court can order any other appropriate placement authorized under the laws of the court's state. Placement with the petitioner may not be indicated if there is a likelihood that the petitioner also will flee the jurisdiction. Placement with the petitioner may not be practical if the petitioner is proceeding through an attorney and is not present before the court.

This section authorizes the court to utilize whatever means are available under local law to ensure the appearance of the petitioner and child at the enforcement hearing. Such means might include cash bonds, a surrender of a passport, or whatever the court determines is necessary.

§ 152.312. Costs, Fees, and Expenses

(a) The court shall award the prevailing party, including a state, necessary and reasonable expenses incurred by or on behalf of the party, including costs, communication expenses, attorney's fees, investigative fees, expenses for witnesses, travel expenses, and child care during the course of the proceedings, unless the party from whom fees or expenses are sought establishes that the award would be clearly inappropriate.

(b) The court may not assess fees, costs, or expenses against a state unless authorized by law other than this chapter.

Commissioners' Comment

This section is derived from the International Child Abduction Remedies Act, 42 U.S.C. § 11607(b)(3). Normally the court will award fees and costs against the non-prevailing party. Included as expenses are the amount of investigation fees incurred by private persons or by public officials as well as the cost of child placement during the proceedings.

The non-prevailing party has the burden of showing that such an award would be clearly inappropriate. Fees and costs may be inappropriate if their payment would cause the parent and child to seek public assistance.

This section implements the policies of Section 8(c) of Pub. L. 96–611 (part of the PKPA) which provides that:

> In furtherance of the purposes of section 1738A of title 28, United States Code [this section], as added by Subsection (a) of this section, state courts are encouraged to—
>
> (2) award to the person entitled to custody or visitation pursuant to a custody determination which is consistent with the provisions of such section 1738A [this section], necessary travel expenses, attorneys' fees, costs of private investigations, witness fees or expenses, and other expenses incurred in connection with such custody determination....

The term "prevailing party" is not given a special definition for this Act. Each state will apply its own standard.

Subsection (b) was added to ensure that this section would not apply to the state unless otherwise authorized. The language is taken from UIFSA § 313 (court may assess costs against obligee or support enforcement agency only if allowed by local law).

§ 152.313. Recognition and Enforcement

A court of this state shall accord full faith and credit to an order issued by another state and consistent with this chapter which enforces a child custody determination by a court of another state unless the order has been vacated, stayed, or modified by a court having jurisdiction to do so under Subchapter C.

Commissioners' Comment

The enforcement order, to be effective, must also be enforced by other states. This section requires courts of this state to enforce and not modify enforcement orders issued by other states when made consistently with the provisions of this Act.

§ 152.314. Appeals

An appeal may be taken from a final order in a proceeding under this subchapter in accordance with expedited appellate procedures in other civil cases. Unless the court enters a temporary emergency order under Section 152.204, the enforcing court may not stay an order enforcing a child custody determination pending appeal.

Commissioners' Comment

The order may be appealed as an expedited civil matter. An enforcement order should not be stayed by the court. Provisions for a stay would defeat the purpose of having a quick enforcement procedure. If there is a risk of serious mistreatment or abuse to the child, a petition to assume emergency jurisdiction must be filed under Section 204. This section leaves intact the possibility of obtaining an extraordinary remedy such as mandamus or prohibition from an appellate court to stay the court's enforcement action. In many states, it is not possible to limit the constitutional authority of appellate courts to issue a stay. However, unless the information before the appellate panel indicates that emergency jurisdiction would be assumed under Section 204, there is no reason to stay the enforcement of the order pending appeal.

§ 152.315. Role of Prosecutor or Public Official

(a) In a case arising under this chapter or involving the Hague Convention on the Civil Aspects of International Child Abduction, the prosecutor or other appropriate public official may take any lawful action, including resorting to a proceeding under this subchapter or any other available civil proceeding to locate a child, obtain the return of a child, or enforce a child custody determination if there is:

(1) an existing child custody determination;

(2) a request to do so from a court in a pending child custody proceeding;

(3) a reasonable belief that a criminal statute has been violated; or

(4) a reasonable belief that the child has been wrongfully removed or retained in violation of the Hague Convention on the Civil Aspects of International Child Abduction.

(b) A prosecutor or appropriate public official acting under this section acts on behalf of the court and may not represent any party.

Commissioners' Comment

Sections 315–317 are derived from the recommendations of the *Obstacles Study* that urge a role for public authorities in civil enforcement of custody and visitation determinations. One of the basic policies behind this approach is that, as is the case with child support, the involvement of public authorities will encourage the parties to abide by the terms of the court order. The prosecutor usually would be the most appropriate public official to exercise authority under this section. However, states may locate the authority described in the section in the most appropriate public office for their governmental structure. The authority could be, for example, the Friend of the Court Office or the Attorney General. If the parties know that prosecutors and law enforcement officers are available to help secure the return of a child, the parties may be deterred from interfering with the exercise of rights established by court order.

The use of public authorities should provide a more effective method of remedying violations of the custody determination. Most parties do not have the resources to enforce a custody determination in another jurisdiction. The availability of the prosecutor or other government official as an enforcement agency will help ensure that remedies of this Act can be made available regardless of income level. In addition, the prosecutor may have resources to draw on that are unavailable to the average litigant.

The role of the public authorities should generally not begin until there is a custody determination that is sought to be enforced. The Act does not authorize the public authorities to be involved in the action leading up to the making of the custody determination, except when requested by the court, when there is a violation the Hague Convention on the Civil Aspects of International Child Abduction, or when the person holding the child has violated a criminal statute. This Act does not mandate that the public authorities be involved in all cases referred to it. There is only so much time and money available for enforcement proceedings. Therefore, the public authorities eventually will develop guidelines to determine which cases will receive priority.

The use of civil procedures instead of, or in addition to, filing and prosecuting criminal charges enlarges the prosecutor's options and may provide a more economical and less disruptive means of solving problems of criminal abduction and retention. With the use of criminal proceedings alone, the procedure may be inadequate to ensure the return of the child. The civil options would permit the prosecutor to resolve that recurring and often frustrating problem.

A concern was expressed about whether allowing the prosecutor to use civil means as a method of settling a child abduction violated either DR 7—105(A) of the Code of Professional Responsibility or Model Rule of Professional Responsibility 4.4. Both provisions either explicitly or implicitly disapprove of a lawyer threatening criminal action to gain an advantage in a civil case. However, the prohibition relates to threats that are solely to gain an advantage in a civil case. If the prosecutor has a good faith reason for pursuing the criminal action, there is no ethical violation. *See Committee on Legal Ethics v. Printz*, 416 S.E. 2d 720 (W.Va. 1992) (lawyer can threaten to press criminal charges against a client's former employee unless employee made restitution).

It must be emphasized that the public authorities do not become involved in the merits of the case. They are authorized only to locate the child and enforce the custody determination. The public authority is authorized by this section to utilize any civil proceeding to secure the enforcement of the custody determination. In most jurisdictions, that would be a proceeding under this Act. If the prosecutor proceeds pursuant to this Act, the prosecutor is subject to its provisions. There is nothing in this Act that would prevent a state from authorizing the prosecutor or other public official to use additional remedies beyond those provided in this Act.

The public authority does not represent any party to the custody determination. It acts as a "friend of the court." Its role is to ensure that the custody determination is enforced.

Sections 315–317 are limited to cases covered by this Act, i.e. interstate cases. However, states may, if they wish, extend this part of the Act to intrastate cases.

It should also be noted that the provisions of this section relate to the civil enforcement of child custody determinations. Nothing in this section is meant to detract from the ability of the prosecutor to use criminal provisions in child abduction cases.

§ 152.316. Role of Law Enforcement

At the request of a prosecutor or other appropriate public official acting under Section 152.315, a law enforcement officer may take any lawful action reasonably necessary to locate a child or a party and assist a prosecutor or appropriate public official with responsibilities under Section 152.315.

Commissioners' Comment

This section authorizes law enforcement officials to assist in locating a child and enforcing a custody determination when requested to do so by the public authorities. It is to be read as an enabling provision. Whether law enforcement officials have discretion in responding to a request by the prosecutor or other public official is a matter of local law.

§ 152.317. Costs and Expenses

If the respondent is not the prevailing party, the court may assess against the respondent all direct expenses and costs incurred by the prosecutor or other appropriate public official and law enforcement officers under Section 152.315 or 152.316.

Commissioners' Comment

One of the major problems of utilizing public officials to locate children and enforce custody and visitation determinations is cost. This section authorizes the prosecutor and law enforcement to recover costs against the non-prevailing party. The use of the term "direct" indicates that overhead is not a recoverable cost. This section cannot be used to recover the value of the time spent by the public authorities' attorneys.

CHAPTER 153. CONSERVATORSHIP, POSSESSION, AND ACCESS

SUBCHAPTER A. GENERAL PROVISIONS

SUBCHAPTER B. PARENT APPOINTED AS CONSERVATOR: IN GENERAL

SUBCHAPTER C. PARENT APPOINTED AS SOLE OR JOINT MANAGING CONSERVATOR

SUBCHAPTER D. PARENT APPOINTED AS POSSESSORY CONSERVATOR

SUBCHAPTER E. GUIDELINES FOR THE POSSESSION OF A CHILD BY A PARENT NAMED AS POSSESSORY CONSERVATOR

SUBCHAPTER F. STANDARD POSSESSION ORDER

SUBCHAPTER G. APPOINTMENT OF NONPARENT AS CONSERVATOR

SUBCHAPTER H. RIGHTS OF GRANDPARENT, AUNT, OR UNCLE

SUBCHAPTER I. PREVENTION OF INTERNATIONAL PARENTAL CHILD ABDUCTION

SUBCHAPTER J. RIGHTS OF SIBLINGS

SUBCHAPTER K. PARENTING PLAN, PARENTING COORDINATOR, AND PARENTING FACILITATOR

SUBCHAPTER L. MILITARY DUTY

Introductory Comment

Chapter 153 is the primary source of substantive law for a SAPCR involving litigation between the parents of a child. It undoubtedly is the most important, and most contested chapter in private litigation. Subchapter A provides the major guiding principles for the issues of sole and joint managing conservatorship, possessory conservatorship, and possession of and access to the child, a.k.a., custody and visitation. Effective January 1, 1974, original Chapter 14 of the newly minted Title 2 of Texas Family Code contained but six sections on four pages creating and dealing with conservatorship. Chapter 14 also contained four more sections on three pages to cover child support, modification, enforcement, and habeas corpus. Over the last 35 years magnitudes of expansion have occurred with detailed specificity as Title 2 morphed into Titles 4 and 5. Insofar as private litigation is concerned, this is best illustrated by the attention paid to the exercise and enforcement of the rights and duties of the noncustodial parent, whether denominated as the possessory conservator or as a joint managing conservator. As a practical matter, if both parents are fit, or perhaps rather if each parent is not unfit, beginning in 1995 the title routinely given to each parent is joint managing conservator (JMC). In short, litigation between the parents is over rights and duties of each JMC. Distinguishing between parents as a sole managing conservator and a possessory conservator is passé.

During this century the march of statutory micromanagement has not abated. It can be measured by the creation of new methods or new subchapters dealing with aspects of decision making. The 2001 addition of Collaborative Law, Section 153.0072, has had a significant impact on the practice of family law. Less crucial, in 2003, Subchapter I was enacted in an attempt to prevent international parental child abduction, and in 2005, Subchapter J dealt with the rights of a sibling when siblings are separated by an action of the Department of Family and Protective Services. That same year, however, now-Subchapter K was enacted to require parents to think through and develop a parenting plan designed to minimize future litigation between the parents. Moreover, a role for a "parenting coordinator" was created to assist the parties in reaching an agreement. Apparently 2007 was an off-year because no additional subchapter was created. In 2009, the legislature got back on track by creating Subchapter L, which establishes very detailed rights and duties when a parent is in the U.S. armed forces and the servicemember's family is affected by a military assignment that interferes with the rights and duties assigned to that parent by an existing court order. The 81st legislature also came to grips with the considerable controversy generated by Subchapter K, which had gone unresolved in 2007. The 2009 session saw extensive amendments of the parenting plan established in Subchapter K, not coincidentally adding the role of "parenting facilitator."

CLE/Other Legal Publications

Possession and access for children under three. Diana S. Friedman, 2011 Adv. Fam. L.

Issues for the disabled or special needs child. Keith D. Maples, 2011 Adv. Fam. L.

Rights, powers and duties of conservators. Richard L. Robertson, 2011 Marriage Dissolution

Strategies for proving best interest. Chris Nickelson & Judy L. Warne, 2011 U.T. Advanced Parent-Child Relationships

Trial tactics and evidence. Joseph Indelicato, Jr. & Robert J. Kern, 2011 U.T. Advanced Parent-Child Relationships

Conservatorship and presumptions: the starting line. Jonathan J. Bates, 2011 U.T. Fam. L. Front Lines

Trial tactics and evidence. Joseph Indelicato, Jr. & Robert J. Kern, 2011 U.T. Advanced Parent-Child Relationships

Parent coordination and facilitation. Christy Bradshaw Schmidt & Jody L. Johnson, 2011 U.T. Fam. L. Front Lines

Child custody case law update. Sallee S. Smyth, 2011 Marriage Dissolution

The impact of domestic violence on a divorce. Doug Warne, Scott A. Beauchamp & Judith G. Wells, 2011 Marriage Dissolution

Possession and access to children under the age of three. Diana S. Friedman & Jonathan Gould, 2011 Marriage Dissolution

Factors to consider with special needs children during divorce. Lisa M. Walker, 2011 Marriage Dissolution

Procedural concerns: commonly overlooked rules. Chris Nickelson, 2011 U.T. Parent-Child Relationships: Basics

Conservatorship and Possession: Primer on JMC, sole MC, and parenting time. Patricia N. Carter, 2011 U.T. Parent-Child Relationships: Basics

Evidentiary concerns: commonly overlooked rules of evidence in SAPCR's. Jack W. Marr, 2011 U.T. Parent-Child Relationships: Basics

Plutoed parents: preventing and overcoming parental alienation. Diana S. Friedman & Richard Warshak, 2011 U.T. Fam. L. Front Lines

Conservatorship and presumptions: the starting line. Jonathan J. Bates, 2011 U.T. Fam. L. Front Lines

Parent coordination and facilitation. Christy Bradshaw Schmidt & Jody L. Johnson, 2011 U.T. Fam. L. Front Lines

Strategies for proving best interest. Chris Nickelson & Judy L. Warne, 2011 U.T. Advanced Parent-Child Relationships

SAPCR caselaw update. Eva Guzman, 2010 Adv. Fam. L.

Cases involving foreign nationals. Larry H. Schwartz, 2010 Adv. Fam. L.

Trying the SAPCR case on a shoestring. Cynthia J. Barela Graham, 2010 Adv. Fam. L.

SAPCR's for same sex partners. Barbara D. Nunneley, 2010 Adv. Fam. L.

Keeping up with the kiddos: case law update. Sallee S. Smyth, 2010 Marriage Dissolution

Creative possession schedules. Kimberly M. Naylor & Stephen J. Naylor, 2010 Adv. Fam. L. Drafting

Dealing with ethnic and religious issues in a SAPCR. Laura D. Dale, 2010 U.T. Parent-Child Relationships

Preparing for trial—children's issues. Charlotte D. Rainwater, 2010 So. Tex. Fam. L. Conf.

Final trial. Mike Gregory, 2010 Fam. L. Boot Camp

See Accompanying CD–ROM for Additional CLE/Other Legal Publications.

Cross Reference

TX FCA Penal § 25.03. Interference with Child Custody, *infra*.

SUBCHAPTER A. GENERAL PROVISIONS

§ 153.001. Public Policy

(a) The public policy of this state is to:

(1) assure that children will have frequent and continuing contact with parents who have shown the ability to act in the best interest of the child;

(2) provide a safe, stable, and nonviolent environment for the child; and

(3) encourage parents to share in the rights and duties of raising their child after the parents have separated or dissolved their marriage.

(b) A court may not render an order that conditions the right of a conservator to possession of or access to a child on the payment of child support.

Comment

Subsection (b) codifies the court-originated rule that support and custody are independent rights and duties.

Leading Case

In re A.N.H., 70 S.W.3d 918 (Tex. App.—Amarillo 2002, no pet.) (support order conditioned on obligor's right to visitation violates public policy and is void)

§ 153.002. Best Interest of Child

The best interest of the child shall always be the primary consideration of the court in determining the issues of conservatorship and possession of and access to the child.

Comment

This is the most quoted section in the Family Code. However, it does not provide much guidance to predict the outcome of a case. Discretion of the trial court is extraordinarily broad; "best interest" is in the eye of the beholder, the trier of fact, judge or jury.

CLE/Other Legal Publications

Strategies for proving best interest. Chris Nickelson & Judy L. Warne, 2011 U.T. Advanced Parent–Child Relationships

Trial tactics and evidence. Joseph Indelicato, Jr. & Robert J. Kern, 2011 U.T. Advanced Parent–Child Relationships

Leading Cases

Holley v. Adams, 544 S.W.2d 367 (Tex. 1976) (factors in "best interest" listed in a private termination of parental rights case, not a custody case; on 6/01/11 a Westlaw search of "tx cs-all" found *Holley* had been cited in 886 documents)

Gillespie v. Gillespie, 644 S.W.2d 449 (Tex. 1982) (trial court determination of best interest reversible only if court abused its discretion)

Bukovich v. Bukovich, 399 S.W.2d 528 (Tex. 1966) (desires, acts and claims of parents secondary consideration to best interest of the child)

In re S.K., 198 S.W.3d 899 (Tex. App.—Dallas 2006, rev. denied) (love is not enough to offset bad parenting)

Rogers v. DFPS, 175 S.W.3d 370 (Tex. App.—Houston [1st Dist.] 2005, rev. dismissed) (jury charge containing best interest factors not abuse of discretion)

In re K.L.R., 162 S.W.3d 291 (Tex. App.—Tyler 2005, no pet.) (evidence of arrests was admissible on best interest issue)

Coleman v. Coleman, 109 S.W.3d 108 (Tex. App.—Austin 2003, no pet.) (clear and compelling reasons must be articulated by trial court to affirm splitting custody of siblings)

Edwards v. Edwards, 79 S.W.3d 88 (Tex. App.—Texarkana 2002, no pet.) (trial court directed to explain "best interest" finding to appellate court when naming father sole managing conservator)

Lohmann v. Lohmann, 62 S.W.3d 875 (Tex. App.—El Paso 2001, no pet.) (court with jurisdiction over child has duty to exercise equitable powers to make proper disposition of all matters; therefore, technical rules of pleading and practice of little importance in determining child custody issues)

---

§ 153.003. No Discrimination Based on Sex or Marital Status

The court shall consider the qualifications of the parties without regard to their marital status or to the sex of the party or the child in determining:

(1) which party to appoint as sole managing conservator;

(2) whether to appoint a party as joint managing conservator; and

(3) the terms and conditions of conservatorship and possession of and access to the child.

Comment

When the court or jury is called upon to decide issues of conservatorship and possession of and access to a child, the legal equality of the parents is now well-established (at least in the statutory law) with regard to their sex or marital status. Gone are the days when, under certain fact situations, either the mother or the father was automatically presumed to be the best choice for custody. Decreeing that unmarried parents should also be treated equally in custody matters is of somewhat more recent vintage, i.e., something that did not receive statutory recognition in Texas until 1995.

---

§ 153.004. History of Domestic Violence

(a) In determining whether to appoint a party as a sole or joint managing conservator, the court shall consider evidence of the intentional use of abusive physical force by a party against the party's spouse, a parent of the child, or any person younger than 18 years of age committed within a two-year period preceding the filing of the suit or during the pendency of the suit.

(b) The court may not appoint joint managing conservators if credible evidence is presented of a history or pattern of past or present child neglect, or physical or sexual abuse by one parent directed against the other parent, a spouse, or a child, including a sexual assault in violation of Section 22.011 or 22.021, Penal Code, that results in the other parent becoming pregnant with the child. A history of sexual abuse includes a sexual assault that results in the other parent becoming pregnant with the child, regardless of the prior relationship of the parents. It is a rebuttable presumption that the appointment of a parent as the sole managing conservator of a child or as the conservator who has the exclusive right to determine the primary residence of a child is not in the best interest of the child if credible evidence is presented of a history or pattern of past or present child neglect, or physical or sexual abuse by that parent directed against the other parent, a spouse, or a child.

(c) The court shall consider the commission of family violence in determining whether to deny, restrict, or limit the possession of a child by a parent who is appointed as a possessory conservator.

(d) The court may not allow a parent to have access to a child for whom it is shown by a preponderance of the evidence that there is a history or pattern of committing family violence during the two years preceding the date of the filing of the suit or during the pendency of the suit, unless the court:

(1) finds that awarding the parent access to the child would not endanger the child's physical health or emotional welfare and would be in the best interest of the child; and

(2) renders a possession order that is designed to protect the safety and well-being of the child and any other person who has been a victim of family violence committed by the parent and that may include a requirement that:

(A) the periods of access be continuously supervised by an entity or person chosen by the court;

(B) the exchange of possession of the child occur in a protective setting;

(C) the parent abstain from the consumption of alcohol or a controlled substance, as defined by Chapter 481, Health and Safety Code, within 12 hours prior to or during the period of access to the child; or

(D) the parent attend and complete a battering intervention and prevention program as provided by Article 42.141, Code of Criminal Procedure, or, if such a program is not available, complete a course of treatment under Section 153.010.

(e) It is a rebuttable presumption that it is not in the best interest of a child for a parent to have unsupervised visitation with the child if credible evidence is presented of a history or pattern of past or present child neglect or physical or sexual abuse by that parent directed against the other parent, a spouse, or a child.

(f) In determining under this section whether there is credible evidence of a history or pattern of past or present child neglect or physical or sexual abuse by a parent directed against the other parent, a spouse, or a child, the court shall consider whether a protective order was rendered under Chapter 85, Title 4, against the parent during the two-year period preceding the filing of the suit or during the pendency of the suit.

Comment

The test for whether there is "credible evidence of a history or pattern of past or present child neglect or physical or sexual abuse by a parent" previously has been left to a case by case determination by the court. Subsection (f) provides a nonexclusive test regarding whether such a history exists. That is, whether a protective order was rendered against the respondent in the preceding two year period. Arguably, rendition of a single protective order within the past two years is not necessarily proof of a "pattern," but it surely is a good start on proof of a "history."

CLE/Other Legal Publications

Protective orders. Sally H. Emerson, 2011 Adv. Fam. L.

Protective orders: who needs them and how to get them. Carlos Guillermo Salinas, 2011 U.T. Fam. L. Front Lines

Protective orders: the nuts and bolts. Lynn Bradshaw-Hull, 2011 So. Tex. Fam. L.

Family violence protective orders: collateral consequences—civil and criminal. Frederick S. Adams, Jr., 2010 Adv. Fam. L.

Domestic violence and protective orders. Judy L. Warne, 2010 Adv. Fam. L. Drafting

The impact of domestic violence on the child: understanding the impact of domestic violence on the child as it effects development of the legal case. Jeana Lungwitz, 2009 Adv. Fam. L.

See Accompanying CD-ROM for Additional CLE/Other Legal Publications.

11/20

Leading Cases

Peña v. Peña, 8 S.W.3d 639 (Tex. 1999) (major issue of physical abuse or history or pattern of domestic violence is not dependent on its cause, but on whether it happened)

Lewelling v. Lewelling, 796 S.W.2d 164 (Tex. 1990) (preferences for nonviolent parent; since abuser cannot take advantage of abuse, neither can the abuser's parents)

Anderson v. Rogers, 247 S.W.3d 757 (Tex. App.—Dallas 2008, no pet.) (issuance of protective order is to be considered in determining managing conservatorship, but is not completely dispositive)

In re D.R., 177 S.W.3d 574 (Tex. App.—Houston [1st Dist.] 2005, no pet.) (jury charge improper to suggest that father could not be sole MC if history of family violence in his home)

In re R.T.H., 175 S.W.3d 519 (Tex. App.—Fort Worth 2005, no pet.) (family violence incident by JMC/mother did not justify modification of primary residence to JMC/father)

Burns v. Burns, 116 S.W.3d 916 (Tex. App.—Dallas 2003, no pet.) (family violence rebuts joint managing conservatorship presumption)

In re J.R.P., 55 S.W.3d 147 (Tex. App.—Corpus Christi 2001, pet. denied) (consider whether a potential family for placement has a history of physical and substance abuse, and whether others with access to the home pose a physical threat to the children)

11/20/12

§ 153.005. Appointment of Sole or Joint Managing Conservator

(a) In a suit, the court may appoint a sole managing conservator or may appoint joint managing conservators. If the parents are or will be separated, the court shall appoint at least one managing conservator.

(b) A managing conservator must be a parent, a competent adult, an authorized agency, or a licensed child-placing agency.

11/20/12

§ 153.006. Appointment of Possessory Conservator

(a) If a managing conservator is appointed, the court may appoint one or more possessory conservators.

(b) The court shall specify the rights and duties of a person appointed possessory conservator.

(c) The court shall specify and expressly state in the order the times and conditions for possession of or access to the child, unless a party shows good cause why specific orders would not be in the best interest of the child.

§ 153.007. Agreed Parenting Plan

(a) To promote the amicable settlement of disputes between the parties to a suit, the parties may enter into a written agreed parenting plan containing provisions for conservatorship and possession of the child and for modification of the parenting plan, including variations from the standard possession order.

(b) If the court finds that the agreed parenting plan is in the child's best interest, the court shall render an order in accordance with the parenting plan.

(c) Terms of the agreed parenting plan contained in the order or incorporated by reference regarding conservatorship or support of or access to a child in an order may be enforced by all remedies available for enforcement of a judgment, including contempt, but are not enforceable as a contract.

(d) If the court finds the agreed parenting plan is not in the child's best interest, the court may request the parties to submit a revised parenting plan. If the parties do not submit a revised parenting plan satisfactory to the court, the court may, after notice and hearing, order a parenting plan that the court finds to be in the best interest of the child.

Comment

Originally derived from the Uniform Marriage and Divorce Act, this section long bedeviled Texas lawyers. Prior to September 1, 1995, the Law of Contracts applied to an agreement concerning conservatorship, while the Law of Judgments applied to a court decree. Remedial actions available to a dissatisfied party could vary, depending on whether a contract or a judgment was involved. But since that date, Subsection (c) places all remedies under the aegis of the Law of Judgments. *See* comment to Section 154.124. Contracts entered into before September 1, 1995 remain enforceable on that basis, but should all expire in the next few years.

CLE/Other Legal Publications

Finalizing the deal: Rule 11 and the importance of getting orders timely signed. Chris Nickelson & Gary L. Nickelson, 2010 Marriage Dissolution

Negotiation techniques for getting the case settled. Larry H. Schwartz, 2010 Marriage Dissolution

The new parent coordination/facilitation statute: what's in, what's out? Christy Bradshaw Schmidt & Diana S. Friedman, 2010 Marriage Dissolution

Negotiation and parenting issues: Do your clients know what you think they know? Principles and strategies to help clients in difficult negotiations. Mark R. Otis, 2009 Adv. Fam. L.

Negotiation workshop. Guhan Subramanian, 2009 Adv. Fam. L.

Negotiation: How to get the most marbles for your client. Guhan Subramanian, 2009 Adv. Fam. L.

Techniques in negotiation. Christopher K. Wrampelmeier, 2009 Marriage Dissolution

Leading Cases

Elfeldt v. Elfeldt, 730 S.W.2d 657 (Tex. 1987) (agreement must specify terms to be enforceable as contract) (apparently overruled by statute)

Ex parte Gorena, 595 S.W.2d 841 (Tex. 1979) (agreement incorporated in decree enforceable as judgment)

Beyers v. Roberts, 199 S.W.3d 354 (Tex. App.—Houston [1st Dist.] 2006, rev. denied) (requirement to enforce mediated settlement agreement trumps § 153.133 requirements of certain terms to be included in JMC agreements)

In re Burtch, 972 S.W.2d 882 (Tex. App.—Austin 1998, no pet.) (agreement to pay college expenses enforceable as a contract, not to be confused with child support)

Stein v. Stein, 868 S.W.2d 902 (Tex. App.—Houston [14th Dist.] 1994, no writ) (wife timely withdrew consent to settlement agreement given to associate judge)

Hill v. Hill, 819 S.W.2d 570 (Tex. App.—Dallas 1991, writ denied) (public policy prohibits enforcement of contracts seeking to fix child support permanently); *see also* Hibler v. Hibler, 813 S.W.2d 524 (Tex. App.—San Antonio 1991, writ denied) *and* Leonard v. Lane, 821 S.W.2d 275 (Tex. App.—Houston [1st Dist.] 1991, writ denied)

Pettit v. Pettit, 818 S.W.2d 561 (Tex. App.—Beaumont 1991, no writ) (child support provision incorporated in consent decree subject to modification)

---

§ 153.0071. Alternate Dispute Resolution Procedures

(a) On written agreement of the parties, the court may refer a suit affecting the parent-child relationship to arbitration. The agreement must state whether the arbitration is binding or non-binding.

(b) If the parties agree to binding arbitration, the court shall render an order reflecting the arbitrator's award unless the court determines at a non-jury hearing that the award is not in the best interest of the child. The burden of proof at a hearing under this subsection is on the party seeking to avoid rendition of an order based on the arbitrator's award.

(c) On the written agreement of the parties or on the court's own motion, the court may refer a suit affecting the parent-child relationship to mediation.

(d) A mediated settlement agreement is binding on the parties if the agreement:

(1) provides, in a prominently displayed statement that is in boldfaced type or capital letters or underlined, that the agreement is not subject to revocation;

(2) is signed by each party to the agreement; and

(3) is signed by the party's attorney, if any, who is present at the time the agreement is signed.

(e) If a mediated settlement agreement meets the requirements of Subsection (d), a party is entitled to judgment on the mediated settlement agreement notwithstanding Rule 11, Texas Rules of Civil Procedure, or another rule of law.

(e–1) Notwithstanding Subsections (d) and (e), a court may decline to enter a judgment on a mediated settlement agreement if the court finds that:

(1) a party to the agreement was a victim of family violence, and that circumstance impaired the party's ability to make decisions; and

(2) the agreement is not in the child's best interest.

(f) A party may at any time prior to the final mediation order file a written objection to the referral of a suit affecting the parent-child relationship to mediation on the basis of family violence having been committed by another party against the objecting party or a child who is the subject of the suit. After an objection is filed, the suit may not be referred to mediation unless, on the request of a party, a hearing is held and the court finds that a preponderance of the evidence does not support the objection. If the suit is referred to mediation, the court shall order appropriate measures be taken to ensure the physical and emotional safety of the party who filed the objection. The order shall provide that the parties not be required to have face-to-face contact and that the parties be placed in separate rooms during mediation. This subsection does not apply to suits filed under Chapter 262.

(g) The provisions for confidentiality of alternative dispute resolution procedures under Chapter 154, Civil Practice and Remedies Code, apply equally to the work of a parenting coordinator, as defined by Section 153.601, and to the parties and any other person who participates in the parenting coordination. This subsection does not affect the duty of a person to report abuse or neglect under Section 261.101.

Comment

Subsections (a) and (b) recognize the validity of arbitration in suits affecting the parent child relationship. These provisions reflect the majority rule in American law—family law arbitration is valid, subject to court review.

Subsections (c)-(e) adopt the majority rule in Texas law that mediated settlement agreements are binding and not subject to revocation. However, mediated settlement agreements may be set aside by the court upon a finding that domestic violence impaired the party's ability to make decisions and that the agreement is not in the best interest of the child.

Subsection (f) responds to complaints that mediation is inappropriate if the parent child relationship, or the parent-parent relationship, has been scarred by domestic violence. If the court finds an allegation of violence to be true, mediation is not to be ordered. But if mediation is ordered after an objection is overruled, the court is directed to ensure the safety of the parties by ordering that face to face contact between the parties is prohibited. This restriction seems a bit strange given the fact that, by definition, mediation can be ordered only if the court has rejected an objection to mediation based on alleged violence—presumptively such an order is based on a finding that the movant did not produce a preponderance of the evidence that violence occurred. Finally, if an objection is made based on past family violence, the subsection excuses a CPS suit alleging child abuse and neglect from mediation. This too is strange, given the fact that much CPS litigation is settled through mediation.

For CLE/Other Legal Publications *re* Alternative Dispute Resolution, *see* Title 1, Subtitle G. (§§6.601-.604), *supra*, and Accompanying CD–ROM.

Leading Cases

Beyers v. Roberts, 199 S.W.3d 354 (Tex. App.—Houston [1st Dist.] 2006, rev. denied) (court must enforce terms of mediated settlement agreement, even if they don't comply with § 153.133 requirements for agreements regarding JMC)

In re K.A.R., 171 S.W.3d 705 (Tex. App.—Houston [14th Dist.] 2005, no pet.) (significant sanctions against attorney and client for no-show at ordered mediation upheld)

Ricks v. Ricks, 169 S.W.3d 523 (Tex. App.—Dallas 2005, no pet.) (wife failed to preserve error that mediated settlement agreement unenforceable under statute)

In re T.M.G.R., 164 S.W.3d 851 (Tex. App.—Beaumont 2005, no pet.) (without copy of "original" mediated settlement agreement, no way to tell if signed document varies from order signed by judge)

Lee v. Lee, 158 S.W.3d 612 (Tex. App.—Fort Worth 2005, no pet.) (enforcement as a mediated settlement agreement actually requires mediation and a mediator)

Garcia-Udall v. Udall, 141 S.W.3d 323 (Tex. App.—Dallas 2004, no pet.) (trial court has no authority to modify terms of mediated settlement agreement)

Goetz v. Goetz, 130 S.W.3d 359 (Tex. App.—Houston [14th Dist.] 2004, pet. denied) (trial court may appoint arbitrator when arbitration agreement does not specify method for appointment)

In re A.H., 114 S.W.3d 750 (Tex. App.—Dallas 2003, no pet.) (mediated settlement agreement with notice as to irrevocability terminating parental rights binding on parent)

Jabri v. Qaddura, 108 S.W.3d 404 (Tex. App.—Fort Worth 2003, no pet.) (agreement to arbitrate all family law claims enforceable; trial court must defer to arbitrator)

In re Cartwright, 104 S.W.3d 706 (Tex. App.—Houston [1st Dist.] 2003, no pet.) (trial court abused its discretion in appointing mediator as arbitrator)

Stieren v. McBroom, 103 S.W.3d 602 (Tex. App.—San Antonio 2003, pet. denied) (arbitrator's validation of obligor's double-cross of a deal he made one year earlier reversed on best interest test—but case goes back to arbitration as trial court lacks authority to decide motion to modify)

In re Calderon, 96 S.W.3d 711 (Tex. App.—Tyler 2003, orig. proceeding) (mandatory transfer of SAPCR not trumped by mediated settlement agreement signed over 18 months earlier)

Cross References

TX FCA Family §§ 6.601 to 6.602, Alternative Dispute Resolution Procedures, *infra*.
TX FCA Civ Prac & Rem § 154.001 *et seq.*, Alternative Dispute Resolution Procedures, *infra.*
Tex. Civ. Prac. & Rem. Code Ann. § 171.001 *et seq.*, General Arbitration Law.

§ 153.00715. Determination of Validity and Enforceability of Contract Containing Agreement to Arbitrate

(a) If a party to a suit affecting the parent-child relationship opposes an application to compel arbitration or makes an application to stay arbitration and asserts that the contract containing the agreement to arbitrate is not valid or enforceable, notwithstanding any provision of the contract to the contrary, the court shall try the issue promptly and may order arbitration only if the court determines that the contract containing the agreement to arbitrate is valid and enforceable against the party seeking to avoid arbitration.

(b) A determination under this section that a contract is valid and enforceable does not affect the court's authority to stay arbitration or refuse to compel arbitration on any other ground provided by law.

(c) This section does not apply to:

(1) a court order;

(2) an agreed parenting plan described by Section 153.007;

(3) a mediated settlement agreement described by Section 153.0071;

(4) a collaborative law agreement described by Section 153.0072; or

(5) any other agreement between the parties that is approved by a court.

Added by Acts 2011, 82nd Leg., ch. 1088 (S.B. 1216), § 2, eff. June 17, 2011.

Comment

Subsection (a) of this new statute requires a court to promptly determine the validity and enforceability of a contract containing an agreement to arbitrate notwithstanding the arbitration agreement. It further mandates that a court may compel arbitration only if the contract is valid and enforceable. However, subsection (b) clarifies that a finding of validity and enforceability of a contract does not abrogate a courts ability to either stay arbitration or refuse to compel arbitration on another ground of law.

This new section of the Texas Family Code is a departure from the general standard for challenging a contract containing an arbitration agreement under the Texas Civil Practice and Remedies Code. Chapter 171 of the Civil Practice and Remedies Code provides that a court may determine the validity of an agreement to arbitrate; however, it does not provide for a court to determine the validity or enforceability of the contract that contains such an agreement in its entirety. Tex. Civ. Prac. & Rem. Code ch. 171. Reflecting the lack of such provisions, the Texas Supreme Court has ruled that when a challenge is to the entirety of a contract containing an arbitration agreement as well as to the agreement itself, the challenge must be taken to arbitration, not court. *In re* Labatt Food Service, L.P., 279 S.W.3d 640 (Tex. 2009).

Of note, the bill analysis of this statute reflects the underlying concern that parties may be forced into an agreement to arbitrate as a part of a larger contract. The example given was that of a party having a gun held to his or her head while signing a contract containing an arbitration agreement or clause. The analysis likewise expresses concern that a party forced to enter an agreement for arbitration as the part of a larger contract would have difficulty obtaining a fair outcome in arbitration. However, provisions requiring arbitration in divorce decrees and other settlement documents or court orders are not subject to this court review.

~~§ 153.0072. Collaborative Law~~

~~(a) On a written agreement of the parties and their attorneys, a suit affecting the parent-child relationship may be conducted under collaborative law procedures.~~

~~(b) Collaborative law is a procedure in which the parties and their counsel agree in writing to use their best efforts and make a good faith attempt to resolve the suit affecting the parent-child relationship on an agreed basis without resorting to judicial intervention except to have the court approve the settlement agreement, make the legal pronouncements, and sign the orders required by law to effectuate the agreement of the parties as the court determines appropriate. The parties' counsel may not serve as litigation counsel except to ask the court to approve the settlement agreement.~~

~~(c) A collaborative law agreement must include provisions for:~~

~~(1) full and candid exchange of information between the parties and their attorneys as necessary to make a proper evaluation of the case;~~

~~(2) suspending court intervention in the dispute while the parties are using collaborative law procedures;~~

(3) hiring experts, as jointly agreed, to be used in the procedure;

(4) withdrawal of all counsel involved in the collaborative law procedure if the collaborative law procedure does not result in settlement of the dispute; and

(5) other provisions as agreed to by the parties consistent with a good faith effort to collaboratively settle the matter.

(d) Notwithstanding Rule 11, Texas Rules of Civil Procedure, or another rule or law, a party is entitled to judgment on a collaborative law settlement agreement if the agreement:

(1) provides, in a prominently displayed statement that is boldfaced, capitalized, or underlined, that the agreement is not subject to revocation; and

(2) is signed by each party to the agreement and the attorney of each party.

(e) Subject to Subsection (g), a court that is notified 30 days before trial that the parties are using collaborative law procedures to attempt to settle a dispute may not, until a party notifies the court that the collaborative law procedures did not result in a settlement:

(1) set a hearing or trial in the case;

(2) impose discovery deadlines;

(3) require compliance with scheduling orders; or

(4) dismiss the case.

(f) The parties shall notify the court if the collaborative law procedures result in a settlement. If they do not, the parties shall file:

(1) a status report with the court not later than the 180th day after the date of the written agreement to use the procedures; and

(2) a status report on or before the first anniversary of the date of the written agreement to use the procedures, accompanied by a motion for continuance that the court shall grant if the status report indicates the desire of the parties to continue to use collaborative law procedures.

(g) If the collaborative law procedures do not result in a settlement on or before the second anniversary of the date that the suit was filed, the court may:

(1) set the suit for trial on the regular docket; or

(2) dismiss the suit without prejudice.

(h) The provisions for confidentiality of alternative dispute resolution procedures as provided in Chapter 154, Civil Practice and Remedies Code, apply equally to collaborative law procedures under this section.

Repealed by Acts 2011, 82nd Leg., ch. 1048 (H.B. 3833), § 2, eff. Sept. 1, 2011

Comment

Title 1A of the Texas Family Code is added in 2011 adopting the Uniform Collaborative Law Act in Texas. Henceforth, all of the provisions for collaborative law are contained in its own title.

To access the statutory text of the Uniform Collaborative Law Act, and related CLE/Other Legal Publications and Leading Cases, *see* Title 1A, §§ 15.001-.116, *supra*, and Accompanying CD–ROM.

---

§ 153.008. Repealed.

Comment

This controversial section, "Child's Preference of Person to Designate Residence," was repealed in 2009; to make sure it would really be gone, two separate bills were enacted to do the job. In large part, the controversy is inherent to the nature of family law litigation. The perspective that a lawyer naturally brings to a case involving managing conservatorship and the primary residence of the child is the client's perspective. It is obvious the attorney's parent-client should decide the issue and the other parent should agree. An attorney ad litem appointed to represent the child similarly is duty bound to see that the child has a voice in the issue, while an amicus attorney is to determine and advocate the child's best interest. As a result of the repeal of Section 153.008, the child no longer is authorized to file with the court the name of the person preferred to provide the primary residence of the child, of course subject to the approval of the court. This leaves the interview of the child under Section 153.009 as the means whereby a child is able to communicate a preference on the issue.

A brief history of this section illustrates the depth and breadth of the controversy, presently settled (at least temporarily). The story began at age 14, followed a steady progression of reducing the age for a child to "express a preference regarding managing conservatorship," which culminated in 1999 when the age was reduced to 10. Critics of that amendment were outraged, asserting that a child of 10 would be subject to undue parental pressure if the child attempted to announce a choice of managing conservator. Whether the choice was freely given would always remain a question, no matter what age is chosen by statute. Implicit in the 2001 amendment, which changed the "age of reason" to 12 or older, is the assumption that free choice would be available to a 12-year-old while unavailable to a 10-year-old. With only a couple of exceptions, age 12 was established throughout Title 5 as the touchstone for a child's autonomy. Implicit in this the idea that the law can regulate parental advice, consultation, and thereby control out-of court "undue pressure." This conclusion is to be made in the context of the parents disputing custody to the point of what is commonly called a "custody battle."

In 2003 this section was clarified to allow children 12 and over to file in writing the preference for which person would provide the primary residence, subject to the approval of the court. Rather than relieving parental pressure, what allegedly was triggered was a phenomenon known as dueling affidavits. It seems unlikely that this result was actually confusing to the courts. A judge confronted with dueling affidavits could rightly conclude that the affidavits were the result of parental consultation, advice, or indeed what might be viewed as undue pressure or bullying. It also seems unlikely that a judge could cure the problem, but rather would be forced to take the parents as they are and decide the case on evidence other than the affidavits.

No change was made to Section 153.009, which regulates the interview of a child in chambers. Insofar as the initial decision on conservatorship, the interview will usually be the only way a child's voice will be heard. Calling a child as a witness to testify on this subject is regarded as unthinkable.

---

§ 153.009. Interview of Child in Chambers

(a) In a nonjury trial or at a hearing, on the application of a party, the amicus attorney, or the attorney ad litem for the child, the court shall interview in chambers a child 12 years of age or older and may interview in chambers a child under 12 years of age to determine the child's wishes as to conservatorship or as to the person who shall have the exclusive right to determine the child's primary residence. The court may also interview a child in chambers on the court's own motion for a purpose specified by this subsection.

(b) In a nonjury trial or at a hearing, on the application of a party, the amicus attorney, or the attorney ad litem for the child or on the court's own motion, the court may interview the child in chambers to determine the child's wishes as to possession, access, or any other issue in the suit affecting the parent-child relationship.

(c) Interviewing a child does not diminish the discretion of the court in determining the best interests of the child.

(d) In a jury trial, the court may not interview the child in chambers regarding an issue on which a party is entitled to a jury verdict.

(e) In any trial or hearing, the court may permit the attorney for a party, the amicus attorney, the guardian ad litem for the child, or the attorney ad litem for the child to be present at the interview.

(f) On the motion of a party, the amicus attorney, or the attorney ad litem for the child, or on the court's own motion, the court shall cause a record of the interview to be made when the child is 12 years of age or older. A record of the interview shall be part of the record in the case.

Comment

A mandatory interview of a child age 12 or over in chambers, on request from a party, amicus attorney, or attorney ad litem, is an important step in giving a child a voice in a lawsuit in which the child is "the real party in interest." An interview with a child under 12 years of age is discretionary with the judge. However, hearing the child's voice does not in any way diminish the trial court's discretion to decide the issues without being bound by the child's wishes. Additionally, in a jury trial the court may not interview the child with regard to any issue on which the jury is to decide. *See also* Sections 156.006 and 156.101-.102.

The repeal of Section 153.008 will place an even more intense focus on an interview of a child in chambers. The mechanics of that interview are not described in the statute; thus, the procedure to be followed is the responsibility of the judge to formulate. One thing is clear from the first sentence of Subsection (a); the interview of a child 12 or over is mandatory only on "the application of a party, the amicus attorney, or the attorney ad litem for the child . . . ."

In suits involving alleged abuse or neglect filed by the Department of Family and Protective Services, if the litigation lasts more than six months the presence of the child in court will be routine. Unless the child is specifically excused, Section 263.302 directs the child's attendance at the six-month and ten-month permanency hearings (and at hearings thereafter, if any). In DFPS cases the child's presence in court facilitates the judge speaking with the child on a routine basis, sometimes in open court and sometimes in chambers. The discussion with the child in chambers often would not fit the definition of an "interview" (if one was provided by the statute). Note there is no stated minimum age which automatically excuses a child's attendance. The consequence is that judges with a CPS docket become quite accustomed to speaking with children past preschool age. Presence of the child in court in a custody battle is, of course, not an expected standard, but rather an event scheduled in advance.

CLE/Legal Publications

The child's voice in court: in camera interviews and child hearsay. Latrelle Bright Joy, 2010 ADV. FAM. L.

Life after the child preference: where do we go from here? Dean Rucker, Stephen J. Naylor & JoAl Cannon Sheridan, 2010 U.T. PARENT-CHILD RELATIONSHIPS

When it's right for the child to decide. Wendy S. Burgower, 2010 MARRIAGE DISSOLUTION

The sixth sense: I hear voices, but is the child being heard? (Which perspective really matters to the court?) Diana S. Friedman & Christy Bradshaw Schmidt, 2009 U.T. PARENT-CHILD RELATIONSHIPS

In chambers conferences: making them count. Heather L. King, 2008 U.T. FAM. L. FRONT LINES

Giving the kids a voice in the courtroom. Wendy S. Burgower, 2008 ADV. FAM. L.

Leading Cases

Ellason v. Ellason, 162 S.W.3d 883 (Tex. App.—Dallas 2005, no pet.) (mother waived appellate review of court's interview with child by failing to request record of interview)

Long v. Long, 144 S.W.3d 64 (Tex. App.—El Paso 2004, no pet.) (interview with children in chambers presumed to have furnished basis for modification of principal residence to father)

---

§ 153.010. Order for Family Counseling

(a) If the court finds at the time of a hearing that the parties have a history of conflict in resolving an issue of conservatorship or possession of or access to the child, the court may order a party to:

(1) participate in counseling with a mental health professional who:

(A) has a background in family therapy;

(B) has a mental health license that requires as a minimum a master's degree; and

(C) has training in domestic violence if the court determines that the training is relevant to the type of counseling needed; and

(2) pay the cost of counseling.

(b) If a person possessing the requirements of Subsection (a)(1) is not available in the county in which the court presides, the court may appoint a person the court believes is qualified to conduct the counseling ordered under Subsection (a).

§ 153.011. Security Bond

If the court finds that a person who has a possessory interest in a child may violate the court order relating to the interest, the court may order the party to execute a bond or deposit security. The court shall set the amount and condition the bond or security on compliance with the order.

§ 153.012. Right to Privacy; Deletion of Personal Information in Records

The court may order the custodian of records to delete all references in the records to the place of residence of either party appointed as a conservator of the child before the release of the records to another party appointed as a conservator.

§ 153.013. False Report of Child Abuse

(a) If a party to a pending suit affecting the parent-child relationship makes a report alleging child abuse by another party to the suit that the reporting party knows lacks a factual foundation, the court shall deem the report to be a knowingly false report.

(b) Evidence of a false report of child abuse is admissible in a suit between the involved parties regarding the terms of conservatorship of a child.

(c) If the court makes a finding under Subsection (a), the court shall impose a civil penalty not to exceed $500.

§ 153.014. Visitation Centers and Visitation Exchange Facilities

A county may establish a visitation center or a visitation exchange facility for the purpose of facilitating the terms of a court order providing for the possession of or access to a child.

§ 153.015. Electronic Communication with Child by Conservator

(a) In this section, "electronic communication" means any communication facilitated by the use of any wired or wireless technology via the Internet or any other electronic media. The term includes communication facilitated by the use of a telephone, electronic mail, instant messaging, videoconferencing, or webcam.

(b) If a conservator of a child requests the court to order periods of electronic communication with the child under this section, the court may award the conservator reasonable periods of electronic communication with the child to supplement the conservator's periods of possession of the child. In determining whether to award electronic communication, the court shall consider:

(1) whether electronic communication is in the best interest of the child;

(2) whether equipment necessary to facilitate the electronic communication is reasonably available to all parties subject to the order; and

(3) any other factor the court considers appropriate.

(c) If a court awards a conservator periods of electronic communication with a child under this section, each conservator subject to the court's order shall:

(1) provide the other conservator with the e-mail address and other electronic communication access information of the child;

(2) notify the other conservator of any change in the e-mail address or other electronic communication access information not later than 24 hours after the date the change takes effect; and

(3) if necessary equipment is reasonably available, accommodate electronic communication with the child, with the same privacy, respect, and dignity accorded all other forms of access, at a reasonable time and for a reasonable duration subject to any limitation provided by the court in the court's order.

(d) The court may not consider the availability of electronic communication as a factor in determining child support. The availability of electronic communication under this section is not intended as a substitute for physical possession of or access to the child, where otherwise appropriate.

(e) In a suit in which the court's order contains provisions related to a finding of family violence in the suit, including supervised visitation, the court may award periods of electronic communication under this section only if:

(1) the award and terms of the award are mutually agreed to by the parties; and

(2) the terms of the award:

(A) are printed in the court's order in boldfaced, capitalized type; and

(B) include any specific restrictions relating to family violence or supervised visitation, as applicable, required by other law to be included in a possession or access order.

Comment

After hearing stories of one parent not allowing children to speak to have contact with the other parent during the first parent's periods of possession, the legislature authorized the court to order contact via telephone, email, instant messaging or webcam.

SUBCHAPTER B. PARENT APPOINTED AS CONSERVATOR: IN GENERAL

Introductory Comment

The Family Code originally allocated powers of conservators along the lines of managing and possessory conservators. The parent managing conservator had "all the rights of a parent" to the exclusion of the parent possessory conservator, except for those rights specifically allocated to the possessory conservator. Gradually, the lines became blurred with the rise, first of the ability of parents to agree to joint conservatorship, then of the power of a court to order joint conservatorship. Since 1995, however, there is a statutory presumption of joint managing conservatorship. Accordingly, the various rights and duties of conservators must now be allocated to the parties as independent, joint, or exclusive rights. This subchapter defines certain rights to exist at all times and other rights that exist only when the child is with the conservator.

CLE/Other Legal Publications

SAPCR caselaw update. Eva Guzman, 2010 Adv. Fam. L.

Keeping up with the kiddos: case law update. Sallee S. Smyth, 2010 Marriage Dissolution

Application of child development research to crafting age-appropriate possession orders for children under three. Diana S. Friedman & Jonathan W. Gould, 2010 Fam. L. Front Lines

Understanding mental health evaluations and the mental health process. Bruce R. Steffler, 2010 So. Tex. Fam. L. Conf.

***See* Accompanying CD–ROM for Additional CLE/Other Legal Publications.**

Leading Cases

Phillips v. Beaber, 995 S.W.2d 655 (Tex. 1999), *reversing*, 971 S.W.2d 127 (parent with right to establish principle residence is equivalent of sole MC, modification of terms of JMC constitutes a suit to modify custody)

11/20

Lewelling v. Lewelling, 796 S.W.2d 164 (Tex. 1990) (statutory parental preference creates strong presumption)

Urbish v. 127th Judicial District Court, 708 S.W.2d 429 (Tex. 1986) (noncustodial parent's right to maintain suit on behalf of minor child upheld when MC slow to object)

Ex parte Rhodes, 352 S.W.2d 249 (Tex. 1961) (restrictions on custodian's power to choose domicile of child upheld)

In re R.C.S., 167 S.W.3d 145 (Tex. App.—Dallas 2005, pet. denied) (court should designate someone to have right to designate primary residence of the children)

In re K.L.R., 162 S.W.3d 291 (Tex. App.—Tyler 2005, no pet.) (evidence of arrests was admissible on best interest issue)

Chavez v. Chavez, 148 S.W.3d 449 (Tex. App.—El Paso 2004, no pet.) (grandparents must overcome constitutionally-based parental presumption, even if they would be better option for raising children)

In re Jeffries, 144 S.W.3d 636 (Tex. App.—Texarkana 2004, no pet.) (court's discretion not abused by granting JMC mother right to determine child's residence in light of conflicting evidence between mother and father)

In re D.R.S., 138 S.W.3d 467 (Tex. App.—Houston [14th Dist.] 2004, pet. denied) (jury, not judge, decides geographical restriction on primary conservator's establishment of child's primary residence)

Lide v. Lide, 116 S.W.3d 147 (Tex. App.—El Paso 2003, no pet.) (JMC presumption rebutted affirming mom's appointment as sole MC)

In re Ostrofsky, 112 S.W.3d 925 (Tex. App.—Houston [14th] 2003, orig. proceeding) (temporary order placing children in boarding school deprives mother of possession of children and her right to determine primary residence)

In re Z.B.P., 109 S.W.3d 772 (Tex. App.—Fort Worth 2003, no pet.) (traditional household in children's best interest)

In re S.W.H., 72 S.W.3d 772 (Tex. App.—Fort Worth 2002, no pet.) (parental presumption prevails; court improperly appointed nonparent as conservator)

---

§ 153.071. Court to Specify Rights and Duties of Parent Appointed a Conservator

If both parents are appointed as conservators of the child, the court shall specify the rights and duties of a parent that are to be exercised:

(1) by each parent independently;

(2) by the joint agreement of the parents; and

(3) exclusively by one parent.

§ 153.072. Written Finding Required to Limit Parental Rights and Duties

The court may limit the rights and duties of a parent appointed as a conservator if the court makes a written finding that the limitation is in the best interest of the child.

11/20

§ 153.073. Rights of Parent at All Times

(a) Unless limited by court order, a parent appointed as a conservator of a child has at all times the right:

(1) to receive information from any other conservator of the child concerning the health, education, and welfare of the child;

(2) to confer with the other parent to the extent possible before making a decision concerning the health, education, and welfare of the child;

(3) of access to medical, dental, psychological, and educational records of the child;

(4) to consult with a physician, dentist, or psychologist of the child;

(5) to consult with school officials concerning the child's welfare and educational status, including school activities;

(6) to attend school activities;

(7) to be designated on the child's records as a person to be notified in case of an emergency;

(8) to consent to medical, dental, and surgical treatment during an emergency involving an immediate danger to the health and safety of the child; and

(9) to manage the estate of the child to the extent the estate has been created by the parent or the parent's family.

(b) The court shall specify in the order the rights that a parent retains at all times.

Leading Case

Abrams v. Jones, 35 S.W.3d 620 (Tex. 2000) (psychological records do not have to be revealed to parent when psychologist testifies conclusively that disclosure to parent would be harmful to child)

---

§ 153.074. Rights and Duties During Period of Possession 11/20

Unless limited by court order, a parent appointed as a conservator of a child has the following rights and duties during the period that the parent has possession of the child:

(1) the duty of care, control, protection, and reasonable discipline of the child;

(2) the duty to support the child, including providing the child with clothing, food, shelter, and medical and dental care not involving an invasive procedure;

(3) the right to consent for the child to medical and dental care not involving an invasive procedure; and

(4) the right to direct the moral and religious training of the child.

§ 153.075. Duties of Parent Not Appointed Conservator

The court may order a parent not appointed as a managing or a possessory conservator to perform other parental duties, including paying child support.

§ 153.076. Duty to Provide Information

(a) The court shall order that each conservator of a child has a duty to inform the other conservator of the child in a timely manner of significant information concerning the health, education, and welfare of the child.

(b) The court shall order that each conservator of a child has the duty to inform the other conservator of the child if the conservator resides with for at least 30 days, marries, or intends to marry a person who the conservator knows:

(1) is registered as a sex offender under Chapter 62, Code of Criminal Procedure; or

(2) is currently charged with an offense for which on conviction the person would be required to register under that chapter.

(c) The notice required to be made under Subsection (b) must be made as soon as practicable but not later than the 40th day after the date the conservator of the child begins to reside with the person or the 10th day after the date the marriage occurs, as appropriate. The notice must include a description of the offense that is the basis of the person's requirement to register as a sex offender or of the offense with which the person is charged.

(d) A conservator commits an offense if the conservator fails to provide notice in the manner required by Subsections (b) and (c). An offense under this subsection is a Class C misdemeanor.

Comment

Subsection (a) is merely a statement of sound public policy directing civilized behavior between parents after their appointment as conservators. Often the legislature enacts such statements of public policy, even though enforceability may be questionable or impossible. This latter aspect led to some controversy over this particular provision because it appears that the failure to define "timely manner" and "significant information" probably renders the court order unenforceable by contempt.

Subsections (b)–(d) may be criticized because: (1) the behavior described does not sound particularly civilized; (2) the provisions were drafted for very rare instances; and (3) almost surely a parent covered by the statute will disobey it if and when such a fact situation does arise, either consciously or unknowingly.

SUBCHAPTER C. PARENT APPOINTED AS SOLE OR JOINT MANAGING CONSERVATOR

Introductory Comment

Joint managing conservatorship was introduced to Texas law in 1979, when such arrangements were permitted by agreement only. In 1987, the legislature granted the trial court the authority to order a JMC; such an arrangement may be imposed on two unwilling parents. A distinguishing feature of the Texas statute is the fact that, either by agreement or by court order, the process for reaching certain decisions must be included in the decree. Issues that have a heightened likelihood for future controversy must be resolved in advance, such as the method for determining the residence/domicile of the child and where the child will go to school. Either joint managing conservator may be awarded the authority to determine these issues, or the court itself may fix the outcome in advance, *e.g.*, the child resides in Travis County, Texas, and attends public school until further order of the court.

Although there may be many reasons why appointment of a parent is not in the best interest of a child, the statute provides that there is only one satisfactory reason to deny a parent's appointment as a managing conservator (either sole or joint). The "best interest test" is limited by the restriction that a parent should be denied managing conservatorship only if "appointment would significantly impair the child's physical health or emotional development." The fact that another contesting party, most typically a grandparent, would likely be a better custodian is not sufficient to rebut the parental preference. That presumption, however, remains fully rebuttable if the facts warrant a finding of future harm to the child.

In 1995 the Legislature created a legislative presumption of joint managing conservatorship. The amendment, standing alone without amending the details of court-ordered JMC, does little more than change the title of the parents, who are presumptively appointed as JMCs. The relationships between the "custodial" and "noncustodial" parent JMCs remain basically unchanged as far as the balance of the relevant statutes are concerned. The effect on the psychology of the JMC parents may be more significant.

CLE/Other Legal Publications

Shared custody: advocacy and drafting. Ike Vanden Eykel, 2010 Adv. Fam. L.

Rebutting the statutory presumptions: joint managing conservator, parental preference, standard possession orders, and practical presumptions. Ann Coover, H.E. Mendez, James E. Monnig & Judith G. Wells, 2009 Adv. Fam. L.

See Accompanying CD–ROM for Additional CLE/Other Legal Publications.

Leading Cases

Santosky v. Kramer, 455 U.S. 745, 71 L.Ed.2d 599, 102 S.Ct. 1388 (1982) (constitutional dimensions of parent-child relationship)

Phillips v. Beaber, 995 S.W.2d 655 (Tex. 1999), reversing 971 S.W.2d 127 (JMC-parent's right to establish principle residence is equivalent of sole MC; modification of that term of JMC constitutes a suit to modify custody)

Brook v. Brook, 881 S.W.2d 297 (Tex. 1994) (parental preference not offended when one parent named JMC with a nonparent; nonparent may be named as sole M.C. or as J.M.C. with a parent or another nonparent)

Lewelling v. Lewelling, 796 S.W.2d 164 (Tex. 1990) (statutory parental preference creates strong presumption)

Ex parte Rhodes, 352 S.W.2d 249 (Tex. 1961) (restrictions on custodian's power to choose domicile of child)

In re M.M.M., 307 S.W.3d 846 (Tex. App.—Fort Worth 2010, no pet.) (mother named sole M.C. with right to establish child's residence without geographic restriction—father awarded supervised visitation)

In re D.A., 307 S.W.3d 556 (Tex. App.—Dallas 2010, no pet.) (mother sole M.C.; unmarried father given limited visitation with exchanges to be at McDonalds)

In re C.R.S., 2010 WL 1492335 (Tex. App.—San Antonio 2010) (mem. op.) (father named primary joint M.C. by jury, court sua sponte ordered new trial; remand for trial court to specify reasons for refusing to render judgment on jury's verdict)

In re B.A.W., 311 S.W. 3d 544 (Tex. App.—El Paso 2009, no pet.) (trial court has discretion to order neutral point of exchange and keep geographic restriction in place)

In re R.C.S., 167 S.W.3d 145 (Tex. App.—Dallas 2005, pet. denied) (court should designate someone to have right to designate primary residence of the children)

In re K.L.R., 162 S.W.3d 291 (Tex. App.—Tyler 2005, no pet.) (evidence of arrests was admissible on best interest issue)

In re Jeffries, 144 S.W.3d 636 (Tex. App.—Texarkana 2004, no pet.) (court's discretion not abused by granting JMC mother right to determine child's residence in light of conflicting evidence between mother and father)

Lide v. Lide, 116 S.W.3d 147 (Tex. App.—E1 Paso 2003, no pet.) (JMC presumption rebutted)

In re Ostrofsky, 112 S.W.3d 925 (Tex. App.—Houston [14th Dist.] 2003, no pet.) (temporary order sending children to boarding school deprived joint managing conservator of right to determine primary residence)

Robinson v. Robinson, 16 S.W.3d 451 (Tex. App.—Waco 2000, no pet.) (JMC presumption rebutted by conflict and geographical distance between the parents)

Alaniz v. Alaniz, 867 S.W.2d 54 (Tex. App.—El Paso 1993, no writ) (state cannot prefer one religious belief over another)

11/20

§ 153.131. Presumption That Parent to be Appointed Managing Conservator

(a) Subject to the prohibition in Section 153.004, unless the court finds that appointment of the parent or parents would not be in the best interest of the child because the appointment would significantly impair the child's physical health or emotional development, a parent shall be appointed sole managing conservator or both parents shall be appointed as joint managing conservators of the child.

(b) It is a rebuttable presumption that the appointment of the parents of a child as joint managing conservators is in the best interest of the child. A finding of a history of family violence involving the parents of a child removes the presumption under this subsection.

Comment

In 1995 this section created a rebuttable presumption that the naming of parents as JMCs is in the best interest of the child. The substantive provisions regulating the appointment of joint managing conservators and the terms of joint conservatorship are not affected. The rule regarding the appointment of a parent to furnish the primary residence is continued, § 153.136, and the statutory statement that joint managing conservatorship in Texas does not require "equal or nearly equal periods of physical possession" is unchanged, § 153.135. Undoubtedly there has been a significant psychological impact on many parents due to the legislative declaration that JMC is presumptively in the best interest of the child. Whether that psychological impact has been positive or negative unquestionably has varied greatly from couple to couple.

CLE/Other Legal Publications

Rebutting the statutory presumptions: joint managing conservator, parental preference, standard possession orders, and practical presumptions. Ann Coover, H.E. Mendez, James E. Monnig & Judith G. Wells, 2009 Adv. Fam. L.

Moving Away: Dealing with Residency Restriction Issues. Bret A. Bosker, Kate H. McConnico, 2009 So. Tex. Fam. L. Conf.

Leading Cases

In re J.A.J., 243 S.W.3d 611 (Tex. 2007) (reversal of termination of parental rights does not affect trial court's appointment of DFPS as conservator of the child)

Lewelling v. Lewelling, 796 S.W.2d 164 (Tex. 1990) (test of strong statutory parental preference presumption is not whether a nonparent would be a better custodian of child; test is significant physical or emotional impairment of child if parent is M.C.)

Gray v. Shook, 329 S.W.3d 186 (Tex. App.—Corpus Christi 2010) (possible harm from "uprooting" child from grandmother to live with genetic father insufficient to rebut parental presumption)

Gardner v. Gardner, 229 S.W.3d 747 (Tex. App.—San Antonio 2007, no pet.) (parental presumption does not apply to right to establish primary residence of child), *contra: In re* De La Pena, 999 S.W.2d 521, 534-35 (Tex. App.—El Paso 1999, no pet.)

In re J.P., 196 S.W.3d 434 (Tex. App.—Dallas 2006, no pet.) (termination of father's parentage rights end paternal aunt's standing)

In re G.R.W., 191 S.W.3d 896 (Tex. App.—Texarkana 2006, no pet.) (18-year old father and grandmother lose custody battle with maternal uncle and aunt when parental presumption rebutted)

In re G.R.W., 191 S.W.3d 896 (Tex. App.—Texarkana 2006, no pet.) (evidence sufficient to support appointment of maternal great-aunt and uncle sole MC of child)

Sotelo v. Gonzales, 170 S.W.3d 783 (Tex. App.—El Paso 2005, no pet.) (parental presumption not applicable in modification proceeding)

In re J.R.D., 169 S.W.3d 740 (Tex. App.—Austin 2005, pet. denied) (joint managing conservatorship does not mean equal time)

Corrales v. DFPS, 155 S.W.3d 478 (Tex. App.—El Paso 2004, no pet.) (jury determined DPRS, not grandmother, best option for managing conservator)

Chavez v. Chavez, 148 S.W.3d 449 (Tex. App.—El Paso 2004, no pet.) (grandparents must overcome constitutionally-based parental presumption, even if they would be better option for raising children)

In re C.J.F., 134 S.W.3d 343 (Tex. App.—Amarillo 2003, pet. denied) (parental presumption rebutted)

In re P.D.M., 117 S.W.3d 453 (Tex. App.—Fort Worth 2003, pet. denied) (grandmother's suit after death of managing conservator is not original suit subject to father's parental presumption)

In re K.R.P., 80 S.W.3d 669 (Tex. App.—Houston [1st Dist.] 2002, pet. denied) (former step-parent named sole MC over wishes of unfit parents)

Robinson v. Robinson, 16 S.W.3d 451 (Tex. App.—Waco 2000, no pet.) (joint MC presumption rebutted, jury's choice of father as sole MC stands)

---

§ 153.132. Rights and Duties of Parent Appointed Sole Managing Conservator

Unless limited by court order, a parent appointed as sole managing conservator of a child has the rights and duties provided by Subchapter B and the following exclusive rights:

(1) the right to designate the primary residence of the child;

(2) the right to consent to medical, dental, and surgical treatment involving invasive procedures;

(3) the right to consent to psychiatric and psychological treatment;

(4) the right to receive and give receipt for periodic payments for the support of the child and to hold or disburse these funds for the benefit of the child;

(5) the right to represent the child in legal action and to make other decisions of substantial legal significance concerning the child;

(6) the right to consent to marriage and to enlistment in the armed forces of the United States;

(7) the right to make decisions concerning the child's education;

(8) the right to the services and earnings of the child; and

(9) except when a guardian of the child's estate or a guardian or attorney ad litem has been appointed for the child, the right to act as an agent of the child in relation to the child's estate if the child's action is required by a state, the United States, or a foreign government.

Comment

Throughout the Family Code the right to "establish the primary residence" has been changed to provide the right to "designate" that residence. The change in terminology makes it clear that the person with the right to designate may determine where the child will live.

Leading Case

Lueg v. Lueg, 976 S.W.2d 308 (Tex. App.—Corpus Christi 1998, pet. denied) (error to order sole MC father to pay child support to PC mother)

---

§ 153.133. Parenting Plan for Joint Managing Conservatorship

(a) If a written agreed parenting plan is filed with the court, the court shall render an order appointing the parents as joint managing conservators only if the parenting plan:

(1) designates the conservator who has the exclusive right to designate the primary residence of the child and:

(A) establishes, until modified by further order, the geographic area within which the conservator shall maintain the child's primary residence; or

(B) specifies that the conservator may designate the child's primary residence without regard to geographic location;

(2) specifies the rights and duties of each parent regarding the child's physical care, support, and education;

(3) includes provisions to minimize disruption of the child's education, daily routine, and association with friends;

(4) allocates between the parents, independently, jointly, or exclusively, all of the remaining rights and duties of a parent provided by Chapter 151;

(5) is voluntarily and knowingly made by each parent and has not been repudiated by either parent at the time the order is rendered; and

(6) is in the best interest of the child.

(b) The agreed parenting plan may contain an alternative dispute resolution procedure that the parties agree to use before requesting enforcement or modification of the terms and conditions of the joint conservatorship through litigation, except in an emergency.

(c) Notwithstanding Subsection (a)(1), the court shall render an order adopting the provisions of a written agreed parenting plan appointing the parents as joint managing conservators if the parenting plan:

(1) meets all the requirements of Subsections (a)(2) through (6); and

(2) provides that the child's primary residence shall be within a specified geographic area.

Comment

Added in 2009, Subsection (c) apparently converts an agreement by the parties to a parenting plan into being determinative of the primary residence of the child.

§ 153.134. Court-Ordered Joint Conservatorship

(a) If a written agreed parenting plan is not filed with the court, the court may render an order appointing the parents joint managing conservators only if the appointment is in the best interest of the child, considering the following factors:

(1) whether the physical, psychological, or emotional needs and development of the child will benefit from the appointment of joint managing conservators;

(2) the ability of the parents to give first priority to the welfare of the child and reach shared decisions in the child's best interest;

(3) whether each parent can encourage and accept a positive relationship between the child and the other parent;

(4) whether both parents participated in child rearing before the filing of the suit;

(5) the geographical proximity of the parents' residences;

(6) if the child is 12 years of age or older, the child's preference, if any, regarding the person to have the exclusive right to designate the primary residence of the child; and

(7) any other relevant factor.

(b) In rendering an order appointing joint managing conservators, the court shall:

(1) designate the conservator who has the exclusive right to determine the primary residence of the child and:

(A) establish, until modified by further order, a geographic area within which the conservator shall maintain the child's primary residence; or

(B) specify that the conservator may determine the child's primary residence without regard to geographic location;

(2) specify the rights and duties of each parent regarding the child's physical care, support, and education;

(3) include provisions to minimize disruption of the child's education, daily routine, and association with friends;

(4) allocate between the parents, independently, jointly, or exclusively, all of the remaining rights and duties of a parent as provided by Chapter 151; and

(5) if feasible, recommend that the parties use an alternative dispute resolution method before requesting enforcement or modification of the terms and conditions of the joint conservatorship through litigation, except in an emergency.

Comment

The issue of the right to determine the primary residence of a child by a joint managing conservator has refocused the relocation issue in this context. Recent amendments to this section, and the preceding section dealing with agreements, places the area of conflict exactly where it belongs, between joint conservators. That is, with the same title the real issues are with whom does the child live and which JMC has the right to determine just exactly where that will be? In either the context of an agreed JMC or a court ordered JMC, primary residence is almost always a crucial issue.

CLE/Other Legal Publications

Representing and defending against the impaired parent. Wendy S. Burgower & JoAl Cannon Sheridan, 2008 UT FAM. L. FRONT LINES

Conservatorship: what's the fight about? Janet McCullar Vavra, 2008 MARRIAGE DISSOLUTION

Identifying parental interests in parent child relationships. Kristen A. Algert, 2007 UT DEFINITIVE SAPCR

Parental estrangement and alienation: how do we deal with the aftermath. Jeffrey C. Siegel, 2007 UT DEFINITIVE SAPCR

Parental rights, duties and powers beyond the Family Code. Jana L. Wickham, 2007 UT DEFINITIVE SAPCR

Leading Cases

Phillips v. Beaber, 995 S.W.2d 655 (Tex. 1999), *reversing* 971 S.W.2d 127 (parent with right to establish principle residence is equivalent of sole MC; modification of terms of JMC constitutes a suit to modify custody)

In re R.C.S., 167 S.W.3d 145 (Tex. App.—Dallas 2005, pet. denied) (court should designate someone to have right to designate primary residence of the children)

In re K.L.R., 162 S.W.3d 291 (Tex. App.—Tyler 2005, no pet.) (evidence of arrests was admissible on best interest issue)

In re Jeffries, 144 S.W.3d 636 (Tex. App.—Texarkana 2004, no pet.) (court's discretion not abused by granting JMC mother right to determine child's residence in light of conflicting evidence between mother and father)

In re Ostrofsky, 112 S.W.3d 925 (Tex. App.—Houston [14th Dist.] 2003, no pet.) (temporary order sending children to boarding school deprived joint managing conservator of right to determine primary residence)

London v. London, 94 S.W.3d 139 (Tex. App.—Houston [14th Dist.] 2002, no pet.) (jury determines residency restriction and father's right to make educational decisions for his children)

§ 153.135. Equal Possession Not Required

Joint managing conservatorship does not require the award of equal or nearly equal periods of physical possession of and access to the child to each of the joint conservators.

Leading Case

In re J.R.D., 169 S.W.3d 740 (Tex. App.—Austin 2005, pet. denied) (joint managing conservatorship does not mean equal time)

§ 153.136. Repealed

§ 153.137. Repealed

§ 153.138. Child Support Order Affecting Joint Conservators

The appointment of joint managing conservators does not impair or limit the authority of the court to order a joint managing conservator to pay child support to another joint managing conservator.

SUBCHAPTER D. PARENT APPOINTED AS POSSESSORY CONSERVATOR

Introductory Comment

The Texas Legislature has periodically recalibrated the rights of managing conservators and possessory conservators. Generally this process has resulted in significant expansion of the rights of a possessory conservator. But, the importance of this section has been greatly reduced by the specificity now included in the standard possession order.

***See* CLE/Other Legal Publications following Comment to Subchapter F. Standard Possession Order (§§ 153.311-.317), *infra*.**

Leading Cases

Ex parte MacCallum, 807 S.W.2d 729 (Tex. 1991) (no clear order to return children from weekend visitation)

Ex parte Brister, 801 S.W.2d 833 (Tex. 1990) (visitation order ambiguous, not enforceable by contempt—irregular work schedule)

Martin v. Martin, 776 S.W.2d 572 (Tex. 1989) (terms of possessory conservatorship within court's discretion; jury denied in modification action)

In re J.R.D., 169 S.W.3d 740 (Tex. App.—Austin 2005, pet. denied) (father does not have constitutional right to equal time with children)

In re A.P.S., 54 S.W.3d 493 (Tex. App.—Texarkana 2001, no pet.) (order giving father's complete discretion over possessory-conservator mother's access to children error) (in an order appointing a parent as possessory conservator, the trial court must specifically state the times and conditions for possession of or access to the children)

In re Walters, 39 S.W.3d 280 (Tex. App.—Texarkana 2001, no pet.) (because mother appointed PC, error not to provide specific conditions and times for access and possession)

---

§ 153.191. Presumption that Parent to be Appointed Possessory Conservator

The court shall appoint as a possessory conservator a parent who is not appointed as a sole or joint managing conservator unless it finds that the appointment is not in the best interest of the child and that parental possession or access would endanger the physical or emotional welfare of the child.

§ 153.192. Rights and Duties of Parent Appointed Possessory Conservator

(a) Unless limited by court order, a parent appointed as possessory conservator of a child has the rights and duties provided by Subchapter B and any other right or duty expressly granted to the possessory conservator in the order.

(b) In ordering the terms and conditions for possession of a child by a parent appointed possessory conservator, the court shall be guided by the guidelines in Subchapter E.

§ 153.193. Minimal Restriction on Parent's Possession or Access

The terms of an order that denies possession of a child to a parent or imposes restrictions or limitations on a parent's right to possession of or access to a child may not exceed those that are required to protect the best interest of the child.

SUBCHAPTER E. GUIDELINES FOR THE POSSESSION OF A CHILD BY A PARENT NAMED AS POSSESSORY CONSERVATOR

Introductory Comment

These statutory guidelines apply to a parent named as a possessory conservator or as a sole or joint managing conservator who is not awarded primary possession. Guidelines do not exist for possession of or access to a child by a nonparent possessory conservator. Further, the standard order, *infra*, specifically is applicable only to children three years of age or older; no guidelines exist for a child under three. Very young children, infants through toddlers, at least theoretically must be dealt with individually. However, the standard order is designed to automatically take effect when a child reaches age three. This constitutes legislative approval of a prospective order.

See CLE/Other Legal Publications and Leading Cases following Introductory Comment for Subch. F. Standard Possession Order (§§ 153.3101-.317), _infra_.

---

§ 153.251. Policy and General Application of Guidelines

(a) The guidelines established in the standard possession order are intended to guide the courts in ordering the terms and conditions for possession of a child by a parent named as a possessory conservator or as the minimum possession for a joint managing conservator.

(b) It is the policy of this state to encourage frequent contact between a child and each parent for periods of possession that optimize the development of a close and continuing relationship between each parent and child.

(c) It is preferable for all children in a family to be together during periods of possession.

(d) The standard possession order is designed to apply to a child three years of age or older.

§ 153.252. Rebuttable Presumption

In a suit, there is a rebuttable presumption that the standard possession order in Subchapter F:

(1) provides reasonable minimum possession of a child for a parent named as a possessory conservator or joint managing conservator; and

(2) is in the best interest of the child.

§ 153.253. Standard Possession Order Inappropriate or Unworkable

The court shall render an order that grants periods of possession of the child as similar as possible to those provided by the standard possession order if the work schedule or other special circumstances of the managing conservator, the possessory conservator, or the child, or the year-round school schedule of the child, make the standard order unworkable or inappropriate.

§ 153.254. Child Less Than Three Years of Age

(a) The court shall render an order appropriate under the circumstances for possession of a child less than three years of age. **In rendering the order, the court shall consider evidence of all relevant factors, including:**

(1) the caregiving provided to the child before and during the current suit;

(2) the effect on the child that may result from separation from either party;

(3) the availability of the parties as caregivers and the willingness of the parties to personally care for the child;

(4) the physical, medical, behavioral, and developmental needs of the child;

(5) the physical, medical, emotional, economic, and social conditions of the parties;

(6) the impact and influence of individuals, other than the parties, who will be present during periods of possession;

(7) the presence of siblings during periods of possession;

(8) the child's need to develop healthy attachments to both parents;

(9) the child's need for continuity of routine;

(10) the location and proximity of the residences of the parties;

(11) the need for a temporary possession schedule that incrementally shifts to the schedule provided in the prospective order under Subsection (d) based on:

(A) the age of the child; or

(B) minimal or inconsistent contact with the child by a party;

(12) the ability of the parties to share in the responsibilities, rights, and duties of parenting; and

(13) any other evidence of the best interest of the child.

(b) **Notwithstanding the Texas Rules of Civil Procedure, in rendering an order under Subsection (a), the court shall make findings in support of the order if:**

(1) a party files a written request with the court not later than the 10th day after the date of the hearing; or

(2) a party makes an oral request in court during the hearing on the order.

(c) The court shall make and enter the findings required by Subsection (b) not later than the 15th day after the date the party makes the request.

(d) The court shall render a prospective order to take effect on the child's third birthday, which presumptively will be the standard possession order.

Amended by Acts 2011, 82nd Leg., ch. 86 (S.B. 820), § 1, eff. Sept. 1, 2011.

Comment

Drafting a court order in a final SAPCR decree for possession of and access to a child of whatever age to be in effect over an extended period of time is, by definition, an impossible task to do perfectly. It is not akin to shooting a moving target; rather, it is like firing off one shot at an almost infinite number of targets moving over time. What a court order can do is settle immediate questions between the parties and form a basis for future accommodations between cooperative parents. Alternatively, it can create stress, or even constant strife leading to further attempts to do the impossible. For the most part, periodic return to court for an updating of the order for most parents no longer living together is impracticable in the extreme. Thankfully, only common sense will serve as the best remedy for future changes and difference of opinion.

The drafting difficulties for a standard order are compounded when a court order is needed for a young child, ranging from a newborn infant to one completing the "terrible twos." Never in any person's life do the moving targets of need and development move so swiftly.

The modification of this plain-vanilla section covering the first three years of life is far from the extreme detail in the Texas Standard Order for older children, but the result is most certainly a good faith effort to attack an intractable problem. The enumeration of factors for the court to take into account is a paradigm of common sense. Of course, more factors are always possible to conceive, but focusing on the ones at hand should suffice for the foreseeable future.

CLE/Other Legal Publication

Possession and access to children under the age of three. Diana S. Friedman & Jonathan Gould, 2011 MARRIAGE DISSOLUTION

Visitation with children under three. Doug R. Woodburn, Diana S. Friedman & Jonathan Gould, 2010 ADV. FAM. L.

§ 153.255. Agreement

The court may render an order for periods of possession of a child that vary from the standard possession order based on the agreement of the parties.

§ 153.256. Factors for Court to Consider

In ordering the terms of possession of a child under an order other than a standard possession order, the court shall be guided by the guidelines established by the standard possession order and may consider:

(1) the age, developmental status, circumstances, needs, and best interest of the child;

(2) the circumstances of the managing conservator and of the parent named as a possessory conservator; and

(3) any other relevant factor.

§ 153.257. Means of Travel

In an order providing for the terms and conditions of possession of a child, the court may restrict the means of travel of the child by a legal mode of transportation only after a showing of good cause contained in the record and a finding by the court that the restriction is in the best interest of the child. The court shall specify the duties of the conservators to provide transportation to and from the transportation facilities.

§ 153.258. Request for Findings When Order Varies From Standard Order

Without regard to Rules 296 through 299, Texas Rules of Civil Procedure, in all cases in which possession of a child by a parent is contested and the possession of the child varies from the standard possession order, on written request made or filed with the court not later than 10 days after the date of the hearing or on oral request made in open court during the hearing, the court shall state in the order the specific reasons for the variance from the standard order.

SUBCHAPTER F. STANDARD POSSESSION ORDER

Introductory Comment

The standard possession order contemplates the rendition of a single, uniform order to remain in effect throughout the period of conservatorship. The reality of a child's life does not intrude on the uniformity of the standard order. It is one thing to order regular weekend visitation for a six year old and expect enforcement. It is quite another to expect compliance of an inflexible schedule in dealing with a 16 year old. Fortunately for the child, the very first provision, Section 153.311, provides that the parents may mutually agree to change any aspect of the order. Probably pressure for reasoned change from a 16 year old is more likely to elicit a response favored by the teenager than anything a 6 year-old might request.

In 2009 the standard possession order received a thoroughgoing update and cleanup without making significant change to its basic structure. The provisions designed to cover parents who live "near" to each other, i.e., 100 miles or less apart, and "far apart," i.e., over 100 miles, were unchanged. The basic order is firmed up to indicate that periods of possession begin and end at 6:00 p.m. on the applicable day. Unless a default alternative is selected the parties may rely on the question of beginning and ending time without reference to the actual order. The alternative times for beginning and ending of weekly possession, holidays, and weekends extended by holidays are subject to alternative beginning and ending possession times at the election of the conservator. Of course, the election of an alternative time is overridden if "the court finds that the election is not in the best interest of the child."

The times for possession spelled out for orders involving parents who live over 100 miles apart are not subject to election of alternative times.

CLE/Other Legal Publication

Possession and access to children under the age of three. Diana S. Friedman & Jonathan Gould, 2011 Marriage Dissolution

Conservatorship and Possession: Primer on JMC, sole MC, and parenting time. Patricia N. Carter, 2011 U.T. Parent-Child Relationships: Basics

Visitation with children under three. Doug R. Woodburn, Diana S. Friedman & Jonathan Gould, 2010 Adv. Fam. L.

Shared custody: advocacy and drafting. Ike Vanden Eykel, 2010 Adv. Fam. L.

Possession with bad fact parents: problematic possession orders. David A. Kazen, 2010 Marriage Dissolution

When standard doesn't fit—custom tailored possession orders. Larry L. Martin, 2010 U.T. Parent-Child Relationships

Creative possession schedules. Kimberly M. Naylor & Stephen J. Naylor, 2010 Adv. Fam. L. Drafting

Rebutting the statutory presumptions: joint managing conservator, parental preference, standard possession orders, and practical presumptions. Ann Coover, H.E. Mendez, James E. Monnig & Judith G. Wells, 2009 Adv. Fam. L.

Meaningful Parenting time under unusual circumstances (visitation). Amy A. Geistweidt, 2009 U.T. Parent-Child Relationships

Psychology of a possession order. Mark J. Blotcky, Mary A. Connell & Stephen J. Naylor, 2009 Marriage Dissolution

---

See Accompanying CD-ROM for Additional CLE/Other Legal Publications.

Leading Cases

Peck v. Peck, 172 S.W.3d 26 (Tex. App.—Dallas 2005, pet. denied) (mutual injunction against "overnight guests" upheld, even as a condition of father's visitation)

In re J.R.D., 169 S.W.3d 740 (Tex. App.—Austin 2005, pet. denied) (father does not have constitutional right to equal time with children)

In re A.P.S., 54 S.W.3d 493 (Tex. App.—Texarkana 2001, no pet.) (mother a danger to two daughters, but award of possessory conservatorship means that access cannot be left to sole discretion of father; in an order appointing a parent as PC, the trial court must specifically state the times and conditions for possession of or access to the children)

In re Lemons, 47 S.W.3d 202 (Tex. App.—Beaumont 2001, no pet.) (absolute discretion over mother's "reasonable visitation" by father in temporary order created lack of enforceability by mother which effectively denied the mother's right to visitation with her child)

§ 153.3101. Reference to "School" in Standard Possession Order

In a standard possession order, "school" means the primary or secondary school in which the child is enrolled or, if the child is not enrolled in a primary or secondary school, the public school district in which the child primarily resides.

§ 153.311. Mutual Agreement or Specified Terms for Possession

The court shall specify in a standard possession order that the parties may have possession of the child at times mutually agreed to in advance by the parties and, in the absence of mutual agreement, shall have possession of the child under the specified terms set out in the standard possession order.

Comment

This is the most important substantive provision in the standard order. This crucial section provides that the parties may mutually agree to vary the possession of a child at any time, in any mutually acceptable manner, and that the specific terms set out in the standard order take effect only failing such mutual agreement.

---

§ 153.312. Parents Who Reside 100 Miles or Less Apart

(a) If the possessory conservator resides 100 miles or less from the primary residence of the child, the possessory conservator shall have the right to possession of the child as follows:

(1) on weekends throughout the year beginning at 6 p.m. on the first, third, and fifth Friday of each month and ending at 6 p.m. on the following Sunday; and

(2) on Thursdays of each week during the regular school term beginning at 6 p.m. and ending at 8 p.m., unless the court finds that visitation under this subdivision is not in the best interest of the child.

(b) The following provisions govern possession of the child for vacations and certain specific holidays and supersede conflicting weekend or Thursday periods of possession. The possessory conservator and the managing conservator shall have rights of possession of the child as follows:

(1) the possessory conservator shall have possession in even-numbered years, beginning at 6 p.m. on the day the child is dismissed from school for the school's spring vacation and ending at 6 p.m. on the day before school resumes after that vacation, and the managing conservator shall have possession for the same period in odd-numbered years;

(2) if a possessory conservator:

(A) gives the managing conservator written notice by April 1 of each year specifying an extended period or periods of summer possession, the possessory conservator shall have possession of the child for 30 days beginning not earlier than the day after the child's school is dismissed for the summer vacation and ending not later than seven days before school resumes at the end of the summer vacation, to be exercised in not more than two separate periods of at least seven consecutive days each, with each period of possession beginning and ending at 6 p.m. on each applicable day; or

(B) does not give the managing conservator written notice by April 1 of each year specifying an extended period or periods of summer possession, the possessory conservator shall have possession of the child for 30 consecutive days beginning at 6 p.m. on July 1 and ending at 6 p.m. on July 31;

(3) if the managing conservator gives the possessory conservator written notice by April 15 of each year, the managing conservator shall have possession of the child on any one weekend beginning Friday at 6 p.m. and ending at 6 p.m. on the following Sunday during one period of possession by the possessory conservator under Subdivision (2), provided that the managing conservator picks up the child from the possessory conservator and returns the child to that same place; and

(4) if the managing conservator gives the possessory conservator written notice by April 15 of each year or gives the possessory conservator 14 days' written notice on or after April 16 of each year, the managing conservator may designate one weekend beginning not earlier than the day after the child's school is dismissed for the summer vacation and ending not later than seven days before school resumes at the end of the summer vacation, during which an otherwise scheduled weekend period of possession by the possessory conservator will not take place, provided that the weekend designated does not interfere with the possessory conservator's period or periods of extended summer possession or with Father's Day if the possessory conservator is the father of the child.

Comment

The standard possession order has become a way of life for family law practitioners. Basic acceptance of the terms of the standard order by the bench and bar is widely supported.

There has been little real controversy in the basic right of possession to the child for the noncustodial parent who lives within relatively easy driving distance from the custodial parent and child. The first, third and fifth weekends have remained in place since the initiation of the standard order process. The mid-week possession has undergone some significant change since its first adoption, however. Originally, the Wednesday visit was purely a 6:00 p.m. to 8:00 p.m. affair, a mid-week meal visit. The first major change in this procedure was to provide that, at the non-custodial conservator's election the mid-week possession could be converted into a mid-week overnight visit with the child being returned to the school the following morning. Moreover, the court was directed to approve this process on the request of the possessory conservator unless the court could rule it was "not in the best interest of the child."

In 2003, the Wednesday period was moved to Thursday. The rationale for the change was relatively simple. Thursday overnight means that the first, third and fifth weekend will always be a long weekend since the child will arrive Thursday evening and not return to the custodial parent's custody until the following Monday after school, and if Monday is a holiday it will be Tuesday after school before the child returns.

§ 153.313. Parents Who Reside Over 100 Miles Apart

If the possessory conservator resides more than 100 miles from the residence of the child, the possessory conservator shall have the right to possession of the child as follows:

(1) either regular weekend possession beginning on the first, third, and fifth Friday as provided under the terms applicable to parents who reside 100 miles or less apart or not more than one weekend per month of the possessory conservator's choice beginning at 6 p.m. on the day school recesses for the weekend and ending at 6 p.m. on the day before school resumes after the weekend, provided that the possessory conservator gives the managing conservator 14 days' written or telephonic notice preceding a designated weekend, and provided that the possessory conservator elects an option for this alternative period of possession by written notice given to the managing conservator within 90 days after the parties begin to reside more than 100 miles apart, as applicable;

(2) each year beginning at 6 p.m. on the day the child is dismissed from school for the school's spring vacation and ending at 6 p.m. on the day before school resumes after that vacation;

(3) if the possessory conservator:

(A) gives the managing conservator written notice by April 1 of each year specifying an extended period or periods of summer possession, the possessory conservator shall have possession of the child for 42 days beginning not earlier than the day after the child's school is dismissed for the summer vacation and ending not later than seven days before school resumes at the end of the summer vacation, to be exercised in not more than two separate periods of at least seven consecutive days each, with each period of possession beginning and ending at 6 p.m. on each applicable day; or

(B) does not give the managing conservator written notice by April 1 of each year specifying an extended period or periods of summer possession, the possessory conservator shall have possession of the child for 42 consecutive days beginning at 6 p.m. on June 15 and ending at 6 p.m. on July 27;

(4) if the managing conservator gives the possessory conservator written notice by April 15 of each year the managing conservator shall have possession of the child on one weekend beginning Friday at 6 p.m. and ending at 6 p.m. on the following Sunday during one period of possession by the possessory conservator under Subdivision (3), provided that if a period of possession by the possessory conservator exceeds 30 days, the managing conservator may have possession of the child under the terms of this subdivision on two nonconsecutive weekends during that time period, and further provided that the managing conservator picks up the child from the possessory conservator and returns the child to that same place; and

(5) if the managing conservator gives the possessory conservator written notice by April 15 of each year, the managing conservator may designate 21 days beginning not earlier than the day after the child's school is dismissed for the summer vacation and ending not later than seven days before school resumes at the end of the summer vacation, to be exercised in not more than two separate periods of at least seven consecutive days each, with each period of possession beginning and ending at 6 p.m. on each applicable day, during which the possessory conservator may not have possession of the child, provided that the period or periods so designated do not interfere with the possessory conservator's period or periods of extended summer possession or with Father's Day if the possessory conservator is the father of the child.

§ 153.314. Holiday Possession Unaffected by Distance Parents Reside Apart

The following provisions govern possession of the child for certain specific holidays and supersede conflicting weekend or Thursday periods of possession without regard to the distance the parents reside apart. The possessory conservator and the managing conservator shall have rights of possession of the child as follows:

(1) the possessory conservator shall have possession of the child in even-numbered years beginning at 6 p.m. on the day the child is dismissed from school for the Christmas school vacation and ending at noon on December 28, and the managing conservator shall have possession for the same period in odd-numbered years;

(2) the possessory conservator shall have possession of the child in odd-numbered years beginning at noon on December 28 and ending at 6 p.m. on the day before school resumes after that vacation, and the managing conservator shall have possession for the same period in even-numbered years;

(3) the possessory conservator shall have possession of the child in odd-numbered years, beginning at 6 p.m. on the day the child is dismissed from school before Thanksgiving and ending at 6 p.m. on the following Sunday, and the managing conservator shall have possession for the same period in even-numbered years;

(4) the parent not otherwise entitled under this standard possession order to present possession of a child on the child's birthday shall have possession of the child beginning at 6 p.m. and ending at 8 p.m. on that day, provided that the parent picks up the child from the residence of the conservator entitled to possession and returns the child to that same place;

(5) if a conservator, the father shall have possession of the child beginning at 6 p.m. on the Friday preceding Father's Day and ending on Father's Day at 6 p.m., provided that, if he is not otherwise entitled under this standard possession order to present possession of the child, he picks up the child from the residence of the conservator entitled to possession and returns the child to that same place; and

(6) if a conservator, the mother shall have possession of the child beginning at 6 p.m. on the Friday preceding Mother's Day and ending on Mother's Day at 6 p.m., provided that, if she is not otherwise entitled under this standard possession order to present possession of the child,

she picks up the child from the residence of the conservator entitled to possession and returns the child to that same place.

§ 153.315. Weekend Possession Extended by Holiday

(a) If a weekend period of possession of the possessory conservator coincides with a student holiday or teacher in-service day that falls on a Monday during the regular school term, as determined by the school in which the child is enrolled, or with a federal, state, or local holiday that falls on a Monday during the summer months in which school is not in session, the weekend possession shall end at 6 p.m. on Monday.

(b) If a weekend period of possession of the possessory conservator coincides with a student holiday or teacher in-service day that falls on a Friday during the regular school term, as determined by the school in which the child is enrolled, or with a federal, state, or local holiday that falls on a Friday during the summer months in which school is not in session, the weekend possession shall begin at 6 p.m. on Thursday.

§ 153.316. General Terms and Conditions

The court shall order the following general terms and conditions of possession of a child to apply without regard to the distance between the residence of a parent and the child:

(1) the managing conservator shall surrender the child to the possessory conservator at the beginning of each period of the possessory conservator's possession at the residence of the managing conservator;

(2) if the possessory conservator elects to begin a period of possession at the time the child's school is regularly dismissed, the managing conservator shall surrender the child to the possessory conservator at the beginning of each period of possession at the school in which the child is enrolled;

(3) the possessory conservator shall be ordered to do one of the following:

(A) the possessory conservator shall surrender the child to the managing conservator at the end of each period of possession at the residence of the possessory conservator; or

(B) the possessory conservator shall return the child to the residence of the managing conservator at the end of each period of possession, except that the order shall provide that the possessory conservator shall surrender the child to the managing conservator at the end of each period of possession at the residence of the possessory conservator if:

(i) at the time the original order or a modification of an order establishing terms and conditions of possession or access the possessory conservator and the managing conservator lived in the same county, the possessory conservator's county of residence remains the same after the rendition of the order, and the managing conservator's county of residence changes, effective on the date of the change of residence by the managing conservator; or

(ii) the possessory conservator and managing conservator lived in the same residence at any time during a six-month period preceding the date on which a suit for dissolution of the marriage was filed and the possessory conservator's county of residence remains the same and the managing conservator's county of residence changes after they no longer live in the same residence, effective on the date the order is rendered;

(4) if the possessory conservator elects to end a period of possession at the time the child's school resumes, the possessory conservator shall surrender the child to the managing conservator at the end of each period of possession at the school in which the child is enrolled;

(5) each conservator shall return with the child the personal effects that the child brought at the beginning of the period of possession;

(6) either parent may designate a competent adult to pick up and return the child, as applicable; a parent or a designated competent adult shall be present when the child is picked up or returned;

(7) a parent shall give notice to the person in possession of the child on each occasion that the parent will be unable to exercise that parent's right of possession for a specified period;

(8) written notice shall be deemed to have been timely made if received or postmarked before or at the time that notice is due; and

(9) if a conservator's time of possession of a child ends at the time school resumes and for any reason the child is not or will not be returned to school, the conservator in possession of the child shall immediately notify the school and the other conservator that the child will not be or has not been returned to school.

Comment

Subdivisions (1) and (2) set forth the basic rule that the managing conservator is to surrender custody of the child when the possessory conservator arrives for pick-up.

Most of the legislation in this section (and there has been quite a bit) has focused on Subdivision (3). The first major change in the manner in which the parties are to conduct themselves altered the pick-up-and-return process for the noncustodial parent. Now the court is to choose between the pick-up-and-return process and the pick-up-and-pick-up process. That is, each conservator may be required to retrieve the child from the residence of the other conservator at the end of these periods of possession. Parenthetically, requiring the court to make a choice in the standard order has given no little difficulty to inattentive lawyers or judges. That is, many an order has been signed with neither choice being made, leaving the question open as to how the child is to be returned to the primary managing conservator. A second, even more complicated and convoluted problem is provided in (3)(B)(i)-(ii). Those provisions are intended to require a managing conservator who "moved away" to pick up the child at the home of the possessory conservator. The fact situation described automatically by statute modifies a "pick-up and return" into a "pick-up and pick-up" process. This assumes, of course, that the parents are able to fathom the meaning of relatively opaque statutory language copied into a standard order.

Subdivision (4) merely directs the possessory conservator to return the child as the order directs. Thus, each conservator is "ordered" to obey the order, which seems reasonable.

Subdivisions (5) through (9) constitute the "act in a civilized manner please" provisions. Subdivision (5) mandates return of teddy bears and crisp pinafores with the child. The "competent adult" in Subdivision (6) really means "new spouse or significant other of the other conservator." Subdivisions (7)–(9) are directed at providing notice of a problem with the schedule as a matter of common courtesy to facilitate compliance with the standard order.

§ 153.3161. Repealed.

§ 153.3162. Additional Periods of Possession or Access After Conclusion of Military Deployment

(a) In this section, "conservator" means:

(1) a possessory conservator of a child; or

(2) a joint managing conservator of a child without the exclusive right to designate the primary residence of the child.

(b) Not later than the 90th day after the date a conservator who is a member of the armed services concludes the conservator's active military deployment, the conservator may petition the court to:

(1) compute the periods of possession of or access to the child to which the conservator would have otherwise been entitled during the conservator's deployment; and

(2) award the conservator additional periods of possession of or access to the child to compensate for the periods described by Subdivision (1).

(c) If a conservator petitions the court under Subsection (b), the court:

(1) shall compute the periods of possession or access to the child described by Subsection (b)(1); and

(2) may award to the conservator additional periods of possession of or access to the child for a length of time and under terms the court considers reasonable, if the court determines that:

(A) the conservator was deployed in a location where access to the child was not reasonably possible; and

(B) the award of additional periods of possession of or access to the child is in the best interest of the child.

(d) In making the determination under Subsection (c)(2), the court:

(1) shall consider:

(A) the periods of possession of or access to the child to which the conservator would otherwise have been entitled during the conservator's deployment, as computed under Subsection (c)(1);

(B) whether the court provided in an order under Section 153.3161 that a person exercise limited possession of the child during the conservator's deployment; and

(C) any other factor the court considers appropriate; and

(2) is not required to award additional periods of possession of or access to the child that equals the possession or access to which the conservator would have been entitled during the conservator's deployment, as computed under Subsection (c)(1).

(e) After the conservator has exercised all additional periods of possession or access awarded under this section, the rights of all affected parties are governed by the terms of any court order applicable when the conservator is not deployed.

Comment

The amendments to this section are independent of the provisions in Subchapter L of this chapter, which deals comprehensively with military deployment, mobilization, or temporary duty affecting the parental rights and duties of a servicemember. This section and Section 153.709 cover the same ground, i.e., makeup time for the access to and possession of a child missed by a servicemember while deployed on active military service. The language of the two sections is very similar, but not identical; they coexist unless there is a direct conflict. To the extent that there may be a conflict, the principle rule most likely to apply is that the specific controls over the general. For example, the provisions under this section are directed at servicemembers who have active military deployment. The provisions in Section 153.709 apply to a conservator who has been ordered to military deployment, military mobilization, or temporary military duty." The definitions of the three forms of military assignments are more specific and broader, but are not in conflict with the narrower application to only "military deployment."

CLE/Other Legal Publications

Military visitation and conservator issues. Meca Latreice Walker, 2011 MARRIAGE DISSOLUTION

Special problems for military families. David D. Farr, 2011 ADV. FAM. L.

Avoiding conflict at home when there is conflict abroad: military child custody and visitation. Lauren S. Douglass, 43 FAM. L. Q. 315 (2009)

---

§ 153.317. Alternative Beginning and Ending Possession Times

(a) If elected by a conservator, the court shall alter the standard possession order under Sections 153.312, 153.314, and 153.315 to provide for one or more of the following alternative beginning and ending possession times for the described periods of possession, unless the court finds that the election is not in the best interest of the child:

(1) for weekend periods of possession under Section 153.312(a)(1) during the regular school term:

(A) beginning at the time the child's school is regularly dismissed; or

(B) ending at the time the child's school resumes after the weekend;

(2) for Thursday periods of possession under Section 153.312(a)(2):

(A) beginning at the time the child's school is regularly dismissed; or

(B) ending at the time the child's school resumes on Friday;

(3) for spring vacation periods of possession under Section 153.312(b)(1), beginning at the time the child's school is dismissed for those vacations;

(4) for Christmas school vacation periods of possession under Section 153.314(1), beginning at the time the child's school is dismissed for the vacation;

(5) for Thanksgiving holiday periods of possession under Section 153.314(3), beginning at the time the child's school is dismissed for the holiday;

(6) for Father's Day periods of possession under Section 153.314(5), ending at 8 a.m. on the Monday after Father's Day weekend;

(7) for Mother's Day periods of possession under Section 153.314(6):

(A) beginning at the time the child's school is regularly dismissed on the Friday preceding Mother's Day; or

(B) ending at the time the child's school resumes after Mother's Day; or

(8) for weekend periods of possession that are extended under Section 153.315(b) by a student holiday or teacher in-service day that falls on a Friday, beginning at the time the child's school is regularly dismissed on Thursday.

(b) A conservator must make an election under Subsection (a) before or at the time of the rendition of a possession order. The election may be made:

(1) in a written document filed with the court; or

(2) through an oral statement made in open court on the record.

Comment

For parents who live within 100 miles of each other, alternative possession times for Christmas vacation, the other holidays and special days, and Thursday evening possessions are treated in an identical manner. For example, the judge is mandated to accede to the election of a conservator for an alternative order directing that: (1) Thursday possession pickups take place on dismissal of the child's school; or, (2) return of the child is to occur when the school resumes on Friday; or (3) both.

SUBCHAPTER G. APPOINTMENT OF NONPARENT AS CONSERVATOR

Introductory Comment

The parental presumption has always been called "one of the strongest presumptions known." As discussed in the *Lewelling* decision below, that presumption is recognized as such in reality as well as in rhetoric. Nonetheless, there is always a possibility that a nonparent will be named as a sole or joint managing conservator in the best interest of the child. Naming a nonparent as a possessory conservator does not affect the parental preference. Note that a grandparent, uncle, or aunt are nonparents covered by this section. In addition, Subchapter H of this chapter provides special rules of possession and access for these close relatives.

Editor's Note: *See* Sections 153.371-.377 for rights of grandparents.

CLE/Other Legal Publications

Representing relatives. JoAl Cannon Sheridan, 2010 Adv. Fam. L.

The extended family: rights and duties of nonparents. Barbara Nunneley & Stephen Farrar, 2010 U.T. Parent-Child Relationships

Third-party SAPCR issues. William Merritt Reppeto, 2010 U.T. Fam. L. Front Lines

New Chapter 34: authorization agreements for nonparent relatives. Judy L. Warne, 2010 Marriage Dissolution

Joinder of third parties—entities and/or individuals. John F. Nichols, Sr., 2009 Adv. Fam. L.

Getting the information from third parties about kids. Joseph Indelicato, Jr., 2009 U.T. Parent-Child Relationships

Discovery from third parties. Cynthia Barela Graham, Jonathan J. Bates, Kristy D. Piazza & Cindy V. Tinsdale, 2009 Marriage Dissolution

Joinder of third parties—entities and/or individuals. John F. Nichols, Sr., 2009 Adv. Fam. L.

See Accompanying CD–ROM for Additional CLE/Other Legal Publications.

Leading Cases

Brook v. Brook, 881 S.W.2d 297 (Tex. 1994) (parental preference not offended when one parent named JMC with a nonparent)

Lewelling v. Lewelling, 796 S.W.2d 164 (Tex. 1990) (statutory parental preference creates strong presumption)

In re M.K.S-V, 301 S.W.3d 460 (Tex. App.—Dallas 2009, no pet.) (former same-sex partner did not have care, control and possession of partner's child)

In re K.K.C., 299 S.W.3d 788 (Tex. App.—Beaumont 2009, no pet.) (man living with child's mother for seven years did not have standing re care, control and possession)

In re G.R.W., 191 S.W.3d 896 (Tex. App.—Texarkana 2006, no pet.) (evidence sufficient to support appointment of maternal great-aunt and uncle sole MC of child)

Sotelo v. Gonzales, 170 S.W.3d 783 (Tex. App.—El Paso 2005, no pet.) (parental presumption not applicable in modification proceeding)

In re A.J.L., 108 S.W.3d 414 (Tex. App.—Fort Worth 2003, pet. denied) (ex-stepfather lacks standing to obtain visitation with stepchildren by modifying his divorce decree of the prior SAPCR order between his ex and kids' father)

Coons-Andersen v. Andersen, 104 S.W.3d 630 (Tex. App.—Dallas 2003, no pet.) (mother's ex-partner lacked standing to seek conservatorship of child born while the two women were still living together)

In re K.R.P., 80 S.W.3d 669 (Tex. App.—Houston [1st Dist.] 2002, pet. denied) (former step-parent named sole MC over wishes of unfit parents)

§ 153.371. Rights and Duties of Nonparent Appointed as Sole Managing Conservator

Unless limited by court order or other provisions of this chapter, a nonparent, licensed child-placing agency, or authorized agency appointed as a managing conservator of the child has the following rights and duties:

(1) the right to have physical possession and to direct the moral and religious training of the child;

(2) the duty of care, control, protection, and reasonable discipline of the child;

(3) the duty to provide the child with clothing, food, shelter, education, and medical, psychological, and dental care;

(4) the right to consent for the child to medical, psychiatric, psychological, dental, and surgical treatment and to have access to the child's medical records;

(5) the right to receive and give receipt for payments for the support of the child and to hold or disburse funds for the benefit of the child;

(6) the right to the services and earnings of the child;

(7) the right to consent to marriage and to enlistment in the armed forces of the United States;

(8) the right to represent the child in legal action and to make other decisions of substantial legal significance concerning the child;

(9) except when a guardian of the child's estate or a guardian or attorney ad litem has been appointed for the child, the right to act as an agent of the child in relation to the child's estate if the child's action is required by a state, the United States, or a foreign government;

(10) the right to designate the primary residence of the child and to make decisions regarding the child's education; and

(11) if the parent-child relationship has been terminated with respect to the parents, or only living parent, or if there is no living parent, the right to consent to the adoption of the child and to make any other decision concerning the child that a parent could make.

Leading Cases

In re V.L.K., 24 S.W.3d 338 (Tex. 2000) (nonparent sole M.C. has right to establish child's residence and have primary custody)

Brook v. Brook, 881 S.W.2d 297 (Tex. 1994) (appointment of nonparent as sole or joint M.C.)

---

§ 153.372. Nonparent Appointed as Joint Managing Conservator

(a) A nonparent, authorized agency, or licensed child-placing agency appointed as a joint managing conservator may serve in that capacity with either another nonparent or with a parent of the child.

(b) The procedural and substantive standards regarding an agreed or court-ordered joint managing conservatorship provided by Subchapter C apply to a nonparent joint managing conservator.

§ 153.3721. Access to Certain Records by Nonparent Joint Managing Conservator

Unless limited by court order or other provisions of this chapter, a nonparent joint managing conservator has the right of access to the medical records of the child, without regard to whether the right is specified in the order.

§ 153.373. Voluntary Surrender of Possession Rebuts Parental Presumption

The presumption that a parent should be appointed or retained as managing conservator of the child is rebutted if the court finds that:

(1) the parent has voluntarily relinquished actual care, control, and possession of the child to a nonparent, licensed child-placing agency, or authorized agency for a period of one year or more, a portion of which was within 90 days preceding the date of intervention in or filing of the suit; and

(2) the appointment of the nonparent or agency as managing conservator is in the best interest of the child.

§ 153.374. Designation of Managing Conservator in Affidavit of Relinquishment

(a) A parent may designate a competent person, authorized agency, or licensed child-placing agency to serve as managing conservator of the child in an unrevoked or irrevocable affidavit of relinquishment of parental rights executed as provided by Chapter 161.

(b) The person or agency designated to serve as managing conservator shall be appointed managing conservator unless the court finds that the appointment would not be in the best interest of the child.

§ 153.375. Annual Report by Nonparent Managing Conservator

(a) A nonparent appointed as a managing conservator of a child shall each 12 months after the appointment file with the court a report of facts concerning the child's welfare, including the child's whereabouts and physical condition.

(b) The report may not be admitted in evidence in a subsequent suit.

§ 153.376. Rights and Duties of Nonparent Possessory Conservator

(a) Unless limited by court order or other provisions of this chapter, a nonparent, licensed child-placing agency, or authorized agency appointed as a possessory conservator has the following rights and duties during the period of possession:

(1) the duty of care, control, protection, and reasonable discipline of the child;

(2) the duty to provide the child with clothing, food, and shelter; and

(3) the right to consent to medical, dental, and surgical treatment during an emergency involving an immediate danger to the health and safety of the child.

(b) A nonparent possessory conservator has any other right or duty specified in the order.

§ 153.377. Access to Child's Records

A nonparent possessory conservator has the right of access to medical, dental, psychological, and educational records of the child to the same extent as the managing conservator, without regard to whether the right is specified in the order.

SUBCHAPTER H. RIGHTS OF GRANDPARENT, AUNT, OR UNCLE

Introductory Comment

In 1973 the Family Code granted the trial court discretionary power to "grant reasonable visitation rights to either the maternal or paternal grandparents of the child and issue any necessary orders to enforce said decree." Since this relatively modest beginning, the provisions for what is usually called "grandparental visitation" have been amended on several occasions and generally been the source of intermittent tinkering. Along the way, the terminology was inconsistently changed from "visitation" to "possession of and access to the child," or alternatively simply "access." In sum, since 1973 grandparents have had an independent cause of action to request access to their grandchildren.

Because the statutory framework was almost entirely fact driven, until 2002 it operated with relatively little legal controversy. A major shift occurred when the U.S. Supreme Court decided *Troxel v. Granville*, 530 U.S. 57, 120 S.Ct. 2054, 147 L.Ed.2d 49 (2000). The Court has consistently maintained that parents have a fundamental constitutional right to have and raise children without interference from the state except in extraordinary circumstances, e.g., mandatory schooling, mandatory immunization, and abuse and neglect of a child. *Troxel* reaffirmed that principle, finding unconstitutional a Washington State statute that provided for access to a child by third parties over the objection of the parents. The Court ruled that the right of a parent to decide with whom the child would have contact is one of the fundamental rights of parenthood, and that a trial court must presume that a fit parent makes such decisions in the best interest of the child.

The implications of the *Troxel* decision were enormous. This ultimately led Attorney General Abbott to issue opinion GA–0260 in October 2004, addressing the constitutionality of the Texas statutes. Analyzing seven Texas appellate court opinions, the opinion concluded that the statutes could be constitutionally applied. However, the principles expressed in *Troxel* must be observed. In response to *Troxel* and this AG opinion, the provisions for "grandparent (and now aunt and uncle) visitation" were substantially rewritten in 2005.

Dispute over the right of grandparents to have possession of and access to a grandchild continues to be debated at the legislature. Interestingly, the 2009 amendments again raised the bar for grandparental visitation, albeit not by a significant degree. First, the grandparent must file an affidavit alleging, along with supporting facts, that the denial of the grandparental visitation "would significantly impair the child's physical health or emotional well-being." The court is also to make a preliminary determination that the facts stated would, if true, demonstrate the truth of that allegation. Even if the facts are so stated, the court retains discretion to order or refuse to order the access and possession.

Editor's Note: *See* Sections 153.371-.377 for rights of nonparents.

CLE/Other Legal Publications

Grandparents: what's new? Lynn Kamin, 2010 So. Tex. Fam. L. Conf.

Grandparents' program synopsis. Michael Childs, 2009 So. Tex. Fam. L. Conf..

Grandparent rights in Texas: does a grandparent stand a fighting chance? Allen R. Griffin & Holly Frymire Griffin, Fam. L. Sect. Rep. (Spring 2009)

Grandparents and other third parties. Lisa K. Hoppes, 2008 Marriage Dissolution

Grandparents' rights: are there any left after Troxel?. Angela Pence England, 2008 So. Tex. Fam. L. Grandparent & Kinship Care

Leading Cases

Troxel v. Granville, 530 U.S. 57, 120 S.Ct. 2054 (2000) (*see* comment above)

In re Scheller, 325 S.W.3d 640 (Tex. 2010) (trial court abused discretion as grandfather failed to prove father not acting in children's best interests; parent's Troxel rights upheld, but only on 2d mandamus petition) (appointment of psychologist as GAL didn't violate *Troxel*)

In re Chambless, 257 S.W.3d 698 (Tex. 2008) (parent entitled to opportunity to be heard before temporary grandparent visitation may be ordered)

In re Derzapf, 219 S.W.3d 327 (Tex. 2007) (step grandfather has no standing for seeking possession or access to grandchild)

In re Mays-Hooper, 189 S.W.3d 777 (Tex. 2006) (paternal grandmother not entitled to access to grandchild; *Troxel* applies to Texas cases)

In re S.M.D., 329 S.W.3d 8 (Tex. App.—San Antonio 2010, no pet.) (mother abandoned child, but maternal grandmother lacked standing under current version of § 102.004)

In re M.T.C., 299 S.W.3d 474 (Tex. App.—Texarkana 2009, no pet.) (step grandmother lacks standing, as did grandfather)

Critz v. Critz, 297 W.W.3d 464 (Tex. App.—Ft. Worth 2009, no pet.) (grandparents appointed JMCs with parents—the parental presumption should have been applied, which led to remand)

In re J.M.T., 280 S.W.3d 490 (Tex. App.—Eastland 2009, no pet.)(paternal grandparents obtained termination of parents and adopted grandchild; maternal grandparents failed to show impairment to child warranting their visitation)

In re Brown, 277 S.W.3d 474 (Tex. App.—Houston [14th Dist.] 2009, no pet.) (court-ordered psychiatric evaluation based on history of family violence and substance abuse)

In re M.J.G., 248 S.W.3d 753 (Tex. App.—Fort Worth 2008, no pet.) (grandparents lacked standing to file a motion for new trial)

In re B.R.S., 166 S.W.3d 373 (Tex. App.—Waco 2005, no pet.) (grandparent access statutes not unconstitutional)

Corrales v. DFPS, 155 S.W.3d 478 (Tex. App.—El Paso 2004, no pet.) (jury determined DPRS, not grandmother, best option for managing conservator)

Chavez v. Chavez, 148 S.W.3d 449 (Tex. App.—El Paso 2004, no pet.) (grandparents must overcome constitutionally based parental presumption, even if they would be better option for raising children)

In re P.D.M., 117 S.W.3d 453 (Tex. App.—Fort Worth 2003, pet. denied) (grandmother's suit after death of managing conservator is not an original suit and therefore is not subject to father's parental presumption)

In re C.T.H., 112 S.W.3d 262 (Tex. App.—Beaumont 2003, no pet.) (grandparents have justiciable interest in custody modification after caring for child for over six months)

Roby v. Adams, 68 S.W.3d 822 (Tex. App.—El Paso 2002, no pet.) (grandparent seeking visitation rights to grandchildren has the burden to overcome the presumption that a fit parent acts in the best interest of the children)

In re C.R.T., 61 S.W.3d 62 (Tex. App.—Amarillo 2001, pet. denied) (aunt named PMC of three of her druggie sister's children, thereby confirming placement of kids by mom with aunt)

---

§ 153.431. Appointment of Grandparent, Aunt, or Uncle as Managing Conservator

If both of the parents of a child are deceased, the court may consider appointment of a parent, sister, or brother of a deceased parent as a managing conservator of the child, but that consideration does not alter or diminish the discretionary power of the court.

§ 153.432. Suit for Possession or Access by Grandparent

(a) A biological or adoptive grandparent may request possession of or access to a grandchild by filing:

(1) an original suit; or

(2) a suit for modification as provided by Chapter 156.

(b) A grandparent may request possession of or access to a grandchild in a suit filed for the sole purpose of requesting the relief, without regard to whether the appointment of a managing conservator is an issue in the suit.

(c) In a suit described by Subsection (a), the person filing the suit must execute and attach an affidavit on knowledge or belief that contains, along with supporting facts, the allegation that denial of possession of or access to the child by the petitioner would significantly impair the child's physical health or emotional well-being. The court shall deny the relief sought and dismiss the suit unless the court determines that the facts stated in the affidavit, if true, would be sufficient to support the relief authorized under Section 153.433.

Comment

The addition of the term "possession of or" makes the language consistent throughout Subchapter H. For example, the caption of § 153.433 formerly referred to the conjunctive "possession of and access to the child," but the text was limited to "access." The caption of former § 153.434 referred only to "access," but the text applied the disjunctive "possession of or access to." The legislature has settled the conundrum by decreeing that a grandparent may be awarded either possession or access, which under rules of statutory construction also includes an award of both.

---

§ 153.433. Possession of or Access to Grandchild

(a) The court may order reasonable possession of or access to a grandchild by a grandparent if:

(1) at the time the relief is requested, at least one biological or adoptive parent of the child has not had that parent's parental rights terminated;

(2) the grandparent requesting possession of or access to the child overcomes the presumption that a parent acts in the best interest of the parent's child by proving by a preponderance of the

evidence that denial of possession of or access to the child would significantly impair the child's physical health or emotional well-being; and

(3) the grandparent requesting possession of or access to the child is a parent of a parent of the child and that parent of the child:

(A) has been incarcerated in jail or prison during the three-month period preceding the filing of the petition;

(B) has been found by a court to be incompetent;

(C) is dead; or

(D) does not have actual or court-ordered possession of or access to the child.

(b) An order granting possession of or access to a child by a grandparent that is rendered over a parent's objections must state, with specificity that:

(1) at the time the relief was requested, at least one biological or adoptive parent of the child had not had that parent's parental rights terminated;

(2) the grandparent requesting possession of or access to the child has overcome the presumption that a parent acts in the best interest of the parent's child by proving by a preponderance of the evidence that the denial of possession of or access to the child would significantly impair the child's physical health or emotional well-being; and

(3) the grandparent requesting possession of or access to the child is a parent of a parent of the child and that parent of the child:

(A) has been incarcerated in jail or prison during the three-month period preceding the filing of the petition;

(B) has been found by a court to be incompetent;

(C) is dead; or

(D) does not have actual or court-ordered possession of or access to the child.

Comment

Following the U.S. Supreme Court decision in *Troxel v. Granville*, 530 U.S. 57 (2000), opinions varied around the state as to whether the then existing Section 153.433 regarding grandparent access was constitutional. Finally in 2004, an Attorney General's opinion weighted in: Opinion No. GA–0260 states in part:

> Section 153.433 of the Family Code, the Texas Grandparent Access Statute, is constitutional on its face. It may be constitutionally applied, however, only in light of the limitations imposed by *Troxel v. Granville*, 530 U.S. 57 (2000). In order to avoid an unconstitutional application of the statute, a court must require a grandparent to "overcome the presumption that a fit parent acts in the best interest of his or her child." *In re* Pensom, 126 S.W.3d 251, 256 (Tex. App.—San Antonio 2003, no pet.). To overcome the presumption, "a grandparent has the burden to prove, by a preponderance of the evidence, either that the parent is not fit, or that denial of access by the grandparent would significantly impair the child's physical health or emotional well-being."

Because of this perceived potential that the statute could be unconstitutionally applied, the Legislature responded by amending the section in 2005.

§ 153.434. Limitation on Right to Request Possession or Access

A biological or adoptive grandparent may not request possession of or access to a grandchild if:

(1) each of the biological parents of the grandchild has:

(A) died;

(B) had the person's parental rights terminated; or

(C) executed an affidavit of waiver of interest in child or an affidavit of relinquishment of parental rights under Chapter 161 and the affidavit designates an authorized agency, licensed child-placing agency, or person other than the child's stepparent as the managing conservator of the child; and

(2) the grandchild has been adopted, or is the subject of a pending suit for adoption, by a person other than the child's stepparent.

Leading Case

Raines v. Sugg, 930 S.W.2d 912 (Tex. App.—Fort Worth 1996, no writ) (maternal grandparents entitled to access to grandchild despite child's adoption by father's second wife)

SUBCHAPTER I. PREVENTION OF INTERNATIONAL PARENTAL CHILD ABDUCTION

Introductory Comment

Subchapter I adds a statutory basis to ensure that a court attempt to determine the risk of international parental child abduction in certain cases and order preventive measures based on that risk, if the court deems the risk sufficient. The provisions are adapted from a study published by the ABA Center on Children and the Law, and from numerous reports published and disseminated by the U.S. Dept. of State, Office of Children's Issues; the U.S. Dept. of Justice, Office of Juvenile Justice and Delinquency Program; the National Center for Missing and Exploited Children (NCMEC); and other sources. The recommended safeguards have been successfully utilized in some Texas family court cases to discourage or prevent international parental abduction.

Unfortunately, most Texas family courts remain unaware or underestimate various "red flag" indicators and the need for preventive safeguards. As a result, Texas children continue to remain at high risk for international parental child abduction. When the abduction is to a foreign country, the return of the child very often is extremely difficult, and sometimes impossible. This warrants more emphasis on preventing such abductions before they occur. Existing federal law implements the provisions of the Hague Convention on the Civil Aspects of International Child Abduction, *see* International Child Abduction Remedies Act, 42 U.S.C.A. § 11601, *et seq*. The federal act provides remedies for the wrongful removal or retention of a child in cases of international child abduction. Many foreign countries, however, are not parties to the convention. Moreover, even if a country is a signatory, this does not mean that ready compliance is assured.

Both federal and Texas law prohibit the abduction of a child in violation of the right of custody or access of a person. However, many foreign countries refuse to recognize U.S. custody orders. A number of parents succeed in abducting children internationally by avoiding the exit controls established in the United States. For example, some foreign countries (including their embassies and consulates located in the U.S.) issue passports to children they consider to be dual nationals, despite U.S. court orders prohibiting such issuance.

Further, many foreign parents are also U.S. citizens or permanent residents who have resided in the United States for many years. The fact that the parent may have a successful job or business, will lead the courts to mistakenly conclude that they do not pose a risk of child abduction. In many foreign countries there are no legal remedies to enable an American parent to secure the return of a child to the U.S., or to gain access to the child in the foreign country. As a result, many American parents have had their children literally stolen, with little or no recourse available under the law. Consequently, the U.S. Dept. of Justice (OJJDP) recommends that state legislatures pass this statute to prevent parental abductions.

Subchapter I supplements current Texas family law to provide that in any child custody proceeding in which the court is made aware of evidence indicating a possible risk of international abduction of the child, the court shall consider certain factors (a.k.a., "red flags") to determine whether safeguards are needed to prevent such an abduction. If the court determines that the need exists, it may take specified measures to discourage or prevent the abduction of the child.

An amendment in 2009 to Section 152.502 directs the court to consider whether the activities described as possible indicators of risk of international abduction might be "part of a safety plan to flee from family violence."

CLE/Other Legal Publications

International issues/travel. Laura June Dyke Dale, 2010 Adv. Fam. L. Drafting

Cases involving foreign nationals. Larry H. Schwartz, 2010 Adv. Fam. L.

Mexico—a different country but not an insurmountable obstacle in family law proceedings. Michael Rojas, 2010 So. Tex. Fam. L. Conf.

Immigration and multinational issues in divorce. Workshop, 2008 Adv. Fam. L.

Parenting across borders: international issues in the parent-child relationship. Adair Dyer, Jr., 2007 UT Definitive SAPCR

International child issues and the Hague Convention: What Do You Do when You Get One of These Cases? Charles G. Childress, 2007 Adv. Fam. L.

Let's go overseas, or maybe we shouldn't: International child issues & the Hague Convention. Julie Crawford and G. Thomas Vick, Jr., 2006 Adv. Fam. L.

Leading Cases

In re Sigmar, 270 S.W.3d 389 (Tex. App.—Waco 2008, no pet.) (evidence shows risk of international abduction to Mexico by father warranting injunctive orders)

Kogel v. Robertson, 2005 WL 3234627 (Tex. App.—Austin 2005, no pet.) (mother's previous flight with child requires appropriate safeguards to protect against future international abduction)

---

§ 153.501. Necessity of Measures to Prevent International Parental Child Abduction

(a) In a suit, if credible evidence is presented to the court indicating a potential risk of the international abduction of a child by a parent of the child, the court, on its own motion or at the request of a party to the suit, shall determine under this section whether it is necessary for the court to take one or more of the measures described by Section 153.503 to protect the child from the risk of abduction by the parent.

(b) In determining whether to take any of the measures described by Section 153.503, the court shall consider:

(1) the public policies of this state described by Section 153.001(a) and the consideration of the best interest of the child under Section 153.002;

(2) the risk of international abduction of the child by a parent of the child based on the court's evaluation of the risk factors described by Section 153.502;

(3) any obstacles to locating, recovering, and returning the child if the child is abducted to a foreign country; and

(4) the potential physical or psychological harm to the child if the child is abducted to a foreign country.

§ 153.502. Abduction Risk Factors

(a) To determine whether there is a risk of the international abduction of a child by a parent of the child, the court shall consider evidence that the parent:

(1) has taken, enticed away, kept, withheld, or concealed a child in violation of another person's right of possession of or access to the child, unless the parent presents evidence that the parent believed in good faith that the parent's conduct was necessary to avoid imminent harm to the child or the parent;

(2) has previously threatened to take, entice away, keep, withhold, or conceal a child in violation of another person's right of possession of or access to the child;

(3) lacks financial reason to stay in the United States, including evidence that the parent is financially independent, is able to work outside of the United States, or is unemployed;

(4) has recently engaged in planning activities that could facilitate the removal of the child from the United States by the parent, including:

(A) quitting a job;

(B) selling a primary residence;

(C) terminating a lease;

(D) closing bank accounts;

(E) liquidating other assets;

(F) hiding or destroying documents;

(G) applying for a passport or visa or obtaining other travel documents for the parent or the child; or

(H) applying to obtain the child's birth certificate or school or medical records;

(5) has a history of domestic violence that the court is required to consider under Section 153.004; or

(6) has a criminal history or a history of violating court orders.

(a–1) In considering evidence of planning activities under Subsection (a)(4), the court also shall consider any evidence that the parent was engaging in those activities as a part of a safety plan to flee from family violence.

(b) If the court finds that there is credible evidence of a risk of abduction of the child by a parent of the child based on the court's consideration of the factors in Subsection (a), the court shall also consider evidence regarding the following factors to evaluate the risk of international abduction of the child by a parent:

(1) whether the parent has strong familial, emotional, or cultural ties to another country, particularly a country that is not a signatory to or compliant with the Hague Convention on the Civil Aspects of International Child Abduction; and

(2) whether the parent lacks strong ties to the United States, regardless of whether the parent is a citizen or permanent resident of the United States.

(c) If the court finds that there is credible evidence of a risk of abduction of the child by a parent of the child based on the court's consideration of the factors in Subsection (a), the court may also consider evidence regarding the following factors to evaluate the risk of international abduction of the child by a parent:

(1) whether the parent is undergoing a change in status with the United States Immigration and Naturalization Service that would adversely affect that parent's ability to legally remain in the United States;

(2) whether the parent's application for United States citizenship has been denied by the United States Immigration and Naturalization Service;

(3) whether the parent has forged or presented misleading or false evidence to obtain a visa, a passport, a social security card, or any other identification card or has made any misrepresentation to the United States government; or

(4) whether the foreign country to which the parent has ties:

(A) presents obstacles to the recovery and return of a child who is abducted to the country from the United States;

(B) has any legal mechanisms for immediately and effectively enforcing an order regarding the possession of or access to the child issued by this state;

(C) has local laws or practices that would:

(i) enable the parent to prevent the child's other parent from contacting the child without due cause;

(ii) restrict the child's other parent from freely traveling to or exiting from the country because of that parent's gender, nationality, or religion; or

(iii) restrict the child's ability to legally leave the country after the child reaches the age of majority because of the child's gender, nationality, or religion;

(D) is included by the United States Department of State on a list of state sponsors of terrorism;

(E) is a country for which the United States Department of State has issued a travel warning to United States citizens regarding travel to the country;

(F) has an embassy of the United States in the country;

(G) is engaged in any active military action or war, including a civil war;

(H) is a party to and compliant with the Hague Convention on the Civil Aspects of International Child Abduction according to the most recent report on compliance issued by the United States Department of State;

(I) provides for the extradition of a parental abductor and the return of the child to the United States; or

(J) poses a risk that the child's physical health or safety would be endangered in the country because of specific circumstances relating to the child or because of human rights violations committed against children, including arranged marriages, lack of freedom of religion, child labor, lack of child abuse laws, female genital mutilation, and any form of slavery.

§ 153.503. Abduction Prevention Measures

If the court finds that it is necessary under Section 153.501 to take measures to protect a child from international abduction by a parent of the child, the court may take any of the following actions:

(1) appoint a person other than the parent of the child who presents a risk of abducting the child as the sole managing conservator of the child;

(2) require supervised visitation of the parent by a visitation center or independent organization until the court finds under Section 153.501 that supervised visitation is no longer necessary;

(3) enjoin the parent or any person acting on the parent's behalf from:

(A) disrupting or removing the child from the school or child-care facility in which the child is enrolled; or

(B) approaching the child at any location other than a site designated for supervised visitation;

(4) order passport and travel controls, including controls that:

(A) prohibit the parent and any person acting on the parent's behalf from removing the child from this state or the United States;

(B) require the parent to surrender any passport issued in the child's name, including any passport issued in the name of both the parent and the child; and

(C) prohibit the parent from applying on behalf of the child for a new or replacement passport or international travel visa;

(5) require the parent to provide:

(A) to the United States Department of State's Office of Children's Issues and the relevant foreign consulate or embassy:

(i) written notice of the court-ordered passport and travel restrictions for the child; and

(ii) a properly authenticated copy of the court order detailing the restrictions and documentation of the parent's agreement to the restrictions; and

(B) to the court proof of receipt of the written notice required by Paragraph (A)(i) by the United States Department of State's Office of Children's Issues and the relevant foreign consulate or embassy;

(6) order the parent to execute a bond or deposit security in an amount sufficient to offset the cost of recovering the child if the child is abducted by the parent to a foreign country;

(7) authorize the appropriate law enforcement agencies to take measures to prevent the abduction of the child by the parent; or

(8) include in the court's order provisions:

(A) identifying the United States as the country of habitual residence of the child;

(B) defining the basis for the court's exercise of jurisdiction; and

(C) stating that a party's violation of the order may subject the party to a civil penalty or criminal penalty or to both civil and criminal penalties.

SUBCHAPTER J. RIGHTS OF SIBLINGS

§ 153.551. Suit for Access

(a) The sibling of a child who is separated from the child because of an action taken by the Department of Family and Protective Services may request access to the child by filing:

(1) an original suit; or

(2) a suit for modification as provided by Chapter 156.

(b) A sibling described by Subsection (a) may request access to the child in a suit filed for the sole purpose of requesting the relief, without regard to whether the appointment of a managing conservator is an issue in the suit.

(c) The court shall order reasonable access to the child by the child's sibling described by Subsection (a) if the court finds that access is in the best interest of the child.

SUBCHAPTER K. PARENTING PLAN, PARENTING COORDINATOR, AND PARENTING FACILITATOR

Legislative "Finding"

The legislature finds that the use of parenting plans and parenting coordinators in suits affecting the parent-child relationship will assist in promoting the best interest of children and in helping litigants resolve their issues relating to parenting. The legislature further finds that conciliatory forms of dispute resolution, including mediation and the use of parenting coordinators, promote the policy set forth in Section 153.001, Family Code.

Guest Commentary

Gay G. Cox, Dallas
and
Diana S. Friedman, Dallas

The most significant changes arising from the 2009 amendments to the parenting coordinator statute relate to the creation of new sections governing parenting facilitators. Prior to 2009, the term "parenting facilitator," did not appear anywhere in the Texas Family Code and yet, courts throughout the State of Texas were appointing them. This role required one to perform the functions of a parenting coordinator, but also allowed the individual to testify. The absence of a parenting facilitator statute created a situation where there were no qualifications or standards of practice for any person serving in that role. The new statute brings clarity to the titles of persons performing the functions of a parenting coordinator or parenting facilitator, because anyone performing the functions listed and appointed under Subchapter K is governed by it and will be serving in one of the two capacities regardless of the title used in the court order.

If the evidence proffered is admissible under the Rules of Evidence, the parenting facilitator may make a report to the court, make recommendations, and testify regarding the parties' interactions on a variety of parenting issues, but they may not make recommendations about conservatorship or possession of or access to a child or which affect the terms of an existing court order. A parenting coordinator remains barred from testifying under the amendments and can only report whether the process should continue or not. Parenting coordination remains a strictly confidential alternative dispute resolution process.

There is also a requirement for five state agencies, including the State Bar of Texas, to adopt rules setting forth standards of practice for parenting facilitators no later than March 1, 2011. Failure to adopt standards will bar individuals within a given profession from functioning in the role of parenting facilitator after that date, but not from serving as a parenting coordinator. The guidelines that the amended statute now applies to parenting coordinators are the existing Supreme Court Guidelines for Mediators. Parenting facilitators must be licensed professionals and have more hours of training than parenting coordinators. Parenting coordinators are qualified by education, training and experience with high conflict or litigating parents, but are not required to be licensed and some of their training requirements may be waived. This requirement of licensure to serve as a parenting facilitator by one of the five agencies and the additional training requirements do not apply to those employed by Dispute Resolution Organizations who are qualified as parenting coordinators on or before August 31, 2009.

The new law also provides explicit conflict of interest rules for parenting facilitators which prohibit any type of dual role and also requires certain disclosures of relationships with the attorneys, parties, or a child who is the subject of the suit. Some relationships bar the person from serving in the capacity of parenting facilitator. Additionally, a parenting facilitator may not change roles and serve as a parenting coordinator, or vice versa.

While a parenting coordinator or parenting facilitator may assist the parties in attempting to settle parenting issues, they may not make decisions for clients, modify an order or create a Rule 11 agreement, mediated settlement agreement, collaborative law agreement or other settlement agreement. Instead, they may submit a written report describing the parties' statement of intent or proposed joint resolution to the parties and attorneys, but not to the court. The lawyers or pro se parties may then take the terms referenced in the report and draft one of the more formal agreements, which must be incorporated in a signed court order if it is to constitute an agreement.

CLE/Other Legal Publications

The new parent coordination/facilitation statute: what's in, what's out? Christy Bradshaw Schmidt & Diana S. Friedman, 2010 Marriage Dissolution

What's in a name? Parenting Coordination vs. Family Psychotherapy. Aaron Robb, State Bar Section Report: Family Law Vol. 2008-1

Guidelines for parenting coordination. AFCC Task Force on Parenting Coordination, 44:1 Fam. Ct. Rev. 164 (2006)

Using parenting plans to deal with special circumstances. Harry L. Tindall, 2006 U.T. Parenting Plan

---

§ 153.601. Definitions

In this subchapter:

(1) "Dispute resolution process" means:

(A) a process of alternative dispute resolution conducted in accordance with Section 153.0071 of this chapter and Chapter 154, Civil Practice and Remedies Code; or

(B) any other method of voluntary dispute resolution.

(2) "High-conflict case" means a suit affecting the parent-child relationship in which the court finds that the parties have demonstrated an unusual degree of:

(A) repetitiously resorting to the adjudicative process;

(B) anger and distrust; and

(C) difficulty in communicating about and cooperating in the care of their children.

(3) "Parenting coordinator" means an impartial third party:

(A) who, regardless of the title by which the person is designated by the court, performs any function described by Section 153.606 in a suit; and

(B) who:

(i) is appointed under this subchapter by the court on its own motion or on a motion or agreement of the parties to assist parties in resolving parenting issues through confidential procedures; and

(ii) is not appointed under another statute or a rule of civil procedure.

(3–a) "Parenting facilitator" means an impartial third party:

(A) who, regardless of the title by which the person is designated by the court, performs any function described by Section 153.6061 in a suit; and

(B) who:

(i) is appointed under this subchapter by the court on its own motion or on a motion or agreement of the parties to assist parties in resolving parenting issues through procedures that are not confidential; and

(ii) is not appointed under another statute or a rule of civil procedure.

(4) "Parenting plan" means the provisions of a final court order that:

(A) set out rights and duties of a parent or a person acting as a parent in relation to the child;

(B) provide for periods of possession of and access to the child, which may be the terms set out in the standard possession order under Subchapter F and any amendments to the standard possession order agreed to by the parties or found by the court to be in the best interest of the child;

(C) provide for child support; and

(D) optimize the development of a close and continuing relationship between each parent and the child.

§ 153.602. Parenting Plan Not Required in Temporary Order

A temporary order in a suit affecting the parent-child relationship rendered in accordance with Section 105.001 is not required to include a temporary parenting plan. The court may not require the submission of a temporary parenting plan in any case or by local rule or practice.

§ 153.603. Requirement of Parenting Plan in Final Order

(a) Except as provided by Subsection (b), a final order in a suit affecting the parent-child relationship must include a parenting plan.

(b) The following orders are not required to include a parenting plan:

(1) an order that only modifies child support;

(2) an order that only terminates parental rights; or

(3) a final order described by Section 155.001(b).

(c) If the parties have not reached agreement on a final parenting plan on or before the 30th day before the date set for trial on the merits, a party may file with the court and serve a proposed parenting plan.

(d) This section does not preclude the parties from requesting the appointment of a parenting coordinator to resolve parental conflicts.

§ 153.6031. Exception to Dispute Resolution Process Requirement

A requirement in a parenting plan that a party initiate or participate in a dispute resolution process before filing a court action does not apply to an action:

(1) to modify the parenting plan in an emergency;

(2) to modify child support;

(3) alleging that the child's present circumstances will significantly impair the child's physical health or significantly impair the child's emotional development;

(4) to enforce; or

(5) in which the party shows that enforcement of the requirement is precluded or limited by Section 153.0071.

§ 153.604. Repealed.

§ 153.605. Appointment of Parenting Coordinator

(a) In a suit affecting the parent-child relationship, the court may, on its own motion or on a motion or agreement of the parties, appoint a parenting coordinator or assign a domestic relations office under Chapter 203 to appoint an employee or other person to serve as parenting coordinator.

(b) The court may not appoint a parenting coordinator unless, after notice and hearing, the court makes a specific finding that:

(1) the case is a high-conflict case or there is good cause shown for the appointment of a parenting coordinator and the appointment is in the best interest of any minor child in the suit; and

(2) the person appointed has the minimum qualifications required by Section 153.610, as documented by the person, unless those requirements have been waived by the court with the agreement of the parties in accordance with Section 153.610(c).

(c) Notwithstanding any other provision of this subchapter, a party may at any time file a written objection to the appointment of a parenting coordinator on the basis of family violence having been committed by another party against the objecting party or a child who is the subject of the suit. After an objection is filed, a parenting coordinator may not be appointed unless, on the request of a party, a hearing is held and the court finds that a preponderance of the evidence does not support the objection. If a parenting coordinator is appointed, the court shall order appropriate measures be taken to ensure the physical and emotional safety of the party who filed the objection. The order may provide that the parties not be required to have face-to-face contact and that the parties be placed in separate rooms during the parenting coordination.

(d) An individual appointed as a parenting coordinator may not serve in any nonconfidential capacity in the same case, including serving as an amicus attorney, guardian ad litem, or social study evaluator under Chapter 107, as a friend of the court under Chapter 202, or as a parenting facilitator under this subchapter.

§ 153.6051. Appointment of Parenting Facilitator

(a) In a suit affecting the parent-child relationship, the court may, on its own motion or on a motion or agreement of the parties, appoint a parenting facilitator or assign a domestic relations office under Chapter 203 to appoint an employee or other person as a parenting facilitator.

(b) The court may not appoint a parenting facilitator unless, after notice and hearing, the court makes a specific finding that:

(1) the case is a high-conflict case or there is good cause shown for the appointment of a parenting facilitator and the appointment is in the best interest of any minor child in the suit; and

(2) the person appointed has the minimum qualifications required by Section 153.6101, as documented by the person.

(c) Notwithstanding any other provision of this subchapter, a party may at any time file a written objection to the appointment of a parenting facilitator on the basis of family violence having been committed by another party against the objecting party or a child who is the subject of the suit. After an objection is filed, a parenting facilitator may not be appointed unless, on the request of a party, a hearing is held and the court finds that a preponderance of the evidence does not support the objection. If a parenting facilitator is appointed, the court shall order appropriate measures be taken to ensure the physical and emotional safety of the party who filed the objection. The order may provide that the parties not be required to have face-to-face contact and that the parties be placed in separate rooms during the parenting facilitation.

§ 153.606. Duties of Parenting Coordinator

(a) The court shall specify the duties of a parenting coordinator in the order appointing the parenting coordinator. The duties of the parenting coordinator are limited to matters that will aid the parties in:

(1) identifying disputed issues;

(2) reducing misunderstandings;

(3) clarifying priorities;

(4) exploring possibilities for problem solving;

(5) developing methods of collaboration in parenting;

(6) understanding parenting plans and reaching agreements about parenting issues to be included in a parenting plan;

(7) complying with the court's order regarding conservatorship or possession of and access to the child;

(8) implementing parenting plans;

(9) obtaining training regarding problem solving, conflict management, and parenting skills; and

(10) settling disputes regarding parenting issues and reaching a proposed joint resolution or statement of intent regarding those disputes.

(b) The appointment of a parenting coordinator does not divest the court of:

(1) its exclusive jurisdiction to determine issues of conservatorship, support, and possession of and access to the child; and

(2) the authority to exercise management and control of the suit.

(c) The parenting coordinator may not modify any order, judgment, or decree.

(d) Meetings between the parenting coordinator and the parties may be informal and are not required to follow any specific procedures unless otherwise provided by this subchapter.

(e) Repealed by Acts 2007, 80th Leg., ch. 1181, §11(2).

(f) A parenting coordinator appointed under this subchapter shall comply with the Ethical Guidelines for Mediators as adopted by the Supreme Court of Texas (Misc. Docket No. 05–9107, June 13, 2005). On request by the court, the parties, or the parties' attorneys, the parenting coordinator shall sign a statement of agreement to comply with those guidelines and submit the statement to the court on acceptance of the appointment. A failure to comply with the guidelines is grounds for removal of the parenting coordinator.

§ 153.6061. Duties of Parenting Facilitator

(a) The court shall specify the duties of a parenting facilitator in the order appointing the parenting facilitator. The duties of the parenting facilitator are limited to those matters described with regard to a parenting coordinator under Section 153.606(a), except that the parenting facilitator may also monitor compliance with court orders.

(b) A parenting facilitator appointed under this subchapter shall comply with the standard of care applicable to the professional license held by the parenting facilitator in performing the parenting facilitator's duties.

(c) The appointment of a parenting facilitator does not divest the court of:

(1) the exclusive jurisdiction to determine issues of conservatorship, support, and possession of and access to the child; and

(2) the authority to exercise management and control of the suit.

(d) The parenting facilitator may not modify any order, judgment, or decree.

(e) Meetings between the parenting facilitator and the parties may be informal and are not required to follow any specific procedures unless otherwise provided by this subchapter or the standards of practice of the professional license held by the parenting facilitator.

§ 153.607. Presumption of Good Faith; Removal of Parenting Coordinator

(a) It is a rebuttable presumption that a parenting coordinator is acting in good faith if the parenting coordinator's services have been conducted as provided by this subchapter and the Ethical Guidelines for Mediators described by Section 153.606(f).

(a–1) Except as otherwise provided by this section, the court may remove the parenting coordinator in the court's discretion.

(b) The court shall remove the parenting coordinator:

(1) on the request and agreement of all parties;

(2) on the request of the parenting coordinator;

(3) on the motion of a party, if good cause is shown; or

(4) if the parenting coordinator ceases to satisfy the minimum qualifications required by Section 153.610.

§ 153.6071. Presumption of Good Faith; Removal of Parenting Facilitator

(a) It is a rebuttable presumption that a parenting facilitator is acting in good faith if the parenting facilitator's services have been conducted as provided by this subchapter and the standard of care applicable to the professional license held by the parenting facilitator.

(b) Except as otherwise provided by this section, the court may remove the parenting facilitator in the court's discretion.

(c) The court shall remove the parenting facilitator:

(1) on the request and agreement of all parties;

(2) on the request of the parenting facilitator;

(3) on the motion of a party, if good cause is shown; or

(4) if the parenting facilitator ceases to satisfy the minimum qualifications required by Section 153.6101.

§ 153.608. Report of Parenting Coordinator

A parenting coordinator shall submit a written report to the court and to the parties as often as ordered by the court. The report must be limited to a statement of whether the parenting coordination should continue.

§ 153.6081. Report of Parenting Facilitator

A parenting facilitator shall submit a written report to the court and to the parties as ordered by the court. The report may include a recommendation described by Section 153.6082(e) and any other information required by the court, except that the report may not include recommendations regarding the conservatorship of or the possession of or access to the child who is the subject of the suit.

§ 153.6082. Report of Joint Proposal or Statement of Intent; Agreements and Recommendations

(a) If the parties have been ordered by the court to attempt to settle parenting issues with the assistance of a parenting coordinator or parenting facilitator and to attempt to reach a proposed joint resolution or statement of intent regarding the dispute, the parenting coordinator or parenting facilitator, as applicable, shall submit a written report describing the parties' joint proposal or statement to the parties, any attorneys for the parties, and any attorney for the child who is the subject of the suit.

(b) The proposed joint resolution or statement of intent is not an agreement unless the resolution or statement is:

(1) prepared by the parties' attorneys, if any, in a form that meets the applicable requirements of:

(A) Rule 11, Texas Rules of Civil Procedure;

(B) a mediated settlement agreement described by Section 153.0071;

(C) a collaborative law agreement described by Section 153.0072;

(D) a settlement agreement described by Section 154.071, Civil Practice and Remedies Code; or

(E) a proposed court order; and

(2) incorporated into an order signed by the court.

(c) A parenting coordinator or parenting facilitator may not draft a document listed in Subsection (b)(1).

(d) The actions of a parenting coordinator or parenting facilitator under this section do not constitute the practice of law.

(e) If the parties have been ordered by the court to attempt to settle parenting issues with the assistance of a parenting facilitator and are unable to settle those issues, the parenting facilitator may make recommendations, other than recommendations regarding the conservatorship of or possession of or access to the child, to the parties and attorneys to implement or clarify provisions of an existing court order that are consistent with the substantive intent of the court order and in the best interest of the child who is the subject of the suit. A recommendation authorized by this subsection does not affect the terms of an existing court order.

§ 153.6083. Communications and Recordkeeping of Parenting Facilitator

(a) Notwithstanding any rule, standard of care, or privilege applicable to the professional license held by a parenting facilitator, a communication made by a participant in parenting facilitation is subject to disclosure and may be offered in any judicial or administrative proceeding, if otherwise admissible under the rules of evidence. The parenting facilitator may be required to testify in any proceeding relating to or arising from the duties of the parenting facilitator, including as to the basis for any recommendation made to the parties that arises from the duties of the parenting facilitator.

(b) A parenting facilitator shall keep a detailed record regarding meetings and contacts with the parties, attorneys, or other persons involved in the suit.

(c) A person who participates in parenting facilitation is not a patient as defined by Section 611.001, Health and Safety Code, and no record created as part of the parenting facilitation that arises from the parenting facilitator's duties is confidential.

(d) On request, records of parenting facilitation shall be made available by the parenting facilitator to an attorney for a party, an attorney for a child who is the subject of the suit, and a party who does not have an attorney.

(e) A parenting facilitator shall keep parenting facilitation records from the suit until the seventh anniversary of the date the facilitator's services are terminated, unless a different retention period is established by a rule adopted by the licensing authority that issues the professional license held by the parenting facilitator.

§ 153.609. Compensation of Parenting Coordinator

(a) A court may not appoint a parenting coordinator, other than a domestic relations office or a comparable county agency appointed under Subsection (c) or a volunteer appointed under Subsection (d), unless, after notice and hearing, the court finds that the parties have the means to pay the fees of the parenting coordinator.

(b) Any fees of a parenting coordinator appointed under Subsection (a) shall be allocated between the parties as determined by the court.

(c) Public funds may not be used to pay the fees of a parenting coordinator. Notwithstanding this prohibition, a court may appoint the domestic relations office or a comparable county agency to act as a parenting coordinator if personnel are available to serve that function.

(d) If due to hardship the parties are unable to pay the fees of a parenting coordinator, and a **domestic relations office or a comparable county agency** ~~public employee~~ is not available under Subsection (c), the court, if feasible, may appoint a person **who meets the minimum qualifications prescribed by Section 153.610, including an employee of the court,** to act as a parenting coordinator on a volunteer basis **and without compensation**.

Amended by Acts 2011, 82nd Leg., ch. 682 (H.B. 149), § 1, eff. June 17, 2011.

§ 153.6091. Compensation of Parenting Facilitator

Section 153.609 applies to ~~the compensation of~~ a parenting facilitator in the same manner as provided for ~~the compensation of~~ a parenting coordinator, **except that a person appointed in accordance with Section 153.609(d) to act as a parenting facilitator must meet the minimum qualifications prescribed by Section 153.6101**.

Amended by Acts 2011, 82nd Leg., ch. 682 (H.B. 149), § 2, eff. June 17, 2011.

§ 153.610. Qualifications of Parenting Coordinator

(a) The court shall determine the required qualifications of a parenting coordinator, provided that a parenting coordinator must have experience working in a field relating to families, have practical experience with high-conflict cases or litigation between parents, and :

(1) hold at least:

(A) a bachelor's degree in counseling, education, family studies, psychology, or social work; or

(B) a graduate degree in a mental health profession, with an emphasis in family and children's issues; or

(2) be licensed in good standing as an attorney in this state.

(b) In addition to the qualifications prescribed by Subsection (a), a parenting coordinator must complete at least:

(1) eight hours of family violence dynamics training provided by a family violence service provider;

(2) 40 classroom hours of training in dispute resolution techniques in a course conducted by an alternative dispute resolution system or other dispute resolution organization approved by the court; and

(3) 24 classroom hours of training in the fields of family dynamics, child development, family law and the law governing parenting coordination, and parenting coordination styles and procedures.

(c) In appropriate circumstances, a court may, with the agreement of the parties, appoint a person as parenting coordinator who does not satisfy the requirements of Subsection (a) or Subsection (b)(2) or (3) if the court finds that the person has sufficient legal or other professional training or experience in dispute resolution processes to serve in that capacity.

(d) The actions of a parenting coordinator who is not an attorney do not constitute the practice of law.

§ 153.6101. Qualifications of Parenting Facilitator

(a) The court shall determine whether the qualifications of a proposed parenting facilitator satisfy the requirements of this section. On request by a party, an attorney for a party, or any attorney for a child who is the subject of the suit, a person under consideration for appointment as a parenting facilitator in the suit shall provide proof that the person satisfies the minimum qualifications required by this section.

(b) A parenting facilitator must:

(1) hold a license to practice in this state as a social worker, licensed professional counselor, licensed marriage and family therapist, psychologist, or attorney; and

(2) have completed at least:

(A) eight hours of family violence dynamics training provided by a family violence service provider;

(B) 40 classroom hours of training in dispute resolution techniques in a course conducted by an alternative dispute resolution system or other dispute resolution organization approved by the court;

(C) 24 classroom hours of training in the fields of family dynamics, child development, and family law; and

(D) 16 hours of training in the laws governing parenting coordination and parenting facilitation and the multiple styles and procedures used in different models of service.

(c) The actions of a parenting facilitator who is not an attorney do not constitute the practice of law.

§ 153.6102. Parenting Facilitator; Conflicts of Interest and Bias

(a) A person who has a conflict of interest with, or has previous knowledge of, a party or a child who is the subject of a suit must, before being appointed as parenting facilitator in a suit:

(1) disclose the conflict or previous knowledge to the court, each attorney for a party, any attorney for a child, and any party who does not have an attorney; and

(2) decline appointment in the suit unless, after the disclosure, the parties and the child's attorney, if any, agree in writing to the person's appointment as parenting facilitator.

(b) A parenting facilitator who, after being appointed in a suit, discovers that the parenting facilitator has a conflict of interest with, or has previous knowledge of, a party or a child who is the subject of the suit shall:

(1) immediately disclose the conflict or previous knowledge to the court, each attorney for a party, any attorney for a child, and any party who does not have an attorney; and

(2) withdraw from the suit unless, after the disclosure, the parties and the child's attorney, if any, agree in writing to the person's continuation as parenting facilitator.

(c) A parenting facilitator, before accepting appointment in a suit, must disclose to the court, each attorney for a party, any attorney for a child who is the subject of the suit, and any party who does not have an attorney:

(1) a pecuniary relationship with an attorney, party, or child in the suit;

(2) a relationship of confidence or trust with an attorney, party, or child in the suit; and

(3) other information regarding any relationship with an attorney, party, or child in the suit that might reasonably affect the ability of the person to act impartially during the person's service as parenting facilitator.

(d) A person who makes a disclosure required by Subsection (c) shall decline appointment as parenting facilitator unless, after the disclosure, the parties and the child's attorney, if any, agree in writing to the person's service as parenting facilitator in the suit.

(e) A parenting facilitator may not serve in any other professional capacity at any other time with any person who is a party to, or the subject of, the suit in which the person serves as parenting facilitator, or with any member of the family of a party or subject. A person who, before appointment as a parenting facilitator in a suit, served in any other professional capacity with a person who is a party to, or subject of, the suit, or with any member of the family of a party or subject, may not serve as parenting facilitator in a suit involving any family member who is a party to or subject of the suit. This subsection does not apply to a person whose only other service in a professional capacity with a family or any member of a family that is a party to or the subject of a suit to which this section applies is as a teacher of coparenting skills in a class conducted in a group setting. For purposes of this subsection, "family" has the meaning assigned by Section 71.003.

(f) A parenting facilitator shall promptly and simultaneously disclose to each party's attorney, any attorney for a child who is a subject of the suit, and any party who does not have an attorney the existence and substance of any communication between the parenting facilitator and another person, including a party, a party's attorney, a child who is the subject of the suit, and any attorney for a child who is the subject of the suit, if the communication occurred outside of a parenting facilitator session and involved the substance of parenting facilitation.

§ 153.611. Exception for Certain Title IV–D Proceedings

Notwithstanding any other provision of this subchapter, this subchapter does not apply to a proceeding in a Title IV–D case relating to the determination of parentage or establishment, modification, or enforcement of a child support or medical support obligation.

SUBCHAPTER L. MILITARY DUTY

Introductory Comment

The United States has been at war for more than six years in Iraq and even longer on a second front in Afghanistan. Although this fact has not gone unnoticed by the Texas Legislature, in 2009 much greater focus was given to the impact of repeated assignments of servicemembers to those war zones and the effect on their families. This new subchapter attempts to deal comprehensively with the problems of such orders, whether they be labeled deployment, mobilization or temporary duty (hereafter referred to as deployment). First, the appropriate court is authorized to issue temporary orders to deal with the consequences of the deployment. If the servicemember has a court order granting the exclusive right to provide the primary residence of the child, to accommodate the change of circumstances the court is to follow a set pattern preference on a temporary basis only as follows: (1) the conservator without the right to provide the primary residence, i.e., the other parent; (2) the person chosen by the conservator as entitled to provide the primary residence; (3) the person appointed by the court. Each of these appointments, of course, is conditioned on the best interest of the child.

If the servicemember who has been not been providing primary residence is deployed, the court shall "award visitation" to another person designated by the servicemember to exercise visitation to the same degree as the servicemember had. Yes, the term "visitation" has returned to the Texas Family Code after being absent since January 1, 1974.

New Subchapter L touches just about every base possible, including temporary child support, an expedited hearing which is to be given preference over other SAPCRs not involving military duty, enforcement of the orders, and makeup visitation when the servicemember returns, *see* Section 153.3162, *supra*.

As has come to be expected by bench and bar, minor corrections of language to improve its clarity is a hallmark of this code; in 2011, Sections 153.702(a), (c), and 153.703(b) were the beneficiaries of such constant vigilance.

CLE/Other Legal Publications

Military visitation and conservator issues. Meca Latreice Walker, 2011 MARRIAGE DISSOLUTION

Special problems for military families. David D. Farr, 2011 ADV. FAM. L.

Avoiding conflict at home when there is conflict abroad: military child custody and visitation. Lauren S. Douglass, 43 FAM. L. Q. 315 (2009)

Leading Case

In re L.L., 2010 WL 2403579 (Tex. App.—San Antonio 2010) (military deployment may be considered in modification suit as to material and substantial change of circumstances)

---

§ 153.701. Definitions

In this subchapter:

(1) "Designated person" means the person ordered by the court to temporarily exercise a conservator's rights, duties, and periods of possession and access with regard to a child during the conservator's military deployment, military mobilization, or temporary military duty.

(2) "Military deployment" means the temporary transfer of a service member of the armed forces of this state or the United States serving in an active-duty status to another location in support of combat or some other military operation.

(3) "Military mobilization" means the call-up of a National Guard or Reserve service member of the armed forces of this state or the United States to extended active duty status. The term does not include National Guard or Reserve annual training.

(4) "Temporary military duty" means the transfer of a service member of the armed forces of this state or the United States from one military base to a different location, usually another base, for a limited time for training or to assist in the performance of a noncombat mission.

§ 153.702. Temporary Orders

(a) If a conservator is ordered to military deployment, military mobilization, or temporary military duty that involves moving a substantial distance from the conservator's residence so as to materially affect the conservator's ability to exercise the conservator's rights and duties in relation to a child, either conservator may file for an order under this subchapter **without the necessity of showing a material and substantial change of circumstances other than the military deployment, military mobilization, or temporary military duty**.

(b) The court may render a temporary order in a proceeding under this subchapter regarding:

(1) possession of or access to the child; or

(2) child support.

(c) A temporary order rendered by the court under this subchapter may grant rights to and impose duties on a designated person regarding the child, except **that if the designated person is a nonparent,** the court may not require the designated person to pay child support.

(d) After a conservator's military deployment, military mobilization, or temporary military duty is concluded, and the conservator returns to the conservator's usual residence, the temporary orders under this section terminate and the rights of all affected parties are governed by the terms of any court order applicable when the conservator is not ordered to military deployment, military mobilization, or temporary military duty.

Amended by Acts 2011, 82nd Leg., ch. 112 (H.B. 1404), § 1, eff. Sept. 1, 2011.

§ 153.703. Appointing Designated Person for Conservator with Exclusive Right to Designate Primary Residence of Child

(a) If the conservator with the exclusive right to designate the primary residence of the child is ordered to military deployment, military mobilization, or temporary military duty, the court may render a temporary order to appoint a designated person to exercise the exclusive right to designate the primary residence of the child during the military deployment, military mobilization, or temporary military duty in the following order of preference:

(1) the conservator who does not have the exclusive right to designate the primary residence of the child;

(2) if appointing the conservator described by Subdivision (1) is not in the child's best interest, a designated person chosen by the conservator with the exclusive right to designate the primary residence of the child; or

(3) if appointing the conservator described by Subdivision (1) or the person chosen under Subdivision (2) is not in the child's best interest, another person chosen by the court.

(b) A **nonparent appointed as a** designated person ~~named~~ in a temporary order rendered under this section has the rights and duties of a nonparent appointed as sole managing conservator under Section 153.371.

(c) The court may limit or expand the rights of a nonparent named as a designated person in a temporary order rendered under this section as appropriate to the best interest of the child.

Amended by Acts 2011, 82nd Leg., ch. 112 (H.B. 1404), § 2, eff. Sept. 1, 2011.

§ 153.704. Appointing Designated Person to Exercise Visitation for Conservator with Exclusive Right to Designate Primary Residence of Child in certain Circumstances

(a) If the court appoints the conservator without the exclusive right to designate the primary residence of the child under Section 153.703(a)(1), the court may award visitation with the child to a designated person chosen by the conservator with the exclusive right to designate the primary residence of the child.

(b) The periods of visitation shall be the same as the visitation to which the conservator without the exclusive right to designate the primary residence of the child was entitled under the court order in effect immediately before the date the temporary order is rendered.

(c) The temporary order for visitation must provide that:

(1) the designated person under this section has the right to possession of the child for the periods and in the manner in which the conservator without the exclusive right to designate the primary residence of the child is entitled under the court order in effect immediately before the date the temporary order is rendered;

(2) the child's other conservator and the designated person under this section are subject to the requirements of Section 153.316, with the designated person considered for purposes of that section to be the possessory conservator;

(3) the designated person under this section has the rights and duties of a nonparent possessory conservator under Section 153.376(a) during the period that the person has possession of the child; and

(4) the designated person under this section is subject to any provision in a court order restricting or prohibiting access to the child by any specified individual.

(d) The court may limit or expand the rights of a nonparent designated person named in a temporary order rendered under this section as appropriate to the best interest of the child.

§ 153.705. Appointing Designated Person to Exercise Visitation for Conservator without Exclusive Right to Designate Primary Residence of Child

(a) If the conservator without the exclusive right to designate the primary residence of the child is ordered to military deployment, military mobilization, or temporary military duty, the court may award visitation with the child to a designated person chosen by the conservator, if the visitation is in the best interest of the child.

(b) The temporary order for visitation must provide that:

(1) the designated person under this section has the right to possession of the child for the periods and in the manner in which the conservator described by Subsection (a) would be entitled if not ordered to military deployment, military mobilization, or temporary military duty;

(2) the child's other conservator and the designated person under this section are subject to the requirements of Section 153.316, with the designated person considered for purposes of that section to be the possessory conservator;

(3) the designated person under this section has the rights and duties of a nonparent possessory conservator under Section 153.376(a) during the period that the designated person has possession of the child; and

(4) the designated person under this section is subject to any provision in a court order restricting or prohibiting access to the child by any specified individual.

(c) The court may limit or expand the rights of a nonparent designated person named in a temporary order rendered under this section as appropriate to the best interest of the child.

§ 153.706. ~~Temporary Order for Child Support~~

~~A temporary order rendered under this subchapter may result in a change of circumstances sufficient to justify a temporary order modifying the child support obligations of a party.~~

Repealed by Acts 2011, 82nd Leg., ch. 112 (H.B. 1404), § 3, eff. Sept. 1, 2011

§ 153.707. Expedited Hearing

(a) On a motion by the conservator who has been ordered to military deployment, military mobilization, or temporary military duty, the court shall, for good cause shown, hold an expedited hearing if the court finds that the conservator's military duties have a material effect on the conservator's ability to appear in person at a regularly scheduled hearing.

(b) A hearing under this section shall, if possible, take precedence over other suits affecting the parent-child relationship not involving a conservator who has been ordered to military deployment, military mobilization, or temporary military duty.

(c) On a motion by any party, the court shall, after reasonable advance notice and for good cause shown, allow a party to present testimony and evidence by electronic means, including by teleconference or through the Internet.

§ 153.708. Enforcement

Temporary orders rendered under this subchapter may be enforced by or against the designated person to the same extent that an order would be enforceable against the conservator who has been ordered to military deployment, military mobilization, or temporary military duty.

§ 153.709. Additional Periods of Possession or Access

(a) Not later than the 90th day after the date a conservator without the exclusive right to designate the primary residence of the child who is a member of the armed services concludes the conservator's military deployment, military mobilization, or temporary military duty, the conservator may petition the court to:

(1) compute the periods of possession of or access to the child to which the conservator would have otherwise been entitled during the conservator's deployment; and

(2) award the conservator additional periods of possession of or access to the child to compensate for the periods described by Subdivision (1).

(b) If the conservator described by Subsection (a) petitions the court under Subsection (a), the court:

(1) shall compute the periods of possession or access to the child described by Subsection (a)(1); and

(2) may award to the conservator additional periods of possession of or access to the child for a length of time and under terms the court considers reasonable, if the court determines that:

(A) the conservator was on military deployment, military mobilization, or temporary military duty in a location where access to the child was not reasonably possible; and

(B) the award of additional periods of possession of or access to the child is in the best interest of the child.

(c) In making the determination under Subsection (b)(2), the court:

(1) shall consider:

(A) the periods of possession of or access to the child to which the conservator would otherwise have been entitled during the conservator's military deployment, military mobilization, or temporary military duty, as computed under Subsection (b)(1);

(B) whether the court named a designated person under Section 153.705 to exercise limited possession of the child during the conservator's deployment; and

(C) any other factor the court considers appropriate; and

(2) is not required to award additional periods of possession of or access to the child that equals the possession or access to which the conservator would have been entitled during the conservator's military deployment, military mobilization, or temporary military duty, as computed under Subsection (b)(1).

(d) After the conservator described by Subsection (a) has exercised all additional periods of possession or access awarded under this section, the rights of all affected parties are governed by the terms of the court order applicable when the conservator is not ordered to military deployment, military mobilization, or temporary military duty.

CHAPTER 154. CHILD SUPPORT

SUBCHAPTER A. COURT–ORDERED CHILD SUPPORT

SUBCHAPTER B. COMPUTING NET RESOURCES AVAILABLE FOR PAYMENT OF CHILD SUPPORT

SUBCHAPTER C. CHILD SUPPORT GUIDELINES

SUBCHAPTER D. MEDICAL SUPPORT FOR CHILD

SUBCHAPTER E. LOCAL CHILD SUPPORT REGISTRY

SUBCHAPTER F. SUPPORT FOR A MINOR OR ADULT DISABLED CHILD

Editors' Note: *This chapter contains guest comments by Alicia Gray Key, Deputy Attorney General and Title IV-D Director, and H. Patrick Sullivan, Deputy Director for State and Federal Operations, Child Support Division, Office of the Attorney General, identified as (A.G.K. & H.P.S.).*

Introductory Comment

Texas receives a substantial federal subsidy for the state's child support enforcement program (as do all other states). The Child Support Division of the Office of Attorney General, hereafter Title IV-D agency, is responsible for establishing paternity and establishing, enforcing, and modifying child support orders in public assistance cases referred to it, and on the request of an applicant for services, in non public assistance cases. The history of the IV D agency, so named after the part of the Social Security Act, 42 U.S.C. § 651 etc. A wealth of further information is available at http://www.oag.state.tx.us/sitesearch.shtml.

CLE/Other Legal Publications

Child support. Kyle W. Sanders, 2011 Adv. Fam. L.

Post-divorce medical benefits (now you see it, now you don't). James N. Higdon, 2011 Adv. Fam. L.

Case law update—SAPCR. Jack W. Marr & Stephen J. Naylor, 2011 Adv. Fam. L.

Above guideline child support. Angela G. Pence England, 2011 U.T. Advanced Parent-Child Relationships

Primer on child support calculation and collection. Angela G. Pence England, 2011 U.T. Parent-Child Relationships: Basics

Child support. Angela Stout, 2011 So. Tex. Fam. L.

To Infinity and Beyond the Guidelines: Child Support Cases Every Space Ranger Should Know. Michael D. Wysocki, Fam. L. Sect. Rpt. (Spring 2011)

Collecting child support. Cindy V. Tisdale, 2010 ADV. FAM. L.

Creative approaches to child support. Jack W. Marr, 2010 ADV. FAM. L.

SAPCR caselaw update. Eva Guzman, 2010 ADV. FAM. L.

Parentage testing and child support in CPS cases. Alicia G. Key, 2010 ADV. FAM. L.

Hidden child support resources. Patricia A. Wicoff, 2010 U.T. PARENT-CHILD RELATIONSHIPS

Advocating and defending unusual child support requests. Cindy Venise Tisdale, 2010 U.T. FAM. L. FRONT LINES

AG and CPS. Frederick S. Adams, Jr. & Alicia G. Key, 2010 ADV. FAM. L. DRAFTING

Obtaining child support. Barry J. Brooks & Karen L. Marvel, 2009 U.T. PARENT-CHILD RELATIONSHIPS

See Accompanying CD–ROM for Additional CLE/Other Legal Publications.

Leading Cases

Iliff v. Iliff, 339 S.W.3d 74 (Tex. 2011) (when child support obligor is intentionally unemployed or underemployed, intent to avoid child support need not be proven for court to apply the child support guidelines to obligor's earning potential earnings instead of to actual earnings, disapproving two appellate decisions) (court may properly consider an obligor's intent to avoid child support as a factor, along with other relevant facts, in analyzing whether obligor is intentionally unemployed or underemployed) (court did not abuse its discretion finding husband was intentionally underemployed and in basing his child support obligation on earning potential of $60,000 yearly)

In re A.M., 192 S.W.3d 570 (Tex. 2006) (obligor having actual custody of child may seek reimbursement of support paid, or offset against support ordered, but not both)

Bruni v. Bruni, 924 S.W.2d 366 (Tex. 1996) (parents' agreement for obligor to provide support for children until age 21 enforceable as contract; agreement survives the expiration of enforceable decree)

Elfeldt v. Elfeldt, 730 S.W.2d 657 (Tex. 1987) (agreement must specify terms enforceable as contract)

In re K.J.D., 299 S.W. 3d 517 (Tex. App.—Dallas 2009, no pet.) (attorney's fees in modification suit cannot be classified as child support; remedy limited to money judgment)

In re R.C.T., 294 S.W.3d 238 (Tex. App.—Houston [14 Dist.] 2009, pet. denied) (child support "due and owing" based on retroactive modification; lien proper but IRS intercept not because installments not delinquent)

In re B.N.A. 278 S.W. 3d 530 (Tex. App.—Dallas 2009, no pet.) (trial court's sanctions against OAG restricting enforcement of child support and imposing costs were error; OAG did not preserve appeal regarding confirmation of child support arrearage)

Garner v. Garner, 200 S.W.3d 303 (Tex. App.—Dallas 2006, no pet.) (musician's expenses were $2,600 monthly on allegedly zero income—trial court's directive to get a job to pay child support upheld)

In re A.B., 207 S.W.3d 434 (Tex. App.—Dallas 2006, no pet.) (old default judgment taken by A.G. for child support based on publication service sustained as establishing personal jurisdiction over obligor)

In re V.R.N., 188 S.W.3d 835 (Tex. App.—Eastland 2006, pet denied) (periodic wage withholdings keep 1989 judgment for arrears alive, not dormant) .

Gaxiola v. Garcia, 169 S.W.3d 426 (Tex. App.—El Paso 2005, no pet.) (evidence was sufficient to support trial court's finding that father was not intentionally underemployed)

Cameron v. Cameron, 158 S.W.3d 680 (Tex. App.—Dallas 2005, pet. denied) (above guideline support order approved based upon alleged underemployment of father obligor)

Cross References

Federal IV–D Child Support Program. 42 U.S.C.A. § 651 *et seq.*

TX FCA Const. Art. 16, § 28. Garnishment of Wages, *infra*.

SUBCHAPTER A. COURT–ORDERED CHILD SUPPORT

§ 154.001. Support of Child

(a) The court may order either or both parents to support a child in the manner specified by the order:

(1) until the child is 18 years of age or until graduation from high school, whichever occurs later;

(2) until the child is emancipated through marriage, through removal of the disabilities of minority by court order, or by other operation of law;

(3) until the death of the child; or

(4) if the child is disabled as defined in this chapter, for an indefinite period.

(a–1) The court may order each person who is financially able and whose parental rights have been terminated with respect to a child in substitute care for whom the department has been appointed managing conservator to support the child in the manner specified by the order:

(1) until the earliest of:

(A) the child's adoption;

(B) the child's 18th birthday or graduation from high school, whichever occurs later;

(C) removal of the child's disabilities of minority by court order, marriage, or other operation of law; or

(D) the child's death; or

(2) if the child is disabled as defined in this chapter, for an indefinite period.

(b) The court may order either or both parents to make periodic payments for the support of a child in a proceeding in which the Department of Protective and Regulatory Services is named temporary managing conservator. In a proceeding in which the Department of Protective and Regulatory Services is named permanent managing conservator of a child whose parents' rights have not been terminated, the court shall order each parent that is financially able to make periodic payments for the support of the child.

(c) In a Title IV–D case, if neither parent has physical possession or conservatorship of the child, the court may render an order providing that a nonparent or agency having physical possession may receive, hold, or disburse child support payments for the benefit of the child.

Comment

Subsection (a) is as simple and straightforward as any provision in the Family Code. It mandates that either or both parents must support their child and, by virtue of the maximum *inclusio unius est exclusio alterius*, only the parents may be ordered to support their child. That means that grandparents, nonparent conservators, and former managing conservators have no obligation to support a child. Section (a–1) allows the court to order certain terminated parents to continue to support their child.

Subsection (b) is designed to ensure that DFPS may be awarded child support after the department is named temporary managing conservator if the parents are financially able to pay. Note that the phrasing of the statute converts to the mandatory "shall order" language when DFPS is named permanent managing conservator.

Subsection (c) states the obvious; if a parent does not have possession of a child or conservatorship the court may redirect payments to a nonparent who has possession of the child, or to an agency. Obviously, payments are for the benefit of the child.

§ 154.002. Child Support Through High School Graduation

(a) The court may render an original support order, or modify an existing order, providing child support past the 18th birthday of the child to be paid only if the child is:

(1) enrolled:

(A) under Chapter 25, Education Code, in an accredited secondary school in a program leading toward a high school diploma;

(B) under Section 130.008, Education Code, in courses for joint high school and junior college credit; or

(C) on a full-time basis in a private secondary school in a program leading toward a high school diploma; and

(2) complying with:

(A) the minimum attendance requirements of Subchapter C, Chapter 25, Education Code; or

(B) the minimum attendance requirements imposed by the school in which the child is enrolled, if the child is enrolled in a private secondary school.

(b) The request for a support order through high school graduation may be filed before or after the child's 18th birthday.

(c) The order for periodic support may provide that payments continue through the end of the month in which the child graduates.

Comment

A fair amount of litigation has been generated regarding what graduation from high school entails. One thing is clear; graduation must take place prior to the child's 21st birthday before September 1 of any year. Over the years the detail in the section has expanded in the attempt to resolve as many additional questions as possible, and thus eliminate repeated litigation on the subject.

Leading Cases

In re J.A.B., 13 S.W.3d 813 (Tex. App.—Fort Worth 2000, no pet.) (child fully enrolled despite multiple unexcused absences)

Crocker v. Attorney General of Texas, 3 S.W.3d 650 (Tex. App.—Austin 1999, no pet.) (modification to continue support past 18 may be valid if child still fully enrolled in high school)

In re A.B., 994 S.W.2d 229 (Tex. App.—Eastland 1999, pet. denied) ("fully enrolled" does not require that post-18 high school student is passing—just trying to pass)

§ 154.003. Manner of Payment

The court may order that child support be paid by:

(1) periodic payments;

(2) a lump-sum payment;

(3) an annuity purchase;

(4) the setting aside of property to be administered for the support of the child as specified in the order; or

(5) any combination of periodic payments, lump-sum payments, annuity purchases, or setting aside of property.

Leading Case

Moroch v. Collins, 174 S.W.3d 849 (Tex. App.—Dallas 2005, pet. denied) (lump-sum child support award approved for children aged 16 and 19)

§ 154.004. Place of Payment

(a) The court shall order the payment of child support to the state disbursement unit as provided by Chapter 234.

(b) In a Title IV–D case, the court or the Title IV–D agency shall order that income withheld for child support be paid to the state disbursement unit of this state or, if appropriate, to the state disbursement unit of another state.

(c) This section does not apply to a child support order that:

(1) was initially rendered by a court before January 1, 1994; and

(2) is not being enforced by the Title IV–D agency.

Comment

With the establishment of the state disbursement unit required by federal law, certain child support payments must be directed to that unit as provided by § 234.007(a). These include payments in all cases being enforced by the Title IV D agency and in all other cases in which the support order was initially issued on or after January 1, 1994, and in which the obligor is subject to income withholding. While this reflects the requirements of federal law (42 U.S.C. 654b(1)), through cooperative agreements between the Title IV-D agency and counties virtually all child support payments under pre-1994 non-IV-D orders rendered in the state are also processed through the state disbursement unit. Subsection (b) enables the court or the IV D agency to redirect support payments to the disbursement of another state if the obligee has relocated. This conforms to § 159.319(b). *(A.G.K. & H.P.S.)*

---

§ 154.005. Payments of Support Obligation by Trust

(a) The court may order the trustees of a spendthrift or other trust to make disbursements for the support of a child to the extent the trustees are required to make payments to a beneficiary who is required to make child support payments as provided by this chapter.

(b) If disbursement of the assets of the trust is discretionary, the court may order child support payments from the income of the trust but not from the principal.

§ 154.006. Termination of Duty of Support

(a) Unless otherwise agreed in writing or expressly provided in the order or as provided by Subsection (b), the child support order terminates on:

(1) the marriage of the child;

(2) the removal of the child's disabilities for general purposes;

(3) the death of the child;

(4) a finding by a court that the child:

(A) is 18 years of age or older; and

(B) has failed to comply with the enrollment or attendance requirements described by Section 154.002(a); ~~or~~

(5) **the issuance under Section 161.005(h) of an order terminating the parent-child relationship between the obligor and the child based on the results of genetic testing that exclude the obligor as the child's genetic father; or**

(6) if the child enlists in the armed forces of the United States, the date on which the child begins active service as defined by 10 U.S.C. Section 101.

(b) Unless a nonparent or agency has been appointed conservator of the child under Chapter 153, the order for current child support, and any provision relating to conservatorship, possession, or access terminates on the marriage or remarriage of the obligor and obligee to each other.

Amended by Acts 2011, 82nd Leg., ch. 54 (S.B. 785), § 1, eff. May 12, 2011.

Comment

In 2011 an additional basis for terminating child support authorizes an adjudicated or acknowledged father to terminate his parental rights due to mistaken paternity, *see* § 161.005, *infra*.

Note that beginning in 2007 the duty of support does not terminate on the death of the obligor. Fundamentally this makes the unpaid, prospective support obligation a debt of the obligor's estate to the extent it cannot be satisfied by benefits to which the child would be entitled as a result of the obligor's death (e.g., life insurance proceeds) or other financial resources available for the support of the child. *See* § 154.015 and § 154.016.

Subsection (a)(5) provides that the duty of support ends on the date a child who has enlisted in the armed forces begins active service. "Active service" is distinguished from enlistment alone, inasmuch as enlistment can occur months before the child actually reports for full time active duty (including full time national guard service). The child may during that period continue to reside with the custodial parent as a minor dependent.

Leading Cases

Newberry v. Newberry, 146 S.W.3d 233 (Tex. App.—Houston [14th Dist.] 2004, no pet.) (failure to reduce child support order for two kids after only one is entitled to support is reversible error)

Deltuva v. Deltuva, 113 S.W.3d 882 (Tex. App.—Dallas 2003, no pet.) (failure to reduce child support as children age-out is reversible error)

§ 154.007. Order to Withhold Child Support From Income

(a) In a proceeding in which periodic payments of child support are ordered, modified, or enforced, the court or Title IV-D agency shall order that income be withheld from the disposable earnings of the obligor as provided by Chapter 158.

(b) If the court does not order income withholding, an order for support must contain a provision for income withholding to ensure that withholding may be effected if a delinquency occurs.

(c) A child support order must be construed to contain a withholding provision even if the provision has been omitted from the written order.

(d) If the order was rendered or last modified before January 1, 1987, the order is presumed to contain a provision for income withholding procedures to take effect in the event a delinquency occurs without further amendment to the order or future action by the court.

Comment

This section mandates that an income withholding order is to be rendered in every case, without exception. This does not necessarily mean that an income withholding order will be served on the obligor's employer. *See* § 158.002. It does mean that an income withholding order will be available in the courthouse file in every case without requiring a return to court.

§ 154.008. Provision for Medical Support

The court shall order medical support for the child as provided by Subchapters B and D.

CLE/Other Legal Publications

Post-divorce medical benefits (now you see it, now you don't). James N. Higdon, 2011 Adv. Fam. L.

General medicine: medical care, invasive vs. non-invasive, parental rights, medications, etc. Kelly Larkin, 2011 U.T. Advanced Parent–Child Relationships

HIPAA and other releases. Bridget Danielle Burke & Gabe Thomas Vick III, 2011 Adv. Fam. L.

§ 154.009. Retroactive Child Support

(a) The court may order a parent to pay retroactive child support if the parent:

(1) has not previously been ordered to pay support for the child; and

(2) was not a party to a suit in which support was ordered.

(b) In ordering retroactive child support, the court shall apply the child support guidelines provided by this chapter.

(c) Unless the Title IV–D agency is a party to an agreement concerning support or purporting to settle past, present, or future support obligations by prepayment or otherwise, an agreement between the parties does not reduce or terminate retroactive support that the agency may request.

(d) Notwithstanding Subsection (a), the court may order a parent subject to a previous child support order to pay retroactive child support if:

(1) the previous child support order terminated as a result of the marriage or remarriage of the child's parents;

(2) the child's parents separated after the marriage or remarriage; and

(3) a new child support order is sought after the date of the separation.

(e) In rendering an order under Subsection (d), the court may order retroactive child support back to the date of the separation of the child's parents.

Comment

Subsection (d) provides an exception to the rule that an obligor may not be ordered to pay retroactive support if the obligor had previously been ordered to pay support for the same child. The exception arises where the earlier support order terminated upon the marriage or remarriage of the parties and the parties subsequently separate. When that happens, the court may order the obligor to pay support back to the time of separation. Of course, this scenario could be replayed more than once. (*H.P.S.*)

Leading Cases

In re B.R., 327 S.W. 3d 208 (Tex. App.—San Antonio 2010) (retroactive support not limited to four-year period)

In re Sanders, 159 S.W.3d 797 (Tex. App.—Amarillo 2005, no pet.) (retroactive support must be based upon child support guidelines as applied to income for retroactive time period)

---

§ 154.010. No Discrimination Based on Marital Status of Parents or Sex

The amount of support ordered for the benefit of a child shall be determined without regard to:

(1) the sex of the obligor, obligee, or child; or

(2) the marital status of the parents of the child.

§ 154.011. Support Not Conditioned on Possession or Access

A court may not render an order that conditions the payment of child support on whether a managing conservator allows a possessory conservator to have possession of or access to a child.

Leading Case

In re A.N.H., 70 S.W.3d 918 (Tex. App.—Amarillo 2002, no pet.) (support order conditioned on obligor's right to visitation violates public policy and is void)

---

§ 154.012. Support Paid in Excess of Support Order

(a) If an obligor is not in arrears and the obligor's child support obligation has terminated, the obligee shall return to the obligor a child support payment made by the obligor that exceeds the amount of support ordered, regardless of whether the payment was made before, on, or after the date the child support obligation terminated.

(b) An obligor may file a suit to recover a child support payment under Subsection (a). If the court finds that the obligee failed to return a child support payment under Subsection (a), the court shall order the obligee to pay to the obligor attorney's fees and all court costs in addition to the amount of support paid after the date the child support order terminated. For good cause shown, the court may waive the requirement that the obligee pay attorney's fees and costs if the court states the reasons supporting that finding.

Comment

Under this section, if a support obligation has terminated and no arrearages are owed, an obligor is due any amounts paid the obligee in excess of the ordered child support amount, no matter when the excess payments may have been made. An obligee who refuses or otherwise fails to return any such amounts to the obligor may be forced to do so by the court, as well as to pay any costs and fees. While this seems and, undoubtedly in most cases, is equitable, there is always the possibility that an obligor may have, for whatever good-hearted reasons, intentionally paid excess support, only to lay claim to such excess payment under this section after a change of heart. *(H.P.S.)*

§ 154.013. Continuation of Duty to Pay Support After Death of Obligee

(a) A child support obligation does not terminate on the death of the obligee but continues as an obligation to the child named in the support order, as required by this section.

(b) Notwithstanding any provision of the Probate Code, a child support payment held by the Title IV-D agency, a local registry, or the state disbursement unit or any uncashed check or warrant representing a child support payment made before, on, or after the date of death of the obligee shall be paid proportionately for the benefit of each surviving child named in the support order and not to the estate of the obligee. The payment is free of any creditor's claim against the deceased obligee's estate and may be disbursed as provided by Subsection (c).

(c) On the death of the obligee, current child support owed by the obligor for the benefit of the child or any amount described by Subsection (b) shall be paid to:

(1) a person, other than a parent, who is appointed as managing conservator of the child;

(2) a person, including the obligor, who has assumed actual care, control, and possession of the child, if a managing conservator or guardian of the child has not been appointed;

(3) the county clerk, as provided by Section 887, Texas Probate Code, in the name of and for the account of the child for whom the support is owed;

(4) a guardian of the child appointed under Chapter XIII, Texas Probate Code, as provided by that code; or

(5) the surviving child, if the child is an adult or has otherwise had the disabilities of minority removed.

(d) On presentation of the obligee's death certificate, the court shall render an order directing payment of child support paid but not disbursed to be made as provided by Subsection (c). A copy of the order shall be provided to:

(1) the obligor;

(2) as appropriate:

(A) the person having actual care, control, and possession of the child;

(B) the county clerk; or

(C) the managing conservator or guardian of the child, if one has been appointed;

(3) the local registry or state disbursement unit and, if appropriate, the Title IV-D agency; and

(4) the child named in the support order, if the child is an adult or has otherwise had the disabilities of minority removed.

(e) The order under Subsection (d) must contain:

(1) a statement that the obligee is deceased and that child support amounts otherwise payable to the obligee shall be paid for the benefit of a surviving child named in the support order as provided by Subsection (c);

(2) the name and age of each child named in the support order; and

(3) the name and mailing address of, as appropriate:

(A) the person having actual care, control, and possession of the child;

(B) the county clerk; or

(C) the managing conservator or guardian of the child, if one has been appointed.

(f) On receipt of the order required under this section, the local registry, state disbursement unit, or Title IV-D agency shall disburse payments as required by the order.

Comment

The death of the obligee does not affect the continuing duty of support owed by the obligor to a child named in an order. Under this section, any current support, including amounts that have been collected but not disbursed at the time of an obligee's death, as well as any subsequent support payments, are not to be treated as part of the obligee's estate or subject to any creditor's claims against the estate, but are to be paid over for the benefit of each surviving child named in the support order. By court order, payment would be made to the child's caretaker, including through an account administered by the county clerk. Presumably, if the caretaker changed, the court could be petitioned to redirect support payments to the successor caretaker.

If the obligor is the new caretaker—as likely will be the case—any undisbursed collections would be returned to the obligor, and no further payments would be made—at least, for as long as the obligor continued to have actual care, control, and possession of the child. If a surviving child is no longer a minor, that child would be entitled to a proportionate share of any collected, but undisbursed, support collections at the time of the death of the obligee. The section does not address the more complex issue of support arrearages which may have accrued at the time of the obligee's death, including the question of ownership of those arrearages. *(H.P.S.)*

§ 154.014. Payments in Excess of Court-Ordered Amount

(a) If a child support agency or local child support registry receives from an obligor who is not in arrears a child support payment in an amount that exceeds the court-ordered amount, the agency or registry, to the extent possible, shall give effect to any expressed intent of the obligor for the application of the amount that exceeds the court-ordered amount.

(b) If the obligor does not express an intent for the application of the amount paid in excess of the court-ordered amount, the agency or registry shall:

(1) credit the excess amount to the obligor's future child support obligation; and

(2) promptly disburse the excess amount to the obligee.

(c) This section does not apply to an obligee who is a recipient of public assistance under Chapter 31, Human Resources Code.

Comment

This section addresses the situation in which a child support registry receives a support payment exceeding the court-ordered amount. Lacking instruction from the obligor, the registry might treat the overpayment as a gift to the obligee, hold it to be disbursed along with the next periodic support payment, or simply return the excess amount to the obligor. This section directs the registry, in the absence of any expressed intent of the obligor, to credit the excess amount towards future child support payments and promptly to disburse the full amount paid by the obligor to the obligee. *(H.P.S.)*

§ 154.015. Acceleration of Unpaid Child Support Obligation

(a) In this section, "estate" has the meaning assigned by Section 3, Texas Probate Code.

(b) If the child support obligor dies before the child support obligation terminates, the remaining unpaid balance of the child support obligation becomes payable on the date the obligor dies.

(c) For purposes of this section, the court of continuing jurisdiction shall determine the amount of the unpaid child support obligation for each child of the deceased obligor. In determining the amount of the unpaid child support obligation, the court shall consider all relevant factors, including:

(1) the present value of the total amount of monthly periodic child support payments that would become due between the month in which the obligor dies and the month in which the child turns 18 years of age, based on the amount of the periodic monthly child support payments under the child support order in effect on the date of the obligor's death;

(2) the present value of the total amount of health insurance premiums payable for the benefit of the child from the month in which the obligor dies until the month in which the child turns 18 years of age, based on the cost of health insurance for the child ordered to be paid on the date of the obligor's death;

(3) in the case of a disabled child under 18 years of age or an adult disabled child, an amount to be determined by the court under Section 154.306;

(4) the nature and amount of any benefit to which the child would be entitled as a result of the obligor's death, including life insurance proceeds, annuity payments, trust distributions, social security death benefits, and retirement survivor benefits; and

(5) any other financial resource available for the support of the child.

(d) If, after considering all relevant factors, the court finds that the child support obligation has been satisfied, the court shall render an order terminating the child support obligation. If the court finds that the child support obligation is not satisfied, the court shall render a judgment in favor of the obligee, for the benefit of the child, in the amount of the unpaid child support obligation determined under Subsection (c). The order must designate the obligee as constructive trustee, for the benefit of the child, of any money received in satisfaction of the judgment.

(e) The obligee has a claim, on behalf of the child, against the deceased obligor's estate for the unpaid child support obligation determined under Subsection (c). The obligee may present the claim in the manner provided by the Texas Probate Code.

(f) If money paid to the obligee for the benefit of the child exceeds the amount of the unpaid child support obligation remaining at the time of the obligor's death, the obligee shall hold the excess amount as constructive trustee for the benefit of the deceased obligor's estate until the obligee delivers the excess amount to the legal representative of the deceased obligor's estate.

Comment

This section makes any unpaid, prospective child support a claim against a deceased obligor's estate to the extent that the unpaid amount cannot be satisfied by benefits to which the child would be entitled as a result of the obligor's death (such as life insurance taken out to cover unpaid support, as provided under § 154.016) or other financial resources available for the support of the child. It is unclear what is intended by "other financial resources." Conceivably, at the discretion of the court, they could include the obligee's income or other assets of the obligee or the willing generosity of grandparents or other family members.

Prior to 2007, child support arrearages constituted a claim against a decedent's estate with a Class 4 priority, but the parties could agree in writing or the court could order that the prospective obligation survive the obligor's death. This section, with conforming changes to the Probate Code, now ensures that the unpaid balance of the support obligation may be pursued against the obligor's estate if it cannot be satisfied otherwise. The court must do some considerable computation, including factoring in health insurance premiums, to determine what amount, if any, remains to be paid from the estate. The presumption is that the child will live until the age of 18 years and not be legally emancipated before that age. If the obligee does end up with a viable claim against the estate, the whole matter shifts to the arena of the probate court for settlement. Presumably the obligee's claim stands apart from any bequest made the child under the obligor's will or any amount of the estate that the child might otherwise be entitled under the probate code. *(A.G.K. & H.P.S.)*

---

§ 154.016. Provision of Support in Event of Death of Parent

(a) The court may order a child support obligor to obtain and maintain a life insurance policy, including a decreasing term life insurance policy, that will establish an insurance-funded trust or an annuity payable to the obligee for the benefit of the child that will satisfy the support obligation under the child support order in the event of the obligor's death.

(b) In determining the nature and extent of the obligation to provide for the support of the child in the event of the death of the obligor, the court shall consider all relevant factors, including:

(1) the present value of the total amount of monthly periodic child support payments from the date the child support order is rendered until the month in which the child turns 18 years of age, based on the amount of the periodic monthly child support payment under the child support order;

(2) the present value of the total amount of health insurance premiums payable for the benefit of the child from the date the child support order is rendered until the month in which the child turns 18 years of age, based on the cost of health insurance for the child ordered to be paid; and

(3) in the case of a disabled child under 18 years of age or an adult disabled child, an amount to be determined by the court under Section 154.306.

(c) The court may, on its own motion or on a motion of the obligee, require the child support obligor to provide proof satisfactory to the court verifying compliance with the order rendered under this section.

Comment

This section authorizes the court to order an obligor to take out a suitable life insurance policy to cover any unpaid support remaining beyond the obligor's death. The presumption here, as under § 154.015, is that the child will live until the age of 18 years and not be legally emancipated before that age. If there is no life insurance policy in effect at the time of the obligor's death or no policy or other assets and resources that adequately cover any unpaid, prospective support, the prospective support is immediately accelerated, as provided under § 154.015, to become a debt of the obligor's estate. *(A.G.K. & H.P.S.)*

SUBCHAPTER B. COMPUTING NET RESOURCES AVAILABLE FOR PAYMENT OF CHILD SUPPORT

***See* CLE/Other Legal Publications following Introductory Comment to this Chapter, *supra*.**

---

§ 154.061. Computing Net Monthly Income

(a) Whenever feasible, gross income should first be computed on an annual basis and then should be recalculated to determine average monthly gross income.

(b) The Title IV–D agency shall annually promulgate tax charts to compute net monthly income, subtracting from gross income social security taxes and federal income tax withholding for a single person claiming one personal exemption and the standard deduction.

Leading Case

Norris v. Norris, 56 S.W.3d 333 (Tex. App.—El Paso 2001, no pet.) (to reach correct result in computing child support, yearly income swings should be averaged to calculate the most likely future income)

2011 CHILD SUPPORT TAX CHARTS FOR CALCULATING CHILD SUPPORT ORDERS

OFFICE OF THE ATTORNEY GENERAL 2011 TAX CHARTS

Pursuant to § 154.061(b) of the Texas Family Code, the Office of the Attorney General of Texas, as the Title IV–D agency, has promulgated the following tax charts to assist courts in establishing the amount of a child support order. These tax charts are applicable to employed and self-employed persons in computing net monthly income.

Editor's note: *We doubt that anyone, even the A.G., will chase after child support from potential obligors for the first few entries in the official charts, i.e., $100 to $800, which fall below the minimum wage rate.*

INSTRUCTIONS FOR USE

To use these tables, first compute the obligor's annual gross income. Then recompute to determine the obligor's average monthly gross income. These tables provide a method for calculating "monthly net income" for child support purposes, subtracting from monthly gross income the social security taxes and the federal income tax withholding for a single person claiming one personal exemption and the standard deduction.

Thereafter, in many cases the guidelines call for a number of additional steps to complete the necessary calculations. For example, §§ 154.061–154.070 provide for appropriate additions to "income" as that term is defined for federal income tax purposes, and for certain subtractions from monthly net income, in order to arrive at the net resources of the obligor available for child support purposes. If necessary, one may compute an obligee's net resources using similar steps.

EMPLOYED PERSONS 2011 TAX CHART

	Social Security Taxes			
Monthly Gross Wages	Old-Age, Survivors and Disability Insurance Taxes (4.2%)[1]	Hospital (Medicare) Insurance Taxes (1.45%)[1]	Federal Income Taxes[2]	Net Monthly Income
100.00	4.20	1.45	0.00	94.35
200.00	8.40	2.90	0.00	188.70
300.00	12.60	4.35	0.00	283.05
400.00	16.80	5.80	0.00	377.40
500.00	21.00	7.25	0.00	471.75
600.00	25.20	8.70	0.00	566.10
700.00	29.40	10.15	0.00	660.45
800.00	33.60	11.60	0.83	753.97
900.00	37.80	13.05	10.83	838.32
1,000.00	42.00	14.50	20.83	922.67
1,100.00	46.20	15.95	30.83	1,007.02
1,200.00	50.40	17.40	40.83	1,091.37
1,256.67[3]	52.78	18.22	46.50	1,139.17
1,300.00	54.60	18.85	50.83	1,175.72
1,400.00	58.80	20.30	60.83	1,260.07
1,500.00	63.00	21.75	70.83	1,344.42
1,600.00	67.20	23.20	85.83	1,423.77
1,700.00	71.40	24.65	100.83	1,503.12
1,800.00	75.60	26.10	115.83	1,582.47
1,900.00	79.80	27.55	130.83	1,661.82
2,000.00	84.00	29.00	145.83	1,741.17

Monthly Gross Wages	Social Security Taxes: Old–Age, Survivors and Disability Insurance Taxes (4.2%)[1]	Social Security Taxes: Hospital (Medicare) Insurance Taxes (1.45%)[1]	Federal Income Taxes[2]	Net Monthly Income
2,100.00	88.20	30.45	160.83	1,820.52
2,200.00	92.40	31.90	175.83	1,899.87
2,300.00	96.60	33.35	190.83	1,979.22
2,400.00	100.80	34.80	205.83	2,058.57
2,500.00	105.00	36.25	220.83	2,137.92
2,600.00	109.20	37.70	235.83	2,217.27
2,700.00	113.40	39.15	250.83	2,296.62
2,800.00	117.60	40.60	265.83	2,375.97
2,900.00	121.80	42.05	280.83	2,455.32
3,000.00	126.00	43.50	295.83	2,534.67
3,100.00	130.20	44.95	310.83	2,614.02
3,200.00	134.40	46.40	325.83	2,693.37
3,300.00	138.60	47.85	340.83	2,772.72
3,400.00	142.80	49.30	355.83	2,852.07
3,500.00	147.00	50.75	370.83	2,931.42
3,600.00	151.20	52.20	385.83	3,010.77
3,700.00	155.40	53.65	404.17	3,086.78
3,800.00	159.60	55.10	429.17	3,156.13
3,900.00	163.80	56.55	454.17	3,225.48
4,000.00	168.00	58.00	479.17	3,294.83
4,250.00	178.50	61.63	541.67	3,468.20
4,500.00	189.00	65.25	604.17	3,641.58
4,750.00	199.50	68.88	666.67	3,814.95
5,000.00	210.00	72.50	729.17	3,988.33
5,250.00	220.50	76.13	791.67	4,161.70
5,500.00	231.00	79.75	854.17	4,335.08
5,750.00	241.50	83.38	916.67	4,508.45
6,000.00	252.00	87.00	979.17	4,681.83
6,250.00	262.50	90.63	1,041.67	4,855.20
6,500.00	273.00	94.25	1,104.17	5,028.58
6,750.00	283.50	97.88	1,166.67	5,201.95
7,000.00	294.00	101.50	1,229.17	5,375.33
7,500.00	315.00	108.75	1,354.17	5,722.08
8,000.00	336.00	116.00	1,486.42	6,061.58
8,500.00	357.00	123.25	1,626.42	6,393.33
9,000.00	373.80[4]	130.50	1,766.42	6,729.28
10,092.44[5]	373.80	146.34	2,072.30	7,500.00
10,500.00	373.80	152.25	2,186.42	7,787.53
11,000.00	373.80	159.50	2,326.42	8,140.28
11,500.00	373.80	166.75	2,466.42	8,493.03
12,000.00	373.80	174.00	2,606.42	8,845.78
12,500.00	373.80	181.25	2,746.42	9,198.53
13,000.00	373.80	188.50	2,886.42	9,551.28
13,500.00	373.80	195.75	3,026.42	9,904.03
14,000.00	373.80	203.00	3,166.42	10,256.78
14,500.00	373.80	210.25	3,306.42	10,609.53
15,000.00	373.80	217.50	3,446.42	10,962.28

Footnotes to Employed Persons 2011 Tax Chart:

1. An employed person not subject to the Old–Age, Survivors and Disability Insurance/Hospital (Medicare) Insurance taxes will be allowed the reductions reflected in these columns, unless it is shown that such person has no similar contributory plan such as teacher retirement, federal railroad retirement, federal civil service retirement, etc.

2. These amounts represent one-twelfth (1/12) of the annual federal income tax calculated for a single taxpayer claiming one personal exemption ($3,700.00), and taking the standard deduction ($5,800.00).

3. The amount represents one-twelfth (1/12) of the gross income of an individual earning the federal minimum wage ($7.25 per hour) for a 40–hour week for a full year. $7.25 per hour x 40 hours per week x 52 weeks per year equals $15,080.00 per year. One-twelfth (1/12) of $15,080.00 equals $1,256.67.

4. For annual gross wages above $106,800.00, this amount represents a monthly average of the Old–Age, Survivors and Disability Insurance tax based on the 2011 maximum Old–Age, Survivors and Disability Insurance tax of $4,485.60 per person (4.2% of the first $106,800.00 of annual gross wages equals $4,485.60). One-twelfth (1/12) of $4,485.60 equals $373.80.

5. This amount represents the point where the monthly gross wages of an employed individual would result in $7,500.00 of net resources.

* *

References Relating to Employed Persons 2011 Tax Chart:

1. Old–Age, Survivors and Disability Insurance Tax
   (a) Contribution Base
      (1) Social Security Administration's notice dated November 19, 2010, and appearing in 75 Fed. Reg. 74123 (November 30, 2010)
      (2) Section 3121(a) of the Internal Revenue Code of 1986, as amended (26 U.S.C. § 3121(a))
      (3) Section 230 of the Social Security Act, as amended (42 U.S.C. § 430)
   (b) Tax Rate
      (1) Section 3101(a) of the Internal Revenue Code of 1986, as amended (26 U.S.C. § 3101(a))
2. Hospital (Medicare) Insurance Tax
   (a) Contribution Base
      (1) Section 3121(a) of the Internal Revenue Code of 1986, as amended (26 U.S.C. § 3121(a))
      (2) Omnibus Budget Reconciliation Act of 1993, Pub.L.No. 103–66, § 13207, 107 Stat. 312, 467–69 (1993)
   (b) Tax Rate
      (1) Section 3101(b) of the Internal Revenue Code of 1986, as amended (26 U.S.C. § 3101(b))
3. Federal Income Tax
   (a) Tax Rate Schedule for 2011 for Single Taxpayers
      (1) Revenue Procedure 2011–12, Section 2.01, Table 3 which appears in Internal Revenue Bulletin 2011–02, dated January 10, 2011
      (2) Section 1(c), (f) and (i) of the Internal Revenue Code of 1986, as amended (26 U.S.C. § 1(c), 1(f) and 1(i))
   (b) Standard Deduction
      (1) Revenue Procedure 2011–12, Section 2.05(1), which appears in Internal Revenue Bulletin 2011–02 dated January 10, 2011
      (2) Section 63(c) of the Internal Revenue Code of 1986, as amended (26 U.S.C. § 63(c))
   (c) Personal Exemption
      (1) Revenue Procedure 2011–12, Section 2.07, which appears in Internal Revenue Bulletin 2011–02, dated January 10, 2011
      (2) Section 151(d) of the Internal Revenue Code of 1986, as amended (26 U.S.C. § 151(d))

SELF–EMPLOYED PERSONS 2011 TAX CHART

Social Security Taxes

Monthly Net Earnings From Self–Employment[1]	Old–Age, Survivors and Disability Insurance Taxes (10.4%)[2]	Hospital (Medicare) Insurance Taxes (2.9%)[2]	Federal Income Taxes[3]	Net Monthly Income
100.00	9.60	2.68	0.00	87.72
200.00	19.21	5.36	0.00	175.43
300.00	28.81	8.03	0.00	263.16
400.00	38.42	10.71	0.00	350.87
500.00	48.02	13.39	0.00	438.59
600.00	57.63	16.07	0.00	526.30
700.00	67.23	18.75	0.00	614.02
800.00	76.84	21.43	0.00	701.73
900.00	86.44	24.10	4.48	784.98
1,000.00	96.04	26.78	13.77	863.41
1,100.00	105.65	29.46	23.06	941.83
1,200.00	115.25	32.14	32.36	1,020.25
1,300.00	124.86	34.82	41.65	1,098.67
1,400.00	134.46	37.49	50.95	1,177.10
1,500.00	144.07	40.17	60.24	1,255.52
1,600.00	153.67	42.85	69.53	1,333.95

Monthly Net Earnings From Self-Employment[1]	Social Security Taxes: Old-Age, Survivors and Disability Insurance Taxes (10.4%)[2]	Social Security Taxes: Hospital (Medicare) Insurance Taxes (2.9%)[2]	Federal Income Taxes[3]	Net Monthly Income
1,700.00	163.27	45.53	82.82	1,408.38
1,800.00	172.88	48.21	96.76	1,482.15
1,900.00	182.48	50.88	110.70	1,555.94
2,000.00	192.09	53.56	124.64	1,629.71
2,100.00	201.69	56.24	138.58	1,703.49
2,200.00	211.30	58.92	152.52	1,777.26
2,300.00	220.90	61.60	166.46	1,851.04
2,400.00	230.51	64.28	180.40	1,924.81
2,500.00	240.11	66.95	194.35	1,998.59
2,600.00	249.71	69.63	208.29	2,072.37
2,700.00	2599.32	72.31	222.23	2,146.14
2,800.00	268.92	74.99	236.17	2,219.92
2,900.00	278.53	77.67	250.11	2,293.69
3,000.00	288.13	80.34	264.05	2,367.48
3,100.00	297.74	83.02	277.99	2,441.25
3,200.00	307.34	85.70	291.93	2,515.03
3,300.00	316.95	88.38	305.87	2,588.80
3,400.00	326.55	91.06	319.81	2,662.58
3,500.00	336.15	93.74	333.75	2,736.36
3,600.00	345.76	96.41	347.69	2,810.14
3,700.00	355.36	99.09	361.63	2,883.92
3,800.00	364.97	101.77	375.57	2,957.69
3,900.00	374.57	104.45	389.51	3,031.47
4,000.00	384.18	107.13	408.53	3,100.16
4,250.00	408.19	113.82	466.62	3,261.37
4,500.00	432.20	120.52	524.70	3,422.58
4,750.00	456.21	127.21	582.79	3,583.79
5,000.00	480.22	133.91	640.88	3,744.99
5,250.00	504.23	140.60	698.96	3,906.21
5,500.00	528.24	147.30	757.05	4,067.41
5,750.00	552.25	153.99	815.13	4,228.63
6,000.00	576.26	160.69	873.22	4,389.83
6,250.00	600.28	167.38	931.30	4,551.04
6,500.00	624.29	174.08	989.39	4,712.24
6,750.00	648.30	180.78	1,047.47	4,873.45
7,000.00	672.31	187.47	1,105.56	5,034.66
7,500.00	720.33	200.86	1,221.73	5,357.08
8,000.00	768.35	214.25	1,337.90	5,679.50
8,500.00	816.37	227.64	1,458.31	5,997.68
9,000.00	864.40	241.03	1,588.42	6,306.15
9,500.00	912.42	254.42	1,718.53	6,614.63
10,000.00	925.60[4]	267.82	1,854.46	6,952.12
10,500.00	925.60	281.21	1,992.58	7,300.61
11,786.08[5]	925.60	288.87	2,071.61	7,500.00
11,000.00	925.60	294.60	2,130.71	7,649.09
11,500.00	925.60	307.99	2,268.83	7,997.58
12,000.00	925.60	321.38	2,406.96	8,346.06
12,500.00	925.60	334.77	2,545.08	8,694.55
13,000.00	925.60	348.16	2,683.21	9,043.03
13,500.00	925.60	361.55	2,821.34	9,391.51
14,000.00	925.60	374.94	2,959.46	9,740.00
14,500.00	925.60	388.33	3,097.59	10,088.48
15,000.00	925.60	401.72	3,235.71	10,436.97

Footnotes to Self-Employed Persons 2011 Tax Chart:

1. Determined without regard to Section 1402(a)(12) of the Internal Revenue Code of 1986, as amended (26 U.S.C. § 1402(a)(12)) (the "Code").

2. In calculating each of the Old-Age, Survivors and Disability Insurance tax and the Hospital (Medicare) Insurance tax, net earnings from self-employment are reduced by the deduction under Section 1402(a)(12) of the Code. The deduction under Section 1402(a)(12) of the Code is equal to net earnings from self-employment (determined without regard to Section 1402(a)(12) of the Code) multiplied by one-half (1/2) of the sum of the Old-Age, Survivors and Disability Insurance tax rate (determined without regard to the temporary employee

payroll tax cut as described by section 601(b)(1) of the "Tax Relief, Unemployment Insurance Reauthorization, and Job Creation Act of 2010") (12.4%) and the Hospital (Medicare) Insurance tax rate (2.9%). The sum of these rates is 15.3% (12.4% + 2.9% = 15.3%). One-half (1/2) of the combined rate is 7.65% (15.3% x 1/2 = 7.65%). The deduction can be computed by multiplying the net earnings from self-employment (determined without regard to Section 1402(a)(12) of the Code) by 92.35%. This gives the same deduction as multiplying the net earnings from self-employment (determined without regard to Section 1402(a)(12) of the Code) by 7.65% and then subtracting the result.

For example, the Social Security taxes imposed on monthly net earnings from self-employment (determined without regard to Section 1402(a)(12) of the Code) of $2,500.00 are calculated as follows:
(i) Old–Age, Survivors and Disability Insurance Taxes:
$2,500.00 × 92.35% × 10.4% = $240.11
(ii) Hospital (Medicare) Insurance Taxes:
$2,500.00 × 92.35% × 2.9% = $66.95

3. These amounts represent one-twelfth (1/12) of the annual federal income tax calculated for a single taxpayer claiming one personal exemption ($3,700.00) and taking the standard deduction ($5,800.00).

In calculating the annual federal income tax, gross income is reduced by the deduction under Section 164(f) of the Code. The deduction under Section 164(f) of the Code for 2011 is computed at the rate of 59.6 percent of the OASDI tax paid plus one half of the Hospital (Medicare) Insurance tax paid as described by section 601(b)(2) of the "Tax Relief, Unemployment Insurance Reauthorization, and Job Creation Act of 2010." For example, monthly net earnings from self-employment of $8,500.00 times 12 months equals $102,000.00. The Old–Age, Survivors and Disability Insurance taxes imposed by Section 1401 of the Code for the taxable year equal $9,796.49 ($102,000.00 x .9235 x 10.4% = $9,796.49). The Hospital (Medicare) Insurance taxes imposed by Section 1401 of the Code for the taxable year equal $2,731.71 ($102,000.00 x .9235 x 2.9% = $2,731.71). The deduction under Section 164(f) of the Code for 2011 is equal to $7,204.57 (($9,796.49 x 0.596) + ($2,731.72 x 0.5) = $7,204.57).

4. For annual net earnings from self-employment (determined with regard to Section 1402(a)(12) of the Code) above $106,800.00, this amount represents a monthly average of the Old–Age, Survivors and Disability Insurance tax based on the 2011 maximum Old–Age, Survivors and Disability Insurance tax of $11,107.20 per person (10.4% of the first $106,800.00 of net earnings from self-employment (determined with regard to Section 1402(a)(12) of the Code) equals $11,107.20). One-twelfth (1/12) of $11,107.20 equals $925.60.

5. This amount represents the point where the monthly net earnings from self-employment of a self-employed individual would result in $7,500.00 of net resources.

* *

References Relating to Self-Employed Persons 2011 Tax Chart:

1. Old–Age, Survivors and Disability Insurance Tax
   (a) Contribution Base
      (1) Social Security Administration's notice dated November 19, 2010 appearing in 75 Fed. Reg. 74123 (November 30, 2010)
      (2) Section 1402(b) of the Internal Revenue Code of 1986, as amended (26 U.S.C. § 1402(b))
      (3) Section 230 of the Social Security Act, as amended (42 U.S.C. § 430)
   (b) Tax Rate
      (1) Section 1401(a) of the Internal Revenue Code of 1986, as amended (26 U.S.C. § 1401(a))
   (c) Deduction Under Section 1402(a)(12)
      (1) Section 1402(a)(12) of the Internal Revenue Code of 1986, as amended (26 U.S.C. § 1402(a)(12))
2. Hospital (Medicare) Insurance Tax
   (a) Contribution Base
      (1) Section 1402(b) of the Internal Revenue Code of 1986, as amended (26 U.S.C. § 1402(b))
      (2) Omnibus Budget Reconciliation Act of 1993, Pub. L. No. 103–66, § 13207, 107 Stat. 312, 467–69 (1993)
   (b) Tax Rate
      (1) Section 1401(b) of the Internal Revenue Code of 1986, as amended (26 U.S.C. § 1401(b))
   (c) Deduction Under Section 1402(a)(12)
      (1) Section 1402(a)(12) of the Internal Revenue Code of 1986, as amended (26 U.S.C. § 1402(a)(12))

3. Federal Income Tax
   (a) Tax Rate Schedule for 2011 for Single Taxpayers
      (1) Revenue Procedure 2011–12, Section 2.01, Table 3 which appears in Internal Revenue Bulletin 2011–02, dated January 10, 2011
      (2) Section 1(c), (f) and (i) of the Internal Revenue Code of 1986, as amended (26 U.S.C. § 1(c), 1(f), 1(i))
   (b) Standard Deduction
      (1) Revenue Procedure 2011–12, Section 2.05(1), which appears in Internal Revenue Bulletin 2011–02, dated January 10, 2011
      (2) Section 63(c) of the Internal Revenue Code of 1986, as amended (26 U.S.C. § 63(c))
   (c) Personal Exemption
      (1) Revenue Procedure 2011–12, Section 2.07, which appears in Internal Revenue Bulletin 2011–02, dated January 10, 2011
      (2) Section 151(d) of the Internal Revenue Code of 1986, as amended (26 U.S.C. § 151(d))
   (d) Deduction Under Section 164(f)
      (1) Section 164(f) of the Internal Revenue Code of 1986, as amended (26 U.S.C. § 164(f))

§ 154.062. Net Resources

(a) The court shall calculate net resources for the purpose of determining child support liability as provided by this section.

(b) Resources include:

(1) 100 percent of all wage and salary income and other compensation for personal services (including commissions, overtime pay, tips, and bonuses);

(2) interest, dividends, and royalty income;

(3) self-employment income;

(4) net rental income (defined as rent after deducting operating expenses and mortgage payments, but not including noncash items such as depreciation); and

(5) all other income actually being received, including severance pay, retirement benefits, pensions, trust income, annuities, capital gains, social security benefits other than supplemental security income, unemployment benefits, disability and workers' compensation benefits, interest income from notes regardless of the source, gifts and prizes, spousal maintenance, and alimony.

(c) Resources do not include:

(1) return of principal or capital;

(2) accounts receivable;

(3) benefits paid in accordance with the Temporary Assistance for Needy Families program **or another** federal public assistance **program** ~~programs~~; or

(4) payments for foster care of a child.

Text of subsec. (d) effective until Sept. 1, 2012

(d) The court shall deduct the following items from resources to determine the net resources available for child support:

(1) social security taxes;

(2) federal income tax based on the tax rate for a single person claiming one personal exemption and the standard deduction;

(3) state income tax;

(4) union dues; and

(5) expenses for the cost of health insurance or cash medical support for the obligor's child ordered by the court under Section 154.182.

Text of subsec. (d) effective Sept. 1, 2012

(d) The court shall deduct the following items from resources to determine the net resources available for child support:

(1) social security taxes;

(2) federal income tax based on the tax rate for a single person claiming one personal exemption and the standard deduction;

(3) state income tax;

(4) union dues; ~~and~~

(5) expenses for the cost of health insurance or cash medical support for the obligor's child ordered by the court under Section 154.182**; and**

(6) if the obligor does not pay social security taxes, nondiscretionary retirement plan contributions.

(e) In calculating the amount of the deduction for health care coverage for a child under Subsection (d)(5), if the obligor has other minor dependents covered under the same health insurance plan, the court shall divide the total cost to the obligor for the insurance by the total number of minor dependents, including the child, covered under the plan.

Text of subsec. (f) effective Sept. 1, 2012

(f) For purposes of Subsection (d)(6), a nondiscretionary retirement plan is a plan to which an employee is required to contribute as a condition of employment.

Amended by Acts 2011, 82nd Leg., ch. 91 (S.B. 1303), § 9.001, eff. Sept. 1, 2011; Acts 2011, 82nd Leg., ch. 932 (S.B. 1751), § 1, eff. Sept. 1, 2012.

Comment

The "100 percent of all wage and salary income" of Subsection (b)(1) specifically includes the obvious, such as overtime pay, commissions, tips, and bonuses. While some of these items may be irregular. whether the pay is regular or somewhat unpredictable the court must seek to even out irregularities in wages or salary and take the long view of the obligor's ability to pay. Considering the past year of employment often will yield a more accurate profile than considering the last paycheck or two.

An amendment in 2009 to (b)(5) specifically excludes supplemental security income (SSI) from the net resources of an obligor in setting of the support obligation. This follows case law that noted SSI is an entitlement paid to disabled individuals who do not qualify for earnings-based Social Security Disability Insurance benefits (SSDI). Such SSI payments are akin to other federal public assistance excluded from net resources under (c)(3), which are typically small and in themselves barely sufficient for the subsistence of the recipient.

Subsection (c) excludes from the net resources of an obligor any amounts paid to the obligor for the foster care of a child. This exclusion accords with the federal income tax exclusion of foster care payments from taxable income of the individual to whom the payments are made.

Subsection (d)(5) includes "cash medical support" in addition to the cost of health insurance for the child as among the items to be deducted by the court to arrive at the net resources of the obligor against which the guidelines would be applied. This reflects the change in the medical support provisions under § 154.182. Subsection (e) is to ensure that the obligor receives a deduction for health care costs only for the child for which the obligor is responsible, and not for any other minor dependents that might be covered under the same insurance policy. *(A.G.K. & H.P.S.)*

CLE/Other Legal Publications

Post-divorce medical benefits (now you see it, now you don't). James N. Higdon, 2011 ADV. FAM. L.

Above guidelines child support. Angela G. Pence England, 2011 U.T. ADVANCED PARENT-CHILD RELATIONSHIPS

Primer on child support calculation and collection. Angela G. Pence England, 2011 U.T. PARENT-CHILD RELATIONSHIPS: BASICS

To Infinity and Beyond the Guidelines: Child Support Cases Every Space Ranger Should Know. Michael D. Wysocki, FAM. L. SECT. RPT. (Spring 2011)

Leading Cases

Iliff v. Iliff, 339 S.W.3d 74 (Tex. 2011) (when child support obligor is intentionally unemployed or underemployed, intent to avoid child support need not be proven for court to apply the child support guidelines to obligor's earning potential earnings instead of to actual earnings, disapproving two appellate decisions) (court may properly consider an obligor's intent to avoid child support as a factor, along with other relevant facts, in analyzing whether obligor is intentionally unemployed or underemployed) (court did not abuse its discretion finding husband was intentionally underemployed and in basing his child support obligation on earning potential of $60,000 yearly)

Burney v. Burney, 225 S.W.3d 208 (Tex. App.—El Paso 2006, no pet.) (trial court looks to unexplained deposits in bank accounts to increase net resources beyond salary)

Moroch v. Collins, 174 S.W.3d 849 (Tex. App.—Dallas 2005, no pet.) (child support calculations based on imputed income to obligor)

Knight v. Knight, 131 S.W.3d 535 (Tex. App.—El Paso 2004, no pet.) (child support based on husband's income from prior year rather than alleged current income)

In re E.A.S., 123 S.W.3d 565 (Tex. App.—El Paso 2003, pet. denied) (court finds obligor intentionally underemployed with undisclosed financial resources)

In re Knott, 118 S.W.3d 899 (Tex. App.—Texarkana 2003, no pet.) (new spouse's income not to be included in parent's net resources; no reason found to deviate from guideline support)

In re L.R.P., 98 S.W.3d 312 (Tex. App.—Houston [1st Dist.] 2003, pet. dism'd) (monetary gifts from parents and scholarship funds received included in student father's income for net resources)

---

§ 154.063. Party to Furnish Information

The court shall require a party to:

(1) furnish information sufficient to accurately identify that party's net resources and ability to pay child support; and

(2) produce copies of income tax returns for the past two years, a financial statement, and current pay stubs.

§ 154.064. Medical Support for Child Presumptively Provided by Obligor

The guidelines for support of a child are based on the assumption that the court will order the obligor to provide medical support for the child in addition to the amount of child support calculated in accordance with those guidelines.

Comment

The application of the support guidelines assume that the obligor will be ordered to provide medical support for the child. The manner in which medical support is provided is left to the court, depending on the availability of health insurance to either party, but at "reasonable cost" to the obligor, as that is defined under § 154.181(e), *infra. (A.G.K. & H.P.S.)*

CLE/Other Legal Publications

Post-divorce medical benefits (now you see it, now you don't). James N. Higdon, 2011 ADV. FAM. L.

General medicine: medical care, invasive vs. non-invasive, parental rights, medications, etc. Kelly Larkin, 2011 U.T. ADVANCED PARENT-CHILD RELATIONSHIPS

---

§ 154.065. Self-Employment Income

(a) Income from self-employment, whether positive or negative, includes benefits allocated to an individual from a business or undertaking in the form of a proprietorship, partnership, joint venture, close corporation, agency, or independent contractor, less ordinary and necessary expenses required to produce that income.

(b) In its discretion, the court may exclude from self-employment income amounts allowable under federal income tax law as depreciation, tax credits, or any other business expenses shown by the evidence to be inappropriate in making the determination of income available for the purpose of calculating child support.

§ 154.066. Intentional Unemployment or Underemployment

If the actual income of the obligor is significantly less than what the obligor could earn because of intentional unemployment or underemployment, the court may apply the support guidelines to the earning potential of the obligor.

Leading Cases

McLane v. McLane, 263 S.W.3d 358 (Tex. App.—Houston [1st Dist.] 2008, pet. denied) (finding of intentional underemployment supported by evidence)

Swaab v. Swaab, 282 S.W.3d 519 (Tex. App.—Houston [14th Dist.] 2008, dism. w.o.j.) (court properly determined approximate net monthly resources by averaging annual self-employment income over appropriate time period)

Cameron v. Cameron, 158 S.W.3d 680 (Tex. App.—Dallas 2005, pet. denied) (evidence sufficient for above guideline support based upon potential underemployment)

Gaxiola v. Garcia, 169 S.W.3d 426 (Tex. App.—El Paso 2005, no pet.) (obligor's move from Phoenix to El Paso for less money but to be closer to child does not support finding of underemployment)

In re E.A.S., 123 S.W.3d 565 (Tex. App.—El Paso 2003, pet. denied) (court finds obligor intentionally underemployed with undisclosed financial resources)

§ 154.067. Deemed Income

(a) When appropriate, in order to determine the net resources available for child support, the court may assign a reasonable amount of deemed income attributable to assets that do not currently produce income. The court shall also consider whether certain property that is not producing income can be liquidated without an unreasonable financial sacrifice because of cyclical or other market conditions. If there is no effective market for the property, the carrying costs of such an investment, including property taxes and note payments, shall be offset against the income attributed to the property.

(b) The court may assign a reasonable amount of deemed income to income-producing assets that a party has voluntarily transferred or on which earnings have intentionally been reduced.

§ 154.068. Wage and Salary Presumption

In the absence of evidence of the wage and salary income of a party, the court shall presume that the party has wages or salary equal to the federal minimum wage for a 40–hour week.

Comment

This section provides a benchmark for calculating an appropriate child support order in the absence of reliable information about the obligor's financial circumstances, to wit, the federal minimum wage.

Leading Case

In re B.R.G., 48 S.W.3d 812 (Tex. App.—El Paso 2001, no pet.), *see also* 37 S.W.3d 542 (without proof to the contrary, father may be presumed to have earned minimum wage since birth of child)

§ 154.069. Net Resources of Spouse

(a) The court may not add any portion of the net resources of a spouse to the net resources of an obligor or obligee in order to calculate the amount of child support to be ordered.

(b) The court may not subtract the needs of a spouse, or of a dependent of a spouse, from the net resources of the obligor or obligee.

Leading Cases

In re J.C.K., 143 S.W.3d 131 (Tex. App.—Waco 2004, no pet.) (improper to consider stepmother's sole management community property in calculating net resources)

In re Knott, 118 S.W.3d 899 (Tex. App.—Texarkana 2003, no pet.) (new spouse's income not to be included in parent's net resources)

§ 154.070. Child Support Received by Obligor

In a situation involving multiple households due child support, child support received by an obligor shall be added to the obligor's net resources to compute the net resources before determining the child support credit or applying the percentages in the multiple household table in this chapter.

SUBCHAPTER C. CHILD SUPPORT GUIDELINES

Comment

The Texas Legislature has assumed the major role regarding child support guidelines. Undoubtedly, the most significant aspect of the legislatively mandated guidelines is that they are applicable in every case and rebuttably presumed to be in the best interest of the child.

***See* CLE/Other Legal Publications following Introductory Comment to this Chapter, *supra*.**

Leading Cases

Cameron v. Cameron, 158 S.W.3d 680 (Tex. App.—Dallas 2005, pet. denied) (above guideline support order approved based upon alleged underemployment of father obligor)

Yarbrough v. Yarbrough, 151 S.W.3d 687 (Tex. App.—Waco 2004, no pet.) (above guidelines support approved considering cost of child's school lunches and uninsured medical expenses)

In re J.C.K., 143 S.W.3d 131 (Tex. App.—Waco 2004, no pet.) (improper to consider community property subject to sole management and control of father's wife in calculating net resources for purposes of child support payments)

In re Knott, 118 S.W.3d 899 (Tex. App.—Texarkana 2003, no pet.) (new spouse's income not to be included in parent's net resources; no reason found to deviate from guideline support)

Lide v. Lide, 116 S.W.3d 147 (Tex. App.—El Paso 2003, no pet.) (above guideline support affirmed based on funds available to obligor and children's needs)

§ 154.121. Guidelines for the Support of a Child

The child support guidelines in this subchapter are intended to guide the court in determining an equitable amount of child support.

§ 154.122. Application of Guidelines Rebuttably Presumed in Best Interest of Child

(a) The amount of a periodic child support payment established by the child support guidelines in effect in this state at the time of the hearing is presumed to be reasonable, and an order of support conforming to the guidelines is presumed to be in the best interest of the child.

(b) A court may determine that the application of the guidelines would be unjust or inappropriate under the circumstances.

Comment

The child support guidelines determining the amount of support are explicitly presumed to be in the best interest of the child. The trial court may determine the presumed amount is "unjust or inappropriate," but if that conclusion is reached, the court must have a specific explanation to justify it. *See* § 154.130.

---

§ 154.123. Additional Factors for Court to Consider

(a) The court may order periodic child support payments in an amount other than that established by the guidelines if the evidence rebuts the presumption that application of the guidelines is in the best interest of the child and justifies a variance from the guidelines.

(b) In determining whether application of the guidelines would be unjust or inappropriate under the circumstances, the court shall consider evidence of all relevant factors, including:

(1) the age and needs of the child;

(2) the ability of the parents to contribute to the support of the child;

(3) any financial resources available for the support of the child;

(4) the amount of time of possession of and access to a child;

(5) the amount of the obligee's net resources, including the earning potential of the obligee if the actual income of the obligee is significantly less than what the obligee could earn because the obligee is intentionally unemployed or underemployed and including an increase or decrease in the income of the obligee or income that may be attributed to the property and assets of the obligee;

(6) child care expenses incurred by either party in order to maintain gainful employment;

(7) whether either party has the managing conservatorship or actual physical custody of another child;

(8) the amount of alimony or spousal maintenance actually and currently being paid or received by a party;

(9) the expenses for a son or daughter for education beyond secondary school;

(10) whether the obligor or obligee has an automobile, housing, or other benefits furnished by his or her employer, another person, or a business entity;

(11) the amount of other deductions from the wage or salary income and from other compensation for personal services of the parties;

(12) provision for health care insurance and payment of uninsured medical expenses;

(13) special or extraordinary educational, health care, or other expenses of the parties or of the child;

(14) the cost of travel in order to exercise possession of and access to a child;

(15) positive or negative cash flow from any real and personal property and assets, including a business and investments;

(16) debts or debt service assumed by either party; and

(17) any other reason consistent with the best interest of the child, taking into consideration the circumstances of the parents.

Comment

Deviation from the amount "suggested" by the guidelines is permissible, of course, and may be based on any of the wide variety of factors enumerated.

Leading Cases

In re J.R.D., 169 S.W.3d 740 (Tex. App.—Austin 2005, pet. denied) (no reduction in support even though mother had the same or similar financial resources as he did)

Lide v. Lide, 116 S.W.3d 147 (Tex. App.—El Paso 2003, no pet.) (above guideline support affirmed based on funds available to obligor and children's needs)

McGuire v. McGuire, 4 S.W.3d 382 (Tex. App.—Houston [1st Dist.] 1999, no pet.) (obligor went into business that yields less income—underemployment allegation for trial court to evaluate)

Thomas v. Thomas, 895 S.W.2d 895 (Tex. App.—Waco 1995, writ denied) (expiration of contractual alimony constitutes material change in obligee's financial circumstances)

§ 154.124. Agreement Concerning Support

(a) To promote the amicable settlement of disputes between the parties to a suit, the parties may enter into a written agreement containing provisions for support of the child and for modification of the agreement, including variations from the child support guidelines provided by Subchapter C.

(b) If the court finds that the agreement is in the child's best interest, the court shall render an order in accordance with the agreement.

(c) Terms of the agreement pertaining to child support in the order may be enforced by all remedies available for enforcement of a judgment, including contempt, but are not enforceable as a contract.

(d) If the court finds the agreement is not in the child's best interest, the court may request the parties to submit a revised agreement or the court may render an order for the support of the child.

Comment

Subsection (c) specifically recognizes that most disputes over child support are settled by agreement of the parties. This does not mean that the agreement reached is a contract. Indeed, contractual enforcement of agreements for child support is not an available remedy. Previously, if an agreement was reached it could provide that it was "enforceable as a contract." This often created conflict between a court ordered downward modification and the "contract" reached earlier by the parties. This statute takes dead aim at the former anomaly that a court decision was effective in one context—statutory enforcement—but contractually enforceable in a manner that could, at least in partial effect, trump the court order. Under this statute the downward modification of a child support order does not leave a contractual obligation enforceable at the pre modification amount. Because the change in the law was prospective only, contracts entered before September 1, 1995, remain enforceable.

Leading Cases

Bruni v. Bruni, 924 S.W.2d 366 (Tex. 1996) (parents' agreement for obligor to provide support for children until age 21 enforceable as contract)

Espeche v Ritzell, 123 S.W.3d 657 (Tex. App.—Houston [14th Dist.] 2003, no pet.) (child's breach of contract suit for agreed-upon support against former stepfather not barred by mother's res judicata)

§ 154.125. Application of Guidelines to Net Resources

(a) The guidelines for the support of a child in this section are specifically designed to apply to situations in which the obligor's monthly net resources are not greater than $7,500 or the adjusted amount determined under Subsection (a–1), whichever is greater.

(a–1) The dollar amount prescribed by Subsection (a) is adjusted every six years as necessary to reflect inflation. The Title IV–D agency shall compute the adjusted amount, to take effect beginning September 1 of the year of the adjustment, based on the percentage change in the consumer price index during the 72–month period preceding March 1 of the year of the adjustment, as rounded to the nearest $50 increment. The Title IV–D agency shall publish the adjusted amount in the Texas Register before September 1 of the year in which the adjustment takes effect. For purposes of this subsection, "consumer price index" has the meaning assigned by Section 341. 201, Finance Code.

Text of subsec. (a–2) effective until September 1, 2014

(a–2) The initial adjustment required by Subsection (a–1) shall take effect September 1, 2013. This subsection expires September 1, 2014.

(b) If the obligor's monthly net resources are not greater than the amount provided by Subsection (a), the court shall presumptively apply the following schedule in rendering the child support order:

CHILD SUPPORT GUIDELINES
BASED ON THE MONTHLY NET RESOURCES OF THE OBLIGOR

1 child	20% of Obligor's Net Resources
2 children	25% of Obligor's Net Resources
3 children	30% of Obligor's Net Resources
4 children	35% of Obligor's Net Resources
5 children	40% of Obligor's Net Resources
6+ children	Not less than the amount for 5 children

Comment

In 1993 the presumptive amount of net resources to which the statutory guidelines are to be applied, commonly known somewhat inaccurately as "the cap," was raised from $4,000 to $6,000. After 14 years of increases in both expenses and income, the amount was raised to $7,500 in 2007. Notwithstanding the wounded cries from the dedicated opponents of the change, for the vast majority of children this amendment will have absolutely no effect. On the other hand, what might be called the lower range of the well to do obligors will feel a pinch. Under the former "cap," employed individuals maxed out at $98,940, and the self-employed at $106,188 (higher Social Security taxes for the latter, as many of our readers are well acquainted with). Because the presumptive amount has been raised by 25%, it is not surprising that "complaints were heard," i.e., maximum net resources of $124,317 and $132,084, respectively. And remember, the more children and the more families an obligor has, the greater the pain. No wonder one and two are such popular numbers for having children these days.

The Texas child support guidelines have the effect of subjecting the total net resources of well over 95% of all potential obligors to the presumptive application of the guidelines. As before, the child support guidelines also deal with multiple families, thereby resolving a set of problems that once had bedeviled Texas courts. *(A.G.K. & H.P.S.)*

§ 154.126. Application of Guidelines to Additional Net Resources

(a) If the obligor's net resources exceed the amount provided by Section 154.125(a), the court shall presumptively apply the percentage guidelines to the portion of the obligor's net resources that does not exceed that amount. Without further reference to the percentage recommended by these guidelines, the court may order additional amounts of child support as appropriate, depending on the income of the parties and the proven needs of the child.

(b) The proper calculation of a child support order that exceeds the presumptive amount established for the portion of the obligor's net resources provided by Section 154.125(a) requires that the entire amount of the presumptive award be subtracted from the proven total needs of the child. After the presumptive award is subtracted, the court shall allocate between the parties the responsibility to meet the additional needs of the child according to the circumstances of the parties. However, in no event may the obligor be required to pay more child support than the greater of the presumptive amount or the amount equal to 100 percent of the proven needs of the child.

Leading Cases

Scott v. Younts, 926 S.W.2d 415 (Tex. App.—Corpus Christi 1996, writ denied) (obligor earning $300,000 ordered to pay $2,500 monthly support)

Zajac v. Penkava, 924 S.W.2d 405 (Tex. App.—San Antonio 1996, no writ) (doctor-obligor should pay monthly child support of $3,000 on net resources of $13,000 monthly when children's proven needs nearly $8,400)

Panozzo v. Panozzo, 904 S.W.2d 780 (Tex. App.—Corpus Christi 1995, no writ) ($10,000 per month child support is abuse of discretion)

§ 154.127. Partial Termination of Support Obligation

(a) A child support order for more than one child shall provide that, on the termination of support for a child, the level of support for the remaining child or children is in accordance with the child support guidelines.

(b) A child support order is in compliance with the requirement imposed by Subsection (a) if the order contains a provision that specifies:

(1) the events, including a child reaching the age of 18 years or otherwise having the disabilities of minority removed, that have the effect of terminating the obligor's obligation to pay child support for that child; and

(2) the reduced total amount that the obligor is required to pay each month after the occurrence of an event described by Subdivision (1).

Comment

Subsection (b) identifies the details of the "step down" order required under Subsection (a) in situations in which more than one child is covered by the order. The order is directed to recite the reduced total amount of support owed by the obligor as a child "ages out" or otherwise ceases to be the financial responsibility of the obligor. Note the apparent legislative drafting oversight in (b)(1) which fails to recognize that child support is due until an able bodied child reaches 18 *or graduates from high school, whichever is later*, §§ 154.001–.002.

§ 154.128. Computing Support for Children in More Than One Household

(a) In applying the child support guidelines for an obligor who has children in more than one household, the court shall apply the percentage guidelines in this subchapter by making the following computation:

(1) determine the amount of child support that would be ordered if all children whom the obligor has the legal duty to support lived in one household by applying the schedule in this subchapter;

(2) compute a child support credit for the obligor's children who are not before the court by dividing the amount determined under Subdivision (1) by the total number of children whom the obligor is obligated to support and multiplying that number by the number of the obligor's children who are not before the court;

(3) determine the adjusted net resources of the obligor by subtracting the child support credit computed under Subdivision (2) from the net resources of the obligor; and

(4) determine the child support amount for the children before the court by applying the percentage guidelines for one household for the number of children of the obligor before the court to the obligor's adjusted net resources.

(b) For the purpose of determining a child support credit, the total number of an obligor's children includes the children before the court for the establishment or modification of a support order and any other children, including children residing with the obligor, whom the obligor has the legal duty of support.

(c) The child support credit with respect to children for whom the obligor is obligated by an order to pay support is computed, regardless of whether the obligor is delinquent in child support payments, without regard to the amount of the order.

Comment

This cleverly devised formula provides a method for computing support for obligors with multiple families, *i.e.,* with children who reside in more than one household. Most practitioners will skip the textual statement for calculating the formula and go directly to the chart provided in the next section.

---

§ 154.129. Alternative Method of Computing Support for Children in More Than One Household

In lieu of performing the computation under the preceding section, the court may determine the child support amount for the children before the court by applying the percentages in the table below to the obligor's net resources:

MULTIPLE FAMILY ADJUSTED GUIDELINES
(% OF NET RESOURCES)

		Number of children before the court						
		1	2	3	4	5	6	7
Number of	0	20.00	25.00	30.00	35.00	40.00	40.00	40.00
other	1	17.50	22.50	27.38	32.20	37.33	37.71	38.00
children for	2	16.00	20.63	25.20	30.33	35.43	36.00	36.44
whom the	3	14.75	19.00	24.00	29.00	34.00	34.67	35.20
obligor	4	13.60	18.33	23.14	28.00	32.89	33.60	34.18
has a	5	13.33	17.86	22.50	27.22	32.00	32.73	33.33
duty of	6	13.14	17.50	22.00	26.60	31.27	32.00	32.62
support	7	13.00	17.22	21.60	26.09	30.67	31.38	32.00

§ 154.130. Findings in Child Support Order

(a) Without regard to Rules 296 through 299, Texas Rules of Civil Procedure, in rendering an order of child support, the court shall make the findings required by Subsection (b) if:

(1) a party files a written request with the court not later than 10 days after the date of the hearing;

(2) a party makes an oral request in open court during the hearing; or

(3) the amount of child support ordered by the court varies from the amount computed by applying the percentage guidelines under Section 154.125 or 154.129, as applicable.

(a–1) If findings under this section are required as a result of the request by a party under Subsection (a)(1) or (2), the court shall make and enter the findings not later than the 15th day after the date of the party's request.

(b) If findings are required by this section, the court shall state whether the application of the guidelines would be unjust or inappropriate and shall state the following in the child support order:

"(1) the net resources of the obligor per month are $__________;

"(2) the net resources of the obligee per month are $__________;

"(3) the percentage applied to the obligor's net resources for child support is __________%; and

"(4) if applicable, the specific reasons that the amount of child support per month ordered by the court varies from the amount computed by applying the percentage guidelines under Section 154.125 or 154.129, as applicable."

(c) Repealed by Acts 2009, 81st Leg., ch. 767, § 37.

Comment

The request for findings in a child support order is specifically placed outside the range of Texas Rules of Civil Procedure 296–299. Response to a request for an explanation is mandatory; failure to justify the deviation from the amount suggested by the guidelines constitutes reversible error. Subsection (b) requires the court to explain its deviation from the guidelines whenever the guidelines would yield an amount different from the sum actually ordered.

Leading Cases

Tenery v. Tenery, 932 S.W.2d 29 (Tex. 1996) (obligor has right to demand findings and conclusions when trial court deviates from child support guidelines)

Haney v. Haney, 834 S.W.2d 490 (Tex. App.—Houston [14th Dist.] 1992, writ denied) (required findings recorded on docket sheet satisfy requirement even though not stated in order)

Hanna v. Hanna, 813 S.W.2d 626 (Tex. App.—Houston [1st Dist.] 1991, no writ) (failure to make requested findings on net resources reversible error)

Chamberlain v. Chamberlain, 788 S.W.2d 455 (Tex. App.—Houston [1st Dist.] 1990, writ denied) (trial court's failure to explain deviation from guidelines after request is reversible error)

Cross References

Tex. R. Civ. P. 296, Requests for Findings of Facts and Conclusions of Law; Tex. R. Civ. P. 297, Time to File Findings of Facts and Conclusions of Law.

---

§ 154.131. Retroactive Child Support

(a) The child support guidelines are intended to guide the court in determining the amount of retroactive child support, if any, to be ordered.

(b) In ordering retroactive child support, the court shall consider the net resources of the obligor during the relevant time period and whether:

(1) the mother of the child had made any previous attempts to notify the obligor of his paternity or probable paternity;

(2) the obligor had knowledge of his paternity or probable paternity;

(3) the order of retroactive child support will impose an undue financial hardship on the obligor or the obligor's family; and

(4) the obligor has provided actual support or other necessaries before the filing of the action.

(c) It is presumed that a court order limiting the amount of retroactive child support to an amount that does not exceed the total amount of support that would have been due for the four years preceding the date the petition seeking support was filed is reasonable and in the best interest of the child.

(d) The presumption created under this section may be rebutted by evidence that the obligor:

(1) knew or should have known that the obligor was the father of the child for whom support is sought; and

(2) sought to avoid the establishment of a support obligation to the child.

(e) An order under this section limiting the amount of retroactive support does not constitute a variance from the guidelines requiring the court to make specific findings under Section 154.130.

(f) Notwithstanding any other provision of this subtitle, the court retains jurisdiction to render an order for retroactive child support in a suit if a petition requesting retroactive child support is filed not later than the fourth anniversary of the date of the child's 18th birthday.

Comment

This section provides a method for calculating arrears when a parentage suit determines retroactive support is due. *See* Chapter 160, Uniform Parentage Act, *infra*.

Subsection (c) reflects a concern expressed by public policy groups that large amounts of retroactive support may diminish the ability of many child support obligors to stay current in payment of their support obligations. There was also the sense among lawmakers that an obligor ignorant of having fathered a child—perhaps because of deliberate concealment of the fact by the mother—or an obligor knowing he was the father, but being told by the obligee that his support was not needed or wanted, would be unfairly burdened with a child support obligation reaching back many years. Although the code already clearly provided the court with discretion in determining whether, and how much, retroactive support should be ordered, Subsection (c) rebuttably limits retroactive support to an amount not exceeding the amount of support that would have been due under the support guidelines for the four-year period preceding the filing of the petition. In effect, it creates an estoppel by laches defense with the burden of refutation falling upon the obligee or the state, as the case may be.

Subsection (f) specifically limits the time in which the court retains jurisdiction for ordering retroactive support to the child's 22 birthday. For example, this provision would prevent an abandoned parent, whether divorced, separated, or unmarried, from seeking retroactive support for a child well beyond the minority of a child if the other parent had not previously been ordered to pay support. *See* § 154.009. This time limitation also bars an adult disabled child, or the caretaker of that child, from seeking post-minority support of the child under Subchapter F. The purpose of the subsection is rather narrow, i.e., to address the ordering of retroactive support in the context of the establishment of paternity. *(A.G.K. & H.P.S.)*

Leading Cases

Martinez v. Martinez, 61 S.W.3d 589 (Tex. App.—San Antonio 2001, pet. denied) (order awarding retroactive child support is void without specific notice it is being sought)

Garza v. Blanton, 55 S.W.3d 708 (Tex. App.—Corpus Christi 2001, no pet.) (order for retroactive support in paternity suit discretionary with the court—payments made pre-parentage determination seriously mitigate against such an order)

In re A.P., 46 S.W.3d 347 (Tex. App.—Corpus Christi 2001, no pet.) (court ordered 18 years of retroactive child support for the child before she turned age 20)

§ 154.132. Application of Guidelines to Children of Certain Disabled Obligors

In applying the child support guidelines for an obligor who has a disability and who is required to pay support for a child who receives benefits as a result of the obligor's disability, the court shall apply the guidelines by determining the amount of child support that would be ordered under the child support guidelines and subtracting from that total the amount of benefits or the value of the benefits paid to or for the child as a result of the obligor's disability.

Comment

Courts had taken different positions as to whether a disabled obligor is entitled to a credit for the amount of payments received by a child as a result of the obligor's disability when the support guidelines are applied. This provision makes it clear that the obligor is entitled to such a credit.

§ 154.133. Application of Guidelines to Children of Obligors Receiving Social Security

In applying the child support guidelines for an obligor who is receiving social security old age benefits and who is required to pay support for a child who receives benefits as a result of the obligor's receipt of social security old age benefits, the court shall apply the guidelines by determining the amount of child support that would be ordered under the child support guidelines and subtracting from that total the amount of benefits or the value of the benefits paid to or for the child as a result of the obligor's receipt of social security old age benefits.

Comment

The net resources of the obligor to which the court applies the guidelines in determining the child support obligation include any social security benefits, see § 154.062, *supra*. Under federal social security law, a minor child or an adult disabled child of an obligor receiving social security old age (retirement) benefits is also entitled to receive dependent benefits. This section requires the court to deduct from the amount of child support that would be ordered by the application of the guidelines to the obligor's net resources the amount of dependent benefits received by the child as a result of the obligor's eligibility to social security old age benefits. The provision complements § 154.132, *supra,* which accords the obligor a similar credit with respect to disability benefits. *(H.P.S.)*

SUBCHAPTER D. MEDICAL SUPPORT FOR CHILD

Comment

The trial court has great flexibility to fashion an appropriate order to ensure that health insurance is available to the child. While the cost of health insurance is assumed to be borne by the obligor, in some circumstances this is impractical or impossible. If the obligee bears the cost of health insurance, a recalculation of the periodic payments of child support is appropriate.

CLE/Other Legal Publications

Obtaining child support. Barry J. Brooks & Karen L. Marvel, 2009 U.T. Parent-Child Rel.

Child Support and Health Care—Over, Above, and Beyond. Hon. Conrad L. Moren. 2009 So. Tex. Fam. L. Conf.

Dealing with special needs children (electronic visitation statute, disabled adult children) governmental benefits for children (SSI). Sally H. Emerson & Karen L. Marvel, 2008 Marriage Dissolution

Health care options for former military spouses: Tricare and the Continued Health Care Benefit Program (CHCBP). William J. Camp, 43 Fam. L. Q. 227

Leading Case

State v. Hernandez, 802 S.W.2d 894 (Tex. App.—San Antonio 1991, no writ) (court erred in not ordering health insurance)

Cross References

Continuation of Medical Coverage (COBRA). 29 U.S.C.A. § 1161 *et seq.*

Qualified Medical Child Support Order (QMCSO), 29 U.S.C.A. § 1169.

Tex. Ins. Code Ann. § 1251.001 *et seq.*, Group and Blanket Health Insurance.

§ 154.181. Medical Support Order

(a) The court shall render an order for the medical support of the child as provided by this section and Section 154.182 in:

(1) a proceeding in which periodic payments of child support are ordered under this chapter or modified under Chapter 156;

(2) any other suit affecting the parent-child relationship in which the court determines that medical support of the child must be established, modified, or clarified; or

(3) a proceeding under Chapter 159.

(b) Before a hearing on temporary orders or a final order, if no hearing on temporary orders is held, the court shall require the parties to the proceedings to disclose in a pleading or other statement:

(1) if private health insurance is in effect for the child, the identity of the insurance company providing the coverage, the policy number, which parent is responsible for payment of any insurance premium for the coverage, whether the coverage is provided through a parent's employment, and the cost of the premium; or

(2) if private health insurance is not in effect for the child, whether:

(A) the child is receiving medical assistance under Chapter 32, Human Resources Code;

(B) the child is receiving health benefits coverage under the state child health plan under Chapter 62, Health and Safety Code, and the cost of any premium; and

(C) either parent has access to private health insurance at reasonable cost to the obligor.

(c) In rendering temporary orders, the court shall, except for good cause shown, order that any health insurance coverage in effect for the child continue in effect pending the rendition of a final order, except that the court may not require the continuation of any health insurance that is not available to the parent at reasonable cost to the obligor. If there is no health insurance coverage in effect for the child or if the insurance in effect is not available at a reasonable cost to the obligor, the court shall, except for good cause shown, order health care coverage for the child as provided under Section 154.182.

(d) On rendering a final order the court shall:

(1) make specific findings with respect to the manner in which health care coverage is to be provided for the child, in accordance with the priorities identified under Section 154.182; and

(2) except for good cause shown or on agreement of the parties, require the parent ordered to provide health care coverage for the child as provided under Section 154.182 to produce evidence to the court's satisfaction that the parent has applied for or secured health insurance or has otherwise taken necessary action to provide for health care coverage for the child, as ordered by the court.

(e) In this section, "reasonable cost" means the cost of health insurance coverage for a child that does not exceed nine percent of the obligor's annual resources, as described by Section 154.062(b), if the obligor is responsible under a medical support order for the cost of health insurance coverage for only one child. If the obligor is responsible under a medical support order for the cost of health insurance coverage for more than one child, "reasonable cost" means the total cost of health insurance coverage for all children for which the obligor is responsible under a medical support order that does not exceed nine percent of the obligor's annual resources, as described by Section 154.062(b).

Comment

Subsection (a) clarifies that a medical support order is not required in every SAPCR, but only in those proceedings which address child support or medical support or in a UIFSA proceeding. Health care coverage of a child is considered an integral part of the child support obligation and must ordinarily be ordered along with financial support. The court, however, must determine how health care coverage will be provided, either by private or government plans. This section lays out a process by which the court is to consider the availability to either parent of affordable coverage for the child. Although at one time it was assumed that insurance coverage of a child through a parent's place of employment was available "at reasonable cost," in 2001 the legislature established a criterion of "reasonable cost" under Subsection (e).

Subsection (d) requires the court to make specific findings with respect to the manner in which health care coverage for the child would be provided, in accordance with the priorities laid out under § 154.182. The standard of "reasonable cost" under Subsection (e) is nine percent of that parent's annual resources. There were two reasons for this change. The Tax Charts promulgated by the Office of the Attorney General identify a "net monthly income," which denotes an amount remaining after the deduction of federal income and social security taxes from the obligor's "monthly gross wages." "Resources," on the other hand, is spelled out in § 154.062(b) and includes all income, not just wage or salary income. Federal rules implementing provisions of the Deficit Reduction Act of 2005 require each state to use an income based numeric standard, defined by the state, in setting a medical support obligation that may be considered reasonable in cost. "Resources," as identified under 154.062(b) accords with the federal definition of "income" (42 U.S.C. § 666(b)(8)). In 2007 the legislature determined that nine percent of "resources" for medical support was a reasonable cost.

In 2009 Subsection (e) was amended to clarify that the standard of "reasonable cost" applied to the annual resources of the obligor under the support order, not to the parent ordered to include the child in a health insurance plan available to that parent. It also provided, quite reasonably, that, no matter the number of children for which the obligor is required to provide health insurance coverage under a medical support order, the total cost to the obligor of the coverage may not exceed nine percent of the obligor's annual resources. *(A.G.K. & H.P.S.)*

§ 154.182. Health Care Coverage for Child

(a) The court shall consider the cost, accessibility, and quality of health insurance coverage available to the parties and shall give priority to health insurance coverage available through the employment of one of the parties if the coverage is available at a reasonable cost to the obligor.

(b) In determining the manner in which health care coverage for the child is to be ordered, the court shall render its order in accordance with the following priorities, unless a party shows good cause why a particular order would not be in the best interest of the child:

(1) if health insurance is available for the child through a parent's employment or membership in a union, trade association, or other organization at reasonable cost, the court shall order that parent to include the child in the parent's health insurance;

(2) if health insurance is not available for the child under Subdivision (1) but is available to a parent at a reasonable cost from another source, including the program under Section 154.1826 to provide health insurance in Title IV-D cases, the court may order that parent to provide health insurance for the child; or

(3) if health insurance coverage is not available for the child under Subdivision (1) or (2), the court shall order the obligor to pay the obligee, in addition to any amount ordered under the guidelines for child support, an amount, not to exceed nine percent of the obligor's annual resources, as described by Section 154.062(b), as cash medical support for the child.

(b–1) If the parent ordered to provide health insurance under Subsection (b)(1) or (2) is the obligee, the court shall order the obligor to pay the obligee, as additional child support, an amount equal to the actual cost of health insurance for the child, but not to exceed a reasonable cost to the obligor. In calculating the actual cost of health insurance for the child, if the obligee has other minor dependents covered under the same health insurance plan, the court shall divide the total cost to the obligee for the insurance by the total number of minor dependents, including the child covered under the plan.

(b–2) If the court finds that neither parent has access to private health insurance at a reasonable cost to the obligor, the court shall order the parent awarded the exclusive right to designate the child's primary residence or, to the extent permitted by law, the other parent to apply immediately on behalf of the child for participation in a government medical assistance program or health plan. If the child participates in a government medical assistance program or health plan, the court shall order cash medical support under Subsection (b)(3).

(b–3) An order requiring the payment of cash medical support under Subsection (b)(3) must allow the obligor to discontinue payment of the cash medical support if:

(1) health insurance for the child becomes available to the obligor at a reasonable cost; and

(2) the obligor:

(A) enrolls the child in the insurance plan; and

(B) provides the obligee and, in a Title IV–D case, the Title IV–D agency, the information required under Section 154.185.

(c) In this section:

(1) "Accessibility" means the extent to which health insurance coverage for a child provides for the availability of medical care within a reasonable traveling distance and time from the child's primary residence, as determined by the court.

(2) "Reasonable cost" has the meaning assigned by Section 154.181(e).

(d) Repealed by Acts 2009, 81st Leg., ch. 767, § 37.

Comment

The guidelines used by the court in determining the amount of child support are based on the assumption that the obligor will be providing the cost of health care coverage for the child. In 2007, the legislature rewrote this section, with its recitation of priorities to be followed by the court in setting a medical support obligation, to reflect certain federal requirements under the Deficit Reduction Act of 2005. Either parent may be ordered to provide health insurance for the child, depending on which parent has access to health insurance for the child at "reasonable cost" through employment or union or trade association membership. If neither parent has access to such health insurance for the child through employment or union membership, but one of them can secure it from another source, then that parent must provide the coverage. If employment based or other private insurance is not available to the obligor, then the obligor must pay the obligee, as additional child support, cash medical support, not to exceed nine percent of the obligor's monthly resources. If the obligee is ordered to provide health insurance for the child, the obligor must pay the obligee, as additional child support, the actual cost of the insurance but on a prorated basis if there are other minor dependents of the obligee covered under the same insurance policy. If coverage is not available at "reasonable cost" to either parent through a private plan, the custodial parent (or, depending on eligibility requirements, the noncustodial parent) must apply for the participation of the child in Medicaid or CHIP. If the child does participate in one of these government programs, the obligor must pay cash medical support, not to exceed nine percent of the obligor's monthly resources. The obligation to pay the cash medical support amount ceases, however, if the obligor is able to find health insurance for the child at reasonable cost. Whichever way these priorities play out, up to nine percent of the obligor's monthly resources will go for medical support.

In 2009, the legislature amended Subsection (a) to add "accessibility" (defined under a new Subsection c(1)) of health insurance coverage as among the factors the court had to consider in ordering insurance coverage for the child. Also, Subsection (b)(2) identifies an insurance plan for children in Title IV-D cases, authorized under 154.1826 *infra*, as "another source" of insurance coverage, if neither parent has access to coverage for the child through employment or membership in a union or other organization. *(A.G.K. & H.P.S.)*

---

§ 154.1826. Health Care Program for Certain Children in Title IV–D Cases

(a) In this section:

(1) "Health benefit plan issuer" means an insurer, health maintenance organization, or other entity authorized to provide health benefits coverage under the laws of this state.

(2) "Health care provider" means a physician or other person who is licensed, certified, or otherwise authorized to provide a health care service in this state.

(3) "Program" means the child health care program developed under this section.

(4) "Reasonable cost" has the meaning assigned by Section 154.181(e).

(5) "Third-party administrator" means a person who is not a health benefit plan issuer or agent of a health benefit plan issuer and who provides administrative services for the program, including processing enrollment of eligible children in the program and processing premium payments on behalf of the program.

(b) In consultation with the Texas Department of Insurance, the Health and Human Services Commission, and representatives of the insurance industry in this state, the Title IV–D agency shall develop and implement a statewide program to address the health care needs of children in Title IV–D cases for whom health insurance is not available to either parent at reasonable cost under Section 154.182(b)(1) or under Section 154.182(b)(2) from a source other than the program.

(c) The director of the Title IV–D agency may establish an advisory committee to consult with the director regarding the implementation and operation of the program. If the director establishes an advisory committee, the director may appoint any of the following persons to the advisory committee:

(1) representatives of appropriate public and private entities, including state agencies concerned with health care management;

(2) members of the judiciary;

(3) members of the legislature; and

(4) representatives of the insurance industry.

(d) The principal objective of the program is to provide basic health care services, including office visits with health care providers, hospitalization, and diagnostic and emergency services, to eligible children in Title IV–D cases at reasonable cost to the parents obligated by court order to provide medical support for the children.

(e) The Title IV–D agency may use available private resources, including gifts and grants, in administering the program.

(f) The Title IV–D agency shall adopt rules as necessary to implement the program. The Title IV–D agency shall consult with the Texas Department of Insurance and the Health and Human Services Commission in establishing policies and procedures for the administration of the program and in determining appropriate benefits to be provided under the program.

(g) A health benefit plan issuer that participates in the program may not deny health care coverage under the program to eligible children because of preexisting conditions or chronic illnesses. A child who is determined to be eligible for coverage under the program continues to be eligible until the termination of the parent's duty to pay child support as specified by Section 154.006. Enrollment of a child in the program does not preclude the subsequent enrollment of the child in another health care plan that becomes available to the child's parent at reasonable cost, including a health care plan available through the parent's employment or the state child health plan under Chapter 62, Health and Safety Code.

(h) The Title IV–D agency shall contract with an independent third-party administrator to provide necessary administrative services for operation of the program.

(i) A person acting as a third-party administrator under Subsection (h) is not considered an administrator for purposes of Chapter 4151, Insurance Code.

(j) The Title IV–D agency shall solicit applications for participation in the program from health benefit plan issuers that meet requirements specified by the agency. Each health benefit plan issuer that participates in the program must hold a certificate of authority issued by the Texas Department of Insurance.

(k) The Title IV–D agency shall promptly notify the courts of this state when the program has been implemented and is available to provide for the health care needs of children described by Subsection (b). The notification must specify a date beginning on which children may be enrolled in the program.

(*l*) On or after the date specified in the notification required by Subsection (k), a court that orders health care coverage for a child in a Title IV–D case shall order that the child be enrolled in the program authorized by this section unless other health insurance is available for the child at reasonable cost, including the state child health plan under Chapter 62, Health and Safety Code.

(m) Payment of premium costs for the enrollment of a child in the program may be enforced by the Title IV–D agency against the obligor by any means available for the enforcement of a child support obligation, including income withholding under Chapter 158.

(n) The program is not subject to any provision of the Insurance Code or other law that requires coverage or the offer of coverage of a health care service or benefit.

(*o*) Any health information obtained by the program, or by a third-party administrator providing program services, that is subject to the Health Insurance Portability and Accountability Act of 1996 (42 U.S.C. Section 1320d et seq.) or Chapter 181, Health and Safety Code, is confidential and not open to public inspection. Any personally identifiable financial information or supporting documentation of a parent whose child is enrolled in the program that is obtained by the program, or by a third-party administrator providing program services, is confidential and not open to public inspection.

Comment

In 2009 the creation of a new health insurance program authorized coverage of children in Title IV-D cases for whom health care insurance is not available to either parent through employment or other private sources at reasonable cost to the obligor. Although the IV-D agency is responsible for the development, implementation, and administration of the new program, the insurance coverage will be provided by private insurers at premium rates not exceeding reasonable cost to the obligors in the eligible cases and will not entail the expenditure of any taxpayer dollars. The intent of the legislation authorizing the insurance program was that it would provide a "private" source of insurance coverage in which the court will order the enrollment of a child, if enrollment is available at reasonable cost to the obligor and unless the child is already enrolled in private insurance available through another source or the child is enrolled in CHIP. As ordered medical support, premiums for the enrollment of the child in the Title IV-D insurance plan may be enforced by any means available for the enforcement of a child support obligation, including income withholding. A third-party administrator, however, will be responsible for the actual processing of premium payments and on-going administration of the program (e.g., negotiating and resolving claim disputes). *(A.G.K. & H.P.S.)*

---

§ 154.1827. Administrative Adjustment of Medical Support Order

(a) In each Title IV–D case in which a medical support order requires that a child be enrolled in a health care program under Section 154.1826, the Title IV–D agency may administratively adjust the order as necessary on an annual basis to reflect changes in the amount of premium costs associated with the child's enrollment.

(b) The Title IV–D agency shall provide notice of the administrative adjustment to the obligor and the clerk of the court that rendered the order.

Comment

This section, added in 2009, complements 154.1826 authorizing the creation of a health insurance program for certain children in Title IV-D cases. Inasmuch as the premiums for coverage under this program may be subject to annual adjustments by the private insurers participating in the program, this section enables the Title IV-D agency to make administrative adjustments to the medical support order to reflect a change in the premium rate. This obviates the need for potentially voluminous suits for modification and corresponds in character to the administrative authority of the IV-D agency to modify writs of income withholding under Chapter 158. *(A.G.K. & H.P.S.)*

---

§ 154.183. Medical Support Additional Support Duty of Obligor

(a) An amount that an obligor is ordered to pay as medical support for the child under this chapter, including the costs of health insurance coverage or cash medical support under Section 154.182:

(1) is in addition to the amount that the obligor is required to pay for child support under the guidelines for child support;

(2) is a child support obligation; and

(3) may be enforced by any means available for the enforcement of child support, including withholding from earnings under Chapter 158.

(b) If the court finds and states in the child support order that the obligee will maintain health insurance coverage for the child at the obligee's expense, the court shall increase the amount of child support to be paid by the obligor in an amount not exceeding the actual cost to the obligee for maintaining health insurance coverage, as provided under Section 154.182(b–1).

(c) As additional child support, the court shall allocate between the parties, according to their circumstances:

(1) the reasonable and necessary health care expenses, including vision and dental expenses, of the child that are not reimbursed by health insurance or are not otherwise covered by the amount of cash medical support ordered under Section 154.182(b)(3); and

(2) amounts paid by either party as deductibles or copayments in obtaining health care services for the child covered under a health insurance policy.

§ 154.184. Effect of Order

(a) Receipt of a medical support order requiring that health insurance be provided for a child shall be considered a change in the family circumstances of the employee or member, for health insurance purposes, equivalent to the birth or adoption of a child.

(b) If the employee or member is eligible for dependent health coverage, the employer shall automatically enroll the child for the first 31 days after the receipt of the order or notice of the medical support order under Section 154.186 on the same terms and conditions as apply to any other dependent child.

(c) The employer shall notify the insurer of the automatic enrollment.

(d) During the 31–day period, the employer and insurer shall complete all necessary forms and procedures to make the enrollment permanent or shall report in accordance with this subchapter the reasons the coverage cannot be made permanent.

§ 154.185. Parent to Furnish Information

(a) The court shall order a parent providing health insurance to furnish to either the obligee, obligor, or child support agency the following information not later than the 30th day after the date the notice of rendition of the order is received:

(1) the social security number of the parent;

(2) the name and address of the parent's employer;

(3) whether the employer is self-insured or has health insurance available;

(4) proof that health insurance has been provided for the child;

(5) if the employer has health insurance available, the name of the health insurance carrier, the number of the policy, a copy of the policy and schedule of benefits, a health insurance membership card, claim forms, and any other information necessary to submit a claim; and

(6) if the employer is self-insured, a copy of the schedule of benefits, a membership card, claim forms, and any other information necessary to submit a claim.

(b) The court shall also order a parent providing health insurance to furnish the obligor, obligee, or child support agency with additional information regarding health insurance coverage not later than the 15th day after the date the information is received by the parent.

§ 154.186. Notice to Employer Concerning Medical Support

(a) The obligee, obligor, or a child support agency of this state or another state may send to the employer a copy of the order requiring an employee to provide health insurance coverage for a child or may include notice of the medical support order in an order or writ of withholding sent to the employer in accordance with Chapter 158.

(b) In an appropriate Title IV–D case, the Title IV–D agency of this state or another state shall send to the employer the national medical support notice required under Part D, Title IV of the federal Social Security Act (42 U.S.C. Section 651 et seq.), as amended. The notice may be used in any other suit in which an obligor is ordered to provide health insurance coverage for a child.

(c) The Title IV–D agency by rule shall establish procedures consistent with federal law for use of the national medical support notice and may prescribe forms for the efficient use of the notice. The agency shall provide the notice and forms, on request, to obligees, obligors, domestic relations offices, friends of the court, and attorneys.

Comment

Congress has attempted to remove some of the impediments to the attempts of state IV–D agencies to secure and enforce medical coverage for children in IV–D cases (OBRA 1993; Pub. L. 103–66). OBRA contained many improvements that facilitated obtaining and enforcing medical coverage, including the creation of "qualified medical child support orders" (QMCSOs) to obtain coverage for dependent children of employees from group health plans subject to the Employee Retirement Income Security Act of 1974 (ERISA). Despite improved state procedures mandated by federal law for the establishment and enforcement of medical support for children, states continued to experience difficulty in satisfying specific conditions of ERISA, particularly with respect to informational requirements and restrictions against requiring new types or forms of benefits. To more fully address the needs and concerns of sponsors and administrators of group health plans, Congress required the Secretaries of the federal departments of Health and Human Services and Labor to develop and promulgate a federal "national medical support notice" for the enforcement of medical support obligations in IV–D cases, P.L. 105–200. There is a federal mandate for IV–D cases and, in addition, authorization, but no mandate, for the use of the federal notice in non IV–D cases. *(A.G.K. & H.P.S.)*

---

§ 154.187. Duties of Employer

(a) An order or notice under this subchapter to an employer directing that health insurance coverage be provided to a child of an employee or member is binding on a current or subsequent employer on receipt without regard to the date the order was rendered. If the employee or member is eligible for dependent health coverage for the child, the employer shall immediately enroll the child in a health insurance plan regardless of whether the employee is enrolled in the plan. If dependent coverage is not available to the employee or member through the employer's health insurance plan or enrollment cannot be made permanent or if the employer is not responsible or otherwise liable for providing such coverage, the employer shall provide notice to the sender in accordance with Subsection (c).

(b) If additional premiums are incurred as a result of adding the child to the health insurance plan, the employer shall deduct the health insurance premium from the earnings of the employee in accordance with Chapter 158 and apply the amount withheld to payment of the insurance premium.

(c) An employer who has received an order or notice under this subchapter shall provide to the sender, by first class mail not later than the **40th** ~~30th~~ day after the date the employer receives the order or notice, a statement that the child:

(1) has been enrolled in the employer's health insurance plan or is already enrolled in another health insurance plan in accordance with a previous child support or medical support order to which the employee is subject; or

(2) cannot be enrolled or cannot be enrolled permanently in the employer's health insurance plan and provide the reason why coverage or permanent coverage cannot be provided.

(d) If the employee ceases employment or if the health insurance coverage lapses, the employer shall provide to the sender, by first class mail not later than the 15th day after the date of the termination of employment or the lapse of the coverage, notice of the termination or lapse and of the availability of any conversion privileges.

(e) On request, the employer shall release to the sender information concerning the available health insurance coverage, including the name of the health insurance carrier, the policy number, a copy of the policy and schedule of benefits, a health insurance membership card, and claim forms.

(f) In this section, "sender" means the person sending the order or notice under Section 154.186.

(g) An employer who fails to enroll a child, fails to withhold or remit premiums or cash medical support, or discriminates in hiring or employment on the basis of a medical support order or notice under this subchapter shall be subject to the penalties and fines in Subchapter C, Chapter 158.

(h) An employer who receives a national medical support notice under Section 154.186 shall comply with the requirements of the notice.

Amended by Acts 2011, 82nd Leg., ch. 508 (H.B. 1674), § 1, eff. Sept. 1, 2011.

Comment

Medical insurance coverage after divorce is a crucial element in the Texas child support scheme. Subsection (g) puts some teeth in the mandate that employers take steps to ensure such coverage. Subsection (h) requires an employer to comply with the federal notice authorized under § 154.186.

A 2009 amendment to Subsection (c)(1) provided that the employer is not required to enroll the child in the employer's plan if, in compliance with a prior order, the employee had already enrolled the child in another plan (e.g., a union insurance plan or dual employment). Somehow the employee (obligor) would have to make this fact known to the employer in order to avoid redundant insurance coverage for the child. In a small business situation that might be easily achieved, but in a large corporation it could be far more difficult to have the child removed from insurance enrollment once coverage had begun and premium costs had been deducted from the employee's income. Also, the employer would need more than just the employee's word that the child was already covered under another plan and that employer had no responsibility for providing the insurance coverage. *(H.P.S.)*

§ 154.188. Failure to Provide or Pay For Required Health Insurance

A parent ordered to provide health insurance or to pay the other parent additional child support for the cost of health insurance who fails to do so is liable for:

(1) necessary medical expenses of the child, without regard to whether the expenses would have been paid if health insurance had been provided; and

(2) the cost of health insurance premiums or contributions, if any, paid on behalf of the child.

Comment

Under § 154.182(b) an obligor may be ordered to provide health insurance for a child through the obligor's employment or, if such insurance is not available to the obligor at "reasonable cost" but is available to the obligee, to reimburse the obligee the cost of the coverage as additional child support. This section addresses an obligor's liability for failure either to secure ordered coverage for a child or to reimburse the other parent the costs of coverage provided by that parent. The protection afforded the obligee under this section is particularly important in the event the obligor becomes delinquent in payment of support and the obligee faces not only the loss of the additional support to cover health insurance premiums but also medical expenses of the child not covered by health insurance, on top of the unpaid "regular" child support. *(A.G.K. & H.P.S.)*

§ 154.189. Notice of Termination or Lapse of Insurance Coverage

(a) An obligor ordered to provide health insurance coverage for a child must notify the obligee and any child support agency enforcing a support obligation against the obligor of the:

(1) termination or lapse of health insurance coverage for the child not later than the 15th day after the date of a termination or lapse; and

(2) availability of additional health insurance to the obligor for the child after a termination or lapse of coverage not later than the 15th day after the date the insurance becomes available.

(b) If termination of coverage results from a change of employers, the obligor, the obligee, or the child support agency may send the new employer a copy of the order requiring the employee to provide health insurance for a child or notice of the medical support order as provided by this subchapter.

§ 154.190. Reenrolling Child for Insurance Coverage

After health insurance has been terminated or has lapsed, an obligor ordered to provide health insurance coverage for the child must enroll the child in a health insurance plan at the next available enrollment period.

§ 154.191. Remedy Not Exclusive

(a) This subchapter does not limit the rights of the obligor, obligee, local domestic relations office, or Title IV–D agency to enforce, modify, or clarify the medical support order.

(b) This subchapter does not limit the authority of the court to render or modify a medical support order to provide for payment of uninsured health expenses, health care costs, or health insurance premiums in a manner consistent with this subchapter.

§ 154.192. Cancellation or Elimination of Insurance Coverage for Child

(a) Unless the employee or member ceases to be eligible for dependent coverage, or the employer has eliminated dependent health coverage for all of the employer's employees or members, the employer may not cancel or eliminate coverage of a child enrolled under this subchapter until the employer is provided satisfactory written evidence that:

(1) the court order or administrative order requiring the coverage is no longer in effect; or

(2) the child is enrolled in comparable health insurance coverage or will be enrolled in comparable coverage that will take effect not later than the effective date of the cancellation or elimination of the employer's coverage.

§ 154.193. Medical Support Order Not Qualified

(a) If a plan administrator or other person acting in an equivalent position determines that a medical support order issued under this subchapter does not qualify for enforcement under federal law, the tribunal may, on its own motion or the motion of a party, render an order that qualifies for enforcement under federal law.

(b) The procedure for filing a motion for enforcement of a final order applies to a motion under this section. Service of citation is not required, and a person is not entitled to a jury in a proceeding under this section.

(c) The employer or plan administrator is not a necessary party to a proceeding under this section.

Comment

The provisions of this section are largely superseded by the use of the federal "national medical support notice" under § 154.186. Should a group health plan administrator reject a medical support order as not satisfying the requirements of federal law (ERISA), the IV–D agency or, in non IV–D cases, an obligee, obligor, friend of the court, domestic relations office or private attorney, may send the federal notice that, by the will of Congress, does satisfy the requirements of federal law. *(A.G.K. & H.P.S.)*

SUBCHAPTER E. LOCAL CHILD SUPPORT REGISTRY

Comment

The Family Code regulates some aspects of the practices of local child support registries. With the implementation of the state disbursement unit (SDU) under Chapter 234 the scope of operations of the local registries has been significantly changed.

Leading Case

In re Pierre, 50 S.W.3d 554 (Tex. App.—El Paso 2001, no pet.) (without evidence of drug use it is abuse of discretion to require drug and alcohol testing of obligor as supervision officer may direct)

---

§ 154.241. Local Registry

(a) A local registry shall receive a court-ordered child support payment or a payment otherwise authorized by law and shall forward the payment, as appropriate, to the Title IV–D agency, local domestic relations office, or obligee within two working days after the date the local registry receives the payment.

(b) A local registry may not require an obligor, obligee, or other party or entity to furnish a certified copy of a court order as a condition of processing child support payments and shall accept as sufficient authority to process the payments a photocopy, facsimile copy, or conformed copy of the court's order.

(c) A local registry shall include with each payment it forwards to the Title IV–D agency the date it received the payment and the withholding date furnished by the employer.

(d) A local registry shall accept child support payments made by personal check, money order, or cashier's check. A local registry may refuse payment by personal check if a pattern of abuse regarding the use of personal checks has been established. Abuse includes checks drawn on insufficient funds, abusive or offensive language written on the check, intentional mutilation of the instrument, or other actions that delay or disrupt the registry's operation.

(e) Subject to Section 154.004, at the request of an obligee, a local registry shall redirect and forward a child support payment to an address and in care of a person or entity designated by the obligee. A local registry may require that the obligee's request be in writing or be made on a form provided by the local registry for that purpose, but may not charge a fee for receiving the request or redirecting the payments as requested.

(f) A local registry may accept child support payments made by credit card, debit card, or automatic teller machine card.

(g) Notwithstanding any other law, a private entity may perform the duties and functions of a local registry under this section either under a contract with a county commissioners court or domestic relations office executed under Section 204.002 or under an appointment by a court.

Comment

The ability of local registries to process child support payments and the facility of obligors to make such payment is enhanced through the use of modern technology under Subsection (f), which complements payment by electronic funds transfer under § 154.242. *(A.G.K. & H.P.S.)*

---

§ 154.242. Payment or Transfer of Child Support Payments by Electronic Funds Transfer

(a) A child support payment may be made by electronic funds transfer to:

(1) the Title IV–D agency;

(2) a local registry if the registry agrees to accept electronic payment; or

(3) the state disbursement unit.

(b) A local registry may transmit child support payments to the Title IV–D agency by electronic funds transfer. Unless support payments are required to be made to the state disbursement unit, an obligor may make payments, with the approval of the court entering the order, directly to the bank account of the obligee by electronic transfer and provide verification of the deposit to the local registry. A local registry in a county that makes deposits into personal bank accounts by electronic funds transfer as of April 1, 1995, may transmit a child support payment to an obligee by electronic funds transfer if the obligee maintains a bank account and provides the local registry with the necessary bank account information to complete electronic payment.

§ 154.243. Production of Child Support Payment Record

The Title IV–D agency, a local registry, or the state disbursement unit may comply with a subpoena or other order directing the production of a child support payment record by sending a certified copy of the record or an affidavit regarding the payment record to the court that directed production of the record.

SUBCHAPTER F. SUPPORT FOR A MINOR OR ADULT DISABLED CHILD

Comment

This subchapter allows a suit seeking post-majority support of a disabled child or a disabled adult to be brought at any time, provided that the disability existed on or before the individual's 18th birthday. The statute does not create a method for the state to be reimbursed by an individual's parents for expenditures incurred on behalf of the institutionalized adult. However, the statute does allow an assignment of the support to the Title IV–D agency.

The support obligor may seek possession of and access to the adult disabled child. Because the person is an adult, however, the possession and access may be refused by the disabled person.

Sections 154.302–.303 have expanded the possibilities for support of an adult disabled child. Heretofore an action would lie only between the two parents, one of whom maintained possession of the adult disabled child and the other of whom could be required to assist by providing financial support. The cause of action has been expanded to allow persons other than a parent to provide the actual care and custody of the adult disabled child and seek support from a parent, or from both the parents. Likely candidates as caretakers are close relatives, such as adult siblings or grandparents, although the statutory coverage is not limited to relatives of the adult disabled child. In fact, the adult child may receive the support directly from the parent if the disability does not impair the adult child's ability to manage his or her financial affairs.

CLE/Legal Publications

Issues for the disabled or special needs child. Keith D. Maples, 2011 Adv. Fam. L.

Child support for children with disabilities. Keith D. Maples & Pi-Yi Mayo, 2010 Adv. Fam. L.

Paying special attention to special needs cases. Patricia N. Carter, 2010 U.T. Parent-Child Relationships

Obtaining child support. Barry J. Brooks & Karen L. Marvel, 2009 U.T. Parent-Child Rel.

Dealing with special needs children (electronic visitation statute, disabled adult children) governmental benefits for children (SSI). Sally H. Emerson & Karen L. Marvel, 2008 Marriage Dissolution

The kids really need more, judge—Above guideline support and providing for special needs and disabled children. Wendy S. Burgower, 2006 Adv. Fam. L.

Leading Cases

Worford v. Stamper, 801 S.W.2d 108 (Tex. 1990) (increase in support for disabled child)

In re M.W.T., 12 S.W.3d 598 (Tex. App.—San Antonio 2000, pet. denied) (adult disabled child entitled to post-18 support from genetic father; child able to work but Oppositional Defiant Disorder will interfere if it continues)

Garland v. Garland, 868 S.W.2d 847 (Tex. App.—Dallas 1993, no writ) (guardianship belongs exclusively to probate court; CEJ over support does not preempt probate jurisdiction)

In re Frost, 815 S.W.2d 890 (Tex. App.—Amarillo 1991, no writ) (enrollment of learning disabled student in local college program justifies support beyond age 18)

§ 154.301. Definitions

In this subchapter:

(1) "Adult child" means a child 18 years of age or older.

(2) "Child" means a son or daughter of any age.

§ 154.302. Court-Ordered Support for Disabled Child

(a) The court may order either or both parents to provide for the support of a child for an indefinite period and may determine the rights and duties of the parents if the court finds that:

(1) the child, whether institutionalized or not, requires substantial care and personal supervision because of a mental or physical disability and will not be capable of self-support; and

(2) the disability exists, or the cause of the disability is known to exist, on or before the 18th birthday of the child.

(b) A court that orders support under this section shall designate a parent of the child or another person having physical custody or guardianship of the child under a court order to receive the support for the child. The court may designate a child who is 18 years of age or older to receive the support directly.

§ 154.303. Standing to Sue

(a) A suit provided by this subchapter may be filed only by:

(1) a parent of the child or another person having physical custody or guardianship of the child under a court order; or

(2) the child if the child:

(A) is 18 years of age or older;

(B) does not have a mental disability; and

(C) is determined by the court to be capable of managing the child's financial affairs.

(b) The parent, the child, if the child is 18 years of age or older, or other person may not transfer or assign the cause of action to any person, including a governmental or private entity or agency, except for an assignment made to the Title IV–D agency **under Section 231.104 or in the provision of child support enforcement services under Section 159.307**.

Amended by Acts 2011, 82nd Leg., ch. 508 (H.B. 1674), § 2, eff. Sept. 1, 2011.

Comment

A ruling by a Texas appeals court required the legislature in 2011 to clarify in Subsection (b) that existing provisions of the Family Code under § 231.104 and, in interstate cases, under § 159.307 provide the Title IV-D agency with sufficient standing to seek post-majority support of a disabled child and that a specific assignment of the right to sue to establish that support is not required, as the appeals court had ruled. (*See* Office of Attorney General of Texas v. Crawford, 2010 WL 3448053 (Tex. App.—Houston [1st Dist.], no pet.) *(A.G.K. & H.P.S.)*

---

§ 154.304. General Procedure

Except as otherwise provided by this subchapter, the substantive and procedural rights and remedies in a suit affecting the parent-child relationship relating to the establishment, modification, or enforcement of a child support order apply to a suit filed and an order rendered under this subchapter.

§ 154.305. Specific Procedures

(a) A suit under this subchapter may be filed:

(1) regardless of the age of the child; and

(2) as an independent cause of action or joined with any other claim or remedy provided by this code.

(b) If no court has continuing, exclusive jurisdiction of the child, an action under this subchapter may be filed as an original suit affecting the parent-child relationship.

(c) If there is a court of continuing, exclusive jurisdiction, an action under this subchapter may be filed as a suit for modification as provided by Chapter 156.

§ 154.306. Amount of Support After Age 18

In determining the amount of support to be paid after a child's 18th birthday, the specific terms and conditions of that support, and the rights and duties of both parents with respect to the support of the child, the court shall determine and give special consideration to:

(1) any existing or future needs of the adult child directly related to the adult child's mental or physical disability and the substantial care and personal supervision directly required by or related to that disability;

(2) whether the parent pays for or will pay for the care or supervision of the adult child or provides or will provide substantial care or personal supervision of the adult child;

(3) the financial resources available to both parents for the support, care, and supervision of the adult child; and

(4) any other financial resources or other resources or programs available for the support, care, and supervision of the adult child.

§ 154.307. Modification and Enforcement

An order provided by this subchapter may contain provisions governing the rights and duties of both parents with respect to the support of the child and may be modified or enforced in the same manner as any other order provided by this title.

§ 154.308. Remedy Not Exclusive

(a) This subchapter does not affect a parent's:

(1) cause of action for the support of a disabled child under any other law; or

(2) ability to contract for the support of a disabled child.

(b) This subchapter does not affect the substantive or procedural rights or remedies of a person other than a parent, including a governmental or private entity or agency, with respect to the support of a disabled child under any other law.

§ 154.309. Possession of or Access to Adult Disabled Child

(a) A court may render an order for the possession of or access to an adult disabled child that is appropriate under the circumstances.

(b) Possession of or access to an adult disabled child is enforceable in the manner provided by Chapter 157. An adult disabled child may refuse possession or access if the adult disabled child is mentally competent.

(c) A court that obtains continuing, exclusive jurisdiction of a suit affecting the parent-child relationship involving a disabled person who is a child retains continuing, exclusive jurisdiction of subsequent proceedings involving the person, including proceedings after the person is an adult. Notwithstanding this subsection and any other law, a probate court may exercise jurisdiction in a guardianship proceeding for the person after the person is an adult.

Comment

Complaint was made to the legislature that after a disabled adult child reaches majority the custodial parent often prevents possession of or access to that child by the other parent. This takes that decision out of the custodian's hands and also provides that a disabled adult child may exercise adult prerogatives.

CHAPTER 155. CONTINUING, EXCLUSIVE JURISDICTION; TRANSFER

SUBCHAPTER A. CONTINUING, EXCLUSIVE JURISDICTION

SUBCHAPTER B. IDENTIFICATION OF COURT OF CONTINUING, EXCLUSIVE JURISDICTION

SUBCHAPTER C. TRANSFER OF CONTINUING, EXCLUSIVE JURISDICTION

SUBCHAPTER D. TRANSFER OF PROCEEDINGS WITHIN THE STATE WHEN PARTY OR CHILD RESIDES OUTSIDE THE STATE

SUBCHAPTER A. CONTINUING, EXCLUSIVE JURISDICTION

Introductory Comment

A major innovation of the Family Code is the principle that the court of original rendition retains continuing, exclusive jurisdiction over all subsequent matters arising out a SAPCR. All further action must begin in that court, even when the fact circumstances dictate that the suit should ultimately be transferred to a more convenient forum. The transferring court is authorized to continue to enforce its temporary orders and to receive and distribute child support payments until the transferee court dockets the case. At that time the transitional period ends, the transferring court loses all jurisdiction, and any further payments received should be forwarded to the transferee court (assuming payments are directed to the court registry).

CLE/Other Legal Publications

Jurisdiction/standing. Christopher K. Wrampelmeier, 2011 Adv. Fam. L.

Venue/jurisdiction: where to file a SAPCR. Harry L. Tindall, 2011 U.T. Parent—Child Relationships: Basics

Jurisdiction and standing. Angela Pence England & Harry L. Tindall, 2011 So. Tex. Fam. L.

Venue, standing and jurisdiction. Stephen J. Naylor, 2011 MARRIAGE DISSOLUTION

International and domestic jurisdiction issues: UIFSA, UCCJEA, UCAPA, PKPA, FFCCSOA, ICARA. Karl E. Hays & Janet McCullar Vavra, 2011 U.T. FAM. L. FRONT LINES

Caution! Acronyms ahead: traveling on the interstate case highway. Karen L. Marvel & John Christopher Nickelson, 2010 U.T. PARENT-CHILD RELATIONSHIPS

Follow the yellow brick road: jurisdiction and venue issues. JoAl Cannon Sheridan, 2010 MARRIAGE DISSOLUTION

Standing and other nonparent issues. Heather L. King, 2009 MARRIAGE DISSOLUTION

Jurisdiction and venue. Brad M. LaMorgese, 2009 MARRIAGE DISSOLUTION

Jurisdiction, standing, venue, and more: special appearances, UCCJEA, 3rd party standing, Hague. JoAl Cannon Sheridan, 2009 ADV. FAM. L.

UCCJEA and UIFSA —Can they be modified? Angela Pence England. 2009 SO. TEX. FAM. L. CONF.

Uniform Interstate Family Support Act (2001) with prefatory note and comments (with still more unofficial annotations). John J. Sampson and Barry J. Brooks, 36 FAM. L.Q. 329 (2002)

Uniform Child-Custody Jurisdiction and Enforcement Act (with prefatory notes and comment). Robert G. Spector, 32 FAM. L.Q. 301 (1998)

***See* Accompanying CD–ROM for Additional CLE/Other Legal Publications.**

Leading Cases

Alexander v. Russell, 699 S.W.2d 209 (Tex. 1985) (judge must act in capacity as court of continuing jurisdiction)

Curtis v. Gibbs, 511 S.W.2d 263 (Tex. 1974) (court acquiring dominant jurisdiction prevents another court from asserting jurisdiction)

In re Compton, 185 S.W.3d 526 (Tex. App.—Houston [14th Dist.] 2006, orig. proceeding) (transfer motion timely filed as long as before answer date, even if after appearance at temporary orders hearing)

In re Wheeler, 177 S.W.3d 350 (Tex. App.—Houston [1st Dist.] 2005, orig. proceeding) (transfer of SAPCR involving one child ministerial but transfer related to second child requires hearing based upon filing of a controverting affidavit)

In re Ferguson, 172 S.W.3d 122 (Tex. App.—Beaumont 2005, orig. proceeding) (mandatory transfer of SAPCR to county of child's residence does not recognize "dual residence" concept)

Cross Reference

TX FCA FAMILY § 103.001 *et seq.*, Venue and Transfer of Original Proceedings, *supra.*

---

§ 155.001. Acquiring Continuing, Exclusive Jurisdiction

(a) Except as otherwise provided by this section, a court acquires continuing, exclusive jurisdiction over the matters provided for by this title in connection with a child on the rendition of a final order.

(b) The following final orders do not create continuing, exclusive jurisdiction in a court:

(1) a voluntary or involuntary dismissal of a suit affecting the parent-child relationship;

(2) in a suit to determine parentage, a final order finding that an alleged or presumed father is not the father of the child, except that the jurisdiction of the court is not affected if the child was subject to the jurisdiction of the court or some other court in a suit affecting the parent-child relationship before the commencement of the suit to adjudicate parentage; and

(3) a final order of adoption, after which a subsequent suit affecting the child must be commenced as though the child had not been the subject of a suit for adoption or any other suit affecting the parent-child relationship before the adoption.

(c) If a court of this state has acquired continuing, exclusive jurisdiction, no other court of this state has jurisdiction of a suit with regard to that child except as provided by this chapter or Chapter 262.

(d) Unless a final order has been rendered by a court of continuing, exclusive jurisdiction, a subsequent suit shall be commenced as an original proceeding.

§ 155.002. Retaining Continuing, Exclusive Jurisdiction

Except as otherwise provided by this subchapter, a court with continuing, exclusive jurisdiction retains jurisdiction of the parties and matters provided by this title.

§ 155.003. Exercise of Continuing, Exclusive Jurisdiction

(a) Except as otherwise provided by this section, a court with continuing, exclusive jurisdiction may exercise its jurisdiction to modify its order regarding managing conservatorship, possessory conservatorship, possession of and access to the child, and support of the child.

(b) A court of this state may not exercise its continuing, exclusive jurisdiction to modify managing conservatorship if:

(1) the child's home state is other than this state; or

(2) modification is precluded by Chapter 152.

(c) A court of this state may not exercise its continuing, exclusive jurisdiction to modify possessory conservatorship or possession of or access to a child if:

(1) the child's home state is other than this state and all parties have established and continue to maintain their principal residence outside this state; or

(2) each individual party has filed written consent with the tribunal of this state for a tribunal of another state to modify the order and assume continuing, exclusive jurisdiction of the suit.

(d) A court of this state may not exercise its continuing, exclusive jurisdiction to modify its child support order if modification is precluded by Chapter 159.

§ 155.004. Loss of Continuing, Exclusive Jurisdiction

(a) A court of this state loses its continuing, exclusive jurisdiction to modify its order if:

(1) an order of adoption is rendered after the court acquires continuing, exclusive jurisdiction of the suit;

(2) the parents of the child have remarried each other after the dissolution of a previous marriage between them and file a suit for the dissolution of their subsequent marriage combined with a suit affecting the parent-child relationship as if there had not been a prior court with continuing, exclusive jurisdiction over the child; or

(3) another court assumed jurisdiction over a suit and rendered a final order based on incorrect information received from the bureau of vital statistics that there was no court of continuing, exclusive jurisdiction.

(b) This section does not affect the power of the court to enforce its order for a violation that occurred before the time continuing, exclusive jurisdiction was lost under this section.

§ 155.005. Jurisdiction Pending Transfer

(a) During the transfer of a suit from a court with continuing, exclusive jurisdiction, the transferring court retains jurisdiction to render temporary orders.

(b) The jurisdiction of the transferring court terminates on the docketing of the case in the transferee court.

Leading Case

Bigham v. Dempster, 901 S.W.2d 424 (Tex. 1995) (case docketed when transferee court receives transfer order and asserts jurisdiction, or when files transferred, whichever is first)

SUBCHAPTER B. IDENTIFICATION OF COURT OF CONTINUING, EXCLUSIVE JURISDICTION

Introductory Comment

The request for the identification of the court of continuing jurisdiction is permissive. But, if such a court does exist, it must be identified, because its jurisdiction is not just continuing, it is also exclusive. Failure to properly identify the correct court can result in a voidable decree.

---

§ 155.101. Request for Identification of Court of Continuing, Exclusive Jurisdiction

(a) The petitioner or the court shall request from the bureau of vital statistics identification of the court that last had continuing, exclusive jurisdiction of the child in a suit unless:

(1) the petition alleges that no court has continuing, exclusive jurisdiction of the child and the issue is not disputed by the pleadings; or

(2) the petition alleges that the court in which the suit or petition to modify has been filed has acquired and retains continuing, exclusive jurisdiction of the child as the result of a prior proceeding and the issue is not disputed by the pleadings.

(b) The bureau of vital statistics shall, on the written request of the court, an attorney, or a party:

(1) identify the court that last had continuing, exclusive jurisdiction of the child in a suit and give the docket number of the suit; or

(2) state that the child has not been the subject of a suit.

(c) The child shall be identified in the request by name, birthdate, and place of birth.

(d) The bureau of vital statistics shall transmit the information not later than the 10th day after the date on which the request is received.

Cross Reference

TX FCA FAMILY § 108.001, Transmittal of Records of Suit by Clerk, *supra*; TX FCA FAMILY § 108.006, Fees, *supra*.

---

§ 155.102. Dismissal

If a court in which a suit is filed determines that another court has continuing, exclusive jurisdiction of the child, the court in which the suit is filed shall dismiss the suit without prejudice.

§ 155.103. Reliance on Bureau of Vital Statistics Information

(a) A court shall have jurisdiction over a suit if it has been, correctly or incorrectly, informed by the bureau of vital statistics that the child has not been the subject of a suit and the petition states that no other court has continuing, exclusive jurisdiction over the child.

(b) If the bureau of vital statistics notifies the court that the bureau has furnished incorrect information regarding the existence of another court with continuing, exclusive jurisdiction before the rendition of a final order, the provisions of this chapter apply.

§ 155.104. Voidable Order

(a) If a request for information from the bureau of vital statistics relating to the identity of the court having continuing, exclusive jurisdiction of the child has been made under this subchapter, a final order, except an order of dismissal, may not be rendered until the information is filed with the court.

(b) If a final order is rendered in the absence of the filing of the information from the bureau of vital statistics, the order is voidable on a showing that a court other than the court that rendered the order had continuing, exclusive jurisdiction.

SUBCHAPTER C. TRANSFER OF CONTINUING, EXCLUSIVE JURISDICTION

Introductory Comment

Transfer in conjunction with the original filing of a SAPCR is appropriate in situations involving improper venue or dominant divorce venue; in such cases the transfer is governed by Chapter 103, *supra*. This subchapter describes the second basic fact situation that calls for a transfer of a SAPCR lawsuit from one Texas court to another Texas court. Note, there is no provision in the Family Code for transfer of a SAPCR to a sister-state court, although a Texas child support order may be enforced out-of-state under UIFSA, *infra.*

Under the provisions of this subchapter, a transfer is required when, after an original SAPCR decree has established a court of continuing, exclusive jurisdiction, a.k.a. CEJ, the child has moved from one county in Texas to another. Current information and evidence about the circumstances of the child is best obtained in the child's home county. Thus, on motion this subchapter mandates a transfer to the county the child makes his home after a period of six months has elapsed. Almost all of the reported litigation has revolved around this aspect of CEJ. Finally, the transferring court is directed to order the obligor to make child support payments to the transferee court in order to facilitate the transfer of CEJ to the new court.

Leading Cases

Bigham v. Dempster, 901 S.W.2d 424 (Tex. 1995) (case docketed when transferee court receives transfer order and asserts jurisdiction, or when files transferred, whichever is first)

Tippy v. Walker, 865 S.W.2d 928 (Tex. 1993) (computation of six months residence in county for mandatory transfer begins with actual change of residence, not from signing of order)

Proffer v. Yates, 734 S.W.2d 671 (Tex. 1987) (mandamus issued when court fails to transfer after child resides in new county for six months)

Leonard v. Paxson, 654 S.W.2d 440 (Tex. 1983) (settlement agreement cannot establish venue for SAPCR)

Seay v. Valderas, 643 S.W.2d 395 (Tex. 1982) (after case transferred, transferor court cannot order return of case)

Arias v. Spector, 623 S.W.2d 312 (Tex. 1981) (transfer mandatory)

Ex parte Barnett, 600 S.W.2d 252 (Tex. 1980) (transferee court enforces with full jurisdiction)

Brines v. McIlhaney, 596 S.W.2d 519 (Tex. 1980) (divorce appointing temporary managing conservator doesn't negate mandatory transfer)

Brod v. Baker, 591 S.W.2d 457 (Tex. 1979) (mandatory transfer to county where children reside)

Cassidy v. Fuller, 568 S.W.2d 845 (Tex. 1978) (automatic transfer provisions are enforceable by mandamus)

***See* Accompanying CD–ROM for Cases Linked to Westlaw and Additional Leading Cases.**

Cross Reference

TX FCA FAMILY § 103.001 *et seq.*, Venue and Transfer of Original Proceedings, *supra.*

§ 155.201. Mandatory Transfer

(a) On the filing of a motion showing that a suit for dissolution of the marriage of the child's parents has been filed in another court and requesting a transfer to that court, the court having continuing, exclusive jurisdiction of a suit affecting the parent-child relationship shall, within the time required by Section 155.204, transfer the proceedings to the court in which the dissolution of the marriage is pending. The motion must comply with the requirements of Section 155.204(a).

(b) If a suit to modify or a motion to enforce an order is filed in the court having continuing, exclusive jurisdiction of a suit, on the timely motion of a party the court shall, within the time required by Section 155. 204, transfer the proceeding to another county in this state if the child has resided in the other county for six months or longer.

(c) If a suit to modify or a motion to enforce an order is pending at the time a subsequent suit to modify or motion to enforce is filed, the court may transfer the proceeding as provided by Subsection (b) only if the court could have transferred the proceeding at the time the first motion or suit was filed.

§ 155.202. Discretionary Transfer

(a) If the basis of a motion to transfer a proceeding under this subchapter is that the child resides in another county, the court may deny the motion if it is shown that the child has resided in that county for less than six months at the time the proceeding is commenced.

(b) For the convenience of the parties and witnesses and in the interest of justice, the court, on the timely motion of a party, may transfer the proceeding to a proper court in another county in the state.

Leading Cases

In re Leyva, 333 S.W.3d 315 (Tex. App.—San Antonio 2010) (mandamus proper remedy when venue not transferred in timely manner)

In re Cooper, 320 S.W.3d 905 (Tex. App.—Texarkana 2010) (transfer mandatory on six-months rule; parties had agreed on modification of relocation prohibition to allow mother to move, but father didn't file papers, *distinguishing* Huey v. Huey)

Huey v. Huey, 200 S.W.3d 851 (Tex. App.—Dallas 2006, no pet.) (mother forfeited her rights under the mandatory venue provision by intentionally violating final decree that "expressly restricted her choice of residence to" forum county)

Hathorn v. Sivers, 962 S.W.2d 284 (Tex. App.—Houston [14th Dist.] 1998, no pet.) (intra-county transfer from district court to county court at law upheld)

---

§ 155.203. Determining County of Child's Residence

In computing the time during which the child has resided in a county, the court may not require that the period of residence be continuous and uninterrupted but shall look to the child's principal residence during the six-month period preceding the commencement of the suit.

Leading Case

In re Ferguson, 172 S.W.3d 122 (Tex. App.—Beaumont 2005, orig. proceeding) (mandatory transfer of SAPCR to county of child's residence does not recognize "dual residence" concept)

---

§ 155.204. Procedure for Transfer

(a) A motion to transfer under Section 155.201(a) may be filed at any time. The motion must contain a certification that all other parties, including the attorney general, if applicable, have been informed of the filing of the motion.

(b) Except as provided by Subsection (a) or Section 262.203, a motion to transfer by a petitioner or movant is timely if it is made at the time the initial pleadings are filed. A motion to transfer by another party is timely if it is made on or before the first Monday after the 20th day after the date of service of citation or notice of the suit or before the commencement of the hearing, whichever is sooner.

(c) If a timely motion to transfer has been filed and no controverting affidavit is filed within the period allowed for its filing, the proceeding shall, not later than the 21st day after the final date of the period allowed for the filing of a controverting affidavit, be transferred without a hearing to the proper court.

(d) On or before the first Monday after the 20th day after the date of notice of a motion to transfer is served, a party desiring to contest the motion must file a controverting affidavit denying that grounds for the transfer exist.

(e) If a controverting affidavit contesting the motion to transfer is filed, each party is entitled to notice not less than 10 days before the date of the hearing on the motion to transfer.

(f) Only evidence pertaining to the transfer may be taken at the hearing.

(g) If the court finds after the hearing on the motion to transfer that grounds for the transfer exist, the proceeding shall be transferred to the proper court not later than the 21st day after the date the hearing is concluded.

(h) An order transferring or refusing to transfer the proceeding is not subject to interlocutory appeal.

(i) If a transfer order has been signed by a court exercising jurisdiction under Chapter 262, a party may file the transfer order with the clerk of the court of continuing, exclusive jurisdiction. On receipt and without a hearing, the clerk of the court of continuing, exclusive jurisdiction shall transfer the files as provided by this subchapter.

Leading Case

Alexander v. Russell, 699 S.W.2d 209 (Tex. 1985) (the procedure for motion and ruling established in this section must be followed or a transfer is without authority)

§ 155.205. Transfer of Child Support Registry

(a) On rendition of an order transferring continuing, exclusive jurisdiction to another court, the transferring court shall also order that all future payments of child support be made to the local registry of the transferee court or, if payments have previously been directed to the state disbursement unit, to the state disbursement unit.

(b) The transferring court's local registry or the state disbursement unit shall continue to receive, record, and forward child support payments to the payee until it receives notice that the transferred case has been docketed by the transferee court.

(c) After receiving notice of docketing from the transferee court, the transferring court's local registry shall send a certified copy of the child support payment record to the clerk of the transferee court and shall forward any payments received to the transferee court's local registry or to the state disbursement unit, as appropriate.

§ 155.206. Effect of Transfer

(a) A court to which a transfer is made becomes the court of continuing, exclusive jurisdiction and all proceedings in the suit are continued as if it were brought there originally.

(b) A judgment or order transferred has the same effect and shall be enforced as if originally rendered in the transferee court.

(c) The transferee court shall enforce a judgment or order of the transferring court by contempt or by any other means by which the transferring court could have enforced its judgment or order. The transferee court shall have the power to punish disobedience of the transferring court's order, whether occurring before or after the transfer, by contempt.

(d) After the transfer, the transferring court does not retain jurisdiction of the child who is the subject of the suit, nor does it have jurisdiction to enforce its order for a violation occurring before or after the transfer of jurisdiction.

§ 155.207. Transfer of Court Files

(a) On the signing of an order of transfer, the clerk of the court transferring a proceeding shall send to the proper court in the county to which transfer is being made:

(1) the pleadings in the pending proceeding and any other document specifically requested by a party;

(2) certified copies of all entries in the minutes; and

(3) a certified copy of each final order.

(b) The clerk of the transferring court shall keep a copy of the transferred pleadings and other requested documents. If the transferring court retains jurisdiction of another child who was the subject of the suit, the clerk shall send a copy of the pleadings and other requested documents to the court to which the transfer is made and shall keep the original pleadings and other requested documents.

(c) On receipt of the pleadings, documents, and orders from the transferring court, the clerk of the transferee court shall docket the suit and shall notify all parties, the clerk of the transferring court, and, if appropriate, the transferring court's local registry that the suit has been docketed.

(d) The clerk of the transferring court shall send a certified copy of the order directing payments to the transferee court, to any party or employer affected by that order, and, if appropriate, to the local registry of the transferee court.

SUBCHAPTER D. TRANSFER OF PROCEEDINGS WITHIN THE STATE WHEN PARTY OR CHILD RESIDES OUTSIDE THE STATE

§ 155.301. Authority to Transfer

(a) A court of this state with continuing, exclusive jurisdiction over a child custody proceeding under Chapter 152 or a child support proceeding under Chapter 159 shall transfer the proceeding to the county of residence of the resident party if one party is a resident of this state and all other parties including the child or all of the children affected by the proceeding reside outside this state.

(b) If one or more of the parties affected by the proceedings reside outside the state and if more than one party or one or more children affected by the proceeding reside in this state in different counties, the court shall transfer the proceeding according to the following priorities:

(1) to the court of continuing, exclusive jurisdiction, if any;

(2) to the county of residence of the child, if applicable, provided that:

(A) Subdivision (1) is inapplicable; or

(B) the court of continuing, exclusive jurisdiction finds that neither a party nor a child affected by the proceeding resides in the county of the court of continuing, exclusive jurisdiction; or

(3) if Subdivisions (1) and (2) are inapplicable, to the county most appropriate to serve the convenience of the resident parties, the witnesses, and the interest of justice.

(c) Except as otherwise provided by this subsection, if a transfer of continuing, exclusive jurisdiction is sought under this section, the procedures for determining and effecting a transfer of proceedings provided by this chapter apply. If the parties submit to the court an agreed order for transfer, the court shall sign the order without the need for other pleadings.

Comment

The Uniform Child Custody Jurisdiction and Enforcement Act, Chapter 152, and the Uniform Interstate Family Support Act, Chapter 159, both incorporate the concept of continuing, exclusive jurisdiction as the touchstone of authority. The enactment of these uniform acts necessitated these conforming provisions to allow for intrastate transfer of UCCJEA and UIFSA proceedings if an original litigant lives in another state and the other litigant continues to reside in Texas, but has moved from the CEJ county in which the custody or support decree was rendered.

Subsection (c) simplifies the process for intrastate transfer by removing the need for pleadings otherwise required for effecting transfer if the parties submit an agreed order for transfer to the court.

Leading Case

In re Casseb, 119 S.W.3d 841 (Tex. App.—San Antonio 2003, no pet.) (transfer of child support proceeding was mandated when child had moved out of state and father had moved counties)

CHAPTER 156. MODIFICATION

SUBCHAPTER A. GENERAL PROVISIONS

SUBCHAPTER B. MODIFICATION OF CONSERVATORSHIP, POSSESSION AND ACCESS, OR DETERMINATION OF RESIDENCE

SUBCHAPTER C. MODIFICATION OF JOINT MANAGING CONSERVATORSHIP [REPEALED]

SUBCHAPTER D. MODIFICATION OF POSSESSION OF OR ACCESS TO CHILD [REPEALED]

SUBCHAPTER E. MODIFICATION OF CHILD SUPPORT

SUBCHAPTER A. GENERAL PROVISIONS

CLE/Other Legal Publications

Relocation in the age of technology. Marty Carden & Travis Rodmon, 2010 U.T. PARENT-CHILD RELATIONSHIPS

Post judgment: enforcement of judgments and modifications. Karl E. Hays, 2010 MARRIAGE DISSOL. BOOT CAMP.

Relocation update. Larry L. Martin, 2009 PARENT-CHILD RELATIONSHIPS

Moving away: dealing with residency restriction issues. Bret A. Bosker & Kate H. McConnico, 2009 SO. TEX. FAM. L. CONF.

UCCJEA and UIFSA—can they be modified? Angela Pence England. 2009 SO. TEX. FAM. L. CONF.

See **Accompanying CD–ROM for Additional CLE/Other Legal Publications.**

---

§ 156.001. Orders Subject to Modification

A court with continuing, exclusive jurisdiction may modify an order that provides for the conservatorship, support, or possession of and access to a child.

§ 156.002. Who Can File

(a) A party affected by an order may file a suit for modification in the court with continuing, exclusive jurisdiction.

(b) A person or entity who, at the time of filing, has standing to sue under Chapter 102 may file a suit for modification in the court with continuing, exclusive jurisdiction.

(c) The sibling of a child who is separated from the child because of the actions of the Department of Family and Protective Services may file a suit for modification requesting access to the child in the court with continuing, exclusive jurisdiction.

§ 156.003. Notice

A party whose rights and duties may be affected by a suit for modification is entitled to receive notice by service of citation.

§ 156.004. Procedure

The Texas Rules of Civil Procedure applicable to the filing of an original lawsuit apply to a suit for modification under this chapter.

§ 156.005. Frivolous Filing of Suit for Modification

If the court finds that a suit for modification is filed frivolously or is designed to harass a party, the court shall tax attorney's fees as costs against the offending party.

Leading Case

D.R. v. J.A.R., 894 S.W.2d 91 (Tex. App.—Fort Worth 1995, writ denied) (frivolous modification suit leads to large attorney's fees award)

---

§ 156.006. Temporary Orders

(a) Except as provided by Subsection (b), the court may render a temporary order in a suit for modification.

(b) While a suit for modification is pending, the court may not render a temporary order that has the effect of changing the designation of the person who has the exclusive right to designate the primary residence of the child under the final order unless the temporary order is in the best interest of the child and:

(1) the order is necessary because the child's present circumstances would significantly impair the child's physical health or emotional development;

(2) the person designated in the final order has voluntarily relinquished the primary care and possession of the child for more than six months; or

(3) the child is 12 years of age or older and has expressed to the court in chambers as provided by Section 153.009 the name of the person who is the child's preference to have the exclusive right to designate the primary residence of the child.

(c) Subsection (b)(2) does not apply to a conservator who has the exclusive right to designate the primary residence of the child and who has temporarily relinquished the primary care and possession of the child to another person during the conservator's military deployment, military mobilization, or temporary military duty, as those terms are defined by Section 153.701.

Comment

The 2009 amendment to this section eliminates the opportunity for a child to file a document with the court expressing the child's preference for a person to provide the primary residence. Henceforth, an expression of the child's preference is to be limited to a communication to the court in chambers. This process is tied to Section 153.009, which provides for a mandatory interview of a child 12 years of age or older, and a discretionary interview of a child younger than 12. In the context of temporary orders, interviewing a child in chambers may prove to be a mischief-maker. Hypothetically, a lawyer seeking modification might arrive in the courtroom with the child in tow to request an interview of the child to elicit temporary orders. However, temporary orders in the context of modification of conservatorship is seldom, if ever, an emergency order. If an emergency exists, either the police or a DFPS caseworker are the appropriate responders to reports of abuse or neglect. *See* Section 261.101.

See Section 105.001, supra, CLE/Other Legal Publications.

Leading Cases

In re Levay, 179 S.W.3d 93 (Tex. App.—San Antonio 2005, orig. proceeding) (temporary order placing child in mental health facility improperly deprived father's right to determine child's primary residence)

In re K.L.R., 162 S.W.3d 291 (Tex. App.—Tyler 2005, no pet.) (affidavit and evidence supported temporary order and injunctions)

In re Ostrofsky, 112 S.W.3d 925 (Tex. App.—Houston [14th] 2003, orig. proceeding) (temporary order placing children in boarding school deprives mother of possession of, and right to determine primary residence of children)

SUBCHAPTER B. MODIFICATION OF CONSERVATORSHIP, POSSESSION AND ACCESS, OR DETERMINATION OF RESIDENCE

Introductory Comment

When the Family Code became effective Jan. 1, 1974, modification of (sole) managing conservatorship (there was no "joint") was measured by tests of "a material and substantial change of circumstances" and "best interest." In 1975, the hurdle to modify custody was significantly raised by the addition of a three prong test. This was perfectly consistent with the thinking of the time that stability for child placement was all-important, and that the initial "winner" in a custody battle "retains all the rights, privileges, duties, and powers of a parent to the exclusion of the other parent . . . "[old § 14.02(a), amended in 1993].

Over time, principles and practices have really changed. Beginning in 1983, the legislature determined that an order of "reasonable visitation," to a noncustodial parent should be discouraged. All such an order truly meant was that the noncustodial parent had no actual time where possession of the child was his by right. Rather, visitation was at the sufferance of the custodial parent. The initial action by the legislature was merely to suggest that the courts themselves create advisory guidelines for possession of and access to the child by the noncustodial parent. When only a few courts responded to this prodding, guidelines were ultimately promulgate through a statewide standard order stated to be presumptively in the child's best interest. The allocation of all rights to the managing conservator has been replaced by a list of rights of conservators; at all times when in possession, and when exclusive rights are appropriate. The nonexistence of joint managing conservatorship was altered, first into JMC by agreement, and then by court order, theoretically even over the objection of the parties, and finally by presumption that JMC is in the child's best interest, § 153.131, *supra*.

Although this subchapter is phrased in terms of "orders subject to modification," reopening of a matter "finally adjudicated" in a prior proceeding more closely resembles the initiation of a new lawsuit than motion practice in ongoing litigation. Modification has long been the most discussed, controversial, and highly litigated aspect of sole and joint managing conservatorships, possessory conservatorships, and child support. Of these, modification from one sole conservator to another was for many years the most highly visible; that winner take all formula used a then familiar three prong test. But, since 1995 a sole to sole action has been governed by a "two prong test," which included "material and significant change," and "positive improvement." In the never ending battle of the sexes waged each legislative session, this formulation was regarded by many as the ultimate triumph for fathers' rights organizations over feminist spokespersons.

Much of the complexity was washed away in 2001; that process has continued through 2009. This chapter provides a set of uniform standards for modification of all the many varieties of conservatorship. The sweeping change was directed at simplifying the law, and saw the repeal of provisions relating to voluntary relinquishment, modification from sole managing conservatorship to joint managing conservatorship and vice versa, elimination of statutory definitions of change of circumstance, specific provisions for the modification of joint managing conservatorship, and for modification of possession of or access to a child.

---

§ 156.101. Grounds for Modification of Order Establishing Conservatorship or Possession and Access

(a) The court may modify an order that provides for the appointment of a conservator of a child, that provides the terms and conditions of conservatorship, or that provides for the possession of or access to a child if modification would be in the best interest of the child and:

(1) the circumstances of the child, a conservator, or other party affected by the order have materially and substantially changed since the earlier of:

(A) the date of the rendition of the order; or

(B) the date of the signing of a mediated or collaborative law settlement agreement on which the order is based;

(2) the child is at least 12 years of age and has expressed to the court in chambers as provided by Section 153.009 the name of the person who is the child's preference to have the exclusive right to designate the primary residence of the child; or

(3) the conservator who has the exclusive right to designate the primary residence of the child has voluntarily relinquished the primary care and possession of the child to another person for at least six months.

(b) Subsection (a)(3) does not apply to a conservator who has the exclusive right to designate the primary residence of the child and who has temporarily relinquished the primary care and possession of the child to another person during the conservator's military deployment, military mobilization, or temporary military duty, as those terms are defined by Section 153.701.

Comment

Section 156.101(a) attempts to accommodate all (or at least almost all) of the wide variety of scenarios for modification of conservatorships. Section 156.101 establishes a two prong test, best interest and one of three "second prongs." The vast majority of modifications will undoubtedly be based on the "best interest" test and a showing of "material and substantial changed circumstances." Note this two prong test applies to modification of sole managing, joint managing, or possessory conservatorships, and of the terms of any of those.

Two other "two prong tests" are established in this section. First, Subsection (2) retains the contentious "choice of child," coupled with best interest. And, Subsection (3) continues the "voluntary relinquishment" basis for modification, now tied to the conservator who has the right to provide the primary residence of the child, again coupled with best interest. The same two prong tests are applicable in situations in which less than one year has elapsed since the order sought to be modified, with the extra affidavit required under the prior law reworded without significant change.

Conviction or deferred adjudication for an offense involving sexual abuse, aggravated sexual abuse, or indecency with a child is sufficient to justify a temporary order and modification of an existing order that provides for the appointment of a conservator or possession of or access to a child. A person who knowingly files a false motion to modify an order or portion of a decree based on the above grounds commits a Class B misdemeanor, § 156.104.

The chapter now makes uniform references to a person who has the exclusive right to determine the primary residence of the child in provisions relating to temporary orders, §§ 156.006, 156.101, 156.102, and 156.409.

In 2009 the legislature repealed Section 153.008, which provided that a child of 12 or older could "file with the court in writing" a preference for a person to provide child's primary residence. This option was heavily criticized as placing undue stress on the child, particularly when dueling affidavits were presented to the court. This section had provided a comparable option in the context of modification of conservatorship. The 2009 amendment retains a modicum of choice for the child, who may inform the judge of the preference for the person to designate the primary residence. But, that opinion may be given to the judge in chambers, *see* Section 153.009.

Leading Cases

Lenz v. Lenz, 79 S.W.3d 10 (Tex. 2002) (evidence presented legally sufficient to support modification of decree to allow mother to relocate to Germany)

In re V.L.K., 24 S.W.3d 338 (Tex. 1999) (parental presumption for custody in original action does not apply in modification litigation—nonparent seeking conservatorship has higher burden); *recently cited by In re* C.D.W., 2010 WL 156294 (Tex. App.—Fort Worth, 2010, no pet.); *but see*, Troxel v. Granville, 530 U.S. 57 (2000) (parents have a fundamental constitutional right to have and raise children without interference from the state except in extraordinary circumstances, *see* Introductory Comment to §§ 153.431–.434)

Martin v. Martin, 776 S.W.2d 572 (Tex. 1989) (modification of terms of possessory conservatorship within court's discretion—jury denied)

In re N.L.V., 2011 WL 1734228 (Tex. App.—San Antonio) (citing *V.L.K.* for proposition that parental preference not applicable in modification suit; after custodial mother died adult sister and maternal aunt awarded right to determine primary residence of three minor girls and JMC with father)

In re R.T.H., 175 S.W.3d 519 (Tex. App.—Fort Worth 2005, no pet.) (one time act of family violence by JMC/mother did not justify modification of primary residence to JMC/father)

Ellason v. Ellason, 162 S.W.3d 883 (Tex. App.—Dallas 2005, no pet.) (Evidence supports modification granting father exclusive right to determine 15 year old child's residency)

In re K.L.R., 162 S.W.3d 291 (Tex. App.—Tyler 2005, no pet.) (mom's declining health, remarriage and divorce, and felony arrests since prior order sufficient change of circumstance to warrant change of primary residence)

§ 156.102. Modification of Exclusive Right to Determine Primary Residence of Child Within One Year of Order

(a) If a suit seeking to modify the designation of the person having the exclusive right to designate the primary residence of a child is filed not later than one year after the earlier of the date of the rendition of the order or the date of the signing of a mediated or collaborative law settlement agreement on which the order is based, the person filing the suit shall execute and attach an affidavit as provided by Subsection (b).

(b) The affidavit must contain, along with supporting facts, at least one of the following allegations:

(1) that the child's present environment may endanger the child's physical health or significantly impair the child's emotional development;

(2) that the person who has the exclusive right to designate the primary residence of the child is the person seeking or consenting to the modification and the modification is in the best interest of the child; or

(3) that the person who has the exclusive right to designate the primary residence of the child has voluntarily relinquished the primary care and possession of the child for at least six months and the modification is in the best interest of the child.

(c) The court shall deny the relief sought and refuse to schedule a hearing for modification under this section unless the court determines, on the basis of the affidavit, that facts adequate to support an allegation listed in Subsection (b) are stated in the affidavit. If the court determines that the facts stated are adequate to support an allegation, the court shall set a time and place for the hearing.

(d) Subsection (b)(3) does not apply to a person who has the exclusive right to designate the primary residence of the child and who has temporarily relinquished the primary care and possession of the child to another person during the conservator's military deployment, military mobilization, or temporary military duty, as those terms are defined by Section 153.701.

Leading Case

In re A.S.M., 172 S.W.3d 710 (Tex. App.—Fort Worth 2005, no pet.) (petition to modify without affidavit filed one month after agreed order elicits dismissal and $5,000 in respondent's attorney's fees)

---

§ 156.103. Increased Expenses Because of Change of Residence

(a) If a change of residence results in increased expenses for a party having possession of or access to a child, the court may render appropriate orders to allocate those increased expenses on a fair and equitable basis, taking into account the cause of the increased expenses and the best interest of the child.

(b) The payment of increased expenses by the party whose residence is changed is rebuttably presumed to be in the best interest of the child.

(c) The court may render an order without regard to whether another change in the terms and conditions for the possession of or access to the child is made.

Comment

The court is authorized to render appropriate orders to allocate increased expenses of a child on a fair and equitable basis. In particular, the court should take note of whether a change in the residence of the child results in increased expenses for the noncustodial parent. Payment of those increased expenses by the party whose residence has changed is rebuttably presumed to be in the best interest of the child.

---

§ 156.104. Modification of Order on Conviction for Child Abuse; Penalty

(a) Except as provided by Section 156.1045, the conviction of a conservator for an offense under Section 21.02, Penal Code, or the conviction of a conservator or an order deferring adjudication with regard to the conservator, for an offense involving the abuse of a child under Section 21.11, 22.011, or 22.021, Penal Code, is a material and substantial change of circumstances sufficient to justify a temporary order and modification of an existing court order or portion of a decree that provides for the appointment of a conservator or that sets the terms and conditions of conservatorship or for the possession of or access to a child.

(b) A person commits an offense if the person files a suit to modify an order or portion of a decree based on the grounds permitted under Subsection (a) and the person knows that the person against whom the motion is filed has not been convicted of an offense, or received deferred adjudication for an offense, under Section 21.02, 21.11, 22.011, or 22.021, Penal Code. An offense under this subsection is a Class B misdemeanor.

§ 156.1045. Modification of Order on Conviction for Family Violence

(a) The conviction or an order deferring adjudication of a person who is a possessory conservator or a sole or joint managing conservator for an offense involving family violence is a material and substantial change of circumstances sufficient to justify a temporary order and modification of an existing court order or portion of a decree that provides for the appointment of a conservator or that sets the terms and conditions of conservatorship or for the possession of or access to a child to conform the order to the requirements of Section 153.004(d).

(b) A person commits an offense if the person files a suit to modify an order or portion of a decree based on the grounds permitted under Subsection (a) and the person knows that the person against whom the motion is filed has not been convicted of an offense, or received deferred adjudication for an offense, involving family violence. An offense under this subsection is a Class B misdemeanor.

§ 156.105. Modification of Order Based on Military Duty

The military duty of a conservator who is ordered to military deployment, military mobilization, or temporary military duty, as those terms are defined by Section 153.701, does not by itself constitute a material and substantial change of circumstances sufficient to justify a modification of an existing court order or portion of a decree that sets the terms and conditions for the possession of or access to a child except that the court may render a temporary order under Subchapter L, Chapter 153.

SUBCHAPTER C. MODIFICATION OF JOINT MANAGING CONSERVATORSHIP [REPEALED]

SUBCHAPTER D. MODIFICATION OF POSSESSION OF OR ACCESS TO CHILD [REPEALED]

SUBCHAPTER E. MODIFICATION OF CHILD SUPPORT

Editors' Note: *This subchapter contains guest comments by Alicia G. Key, Deputy Attorney General and H. Patrick Sullivan, Deputy Director for State and Federal Operations, Child Support Division, Office of the Attorney General, identified as* (A.G.K. & H.P.S.)

CLE/Other Legal Publications

See CLE/Other Legal Publications for Chapter 154, *supra*, and Chapter 158, *infra*.

Leading Cases

In re S.A.V., 837 S.W.2d 80 (Tex. 1992) (Texas had minimum contacts to modify child support paid by nonresident)

In re E.V., 255 S.W.3d 389 (Tex. App.—El Paso 2008, no pet.) (evidence of a material and substantial change in circumstances must be presented to warrant increase in child support)

In re J.D.M., 221 S.W.3d 740 (Tex. App.—Waco 2007, no pet.) (finding of best interest not required when court is not setting or modifying support)

In re Naylor, 160 S.W.3d 292 (Tex. App.—Texarkana 2005, pet. denied) (retroactive reduction of child support order may go back to filing date of modification motion or sometime thereafter at trial court's discretion)

Cameron v. Cameron, 158 S.W.3d 680 (Tex. App.—Dallas 2005, pet. denied) (father seeking to reduce child support carried burden of showing material and substantial change)

---

§ 156.401. Grounds for Modification of Child Support

(a) Except as provided by Subsection (a–1), **(a–2),** or (b), the court may modify an order that provides for the support of a child, including an order for health care coverage under Section 154.182, if:

(1) the circumstances of the child or a person affected by the order have materially and substantially changed since the earlier of:

(A) the date of the order's rendition; or

(B) the date of the signing of a mediated or collaborative law settlement agreement on which the order is based; or

(2) it has been three years since the order was rendered or last modified and the monthly amount of the child support award under the order differs by either 20 percent or $100 from the amount that would be awarded in accordance with the child support guidelines.

(a–1) If the parties agree to an order under which the amount of child support differs from the amount that would be awarded in accordance with the child support guidelines, the court may modify the order only if the circumstances of the child or a person affected by the order have materially and substantially changed since the date of the order's rendition.

(a–2) A court or administrative order for child support in a Title IV–D case may be modified as provided under Section 233.013(c) to provide for medical support of a child.

(b) A support order may be modified with regard to the amount of support ordered only as to obligations accruing after the earlier of:

(1) the date of service of citation; or

(2) an appearance in the suit to modify.

(c) An order of joint conservatorship, in and of itself, does not constitute grounds for modifying a support order.

(d) Release of a child support obligor from incarceration is a material and substantial change in circumstances for purposes of this section if the obligor's child support obligation was abated, reduced, or suspended during the period of the obligor's incarceration.

Amended by Acts 2011, 82nd Leg., ch. 508 (H.B. 1674), § 3, eff. Sept. 1, 2011.

Comment

A deviation from the child support guidelines may be sufficient cause to modify child support. Periodic review of the support amount every three years, plus a fixed deviation of relatively narrow scope, authorizes the court to modify support. Note that the required 20% deviation does not equal the flat amount until it reaches $100 per month on a $500 monthly order or more. Any order over $500 requires at least a $100 per month deviation to trigger a modification. Orders for a smaller monthly amount will require a smaller deviation in absolute dollars, e.g. a child support order for $250 per month will require only a $50 per month variation from the support guidelines to warrant a modification. However, if parties agree to a child support amount that deviates from guidelines, future modifications will require a showing of a material and substantial change of circumstances of the child or of the parties.

Leading Cases

In re D.S., 76 S.W.3d 512 (Tex. App.—Houston [14th Dist.] 2002, no pet.) (agreed schedule for present and future child support based on anticipated career not modified just because he changed his plans)

In re H.S.N., 69 S.W.3d 829 (Tex. App.—Corpus Christi 2002, no pet.) (support order more than three years old and not within 20% or $100 of amount due; review and modification appropriate)

In re J.G.Z., 963 S.W.2d 144 (Tex. App.—Texarkana 1998, no pet.) (retroactive child support ordered back only to time of motion)

---

§ 156.402. Effect of Guidelines

(a) The court may consider the child support guidelines for single and multiple families under Chapter 154 to determine whether there has been a material or substantial change of circumstances under this chapter that warrants a modification of an existing child support order if the modification is in the best interest of the child.

(b) If the amount of support contained in the order does not substantially conform with the guidelines for single and multiple families under Chapter 154, the court may modify the order to substantially conform with the guidelines if the modification is in the best interest of the child. A court may consider other relevant evidence in addition to the factors listed in the guidelines.

Comment

The child support guidelines may be considered in modifying a prior support order, but the income of a new spouse shall not be considered in calculating the net resources of the obligor or obligee. The guideline formula for multiple family situations applies in a suit for modification.

---

§ 156.403. Voluntary Additional Support

A history of support voluntarily provided in excess of the court order does not constitute cause to increase the amount of an existing child support order.

§ 156.404. Net Resources of New Spouse

(a) The court may not add any portion of the net resources of a new spouse to the net resources of an obligor or obligee in order to calculate the amount of child support to be ordered in a suit for modification.

(b) The court may not subtract the needs of a new spouse, or of a dependent of a new spouse, from the net resources of the obligor or obligee in a suit for modification.

§ 156.405. Change in Lifestyle

An increase in the needs, standard of living, or lifestyle of the obligee since the rendition of the existing order does not warrant an increase in the obligor's child support obligation.

§ 156.406. Use of Guidelines for Children in More Than One Household

In applying the child support guidelines in a suit under this subchapter, if the obligor has the duty to support children in more than one household, the court shall apply the percentage guidelines for multiple families under Chapter 154.

§ 156.407. Assignment of Child Support Right

A notice of assignment filed under Chapter 231 does not constitute a modification of an order to pay child support.

§ 156.408. Modification of Support Order Rendered by Another State

(a) Unless both parties and the child reside in this state, a court of this state may modify an order of child support rendered by an appropriate tribunal of another state only as provided by Chapter 159.

(b) If both parties and the child reside in this state, a court of this state may modify an order of child support rendered by an appropriate tribunal of another state after registration of the order as provided by Chapter 159.

Comment

This section conforms to the UIFSA jurisdictional principles found in § 159.613 for the modification of a child support order by a court of this state where the issuing state has lost exclusive jurisdiction and both parties and the child reside in this state. Nonmodifiable aspects of the controlling order—such as the duration of support—remain in effect as required in § 159.611(c). *(H.P.S.)*

---

§ 156.409. Change in Physical Possession

(a) The court shall, on the motion of a party or a person having physical possession of the child, modify an order providing for the support of the child to provide that the person having physical possession of the child for at least six months shall have the right to receive and give receipt for payments of support for the child and to hold or disburse money for the benefit of the child if the sole managing conservator of the child or the joint managing conservator who has the exclusive right to determine the primary residence of the child has:

(1) voluntarily relinquished the primary care and possession of the child;

(2) been incarcerated or sentenced to be incarcerated for at least 90 days; or

(3) relinquished the primary care and possession of the child in a proceeding under Title 3 or Chapter 262.

(a–1) If the court modifies a support order under this section, the court shall order the obligor to pay the person or entity having physical possession of the child any unpaid child support that is not subject to offset or reimbursement under Section 157.008 and that accrues after the date the sole or joint managing conservator:

(1) relinquishes possession and control of the child, whether voluntarily or in a proceeding under Title 3 or Chapter 262; or

(2) is incarcerated.

(a–2) This section does not affect the ability of the court to render a temporary order for the payment of child support that is in the best interest of the child.

(a–3) An order under this section that modifies a support order because of the incarceration of the sole or joint managing conservator of a child must provide that on the conservator's release from incarceration the conservator may file an affidavit with the court stating that the conservator has been released from incarceration, that there has not been a modification of the conservatorship of the child during the incarceration, and that the conservator has resumed physical possession of the child. A copy of the affidavit shall be delivered to the obligor and any other party, including the Title IV–D agency if appropriate. On receipt of the affidavit, the court on its own motion shall order the obligor to make support payments to the conservator.

(b) Notice of a motion for modification under this section may be served in the manner for serving a notice under Section 157.065.

Comment

This section addresses situations, other than voluntary relinquishment, in which the child is no longer in the physical possession of the sole or joint managing conservator and child support should be directed to the person who has had physical possession of the child for at least six months. In fact, however, under Subsection (a–2) the court is not constrained from acting sooner than six months and may, on the motion of a party, render a temporary order for the redirection of support, if it in the best interest of the child. This would mean, for example, that a relative caretaker or a government entity could move quickly to have support, including payment on any arrearages, redirected for the care of a child abandoned by, or removed from the possession of a parent. A conservator who loses physical possession of the child because of incarceration may, on release, file an affidavit with the court to undo the redirection of support, provided the conservator has actual possession of the child and conservatorship had not been modified during the term of incarceration. No similar procedure for returning payment of support to the obligee under the original order is available under this section for the conservator who for a limited period of time voluntarily relinquishes possession of the child or who loses possession through the action of a government entity. A notice of a motion for modification may be served by first class mail under the limited circumstances described in Subsection (a). The intent of the exception is to allow the court to move forward with an order directing payment of support to the actual caretaker of the child in cases in which the child is no longer in the physical possession of the custodial parent. *(A.G.K & H.P.S.)*

CHAPTER 157. ENFORCEMENT

SUBCHAPTER A. PLEADINGS AND DEFENSES

SUBCHAPTER B. PROCEDURE

SUBCHAPTER C. FAILURE TO APPEAR; BOND OR SECURITY

SUBCHAPTER D. HEARING AND ENFORCEMENT ORDER

SUBCHAPTER E. COMMUNITY SUPERVISION

SUBCHAPTER F. JUDGMENT AND INTEREST

SUBCHAPTER G. CHILD SUPPORT LIEN

SUBCHAPTER H. HABEAS CORPUS

SUBCHAPTER I. CLARIFICATION OF ORDERS

Editors' Note: *This chapter contains guest comments by Alicia Gray Key, Deputy Attorney General and Title IV-D Director, and H. Patrick Sullivan, Deputy Director for State and Federal Operations, Child Support Division, Office of the Attorney General, identified as (*A.G.K. & H.P.S.*).*

Introductory Comment

In 1983 the only remedies to enforce child support provided in the Family Code were contempt and rendition of a money judgment for arrears. That year, the Texas Legislature provided for a constitutional amendment authorizing wage withholding for child support, which was overwhelmingly approved by the voters. The next major event in the evolutionary process of reforming the enforcement remedies available occurred with the enactment of the federal Child Support Enforcement Amendments of 1984. In the next decade, the legislature enacted as wide an array of remedies as are available in any state. During this same time, Texas moved from a system in which child support orders were wholly within the discretion of the trial court—with the attendant unpredictability—to a highly regulated, predictable system based on child support guidelines rebuttably presumed to be in the child's best interest.

Texas can now claim to be in the first rank of states insofar as the legal remedies available to enforce court-ordered support. The last piece fell into place with the enactment of Chapter 232, Suspension of License for Failure To Pay Child Support, *infra.* Chapters 157 and 158 gather together in one place almost all of the other post-decree enforcement remedies and procedures for SAPCR's.

Subchapters A and B present fourteen detailed statutes, comprising the procedural portion of this chapter. A common structure is established for every motion to enforce an existing final order, whether for child support or for possession of and access to a child.

"Contempt of court" historically has been the chief enforcement remedy. In large part the prior law of contempt has been continued, albeit with the addition of nonsubstantive details lacking in prior statutes which recognize jurisprudential developments in constitutional due process. An important example of innovative thinking is found in §§ 157.006–157.008, modeled after the Penal Code provision for criminal nonsupport, TEX. PEN. CODE § 25.05, *infra*. The burden of persuasion regarding "inability to pay" is allocated to the respondent as an affirmative defense.

Civil and coercive contempt is the process by which a court exerts authority to compel obedience to its orders. Punishment for civil contempt may also be characterized as remedial in nature and is generally assessed for the benefit of the movant. Criminal or punitive contempt is designed to punish the contemnor for disobedience of a court order so as to protect the dignity of the judicial system. It is most easily identified by its determinate sentence, e.g. "six months in jail as punishment for failure to comply with the court's order." In sum, the contemnor may purge himself of coercive contempt, but not of punitive contempt because the contumacious act has been completed and cannot be undone. To further complicate matters, a finding of contempt may involve elements of contempt both coercive and punitive. The goal of both forms of contempt, in reality, is almost always to ensure future compliance with the obligation of supporting a child.

CLE/Other Legal Publications

Enforcement. Randall Scott Downing, 2011 ADV. FAM. L.

Enforcement. Katherine A. Kinser, 2011 ADV. FAM. L.

Enforcement: how to make it stick or get it unstuck. Michelle May O'Neil, 2011 MARRIAGE DISSOLUTION

Contempt and enforcement. David D. Farr, 2011 SO. TEX. FAM. L.

Enforcement. Brenda Hull Thompson, 2010 FAM. L. BOOT CAMP

Confused about contempt? Prosecuting and defending enforcement cases. Daniel J. Lemkuil & Alyssa P. Lemkuil, 2010 U.T. PARENT-CHILD RELATIONSHIPS

Temporary orders: what you can get and how to get it. Thomas L. Ausley & John T. Eck, 2010 MARRIAGE DISSOL. BOOT CAMP

Enforcement: nuts and bolts. Hon. Roy L. Moore, 2010 SO. TEX. FAM. L. CONF.

Temporary orders on the fly. Maisie Barringer, 2010 SO. TEX. FAM. L. CONF.

Child support workshop: UIFSA, above guideline child support, effective use of financial documents, utilization of QDRO's and child support liens; enforcement techniques. (Panel), 2009 ADV. FAM. L.

Enforcement. Warren Cole, 2009 FAM. L. BOOT CAMP

Enforcement of child related issues. John F. (Bo) Nichols, Jr., 2009 U.T. FAM. L. FRONT LINES

Tips for drafting motions for enforcement. Hon. David D. Farr. 2009 SO. TEX. FAM. L. CONF.

***See* Accompanying CD–ROM for Additional CLE/Other Legal Publications.**

Cross References

TX FCA FAMILY § 232.001 *et seq.*, Suspension of License for Failure To Pay Child Support, *infra*.

TEX. GOV'T CODE ANN. § 21.002, Contempt of Court.

TX FCA PENAL § 25.05, Criminal Nonsupport, *infra*.

IV–D Child Support Enforcement, 42 U.S.C.A. § 651 *et seq.*

Family Support Act of 1988, Pub. L. 100–485, 102 Stat. 2343, *see* 5 U.S. Code Cong. & Admin. News 2776 (1988) (last federal legislative action to regulate state enforcement efforts)

Child Support Enforcement Amendments of 1984 [CSEA]. Pub. L. No. 98–378, 98 Stat. 1305, *see* 4 U.S. Code Cong. & Admin. News 2397 (1984) (federal act creating present system), codified at 42 U.S.C.A. § 651 *et seq.* (especially § 666, *see* 45 C.F.R. § 303)

42 U.S.C.A. §§ 651–665, P. L. 93–647, 88 Stat. 2351 (first federal intervention in child support enforcement, recoupment of AFDC payments the goal)

SUBCHAPTER A. PLEADINGS AND DEFENSES

§ 157.001. Motion for Enforcement

(a) A motion for enforcement as provided in this chapter may be filed to enforce a final order for conservatorship, child support, possession of or access to a child, or other provisions of a final order.

(b) The court may enforce by contempt a final order for possession of and access to a child as provided in this chapter.

(c) The court may enforce a final order for child support as provided in this chapter or Chapter 158.

(d) A motion for enforcement shall be filed in the court of continuing, exclusive jurisdiction.

§ 157.002. Contents of Motion

(a) A motion for enforcement must, in ordinary and concise language:

(1) identify the provision of the order allegedly violated and sought to be enforced;

(2) state the manner of the respondent's alleged noncompliance;

(3) state the relief requested by the movant; and

(4) contain the signature of the movant or the movant's attorney.

(b) A motion for enforcement of child support:

(1) must include the amount owed as provided in the order, the amount paid, and the amount of arrearages;

(2) if contempt is requested, must include the portion of the order allegedly violated and, for each date of alleged contempt, the amount due and the amount paid, if any;

(3) may include as an attachment a copy of a record of child support payments maintained by the Title IV-D registry or a local registry; and

(4) if the obligor owes arrearages for a child receiving assistance under Part A of Title IV of the federal Social Security Act (42 U.S.C. Section 601 et seq.), may include a request that:

(A) the obligor pay the arrearages in accordance with a plan approved by the court; or

(B) if the obligor is already subject to a plan and is not incapacitated, the obligor participate in work activities, as defined under 42 U.S.C. Section 607(d), that the court determines appropriate.

(c) A motion for enforcement of the terms and conditions of conservatorship or possession of or access to a child must include the date, place, and, if applicable, the time of each occasion of the respondent's failure to comply with the order.

(d) The movant is not required to plead that the underlying order is enforceable by contempt to obtain other appropriate enforcement remedies.

(e) The movant may allege repeated past violations of the order and that future violations of a similar nature may occur before the date of the hearing.

§ 157.003. Joinder of Claims and Remedies; No Election of Remedies

(a) A party requesting enforcement may join in the same proceeding any claim and remedy provided for in this chapter, other provisions of this title, or other rules of law.

(b) A motion for enforcement does not constitute an election of remedies that limits or precludes:

(1) the use of any other civil or criminal proceeding to enforce a final order; or

(2) a suit for damages under Chapter 42.

§ 157.004. Time Limitations; Enforcement of Possession

The court retains jurisdiction to render a contempt order for failure to comply with the order of possession and access if the motion for enforcement is filed not later than the sixth month after the date:

(1) the child becomes an adult; or

(2) on which the right of possession and access terminates under the order or by operation of law.

§ 157.005. Time Limitations; Enforcement of Child Support

(a) The court retains jurisdiction to render a contempt order for failure to comply with the child support order if the motion for enforcement is filed not later than the second anniversary of the date:

(1) the child becomes an adult; or

(2) on which the child support obligation terminates under the order or by operation of law.

(b) The court retains jurisdiction to confirm the total amount of child support arrearages and render a cumulative money judgment for past-due child support, as provided by Section 157.263, if a motion for enforcement requesting a cumulative money judgment is filed not later than the 10th anniversary after the date:

(1) the child becomes an adult; or

(2) on which the child support obligation terminates under the child support order or by operation of law.

Comment

As of 2005, an action for confirmation and judgment may be brought no later than 10 years after the child becomes an adult or the child support obligation terminates. This is a departure from the prior statute which allowed for confirmation of the arrearage and a judgment for as long as support payments, interest, fees and costs went unpaid.

Leading Case

In re A.D., 73 S.W.3d 244 (Tex. 2002) (issuance of administrative writ of withholding over 4 years after child turned 18 not violation of constitutional prohibition on retroactive laws)

§ 157.006. Affirmative Defense to Motion for Enforcement

(a) The issue of the existence of an affirmative defense to a motion for enforcement does not arise unless evidence is admitted supporting the defense.

(b) The respondent must prove the affirmative defense by a preponderance of the evidence.

§ 157.007. Affirmative Defense to Motion for Enforcement of Possession or Access

(a) The respondent may plead as an affirmative defense to contempt for failure to comply with an order for possession or access to a child that the movant voluntarily relinquished actual possession and control of the child.

(b) The voluntary relinquishment must have been for the time encompassed by the court-ordered periods during which the respondent is alleged to have interfered.

§ 157.008. Affirmative Defense to Motion for Enforcement of Child Support

(a) An obligor may plead as an affirmative defense in whole or in part to a motion for enforcement of child support that the obligee voluntarily relinquished to the obligor actual possession and control of a child.

(b) The voluntary relinquishment must have been for a time period in excess of any court-ordered periods of possession of and access to the child and actual support must have been supplied by the obligor.

(c) An obligor may plead as an affirmative defense to an allegation of contempt or of the violation of a condition of community service requiring payment of child support that the obligor:

(1) lacked the ability to provide support in the amount ordered;

(2) lacked property that could be sold, mortgaged, or otherwise pledged to raise the funds needed;

(3) attempted unsuccessfully to borrow the funds needed; and

(4) knew of no source from which the money could have been borrowed or legally obtained.

(d) An obligor who has provided actual support to the child during a time subject to an affirmative defense under this section may request reimbursement for that support as a counter-claim or offset against the claim of the obligee.

(e) An action against the obligee for support supplied to a child is limited to the amount of periodic payments previously ordered by the court.

Leading Cases

In re Coppock, 277 S.W.3d 417 (Tex. 2009) (divorce judgment must have command language to be enforced by contempt, i.e., "coarse and offensive communication" not specifically prohibited in divorce decree)

In re A.M., 192 S.W.3d 570 (Tex. 2006) (obligor not required to provide evidence of his expenses for actual support during periods of excess possession)

Ex parte Rojo, 925 S.W.2d 654 (Tex. 1996) (inability to pay valid defense to civil contempt)

Ex parte Dustman, 538 S.W.2d 409 (Tex. 1976) (uncontroverted evidence of contemnor's inability to pay arrearage)

Pedregon v. Pedregon, 234 S.W.3d 90 (Tex. App.—El Paso 2007, no pet.) (claim of offset must be proven by party seeking offset)

In re Lausch, 177 S.W.3d 144 (Tex. App.—Houston [1st Dist.] 2005, no pet.) (father's inability to pay child support not established)

Beck v. Walker, 154 S.W.3d 895 (Tex. App.—Dallas 2005, no pet.) (offset against child support order for time child in obligor's actual custody allowed even without expense receipts)

§ 157.009. Credit for Payment of Disability Benefits

In addition to any other credit or offset available to an obligor under this title, if a child for whom the obligor owes child support receives a lump-sum payment as a result of the obligor's disability and that payment is made to the obligee as the representative payee of the child, the obligor is entitled to a credit. The credit under this section is equal to the amount of the lump-sum payment and shall be applied to any child support arrearage and interest owed by the obligor on behalf of that child at the time the payment is made.

Comment

This section, added in 2009, provides a statutory resolution to an issue appeals courts left to the legislature to decide: whether the court's applying a credit against support arrearages in the amount of a lump-sum payment to the child resulting from the obligor's disability would violate the prohibition against retroactive modification of a child support obligation under 157.262(a) *infra*. The legislature determined that the obligor should receive credit for the payment. This brings full circle the provision under 154.131 that in the setting of a support obligation the court may give an obligor prospective credit in the setting of a support obligation for benefits received by the child as a result of the obligor's disability. Under 157.009 an obligor who becomes disabled is entitled to a credit against support arrearages in the full amount of a lump-sum disability benefit paid the obligee as representative payee of the child. The fine point here is that this credit is akin to any other permissible offset or counterclaim against the claim of the obligee (as, e.g., under 157.008 *supra*) and is not, in fact, a retroactive modification of the support order. What some may find troubling is that the credit under this section is to be applied to all support arrearages (and accrued interest) owed by the obligor, not just those amounts which arose during the term of the obligor's disability and may reasonably be attributed to the disability. *(A.G.K. and H.P.S.)*

SUBCHAPTER B. PROCEDURE

§ 157.061. Setting Hearing

(a) On filing a motion for enforcement requesting contempt, the court shall set the date, time, and place of the hearing and order the respondent to personally appear and respond to the motion.

(b) If the motion for enforcement does not request contempt, the court shall set the motion for hearing on the request of a party.

(c) The court shall give preference to a motion for enforcement of child support in setting a hearing date and may not delay the hearing because a suit for modification of the order requested to be enforced has been or may be filed.

§ 157.062. Notice of Hearing

(a) The notice of hearing must include the date, time, and place of the hearing.

(b) The notice of hearing need not repeat the allegations contained in the motion for enforcement.

(c) Notice of hearing on a motion for enforcement of an existing order providing for child support or possession of or access to a child shall be given to the respondent by personal service of a copy of the motion and notice not later than the 10th day before the date of the hearing.

(d) If a motion for enforcement is joined with another claim:

(1) the hearing may not be held before 10 a.m. on the first Monday after the 20th day after the date of service; and

(2) the provisions of the Texas Rules of Civil Procedure applicable to the filing of an original lawsuit apply.

Leading Cases

In re Digges, 981 S.W.2d 445 (Tex. App.—San Antonio 1998, no pet.) (default judgment taken before time to answer is void)

In re Hathcox, 981 S.W.2d 422 (Tex. App.—Texarkana 1998, no pet.) (new causes of action added to enforcement motion require new answer date before taking default judgment)

§ 157.063. Appearance

A party makes a general appearance for all purposes in an enforcement proceeding if:

(1) the party appears at the hearing or is present when the case is called; and

(2) the party does not object to the court's jurisdiction or the form or manner of the notice of hearing.

§ 157.064. Special Exception

(a) If a respondent specially excepts to the motion for enforcement or moves to strike, the court shall rule on the exception or the motion to strike before it hears the motion for enforcement.

(b) If an exception is sustained, the court shall give the movant an opportunity to replead and continue the hearing to a designated date and time without the requirement of additional service.

§ 157.065. Notice of Hearing, First Class Mail

(a) If a party has been ordered under Chapter 105 to provide the court and the state case registry with the party's current mailing address, notice of a hearing on a motion for enforcement may be served by mailing a copy of the notice to the respondent, together with a copy of the motion, by first class mail to the last mailing address of the respondent on file with the court and the registry.

(b) The notice may be sent by the clerk of the court, the movant's attorney, or any person entitled to the address information as provided in Chapter 105.

(c) A person who sends the notice shall file of record a certificate of service showing the date of mailing and the name of the person who sent the notice.

§ 157.066. Failure to Appear

If a respondent who has been personally served with notice to appear at a hearing does not appear at the designated time, place, and date to respond to a motion for enforcement of an existing court order, regardless of whether the motion is joined with other claims or remedies, the court may not hold the respondent in contempt but may, on proper proof, grant a default judgment for the relief sought and issue a capias for the arrest of the respondent.

Comment

Personal service of notice is required if the court is to order the issuance of a capias for the arrest of the respondent when the respondent fails to show up as ordered for a hearing. A person may not be adjudicated in contempt in absentia, but other remedies may be invoked by default, a capias (bench warrant) may issue to bring the no show physically to the courthouse.

Leading Cases

In re Sheard, 102 S.W.3d 808 (Tex. App.—Beaumont 2003, orig. proceeding) (contempt finding inappropriate when only violation was failure to appear at hearing)

In re White, 45 S.W.3d 787 (Tex. App.—Waco 2001, no pet.) (respondent who fails to personally appear at a hearing regarding enforcement of a previous court support order cannot be held in contempt)

In re Aguilera, 37 S.W.3d 43 (Tex. App.—El Paso 2000, no pet.) (capias valid for arrest of no-show even though show-cause to appear on motion for contempt did not provide 10–day notice)

SUBCHAPTER C. FAILURE TO APPEAR; BOND OR SECURITY

Introductory Comment

The capias procedure deals with recalcitrant child support obligors who refuse or neglect to appear at hearings. The procedure required for issuance of the capias and after the execution of an arrest has continued with little substantive change. The basic principle is the requirement that a "reasonable" bond be established at the time a capias is issued. There is a statutory presumption that $1,000 is a reasonable amount, but this can be rebutted if the alleged arrearages are in excess of that sum, or if the respondent has a record of prior contempt adjudications.

Release on an appearance bond is conditioned on the respondent's promise to appear; this is analogous to criminal law procedure under which it is the duty of the defendant to appear at a scheduled hearing without further official notice of the time and place of that hearing. If the respondent cannot post an appearance bond or other satisfactory security, his release may still be secured by other means, *i.e.,* personal recognizance. An expedited hearing is provided if the respondent cannot be released on his own recognizance and cannot or will not post an appearance bond.

This subchapter also attempts to deal with the dilemma of enforcing child support orders against such disparate obligors as day-laborers and the self-employed. Because withholding from earnings is either impractical or entirely useless in a variety of employment contexts, posting security or a bond to secure ordered periodic payments "may" be required by the court. Unfortunately, only in rare instances is there a possibility that a working class, or sometimes middle class, obligor will be in a financial position to post an adequate bond or other satisfactory security to ensure that support payments will be made.

§ 157.101. Bond or Security for Release of Respondent

(a) When the court orders the issuance of a capias as provided in this chapter, the court shall also set an appearance bond or security, payable to the obligee or to a person designated by the court, in a reasonable amount.

(b) An appearance bond or security in the amount of $1,000 or a cash bond in the amount of $250 is presumed to be reasonable. Evidence that the respondent has attempted to evade service of process, has previously been found guilty of contempt, or has accrued arrearages over $1,000 is sufficient to rebut the presumption. If the presumption is rebutted, the court shall set a reasonable bond.

Leading Case

In re Gawerc, 165 S.W.3d 314 (Tex. 2005) (improper to keep obligor confined just because he did not have ability to purge himself of civil contempt by posting bond to secure future payments)

§ 157.102. Capias or Warrant; Duty of Law Enforcement Officials

Law enforcement officials shall treat a capias or arrest warrant ordered under this chapter in the same manner as an arrest warrant for a criminal offense and shall enter the capias or warrant in the computer records for outstanding warrants maintained by the local police, sheriff, and Department of Public Safety. The capias or warrant shall be forwarded to and disseminated by the Texas Crime Information Center and the National Crime Information Center.

§ 157.103. Capias Fees

(a) The fee for issuing a capias as provided in this chapter is the same as the fee for issuance of a writ of attachment.

(b) The fee for serving a capias is the same as the fee for service of a writ in civil cases generally.

§ 157.104. Conditional Release

If the respondent is taken into custody and released on bond, the court shall condition the bond on the respondent's promise to appear in court for a hearing as required by the court without the necessity of further personal service of notice on the respondent.

§ 157.105. Release Hearing

(a) If the respondent is taken into custody and not released on bond, the respondent shall be brought before the court that issued the capias on or before the third working day after the arrest. The court shall determine whether the respondent's appearance in court at a designated time and place can be assured by a method other than by posting the bond or security previously established.

(b) If the respondent is released without posting bond or security, the court shall set a hearing on the alleged contempt at a designated date, time, and place and give the respondent notice of hearing in open court. No other notice to the respondent is required.

(c) If the court is not satisfied that the respondent's appearance in court can be assured and the respondent remains in custody, a hearing on the alleged contempt shall be held as soon as practicable, but not later than the seventh day after the date that the respondent was taken into custody, unless the respondent and the respondent's attorney waive the accelerated hearing.

§ 157.106. Cash Bond as Support

(a) If the respondent has posted a cash bond and is found to be in arrears in the payment of court-ordered child support, the court shall order that the proceeds of the cash bond be paid to the child support obligee or to a person designated by the court, not to exceed the amount of child support arrearages determined to exist.

(b) This section applies without regard to whether the respondent appears at the hearing.

§ 157.107. Appearance Bond or Security Other Than Cash Bond as Support

(a) If the respondent fails to appear at the hearing as directed, the court shall order that the appearance bond or security be forfeited and that the proceeds of any judgment on the bond or security, not to exceed the amount of child support arrearages determined to exist, be paid to the obligee or to a person designated by the court.

(b) The obligee may file suit on the bond.

§ 157.108. Cash Bond as Property of Respondent

A court shall treat a cash bond posted for the benefit of the respondent as the property of the respondent. A person who posts the cash bond does not have recourse in relation to an order regarding the bond other than against the respondent.

§ 157.109. Security for Compliance With Order

(a) The court may order the respondent to execute a bond or post security if the court finds that the respondent:

(1) has on two or more occasions denied possession of or access to a child who is the subject of the order; or

(2) is employed by an employer not subject to the jurisdiction of the court or for whom income withholding is unworkable or inappropriate.

(b) The court shall set the amount of the bond or security and condition the bond or security on compliance with the court order permitting possession or access or the payment of past-due or future child support.

(c) The court shall order the bond or security payable through the registry of the court:

(1) to the obligee or other person or entity entitled to receive child support payments designated by the court if enforcement of child support is requested; or

(2) to the person who is entitled to possession or access if enforcement of possession or access is requested.

§ 157.110. Forfeiture of Security for Failure to Comply With Order

(a) On the motion of a person or entity for whose benefit a bond has been executed or security deposited, the court may forfeit all or part of the bond or security deposit on a finding that the person who furnished the bond or security:

(1) has violated the court order for possession of and access to a child; or

(2) failed to make child support payments.

(b) The court shall order the registry to pay the funds from a forfeited bond or security deposit to the obligee or person or entity entitled to receive child support payments in an amount that does not exceed the child support arrearages or, in the case of possession of or access to a child, to the person entitled to possession or access.

(c) The court may order that all or part of the forfeited amount be applied to pay attorney's fees and costs incurred by the person or entity bringing the motion for contempt or motion for forfeiture.

§ 157.111. Forfeiture Not Defense to Contempt

The forfeiture of bond or security is not a defense in a contempt proceeding.

§ 157.112. Joinder of Forfeiture and Contempt Proceedings

A motion for enforcement requesting contempt may be joined with a forfeiture proceeding.

§ 157.113. Application of Bond Pending Writ

If the obligor requests to execute a bond or to post security pending a hearing by an appellate court on a writ, the bond or security on forfeiture shall be payable to the obligee.

§ 157.114. Failure to Appear

The court may order a capias to be issued for the arrest of the respondent if:

(1) the motion for enforcement requests contempt;

(2) the respondent was personally served; and

(3) the respondent fails to appear.

§ 157.115. Default Judgment

(a) The court may render a default order for the relief requested if the respondent:

(1) has been personally served, has filed an answer, or has entered an appearance; and

(2) does not appear at the designated time, place, and date to respond to the motion.

(b) If the respondent fails to appear, the court may not hold the respondent in contempt but may order a capias to be issued.

SUBCHAPTER D. HEARING AND ENFORCEMENT ORDER

Introductory Comment

Two major principles of constitutional due process are codified in this subchapter: (1) the right to remain silent under the 5th Amendment (as applicable in the contempt context); and, (2) the right to appointed counsel of an indigent, alleged contemnor who faces possible incarceration. Note the statute does not specify the length of time of the possible incarceration.

Insofar as the Family Code is concerned, contempt and other remedies apply equally to a violation of an order to pay child support and interference with the noncustodial parent's right of possession of and access to the child. Although a possessory conservator obligor theoretically has almost identical remedies for violation of court orders to those afforded a managing conservator obligee, actual practice has not caught up with the letter of the law (and probably never will).

Leading Cases

Commitment Order

Ex parte Swate, 922 S.W.2d 122 (Tex. 1996) (commitment order increasing punishment imposed by contempt order is void)

Ex parte Jordan, 865 S.W.2d 459 (Tex. 1993) (three days is too long to hold contemnor without written commitment order)

Ex parte Amaya, 748 S.W.2d 224 (Tex. 1988) (contempt commitment order must be signed within reasonable time; over the weekend is too long)

Contempt Order

In re Gawerc, 165 S.W.3d 314 (Tex. 2005) (inability to post bond ($50,000) voids incarceration for contempt)

Ex parte Hernandez, 827 S.W.2d 858 (Tex. 1992) (civil contempt requires both written judgment of contempt and written order of commitment)

Ex parte Strickland, 723 S.W.2d 668 (Tex. 1987) (incarceration requires written judgment of contempt or written order of commitment)

In re Mann, 162 S.W.3d 429 (Tex. App.—Fort Worth 2005, orig. proceeding) (failure to specify contemptuous acts violates child support obligor's due process rights)

Due Process Rights

Ex parte Acker, 949 S.W.2d 314 (Tex. 1997) (party must be advised of right to counsel)

Ex parte Keene, 909 S.W.2d 507 (Tex. 1995) (without record or instruction regarding right to counsel, alleged child support contemnor cannot be adjudicated in contempt)

Ex parte Sproull, 815 S.W.2d 250 (Tex. 1991); *Ex parte* Gunther, 758 S.W.2d 226 (Tex. 1988) (alleged contemnor facing "serious punishment," *i.e.*, possible sentence of more than six months incarceration, has right to jury trial)

Fifth Amendment

Ex parte Werblud, 536 S.W.2d 542 (Tex. 1976) (Fifth Amendment privilege in civil case)

Probation

Ex parte Spikes, 909 S.W.2d 245 (Tex. App.—Amarillo 1995, no writ) (probation on contempt finding may not extend beyond five years—revocation thereafter a nullity)

Ex parte Balderas, 804 S.W.2d 261 (Tex. App.—Houston [1st Dist.] 1991, no writ) (court cannot increase punishment originally imposed at later compliance hearing)

Punishment

Rosser v. Squier, 902 S.W.2d 962 (Tex. 1995) ($45,000 fine for contempt summarily reversed)

Ex parte Roosth, 881 S.W.2d 300 (Tex. 1994) (trial court cannot limit the operation of good time behavior credit in punitive contempt sentence)

Ex parte Sproull, 815 S.W.2d 250 (Tex. 1991) (22 year sentence for contempt reversed)

Ex parte Acly, 711 S.W.2d 627 (Tex. 1986) (equal protection requires good time credits for contemnor)

Reasonable Notice

Ex parte Anderson, 900 S.W.2d 333 (Tex. 1995); *Ex parte* Delcourt, 888 S.W.2d 811 (Tex. 1994) (new commitment order requires notice and hearing)

Release from Contempt

Ex parte Padron, 565 S.W.2d 921 (Tex. 1978) (civil contemnor has the keys to the jailhouse door to purge coercive contempt)

Specificity of SAPCR Order

Ex parte Acker, 949 S.W.2d 314 (Tex. 1997) (payments beginning in "June" not specific enough for contempt)

Ex parte MacCallum, 807 S.W.2d 729 (Tex. 1991) (visitation order not sufficiently specific to be enforced by contempt)

Ex parte Brister, 801 S.W.2d 833 (Tex. 1990) (ambiguous visitation order not enforceable by contempt)

Ex parte Garcia, 795 S.W.2d 740 (Tex. 1990); *Ex parte* Holland, 790 S.W.2d 568 (Tex. 1990) (specificity of underlying order required to sustain contempt)

Ex parte Davila, 718 S.W.2d 281 (Tex. 1986) (no incarceration for failure to pay overdue medical expenses)

Ex parte Slavin, 412 S.W.2d 43 (Tex. 1967) (ambiguous decree not enforceable by contempt—probably most cited case on subject)

Written Complaint Alleging Specific Violation

In re Mann, 162 S.W.3d 429 (Tex. App.—Fort Worth 2005, orig. proceeding) (failure to specify contemptuous acts violates child support obligor's due process rights)

Ex parte Barlow, 899 S.W.2d 791 (Tex. App.—Houston [14th Dist.] 1995, no writ) (contempt order based on nonconforming motion to enforce support voids order)

§ 157.161. Record

(a) Except as provided by Subsection (b), a record of the hearing in a motion for enforcement shall be made by a court reporter or as provided by Chapter 201.

(b) A record is not required if:

(1) the parties agree to an order; or

(2) the motion does not request incarceration and the parties waive the requirement of a record at the time of hearing, either in writing or in open court, and the court approves waiver.

§ 157.162. Proof

(a) The movant is not required to prove that the underlying order is enforceable by contempt to obtain other appropriate enforcement remedies.

(b) A finding that the respondent is not in contempt does not preclude the court from ordering any other enforcement remedy, including rendering a money judgment, posting a bond or other security, or withholding income.

(c) **The movant may attach to the motion a** ~~A~~copy of **a** ~~the~~ payment record. **The movant may subsequently update that payment record at the hearing. If a payment record was attached to the motion as authorized by this subsection, the payment record, as updated if applicable,** ~~attached to the motion is evidence of the facts asserted in the payment record and~~is admissible to **prove:**

(1) the dates and in what amounts payments were made;

(2) the amount of any accrued interest;

(3) the cumulative arrearage over time; and

(4) the cumulative arrearage as of the final date of the record.

(c-1) A ~~show whether payments were made. The~~ respondent may offer ~~controverting~~evidence **controverting the contents of a payment record under Subsection (c).**

(d) The court may not find a respondent in contempt of court for failure to pay child support if the respondent appears at the hearing with a copy of the payment record or other evidence satisfactory to the court showing that the respondent is current in the payment of child support as ordered by the court.

(e) Notwithstanding Subsection (d), the court may award the petitioner costs of court and reasonable attorney's fees in a proceeding described by that subsection if the court finds that:

(1) on the date the motion for enforcement was filed, the respondent was not current in the payment of child support as ordered by the court; and

(2) the respondent made the child support payments described by Subsection (d) after the date the respondent was served notice of the motion or otherwise discovered that the motion for enforcement had been filed.

Amended by Acts 2011, 82nd Leg., ch. 508 (H.B. 1674), § 4, eff. Sept. 1, 2011.

Comment

In 2011, the legislature both amplified and divided Subsection (c), creating a new Subsection (c–1) with respect to the respondent's being able to offer controverting evidence. The remaining part of the subsection was amended in two important ways. First, the payment record attached to the motion for enforcement is admissible to prove not just whether payments were made, but also the amounts of any accrued interest, as well as the cumulative arrearage both over time and as of the final date of the record. The significance of the articulation of these details lies in an appeals court's decision that the payment record is admissible to show only whether payments were made, not the amount of accrued interest or cumulative arrearage. *In re* K.R. No. 05-06-00885-CV, 2007 WL 2081453 (Tex. App.—Dallas July 23, 2007, pet. denied).

The second important aspect of the 2011 amendment is the provision that the movant may update the payment record at the hearing, filling the gap in the record from the time the motion is filed to the time it is heard. Although not stated in Subsections (c) and (d), it is reasonable to assume that the payment record presented by either the movant or respondent will be one that passes the scrutiny of the court as being, in some manner, an "official" record (as under §234.009 *infra*).

Subsection (d) provides an obligor in arrears on the child support order with an opportunity to avoid a finding of contempt by appearing at a hearing on a motion for enforcement with a payment record or other evidence showing that the obligor was at that time current in payments of support—no matter how many times before, or for how long the obligor had violated the court's support order. In 2009, this section was further amended to provide under Subsection (e) that although the obligor may escape being found in contempt for failing to pay support as ordered, the court may yet award the petitioner in the motion for enforcement court costs and reasonable attorney fees, but only if the obligor was not current in support on the date the motion was filed and the obligor paid the support arrearages after being served notice of the motion or otherwise knew the motion had been filed. Thus, it is left to the threat of legal action to coerce compliance. An obligee who has engaged an attorney and paid some amount of fees will not be recompensed if the obligor had posted a check in the mail before a motion for enforcement had been filed. It seems that under §157.167(a) the court may still order payment of attorney's fees and court costs on a finding that the obligor failed to make ordered child support payments, notwithstanding the fact that the respondent appears at a hearing on a motion for enforcement with evidence of then being current in paying support. (*A.G.K. and H.P.S.*)

Leading Case

In re Ezukanma, 336 S.W.3d 389 (Tex. App.–Fort Worth 2011) (avoidance of contempt for nonpayment under (d) based on obligor's response to make missed payments in full, albeit late, reflects legislature's favoring $$ over punishment) (court may award the petitioner costs and attorney's under (e) when obligor pays up late after contempt sought)

§ 157.163. Appointment of Attorney

(a) In a motion for enforcement or motion to revoke community service, the court must first determine whether incarceration of the respondent is a possible result of the proceedings.

(b) If the court determines that incarceration is a possible result of the proceedings, the court shall inform a respondent not represented by an attorney of the right to be represented by an attorney and, if the respondent is indigent, of the right to the appointment of an attorney.

(c) If the court determines that the respondent will not be incarcerated as a result of the proceedings, the court may require a respondent who is indigent to proceed without an attorney.

(d) If the respondent claims indigency and requests the appointment of an attorney, the court shall require the respondent to file an affidavit of indigency. The court may hear evidence to determine the issue of indigency.

(e) Except as provided by Subsection (c), the court shall appoint an attorney to represent the respondent if the court determines that the respondent is indigent.

(f) If the respondent is not in custody, an appointed attorney is entitled to not less than 10 days from the date of the attorney's appointment to respond to the movant's pleadings and prepare for the hearing.

(g) If the respondent is in custody, an appointed attorney is entitled to not less than five days from the date the respondent was taken into custody to respond to the movant's pleadings and prepare for the hearing.

(h) The court may shorten or extend the time for preparation if the respondent and the respondent's attorney sign a waiver of the time limit.

(i) The scope of the court appointment of an attorney to represent the respondent is limited to the allegation of contempt or of violation of community supervision contained in the motion for enforcement or motion to revoke community supervision.

§ 157.164. Payment of Appointed Attorney

(a) An attorney appointed to represent an indigent respondent is entitled to a reasonable fee for services within the scope of the appointment in the amount set by the court.

(b) The fee shall be paid from the general funds of the county according to the schedule for the compensation of counsel appointed to defend criminal defendants as provided in the Code of Criminal Procedure.

(c) For purposes of this section, a proceeding in a court of appeals or the Supreme Court of Texas is considered the equivalent of a bona fide appeal to the Texas Court of Criminal Appeals.

§ 157.165. Probation of Contempt Order

The court may place the respondent on community supervision and suspend commitment if the court finds that the respondent is in contempt of court for failure or refusal to obey an order rendered as provided in this title.

§ 157.166. Contents of Enforcement Order

(a) An enforcement order must include:

(1) in ordinary and concise language the provisions of the order for which enforcement was requested;

(2) the acts or omissions that are the subject of the order;

(3) the manner of the respondent's noncompliance; and

(4) the relief granted by the court.

(b) If the order imposes incarceration or a fine for criminal contempt, an enforcement order must contain findings identifying, setting out, or incorporating by reference the provisions of the order for which enforcement was requested and the date of each occasion when the respondent's failure to comply with the order was found to constitute criminal contempt.

(c) If the enforcement order imposes incarceration for civil contempt, the order must state the specific conditions on which the respondent may be released from confinement.

§ 157.167. Respondent to Pay Attorney's Fees and Costs

(a) If the court finds that the respondent has failed to make child support payments, the court shall order the respondent to pay the movant's reasonable attorney's fees and all court costs in addition to the arrearages. Fees and costs ordered under this subsection may be enforced by any means available for the enforcement of child support, including contempt.

(b) If the court finds that the respondent has failed to comply with the terms of an order providing for the possession of or access to a child, the court shall order the respondent to pay the movant's reasonable attorney's fees and all court costs in addition to any other remedy. If the court finds that the enforcement of the order with which the respondent failed to comply was necessary to ensure the child's physical or emotional health or welfare, the fees and costs ordered under this subsection may be enforced by any means available for the enforcement of child support, including contempt, but not including income withholding.

(c) Except as provided by Subsection (d), for good cause shown, the court may waive the requirement that the respondent pay attorney's fees and costs if the court states the reasons supporting that finding.

(d) If the court finds that the respondent is in contempt of court for failure or refusal to pay child support and that the respondent owes $20,000 or more in child support arrearages, the court may not waive the requirement that the respondent pay attorney's fees and costs unless the court also finds that the respondent:

(1) is involuntarily unemployed or is disabled; and

(2) lacks the financial resources to pay the attorney's fees and costs.

Comment

This section includes attorney fees and costs in the enforcement of an order for possession or access, if that enforcement is necessary for the child's well-being. All of the enforcement remedies available for the enforcement of child support may be applied, except for income withholding. Under the exception to the state constitutional prohibition against garnishment of wages, TEX. CONST. art. 16, § 28, income withholding is limited to the enforcement of child support and spousal maintenance. Although contempt is readily available, totally clear directions are not supplied on how the other child support enforcement remedies might be employed. The child support lien and levy processes in Subchapter G of this chapter, and license suspension in Chapter 232, do not contain conforming amendments to the pertinent code provisions. Nonetheless, collecting attorney fees and costs is not fundamentally different than collecting current and past due child support. In fact, these sums may be viewed as an integral aspect of the child support obligation.

At one time a trial judge had considerable latitude to find good cause for not requiring a respondent to pay attorney fees and costs as ordered under this section. In 2003 the discretion of the court was significantly abridged by requiring payment of the fees and costs if the respondent has been found in contempt for failure or refusal to pay support and owes support arrearages of $20,000 or more. Even under those circumstances, the court may waive the requirement upon finding that the respondent was unable to pay the fees and costs for reasons similar to the affirmative defense under § 157.008 to a motion for enforcement. *(A.G.K. & H.P.S.)*

Leading Cases

In re A.C.J., 146 S.W.3d 323 (Tex. App.—Beaumont 2004, no pet.) (child support obligee entitled to attorney's fee both for support and for defending against claim unrelated to support enforcement)

In re Villanueva, 56 S.W.3d 905 (Tex. App.—Houston [1st Dist.] 2001, no pet.) (contempt is one appropriate means to enforce fees and costs in child support case, but trial court abused discretion in setting huge cost bond)

---

§ 157.168. Additional Periods of Possession or Access

(a) A court may order additional periods of possession of or access to a child to compensate for the denial of court-ordered possession or access. The additional periods of possession or access:

(1) must be of the same type and duration of the possession or access that was denied;

(2) may include weekend, holiday, and summer possession or access; and

(3) must occur on or before the second anniversary of the date the court finds that court-ordered possession or access has been denied.

(b) The person denied possession or access is entitled to decide the time of the additional possession or access, subject to the provisions of Subsection (a)(1).

Comment

Make-up visitation long has been a goal for noncustodial parents, many of whom have testified to the legislature about unjustified denials of court-ordered possession. Specifying the details of how make-up time is to be computed and exercised seems logical. But keeping track of alleged violations and a make-up schedule will be a daunting task to any court that actually becomes involved in trying to enforce this provision. In short, while this may be a good idea theoretically, absent voluntary compliance by apparently hostile parties it will be very difficult to implement, especially given the costs to enforce.

SUBCHAPTER E. COMMUNITY SUPERVISION

§ 157.211. Conditions of Community Supervision

If the court places the respondent on community supervision and suspends commitment, the terms and conditions of community supervision may include the requirement that the respondent:

(1) report to the community supervision officer as directed;

(2) permit the community supervision officer to visit the respondent at the respondent's home or elsewhere;

(3) obtain counseling on financial planning, budget management, conflict resolution, parenting skills, alcohol or drug abuse, or other matters causing the respondent to fail to obey the order;

(4) pay required child support and any child support arrearages;

(5) pay court costs and attorney's fees ordered by the court;

(6) seek employment assistance services offered by the Texas Workforce Commission under Section 302.0035, Labor Code, if appropriate; and

(7) participate in mediation or other services to alleviate conditions that prevent the respondent from obeying the court's order.

§ 157.212. Term of Community Supervision

The initial period of community supervision may not exceed 10 years. The court may continue the community supervision beyond 10 years until the earlier of:

(1) the second anniversary of the date on which the community supervision first exceeded 10 years; or

(2) the date on which all child support, including arrearages and interest, has been paid.

Comment

This section allows the court to extend the period of community service if child support arrears remained unpaid at the end of the initial period of ten years. A possible additional two years of community service likely will not make much difference to obligors who are unable to pay off support arrearages within ten years. *(A.G.K. & H.P.S.)*

---

§ 157.213. Community Supervision Fees

(a) The court may require the respondent to pay a fee to the court in an amount equal to that required of a criminal defendant subject to community supervision.

(b) The court may make payment of the fee a condition of granting or continuing community supervision.

(c) The court shall deposit the fees received under this subchapter as follows:

(1) if the community supervision officer is employed by a community supervision and corrections department, in the special fund of the county treasury provided by the Code of Criminal Procedure to be used for community supervision; or

(2) if the community supervision officer is employed by a domestic relations office, in one of the following funds, as determined by the office's administering entity:

(A) the general fund for the county in which the domestic relations office is located; or

(B) the office fund established by the administering entity for the domestic relations office.

§ 157.214. Motion to Revoke Community Supervision

A prosecuting attorney, the Title IV-D agency, a domestic relations office, or a party affected by the order may file a verified motion alleging specifically that certain conduct of the respondent constitutes a violation of the terms and conditions of community supervision.

§ 157.215. Arrest for Alleged Violation of Community Supervision

(a) If the motion to revoke community supervision alleges a prima facie case that the respondent has violated a term or condition of community supervision, the court may order the respondent's arrest by warrant.

(b) The respondent shall be brought promptly before the court ordering the arrest.

§ 157.216. Hearing on Motion to Revoke Community Supervision

(a) The court shall hold a hearing without a jury not later than the third working day after the date the respondent is arrested under Section 157.215. If the court is unavailable for a hearing on that date, the hearing shall be held not later than the third working day after the date the court becomes available.

(b) The hearing under this section may not be held later than the seventh working day after the date the respondent is arrested.

(c) After the hearing, the court may continue, modify, or revoke the community supervision.

§ 157.217. Discharge From Community Supervision

(a) When a community supervision period has been satisfactorily completed, the court on its own motion shall discharge the respondent from community supervision.

(b) The court may discharge the respondent from community supervision on the motion of the respondent if the court finds that the respondent:

(1) has satisfactorily completed one year of community supervision; and

(2) has fully complied with the community supervision order.

SUBCHAPTER F. JUDGMENT AND INTEREST

Introductory Comment

Since the Family Code was enacted, a support obligee has had the option to seek a money judgment for delinquent child support. This subchapter continues this remedy with quite a number of alterations to the original version. Most importantly, it is now the duty of a court to render a money judgment for proven arrears; the court does not have the authority to order a retroactive modification of the accrued obligation. This is a nationwide rule: the U.S. Congress directed that child support orders must be final and not retroactively modifiable if a state desires federal financial assistance to enforce child support, 42 U.S.C. § 666(a)(9) ("the Bradley Amendment").

This subchapter adds, or at least clarifies, yet another remedy to the ever growing arsenal for enforcement of child support orders. In 1993 the complexity of calculating compound interest implicit in the prior statute was removed by providing for 12% simple interest, which apparently seemed reasonable at the time. But time has proved otherwise. In 2001 the legislature determined that imposing an interest rate on unpaid child support arrears far beyond market rate was counterproductive. That approach may well have resulted in a greater level of noncompliance. Accordingly, the legislature reduced the future interest rate to a more reasonable 6%, *see* § 157.265. The conflict between the various interest rates is hopefully resolved by Section 157.265.

Effective January 1, 2002, the interest rate charged on child support arrears was reduced from 12 percent to 6 percent for every child support payment that became due on or after the effective date, and for all existing, but unconfirmed support arrears. It did not, however, affect the rate—12 percent simple—for an existing judgment on such arrears. In effect, the stated interest rate on the judgment was res judicata. A cumulative money judgment under Section 157.263, however, rendered on or after the effective date, reduced the 12 percent interest rate to 6 percent on any balance owed under an existing judgment. In an effort to eliminate any confusion that the change of rates has caused,

Section 157.265 was further amended in 2005 to make clear that any unconfirmed child support arrearages owed before January 1, 2002, accrue interest at the rate in effect at the time the child support payment became delinquent, and that any unpaid balance of child support (including interest) owed on January 1, 2002 accrues interest at the 6 percent rate from that date forward. A money judgment for child support rendered before January 1, 2002 is subject to the rate in effect at the time the judgment was rendered, while a money judgment for child support rendered on or after that date is subject to the new rate. *(A.G.K. & H.P.S.)*

CLE/Other Legal Publications

Child support. Kyle W. Sanders, 2011 Adv. Fam. L.

Primer on child support calculation and collection. Angela G. Pence England, 2011 U.T. Parent-Child Relationships: Basics

Child support. Angela Stout, 2011 So. Tex. Fam. L.

Creative approaches to child support. Jack W. Marr, 2010 Adv. Fam. L.

SAPCR caselaw update. Eva Guzman, 2010 Adv. Fam. L.

Hidden child support resources. Patricia A. Wicoff, 2010 U.T. Parent-Child Relationships

Advocating and defending unusual child support requests. Cindy Venise Tisdale, 2010 U.T. Fam. L. Front Lines

Collecting child support. Cindy V. Tisdale, 2010 Adv. Fam. L.

Obtaining child support. Barry J. Brooks & Karen L. Marvel, 2009 U.T. Parent-Child Relationships

Versus the AG: why can't we just get along? Alicia G. Key, Jack W. Marr, 2009 Adv. Fam. L.

AG Office: things you should know. Cynthia J. Barela & Laura D. Hamilton, 2009 U.T. Fam. L. Front Lines

Creative ways to collect and defend child support claims. Karen L. Marvel, 2009 Marriage Dissolution

Child support workshop: UIFSA, above guideline child support, effective use of financial documents, utilization of QDRO's and child support liens; enforcement techniques. (Panel), 2009 Adv. Fam. L.

Leading Cases

Arrearage Judgment

Williams v. Patton, 821 S.W.2d 141 (Tex. 1991) (settlement of claim for child support arrears must be approved by court)

Huff v. Huff, 648 S.W.2d 286 (Tex. 1983) (pre-statute disapproval of automatic judgments for arrears)

In re M.K.R., 216 S.W.3d 58 (Tex. App.—Fort Worth 2007, no pet.) (determination of arrearage is res judicata)

Beck v. Walker, 154 S.W.3d 895 (Tex. App.—Dallas 2005, no pet.) (court cannot reduce or modify arrearage amount in action to enforce payment of child support)

Interest

In re M.C.C., 187 S.W.3d 383 (Tex. 2006) (statutory amendment to interest rate on child support arrearages not retroactive)

Cross Reference

IV–D Enforcement Procedures. 42 U.S.C.A. § 666(a)(9)

§ 157.261. Unpaid Child Support as Judgment

(a) A child support payment not timely made constitutes a final judgment for the amount due and owing, including interest as provided in this chapter.

(b) For the purposes of this subchapter, interest begins to accrue on the date the judge signs the order for the judgment unless the order contains a statement that the order is rendered on another specific date.

§ 157.262. ~~Reduction of Arrearages; Abeyance of Enforcement~~

~~(a) Except as provided by this section, in a contempt proceeding or in rendering a money judgment, the court may not reduce or modify the amount of child support arrearages.~~

~~(b) In an enforcement action under this chapter, the court may, with the agreement of the Title IV-D agency, hold in abeyance the enforcement of any arrearages, including interest, assigned to the Title IV-D agency under Section 231.104(a) if, for the period of the court's order of abeyance of enforcement, the obligor:~~

~~(1) timely and fully pays the obligor's current child support under a court or administrative order; and~~

~~(2) is involved in the life of the child for whom support is ordered through the exercise of the obligor's right of possession of or access to the child.~~

~~(c) If the court orders an abeyance of enforcement of arrearages under this section, the court may require the obligor to obtain counseling on parenting skills, work skills, job placement, financial planning, conflict resolution, substance abuse, or other matters causing the obligor to fail to obey the child support order.~~

~~(d) If the court finds in a subsequent hearing that the obligor has not met the conditions set by the court's order under this section, the court shall terminate the abeyance of enforcement of the arrearages.~~

~~(e) On the expiration of the child support order, the court may, with the agreement of the Title IV-D agency, reduce the amount of the arrearages assigned to the Title IV-D agency under Section 231.104(a) if the court finds that the obligor has complied with the conditions set by the court under this section.~~

~~(f) The money judgment for arrearages rendered by the court may be subject to a counterclaim or offset as provided by this title.~~

Repealed by Acts 2011, 82nd Leg., ch. 508 (H.B. 1674), § 24, eff. Sept. 1, 2011

Editors' Note: *See* Section 157.263(b–1) and accompanying comment, *infra*, for basis of repeal of this section.

§ 157.263. Confirmation of Arrearages

(a) If a motion for enforcement of child support requests a money judgment for arrearages, the court shall confirm the amount of arrearages and render one cumulative money judgment.

(b) A cumulative money judgment includes:

(1) unpaid child support not previously confirmed;

(2) the balance owed on previously confirmed arrearages or lump sum or retroactive support judgments;

(3) interest on the arrearages; and

(4) a statement that it is a cumulative judgment.

(b–1) In rendering a money judgment under this section, the court may not reduce or modify the amount of child support arrearages but, in confirming the amount of arrearages, may allow a counterclaim or offset as provided by this title.

(c) If the amount of arrearages confirmed by the court reflects a credit to the obligor for support arrearages collected from a federal tax refund under 42 U.S.C. Section 664, and, subsequently, the amount of that credit is reduced because the refund was adjusted because of an injured spouse claim by a jointly filing spouse, the tax return was amended, the return was audited by the Internal Revenue Service, or for another reason permitted by law, the court shall render a new cumulative judgment to include as arrearages an amount equal to the amount by which the credit was reduced.

Amended by Acts 2011, 82nd Leg., ch. 508 (H.B. 1674), § 5, eff. Sept. 1, 2011.

Comment

Subsection (c) relates to the use of an enforcement remedy available only in cases enforced by the IV–D agency; that is, through interception of federal income tax refunds under 42 U.S.C. 664 for payment of past due child support. The IV–D agency certifies to the Secretary of the Treasury the names of support obligors owing past due support and the amounts owed. An allegedly delinquent obligor has an opportunity for contest. In turn, Treasury deducts from income tax refunds that are due delinquent obligors amounts equal to the past due support they owe and forwards those amounts to appropriate state IV–D agencies. If a joint return has been filed, the obligor's innocent spouse is afforded an opportunity to claim an appropriate share of the refund. The obligor may, however, already have received credit under a cumulative money judgment for the full amount of the refund. Should that happen, the court must, upon request, render a new cumulative judgment that does not include any of the refund ultimately paid to the obligor's innocent spouse.

This section includes other circumstances in which a credit provided an obligor through an IRS refund was reduced subsequent to the confirmation of arrearages. Besides an injured spouse claim, the amount of refund actually available to the obligor might have been reduced through an IRS audit of the tax return or the filing of an amended return, among other possibilities.

In 2011 the legislature added Subsection (b–1) which was intended to capture two important elements in repealed §157.262 (Reduction of Arrearages; Abeyance of Enforcement). The first, under repealed §157.262(a), is the federal prohibition on retroactive modification of a child support obligation—the "Bradley Amendment" enacted by Congress under the Omnibus Budget Reconciliation Act of 1986 [P.L. 99–509; codified at 42 U.S.C. §666(a)(9)]. The second element was contained in repealed §157.262(f) which provided that a money judgment for arrearages may be subject to a counterclaim or offset, although the amending language in Subsection (b–1) may suggest that any counterclaim or offset may be allowed before the court has actually rendered judgment—which is not the intent of the provision. *(A.G.K. & H.P.S.)*

Leading Cases

In re B.A.C., 144 S.W.3d 8 (Tex. App.—Waco 2004, no pet.) (mother entitled to judgment for child support arrears accumulated prior to child living with maternal grandfather/managing conservator)

In re Gonzalez, 981 S.W.2d 313 (Tex. App.—San Antonio 1998, no pet.) (obligee entitled to have arrearages reduced to judgment)

---

§ 157.264. Enforcement of Judgment

(a) A money judgment rendered as provided in this subchapter may be enforced by any means available for the enforcement of a judgment for debts.

(b) The court shall render an order requiring that the obligor make periodic payments on the judgment, including by income withholding under Chapter 158 if the obligor is subject to income withholding.

(c) An order rendered under Subsection (b) does not preclude or limit the use of any other means for enforcement of the judgment.

Comment

Income withholding is an especially effective enforcement mechanism in the collection of child support arrearages, as well as current support. Not all child support obligors, however, have incomes subject to withholding for child support. The section specifically requires, rather than authorizes, the court to order periodic payments on a money judgment for arrearages, even if income withholding is not an available enforcement remedy. The 2009 addition of Subsection (c) seeks to address a too narrow reading of Subsection (b) by indicating that an income withholding order was not an exclusive mechanism for enforcing a cumulative money judgment for support. *(A.G.K. & H.P.S.)*

---

§ 157.265. Accrual of Interest on Child Support

(a) Interest accrues on the portion of delinquent child support that is greater than the amount of the monthly periodic support obligation at the rate of six percent simple interest per year from the date the support is delinquent until the date the support is paid or the arrearages are confirmed and reduced to money judgment.

(b) Interest accrues on child support arrearages that have been confirmed and reduced to money judgment as provided in this subchapter at the rate of six percent simple interest per year from the date the order is rendered until the date the judgment is paid.

(c) Interest accrues on a money judgment for retroactive or lump-sum child support at the annual rate of six percent simple interest from the date the order is rendered until the judgment is paid.

(d) Subsection (a) applies to a child support payment that becomes due on or after January 1, 2002.

(e) Child support arrearages in existence on January 1, 2002, that were not confirmed and reduced to a money judgment on or before that date accrue interest as follows:

(1) before January 1, 2002, the arrearages are subject to the interest rate that applied to the arrearages before that date; and

(2) on and after January 1, 2002, the cumulative total of arrearages and interest accumulated on those arrearages described by Subdivision (1) is subject to Subsection (a).

(f) Subsections (b) and (c) apply to a money judgment for child support rendered on or after January 1, 2002. A money judgment for child support rendered before that date is governed by the law in effect on the date the judgment was rendered, and the former law is continued in effect for that purpose.

Comment

In 2001, the legislature amended this section to change the rate of interest on unpaid child support from 12 percent to 6 percent. The intent of the legislature was that the new rate be applied prospectively to unpaid child support accruing after January 1, 2002. The wording of the effective date provisions of the 2001 amendment, however, quickly gave rise to disagreement not only among members of the bar, but also among appellate courts as to the application of the new 6 percent rate. In 2005, the legislature further amended the section by adding Subsections (d)–(f) to make clear to all that any unconfirmed child support arrearages owed *before* January 1, 2002 accrue interest at the rate in effect at the time the child support payment became delinquent and that any unpaid balance of child support (including interest) owed on January 1, 2002 accrues interest at the 6 percent rate from that date forward. A money judgment for child support rendered before January 1, 2002 is subject to the rate in effect at the time the judgment was rendered, while a money judgment for child support rendered on or after that date is subject to the new rate.

Subsection (a) provides that a full month's child support must be delinquent before interest accrues, regardless of the frequency of support payments over the course of a month (*e.g.*, biweekly). Subsection (c) extends the principle that interest is due on the principal even when acquired by a retroactive lump-sum award. *(A.G.K. & H.P.S.)*

Leading Case

In re M.C.C., 187 S.W.3d 383 (Tex. 2006) (statutory amendment to interest rate on child support arrearages not retroactive)

---

§ 157.266. Date of Delinquency

(a) A child support payment is delinquent for the purpose of accrual of interest if the payment is not received before the 31st day after the payment date stated in the order by:

(1) the local registry, Title IV-D registry, or state disbursement unit; or

(2) the obligee or entity specified in the order, if payments are not made through a registry.

(b) If a payment date is not stated in the order, a child support payment is delinquent if payment is not received by the registry or the obligee or entity specified in the order on the date that an amount equal to the support payable for one month becomes past due.

§ 157.267. Interest Enforced as Child Support

Accrued interest is part of the child support obligation and may be enforced by any means provided for the collection of child support.

§ 157.268. Application of Child Support Payment

Child support collected shall be applied in the following order of priority:

(1) current child support;

(2) non-delinquent child support owed;

(3) the principal amount of child support that has not been confirmed and reduced to money judgment;

(4) the principal amount of child support that has been confirmed and reduced to money judgment;

(5) interest on the principal amounts specified in Subdivisions (3) and (4); and

(6) the amount of any ordered attorney's fees or costs, or Title IV–D service fees authorized under Section 231.103 for which the obligor is responsible.

Comment

The purpose of this section is to provide an equitable ordering of priorities in the application of a child support payment. Because the primary intent of a child support payment is to recompense the obligee for the costs of maintaining the child, attorney's fees or costs are last in the application of a payment and will be paid (when collected as part of the child support obligation) only after all amounts due the obligee have been paid.

A 2009 amendment dramatically changed the ordering of priorities by placing payment on accrued interest below payment on principal. This reflected a significant shift in public policy by an acknowledgment that obligors—particularly low-income obligors—are caught in paying off great amounts of support interest over lengthy periods of time before they can ever begin to effectively reduce the principal amount of support owed. In sum, a payment goes to current support, then to past-due child support, and only finally to interest on the arrears. *(A.G.K. & H.P.S.)*

§ 157.269. Retention of Jurisdiction

A court that renders an order providing for the payment of child support retains continuing jurisdiction to enforce the order, including by adjusting the amount of the periodic payments to be made by the obligor or the amount to be withheld from the obligor's disposable earnings, until all current support and medical support and child support arrearages, including interest and any applicable fees and costs, have been paid.

Comment

Unless otherwise provided by this Code, this section provides a court that rendered a support order retains jurisdiction to enforce the order until the support obligation has been fully satisfied, and that the amounts of periodic payments on current support or arrearages may be "adjusted" in subsequent enforcement actions. Thus, the support order does not act as res judicata with respect to subsequent action to enforce the order—such as a federal income tax intercept, income withholding orders, or lien and levy. In other words, the amounts of periodic payments on arrearages identified in the original support order are not "fixed" as though they were installment payments on a money judgment. While the time limitations under § 157.005 affect the jurisdiction of the court to render a judgment for past due support, the provisions of this section make clear that the court continues to have jurisdiction to enforce a judgment for past due support until the total amount has been paid by the obligor. In 2009, the legislature amended Section 34.001 of the Civil Practice and Remedies Code, to clarify that the judgment dormancy provisions of that code do not apply to a judgment for child support under the Family Code. Hence, no limitations are imposed on the jurisdiction of the court to enforce a judgment for accrued arrearages and interest on a child-support order. *(A.G.K. & H.P.S.)*

SUBCHAPTER G. CHILD SUPPORT LIEN

Introductory Comment

Since 1984, federal law has required states to have statutory procedures for imposing liens on the real or personal property of an obligor for past-due child support. The "Personal Responsibility and Work Opportunity Reconciliation Act of 1996" (PRWORA) extended the lien requirements to mandate that liens for child support must arise by operation of law and that liens arising in one state may be enforced in any other state in accordance with the procedural rules of the other state. Also, under PRWORA, state Title IV–D agencies must have the authority to take administrative action to attach and seize assets of an obligor held in financial institutions, to attach public and private retirement funds of an obligor, to impose liens and, in appropriate cases, to force sale of property and distribution of proceeds.

The lien process contains very specific procedures for execution and levy on the financial assets of an obligor. Virtually every financial asset of a delinquent obligor may be subject to levy—not just depository accounts, but also proceeds of life insurance policies, retirement accounts owned by the obligor, insurance settlements or awards for negligent torts or personal injury, or even workers' compensation due the obligor. Together, the lien and levy processes constitute a very effective mechanism for the enforcement of past due child support and, like license suspension, are particularly valuable in cases in which the obligor has income not subject to withholding, e.g., professionals and the self-employed. *(A.G.K. & H.P.S.)*

Leading Case

Dryden v. Dryden, 97 S.W.3d 863 (Tex. App.—Corpus Christi 2003, pet. denied) (exempt protection of certain personal property not applicable to collection of child support; constitutional because "it's not a debt")

§ 157.311. Definitions

In this subchapter:

(1) "Account" means:

(A) any type of a demand deposit account, checking or negotiable withdrawal order account, savings account, time deposit account, ~~money market~~ mutual fund account, certificate of deposit, or any other instrument of deposit in which an individual has a beneficial ownership either in its entirety or on a shared or multiple party basis, including any accrued interest and dividends; and

(B) **an** ~~a life~~ insurance policy**, including a life insurance policy or annuity contract,** in which an individual has a beneficial ownership or ~~liability insurance~~ against which an individual **may file** ~~has filed~~ a claim or counterclaim.

(2) "Claimant" means:

(A) the obligee or a private attorney representing the obligee;

(B) the Title IV-D agency providing child support services;

(C) a domestic relations office or local registry; or

(D) an attorney appointed as a friend of the court.

(3) "Court having continuing jurisdiction" is the court of continuing, exclusive jurisdiction in this state or a tribunal of another state having jurisdiction under the Uniform Interstate Family Support Act or a substantially similar act.

(4) "Financial institution" has the meaning assigned by 42 U.S.C. Section 669a(d)(1) and includes a depository institution, **depository institution holding company as defined by 12 U.S.C. Section 1813(w),** credit union, benefit association, ~~liability or life~~insurance company, ~~money market~~mutual fund, and any similar entity authorized to do business in this state.

(5) "Lien" means a child support lien issued in this or another state.

Amended by Acts 2011, 82nd Leg., ch. 508 (H.B. 1674), § 6, eff. Sept. 1, 2011.

Comment

As a replacement for lost earned income, workers' compensation benefits are available for child support only through an order or writ of income withholding under Chapter 158, as provided by TEX. LAB. CODE § 408.203(b).

§ 157.312. General Provisions

(a) A claimant may enforce child support by a lien as provided in this subchapter.

(b) The remedies provided by this subchapter do not affect the availability of other remedies provided by law.

(c) The lien is in addition to any other lien provided by law.

(d) A child support lien arises by operation of law against real and personal property of an obligor for all amounts of child support due and owing, including any accrued interest, regardless of whether the amounts have been adjudicated or otherwise determined, subject to the requirements of this subchapter for perfection of the lien.

(e) A child support lien arising in another state may be enforced in the same manner and to the same extent as a lien arising in this state.

(f) A foreclosure action under this subchapter is not required as a prerequisite to levy and execution on a judicial or administrative determination of arrearages as provided by Section 157.327.

(g) A child support lien under this subchapter may not be directed to an employer to attach to the disposable earnings of an obligor paid by the employer.

Comment

The lien process is not an exclusive remedy, but may be used in concert with other procedures for enforcement of arrearages, including income withholding and license suspension. A specific lien, however, applies not just to the amount of arrearages in existence at the time the lien notice is issued and the lien is perfected, but to all arrearages that accrue up to the time of foreclosure or execution and levy. Moreover, levy and execution may proceed based upon either a judicial or, in Title IV–D cases, an administrative determination of the arrearages, without the requirement of a foreclosure hearing. Subsection (g) clarifies that a child support lien may not be used in place of an order or writ of income withholding. *(A.G.K., & H.P.S.)*

§ 157.313. Contents of Child Support Lien Notice

(a) Except as provided by Subsection (e), a child support lien notice must contain:

(1) the name and address of the person to whom the notice is being sent;

(2) the style, docket or cause number, and identity of the tribunal of this or another state having continuing jurisdiction of the child support action and, if the case is a Title IV–D case, the case number;

(3) the full name, address, and, if known, the birth date, driver's license number, social security number, and any aliases of the obligor;

(4) the full name and, if known, social security number of the obligee;

(5) the amount of the current or prospective child support obligation, the frequency with which current or prospective child support is ordered to be paid, and the amount of child support arrearages owed by the obligor and the date of the signing of the court order, administrative order, or writ that determined the arrearages or the date and manner in which the arrearages were determined;

(6) the rate of interest specified in the court order, administrative order, or writ or, in the absence of a specified interest rate, the rate provided for by law;

(7) the name and address of the person or agency asserting the lien;

(8) the motor vehicle identification number as shown on the obligor's title if the property is a motor vehicle;

(9) a statement that the lien attaches to all nonexempt real and personal property of the obligor that is located or recorded in the state, including any property specifically identified in the notice and any property acquired after the date of filing or delivery of the notice;

(10) a statement that any ordered child support not timely paid in the future constitutes a final judgment for the amount due and owing, including interest, and accrues up to an amount that may not exceed the lien amount; and

(11) a statement that the obligor is being provided a copy of the lien notice and that the obligor may dispute the arrearage amount by filing suit under Section 157.323.

(b) A claimant may include any other information that the claimant considers necessary.

(c) Except as provided by Subsection (e), the lien notice must be verified.

(d) A claimant must file a notice for each after-acquired motor vehicle.

(e) A notice of a lien for child support under this section may be in the form authorized by federal law or regulation. The federal form of lien notice does not require verification when used by the Title IV–D agency.

(f) The requirement under Subsections (a)(3) and (4) to provide a social security number, if known, does not apply to a lien notice for a lien on real property.

Comment

Notice of a child support lien states the amount of arrearages owed at the time the notice is filed or delivered, by whatever means that amount was determined. The lien also prospectively engages the possibility of a greater amount of arrearages being owed at the time of foreclosure on the lien or, in the case of financial assets, execution and levy. Subsection (a)(9) provides the lien attaches to all after acquired nonexempt property of the obligor. Subsection (f) also removes the requirement that the social security numbers of the obligee and obligor, if known, be recorded on a lien notice for a lien on real property, thereby protecting that personal information from disclosure in the public records of the county clerk's office in which the lien notice is filed *(A.G.K. & H.P.S.)*

§ 157.314. Filing Lien Notice or Abstract of Judgment; Notice to Obligor

(a) A child support lien notice or an abstract of judgment for past due child support may be filed by the claimant with the county clerk of:

(1) any county in which the obligor is believed to own nonexempt real or personal property;

(2) the county in which the obligor resides; or

(3) the county in which the court having continuing jurisdiction has venue of the suit affecting the parent-child relationship.

(b) A child support lien notice may be filed with or delivered to the following, as appropriate:

(1) the clerk of the court in which a claim, counterclaim, or suit by, or on behalf of, the obligor, including a claim or potential right to proceeds from an estate as an heir, beneficiary, or creditor, is pending, provided that a copy of the lien is mailed to the attorney of record for the obligor, if any;

(2) an attorney who represents the obligor in a claim or counterclaim that has not been filed with a court;

(3) any other individual or organization believed to be in possession of real or personal property of the obligor; or

(4) any governmental unit or agency that issues or records certificates, titles, or other indicia of property ownership.

(c) Not later than the 21st day after the date of filing or delivering the child support lien notice, the claimant shall provide a copy of the notice to the obligor by first class or certified mail, return receipt requested, addressed to the obligor at the obligor's last known address. If another person is known to have an ownership interest in the property subject to the lien, the claimant shall provide a copy of the lien notice to that person at the time notice is provided to the obligor.

(d) If a child support lien notice is delivered to a financial institution with respect to an account of the obligor, the institution shall immediately:

(1) provide the claimant with the last known address of the obligor; and

(2) notify any other person having an ownership interest in the account that the account has been frozen in an amount not to exceed the amount of the child support arrearage identified in the notice.

Comment

As specified in this section, the filing or delivery of a lien notice has the effect of perfecting the lien. In the case of a financial institution, this means that all assets of the obligor held by that institution are frozen up to the amount stated in the lien notice. This does not mean, however, that a greater amount may not finally be subject to levy. At the time of levy, the amount subject to seizure is the amount determined by the court or the Title IV–D agency to be the arrearages owed at that point—which may be greater or lesser than the amount stated in the lien notice. The claimant is responsible for sending a copy of the lien notice to any known co-owners of the property affected by the lien, as well as to the obligor at a last known address. If the property is an account in a financial institution which may be levied upon, the institution must provide the claimant with the obligor's last known address, in addition to notifying any co-owner of the account. Presumably a financial institution knows who the owners and co-owners of accounts are and has their correct addresses. *(A.G.K. & H.P.S.)*

§ 157.3145. Service on Financial Institution

(a) Service of a child support lien notice on a financial institution relating to property held by the institution in the name of, or in behalf of, an obligor is governed by Section 59.008, Finance Code, if the institution is subject to that law, or may be delivered to the registered agent, the institution's main business office in this state, or another address provided by the institution under Section 231.307.

(b) A financial institution doing business in this state shall comply with the notice of lien and levy under this section regardless of whether the institution's corporate headquarters is located in this state.

Comment

This section allows service on a financial institution not just at an in state location, but also at any out of state location designated by the institution, such as a central administrative office maintained by a multi-state institution in another state. Moreover, with respect to compliance with a notice of lien and levy it does not matter that the corporate headquarters of a financial institution doing business in this state are located out of state. This section also connects the lien and levy processes under this subchapter with the financial institution data matches—including matches with multi state institutions—required of the Title IV–D agency under § 231.307. It means, finally, that the Title IV–D agency in particular may go after the financial assets of a delinquent obligor wherever they may be located—at least in the United States. *(A.G.K., & H.P.S.)*

§ 157.315. Recording and Indexing Lien

(a) On receipt of a child support lien notice, the county clerk shall immediately record the notice in the county judgment records as provided in Chapter 52, Property Code.

(b) The county clerk may not charge the Title IV-D agency, a domestic relations office, a friend of the court, or any other party a fee for recording the notice of a lien. To qualify for this exemption, the lien notice must be styled "Notice of Child Support Lien" or be in the form authorized by federal law or regulation.

(c) The county clerk may not charge the Title IV-D agency, a domestic relations office, or a friend of the court a fee for recording the release of a child support lien. The lien release must be styled "Release of Child Support Lien."

§ 157.316. Perfection of Child Support Lien

(a) Except as provided by Subsection (b), a child support lien is perfected when an abstract of judgment for past due child support or a child support lien notice is filed or delivered as provided by Section 157.314.

(b) If a lien established under this subchapter attaches to a motor vehicle, the lien must be perfected in the manner provided by Chapter 501, Transportation Code, and the court or Title IV–D agency that rendered the order of child support shall include in the order a requirement that the obligor surrender to the court or Title IV–D agency evidence of the legal ownership of the motor vehicle against which the lien may attach. A lien against a motor vehicle under this subchapter is not perfected until the obligor's title to the vehicle has been surrendered to the court or Title IV–D agency and the Texas Department of Motor Vehicles has issued a subsequent title that discloses on its face the fact that the vehicle is subject to a child support lien under this subchapter.

§ 157.317. Property to Which Lien Attaches

(a) A child support lien attaches to all real and personal property not exempt under the Texas Constitution or other law, including:

(1) an account in a financial institution;

(2) a retirement plan, including an individual retirement account; ~~and~~

(3) the proceeds of **an** ~~a life~~ insurance policy, **including the proceeds from a life insurance policy or annuity contract and the proceeds from the sale or assignment of life insurance or annuity benefits,** a claim for **compensation** ~~negligence or personal injury~~, or **a** ~~an insurance~~ settlement or award for the claim **for compensation**, due to or owned by the obligor**; and**

(4) property seized and subject to forfeiture under Chapter 59, Code of Criminal Procedure.

(a–1) A lien attaches to all property owned or acquired on or after the date the lien notice or abstract of judgment is filed with the county clerk of the county in which the property is located, with the court clerk as to property or claims in litigation, or, as to property of the obligor in the possession or control of a third party, from the date the lien notice is delivered to that party.

(b) A lien attaches to all nonhomestead real property of the obligor but does not attach to a homestead exempt under the Texas Constitution or the Property Code.

Amended by Acts 2011, 82nd Leg., ch. 508 (H.B. 1674), § 7, eff. Sept. 1, 2011.

Comment

While this section is broadly cast with respect to the property to which a child support lien may attach, the 'other law' exception under Subsection (a) alludes to the possibility that certain property owned or in the control of an obligor may be exempt from attachment under either state or federal law and, hence, beyond the reach of this enforcement remedy.

In 2011, the legislature both clarified and expanded the items identified under Subsection (a) to which a child support lien may attach. Proceeds from "insurance" now include not just those from life insurance but also those yielded by annuities, as well as proceeds from the sale or assignment of benefits. Moreover, the legislature added §1108.101(b) to the Insurance Code to provide that, if an obligor is subject to a child support lien, benefits from an insurance policy or annuity assigned by the obligor continue to be subject to the lien to secure payment of all support arrearages owed by the obligor, including those which accrue after the date of assignment. Also, in 2011, the legislature extended the child support lien to property seized and subject to forfeiture. Furthermore, the legislature amended Art. 59.06(a), Code of Criminal Procedure, to authorize the distribution to the Title IV-D agency of proceeds from public sale of forfeited property to satisfy a child support lien after appropriate distribution of proceeds is made to any holder of an interest in the property. *(A.G.K. & H.P.S.)*

§ 157.3171. Release of Lien on Homestead Property

(a) An obligor who believes that a child support lien has attached to real property of the obligor that is the obligor's homestead, as defined by Section 41.002, Property Code, may file an affidavit to release the lien against the homestead in the same manner that a judgment debtor may file an affidavit under Section 52.0012, Property Code, to release a judgment lien against a homestead.

(b) Except as provided by Subsection (c), the obligor must comply with all requirements imposed by Section 52.0012, Property Code. For purposes of complying with that section, the obligor is considered to be a judgment debtor under that section and the claimant under the child support lien is considered to be a judgment creditor under that section.

(c) For purposes of Section 52.0012(d)(2), Property Code, and the associated text in the affidavit required by Section 52.0012(f), Property Code, the obligor is required only to send the letter and affidavit described in those provisions to the claimant under the child support lien at the claimant's last known address.

(d) The claimant under the child support lien may dispute the obligor's affidavit by filing a contradicting affidavit in the manner provided by Section 52.0012(e), Property Code.

(e) Subject to Subsection (f), an affidavit filed by an obligor under this section has the same effect with respect to a child support lien as an affidavit filed under Section 52.0012, Property Code, has with respect to a judgment lien.

(f) If the claimant files a contradicting affidavit as described by Subsection (d), the issue of whether the real property is subject to the lien must be resolved in an action brought for that purpose in the district court of the county in which the real property is located and the lien was filed.

Comment

This section, added in 2009, adopts a procedure under the Property Code to provide for the release of a child support lien on property an obligor claims is homestead property and, hence, exempt from lien. The procedure is simple enough. The obligor files an affidavit with the clerk of the county in which the property is located, stating that the property against which the child support lien has been asserted is the obligor's homestead. At least 30 days before filing the affidavit the obligor must have sent a copy of the affidavit and a letter announcing the obligor's intent to file the affidavit to the lien claimant. The claimant may file a contradicting affidavit asserting that the obligor's affidavit is untrue or that there is another reason why the obligor's property is subject to lien. The issue must then be resolved in the district court in which the property is located. If the claimant fails to file a contradicting affidavit before the filing of the obligor's affidavit, the obligor's affidavit serves to release the child support lien on the property. While the procedure is relatively simple, it is likely that any contest in court between the lien claimant and the support obligor will be complex, requiring the production and verification of property records, perhaps in some cases going back several generations. *(A.G.K. & H. P.S.)*

§ 157.318. Duration and Effect of Child Support Lien

(a) Subject to Subsection (d), a lien is effective until all current support and child support arrearages, including interest, any costs and reasonable attorney's fees, and any Title IV–D service fees authorized under Section 231.103 for which the obligor is responsible, have been paid or the lien is otherwise released as provided by this subchapter.

(b) The lien secures payment of all child support arrearages owed by the obligor under the underlying child support order, including arrearages that accrue after the lien notice was filed or delivered as provided by Section 157.314.

(c) The filing of a lien notice or abstract of judgment with the county clerk is a record of the notice and has the same effect as any other lien notice with respect to real property records.

(d) A lien is effective with respect to real property until the 10th anniversary of the date on which the lien notice was filed with the county clerk. A lien subject to the limitation prescribed by this subsection may be renewed for subsequent 10–year periods by filing a renewed lien notice in the same manner as the original lien notice. For purposes of establishing priority, a renewed lien notice filed before the applicable 10th anniversary relates back to the date the original lien notice was filed. A renewed lien notice filed on or after the applicable 10th anniversary has priority over any other lien recorded with respect to the real property only on the basis of the date the renewed lien notice is filed.

Comment

In 2009, the legislature added Subsection (d) which imposes a specific time limitation on the duration of a child support lien on real property unless the lien is timely renewed by the claimant. The problem addressed by this subsection is the difficulty of transferring clear title on real property against which a child support lien has been asserted but where, because of the passage of time, it is difficult, if not impossible, to accurately document existing support arrearages (including accrued interest). This time limitation on the duration of a child support lien on real property corresponds to the duration of a judgment lien under § 52.006, Property Code. *(A.G.K. & H.P.S.)*

---

§ 157.319. Effect of Lien Notice

(a) If a person having actual notice of the lien possesses nonexempt personal property of the obligor that may be subject to the lien, the property may not be paid over, released, sold, transferred, encumbered, or conveyed unless:

(1) a release of lien signed by the claimant is delivered to the person in possession; or

(2) a court, after notice to the claimant and hearing, has ordered the release of the lien because arrearages do not exist.

(b) A person having notice of a child support lien who violates this section may be joined as a party to a foreclosure action under this chapter and is subject to the penalties provided by this subchapter.

(c) This section does not affect the validity or priority of a lien of a health care provider, a lien for attorney's fees, or a lien of a holder of a security interest. This section does not affect the assignment of rights or subrogation of a claim under Title XIX of the federal Social Security Act (42 U.S.C. Section 1396 et seq.), as amended.

§ 157.320. Priority of Lien as to Real Property

(a) A lien created under this subchapter does not have priority over a lien or conveyance of an interest in the nonexempt real property recorded before the child support lien notice is recorded in the county where the real property is located.

(b) A lien created under this subchapter has priority over any lien or conveyance of an interest in the nonexempt real property recorded after the child support lien notice is recorded in the county clerk's office in the county where the property of the obligor is located.

(c) A conveyance of real property by the obligor after a lien notice has been recorded in the county where the real property is located is subject to the lien and may not impair the enforceability of the lien against the real property.

(d) A lien created under this subchapter is subordinate to a vendor's lien retained in a conveyance to the obligor.

§ 157.321. Discretionary Release of Lien

A child support lien claimant may at any time release a lien on all or part of the property of the obligor or return seized property, without liability, if assurance of payment is considered adequate by the claimant or if the release or return will facilitate the collection of the arrearages. The release or return may not operate to prevent future action to collect from the same or other property owned by the obligor.

§ 157.322. Mandatory Release of Lien

(a) On payment in full of the amount of child support due, together with any costs and reasonable attorney's fees, the child support lien claimant shall execute and deliver to the obligor or the obligor's attorney a release of the child support lien.

(b) The release of the child support lien is effective when:

(1) filed with the county clerk with whom the lien notice or abstract of judgment was filed; or

(2) delivered to any other individual or organization that may have been served with a lien notice under this subchapter.

§ 157.323. Foreclosure or Suit to Determine Arrearages

(a) In addition to any other remedy provided by law, an action to foreclose a child support lien, to dispute the amount of arrearages stated in the lien, or to resolve issues of ownership interest with respect to property subject to a child support lien may be brought in:

(1) the court in which the lien notice was filed under Section 157. 314(b)(1);

(2) the district court of the county in which the property is or was located and the lien was filed; or

(3) the court of continuing jurisdiction.

(b) The procedures provided by Subchapter B apply to a foreclosure action under this section, except that a person or organization in possession of the property of the obligor or known to have an ownership interest in property that is subject to the lien may be joined as an additional respondent.

(c) If arrearages are owed by the obligor, the court shall:

(1) render judgment against the obligor for the amount due, plus costs and reasonable attorney's fees;

(2) order any official authorized to levy execution to satisfy the lien, costs, and attorney's fees by selling any property on which a lien is established under this subchapter; or

(3) order an individual or organization in possession of nonexempt personal property or cash owned by the obligor to dispose of the property as the court may direct.

(d) For execution and sale under this section, publication of notice is necessary only for three consecutive weeks in a newspaper published in the county where the property is located or, if there is no newspaper in that county, in the most convenient newspaper in circulation in the county.

§ 157.324. Liability for Failure to Comply With Order or Lien

A person who knowingly disposes of property subject to a child support lien or who, after a foreclosure hearing, fails to surrender on demand nonexempt personal property as directed by a court under this subchapter is liable to the claimant in an amount equal to the value of the property disposed of or not surrendered, not to exceed the amount of the child support arrearages for which the lien or foreclosure judgment was issued.

Comment

This section does not apply to noncompliance with a notice of levy. The extent of the liability—the value of the property disposed of or not surrendered is not to exceed the amount of the arrearages identified in the court's order or the lien notice. *(A.G.K. & H.P.S.)*

---

§ 157.325. Release of Excess Funds to Debtor or Obligor

(a) If a person has in the person's possession earnings, deposits, accounts, balances, or other funds or assets of the obligor, including the proceeds of a judgment or other settlement of a claim or counterclaim due to the obligor that are in excess of the amount of arrearages specified in the child support lien, the holder of the nonexempt personal property or the obligor may request that the claimant release any excess amount from the lien. The claimant shall grant the request and discharge any lien on the excess amount unless the security for the arrearages would be impaired.

(b) If the claimant refuses the request, the holder of the personal property or the obligor may file suit under this subchapter for an order determining the amount of arrearages and discharging excess personal property or money from the lien.

§ 157.326. Interest of Obligor's Spouse or Another Person Having Ownership Interest

(a) A spouse of an obligor or another person having an ownership interest in property that is subject to a child support lien may file suit under Section 157.323 to determine the extent, if any, of the spouse's or other person's interest in real or personal property that is subject to:

(1) a lien perfected under this subchapter; or

(2) an action to foreclose under this subchapter.

(b) After notice to the obligor, the obligor's spouse, any other person alleging an ownership interest, the claimant, and the obligee, the court shall conduct a hearing and determine the extent, if any, of the ownership interest in the property held by the obligor's spouse or other person. If the court finds that:

(1) the property is the separate property of the obligor's spouse or the other person, the court shall order that the lien against the property be released and that any action to foreclose on the property be dismissed;

(2) the property is jointly owned by the obligor and the obligor's spouse, the court shall determine whether the sale of the obligor's interest in the property would result in an unreasonable hardship on the obligor's spouse or family and:

(A) if so, the court shall render an order that the obligor's interest in the property not be sold and that the lien against the property should be released; or

(B) if not, the court shall render an order partitioning the property and directing that the property be sold and the proceeds applied to the child support arrearages; or

(3) the property is owned in part by another person, other than the obligor's spouse, the court shall render an order partitioning the property and directing that the obligor's share of the property be applied to the child support arrearages.

(c) In a proceeding under this section, the spouse or other person claiming an ownership interest in the property has the burden to prove the extent of that ownership interest.

§ 157.327. Execution and Levy on Financial Assets of Obligor

(a) Notwithstanding any other provision of law, if a judgment or administrative determination of arrearages has been rendered, a claimant may deliver a notice of levy to any financial institution possessing or controlling assets or funds owned by, or owed to, an obligor and subject to a child support lien, including a lien for child support arising in another state.

(b) The notice under this section must:

(1) identify the amount of child support arrearages owing at the time the amount of arrearages was determined or, if the amount is less, the amount of arrearages owing at the time the notice is prepared and delivered to the financial institution; and

(2) direct the financial institution to pay to the claimant, not earlier than the 15th day or later than the 21st day after the date of delivery of the notice, an amount from the assets of the obligor or from funds due to the obligor that are held or controlled by the institution, not to exceed the amount of the child support arrearages identified in the notice, unless:

(A) the institution is notified by the claimant that the obligor has paid the arrearages or made arrangements satisfactory to the claimant for the payment of the arrearages;

(B) the obligor or another person files a suit under Section 157.323 requesting a hearing by the court; or

(C) if the claimant is the Title IV–D agency, the obligor has requested an agency review under Section 157.328.

(c) A financial institution that receives a notice of levy under this section may not close an account in which the obligor has an ownership interest, permit a withdrawal from any account the obligor owns, in whole or in part, or pay funds to the obligor so that any amount remaining in the account is less than the amount of the arrearages identified in the notice, plus any fees due to the institution and any costs of the levy identified by the claimant.

(d) A financial institution that receives a notice of levy under this section shall notify any other person having an ownership interest in an account in which the obligor has an ownership interest that the account has been levied on in an amount not to exceed the amount of the child support arrearages identified in the notice of levy.

(e) The notice of levy may be delivered to a financial institution as provided by Section 59.008, Finance Code, if the institution is subject to that law or may be delivered to the registered agent, the institution's main business office in this state, or another address provided by the institution under Section 231.307.

(f) A financial institution may deduct the fees and costs identified in Subsection (c) from the obligor's assets before paying the appropriate amount to the claimant.

Comment

Subsection (b)(1) draws an important distinction between the amount of the support arrearages at the time that amount was determined (by the court or the Title IV D agency) and the amount of arrearages actually owing at the time the notice of levy is prepared and delivered to the financial institution. Clearly, the financial institution should not pay to the claimant an amount that is greater than the balance of the unpaid arrearages. *(A.G.K. & H.P.S.)*

---

§ 157.3271. Levy on Financial Institution Account of Deceased Obligor

(a) Subject to Subsection (b), the Title IV–D agency may, not earlier than the 90th day after the date of death of an obligor in a Title IV–D case, deliver a notice of levy to a financial institution in which the obligor was the sole owner of an account, regardless of whether the Title IV–D agency has issued a child support lien notice regarding the account.

(b) The Title IV–D agency may not deliver a notice of levy under this section if probate proceedings relating to the obligor's estate have commenced.

(c) The notice of levy must:

(1) identify the amount of child support arrearages determined by the Title IV–D agency to be owing and unpaid by the obligor on the date of the obligor's death; and

(2) direct the financial institution to pay to the Title IV–D agency, not earlier than the 45th day or later than the 60th day after the date of delivery of the notice, an amount from the assets of the obligor or from funds due to the obligor that are held or controlled by the institution, not to exceed the amount of the child support arrearages identified in the notice.

(d) Not later than the 35th day after the date of delivery of the notice, the financial institution must notify any other person asserting a claim against the account that:

(1) the account has been levied on for child support arrearages in the amount shown on the notice of levy; and

(2) the person may contest the levy by filing suit and requesting a court hearing in the same manner that a person may challenge a child support lien under Section 157.323.

(e) A person who contests a levy under this section, as authorized by Subsection (d)(2), may bring the suit in:

(1) the district court of the county in which the property is located or in which the obligor resided; or

(2) the court of continuing jurisdiction.

(f) The notice of levy may be delivered to a financial institution as provided by Section 59.008, Finance Code, if the institution is subject to that law or may be delivered to the registered agent, the institution's main business office in this state, or another address provided by the institution under Section 231.307.

(g) A financial institution may deduct its fees and costs, including any costs for complying with this section, from the deceased obligor's assets before paying the appropriate amount to the Title IV–D agency.

Added by Acts 2011, 82nd Leg., ch. 508 (H.B. 1674), § 8, eff. Sept. 1, 2011.

Comment

Added in 2011, this section complements the levy process laid out in §157.328. Under that process the obligor must be served with a copy of the notice of levy delivered to the financial institution possessing or controlling the obligor's assets. Section 157.3271 addresses the use of levy on financial assets—although only in Title IV–D cases—where the obligor has died. The Title IV–D agency has to act in measured fashion to levy the deceased obligor's assets: not too soon and not too late. It may not deliver a notice of levy to a financial institution earlier than 90 days after the death of the obligor, but it must deliver the notice before probate proceedings have commenced. Once probate has begun, the agency must wait its turn to assert a claim against the decedent's estate (a "Class 4" claim under §322, Probate Code). If there is no hindrance posed by probate proceedings, the financial institution must respond to the levy with some dispatch. As under §157.327, this section provides amply for the interests of others who may lay claim to the deceased obligor's assets, as it does also for fees and costs the financial institution may incur in complying with the notice. *(A.G.K. & H.P.S.)*

---

§ 157.328. Notice of Levy Sent to Obligor

(a) At the time the notice of levy under Section 157.327 is delivered to a financial institution, the claimant shall serve the obligor with a copy of the notice.

(b) The notice of levy delivered to the obligor must inform the obligor that:

(1) the claimant will not proceed with levy if, not later than the 10th day after the date of receipt of the notice, the obligor pays in full the amount of arrearages identified in the notice or otherwise makes arrangements acceptable to the claimant for the payment of the arrearage amounts; and

(2) the obligor may contest the levy by filing suit under Section 157.323 not later than the 10th day after the date of receipt of the notice.

(c) If the claimant is the Title IV-D agency, the obligor receiving a notice of levy may request review by the agency not later than the 10th day after the date of receipt of the notice to resolve any issue in dispute regarding the existence or amount of the arrearages. The agency shall provide an opportunity for a review, by telephone conference or in person, as appropriate to the circumstances, not later than the fifth business day after the date an oral or written request from the obligor for the review is received. If the review fails to resolve any issue in dispute, the obligor may file suit under Section 157.323 for a hearing by the court not later than the fifth day after the date of the conclusion of the agency review. If the obligor fails to timely file suit, the Title IV-D agency may request the financial institution to release and remit the funds subject to levy.

(d) The notice under this section may be delivered to the last known address of the obligor by first class mail, certified mail, or registered mail.

Comment

The levy process moves rather swiftly. The obligor has to respond with dispatch to the notice, with only ten days within which either to pay the full amount of the arrearages or make arrangements for payment satisfactory to the claimant or to file suit to contest. In a Title IV–D case, however, within 10 days of receipt of the notice, the obligor may request an administrative review before turning to the court to contest the levy. But even then, from the time of receipt of the notice, the obligor has—at the most—only twenty days within which to put the levy on hold by filing suit. *(A.G.K. & H.P.S.)*

---

§ 157.329. No Liability for Compliance With Notice of Levy

A financial institution that possesses or has a right to an obligor's assets for which a notice of levy has been delivered and that surrenders the assets or right to assets to a child support lien claimant is not liable to the obligor or any other person for the property or rights surrendered.

§ 157.330. Failure to Comply With Notice of Levy

(a) A person who possesses or has a right to property that is the subject of a notice of levy delivered to the person and who refuses to surrender the property or right to property to the claimant on demand is liable to the claimant in an amount equal to the value of the property or right to property not surrendered but that does not exceed the amount of the child support arrearages for which the notice of levy has been filed.

(b) A claimant may recover costs and reasonable attorney's fees incurred in an action under this section.

§ 157.331. Additional Levy to Satisfy Arrearages

If the property or right to property on which a notice of levy has been filed does not produce money sufficient to satisfy the amount of child support arrearages identified in the notice of levy, the claimant may proceed to levy on other property of the obligor until the total amount of child support due is paid.

Comment

Delivery of either the notice of lien or notice of levy to a financial institution has the effect of freezing the assets of the obligor in an account held by that institution. Receipt of either notice requires the institution to notify any other person having an ownership interest in the frozen account of the existence of the lien or the impending levy. The difference between the two notices is that the lien notice does not announce, as does the levy notice, that the frozen assets are about to be seized. The lien may encumber the account indefinitely; the levy may exhaust it almost immediately. (*A.G.K. & H.P.S.*)

SUBCHAPTER H. HABEAS CORPUS

Introductory Comment

Before the enactment of the Family Code, the merits of a child custody dispute were often litigated in the context of a habeas corpus proceeding. The Code put an end to that, substituting what has come to be known as "automatic habeas corpus." The sole issue in almost all habeas corpus proceedings is whether the relator is currently entitled to possession of a child by virtue of a valid court order.

For a considerable time trial courts demonstrated great reluctance in accepting this principle, unwillingly yielding considerable judicial discretion. But, thanks to numerous, repeated decisions by the supreme court, the message finally got through to the trial bench. Automatic habeas is now widely accepted in Texas jurisprudence. The primary (theoretical) exception to the summary nature of the writ, the "serious immediate question" of § 157.374 is often argued, but seldom found to exist. Finally, while habeas corpus is not available between parents in the absence of a prior order, the writ has validity when a parent seeks to recover possession of a child from a nonparent.

With the enactment of the Uniform Child Custody Jurisdiction and Enforcement Act in 1999, the remedy of this subchapter has been somewhat upstaged by the so-called "turbo" writ now provided in Ch. 152, Subch. D, *supra*.

Leading Cases

Nature of Writ

Mergerson v. Daggett, 644 S.W.2d 451 (Tex. 1982) (writ improperly granted, custody covered by existing court order)

Gray v. Rankin, 594 S.W.2d 409 (Tex. 1980) (granting of habeas corpus not appealable order)

Strobel v. Thurman, 565 S.W.2d 238 (Tex. 1978) ("grant of the writ should be automatic, immediate, and ministerial . . . upon proof of the bare legal right to possession")

Trader v. Dear, 565 S.W.2d 233 (Tex. 1978) (relator has choice of forums—where child found or in court of continuing jurisdiction)

Lamphere v. Chrisman, 554 S.W.2d 935 (Tex. 1977) (mandamus proper remedy to enforce relator's rights)

Out-of-State Order

Rush v. Stansbury, 668 S.W.2d 690 (Tex. 1984) (automatic habeas applies to sister state decrees)

Silver v. Storey, 677 S.W.2d 504 (Tex. 1984) (PA order entered without service on respondent establishes that father evaded service)

Perry v. Scoggins, 626 S.W.2d 302 (Tex. 1981) (Missouri custody order entitles father to habeas)

Marshall v. Wilson, 616 S.W.2d 932 (Tex. 1981) (out-of-state custody order enforced by habeas; relator immune from countersuit)

Serious Immediate Question

Schoenfeld v. Onion, 647 S.W.2d 954 (Tex. 1983) (absent dire emergency, habeas automatic, immediate, & ministerial)

Wise v. Yates, 639 S.W.2d 460 (Tex. 1982) (possibility that custodial parent would take children to Taiwan does not present serious immediate danger)

Forbes v. Wettman, 598 S.W.2d 231 (Tex. 1980) (fungus on finger and minor weight loss not serious immediate question)

Parent versus Nonparent

Rodriguez v. McFall, 658 S.W.2d 150 (Tex. 1983) (mother entitled to return of child from paternal grandparents)

Whatley v. Bacon, 649 S.W.2d 297 (Tex. 1983) (surviving father entitled to habeas against maternal grandparents)

Armstrong v. Reiter, 628 S.W.2d 439 (Tex. 1982) (natural mother entitled to recover child from guardian)

Trevino v. Garcia, 627 S.W.2d 147 (Tex. 1982) (habeas overcomes claim of adoption by estoppel)

Saucier v. Pena, 559 S.W.2d 654 (Tex. 1977) (surviving father entitled to return of children from maternal grandparents)

Restrictions on Granting Writ

Greene v. Schuble, 654 S.W.2d 436 (Tex. 1983) (automatic habeas means temporary custody issue may not be combined with habeas hearing)

Elliott v. Bradshaw, 587 S.W.2d 108 (Tex. 1978) (temporary order cannot defeat right to habeas corpus)

Standley v. Stewart, 539 S.W.2d 882 (Tex. 1976) (court cannot join hearing to modify conservatorship during habeas proceeding)

Cross Reference

Parental Kidnapping Prevention Act. TX FCA 28 USCA § 1738A, *infra*.

---

§ 157.371. Jurisdiction

(a) The relator may file a petition for a writ of habeas corpus in either the court of continuing, exclusive jurisdiction or in a court with jurisdiction to issue a writ of habeas corpus in the county in which the child is found.

(b) Although a habeas corpus proceeding is not a suit affecting the parent-child relationship, the court may refer to the provisions of this title for definitions and procedures as appropriate.

§ 157.372. Return of Child

(a) Subject to Chapter 152 and the Parental Kidnapping Prevention Act (28 U.S.C. Section 1738A), if the right to possession of a child is governed by a court order, the court in a habeas corpus proceeding involving the right to possession of the child shall compel return of the child to the relator only if the court finds that the relator is entitled to possession under the order.

(b) If the court finds that the previous order was granted by a court that did not give the contestants reasonable notice of the proceeding and an opportunity to be heard, the court may not render an order in the habeas corpus proceeding compelling return of the child on the basis of that order.

§ 157.373. Relator Relinquished Possession; Temporary Orders

(a) If the relator has by consent or acquiescence relinquished actual possession and control of the child for not less than 6 months preceding the date of the filing of the petition for the writ, the court may either compel or refuse to order return of the child.

(b) The court may disregard brief periods of possession and control by the relator during the 6-month period.

(c) In a suit in which the court does not compel return of the child, the court may issue temporary orders under Chapter 105 if a suit affecting the parent-child relationship is pending and the parties have received notice of a hearing on temporary orders set for the same time as the habeas corpus proceeding.

§ 157.374. Welfare of Child

Notwithstanding any other provision of this subchapter, the court may render an appropriate temporary order if there is a serious immediate question concerning the welfare of the child.

Leading Case

Whatley v. Bacon, 649 S.W.2d 297 (Tex. 1983) (giving grandparents temporary possession of child from sole surviving parent inappropriate; only serious, immediate question of child's welfare could justify habeas corpus writ)

§ 157.375. Immunity to Civil Process

(a) While in this state for the sole purpose of compelling the return of a child through a habeas corpus proceeding, the relator is not amenable to civil process and is not subject to the jurisdiction of any civil court except the court in which the writ is pending. The relator is subject to process and jurisdiction in that court only for the purpose of prosecuting the writ.

(b) A request by the relator for costs, attorney's fees, and necessary travel and other expenses under Chapter 106 or 152 is not a waiver of immunity to civil process.

§ 157.376. No Existing Order

(a) If the right to possession of a child is not governed by an order, the court in a habeas corpus proceeding involving the right of possession of the child:

(1) shall compel return of the child to the parent if the right of possession is between a parent and a nonparent and a suit affecting the parent-child relationship has not been filed; or

(2) may either compel return of the child or issue temporary orders under Chapter 105 if a suit affecting the parent-child relationship is pending and the parties have received notice of a hearing on temporary orders set for the same time as the habeas corpus proceeding.

(b) The court may not use a habeas corpus proceeding to adjudicate the right of possession of a child between two parents or between two or more nonparents.

SUBCHAPTER I. CLARIFICATION OF ORDERS

Introductory Comment

These provisions are directly modeled after the clarification procedure found in Title 1, § 9.008 *et seq.* The court of continuing jurisdiction has the opportunity to clarify or rectify errors or ambiguities in an order without reference to the nunc pro tunc test, and without the necessity of meeting the standards for a modification of an original order, *e.g.,* substantial change of circumstances, multi-prong test, etc.

Leading Cases

McGehee v. Epley, 661 S.W.2d 924 (Tex. 1983) (clarification order cannot affect substance of original order)

Horton v. Horton, 335 S.W.3d 862 ((Tex. App.—Beaumont 2011) (obligor's social security retirement benefits were subject to withholding)

Cross Reference

TEX. R. CIV. P. 316. Correction of Clerical Mistakes in Judgment Record.

---

§ 157.421. Clarifying Nonspecific Order

(a) A court may clarify an order rendered by the court in a proceeding under this title if the court finds, on the motion of a party or on the court's own motion, that the order is not specific enough to be enforced by contempt.

(b) The court shall clarify the order by rendering an order that is specific enough to be enforced by contempt.

(c) A clarified order does not affect the finality of the order that it clarifies.

§ 157.422. Procedure

(a) The procedure for filing a motion for enforcement of a final order applies to a motion for clarification.

(b) A person is not entitled to a jury in a proceeding under this subchapter.

§ 157.423. Substantive Change Not Enforceable

(a) A court may not change the substantive provisions of an order to be clarified under this subchapter.

(b) A substantive change made by a clarification order is not enforceable.

§ 157.424. Relation to Motion for Contempt

The court may render a clarification order before a motion for contempt is made or heard, in conjunction with a motion for contempt, or after the denial of a motion for contempt.

§ 157.425. Order Not Retroactive

The court may not provide that a clarification order is retroactive for the purpose of enforcement by contempt.

§ 157.426. Time Allowed to Comply

(a) In a clarification order, the court shall provide a reasonable time for compliance.

(b) The clarification order may be enforced by contempt after the time for compliance has expired.

CHAPTER 158. WITHHOLDING FROM EARNINGS FOR CHILD SUPPORT

SUBCHAPTER A. INCOME WITHHOLDING REQUIRED; GENERAL PROVISIONS

SUBCHAPTER B. PROCEDURE

SUBCHAPTER C. RIGHTS AND DUTIES OF EMPLOYER

SUBCHAPTER D. JUDICIAL WRIT OF WITHHOLDING ISSUED BY CLERK

SUBCHAPTER E. MODIFICATION, REDUCTION, OR TERMINATION OF WITHHOLDING

SUBCHAPTER F. ADMINISTRATIVE WRIT OF WITHHOLDING

Editors' Note: This chapter contains guest comments by Alicia Gray Key, Deputy Attorney General and Title IV-D Director, and H. Patrick Sullivan, Deputy Director for State and Federal Operations, Child Support Division, Office of the Attorney General, identified as *(A.G.K. & H.P.S.)*.

Introductory Comment

Income withholding has become the primary tool for collecting child support and is mandated to be available for all cases. The employer community has quietly accepted the burden of collecting and remitting support without much controversy. Moreover, there has been very little appellate litigation reported on this crucial subject. Federally mandated withholding forms have been implemented to assist employers in processing the paperwork.

CLE/Other Legal Publications

Obtaining child support. Barry J. Brooks & Karen L. Marvel, 2009 U.T. Parent-Child Relationships

AG Office: Things you should know. Cynthia J. Barela & Laura D. Hamilton, 2009 U.T. Fam. L. Front Lines

Versus the AG: Why Can't We Just Get Along? Alicia G. Key, Jack W. Marr, 2009 Adv. Fam. L.

Cross References

Family Support Act of 1988, Pub. L. 100–485, 102 Stat. 2343, *see* 5 U.S. Code Cong. & Admin. News 2776 (1988) (last federal legislative action to regulate state enforcement efforts)

IV–D Child Support Enforcement. 42 U.S.C.A. § 651 *et seq.*

Tex. FCA Const. Art. 16, § 28. Garnishment of Wages.

SUBCHAPTER A. INCOME WITHHOLDING REQUIRED; GENERAL PROVISIONS

§ 158.001. Income Withholding; General Rule

In a proceeding in which periodic payments of child support are ordered, modified, or enforced, the court or the Title IV-D agency shall order that income be withheld from the disposable earnings of the obligor as provided by this chapter.

§ 158.002. Suspension Of Income Withholding

Except in a Title IV-D case, the court may provide, for good cause shown or on agreement of the parties, that the order withholding income need not be issued or delivered to an employer until:

(1) the obligor has been in arrears for an amount due for more than 30 days;

(2) the amount of the arrearages is an amount equal to or greater than the amount due for a one-month period; or

(3) any other violation of the child support order has occurred.

Comment

Section 154.007 provides that every SAPCR order involving child support must include an order for income withholding. This section restates that rule. However, the order need not be delivered to the obligor's employer if good cause for restraint is found by the court. It is commonplace for an order not be delivered in an up-scale case. Note, however, good cause to sit on a withholding order does not exist for a IV–D case. *See* § 158.006.

---

§ 158.003. Withholding for Arrearages in Addition to Current Support

(a) In addition to income withheld for the current support of a child, income shall be withheld from the disposable earnings of the obligor to be applied toward the liquidation of any child support arrearages, including accrued interest as provided in Chapter 157.

(b) The additional amount to be withheld for arrearages shall be an amount sufficient to discharge those arrearages in not more than two years or an additional 20 percent added to the amount of the current monthly support order, whichever amount will result in the arrearages being discharged in the least amount of time.

§ 158.004. Withholding for Arrearages When no Current Support is Due

If current support is no longer owed, the court or the Title IV–D agency shall order that income be withheld for arrearages, including accrued interest as provided in Chapter 157, in an amount sufficient to discharge those arrearages in not more than two years.

§ 158.005. Withholding to Satisfy Judgment for Arrearages

In rendering a cumulative judgment for arrearages, the court shall order that a reasonable amount of income be withheld from the disposable earnings of the obligor to be applied toward the satisfaction of the judgment.

§ 158.0051. Order for Withholding for Costs and Fees

(a) In addition to an order for income to be withheld for child support, including child support and child support arrearages, the court may render an order that income be withheld from the disposable earnings of the obligor to be applied towards the satisfaction of any ordered attorney's fees and costs resulting from an action to enforce child support under this title.

(b) An order rendered under this section is subordinate to an order or writ of withholding for child support under this chapter and is subject to the maximum amount allowed to be withheld under Section 158.009.

(c) The court shall order that amounts withheld for fees and costs under this section be remitted directly to the person entitled to the ordered attorney's fees or costs or be paid through a local registry for disbursement to that person.

§ 158.006. Income Withholding in Title IV-D Suits

In a Title IV-D case, the court or the Title IV-D agency shall order that income be withheld from the disposable earnings of the obligor and may not suspend, stay, or delay issuance of the order or of a judicial or administrative writ of withholding.

Comment

Comment to § 158.002, *supra,* is applicable to this section as well.

---

§ 158.007. Extension of Repayment Schedule by Court or Title IV–D Agency; Unreasonable Hardship

If the court or the Title IV–D agency finds that the schedule for discharging arrearages would cause the obligor, the obligor's family, or children for whom support is due from the obligor to suffer unreasonable hardship, the court or agency may extend the payment period for a reasonable length of time.

Leading Cases

In re Chambers, 5 S.W.3d 341 (Tex. App.—San Antonio 1999, no pet.) (no minimum amount required to withhold to collect arrears—$150 per month to collect nearly $21,000 affirmed)

In re Digges, 981 S.W.2d 445 (Tex. App.—San Antonio 1998, no pet.) (income withholding remedy not limited by time or due process defenses applicable to contempt proceedings)

---

§ 158.008. Priority of Withholding

An order or writ of withholding has priority over any garnishment, attachment, execution, or other assignment or order affecting disposable earnings.

§ 158.009. Maximum Amount Withheld From Earnings

An order or writ of withholding shall direct that any employer of the obligor withhold from the obligor's disposable earnings the amount specified up to a maximum amount of 50 percent of the obligor's disposable earnings.

§ 158.010. Order or Writ Binding on Employer Doing Business in State

An order or writ of withholding issued under this chapter and delivered to an employer doing business in this state is binding on the employer without regard to whether the obligor resides or works outside this state.

§ 158.011. Voluntary Withholding by Obligor

(a) An obligor may file with the clerk of the court a notarized or acknowledged request signed by the obligor and the obligee for the issuance and delivery to the obligor's employer of a writ of withholding. A notarized or acknowledged request may be filed under this section regardless of whether a writ or order has been served on any party or of the existence or amount of an arrearage.

(b) On receipt of a request under this section, the clerk shall issue and deliver a writ of withholding in the manner provided by this chapter.

(c) An employer that receives a writ of withholding issued under this section may request a hearing in the same manner and according to the same terms provided by Section 158.205.

(d) An obligor whose employer receives a writ of withholding issued under this section may request a hearing in the manner provided by Section 158.309.

(e) An obligee may contest a writ of withholding issued under this section by requesting, not later than the 180th day after the date on which the obligee discovers that the writ has been issued, a hearing in the manner provided by Section 158.309.

(f) A writ of withholding under this section may not reduce the total amount of child support, including arrearages, owed by the obligor.

Comment

An obligor may wish to have wages withheld to ensure proper payment and to make life less complicated.

SUBCHAPTER B. PROCEDURE

§ 158.101. Applicability of Procedure

Except as otherwise provided in this chapter, the procedure for a motion for enforcement of child support as provided in Chapter 157 applies to an action for income withholding.

§ 158.102. Time Limitations

An order or writ for income withholding under this chapter may be issued until all current support and child support arrearages, interest, and any applicable fees and costs, including ordered attorney's fees and court costs, have been paid.

Comment

Until a 1999 amendment, § 157.005 imposed a four-year limitation on obtaining a judgment to collect child support after a child became an adult. With the elimination of that limitation, both the judgment remedy and the income withholding remedy for collecting current and past due support, plus interest, continue indefinitely.

Leading Case

In re A.D., 73 S.W.3d 244 (Tex. 2002) (1997 amendment repealing four-year limitation on court's jurisdiction to order withholding for child support constitutional, unlimited time for enforcement not a retroactive law)

---

§ 158.103. Contents of Order or Writ of Withholding

An order of withholding or writ of withholding issued under this chapter must contain the information required by the forms prescribed by the Title IV-D agency under Section 158.106.

§ 158.104. Request for Issuance of Order or Judicial Writ of Withholding

A request for issuance of an order or judicial writ of withholding may be filed with the clerk of the court by the prosecuting attorney, the Title IV–D agency, the friend of the court, a domestic relations office, the obligor, the obligee, or an attorney representing the obligee or obligor.

§ 158.105. Issuance and Delivery of Order or Judicial Writ of Withholding

(a) On filing a request for issuance of an order or judicial writ of withholding, the clerk of the court shall cause a certified copy of the order or writ to be delivered to the obligor's current employer or to any subsequent employer of the obligor.

(b) The clerk shall issue and deliver the certified copy of the order or judicial writ not later than the fourth working day after the date the order is signed or the request is filed, whichever is later.

(c) An order or judicial writ of withholding shall be delivered to the employer by first class mail or, if requested, by certified or registered mail, return receipt requested, by electronic transmission, including electronic mail or facsimile transmission, or by service of citation to:

(1) the person authorized to receive service of process for the employer in civil cases generally; or

(2) a person designated by the employer, by written notice to the clerk, to receive orders or writs of withholding.

(d) The clerk may deliver an order or judicial writ of withholding under Subsection (c) by electronic mail if the employer has an electronic mail address or by facsimile transmission if the employer is capable of receiving documents transmitted in that manner. If delivery is accomplished by electronic mail, the clerk must request acknowledgment of receipt from the employer or use an electronic mail system with a read receipt capability. If delivery is accomplished by facsimile transmission, the clerk's facsimile machine must create a delivery confirmation report.

Comment

The issuance and delivery to an employer of a judicial order or writ of income withholding is a relatively simple ministerial process executed by the clerk, for which the clerk may—and, without exception, does—charge the fee authorized under § 110.004. The original purpose of the fee was, in part, to cover the costs of delivering the order or writ by certified or registered mail. But a 2001 amendment made that mode of delivery dependent upon the specific request of the party requesting issuance. While in general first-class mail may be reliable, that method of delivery provides no way of monitoring whether an employer has actually received the order or writ. Anyone requesting issuance should probably request that this important document be delivered by certified or registered mail. (*A.G.K. & H.P.S.*)

§ 158.106. Forms for Income Withholding

(a) The Title IV-D agency shall prescribe forms as required by federal law in a standard format entitled order or notice to withhold income for child support.

(b) The Title IV–D agency shall make the appropriate forms available to obligors, obligees, domestic relations offices, friends of the court, and private attorneys.

(c) The Title IV–D agency may prescribe additional forms for the efficient collection of child support and to promote the administration of justice for all parties.

(d) The forms prescribed by the Title IV–D agency under this section may be used to request voluntary withholding under Section 158.011.

SUBCHAPTER C. RIGHTS AND DUTIES OF EMPLOYER

Leading Case

Casino Magic Corp. v. King, 43 S.W.3d 14 (Tex. App.—Dallas 2001, no pet.) (Louisiana business served with income withholding order escapes money judgment only because no evidence presented to establish liability)

§ 158.201. Order or Writ Binding on Employer

(a) An employer required to withhold income from earnings is not entitled to notice of the proceedings before the order is rendered or writ of withholding is issued.

(b) An order or writ of withholding is binding on an employer regardless of whether the employer is specifically named in the order or writ.

§ 158.202. Effective Date of and Duration of Withholding

An employer shall begin to withhold income in accordance with an order or writ of withholding not later than the first pay period following the date on which the order or writ was delivered to the employer and shall continue to withhold income as required by the order or writ as long as the obligor is employed by the employer.

§ 158.203. Remitting Withheld Payments

(a) The employer shall remit the amount to be withheld to the person or office named in the order or writ on each pay date. The payment must include the date on which the withholding occurred.

(b) An employer with **50** ~~250~~or more employees shall remit a payment required under this section by electronic funds transfer or electronic data interchange not later than the second business day after the pay date.

(b–1) An employer with fewer than **50** ~~250~~employees may remit a payment required under this section by electronic funds transfer or electronic data interchange. A payment remitted by the employer electronically must be remitted not later than the date specified by Subsection (b).

(c) The employer shall include with each payment transmitted:

(1) the number assigned by the Title IV–D agency, if available, and the county identification number, if available;

(2) the name of the county or the county's federal information processing standard code;

(3) the cause number of the suit under which withholding is required;

(4) the payor's name and social security number; and

(5) the payee's name and, if available, social security number, unless the payment is transmitted by electronic funds transfer.

(d) In a case in which an obligor's income is subject to withholding, the employer shall remit the payment of child support directly to a local registry, the Title IV–D agency, or to the state disbursement unit.

Amended by Acts 2011, 82nd Leg., ch. 508 (H.B. 1674), § 9, eff. Sept. 1, 2011.

§ 158.204. Employer May Deduct Fee From Earnings

An employer may deduct an administrative fee of not more than $10 each month from the obligor's disposable earnings in addition to the amount to be withheld as child support.

§ 158.205. Hearing Requested by Employer

(a) Not later than the 20th day after the date an order or writ of withholding is delivered, the employer may, as appropriate, file a motion with the court or file a request with the Title IV-D agency for a hearing on the applicability of the order or writ to the employer. The Title IV-D agency by rule shall establish procedures for an agency hearing under this section.

(b) The hearing under this section shall be held not later than the 15th day after the date the motion or request was made.

(c) An order or writ of withholding remains binding and payments shall continue to be made pending further order of the court or, in the case of an administrative writ, action of the Title IV-D agency.

§ 158.206. Liability and Obligation of Employer; Workers' Compensation Claims

(a) An employer receiving an order or a writ of withholding under this chapter, including an order or writ directing that health insurance be provided to a child, who complies with the order or writ is not liable to the obligor for the amount of income withheld and paid as required by the order or writ.

(b) An employer receiving an order or writ of withholding who does not comply with the order or writ is liable:

(1) to the obligee for the amount not paid in compliance with the order or writ, including the amount the obligor is required to pay for health insurance under Chapter 154;

(2) to the obligor for:

(A) the amount withheld and not paid as required by the order or writ; and

(B) an amount equal to the interest that accrues under Section 157.265 on the amount withheld and not paid; and

(3) for reasonable attorney's fees and court costs.

(c) If an obligor has filed a claim for workers' compensation, the obligor's employer shall send a copy of the income withholding order or writ to the insurance carrier with whom the claim has been filed in order to continue the ordered withholding of income.

Comment

Tex. Labor Code § 408.203 authorizes the garnishment of workers' compensation benefits for child support. Subsection (c) makes the employer responsible for seeing that there is no break in income withholding if an employee files a claim for those benefits. There is no need for the clerk in this instance to issue, deliver, or file a copy of the original writ or order, thereby saving time and expense to the party who originally filed an application for the writ or order. (*A.G.K. & H.P.S.*)

§ 158.207. Employer Receiving More Than One Order or Writ

(a) An employer receiving two or more orders or writs for one obligor shall comply with each order or writ to the extent possible.

(b) If the total amount due under the orders or writs exceeds the maximum amount allowed to be withheld under Section 158.009, the employer shall pay an equal amount towards the current support in each order or writ until the employer has complied fully with each current support obligation and, thereafter, equal amounts on the arrearages until the employer has complied with each order or writ, or until the maximum total amount of allowed withholding is reached, whichever occurs first.

(c) An employer who receives more than one order or writ of withholding that combines withholding for child support and spousal maintenance as provided by Section 8.101 shall withhold income and pay the amount withheld in accordance with Section 8.207.

§ 158.208. Employer may Combine Amounts Withheld

An employer required to withhold from more than one obligor may combine the amounts withheld and make a single payment to each agency designated if the employer separately identifies the amount of the payment that is attributable to each obligor.

§ 158.209. Employer's Penalty for Discriminatory Hiring or Discharge

(a) An employer may not use an order or writ of withholding as grounds in whole or part for the termination of employment or for any other disciplinary action against an employee.

(b) An employer may not refuse to hire an employee because of an order or writ of withholding.

(c) If an employer intentionally discharges an employee in violation of this section, the employer continues to be liable to the employee for current wages and other benefits and for reasonable attorney's fees and court costs incurred in enforcing the employee's rights as provided in this section.

(d) An action under this section may be brought by the employee, a friend of the court, the domestic relations office, or the Title IV-D agency.

§ 158.210. Fine for Noncompliance

(a) In addition to the civil remedies provided by this subchapter or any other remedy provided by law, an employer who knowingly violates the provisions of this chapter may be subject to a fine not to exceed $200 for each occurrence in which the employer fails to:

(1) withhold income for child support as instructed in an order or writ issued under this chapter; or

(2) remit withheld income within the time required by Section 158.203 to the payee identified in the order or writ or to the state disbursement unit.

(b) A fine recovered under this section shall be paid to the county in which the obligee resides and shall be used by the county to improve child support services.

§ 158.211. Notice of Termination of Employment and of New Employment

(a) If an obligor terminates employment with an employer who has been withholding income, both the obligor and the employer shall notify the court or the Title IV–D agency and the obligee of that fact not later than the seventh day after the date employment terminated and shall provide the obligor's last known address and the name and address of the obligor's new employer, if known.

(b) The obligor has a continuing duty to inform any subsequent employer of the order or writ of withholding after obtaining employment.

§ 158.212. Improper Payment

An employer who remits a payment to an incorrect office or person shall remit the payment to the agency or person identified in the order of withholding not later than the second business day after the date the employer receives the returned payment.

§ 158.213. Withholding From Workers' Compensation Benefits

(a) An insurance carrier that receives an order or writ of withholding under Section 158.206 for workers' compensation benefits payable to an obligor shall withhold an amount not to exceed the maximum amount allowed to be withheld from income under Section 158.009 regardless of whether the benefits payable to the obligor for lost income are paid as lump sum amounts or as periodic payments.

(b) An insurance carrier subject to this section shall send the amount withheld for child support to the place of payment designated in the order or writ of withholding.

Comment

Workers' compensation benefits replace lost earned income; it follows that the benefits are subject to the provisions on income withholding for child support prescribed by federal law (42 U.S.C. 666(b)(1)) and § 158.009. An order or writ of income withholding sent to a workers' compensation insurance carrier operates just as if sent to an employer. The insurer must comply with the terms of the order or writ and remit the portion of the benefits subject to the order or writ to the place of payment designated. *(A.G.K. & H.P.S.)*

§ 158.214. Withholding From Severance Pay

(a) In this section, "severance pay" means income paid on termination of employment in addition to the employee's usual earnings from the employer at the time of termination.

(b) An employer receiving an order or writ of withholding under this chapter shall withhold from any severance pay owed an obligor an amount equal to the amount the employer would have withheld under the order or writ if the severance pay had been paid as the obligor's usual earnings as a current employee.

(c) The total amount that may be withheld under this section is subject to the maximum amount allowed to be withheld under Section 158.009.

Comment

Although this chapter provides for withholding from "earnings" for child support, prior to the addition in 2007 of § 158.214 and § 158.215 there were no specific procedures in the chapter for withholding from severance pay and from lump-sum, both of these payments made by an employer to an obligor being identified under § 101.011 as forms of "earnings." This section treats severance pay as prospective earnings of the obligor, representing periodic payments the obligor would have received, had employment not been terminated, and, thus, subject to the same withholding processes as on-going wages, with the maximum amount withheld limited to the cap under § 158.009, *supra*. *(A.G.K. & H.P.S.)*

§ 158.215. Withholding From Lump–Sum Payments

(a) In this section, "lump-sum payment" means income in the form of a bonus or an amount paid in lieu of vacation or other leave time. The term does not include an employee's usual earnings or an amount paid as severance pay on termination of employment.

(b) This section applies only to an employer who receives an administrative writ of withholding in a Title IV–D case.

(c) An employer to whom this section applies may not make a lump-sum payment to the obligor in the amount of $500 or more without first notifying the Title IV–D agency to determine whether all or a portion of the payment should be applied to child support arrearages owed by the obligor.

(d) After notifying the Title IV–D agency in compliance with Subsection (c), the employer may not make the lump-sum payment before the earlier of:

(1) the 10th day after the date on which the employer notified the Title IV–D agency; or

(2) the date on which the employer receives authorization from the Title IV–D agency to make the payment.

(e) If the employer receives a timely authorization from the Title IV–D agency under Subsection (d)(2), the employer may make the payment only in accordance with the terms of that authorization.

Comment

A form of "earnings" (*see* § 101.011), certain lump sum payments (such as bonuses) are amounts paid by an employer that fall outside the categories of regular (viz., periodic) earnings and severance pay (*see* § 158.214). They are, therefore, not subject to the usual withholding procedures. Moreover, under this section added in 2007 and amended in 2009, lump sum payments may be intercepted only by the Title IV–D agency to be applied to arrearages owed by an obligor in a case in which the agency has already issued an administrative writ of withholding. The administrative process established in this section will be effective only to the extent that employers report lump sum payments, as required under the process. There is no sure way, however, of enforcing this employer duty, and likely many bonuses and commissions will go unreported. *(A.G.K. & H.P.S.)*

SUBCHAPTER D. JUDICIAL WRIT OF WITHHOLDING ISSUED BY CLERK

Introductory Comment

This statute has not been the subject of an authoritative appellate decision. The only attention it has received from the legislature has been by way of technical amendments.

Leading Case

Atty. Gen.'s Office on behalf of State v. Mitchell, 819 S.W.2d 556 (Tex. App.—Dallas 1991, no writ) (time expired to challenge writ of withholding)

Cross Reference

IV–D Child Support and Enforcement. 42 U.S.C.A. § 651 *et seq.*

§ 158.301. Notice of Application for Judicial Writ Of Withholding; Filing

(a) A notice of application for judicial writ of withholding may be filed if:

(1) a delinquency occurs in child support payments in an amount equal to or greater than the total support due for one month; or

(2) income withholding was not ordered at the time child support was ordered.

(b) The notice of application for judicial writ of withholding may be filed in the court of continuing jurisdiction by:

(1) the Title IV-D agency;

(2) the attorney representing the local domestic relations office;

(3) the attorney appointed a friend of the court as provided in Chapter 202;

(4) the obligor or obligee; or

(5) a private attorney representing the obligor or obligee.

(c) The Title IV-D agency may in a Title IV-D case file a notice of application for judicial writ of withholding on request of the obligor or obligee.

§ 158.302. Contents of Notice of Application for Judicial Writ Of Withholding

The notice of application for judicial writ of withholding shall be verified and:

(1) state the amount of monthly support due, including medical support, the amount of arrearages or anticipated arrearages, including accrued interest, and the amount of wages that will be withheld in accordance with a judicial writ of withholding;

(2) state that the withholding applies to each current or subsequent employer or period of employment;

(3) state that if the obligor does not contest the withholding within 10 days after the date of receipt of the notice, the obligor's employer will be notified to begin the withholding;

(4) describe the procedures for contesting the issuance and delivery of a writ of withholding;

(5) state that if the obligor contests the withholding, the obligor will be afforded an opportunity for a hearing by the court not later than the 30th day after the date of receipt of the notice of contest;

(6) state that the sole ground for successfully contesting the issuance of a writ of withholding is a dispute concerning the identity of the obligor or the existence or amount of the arrearages, including accrued interest;

(7) describe the actions that may be taken if the obligor contests the notice of application for judicial writ of withholding, including the procedures for suspending issuance of a writ of withholding; and

(8) include with the notice a suggested form for the motion to stay issuance and delivery of the judicial writ of withholding that the obligor may file with the clerk of the appropriate court.

§ 158.303. Interstate Request for Income Withholding

(a) The registration of a foreign support order as provided in Chapter 159 is sufficient for the filing of a notice of application for judicial writ of withholding.

(b) The notice shall be filed with the clerk of the court having venue as provided in Chapter 159.

(c) Notice of application for judicial writ of withholding may be delivered to the obligor at the same time that an order is filed for registration under Chapter 159.

§ 158.304. Additional Arrearages

If the notice of application for judicial writ of withholding states that the obligor has repeatedly failed to pay support in accordance with the underlying support order, the judicial writ may include arrearages that accrue between the filing of the notice and the date of the hearing or the issuance of a judicial writ of withholding.

§ 158.305. Repealed

§ 158.306. Delivery of Notice of Application for Judicial Writ Of Withholding; Time of Delivery

(a) A notice of application for judicial writ of withholding may be delivered to the obligor by:

(1) hand delivery by a person designated by the Title IV-D agency or local domestic relations office;

(2) first-class or certified mail, return receipt requested, addressed to the obligor's last known address or place of employment; or

(3) by service of citation as in civil cases generally.

(b) If the notice is delivered by mailing or hand delivery, the party who filed the notice shall file with the court a certificate stating the name, address, and date on which the mailing or hand delivery was made.

(c) Notice is considered to have been received by the obligor:

(1) if hand delivered, on the date of delivery;

(2) if mailed by certified mail, on the date of receipt;

(3) if mailed by first-class mail, on the 10th day after the date the notice was mailed; or

(4) if delivered by service of citation, on the date of service.

§ 158.307. Motion to Stay Issuance of Writ of Withholding

(a) The obligor may stay issuance of a judicial writ of withholding by filing a motion to stay with the clerk of court not later than the 10th day after the date the notice of application for judicial writ of withholding was received.

(b) The grounds for filing a motion to stay issuance are limited to a dispute concerning the identity of the obligor or the existence or the amount of the arrearages.

(c) The obligor shall verify that statements of fact in the motion to stay issuance of the writ are true and correct.

§ 158.308. Effect of Filing Motion to Stay

The filing of a motion to stay by an obligor in the manner provided by Section 158.307 prohibits the clerk of court from delivering the judicial writ of withholding to any employer of the obligor before a hearing is held.

§ 158.309. Hearing on Motion to Stay

(a) If a motion to stay is filed in the manner provided by Section 158.307, the court shall set a hearing on the motion and the clerk of court shall notify the obligor, obligee, or their authorized representatives, and the party who filed the application for judicial writ of withholding of the date, time, and place of the hearing.

(b) The court shall hold a hearing on the motion to stay not later than the 30th day after the date the motion was filed, except that a hearing may be held later than the 30th day after filing if both the obligor and obligee agree and waive the right to have the motion heard within 30 days.

(c) Upon hearing, the court shall:

(1) render an order for income withholding that includes a determination of the amount of child support arrearages, including medical support and interest; or

(2) grant the motion to stay.

§ 158.310. Special Exceptions

(a) A defect in a notice of application for judicial writ of withholding is waived unless the respondent specially excepts in writing and cites with particularity the alleged defect, obscurity, or other ambiguity in the notice.

(b) A special exception under this section must be heard by the court before hearing the motion to stay issuance.

(c) If the court sustains an exception, the court shall provide the party filing the notice an opportunity to refile and the court shall continue the hearing to a date certain without the requirement of additional service.

§ 158.311. Arrearages

(a) Payment of arrearages after receipt of notice of application for judicial writ of withholding may not be the sole basis for the court to refuse to order withholding.

(b) The court shall order that a reasonable amount of income be withheld to be applied toward the liquidation of arrearages, even though a judgment confirming arrearages has been rendered against the obligor.

§ 158.312. Request for Issuance and Delivery of Writ of Withholding

(a) If a notice of application for judicial writ of withholding is delivered and a motion to stay is not filed within the time limits provided by Section 158.307, the party who filed the notice shall file with the clerk of the court a request for issuance of the writ of withholding stating the amount of current support, including medical support, the amount of arrearages, and the amount to be withheld from the obligor's income.

(b) The request for issuance may not be filed before the 11th day after the date of receipt of the notice of application for judicial writ of withholding by the obligor.

§ 158.313. Issuance and Delivery of Writ of Withholding

(a) On the filing of a request for issuance of a writ of withholding, the clerk of the court shall issue the writ.

(b) The writ shall be delivered as provided by Subchapter B.

(c) The clerk shall issue and mail the writ not later than the second working day after the date the request is filed.

§ 158.314. Contents of Writ of Withholding

The judicial writ of income withholding issued by the clerk must direct that the employer or a subsequent employer withhold from the obligor's disposable income for current child support, including medical support, and child support arrearages an amount that is consistent with the provisions of this chapter regarding orders of withholding.

§ 158.315. Extension of Repayment Schedule by Party; Unreasonable Hardship

If the party who filed the notice of application for judicial writ of withholding finds that the schedule for repaying arrearages would cause the obligor, the obligor's family, or the children for whom the support is due from the obligor to suffer unreasonable hardship, the party may extend the payment period in the writ.

§ 158.316. Payment of Amount to be Withheld

The amount to be withheld shall be paid to the person or office named in the writ on each pay date and shall include with the payment the date on which the withholding occurred.

§ 158.317. Failure to Receive Notice of Application for Judicial Writ Of Withholding

(a) Not later than the 30th day after the date of the first pay period following the date of delivery of the writ of withholding to the obligor's employer, the obligor may file an affidavit with the court that a motion to stay was not timely filed because the notice of application for judicial writ of withholding was not received by the obligor and that grounds exist for a motion to stay.

(b) Concurrently with the filing of the affidavit, the obligor may file a motion to withdraw the writ of withholding and request a hearing on the applicability of the writ.

(c) Income withholding may not be interrupted until after the hearing at which the court renders an order denying or modifying withholding.

§ 158.318. [Blank]

§ 158.319. Issuance and Delivery of Judicial Writ of Withholding to Subsequent Employer

(a) After the issuance of a judicial writ of withholding by the clerk, a party authorized to file a notice of application for judicial writ of withholding under this subchapter may issue the judicial writ of withholding to a subsequent employer of the obligor by delivering to the employer by certified mail a copy of the writ.

(b) The judicial writ of withholding must include the name, address, and signature of the party and clearly indicate that the writ is being issued to a subsequent employer.

(c) The party shall file a copy of the judicial writ of withholding with the clerk not later than the third working day following delivery of the writ to the subsequent employer. The party shall pay the clerk a fee of $15 at the time the copy of the writ is filed.

(d) The party shall file the postal return receipt from the delivery to the subsequent employer not later than the third working day after the party receives the receipt.

SUBCHAPTER E. MODIFICATION, REDUCTION, OR TERMINATION OF WITHHOLDING

Leading Cases

In re A.D., 73 S.W.3d 244 (Tex. 2002) (administrative writ proper enforcement tool that removed bar to exercise of court's jurisdiction and therefore is not a retroactive law)

Attorney General v. Redding, 60 S.W.3d 891 (Tex. App.—Dallas 2001, no pet.) (*see In re* A.D., *supra*) (father subject to administrative writ; application of an extended statute of limitations to a claim for support arrears that is not yet barred by limitations does not implicate the vested rights of the obligor)

---

§ 158.401. Modifications to or Termination of Withholding by Title IV–D Agency

(a) The Title IV–D agency shall establish procedures for the reduction in the amount of or termination of withholding from income on the liquidation of an arrearages or the termination of the obligation of support in Title IV–D cases. The procedures shall provide that the payment of overdue support may not be used as the sole basis for terminating withholding.

(b) At the request of the Title IV-D agency, the clerk of the court shall issue a judicial writ of withholding to the obligor's employer reflecting any modification or changes in the amount to be withheld or the termination of withholding.

§ 158.402. Agreement by Parties Regarding Amount or Duration of Withholding

(a) An obligor and obligee may agree on a reduction in or termination of income withholding for child support on the occurrence of one of the following contingencies stated in the order:

(1) the child becomes 18 years of age or is graduated from high school, whichever is later;

(2) the child's disabilities of minority are removed by marriage, court order, or other operation of law; or

(3) the child dies.

(b) The obligor and obligee may file a notarized or acknowledged request with the clerk of the court under Section 158.011 for a revised judicial writ of withholding, including the termination of withholding.

(c) The clerk shall issue and deliver to an employer of the obligor a judicial writ of withholding that reflects the agreed revision or termination of withholding.

(d) An agreement by the parties under this section does not modify the terms of a support order.

§ 158.403. Modifications to or Termination of Withholding in Voluntary Withholding Cases

(a) If an obligor initiates voluntary withholding under Section 158.011, the obligee or an agency providing child support services may file with the clerk of the court a notarized request signed by the obligor and the obligee or agency, as appropriate, for the issuance and delivery to the obligor of a:

(1) modified writ of withholding that reduces the amount of withholding; or

(2) notice of termination of withholding.

(b) On receipt of a request under this section, the clerk shall issue and deliver a modified writ of withholding or notice of termination in the manner provided by Section 158.402.

(c) The clerk may charge a reasonable fee not to exceed $15 for filing the request.

(d) An obligee may contest a modified writ of withholding or notice of termination issued under this section by requesting a hearing in the manner provided by Section 158.309 not later than the 180th day after the date the obligee discovers that the writ or notice has been issued.

§ 158.404. Delivery of Order of Reduction or Termination of Withholding

If a court has rendered an order that reduces the amount of child support to be withheld or terminates withholding for child support, any person or governmental entity may deliver to the employer a certified copy of the order without the requirement that the clerk of the court deliver the order.

§ 158.405. Liability of Employers

The provisions of this chapter regarding the liability of employers for withholding apply to an order that reduces or terminates withholding.

SUBCHAPTER F. ADMINISTRATIVE WRIT OF WITHHOLDING

Introductory Comment

Under the federal welfare reform act of 1996 a state Title IV–D agency must have statutory authority to take certain administrative actions to enforce support without the necessity of a court order. Among these actions is income withholding. This subchapter implements the federal requirement by providing the Title IV–D agency with the ability to issue a writ of withholding directly instead of having to request the issuance of a writ by the clerk. Once delivered to an employer the administrative writ is filed for the record with the clerk of the court of continuing, exclusive jurisdiction.

Although an administrative writ may be contested on the same grounds as a writ issued by the clerk, the issuance of an administrative writ, unlike a judicial writ, may not be stayed. As required by federal law, the obligor is given notice of the administrative writ only after it has been issued and withholding has commenced. An obligor may contest an administrative writ by first requesting an agency review and, then, should any issue remain unresolved, by requesting judicial review. Once all current support, including medical support, and any arrears have been satisfied, the agency may issue a writ terminating withholding.

The administrative writ process is available to domestic relations offices [DRO's] to assist those agencies to enforce their child support cases. Prior to 2005, issuance of an administrative income withholding writ was the only enforcement remedy in the Family Code restricted to the Title IV–D agency. The decision that all of the wide variety of enforcement methods should be in the arsenal of whichever entity is charged with the duty of collecting a child support order seems eminently practical. *(A.G.K. & H.P.S.)*

---

§ 158.501. Issuance of Administrative Writ of Withholding

(a) The Title IV–D agency may initiate income withholding by issuing an administrative writ of withholding for the enforcement of an existing order as authorized by this subchapter.

(b) Except as provided by Subsection (d), the Title IV–D agency is the only entity that may issue an administrative writ under this subchapter.

(c) The Title IV-D agency may use the procedures authorized by this subchapter to enforce a support order rendered by a tribunal of another state regardless of whether the order has been registered under Chapter 159.

(d) A domestic relations office may issue an administrative writ of withholding under this chapter in a proceeding in which the office is providing child support enforcement services. A reference in this code to the Title IV–D agency that relates to an administrative writ includes a domestic relations office, except that the writ must be in the form prescribed by the Title IV–D agency under Section 158.504.

Comment

This section conforms the use of the administrative writ procedures to UIFSA for administrative enforcement of an interstate order by the Title IV–D agency without initially being required to register the order. It also authorizes a domestic relations office to use the administrative writ process in cases in which the DRO is enforcing child support. *See* respectively §159.507(b) and §203.004. *(A.G.K. & H.P.S.)*

---

§ 158.502. When Administrative Writ of Withholding May be Issued

(a) An administrative writ of withholding under this subchapter may be issued by the Title IV–D agency at any time until all current support, including medical support, and child support arrearages, and Title IV–D service fees authorized under Section 231.103 for which the obligor is responsible, have been paid. The writ issued under this subsection may be based on an obligation in more than one support order.

(b) The Title IV–D agency may issue an administrative writ of withholding that directs that an amount be withheld for an arrearage or adjusts the amount to be withheld for an arrearage. An administrative writ issued under this subsection may be contested as provided by Section 158.506.

(c) The Title IV-D agency may issue an administrative writ of withholding as a reissuance of an existing withholding order on file with the court of continuing jurisdiction or a tribunal of another state. The administrative writ under this subsection is not subject to the contest provisions of Sections 158.505(a)(2) and 158.506.

(d) The Title IV–D agency may issue an administrative writ of withholding to direct child support payments to the state disbursement unit of another state.

Comment

Subsection (d) enables the IV–D agency to redirect income withheld for child support to the disbursement unit of a state to which the obligee has relocated. This conforms to the provisions under § 159.319 (UIFSA) for redirection of support payments in interstate enforcement. *(A.G.K. & H.P.S.)*

Leading Cases

In re A.D., 73 S.W.3d 244 (Tex. 2002) (1997 amendment repealing four-year limitation on court's jurisdiction to order withholding for child support constitutional, unlimited time for enforcement not a retroactive law)

In re A.C.B., 103 S.W.3d 570 (Tex. App.—San Antonio 2003, no pet.) (AG sanctioned for administrative writ of withholding)

---

§ 158.503. Delivery of Administrative Writ to Employer; Filing With Court or Maintaining Record

(a) An administrative writ of withholding issued under this subchapter may be delivered to an ~~obligor, obligee, and~~employer by mail or by electronic transmission.

(b) **The Title IV–D agency shall:**

(1) not ~~Not~~later than the third business day after the date of delivery of the administrative writ of withholding to an employer, ~~the Title IV–D agency shall~~file a copy of the writ, together with a signed certificate of service, in the court of continuing jurisdiction**; or**

(2) maintain a record of the writ until all support obligations of the obligor have been satisfied or income withholding has been terminated as provided by this chapter.

(b–1) The certificate of service **required under Subsection (b)(1)** may be signed electronically. ~~This subsection does not apply to the enforcement under Section 158.501(c) of a support order rendered by a tribunal of another state.~~

(c) The copy of the administrative writ of withholding filed with the clerk of court must include:

(1) the name, address, and signature of the authorized attorney or individual that issued the writ;

(2) the name and address of the employer served with the writ; and

(3) a true copy of the information provided to the employer.

(d) The clerk of the court may charge a reasonable fee not to exceed $15 for filing an administrative writ under this section.

Amended by Acts 2011, 82nd Leg., ch. 508 (H.B. 1674), §§ 10, 11, eff. Sept. 1, 2011.

Comment

The only value of the filing of an administrative writ with the clerk may be that it provides counties with income through the fee required under Subsection (d). While the Title IV–D agency must pay the filing fee out of its own funds, a domestic relations office may recover the amount of the fee from the obligor. (*See infra* § 203.005(a)(9)). *(A.G.K. & H.P.S.)*

---

§ 158.504. Contents of Administrative Writ of Withholding

(a) The administrative writ of withholding must be in the form prescribed by the Title IV-D agency as required by this chapter and in a standard format authorized by the United States Department of Health and Human Services.

(b) An administrative writ of withholding issued under this subchapter may contain only the information that is necessary for the employer to withhold income for child support and medical support and shall specify the place where the withheld income is to be paid.

§ 158.505. Notice to Obligor

(a) On issuance of an administrative writ of withholding, the Title IV-D agency shall send the obligor:

(1) notice that the withholding has commenced, including, if the writ is issued as provided by Section 158.502(b), the amount of the arrearages, including accrued interest;

(2) except as provided by Section 158.502(c), notice of the procedures to follow if the obligor desires to contest withholding on the grounds that the identity of the obligor or the existence or amount of arrearages is incorrect; and

(3) a copy of the administrative writ, including the information concerning income withholding provided to the employer.

(b) The notice required under this section may be sent to the obligor by:

(1) personal delivery by a person designated by the Title IV-D agency;

(2) first-class mail or certified mail, return receipt requested, addressed to the obligor's last known address; or

(3) service of citation as in civil cases generally.

§ 158.506. Contest by Obligor to Administrative Writ of Withholding

(a) Except as provided by Section 158.502(c), an obligor receiving the notice under Section 158.505 may request a review by the Title IV–D agency to resolve any issue in dispute regarding the identity of the obligor or the existence or amount of arrearages. The Title IV–D agency shall provide an opportunity for a review, by telephonic conference or in person, as may be appropriate under the circumstances.

(b) After a review under this section, the Title IV-D agency may issue a new administrative writ of withholding to the employer, including a writ modifying the amount to be withheld or terminating withholding.

(c) If a review under this section fails to resolve any issue in dispute, the obligor may file a motion with the court to withdraw the administrative writ of withholding and request a hearing with the court not later than the 30th day after receiving notice of the agency's determination. Income withholding may not be interrupted pending a hearing by the court.

(d) If an administrative writ of withholding issued under this subchapter is based on an order of a tribunal of another state that has not been registered under Chapter 159, the obligor may file a motion with an appropriate court in accordance with Subsection (c).

§ 158.507. Administrative Writ Terminating Withholding

An administrative writ to terminate withholding may be issued and delivered to an employer by the Title IV–D agency when all current support, including medical support, and child support arrearages, and Title IV–D service fees authorized under Section 231.103 for which the obligor is responsible, have been paid.

CHAPTER 159. UNIFORM INTERSTATE FAMILY SUPPORT ACT

***Editors' Note**: Explanation of UIFSA Cross References. To assist bench and bar in construing UIFSA, the "Prefatory Note" and the "Commissioners' Official Comments" regarding provisions of the Act which accompany the official version are reprinted after each section. The section numbers of the uniform act, e.g., UIFSA § 101, correspond to the numbers of the sections in the Texas Family Code, e.g., § 159.101, etc. To avoid confusion for the reader, references in the Commissioners' Official Comments have been edited to reflect the enactment of the Act in Texas. For example, the comments often refer to changes made in the "2001" version of the Act. Such references are edited here to reflect the fact that version did not become effective in Texas until 9/01/2003.*

UIFSA (2001) has the following enabling clause:

History: Amended by 78th Legis., Reg. Sess. (2003), S.B. 1805, eff. Sept. 1, 2003. (a) The changes in law made by this Act to Section 154.004, Family Code, apply only to a court order or a portion of a decree that provides for the support of a child that is rendered on or after the effective date of this Act. An order or decree rendered before the effective date of this Act is governed by the law in effect on the date the order or decree was rendered, and the former law is continued in effect for that purpose. (b) Except as provided by Subsection (a) of this section, the changes in law made by this Act apply only to an interstate proceeding to establish, modify, or enforce a support obligation or to determine if parentage began on or after the effective date of this Act. A proceeding begun before the effective date is governed by the law in effect on the date the proceeding began, and the former law is continued in effect for that purpose.

SUBCHAPTER A. CONFLICTS BETWEEN PROVISIONS

SUBCHAPTER B. GENERAL PROVISIONS

SUBCHAPTER C. JURISDICTION

SUBCHAPTER D. CIVIL PROVISIONS OF GENERAL APPLICATION

SUBCHAPTER E. ESTABLISHMENT OF SUPPORT ORDER

SUBCHAPTER F. ENFORCEMENT OF ORDER OF ANOTHER STATE WITHOUT REGISTRATION

SUBCHAPTER G. REGISTRATION, ENFORCEMENT, AND MODIFICATION OF SUPPORT ORDER

SUBCHAPTER H. DETERMINATION OF PARENTAGE

SUBCHAPTER I. INTERSTATE RENDITION

SUBCHAPTER J. MISCELLANEOUS PROVISIONS

§ 159.901. Uniformity of Application and Construction.

Introductory Comment

The brief history of the Uniform Interstate Family Support Act (*UIFSA*) is as follows. Beginning in 1950, the National Conference of Commissioners on Uniform State Laws (NCCUSL), now also known as the Uniform Law Commission (ULC), set forth down a long, winding road to facilitate interstate enforcement of child support orders. The first steps began with the Uniform Reciprocal Enforcement of Support Act (URESA), which led to its Revised act (RURESA) in 1968. Ultimately, all states had their own version of one of these two versions of the uniform act.

In 1992 NCCUSL promulgated the Uniform Interstate Family Support Act (UIFSA) to replace the existing laws. Effective Sept. 1, 1993, Texas was the second state to enact UIFSA (perhaps due in part to the involvement of the editors in its drafting). In 1996, NCCUSL approved a comprehensive set of amendments to the 1992 act. Also in 1996, Congress enacted the Personal Responsibility and Work Opportunity Reconciliation Act (PRWORA), which mandated enactment of the amended UIFSA by all U.S. jurisdictions by January 1, 1998. Texas passed the amended act in 1997; by May 1, 1998 all states, the District of Columbia, and the U.S. territories had adopted UIFSA (1996).

In August 2001, UIFSA was once again revised by the National Conference. Once again, the Texas Legislature enacted the latest version at the earliest opportunity, *i.e.*, the 2003 session.

One of the most interesting aspects of the continued attention to detail evidenced by the repeated updating of the act is the very little appellate caselaw generated over the years. Despite the fact that the Child Support Division of the Office of the Texas Attorney General has processed many thousands of cases, both incoming and outgoing, there are only 25 Texas cases reported on Westlaw as of June 30, 2010. Arguably this may be attributed to the fact that UIFSA is a masterpiece of drafting.

Finally, in 2008 yet another version of UIFSA was promulgated, designed to accommodate international enforcement of child support orders in the expectation that a new Hague Convention on the International Recovery of Child Support and Other Forms of Family Maintenance (2008) will be adopted by the United States. The exact timing of entry into force of the treaty is beyond the ability of the editors to predict.

As this 2011 edition goes to print, 18 jurisdictions have enacted the 2001 version of UIFSA, 24 have continued to rely on the (1996) version, and nine have adopted the (2008) offering. The latest list of enacting jurisdictions may be found on the website of the National Conference of Commissioners on Uniform State Laws; *www.nccusl.org*

CLE/Other Legal Publications

UCCJEA/UIFSA. Harry L. Tindall, 2011 U.T. Advanced Parent–Child Relationships

Ding! You are now free to move about the country: UCCJEA and UIFSA. JoAl Cannon Sheridan, 2011 Adv. Fam. L.

International and domestic jurisdiction issues: UIFSA, UCCJEA, UCAPA, PKPA, FFCCSOA, ICARA. Karl E. Hays & Janet McCullar Vavra, 2011 U.T. Fam. L. Front Lines

Caution! Acronyms ahead: traveling on the interstate case highway. Karen L. Marvel & John Christopher Nickelson, 2010 U.T. Parent-Child Relationships

Uniform Interstate Family Support Act (2001) with Prefatory Note and Comments (with Still More Unofficial Annotations). John J. Sampson and Barry J. Brooks, 36 Fam. L.Q. 329 (2002)

A guide for assisting military families with the Uniform Interstate Family Support Act (UIFSA). Joseph W. Booth, 43 Fam. L.Q. 203 (2009)

Child Support Workshop: UIFSA, Above Guideline Child Support, Effective Use of Financial Documents, Utilization of QDRO's and Child Support Liens; Enforcement Techniques, (Panel). 2009 ADV. FAM. L.

UCCJEA and UIFSA —can they be modified. Angela Pence England, 2009 SO. TEX. FAM. L. CONF.

Leading Cases

In re T.L., 316 S.W.3d 78 (Tex. App.—Houston [14th Dist.] 2010, no pet.) (Texas did not lose continuing, exclusive jurisdiction under UIFSA to enforce Texas child support; LA lacked jurisdiction to modify order)

In re V.L.C., 225 S.W.3d 221 (Tex. App.—El Paso 2006, no pet.) (UIFSA inapplicable, no out of state order—Sinaloa, Mexico not a reciprocating "state")

In re G.L.A., 195 S.W.3d 787 (Tex. App.—Beaumont, 2006, pet. denied) (trial court cannot refuse to enforce another state's child support order—forum non conveniens doesn't apply, but UIFSA and Full Faith and Credit do)

In re M.G.M., 163 S.W.3d 191 (Tex. App.—Beaumont 2005, no pet.) (father did not waive special appearance in challenge to personal jurisdiction)

See Accompanying CD–ROM for Cases Linked to Westlaw and Additional Leading Cases.

COMMISSIONERS' PREFATORY NOTE

I. BACKGROUND INFORMATION

In 1992 the National Conference of Commissioners on Uniform State Laws [hereafter NCCUSL, the Conference, or Uniform Law Commissioners] promulgated the UNIFORM INTERSTATE FAMILY SUPPORT ACT [hereafter UIFSA] as a complete replacement for the two then-existing uniform interstate support acts, the UNIFORM RECIPROCAL ENFORCEMENT OF SUPPORT ACT [URESA] and its revised version [RURESA]. In 1993 two States, Arkansas and Texas, enacted UIFSA. By the summer of 1996, 35 States had adopted the new Uniform Act. That year was a very eventful one in the history of UIFSA. First, a Drafting Committee was convened in Spring 1996 in response to requests from representatives of employer groups for more specific statutory directions regarding interstate child-support withholding orders. Second, the child-support community (primarily the IV–D programs funded by federal subsidies) requested review of the substantive and procedural provisions. As a result, significant amendments to UIFSA were adopted by the Conference in July, 1996.

The Conference promulgated UIFSA in July, 1996. Less than one month later, the U.S. Congress assured that nationwide acceptance of the amended Act was virtually certain. In the "welfare reform" legislation passed in August 1996, officially known as the PERSONAL RESPONSIBILITY AND WORK OPPORTUNITY RECONCILIATION ACT OF 1996 (PRWORA), the enactment of UIFSA, as amended, was mandated as a condition of state eligibility for the federal funding of child support enforcement, as follows:

> Sec. 321. ADOPTION OF UNIFORM STATE LAWS [42 U.S.C. Section 666] is amended by adding at the end the following new subsection:
>
> > "(f) Uniform Interstate Family Support Act.—In order to satisfy [42 U.S.C. 654(20)(A)], on and after January 1, 1998, each State must have in effect the Uniform Interstate Family Support Act, as approved by the American Bar Association on February 9, 1993, together with any amendments officially adopted before January 1, 1998, by the National Conference of Commissioners on Uniform State Laws." P.L. 104–193, Section 321, 110 Stat. 2221.

For a comprehensive history of the events leading up to the replacement of URESA and RURESA by UIFSA, *see* the Prefatory Notes to the 1992 and 1996 versions of the Act found in 9 UNIFORM LAWS ANNOTATED 253, 393 (2000), or John J. Sampson, *Uniform Interstate Family Support Act with Unofficial Annotations*, 27 FAM. L.Q. 91 (1993), and John J. Sampson, *Uniform Interstate Family*

Support Act (1996), Statutory Text, Prefatory Note, and Commissioners Comments (with More Unofficial Annotations), 32 FAM. L.Q. 385 (1998).

In accordance with the congressional mandate, by 1998 all U.S. jurisdictions had enacted UIFSA. Thus, the several states have had between four and eight years of experience with the various iterations of the Act. Moreover, there has been an extraordinary amount of comprehensive training about the Act by the child support enforcement agencies throughout the nation and associated agencies and organizations of those agencies, *e.g.*: U.S. Department of Health and Human Services, Office of Child Support Enforcement (OCSE); National Child Support Enforcement Association (NCSEA); Eastern Regional Interstate Child Support Association (ERICSA); and, Western Interstate Child Support Enforcement Council (WICSEC). As a consequence, the provisions of UIFSA are far more familiar to those who must administer it than ever was true of its predecessor acts, URESA and RURESA.

In 2000 the child-support community again requested that the Act be reviewed and amendments suggested as appropriate. In response to this request, the Conference leadership appointed a new Drafting Committee (the earlier Committee had been disbanded). A single meeting in March 2001 led to significant substantive and procedural amendments that ultimately were approved by the Conference at its Annual Meeting in August, 2001. None of the amendments, however, make a fundamental change in the policies and procedures established in UIFSA 1996. The widespread acceptance of UIFSA is due primarily to the fact that representatives of the child support enforcement community mentioned above participated actively in the drafting of each version of the Act, including the amendments of 2001. In sum, although two sets of amendments have been propounded since the initial 1992 version of UIFSA, its basic principles have remained constant.

II. BASIC PRINCIPLES OF UIFSA

A. In General

1. RECIPROCITY NOT REQUIRED BETWEEN STATES. Reciprocal laws, the hallmark of RURESA and URESA, are not required under UIFSA. Although reciprocity became irrelevant in this country with the universal adoption of UIFSA, reciprocity continues to be an issue with regard to the recognition and enforcement of support orders of foreign countries and their political subdivisions, Sections 102(21), 104, 308. Respect and tolerance for the laws of other states and nations in order to facilitate child support enforcement is another prime goal of the Act. The 2001 amendments continue this perspective by explicitly recognizing that tribunals may extend the principle of comity to foreign support orders, Sections 104 and 210.

2. LONG–ARM JURISDICTION. UIFSA contains a broad provision for asserting long-arm jurisdiction to provide a tribunal in the State of residence of the spouse or a child entitled to support with the maximum possible opportunity to secure personal jurisdiction over an absent respondent, Section 201. This converts what otherwise would be a two-state proceeding into a one-state proceeding. When jurisdiction over a nonresident is obtained, the tribunal may obtain evidence, provide for discovery, and elicit testimony through use of the same "information route" provided for two-state proceedings, Sections 210, 316–318. Amendments in 2001 to the basic long-arm provision, Section 201, clarified and strengthened the interrelationship between the assertion of such jurisdiction and the continuing nature of personal jurisdiction for enforcement and modification of a support order, Sections 205 and 206.

B. Establishing a Support Order

1. FAMILY SUPPORT. The Act may be used only for proceedings involving the support of a child or spouse of the support obligor; it does not include enforcement of other duties of support found in the statutes of a few states, such as requiring support of an elderly or disabled parent by an adult child, Sections 101(2),(18).

2. LOCAL LAW. UIFSA provides that the procedures and law of the forum apply, with some significant additions or exceptions:

(a) Certain procedures are prescribed for interstate cases even if they are not consistent with local law, i.e.: the contents of interstate petitions, Sections 311 and 602; the nondisclosure of certain sensitive information, Section 312; authority to award fees and costs including attorney's fees, Section 313; elimination of certain testimonial immunities, Section 314; and, limits on the assertion of nonparentage as a defense to support enforcement, Section 315.

(b) Visitation issues cannot be raised in child support proceedings, Section 305(d).

(c) Special rules for the interstate transmission of evidence and discovery are added to help place the maximum amount of information before the deciding tribunal. These procedures are available in cases in which the tribunal asserts jurisdiction over a nonresident, (Sections 210, 316–318), and may have the effect of amending local law in long-arm cases.

(d) The choice-of-law rule for the interpretation of a registered order is that the law of the issuing State governs the underlying terms of the controlling support order. One important exception exists; if the registering and issuing State have different statutes of limitation for enforcement, the longer time limit applies, Section 604.

3. CONTINUING EXCLUSIVE JURISDICTION AND THE ONE–ORDER SYSTEM. Under URESA and RURESA the majority of support proceedings were de novo. Even when an existing order of one State was "registered" in a second State, the registering State often asserted the right to modify the registered order. This meant that multiple support orders could be in effect in several states. As far as is possible, under UIFSA the principle of continuing, exclusive jurisdiction aims to recognize that only one valid support order may be effective at any one time, Sections 205–207. This principle is carried out in Sections 203–211.

4. PRIVATE ATTORNEYS. UIFSA explicitly authorizes parties to retain private legal counsel in support proceedings, Section 309, as well as to use the services of a state support enforcement agency, Section 307(a). The Act expressly takes no position on whether the support enforcement agency's assistance of a supported family establishes an attorney-client relationship with the applicant, Section 307(c).

5. EFFICIENCY. UIFSA streamlines interstate proceedings as follows:

(a) Proceedings may be initiated by or referred to administrative agencies rather than to courts in those states that use those agencies to establish support orders, Section 101(22).

(b) Under the old system, the process began by requiring a local "initiating tribunal" to make a preliminary (and nonbinding) determination of a duty to support, and then forwarding the documents to a "responding tribunal" for a binding decision. Under UIFSA an individual party or support enforcement agency in the initiating State may file a proceeding directly in a tribunal in the responding State, Section 301. This innovation by UIFSA has proven to be a major contribution to efficient case management. In the unlikely event that some local action is needed, initiation of an interstate case in the initiating State is expressly made ministerial rather than a matter for adjudication or review by a tribunal.

(c) To facilitate efficient interstate establishment, enforcement, and modification of child support orders, forms sanctioned by the federal Office of Child Support Enforcement are available. Although developed in conjunction with the federal IV–D program, private parties and their attorneys who are engaged in an interstate child support case are well advised to use the appropriate forms for transmission of information to the responding State, Section 311(b). The information in those forms is declared to be admissible evidence, Section 316(b).

(d) Authority is provided for the transmission of information and documents through electronic and other modern means of communication, Section 316(e).

(e) Tribunals are directed to permit an out-of-state party or witness to be deposed or to testify by telephone conference, Section 316(f).

(f) Tribunals are required to cooperate in the discovery process for use in a tribunal in another State, Section 318.

(g) A tribunal and a support enforcement agency providing services to a supported family must keep the parties informed about all important developments in a case, Sections 305 and 307.

(h) A registered support order is confirmed and immediately enforceable unless the respondent files an objection in a record within a fixed period of time, almost invariably the 20 days suggested originally, Sections 603 and 607.

6. INTERSTATE PARENTAGE. UIFSA authorizes establishment of parentage in an interstate proceeding, even if not coupled with a proceeding to establish support, Section 701.

C. Enforcing a Support Order

1. DIRECT ENFORCEMENT. UIFSA provides two direct enforcement procedures that do not require assistance from a tribunal. First, a notice may be sent directly to the obligor's employer in another State, Section 501, which triggers income withholding by that employer without the necessity of a hearing unless the employee objects. The Act details the procedure to be followed by the employer in response to an interstate request for direct income withholding, Sections 502–506. Additionally, the Act provides for direct administrative enforcement by the support enforcement agency of the obligor's State, Section 507.

2. REGISTRATION. Enforcement of a support order of another State or nation involving a tribunal of the forum State begins with the registration of the existing support order in a tribunal of the responding State, Sections 601–604. However, the registered order continues to be the order of the issuing State, Sections 605–608. The role of the responding State is limited to enforcing that order except in the very limited circumstances under which modification is permitted, *infra.*

D. Modifying a Support Order

1. REGISTRATION. The first step for a party (whether obligor or obligee) requesting a tribunal of another State to modify an existing child support order is to follow the identical procedure for registration as when enforcement is sought. All modification requests are subject to strict rules, *infra*, although different sequences are allowable: *i.e.*, registration for enforcement and a later request for modification; or, a request for contemporaneous modification and enforcement.

2. MODIFICATION STATUTORILY RESTRICTED. Under UIFSA, the only tribunal that can modify a support order is one having continuing, exclusive jurisdiction over the support issue. As an initial matter, this is the tribunal that first acquires personal and subject matter jurisdiction over the parties and the support obligation. If modification of the order by the issuing tribunal is no longer appropriate, another tribunal may become vested with the continuing, exclusive jurisdiction necessary to modify the order. Primarily this occurs when neither the individual parties nor the child reside in the issuing State, or when the parties agree in a record that another tribunal may assume modification jurisdiction. Only then may another tribunal with personal jurisdiction over the parties assume continuing, exclusive jurisdiction and have jurisdiction to modify the order, Sections 205, 206, 603(c), 609–612. Further, except for modification by agreement, Section 205 and 207, or when the parties have all moved to the same new State, Section 613, the party petitioning for modification must be a nonresident of the responding State and must submit himself or herself to the forum State, which must have personal jurisdiction over the respondent, Section 611. The vast majority of the time this is the State in which the respondent resides. A colloquial short-hand summary of the principle is that ordinarily the movant for modification of a child support order "must play an away game."

A 2001 amendment adds that even if the parties and child have moved from the issuing State they may agree that the tribunal that issued the controlling order will continue to exercise its continuing, exclusive jurisdiction, Section 205. This recognizes the fact that it may be preferable for the parties to return to a tribunal familiar with the issues rather than to be required to fully inform another tribunal of all the facts and issues that have been previously litigated. This exception may be particularly appropriate if both child-support and spousal-support are involved in the same case; under this Act, jurisdiction to modify the spousal support order is exclusively reserved to the issuing tribunal, regardless of where the parties reside.

Section 613 makes an obvious exception to the nonresident petitioner rule: if the child no longer resides in the issuing State and the parties have moved from the issuing State and by coincidence or design currently reside in the same State, that State has jurisdiction to modify the existing order and assume continuing, exclusive jurisdiction over the child support order.

Section 614 places the duty on the party obtaining a modification to provide notice of the new order to all interested tribunals, and grants the tribunal authority to sanction a party who fails to perform this duty of notice.

To facilitate modification across international borders, another exception to the nonresident petitioner rule was added in 1996 for child support orders issued by foreign jurisdictions. The amendments of 2001 recodified this procedure in a wholly new provision. Section 615 expands on the right of a tribunal of one of the several states to modify a child support order of a foreign country or political subdivision if that jurisdiction is prevented from modifying its order under its local law and the modification would be consistent with standards of due process.

SUBCHAPTER A. CONFLICTS BETWEEN PROVISIONS

§ 159.001. Conflicts Between Provisions

If a provision of this chapter conflicts with a provision of this title or another statute or rule of this state and the conflict cannot be reconciled, this chapter prevails.

SUBCHAPTER B. GENERAL PROVISIONS

§ 159.101. Short Title

This chapter may be cited as the Uniform Interstate Family Support Act.

§ 159.102. Definitions

In this chapter:

(1) "Child" means an individual, whether over or under the age of majority, who:

(A) is or is alleged to be owed a duty of support by the individual's parent; or

(B) is or is alleged to be the beneficiary of a support order directed to the parent.

(2) "Child support order" means a support order for a child, including a child who has attained the age of majority under the law of the issuing state.

(3) "Duty of support" means an obligation imposed or imposable by law to provide support for a child, spouse, or former spouse, including an unsatisfied obligation to provide support.

(4) "Home state" means the state in which a child lived with a parent or a person acting as parent for at least six consecutive months preceding the time of filing of a petition or a comparable pleading for support and, if a child is less than six months old, the state in which the child lived with a parent or a person acting as parent from the time of birth. A period of temporary absence of any of them is counted as part of the six-month or other period.

(5) "Income" includes earnings or other periodic entitlements to money from any source and any other property subject to withholding for support under the law of this state.

(6) "Income–withholding order" means an order or other legal process directed to an obligor's employer, as provided in Chapter 158, to withhold support from the income of the obligor.

(7) "Initiating state" means a state from which a proceeding is forwarded or in which a proceeding is filed for forwarding to a responding state under this chapter or a law or procedure substantially similar to this chapter.

(8) "Initiating tribunal" means the authorized tribunal in an initiating state.

(9) "Issuing state" means the state in which a tribunal issues a support order or renders a judgment determining parentage.

(10) "Issuing tribunal" means the tribunal that issues a support order or renders a judgment determining parentage.

(11) "Law" includes decisional and statutory law and rules and regulations having the force of law.

(12) "Obligee" means:

(A) an individual to whom a duty of support is or is alleged to be owed or in whose favor a support order has been issued or a judgment determining parentage has been rendered;

(B) a state or political subdivision to which the rights under a duty of support or support order have been assigned or that has independent claims based on financial assistance provided to an individual obligee; or

(C) an individual seeking a judgment determining parentage of the individual's child.

(13) "Obligor" means an individual or the estate of a decedent:

(A) who owes or is alleged to owe a duty of support;

(B) who is alleged but has not been adjudicated to be a parent of a child; or

(C) who is liable under a support order.

(14) "Person" means an individual, corporation, business trust, estate, trust, partnership, limited liability company, association, joint venture, government, governmental subdivision, agency, instrumentality, public corporation, or any other legal or commercial entity.

(15) "Record" means information that is:

(A) inscribed on a tangible medium or stored in an electronic or other medium; and

(B) retrievable in a perceivable form.

(16) "Register" means to file a support order or judgment determining parentage in the registry of foreign support orders.

(17) "Registering tribunal" means a tribunal in which a support order is registered.

(18) "Responding state" means a state in which a proceeding is filed or to which a proceeding is forwarded for filing from an initiating state under this chapter or a law or procedure substantially similar to this chapter.

(19) "Responding tribunal" means the authorized tribunal in a responding state.

(20) "Spousal support order" means a support order for a spouse or former spouse of the obligor.

(21) "State" means a state of the United States, the District of Columbia, Puerto Rico, the United States Virgin Islands, or any territory or insular possession subject to the jurisdiction of the United States. The term includes:

(A) an Indian tribe; and

(B) a foreign country or political subdivision that has:

(i) been declared to be a foreign reciprocating country or political subdivision under federal law;

(ii) established a reciprocal arrangement for child support with this state as provided by Section 159.308; or

(iii) enacted a law or established procedures for issuance and enforcement of support orders that are substantially similar to the procedures under this chapter.

(22) "Support enforcement agency" means a public official or agency authorized to seek:

(A) enforcement of support orders or laws relating to the duty of support;

(B) establishment or modification of child support;

(C) determination of parentage;

(D) the location of obligors or their assets; or

(E) determination of the controlling child support order.

"Support enforcement agency" does not include a domestic relations office unless that office has entered into a cooperative agreement with the Title IV–D agency to perform duties under this chapter.

(23) "Support order" means a judgment, decree, order, or directive, whether temporary, final, or subject to modification, issued by a tribunal for the benefit of a child, a spouse, or a former spouse that provides for monetary support, health care, arrearages, or reimbursement and may include related costs and fees, interest, income withholding, attorney's fees, and other relief.

(24) "Tribunal" means a court, administrative agency, or quasi-judicial entity authorized to establish, enforce, or modify support orders or to determine parentage.

Commissioners' Official Comment to UIFSA Section 102

The terms defined in UIFSA have undergone relatively little amendment since its original promulgation in 1992. Two new terms were added in 2003—"person" and "record," found in Subsections (14) and (15), respectively. Other definitions have been amended slightly over the years, but none as significantly as the 2003 amendments to the definition of "State" in Subsection (21).

Many crucial definitions continue to be left to local law. For example, the definitions of "child" and "child-support order" provided by Subsections (1) and (2) refer to "the age of majority" without further elaboration. The exact age at which a child becomes an adult for different purposes is a matter for the law of each State, as is the age at which a parent's duty to furnish child support terminates. Similarly, a wide variety of other terms of art are implicitly left to state law. For example, Subsection (23) refers inter alia to "health care, arrearages, or reimbursement ." All of these terms are subject to individualized definitions on a state-by-state basis.

Subsection (3) defines "duty of support" to mean the legal obligation to provide support, whether or not that duty has been the subject of an order by a tribunal. This broad definition includes both prospective and retrospective obligations to the extent they are imposed by the relevant state law.

For the limited purpose of resolving certain conflicts in the exercise of jurisdiction, Subsection (4) borrows the concept of the "home State of a child" from the UNIFORM CHILD CUSTODY JURISDICTION ACT (UCCJA) and its successor, the UNIFORM CHILD CUSTODY JURISDICTION AND ENFORCEMENT ACT (UCCJEA), versions of which have been adopted in all 50 states, and incorporated into the federal Parental Kidnapping Prevention Act, 42 U.S.C. Section 1738A (PKPA).

Subsection (6) is written broadly to include an "income withholding order" based on "other legal process," as distinguished from "by order of a tribunal." Some states issue such orders administratively, which are entitled to enforcement notwithstanding the fact that no judicial or quasi-judicial process is involved. Federal law requires that, in order to be eligible for federal subsidy monies, each State must provide for income withholding "without the necessity of any application therefor, or for any further action by the court or other entity which issued such order ." 42 U.S.C. Section 666(b)(2). States have complied with this requirement in a variety of ways.

From its beginning UIFSA has permitted direct filing of an interstate proceeding in a responding State without an initial filing in an initiating tribunal. This has become the standard operating procedure for child support enforcement agencies. Thus, a petitioner in one State may seek to establish, enforce, or modify a support order in a second State by either filing in the responding state's tribunal or by directly seeking the assistance of the support enforcement agency in the second State. Although Subsections (7), (8), (18) and (19) supply definitions for "initiating and responding State" and "initiating and responding tribunal," the procedure of "initiation and response" established by the predecessor acts of URESA and RURESA has become an anachronism since the universal enactment of UIFSA.

Until the 2003 amendments, the relationship between UIFSA and the prior uniform acts was captured in the reference to URESA and RURESA as "substantially similar" acts. This phrasing in Subsections (7), (18) and (21), and repeated several times throughout the Act, has been deleted everywhere it appears to avoid confusion that might arise from appearing to incorporate statutes that have been replaced. This is not to suggest in any way that support orders issued under URESA or RURESA are not fully enforceable under UIFSA. Until valid orders issued under those laws expire of their own terms or are replaced by new UIFSA orders, the support orders themselves will continue to have vitality, *see* Sections 201–211, *infra*. In short, UIFSA is specifically designed to function with the earlier acts without conflict. Support orders issued under one of the earlier acts should be honored and enforced in every State. But, despite their common roots, neither URESA nor RURESA can be said to be "substantially similar" with regard to the continuing, exclusive jurisdiction/one-order system established in UIFSA. States are directed to accord full enforcement remedies to support orders issued under the prior acts, but they must apply UIFSA restraint regarding modification. In situations involving multiple orders created under the former system, UIFSA mandates the application of its one-order rules to determine the single order that is entitled to prospective enforcement, *see* Section 207, *infra.*

The term "obligee" in Subsection (12) is defined in a broad manner, which is consistent with common usage. In instances of spousal support, the person owed the duty of support and the person receiving the payments are almost always the same. Use of the term is more complicated in the context of child support. The child is the person to whom the duty of support is owed, and therefore can be viewed as the ultimate obligee. However, "obligee" usually refers to the individual receiving the payments. While this is most commonly the custodial parent or other legal custodian, the "obligee" may be a support enforcement agency that has been assigned the right to receive support payments in order to recoup Temporary Assistance for Needy Families (TANF), 42 U.S.C. Section 601 *et seq.*, formerly known as Aid to Families with Dependent Children (AFDC). Even in the absence of such an assignment, a State may have an independent statutory claim for reimbursement for general assistance provided to a spouse, a former spouse, or a child of an obligor. The Act also uses "obligee" to identify an individual who is asserting a claim for support, not just for a person whose right to support is unquestioned, presumed, or has been established in a legal proceeding.

Subsection (13) provides the correlative definition of an "obligor," which includes an individual who is alleged to owe a duty of support as well as a person whose obligation has previously been determined.

The terms "obligor" and "obligee" inherently contain the legal obligation to pay or receive support, and both terms also implicitly refer to the individuals with a duty to support a child. The one-order system of UIFSA can succeed only if the respective obligations of support are adjusted as the physical possession of a child changes between parents or involves a third party caretaker. This must be accomplished in the context of modification, and not by the creation of multiple orders attempting to reflect each changing custody scenario. Obviously this issue is of concern not only to interstate child-support orders, but applies to intrastate orders as well.

The definition of "record" in new Subsection (14) conforms UIFSA to the Conference standard for legal documentation as established in the UNIFORM ELECTRONIC TRANSACTIONS ACT Section 102(13) [hereafter UETA]. Henceforth, the phrase "in a record" will replace the terminology "in writing" as the appropriate manner to recognize that electronic transmissions and signatures are increasingly appropriate substitutes for more traditional documentation.

The definitions of "responding State" and "responding tribunal" in Subsections (18) and (19) accommodate the direct filing of a petition under UIFSA without the intervention of an initiating tribunal. Both definitions acknowledge the possibility that there may be a responding State and a responding tribunal in a situation where there is no initiating State or initiating tribunal.

Subsection (21) no longer requires reciprocity between the several states, formerly a cornerstone of RURESA and URESA. Public policy favoring enforcement of child support orders is sufficiently strong to warrant waiving any quid pro quo requirement between U.S. jurisdictions. This was true even before the issue was mooted by the enactment of UIFSA by all states by 1998.

The 1996 amendment to Subsection (21) clarified the position that UIFSA, like RURESA before it, does not waive reciprocity in the international context. A major amendment to the text of Subsection (21) was made in 2003 to make clear that a foreign country or political subdivision is defined as a "State" under the Act in three situations. First, a declaration by the U.S. State Department that a foreign jurisdiction is a reciprocating country or political subdivision is controlling for all states. Second, in the absence of such a declaration, each of the several states can make an arrangement with a foreign country or political subdivision for reciprocal enforcement of child support. Finally, a finding may be made that a foreign jurisdiction has a law or procedure substantially similar to UIFSA. That is, a tribunal may consider whether the foreign jurisdiction also has laws and procedures that allow for a U.S. order to be recognized in that foreign jurisdiction independent of a formal reciprocity agreement. The inclusion of foreign political subdivisions is necessary because in some countries the central government will not or cannot bind the subdivisions. For example, reciprocal arrangements with Canada are made on the province level and not with the Canadian federal government.

Although the vast bulk of child support establishment, enforcement, and modification in the United States is performed by the state IV–D agencies, *see* Part IV–D, Social Security Act, 42 U.S.C. Section 651 *et seq.*, Subsection (22) defines the term "support enforcement agency" to include not only those entities, but also any other state or local governmental entities charged with establishing or enforcing support. The 2003 amendment simply adds another key task to the list of powers, that is, determination of the controlling order in multiple order situations.

In 1992 Subsection (24) introduced a completely new term, "tribunal," which replaced the term "court" used in RURESA. With the advent of federally-funded IV–D programs, a number of states have delegated various aspects of child support establishment and enforcement to quasi-judicial bodies and administrative agencies. The term "tribunal" accounts for the breadth of state variations in dealing with support orders. By 2003 the usage has become the standard in the child support enforcement community, although private practitioners who only rarely are involved in such cases may still find the term unfamiliar.

Editors' Comment on Texas Version of Section 102

The second paragraph of § 159.101(20) [UIFSA § 101(20)] relating to the exception of a domestic relations office from the definition of a "support enforcement agency" was added by the Texas Legislature. Local DRO's have a long history of independent operation in this state. Texas domestic relations offices are funded from local fees to enforce child support and visitation; the Texas Legislature was unwilling to impose this additional requirement without some funding source. The variant language is intended to exempt such offices from a duty to provide services in interstate cases unless such services are eligible for federal financial participation through the Title IV–D agency (the attorney general).

Editors' Comment on International Child Support Orders

Sections 159.102(21) and 159.104 deal with the possibility of enforcement of international child support orders. In the federal "welfare reform" legislation passed in August 1996, officially known as the PERSONAL RESPONSIBILITY AND WORK OPPORTUNITY RECONCILIATION ACT OF 1996 (PRWORA), the U.S. Congress authorized the Secretary of State, with the concurrence of the Secretary of HHS (Health and Human Services), to declare foreign nations or their political subdivisions to be "reciprocating countries," whose child support orders are entitled to be treated as if they are orders of sister states, [42 U.S.C. Section 659a]. As of June 30, 2010, the following have been so designated:

FOREIGN RECIPROCATING COUNTRIES

Australia; Canada (all of the individual provinces except Quebec); Czech Republic; El Salvador; Finland; Hungary; Ireland; Israel; Netherlands; Norway; Poland; Portugal; Slovak Republic; Switzerland; and United Kingdom of Great Britain and Northern Ireland.

http://www.acf.dhhs.gov/programs/cse/international/index.html

The federal IV–D also statute provides that "States may enter into reciprocal arrangements for the establishment and enforcement of support obligations with foreign countries that are not the subject of a declaration [of reciprocity by the federal government] to the extent consistent with Federal law," 42 U.S.C.A. § 659a(d). The details for a state plan providing for an agreement with a foreign jurisdiction are supplied in 42 U.S.C.A. § 654 ¶ 32(A). Texas has agreements with a number of countries not on the "official list" above, Germany being by far the most important of these.

§ 159.103. Tribunal of State

The court is the tribunal of this state.

Commissioners' Official Comment to UIFSA Section 103

The enacting state must identify the court, administrative agency, or the combination of those entities, which constitute the tribunal or tribunals authorized to deal with family support. In a particular state there may be several different such entities authorized to determine family support matters.

§ 159.104. Remedies Cumulative

(a) Remedies provided in this chapter are cumulative and do not affect the availability of remedies under other law, including the recognition of a support order of a foreign country or political subdivision on the basis of comity.

(b) This chapter does not:

(1) provide the exclusive method of establishing or enforcing a support order under the law of this state; or

(2) grant a tribunal of this state jurisdiction to render a judgment or issue an order relating to child custody or visitation in a proceeding under this chapter.

Commissioners' Official Comment to UIFSA Section 104

The existence of procedures for interstate establishment, enforcement, or modification of support or a determination of parentage in UIFSA does not preclude the application of the general law of the forum. Even if the parents live in different states, for example, a petitioner may decide to file an original proceeding for child support (and most likely for other relief as well) directly in the State of residence of the respondent and proceed under that forum's generally applicable support law. In so doing, the petitioner thereby submits to the personal jurisdiction of the forum and foregoes reliance on UIFSA. Once a child support order has been issued, this option is no longer available to interstate parties. Under UIFSA, a State may not permit a party to proceed to obtain a second support order; rather, in further litigation the tribunal must apply the Act's provisions for enforcement of an existing order and limit modification to the strict standards of UIFSA.

The 2003 addition to Subsection (a) specifically recognizes the doctrine of comity as a legitimate function of state law that on a proper showing provides for the recognition of a foreign support order, *see Mississippi Dept. Human Svcs. v. Shelnut*, 772 So.2d 1041 (Miss. 2000). Although the determination by the U.S. State Department that a foreign nation is a reciprocating country is binding on all states, recognition of foreign support orders through comity is dependent on the law of each UIFSA State. The reference to "remedies under other law" is intended to recognize the principle of comity as developed in the forum State by statutory or common law, rather than to create a substantive right independent of that law.

New Subsection (b)(1) gives notice that UIFSA is not the only means for establishing or enforcing a support order with an interstate aspect. Examples abound. A potential child-support obligee may voluntarily submit to the jurisdiction of another State to seek the full range of desired relief under the law of that State using intrastate procedures, rather than resorting to the interstate procedure provided by UIFSA. A nonresident married parent may choose to file a proceeding in the forum State for dissolution of the marriage, including property division and spousal support, and in conjunction seek an order regarding child custody and visitation and child support. A parent may submit to the jurisdiction of another State for a determination of parentage and child support. A support order resulting from each of these scenarios implicates UIFSA. Invariably the issuing tribunal will have continuing, exclusive jurisdiction over its controlling child or spousal support orders as provided by Sections 205, 207, 211, *infra*, with all of the attendant application of the Act to those orders.

On the other hand, Subsection (b)(2) states what is clear under U.S. Supreme Court decisions; the bases of jurisdiction for child custody and visitation orders and the jurisdiction for child-support orders run on separate tracks, compare *May v. Anderson*, 345 U.S. 528 (1953) with *Kulko v. Superior Court*, 436 U.S. 84 (1978). If the child-support order is sought under the authority of UIFSA, the most important aspect of this rule is that a child-support obligee utilizing the provisions of UIFSA to establish child support across State lines submits to jurisdiction for child support only, and does not submit to the jurisdiction of the responding State with regard to child custody or visitation.

SUBCHAPTER C. JURISDICTION

Leading Case

Cotton v. Cotton, 57 S.W.3d 506 (Tex. App.—Waco 2001, no pet.) (where there is no basis for in personam jurisdiction of a parent, a trial court lacks the authority to render any judgment or child support payments against the parent)

---

§ 159.201. Bases for Jurisdiction over Nonresident

(a) In a proceeding to establish or enforce a support order or to determine parentage, a tribunal of this state may exercise personal jurisdiction over a nonresident individual or the individual's guardian or conservator if:

(1) the individual is personally served with citation in this state;

(2) the individual submits to the jurisdiction of this state by consent, by entering a general appearance, or by filing a responsive document having the effect of waiving any contest to personal jurisdiction;

(3) the individual resided with the child in this state;

(4) the individual resided in this state and provided prenatal expenses or support for the child;

(5) the child resides in this state as a result of the acts or directives of the individual;

(6) the individual engaged in sexual intercourse in this state and the child may have been conceived by that act of intercourse;

(7) the individual asserted parentage in the paternity registry maintained in this state by the bureau of vital statistics; or

(8) there is any other basis consistent with the constitutions of this state and the United States for the exercise of personal jurisdiction.

(b) A tribunal of this state may not use the bases of personal jurisdiction listed in Subsection (a) or in any other law of this state to acquire personal jurisdiction to modify a child support order of another state unless the requirements of Section 159.611 or 159.615 are satisfied.

Commissioners' Official Comment to UIFSA Section 201

Sections 201 and 202 assert what is commonly described as long-arm jurisdiction over a nonresident respondent for purposes of establishing a support order or determining parentage. Inclusion of this long-arm provision in this interstate Act is justified because residents of two separate states are involved in the litigation, both of whom are subject to the personal jurisdiction of the forum. Thus, the case has a clear interstate aspect, despite the fact that only the law of the forum State is applicable. Moreover, this is sufficient to invoke additional UIFSA provisions in an otherwise intrastate proceeding. *See* Sections 202, 316, and 318, *infra*. The intent is to insure that every enacting State has a long-arm statute that is as broad as constitutionally permitted. In situations in which the long-arm statute can be satisfied, the petitioner (either the obligor or the obligee) has two options: (1) utilize the long-arm statute to obtain personal jurisdiction over the respondent; or (2) initiate a two-state proceeding under the succeeding provisions of UIFSA seeking to establish a support order in the respondent's State of residence. Of course, a third option is available that does not implicate UIFSA; a petitioner may file a proceeding in the respondent's State of residence (perhaps to settle all issues between the parties in a single proceeding).

This long-arm statute applies to an order for spousal support as well as an order for child support. However, almost all of the specific provisions relate to child support orders or determinations of parentage. This derives from the fact that the focus of UIFSA is primarily on child support. Only Subsections (1), (2) and (8) are applicable to an action for spousal support asserting long-arm jurisdiction over a nonresident. The first two subsections are wholly noncontroversial insofar as an assertion of personal jurisdiction is concerned. Moreover, assertion of personal jurisdiction under Subsections (1), (2), or (8) will doubtless yield jurisdiction over all matters to be decided between the spouses, including division of property on divorce. Thus, the most obvious possible basis for asserting long-arm jurisdiction over spousal support, *i.e.*, "last matrimonial domicile," is not included in Section 201 to avoid the potential problem of another instance of bifurcated jurisdiction. This restraint avoids a situation in which UIFSA grants long-arm jurisdiction for a spousal support order when the forum State has no correlative statute for property division in divorce.

Under RURESA, multiple support orders affecting the same parties were commonplace. UIFSA creates a structure designed to provide for only one support order at a time. The new one-order regime is facilitated and combined with a broad assertion of personal jurisdiction under this long-arm provision. The frequency of a two-state procedure involving the participation of tribunals in both states should be substantially reduced by the introduction of this long-arm statute.

Subsections (1) through (8) are derived from a variety of sources, including the UNIFORM PARENTAGE ACT (1973) Section 8, TEXAS FAMILY CODE Section 102.011, and NEW YORK FAMILY COURT ACT Section 154.

Subsection (1) codifies the holding of *Burnham v. Superior Court*, 495 U.S. 604 (1990), which reaffirms the constitutional validity of asserting personal jurisdiction based on personal service within a State.

Subsection (2) expresses the principle that a nonresident party concedes personal jurisdiction by seeking affirmative relief or by submitting to the jurisdiction by answering or entering an appearance. However, the power to assert jurisdiction over a support issue under the Act does not extend the tribunal's jurisdiction to other matters.

Subsections (3) through (6) identify specific fact situations justifying the assertion of long-arm jurisdiction over a nonresident. Each provides an appropriate affiliating nexus for such an assertion, when judged on a case-by-case basis with an eye on procedural and substantive due process. Further, each subsection does contain a possibility that an overly literal construction of the terms of the statute will overreach due process. For example, Subsection (3) provides that long-arm jurisdiction to establish a support order may be asserted if "the individual resided with the child in this State." The typical scenario contemplated by the statute is that the parties lived as a family unit in the forum State, separated, and one of the parents subsequently moved to another State while the other parent and the child continued to reside in the forum. No time frame is stated for filing a proceeding; this is based on the fact that the absent parent has a support obligation that extends for at least the minority of the child (and often longer in many states).

On the other hand, suppose that the two parents and their child lived in State A for many years, and then decided to move the family to State B to seek better employment opportunities. Those opportunities did not materialize and, after several weeks or a few months of frustration with the situation, one of the parents returned with the child to State A. Under these facts a tribunal of State A may conclude it has long-arm jurisdiction to establish the support obligation of the absent parent. But, suppose that the family's sojourn in State B lasted for many years, and then one parent unilaterally decides to return to State A. It is a reasonable expectation that all tribunals will conclude that assertion of personal jurisdiction over the absent parent immediately after the return based on Subsection (3) would offend due process. The interstate provisions of UIFSA are available to the returning parent to establish child support. Note that State B will have long-arm jurisdiction to establish support under Section 201. *See also* Section 204, *infra*, for the resolution of simultaneous proceedings provided by the Act.

The factual situations catalogued in the first seven subsections are appropriate and constitutionally acceptable grounds upon which to exercise personal jurisdiction over an individual. Subsection (7) is bracketed because not all states maintain putative father registries.

Finally, Subsection (8) tracks the broad, catch-all provisions found in many state statutes, including CALIFORNIA, CIV. P. CODE Section 410.10 (1973); New York, *supra*; and Texas, *supra*. Note, however, that the California provision, standing alone, was found to be inadequate to sustain a child support order under the facts presented in *Kulko v. Superior Court,* 436 U.S. 84 (1978).

When read together, the 2003 amendments to Subsection(a) deleting the term "modify" and the addition of new Subsection (b) are designed to preclude a tribunal of the forum from ignoring the restrictions on modification of child-support orders established by UIFSA. Some courts broadly construed the former reference to "modify" to justify ignoring the requirement of Section 611 that, absent agreement of the parties, a petitioner for modification of a child-support order of an issuing State when all parties have left that State must be a nonresident of the forum. The 2003 amendments make clear that a tribunal may not apply the long-arm provisions of Subsection (a), or any other law of the forum, and thereby assert that personal jurisdiction over both individual parties to a support order of another State is sufficient to modify that order. The limitations on the exercise of subject matter jurisdiction provided by Sections 611 and 615 must be observed irrespective of the existence of personal jurisdiction over the parties. Long-arm personal jurisdiction over the respondent, standing alone, is not sufficient to grant subject matter jurisdiction over a proposed modification to a tribunal of the State of residence of the petitioner, *see LeTellier v. LeTellier*, 40 S.W.3d 490, 90 A.L.R.5th 707 (Tenn. 2001), *reversing* 1999 WL 732487 (Tenn. App. 1999).

Subsection (b) is intended to cement the principle that modification of an existing order is not subject solely to the usual rules of personal jurisdiction over both parties. Even if a tribunal has personal jurisdiction over both parties, absent agreement of the parties it does not have subject matter jurisdiction to modify a support order of another State if one of the parties or the child reside in the issuing State at the time the modification proceeding is filed, *see* Section 207, *infra*. Even if everyone has moved away from the issuing State, a tribunal having personal jurisdiction over both parties may not modify the order if the petitioner is a resident of the tribunal forum—unless both parties are residents of the forum, *see* Sections 611 and 613, *infra*. Absent an agreement of the parties, in all other cases the movant must be a nonresident, and the tribunal must have personal jurisdiction over the respondent. Almost invariably the respondent will be a resident of the forum.

On rare occasion, however, the required personal jurisdiction over the respondent may be available only by virtue of the long-arm provisions of this section, which explains why Sections 201, 205, 207, 611 and 615 must read in conjunction with one another. An example of such a situation is as follows: the controlling child-support order was issued by a tribunal in State A, which of course had personal jurisdiction over the parties when it issued its order; the obligee and child presently reside in State B (a State the obligor has never even visited); the obligor presently is employed and resides in Nation X, although the obligor's "home base" in the United States can be identified as State C where the headquarters of the obligor's employer is located; and, finally, other than Nation X, the only states that can claim a nexus with the obligor sufficient to assert personal jurisdiction over him are State C and perhaps State A. Under this fact situation, it is necessary to invoke one of the long-arm bases of Section 201 to assert the personal jurisdiction over the obligor necessary to modify the order. Note that the long-arm statute may not be asserted in State B where the movant resides due to the restriction provided in Section 611, even if a basis exists for assertion of long-arm jurisdiction in that State. The employment connection in State C is likely to permit a tribunal in that State to assert jurisdiction to modify the support order based on the catch-all provision, Subsection (a)(8). Further, a tribunal in State A might also find that it has retained jurisdiction to modify the order under Subsection (a)(8) (remember both parties are nonresidents) given the absence or paucity of other U.S. jurisdictions with a nexus to the obligor, *see Phillips v. Phillips*, 826 S.W.2d 746 (Tex. App.–Houston [14th Dist.] 1992, no writ). Note, however, that such an action by the original issuing State must be exercised with extreme restraint or the restriction on modification in Section 611 will become a nullity. Concern that long-arm jurisdiction will be asserted in less compelling circumstances than presented in this hypothetical situation is not substantiated by experience with Section 201 in establishment cases filed since the enactment of UIFSA. In fact, overreaching assertions of long-arm jurisdiction have been dealt with satisfactorily on a case-by-case basis using due process constitutional or forum non conveniens grounds. *Rains v. Dept. of Social & Health Serv.*, 989 P.2d 558 (Wash. App. 1998); *Phillips v. Fallen*, 6 S.W.3d 862 (Mo.1999), reversing 1999 WL 50159 (Mo. App. 1999); *Abu-Dalbouh v. Abu–Dalbouh*, 547 N.W.2d 700 (Minn. Ct. App. 1996)

Editors' Comment

The Texas Legislature originally omitted Subsection (7) of § 201 of the Uniform Act. However, the 1997 Legislature added a paternity registry to Texas law. *See* §§ 160.401–.423, *infra*. Consequently, § 159.201 was amended to recognize this fact.

CLE/Other Legal Publications

Caution! Acronyms ahead: traveling on the interstate case highway. Karen L. Marvel & John Christopher Nickelson, 2010 U.T. PARENT-CHILD RELATIONSHIPS

Jurisdiction jeopardy! Jurisdiction, standing, venue and more: special appearances, UCCJEA, 3'd Party Standing, Hague. JoAl Cannon Sheridan, 2009 ADV. FAM. L.

Jurisdiction and venue. Brad M. LaMorgese, 2009 MARRIAGE DISSOLUTION

UCCJEA and UIFSA—can they be modified. Angela Pence England, 2009 SO. TEX. FAM. L. CONF.

The ABCs of interstate family support jurisdiction. Angela G. Pence, 2003 ADV. FAM. L.

Leading Cases

Burnham v. Superior Court of California, 495 U.S. 604, 109 L.Ed.2d 631, 110 S.Ct. 2105 (1990) (in personam jurisdiction obtained by service of citation in forum state on transient respondent)

Kulko v. Superior Court of California, 436 U.S. 84, 56 L.Ed.2d 132, 98 S.Ct. 1690 (1978) (application of California long-arm statute did not conform to constitutional requirements)

Cotton v. Cotton, 57 S.W.3d 506 (Tex. App.—Waco 2001, no pet.) (without personal jurisdiction over parent, court may not order child support payments; where there is no basis for in personam jurisdiction of a parent, a trial court lacks the authority to render judgment against the parent)

---

§ 159.202. Duration of Personal Jurisdiction

Personal jurisdiction acquired by a tribunal of this state in a proceeding under this chapter or other law of this state relating to a support order continues as long as the tribunal has continuing, exclusive jurisdiction to modify its order or continuing jurisdiction to enforce its order under Sections 159.205, 159.206, and 159.211.

Commissioners' Official Comment to UIFSA Section 202

This section can be said to state a legal truism, albeit a useful one. That is, once a tribunal issues a support order binding on the parties, which must be based on personal jurisdiction by virtue of *Kulko v. Superior Court*, 436 U.S. 84 (1978) and *Vanderbilt v. Vanderbilt*, 354 U.S. 416 (1957), jurisdiction in personam continues absent the statutorily specified reasons for its termination. The rule established by UIFSA is that the personal jurisdiction necessary to sustain enforcement or modification of an order of child support or spousal support persists as long as the order is in force and effect, even as to arrears, *see* Sections 205–207, 211, *infra*. This is true irrespective of the context in which the support order arose, *e.g.*, divorce, UIFSA support establishment, parentage establishment, modification of prior controlling order, etc. Insofar as a child-support order is concerned, depending on specific factual circumstances a distinction is made between continuing, exclusive jurisdiction to modify an order and continuing jurisdiction to enforce an order, *see* Sections 205 and 206, *infra*. Authority to modify a spousal support order is permanently reserved to the issuing tribunal, Section 211, *infra*.

---

§ 159.203. Initiating and Responding Tribunal of State

Under this chapter, a tribunal of this state may serve as an initiating tribunal to forward proceedings to another state and as a responding tribunal for proceedings initiated in another state.

Commissioners' Official Comment to UIFSA Section 203

This section identifies the various roles a tribunal of the forum may serve; as appropriate, it may act as either an initiating or a responding tribunal. Under UIFSA a tribunal may serve as a responding tribunal even when there is no initiating tribunal in another State. This accommodates the direct filing of a proceeding in a responding tribunal by a nonresident.

---

§ 159.204. Simultaneous Proceedings

(a) A tribunal of this state may exercise jurisdiction to establish a support order if the petition or comparable pleading is filed after a pleading is filed in another state only if:

(1) the petition or comparable pleading in this state is filed before the expiration of the time allowed in the other state for filing a responsive pleading challenging the exercise of jurisdiction by the other state;

(2) the contesting party timely challenges the exercise of jurisdiction in the other state; and

(3) if relevant, this state is the home state of the child.

(b) A tribunal of this state may not exercise jurisdiction to establish a support order if the petition or comparable pleading is filed before a petition or comparable pleading is filed in another state if:

(1) the petition or comparable pleading in the other state is filed before the expiration of the time allowed in this state for filing a responsive pleading challenging the exercise of jurisdiction by this state;

(2) the contesting party timely challenges the exercise of jurisdiction in this state; and

(3) if relevant, the other state is the home state of the child.

Commissioners' Official Comment to UIFSA Section 204

Under the one-order system established by UIFSA, it is necessary to provide a new procedure to eliminate the multiple orders so common under RURESA and URESA. This requires cooperation between, and deference by, sister-state tribunals in order to avoid issuance of competing support orders. To this end, tribunals are expected to take an active role in seeking out information about support proceedings in other States concerning the same child. Depending on the circumstances, one or the other of two tribunals considering the same support obligation should decide to defer to the other. In 1992 UIFSA took a significant departure from the approach adopted by the UCCJA ("first filing"), by choosing the "home State of the child" as the primary method for resolving competing jurisdictional disputes, thereby adopting the choice of the federal PARENTAL KIDNAPPING PREVENTION ACT, 28 U.S.C. 1238A Section (C). Given the pre-emptive nature of the PKPA, and the possibility that custody and support will both be involved in some cases, the PKPA/UIFSA choice for resolving disputes between competing jurisdictional assertions was followed in 1997 by the decision of the Conference to replace the UCCJA with the UCCJEA. If the child has no home State, however, "first filing" will continue to control.

---

§ 159.205. Continuing, Exclusive Jurisdiction to Modify Child Support Order

(a) A tribunal of this state that has issued a child support order consistent with the law of this state has and shall exercise continuing, exclusive jurisdiction to modify its order if the order is the controlling order and:

(1) at the time a request for modification is filed, this state is the state of residence of the obligor, the individual obligee, or the child for whose benefit the support order is issued; or

(2) the parties consent in a record or in open court that the tribunal of this state may continue to exercise jurisdiction to modify its order.

(b) A tribunal of this state that has issued a child support order consistent with the law of this state may not exercise continuing, exclusive jurisdiction to modify the order if:

(1) each party who is an individual files a consent in a record with the tribunal of this state that a tribunal of another state that has jurisdiction over at least one of the parties who is an individual or that is located in the state of residence of the child may modify the order and assume continuing, exclusive jurisdiction; or

(2) the order is not the controlling order.

(c) A tribunal of this state shall recognize the continuing, exclusive jurisdiction of a tribunal of another state if the tribunal of the other state has issued a child support order that modifies a child support order of a tribunal of this state under a law substantially similar to this chapter.

(d) A tribunal of this state that does not have continuing, exclusive jurisdiction to modify a child support order may serve as an initiating tribunal to request a tribunal of another state to modify a support order issued in that state.

(e) A temporary support order issued ex parte or pending resolution of a jurisdictional conflict does not create continuing, exclusive jurisdiction in the issuing tribunal.

(f) Repealed by Acts 2003, 78th Leg., ch. 1247, § 46.

Commissioners' Official Comment to UIFSA Section 205

This section is perhaps the most crucial provision in UIFSA. Drawing on the precedent of the federal Parental Kidnapping Prevention Act, 28 U.S.C. Section 1738A, the issuing tribunal retains continuing, exclusive jurisdiction over a child support order, except in very narrowly defined circumstances. First introduced by UIFSA in 1992, this principle is understood and widely accepted in all jurisdictions. "CEJ," as it is known in the child-support enforcement world, is fundamental to the one-child-support-order-at-a-time principle of UIFSA. At first glance this section appears to have been significantly rewritten; certainly minor adjustments have been made to the substantive rules established. But, with the exception of the addition of and entirely new Subsection (a)(2), the sole intent and effect of the 2003 amendments is to reorganize the statutory language for greater clarity. The basic concept that the tribunal issuing a support order retains continuing, exclusive jurisdiction to modify that order remains the cornerstone of the Act.

As long as one of the individual parties or the child continues to reside in the issuing State, and as long as the parties do not agree to the contrary, the issuing tribunal has continuing, exclusive jurisdiction over its child-support order—which in practical terms means that it may modify its order. The statute attempts to be even-handed. The identity of the remaining party—obligor or obligee—does not matter. If the individual parties have left the issuing State but the child remains behind, continuing, exclusive jurisdiction [a.k.a. CEJ] remains with the issuing State. Even if all parties and the child no longer reside in the State, the support order continues in existence and is fully enforceable unless and until a modification takes place in accordance with the requirements of Article 6, *infra*. Note, however, that the CEJ of the issuing State over a spousal support order is permanent, *see* Section 211, *infra*.

In 2003 a significant, albeit subtle amendment was made to Subsection (a)(1). The intent was not to make a substantive change, but rather to clarify the original intent of the Drafting Committee. First, the time to measure whether the issuing tribunal has continuing, exclusive jurisdiction to modify its order, or whether all parties and child have left the State, is explicitly stated to be at the time of filing a proceeding to modify the child support order. Second, substitution of the term "is the residence" for the term "remains the residence" makes clear that any interruption of residence of a party between the date of the issuance of the order and the date of filing the request for modification does not affect jurisdiction to modify. Thus, if there is but one order, it is the controlling order in effect and enforceable throughout the United States, notwithstanding the fact that everyone has left the issuing State. If the order is not modified during this time of absence, a return to reside in the issuing State by a party or child will immediately identify the proper forum at the time of filing a proceeding for modification. Although the statute does not speak explicitly to the issue, temporary absence should be treated in a similar fashion. Temporary employment in another State may not forfeit a claim of residence in the issuing State, *State ex rel. Havlin v. Jamison*, 971 S.W.2d 938 (Mo. App. 1998). Of course, residence is a fact question for the trial court, keeping in mind that the question is residence, not domicile.

A substantive change is made by the 2003 amendment that adds entirely new language to Subsection (a)(2). From the beginning of the implementation of the CEJ principle, questions have been raised about why a tribunal may not modify its own order if the parties agree that it should do so even after both parties have left the State. The move of the parties and the child from the State may have been of a very short distance and, although the parties reside outside the issuing State, they may prefer to continue to be governed by the same issuing tribunal because they continue to have a strong affiliation with the issuing tribunal. For example, the child-support order may have been issued by a tribunal of Washington, D.C. Subsequently the obligee and child have moved to Virginia, the obligor now resides in Maryland, and perhaps one or both parties continue to be employed in Washington. The possibility that under such circumstances the parties reasonably may prefer to continue to deal with the issuing tribunal convinced the Drafting Committee to add this exception to the basic principle of CEJ to modify.

The other side of the coin follows logically. Just as Subsection (a) defines the retention of continuing, exclusive jurisdiction, by clear implication the subsection also identifies how jurisdiction to modify may be lost. That is, if all the relevant persons—the obligor, the individual obligee, and the child—have permanently left the issuing State, the issuing State no longer has an appropriate nexus with the parties or child to justify the exercise of jurisdiction to modify its child-support order. *See In re Marriage of Erickson*, Wash. App. Div. 3 2000, 991 P.2d 123, 98 (Wash. App. 2000); *Groseth v. Groseth*, 600 N.W.2d 159 (Neb. 1999). Further, the issuing tribunal has no current information about the factual circumstances of anyone involved, and the taxpayers of that State have no reason to expend public funds on the process. Note, however, that the original order of the issuing tribunal remains valid and enforceable. That order is in effect not only in the issuing State but also in those States in which the order has been registered. It also may be registered and enforced in additional States even after the issuing State has lost its power to modify its order, *see* Sections 601–604, *infra*. The original order remains in effect until it is properly modified in accordance with the narrow terms of Sections 609–612, *infra*.

Subsection (b)(1), reworded in 2003, explicitly states that the issuing State may also lose its continuing, exclusive jurisdiction to modify if the parties consent in a record for another State to assume jurisdiction to modify (even though one of the parties or the child continues to reside in the issuing State). Filing of the record in the issuing State divests the issuing tribunal of its CEJ. *See Peace v. Peace*, 737 A.2d 1164 (N.J. Super. 1999). The Drafting Committee anticipated that such an agreement would seldom occur because of the almost universal desire of each party to prefer his or her local tribunal; but, the Committee also believed that the parties should be allowed to agree upon an alternate forum if they choose to do so. The 2003 rewording of this provision also makes this procedure available in a situation in which all the parties and the child have left the issuing State and are in agreement that a tribunal of the State in which only the movant resides shall assume modification jurisdiction.

Although Subsections (a) and (b) identify the methods for the retention and the loss of continuing, exclusive jurisdiction by the issuing tribunal, this section does not confer jurisdiction to modify on another tribunal. Modification requires that a tribunal have personal jurisdiction over the parties and meet other criteria as provided in Sections 609 through 615, *infra*.

Leading Case

Thompson v. Thompson, 893 S.W.2d 301 (Tex. App.—Houston [1st Dist.] 1995, no writ) (Texas cannot modify URESA support order because Indiana has continuing jurisdiction)

---

§ 159.206. Continuing Jurisdiction to Enforce Child Support Order

(a) A tribunal of this state that has issued a child support order consistent with the law of this state may serve as an initiating tribunal to request a tribunal of another state to enforce:

(1) the order, if the order:

(A) is the controlling order; and

(B) has not been modified by a tribunal of another state that assumed jurisdiction under the Uniform Interstate Family Support Act; or

(2) a money judgment for support arrearages and interest on the order accrued before a determination that an order of another state is the controlling order.

(b) A tribunal of this state having continuing jurisdiction over a support order may act as a responding tribunal to enforce the order.

Commissioners' Official Comment to UIFSA Section 206

This section is the correlative of the continuing, exclusive jurisdiction asserted in the preceding section. It makes the relatively subtle distinction between the CEJ "to modify a support order" established in Section 205 and the "continuing jurisdiction to enforce" established in this section. A keystone of UIFSA is that the power to enforce the order of the issuing State is not "exclusive" with that State. Rather, on request one or more responding States may also exercise authority to enforce the order of the issuing State. Secondly, under the one-order-at-a-time system, the validity and enforceability of the controlling order continues unabated until it is fully complied with, unless it is replaced by a modified order issued in accordance with the standards established by Sections 609–615. That is, even if the individual parties and the child no longer reside in the issuing State, the controlling order remains in effect and may be enforced by the issuing State or any responding State without regard to the fact that the potential for its modification and replacement exists. The 2003 amendments to Subsection (a) authorize the issuing tribunal to initiate a request for enforcement of its order by a tribunal of another State if its order is controlling, *see* Section 207, or to request reconciliation of the arrears and interest due on its order if another order is controlling.

Subsection (b) reiterates that the issuing State has jurisdiction to serve as a responding State to enforce its own order at the request of another State.

The 2003 amendments moved the second sentence in Subsection (b) to Section 210, *infra*, and moved Subsection (c) to Section 211, *infra*.

---

§ 159.207. Determination of Controlling Child Support Order

(a) If a proceeding is brought under this chapter and only one tribunal has issued a child support order, the order of that tribunal controls and must be so recognized.

(b) If a proceeding is brought under this chapter and two or more child support orders have been issued by tribunals of this state or another state with regard to the same obligor and same child, a tribunal of this state having personal jurisdiction over both the obligor and individual obligee shall apply the following rules to determine by order which order controls:

(1) if only one of the tribunals would have continuing, exclusive jurisdiction under this chapter, the order of that tribunal controls and must be so recognized;

(2) if more than one of the tribunals would have continuing, exclusive jurisdiction under this chapter:

(A) an order issued by a tribunal in the current home state of the child controls if an order is issued in the current home state of the child; or

(B) the order most recently issued controls if an order has not been issued in the current home state of the child; and

(3) if none of the tribunals would have continuing, exclusive jurisdiction under this chapter, the tribunal of this state shall issue a child support order that controls.

(c) If two or more child support orders have been issued for the same obligor and same child, on request of a party who is an individual or a support enforcement agency, a tribunal of this state having personal jurisdiction over both the obligor and the obligee who is an individual shall determine which order controls under Subsection (b). The request may be filed:

(1) with a registration for enforcement or registration for modification under Subchapter G; or

(2) as a separate proceeding.

(d) A request to determine the controlling order must be accompanied by a copy of each child support order in effect and the applicable record of payments. The requesting party shall give notice of the request to each party whose rights may be affected by the determination.

(e) The tribunal that issued the controlling order under Subsection (a), (b), or (c) has continuing jurisdiction to the extent provided under Section 159.205 or 159.206.

(f) A tribunal of this state that determines by order which order is the controlling order under Subsection (b)(1) or (2) or Subsection (c) or that issues a new controlling order under Subsection (b)(3) shall state in that order:

(1) the basis upon which the tribunal made its determination;

(2) the amount of prospective child support, if any; and

(3) the total amount of consolidated arrearages and accrued interest, if any, under the orders after all payments are credited under Section 159.209.

(g) Within 30 days after issuance of an order determining which order is the controlling order, the party obtaining the order shall file a certified copy of the controlling order in each tribunal that issued or registered an earlier order of child support. A party or support enforcement agency that obtains the order and fails to file a certified copy of the order is subject to appropriate sanctions by a tribunal in which the issue of failure to file arises. The failure to file does not affect the validity or enforceability of the controlling order.

(h) An order that has been determined to be the controlling order, or a judgment for consolidated support arrearages and interest issued under this section, must be recognized in a proceeding under this chapter.

Commissioners' Official Comment to UIFSA Section 207

Next to the introduction of the concept of continuing exclusive jurisdiction in Section 205, *supra*, the most dramatic founding principle of UIFSA was to establish a system whereby the multiple orders created by URESA and RURESA could be reconciled in the transition from a world with multiple child-support orders to a one-order-at-a-time world. This principle introduced by Section 207 was subsequently incorporated into the requirements of 28 U.S.C. 1738B, Full Faith and Credit for Child Support Orders, a.k.a. FFCCSOA.

Sections 207 and 209–210 are designed to span the gulf between the one-order system created by UIFSA and the multiple-order system previously in place under RURESA and URESA. UIFSA necessarily must provide transitional procedures for the eventual elimination of existing multiple support orders in an expeditious and efficient manner. But, even though all U.S. jurisdictions enacted UIFSA by 1998, many years will pass before its one-order system will be completely in place. Multiple orders covering the same parties and child number in the hundreds of thousands; it can be reasonably anticipated that some of these orders will continue in effect until nearly 2020. To begin the journey toward a one-order system, however, this section provides a relatively simple procedure designed to identify a single viable order that will be entitled to prospective enforcement in every UIFSA State.

Subsection (a) declares that if only one child support order exists, it is to be denominated the controlling order, irrespective of when and where it was issued and whether any of the individual parties or the child continue to reside in the issuing State.

Subsection (b) establishes the priority scheme for recognition and prospective enforcement of a single order among existing multiple orders regarding the same obligor, obligee, and child. The 2003 amendment to Subsection (b) clarifies that a tribunal requested to sort out the multiple orders and determine which one will be prospectively controlling of future payments must have personal jurisdiction over the litigants in order to ensure that its decision is binding on all concerned. For UIFSA to function, one order must be denominated as the controlling order, and its issuing tribunal must be recognized as having continuing, exclusive jurisdiction. In choosing among existing multiple orders, none of which can be distinguished as being in conflict with the principles of UIFSA, Subsection (b)(1) gives first priority to an order issued by the only tribunal that is entitled to continuing, exclusive jurisdiction under the terms of UIFSA, *i.e.,* an individual party or the child continues to reside in that State and no other issuing State meets this criterion. If two or more tribunals would have continuing, exclusive jurisdiction under the Act, Subsection (b)(2) first looks to the tribunal of the child's current home State. If that State has not issued a support order, Subsection (b)(2) looks next to the order most recently issued. Finally, Subsection (b)(3) provides that if none of the existing multiple orders are entitled to be denominated as the controlling order because none of the preceding priorities apply, the forum tribunal is directed to issue a new order, given that it has personal jurisdiction over the obligor and obligee. The new order becomes the controlling order, establishes the continuing, exclusive jurisdiction of the tribunal, and fixes the support obligation and its nonmodifiable aspects, primarily duration of support, *see* Sections 604 and 611(c), *infra*. The rationale for creating a new order to replace existing multiple orders is that there is no valid reason to prefer the terms of any one of the multiple orders over another in the absence of a fact situation described in Subsections (b)(1) or (b)(2).

As originally promulgated, UIFSA did not come to grips with whether existing multiple orders issued by different States might be entitled to full faith and credit without regard to the determination of the controlling order under the Act. The drafters took the position that state law, however uniform, could not interfere with the ultimate interpretation of a constitutional directive. Fortunately, this question has almost certainly been mooted by the 1996 amendment to 28 U.S.C. Section 1738B, Full Faith and Credit for Child Support Orders. Congress incorporated the multiple order recognition provisions of Section 207 of UIFSA into FFCCSOA virtually word for word in the PERSONAL RESPONSIBILITY AND WORK OPPORTUNITY RECONCILIATION ACT OF 1996. Pub. L. 104–193, Aug. 22, 1996, 110 Stat. 2221.

It is not altogether clear whether the terms of UIFSA apply to a strictly intrastate case; that is, a situation in which multiple child support orders have been issued by multiple tribunals of a single State and all parties and the child continue to reside in that State. This is not an uncommon situation, often traceable to the intrastate applicability of RURESA. A literal reading of the statutory language suggests the section applies. Further, FFCCSOA does not make a distinction regarding the tribunals that issued multiple orders. If multiple orders have been issued by different tribunals in the home State of the child, most likely the most recent will be recognized as the controlling order, notwithstanding the fact that UIFSA Section 207(b)(2)(B) and FFCCSOA 42 U.S.C. Section 1738B(f)(3) literally do not apply. At the very least, this section, together with FFCCSOA, provide a template for resolving such conflicts.

Subsection (c), added in 1996, clarifies that any party or a support enforcement agency may request a tribunal of the forum State to identify the controlling order. That party is directed to fully inform the tribunal of all existing child support orders.

The 2003 addition of new Subsection (d) is to assure the tribunal is furnished with all the information needed to make a proper determination of the controlling order as well as the information needed to make a calculation of the consolidated arrears. The party or support enforcement agency requesting the determination of controlling order and determination of consolidated arrears is also required to notify all other parties and entities who may have an interest in either of those determinations. Those with such an interest most likely are support agencies and the obligee.

Relettered Subsection (e) provides that the determination of the controlling order under this section has the effect of establishing the tribunal with continuing, exclusive jurisdiction; only the order of that tribunal is entitled to prospective enforcement by a sister State.

Relettered Subsection (f) directs the forum tribunal to identify the details upon which it makes its determination of the controlling order. In addition, the tribunal is also directed to state specifically the amount of the prospective support, and to reconcile and consolidate the arrears and interest due on all of the multiple orders to the extent possible.

The party obtaining the determination is directed by relettered Subsection (g) to notify all interested tribunals of the decision after the fact. Although tribunals need not be given original notice of the proceeding, all tribunals that have contributed an order to the determination must be informed regarding which order was determined to be controlling, and should also be informed of the consolidated arrears and interest so that the extent of possible subsequent enforcement will be known with regard to each of the orders. The Act does not deal with the resolution of potential conflicting claims regarding arrears; this is left to case-by-case decisions or to federal regulation.

Section 207 presumes that the parties are accorded notice and opportunity to be heard by the tribunal. It also presumes that the tribunal will be fully informed about all existing orders when it is requested to determine which one of the existing multiple child support orders is to be accorded prospective enforcement. If this does not occur and one or more existing orders is not considered by the tribunal, the finality of its decision is likely to turn on principles of estoppel on a case-by-case basis. Finally, new Subsection (h), added in 2003, affirms the concept that when a fully informed tribunal makes a determination of the controlling order for prospective enforcement, or renders a judgment for the amount of the consolidated arrears, the decision is entitled to full faith and credit.

§ 159.208. Child Support Orders for Two or More Obligees

In responding to registrations or petitions for enforcement of two or more child support orders in effect at the same time with regard to the same obligor and different individual obligees, at least one of which was issued by a tribunal of another state, a tribunal of this state shall enforce those orders in the same manner as if the orders had been issued by a tribunal of this state.

Commissioners' Official Comment to UIFSA Section 208

Multiple orders may involve two or more families of the same obligor. Although all such orders are entitled to enforcement, practical difficulties frequently exist. For example, full enforcement of each of the multiple orders may exceed the maximum allowed for income withholding. The federal statute, 42 U.S.C. Section 666(b)(1), requires that to be eligible for the federal funding for enforcement, States must provide a ceiling for child support withholding expressed in a percentage that may not exceed the federal consumer credit code limitations on wage garnishment, 15 U.S.C. Section 1673(b). In order to allocate resources between competing families, UIFSA refers to state law. The basic principle is that one or more foreign orders for the support of an out-of-state family of the obligor, and one or more orders for an in-state family, are all of equal dignity. In allocating payments to different obligees, every child support order should be treated as if it had been issued by a tribunal of the forum State.

§ 159.209. Credit for Payments

A tribunal of this state shall credit amounts collected for a particular period under a support order against the amounts owed for the same period under any other child support order for support of the same child issued by a tribunal of this or another state.

Commissioners' Official Comment to UIFSA Section 209

Because of the multiple orders possible under the former reciprocal acts, RURESA and URESA, the predecessor section was nominally concerned with insuring that payments made on a particular order were credited toward the amounts due on all other orders. As a practical matter, however, very little attention was paid to that provision. No mechanism was available to reconcile payments on multiple orders other than the obligor's record keeping, if any.

Quite a different situation is currently in place throughout the nation. The advent and development of IV–D agencies has brought collection of arrears and interest on those arrears to the forefront. Computerized exchange of complex information is now almost instantaneously available in many cases. Thus, deciphering the financial information available to accord credit for payment on one order against other orders is possible to a degree unknown in the days of RURESA. For example, full payment of $300 on an order of State C earns a 100% pro tanto discharge of the current support owed on a $200 order of State A, and a 75% credit against a $400 order of State B. Crediting payments against arrears on multiple orders is more complex, and is subject to different constructions in various states.

Under the one-order system of UIFSA, an obligor ultimately will be ordered to pay only one sum-certain amount for current support, and a sum certain to reduce arrears and interest, if any. Nonetheless, multiple orders will exist for several years into the future. Moreover, even under a one-order system, more than one entity may be engaged in collecting past arrears. Ultimately those collections must be reported to a single entity with final accounting responsibility. Finally, because the nature of human enterprise is such that mistakes are inevitable, at least on occasion multiple orders will continue to be issued in error.

The issuing tribunal is ultimately responsible for the overall control of the enforcement methods employed and for accounting for the payments made on its order from multiple sources. Until that scheme is fully in place, however, it will be necessary to continue to mandate pro tanto credit for actual payments made against all existing orders.

The rewording of this section in 2003 reaffirms the simultaneous accrual and simultaneous credit approach, and provides further substance to the directive in Section 207(f) that a tribunal making a determination of the consolidated arrears must use this approach.

§ 159.210. Applicability to Nonresident Subject to Personal Jurisdiction

(a) Except as provided by Subsection (b), Subchapters D–H do not apply to a tribunal of this state exercising personal jurisdiction over a nonresident in a proceeding under this chapter or under other law of this state relating to a support order or recognizing a support order of a foreign country or political subdivision on the basis of comity. The tribunal shall apply the procedural and substantive law of this state in a proceeding described by this subsection.

(b) Notwithstanding Subsection (a), a tribunal of this state exercising personal jurisdiction over a nonresident in a proceeding under this chapter or under other law of this state relating to a support order or recognizing a support order of a foreign country or political subdivision on the basis of comity may:

(1) receive evidence from another state as provided by Section 159.316;

(2) communicate with a tribunal of another state as provided by Section 159.317; and

(3) obtain discovery through a tribunal of another state as provided by Section 159.318.

Commissioners' Official Comment to UIFSA Section 210

Although this section is a product of the 2003 amendments, in fact it combines provisions formerly found in Sections 202 and 206(b) into a single, comprehensive provision. Section 202 took account of the fact that assertion of long-arm jurisdiction over a nonresident results in a one-state proceeding, notwithstanding the fact that the parties reside in different States. Section 206(b) made a vital contribution to the exercise of continuing, exclusive jurisdiction to modify and continuing jurisdiction to enforce support orders if one of the parties to an original proceeding in the forum State subsequently left the State after the initial support order was issued. Indeed, it is far more common for a support order to be issued in conjunction with a divorce or determination of parentage in which both the obligor and obligee are residents of the forum than to be issued as a result of an assertion of long-arm jurisdiction. Note that either the petitioner or the respondent may be the nonresident party (either of whom may be the obligor or the obligee). And, also note that absent this provision the ordinary intrastate substantive and procedural law of the forum would apply to either fact situation without reference to the fact that one of the parties is a nonresident. In sum, whether the matter at hand involves establishment of an original support order or enforcement or modification of an existing order. If one of the parties resides outside the forum State, the nonresident may avail himself or herself of the special evidentiary and discovery provisions provided by UIFSA.

Except for the three sections specified, the provisions of UIFSA—its title labels it an interstate act—are not applicable to an intrastate proceeding. The first exception allows the tribunal to apply the special rules of evidence and procedure of Section 316 in order to facilitate decision-making when one party resides in another State. The improved interstate exchange of information enables the nonresident to participate as fully as possible in the proceedings without the necessity of personally appearing in the forum State. The same considerations account for authorizing inter-tribunal communications as per Section 317. Finally, the two-state discovery procedures of Section 318 are made applicable in a one-state proceeding when a foreign tribunal can assist in that process. In all other situations, the ordinary substantive and procedural law of the forum State applies to a one-state proceeding. In sum, the parties and the tribunal in a one-state case may utilize those two-state procedures that contribute to economy, efficiency, and fair play.

Finally, the 2003 amendment recognizes and extends the operation of these evidentiary and discovery provisions to a case involving a foreign support order recognized on the basis of comity.

§ 159.211. Continuing, Exclusive Jurisdiction to Modify Spousal Support Order

(a) A tribunal of this state issuing a spousal support order consistent with the law of this state has continuing, exclusive jurisdiction to modify the spousal support order throughout the existence of the support obligation.

(b) A tribunal of this state may not modify a spousal support order issued by a tribunal of another state having continuing, exclusive jurisdiction over that order under the law of that state.

(c) A tribunal of this state that has continuing, exclusive jurisdiction over a spousal support order may serve as:

(1) an initiating tribunal to request a tribunal of another state to enforce the spousal support order issued in this state; or

(2) a responding tribunal to enforce or modify its own spousal support order.

Commissioners' Official Comment to UIFSA Section 211

This is not new language; a 2003 amendment moved former Section 205(f) to this stand-alone section. Complimentary provisions with regard to other aspects of CEJ over a spousal support order are also moved. An order for spousal support is treated differently than an order for child support. The issuing tribunal retains continuing, exclusive jurisdiction over an order of spousal support throughout the entire existence of the support obligation. Sections 205(f) and 206(c) state that the procedures of UIFSA are not available to a responding tribunal to modify the existing spousal support order of the issuing State. This marks a radical departure from RURESA, which treated spousal and child support orders identically. Under UIFSA, "interstate" modification of spousal support is limited to a procedure whereby a proceeding may be initiated outside of the issuing State, but only the tribunal in the original issuing State may modify the order under its law. This approach was expected to have minimal effect on actual practice, a prediction that appears to have been accurate. Interstate modification of pure spousal support was relatively rare under RURESA, and plays almost no part in the activities of support enforcement agencies.

The prohibition of modification of spousal support by a nonissuing state tribunal under UIFSA is consistent with the principle that a tribunal should apply local law to such cases to insure efficient handling and to minimize choice of law problems. Avoiding conflict of law problems is almost impossible if spousal support orders are subject to modification in a second State. For example, States take widely varying views of the effect on a spousal support order of the obligee's remarriage or nonmarital cohabitation. Making a distinction between spousal and child support is further justified because the standards for modification of child support and spousal support are very different. In most jurisdictions a dramatic improvement in the obligor's economic circumstances will have little or no relevance in a proceeding seeking an upward modification of spousal support, while a similar change in an obligor's situation typically is the primary basis for an increase in child support. This disparity is founded on a policy choice that post-divorce success of an obligor-parent should benefit the obligor's child, but not the obligor's ex-spouse.

Finally, UIFSA does not provide for shifting the continuing, exclusive jurisdiction over a spousal-support order by mutual agreement. That procedure is limited to child support under Section 205(b)(1). Note that the Act is silent rather than preclusive on the subject. If the parties wish to enter into such an agreement, it is up to the individual States to decide whether to recognize it. A waiver of continuing, exclusive jurisdiction and subsequent modification of spousal support by a tribunal of another State simply is not authorized by UIFSA, rather than prohibited.

SUBCHAPTER D. CIVIL PROVISIONS OF GENERAL APPLICATION

§ 159.301. Proceedings Under Chapter

(a) Except as otherwise provided in this chapter, this subchapter applies to all proceedings under this chapter.

(b) Repealed by Acts 2003, 78th Leg., ch. 1247, § 46.

(c) An individual or a support enforcement agency may initiate a proceeding authorized under this chapter by filing a petition in an initiating tribunal for forwarding to a responding tribunal or by filing a petition or a comparable pleading directly in a tribunal of another state that has or that can obtain personal jurisdiction over the respondent.

Commissioners' Official Comment to UIFSA Section 301

Subsection (a) mandates application of the general provisions of this article to all UIFSA proceedings.

Subsection (b), the once controversial "road map" originally thought by the 1992 Drafting Committee to be required in order to introduce the large number of non-lawyer administrators employed by child support enforcement agencies to the intricacies of UIFSA. Given the extensive training on the Act throughout the nation, the road map no longer can be viewed as necessary.

Subsection (c) continues in a new form the basic two-state procedure long-employed by the former reciprocal acts to establish a support order in the interstate context. Direct filing of a petition in the responding State by an individual or a support enforcement agency without reference to an initiating tribunal State was introduced by UIFSA 1992. Although filing of a petition in an initiating tribunal to be forwarded to a responding tribunal is still recognized as a possible procedure, the direct filing procedure has proven to be one of the most significant improvements in efficient interstate case management. The promulgation and use of the federally mandated forms, Section 311(b), further serves to eliminate any role for the initiating tribunal.

§ 159.302. Proceeding by Minor Parent

A minor parent or a guardian or other legal representative of a minor parent may maintain a proceeding on behalf of or for the benefit of the minor's child.

Commissioners' Official Comment to UIFSA Section 302

A minor parent may maintain a proceeding under UIFSA without the appointment of a guardian ad litem, even if the law of the forum jurisdiction requires a guardian for an in-state case. If a guardian or legal representative has been appointed, he or she may act on behalf of the minor's child in seeking support.

§ 159.303. Application of Law of State

Except as otherwise provided in this chapter, a responding tribunal of this state shall:

(1) apply the procedural and substantive law generally applicable to similar proceedings originating in this state and may exercise all powers and provide all remedies available in those proceedings; and

(2) determine the duty of support and the amount payable in accordance with the law and support guidelines of this state.

Commissioners' Official Comment to UIFSA Section 303

Historically States have insisted that forum law be applied to support cases whenever possible. This continues as a key principle of UIFSA. In general, a responding tribunal has the same powers in a proceeding involving interstate parties as it has in an intrastate case. This inevitably means that the Act is not self-contained; rather, it is supplemented by the forum's statutes and procedures governing support orders. To insure the efficient processing of the huge number of interstate support cases, it is vital that decision-makers apply familiar rules of local law to the maximum degree possible. This must be accomplished in a manner consistent with the overriding principle of UIFSA that enforcement is of the issuing tribunal's order, and that the responding State does not make the order its own as a condition of enforcing it.

Prior to the 2003 amendments, choice of law rules of the forum State were specifically invoked in three places; henceforth Section 604 is the sole reference to the issue.

Leading Case

In re B.C., 52 S.W.3d 926 (Tex. App.—Beaumont 2001, no pet.) (in a proceeding for arrearages, the statute of limitations of Texas or the issuing state, whichever is longer, governs)

---

§ 159.304. Duties of Initiating Tribunal

(a) On the filing of a petition authorized by this chapter, an initiating tribunal of this state shall forward the petition and its accompanying documents:

(1) to the responding tribunal or appropriate support enforcement agency in the responding state; or

(2) if the identity of the responding tribunal is unknown, to the state information agency of the responding state with a request that they be forwarded to the appropriate tribunal and that receipt be acknowledged.

(b) If requested by the responding tribunal, a tribunal of this state shall issue a certificate or other document and make findings required by the law of the responding state. If the responding state is a foreign country or political subdivision, the tribunal shall specify the amount of support sought, convert that amount into the equivalent amount in the foreign currency under the applicable official or market exchange rate as publicly reported, and provide any other documents necessary to satisfy the requirements of the responding state.

Commissioners' Official Comment to UIFSA Section 304

Under UIFSA the role of the initiating tribunal consists of the ministerial function of forwarding the documents to the appropriate entity in the responding State for action. The initiating tribunal has no substantive legal task to perform.

Subsection (b) was designed primarily to facilitate interstate enforcement between UIFSA States and URESA and RURESA States, with some applicability to cases involving foreign jurisdictions. After the nationwide enactment of UIFSA by 1998, *see* Prefatory Note, *supra*, the subsection retains its utility only with regard to support orders of foreign nations. Supplying documentation required by a foreign jurisdiction which is not otherwise required by UIFSA procedure will continue to be appropriate in the international context for the foreseeable future. An initiating tribunal is authorized to cooperate and provide whatever information or documentation is required or requested by a foreign jurisdiction. For example, a statement of the amount of support being requested is required by Canadian provinces before a tribunal will establish a support order. The 2003 amendment adds a duty for the initiating tribunal to state the amount of foreign currency equivalent to that request; there is a corresponding duty of a responding tribunal to convert the foreign currency into dollars if the foreign initiating tribunal does not, Section 305(f).

The reference to "the applicable official or market exchange rate" takes into account the present practices of international money markets. A few countries continue to maintain an official exchange rate for their currency. The vast majority of countries recognize the fact that the value of their currency is subject to daily market fluctuations that are reported on the financial pages of many daily newspapers. Thus, in the example described above, a request for a specific amount of support in U.S. dollars, which is to be translated into Canadian dollars on a specific date, will inevitably have a variable value as the foreign currency rises or falls against the U.S. dollar.

---

§ 159.305. Duties and Powers of Responding Tribunal

(a) When a responding tribunal of this state receives a petition or comparable pleading from an initiating tribunal or directly under Section 159.301(c), the responding tribunal shall cause the petition or pleading to be filed and notify the petitioner where and when it was filed.

(b) Except as prohibited by other law, a responding tribunal of this state may do one or more of the following:

(1) issue or enforce a support order, modify a child support order, determine the controlling child support order, or determine parentage;

(2) order an obligor to comply with a support order and specify the amount and the manner of compliance;

(3) order income withholding;

(4) determine the amount of any arrearages and specify a method of payment;

(5) enforce orders by civil or criminal contempt, or both;

(6) set aside property for satisfaction of the support order;

(7) place liens and order execution on the obligor's property;

(8) order an obligor to keep the tribunal informed of the obligor's current residential address, telephone number, employer, address of employment, and telephone number at the place of employment;

(9) issue a bench warrant or capias for an obligor who has failed after proper notice to appear at a hearing ordered by the tribunal and enter the bench warrant or capias in any local and state computer systems for criminal warrants;

(10) order the obligor to seek appropriate employment by specified methods;

(11) award reasonable attorney's fees and other fees and costs; and

(12) grant any other available remedy.

(c) A responding tribunal of this state shall include in a support order issued under this chapter, or in the documents accompanying the order, the calculations on which the support order is based.

(d) A responding tribunal of this state may not condition the payment of a support order issued under this chapter on compliance by a party with provisions for visitation.

(e) If a responding tribunal of this state issues an order under this chapter, the tribunal shall send a copy of the order to the petitioner and the respondent and to the initiating tribunal, if any.

(f) If requested to enforce a support order, arrearages, or a judgment or to modify a support order stated in a foreign currency, a responding tribunal of this state shall convert the amount stated in the foreign currency to the equivalent amount in dollars under the applicable official or market exchange rate as publicly reported.

Commissioners' Official Comment to UIFSA Section 305

This section establishes a wide variety of duties for a responding tribunal. It contains: ministerial functions, Subsection (a); judicial functions, Subsection (b); and, substantive rules applicable to interstate cases, Subsections (c)-(e). Because a responding tribunal may be an administrative agency rather than a court, the Act explicitly states that a tribunal is not granted powers that it does not otherwise possess under state law. For example, authority to enforce a support order by contempt generally is limited to courts.

Subsection (a) directs the filing of the documents received without regard to whether an initiating tribunal in another State was involved in forwarding the documentation. It also directs that the individual or entity requesting the filing be notified, but leaves the means of that notification to local law. The advent of a variety of swifter, and perhaps even more reliable, forms of notice in the modern era justifies the deletion of a particular form of notice. For example, many States now authorize notice by telephone facsimile (FAX), or by an express delivery service. Already many legal documents are transmitted by electronic mail (email).

Subsection (b) lists duties that, if possessed under state law in connection with in-state cases, are allocated to the responding tribunal in UIFSA cases. Thus, each subdivision purposefully avoids mention of substantive rules. For example, Subsection (b)(7) does not identify the type, nature, or priority of liens that may be issued under UIFSA. As is generally true under the Act, those details will be determined by applicable state law concerning support enforcement remedies of local orders.

Subsection (c) clarifies that the details of calculating the child support order are to be included along with the order. Local law generally requires that variation from the child support guidelines must be explained, *see* 42 U.S.C. Section 667; this requirement is extended to interstate cases.

Subsection (d) states that an interstate support order may not be conditioned on compliance with a visitation order. *Chaisson v. Ragsdale*, 914 S.W.2d 739 (Ark. 1996). While this may be at variance with state law governing intrastate cases, under a UIFSA proceeding the petitioner generally is not present before the tribunal. This distinction justifies prohibiting visitation issues from being litigated in the context of a support proceeding. All States have enacted some version of either the UCCJA or the UCCJEA providing for resolution of visitation issues in interstate cases.

Subsection (e) introduces the policy determination that the petitioner, the respondent, and the initiating tribunal, if any, shall be kept informed about actions taken by the responding tribunal.

Subsection (f) is designed to facilitate enforcement of foreign support orders.

§ 159.306. Inappropriate Tribunal

If a petition or comparable pleading is received by an inappropriate tribunal of this state, that tribunal shall forward the pleading and accompanying documents to an appropriate tribunal in this state or another state and notify the petitioner where and when the pleading was sent.

Commissioners' Official Comment to UIFSA Section 306

This section directs a tribunal receiving UIFSA documents in error to forward the original documents to their proper destination without undue delay, whether the appropriate tribunal is located in the same State or elsewhere. This section was originally intended to apply both to initiating and responding tribunals receiving such documents, but the practical elimination of the role of initiating tribunals under modern practice now limits the notice requirement to the petitioner, *i.e.*, the individual party or support enforcement agency, that filed (or misfiled) the document directly. For example, if a tribunal is inappropriately designated as the responding tribunal, it shall forward the petition to the appropriate responding tribunal wherever located, if known, and notify the petitioner of its action. Such a procedure is much to be preferred to returning the documents to the petitioner to begin the process anew. Cooperation of this sort will facilitate the ultimate goals of the Act.

§ 159.307. Duties of Support Enforcement Agency

(a) A support enforcement agency of this state, on request, shall provide services to a petitioner in a proceeding under this chapter.

(b) A support enforcement agency of this state that provides services to the petitioner shall:

(1) take all steps necessary to enable an appropriate tribunal in this state or another state to obtain jurisdiction over the respondent;

(2) request an appropriate tribunal to set a date, time, and place for a hearing;

(3) make a reasonable effort to obtain all relevant information, including information as to income and property of the parties;

(4) not later than the second day, excluding Saturdays, Sundays, and legal holidays, after the date of receipt of a written notice in a record from an initiating, responding, or registering tribunal, send a copy of the notice to the petitioner;

(5) not later than the second day, excluding Saturdays, Sundays, and legal holidays, after the date of receipt of a written communication in a record from the respondent or the respondent's attorney, send a copy of the communication to the petitioner; and

(6) notify the petitioner if jurisdiction over the respondent cannot be obtained.

(c) A support enforcement agency of this state that requests registration of a child support order in this state for enforcement or for modification shall make reasonable efforts to ensure that:

(1) the order to be registered is the controlling order; or

(2) a request for a determination of which order is the controlling order is made in a tribunal having jurisdiction to make the determination, if two or more child support orders have been issued and a determination of the controlling order has not been made.

(d) A support enforcement agency of this state that requests registration and enforcement of a support order, arrearages, or a judgment stated in a foreign currency shall convert the amount stated in the foreign currency to the equivalent amount in dollars under the applicable official or market exchange rate as publicly reported.

(e) A support enforcement agency of this state shall issue, or request a tribunal of this state to issue, a child support order and an income-withholding order that redirects payment of current support, arrearages, and interest if requested to do so by a support enforcement agency of another state under Section 159.319.

(f) This chapter does not create or negate a relationship of attorney and client or other fiduciary relationship between a support enforcement agency or the attorney for the agency and the individual being assisted by the agency.

Commissioners' Official Comment to UIFSA Section 307

The focus of Subsection (a) is on providing services to a petitioner, and not merely on "representing" the obligee. Care should be exercised in the use of terminology given this substantial alteration of past practice under RURESA. Not only may either the obligee or the obligor request services, but that request may be in the context of the establishment of an initial child-support order, enforcement or review and adjustment of an existing child-support order, or a modification of that order (upward or downward). Note that the Act does not distinguish between child support and spousal support for purposes of providing services. Note also, that the services available may differ significantly; for example, modification of spousal support is limited to the issuing State, *see* Section 205(f), *supra*.

Subsection (b) responds to the past complaints of many petitioners that they were not properly kept informed about the progress of their requests for services.

The 2003 additions of Subsections (c) and (d) are procedural clarifications reflecting actual practice of the support agencies developed after years of experience with the Act. Subsection (c) imposes a duty on all support enforcement agencies to facilitate the UIFSA one-order world by actively searching for cases with multiple orders and obtaining a determination of the controlling order as expeditiously as possible. This agency duty correlates to new Subsection 602(d) regarding the registration process and cases with multiple orders.

Read in conjunction with Section 319, *infra*, new Subsection (e) requires the state support enforcement agency to facilitate redirection of the stream of child support in order that the payments be more efficiently received by the obligee.

Subsection (f) explicitly states that UIFSA neither creates nor rejects the establishment of an attorney-client or fiduciary relationship between the support enforcement agency and a petitioner receiving services from that agency. This highly controversial issue is left to otherwise applicable state law.

§ 159.308. Duty of Certain State Officials

(a) If the attorney general determines that the support enforcement agency is neglecting or refusing to provide services to an individual, the attorney general may order the agency to perform its duties under this chapter or may provide those services directly to the individual.

(b) The governor may determine that a foreign country or political subdivision has established a reciprocal arrangement for child support with this state and take appropriate action for notification of the determination.

Commissioners' Official Comment to UIFSA Section 308

In a carryover from RURESA, Subsection (a) provides that the State Attorney General, or an alternative designated by state law, is given oversight responsibility for the diligent provision of services by the support enforcement agency and the power to seek compliance with the Act.

The 2003 addition of Subsection (b) makes clear that a State has a variety of options in determining the scope of its support enforcement program. In the absence of controlling federal action declaring a foreign jurisdiction to be a reciprocating country or political subdivision, *see* Section 102(21)(B)(i), *supra*, each State may designate an official with authority to make a statewide, binding determination recognizing a foreign country or political subdivision as having a reciprocal arrangement with the that State.

§ 159.309. Private Counsel

An individual may employ private counsel to represent the individual in proceedings authorized by this chapter.

Commissioners' Official Comment to UIFSA Section 309

The right of a party to retain private counsel in a proceeding brought under UIFSA is explicitly recognized. The failure to clearly recognize that power under the prior uniform acts led to confusion and inconsistent decisions.

§ 159.310. Duties of State Information Agency

(a) The Title IV–D agency is the state information agency under this chapter.

(b) The state information agency shall:

(1) compile and maintain a current list, including addresses, of the tribunals in this state that have jurisdiction under this chapter and any support enforcement agencies in this state and send a copy to the state information agency of every other state;

(2) maintain a register of names and addresses of tribunals and support enforcement agencies received from other states;

(3) forward to the appropriate tribunal in the county in this state where the obligee who is an individual or the obligor resides, or where the obligor's property is believed to be located, all documents concerning a proceeding under this chapter received from an initiating tribunal or the state information agency of the initiating state; and

(4) obtain information concerning the location of the obligor and the obligor's property in this state not exempt from execution, by such means as postal verification and federal or state locator services, examination of telephone directories, requests for the obligor's address from employers, and examination of governmental records, including, to the extent not prohibited by other law, those relating to real property, vital statistics, law enforcement, taxation, motor vehicles, driver's licenses, and social security.

Commissioners' Official Comment to UIFSA Section 310

Subsection (a) identifies the central information agency. Subsection (b) details the duties of that agency insofar as interstate proceedings are concerned. Subsection (b)(4) does not provide independent access to the information sources or to the governmental documents listed. Because States have different requirements and limitations concerning such access based on differing views of the privacy interests of individual citizens, the agency is directed to use all lawful means under the relevant state law to obtain and disseminate information.

§ 159.311. Pleadings and Accompanying Documents

(a) In a proceeding under this chapter, a petitioner seeking to establish a support order, to determine parentage, or to register and modify a support order of another state must file a petition. Unless otherwise ordered under Section 159.312, the petition or accompanying documents must provide, so far as known, the name, residential address, and social security numbers of the obligor and the obligee or the parent and alleged parent and the name, sex, residential address, social security number, and date of birth of each child for whose benefit support is sought or whose parentage is to be determined. Unless filed at the time of registration, the petition must be accompanied by a copy of any support order known to have been issued by another tribunal. The petition may include any other information that may assist in locating or identifying the respondent.

(b) The petition must specify the relief sought. The petition and accompanying documents must conform substantially with the requirements imposed by the forms mandated by federal law for use in cases filed by a support enforcement agency.

Commissioners' Official Comment to UIFSA Section 311

This section establishes the basic requirements for drafting and filing interstate pleadings. Subsection (a) should be read in conjunction with Section 312, which provides for the confidentiality of certain information if disclosure is likely to result in harm to a party or a child. The 2003 amendments are directed at improving the efficiency of the process. Illustrative of that goal is the requirement that all known support orders be attached to the petition for relief, coupled with the elimination of the requirement that such copies be certified. If a dispute arises over the authenticity of a purported order, the tribunal must, of necessity, sort out conflicting claims at that time. Another improvement is the deletion of the requirement for verified pleadings originated in URESA and carried forward in the original version of UIFSA.

Subsection (b) provides authorization for the use of the federally authorized forms promulgated in connection with the IV–D child support enforcement program and mandates substantial compliance with those forms. Although the use of other forms is not prohibited, standardized documents have resulted in substantial improvement in the efficient processing of UIFSA proceedings.

---

§ 159.312. Nondisclosure of Information in Exceptional Circumstances

If a party alleges in an affidavit or pleading under oath that the health, safety, or liberty of a party or child would be jeopardized by disclosure of specific identifying information regarding the party or the child, the identifying information shall be sealed and may not be disclosed to the other party or to the public. After a hearing in which a tribunal considers the health, safety, or liberty of the party or the child, the tribunal may order disclosure of information if the tribunal determines that the disclosure serves the interests of justice.

Commissioners' Official Comment to UIFSA Section 312

Derived from the UNIFORM CHILD CUSTODY JURISDICTION AND ENFORCEMENT ACT, Section 209. Information To Be Submitted to Court. This section is the latest version of the statutory formulation originally developed in UIFSA 1992. Public awareness of and sensitivity to the dangers of domestic violence has significantly increased since interstate enforcement of support originated. This section authorizes confidentiality in instances where there is a serious risk of domestic violence or child abduction. Although local law generally governs the conduct of the forum tribunal, state law may not provide for maintaining secrecy about the exact whereabouts of a litigant or other information ordinarily required to be disclosed under state law, *i.e.*, Social Security number of the parties or the child. If so, this section creates a confidentiality provision that is particularly appropriate in the light of the intractable problems associated with interstate parental kidnapping, *see* the Parental Kidnapping Prevention Act (PKPA), 28 U.S.C. Section 1738A.

---

§ 159.313. Costs and Fees

(a) The petitioner may not be required to pay a filing fee or other costs.

(b) If an obligee prevails, a responding tribunal may assess against an obligor filing fees, reasonable attorney's fees, other costs, and necessary travel and other reasonable expenses incurred by the obligee and the obligee's witnesses. The tribunal may not assess fees, costs, or expenses against the obligee or the support enforcement agency of either the initiating state or the responding state, except as provided by other law. Attorney's fees may be taxed as costs and may be ordered paid directly to the attorney, who may enforce the order in the attorney's own name. Payment of support owed to the obligee has priority over fees, costs, and expenses.

(c) The tribunal shall order the payment of costs and reasonable attorney's fees if it determines that a hearing was requested primarily for delay. In a proceeding pursuant to Sections 159.601 through 159.608, a hearing is presumed to have been requested primarily for delay if a registered support order is confirmed or enforced without change.

Commissioners' Official Comment to UIFSA Section 313

Under UIFSA either the obligor or the obligee may file a proceeding or seek services from a support enforcement agency, Subsection (a) permits either party to file without payment of a filing fee or other costs. Subsection (b), however, provides that only the support obligor may be assessed the authorized costs and fees.

Subsection (c) provides a sanction to deal with a frivolous contest regarding compliance with an interstate withholding order, registration of a support order, or comparable delaying tactics regarding an appropriate enforcement remedy.

§ 159.314. Limited Immunity of Petitioner

(a) Participation by a petitioner in a proceeding under this chapter before a responding tribunal, whether in person, by private attorney, or through services provided by the support enforcement agency, does not confer personal jurisdiction over the petitioner in another proceeding.

(b) A petitioner is not amenable to service of civil process while physically present in this state to participate in a proceeding under this chapter.

(c) The immunity granted by this section does not extend to civil litigation based on acts unrelated to a proceeding under this chapter committed by a party while present in this state to participate in the proceeding.

Commissioners' Official Comment to UIFSA Section 314

Under Subsection (a), direct or indirect participation in a UIFSA proceeding does not subject a petitioner to an assertion of personal jurisdiction over the petitioner by the forum State in other litigation between the parties. The primary object of this prohibition is to preclude joining disputes over child custody and visitation with the establishment, enforcement, or modification of child support. This prohibition strengthens the ban on visitation litigation established in Section 305(d). A petition for affirmative relief under UIFSA limits the jurisdiction of the tribunal to the boundaries of the support proceeding. In sum, proceedings under UIFSA are not suitable vehicles for the relitigation of all of the issues arising out of a foreign divorce or custody cases. Only enforcement or modification of the support portion of such decrees or orders are relevant. Other issues, such as custody and visitation, or matters relating to other aspect of the divorce decree, are collateral and have no place in a UIFSA proceeding. *Chaisson v. Ragsdale*, 914 S.W.2d 739 (Ark. 1996).

Subsection (b) grants a litigant a variety of limited immunity from service of process during the time that party is physically present in a State for a UIFSA proceeding. The immunity provided is in no way comparable to diplomatic immunity, however, which should be clear from reading Subsection (c) in conjunction with the other subsections.

Subsection (c) does not extend immunity to civil litigation unrelated to the support proceeding which stems from contemporaneous acts committed by a party while present in the State for the support litigation. For example, a petitioner involved in an automobile accident or a contract dispute over the cost of lodging while present in the State does not have immunity from a civil suit on those issues.

§ 159.315. Nonparentage as Defense

A party whose parentage of a child has been previously determined by or under law may not plead nonparentage as a defense to a proceeding under this chapter.

Commissioners' Official Comment to UIFSA Section 315

Arguably this section does no more than restate the basic principle of *res judicata*. However, there is a great variety of state law regarding presumptions of parentage and available defenses after a prior determination of parentage. As long as a proceeding is brought in an appropriate forum, this section is intended neither to discourage nor encourage collateral attacks in situations in which the law of a foreign jurisdiction is at significant odds with local law. If a collateral attack on a parentage decree is permissible under the law of the issuing jurisdiction, such a proceeding must be pursued in that forum and not in a UIFSA proceeding.

In sum, this section mandates that a parentage decree rendered by another tribunal "pursuant to law" is not subject to collateral attack in a UIFSA proceeding. *State v. Hanson*, 725 So.2d 514 (La. App. 1998). Of course, an attack on an alleged final order based on a fundamental constitutional defect in the parentage decree is permissible in the forum State. For example, a responding tribunal may find that a foreign tribunal acted unconstitutionally by denying a party due process because of a failure of notice and opportunity to be heard or a lack of personal jurisdiction over a party who did not answer or appear. Insofar as the latter ground is concerned, the universal enactment of the long-arm statute asserting personal jurisdiction over a respondent if the child "may have been conceived" in the forum State may greatly reduce successful attacks on a parentage determinations, *see* Section 201(a)(6), *supra*.

Similarly, the law of the issuing State may provide for a determination of parentage based on certain specific acts of the obligor, such as voluntarily acknowledging parentage as a substitute for a decree. UIFSA also is neutral regarding a collateral attack on such a parentage determination filed in the issuing State. In the meantime, however, the responding tribunal must give effect to such an act of acknowledgment of parentage if it is recognized as determinative in the issuing State. The consistent theme is that a collateral attack on a parentage determination cannot be made in a UIFSA proceeding other than on fundamental due process grounds.

§ 159.316. Special Rules of Evidence and Procedure

(a) The physical presence of a nonresident party who is an individual in a tribunal of this state is not required for the establishment, enforcement, or modification of a support order or the rendition of a judgment determining parentage.

(b) An affidavit, a document substantially complying with federally mandated forms, or a document incorporated by reference in an affidavit or document, that would not be under the hearsay rule if given in person, is admissible in evidence if given under penalty of perjury by a party or witness residing in another state.

(c) A copy of the record of child support payments certified as a true copy of the original by the custodian of the record may be forwarded to a responding tribunal. The copy is evidence of facts asserted in it and is admissible to show whether payments were made.

(d) Copies of bills for testing for parentage and for prenatal and postnatal health care of the mother and child that are furnished to the adverse party not less than 10 days before the date of trial are admissible in evidence to prove the amount of the charges billed and that the charges were reasonable, necessary, and customary.

(e) Documentary evidence transmitted from another state to a tribunal of this state by telephone, telecopier, or another means that does not provide an original record may not be excluded from evidence on an objection based on the means of transmission.

(f) In a proceeding under this chapter, a tribunal of this state shall permit a party or witness residing in another state to be deposed or to testify by telephone, audiovisual means, or other electronic means at a designated tribunal or other location in that state. A tribunal of this state shall cooperate with a tribunal of another state in designating an appropriate location for the deposition or testimony.

(g) If a party called to testify at a civil hearing refuses to answer on the ground that the testimony may be self-incriminating, the trier of fact may draw an adverse inference from the refusal.

(h) A privilege against disclosure of communications between spouses does not apply in a proceeding under this chapter.

(i) The defense of immunity based on the relationship of husband and wife or parent and child does not apply in a proceeding under this chapter.

(j) A voluntary acknowledgment of paternity, certified as a true copy, is admissible to establish parentage of the child.

Commissioners' Official Comment to UIFSA Section 316

This section combines many time-tested procedures with additional innovative methods for gathering evidence in interstate cases. The amendment to Subsection (a) ensures that a nonresident petitioner or a nonresident respondent may fully participate in a proceeding under the Act without being required to appear personally. This was always the intent of the provision, but the text was ambiguous in this regard.

Subsections (b) through (f) greatly expand the special rules of evidence originally propounded in RURESA which are designed to take into account the virtually unique nature of the interstate proceedings under this Act. These sections provide exceptions to the otherwise guiding principle of UIFSA, *i.e.*, local procedural and substantive law should apply. Because the out-of-state party, and that party's witnesses, necessarily do not ordinarily appear in person at the hearing, deviation from the ordinary rules of evidence is justified in order to assure that the tribunal will have available to it the maximum amount of information on which to base its decision. The intent throughout these subsections is to eliminate by statute as many potential hearsay problems as possible in interstate litigation, with the goal of providing each party with the means to present evidence, even if not physically present. *See Attorney General v. Litten*, 999 S.W.2d 74 (Tex. App.—Houston [14th Dist.] 1999, no pet.); *State ex rel. T.L.R. v. R.W.T.*, 737 So.2d 688 (La. 1999).

Subsection (d) provides a simplified means for proving health care expenses related to the birth of a child. Because ordinarily these charges are not in dispute, this is designed to obviate the cost of having health care providers appear in person or of obtaining affidavits of business records from each provider.

Perhaps the most dramatic of the 2003 amendments affecting these special rules of evidence is the change of a single word. The authorization in Subsection (f) of telephonic or audiovisual testimony in depositions and in hearing now substitutes the word "shall" for the word "may." Adoption by the States may herald the day when every relevant court room will be equipped with a speaker phone, at the minimum, if not cameras and audiovisual receivers. This amendment will also eliminate decisions such as *Schwier v. Bernstein*, 734 So.2d 531 (Fla. App. 1999), which construed the use of electronic transmission of testimony to be wholly within the discretion of the tribunal. On a related track, the 2003 amendments to Subsection (b): (1) recognize the pervasive effect of the federal forms promulgated by the Office of Child Support Enforcement, HHS; and (2) replace the necessity of swearing to a document "under oath" with the simpler requirement that the document be provided "under penalty of perjury," as is required by federal income tax form 1040.

Subsections (e) and (f) encourage tribunals and litigants to take advantage of modern methods of communication in interstate support litigation; most dramatically, the out-of-state party is authorized to testify by telephone and supply documents by fax. One of the most useful applications of these subsections has been the combining of (c) and (e) to provide an enforcing tribunal with up-to-date information concerning the amount of arrears.

Subsection (g) codifies the rule in effect in many States that in civil litigation an adverse inference may be drawn from a litigant's silence. If a party refuses to submit to genetic testing, the refusal may be admitted into evidence and the court may resolve the question of paternity against that party on the basis of an inference that the results of the tests would have been unfavorable to the interests of the refusing party.

---

§ 159.317. Communications Between Tribunals

A tribunal of this state may communicate with a tribunal of another state or of a foreign country or political subdivision in a record, by telephone, or by other means, to obtain information concerning the laws, the legal effect of a judgment, decree, or order of that tribunal, and the status of a proceeding in the other state, foreign country, or political subdivision. A tribunal of this state may furnish similar information by similar means to a tribunal of another state or of a foreign country or political subdivision.

Commissioners' Official Comment to UIFSA Section 317

This section authorizes communications between tribunals in order to facilitate decisions. The 2003 amendments extend the coverage of the section to tribunals of foreign nations. Broad cooperation between tribunals is permitted to expedite establishment and enforcement of a support order.

---

§ 159.318. Assistance With Discovery

A tribunal of this state may:

(1) request a tribunal of another state to assist in obtaining discovery; and

(2) on request, compel a person over whom the tribunal has jurisdiction to respond to a discovery order issued by a tribunal of another state.

Commissioners' Official Comment to UIFSA Section 318

This section takes another logical step to facilitate interstate cooperation by enlisting the power of the forum to assist a tribunal of another State with the discovery process. The grant of authority is quite broad, enabling the tribunal of the enacting State to fashion its remedies to facilitate discovery consistent with local practice.

---

§ 159.319. Receipt and Disbursement of Payments

(a) A support enforcement agency or tribunal of this state shall disburse promptly any amounts received under a support order, as directed by the order. The agency or tribunal shall furnish to a requesting party or tribunal of another state a certified statement by the custodian of the record of the amounts and dates of all payments received.

(b) If the obligor, the obligee who is an individual, and the child do not reside in this state, on request from the support enforcement agency of this state or another state, the support enforcement agency of this state or a tribunal of this state shall:

(1) direct that the support payment be made to the support enforcement agency in the state in which the obligee is receiving services; and

(2) issue and send to the obligor's employer a conforming income-withholding order or an administrative notice of change of payee reflecting the redirected payments.

(c) The support enforcement agency of this state on receiving redirected payments from another state under a law similar to Subsection (b) shall provide to a requesting party or a tribunal of the other state a certified statement by the custodian of the record of the amount and dates of all payments received.

Commissioners' Official Comment to UIFSA Section 319

The first sentence of Subsection (a) is truly hortatory in nature, although its principle is implemented insofar as support enforcement agencies are concerned by federal regulations promulgated by the Office of Child Support Enforcement. The second sentence confirms the duty of the agency or tribunal to furnish payment information in interstate cases.

The 2003 amendments to Subsections (b) and (c) were inspired by the federal Office of Child Support Enforcement (OCSE), U.S. Department of Health and Human Services. Support enforcement agencies are directed to cooperate in the efficient and expeditious collection and transfer of child support from obligor to obligee. States may choose whether only a tribunal may order redirection of support payments, or whether a support enforcement agency of the State is also authorized to render such an order. Under either approach, the request for such redirection that must be acted upon may only be made by a support enforcement agency in either the issuing State or another State. The basic idea is that redirection of payments will be facilitated, with the proviso that the issuing tribunal be kept informed as to the disposition of the payments made under its order.

SUBCHAPTER E. ESTABLISHMENT OF SUPPORT ORDER

§ 159.401. Petition to Establish Support Order

(a) If a support order entitled to recognition under this chapter has not been issued, a responding tribunal of this state may issue a support order if:

(1) the individual seeking the order resides in another state; or

(2) the support enforcement agency seeking the order is located in another state.

(b) The tribunal may issue a temporary child support order if the tribunal determines that the order is appropriate and the individual ordered to pay is:

(1) a presumed father of the child;

(2) a man petitioning to have his paternity adjudicated;

(3) a man identified as the father of the child through genetic testing;

(4) an alleged father who has declined to submit to genetic testing;

(5) a man shown by clear and convincing evidence to be the father of the child;

(6) an acknowledged father as provided by applicable state law;

(7) the mother of the child; or

(8) an individual who has been ordered to pay child support in a previous proceeding and the order has not been reversed or vacated.

(c) On finding, after notice and an opportunity to be heard, that an obligor owes a duty of support, the tribunal shall issue a support order directed to the obligor and may issue other orders under Section 159.305.

Commissioners' Official Comment to UIFSA Section 401

This section authorizes a tribunal of the responding State to issue temporary and permanent support orders binding on an obligor over whom the tribunal has personal jurisdiction. UIFSA does not permit such orders to be issued when another support order exists, thereby prohibiting a second tribunal from establishing another support order and the accompanying continuing, exclusive jurisdiction over the matter, *see* Sections 205 and 206.

The 2003 rewording of Subsection (b) conforms the language to the provisions of the UNIFORM PARENTAGE ACT (2000) regarding the individual party who may be ordered to pay temporary support.

SUBCHAPTER F. ENFORCEMENT OF ORDER OF ANOTHER STATE WITHOUT REGISTRATION

§ 159.501. Employer's Receipt of Income–Withholding Order of Another State

An income-withholding order issued in another state may be sent by or on behalf of the obligee or by the support enforcement agency to the person defined as the obligor's employer under Chapter 158 without first filing a petition or comparable pleading or registering the order with a tribunal of this state.

Commissioners' Official Comment to UIFSA Section 501

In 1984 Congress mandated that all States adopt procedures for enforcing income-withholding orders of sister States. Direct recognition by the out-of-state obligor's employer of a withholding order issued by another State long was sought by support enforcement associations and other advocacy groups. In 1992 UIFSA recognized such a procedure. The article was extensively amended in 1996, but was the subject only of clarifying amendments in 2003.

Section 501 is deliberately written in the passive voice; the Act does not restrict those who may send an income-withholding order across state lines. Although the sender will ordinarily be a child support enforcement agency or the obligee, the obligor or any other person may supply an employer with the income-withholding order. "Sending a copy" of a withholding order to an employer is clearly distinguishable from "service" of that order on the same employer. Service of an order necessarily intends to invoke a tribunal's authority over an employer doing business in the State. Thus, for there to be valid "service" of a withholding order on an employer in a State, the tribunal must have authority to bind the employer. In most cases, this requires the assertion of the authority of a local responding tribunal in a "registration for enforcement" proceeding. In short, the formality of "service" defeats the whole purpose of direct income withholding across state lines.

In sum, the process contemplated in this article is direct "notification" of an employer in another State of a withholding order without the involvement of initiating or responding tribunals. Therefore, receipt of a copy of a withholding order by facsimile, regular first class mail, registered or certified mail, or any other type of direct notice is sufficient to provide the requisite notice to trigger direct income withholding in the absence of a contest by the employee-obligor.

The 2003 amendments acknowledge that this process is now widely used by not only child support enforcement agencies, but also by private collection agencies or private attorneys acting on behalf of obligees.

---

§ 159.502. Employer's Compliance With Income-Withholding Order of Another State

(a) On receipt of an income-withholding order, the obligor's employer shall immediately provide a copy of the order to the obligor.

(b) The employer shall treat an income-withholding order issued in another state that appears regular on its face as if the order had been issued by a tribunal of this state.

(c) Except as otherwise provided in Subsection (d) and Section 159.503, the employer shall withhold and distribute the funds as directed in the withholding order by complying with terms of the order that specify:

(1) the duration and amount of periodic payments of current child support, stated as a sum certain;

(2) the person designated to receive payments and the address to which the payments are to be forwarded;

(3) medical support, whether in the form of periodic cash payments, stated as a sum certain, or ordering the obligor to provide health insurance coverage for the child under a policy available through the obligor's employment;

(4) the amount of periodic payments of fees and costs for a support enforcement agency, the issuing tribunal, and the obligee's attorney, stated as sums certain; and

(5) the amount of periodic payments of arrearages and interest on arrearages, stated as sums certain.

(d) An employer shall comply with the law of the state of the obligor's principal place of employment for withholding from income with respect to:

(1) the employer's fee for processing an income-withholding order;

(2) the maximum amount permitted to be withheld from the obligor's income; and

(3) the times within which the employer must implement the withholding order and forward the child support payment.

Commissioners' Official Comment to UIFSA Section 502

In 1996 major employers and national payroll associations urged NCCUSL to supply more detail regarding the rights and duties of an employer on receipt of an income-withholding order from another State. The Conference obliged with amendments to UIFSA establishing a series of steps for employers to track.

When an employer receives an income withholding order from another State, the first step is to notify the employee that an income withholding order has been received naming the employee as the obligor of child support, and that income withholding will begin within the time frame specified by local law. In other words, the employer will initially proceed just as if the withholding order had been received from a tribunal of the employer's State. It is the responsibility of the employee to take whatever protective measures are necessary to prevent the withholding if the employee asserts a defense as provided in Section 506, *infra*.

At this point neither an initiating nor a responding tribunal is directly involved. The withholding order may have been forwarded by the obligee, the obligee's attorney, or the out-of-state IV–D agency. In fact, there is no prohibition against anyone sending a valid copy of an income-withholding order, even a stranger to the litigation, such as the child's grandparent. Subsection (a) does not specify the method for sending this relatively informal notice for direct income withholding, but rather makes the assumption that the employer's communication to the employee regarding receipt of the order will cause an employee-obligor to act to prevent a wrongful invasion of his or her income if it is not owed as current child support or arrears.

Subsection (b) directs an employer of the enacting State to recognize a withholding order of a sister State, subject to the employee's right to contest the validity of the order or its enforcement. Prior to the promulgation of UIFSA, agencies in several States adopted a procedure of sending direct withholding requests to out-of-state employers. A contemporaneous study by the federal General Accounting Office reported that employers in a second State routinely recognized withholding orders of sister States despite an apparent lack of statutory authority to do so. UIFSA marked the first official sanction of this practice. Subsection (b) does not define "regular on its face," but the term should be liberally construed, *see U.S. v. Morton*, 467 U.S. 822 (1984) ("legal process regular on its face"). The rules governing intrastate procedure and defenses for withholding orders will apply to interstate orders.

Subsection (c) answered employers' complaints that insufficient direction for action was given by the original UIFSA. Prior to the 1996 amendments an employer was merely told to "distribute the funds as directed in the withholding order." This section clarifies the terms of the out-of-state order with which the employer must strictly comply. As a general principle, an employer is directed to comply with the specific terms contained in the order, but there are exceptions. Moreover, many income-withholding orders received at that time did not provide the detail necessary for the employer to comply with every directive. Since then, however, the long-anticipated federal forms were promulgated throughout 1997 and 1998, with periodic updates to the present time. Most recently, the text of income withholding orders for child support is fast becoming subject to a nationwide norm. To the extent that an order is silent, the employer is not required to respond to unstated demands of the issuing State. Formerly, employers often were so concerned about ambiguous or incomplete orders that they telephoned child support enforcement agencies in other States to attempt to understand and comply with unstated terms. Employers should not be expected to become investigators or shoulder the responsibility of learning the law of 50 States.

Subsection (c)(1) directs that the amount and duration of periodic payments of current child support must be stated in a sum certain in order to elicit compliance. The duration of the support obligation is fixed by the controlling order and should be stated in the withholding order so that the employer is informed of the date on which the withholding is anticipated to terminate. The "sum certain" requirement is crucial to facilitating the employer's compliance. For example, an order for a "percentage of the obligor's net income," does not satisfy this requirement and is not entitled to compliance from an employer receiving an such an interstate income-withholding order.

Subsection (c)(2) states the obvious: information necessary for compliance must be clearly stated. For example, the destination of the payments must correspond to the destination originally designated or subsequently authorized by the issuing tribunal, such as by the redirection of payments pursuant to Section 319, *supra*. Absent such action by the issuing tribunal, no redirection by any support enforcement agency or other person or entity is authorized by this section.

Subsection (c)(3) provides that medical support for the child must be stated either by a periodic cash payment or, alternatively, by an order directing the employee-obligor to provide health insurance coverage from his employment. In the absence of an order for payment of a sum certain, an order for medical support as child support requires the employer to enroll the obligor's child for coverage if medical insurance is available through the obligor's employment. Failure to enroll the child should elicit, at the least, registration of the order for enforcement in the responding State, to be implemented by an order of a tribunal directing the employer to comply. Because the employer is so directed by the medical support order, enrollment of the child in the health care plan at the employee-obligor's expense is not dependent on the obligor's consent, any more than withholding a sum certain from the obligor's income is subject to a veto. It is up to the employee-obligor to assert any defense to prevent the employer from abiding by the medical support order.

Subsection (c)(4) identifies certain costs and fees incurred in conjunction with the support enforcement that may be added to the withholding order.

Subsection (c)(5) requires that the amount of periodic payments for arrears and interest on arrears also must be stated as a sum certain. If the one-order system is to function properly, the issuing State ultimately must be responsible to account for payments and maintain the record of arrears and interest rate on arrears. Full compliance with the support order will only be achieved when the issuing State determines that the obligation no longer exists.

Subsection (d) identifies those narrow provisions in which the law of the employee's work State applies, rather than the law of the issuing State. A large employer will almost certainly have a number of employees subject to income-withholding orders. From the employer's perspective, the procedural requirements for compliance should be uniform for all of those employees. Certain issues should be matters for the law of the employee's work State, such as the employer's fee for processing, the maximum amount to be withheld, and the time in which to comply. The latter necessarily includes the frequency with which income withholding must occur. This is also consistent with regard to the tax consideration imposed by choice of law considerations. The only element in the list of local laws identified in Subsection (d) which stirred any controversy whatsoever was the fact that the maximum amount permitted to be withheld is to be subject to the law of the employee's work State. Demands of equal treatment for all citizens of the responding State, plus the practical concern that large employers require uniform computer programming mandate this solution.

§ 159.503. Employer's Compliance with Two or More Income–Withholding Orders

If an obligor's employer receives two or more income-withholding orders with respect to the earnings of the same obligor, the employer satisfies the terms of the orders if the employer complies with the law of the state of the obligor's principal place of employment to establish the priorities for withholding and allocating income withheld for two or more child support obligees.

Commissioners' Official Comment to UIFSA Section 503

Consistent with the Act's general problem-solving approach, the employer is directed to deal with multiple income orders for multiple families in the same manner as required by local law for orders of the forum State.

---

§ 159.504. Immunity From Civil Liability

An employer who complies with an income-withholding order issued in another state in accordance with this subchapter is not subject to civil liability to an individual or agency with regard to the employer's withholding of child support from the obligor's income.

Commissioners' Official Comment to UIFSA Section 504

Because employer cooperation is a key element in interstate child support enforcement, it is sound policy to state explicitly that an employer who complies with an income-withholding order from another State is immune from civil liability.

---

§ 159.505. Penalties for Noncompliance

An employer who wilfully fails to comply with an income-withholding order issued by another state and received for enforcement is subject to the same penalties that may be imposed for noncompliance with an order issued by a tribunal of this state.

Commissioners' Official Comment to UIFSA Section 505

Only an employer who willfully fails to comply with an interstate order will be subject to enforcement procedures. Local law is the appropriate source for the applicable sanctions and other remedies available under state law.

---

§ 159.506. Contest by Obligor

(a) An obligor may contest the validity or enforcement of an income-withholding order issued in another state and received directly by an employer in this state by registering the order in a tribunal of this state and:

(1) filing a contest to that order under Subchapter G; or

(2) contesting the order in the same manner as if the order had been issued by a tribunal of this state.

(b) The obligor shall give notice of the contest to:

(1) a support enforcement agency providing services to the obligee;

(2) each employer that has directly received an income-withholding order relating to the obligor; and

(3) the person designated to receive payments in the income-withholding order or to the obligee, if no person is designated.

Commissioners' Official Comment to UIFSA Section 506

This section incorporates into the interstate context the law regarding defenses an employee-obligor may raise to an intrastate withholding order. Generally, States have accepted the IV–D requirement that the only viable defense is a "mistake of fact." 42 U.S.C. Section 666(b)(4)(A). This apparently includes "errors in the amount of current support owed, errors in the amount of accrued arrearage or mistaken identity of the alleged obligor" while excluding "other grounds, such as the inappropriateness of the amount of support ordered to be paid, changed financial circumstances of the obligor, or lack of visitation." H.R. Rep. No. 98–527, 98th Cong., 1st Sess. 33 (1983). The latter claims must be pursued in a separate proceeding in the appropriate State, not in a UIFSA proceeding.

This procedure is based on the assumption that valid defenses to income withholding for child support are few and far between. Experience has shown that in relatively few cases does an employee-obligor have a complete defense, *e.g.*, the child has died, another contingency ending the support has occurred, the order has been superseded, or there is a case of mistaken identity and the employee is not the obligor. An employee's complaint that "The child support is too high" must be ignored.

However, situations do arise where an employer has received multiple withholding notices regarding the obligor-employee and the same obligee. The notices may even allege conflicting amounts due, especially for payments on arrears. Additionally, many employees claim to have only learned of default orders when the withholding notice Is delivered to the employer; this leads to claims that the order being enforced through income withholding was entered without personal jurisdiction over the obligor-employee.

The 2003 rewording of Subsection (a) affirms that a simple. efficient, and cost-effective method for an employee-alleged obligor to assert a defense is to register the withholding order with a local tribunal and seek protection from that tribunal pending resolution of the contest. This may be accomplished through the obligor's employment of private counsel or by a request for services made to the child support enforcement agency of the responding State. Some States provide administrative procedures for challenging the income withholding that may provide quicker resolution of a dispute than a judicially-based registration and hearing process. In the absence of expeditious action by the employee to assert a defense and contest the direct filing of a notice for withholding, however, the employer must begin income withholding in a timely fashion.

In contrast to the multiple-order system of RURESA, another issue the employee-obligor may raise is that the withholding order received by the employer is not based on the controlling child support order issued by the tribunal with continuing, exclusive jurisdiction, *see* Section 207, *supra*. Such a claim does not constitute a defense to the obligation of child support, but does put at issue the identity of the order to which the employer must respond. Clearly the employer is in no position to make such a decision. When multiple orders involve the same employee-obligor and child, as a practical matter resort to a responding tribunal to resolve a dispute over apportionment almost certainly is necessary.

§ 159.507. Administrative Enforcement of Orders

(a) A party or support enforcement agency seeking to enforce a support order or an income-withholding order, or both, issued by a tribunal of another state may send the documents required for registering the order to a support enforcement agency of this state.

(b) On receipt of the documents, the support enforcement agency, without initially seeking to register the order, shall consider and, if appropriate, use any administrative procedure authorized by the law of this state to enforce a support order or an income-withholding order, or both. If the obligor does not contest administrative enforcement, the order need not be registered. If the obligor contests the validity or administrative enforcement of the order, the support enforcement agency shall register the order under this chapter.

Commissioners' Official Comment to UIFSA Section 507

This section authorizes summary enforcement of an interstate child support order through the administrative means available for intrastate orders. Under Subsection (a), an interested party in another State, which necessarily may include a private attorney or a support enforcement agency, may forward a support order or income-withholding order to a support enforcement agency of the responding State. The term "responding State" in this context does not necessarily contemplate resort to a tribunal as an initial step.

Subsection (b) directs the support enforcement agency in the responding State to employ that State's regular administrative procedures to process an out-of-state order. Thus, a local employer accustomed to dealing with the local agency need not change its procedure to comply with an out-of-state order. Similarly, the administrative agency is authorized to apply its ordinary rules equally to both intrastate and interstate orders. For example, if the administrative hearing procedure must be exhausted for an intrastate order before a contesting party may seek relief in a tribunal, the same rule applies to an interstate order received for administrative enforcement.

SUBCHAPTER G. REGISTRATION, ENFORCEMENT, AND MODIFICATION OF SUPPORT ORDER

§ 159.601. Registration of Order for Enforcement

A support order or income-withholding order issued by a tribunal of another state may be registered in this state for enforcement.

Commissioners' Official Comment to UIFSA Section 601

Sections 601 through 604 establish the basic procedure for the registration of interstate support orders. Formerly, the common practice under RURESA was to initiate a new proceeding for the establishment of a support order, even though there was an existing order for child support. That practice was specifically rejected by UIFSA; the fact that RURESA permitted (really encouraged) initiation of new proceedings under those circumstances led to the multiple support order system that UIFSA is designed to eliminate.

Under the one-order system of UIFSA, only one existing order is to be enforced prospectively. If more than one child-support order exists, Section 207 is designed to resolve the conflict by determining which order is controlling. Registration of an order in a tribunal of the responding State is the first step to enforce a child-support order of another State. Similarly, it is the first step for modification of another State's child-support order and may be the same for identification of the controlling order. Rather than being an optional procedure, as was the case under RURESA, registration under UIFSA is the primary method for interstate enforcement or modification of a child-support order by a tribunal of a responding State. If the prior support order has been validly issued by a tribunal with continuing, exclusive jurisdiction, *see* Section 205, that order is to be prospectively enforced against the obligor in the absence of narrow, strictly-defined fact situations in which an existing order may be modified, *see* Sections 609 through 612. Until that order is modified, however, it is fully enforceable in the responding State.

Although registration that is not accompanied by a request for the affirmative relief of enforcement or modification is not prohibited, the Act does not contemplate registration as serving a purpose in itself.

§ 159.602. Procedure to Register Order for Enforcement

(a) A support order or income-withholding order of another state may be registered in this state by sending to the appropriate tribunal in this state:

(1) a letter of transmittal to the tribunal requesting registration and enforcement;

(2) two copies, including one certified copy, of the order to be registered, including any modification of the order;

(3) a sworn statement by the person requesting registration or a certified statement by the custodian of the records showing the amount of any arrearage;

(4) the name of the obligor and, if known:

(A) the obligor's address and social security number;

(B) the name and address of the obligor's employer and any other source of income of the obligor; and

(C) a description of and the location of property of the obligor in this state not exempt from execution; and

(5) except as otherwise provided by Section 159.312, the name of the obligee and, if applicable, the person to whom support payments are to be remitted.

(b) On receipt of a request for registration, the registering tribunal shall cause the order to be filed as a foreign judgment, together with one copy of the documents and information, regardless of their form.

(c) A petition or comparable pleading seeking a remedy that must be affirmatively sought under other law of this state may be filed at the same time as the request for registration or later. The pleading must specify the grounds for the remedy sought.

(d) If two or more orders are in effect, the person requesting registration shall:

(1) provide to the tribunal a copy of each support order and the documents specified in this section;

(2) identify the order alleged to be the controlling order, if any; and

(3) state the amount of consolidated arrearages, if any.

(e) A request for a determination of which order is the controlling order may be filed separately from or with a request for registration and enforcement or for registration and modification. The person requesting registration shall give notice of the request to each party whose rights may be affected by the determination.

Commissioners' Official Comment to UIFSA Section 602

Subsection (a) outlines the mechanics for registration of an interstate order. Substantial compliance with the requirements is expected, *Twaddell v. Anderson*, 523 S.E.2d 710 (N.C. App. 1999); *In re Chapman*, 973 S.W.2d 346 (Tex. App.—Amarillo 1998, no pet.).

Subsection (b) confirms that the order being registered is not converted into an order of the responding State, but rather continues to be an order of the issuing State.

Subsection (c) warns that if a particular enforcement remedy must be specifically sought under local law, the same rule of pleading is applicable as in an interstate case. For example, if license suspension or revocation is sought as a remedy for alleged noncompliance with the terms of the order, the substantive and procedural rules of the responding State apply. Whether the range of application of the remedy in the responding State is wider or narrower than that available in the issuing State is irrelevant. The responding tribunal will apply the familiar law of its State, and is neither expected nor authorized to consider the law of the issuing State. In short, the path in enforcing the order of a tribunal of another State is identical to the path followed for enforcing an order of the responding State. The authorization of a later filing to comply with local law contemplates that interstate pleadings may be liberally amended to conform to local practice.

The 2003 amendments adding Subsections (d) and (e) amplify the procedures to be followed when two or more child-support orders exist and registration for enforcement or modification is sought. In such instances, the requester is directed to furnish the tribunal with sufficient information and documentation so that the tribunal may make determinations of the controlling order and of the amount of consolidated arrears and interest as provided by Section 207, *supra*.

Leading Case

In re Chapman, 973 S.W.2d 346 (Tex. App.—Amarillo 1998, no pet.) (missing sworn statement precludes UIFSA registration)

---

§ 159.603. Effect of Registration for Enforcement

(a) A support order or income-withholding order issued in another state is registered when the order is filed in the registering tribunal of this state.

(b) A registered order issued in another state is enforceable in the same manner and is subject to the same procedures as an order issued by a tribunal of this state.

(c) Except as otherwise provided in this subchapter, a tribunal of this state shall recognize and enforce, but may not modify, a registered order if the issuing tribunal had jurisdiction.

Commissioners' Official Comment to UIFSA Section 603

Until the advent of the 2003 amendments, the registration procedure under UIFSA was nearly identical to that of RURESA. But, the underlying intent of UIFSA registration has always been radically different. Under RURESA, once an order of State A was registered in State B, it became an order of the latter. Under UIFSA, the order continues to be an order of State A, which is to be enforced by a tribunal of State B. The rules of evidence and procedure of State B apply to hearings, except as local law is supplemented or specifically superseded by the Act. The purpose of the 2003 amendments to the registration procedure set forth in Sections 601 through 604 is to confirm and clarify that the order being registered remains a State A order unless and until modification is accomplished.

RURESA specifically subjected a registered order to "proceedings for reopening, vacating, or staying as a support order of this State." These procedures are not authorized under UIFSA. Subsection (b) states that an interstate support order is to be enforced and satisfied in the same manner as if it had been issued by a tribunal of the registering State, although it remains an order of the issuing State. Conceptually, the responding State is enforcing the order of another State, not its own order.

Subsection (c) mandates enforcement of the registered order, *see* also Sections 606 through 608, *infra*. This is at sharp variance with the common interpretation of RURESA, which was generally construed as converting the foreign order into an order of the registering State. Once the registering court concluded that it was enforcing its own order, the next logical step was to issue an order as the court deemed appropriate. Although quite often couched in terms of a "modification," this procedure resulted in yet another order and was a major contributor to the multiple-order system. UIFSA mandates an end to this process. Under UIFSA there will be only one order in existence at any one time. That order is enforceable in a responding State irrespective of whether the order may be modified. In most instances, the support order will be subject to the continuing, exclusive jurisdiction of the issuing State. But sometimes the issuing State will not be able to exercise its authority to modify the order because neither the child nor the parties reside in the issuing State. Nonetheless, the order may be registered and is fully enforceable in a responding State until the potential for modification actually occurs in accordance with the strict terms for such a proceeding, *see* Sections 609–612, *infra*. Thus, the registering tribunal always must bear in mind that the enforcement procedures taken, whether to enforce current support or to assist collecting current and future arrears and interest are made on behalf of the issuing State, and are not to be viewed as modifications of the controlling order.

§ 159.604. Choice of Law

(a) Except as provided by Subsection (d), the law of the issuing state governs:

(1) the nature, extent, amount, and duration of current payments under a registered support order;

(2) the computation and payment of arrearages and accrual of interest on the arrearages under the support order; and

(3) the existence and satisfaction of other obligations under the support order.

(b) In a proceeding for arrearages under a registered support order, the statute of limitation of this state or of the issuing state, whichever is longer, applies.

(c) A responding tribunal in this state shall apply the procedures and remedies of this state to enforce current support and collect arrearages and interest due on a support order of another state registered in this state.

(d) After a tribunal of this or another state determines which order is the controlling order and issues an order consolidating arrearages, if any, the tribunal of this state shall prospectively apply the law of the state issuing the controlling order, including that state's law on interest on arrearages, current and future support, and consolidated arrearages.

Commissioners' Official Comment to UIFSA Section 604

This section identifies situations in which local law is inapplicable. A basic principle of UIFSA is that throughout the process the controlling order remains the order of the issuing State, and that responding States only assist in the enforcement of that order. Absent a loss of continuing, exclusive jurisdiction and a subsequent modification of the order, the order never becomes an "order of the responding State." Ultimate responsibility for enforcement and final resolution of the obligor's compliance with all aspects of the support order belongs to the issuing State. Thus, calculation of whether the obligor has fully complied with the payment of current support, arrears, and interest on arrears is the duty of the issuing State. For example, under Subsection (a) the responding State must recognize and enforce an order of the issuing State for the support of a child until age 21, notwithstanding the fact that the duty of support of a child ends at age 18 under the law of the responding State, *see Robdau v. Commonwealth, Virginia Dept. Social Serv.*, 543 S.E.2d 602 (Va. App. 2001); *State ex rel. Harnes v. Lawrence*, 538 S.E.2d 223 (N.C. App. 2000). Similarly, the law of the issuing State governs whether a payment made for the benefit of a child, such as a Social Security benefit for a child of a disabled obligor, should be credited against the obligor's child support obligation.

The amendments of 2003 to Subsection (a) are intended to clarify the range of subjects that are governed by the choice of law rules established in this section.

Subsection (b) contains another choice of law provision that may diverge from local law. In situations in which the statutes of limitation differ from State to State, the statute with the longer term is to be applied. *Attorney General v. Litten*, 999 S.W.2d 74 (Tex. App.—Houston [14th Dist.] 1999, no pet.). In interstate cases, arrearages often will have accumulated over a considerable period of time before enforcement is perfected. The rationale for this exception to the general rule is that the obligor should not gain an undue benefit from the choice of residence if the forum State has a shorter statute of limitations for arrearages than does the controlling order State. On the other side of the coin, i.e., the forum has a longer statute of limitations, the obligor will be treated in an identical manner as all other obligors in that State.

Subsection (c) mandates that local law controls with regard to enforcement procedures. For example, if the issuing State has enacted a wide variety of license suspension or revocation statutes, while the responding State has a much narrower list of licenses subject to suspension or revocation, local law prevails.

Subsection (d) may appear to state another truism–the law of the State that issued the controlling order is superior with regard to the terms of the support order itself. However, the last clause in the sentence provides a very important clarifying provision; that is, the law of the issuing State is to be applied to the consolidated arrears, even if the support orders of other States contributed a portion to those arrears.

In sum, the local tribunal applies its own familiar procedures to enforce a support order, but it is clearly enforcing an order of another State and not an order of the forum.

---

§ 159.605. Notice of Registration of Order

(a) When a support order or income-withholding order issued in another state is registered, the registering tribunal shall notify the nonregistering party. The notice must be accompanied by a copy of the registered order and the documents and relevant information accompanying the order.

(b) A notice under this section must inform the nonregistering party:

(1) that a registered order is enforceable as of the date of registration in the same manner as an order issued by a tribunal of this state;

(2) that a hearing to contest the validity or enforcement of the registered order must be requested within 20 days after notice;

(3) that failure to contest the validity or enforcement of the registered order in a timely manner:

(A) will result in confirmation of the order and enforcement of the order and the alleged arrearages; and

(B) precludes further contest of that order with respect to any matter that could have been asserted; and

(4) of the amount of any alleged arrearages.

(c) If the registering party asserts that two or more orders are in effect, the notice under this section must also:

(1) identify:

(A) the orders, including which order is alleged by the registering person to be the controlling order; and

(B) the consolidated arrearages, if any;

(2) notify the nonregistering party of the right to a determination of which order is the controlling order;

(3) state that the procedures provided in Subsection (b) apply to the determination of which order is the controlling order; and

(4) state that failure to contest the validity or enforcement of the order alleged to be the controlling order in a timely manner may result in confirmation that the order is the controlling order.

(d) On registration of an income-withholding order for enforcement, the registering tribunal shall notify the obligor's employer under Chapter 158.

Commissioners' Official Comment to UIFSA Section 605

Sections 605–608 provide the procedure for the nonregistering party to contest registration of an order, either because the order is allegedly invalid, superseded, or no longer in effect, or because the enforcement remedy being sought is opposed by the nonregistering party.

Subsections (a) and (b) direct that the nonregistering party be fully informed of the effect of registration. After such notice is given, absent a successful contest by the nonregistering party, the order will be confirmed and future contest will be precluded.

Subsection (c), with new text in 2003, is the correlative to Section 602(d) and (e) regarding the notice to be given to the nonregistering party if a controlling order determination must be made because of the existence of two or more child-support orders. The petitioner requesting this affirmative relief is directed to identify the order alleged to be controlling under Section 207, *supra*. If the nonregistering party does not contest this allegation, either by default or agreement, the order identified as controlling will be confirmed by operation of law by the following section.

Relettered Subsection (d) states the obvious; the obligor's employer must also be notified if income is to be withheld.

---

§ 159.606. Procedure to Contest Validity or Enforcement of Registered Order

(a) A nonregistering party seeking to contest the validity or enforcement of a registered order in this state shall request a hearing within 20 days after notice of the registration. The nonregistering party may seek under Section 159.607 to:

(1) vacate the registration;

(2) assert any defense to an allegation of noncompliance with the registered order; or

(3) contest the remedies being sought or the amount of any alleged arrearages.

(b) If the nonregistering party fails to contest the validity or enforcement of the registered order in a timely manner, the order is confirmed by operation of law.

(c) If a nonregistering party requests a hearing to contest the validity or enforcement of the registered order, the registering tribunal shall schedule the matter for hearing and give notice to the parties of the date, time, and place of the hearing.

Commissioners' Official Comment to UIFSA Section 606

Subsection (a) directs the "nonregistering party" to contest the registration of a foreign order within a short period of time or forfeit the opportunity to contest. UIFSA provides that either the obligor, the obligee, or a state enforcement agency, may seek to register a foreign support order. In fact, even a stranger to the litigation, for example a grandparent or an employer of an alleged obligor, may register a support order. Thereafter, the nonregistering party is put on notice of the registration and is required to assert any existing defense to the alleged order or forfeit the opportunity. Note that either the obligor or the obligee may have objections to the registered order, although in the vast majority of cases doubtless the obligor will be the nonregistering party. For example, there is a possibility that in multiple order situations either party may register the order most favorable to that party rather than the likely controlling order, thus triggering a contest. However, such chicanery is contrary to Subsection 605(c) and is specifically forbidden for a support enforcement agency, Subsection 307(c).

Subsection (a) is philosophically very different from RURESA which directed that a registered order "shall be treated in the same manner as a support order issued by a court of this State." Under UIFSA a contest of the fundamental provisions of the registered order is not permitted in the responding State. The nonregistering party must return to the issuing State to prosecute such a contest (obviously only as the law of that State permits). The procedure adopted here is akin to the prohibition found in Section 315 against asserting a nonparentage defense in a UIFSA proceeding. In short, raising a collateral issue in a UIFSA proceeding is prohibited, but no attempt is made to preclude the issue from being litigated in another, more appropriate forum if otherwise allowed by that forum.

On the other hand, a nonregistering obligor may assert defenses such as "payment" or "the obligation has terminated" in response to allegations of noncompliance with the registered order. Similarly, a constitutionally-based attack may be asserted, *i.e.*, an alleged lack of personal jurisdiction by the issuing tribunal over a party. There is no defense, however, to registration of a valid foreign support order.

Subsection (b) precludes an untimely contest of a registered support order. As noted above, the nonregistering party is free to seek redress in the issuing State from the tribunal with continuing, exclusive jurisdiction over the support order.

Subsection (c) directs that a hearing be scheduled when the nonregistering party contests some aspect of the registration. At present, federal regulations govern the allowable time frames for contesting income withholding in IV–D cases, see 42 U.S.C. Section 666(b). Additional codification of the procedure process is unwise.

Leading Case

In re Kuykendall, 957 S.W.2d 907 (Tex. App.—Texarkana 1997, no writ) (Kansas decree wording "shall" pay sufficient for monetary judgment in Texas)

---

§ 159.607. Contest of Registration or Enforcement

(a) A party contesting the validity or enforcement of a registered order or seeking to vacate the registration has the burden of proving one or more of the following defenses:

(1) the issuing tribunal lacked personal jurisdiction over the contesting party;

(2) the order was obtained by fraud;

(3) the order has been vacated, suspended, or modified by a later order;

(4) the issuing tribunal has stayed the order pending appeal;

(5) there is a defense under the law of this state to the remedy sought;

(6) full or partial payment has been made;

(7) the statute of limitation under Section 159.604 precludes enforcement of some or all of the alleged arrearages; or

(8) the alleged controlling order is not the controlling order.

(b) If a party presents evidence establishing a full or partial defense under Subsection (a), a tribunal may stay enforcement of the registered order, continue the proceeding to permit production of additional relevant evidence, and issue other appropriate orders. An uncontested portion of the registered order may be enforced by all remedies available under the law of this state.

(c) If the contesting party does not establish a defense under Subsection (a) to the validity or enforcement of the order, the registering tribunal shall issue an order confirming the order.

Commissioners' Official Comment to UIFSA Section 607

Subsection (a) places the burden on the nonregistering party to assert narrowly defined defenses to registration of a support order. The 2003 amendment added an obvious defense that was inadvertently omitted from the original list of defenses. In a multiple order situation, if the nonregistering party contests the allegation regarding the controlling order, either because it allegedly has not been registered or because another order has been misidentified as such, the nonregistering party may defend against enforcement of another order by asserting the existence of a controlling order. Presumably the defense must be substantiated by registration of the other alleged controlling order to be effective.

If the obligor is liable for current support, in the absence of a valid defense under Subsection (b) the registering tribunal must enter an order to enforce that obligation. *State Dept. of Revenue ex rel. Rochell v. Morris*, 736 So. 2d 41 (Fla. App. 1999); *Welsher v. Rager*, 491 S.E.2d 661 (N.C. App. 1997); *Cowan v. Moreno*, 903 S.W.2d 119 (Tex. App.—Austin 1995, no writ). Proof of arrearages must result in enforcement; under the Bradley Amendment, 42 U.S.C. Section 666(a)(10), all States are required to treat child support payments as final judgments as they come due (or lose federal funding). Therefore, such arrearages are not subject to retroactive modification.

Subsection (c) provides that failure to successfully contest a registered order requires the tribunal to confirm the validity of the registered order. Although the statute is silent on the subject, it seems likely that *res judicata* requires that both the registering and nonregistering party who fail to register the "true" controlling order will be estopped from subsequently collaterally attacking the confirmed order on the basis that the unmentioned "true order should have been confirmed instead."

§ 159.608. Confirmed Order

Confirmation of a registered order, whether by operation of law or after notice and hearing, precludes further contest of the order with respect to any matter that could have been asserted at the time of registration.

Commissioners' Official Comment to UIFSA Section 608

If the nonregistering party fails to contest, the registered support order is confirmed by operation of law and no tribunal action is necessary. If contested, a registered support order must be confirmed by the forum tribunal if the defense authorized in Section 607 is rejected after a hearing. Either result precludes the nonregistering party from raising any issue that could have been asserted in a hearing. Confirmation of a foreign support order validates both the terms of the order and the asserted arrearages.

§ 159.609. Procedure to Register Child Support Order of Another State for Modification

A party or support enforcement agency seeking to modify or to modify and enforce a child support order issued in another state shall register that order in this state in the same manner provided in Sections 159.601–159.604 if the order has not been registered. A petition for modification may be filed at the same time as a request for registration or later. The pleading must specify the grounds for modification.

Commissioners' Official Comment to UIFSA Section 609

Sections 609 through 615 deal with situations in which it is permissible for a registering State to modify the existing child-support order of another State. A petitioner wishing to register a support order of another State for purposes of modification must conform to the general requirements for pleadings in Section 311 (Pleadings and Accompanying Documents), and follow the procedure for registration set forth in Section 602 (Procedure To Register Order for Enforcement). If the tribunal has the requisite personal jurisdiction over the parties as established in Sections 611, 613, or 615, modification may be sought in conjunction with registration and enforcement, or at a later date after the order has been registered, confirmed, and enforced.

§ 159.610. Effect of Registration for Modification

A tribunal of this state may enforce a child support order of another state registered for purposes of modification in the same manner as if the order had been issued by a tribunal of this state, but the registered order may be modified only if the requirements of Section 159.611, 159.613, or 159.615 have been met.

Commissioners' Official Comment to UIFSA Section 610

An order registered for purposes of modification may be enforced in the same manner as an order registered for purposes of enforcement. But, the power of the forum tribunal to modify a child-support order of another tribunal is limited by the specific factual preconditions set forth in Sections 611, 613, and 615.

§ 159.611. Modification of Child Support Order of Another State

(a) Except as provided by Section 159.615, on petition a tribunal of this state may modify a child support order issued in another state and registered in this state only if Section 159.613 does not apply and after notice and hearing the tribunal finds that:

(1) the following requirements are met:

(A) the child, the obligee who is an individual, and the obligor do not reside in the issuing state;

(B) a petitioner who is a nonresident of this state seeks modification; and

(C) the respondent is subject to the personal jurisdiction of the tribunal of this state; or

(2) this state is the state of residence of the child, or a party who is an individual is subject to the personal jurisdiction of the tribunal of this state, and all of the parties who are individuals have filed consents in a record in the issuing tribunal for a tribunal of this state to modify the support order and assume continuing, exclusive jurisdiction.

(b) Modification of a registered child support order is subject to the same requirements, procedures, and defenses that apply to the modification of an order issued by a tribunal of this state, and the order may be enforced and satisfied in the same manner.

(c) Except as provided by Section 159.615, a tribunal of this state may not modify any aspect of a child support order, including the duration of the obligation of support, that may not be modified under the law of the issuing state. If two or more tribunals have issued child support orders for the same obligor and same child, the order that controls and must be recognized under Section 159.207 establishes the aspects of the support order that are nonmodifiable.

(d) On issuance of an order by a tribunal of this state modifying a child support order issued in another state, the tribunal of this state becomes the tribunal of continuing, exclusive jurisdiction.

(e) In a proceeding to modify a child support order, the law of the state that is determined to have issued the initial controlling order governs the duration of the obligation of support. The obligor's fulfillment of the duty of support established by that order precludes imposition of a further obligation of support by a tribunal of this state.

Commissioners' Official Comment to UIFSA Section 611

Under the procedure established by RURESA, after a support order was registered for the purpose of enforcement it was treated as if it had originally been issued by the registering tribunal. Most States interpreted these registration provisions as also authorizing prospective "modification" of the registered order. However, except in circumstances in which both States had the same version of RURESA and the formalities were scrupulously followed, the registering tribunal did not have the legal authority to replace the original order with its own order. In short, most often the purported modification in essence established a new obligation. In sum, by its very terms RURESA contemplated, or even encouraged, the existence of multiple support orders, none of which were directly related to any of the others. Although the issuing tribunal under RURESA retained a version of continuing, exclusive jurisdiction to modify its own order, that power was not exclusive. The typical scenario of those days was that an obligee would seek assistance from a local court, which would determine a duty of support existed and forward a certificate and order and petition to a responding court. The subsequent proceeding in the responding State would bring the obligor before the court. The obligor typically sought modification of the support obligation (which almost always was not being paid) in a forum which presented him with the "hometown advantage." Thus arose the common practice of the issuance of a new, lower child-support order.

Under UIFSA, as long as the issuing State has continuing, exclusive jurisdiction over its child-support order, *see* Section 205(a), *supra*, a registering sister State is precluded from modifying that order. Without doubt, this is the most significant departure from the multiple-order system established by the prior Uniform Act. However, if the issuing State no longer has a sufficient interest in the modification of its order under the factual circumstances described in Section 205(b), *supra*, and restated in this section, after registration the responding State may assume the power to modify the controlling order.

Registration is subdivided into distinct categories: registration for enforcement, for modification, or both. UIFSA is based on recognizing the truism that when an out-of-state support order is registered, the rights and duties of the parties affected have been previously litigated. Because the obligor already has had a day before an appropriate tribunal, an enforcement remedy may be summarily invoked. On the other hand, modification of an existing order presupposes a change in the rights or duties of the parties. The requirements for modification of a child-support order are much more explicit under UIFSA, which allows a tribunal to modify an existing child-support order of another State only if certain quite limited conditions are met. First, the tribunal must have all the prerequisites for the exercise of personal jurisdiction required for rendition of an original support order. Second, one of the restricted fact situations described in Subsection (a) must be present. This section, which is a counterpart to Section 205(a), establishes the conditions under which the continuing, exclusive jurisdiction of the issuing tribunal is released.

Under Subsection (a)(1), before a tribunal in a new forum may modify the controlling order three specific criteria must be satisfied. First, the individual parties affected by the controlling order and the child must no longer reside in the issuing State. Second, the party seeking modification must register the order in a new forum, almost invariably the State of residence of the other party. A colloquial (but easily understood) description of this requirement is that the modification movant must "play an away game on the other party's home field." This rule applies to either obligor or obligee, depending on which of those parties seeks to modify. Proof of the fact that neither individual party nor the child continues to reside in the issuing State may be made directly in the registering State; no purpose would be served by requiring the petitioner to return to the original issuing State for a document to confirm the fact that none of the relevant persons still lives there. Third, the forum must have personal jurisdiction over the parties. This is supplied by the movant submitting to the personal jurisdiction of the forum by seeking affirmative relief, almost always coupled with the fact that the respondent resides in the forum. On rare occasion, the personal jurisdiction over the respondent may be supplied by other factors, *see* Section 201 and the comment thereto, *supra*.

The policies underlying the change affected by Subsection (a)(1) contemplate that the issuing State no longer has an interest in exercising its continuing, exclusive jurisdiction to modify its order. This restriction attempts to achieve a rough justice between the parties in the majority of cases by preventing a litigant from choosing to seek modification in a local tribunal to the marked disadvantage of the other party. For example, an obligor visiting the children at the residence of the obligee cannot be validly served with citation accompanied by a motion to modify the support order. Even though such personal service of the obligor in the obligee's home State is consistent with the jurisdictional requisites of *Burnham v. Superior Court*, 495 U.S. 604 (1990), the motion to modify does not fulfill the requirement of being brought by "a [petitioner] who is a nonresident of this State ." In short, the obligee is required to register the existing order and seek modification of that order in a State that has personal jurisdiction over the obligor other than the State of the obligee's residence. Again, almost invariably this will be the State of residence of the obligor. Similarly, fairness requires that an obligee seeking to modify or modify and enforce the existing order in the State of residence of the obligor will not be subject to a cross-motion to modify custody or visitation merely because the issuing State has lost its continuing, exclusive jurisdiction over the support order. The same is true of the obligor, who also is required to make a motion to modify support in a State other than that of his or her residence. Yet another benefit is supplied by the procedure mandated in this section. The most typical case is a motion to increase child support by the obligee, the enforcement of which ultimately will primarily, if not exclusively, take place in the obligor's State of residence. Modification and enforcement in the same forum promotes efficiency.

Several arguments sustain the jurisdictional choice made by UIFSA. First, "jurisdiction by ambush" will be avoided. That is, personal service on either the custodial or noncustodial party found within the state borders will not yield jurisdiction to modify. Thus, a parent seeking to exercise rights of visitation, delivering or picking-up the child for such visitation, or engaging in unrelated business activity in the State, will not be involuntarily subjected to protracted litigation in an inconvenient forum. The rule avoids the possible chilling effect on the exercise of parental contact with the child that the possibility of such litigation might have. Second, almost all disputes about whether the tribunal has jurisdiction will be eliminated; submission by the petitioner to the State of residence of the respondent alleviates this issue completely. Finally, because there is an existing order the primary focus will shift to enforcement, thereby curtailing to a degree unnecessary, time-consuming modification efforts. The array of enforcement procedures available administratively to support enforcement agencies may be invoked without resort to action by a tribunal, which had constituted a bottleneck under RURESA and URESA.

There are two exceptions to the rule of Subsection (a)(1) requiring the petitioner to be a nonresident of the forum in which modification is sought. First, under Subsection (a)(2) the parties may agree that a particular forum may serve to modify the order. Second, Section 613, *infra*, applies if all parties have left the original issuing State and now reside in the same new forum State. Subsection (a)(2), which authorizes the parties to terminate the continuing, exclusive jurisdiction of the issuing State by agreement, is based on several implicit assumptions. First, the subsection applies even if the issuing tribunal has continuing, exclusive jurisdiction because one of the parties or the child continues to reside in that State. Subsection (a)(2) also is applicable if the individual parties and the child no longer reside in the issuing State, but agree to submit the modification issue to a tribunal in the petitioner's State of residence. Also implicit in a shift of jurisdiction over the child-support order is that the agreed-upon tribunal must have subject matter jurisdiction and personal jurisdiction over at least one of the parties or the child, and that the other party submits to the personal jurisdiction of that forum. In short, UIFSA does not contemplate that absent parties can agree to confer jurisdiction on a tribunal without a nexus to the parties or the child. But if the other party agrees, either the obligor or the obligee may seek assertion of jurisdiction to modify by a tribunal of the State of residence of either party.

The requirements of Subsection (a) are demonstrated to the tribunal being asked to assume continuing, exclusive jurisdiction. No action to transfer, surrender, or otherwise participate is required or anticipated by the original order-issuing tribunal. The Act does not grant discretion to refuse to yield jurisdiction to the issuing tribunal; nor does it extend discretion to refuse to accept jurisdiction to the assuming tribunal when the statutory requisites are met. However, there is a distinction between the processes involved under Subsection (a)(1) and (a)(2). Once the requirements of (a)(1) or Section 613 have been met for assumption of jurisdiction, the assuming jurisdiction acts on the modification and then notifies the tribunal whose order has been replaced by the order of the assuming tribunal, *see* Section 614, *infra*. In contrast, for a tribunal of another State to assume modification jurisdiction under Subsection (a)(2) it is necessary that the individual parties first agree in a record to submit modification of child support to that tribunal and file their agreement with the issuing tribunal. Thereafter they may then proceed to petition the assuming tribunal to take jurisdiction.

Modification of child support under Subsections (a)(1) and (a)(2) is distinct from custody modification under the federal Parental Kidnapping Prevention Act, 42 U.S.C. Section 1738A, which provides that the court of continuing, exclusive jurisdiction may "decline jurisdiction." Similar provisions are found in the UCCJA, Section 14. In those statutes the methodology for the declination of jurisdiction is not spelled out, but rather is left to the discretion of possibly competing courts for case-by-case determination. The privilege of declining jurisdiction, thereby creating the potential for a vacuum, is not authorized under UIFSA, *see Rosen v. Lantos*, 938 P.2d 729, 734 (N.M. App. 1997). Once a controlling initial child-support order is established under UIFSA, at all times thereafter there is an existing order in effect to be enforced. Even if the issuing tribunal no longer has continuing, exclusive jurisdiction, its order remains fully enforceable until a tribunal with modification jurisdiction issues a new order in conformance with this article.

The degree to which the new standards of one tribunal with continuing, exclusive jurisdiction has been accepted is illustrated by comparing UIFSA to the UNIFORM CHILD CUSTODY JURISDICTION ACT, Sections 12–14, and UNIFORM CHILD CUSTODY JURISDICTION AND ENFORCEMENT ACT Sections 201–202. The UCCJA provides general principles for the judicial determination of an appropriate fact situation for subsequent modification of an existing custody order by another court. In contrast, UIFSA establishes a set of "bright line" rules which must be met before a tribunal may modify an existing child-support order. The intent is to eliminate multiple support orders to the maximum extent possible consistent with the principle of continuing, exclusive jurisdiction that pervades the Act. The UCCJEA borrows heavily, but not identically, from UIFSA. Both UIFSA and UCCJEA seek a world in which there is but one-order-at-a-time for child support and custody and visitation. Both have similar restrictions on the ability of a tribunal to modify the existing order. The major difference between the two acts results from the fact that the basic jurisdictional nexus of each is founded on different consideration. UIFSA has its focus on the personal jurisdiction necessary to bind the obligor to payment of a child-support order. UCCJEA places its focus on the factual circumstances of the child, primarily the "home State" of the child; personal jurisdiction over a parent in order to bind that parent to the custody decree is not required. An example of the disparate consequences of this difference is the fact that a return to the decree State does "not reestablish" continuing jurisdiction under the custody jurisdiction Act, *see* comment to UCCJEA Section 202. But, under UIFSA similar facts permit the issuing State to exercise continuing, exclusive jurisdiction to modify its child-support order if at the time the proceeding is filed the issuing State "is the residence" of one of the individual parties or the child, *see* Section 205(a), *supra*.

Subsection (b) states that when the forum has assumed modification jurisdiction because the issuing State has lost continuing, exclusive jurisdiction, the proceedings will generally follow local law with regard to modification of child-support orders.

The 2003 amendment to Subsection (c) and the addition of Subsection (d) are designed to eliminate scattered attempts to subvert a significant policy decision made when UIFSA was first promulgated. Prior to 1993, American case law was thoroughly in chaos regarding modification of the duration of a child-support obligation when an obligor or obligee moved from one State to another with different ages regarding the duration of the child-support obligation. In those circumstances, whether the obligation ended, extended, or was curtailed was left almost to chance. In a RURESA proceeding, on the obligee's motion some States would increase the duration of the support obligation when the obligor resided in a State with a higher age for the child support obligation. Other States decreased the obligor's duration of child support when the obligor countered with a motion that the new RURESA support order should reflect a shorter duration of the obligation in accordance with local law. Multiple durations of the support obligation, as well as multiple support amounts, were both major problem areas addressed by UIFSA.

From its original promulgation UIFSA determined that the duration of child-support obligation should be fixed by the controlling order, *see Robdau v. Commonwealth, Virginia Dept. Social Serv.*, 543 S.E.2d 602 (Va. App. 2001). If the language was insufficiently specific before the 2003, the amendments should make this decision absolutely clear. The original time frame for support is not modifiable unless the law of the issuing State provides for modification of its duration. Some courts have sought to subvert this policy by holding that completion of the obligation to support a child through age 18 established by the now-completed controlling order does not preclude the imposition of a new obligation thereafter to support the child through age 21 or even to age 23 if the child is enrolled in higher education. Subsection (d) is designed to eliminate these attempts to create multiple, albeit successive, support obligations. Consistent with this principle, if a domestic violence protective order has been entered with a child-support provision that has a duration less than the general child support law of the State that issues the controlling order, the law of that State determines the maximum duration. In sum, absent tribunal error the first child-support order issued under UIFSA will invariably be the initial controlling order. The initial controlling order may be modified and replaced by a new controlling order in accordance with the terms of Sections 609–615, but the duration of the child-support obligation remains constant, even though virtually every other aspect of the original order may be changed. This is also the standard in situations involving multiple valid child-support orders—a problem that will progressively decrease over time as RURESA multiple orders expire or a determination of the initial controlling order is made under Section 207, *supra*. Once a controlling order is identified under these standards, the duration of the support obligation is fixed.

Relettered Subsection (e) provides that upon modification the new order becomes the one order to be recognized by all UIFSA States, and the issuing tribunal acquires continuing, exclusive jurisdiction. Good practice mandates that the tribunal should explicitly state in its order that it is assuming responsibility for the controlling child-support order. Neither the parties nor other tribunals should be required to speculate about the effect of the action taken by the tribunal under this section.

Leading Cases

In re B.O.G., 48 S.W.3d 312 (Tex. App.—Waco 2001, pet. denied) (trial court lacked jurisdiction over father's motion to modify child support—everyone has left Texas)

Link v. Alvarado, 929 S.W.2d 674 (Tex. App.—San Antonio 1996, writ dism'd w.o.j.) (Hawaii's continuing, exclusive jurisdiction over child support order prevents Texas court from modifying child support)

§ 159.612. Recognition of Order Modified in Another State

If a child support order issued by a tribunal of this state is modified by a tribunal of another state that assumed jurisdiction under the Uniform Interstate Family Support Act, a tribunal of this state:

(1) may enforce the order that was modified only as to arrearages and interest accruing before the modification;

(2) may provide appropriate relief for violations of the order that occurred before the effective date of the modification; and

(3) shall recognize the modifying order of the other state, on registration, for the purpose of enforcement.

Commissioners' Official Comment to UIFSA Section 612

A key aspect of UIFSA is the deference to the controlling child-support order of a sister State demanded from a tribunal of the forum State. This applies not just to the original order, but also to a modified child-support order issued by a second State under the standards established by Section 611, 613, and 615. For the Act to function properly, the original issuing State must recognize and accept the modified order as controlling, and must regard its prior order as prospectively inoperative. Because the UIFSA system is based on an interlocking series of state laws, it is fundamental that a modifying tribunal of one State lacks the authority to direct the original issuing State to release its continuing, exclusive jurisdiction. That result is accomplished through the enactment of UIFSA by all States, which empowers a modifying tribunal to assume continuing, exclusive jurisdiction from the original issuing State and requires an issuing State to recognize such an assumption of jurisdiction. This explains why the U.S. Congress took the extraordinary measure in PRWORA of mandating universal passage of UIFSA 1996, as amended, *see* Prefatory Note.

The original issuing tribunal retains authority post-modification to take remedial actions directly connected to its now-modified order.

§ 159.613. Jurisdiction to Modify Child Support Order of Another State When Individual Parties Reside in This State

(a) If all of the parties who are individuals reside in this state and the child does not reside in the issuing state, a tribunal of this state has jurisdiction to enforce and to modify the issuing state's child support order in a proceeding to register that order.

(b) A tribunal of this state exercising jurisdiction under this section shall apply the provisions of Sections 159.101 through 159.209 and 159.601 through 159.614 and the procedural and substantive law of this state to the proceeding for enforcement or modification. Sections 159.301 through 159.507 and 159.701 through 159.802 do not apply.

Commissioners' Official Comment to UIFSA Section 613

A 1996 amendment explicitly dealt with the possibility that the parties and the child subject to a child-support order no longer reside in the issuing State and that the individual parties have moved to the same new State. This section makes it clear that, when the issuing State no longer has continuing, exclusive jurisdiction to modify its order, a tribunal of the State of mutual residence of the individual parties has jurisdiction to modify the child-support order and assume continuing, exclusive jurisdiction. Although the individual parties must reside in the forum State, there is no requirement that the child must also reside in the forum State (although the child must have moved from the issuing State).

Finally, because modification of the child-support order when all parties reside in the forum is essentially an intrastate matter, Subsection (b) withdraws authority to apply most of the substantive and procedural provisions of UIFSA, *i.e.*, those found in the Act other than in Articles 1, 2, and 6. Note, however, that the provision in Section 611(c) forbidding modification of nonmodifiable aspects of the controlling order applies. For example, the duration of the support obligation remains fixed by the original controlling order despite the subsequent residence of all parties in a new State. The fact that the State of the new controlling order has a different duration of for child support is specifically declared to be irrelevant by UIFSA, see Section 611, *supra*. Note that the even-handed approach of the Act is sustained; neither an increase nor a decrease in the duration in the obligation of child support is permitted.

§ 159.614. Notice to Issuing Tribunal of Modification

Within 30 days after issuance of a modified child support order, the party obtaining the modification shall file a certified copy of the order with the issuing tribunal that had continuing, exclusive jurisdiction over the earlier order and in each tribunal in which the party knows the earlier order has been registered. A party who obtains the order and fails to file a certified copy is subject to appropriate sanctions by a tribunal in which the issue of failure to file arises. The failure to file does not affect the validity or enforceability of the modified order of the new tribunal having continuing, exclusive jurisdiction.

Commissioners' Official Comment to UIFSA Section 614

This stand-alone provision is designed to clarify the organization of the Act; it states the crucial proposition that the prevailing party must inform the original issuing tribunal about its loss of continuing, exclusive jurisdiction over its child-support order. Thereafter, the original tribunal may not modify, or review and adjust, the amount of child support. Notice to the issuing tribunal and other affected tribunals that the continuing, exclusive jurisdiction of the former controlling order has been modified is crucial to avoid the confusion and chaos of the multiple-order system UIFSA is designed to replace.

Additionally, the tribunal has authority to impose sanctions on a party who fails to comply with the requirement to give notice of a modification to all interested tribunals. Note, however, that failure to notify a displaced tribunal of a modification of its order does not affect the validity of the modified order.

---

§ 159.615. Jurisdiction to Modify Child Support Order of Foreign Country or Political Subdivision

(a) If a foreign country or political subdivision that is a state refuses to modify its order or may not under its law modify its order, a tribunal of this state may assume jurisdiction to modify the child support order and bind all individuals subject to the personal jurisdiction of the tribunal regardless of whether:

(1) consent to modification of a child support order has been given under Section 159.611; or

(2) the individual seeking modification is a resident of this state or of the foreign country or political subdivision.

(b) An order issued under this section is the controlling order.

Commissioners' Official Comment to UIFSA Section 615

The amendments of 2003 added Section 615, which expands upon language moved from Section 611 (a)(2). A tribunal of one of the several States may modify a support order of a foreign country or political subdivision when a tribunal of the foreign jurisdiction would have jurisdiction to modify its order under the standards of UIFSA, but under the law or procedure of that foreign jurisdiction the tribunal will not or may not exercise that jurisdiction to modify its order. The standard example cited for the necessity of this special rule involves the conundrum posed to a tribunal of a foreign country having a requirement that the parties be physically present in order to sustain a modification of child support, and lacking the authority to compel a party residing outside of the borders of the country to appear. In such an instance, a tribunal of the forum State may modify the order if it has personal jurisdiction over both parties, including jurisdiction over the absent party who has submitted to the jurisdiction of the forum by making a request for modification of the support order.

SUBCHAPTER H. DETERMINATION OF PARENTAGE

§ 159.701. Proceeding to Determine Parentage

A court of this state authorized to determine the parentage of a child may serve as a responding tribunal in a proceeding to determine parentage brought under this chapter or a law substantially similar to this chapter.

Commissioners' Official Comment to UIFSA Section 701

This article authorizes a "pure" parentage action in the interstate context, *i.e.*, an action not joined with a claim for support. Either the mother or a man alleging himself to be the father of a child may bring such an action. Typically, an action to determine parentage across state lines will also seek to establish a support order under the Act, *see* Section 401. An action to establish parentage under UIFSA is to be treated identically to such an action brought in the responding State. Note that in a departure from the rest of this Act, the term "tribunal" is replaced by "court." Although in the several States there are various combinations of judicial and administrative entities that are authorized to establish, enforce, and modify child-support orders, the UNIFORM PARENTAGE ACT (2000) restricts parentage determinations to "a court," *see* UPA (2000) Section 104. The view that only a judicial officer should determine parentage is based on what the Conference believes is sound public policy.

SUBCHAPTER I. INTERSTATE RENDITION

§ 159.801. Grounds for Rendition

(a) In this subchapter, "governor" includes an individual performing the functions of governor or the executive authority of a state covered by this chapter.

(b) The governor of this state may:

(1) demand that the governor of another state surrender an individual found in the other state who is charged criminally in this state with having failed to provide for the support of an obligee; or

(2) on the demand of the governor of another state, surrender an individual found in this state who is charged criminally in the other state with having failed to provide for the support of an obligee.

(c) A provision for extradition of individuals not inconsistent with this chapter applies to the demand even if the individual whose surrender is demanded was not in the demanding state when the crime was allegedly committed and has not fled from that state.

Commissioners' Official Comment to UIFSA Section 801

This section has not been amended substantively since 1968. Virtually no controversy has been generated regarding this procedure. Arguably application of Subsection (c) is problematic in situations in which the obligor neither was present in the demanding State at the time of the commission of the crime nor fled from the demanding State. The possibility that an individual may commit a crime in a State without ever being physically present there has elicited considerable discussion and some case law. *See* L. BRILMAYER, AN INTRODUCTION TO JURISDICTION IN THE AMERICAN FEDERAL SYSTEM, 329–335 (1986) (discussing minimum contacts theory for criminal jurisdiction); Rotenberg, *Extraterritorial Legislative Jurisdiction and the State Criminal Law*, 38 TEX. L. REV. 763, 784–87 (1960) (due process requires that the behavior of the defendant must be predictably subject to State's criminal jurisdiction); *cf. Ex parte Boetscher*, 812 S.W.2d 600 (Tex. Crim. App. 1991) (Equal Protection Clause limits disparate treatment of nonresident defendants); *In re King*, 3 Cal.3d 226, 90 Cal. Rptr. 15, 474 P.2d 983 (1970), cert. denied 403 U.S. 931 (enhanced offense for nonresidents impacts constitutional right to travel).

§ 159.802. Conditions of Rendition

(a) Before making a demand that the governor of another state surrender an individual charged criminally in this state with having failed to provide for the support of an obligee, the governor may require a prosecutor of this state to demonstrate:

(1) that not less than 60 days before the date of the demand, the obligee had initiated proceedings for support under this chapter; or

(2) that initiating the proceeding would be of no avail.

(b) If, under this chapter or a law substantially similar to this chapter, the governor of another state makes a demand that the governor of this state surrender an individual charged criminally in that state with having failed to provide for the support of a child or other individual to whom a duty of support is owed, the governor may require a prosecutor to investigate the demand and report whether a proceeding for support has been initiated or would be effective. If it appears that a proceeding would be effective but has not been initiated, the governor may delay honoring the demand for a reasonable time to permit the initiation of a proceeding.

(c) If a proceeding for support has been initiated and the individual whose rendition is demanded prevails, the governor may decline to honor the demand. If the petitioner prevails and the individual whose rendition is demanded is subject to a support order, the governor may decline to honor the demand if the individual is complying with the support order.

Commissioners' Official Comment to UIFSA Section 802

This section has not undergone significant change since 1968. Interstate rendition remains the last resort for support enforcement, in part because a governor may exercise considerable discretion in deciding whether to honor a demand for rendition of an obligor.

SUBCHAPTER J. MISCELLANEOUS PROVISIONS

§ 159.901. Uniformity of Application and Construction

In applying and construing this chapter, consideration must be given to the need to promote uniformity of the law with respect to the subject matter of this chapter among states that enact a law similar to this chapter.

***Editors' Note**: In 2010 the U.S. Senate gave its advice and consent regarding the Hague Convention on the International Recovery of Child Support and Other Forms of Family Maintenance of November 23, 2007. This was the first step toward that treaty entering into force in the United States. Many further steps, however, will be necessary before the treaty will go into force between the United States and other participating countries. One requirement certain to be a prerequisite for this to happen will be the enactment of federal legislation directing states to enact a new version state law to accommodate the terms of the new treaty, to wit, UIFSA (2008). The new version of the uniform act is designed to conform the obligations of the United states under the treaty through the operation of state law. As before, the federal law will not be substantive in the literal sense, but will be tied to the continued receipt of the significant federal subsidy for child support enforcement.*

As of press time for this book, eight states have enacted UIFSA (2008)—primarily contingently; the new version has been introduced in another five states for consideration in 2011.

Thus, the following materials are information primarily for future reference, which become more relevant after Congress acts (perhaps that should say "when and if").

SYMPOSIUM ON INTERNATIONAL ENFORCEMENT OF CHILD SUPPORT

The new Hague Child Support Convention: goals and outcomes of the negotiations. William Duncan, 43 FAM. L.Q. 1 (2009)

United States perspective on the new Hague Convention on the International Recovery of Child Support and Other Forms of Family Maintenance. Mary Helen Carlson, 43 FAM. L.Q. 21 (2009)

Child support at home and abroad: road to the Hague. Marilyn Ray Smith, 43 FAM. L.Q. 37 (2009)

Integrating an international convention into state law: The UIFSA experience. Battle Rankin Robinson, 43 FAM. L.Q. 61 (2009)

Uniform Interstate Family Support Act (2008) with Prefatory Note and Comments (with Afterword by John J. Sampson), 43 FAM. L.Q. 75 (2009)

CHAPTER 160. UNIFORM PARENTAGE ACT

SUBCHAPTER A. APPLICATION AND CONSTRUCTION

SUBCHAPTER B. GENERAL PROVISIONS

SUBCHAPTER C. PARENT-CHILD RELATIONSHIP

SUBCHAPTER D. VOLUNTARY ACKNOWLEDGMENT OF PATERNITY

SUBCHAPTER E. REGISTRY OF PATERNITY

SUBCHAPTER F. GENETIC TESTING

SUBCHAPTER G. PROCEEDING TO ADJUDICATE PARENTAGE

SUBCHAPTER H. CHILD OF ASSISTED REPRODUCTION

SUBCHAPTER I. GESTATIONAL AGREEMENTS

Editors' Introductory Comment

Texas can rightly claim to have the most progressive parentage legislation of any state. Effective June 14, 2001, Texas adopted the *Uniform Parentage Act (2000)*, replacing former Chapter 160, *Determination of Parentage*. The *Uniform Parentage Act* was approved by the National Conference of Commissioners on Uniform State Laws in 2000 and recommended for approval by all states. Texas was the first state to adopt this uniform act, followed by enactments in Alabama, Delaware, New Mexico, North Dakota, Oklahoma, Utah, Washington, and Wyoming. In 2003 amendments were enacted to clarify provisions in Subchapters A-H and to add Subchapter I. In 2011 comprehensive amendments were made to ten separate sections relating to the substance and procedures for acknowledgment and denial of paternity and the rescission a or challenge of those actions.

Subchapter F, dealing with genetic testing, moved Texas from an "exclusionary" approach to a "rebuttably identified" approach in paternity proceedings. Testing did not change, but the test results now read differently and places Texas with the majority of other jurisdictions.

Subchapter G brought change to Texas law, mostly limiting times to challenge presumptions of paternity and clearly defining those individuals who are bound by earlier determinations of paternity. The Texas enactment increases the time from two years for challenge in the uniform act to four years. Existing Texas case law on challenging paternity in the marital context will be of limited significance under amended Chapter 160. On the other hand, the Act eliminates time limitations for children with no presumed father for bringing an action to determine parentage. Section 160.608 introduced paternity by estoppel to Texas statutory law for the first time. Suits for paternity cannot be dismissed with prejudice for want of prosecution.

Subchapter H, dealing with assisted reproduction, was similar to then-existing Texas law. However, default provisions for an assisted reproduction action after divorce or the death of a spouse are a first in Texas law.

Subchapter I dealing with gestational agreements was originally omitted in the enactment of the UPA. Its addition in 2003 completed Texas adoption of the uniform act, subject only to variations that are noted in the Comments, and further amendments periodically.

CLE/Leading Publications

Parentage and paternity fraud. Cynthia J. Barela Graham, 2011 Adv. Fam. L.

DNA/Genetics. Anthony Carter, 2011 U.T. Advanced Parent–Child Relationships

"Are you my daddy?" Paternity fraud and related issues. Holly D. Friedman, 2011 U.T. Fam. L. Front Lines

Parentage: suits and Uniform Parentage Act. Judy L. Warne, 2011 U.T. Parent–Child Relationships: Basics

Parentage testing and child support in CPS cases. Alicia G. Key, 2010 Adv. Fam. L.

Selected issues in parentage and termination. Ellen A. Yarrell, 2010 Adv. Fam. L.

Paternity and extra-marital children. K. Nicole Voyles, 2010 Adv. Fam. L. Drafting

Who's your daddy?: paternity fraud. (Panel), 2010 U.T. Fam. L. Front Lines

Same time, same place, same sex: interesting issues concerning same sex parenting. Joan S. Anderson & Ellen A. Yarrell, 2010 U.T. Parent-Child Relationships

Parentage? A question of truth or consequences. Ellen A. Yarrell, 2010 Marriage Dissolution

Uniform Parentage Act (2000) with Prefatory Note and Comments (and with Unofficial Annotations). John J. Sampson, 35 Fam. L.Q. 83 (2001)

See CLE/Other Legal Publications relating to assisted reproductive technology immediately before § 160.701, *infra*.

See Accompanying CD–ROM for Additional CLE/Other Legal Publications

Leading U.S. Supreme Court Cases

Michael H. v. Gerald D., 491 U.S. 110, 109 S.Ct. 2333, 105 L.Ed.2d 91 (1989) (U.S. Const. does not mandate right of man to establish his paternity of child born to married woman)

Reed v. Campbell, 476 U.S. 852, 90 L.Ed.2d 858, 106 S.Ct. 2234 (1986) (Texas Probate Code held unconstitutional discrimination against illegitimate child)

Lehr v. Robertson, 463 U.S. 248, 77 L.Ed.2d 614, 103 S.Ct. 2985 (1983) (state may restrict claim of biological father to procedure required for paternity registry)

Little v. Streater, 454 U.S. 1, 68 L.Ed.2d 627, 101 S.Ct. 2202 (1981) (indigent respondent has U.S. Const. right to parentage testing in paternity suit brought by state)

Caban v. Mohammed, 441 U.S. 380, 60 L.Ed.2d 297, 99 S.Ct. 1760 (1979) (biological father's actual relationship with child is crucial to determining his rights)

Gomez v. Perez, 409 U.S. 535, 35 L.Ed.2d 56, 93 S.Ct. 872 (1973) (unconstitutional to discriminate between legitimate and illegitimate children regarding father's duty to support)

Stanley v. Illinois, 405 U.S. 645, 31 L.Ed.2d 551, 92 S.Ct. 1208 (1972) (state statute may not presume away father's rights)

Leading Texas Supreme Court Cases

In re R.A.H., 130 S.W.3d 68 (Tex. 2004) (man claiming to be genetic father has four-year time period to file paternity contest after adjudication or acknowledgment)

In re Z.L.T., 124 S.W.3d 163 (Tex. 2003) (not error to implicitly deny bench warrant to transport prison inmate to paternity trial)

Texas Dept. of Protective & Regulatory Services v. Sherry, 46 S.W.3d 857 (Tex. 2001) (man lacks standing to obtain paternity determination for child who already has adjudicated father)

In re B.I.V., 923 S.W.2d 573 (Tex. 1996) (mother has standing to appeal child support order agreed upon by A.G. and father in connection with paternity suit)

In re J.W.T., 872 S.W.2d 189 (Tex. 1994) (if he acts expeditiously, biological father has Tex. Const. right to establish his paternity over objections of mother and her husband)

Dickson v. Simpson, 807 S.W.2d 726 (Tex. 1991) (nonmarital child must be guaranteed fair opportunity to establish heirship)

In re Baby McLean, 725 S.W.2d 696 (Tex. 1987) (Texas ERA protects rights of biological father in a case where there is no presumed father)

Holick v. Smith, 685 S.W.2d 18 (Tex. 1985), and *In re* G.M., 596 S.W.2d 846 (Tex. 1980) (parenthood is a fundamental, natural, basic civil right)

Davis v. Davis, 521 S.W.2d 603 (Tex.1975) (striking down Lord Mansfield's Rule created virtually non-rebuttable presumption that mother's husband is father of child born during marriage—child may have claim against genetic father)

See Accompanying CD–ROM for Cases Linked to Westlaw and Additional Leading Cases.

Cross Reference

TEX. PROBATE CODE ANN. § 42. Inheritance Rights of Children.

COMMISSIONERS' PREFATORY NOTE TO UPA

The promulgation of the Uniform Parentage Act in 2000, as amended in 2002, is now the official recommendation of the National Conference of Commissioners on Uniform State Laws on the subject of parentage. This Act relegates to history all of the earlier uniform acts dealing with parentage, to wit, the replaced Uniform Parentage Act, hereafter UPA (1973), and two withdrawn acts, the Uniform Putative and Unknown Fathers Act, hereafter UPUFA (1988), and the Uniform Status of Children of Assisted Conception Act, hereafter USCACA (1988). The amendments of 2002 are the end-result of objections lodged by the American Bar Association Section of Individual Rights and Responsibilities and the ABA Committee on the Unmet Legal Needs of Children, based on the view that in certain respects the 2000 version did not adequately treat a child of unmarried parents equally with a child of married parents. Because equal treatment of nonmarital children was a hallmark of the 1973 Act, the objections caused the drafters of the 2000 version to reconsider certain sections of the Act. Through extended discussion and a meeting of representatives of all the entities involved, a determination was made that the objections had merit. As a result of this process, the amendments shown in this Act were presented by mail ballot to the Commissioners and unanimously approved in November 2002.

In brief outline, UPA (2002) is structured as follows: Subchapter B, General Provisions, adds many definitions to clarify the participants in determinations of parentage and adapt the Act to recent scientific developments. Subchapter C, Parent–Child Relationship, will look familiar to past users of UPA (1973) because it continues a number of the 1973 provisions with little or no change, while eliminating the ambiguous term "natural" to describe a genetic parent. Subchapter D, Voluntary Acknowledgment of Paternity, is driven by federal mandates that states provide simplified nonjudicial means to establish paternity, especially for newborns and young children. Subchapter E, Registry of Paternity, incorporates a tightly integrated registry law to deal with the rights of a man who is neither an acknowledged, presumed or adjudicated father. A primary goal of this article is to facilitate adoption proceedings. Subchapter F, Genetic Testing, comprehensively covers that subject in ten separate sections (the 1973 Act had one section on the subject). Subchapter G, Proceeding to Adjudicate Parentage, sets forth the parties to, and the procedures for, adjudicating parentage and challenging acknowledgments, presumptions, and judgments. Subchapter H, Child of Assisted Reproduction, recodifies USCACA (1988), but applies its provisions to nonmarital as well as marital children born as a result of assisted reproductive technologies. Subchapter I, Gestational Agreements, is based upon USCACA (1988), but follows only the option that permits enforcement of a gestational agreement. Among the departures from the uniform act, the Texas version is restricted to married couples.

Finally, Uniform Parentage Act (2002) is consistent with the provisions of two other uniform acts of great significance, namely the Uniform Interstate Family Support Act [UIFSA (1996) and UIFSA (2001)] and the Uniform Child Custody Jurisdiction and Enforcement Act [UCCJEA (1997)].

Editors' Note: *The Texas enactment departs from the uniform version in a few sections; the Commissioners' Commentary has been edited to reflect those changes. The full act, with unedited Commissioners' Commentary, is found at National Conference of Commissioners on Uniform State Laws website: www.nccusl.org.*

SUBCHAPTER A. APPLICATION AND CONSTRUCTION

§ 160.001. Application and Construction

This chapter shall be applied and construed to promote the uniformity of the law among the states that enact the Uniform Parentage Act.

§ 160.002. Conflicts Between Provisions

If a provision of this chapter conflicts with another provision of this title or another state statute or rule and the conflict cannot be reconciled, this chapter prevails.

Editors' Comment

Subchapter A is not an official part of the Uniform Parentage Act but was added by the Legislature to make certain that this chapter prevailed over any inconsistency that may exist elsewhere in the Family Code. Similar provisions are found in Chapter 152, the *Uniform Child Custody Jurisdiction and Enforcement Act*, and Chapter 159, the *Uniform Interstate Family Support Act*.

SUBCHAPTER B. GENERAL PROVISIONS

§ 160.101. Short Title

This chapter may be cited as the Uniform Parentage Act.

§ 160.102. Definitions

In this chapter:

(1) "Adjudicated father" means a man who has been adjudicated by a court to be the father of a child.

(2) "Assisted reproduction" means a method of causing pregnancy other than sexual intercourse. The term includes:

(A) intrauterine insemination;

(B) donation of eggs;

(C) donation of embryos;

(D) in vitro fertilization and transfer of embryos; and

(E) intracytoplasmic sperm injection.

(3) "Child" means an individual of any age whose parentage may be determined under this chapter.

(4) "Commence" means to file the initial pleading seeking an adjudication of parentage in a court of this state.

(5) "Determination of parentage" means the establishment of the parent-child relationship by the signing of a valid acknowledgment of paternity under Subchapter D or by an adjudication by a court.

(6) "Donor" means an individual who provides eggs or sperm to a licensed physician to be used for assisted reproduction, regardless of whether the eggs or sperm are provided for consideration. The term does not include:

(A) a husband who provides sperm or a wife who provides eggs to be used for assisted reproduction by the wife;

(B) a woman who gives birth to a child by means of assisted reproduction; or

(C) an unmarried man who, with the intent to be the father of the resulting child, provides sperm to be used for assisted reproduction by an unmarried woman, as provided by Section 160.7031.

(7) "Ethnic or racial group" means, for purposes of genetic testing, a recognized group that an individual identifies as all or part of the individual's ancestry or that is identified by other information.

(8) "Genetic testing" means an analysis of an individual's genetic markers to exclude or identify a man as the father of a child or a woman as the mother of a child. The term includes an analysis of one or more of the following:

(A) deoxyribonucleic acid; and

(B) blood-group antigens, red-cell antigens, human-leukocyte antigens, serum enzymes, serum proteins, or red-cell enzymes.

(9) "Intended parents" means individuals who enter into an agreement providing that the individuals will be the parents of a child born to a gestational mother by means of assisted reproduction, regardless of whether either individual has a genetic relationship with the child.

(10) "Man" means a male individual of any age.

(11) "Parent" means an individual who has established a parent-child relationship under Section 160.201.

(12) "Paternity index" means the likelihood of paternity determined by calculating the ratio between:

(A) the likelihood that the tested man is the father of the child, based on the genetic markers of the tested man, the mother of the child, and the child, conditioned on the hypothesis that the tested man is the father of the child; and

(B) the likelihood that the tested man is not the father of the child, based on the genetic markers of the tested man, the mother of the child, and the child, conditioned on the hypothesis that the tested man is not the father of the child and that the father of the child is of the same ethnic or racial group as the tested man.

(13) "Presumed father" means a man who, by operation of law under Section 160.204, is recognized as the father of a child until that status is rebutted or confirmed in a judicial proceeding.

(14) "Probability of paternity" means the probability, with respect to the ethnic or racial group to which the alleged father belongs, that the alleged father is the father of the child, compared to a random, unrelated man of the same ethnic or racial group, expressed as a percentage incorporating the paternity index and a prior probability.

(15) "Record" means information that is inscribed on a tangible medium or that is stored in an electronic or other medium and is retrievable in a perceivable form.

(16) "Signatory" means an individual who authenticates a record and is bound by its terms.

(17) "Support enforcement agency" means a public official or public agency authorized to seek:

(A) the enforcement of child support orders or laws relating to the duty of support;

(B) the establishment or modification of child support;

(C) the determination of parentage;

(D) the location of child-support obligors and their income and assets; or

(E) the conservatorship of a child or the termination of parental rights.

Commissioners' Comment to UPA Section 102

Subsection (4) is derived from the UCCJEA (1997) § 102(5).

Subsection (7) defines the "ethnic or racial group" of the individual being tested only for purposes of the genetic testing. The genetic tests themselves do not determine the race or ethnic group of the individual; rather, for the individual who is not excluded, the race or ethnic group provided is used in the paternity calculations. This is done because the use of the race or ethnic group of the tested individual gives the most conservative calculations, that is, those most favoring non-paternity.

Subsection (8) contemplates that the genetic testing used in paternity testing is broad and includes all of the traditional genetic tests, such as blood types and HLA (Human Leukocyte Antigen), as well as newer DNA technologies. In the past the term "blood test" was commonly applied to paternity testing. However, this usage actually referred to the sample collected; in fact, the tests were genetic tests performed on blood samples. The Act uses the scientific term "deoxyribonucleic acid." This is to accommodate the changes in technology used to evaluate the DNA. Early DNA testing involved RFLP technology (Restriction Fragment Length Polymorphism), followed by PCR techniques (Polymerase Chain Reaction); these may be replaced by newer technology, such as SNP (Single Nucleotide Polymorphisms). The type of DNA technology to be employed is best left to scientific bodies, such as accreditation agencies, *see* Section 503(a).

Subsection (10) is derived from the Uniform Putative and Unknown Fathers Act (UPUFA). Defining "man" to include all male humans eliminates the connotation of adulthood, thereby satisfying the obvious need for the Act to cover under-age progenitors as well as adults. Although objection to calling a 14–year-old father a "man" was raised when UPUFA was considered by the Conference, for purposes of procreation such an individual is a man.

Subsection (12) defines a complex concept, the "paternity index." Note that the definition includes statistical measures of the mother and tested man. The tested man may be an alleged father, or any other potential biological father. In fact, under appropriate circumstances Article 5 provides for testing without samples from the mother or the alleged father. In these cases the expert statistically reconstructs the missing potential mother or biological father from genetic testing of samples from their relatives. Therefore the definition is correct even in cases involving a missing parent.

Subsection (15) is derived from the Uniform Electronic Transactions Act § 102(13), which establishes a standard for either paper or electronic record keeping. [TEX. BUS. & COM. CODE ANN. ch. 43]

Editors' Comment

UPA (2000) contains definitions for "acknowledged father," "alleged father," and "parent child relationship"; under its drafting guidelines, the Texas Legislative Council placed those definitions in Chapter 101.

Subsection (6), "donor," is not standard issue of the official UPA. In it, and in an earlier act on the subject, the commissioners determined not to make involvement of a licensed physician to be a specific requirement for ART States, of course, are free to decide otherwise—and the Texas Legislature has done so by defining "a donor" as a person who provides gametes "to a licensed physician to be used for assisted reproduction." There are only three exceptions to the definition of who is a donor, *i.e.*, the husband of the mother, the birth mother herself, and an unmarried man who provides sperm with the intent to be the father of a resulting child, with the agreement of the unmarried woman who will be the mother. The process of agreement is specifically detailed in § 160.7031. Note that activity outside of this definition, *e.g.*, so called informal providing sperm via the "turkey baster" method is not covered by the definition.

§ 160.103. Scope of Chapter; Choice of Law

(a) Except as provided by Chapter 233, this chapter governs every determination of parentage in this state.

(b) The court shall apply the law of this state to adjudicate the parent-child relationship. The applicable law does not depend on:

(1) the place of birth of the child; or

(2) the past or present residence of the child.

(c) This chapter does not create, enlarge, or diminish parental rights or duties under another law of this state.

Commissioners' Comment to UPA Section 103

UPA conforms to the requirement of 42 U.S.C. § 666(a)(5)(A), that a state must provide that parentage proceedings be available at any time before a child attains 18 years of age or suffer the potential penalty of forfeiture of the federal funds that subsidize child support enforcement by the state.

Subsection (b) is derived from the UIFSA (1996) § 303 and UPA (1973) § 8(b). This section simplifies choice of law principles; the local court is directed to apply local law. If in fact this state is an inappropriate forum, dismissal for forum non conveniens may be appropriate.

§ 160.104. Authorized Courts

The following courts are authorized to adjudicate parentage under this chapter:

(1) a court with jurisdiction to hear a suit affecting the parent-child relationship under this title; or

(2) a court with jurisdiction to adjudicate parentage under another law of this state.

Commissioners' Comment to UPA Section 104

Source: Uniform Parentage Act (1973) § 8(a).

Although a proceeding to determine parentage is most often associated with an action to establish a child support order, the Act departs from the choice made by the UIFSA (1996) § 102, [Texas Family Code § 159.102] which allows for the establishment of a child support order by an administrative agency. Insofar as establishment of parentage is concerned, UPA (2000) makes the deliberate decision to require a judicial proceeding. This decision is consistent with the practice of most States; in fact, very few States provide for the resolution of disputed paternity through administrative processes. The use of the term "tribunal, as found in UIFSA, was deliberately rejected. Joinder of a parentage proceeding with an action for divorce, annulment, separate maintenance, or child support and custody is left to state law.

§ 160.105. Protection of Participants

A proceeding under this chapter is subject to the other laws of this state governing the health, safety, privacy, and liberty of a child or any other individual who may be jeopardized by the disclosure of identifying information, including the person's address, telephone number, place of employment, and social security number and the name of the child's day-care facility and school.

Commissioners' Comment to UPA Section 105

Source: UCCJEA (1997) § 209(e). [Texas Family Code § 152.209 (e)]

§ 160.106. Determination of Maternity

The provisions of this chapter relating to the determination of paternity apply to a determination of maternity.

Commissioners' Comment to UPA Section 106

Source: UPA (1973) § 21.

This section provides for a determination of the mother-child relationship if that issue is in dispute. Except in circumstances involving immigration, cases involving disputed maternity are extraordinarily rare. Therefore UPA (2000) is otherwise written in terms applicable to the determination of paternity. While certain provisions found in the balance of the Act do not apply in a proceeding to establish maternity, the Act continues the decision made in UPA (1973) not to burden these already complex provisions with unnecessary references to the ascertainment of maternity. Section 160.201(a) is the sole provision in the act specifically relating to the mother-child relationship. In any given case, a judge facing a claim for the determination of the mother-child relationship should have little difficulty deciding which portions of the Act should be applied.

SUBCHAPTER C. PARENT-CHILD RELATIONSHIP

Editors' Comment

As part of a social and legal reform in this country during the 70's and 80's, Texas has had laws in place since 1989 forbidding any form of legal discrimination against a child born to unmarried parents.

See CLE/Other Legal Publications and Leading Cases following Editors' Introductory Comment beginning Chapter 160, *supra*

§ 160.201. Establishment of Parent-Child Relationship

(a) The mother-child relationship is established between a woman and a child by:

(1) the woman giving birth to the child;

(2) an adjudication of the woman's maternity; or

(3) the adoption of the child by the woman.

(b) The father-child relationship is established between a man and a child by:

(1) an unrebutted presumption of the man's paternity of the child under Section 160.204;

(2) an effective acknowledgment of paternity by the man under Subchapter D, unless the acknowledgment has been rescinded or successfully challenged;

(3) an adjudication of the man's paternity;

(4) the adoption of the child by the man; or

(5) the man's consenting to assisted reproduction by his wife under Subchapter H, which resulted in the birth of the child.

Commissioners' Comment to UPA Section 201

Source: UPA (1973), § 4; expanded to include all possible bases of the parent-child relationship.

§ 160.202. No Discrimination Based on Marital Status

A child born to parents who are not married to each other has the same rights under the law as a child born to parents who are married to each other.

Commissioners' Comment to UPA Section 202

Source: UPA (1973) § 2 and Massachusetts Gen. Laws ch. 209C, § 1.

From a legal and social policy perspective, this is one of the most significant substantive provisions of the Act, reaffirming the principle that regardless of the marital status of the parents, children and parents have equal rights with respect to each other. As discussed in the Prefatory Note, U.S. Supreme Court decisions and lower federal and state court decisions require equality of treatment for a child without a presumed father with regard to most areas of substantive law.

The broad statement according equal treatment to a nonmarital child regarding his or her parents is not to be construed as eliminating all possible distinctions in all aspects of the lives of the nonmarital child and parents. For example, Uniform Probate Code (1993) § 2–705(b), states that "in construing a dispositive provision of a transferor who is not a natural parent, an individual born to the natural parent is not considered a child of that parent unless the individual while a minor lived as a regular member of the household of that parent or of that parent's parent, brother, sister, spouse, or surviving spouse." In short, the UPC (1993) provides that an individual is presumed not to be included in a class gift from someone other than the child's parent unless that individual lived as a member of the parent's family during childhood. This presumed intent of the donor is rebuttable. Although this provision probably has a disproportionate effect on nonmarital children, the disparity is not based on the circumstances of birth, but rather on post-birth living conditions.

§ 160.203. Consequences of Establishment of Parentage

Unless parental rights are terminated, a parent-child relationship established under this chapter applies for all purposes, except as otherwise provided by another law of this state.

Commissioners' Comment to UPA Section 203

Source: USCACA (1988) § 10.

This section may seem to state the obvious, but both the statement and the qualifier are necessary because without this explanation a literal reading of §§ 160.201–160.203 could lead to erroneous statutory constructions. The basic purpose of the section is to make clear that a mother, as defined in § 160.201(a), is not a parent once her parental rights have been terminated. Similarly, a man whose paternity has been established by acknowledgment or by court adjudication may subsequently have his parental rights terminated.

The qualifier, "as otherwise provided by another law of this state," is necessary because other statutes may restrict rights of a parent. For example, UPC (1993) § 2–114(c) precludes a parent of a child (and the parent's family) from inheriting from the child by intestate succession "unless that natural parent has openly treated the child as his [or hers] and has not refused to support the child." Similarly, as discussed in the preceding Comment, UPC (1993) § 2–705(b) affects the right of the child to take under class gifts from persons who are not the parents of the child.

---

§ 160.204. Presumption of Paternity

(a) A man is presumed to be the father of a child if:

(1) he is married to the mother of the child and the child is born during the marriage;

(2) he is married to the mother of the child and the child is born before the 301st day after the date the marriage is terminated by death, annulment, declaration of invalidity, or divorce;

(3) he married the mother of the child before the birth of the child in apparent compliance with law, even if the attempted marriage is or could be declared invalid, and the child is born during the invalid marriage or before the 301st day after the date the marriage is terminated by death, annulment, declaration of invalidity, or divorce;

(4) he married the mother of the child after the birth of the child in apparent compliance with law, regardless of whether the marriage is or could be declared invalid, he voluntarily asserted his paternity of the child, and:

(A) the assertion is in a record filed with the bureau of vital statistics;

(B) he is voluntarily named as the child's father on the child's birth certificate; or

(C) he promised in a record to support the child as his own; or

(5) during the first two years of the child's life, he continuously resided in the household in which the child resided and he represented to others that the child was his own.

(b) A presumption of paternity established under this section may be rebutted only by:

(1) an adjudication under Subchapter G; or

(2) the filing of a valid denial of paternity by a presumed father in conjunction with the filing by another person of a valid acknowledgment of paternity as provided by Section 160.305.

Commissioners' Comment to UPA Section 204

Source: UPA (1973) § 4.

A network of presumptions was established by UPA (1973) for application to cases in which proof of external circumstances indicate a particular man to be the probable father. The simplest of these is also the best known—birth of a child during the marriage between the mother and a man. When promulgated in 1973, the contemporaneous commentary noted that:

> While perhaps no one state now includes all these presumptions in its law, the presumptions *are* based on existing presumptions of "legitimacy" in state laws and do not represent a serious departure. Novel is that they have been collected under one roof. All presumptions of paternity are rebuttable in appropriate circumstances. UNIFORM PARENTAGE ACT (1973), Prefatory Note, 9B U.L.A. 379 (2001).

After amendments adopted in 2002, the Uniform Parentage Act retains all but one of the original presumptions of paternity contained in UPA § 4 (1973). Originally the 2000 version of the Act limited presumptions of paternity to those related to marriage. The objection by the ABA Steering Committee on the Unmet Legal Needs of Children and the Section of Individual Rights and Responsibilities that this could result in differential treatment of children born to unmarried parents resulted in the revision to this section.

Subsection (1) deals with a child born during a marriage; Subsection (2) deals with a child conceived during marriage but born after its termination; Subsection (3) deals with a child conceived or born during an invalid marriage; and, Subsection (4) deals with a child born before a valid or invalid marriage, accompanied by other facts indicating the husband is the father.

Added by amendment in 2002, Subsection (5), is a significant revision of UPA § 4(4) (1973), which created a presumption of paternity if a man "receives the child into his home and openly holds out the child as his natural child ...." Because there was no time frame specified in the 1973 act, the language fostered uncertainty about whether the presumption could arise if the receipt of the child into the man's home occurred for a short time or took place long after the child's birth. To more fully serve the goal of treating nonmarital and marital children equally, the "holding out" presumption is restored, subject to an express durational requirement that the man reside with the child for the first two years of the child's life. This mirrors the presumption applied to a married man established by § 607. Once this presumption arises, it is subject to attack only under the limited circumstances set forth in § 607 for challenging a marital presumption, and is similarly subject to the estoppel principles of § 608.

One presumption found in UPA (1973) is not repeated in the Act. Former UPA § 4(5) created a presumption of paternity if the man "acknowledges his paternity of the child in a writing filed with [named agency] [and] ... the mother ... does not dispute the acknowledgment within a reasonable time ...." This presumption was eliminated because it conflicts with Article 3, Voluntary Acknowledgment of Paternity, under which a valid acknowledgment establishes paternity rather than a presumption of paternity.

Finally, Subsection (b) is a complete rewrite of UPA (1973) § 4(b). The requirement that a presumption "may be rebutted ... only by clear and convincing evidence" was eliminated from the Act. The same fate was accorded the statement that: "If two or more presumptions arise which conflict with each other, the presumption which on the facts is founded on the weightier considerations of policy and logic controls." Nowadays the existence of modern genetic testing obviates this old approach to the problem of conflicting presumptions when a court is to determine paternity. Nowadays, genetic testing makes it possible in most cases to resolve competing claims to paternity. Moreover, courts may use the estoppel principles in § 608 in appropriate circumstances to deny requests for genetic testing in the interests of preserving a child's ties to the presumed or acknowledged father who openly held himself out as the child's father regardless of whether he is in fact the genetic father.

Editors' Comment

Subsection (b) provides that a presumption of paternity may be rebutted by either an adjudication of another man's paternity or by the execution of a valid acknowledgment of paternity. This is a slight variation from the uniform act that provides that only an adjudication can rebut a presumption of paternity. However, an acknowledgment of paternity is deemed to be the legal equivalent of an adjudication. See Section 160.305.

See CLE/Other Legal Publications following Editors' Introductory Comment beginning Chapter 160, *supra*

Leading Cases

In re J.W.T., 872 S.W.2d 189 (Tex. 1994) (if he acts expeditiously, biological father has Tex. Const. right to establish his paternity over objections of mother and her husband)

In re B.I.V., 870 S.W.2d 12 (Tex. 1994) (failure to join presumed father in paternity proceeding should be challenged by plea in abatement, not by dismissal)

In re S.C.V., 750 S.W.2d 762 (Tex. 1988) (mother rebutted presumption of husband's paternity by blood test exclusion)

Davis v. Davis, 521 S.W.2d 603 (Tex. 1975) (Lord Mansfield's Rule struck down; spouses may testify about nonaccess)

In re Sullivan, 157 S.W.3d 911 (Tex. App.—Houston [14th Dist.] 2005, orig. proceeding) (man furnishing sperm for artificial insemination with intent to be child's father has standing to adjudicate parentage)

Cross Reference

Tex. Prob. Code Ann. § 42. Inheritance Rights of Children.

SUBCHAPTER D. VOLUNTARY ACKNOWLEDGMENT OF PATERNITY

Commissioners' Prefatory Note to Subchapter D

Voluntary acknowledgment of paternity has long been an alternative to a contested paternity suit. Under UPA (1973) § 4, the inclusion of a man's name on the child's birth certificate created a presumption of paternity, which could be rebutted. A relatively recent enactment of the U.S. Congress has made necessary a fundamental change in the acknowledgment procedure. In the Personal Responsibility and Work Opportunity Reconciliation Act of 1996 (PRWORA, also known as the Welfare Reform Act) Congress conditioned federal child support enforcement funds on a requirement that a state enact laws that greatly strengthen the effect of a man's voluntary acknowledgment of paternity, 42 U.S.C. § 666(a)(5)(C). In brief, a valid, unrescinded, unchallenged acknowledgment of paternity is to be considered equivalent to a judicial determination of paternity.

A comprehensive approach to comply with the congressional mandate is required because the federal act is nonspecific in many respects. Primary among the issues that Congress did not take into account was the fact that a mother who, in cooperation with the actual father of a child, seeks to have that man acknowledge paternity of the child may, in fact, be married to another man. By virtue of parentage laws that are in universal effect, including UPA (2000), the husband of the mother is the presumed father of the child, *see* § 204, *supra*. By ignoring the real possibility that there will be both an acknowledged father and a presumed father, Congress left it to the states to sort out the difficulties inherent in such a fact situation.

Further, PRWORA does not mention that a person acknowledging parentage asserts genetic parentage of the child. Section 301 is designed to prevent circumvention of adoption laws by demanding a sworn assertion of actual parentage of the child through sexual intercourse in support of an acknowledgment under this article.

Sections 302–305 clarify that if a child who is the subject of an acknowledgment also has a presumed father, that man must cooperate by filing a denial of paternity in conjunction with the acknowledgment; if not, the document is void. If the presumed father is unwilling to cooperate, or his whereabouts are unknown, a court proceeding is necessary to resolve the issue of parentage.

Congress also directed that the acknowledgment can be "rescinded" within a particular timeframe, and subsequently can be "challenged"–without stating a timeframe. These procedures are dealt with in Sections 307–309.

Editors' Comment to Subchapter D of UPA

As the Commissioner's Comments indicate, the provisions for voluntary acknowledgment of paternity (known as an AOP in Texas and as a VAP in many other states) were created by Congress without much experience with, or knowledge about, the facts of life on the street regarding determinations of paternity. It was left to the drafters of the uniform act to fashion workable rules for an AOP by a man willing to admit or to claim paternity. For the first time in the ten years since its adoption in 2001, the AOP procedure received a serious second look, resulting in a substantial makeover.

The significant revision in the substance and procedure for making a collateral attack on the signing of an AOP maintains the basic structure intact. Two distinct avenues to dispute an AOP continue to be available, i.e., rescission and challenge. The former is simplicity itself; if timely made, rescission requires no test other than "I take it back." Challenge of an AOP, on the other hand, must be based on a showing of fraud, duress, or mistake of fact.

---

§ 160.301. Acknowledgment of Paternity

The mother of a child and a man claiming to be the biological father of the child may sign an acknowledgment of paternity with the intent to establish the man's paternity.

Commissioners' Comment to UPA Section 301

Source: 42 U.S.C. § 666(a)(5)(C)

PRWORA does not explicitly require that a man acknowledging parentage necessarily is asserting his genetic parentage of the child. In order to prevent circumvention of adoption laws, § 301 corrects this omission by requiring a sworn assertion of genetic parentage of the child. A 2002 amendment provides that a man who signs an acknowledgment of paternity declares that he is the genetic father of the child. Thus both the man and the mother acknowledge his paternity, under penalty of perjury, without requiring the parents to spell out the details of their sexual relations. Further, the amended language also takes into account a situation in which a man, who is unable to have sexual intercourse with his partner, may still have contributed to the conception of the child through the use of his own sperm. Henceforth, a man in that situation will be able to recognize legally his paternity through the voluntary acknowledgment procedure.

---

§ 160.302. Execution of Acknowledgment of Paternity

(a) An acknowledgment of paternity must:

(1) be in a record;

(2) be signed, or otherwise authenticated, under penalty of perjury by the mother and the man seeking to establish paternity;

(3) state that the child whose paternity is being acknowledged:

(A) does not have a presumed father or has a presumed father whose full name is stated; and

(B) does not have another acknowledged or adjudicated father;

(4) state whether there has been genetic testing and, if so, that the acknowledging man's claim of paternity is consistent with the results of the testing; and

(5) state that the signatories understand that the acknowledgment is the equivalent of a judicial adjudication of the paternity of the child and that a challenge to the acknowledgment is permitted only under limited circumstances ~~and is barred after four years~~.

(b) An acknowledgment of paternity is void if it:

(1) states that another man is a presumed father of the child, unless a denial of paternity signed or otherwise authenticated by the presumed father is filed with the bureau of vital statistics;

(2) states that another man is an acknowledged or adjudicated father of the child; or

(3) falsely denies the existence of a presumed, acknowledged, or adjudicated father of the child.

(c) A presumed father may sign or otherwise authenticate an acknowledgment of paternity.

Amended by Acts 2011, 82nd Leg., ch. 1221 (S.B. 502), § 1, eff. Sept. 1, 2011.

Commissioners' Comment to UPA Section 302

Source: 42 U.S.C. § 666(a)(5)(C).

The federal statute cited above declares that receipt by a state of the federal subsidy for its child support enforcement program is dependent on state law providing specific procedures for voluntary acknowledgment of paternity. The principle was simple to mandate; but the application is quite complicated.

Problems most notably include fact situations in which the mother of the child is married to someone other than the man who intends to acknowledge his paternity. With an acknowledgment the child would then have both an acknowledged father and a presumed father. To deal with this circumstance, many states have passed laws allowing the presumed father to sign a denial of paternity, which must be filed as part of the acknowledgment. This Act adopts this common sense solution; otherwise the acknowledgment would have no legal consequence because it cannot affect the legal rights of the presumed father.

At least two other provisions of this section warrant special emphasis. Subsection (a)(2) requires that the acknowledgment be "signed, or otherwise authenticated, under penalty of perjury," just as income tax returns and many other government documents require. Clearly, the potential punishment for false swearing is substantial, and the benefits from avoiding the complication of requiring witnesses and a notary are significant in this context. Mandating greater formality would greatly discourage the in-hospital signatures so earnestly desired in 42 U.S.C. § 666(a)(5)(C)(ii).

Similarly, in an attempt to assure full disclosure and avoid false swearing, Subsection (a)(4) requires information regarding whether there has been genetic testing, and if so, confirmation of the fact that the acknowledgment is consistent with the results of that testing. This provision is designed to avoid a possible subversion of the requirements for an adoption. A would-be "father" whose parentage of a child has been excluded by genetic testing may not validly sign an acknowledgment after that fact has been established.

Editors' Comments to § 160.302

Consistent with the four year limitation on challenging the presumption of paternity under §160.607, and similar limitation in §160.702 to a husband's claim of lack of consent to assisted reproduction, the time frame for a challenge to an acknowledgment of paternity was originally established for that same time period. The four year period was a departure from the two-year limit provided under the NCCUSL/ULC version of the act.

Effective Sept. 1, 2011 the 82nd Legislature removed this four-year limit and replaced it with the provision under § 160.308 that a challenge to an acknowledgment may be made "at any time before the issuance of an order affecting the child identified in the acknowledgment."

The new time frame for making a challenge "under limited circumstances" demanded by PRWORA must be reconsidered in a more complex, and arguably more sophisticated, manner. This could mean that, after the expiration of the period for rescission allowed under § 160.307, the time available for a challenge could be shorter than four years—or, again, it could be longer. All would depend on when or whether any order affecting the child—not just a support order—was issued by a tribunal. Nonetheless, the elimination of the time limit would—absent a court order affecting the child—allow a challenge on the basis of fraud, duress, or material mistake of fact were pertinent evidence (including genetic evidence) to surface after the expiration of four years. Of course, it would still fall to the court to decide in the adjudication of paternity whether facts in the case warranted the ordering of genetic testing. The court could deny testing and find the acknowledged father to be the father of child—and order support for the child, including retroactive support. (See *infra* § 160.608.) (*A.G.K., H.P.S., & J.J.S.*)

---

§ 160.303. Denial of Paternity

A presumed father of a child may sign a denial of his paternity. The denial is valid only if:

(1) an acknowledgment of paternity signed or otherwise authenticated by another man is filed under Section 160.305;

(2) the denial is in a record and is signed or otherwise authenticated under penalty of perjury; and

(3) the presumed father has not previously:

(A) acknowledged paternity of the child, unless the previous acknowledgment has been rescinded under Section 160.307 or successfully challenged under Section 160.308; or

(B) been adjudicated to be the father of the child.

§ 160.304. Rules for Acknowledgment and Denial of Paternity

(a) An acknowledgment of paternity and a denial of paternity may be contained in a single document or in different documents and may be filed separately or simultaneously. If the acknowledgment and denial are both necessary, neither document is valid until both documents are filed.

(b) An acknowledgment of paternity or a denial of paternity may be signed before the birth of the child.

(c) Subject to Subsection (a), an acknowledgment of paternity or denial of paternity takes effect on the date of the birth of the child or the filing of the document with the bureau of vital statistics, whichever occurs later.

(d) An acknowledgment of paternity or denial of paternity signed by a minor is valid if it otherwise complies with this chapter.

Commissioners' Comment to UPA Section 304

Source: 42 U.S.C. § 666(a)(5)(C)(i), requiring a "simple civil process" for voluntary acknowledgment of paternity.

---

§ 160.305. Effect of Acknowledgment or Denial of Paternity

(a) Except as provided by Sections 160.307 and 160.308, a valid acknowledgment of paternity filed with the bureau of vital statistics is the equivalent of an adjudication of the paternity of a child and confers on the acknowledged father all rights and duties of a parent.

(b) Except as provided by Sections 160.307 and 160.308, a valid denial of paternity filed with the bureau of vital statistics in conjunction with a valid acknowledgment of paternity is the equivalent of an adjudication of the nonpaternity of the presumed father and discharges the presumed father from all rights and duties of a parent.

Commissioners' Comment to UPA Section 305

Source: 42 U.S.C. § 666(a)(5)(D)(ii), requiring that an acknowledgment of paternity be "a legal finding of paternity," and 42 U.S.C. § 666(a)(5)(M), directing that acknowledgments be "filed with the State registry of birth records . . . "

---

§ 160.306. Filing Fee Not Required

The bureau of vital statistics may not charge a fee for filing:

(1) an acknowledgment of paternity;

(2) a ~~or~~ denial of paternity; **or**

(3) a rescission of an acknowledgment of paternity or denial of paternity.

Amended by Acts 2011, 82nd Leg., ch. 1221 (S.B. 502), § 2, eff. Sept. 1, 2011.

Editors' Comments to § 160.306

Having changed the process under § 160.307 for rescission of an acknowledgment or denial of paternity from a judicial procedure to an administrative one involving the bureau of vital statistics, the 2011 amendments to this section prohibit the bureau from charging a fee for the filing of a rescission form. A "no fee" mandate is clearly reasonable given the complete revision of the procedure established by the next section.

A conforming amendment was made to § 160.312 to require the bureau to provide the necessary forms for the rescission of an acknowledgment or denial of paternity in addition to the forms for an acknowledgment or denial of paternity. *(A.G.K. & H.P.S.)*

---

§ 160.307. Procedures ~~Proceeding~~ for Rescission

(a) A signatory may rescind an acknowledgment of paternity or denial of paternity **as provided by this section** ~~by commencing a proceeding to rescind~~ before the earlier of:

(1) the 60th day after the effective date of the acknowledgment or denial, as provided by Section 160.304; or

(2) the date ~~of the first hearing in~~ a proceeding to which the signatory is a party **is initiated** before a court to adjudicate an issue relating to the child, including a proceeding that establishes child support.

(b) A signatory seeking to rescind an acknowledgment of paternity or denial of paternity must file with the bureau of vital statistics a completed rescission, on the form prescribed under Section 160.312, in which the signatory declares under penalty of perjury that:

(1) as of the date the rescission is filed, a proceeding has not been held affecting the child identified in the acknowledgment of paternity or denial of paternity, including a proceeding to establish child support;

(2) a copy of the completed rescission was sent by certified or registered mail, return receipt requested, to:

(A) if the rescission is of an acknowledgment of paternity, the other signatory of the acknowledgment of paternity and the signatory of any related denial of paternity; or

(B) if the rescission is of a denial of paternity, the signatories of the related acknowledgment of paternity; and

(3) if a signatory to the acknowledgment of paternity or denial of paternity is receiving services from the Title IV–D agency, a copy of the completed rescission was sent by certified or registered mail to the Title IV–D agency.

(c) On receipt of a completed rescission, the bureau of vital statistics shall void the acknowledgment of paternity or denial of paternity affected by the rescission and amend the birth record of the child, if appropriate.

(d) Any party affected by the rescission, including the Title IV–D agency, may contest the rescission by bringing a proceeding under Subchapter G to adjudicate the parentage of the child.

Amended by Acts 2011, 82nd Leg., ch. 1221 (S.B. 502), § 3, eff. Sept. 1, 2011.

Commissioners' Comment to UPA Section 307

This section reflects a decision to require a judicial adjudicatory process to rescind a voluntary acknowledgment of paternity. A federal statute, 42 U.S.C. § 666(a)(5)(c)(D)(ii), mandates that in order to retain the federal child support subsidy, state law must provide signatories with a right of rescission of an acknowledgment of paternity. However, the federal statute does not prescribe the method for the rescission.

Editors' Comment to UPA § 160.307

Originally the burden placed on the signatory who confirmed his paternity was of a very unusual sort. First, no proof was required to rescind a sworn acknowledgment, and the only consequence of the rescission was that the issue of paternity was restored to a neutral status pending future action. But, this required the signatory to "commence a proceeding," which was not explained. Further, where, what, and how the proceeding was to take place was for the signatory to discern on his own (absent a SAPCR to establish child support, of course). The new version of this section certainly clears up all the mystery previously inherent in the rescission procedure by specifying the details required of the Bureau of Vital Statistics and the signatory regarding time frame, notice, and voidance of the acknowledgment.

Effective Sept. 1, 2011, the judicial adjudicatory procedure prescribed by the UPA under this section for rescission of an acknowledgment or denial of paternity is a fairly simple administrative procedure. The reasoning behind this major change in law was that the acknowledgment of paternity is usually signed in the hospital, in the "glow" of the child's birth and often in the presence of members of the mother's family. Despite prescribed instructions being provided, the man—who will likely have a number of hospital forms to sign—may not immediately or fully understand the significance of the acknowledgment handed him along with other materials. Moreover, the costs of an attorney's services and the prospect of going to court may be daunting to men who have second thoughts about having signed an acknowledgment. Inasmuch as the execution of the acknowledgment is a simple act, so, reasoned the legislature, should the rescission be—especially given the time constraints for commencing a proceeding for rescission. It should be noted, however, that any party affected by the rescission may contest it at any time by filing a suit for adjudication of parentage. Also, the simplified rescission process provided by the 2011 legislature is not just for the man who may want to back out of the acknowledgment; it is also available to the mother who may have her doubts or second thoughts about the paternity of her child and want to void the acknowledgment. *(A.G.K., H.P.S., & J.J.S.)*

---

§ 160.308. Challenge After Expiration of Period for Rescission

(a) After the period for rescission under Section 160.307 has expired, a signatory of an acknowledgment of paternity or denial of paternity may commence a proceeding to challenge the acknowledgment or denial only on the basis of fraud, duress, or material mistake of fact. The proceeding **may** ~~must~~ be commenced **at any time** before the **issuance of an order affecting the child identified in** ~~fourth anniversary of the date~~ the acknowledgment or denial**, including an order relating to support of the child**~~is filed with the bureau of vital statistics unless the signatory was a minor on the date the signatory executed the acknowledgment or denial. If the signatory was a minor on the date the signatory executed the acknowledgment or denial, the proceeding must be commenced before the earlier of the fourth anniversary of the date of: (1) the signatory's 18th birthday; or (2) the removal of the signatory's disabilities of minority by court order, marriage, or by other operation of law~~.

(b) A party challenging an acknowledgment of paternity or denial of paternity has the burden of proof.

(c) Notwithstanding any other provision of this chapter, a collateral attack on an acknowledgment of paternity signed under this chapter may not be maintained after the **issuance of an order affecting the child identified in the acknowledgment, including an order relating to support of the child**~~fourth anniversary of the date the acknowledgment of paternity is filed with the bureau of vital statistics unless the signatory was a minor on the date the signatory executed the acknowledgment. If the signatory was a minor on the date the signatory executed the acknowledgment, a collateral attack on the acknowledgment of paternity may not be maintained after the earlier of the fourth anniversary of the date of: (1) the signatory's 18th birthday; or (2) the removal of the signatory's disabilities of minority by court order, marriage, or by other operation of law~~.

(d) For purposes of Subsection (a), evidence that, based on genetic testing, the man who is the signatory of an acknowledgement of paternity is not rebuttably identified as the father of a child in accordance with Section 160.505 constitutes a material mistake of fact.

Amended by Acts 2011, 82nd Leg., ch. 1221 (S.B. 502), § 4, eff. Sept. 1, 2011.

Commissioners' Comment to UPA Section 308

Congress also added a provision for a "challenge" of an acknowledgment of paternity after the period for rescission of a voluntary acknowledgment of paternity has elapsed. Such a collateral attack is to be limited to a challenge based on alleged "fraud, duress, or material mistake of fact," and according to 42 U.S.C. § 666(a)(5)(c)(D)(iii), must be made "in court." Subsection (d) was added to the Texas version to make clear that genetic exclusion is a material mistake of fact.

Editors' Comments to § 160.308

In 2005, the Legislature departed from the Uniform Parentage Act in providing a tolling of the period for rescission for minors who sign voluntary acknowledgments of paternity. This change in thinking reflects concern that minors do not have the maturity to understand the complete consequences of signing such a legally binding document. Thus, a minor signing an acknowledgment of paternity has until the fourth anniversary following the age of maturity to challenge the acknowledgment. Once challenged, the challenging party must submit to genetic testing. In reality, very few challenges are ever filed.

As noted in the editors' comment to § 160.302, henceforth a proceeding for a challenge of an acknowledgment or denial of paternity may be commenced at any time before, and a collateral attack on an AOP is prohibited from being maintained after the issuance of an order affecting the child identified in the acknowledgment or denial of paternity. This includes an order relating to support of the child. This reverses the prior requirement for the proceeding to commence before, and prohibited a collateral attack from being maintained after the fourth anniversary of the date the acknowledgment or denial. There is no specific time limit by which a proceeding to challenge an AOP or denial is to be commenced. The 2011 Legislature also removed the special provisions added by the 2005 Legislature relating to a signatory who was a minor at the time an acknowledgment or denial was executed.

These changes are primarily intended to address the vexing matter of "paternity fraud, a.k.a. mistaken paternity" where an acknowledged father may discover well beyond the fourth anniversary of his signing the acknowledgment that he was mistakenly led to believe—presumably by the mother who knew the truth of the matter—that he might not be, or certainly is not the child's biological father. *See* § 161.005, *infra*.The challenge puts the signatories into court for an adjudication of parentage. A successful challenge should result in an amendment of the child's birth record (*infra* § 160.309(e)). Principles of estoppel under section 160.608, however, may work to defeat a challenge to an acknowledgment and result in the court's finding the acknowledged father to be the father of the child with all the rights and duties of parentage, including the duty to support the child, of course. *(A.G.K., H.P.S., & J.J.S.)*

§ 160.309. Procedure for ~~Rescission Or~~ Challenge

(a) Each signatory to an acknowledgment of paternity and any related denial of paternity must be made a party to a proceeding to ~~rescind or~~ challenge the acknowledgment or denial of paternity.

(b) For purposes of ~~the rescission of or~~ a challenge to an acknowledgment of paternity or denial of paternity, a signatory submits to the personal jurisdiction of this state by signing the acknowledgment or denial. The jurisdiction is effective on the filing of the document with the bureau of vital statistics.

(c) Except for good cause shown, while a proceeding is pending to ~~rescind or~~ challenge an acknowledgment of paternity or a denial of paternity, the court may not suspend the legal responsibilities of a signatory arising from the acknowledgment, including the duty to pay child support.

(d) A proceeding to ~~rescind or to~~ challenge an acknowledgment of paternity or a denial of paternity shall be conducted in the same manner as a proceeding to adjudicate parentage under Subchapter G.

(e) At the conclusion of a proceeding to ~~rescind or~~ challenge an acknowledgment of paternity or a denial of paternity, the court shall order the bureau of vital statistics to amend the birth record of the child, if appropriate.

Amended by Acts 2011, 82nd Leg., ch. 1221 (S.B. 502), § 5, eff. Sept. 1, 2011.

Commissioners' Comment to UPA Section 309

Although the federal statute does not prescribe the method for "rescission" of an acknowledgment of paternity, it does require a proceeding in court for a subsequent "challenge." Overturning an acknowledgment of paternity is an act of significant legal consequence under either of the prescribed methods allowed. Thus, either method to dispute a prior acknowledgment should require a formal procedure because it may void an otherwise valid legal determination of the child's parentage. A procedure that allows a signatory of an acknowledgment of paternity merely to file a rescission with the state bureau of vital statistics would be an unwise policy choice. Many jurisdictions have come to the same conclusion.

Editors' Comment to § 160.309

The amendments made to this section provide a procedure only for a challenge to an acknowledgment or a denial of paternity, but not one for a rescission. Taking a position opposite to that of the Commissioners (as stated above), the Texas Legislature determined that the procedure for rescinding an acknowledgment or denial of paternity ought to be an administrative matter, rather than a judicial one. *See* § 160.307, *supra*. (*A.G.K. & H.P.S.*)

§ 160.310. Ratification Barred

A court or administrative agency conducting a judicial or administrative proceeding may not ratify an unchallenged acknowledgment of paternity.

Commissioners' Comment to UPA Section 310

Source: 42 U.S.C. § 666(a)(5)(E).

§ 160.311. Full Faith and Credit

A court of this state shall give full faith and credit to an acknowledgment of paternity or a denial of paternity that is effective in another state if the acknowledgment or denial has been signed and is otherwise in compliance with the law of the other state.

Commissioners' Comment to UPA Section 311

Source: 42 U.S.C. § 666(a)(5)(C)(iv).

PRWORA requires states "to give full faith and credit to such an affidavit [of acknowledgment of paternity] signed in any other state according to its procedures." *Id.* And, Subsection (a)(5)(D)(ii) provides that a "signed voluntary acknowledgment is considered a legal finding of paternity." In sum, federal law requires that an acknowledgment of paternity has the same status as a "judgment," 28 U.S.C. § 1738, a "child custody determination," 28 U.S.C. § 1738A, and a "child support order," 28 U.S.C. § 1738B. This section implements these mandates.

§ 160.312. Forms ~~for Acknowledgment and Denial of Paternity~~

(a) To facilitate compliance with this subchapter, the bureau of vital statistics shall prescribe forms for the**:**

(1) acknowledgment of paternity**;**

(2) ~~and the~~ denial of paternity**; and**

(3) rescission of an acknowledgment or denial of paternity.

(b) A valid acknowledgment of paternity**,** ~~or~~ denial of paternity**, or rescission of an acknowledgment or denial of paternity** is not affected by a later modification of the prescribed form.

Amended by Acts 2011, 82nd Leg., ch. 1221 (S.B. 502), § 6, eff. Sept. 1, 2011.

Commissioners' Comment to UPA Section 312

Source: 42 U.S.C. § 666(a)(5)C)(i),(iv).

The federal Office of Child Support Enforcement has issued an Action Transmittal to all IV–D agencies specifying how to ensure that the forms comply with PRWORA, OCSE–AT–98–02, Required Data Elements for Paternity Acknowledgment Affidavits; *see: http://www.acf.dhhs.gov/programs/cse/1998–at.htm*

Editors' Comment

The federal requirements with respect to forms under this section apply only to the form for the acknowledgment of paternity. The forms for a rescission of an acknowledgment or denial of paternity are determined by the vital statistics unit. *(A.G.K. & H.P.S.)*

§ 160.313. Release of Information

The bureau of vital statistics may release information relating to the acknowledgment of paternity or denial of paternity to a signatory of the acknowledgment or denial and to the courts and Title IV-D agency of this or another state.

§ 160.314. Adoption of Rules

The Title IV-D agency and the bureau of vital statistics may adopt rules to implement this subchapter.

Commissioners' Comment to UPA Section 314

States will implement voluntary acknowledgment of paternity procedures in a variety of ways, depending on local practice. This grant of rulemaking authority to carry out the provisions of this article may include electronic transmission of birth and acknowledgment data to the designated state agency.

§ 160.315. Memorandum of Understanding

(a) The Title IV-D agency and the bureau of vital statistics shall adopt a memorandum of understanding governing the collection and transfer of information for the voluntary acknowledgment of paternity.

(b) The Title IV-D agency and the bureau of vital statistics shall review the memorandum semiannually and renew or modify the memorandum as necessary.

SUBCHAPTER E. REGISTRY OF PATERNITY

Commissioners' Prefatory Note to Subchapter E

In *Stanley v. Illinois*, 405 U.S. 645 (1972), the United States Supreme Court held that an unwed father was entitled to a hearing on his fitness as a parent before his children could be taken from him in a dependency proceeding instituted by the state upon the death of the children's mother. That case on its face presented a fairly stable, unwed family situation, although the court did not cite the latter factor as a basis for its decision. The following year, the Conference promulgated the UPA (1973), §§ 24–25 of which dealt with notice of adoption proceedings and proceedings to terminate parental rights in a way that satisfies the *Stanley* requirements.

In *Lehr v. Robertson*, 463 U.S. 248 (1983), the Supreme Court upheld the constitutionality of a New York "putative father registry." The New York statute requires fathers of children born out-of-wedlock to register if they wish to be notified of a termination of parental rights or adoption proceeding. Following a series of well-publicized adoption cases wherein nonmarital fathers had not been given proper notice, legislatures began responding by enacting paternity registries similar to the New York statute. As of May, 2000, at least 28 states had enacted legislation creating paternity registries.

In the view of many commentators, the *Lehr* opinion undercut the rationale of *Stanley* by requiring affirmative action by an alleged father before he would be entitled to notice of a proceeding to terminate his parental rights. The act excepts from registration a man who timely initiates a proceeding for paternity, notwithstanding his failure to register.

Editors' Note: *The Texas enactment of UPA (2000) departs from the official text relating to the registry of paternity in two important ways. First the Texas registry is not limited to children under one year of age and applies to children of all ages whom might be the subject of a termination proceeding or placed for adoption. Secondly, the registry does not waive service on the alleged father if his whereabouts is known. See § 160.404.*

The Texas Paternity Registry came into being almost four years before the Uniform Parentage Act was effective on June 14, 2001. The effective date for the prior paternity registry was August 1, 1997. Because a man could not register as the possible father of a child born before that date, it seems certain that CPS cannot rely on a failure to register to terminate the rights of an alleged father of such a child.

Editors' Comment

Dealing effectively with the rights of alleged fathers in family law matters has long presented a challenge for attorneys and the courts. Attempting to balance the interests of a biological father to establish a legal relationship with his child while, at the same time, facilitating the adoption of children born outside of marriage to a father who does not take action to establish such a relationship is a daunting task. A number of states, including Texas, have responded by establishing paternity registries. Such registries provide a mechanism for a man alleging himself to be the biological father of a child to take action, independent of the mother of the child, to preserve his right to assert parentage and form a relationship with the child. The Bureau of Vital Statistics (BVS) of the Texas Department of Health is charged with administering the paternity registry.

There remains a question as to the constitutionality of the created registry. The U.S. Supreme Court decision of *Lehr v. Robertson*, 463 U.S. 248 (1983), upheld the right of the State of New York to restrict the claim of a biological father to assert his paternal rights when he failed to register his intent to make such a claim in a state-operated paternity registry. The facts of the case were more than a little outrageous; a man asserting himself to be the father was actually litigating the issue in one court, while a termination and adoption for the child was being sought in another court. The adoption court and the litigants there had full knowledge of the man's pending assertion of paternity in the other court. Notwithstanding the fact that his identity and whereabouts were known, the adoption court proceeded to terminate his rights based on the fact that he had failed to register.

According to the Supreme Court, the State of New York had the power to require the registration, and therefore, the man's due process rights were not denied.

Although the New York paternity registry was held not to violate "due process" under the U.S. Constitution, there would be a significant question about the constitutionality of a New York-type registry cutting off all right of a biological father after 30 days for failure to register. Relying on the Texas Constitution's "due course" of law provision, TEX. CONST. Art. I, § 19, the Texas Supreme Court recently dealt with a situation in which a man sought to establish his paternity of a child born to a married woman over the objections of the mother and her husband (the presumed father). The court stated:

> We do not say that our Constitution guarantees a natural father ties with his illegitimate offspring. We do say that one who is arbitrarily prevented from attempting to establish any relationship with his natural child, after making early and unqualified acceptance of parental duties ... is denied due course of law under Section 19 of our Texas Bill of Rights.

In Interest of J.W.T., 872 S.W.2d 189, 198 (Tex. 1994).

In an earlier case, the supreme court held that such rights must extend to a biological father asserting his rights to a child born to an unmarried woman. *In re Baby McLean*, 725 S.W.2d 696 (Tex. 1987). Whether the statutory scheme provided under this subchapter will be deemed to be an arbitrary restriction of the natural father's rights is one that ultimately can only to be resolved in the courts. In this connection, the most objectionable aspects of the New York scheme do not appear in the Texas statute.

Testimony to the Texas legislature indicated that in 1996 some 3,000 men registered with the paternity registry in New York. Also, it was asserted that 17 states have such a registry. The primary value of the registry, of course, is to cut off the rights of biological fathers as soon as possible in order to facilitate adoption. As the bill analysis stated:

> A father may register with the paternity register administered by the Bureau of Vital Statistics by filing a form placed in hospitals, birthing centers, clerk's offices, and other locations. The register protects the parental rights of fathers assuming responsibility for children they may have fathered. The father may not assert any interest in a child if he does not register within 30 days of the child's birth. The mother may contest an alleged father's paternity within 30 days of receipt of a father's paternity registration from the Bureau. Information contained in the registry is confidential and may be released to authorized parties only.

Despite the statement in Section 160.258 that a man asserting a paternity claim must register within 30 days of the birth of the child, the "except" proviso eliminates that time limitation for a known father who decides to assert his claim by way of filing a parentage suit before termination of his rights. Further, an alleged father whose identity and whereabouts are known is entitled to service of the petition and citation. The rights of that man may be terminated only by application of the termination provisions of Chapter 161. On the other hand, if a man's identity or whereabouts are unknown, failure to register intent to assert paternity with the Bureau dispenses with the necessity of service of citation by publication. A search of the registry substitutes for that wholly impractical method of notice.

In sum, the Texas version of the paternity registry is primarily a vehicle for terminating the rights of unknown fathers or fathers whose whereabouts cannot be located after the exercise of due diligence.

Cross Reference

TX FCA FAMILY § 161.109. Requirement of Paternity Registry Certificate, *infra.*

---

§ 160.401. Establishment of Registry

A registry of paternity is established in the bureau of vital statistics.

§ 160.402. Registration for Notification

(a) Except as otherwise provided by Subsection (b), a man who desires to be notified of a proceeding for the adoption of or the termination of parental rights regarding a child that he may have fathered may register with the registry of paternity:

(1) before the birth of the child; or

(2) not later than the 31st day after the date of the birth of the child.

(b) A man is entitled to notice of a proceeding described by Subsection (a) regardless of whether he registers with the registry of paternity if:

(1) a father-child relationship between the man and the child has been established under this chapter or another law; or

(2) the man commences a proceeding to adjudicate his paternity before the court has terminated his parental rights.

(c) A registrant shall promptly notify the registry in a record of any change in the information provided by the registrant. The bureau of vital statistics shall incorporate all new information received into its records but is not required to affirmatively seek to obtain current information for incorporation in the registry.

Commissioners' Comment to UPA Section 402

A registry of paternity protects a claim of paternity from summary termination, but the primary advantage of such a registry is to facilitate infant adoptions through licensed agencies. By registering, a registrant insures that he will receive notice of the possible adoption of a child that he may have fathered if the birth occurs in the state of registration. In this manner, a man may seek to protect his right to assert parentage.

If a state chooses to enact Subsection (b)(2), one of the major criticisms of *Lehr v. Robertson, supra,* will be eliminated. In *Lehr,* although the genetic father did not avail himself of the New York putative fathers registry, he had filed a "visitation and paternity" petition in another local court. The trial judge in the adoption proceeding knew the identity of the biological father, where he could be located, and that he was seeking to establish his paternity in another court. Nonetheless, the court granted the adoption and terminated the genetic father's parental rights without notice to him. Subsection (b)(2) exempts an alleged father from the requirement of registration if the man "commences a proceeding to adjudicate his paternity before the court has terminated his parental rights."

The act of registration submits the man to the personal jurisdiction of the tribunals of the state of registration, *see* UIFSA (1996) § 201(7). [Texas Family Code § 159.201(7)]

Editors' Comment

A man who fails to file a notice of intent to claim paternity before the 30th day after the date of birth of the child may not assert an interest in the child except by filing a suit to establish paternity before the man's parental rights have been terminated. Thus, the Texas scheme differs from the procedure enacted by several other states which bars any action to establish paternity by a man claiming to be the child's father despite the fact that no termination action has taken place. Such a rule apparently was rejected by the Texas Legislature as being overly restrictive and perhaps even unconstitutional under the Texas Constitution.

---

§ 160.403. Notice of Proceeding

Except as provided by Sections 161.002(b)(2), (3), and (4) and (f), notice of a proceeding to adopt or to terminate parental rights regarding a child must be given to a registrant who has timely registered with regard to that child. Notice must be given in a manner prescribed for service of process in a civil action.

Commissioners' Comment to UPA Section 403

This section is the logical conclusion to the legal rationale for establishing a paternity registry. In an adoption of a child or termination of parental rights proceeding, the registry provides a clear procedure for resolving whether a nonmarital father intends to assert his rights with regard to the child. If he registers, termination of his rights and adoption of his child may not proceed without notice to him; this affords him the opportunity to assert his paternity and his claims for custody or visitation.

---

§ 160.404. Termination of Parental Rights: Failure to Register

The parental rights of a man alleged to be the father of a child may be terminated without notice as provided by Section 161.002 if the man:

(1) did not timely register with the bureau of vital statistics; and

(2) is not entitled to notice under Section 160.402 or 161.002.

Editors' Comment to Section 404

In 1997 a paternity registry was added to Chapter 160, then entitled "Determination of Parentage." In so doing, the Texas Legislature rejected the conclusion of the U.S. Supreme Court in *Lehr v. Robertson*, 463 U.S. 248 (1983), that it is constitutionally permissible to terminate the parental rights of a genetic father who has failed to register his interest in a child even when his identity and whereabouts are known. Even more egregious was the fact that the putative father was actually seeking to establish his paternity in one trial court at the time that another trial court, with knowledge of that fact, terminated his parental rights for his failure to register in the New York paternity registry.

When the legislature enacted the Uniform Parentage Act in 2001, it chose to continue this policy. Thus, it rejected UPA Sections 404 and 405, as promulgated by NCCUSL, respectively captioned "Termination of Parental Rights: Child Under One Year of Age" and "Termination of Parental Rights: Child at Least One Year of Age." The UPA provides that notice is not required to terminate the parental rights of an alleged father of an infant less than one year old if he has not registered his interest in the child; notice of a proceeding to terminate or adopt to the alleged father is required as in other civil suit if the child is at least one year old.

Section 160.404, a purely-Texas provision, makes the appropriate cross-references to the relevant provisions in this chapter and Chapter 161, "Termination of the Parent-Child Relationship (TX FCA Family §§ 160.402, 161.002)." In sum, citation in a SAPCR is required in order to bind an alleged genetic father to a termination decree if his identity and whereabouts are known. If his identity or whereabouts are not known, Section 161.002 permits termination of the alleged father's rights without the necessity of "personal service of citation or citation by publication" if a search of the registry yields a certificate attesting to the fact that he has not filed with the registry.

---

§§ 160.405 to 160.410. [Blank]

§ 160.411. Required Form

The bureau of vital statistics shall adopt a form for registering with the registry. The form must require the signature of the registrant. The form must state that:

(1) the form is signed under penalty of perjury;

(2) a timely registration entitles the registrant to notice of a proceeding for adoption of the child or for termination of the registrant's parental rights;

(3) a timely registration does not commence a proceeding to establish paternity;

(4) the information disclosed on the form may be used against the registrant to establish paternity;

(5) services to assist in establishing paternity are available to the registrant through the support enforcement agency;

(6) the registrant should also register in another state if the conception or birth of the child occurred in the other state;

(7) information on registries in other states is available from the bureau of vital statistics; and

(8) procedures exist to rescind the registration of a claim of paternity.

§ 160.412. Furnishing of Information; Confidentiality

(a) The bureau of vital statistics is not required to attempt to locate the mother of a child who is the subject of a registration. The bureau of vital statistics shall send a copy of the notice of the registration to a mother who has provided an address.

(b) Information contained in the registry is confidential and may be released on request only to:

(1) a court or a person designated by the court;

(2) the mother of the child who is the subject of the registration;

(3) an agency authorized by another law to receive the information;

(4) a licensed child-placing agency;

(5) a support enforcement agency;

(6) a party, or the party's attorney of record, to a proceeding under this chapter or a proceeding to adopt or to terminate parental rights regarding a child who is the subject of the registration; and

(7) the registry of paternity in another state.

§ 160.413. Offense: Unauthorized Release of Information

(a) A person commits an offense if the person intentionally releases information from the registry of paternity to another person, including an agency, that is not authorized to receive the information under Section 160.412.

(b) An offense under this section is a Class A misdemeanor.

§ 160.414. Rescission of Registration

A registrant may rescind his registration at any time by sending to the registry a rescission in a record or another manner authenticated by him and witnessed or notarized.

§ 160.415. Untimely Registration

If a man registers later than the 31st day after the date of the birth of the child, the bureau of vital statistics shall notify the registrant that the registration was not timely filed.

§ 160.416. Fees for Registry

(a) A fee may not be charged for filing a registration or to rescind a registration.

(b) Except as otherwise provided by Subsection (c), the bureau of vital statistics may charge a reasonable fee for making a search of the registry and for furnishing a certificate.

(c) A support enforcement agency is not required to pay a fee authorized by Subsection (b).

§ 160.421. Search of Appropriate Registry

(a) If a father-child relationship has not been established under this chapter, a petitioner for the adoption of or the termination of parental rights regarding the child must obtain a certificate of the results of a search of the registry. The petitioner may request a search of the registry on or after the 32nd day after the date of the birth of the child, and the bureau of vital statistics may not by rule impose a waiting period that must elapse before the bureau will conduct the requested search.

(b) If the petitioner for the adoption of or the termination of parental rights regarding a child has reason to believe that the conception or birth of the child may have occurred in another state, the petitioner must obtain a certificate of the results of a search of the paternity registry, if any, in the other state.

§ 160.422. Certificate of Search of Registry

(a) The bureau of vital statistics shall furnish a certificate of the results of a search of the registry on request by an individual, a court, or an agency listed in Section 160.412(b).

(b) The certificate of the results of a search must be signed on behalf of the bureau and state that:

(1) a search has been made of the registry; and

(2) a registration containing the information required to identify the registrant:

(A) has been found and is attached to the certificate; or

(B) has not been found.

(c) A petitioner must file the certificate of the results of a search of the registry with the court before a proceeding for the adoption of or termination of parental rights regarding a child may be concluded.

(d) A search of the registry is not required if a parent-child relationship exists between a man and the child, as provided by Section 160.201(b), and that man:

(1) has been served with citation of the proceeding for termination of the parent-child relationship; or

(2) has signed a relinquishment of parental rights with regard to the child.

§ 160.423. Admissibility of Certificate

A certificate of the results of a search of the registry in this state or of a paternity registry in another state is admissible in a proceeding for the adoption of or the termination of parental rights regarding a child and, if relevant, in other legal proceedings.

SUBCHAPTER F. GENETIC TESTING

§ 160.501. Application of Subchapter

This subchapter governs genetic testing of an individual to determine parentage, regardless of whether the individual:

(1) voluntarily submits to testing; or

(2) is tested under an order of a court or a support enforcement agency.

Commissioners' Comment to UPA Section 501

This section is intended to avoid problems with regard to the admissibility of the result of voluntary genetic testing. Testing is often agreed upon to avoid the cost and delay engendered by requiring a proceeding be filed before the result of genetic testing can be admitted as evidence. If the test excludes the man's paternity, an unnecessary step has been avoided.

§ 160.502. Order for Testing

(a) Except as otherwise provided by this subchapter and by Subchapter G, a court shall order a child and other designated individuals to submit to genetic testing if the request is made by a party to a proceeding to determine parentage.

(b) If a request for genetic testing of a child is made before the birth of the child, the court or support enforcement agency may not order in utero testing.

(c) If two or more men are subject to court-ordered genetic testing, the testing may be ordered concurrently or sequentially.

Commissioners' Comment to UPA Section 502

Source: UPA (1973) § 11; 42 U.S.C. § 666(a)(5)(B)(i) requiring genetic testing in certain cases.

The progress that science has made in understanding molecular genetics since the promulgation of UPA (1973) is phenomenal. Subsection (a) speaks to testing of a "designated individual" other than of the "mother, and alleged or presumed father" to take into account the fact that testing for paternity may proceed without testing the mother. Further, testing may also proceed without testing the alleged father by testing close relatives of that man. Moreover, the right of the court to order testing is not absolute; Sections 607–609 place limitations on genetic testing if the child has a presumed, acknowledged, or adjudicated father.

Subsection (c) is intended to prevent the court from ordering the mother to undergo prenatal testing, such as through amniocentesis or other in utero collection method. These procedures have a measurable risk to the life and health of both the fetus and the mother. If the mother volunteers for such testing, she may undergo prenatal sample collection for parentage determination.

Subsection (d) recognizes that multiple men may be participating in the establishment process. The laboratories prefer to evaluate all persons concurrently, as concurrent testing may prevent multiple sample collections from the child and in rare cases (such as evaluating two non-identical siblings) the laboratory can continue testing until one or both of the tested men are excluded. However, sequential testing is also acceptable.

§ 160.503. Requirements for Genetic Testing

(a) Genetic testing must be of a type reasonably relied on by experts in the field of genetic testing. The testing must be performed in a testing laboratory accredited by:

(1) the American Association of Blood Banks, or a successor to its functions;

(2) the American Society for Histocompatibility and Immunogenetics, or a successor to its functions; or

(3) an accrediting body designated by the federal secretary of health and human services.

(b) A specimen used in genetic testing may consist of one or more samples, or a combination of samples, of blood, buccal cells, bone, hair, or other body tissue or fluid. The specimen used in the testing is not required to be of the same kind for each individual undergoing genetic testing.

(c) Based on the ethnic or racial group of an individual, the testing laboratory shall determine the databases from which to select frequencies for use in the calculation of the probability of paternity of the individual. If there is disagreement as to the testing laboratory's choice:

(1) the objecting individual may require the testing laboratory, not later than the 30th day after the date of receipt of the report of the test, to recalculate the probability of paternity using an ethnic or racial group different from that used by the laboratory;

(2) the individual objecting to the testing laboratory's initial choice shall:

(A) if the frequencies are not available to the testing laboratory for the ethnic or racial group requested, provide the requested frequencies compiled in a manner recognized by accrediting bodies; or

(B) engage another testing laboratory to perform the calculations; and

(3) the testing laboratory may use its own statistical estimate if there is a question regarding which ethnic or racial group is appropriate and, if available, shall calculate the frequencies using statistics for any other ethnic or racial group requested.

(d) If, after recalculation using a different ethnic or racial group, genetic testing does not rebuttably identify a man as the father of a child under Section 160.505, an individual who has been tested may be required to submit to additional genetic testing.

Commissioners' Comment to UPA Section 503

Source: 42 U.S.C. § 666(a)(5)(B)(i)(I)(II) and § 666(a)(5)(F)(i)(I)(II).

As of December 2000, the Secretary of Health and Human Services has not officially designated any accreditation bodies as referenced in Subsection (b)(3). But, Information Memorandum

O.C.S.E.-IM-97-03, April 10, 1997, from the Deputy Director of the Office of Child Support Enforcement identifies the American Association of Blood Banks and American Society for Histocompatibility and Immunogenetics as meeting this requirement. The accreditation requirement assures that the testing will "be of a type reasonably relied upon by experts in the field of genetic testing."

Subsection (b) clarifies that a "specimen" suitable for genetic testing may be composed from one of a wide variety of constituent elements of "body tissue and fluids." This conforms the statutory language to biological terminology to assure common understanding between the scientific community and the legal profession. In states with statutes employing only the broad terms, bench and bar have evidenced confusion about the fact that blood, buccal cells, bone, hair, etc. are "body tissues."

Subsections (c) and (d) are designed to clarify the use of "race or ethnic group" in the paternity calculations. Generally, the individual tested provides the information regarding the ethnic or racial group to use in the calculations. These sections are designed to avoid last minute changes in the racial designation, a scientific version of "forum shopping", and to easily correct any misunderstanding about which race should be used.

§ 160.504. Report of Genetic Testing

(a) A report of the results of genetic testing must be in a record and signed under penalty of perjury by a designee of the testing laboratory. A report made under the requirements of this subchapter is self-authenticating.

(b) Documentation from the testing laboratory is sufficient to establish a reliable chain of custody that allows the results of genetic testing to be admissible without testimony if the documentation includes:

(1) the name and photograph of each individual whose specimens have been taken;

(2) the name of each individual who collected the specimens;

(3) the places in which the specimens were collected and the date of each collection;

(4) the name of each individual who received the specimens in the testing laboratory; and

(5) the dates the specimens were received.

Commissioners' Comment to UPA Section 504

Source: 42 U.S.C. § 666(a)(5)(F) requiring genetic testing in certain cases.

Subsection (b) is designed to indicate that in civil trials only a minimal showing of reliability of the chain of custody is needed. This avoids evidentiary problems, such as arguments modeled on criminal cases in which the chain of evidence is crucial. If an element of the chain is missing, such a defect may be corrected by affidavit or other testimony as to the reliability of the sample. For example, samples from a deceased individual may be obtained from a coroner's office and a picture of the individual need not be taken. In this case, proof of the chain of custody of the body maintained by the coroner may be provided.

§ 160.505. Genetic Testing Results; Rebuttal

(a) A man is rebuttably identified as the father of a child under this chapter if the genetic testing complies with this subchapter and the results disclose:

(1) that the man has at least a 99 percent probability of paternity, using a prior probability of 0.5, as calculated by using the combined paternity index obtained in the testing; and

(2) a combined paternity index of at least 100 to 1.

(b) A man identified as the father of a child under Subsection (a) may rebut the genetic testing results only by producing other genetic testing satisfying the requirements of this subchapter that:

(1) excludes the man as a genetic father of the child; or

(2) identifies another man as the possible father of the child.

(c) Except as otherwise provided by Section 160.510, if more than one man is identified by genetic testing as the possible father of the child, the court shall order each man to submit to further genetic testing to identify the genetic father.

Commissioners' Comment to UPA Section 505

Source: 42 U.S.C. § 666(a)(5)(G) requiring genetic testing in certain cases.

The selection of a probability of paternity of 99.0% and a combined paternity index of 100 to 1 as the rebuttably identified man as father of the child is consistent with the year 2000 standard of practice in the genetic-testing community. Accrediting agencies require the reporting of both of these numbers. As of December, 2000, 27 states have established a presumption at less than this level. However, for several years the standard of practice in the scientific community has been 99.0%. Therefore, raising the genetic presumption to the 99.0% level should have no impact on those states. This number represents a reasonable level of testing, given the breadth of the Act and potential difficulty of working with some specimens in a probate case. It is not intended as a standard of practice for the laboratories, but as a legal presumption to satisfy the legal standard of proof. Given the rapid progress of science, it is likely that accrediting standards will rise over time. If the standard of practice becomes more strict, the newer standards will be made routine by the requirement that laboratories be accredited in order to perform testing under the Act. But, the legal significance of the genetic presumption stated in this section will be unaffected.

Genetic testing results will usually exceed the statutory minimum. During the drafting of UPA (2000) several statutory presumptions were considered, *i.e.*, 95%, 99%, 99.9% and 99.99%. Genetic testing laboratory representatives presented quite persuasive arguments for a variety of choices. The Drafting Committee ultimately chose to settle on the 99% standard because:

(1) the 99% standard reflects the current standard of the American Association of Blood Banks (STANDARDS FOR PARENTAGE TESTING LABORATORIES, 4th Edition 1999), and the proposed standards (5th Edition, 2001);

(2) the standards promulgated by the various accrediting bodies (American Association of Blood Banks and the American Society for Histocompatibility and Immunogenetics) will, in reality, set the benchmark for genetic testing;

(3) the 99% standard is consistent with the standards of the plurality of American jurisdictions as of December, 2000;

(4) a standard higher than 99% could cause evidentiary problems in probate proceedings because of degraded specimens. Similarly, that problem may arise in cases involving one or more missing individuals, *e.g.*, the mother is not available, but the child and alleged father are available;

(5) the percentage is an evidentiary presumption that the respondent may always challenge by requesting a second test under Section 507; and

(6) a proceeding to adjudicate paternity is a civil action based on a preponderance of the evidence, not a criminal action based on evidence beyond reasonable doubt.

§ 160.506. Costs of Genetic Testing

(a) Subject to the assessment of costs under Subchapter G, the cost of initial genetic testing must be advanced:

(1) by a support enforcement agency, if the agency is providing services in the proceeding;

(2) by the individual who made the request;

(3) as agreed by the parties; or

(4) as ordered by the court.

(b) In cases in which the cost of genetic testing is advanced by the support enforcement agency, the agency may seek reimbursement from a man who is rebuttably identified as the father.

Commissioners' Comment to UPA Section 506

Source: UPA (1973) § 11; 42 U.S.C. § 666(a)(5)(B)(ii)(I); Little v. Streater, 454 U.S. 1, (1981).

In general, the party seeking relief from a court must bear the cost of the initial genetic testing. The federal law mandates that the support enforcement agency pay the cost of testing, subject to recoupment. Subsection (a)(3) does present the possibility that a court might order a respondent to pay the initial cost.

§ 160.507. Additional Genetic Testing

The court or the support enforcement agency shall order additional genetic testing on the request of a party who contests the result of the original testing. If the previous genetic testing identified a man as the father of the child under Section 160.505, the court or agency may not order additional testing unless the party provides advance payment for the testing.

Commissioners' Comment to UPA Section 507

Source: UPA (1973) § 11; 42 U.S.C. § 666(a)(5)(B)(ii)(II).

Obviously the opportunity for additional testing should be provided if the original testing is contested in good faith. The requirement that the contestant provide advance payment if prior testing has identified a man as the father is intended to discourage spurious contests. This section provides the most important mechanism for determining the accuracy of a paternity test. While extremely rare, even after initial tests indicate a probability of paternity greater than 99.99% it is theoretically possible that additional testing can result in exclusion of the tested man. Likewise, if there is an error in the chain of custody or testing procedures, exclusion is the expected outcome. The only way to reliably determine whether an error occurred is to obtain a second test.

§ 160.508. Genetic Testing When All Individuals Not Available

(a) Subject to Subsection (b), if a genetic testing specimen for good cause and under circumstances the court considers to be just is not available from a man who may be the father of a child, a court may order the following individuals to submit specimens for genetic testing:

(1) the parents of the man;

(2) any brothers or sisters of the man;

(3) any other children of the man and their mothers; and

(4) other relatives of the man necessary to complete genetic testing.

(b) A court may not render an order under this section unless the court finds that the need for genetic testing outweighs the legitimate interests of the individual sought to be tested.

Commissioners' Comment to UPA Section 508

In some cases, the alleged father may be unavailable for testing. Subsection (a) accommodates those cases by providing for testing of the man's relatives to establish his paternity or nonpaternity of a child. Depending on the proceeding, some of the individuals listed for testing in Subsection (a) will be parties to the paternity proceeding and others will not. If an individual does not volunteer to participate in the testing and is not a party, in the absence of this provision the court would be required to decide whether it has the authority to order the testing and whether testing the objecting individual is necessary. This provision resolves the issues. Given the fact that genetic testing in the modern age is not invasive—use of the buccal swab method means that the intrusion into the privacy of the individual is relatively slight compared to the right of the child to have parentage established. Moreover, the alleged parent also has a right to have that fact determined.

Note that no provision is explicitly made for court-ordered testing of maternal relatives because the establishment of paternity by genetic testing is in no way dependent on testing the mother of the child. However, if maternity is at issue, § 106, Determination of Maternity, directs that this section be construed to test the relatives of the mother.

§ 160.509. Deceased Individual

For good cause shown, the court may order genetic testing of a deceased individual.

Commissioners' Comment to UPA Section 509

In some states, the court with jurisdiction to adjudicate parentage may lack authority to order disinterment of a deceased individual. If so, that authority is provided by this section.

---

§ 160.510. Identical Brothers

(a) The court may order genetic testing of a brother of a man identified as the father of a child if the man is commonly believed to have an identical brother and evidence suggests that the brother may be the genetic father of the child.

(b) If each brother satisfies the requirements of Section 160.505 for being the identified father of the child and there is not another identical brother being identified as the father of the child, the court may rely on nongenetic evidence to adjudicate which brother is the father of the child.

Commissioners' Comment to UPA Section 510

This section refers to "identical brothers" rather than "identical twins" to account for the possibility of identical triplets, etc. In some cases, non-identical brothers (and even other related men) will not be excluded after initial genetic testing. This section should not be used to resolve those cases because more sophisticated genetic testing can differentiate between non-identical siblings. If a case occurs in which, after initial testing, two men are not excluded, both men should be ordered to submit to additional testing as provided in Section 505(c) to determine which is the father. In the extremely rare case in which a competent laboratory exhausts all of its in-house testing and still cannot determine which non-identical sibling is excluded, the common practice is to provide the genetic material to another laboratory for more extensive testing to resolve the case.

Contrasting identical brothers with non-identical brothers, identical brothers can never be differentiated by additional genetic testing. This creates a completely different situation for the court. This section resolves the identical-brother conundrum as much as possible, and is designed to prevent the court from simply dismissing the case.

---

§ 160.511. Offense: Unauthorized Release of Specimen

(a) A person commits an offense if the person intentionally releases an identifiable specimen of another person for any purpose not relevant to the parentage proceeding and without a court order or the written permission of the person who furnished the specimen.

(b) An offense under this section is a Class A misdemeanor.

Commissioners' Comment to UPA Section 511

This section seeks to protect the privacy rights of persons who are tested for a parentage determination. Although the Drafting Committee was not informed of an instance in which a paternity-testing laboratory had released samples or performed unauthorized testing, several states have proposed or passed laws regulating the "genetic privacy" of paternity tests. This section is intended to provide some guidance in this area. The term "identifiable specimen" is included, as there are beneficial uses of samples for anonymous research purposes. For example, the frequency tables used to make calculations are compiled from anonymous data and provide a more precise calculation for all persons involved in paternity testing. On occasion, a court may order the laboratory to release samples. For instance, a man who had been tested in one paternity proceeding and then dies may have his samples utilized in another paternity proceeding if a court orders testing in the second action. Courts have also ordered the release of samples when the tested man has allegedly engaged in criminal conduct. This has occurred when the alleged father has sent an imposter for sample collection. If the state pursues criminal charges, a court might order the laboratory to release the samples to a state crime laboratory for further identification and possible criminal prosecution.

The Drafting Committee was informed that in one case, a grand jury brought indictments for multiple counts of a scheme to defraud, tampering with physical evidence and perjury against the alleged father and the imposter. The results of genetic testing for paternity purposes appear to have no medical or predictive value in any other context. Thus, regulation of the paternity-test results is left to the states. In some states, the records of paternity proceedings are open, thus allowing anyone to obtain the results. A more comprehensive treatment on this subject must necessarily be left to other laws.

The control of the records is left to other state law. In some states paternity records are open to the public, and a fundamental change in handling of the records is beyond the scope of this Act. The accreditation agencies provide guidance on this subject. For example, the American Association of Blood Banks requires that accredited laboratories maintain records for at least five years. Because a laboratory performing testing under this act should be accredited, *see* Section 503(a), *supra*, protection is thus provided to the tested person's records under the accreditation standards.

§ 160.512. Offense: Falsification of Specimen

(a) A person commits an offense if the person alters, destroys, conceals, fabricates, or falsifies genetic evidence in a proceeding to adjudicate parentage, including inducing another person to provide a specimen with the intent to affect the outcome of the proceeding.

(b) An offense under this section is a felony of the third degree.

(c) An order excluding a man as the biological father of a child based on genetic evidence shown to be altered, fabricated, or falsified is void and unenforceable.

Added by Acts 2011, 82nd Leg., ch. 1221 (S.B. 502), § 7, eff. Sept. 1, 2011.

SUBCHAPTER G. PROCEEDING TO ADJUDICATE PARENTAGE

Leading Cases

In re Z.L.T., 124 S.W.3d 163 (Tex. 2003) (not error to implicitly deny bench warrant to transport prison inmate to paternity trial)

In re K.N.P., 179 S.W.3d 717 (Tex. App.—Fort Worth 2005, pet. denied) (paternity action untimely and barred by statute if child has presumed father)

Dickerson v. Doyle, 170 S.W.3d 713 (Tex. App.—El Paso 2005, no pet.) (Texas court appropriately declined jurisdiction over parentage suit based on Alabama more appropriate forum)

In re S.D.E., 170 S.W.3d 642 (Tex. App.—El Paso 2005, no pet.) (bill review leading to set-aside of parentage decree interlocutory in nature and thus not appealable)

In re Sullivan, 157 S.W.3d 911 (Tex. App.—Houston [14th Dist.] 2005, orig. proceeding) (man furnishing sperm for artificial insemination with intent to be child's father has standing to adjudicate parentage)

See CLE/Other Legal Publications following Editors' Introductory Comment beginning Chapter 160, *supra*

§ 160.601. Proceeding Authorized; Rules of Procedure

(a) A civil proceeding may be maintained to adjudicate the parentage of a child.

(b) The proceeding is governed by the Texas Rules of Civil Procedure, except as provided by Chapter 233.

Commissioners' Comment to UPA Section 601

Source: UPA (1973) § 14.

A determination of paternity is governed by the ordinary rules of civil procedure. The party seeking to establish paternity is entitled to full discovery, to compel the testimony of all witnesses, and to have the case tried by a preponderance of the evidence. "The equipoise of the private interests that are at stake in a paternity proceeding supports the conclusion that the standard of proof normally applied in private litigation is also appropriate for these cases." *Rivera v. Minnich*, 483 U.S. 574, 581 (1987).

A corresponding amendment to UPC § 2–114 was not made until the major revision of 1990 (as further revised in 1993). By that time, it had been recognized as illogical and unjust to impose discriminatory burdens on children born out-of-wedlock who were seeking paternal inheritance. It also had been ruled unconstitutional by application of the intermediate scrutiny test formulated under the 14th Amendment. *Reed v. Campbell*, 476 U.S. 852 (1986). Moreover, by 1990 the preponderance of the evidence standard had been widely applied to determinations of paternity and probate proceedings. Against this background, UPC (1993) abandoned the clear and convincing evidence alternative for determining paternal relationships.

§ 160.602. Standing to Maintain Proceeding

(a) Subject to Subchapter D and Sections 160.607 and 160.609 and except as provided by Subsection (b), a proceeding to adjudicate parentage may be maintained by:

(1) the child;

(2) the mother of the child;

(3) a man whose paternity of the child is to be adjudicated;

(4) the support enforcement agency or another government agency authorized by other law;

(5) an authorized adoption agency or licensed child-placing agency;

(6) a representative authorized by law to act for an individual who would otherwise be entitled to maintain a proceeding but who is deceased, is incapacitated, or is a minor;

(7) a person related within the second degree by consanguinity to the mother of the child, if the mother is deceased; or

(8) a person who is an intended parent.

(b) After the date a child having no presumed, acknowledged, or adjudicated father becomes an adult, a proceeding to adjudicate the parentage of the adult child may only be maintained by the adult child.

Commissioners' Comment to UPA Section 602

Source: UPA (1973) § 6.

This section grants standing to a broad range of individuals and agencies to bring a parentage proceeding. But, several limitations on standing to sue are contained within the Act. Subchapter D details the procedures involved in a voluntary acknowledgment of parentage. Sections 607 and 609 establish the ground rules for proceedings involving children with, and without, a presumed father. Subchapter I regulates parentage determinations arising from a gestational agreement.

§ 160.603. Necessary Parties to Proceeding

The following individuals must be joined as parties in a proceeding to adjudicate parentage:

(1) the mother of the child; and

(2) a man whose paternity of the child is to be adjudicated.

Commissioners' Comment to UPA Section 603

Source: UPA (1973) § 9.

This section partially follows and partially rejects the UPA (1973) requirements regarding who must be named as parties in a parentage proceeding. First, contra to UPA (1973), the child is not a necessary party. Few states require children as necessary parties. Further, with the widespread use of DNA testing, such a requirement has outlived its usefulness. On the other hand, failure to join a child as a party may later result in a child's successful collateral attack on the original determination of paternity to be filed by the child. This subject is discussed more fully in the Commissioners' Comment to Section 637, *infra*.

Second, as far as can be determined, no state requires the children born to a woman during marriage to be named as parties in every divorce proceeding; and, those decrees generally serve as res judicata if a later attack on an earlier determination is mounted. *Id.*

---

§ 160.604. Personal Jurisdiction

(a) An individual may not be adjudicated to be a parent unless the court has personal jurisdiction over the individual.

(b) A court of this state having jurisdiction to adjudicate parentage may exercise personal jurisdiction over a nonresident individual or the guardian or conservator of the individual if the conditions in Section 159.201 are satisfied.

(c) Lack of jurisdiction over one individual does not preclude the court from making an adjudication of parentage binding on another individual over whom the court has personal jurisdiction.

Commissioners' Comment to UPA Section 604

Source: UPA (1973) § 6(b).

Although custody and visitation proceedings are considered to be status adjudications, and therefore do not require personal jurisdiction over both parents, Subsection (a) confirms the long-standing view that paternity proceedings require personal jurisdiction.

Subsection (b) incorporates the long-arm provision for establishing personal jurisdiction over an absent respondent set forth in UIFSA (1996), which is in effect in every state.

Subsection (c) makes the best of a situation in which an adjudication will almost inevitably be incomplete because not all the necessary parties are subject to the personal jurisdiction of the court. The most likely scenario for this unfortunate circumstance is one in which the mother and alleged father of the child are subject to the court's jurisdiction, but the mother's absent husband is not. Even if the husband's whereabouts are known, if both the forum court and the court of his residence lacks jurisdiction over all three parties, there still is no court with power to bind all of them to a parentage determination.

Subsection (c) takes the common sense approach that a court should not be dissuaded from making a parentage decision, even if it cannot bind all appropriate parties. In the scenario described above, binding the mother and alleged father to a decision of the man's parentage may not technically bind the husband (the presumed father), but more than likely it will end litigation on the subject.

---

§ 160.605. Venue

Venue for a proceeding to adjudicate parentage is in the county of this state in which:

(1) the child resides or is found;

(2) the respondent resides or is found if the child does not reside in this state; or

(3) a proceeding for probate or administration of the presumed or alleged father's estate has been commenced.

Commissioners' Comment to UPA Section 605

Source: UPA (1973) § 8(c).

The venue provision provides choices proven to be reasonable and convenient since its inclusion in the 1973 Act.

---

§ 160.606. No Time Limitation: Child Having no Presumed, Acknowledged, or Adjudicated Father

A proceeding to adjudicate the parentage of a child having no presumed, acknowledged, or adjudicated father may be commenced at any time, including after the date:

(1) the child becomes an adult; or

(2) an earlier proceeding to adjudicate paternity has been dismissed based on the application of a statute of limitation then in effect.

Commissioners' Comment to UPA Section 606

Source: UPA (1973) §§ 6, 7.

For a state to retain the federal child support enforcement subsidy, 42 U.S.C. § 666(a)(5)(A)(i) mandates that the states must have laws to "permit the establishment of the paternity of a child at any time before the child attains 18 years of age." States have chosen a wide range of age options: age 18 (20 states), age 19 (6 states), age 20 (2 states), age 21 (10 states), age 22 (2 states), age 23 (2 states), and no limitation (9 states). Several states limit the establishment of parental rights to a shorter period.

The UPA directs that an individual whose parentage has not been determined has a civil right to determine his or her own parentage, which should not be subject to limitation except when an estate has been closed. Accordingly, if the action is initiated by the child this section allows a proceeding to adjudicate parentage after the child has reached the age of majority. Such a proceeding is the exclusive province of the child, however.

Editors' Comment

Section 160.602(b) restricts paternity determinations in cases where the child has reached his or her majority. This action can only be maintained by the adult child. This limitation prohibits the filing of an intrusive proceeding by an individual claiming to be a parent of an adult child, or by a legal stranger.

---

§ 160.607. Time Limitation: Child Having Presumed Father

(a) Except as otherwise provided by Subsection (b), a proceeding brought by a presumed father, the mother, or another individual to adjudicate the parentage of a child having a presumed father shall be commenced not later than the fourth anniversary of the date of the birth of the child.

(b) A proceeding seeking to **adjudicate the parentage of a child having a** ~~disprove the father-child relationship between a child and the child's~~ presumed father may be maintained at any time if the court determines that:

(1) the presumed father and the mother of the child did not live together or engage in sexual intercourse with each other during the probable time of conception; **or** ~~and~~

(2) the presumed father **was precluded from commencing a proceeding to adjudicate the parentage of the child before the expiration of the time prescribed by Subsection (a) because of the mistaken belief that he was the child's biological father based on**

misrepresentations that led him to that conclusion ~~never represented to others that the child was his own~~.

Amended by Acts 2011, 82nd Leg., ch. 1221 (S.B. 502), § 8, eff. Sept. 1, 2011.

Commissioners' Comment to UPA Section 607

Source: UPA (1973) § 6; *cf.* UPC (1993) § 2–114(c).

This section deals with difficult issues. First, it establishes the right of a mother or a presumed marital or nonmarital father to challenge the presumption of his paternity established by § 204. Second, it clarifies the right of a third-party male to claim paternity of a child who has an existing presumed father.

This section places a four year limitation on the time in which a proceeding may be brought for the purpose of declaring the nonexistence of the father and child relationship presumed under the act.

The right of an "outsider" to claim paternity of a child born to a married woman varies considerably among the states. Thirty three states allow a man alleging himself to be the father of a child with a presumed father to rebut the marital presumption. Some states have granted this right through legislation, while in other states case law has recognized the alleged father's right to rebut the presumption and establish his paternity. In some states, there is both statutory and common law support for the standing of a man alleging himself to be the father to assert his paternity of a child born to a married woman. Not that long ago, some states imposed an absolute bar on a man commencing a proceeding to establish his paternity if state law provides a statutory presumption of the paternity of another man. *See* Michael H. v. Gerald D., 491 U.S. 110, (1989). It is increasingly clear that those days are coming to an end.

The UPA attempts to establish a middle ground on these exceedingly complex issues. Subsection (a) establishes a four-year limitation for rebutting the presumption of paternity established under § 204 if the mother and presumed father were cohabiting at the time of conception. The presumption of paternity may be attacked by the mother, the presumed father, or a third party male during this limited period; thereafter the presumption is immune from attack by any of those individuals except as provided in subsection (b).

The reverse fact situation is also clear; a presumption of paternity may be challenged at any time if the mother and the presumed father were not cohabiting and did not engage in sexual intercourse at the probable time of conception and the presumed father never openly held out the child as his own.

Under the fact circumstances described in subsection (b), nonpaternity of the presumed father is generally assumed by all the parties as a practical matter. It is inappropriate for the law to assume a presumption known by all those concerned to be untrue.

Editors' Comments to § 160.607

The legislation in 2011 that revised the procedure for rescission or challenge of an acknowledgment or denial of paternity also revised the focus of the litigation regarding actual paternity when a child has a presumed father. Rather than the issue being to disprove the presumption, the proceeding is "to adjudicate parentage." Such a suit may be maintained at any time if the court makes certain specified determinations: (1) the presumed father and the mother of the child did not live together, or engage in sexual intercourse with each other during the probably time of conception; or (2) the presumed father was precluded from commencing a proceeding to adjudicate the parentage of the child before the expiration of the time prescribed by law because of the mistaken belief that he was the child's biological father based on misrepresentations that led him to that conclusion. Gone is the question of whether the presumed father represented to others that the child was his own.

Leading Case

In re Rodriguez, 248 S.W.3d 444 (Tex. App.—Dallas 2008, mandamus granted) (absent statutory exceptions, court cannot order genetic testing to determine parentage outside the 4-year statute of limitations)

§ 160.608. Authority to Deny Motion for Genetic Testing

(a) In a proceeding to adjudicate parentage, a court may deny a motion for an order for the genetic testing of the mother, the child, and the presumed father if the court determines that:

(1) the conduct of the mother or the presumed father estops that party from denying parentage; and

(2) it would be inequitable to disprove the father-child relationship between the child and the presumed father.

(b) In determining whether to deny a motion for an order for genetic testing under this section, the court shall consider the best interest of the child, including the following factors:

(1) the length of time between the date of the proceeding to adjudicate parentage and the date the presumed father was placed on notice that he might not be the genetic father;

(2) the length of time during which the presumed father has assumed the role of father of the child;

(3) the facts surrounding the presumed father's discovery of his possible nonpaternity;

(4) the nature of the relationship between the child and the presumed father;

(5) the age of the child;

(6) any harm that may result to the child if presumed paternity is successfully disproved;

(7) the nature of the relationship between the child and the alleged father;

(8) the extent to which the passage of time reduces the chances of establishing the paternity of another man and a child support obligation in favor of the child; and

(9) other factors that may affect the equities arising from the disruption of the father-child relationship between the child and the presumed father or the chance of other harm to the child.

(c) In a proceeding involving the application of this section, a child who is a minor or is incapacitated must be represented by an amicus attorney or attorney ad litem.

(d) A denial of a motion for an order for genetic testing must be based on clear and convincing evidence.

(e) If the court denies a motion for an order for genetic testing, the court shall issue an order adjudicating the presumed father to be the father of the child.

(f) This section applies to a proceeding to ~~rescind or~~ challenge an acknowledgment of paternity or a denial of paternity as provided by Section 160.309(d).

Amended by Acts 2011, 82nd Leg., ch. 1221 (S.B. 502), § 9, eff. Sept. 1, 2011.

Commissioners' Comment to UPA Section 608

This section incorporates the doctrine of paternity by estoppel, which extends equally to a child with a presumed father or an acknowledged father. In appropriate circumstances, the court may deny genetic testing and find the presumed or acknowledged father to be the father of the child. The most common situation in which estoppel should be applied arises when a man knows that a child is not, or may not be, his genetic child, but the man has affirmatively accepted his role as child's father and both the mother and the child have relied on that acceptance. Similarly, the man may have relied on the mother's acceptance of him as the child's father, and the mother is then estopped to deny the man's presumed parentage.

Subsection (b) delineates the standards for denying genetic testing. Subsection (c) requires the child to be independently represented. Subsection (d) requires an elevated standard of proof before the order for genetic testing can be denied.

Because § 607 places a two-year limitation [four years in Texas] on challenging the presumption of parentage, the application of this section should be applied in those meritorious cases in which the best interest of the child compels the result and the conduct of the mother and presumed or acknowledged father is clear.

Subsection (f) extends principles of estoppel to children of unmarried parents wherein a proceeding is brought to challenge an acknowledgment of paternity.

§ 160.609. Time Limitation: Child Having Acknowledged or Adjudicated Father

(a) If a child has an acknowledged father, a signatory to the acknowledgment or denial of paternity may commence a proceeding **under this chapter** ~~seeking to rescind the acknowledgment or denial or~~ to challenge the paternity of the child only within the time allowed under Section ~~160.307 or~~ 160.308.

(b) If a child has an acknowledged father or an adjudicated father, an individual, other than the child, who is not a signatory to the acknowledgment or a party to the adjudication and who seeks an adjudication of paternity of the child must commence a proceeding not later than the fourth anniversary of the effective date of the acknowledgment or adjudication.

Amended by Acts 2011, 82nd Leg., ch. 1221 (S.B. 502), § 10, eff. Sept. 1, 2011.

Commissioners' Comment to UPA Section 609

A four-year period is prescribed in § 307 for a challenge in which the acknowledged or adjudicated father mistakenly believed himself to be the genetic father. A similar limitation is prescribed in § 607(a) for an individual who was not a signatory or a party to the earlier determination.

Leading Cases

In re R.A.H., 130 S.W.3d 68 (Tex. 2004) (putative father not a party in prior suit has 4 years from date adjudication signed to assert his parentage)

Texas Dept. of Protective & Regulatory Services v. Sherry, 46 S.W.3d 857 (Tex. 2001) (purported father of a child lacks standing to bring a paternity action if a prior, final judgment of paternity has been rendered by a court of competent jurisdiction)

In re K.N.P., 179 S.W.3d 717 (Tex. App.—Fort Worth 2005, pet. denied) (paternity action untimely and barred by statute if child has presumed father)

In re S.D.E., 170 S.W.3d 642 (Tex. App.—El Paso 2005, no pet.) (bill of review leading to set-aside of parentage decree interlocutory in nature and thus not appealable)

§ 160.610. Joinder of Proceedings

(a) Except as provided by Subsection (b), a proceeding to adjudicate parentage may be joined with a proceeding for adoption, termination of parental rights, possession of or access to a child, child support, divorce, annulment, or probate or administration of an estate or another appropriate proceeding.

(b) A respondent may not join a proceeding described by Subsection (a) with a proceeding to adjudicate parentage brought under Chapter 159.

Commissioners' Comment to UPA Section 610

Source: UPA (1973) § 8.

Joinder of paternity proceedings with related matters is common, especially when a child support agency seeks to establish paternity and fix child support.

Subsection (b) restricts counterclaims in those instances in which an initiating state sends a paternity suit to the responding state. Because petitioner is "appearing" in the other forum, to permit counterclaims would serve as a major deterrent to bringing such proceedings. This bar does not prevent a separate action for such matters, but there must be independent jurisdiction not arising from the petitioner's appearance in the paternity proceeding.

§ 160.611. Proceedings Before Birth

(a) A proceeding to determine parentage commenced before the birth of the child may not be concluded until after the birth of the child.

(b) In a proceeding described by Subsection (a), the following actions may be taken before the birth of the child:

(1) service of process;

(2) discovery; and

(3) except as prohibited by Section 160.502, collection of specimens for genetic testing.

Commissioners' Comment to UPA Section 611

This section recognizes that establishing a parental relationship as quickly as possible may be in the best interest of a child. To facilitate that process, some initial steps may be completed prior to the birth of the child.

§ 160.612. Child as Party; Representation

(a) A minor child is a permissible party, but is not a necessary party to a proceeding under this subchapter.

(b) The court shall appoint an amicus attorney or attorney ad litem to represent a child who is a minor or is incapacitated if the child is a party or the court finds that the interests of the child are not adequately represented.

Commissioners' Comment to UPA Section 612

Consistent with § 603, this section rejects the view that the child necessarily has independent standing in a parentage proceeding. On the other hand, if the court determines that the child in fact does have a position at variance with all the other litigants, an attorney may be appointed to represent that interest.

§§ 160.613 to 160.620. [Blank]

§ 160.621. Admissibility of Results of Genetic Testing; Expenses

(a) Except as otherwise provided by Subsection (c), a report of a genetic testing expert is admissible as evidence of the truth of the facts asserted in the report. The admissibility of the report is not affected by whether the testing was performed:

(1) voluntarily or under an order of the court or a support enforcement agency; or

(2) before or after the date of commencement of the proceeding.

(b) A party objecting to the results of genetic testing may call one or more genetic testing experts to testify in person or by telephone, videoconference, deposition, or another method approved by the court. Unless otherwise ordered by the court, the party offering the testimony bears the expense for the expert testifying.

(c) If a child has a presumed, acknowledged, or adjudicated father, the results of genetic testing are inadmissible to adjudicate parentage unless performed:

(1) with the consent of both the mother and the presumed, acknowledged, or adjudicated father; or

(2) under an order of the court under Section 160.502.

(d) Copies of bills for genetic testing and for prenatal and postnatal health care for the mother and child that are furnished to the adverse party on or before the 10th day before the date of a hearing are admissible to establish:

(1) the amount of the charges billed; and

(2) that the charges were reasonable, necessary, and customary.

Commissioners' Comment to UPA Section 621

Source: 42 U.S.C. § 666(a)(5)(F)(ii); UPA (1973) §§ 10,13.

Justification for additional testing is provided by Subsection (a). If the objecting party can state with specificity the grounds for rejecting a genetic test, and those grounds cannot be clarified under Article 5, retesting should be ordered. For example, if the chain of custody is seriously flawed, or the testing laboratory is not accredited, errors of this sort may be corrected by collecting new specimens and repeating the testing. Unlike the samples collected in a potential criminal proceeding which cannot be replaced, such as a blood alcohol test, the samples in a paternity proceedings remain the same no matter when, or how often, the samples are collected. Any flaw in the original test can be corrected by collection of new samples and additional testing of the individuals.

§ 160.622. Consequences of Declining Genetic Testing

(a) An order for genetic testing is enforceable by contempt.

(b) A court may adjudicate parentage contrary to the position of an individual whose paternity is being determined on the grounds that the individual declines to submit to genetic testing as ordered by the court.

(c) Genetic testing of the mother of a child is not a prerequisite to testing the child and a man whose paternity is being determined. If the mother is unavailable or declines to submit to genetic testing, the court may order the testing of the child and each man whose paternity is being adjudicated.

Commissioners' Comment to UPA Section 622

Source: UPA (1973) § 10.

§ 160.623. Admission of Paternity Authorized

(a) A respondent in a proceeding to adjudicate parentage may admit to the paternity of a child by filing a pleading to that effect or by admitting paternity under penalty of perjury when making an appearance or during a hearing.

(b) If the court finds that the admission of paternity satisfies the requirements of this section and that there is no reason to question the admission, the court shall render an order adjudicating the child to be the child of the man admitting paternity.

Commissioners' Comment to UPA Section 623

Source: 42 U.S.C. 666(a)(5)(D)(i)(II).

§ 160.624. Temporary Order

(a) In a proceeding under this subchapter, the court shall render a temporary order for child support for a child if the order is appropriate and the individual ordered to pay child support:

(1) is a presumed father of the child;

(2) is petitioning to have his paternity adjudicated;

(3) is identified as the father through genetic testing under Section 160.505;

(4) is an alleged father who has declined to submit to genetic testing;

(5) is shown by clear and convincing evidence to be the father of the child; or

(6) is the mother of the child.

(b) A temporary order may include provisions for the possession of or access to the child as provided by other laws of this state.

Commissioners' Comment to UPA Section 624

Source: UIFSA (1996) § 401; 42 U.S.C. 666(a)(5)(J).

§§ 160.625 to 160.630. [Blank]

§ 160.631. Rules for Adjudication of Paternity

(a) The court shall apply the rules stated in this section to adjudicate the paternity of a child.

(b) The paternity of a child having a presumed, acknowledged, or adjudicated father may be disproved only by admissible results of genetic testing excluding that man as the father of the child or identifying another man as the father of the child.

(c) Unless the results of genetic testing are admitted to rebut other results of genetic testing, the man identified as the father of a child under Section 160.505 shall be adjudicated as being the father of the child.

(d) Unless the results of genetic testing are admitted to rebut other results of genetic testing, a man excluded as the father of a child by genetic testing shall be adjudicated as not being the father of the child.

(e) If the court finds that genetic testing under Section 160.505 does not identify or exclude a man as the father of a child, the court may not dismiss the proceeding. In that event, the results of genetic testing and other evidence are admissible to adjudicate the issue of paternity.

Commissioners' Comment to UPA Section 631

Source: UPA (1973) § 14.

This section establishes the controlling supremacy of admissible genetic test results in the adjudication of paternity. Other matters such as statute of limitations, equitable estoppel and res judicata may preclude the matter from reaching trial or the court denying genetic testing. However, if test results are admissible, those results control unless other test results create a conflict rebutting the admitted results.

Paragraph (3) is included to ensure that the fact a genetic test does not reach the 99% level decreed in Section 505 will not be perceived as an indicator of an exclusion of paternity. Although test results that do not reach that level do not create a presumption of paternity, the testing should be evaluated as an indicator of paternity along with the other evidence of paternity presented in the proceeding. Presumably expert testimony will be required to provide information about the measure of the weight of a test that does not achieve "at least a 99 percent probability of paternity, using a prior probability of 0.50, as calculated by using the combined paternity index obtained in the testing, and a combined paternity index of at least 100 to 1."

The inclusion of the first clause in paragraph (4) indicates that although a genetic testing exclusion of paternity can be absolute, errors (and sometimes fraud) may occur in testing. Some courts have imposed a rule that a party must first show the test is in error before ordering another test. This imposes an impossible burden because the only accurate method to show that a test is in error is to repeat the testing. Without this clause, some litigants might argue that once an exclusion is obtained it is absolute and no other test can be ordered, even when the first test is shown to be wrong.

---

§ 160.632. Jury Prohibited

The court shall adjudicate paternity of a child without a jury.

Commissioners' Comment to UPA Section 632

Source: 42 U.S.C. § 666(a)(5)(I), requiring state law to provide that "parties to an action to establish paternity are not entitled to trial by jury. . . . "

UPA (1973) § 14[(d)] prohibited jury trials in parentage proceedings on the basis that "The use of a jury is not desirable in the emotional atmosphere of cases of this nature." Congress agreed when it enacted an effectively identical prohibition in PRWORA (1996).

---

§ 160.633. Hearings; Inspection of Records

(a) A proceeding under this subchapter is open to the public as in other civil cases.

(b) Papers and records in a proceeding under this subchapter are available for public inspection.

Commissioners' Comment to UPA Section 633

Source: UPA (1973) § 20.

UPA (1973) § 20 was concerned with the privacy of the parties in a paternity proceeding and required closure of the proceedings. The high caseload and the desensitizing of such proceedings, however, lead to the conclusion that mandating closure of the proceedings is no longer appropriate.

---

§ 160.634. Order on Default

The court shall issue an order adjudicating the paternity of a man who:

(1) after service of process, is in default; and

(2) is found by the court to be the father of a child.

Commissioners' Comment to UPA Section 634

Source: 42 U.S.C. 666(a)(5)(H).

---

§ 160.635. Dismissal for Want of Prosecution

The court may issue an order dismissing a proceeding commenced under this chapter for want of prosecution only without prejudice. An order of dismissal for want of prosecution purportedly with prejudice is void and has only the effect of a dismissal without prejudice.

Commissioners' Comment to UPA Section 635

The child's right to have a determination of paternity is fundamental. This section confirms this right by declaring that the delinquency of another person in prosecuting such a proceeding may not permanently preclude the ultimate conclusion of that determination.

---

§ 160.636. Order Adjudicating Parentage; Costs

(a) The court shall render an order adjudicating whether a man alleged or claiming to be the father is the parent of the child.

(b) An order adjudicating parentage must identify the child by name and date of birth.

(c) Except as otherwise provided by Subsection (d), the court may assess filing fees, reasonable attorney's fees, fees for genetic testing, other costs, and necessary travel and other reasonable expenses incurred in a proceeding under this subchapter. Attorney's fees awarded by the court may be paid directly to the attorney. An attorney who is awarded attorney's fees may enforce the order in the attorney's own name.

(d) The court may not assess fees, costs, or expenses against the support enforcement agency of this state or another state, except as provided by other law.

(e) On request of a party and for good cause shown, the court may order that the name of the child be changed.

(f) If the order of the court is at variance with the child's birth certificate, the court shall order the bureau of vital statistics to issue an amended birth record.

(g) On a finding of parentage, the court may order retroactive child support as provided by Chapter 154 and, on a proper showing, order a party to pay an equitable portion of all of the prenatal and postnatal health care expenses of the mother and the child.

(h) In rendering an order for retroactive child support under this section, the court shall use the child support guidelines provided by Chapter 154, together with any relevant factors.

Commissioners' Comment to UPA Section 636

Source: UIFSA (1996) § 313; UPA (1973) §§ 15, 16; 23.

The UPA (1973) attempted to do more than merely establish parentage. For example, UPA (1973) § 15 provided for a wide range of court orders to be made relating to the child's support, custody, guardianship, visitation privileges, as well as to the payment by the father of the mother's expenses of pregnancy and confinement. This Act leaves such matters to other state law. Only in instances where other state law is likely to be inadequate does this Act specify special treatment for litigants, For example, Subsections (c) and (d) may be required because ordinary civil litigation probably does not provide for the court to apportion the costs of litigation among the parties.

---

§ 160.637. Binding Effect of Determination of Parentage

(a) Except as otherwise provided by Subsection (b) or Section 160.316, a determination of parentage is binding on:

(1) all signatories to an acknowledgment or denial of paternity as provided by Subchapter D; and

(2) all parties to an adjudication by a court acting under circumstances that satisfy the jurisdictional requirements of Section 159.201.

(b) A child is not bound by a determination of parentage under this chapter unless:

(1) the determination was based on an unrescinded acknowledgment of paternity and the acknowledgment is consistent with the results of genetic testing;

(2) the adjudication of parentage was based on a finding consistent with the results of genetic testing and the consistency is declared in the determination or is otherwise shown; or

(3) the child was a party or was represented in the proceeding determining parentage by an attorney ad litem.

(c) In a proceeding to dissolve a marriage, the court is considered to have made an adjudication of the parentage of a child if the court acts under circumstances that satisfy the jurisdictional requirements of Section 159.201, and the final order:

(1) expressly identifies the child as "a child of the marriage" or "issue of the marriage" or uses similar words indicating that the husband is the father of the child; or

(2) provides for the payment of child support for the child by the husband unless paternity is specifically disclaimed in the order.

(d) Except as otherwise provided by Subsection (b), a determination of parentage may be a defense in a subsequent proceeding seeking to adjudicate parentage by an individual who was not a party to the earlier proceeding.

(e) A party to an adjudication of paternity may challenge the adjudication only under the laws of this state relating to appeal, the vacating of judgments, or other judicial review.

Commissioners' Comment to UPA Section 637

A considerable amount of litigation involves exactly who is bound and who is not bound by a final order determining parentage. This section codifies rules regarding the effect of such orders. Subsection (a) provides that, if the order is issued under standards of personal jurisdiction of the UIFSA (1996), the order is binding on all parties to the proceeding. This solves the problem of an order issued without the appropriate jurisdiction, as would be the case of a divorce based on status jurisdiction in which the court lacked the requisite personal jurisdiction over a nonresident party.

Subsection (b) partially resolves the question whether a child is bound by the terms of the order. UPA (1973) required that the child be made a party to a parentage proceeding, and be bound. However, the 1973 Act did not address whether a divorce decree had a legal impact on paternity. A majority of jurisdictions holds that the child is not bound by the divorce decree because the child was not a party to the proceeding. A minority of states holds that the child is bound by the order and that the child is in privity with the parents. In its present formulation, this subsection adopts the majority rule, which does not bind the child during minority unless the parentage order is based on genetic testing or the child was represented by an ad litem.

Subsection (c) resolves whether a divorce decree constitutes a finding of paternity. This subsection provides that a decree is a determination of paternity if the decree states that the child was born of the marriage or grants the husband visitation or custody, or orders support. This is the majority rule in American jurisprudence.

Subsection (d) gives protection to third parties who may claim benefit of an earlier determination of parentage

Finally, the section is silent on whether state IV–D agencies are bound by prior determinations of parentage. This controversial issue is left to other state law. Similarly, issues of collateral attack on final judgments are to be resolved by recourse to other state law, as in civil proceedings generally.

SUBCHAPTER H. CHILD OF ASSISTED REPRODUCTION

Commissioners' Prefatory Note to Subchapter H

Medical science has developed a wide range of assisted reproductive technologies, often referred to as ARTS, which enable childless couples to become parents. Thousands of children are born in the United States each year as the result of ARTS. If a married couple uses their own eggs and sperm to conceive a child born by the wife, the parentage of the child is straightforward. The wife is the mother—by gestation and genetics, the husband is the father—by genetics and presumption, and, insofar as UPA (2000) is concerned, neither fits the definition of a "donor."

If, using assisted reproduction, a wife gives birth to a child conceived using sperm from a man other than her husband, she is the mother and her husband is the presumed father. However, the man providing the sperm might assert his biological paternity, or the husband might seek to rebut the martial presumption of paternity by proving through genetic testing that he is not the genetic father. As was the case in UPA (1973), it is necessary for UPA (2000) to establish the parentage of a child born under these circumstances.

Similarly, assisted reproduction may involve the eggs from a woman other than the wife—perhaps using the husband's sperm, perhaps not. In either event, the Act must clearly exclude the egg donor from claiming maternity. Theoretically, it is even possible that absent legislation the wife could attempt to deny maternity based on her lack of genetic relationship.

Finally, a very common ARTS procedure mixes sperm and eggs to form a pre-zygote that is then frozen for future use. If the couple later divorce or one of them dies, the disposition of these pre-zygotes can be a potential problem on which courts need guidance.

CLE/Leading Publications

Charles P. Kindregan & Maureen Mcbrien, *Assisted Reproductive Technology: A Lawyer's Guide to Emerging Law & Science* (ABA 2nd ed., 2010)

Reaping the harvest: ownership of eggs and sperm. Charles R. Hodges, 2010 Adv. Fam. L.

Drafting for parentage actions: surrogacy and gestational agreements. Ellan A. Yarrell. 2008 Adv. Fam. L. Drafting

Assisted reproduction traps. Ellen A. Yarrell, 2008 Adv. Fam. L.

Clarifying the law of ART: the new American Bar Association Model Act Governing Assisted Reproductive Technology, Charles P. Kindregan & Steven H. Snyder, 42 Fam. L.Q. 203 (2008)

American Bar Association Model Act Governing Assisted Reproductive Technology (February 2008), 42 Fam. L.Q. 171 (2008)

The Quest for the Golden Egg: Gamete Market Reform through Regulation, Marie E. McGrath. 2008-4 (Winter) FAM. L. SEC. REP.

A practical guide to gestational agreements, A.R.T. and adoption issues, Michael J. Heard M.D., F.A., Honorable Cheryl Lee Shannon, Donald R. Royall, Ellen A. Yarrell, 2007 ADV. FAM. L.

The Uniform Parentage Act: will the real parents stand up? Angela Pence England, 2007 U.T. DEFINITIVE SAPCR

Leading Cases

In re Sullivan, 157 S.W.3d 911 (Tex. App.—Houston [14th Dist.] 2005, orig. proceeding) (man furnishing sperm for artificial insemination with intent to be child's father has standing to adjudicate parentage)

In re M.C., 65 S.W.3d 188 (Tex. App.—Amarillo 2001, no pet.) (wife entitled to contest husband's claim of ratification of assisted conception of twins born to her during marriage)

§ 160.701. Scope of Subchapter

This subchapter applies only to a child conceived by means of assisted reproduction.

Commissioners' Comment to UPA Section 701

Article 7 applies only to children born as the result of assisted reproduction technologies; a child conceived by sexual intercourse is not covered by this article, irrespective of the alleged intent of the parties. The bracketed clause relates to gestational agreements under Article 8. If a state enacts Article 8, the brackets should be removed. If a state does not enact Article 8, the bracketed subsection should be omitted.

§ 160.702. Parental Status of Donor

A donor is not a parent of a child conceived by means of assisted reproduction.

Commissioners' Comment to UPA Section 702

Source: UPA (1973) § 5(b); USCACA (1988) § 4(a).

If a child is conceived as the result of assisted reproduction, this section clarifies that a donor (whether of sperm or egg) is not a parent of the resulting child. The donor can neither sue to establish parental rights, nor be sued and required to support the resulting child. In sum, donors are eliminated from the parental equation.

This act does not deal with many of the complex and serious legal problems raised by the practice of assisted reproduction. Issues such as ownership and disposition of embryos, regulation of the medical procedures, insurance coverage, etc., are left to other statutes or common law. Only the issue of parentage falls within the purview of this Act. This was also the case in UPA (1973), which wholly deferred speaking on the subject except to insure the husband's paternal responsibility when he gave his consent to what was then called "artificial insemination" of his wife (now known in the scientific community as "intrauterine insemination").

This act governs the parentage issues in all cases in which the birth mother is also the intended mother of the child. It also insures that if the mother is a married woman, her husband will be the father of the child if he gives his consent to assisted reproduction by his wife, no matter which aspect of the technology is utilized. UPA (1973) § 5(b) specified that a male donor would not be considered the father of a child born of artificial insemination if the sperm was provided to a licensed physician for use in artificial insemination of a married woman other than the donor's wife. The Act does not continue the requirement that the donor provide the sperm to a licensed physician.

This section of UPA (2000) further opts not to limit nonparenthood of a donor to situations in which the donor provides sperm for assisted reproduction by a married woman. This requirement is not realistic in light of present practices in the field of assisted reproduction. Instead, donors are to be shielded from parenthood in all situations in which either a married woman or a single woman conceives a child through assisted reproduction. If a married woman bears a child of assisted reproduction using a donor's sperm, the donor will not be the father in any event. Her husband will be the father unless and until the husband's lack of consent to the assisted reproduction is proven within [four years in Texas] of his learning of the birth, *see* § 705, *infra*. This provides certainty of nonparentage for prospective donors. The comment to USCACA § 4(a) states that "nonparenthood is also provided for those donors who provide sperm for assisted reproduction by unmarried women." Under those circumstances—called a "relatively rare situation" in the 1988 comment—"the child would have no legally recognized father." This result is retained in UPA (2000), although the frequency of unmarried women using assisted reproduction appears to have grown significantly since 1988.

The definition of "donor" in Section 102(8), *supra*, includes persons who provide either sperm or eggs for assisted reproduction. Thus, if a woman provides an egg for assisted reproduction that results in another woman bearing the child, the egg donor is not the child's mother. This does not create a burden on the child because § 201(a)(1), *supra*, declares the general rule that the woman who gives birth to a child is that child's mother. It is clear, however, that a wife who provides eggs for her own conception and a husband who provides sperm for use by his wife in assisted reproduction are not "donors" as defined in Section 102(8).

Editors' Comment

Insofar as unmarried men are concerned, the days are over for the "turkey baster" supplying of sperm for intrauterine insemination to become a donor/father (nothing artificial about that). *See* § 160.7031, *infra*.

---

§ 160.703. Husband's Paternity of Child of Assisted Reproduction

If a husband provides sperm for or consents to assisted reproduction by his wife as provided by Section 160.704, he is the father of a resulting child.

Commissioners' Comment to UPA Section 703

Source: UPA (1973) § 5; USCACA (1988) §§ 1, 3.

The presumptive paternity of the husband of a married woman who bears a child through assisted reproduction reflects a concern for the best interests of the children of assisted reproduction. Of course, a husband who provides sperm for use by his wife in assisted reproduction is the father of any resulting child born to the wife. A similar result is mandated if his sperm is not used when he consents to assisted reproduction by his wife, *see* § 704.

Any uncertainty concerning the identity of the father of such a child ought to be shouldered by the married woman's husband rather than by the child. Thus, the husband (but not someone acting on his behalf, such as a guardian, administrator or executor) has the obligation to file an action aimed at denying paternity through lack of consent to the assisted reproduction rather than the child or mother having an obligation to prove the husband's paternity.

By designating the husband of a woman who bears a child through assisted reproduction as the father, it is intended that he will be considered the father for purposes of any cause of action that arises before the birth of the child. Thus, for example, he would be the father under any state law authorizing a wrongful death action for the death of an unborn child during pregnancy.

---

§ 160.7031. Unmarried Man's Paternity of Child of Assisted Reproduction

(a) If an unmarried man, with the intent to be the father of a resulting child, provides sperm to a licensed physician and consents to the use of that sperm for assisted reproduction by an unmarried woman, he is the father of a resulting child.

(b) Consent by an unmarried man who intends to be the father of a resulting child in accordance with this section must be in a record signed by the man and the unmarried woman and kept by a licensed physician.

Editors' Comment

Insofar as unmarried men and unmarried women are concerned, under this statute their formal agreement determines their status toward the child with certainty. On the other hand, the legal results of the so called "turkey baster" method for supplying sperm for the would be mother to complete intrauterine insemination is settled, but left in a totally indefinite condition that may be decided later by the unilateral decision of one of the participants. The parties to informal ART may, or may not be in the child's life, and the life of the other party, without regard to a previous oral agreement (or probably a written contract for that matter). The issue of standing for a man claiming to be a donor/father has been resolved after two appellate courts reached opposite decisions, compare *In re* H.C.S, 219 S.W.3d 33 (Tex. App.—San Antonio, 2006) (man who provided sperm labeled a "donor" who lacks standing to pursue paternity), *with In re* Sullivan, 157 S.W.3d 911 (Tex. App.—Houston [14th Dist.] 2005, mand. motion denied) (same facts, man allowed to pursue genetic claim of paternity). The statute clearly chooses *Sullivan* as the correct decision—if the strictures of the procedure set forth in the statute are not followed.

Henceforth, the only certain process for a man to guarantee that he will be a parent must include proceeding with ART through a licensed physician, who not only will perform the intrauterine insemination, but also will keep the paperwork of the agreement of the participants in a file cabinet. The other side of the coin is equally guaranteed; the only method for a man to be a "donor," and not a parent, is to adhere to the terms of this statute. This statute does not create an equal rights problem; each party to the informal method of ART takes the risk that their "understanding" will be rejected by the other party. Thus, the only way the mother can ensure that a male sperm provider will not be an unwanted participant in her life, and the life of her child, is to adhere to the process described above. Also note, contrary to the terminology used in *H.C.S.*, the informal male is not a "donor," but a potential litigant in a paternity suit.

§ 160.704. Consent to Assisted Reproduction

(a) Consent by a married woman to assisted reproduction must be in a record signed by the woman and her husband and kept by a licensed physician. This requirement does not apply to the donation of eggs by a married woman for assisted reproduction by another woman.

(b) Failure by the husband to sign a consent required by Subsection (a) before or after the birth of the child does not preclude a finding that the husband is the father of a child born to his wife if the wife and husband openly treated the child as their own.

Commissioners' Comment to UPA Section 704

Source: UPA (1973) § 5; UPC (1993) § 2–114(c).

Subsection (a) continues the requirement that the husband consent to all forms of assisted reproduction. However, the wife is exempted from obtaining her husband's consent if she is acting as an egg donor for another woman.

Subsection (b) provides that even If a husband did not consent to assisted reproduction, he may nonetheless be found to be the father of a child born through that means if he and his wife openly treat the child as their own. This principle is taken from the UNIFORM PROBATE CODE (1993) section cited above, which provides that neither natural parent (nor that natural parent's kindred) inherit from or through a child unless that natural parent, mother or father, has openly treated the child as his or hers and has not refused to support the child. The latter phrase was not carried forward to Subsection (b).

Leading Case

K.B. v. N.B., 811 S.W.2d 634 (Tex. App.—San Antonio 1991, writ denied) (husband's ratification of artificial insemination by conduct substitutes for written consent)

§ 160.705. Limitation on Husband's Dispute of Paternity

(a) Except as otherwise provided by Subsection (b), the husband of a wife who gives birth to a child by means of assisted reproduction may not challenge his paternity of the child unless:

(1) before the fourth anniversary of the date of learning of the birth of the child he commences a proceeding to adjudicate his paternity; and

(2) the court finds that he did not consent to the assisted reproduction before or after the birth of the child.

(b) A proceeding to adjudicate paternity may be maintained at any time if the court determines that:

(1) the husband did not provide sperm for or, before or after the birth of the child, consent to assisted reproduction by his wife;

(2) the husband and the mother of the child have not cohabited since the probable time of assisted reproduction; and

(3) the husband never openly treated the child as his own.

(c) The limitations provided by this section apply to a marriage declared invalid after assisted reproduction.

Commissioners' Comment to UPA Section 705

Source: USCACA (1988) § 3; UPC (1993) § 2–114(c).

Subsection (a) provides for a challenge to a husband's presumed paternity if the conception of the child was through assisted reproduction not consented to by the husband before or after the birth of the child. If a proceeding to establish nonpaternity is timely filed and the husband's lack of consent is demonstrated, the child will be without a legally-recognized father because the sperm donor is not the father under § 702, *supra*. Because the filing of such a nonpaternity proceeding is permitted within [four years in Texas] of the husband's learning of the child's birth, the period of uncertainty concerning the identity of the child's father will be longer than [four years in Texas] in a situation in which an absent husband is not immediately made aware of the child's birth.

Subsection (b) provides an exception to the [four years in Texas] time limit if the husband's sperm was not used, the couple has not cohabited since the probable time of the use of assisted reproduction, and the husband has never openly treated the child as his own.

---

§ 160.706. Effect of Dissolution of Marriage

(a) If a marriage is dissolved before the placement of eggs, sperm, or embryos, the former spouse is not a parent of the resulting child unless the former spouse consented in a record kept by a licensed physician that if assisted reproduction were to occur after a divorce the former spouse would be a parent of the child.

(b) The consent of a former spouse to assisted reproduction may be withdrawn by that individual in a record kept by a licensed physician at any time before the placement of eggs, sperm, or embryos.

Commissioners' Comment to UPA Section 706

This section is entirely new, but is derived from the policy stated in Section 707. If there is to be no liability for a child conceived after death, then there should be no liability for a child conceived or implanted after divorce. If the wife proceeds with assisted reproduction after a divorce, the former husband is *not the legal parent* of the resulting child unless he has consented in a record to post-divorce assisted reproduction. In such a case, the child will have a legal mother under Section 201(a)(1). The child will have a genetic father, but not a legal father. Intention, rather than biology, is the controlling factor. The section is intended to encourage careful drafting of assisted reproduction agreements. The attorney and the parties themselves should discuss the issue and clarify their intent before a problem arises.

This Act does not attempt to resolve issues as to control of frozen embryos following dissolution of marriage. Those matters are left to other state laws, usually in the context of settlement of divorce and regulation of health care facilities.

§ 160.707. Parental Status of Deceased Spouse

If a spouse dies before the placement of eggs, sperm, or embryos, the deceased spouse is not a parent of the resulting child unless the deceased spouse consented in a record kept by a licensed physician that if assisted reproduction were to occur after death the deceased spouse would be a parent of the child.

Commissioners' Comment to UPA Section 707

Source: USCACA (1988) § 4.

Absent consent in a record, the death of a spouse whose genetic material is subsequently used either in conceiving an embryo or in implanting an already existing embryo into a womb ends the potential parenthood of the deceased. This section is designed primarily to avoid the problems of intestate succession which could arise if the posthumous use of a person's genetic material could lead to the deceased being determined to be a parent. Of course, a spouse who wants to explicitly provide for such children in his or her will may do so.

SUBCHAPTER I. GESTATIONAL AGREEMENTS

Editors' Note: *All of the amendments to Subchapter I have the following legislative history:*

History: Enacted by 78th Legis., Reg. Sess. (2003), H.B. 729, eff. Sept. 1, 2003, and "applies to a motion or other request for relief made in a parentage or paternity proceeding that is commenced on or after the effective date of this Act. A motion or other request for relief made in a parentage or paternity proceeding commenced before the effective date of this Act is governed by the law in effect at the time the proceeding was commenced, and the former law is continued in effect for that purpose."

Commissioners' Prefatory Note to Subchapter I

The longstanding shortage of adoptable children in this country has caused many persons to enlist a gestational mother (previously known as a surrogate) in order to have a child of their own genetic making. Assisted reproduction, as regulated by Subchapter H, involves two people who wish to become parents. In contrast, a gestational agreement (previously known as a surrogacy agreement) involves at least three parties; the couple who wish to become parents (the intended mother and father), and a woman who agrees to bear a child for them through the use of assisted reproduction (the gestational mother). Additional persons may be involved. For example, if the proposed gestational mother is married, her husband must be included in the agreement to dispense with his presumptive paternity of a child born to his wife. An egg donor or a sperm donor, or both, may be involved, although neither will be joined as a party to the agreement. Thus, by definition, a child born pursuant to a gestational agreement needs to have his or her *maternity* as well as *paternity* clarified.

The subject of gestational agreements was last addressed by the National Conference of Commissioners on Uniform State Laws in 1988 with the adoption of USCACA (1988). Because some Commissioners believed that such agreements should be prohibited, while others believed that such agreements should be allowed, but regulated, USCACA offered two alternatives on the subject: to regulate such activities through a judicial review process or to void such contracts. Only two states have adopted either version of the Act; Virginia chose to regulate such agreements, while North

Dakota opted to void them. In the twelve years since the promulgation drafting of USCACA, approximately one-half of the states have developed statutory or case law on the issue. Of those, about one-half have recognized such agreements, and the other half has rejected them. In states rejecting such agreements, the legal status of children born pursuant to a gestational agreement is uncertain. Also troubling is the question of whether full faith and credit applies if an agreement was entered into in a state that does recognize such an agreement to be valid. The remaining states do not have adequate laws on the subject.

Voiding or criminalizing gestational agreements will force individuals to find friendly legal forums for the process, which raises a host of legal issues. For example, a couple may return to their home state with a child born as the consequence of a gestational agreement entered into in a state recognizing that agreement. This presents a full faith and credit question if their home state has a statute declaring gestational agreements to be void.

Despite these legal issues, thousands of children are born each year pursuant to gestational agreements. One thing ought to be clear; a child born under these circumstances is entitled to have its status clarified. Nonetheless, in some states, the legislature may feel that it is not yet ready to tackle the issue. For that reason, this article is bracketed: that is, it is optional. For states ready to deal with the issue, the Act provides a model that meets their needs. Those feeling that the issue is still too unsettling may omit this part of UPA(2000) without doing damage to the other provisions.

Despite the lack of acceptance of USCACA, the Conference again finds that the subject is increasingly worthy of legislative attention. Therefore, with some modest modifications, the subject is included in UPA (2000). A relatively minor grammatical change in this version is the elimination of the term "surrogate," which nonetheless has a substantial significance. First, to label a woman who bears a child a "surrogate" does not comply with the dictionary definition of the term under any construction, to wit: "a person appointed to act in the place of another" or "something serving as a substitute." This was especially true when "surrogate" included a woman who supplied both "egg and womb," that is, who is both gestational and genetic mother. The term was eliminated because the assisted reproduction community has generally rejected this pattern to avoid the psychological and legal issues that arise when the "surrogate" changes her mind about the agreement. Further, and of equal importance, the term "surrogate" has acquired a significant negative connotation in American society, which confuses rather than enlightens the discussion.

The single term "gestational mother" is both more accurate and more inclusive, to wit, it covers a woman who, through assisted reproduction, provides the gestational heritage of a child to be raised by the intended parents. A woman who supplies both functions, gestational and genetic, or who only performs the gestational function, is included in the term. The practice of having a woman perform both functions is generally strongly disfavored by the assisted reproduction community. Experience has shown that the gestational mother's genetic link to the child sometimes creates additional emotional and psychological problems in enforcing a gestational agreement.

UPA (2000) takes the position that entering into a gestational agreement is a significant legal act that should be reviewed by a court, just as an adoption is judicially reviewed. The procedure established generally follows that of the 1988 Act, but departs in several important ways. First, nonvalidated gestational agreements are unenforceable (not void), thereby providing a strong incentive for the participants to seek judicial scrutiny. Second, the restriction under USCACA that at least one of the intended parents would be genetically related to the child born of the gestational agreement has been eliminated. Third, individuals who enter into nonvalidated gestational agreements and later refuse to adopt the resulting child may be liable for support of the child.

Assisted reproduction facilities and numerous other entities are involved in the gestational agreement. Internet sites are omnipresent promoting such agreements. As of December, 2000, states take a variety of approaches to gestational agreements: eleven states allow such agreements by statutes or case law; six states void such agreements by statute; eight states statutorily ban compensation to the gestational mother; and two states have judicially refused to recognize such agreements.

Although legal recognition of gestational agreements is undoubtedly controversial, the plain fact is that medical science has raced ahead of the law without heed to the views of the general public—or legislators. Courts have recently come to acknowledge this reality when forced to render decisions regarding collaborative reproduction, noting that artificial insemination, gestational carriers, cloning and gene splicing are part of the present, as well as of the future. One court predicted that even if all forms of assisted reproduction were outlawed in a particular state, its courts would still be called upon to decide on the identity of the lawful parents of a child resulting from those procedures undertaken in less restrictive states.

The intractable issue remains; who must provide the child with maintenance and support? In its opinion, one court stated:

> Again we must call on the Legislature to sort out the parental rights and responsibilities of those involved in artificial reproduction. No matter what one thinks of artificial insemination, traditional and gestational surrogacy (in all of its permutations) and—as now appears in the not-too-distant future, cloning and even gene splicing—courts are still going to be faced with the problem of determining lawful parentage. A child cannot be ignored. Even if all the means of artificial reproduction were outlawed with draconian criminal penalties visited on the doctors and parties involved, courts would still be called upon to decide who the lawful parents are and who—other than the taxpayers—is obligated to provide maintenance and support for the child. These cases will not go away. Again we must call on the Legislature to sort out the parental rights and responsibilities of those involved in artificial reproduction.... Courts can continue to make decisions on an ad hoc basis without necessarily imposing some grand scheme.... Or, the Legislature can act to impose a broader order which, even though it might not be perfect on a case-by-case basis, would bring some predictability to those who seek to make use of artificial reproductive techniques.

In re Buzzanca, 72 Cal. Rptr. 2d 280, 61 Cal. App. 4th 1410 (1998).

Editors' Comment

The Texas adoption of legislation governing gestational agreements is an important advancement for couples desiring to use such methods for having children. The Texas statutes depart in three important ways from the Uniform Parentage Act as amended in 2002. First, Texas restricts the use of validated agreements to married couples. Secondly, the intended mother must demonstrate that she is unable to give birth to a child. Finally, the gestational mother may not contribute her own egg for the embryo, and therefore the gestational mother is not genetically linked to the child.

See CLE/Other Legal Publications cited immediately before § 160.701, *supra*.

---

§ 160.751. Definition

In this subchapter, "gestational mother" means a woman who gives birth to a child conceived under a gestational agreement.

§ 160.752. Scope of Subchapter; Choice of Law

(a) Notwithstanding any other provision of this chapter or another law, this subchapter authorizes an agreement between a woman and the intended parents of a child in which the woman relinquishes all rights as a parent of a child conceived by means of assisted reproduction and that provides that the intended parents become the parents of the child.

(b) This subchapter controls over any other law with respect to a child conceived under a gestational agreement under this subchapter.

§ 160.753. Establishment of Parent–Child Relationship

(a) Notwithstanding any other provision of this chapter or another law, the mother-child relationship exists between a woman and a child by an adjudication confirming the woman as a parent of the child born to a gestational mother under a gestational agreement if the gestational agreement is validated under this subchapter or enforceable under other law, regardless of the fact that the gestational mother gave birth to the child.

(b) The father-child relationship exists between a child and a man by an adjudication confirming the man as a parent of the child born to a gestational mother under a gestational agreement if the gestational agreement is validated under this subchapter or enforceable under other law.

§ 160.754. Gestational Agreement Authorized

(a) A prospective gestational mother, her husband if she is married, each donor, and each intended parent may enter into a written agreement providing that:

(1) the prospective gestational mother agrees to pregnancy by means of assisted reproduction;

(2) the prospective gestational mother, her husband if she is married, and each donor other than the intended parents, if applicable, relinquish all parental rights and duties with respect to a child conceived through assisted reproduction;

(3) the intended parents will be the parents of the child; and

(4) the gestational mother and each intended parent agree to exchange throughout the period covered by the agreement all relevant information regarding the health of the gestational mother and each intended parent.

(b) The intended parents must be married to each other. Each intended parent must be a party to the gestational agreement.

(c) The gestational agreement must require that the eggs used in the assisted reproduction procedure be retrieved from an intended parent or a donor. The gestational mother's eggs may not be used in the assisted reproduction procedure.

(d) The gestational agreement must state that the physician who will perform the assisted reproduction procedure as provided by the agreement has informed the parties to the agreement of:

(1) the rate of successful conceptions and births attributable to the procedure, including the most recent published outcome statistics of the procedure at the facility at which it will be performed;

(2) the potential for and risks associated with the implantation of multiple embryos and consequent multiple births resulting from the procedure;

(3) the nature of and expenses related to the procedure;

(4) the health risks associated with, as applicable, fertility drugs used in the procedure, egg retrieval procedures, and egg or embryo transfer procedures; and

(5) reasonably foreseeable psychological effects resulting from the procedure.

(e) The parties to a gestational agreement must enter into the agreement before the 14th day preceding the date the transfer of eggs, sperm, or embryos to the gestational mother occurs for the purpose of conception or implantation.

(f) A gestational agreement does not apply to the birth of a child conceived by means of sexual intercourse.

(g) A gestational agreement may not limit the right of the gestational mother to make decisions to safeguard her health or the health of an embryo.

Commissioners' Comment to UPA Section 801
[Texas Family Code Section 160.754]

Source: USCACA §§ 1(3), 5, 9.

The previous uniform act on this subject, USCACA, proposed two alternatives, one of which was to declare that gestational agreements were to be void. Subsection (a) rejects that approach. The scientific state of the art and the medical facilities providing the technological capacity to utilize a woman other than the wife as the gestational mother, guarantee that such agreements will continue to be written. Subsection (a) recognizes that certainty and initiates a procedure for its regulation by a judicial officer. All the persons directly involved in the procedure must enter into a written agreement;

this includes the intended parents, the gestational mother, and her husband if she is married. In addition, if there are donors involved, they must also sign the agreement. The agreement must provide that the intended parents will be the parents of any child born pursuant to the agreement while all of the others (gestational mother, her husband, if any, and the donors, as appropriate) relinquish all rights and duties of parenthood.

Under Subsection (b), a valid gestational agreement requires the participation of two intended parents who are married to each other. Although some Commissioners raised objection to not permitting unmarried persons to agree to be intended parents in an enforceable gestational agreement, this decision continues the proscription initiated in USCACA. Given the controversial nature of these agreements, the most worthy fact circumstances meriting legal recognition is the plight of childless married couples. Note that this section simply authorizes such agreements. It does not give them effect in terms of designating parenthood, etc. In order to become enforceable, Subsection (c) demands that the agreement must be validated by the appropriate court under Section 160.756.

Subsection (e) is intended to shield these gestational agreements that include payment of the gestational mother from attack under "baby-selling" statutes that prohibit payment of money to the natural mother in adoptions.

Subsection (f) is intended to acknowledge that the gestational mother, as a pregnant woman, has a constitutionally-recognized right to decide issues regarding her health care and that of the unborn child. In other words, the intended parents have no right to demand that the gestational mother expose herself to undue medical risk.

If the conditions of this section are met, the parties may move forward to a court for approval of their agreement.

Editors' Comment

The 2002 version of the Uniform Parentage Act is not restricted to married couples, but the Texas Legislature chose to adopt the 2000 version of the Act as it pertains to gestational agreements.

---

§ 160.755. Petition to Validate Gestational Agreement

(a) The intended parents and the prospective gestational mother under a gestational agreement may commence a proceeding to validate the agreement.

(b) A person may maintain a proceeding to validate a gestational agreement only if:

(1) the prospective gestational mother or the intended parents have resided in this state for the 90 days preceding the date the proceeding is commenced;

(2) the prospective gestational mother's husband, if she is married, is joined as a party to the proceeding; and

(3) a copy of the gestational agreement is attached to the petition.

Commissioners' Comment to UPA Section 802 [Texas Family Code Section 160.755]

Source: USCACA § 6(a).

Sections 160.755 and 160.756, the core sections of this subchapter, provide for state involvement, through supervision by a court, of the gestational agreement before, during, and after the assisted reproduction process. The purpose of early involvement is to insure that the parties are appropriate for a gestational agreement, that they understand the consequences of what they are about to do, and that the best interests of a child born of the gestational agreement are considered before the arrangement is authorized. The trigger for state involvement is a petition brought by all the parties to the arrangement (including the gestational mother's husband if she is married) in which the parties seek a judicial order authorizing the assisted reproduction contemplated by their agreement. The agreement itself must be submitted to the court.

To discourage forum shopping, Subsection (b)(1) requires that the petition may only be filed to a state in which the intended parents or the gestational mother have been resident for at least 90 days.

§ 160.756. Hearing to Validate Gestational Agreement

(a) A gestational agreement must be validated as provided by this section.

(b) The court may validate a gestational agreement as provided by Subsection (c) only if the court finds that:

(1) the parties have submitted to the jurisdiction of the court under the jurisdictional standards of this chapter;

(2) the medical evidence provided shows that the intended mother is unable to carry a pregnancy to term and give birth to the child or is unable to carry the pregnancy to term and give birth to the child without unreasonable risk to her physical or mental health or to the health of the unborn child;

(3) unless waived by the court, an agency or other person has conducted a home study of the intended parents and has determined that the intended parents meet the standards of fitness applicable to adoptive parents;

(4) each party to the agreement has voluntarily entered into and understands the terms of the agreement;

(5) the prospective gestational mother has had at least one previous pregnancy and delivery and carrying another pregnancy to term and giving birth to another child would not pose an unreasonable risk to the child's health or the physical or mental health of the prospective gestational mother; and

(6) the parties have adequately provided for which party is responsible for all reasonable health care expenses associated with the pregnancy, including providing for who is responsible for those expenses if the agreement is terminated.

(c) If the court finds that the requirements of Subsection (b) are satisfied, the court may render an order validating the gestational agreement and declaring that the intended parents will be the parents of a child born under the agreement.

(d) The court may validate the gestational agreement at the court's discretion. The court's determination of whether to validate the agreement is subject to review only for abuse of discretion.

Commissioners' Comment to UPA Section 803
[Texas Family Code Section 160.756]

Source: USCACA § 6(b).

This pre-conception authorization process for a gestational agreement is roughly analogous to adoption procedures in place in most jurisdictions as of December, 2000. Just as adoption contemplates the transfer of parentage of a child from the natural to the adoptive parents, a gestational agreement involves the transfer from the gestational mother to the intended parents. UPA (2000) is designed to protect the interests of the child to be born under the gestational agreement as well as the interests of gestational mother and the intended parents. It should be noted that in contrast to USCACA (1988) § 1(3), there is no requirement that at least one of the intended parents be genetically related to the child born of a gestational agreement. Given the state of art in the science, this is an unrealistic provision as of the medical science available in 2000. Similarly, the likelihood that the gestational mother will also be the genetic mother is not directly addressed in UPA (2000), while USCACA (1988) virtually assumed that the fact pattern would be typical. Experience with the intractable problems caused by such a combination has dissuaded the majority of fertility laboratories from following that practice. *See In re Baby M.*, 537 A.2d 1227 (N.J. 1988).

Section 160.756 seeks to protect the interests of the child in several ways. The major protection of the child is the authorization procedure itself. By providing for a court order authorizing the assisted reproduction and the gestational agreement, the Act establishes closely supervised gestational arrangements to guarantee the security and well-being of the child. Once a petition has been filed, subsection (a) permits—but does not require—the court to validate a gestational agreement. If validating, the court must declare that the intended parents will be the parents of any child born pursuant to, and during the term of, the agreement.

The court must hold a hearing on the petition. Under subsection (b) the court must make six separate findings before validating the agreement. Subsection (b)(1) requires the court to insure that the 90–day residency requirement of Section 160.755 has been satisfied and that it has jurisdiction over the parties;

The intended parents, who by virtue of subsection (b)(2) are by definition unable to procreate through traditional means, have their interests protected. In addition to the very existence of the court authorization procedure which gives effect to the gestational agreement, help is provided through assurances to them that the gestational mother is capable and is knowingly entering the arrangement. There must be medical evidence that the wife is unable to bear a child or is unable to so without unreasonable risk to her or the child. The clear intent of subsection (b)(2) is to deny validation of a gestational agreement to a couple who are capable of having a child through assisted reproduction or sexual intercourse. This procedure is not created simply to allow a couple to avoid the inconvenience of a pregnancy.

Under subsection(b)(3), the court will be informed of the results of a home study of the intended parents. They must meet the standards imposed upon would-be adoptive parents.

The interests of all the parties are protected by subsection (b)(4), which is designed to protect the individuals involved from the possibility of overreaching or fraud. All must enter into the agreement voluntarily and with full knowledge of the consequences of their actions.

Subsection (b)(5) specifically requires that the court find the gestational mother has had at least one previous pregnancy and delivery. Presumably, such a finding will help insure that she fully understands the nature and experience of pregnancy. Her consent to be the gestational mother is thus with full knowledge of what she has agreed to do, including to relinquish the child born to her to the intended parents. The court must also find the contemplated pregnancy and delivery will not pose unreasonable physical or mental health risks to her. The interest of producing a healthy child is promoted by the additional required finding that the pregnancy will not be unreasonably risky to the child.

The requirement of assurance of health-care expenses until birth imposed by subsection (b)(6) further protects the gestational mother.

Subsection (d) mandates that whether or not to validate the agreement is within the discretion of the court and is subject to review only for abuse of discretion.

Section 160.756, while constructing a detailed set of requirements for the petition and the findings that must be made before an authorizing order can be issued, nowhere states the consequences of violations of the rules. Because of the variety of types of violations that could possibly occur, a bright-line rule concerning the effect of such violations is inappropriate. The question of the consequences of a failure to abide by the rules of Section 160.756 is left to a case-by-case determination. A court should be guided in making such a determination by the narrow purpose of the Act to permit gestational agreements and the equities of a particular situation. Note that Section 160.759 provides a period for termination of the agreement and vacating of the order. The discovery of a failure to abide by the rules of Section 160.756 would certainly provide the occasion for terminating the agreement. On the other hand, if a failure to abide by the rules of Section 160.756 is discovered by a party during a time when Section 160.759 termination would be permissible, failure to terminate might be an appropriate reason to estop the party from later seeking to overturn or ignore the Section 160.756 order.

§ 160.757. Inspection of Records

The proceedings, records, and identities of the parties to a gestational agreement under this subchapter are subject to inspection under the same standards of confidentiality that apply to an adoption under the laws of this state.

Commissioners' Comment to UPA Section 804 [Texas Family Code Section 160.757]

The procedures involved in this subchapter are exceptionally personal, thereby warranting protection from invasions of privacy. Adoption records provide a suitable model for these records.

§ 160.758. Continuing, Exclusive Jurisdiction

Subject to Section 152.201, a court that conducts a proceeding under this subchapter has continuing, exclusive jurisdiction of all matters arising out of the gestational agreement until the date a child born to the gestational mother during the period covered by the agreement reaches 180 days of age.

Commissioners' Comment to UPA Section 805 [Texas Family Code 160.758]

Source: USCACA § 6(e).

This section is designed to minimize the possibility of parallel litigation in different states and the consequent risk of child-napping for strategic purposes. The court that validated the gestational agreement will have authority to enforce the gestational agreement until the child is 180 days old. Note that only the parentage issues and enforcement issues are covered; collateral matters, such as custody, visitation, and child support are not contemplated as subject to the strictures of this chapter.

§ 160.759. Termination of Gestational Agreement

(a) Before a prospective gestational mother becomes pregnant by means of assisted reproduction, the prospective gestational mother, her husband if she is married, or either intended parent may terminate a gestational agreement validated under Section 160.756 by giving written notice of the termination to each other party to the agreement.

(b) A person who terminates a gestational agreement under Subsection (a) shall file notice of the termination with the court. A person having the duty to notify the court who does not notify the court of the termination of the agreement is subject to appropriate sanctions.

(c) On receipt of the notice of termination, the court shall vacate the order rendered under Section 160.756 validating the gestational agreement.

(d) A prospective gestational mother and her husband, if she is married, may not be liable to an intended parent for terminating a gestational agreement if the termination is in accordance with this section.

Commissioners' Comment to UPA Section 806 [Texas Family Code Section 160.759]

Source: USCACA § 7.

Subsection (a) permits a party to terminate a gestational agreement after the authorization order by canceling the arrangement before the pregnancy has been established. This provides for cancellation during a time when the interests of the parties would not be unduly prejudiced by termination. By definition, the procreation process has not begun. The intended parents certainly have an expectation interest during this time, but the nature of this interest is little different from that which they would have while they were attempting to create a pregnancy through traditional means. In contrast to the next subsection, termination of the agreement does not require "good cause."

Under subsection (b) a party who wishes to terminate the agreement must inform the other parties in writing, and must also file notice with the court. The court must then vacate the order validating the agreement. An individual who does not notify the court of his/her termination of the agreement is subject to sanction.

USCACA (1988) provided extensive explanation of termination of an agreement by a gestational mother who has provided the egg for the assisted reproduction. This possibility is not repeated in

UPA (2000) because it is a remote likelihood that an agreement for the gestational mother to furnish the egg will be countenanced in 2001. Assisted reproduction, as conducted as of today, does not approve that practice.

Subsection (d) provides that before pregnancy a gestational mother is not liable to the intended parents for terminating the agreement. UPA (2000) does not speak explicitly to termination of the agreement after pregnancy. Several sections deal with the issue, at least under certain described circumstances. Section 160.754 (g) recognizes that the gestational mother has plenary power to decide issues of her health and the health of the fetus. Sections 160.756(a) and 160.760 direct that the intended parents are in fact the parents of the child with an enforceable right to the possession of the child.

§ 160.760. Parentage Under Validated Gestational Agreement

(a) On the birth of a child to a gestational mother under a validated gestational agreement, the intended parents shall file a notice of the birth with the court not later than the 300th day after the date assisted reproduction occurred.

(b) After receiving notice of the birth, the court shall render an order that:

(1) confirms that the intended parents are the child's parents;

(2) requires the gestational mother to surrender the child to the intended parents, if necessary; and

(3) requires the bureau of vital statistics to issue a birth certificate naming the intended parents as the child's parents.

(c) If a person alleges that a child born to a gestational mother did not result from assisted reproduction, the court shall order that scientifically accepted parentage testing be conducted to determine the child's parentage.

(d) If the intended parents fail to file the notice required by Subsection (a), the gestational mother or an appropriate state agency may file the notice required by that subsection. On a showing that an order validating the gestational agreement was rendered in accordance with Section 160.756, the court shall order that the intended parents are the child's parents and are financially responsible for the child.

Commissioners' Comment to UPA Section 807
[Texas Family Code Section 160.760]

Source: USCACA § 8.

Under subsection (a), parentage of a child born pursuant to an approved gestational agreement within 300 days of the use of assisted reproduction is vested in the intended parents if the order under Section 160.756 is still in effect. Notice of the birth of the child must be filed by the intended parents. The court, upon receipt of the notice, shall issue an order confirming that the intended parents are the legal parents of the child and direct the issuance of a birth certificate to confirm the court's determination. If necessary, the court may also order the gestational mother to surrender the child to the intended parents.

§ 160.761. Effect of Gestational Mother's Marriage After Validation of Agreement

If a gestational mother is married after the court renders an order validating a gestational agreement under this subchapter:

(1) the validity of the gestational agreement is not affected;

(2) the gestational mother's husband is not required to consent to the agreement; and

(3) the gestational mother's husband is not a presumed father of the child born under the terms of the agreement.

Commissioners' Comment to UPA Section 808
[Texas Family Code Section 160.761]

Source: USCACA § 9.

If, after the original court order validates the gestational agreement, the gestational mother marries, the gestational agreement continues to be valid and the consent of her new husband is not required. The new husband is neither a party to the original action nor the presumed father of a resulting child, and therefore ought not be burdened with the status of parent unless he is the genetic father or chooses to adopt the child.

---

§ 160.762. Effect of Gestational Agreement That is Not Validated

(a) A gestational agreement that is not validated as provided by this subchapter is unenforceable, regardless of whether the agreement is in a record.

(b) The parent-child relationship of a child born under a gestational agreement that is not validated as provided by this subchapter is determined as otherwise provided by this chapter.

(c) A party to a gestational agreement that is not validated as provided by this subchapter who is an intended parent under the agreement may be held liable for the support of a child born under the agreement, even if the agreement is otherwise unenforceable.

(d) The court may assess filing fees, reasonable attorney's fees, fees for genetic testing, other costs, and necessary travel and other reasonable expenses incurred in a proceeding under this section. Attorney's fees awarded by the court may be paid directly to the attorney. An attorney who is awarded attorney's fees may enforce the order in the attorney's own name.

Commissioners' Comment to UPA Section 809
[Texas Family Code Section 160. 762]

Source: USCACA §§ 5(b),10.

This section distinguishes between an unenforceable agreement and a prohibited one. Given the widespread use of assisted reproductive technologies in modern society, the Act attempts only to regularize the parentage aspects of the science, not to regulate the practice of assisted reproduction. If individuals choose to ignore the protections afforded gestational agreements by the Act, parentage questions will remain when a child is born as a result of an nonvalidated gestational agreement. The Act provides no assistance to the intended parents; the gestational mother is denominated the mother irrespective of the source of the eggs. While donors of either eggs or sperm are not parents in this circumstance, subsection (c) permits the court to hold the intended parents to an obligation to support the resulting child, even though the balance of the agreement will not be enforced.

Under USCACA (1988), agreements that were not approved were declared "void." Under UPA (2000), a nonapproved agreement is declared "unenforceable." The result may be virtually the same in some instances. As under the prior Act, the gestational mother is the mother of a child conceived through assisted reproduction if the gestational agreement has not been judicially approved as provided in this article. Her husband, if he is a party to such agreement, is presumed to be the father. If the gestational mother's husband is not a party to the agreement, or if she is unmarried, paternity of the child will be left to existing law, if any. If the mother decides to keep the child, the intended parents have no recourse. If the parties agree that the intended parents will raise the child, the only method whereby they may become parents of the child will be through adoption.

---

§ 160.763. Health Care Facility Reporting Requirement

(a) The Texas Department of Health by rule shall develop and implement a confidential reporting system that requires each health care facility in this state at which assisted reproduction procedures are performed under gestational agreements to report statistics related to those procedures.

(b) In developing the reporting system, the department shall require each health care facility described by Subsection (a) to annually report:

(1) the number of assisted reproduction procedures under a gestational agreement performed at the facility during the preceding year; and

(2) the number and current status of embryos created through assisted reproduction procedures described by Subdivision (1) that were not transferred for implantation.

Editors' Comment

This section is not a provision of the Uniform Parentage Act. It was added by the Texas Legislature in order to gather reliable information on the number of gestational agreements undertaken in this state.

CHAPTER 161. TERMINATION OF THE PARENT–CHILD RELATIONSHIP

SUBCHAPTER A. GROUNDS

SUBCHAPTER B. PROCEDURES

SUBCHAPTER C. HEARING AND ORDER

Editors' Note: *In 2003 an amendment to Tex. Gov't Code § 531.001(4)(J), changed the name of the Department of Protective and Regulatory Services, a.k.a. DPRS, to its current name of the Department of Family and Protective Services, a.k.a. DFPS. This change is codified in Family Code § 261.001 and § 264.001. For legislation enacted in 2005 and thereafter, however, the Texas Legislative Council decided to correct the name of the agency only when amending or adding statutes to the Family Code that make reference to the agency, and not to make the corrections throughout the Code. Applying that general rule to the caption of a section is perhaps a minor error.*

Editors' Note: *This chapter contains guest commentary by Charles G. Childress, Clinical Professor (retired), Children's Rights Clinic, University of Texas Law School, formerly Chief*

Attorney, Field Operations, Legal Division, Texas Department of Family and Protective Services, identified as (C.G.C.).

Introductory Comment

The termination of the parent-child relationship might be called the capital punishment of civil law. It constitutes the final, irreversible severance of all legal rights and duties between a parent and child. A termination suit may arise in several very distinct, and distinguishable, contexts: (1) a private termination between one parent and the other, usually to facilitate a stepparent adoption; (2) an intrafamily termination in which relatives of the child seek to terminate the rights of allegedly culpable parents; (3) a termination by an adoption agency to facilitate the adoption of an infant, usually a child without a presumed father; and (4) intervention by the state to terminate allegedly culpable parents on grounds of the abuse or neglect of the child, or on another less frequently alleged statutory ground.

CLE/Other Legal Publications

Beyond D & E—a look at the other 18 grounds for termination of parental rights. Valeria Lee Brock, 2011 ADV. FAM. L.

Interventions in CPS cases. Robin Camille Matthews, 2011 ADV. FAM. L.

Undocumented and abused children. Pamela Kemp Parker, 2011 ADV. FAM. L.

Cross-over youth in CPS cases and juvenile cases. Dustin Rynders, 2011 ADV. FAM. L.

Case law update. Michael C. Shulman & Trevor A. Woodruff, 2010 ADV. FAM. L.

Foster children and their attorneys ad litem: Resources for Children in Care. Carole Hurley, 2010 ADV. FAM. L.

Legal ramifications of emotional abuse. Shelby Moore, 2010 ADV. FAM. L.

Parentage testing and child support in CPS cases. Alicia G. Key, 2010 ADV. FAM. L.

Selected issues in parentage and termination. Ellen A. Yarrell, 2010 ADV. FAM. L.

Representing the parent in CPS cases. Thomas E. Stanton, 2010 ADV. FAM. L.

Constitutional rights of children. Barbara J. Elias-Perciful, 2010 ADV. FAM. L.

Mediation in CPS cases: ethical considerations. Karin Bonicoro, Pam Coffey & Dale A. Rabe, Jr., 2010 ADV. FAM. L.

Navigating through CPS: concerns to anticipate. Lon M. Loveless, 2010 U.T. PARENT CHILD RELATIONSHIPS

Termination and step-parent adoptions. Janet McCullar Vavra, 2010 ADV. FAM. L. DRAFTING

AG and CPS. Frederick S. Adams, Jr. & Alicia G. Key, 2010 ADV. FAM. L. DRAFTING

Nuts and bolts of appointments, protective orders, and working with CPS. Hon. Judy Warne, Hon. Meca Walker, & Amy Allen, 2010 and 2009 SO. TEX. FAM. L. CONF.

Grounds for termination of parental rights.Luisa P. Marrerro, Michael Shulman, Trevor A. Woodruff, Duke Hooten, & Charles G. Childress, FAM. L. SECT. REP. (Fall 2009)

Termination case law update. Luisa P. Marrero, Michael Shulman, Duke Hooten, & Trevor A. Woodruff, 2009 ADV. FAM. L.

Child evidentiary issues and child testimony in CPS cases. Hon. J. Andrew Hathcock, 2009 ADV. FAM. L.

The role of the attorney ad litem on appeal: statutory and ethical duties and responsibilities. Dale A. Rabe, Jr., 2009 ADV. FAM. L.

Children and youth in court: statutory and ethical duties and responsibilities of the appointed attorney. Hon. Karin Bonicoro, 2009 ADV. FAM. L.

Ethical issues for the appointed attorney when representing children. Charles G. Childress, 2009 ADV. FAM. L.

See Accompanying CD–ROM for Additional CLE/Other Legal Publications.

Leading U.S. Supreme Court Cases

M.L.B. v. S.L.J., 519 U.S. 102, 117 S.Ct. 555 (1996) (appeal of termination of parental rights may not be conditioned on payment for trial transcript by indigent mother)

Santosky v. Kramer, 455 U.S. 745, 71 L.Ed.2d 599, 102 S.Ct. 1388 (1982) (clear and convincing evidence needed to terminate parental rights)

Lassiter v. Department of Social Services., 452 U.S. 18, 68 L.Ed.2d 640, 101 S.Ct. 2153 (1981) (no constitutional right to appointed counsel for parent)

Leading Texas Supreme Court/5th Circuit Cases

Gates v. Texas Dept. of Protective and Regulatory Services, 537 F.3d 404 (5th Cir. 2008)(Fourth Amendment applies to warrantless search by CPS in alleged abuse and neglect cases)

In re C.H.C., 331 S.W.3d 426 (Tex. 2011) (trial court erred by failing to order free appellate record to mother whose claim of indigency was uncontested by eligible party, and therefore deemed true by TRAP 20.1)

In re B.G., 317 S.W.3d 250 (Tex. 2010) (accelerated timetable for perfecting appeals of termination of parental rights under this section violated father's due process rights; failure to timely file statement of appellate points cannot be basis for denying indigent parent's right to appellate record)

In re J.H.G., 302 S.W.3d 304 (Tex. 2010) (appellate court may not consider issues not included in points of appeal; remanded on issue raised but not decided) (dismissal date is procedural, not jurisdictional); *accord, In re* Department of Family and Protective Services, 273 S.W.3d 637 (Tex. 2009).

In re J.O.A., 283 S.W.3d 336 (Tex. 2009) (15-day rule for statement of points on appeal unconstitutional as applied, due process requires right to assert ineffective assistance of counsel)

In re Texas Dept. of Family and Protective Serv., 255 S.W.3d 613 (Tex. 2008)(allegation of sexual abuse of post-pubescent girls did not warrant trial court's temporary order to remove all 468 children from allegedly polygamous FLDS ranch—return all children ordered)

In re Texas Dept. of Family and Protective Services, 210 S.W.3d 609 (Tex. 2006) (trial court should have dismissed case after one-year deadline passed—because mother had remedy by accelerated appeal, mandamus improper)

In re H.R.M., 209 S.W.3d 105 (Tex. 2006) (supreme court again validates jury verdict terminating rights of incarcerated father) (on remand termination affirmed, 2007 WL 707553)(Tex. App.—Houston [14th Dist.] 2007)

In re R.R., 209 S.W.3d 112 (Tex. 2006) (default termination decree reversed, new trial granted re *Craddock* test).

In re J.P.B., 180 S.W.3d 570 (Tex. 2005) (court must review all evidence, not just that which supports the judgment, in reviewing legal sufficiency of termination; child had multiple injuries over time, indicating ongoing mistreatment)

In re J.L., 163 S.W.3d 79 (Tex. 2005) (jury verdict is to receive deference if fact-finder could reasonably formed firm belief of factual basis to terminate parental rights—appellate court's consideration of expert testimony not in record is not deference)

In re K.A.F., 160 S.W.3d 923 (Tex. 2005) (timeline for accelerated appeal of termination not affected by post-trial motions); *accord In re* J.L., 163 S.W.3d 79 (Tex. 2005) (but new final order from grant of post-trial motion restarts accelerated appeal time frame)

In re S.A.P., 156 S.W.3d 573 (Tex. 2005) (letters initially finding no abuse or neglect by parents does not estop CPS from later seeking termination)

In re L.M.I., 119 S.W.3d 707 (Tex. 2003) (affidavits of relinquishment of twins by teenage mother and non-English speaking father upheld in bitterly divided 5–4 decision)

In re M.S., 115 S.W.3d 534 (Tex. 2003) (statutory right to counsel in SAPCR embodies right to effective counsel)

In re A.F., 113 S.W.3d 363 (Tex. 2003) (two more broad-form challenges ducked by supreme court on basis of unpreserved complaint)

In re B.L.D., 113 S.W.3d 340 (Tex. 2003) (appellate court reversed jury termination verdict on two grounds, conflict between clients and broad-form charge—both grounds wrong, but for different reasons)

In re A.V., 113 S.W.3d 335 (Tex. 2003) (incarceration "for not less than two years" to be applied prospectively—not retroactive statute)

In re M.S., 115 S.W.3d 534 (Tex. 2003) (attorney's failure to preserve factual sufficiency issue for termination appeal constitutes ineffective assistance of counsel)

In re J.F.C., 96 S.W.3d 256 (Tex. 2002) (finding conclusive proof to establish the (O) ground, the supreme court did not review the parents' constitutional challenge to the broad-form jury charge)

In re C.H., 89 S.W.3d 17 (Tex. 2002) (standard of review for termination is whether evidence is such that fact finder could reasonably form firm belief or conviction about state's allegations)

In re K.R., 63 S.W.3d 796 (Tex. 2001), *reversing and rendering*, 22 S.W.3d 85 (shackling of father at trial harmless error that does not require reversal of jury finding for termination of parental rights)

In re J.W., 52 S.W.3d 730 (Tex. 2001) (terminated parents have right to amend defective affidavits of indigency on appeal)

In re M.C., 917 S.W.2d 268 (Tex. 1996) (neglect that leaves children in potentially dangerous situations sustains termination irrespective of lack of physical abuse)

Texas Dept. of Human Services v. White, 817 S.W.2d 62 (Tex. 1991) (admission in evidence of photo of child with foster family not reversible error)

Texas Dept. of Human Services v. E.B., 802 S.W.2d 647 (Tex. 1990) (broad-form jury question valid—controlling issue whether the parent-child relationship should be terminated, not specific grounds jury found)

Texas Dept. of Human Services v. Boyd, 727 S.W.2d 531 (Tex. 1987) (an actual or concrete threat is not required to establish endangerment; can be inferred from parental misconduct)

In re Unnamed Baby McLean, 725 S.W.2d 696, 698 (Tex. 1987) (Texas ERA applies to genetic father who steps forward, willing and able to shoulder responsibilities of raising a child)

Holick v. Smith, 685 S.W.2d 18 (Tex. 1985) (abandonment ground (C) ground not satisfied—mother made arrangements for adequate support of the children)

Brown v. McLennan County Children's Protective Services, 627 S.W.2d 390 (Tex. 1982) (irrevocable affidavit of relinquishment signed by young mother upheld)

In re G.M., 596 S.W.2d 846 (Tex. 1980) (must prove termination by clear and convincing evidence)

Goffney v. Lowry, 554 S.W.2d 157 (Tex. 1977) (eligibility for pauper's affidavit supports appeal of termination)

Holley v. Adams, 544 S.W.2d 367 (Tex. 1976) (seminal case establishing a non-exhaustive list of factors to be considered in determining best interest)

Wiley v. Spratlan, 543 S.W.2d 349 (Tex. 1976) (one-year period required in (F) means a continuous twelve-month period for both failure to support and ability to pay)

SUBCHAPTER A. GROUNDS

§ 161.001. Involuntary Termination of Parent–Child Relationship

The court may order termination of the parent-child relationship if the court finds by clear and convincing evidence:

(1) that the parent has:

(A) voluntarily left the child alone or in the possession of another not the parent and expressed an intent not to return;

(B) voluntarily left the child alone or in the possession of another not the parent without expressing an intent to return, without providing for the adequate support of the child, and remained away for a period of at least three months;

(C) voluntarily left the child alone or in the possession of another without providing adequate support of the child and remained away for a period of at least six months;

(D) knowingly placed or knowingly allowed the child to remain in conditions or surroundings which endanger the physical or emotional well-being of the child;

(E) engaged in conduct or knowingly placed the child with persons who engaged in conduct which endangers the physical or emotional well-being of the child;

(F) failed to support the child in accordance with the parent's ability during a period of one year ending within six months of the date of the filing of the petition;

(G) abandoned the child without identifying the child or furnishing means of identification, and the child's identity cannot be ascertained by the exercise of reasonable diligence;

(H) voluntarily, and with knowledge of the pregnancy, abandoned the mother of the child beginning at a time during her pregnancy with the child and continuing through the birth, failed to provide adequate support or medical care for the mother during the period of abandonment before the birth of the child, and remained apart from the child or failed to support the child since the birth;

(I) contumaciously refused to submit to a reasonable and lawful order of a court under Subchapter D, Chapter 261;

(J) been the major cause of:

(i) the failure of the child to be enrolled in school as required by the Education Code; or

(ii) the child's absence from the child's home without the consent of the parents or guardian for a substantial length of time or without the intent to return;

(K) executed before or after the suit is filed an unrevoked or irrevocable affidavit of relinquishment of parental rights as provided by this chapter;

(L) been convicted or has been placed on community supervision, including deferred adjudication community supervision, for being criminally responsible for the death or serious injury of a child under the following sections of the Penal Code or adjudicated under Title 3 for conduct that caused the death or serious injury of a child and that would constitute a violation of one of the following Penal Code sections:

(i) Section 19.02 (murder);

(ii) Section 19.03 (capital murder);

(iii) Section 19.04 (manslaughter);

(iv) Section 21.11 (indecency with a child);

(v) Section 22.01 (assault);

(vi) Section 22.011 (sexual assault);

(vii) Section 22.02 (aggravated assault);

(viii) Section 22.021 (aggravated sexual assault);

(ix) Section 22.04 (injury to a child, elderly individual, or disabled individual);

(x) Section 22.041 (abandoning or endangering child);

(xi) Section 25.02 (prohibited sexual conduct);

(xii) Section 43.25 (sexual performance by a child);

(xiii) Section 43.26 (possession or promotion of child pornography); ~~and~~

(xiv) Section 21.02 (continuous sexual abuse of young child or children);

(xv) Section 20A.02(a)(7) or (8) (trafficking of persons); and

(xvi) Section 43.05(a)(2) (compelling prostitution);

(M) had his or her parent-child relationship terminated with respect to another child based on a finding that the parent's conduct was in violation of Paragraph (D) or (E) or substantially equivalent provisions of the law of another state;

(N) constructively abandoned the child who has been in the permanent or temporary managing conservatorship of the Department of Family and Protective Services or an authorized agency for not less than six months, and:

(i) the department or authorized agency has made reasonable efforts to return the child to the parent;

(ii) the parent has not regularly visited or maintained significant contact with the child; and

(iii) the parent has demonstrated an inability to provide the child with a safe environment;

(O) failed to comply with the provisions of a court order that specifically established the actions necessary for the parent to obtain the return of the child who has been in the permanent or temporary managing conservatorship of the Department of Family and Protective Services for not less than nine months as a result of the child's removal from the parent under Chapter 262 for the abuse or neglect of the child;

(P) used a controlled substance, as defined by Chapter 481, Health and Safety Code, in a manner that endangered the health or safety of the child, and:

(i) failed to complete a court-ordered substance abuse treatment program; or

(ii) after completion of a court-ordered substance abuse treatment program, continued to abuse a controlled substance;

(Q) knowingly engaged in criminal conduct that has resulted in the parent's:

(i) conviction of an offense; and

(ii) confinement or imprisonment and inability to care for the child for not less than two years from the date of filing the petition;

(R) been the cause of the child being born addicted to alcohol or a controlled substance, other than a controlled substance legally obtained by prescription, as defined by Section 261.001;

(S) voluntarily delivered the child to a designated emergency infant care provider under Section 262.302 without expressing an intent to return for the child; or

(T) been convicted of:

(i) the murder of the other parent of the child under Section 19.02 or 19.03, Penal Code, or under a law of another state, federal law, the law of a foreign country, or the Uniform Code of Military Justice that contains elements that are substantially similar to the elements of an offense under Section 19.02 or 19.03, Penal Code;

(ii) criminal attempt under Section 15.01, Penal Code, or under a law of another state, federal law, the law of a foreign country, or the Uniform Code of Military Justice that contains elements that are substantially similar to the elements of an offense under Section 15.01, Penal Code, to commit the offense described by Subparagraph (i); or

(iii) criminal solicitation under Section 15.03, Penal Code, or under a law of another state, federal law, the law of a foreign country, or the Uniform Code of Military Justice that contains elements that are substantially similar to the elements of an offense under Section 15.03, Penal Code, of the offense described by Subparagraph (i); and

(2) that termination is in the best interest of the child.

Amended by Acts 2011, 82nd Leg., ch. 1 (S.B. 24), § 4.02, eff. Sept. 1, 2011.

Comment

This section provides the comprehensive laundry list of the culpable conduct grounds that can lead to parental termination. It is a long-standing rule by both statute and constitutionally-based court decisions that the standard of proof in a termination case is "by clear and convincing evidence."

Since the initiation of the code, Subsections (1)(A) through (1)(C) have described discrete species of abandonment of a child by a parent. Time and experience have demonstrated that the length of time necessary to prove "abandonment" varies significantly, depending on the express or implied intent of the parent to abandon the child. When the intent is clear, there is no minimum time requirement, i.e., under (A), (G) or (S). Where the parent's intent to abandon is unclear or only implied, a three months minimum, (B), or a six-months period is required, i.e., (C) or (N). Analogous provisions elsewhere in the code also may apply. For example, delivery of an infant to a designated emergency infant care provider under §§ 263.301–.309 (the "Baby Moses" statute), is a form of abandonment which excuses the department from conducting a search for relatives (§ 262.309), as well as providing a termination ground, *see* § 263.407.

Subsections (1)(D) and (1)(E) are usually referred to as the abuse and neglect, or "endangerment" grounds. They are commonly pled together without further explanation by the Department of Family and Protective Services (DFPS), in cases of state intervention in a family. Note that the terminology of "abuse and neglect" is defined at length in § 261.001 to guide Children's Protective Services staff, but is not utilized in this Chapter.

Subsection (1)(F) is the nonsupport ground customarily used by one parent to terminate the rights of the other parent, particularly to facilitate a stepparent adoption. The one year requirement for nonsupport is strictly construed.

Subsections (1)(G) through (1)(J) seldom, if ever, are applied. Subsection (1)(K) allows for termination based on a voluntary affidavit of relinquishment of parental rights, perhaps the most common procedure to accomplish legal termination.

Subsections (1)(L) and (1)(M), significantly change the statutory scheme from above. Conduct neither directed at, nor directly affecting, a child who is the subject of the suit can form the basis for termination. In short, a ground for termination is available if the parent has been guilty in the past of the requisite culpable conduct directed against another child. Subsection (1)(L) identifies the crimes that create a risk of termination of other children. Subsection (1)(M) covers termination of parental rights based on prior termination of another child of the parent on "endangerment" grounds in this or another state.

Subsection (1)(N) provides a ground to be used in those situations in which a child has been removed from a home before serious damage to the child has occurred, and before a termination ground exists. Thereafter, the "constructive abandonment" ground for termination may come into existence if the parent does not maintain contact with the child and does not take the steps required to convince the court that the child can be safely returned to the parent. Originally, Subsection (1)(N) required at least a year's time to pass before a default in responsible parenting would trigger the ground for termination. In 1997 the legislature set a one-year deadline for cases with children in foster care, shortened the time to prove constructive abandonment by a parent to six months and required the contact that a parent must maintain with the child in DFPS care to be regular and significant. This eliminated irregular or incidental contact with the child as a defense to termination based on this ground.

Several grounds primarily focus on children who end up in the care of DFPS as a result of a report of child abuse or neglect. Subsection (1)(O) is an offshoot of a long term effort by DFPS to convince the legislature to enact a ground for termination based on a parent's failure to cooperate with the caseworkers and with the plans established for the dysfunctional parents by DFPS. Although the legislature has always refused to accept parental noncooperation as a ground for termination, an analogous ground has been accepted. If the parent fails to obey court orders to take the action necessary to obtain the return of the child, a sufficient ground is created if the child remains in the permanent or temporary managing conservatorship of the department for at least nine months.

Subsection (1)(P) is a breakthrough for a long sought-after ground for termination, i.e., the use of controlled substances that damage the child. Additionally, the ground applies if a parent fails to complete a court ordered substance abuse treatment program.

There was a good deal of litigation about the subject matter of Subsection (1)(Q), imprisonment as a ground for termination of parental rights. A legislative clarification and two supreme court opinions make it clear that: (1) the statute is to be applied prospectively, *In re* A.V., 113 S.W.3d 355 (Tex.

2003); and, (2) the evidence can be "clear and convincing" that the parent will remain in prison for at least two years, even if there is some chance of early release, *In re* H.R.M., 209 S.W.3d 105 (Tex. 2006).

Subsection (1)(R) expands on Subsection (1)(P) by dealing with the harm to a child in utero by use of cocaine, crack, or alcohol. Significant damage by way of birth defects or addiction by a newborn is a termination ground.

Subsection (1)(S) is one aspect of the "Baby Moses Law," which encourages a parent (read "mother") not to abandon an infant in an unsafe place. A designated emergency infant care provider may take possession of such an infant, provide care, and deliver the child to DFPS under § 262.302. The parent cannot be detained and is exempt from prosecution for "abandoning or endangering" the child under TEX. PEN. CODE § 22.041. Complying with the statute, however, is grounds for termination of parental rights if the termination is in the infant's best interest.

Subsection (1)(T) precisely identifies yet another course of criminal conduct that warrants termination of parental rights, i.e., murder, attempted murder or soliciting the murder of the child's other parent.

In all cases, a two-step procedure is required. That is, Subsection (2) requires that whenever culpable parental conduct has been proven, it must be independently shown that termination also is in the best interest of the child. In many instances, the evidence for both prongs of the test is similar, if not identical. But, culpable conduct by the parent, including very bad culpable conduct, must be accompanied by evidence that the child's interests will be best served by termination. Indeed, the entire system for the state to combat child abuse and neglect under the authority of Children's Protective Services has as its primary goal the reform and rehabilitation of bad parenting in order to facilitate family functioning and reunification. *(C.G.C. & J.J.S.)*

Leading Cases (Organized by the Following Categories)

Abandonment—Voluntary or Constructive; 161.001(1)(A), (B), (C), (G), (H), (N), (S).

Schiesser v. State, 544 S.W.2d 373 (Tex. 1976) (termination improper; no evidence mother left children without expressing intent to return)

Attorney's Representation of Litigant

See cases cited in Chapter 107. Special Appointments and Social Studies.

In re M.S., 115 S.W.3d 534 (Tex. 2003) (attorney's failure to preserve factual sufficiency issue for appeal constitutes ineffective assistance of counsel)

Valencia v. Texas Dept. of Family and Protective Serv., ___ S.W.3d ___, 2010 WL 1240988 (Tex. App.—Houston [1st Dist.] 2010) (father received no meaningful assistance of counsel; prejudice to his defense presumed).

In re A.H.L., III, 214 S.W.3d 45 (Tex. App.—El Paso 2006, pet. denied) (appointed counsel provided effective representation of incarcerated father who has no right to self-representation (or to attend—bench warrant denied for security reasons)

In re M.R.J.M., 193 S.W.3d 670 (Tex. App.—Fort Worth 2006, no pet.) (statutory restrictions on indigent parents' frivolous appeals are constitutional)

Tex. Att'y Gen. Op. No. GA-0461 (2006) (indigent parent entitled to free transcript in SAPCR to terminate parental rights)

In re T.N.F., 191 S.W.3d 329 (Tex. App.—Waco 2006, pet. denied)(opinion after remand) (mother entitled to remand to develop ineffective assistance claim due to husband's abuse)

In re R.M., 180 S.W.3d 874 (Tex. App.—Texarkana 2005, no pet.) (termination approved because father did not provide support for child to the best of his ability for one year, but he did not abandon child)

In re C.D.S., 172 S.W.3d 179 (Tex. App.—Fort Worth 2005, no pet.) (trial court improperly denied mother indigent status on grounds that her TANF & food stamps provided enough money to hire an attorney)

In re D.E.S., 135 S.W.3d 326 (Tex. App.—Houston [14th Dist.] 2004, no pet.); *In re* K.D., 127 S.W.3d 66 (Tex. App.—Houston [1st Dist.] 2003) (criminal law procedure for filing of *Anders* brief to demonstrate lack of legitimate basis for appeal appropriately extended to appeals of termination of parental rights)

Evidentiary Factors

Holley v. Adams, 544 S.W.2d 367 (Tex. 1976) (list of factors sufficient for court's determination of best interest of child)

Wiley v. Spratlan, 543 S.W.2d 349 (Tex. 1976) (nonsupporting parent's ability to pay must be proven for an entire year to support determination)

In re C.M.B., 204 S.W.3d 886 (Tex. App.—Dallas 2006, pet. denied) (grandparents prevail in private termination case based on parents' bad conduct)

Yonko v. DFPS, 196 S.W.3d 236 (Tex. App.—Houston [1st Dist.] 2006, no pet.) (mother made great progress in jail to improve—trial court ignored effect of termination on child on insufficient evidence of best interest)

In re W.R.E., 167 S.W.3d 636 (Tex. App.—Dallas 2005, pet. denied) (finding of endangerment does not require that conduct be directed at the child or that the child actually suffers injury; rather, it is sufficient that the child is exposed to loss or injury)

Jury Submission or Verdict

In re H.R.M., 209 S.W.3d 105 (Tex. 2006) (supreme court again validates jury verdict terminating rights of incarcerated father) (on remand termination affirmed, 2007 WL 707553)(Tex. App.—Houston [14th Dist.] 2007)

In re C.H., 89 S.W.3d 17 (Tex. 2002) (standard of review for termination is whether evidence is such that fact finder could reasonably form firm belief or conviction about state's allegations)

Texas Dept. of Human Services v. E.B., 802 S.W.2d 647 (Tex. 1990) (upholding broad-form submission to jury)

In re D.N., 172 S.W.3d 303 (Tex. App.—Amarillo 2005, no pet.) (second jury at trial court reverses jury decision before associate judge)

Right to Attend/Right to Record

Jones v. Stayman, 747 S.W.2d 369 (Tex. 1987) (right to a free statement of facts following a termination)

Termination Reversed

In re D.N.C., 252 S.W.3d 317 (Tex. 2008) (reversal of termination order required reversal of underlying conservatorship order)

In re J.W., 52 S.W.3d 730 (Tex. 2001) (terminated parents have right to amend defective indigency affidavits on appeal)

Holick v. Smith, 685 S.W.2d 18 (Tex. 1985) (mother arranged for adequate support for children)

Richardson v. Green, 677 S.W.2d 497 (Tex. 1984) (child's statement regarding abuse not res gestae)

Termination Affirmed

In re J. L., 163 S.W.3d 79 (Tex. 2005) (evidence supported finding that mother knowingly endangered child or allowed him to be endangered)

In re A.V., 113 S.W.3d 335 (Tex. 2003) (incarceration "for not less than two years" to be applied prospectively—not retroactive statute)

In re C.H., 89 S.W.3d 17 (Tex. 2002) (standard of review for termination is whether evidence is such that fact finder could reasonably form firm belief or conviction about state's allegations)

In re K.R., 63 S.W.3d 796 (Tex. 2001), *reversing and rendering*, 22 S.W.3d 85 (shackling of father at trial harmless error that does not require reversal of jury finding for termination of parental rights)

In re M.C., 917 S.W.2d 268 (Tex. 1996) (neglect that leaves children in potentially dangerous situations sustains termination irrespective of lack of physical abuse)

Texas Dept. of Human Services v. White, 817 S.W.2d 62 (Tex. 1991) (admission in evidence of photo of child with foster family not reversible error)

Texas Dept. of Human Services v. Boyd, 727 S.W.2d 531 (Tex. 1987) (criminal conduct resulting in imprisonment defined as endangering conduct; actual harm not necessary)

Brown v. McLennan County Children's Protective Services, 627 S.W.2d 390 (Tex. 1982) (irrevocable affidavit of relinquishment signed by young mother upheld)

Goffney v. Lowry, 554 S.W.2d 157 (Tex. 1977) (eligibility for pauper's affidavit supports appeal of termination)

Dupree v. Texas Dept. of Protective & Regulatory Services, 907 S.W.2d 81 (Tex. App.—Dallas 1995, no writ) (parental rights terminated with regards to cocaine-positive baby)

Spurlock v. Texas Dept. of Protective & Regulatory Services, 904 S.W.2d 152 (Tex. App.—Austin 1995, writ denied) (termination upheld on grounds schizophrenic mother unable to care for children now and in the future)

In re B.R., 822 S.W.2d 103 (Tex. App.—Tyler 1992, writ denied) (mother's rights terminated after failing to protect children against sexual abuse by father)

---

§ 161.002. Termination of the Rights of an Alleged Biological Father

(a) Except as otherwise provided by this section, the procedural and substantive standards for termination of parental rights apply to the termination of the rights of an alleged father.

(b) The rights of an alleged father may be terminated if:

(1) after being served with citation, he does not respond by timely filing an admission of paternity or a counterclaim for paternity under Chapter 160;

(2) the child is over one year of age at the time the petition for termination of the parent-child relationship or for adoption is filed, he has not registered with the paternity registry under Chapter 160, and after the exercise of due diligence by the petitioner:

(A) his identity and location are unknown; or

(B) his identity is known but he cannot be located;

(3) the child is under one year of age at the time the petition for termination of the parent-child relationship or for adoption is filed and he has not registered with the paternity registry under Chapter 160; or

(4) he has registered with the paternity registry under Chapter 160, but the petitioner's attempt to personally serve citation at the address provided to the registry and at any other address for the alleged father known by the petitioner has been unsuccessful, despite the due diligence of the petitioner.

(c) The termination of the rights of an alleged father under Subsection (b)(2) rendered on or after January 1, 1998, and before January 1, 2008, does not require personal service of citation or citation by publication on the alleged father.

(c–1) The termination of the rights of an alleged father under Subsection (b)(2) or (3) rendered on or after January 1, 2008, does not require personal service of citation or citation by publication on the alleged father, and there is no requirement to identify or locate an alleged father who has not registered with the paternity registry under Chapter 160.

(d) The termination of rights of an alleged father under Subsection (b)(4) does not require service of citation by publication on the alleged father.

(e) The court shall not render an order terminating parental rights under Subsection (b)(2) or (3) unless the court receives evidence of a certificate of the results of a search of the paternity registry under Chapter 160 from the bureau of vital statistics indicating that no man has registered the intent to claim paternity.

(f) The court shall not render an order terminating parental rights under Subsection (b)(4) unless the court, after reviewing the petitioner's sworn affidavit describing the petitioner's effort to obtain personal service of citation on the alleged father and considering any evidence submitted by the attorney ad litem for the alleged father, has found that the petitioner exercised due diligence in attempting to obtain service on the alleged father. The order shall contain specific findings regarding the exercise of due diligence of the petitioner.

Comment

Relying on the Texas Equal Rights Amendment, the Texas Supreme Court held that a "father who steps forward, willing and able to shoulder responsibilities of raising a child, should not be required to meet a higher burden of proof solely because he is male." *In re Baby McLean*, 725 S.W.2d 696, 698 (Tex. 1987). This holding greatly strengthened the claims of biological fathers, and, by implication, mandates their involvement in the lawsuit (whether voluntary or not). Subsequently, the supreme court extended this right to a man alleging himself to be the biological father of a child with a presumed father, provided the action is taken expeditiously. *See In re J.W.T.*, 872 S.W.2d 189, 198 (Tex. 1994). The United States Constitution proved not to be so protective of the rights of biological fathers. A biological father who failed to register with a New York paternity registry was not entitled to notice of, or participation in the adoption of his child. *Lehr v. Robertson*, 463 U.S. 248 (1983). There is no federal constitutional right to establish paternity of a child born to a married woman, even if the biological father had an established relationship with his child. *Michael H. v. Gerald D.*, 491 U.S. 110 (1989).

This section reflects some tension between protecting the rights of a biological father and providing an expeditious and effective process for termination and adoption in order to obtain permanency for the child. Under Chapter 160, a biological father has at least four years to bring a parentage action. *See* § 160.607 (Child Having Presumed Father). This section only applies if the alleged father has not established his parentage prior to the filing of the termination suit. This section deals with three categories of alleged biological fathers: (1) those who can be located and personally served; (2) those who have registered with the paternity registry; and, (3) those who have neither registered nor been served.

First, and most importantly, if a man's identity and whereabouts are known (as demonstrated by the fact he was personally served with citation), under (b)(1) his parental rights may be terminated, without the need to otherwise prove his unfitness as a parent if he fails to respond to citation after being personally served, by filing an admission of paternity or a counterclaim to determine parentage. Note that this constitutes a legislative determination that "doing nothing" in this factual context is sufficient culpable conduct to warrant termination of potential parental rights. Unlike § 161.001, this section contains no explicit, separate requirement of proof that termination of the indifferent biological father is in the best interest of the child.

An alleged father who is personally served and simply ignores the suit is not entitled to an appointed attorney ad litem. A default order may be rendered after the answer date on proof that the alleged father was served and that the termination is in the best interest of the child.

This section is intended to encourage the entry of timely default judgments, and to discourage the practice of carrying a defaulting party along with the case until the final trial, which frequently results in a last minute appearance with its inherent complications.

It should be kept in mind that a man who appears and admits paternity or is shown by testing to be the father should immediately be adjudicated to be the father of the child. Once he is adjudicated, he has the same rights and duties as any other parent; he should be required to support his child, and parental rights can be involuntarily terminated only if Chapter 161 grounds for termination are established. His parental rights cannot be terminated under Section 161.002.

The remainder of the section deals with two categories of missing alleged fathers: those rare cases in which the alleged father has registered with the paternity registry, and the much more common unregistered alleged fathers.

A man who has registered with the paternity registry must be served, if possible, at the address provided to the registry or at any other address known to the petitioner. If service of citation is successful, the same default and adjudication rules discussed above apply.

If the petitioner is unable, despite due diligence, to serve the alleged father at the address provided to the registry or at any other address known by the petitioner, the court may issue an order terminating the alleged father's rights without completed service of process after reviewing the petitioner's affidavit of diligent efforts. § 161.002(d) & (f). The court must appoint an attorney ad litem for the alleged father. § 107.013(a)(4). The court must also consider any evidence the AAL may present and find that the petitioner exercised due diligence in attempting to serve the alleged father. The termination decree must include specific findings regarding the due diligence of the petitioner. § 161.002(f).

The much more common scenario occurs when no alleged father has registered with the paternity registry. Under § 161.002(e) the petitioner must obtain and file a certificate from the bureau of vital statistics affirming that fact before the court may render an order terminating the alleged father's rights. If a proper certificate of non-registration is filed, the statute waives both personal service and citation by publication on the biological father.

The statute is inconsistent with respect to whether "due diligence" is required of the petitioner in identifying or locating an alleged father. For a child over one year of age at the time the petition for termination is filed, one provision requires for termination that "after the exercise of due diligence by the petitioner" the alleged father's identity and location are unknown or his identity is known but he cannot be located, § 161.002(b)(2). However, "there is no requirement to identify or locate an alleged father who has not registered with the paternity registry under Chapter 160" § 161.002(c–1). This apparent contradiction may simply reflect a preference for personal service if the father is known to the petitioner, even if the man has not registered with the paternity registry.

The statute is somewhat confusing with respect to the extent to which "due diligence" is required of the petitioner in identifying, locating, and serving an alleged father. The structure of Subsection (b) is largely at fault because is posits four separate and distinct bases for termination of the rights of an alleged father, depending on several interrelated factors. At root of the confusion is the failure to explicitly state the underlying bases for the distinctions. First, and most importantly, if a man's identity and whereabouts are known (as demonstrated by the fact he was served with citation), under (b)(1) his parental rights may be terminated if he does nothing in response to the notice of the lawsuit against him.

As noted, the remaining three bases for sustaining termination involve the paternity registry. Subsection (b)(4) substantially tracks the principle above by requiring the known man who previously registered his interest in the child with the registry to be locatable for service of citation if a lawsuit is filed. If that process turns out to be unsuccessful despite the petitioner's due diligence, the registration substitutes for citation.

Separate rules are supplied dependent on the age of the child. For a child over one year of age at the time the petition for termination is filed, Subsection (b)(3) provides for termination "after the exercise of due diligence by the petitioner" if either the alleged father's identity and location are unknown, or his identity is known but he cannot be located. The man's failure to register is sufficient to substitute for citation. This is made explicit, albeit in a confusing manner by Subsection (c–1), which states "there is no requirement to identify or locate an alleged father who has not registered with the paternity registry under Chapter 160." Finally, the key to understanding the statutory rule for termination of parental right for a child under one year old is a child is to recognize its extreme breadth.

That is, due diligence is not mentioned, nor is whether the alleged father's identity or whereabouts are known, or not! There are no required in attempts to identify and locate an alleged father of a newborn or infant older child. Nonetheless, service of citation, whether personally, or by publication or other substituted service is waived. All that is required to sustain termination of the alleged father's paternal rights is the fact that he did not file in the paternity registry under Chapter 160. In actuality, the aim is to facilitate agency adoptions and avoid the charade and cost associated with service by publication. If any of the paternity registry provisions are used, the court must appoint an attorney ad litem for the absent alleged father who failed to register, § 107.013(a)(3). *(C.G.C. & J.J.S.)*

Leading Cases

O'Connell v. Kirchner, 513 U.S. 1138, 115 S.Ct. 1084, 130 L.Ed.2d 873 (1995) (stay denied in "Baby Richard" case: Illinois adoption invalid, biological father's parental rights not properly terminated, *see In re* Petition of Doe, 638 N.E.2d 181 (1994))

Michael H. v. Gerald D., 491 U.S. 110, 105 L.Ed.2d 91, 109 S.Ct. 2333, (1989) (U.S. Const. does not mandate right of man to establish his paternity of child born to married woman)

In re J.W.T., 872 S.W.2d 189 (Tex. 1994) (under certain factual circumstances, biological father has Tex. Const. right to establish his paternity over objections of mother and her husband)

In re Unnamed Baby McLean, 725 S.W.2d 696 (Tex. 1987) (equal rights for biological fathers)

Toliver v. Texas Dept. of Family and Protective Services, 217 S.W.3d 85 (Tex. App.—Houston [1st Dist.] 2006, no pet.) (alleged biological father's appeared at trial and unequivocally asserted he was child's father—that is admission of paternity to satisfy § 161.002)

---

§ 161.003. Involuntary Termination: Inability to Care for Child

(a) The court may order termination of the parent-child relationship in a suit filed by the Department of Protective and Regulatory Services if the court finds that:

(1) the parent has a mental or emotional illness or a mental deficiency that renders the parent unable to provide for the physical, emotional, and mental needs of the child;

(2) the illness or deficiency, in all reasonable probability, proved by clear and convincing evidence, will continue to render the parent unable to provide for the child's needs until the 18th birthday of the child;

(3) the department has been the temporary or sole managing conservator of the child of the parent for at least six months preceding the date of the hearing on the termination held in accordance with Subsection (c);

(4) the department has made reasonable efforts to return the child to the parent; and

(5) the termination is in the best interest of the child.

(b) Immediately after the filing of a suit under this section, the court shall appoint an attorney ad litem to represent the interests of the parent against whom the suit is brought.

(c) A hearing on the termination may not be held earlier than 180 days after the date on which the suit was filed.

(d) An attorney appointed under Subsection (b) shall represent the parent for the duration of the suit unless the parent, with the permission of the court, retains another attorney.

Comment

This section does not require culpable conduct on the part of a parent who is unable to meet the child's needs due to a persistent mental disability, whether by reason of mental illness or retardation. A parent who is permanently institutionalized, or a parent living in the community who, to the degree that medical science can predict, will not be able to care for the child, may have his or her rights terminated without regard to actual wrongdoing by the parent directed at the child. The protection of parental rights has been strengthened by a requirement that the court must find that DFPS has made reasonable efforts to return the child to the parent.

Subsection (c) prohibits the court from holding a termination hearing sooner than 180 days after the suit is filed. Formerly, Subsection (a)(3) also required that the department have managing conservatorship for six months before filing the petition. Taken together, at a minimum these subsections required two consecutive six-month periods from the filing of the original petition before the case could be heard on the merits. This result was inconsistent with the twelve-month deadline mandated by § 263.401 in order to minimize the time children spend in foster care. Presently, the statute continues to require: (1) the immediate appointment of an attorney for the allegedly disabled parent; (2) the department to prove that reasonable efforts have been made to return the child; and, (3) the child has been in foster care for at least six months preceding trial on the merits. In balancing the competing interests involved, the legislature rationally came down on the side of the innocent child to the theoretical disadvantage of the innocent, but incompetent, parent.

Leading Cases

Adams v. Texas Dept. Family & Protective Services, 236 S.W.3d 271 (Tex. App.—Houston [1 Dist.] 2007, no pet.) (mental illness renders mother incapable of parenting now and in the future)

In re M.F., 173 S.W.3d 220 (Tex. App.—Dallas 2005, no pet.) (mother unable to properly supervise child due to mental illness)

§ 161.004. Termination of Parental Rights After Denial of Prior Petition to Terminate

(a) The court may terminate the parent-child relationship after rendition of an order that previously denied termination of the parent-child relationship if:

(1) the petition under this section is filed after the date the order denying termination was rendered;

(2) the circumstances of the child, parent, sole managing conservator, possessory conservator, or other party affected by the order denying termination have materially and substantially changed since the date that the order was rendered;

(3) the parent committed an act listed under Section 161.001 before the date the order denying termination was rendered; and

(4) termination is in the best interest of the child.

(b) At a hearing under this section, the court may consider evidence presented at a previous hearing in a suit for termination of the parent-child relationship of the parent with respect to the same child.

Comment

This section attempts to codify problems encountered when there has been a prior action by which the court determined that termination was not warranted, whether for reason of a failure of proof of sufficient culpable conduct by the parent or because termination was not in the child's best interest at that time. Subsection (b) makes clear that evidence from a prior proceeding is admissible in a successive action to terminate parental rights.

§ 161.005. Termination When Parent Is Petitioner

(a) A parent may file a suit for termination of the petitioner's parent-child relationship. **Except as provided by Subsection (h), the** ~~The~~ court may order termination if termination is in the best interest of the child.

(b) If the petition designates the Department of Protective and Regulatory Services as managing conservator, the department shall be given service of citation. The court shall notify the department if the court appoints the department as the managing conservator of the child.

(c) Subject to Subsection (d), a man may file a suit for termination of the parent-child relationship between the man and a child if, without obtaining genetic testing, the man signed an acknowledgment of paternity of the child in accordance with Subchapter D, Chapter 160, or was adjudicated to be the father of the child in a previous proceeding under this title in which genetic testing did not occur. The petition must be verified and must allege facts showing that the petitioner:

(1) is not the child's genetic father; and

(2) signed the acknowledgment of paternity or failed to contest parentage in the previous proceeding because of the mistaken belief, at the time the acknowledgment was signed or on the date the court order in the previous proceeding was rendered, that he was the child's genetic father based on misrepresentations that led him to that conclusion.

(d) A man may not file a petition under Subsection (c) if:

(1) the man is the child's adoptive father;

(2) the child was conceived by assisted reproduction and the man consented to assisted reproduction by his wife under Subchapter H, Chapter 160; or

(3) the man is the intended father of the child under a gestational agreement validated by a court under Subchapter I, Chapter 160.

(e) A petition under Subsection (c) must be filed not later than the first anniversary of the date on which the petitioner becomes aware of the facts alleged in the petition indicating that the petitioner is not the child's genetic father.

(e–1) Subsection (e) applies beginning September 1, 2012. Before that date, a petition may be filed under Subsection (c) regardless of the date on which the petitioner became aware of the facts alleged in the petition indicating that the petitioner is not the child's genetic father. This subsection expires September 1, 2013.

(f) In a proceeding initiated under Subsection (c), the court shall hold a pretrial hearing to determine whether the petitioner has established a meritorious prima facie case for termination of the parent-child relationship. If a meritorious prima facie claim is established, the court shall order the petitioner and the child to submit to genetic testing under Subchapter F, Chapter 160.

(g) If the results of genetic testing ordered under Subsection (f) identify the petitioner as the child's genetic father under the standards prescribed by Section 160.505 and the results of any further testing requested by the petitioner and ordered by the court under Subchapter F, Chapter 160, do not exclude the petitioner as the child's genetic father, the court shall deny the petitioner's request for termination of the parent-child relationship.

(h) If the results of genetic testing ordered under Subsection (f) exclude the petitioner as the child's genetic father, the court shall render an order terminating the parent-child relationship.

(i) An order under Subsection (h) terminating the parent-child relationship ends the petitioner's obligation for future support of the child as of the date the order is rendered. The order does not affect the petitioner's obligations for support of the child incurred before that date or the petitioner's obligation to pay interest that accrues after that date on the basis of child support arrearages existing on that date. Those obligations are enforceable until satisfied by any means available for the enforcement of child support other than contempt.

(j) An order under Subsection (h) terminating the parent-child relationship does not preclude:

(1) the initiation of a proceeding under Chapter 160 to adjudicate whether another man is the child's parent; or

(2) if the other man subject to a proceeding under Subdivision (1) is adjudicated as the child's parent, the rendition of an order requiring that man to pay child support for the child under Chapter 154, subject to Subsection (k).

(k) Notwithstanding Section 154.131, an order described by Subsection (j)(2) may not require the other man to pay retroactive child support for any period preceding the date on which the order under Subsection (h) terminated the parent-child relationship between the child and the man seeking termination under this section.

(*l*) At any time before the court renders an order terminating the parent-child relationship under Subsection (h), the petitioner may request that the court also order periods of possession of or access to the child by the petitioner following termination of the parent-child relationship. If requested, the court may order periods of possession of or access to the child only if the court determines that denial of periods of possession of or access to the child would significantly impair the child's physical health or emotional well-being.

(m) The court may include provisions in an order under Subsection (*l*) that require:

(1) the child or any party to the proceeding to participate in counseling with a mental health professional who:

(A) has a background in family therapy; and

(B) holds a professional license that requires the person to possess at least a master's degree; and

(2) any party to pay the costs of the counseling described by Subdivision (1).

(n) Notwithstanding Subsection (m)(1), if a person who possesses the qualifications described by that subdivision is not available in the county in which the court is located, the court may require that the counseling be conducted by another person the court considers qualified for that purpose.

(*o*) During any period of possession of or access to the child ordered under Subsection (*l*) the petitioner has the rights and duties specified by Section 153.074, subject to any limitation specified by the court in its order.

Amended by Acts 2011, 82nd Leg., ch. 54 (S.B. 785), § 2, eff. May 12, 2011.

Comment

From the first days of the Family Code governing the parent-child relationship, in theory a parent may seek to terminate his or her own rights. In practice courts have almost universally opposed such an action, especially if the underlying purpose is to avoid the child support obligation. The last several legislative sessions have elicited an escalating number of complaints from child support obligors (men) about their inability to free themselves of the legal obligations imposed on them for children to whom they discovered they were not biologically related. The duty to support has been imposed either by a final judicial adjudication of paternity, or a dutifully signed acknowledgment of paternity, which has the same legally binding effect, see Chapter 160, *supra*. In short, the determination of paternity in the disputed situations is res judicata, as potent a principle of law as might be imagined (but not insurmountable it turns out). The controversy over the subject has raged nationally for decades, and acquired different labels along the way, depending on which side was speaking. Those defending the finality principle referred to the issue as "disestablishment," *i.e.,* paternity had already been established. The complaining men bound by the "offending" child support order most often described themselves as victims of "paternity fraud," thus, blaming the mother and sometimes dismissing their own failure to respond to the legal system. Admittedly a degree of so-called fraud was almost certainly present because in virtually all cases the mother at least would have known the obligor might not have been the biological father (something the man might not have known or may have known about the possibility but chose not to object). Finally, most recently a new label has come into vogue: "mistaken paternity."

In 2011, the 82nd Legislature took some care to balance res judicata principles with the issue of fairness to adjudicated or acknowledged fathers who are not the biological fathers of their "legal" children. A new termination ground was created, which went into effect immediately on the signing of the legislation by Governor Perry on May 12, 2011. Henceforth, a man who signed an acknowledgment of paternity or who was adjudicated to be the father without genetic testing, may seek to terminate his parental rights, and his child support obligation, if he is not the "child's genetic father" and signed the acknowledgment of paternity or failed to contest the parentage action based on his mistaken belief, induced by misrepresentations, that he was the child's father.

A one-year statute of limitations, running from the date the petitioner "becomes aware of the facts alleged in the petition indicating the petitioner is not the child's genetic father" applies beginning September 1, 2012. Non-fathers have until that date to file suit regardless of when the mistake was made or the error discovered.

The petitioner must file a verified petition and the court must hold a pretrial hearing to determine if the petitioner has a "meritorious prima facie case" for termination under this section. If the petitioner shows a prima facie case, the court must order genetic tests. If those genetic tests do not exclude the petitioner, the termination must be denied. The most likely paths to clearing the "meritorious case" hurdle are: (1) relevant information about nonpaternity received from a reliable source, most likely the mother or perhaps a man asserting actual paternity; or, (2) implementation of a home remedy DNA test by the "father-obligor" obtaining samples from the child and himself. Although a negative result from such a DNA test has zero utility as evidence in court, it seems likely it would generate a court order for controlled scientific testing.

If parentage testing excludes the petitioner, the court must terminate his parental rights. There is no "best interest" test—the petition cannot be denied even if termination is not in the child's best interest.

The order ends the child support obligation of the former father-obligor. *See* § 154.006(a)(5). Termination does not attack res judicata, but is strictly prospective. Thus, it does not affect child support arrears, which continue to be accrue until the rendition of the termination order, and may be collected, with interest, by any means for enforcement of child support, other than contempt, until satisfied.

Termination based on genetic testing excluding the acknowledged or adjudicated father also revives a potential parentage action to adjudicate the child's parentage by another man. Retroactive child support in the subsequent suit cannot include support for any period prior to the termination order.

Although termination may not be denied on "best interest," a variant order on that basis may be rendered; the petitioner may request periods of possession and access following termination of his parental rights. Subsection 160.005(*l*) provides the court may grant the possession and access if denying access would "significantly impair the child's physical health or emotional well-being." The statute does not mention how a court order to that affect will be enforced against a losing, disobedient respondent (mother). Nor does it consider that the child will have but one fit parent, whose constitutional rights to raise her child as she chooses may be affected by a court order affecting those rights on behalf of an unrelated person. *See* Troxel v. Granville, 530 U.S. 57, 120 S.Ct. 2054, 147 L.Ed.2d 49 (2000) (affecting rights of genetic grandparents). The court may also order mental health counseling for the child or any party, to be paid for by "any party" (no indication whether mother, former-father, or both, preferred). *(C.G.C. & J.J.S.)*

§ 161.006. Termination After Abortion

(a) A petition requesting termination of the parent-child relationship with respect to a parent who is not the petitioner may be granted if the child was born alive as the result of an abortion.

(b) In this code, "abortion" means an intentional expulsion of a human fetus from the body of a woman induced by any means for the purpose of causing the death of the fetus.

(c) The court or the jury may not terminate the parent-child relationship under this section with respect to a parent who:

(1) had no knowledge of the abortion; or

(2) participated in or consented to the abortion for the sole purpose of preventing the death of the mother.

§ 161.007. Termination When Pregnancy Results From Criminal Act

The court may order the termination of the parent-child relationship of a parent and a child if the court finds that:

(1) the parent has been convicted of an offense committed under Section 21.02, 22.011, 22.021, or 25.02, Penal Code;

(2) as a direct result of the commission of the offense by the parent, the victim of the offense became pregnant with the parent's child; and

(3) termination is in the best interest of the child.

Comment

This section permits a court to terminate the parental rights of a parent who commits the offense of sexual assault, aggravated sexual assault or prohibited sexual conduct, thereby causing the victim to become pregnant. Termination of the wrongdoer's parental rights must be in the resulting child's best interest, of course, which should go without saying.

SUBCHAPTER B. PROCEDURES

§ 161.101. Petition Allegations

A petition for the termination of the parent-child relationship is sufficient without the necessity of specifying the underlying facts if the petition alleges in the statutory language the ground for the termination and that termination is in the best interest of the child.

§ 161.102. Filing Suit for Termination Before Birth

(a) A suit for termination may be filed before the birth of the child.

(b) If the suit is filed before the birth of the child, the petition shall be styled "In the Interest of an Unborn Child." After the birth, the clerk shall change the style of the case to conform to the requirements of Section 102.008.

Comment

This section is primarily intended to facilitate the placement of newborn infants for adoption by authorized agencies.

---

§ 161.103. Affidavit of Voluntary Relinquishment of Parental Rights

(a) An affidavit for voluntary relinquishment of parental rights must be:

(1) signed after the birth of the child, but not before 48 hours after the birth of the child, by the parent, whether or not a minor, whose parental rights are to be relinquished;

(2) witnessed by two credible persons; and

(3) verified before a person authorized to take oaths.

(b) The affidavit must contain:

(1) the name, county of residence, and age of the parent whose parental rights are being relinquished;

(2) the name, age, and birth date of the child;

(3) the names and addresses of the guardians of the person and estate of the child, if any;

(4) a statement that the affiant is or is not presently obligated by court order to make payments for the support of the child;

(5) a full description and statement of value of all property owned or possessed by the child;

(6) an allegation that termination of the parent-child relationship is in the best interest of the child;

(7) one of the following, as applicable:

(A) the name and county of residence of the other parent;

(B) a statement that the parental rights of the other parent have been terminated by death or court order; or

(C) a statement that the child has no presumed father;

(8) a statement that the parent has been informed of parental rights and duties;

(9) a statement that the relinquishment is revocable, that the relinquishment is irrevocable, or that the relinquishment is irrevocable for a stated period of time;

(10) if the relinquishment is revocable, a statement in boldfaced type concerning the right of the parent signing the affidavit to revoke the relinquishment only if the revocation is made before the 11th day after the date the affidavit is executed;

(11) if the relinquishment is revocable, the name and address of a person to whom the revocation is to be delivered; and

(12) the designation of a prospective adoptive parent, the Department of Family and Protective Services, if the department has consented in writing to the designation, or a licensed child-

placing agency to serve as managing conservator of the child and the address of the person or agency.

(c) The affidavit may contain:

(1) a waiver of process in a suit to terminate the parent-child relationship filed under this chapter or in a suit to terminate joined with a petition for adoption; and

(2) a consent to the placement of the child for adoption by the Department of Protective and Regulatory Services or by a licensed child-placing agency.

(d) A copy of the affidavit shall be provided to the parent at the time the parent signs the affidavit.

(e) The relinquishment in an affidavit that designates the Department of Protective and Regulatory Services or a licensed child-placing agency to serve as the managing conservator is irrevocable. A relinquishment in any other affidavit of relinquishment is revocable unless it expressly provides that it is irrevocable for a stated period of time not to exceed 60 days after the date of its execution.

(f) A relinquishment in an affidavit of relinquishment of parental rights that fails to state that the relinquishment is irrevocable for a stated time is revocable as provided by Section 161.1035.

(g) To revoke a relinquishment under Subsection (e) the parent must sign a statement witnessed by two credible persons and verified before a person authorized to take oaths. A copy of the revocation shall be delivered to the person designated in the affidavit. If a parent attempting to revoke a relinquishment under this subsection has knowledge that a suit for termination of the parent-child relationship has been filed based on the parent's affidavit of relinquishment of parental rights, the parent shall file a copy of the revocation with the clerk of the court.

(h) The affidavit may not contain terms for limited post-termination contact between the child and the parent whose parental rights are to be relinquished as a condition of the relinquishment of parental rights.

Comment

An affidavit of relinquishment is commonly employed as the ground for termination in cases involving a state intervention in the family when a parent ultimately decides to concede the issue. Such affidavits are virtually universal in infant adoptions pursued by an authorized agency, at least insofar as the mother's rights are concerned. The key fact is that an affidavit is irrevocable when given to the state or to an authorized agency, but may be made irrevocable only for a 60–day period when executed in a private case.

A parent (read "mother") may not validly sign an affidavit of relinquishment until at least 48 hours after the birth of a child. This is designed to assure that she has given a knowing, voluntary relinquishment of her parental rights. The statute is primarily designed to foreclose a claim by the mother that the document was signed while she was under the influence of drugs or other medication used in the delivery of the infant.

This restriction was opposed by some agencies because it allegedly would cause problems given the fact that under the then-current hospital practice a new mother often was discharged in less than 48 hours. In response to this insensitive, and sometimes dangerous, cost-cutting procedure, federal and state legislation has intervened to modify this practice by hospitals. Texas Insurance Code, art. 21.53F establishes "required coverage for minimum inpatient stay following birth" for a health benefit plan that provides maternity benefits at "48 hours following an uncomplicated vaginal delivery; and 96 hours following an uncomplicated delivery by caesarean (sic) section."

Subsections (b)-(e) provide additional details about the procedure and contents of an affidavit of relinquishment. Subsections (f) and (g) prescribe a formal method for revoking affidavits that are revocable. If an affidavit fails to state that the relinquishment is irrevocable, revocation is required within a window lasting eleven days. *See* § 161.1035.

Leading Cases

Brown v. McLennan County Children's Protective Services, 627 S.W.2d 390 (Tex. 1982) (irrevocable affidavit signed by young mother is constitutional—waiver of process and notice also irrevocable—signing of affidavit is evidence of best interest)

Rogers v. Searle, 544 S.W.2d 114 (Tex. 1976) (extrinsic fraud regarding affidavit of relinquishment)

Wall v. Texas Dept. Family & Protective Servs., 173 S.W.3d 178 (Tex. App.—Austin 2005) (while mother can't revoke affidavit of relinquishment, she is entitled to hearing on motion for new trial)

§ 161.1031. Medical History Report

(a) A parent who signs an affidavit of voluntary relinquishment of parental rights under Section 161.103 regarding a biological child must also prepare a medical history report that addresses the medical history of the parent and the parent's ancestors.

(b) The Department of Family and Protective Services, in cooperation with the Department of State Health Services, shall adopt a form that a parent may use to comply with this section. The form must be designed to permit a parent to identify any medical condition of the parent or the parent's ancestors that could indicate a predisposition for the child to develop the condition.

(c) The medical history report shall be used in preparing the health, social, educational, and genetic history report required by Section 162.005 and shall be made available to persons granted access under Section 162.006 in the manner provided by that section.

§ 161.1035. Revocability of Certain Affidavits

An affidavit of relinquishment of parental rights that fails to state that the relinquishment or waiver is irrevocable for a stated time is:

(1) revocable only if the revocation is made before the 11th day after the date the affidavit is executed; and

(2) irrevocable on or after the 11th day after the date the affidavit is executed.

Comment

This section provides that an affidavit of relinquishment or affidavit of waiver of interest that fails to state that it is irrevocable for a stated time is revocable. The revocation must be made before the 11th day after execution, after which an unrevoked affidavit becomes irrevocable.

§ 161.104. Rights of Designated Managing Conservator Pending Court Appointment

A person, licensed child-placing agency, or authorized agency designated managing conservator of a child in an irrevocable or unrevoked affidavit of relinquishment has a right to possession of the child superior to the right of the person executing the affidavit, the right to consent to medical, surgical, dental, and psychological treatment of the child, and the rights and duties given by Chapter 153 to a possessory conservator until such time as these rights and duties are modified or terminated by court order.

Comment

This section clarifies that the "designation" of managing conservator in the affidavit of relinquishment does in fact give the designee a right to possession of the child and power to consent to medical care as well as other powers and duties under Chapter 153 pending further court orders. *(C.G.C.)*

§ 161.105. Repealed.

Comment

Notwithstanding the disappearance of the old "Affidavit of Status of Child" from the Family Code, reportedly many courts continue to insist on its completion in order to ensure that the subject of the child and father's relationship is covered in the court records.

§ 161.106. Affidavit of Waiver of Interest in Child

(a) A man may sign an affidavit disclaiming any interest in a child and waiving notice or the service of citation in any suit filed or to be filed affecting the parent-child relationship with respect to the child.

(b) The affidavit may be signed before the birth of the child.

(c) The affidavit shall be:

(1) signed by the man, whether or not a minor;

(2) witnessed by two credible persons; and

(3) verified before a person authorized to take oaths.

(d) The affidavit may contain a statement that the affiant does not admit being the father of the child or having had a sexual relationship with the mother of the child.

(e) An affidavit of waiver of interest in a child may be used in a suit in which the affiant attempts to establish an interest in the child. The affidavit may not be used in a suit brought by another person, licensed child-placing agency, or authorized agency to establish the affiant's paternity of the child.

(f) A waiver in an affidavit under this section is irrevocable.

(g),(h) Repealed.

(i) A copy of the affidavit shall be provided to the person who executed the affidavit at the time the person signs the affidavit.

(j) Repealed.

Comment

This section is designed to give an alleged or probable father an easy out; he may relinquish all of his rights, if any, without acknowledging paternity (or even that he ever met the mother). The affidavit may not be used as evidence of paternity, whether or not the affiant denies being the father. § 161.106(e). Subsection (f) clarifies that a waiver of interest is irrevocable.

---

§ 161.107. Missing Parent or Relative

(a) In this section:

(1) "Parent" means a parent, as defined by Section 160.102, whose parent-child relationship with a child has not been terminated. The term does not include a man who does not have a parent-child relationship established under Chapter 160.

(2) "Relative" means a parent, grandparent, or adult sibling or child.

(b) If a parent of the child has not been personally served in a suit in which the Department of Family and Protective Services seeks termination, the department must make a diligent effort to locate that parent.

(c) If a parent has not been personally served and cannot be located, the department shall make a diligent effort to locate a relative of the missing parent to give the relative an opportunity to request appointment as the child's managing conservator.

(d) If the department is not able to locate a missing parent or a relative of that parent and sufficient information is available concerning the physical whereabouts of the parent or relative, the department shall request the state agency designated to administer a statewide plan for child support to use the parental locator service established under 42 U.S.C. Section 653 to determine the location of the missing parent or relative.

(e) The department shall be required to provide evidence to the court to show what actions were taken by the department in making a diligent effort to locate the missing parent and relative of the missing parent.

Comment

This statute was enacted in response to public criticism of DFPS for failing to search diligently for absent parents and for extended family members before terminating parental rights. By definition the section applies only when the rights of one parent are being terminated. If the rights of the "other parent" are also being terminated, a diligent search is required to serve citation, whether personally or constructively. In point of fact, DFPS must seek to serve an absent parent with citation by its own regulations, by statutory requirement of § 263.202, and to meet constitutional due process. At least in theory, DFPS may not be appointed managing conservator without a clear showing that the agency made diligent efforts to locate the absent parent and the relatives of that parent.

Cross Reference

Federal Parent Locator Service. 42 U.S.C.A. § 65.

§ 161.108. Release of Child From Hospital or Birthing Center

(a) Before or at the time an affidavit of relinquishment of parental rights under Section 161.103 is executed, the mother of a newborn child may authorize the release of the child from the hospital or birthing center to a licensed child-placing agency, the Department of Protective and Regulatory Services, or another designated person.

(b) A release under this section must be:

(1) executed in writing;

(2) witnessed by two credible adults; and

(3) verified before a person authorized to take oaths.

(c) A hospital or birthing center shall comply with the terms of a release executed under this section without requiring a court order.

§ 161.109. Requirement of Paternity Registry Certificate

(a) If a parent-child relationship does not exist between the child and any man, a certificate from the bureau of vital statistics signed by the registrar that a diligent search has been made of the paternity registry maintained by the bureau and that a registration has not been found pertaining to the father of the child in question must be filed with the court before a trial on the merits in the suit for termination may be held.

(b) In a proceeding to terminate parental rights in which the alleged or probable father has not been personally served with citation or signed an affidavit of relinquishment or an affidavit of waiver of interest, the court may not terminate the parental rights of the alleged or probable father, whether known or unknown, unless a certificate from the bureau of vital statistics signed by the registrar states that a diligent search has been made of the paternity registry maintained by the bureau and that a filing or registration has not been found pertaining to the father of the child in question.

Comment

Subsection (a) requires that if a child has no presumed or adjudicated father, a certificate from the paternity registry must be filed with the court prior to a trial on the merits on termination. In the vast majority of instances, the certificate will show that a search of the registry has been made and that BVS did not find anyone who had registered claiming to be the father of the child in question. Subsection (b) waives the requirement if the alleged father has been served or has signed an affidavit of relinquishment or waiver of interest. Some attorneys specializing in the representation of child placing (adoption) agencies have suggested that even if a particular man has executed an affidavit of relinquishment or waiver of interest in the child, the safest practice may be to obtain a certificate from the Bureau of Vital Statistics to ensure that no one else has claimed an interest in the child. In those extremely rare instances in which the certificate discloses that a man has registered a claim of paternity, the petitioner is required to serve him as provided by § 102.009(a)(9), or establish that personal service could not be completed despite due diligence as required by § 161.002(b)(4) and (f).

Cross Reference

TX FCA FAMILY § 160.401 *et seq.*, Uniform Parentage Act, Subchapter E, Registry of Paternity, *infra*.

SUBCHAPTER C. HEARING AND ORDER

§ 161.201. Repealed.

§ 161.2011. Continuance; Access to Child

(a) A parent whose rights are subject to termination in a suit affecting the parent-child relationship and against whom criminal charges are filed that directly relate to the grounds for which termination is sought may file a motion requesting a continuance of the final trial in the suit until the criminal charges are resolved. The court may grant the motion only if the court finds that a continuance is in the best interest of the child. Notwithstanding any continuance granted, the court shall conduct status and permanency hearings with respect to the child as required by Chapter 263 and shall comply with the dismissal date under Section 263.401.

(b) Nothing in this section precludes the court from issuing appropriate temporary orders as authorized in this code.

(c) The court in which a suit to terminate the parent-child relationship is pending may render an order denying a parent access to a child if the parent is indicted for criminal activity that constitutes a ground for terminating the parent-child relationship under Section 161.001. The denial of access under this section shall continue until the date the criminal charges for which the parent was indicted are resolved and the court renders an order providing for access to the child by the parent.

Comment

Subsection (a) now makes clear that a continuance may be granted only if: (1) requested by a parent; and, (2) the delay is in the best interest of the child. It also makes clear that the Chapter 263 deadlines remain in place. Thus, the continuance under this section cannot have the effect of delaying the final termination trial beyond 18 months.

Under Subsection (c) a court may limit access to the child by the parent facing criminal charges when a termination suit and criminal charges related to the termination suit are pending. In effect, the child could become a stranger to the parent, compounding the harm if the ultimate decision were to result in a return of the child to the parent. It seems unlikely such a fact situation will occur with any frequency.

---

§ 161.202. Preferential Setting

In a termination suit, after a hearing, the court shall grant a motion for a preferential setting for a final hearing on the merits filed by a party to the suit or by the amicus attorney or attorney ad litem for the child and shall give precedence to that hearing over other civil cases if:

(1) termination would make the child eligible for adoption; and

(2) discovery has been completed or sufficient time has elapsed since the filing of the suit for the completion of all necessary and reasonable discovery if diligently pursued.

§ 161.2021. Medical History Report

(a) In a termination suit, the court shall order each parent before the court to provide information regarding the medical history of the parent and the parent's ancestors.

(b) A parent may comply with the court's order under this section by completing the medical history report form adopted by the Department of Family and Protective Services under Section 161.1031.

(c) If the Department of Family and Protective Services is a party to the termination suit, the information provided under this section must be maintained in the department records relating to the child and made available to persons with whom the child is placed.

§ 161.203. Dismissal of Petition

A suit to terminate may not be dismissed nor may a nonsuit be taken unless the dismissal or nonsuit is approved by the court. The dismissal or nonsuit approved by the court is without prejudice.

Comment

This section is intended to prevent collusion between parents or other parties which has the effect of hiding relevant facts regarding a danger to the child. Whether the court will ferret out those facts when presented with an agreed order for dismissal is problematic. The intent is to make clear that a dismissal without trial of a suit to terminate does not have res judicata effect.

---

§ 161.204. Termination Based on Affidavit of Waiver of Interest

In a suit for termination, the court may render an order terminating the parent-child relationship between a child and a man who has signed an affidavit of waiver of interest in the child, if the termination is in the best interest of the child.

Comment

This section is intended to prevent the waste of resources inherent in the former common practice of serving process by publication on other "possible fathers" when the alleged father has signed an affidavit of waiver of interest. The waiver of interest has been likened to a quit claim deed because the man is required to admit paternity to sign the waiver. However, like a quit claim deed, it makes no sense to obtain a waiver of interest from man who is not thought to be the genetic father of the child. The court should not render a termination order under this section if the evidence shows there is no parent child relationship to be terminated; if there is no genetic relationship, the proper order would be one declaring non-parentage under Chapter 160. *(C.G.C.)*

---

§ 161.205. Order Denying Termination

If the court does not order termination of the parent-child relationship, the court shall:

(1) deny the petition; or

(2) render any order in the best interest of the child.

Comment

If the finder of fact does not find for termination, the court may either dismiss the petition or may render an order, inter alia, which awards permanent managing conservatorship to DFPS. In short, the state may lose a suit for termination and still prevail on a crucial issue, i.e., custody. However, to prevail on conservatorship, the department would have to rebut the parental preference under § 153.131. Note that the res judicata effect of an order denying termination is not quite what it may appear, since the department may bring a new suit and use the old evidence, at least in part, *see* § 161.004. *(C.G.C.)*

---

§ 161.206. Order Terminating Parental Rights

(a) If the court finds by clear and convincing evidence grounds for termination of the parent-child relationship, it shall render an order terminating the parent-child relationship.

(b) Except as provided by Section 161.2061, an order terminating the parent-child relationship divests the parent and the child of all legal rights and duties with respect to each other, except that the child retains the right to inherit from and through the parent unless the court otherwise provides.

(c) Nothing in this chapter precludes or affects the rights of a biological or adoptive maternal or paternal grandparent to reasonable access under Chapter 153.

(d) An order rendered under this section must include a finding that:

(1) a request for identification of a court of continuing, exclusive jurisdiction has been made as required by Section 155.101; and

(2) all parties entitled to notice, including the Title IV–D agency, have been notified.

Comment

If the court or jury determines that both a culpable ground and best interest exist, termination results. The decree means exactly what it says—a final irrevocable end of the parent-child relationship. The court may, however, order post-termination contact between the terminated parent and the child for a limited time under § 161.2061, or indefinitely under § 161.205(*l*). *(C.G.C)*

Leading Cases

Texas Dept. of Human Services v. E.B., 802 S.W.2d 647 (Tex. 1990) (broad-form submission to jury upheld)

Texas Dept. of Human Services v. Boyd, 727 S.W.2d 531 (Tex. 1987) (criminal conduct resulting in imprisonment defined as endangering conduct; actual harm to child not required)

In re Baby McLean, 725 S.W.2d 696 (Tex. 1987) (equal rights for biological fathers)

Durham v. Barrow, 600 S.W.2d 756 (Tex. 1980) (biological parent has no standing to attack an adoption after termination)

---

§ 161.2061. Terms Regarding Limited Post–termination Contact

(a) If the court finds it to be in the best interest of the child, the court may provide in an order terminating the parent-child relationship that the biological parent who filed an affidavit of voluntary relinquishment of parental rights under Section 161.103 shall have limited post-termination contact with the child as provided by Subsection (b) on the agreement of the biological parent and the Department of Protective and Regulatory Services.

(b) The order of termination may include terms that allow the biological parent to:

(1) receive specified information regarding the child;

(2) provide written communications to the child; and

(3) have limited access to the child.

(c) The terms of an order of termination regarding limited post-termination contact may be enforced only if the party seeking enforcement pleads and proves that, before filing the motion for enforcement, the party attempted in good faith to resolve the disputed matters through mediation.

(d) The terms of an order of termination under this section are not enforceable by contempt.

(e) The terms of an order of termination regarding limited post-termination contact may not be modified.

(f) An order under this section does not:

(1) affect the finality of a termination order; or

(2) grant standing to a parent whose parental rights have been terminated to file any action under this title other than a motion to enforce the terms regarding limited post-termination contact until the court renders a subsequent adoption order with respect to the child.

Leading Case

In re A.G.C., 279 S.W.3d 441 (Tex. App.—Dallas 2005, no pet.) (affidavit of relinquishment upheld; remanded to arbiter to resolve issues relating to post-termination contacts by father re the MSA)

---

§ 161.2062. Provision for Limited Contact Between Biological Parent and Child

(a) An order terminating the parent-child relationship may not require that a subsequent adoption order include terms regarding limited post-termination contact between the child and a biological parent.

(b) The inclusion of a requirement for post-termination contact described by Subsection (a) in a termination order does not:

(1) affect the finality of a termination or subsequent adoption order; or

(2) grant standing to a parent whose parental rights have been terminated to file any action under this title after the court renders a subsequent adoption order with respect to the child.

§ 161.207. Appointment of Managing Conservator on Termination

(a) If the court terminates the parent-child relationship with respect to both parents or to the only living parent, the court shall appoint a suitable, competent adult, the Department of Protective and Regulatory Services, a licensed child-placing agency, or an authorized agency as managing conservator of the child. An agency designated managing conservator in an unrevoked or irrevocable affidavit of relinquishment shall be appointed managing conservator.

(b) The order of appointment may refer to the docket number of the suit and need not refer to the parties nor be accompanied by any other papers in the record.

§ 161.208. Appointment of Department of Protective and Regulatory Services as Managing Conservator

If a parent of the child has not been personally served in a suit in which the Department of Protective and Regulatory Services seeks termination, the court that terminates a parent-child relationship may not appoint the Department of Protective and Regulatory Services as permanent managing conservator of the child unless the court determines that:

(1) the department has made a diligent effort to locate a missing parent who has not been personally served and a relative of that parent; and

(2) a relative located by the department has had a reasonable opportunity to request appointment as managing conservator of the child or the department has not been able to locate the missing parent or a relative of the missing parent.

Editors' Note: *Texas Legislative Council does not correct the name of the department unless there is an amendment to the statute. Applying this general rule to the caption of a section is at least a minor error.*

---

§ 161.209. Copy of Order of Termination

A copy of an order of termination rendered under Section 161.206 is not required to be mailed to parties as provided by Rules 119a and 239a, Texas Rules of Civil Procedure.

§ 161.210. Sealing of File

The court, on the motion of a party or on the court's own motion, may order the sealing of the file, the minutes of the court, or both, in a suit for termination.

§ 161.211. Direct or Collateral Attack on Termination Order

(a) Notwithstanding Rule 329, Texas Rules of Civil Procedure, the validity of an order terminating the parental rights of a person who has been personally served or who has executed an affidavit of relinquishment of parental rights or an affidavit of waiver of interest in a child or whose rights have been terminated under Section 161.002(b) is not subject to collateral or direct attack after the sixth month after the date the order was signed.

(b) Notwithstanding Rule 329, Texas Rules of Civil Procedure, the validity of an order terminating the parental rights of a person who is served by citation by publication is not subject to collateral or direct attack after the sixth month after the date the order was signed.

(c) A direct or collateral attack on an order terminating parental rights based on an unrevoked affidavit of relinquishment of parental rights or affidavit of waiver of interest in a child is limited to issues relating to fraud, duress, or coercion in the execution of the affidavit.

CHAPTER 162. ADOPTION

SUBCHAPTER A. ADOPTION OF A CHILD

SUBCHAPTER B. INTERSTATE COMPACT ON THE PLACEMENT OF CHILDREN

SUBCHAPTER C. INTERSTATE COMPACT ON ADOPTION AND MEDICAL ASSISTANCE

SUBCHAPTER D. ADOPTION SERVICES BY THE DEPARTMENT OF PROTECTIVE AND REGULATORY SERVICES (sic) [in 2003 became the *DEPARTMENT OF FAMILY AND PROTECTIVE SERVICES*]

SUBCHAPTER E. VOLUNTARY ADOPTION REGISTRIES

SUBCHAPTER F. ADOPTION OF AN ADULT

SUBCHAPTER G. MISCELLANEOUS PROVISIONS

Editors' Note: *In 2003 an amendment to Tex. Gov't Code. § 531.001(4)(J), changed the name of the Department of Protective and Regulatory Services, a.k.a. DPRS, to its current name of the Department of Family and Protective Services, a.k.a. DFPS, codified in*

§ 261.001 and § 264.001. For better or ill, in 2005 and thereafter the Texas Legislative Council decided to correct the name of the agency only when amending or adding statutes to the Family Code that make reference to the agency. This decision has avoided Applying this general rule to the caption of a section and a subchapter, as is done in this chapter, seems error to the editors. Some minor corrective action was taken in 2011, but more remains to correct.

Introductory Comment

Adoption legally replaces the biological parents of a child with adoptive parents. All connection with the biological parents must first be severed, either by the death of those parents or by termination of their parental rights. An adoption case may be instituted as a one step procedure by joining the termination and adoption causes of action, or by a two step procedure in which a separate adoption lawsuit follows a termination.

Legal practice of adoption law divides itself into very distinct, dramatically different, categories. What most people probably think of when discussing the subject is the relatively upscale segment involving infant adoption through a private adoption agency, perhaps even from a foreign country. Note, the United States is now a party to the Hague Convention on Protection of Children and Co-operation in Respect of Intercountry Adoption. A lawyer regarded as an "adoption attorney" primarily engages in a variety of private adoptions. A lawyer in the more general practice of family law may well encounter adoption law occasionally as well. For example, it is not uncommon for a married individual to seek to exchange the label of "step-parent" for "adoptive parent" of the child of the spouse. Unfortunately, yet another significant source of adoptions involves abused or neglected children whose parents have had their rights terminated in a SAPCR filed by the Texas Department of Family and Protective Services.

CLE/Other Legal Publications

Termination/adoption: primer on Texas termination and adoption. Victor H. Negron Jr., 2011 U.T. PARENT-CHILD RELATIONSHIPS: BASICS

Adoptions in the 21st Century—new trends in family creation. Ellen Yarrell, 2011 SO. TEX. FAM. L.

Termination and step-parent adoptions. Janet McCullar Vavra, 2010 ADV. FAM. L. DRAFTING

Snowflakes in Texas? Enacting legislation to allow for embryo adoption. Jodi L. Bender, 16 TEX. WESLEYAN L. REV. 413 (2010).

The legal status of same-sex adoption in Texas. Michael J. Ritter, FAM. L. SECT. RPT. (Fall 2010)

Drafting termination and adoption issues. Warren Cole, 2008 ADV. FAM. L. DRAFTING

Leading Cases

In re H.R.M., 209 S.W.3d 105 (Tex. 2006), on remand termination affirmed, 2007 WL 707553 (Tex. App.—Houston [14 Dist.] 2007) (stepfather adoption back on course after jury verdict validated termination of rights of incarcerated father)

In re W.E.R., 669 S.W.2d 716 (Tex. 1984) (single male adoption denied, apparently on best interest test)

Trevino v. Garcia., 627 S.W.2d 147 (Tex. 1982) (adoption by estoppel not recognized; termination and court-decreed adoption is the Texas way), *see In re* Marriage of Eilers, 205 S.W.3d 637 (Tex. App.—Waco,2006 no pet.).

Green v. Remling, 608 S.W.2d 905 (Tex. 1980), *on remand*, 610 S.W.2d 817 (Tex. Civ. App.—Houston [1st Dist.] 1980, no writ) (social study properly considered by trial court in adoption controversy)

Durham v. Barrow, 600 S.W.2d 756 (Tex. 1980) (GAL for child lacked standing to challenge adoption allegedly based on faulty termination attacked via bill of review)

In re A.M., 312 S.W.3d 76 (Tex. App.—San Antonio 2010, no pet.) (petition to adopt by family relatives must be filed within 90 after termination, TFC §102.006(c)); accord, *In re* M.G., 2010 WL 2776566 (whether great-grandparents qualify under grandparents' standing rule left open).

In re M.K.S.-V., 301 S.W.3d 460 (Tex. App.—Dallas 2009, no pet.) (same-sex partner may not adopt child absent mother's consent—but has standing to seek conservatorship).

Goodson v. Castellanos, 214 S.W.3d 741 (Tex. App.—Austin 2007, no pet.) (former same-sex partner adopted other partner's adopted child-former partner named sole MC, original adoptive mother has possession rights and support duty)

In re Mata, 212 S.W.3d 597 (Tex. App.—Austin 2006, no pet.) (mother did not validly consent to termination of parental rights and therefore is entitled to child)

In re C.M.C., 192 S.W.3d 866 (Tex. App.—Texarkana 2006, no pet.) (after termination paternal aunt takes actual custody of children—months later out-of-state grandparents denied standing to seek adoption)

In re C.R.P., 192 S.W.3d 823 (Tex. App.—Fort Worth 2006, no pet.) (terminated former teenage mother cannot attack her child's adoption—challenge must come within 6 months)

In re K.B.S., 172 S.W.3d 152 (Tex. App.—Beaumont 2005, pet. denied) (putative father's assertion of parentage way too late to interfere with adoption of child)

In re Bullock, 146 S.W.3d 783 (Tex. App.—Beaumont 2004, no pet.) (stepparent adoption reversed by Bill of Review after six month limitation for attack had elapsed)

In re E.S.S., 131 S.W.3d 632 (Tex. App.—Fort Worth 2004, no pet.) (father's oral agreement in open court to relinquish parental rights in step-father adoption does not qualify as required affidavit of relinquishment)

Vela v. Marywood, 17 S.W.3d 750 (Tex. App.—Austin 2000, pet. denied per curiam, 2001 WL 459170) (false or misleading representations violated the adoption agency's duty to fully disclose legal effect of open-adoption on biological mother's rights.)

In re M.T., 21 S.W.3d 925 (Tex. App.—Beaumont 2000, no pet.) (DFPS refusal to consent to foster parent adoption withheld without good cause)

In re M.L.P.J., 16 S.W.3d 45 (Tex. App.—Eastland 2000, pet. denied) (equitable adoption will not sustain child support order; doctrine inapplicable to SAPCRs)

In re Hughes, 770 S.W.2d 635 (Tex. App.—Houston [1st Dist.] 1989, no writ) (mother who voluntarily relinquished rights has no vested right to sue for adoption of her natural child)

Cross References

Indian Child Welfare Act. 25 U.S.C.A. §§ 1901–1923.

Intercountry Adoptions. 42 U.S.C.A. §§ 14901-14954

Tex. Health & Safety Code Ann. § 192.001 et seq., Birth Records.

Tex. Hum. Res. Code Ann. § 42.001 et seq., Regulation of Child–Care Facilities.

Tex. Penal Code Ann. § 25.08, Sale or Purchase of Child; § 25.09, Advertising for Placement of Child.

SUBCHAPTER A. ADOPTION OF A CHILD

§ 162.001. Who May Adopt and be Adopted

(a) Subject to the requirements for standing to sue in Chapter 102, an adult may petition to adopt a child who may be adopted.

(b) A child residing in this state may be adopted if:

(1) the parent-child relationship as to each living parent of the child has been terminated or a suit for termination is joined with the suit for adoption;

(2) the parent whose rights have not been terminated is presently the spouse of the petitioner and the proceeding is for a stepparent adoption;

(3) the child is at least two years old, the parent-child relationship has been terminated with respect to one parent, the person seeking the adoption has been a managing conservator or has had actual care, possession, and control of the child for a period of six months preceding the

adoption or is the child's former stepparent, and the nonterminated parent consents to the adoption; or

(4) the child is at least two years old, the parent-child relationship has been terminated with respect to one parent, and the person seeking the adoption is the child's former stepparent and has been a managing conservator or has had actual care, possession, and control of the child for a period of one year preceding the adoption.

(c) If an affidavit of relinquishment of parental rights contains a consent for the Department of Protective and Regulatory Services or a licensed child-placing agency to place the child for adoption and appoints the department or agency managing conservator of the child, further consent by the parent is not required and the adoption order shall terminate all rights of the parent without further termination proceedings.

Comment

Texas law provides adoption agencies with the widest possible range for adoptive placements; any single or married adult is eligible to adopt a child available for adoption.

Subsections (b)(3)–(4) alter the general rule that a child is not eligible for adoption until after the termination of parental rights or death of both parents, or the death or termination of the rights of one parent for a stepparent adoption. Subsection (b)(3) provides that a child may be adopted by a former stepparent if parental rights of one parent have been terminated. The former stepparent must have had actual care, possession, and control of the child for a period of six months if the nonterminated parent consents to the adoption, or for one year if the nonterminated parent does not consent. Compliance with the ICPC (Interstate Compact on Placement of Children) is also necessary.

§ 162.002. Prerequisites to Petition

(a) If a petitioner is married, both spouses must join in the petition for adoption.

(b) A petition in a suit for adoption or a suit for appointment of a nonparent managing conservator with authority to consent to adoption of a child must include:

(1) a verified allegation that there has been compliance with Subchapter B ; or

(2) if there has not been compliance with Subchapter B, a verified statement of the particular reasons for noncompliance.

§ 162.0025. Adoption Sought by Military Service Member

In a suit for adoption, the fact that a petitioner is a member of the armed forces of the United States, a member of the Texas National Guard or the National Guard of another state, or a member of a reserve component of the armed forces of the United States may not be considered by the court, or any person performing a social study or home screening, as a negative factor in determining whether the adoption is in the best interest of the child or whether the petitioner would be a suitable parent.

§ 162.003. Pre–Adoptive and Post–Placement Social Studies

In a suit for adoption, pre-adoptive and post-placement social studies must be conducted as provided in Chapter 107.

§ 162.004. Repealed.

§ 162.0045. Preferential Setting

The court shall grant a motion for a preferential setting for a final hearing on an adoption and shall give precedence to that hearing over all other civil cases not given preference by other law if the social study has been filed and the criminal history for the person seeking to adopt the child has been obtained.

§ 162.005. Preparation of Health, Social, Educational, and Genetic History Report

(a) This section does not apply to an adoption by the child's:

(1) grandparent;

(2) aunt or uncle by birth, marriage, or prior adoption; or

(3) stepparent.

(b) Before placing a child for adoption, the Department of Protective and Regulatory Services, a licensed child-placing agency, or the child's parent or guardian shall compile a report on the available health, social, educational, and genetic history of the child to be adopted.

(c) The report shall include a history of physical, sexual, or emotional abuse suffered by the child, if any.

(d) If the child has been placed for adoption by a person or entity other than the department, a licensed child-placing agency, or the child's parent or guardian, it is the duty of the person or entity who places the child for adoption to prepare the report.

(e) The person or entity who places the child for adoption shall provide the prospective adoptive parents a copy of the report as early as practicable before the first meeting of the adoptive parents with the child. The copy of the report shall be edited to protect the identity of birth parents and their families.

(f) The department, licensed child-placing agency, parent, guardian, person, or entity who prepares and files the original report is required to furnish supplemental medical, psychological, and psychiatric information to the adoptive parents if that information becomes available and to file the supplemental information where the original report is filed. The supplemental information shall be retained for as long as the original report is required to be retained.

§ 162.006. Right to Examine Records

(a) The department, licensed child-placing agency, person, or entity placing a child for adoption shall inform the prospective adoptive parents of their right to examine the records and other information relating to the history of the child. The person or entity placing the child for adoption shall edit the records and information to protect the identity of the biological parents and any other person whose identity is confidential.

(b) The department, licensed child-placing agency, or court retaining a copy of the report shall provide a copy of the report that has been edited to protect the identity of the birth parents and any other person whose identity is confidential to the following persons on request:

(1) an adoptive parent of the adopted child;

(2) the managing conservator, guardian of the person, or legal custodian of the adopted child;

(3) the adopted child, after the child is an adult;

(4) the surviving spouse of the adopted child if the adopted child is dead and the spouse is the parent or guardian of a child of the deceased adopted child; or

(5) a progeny of the adopted child if the adopted child is dead and the progeny is an adult.

(c) A copy of the report may not be furnished to a person who cannot furnish satisfactory proof of identity and legal entitlement to receive a copy.

(d) A person requesting a copy of the report shall pay the actual and reasonable costs of providing a copy and verifying entitlement to the copy.

(e) The report shall be retained for 99 years from the date of the adoption by the department or licensed child-placing agency placing the child for adoption. If the agency ceases to function as a child-placing agency, the agency shall transfer all the reports to the department or, after giving notice to the department, to a transferee agency that is assuming responsibility for the preservation of the agency's adoption records. If the child has not been placed for adoption by the department or a licensed child-placing agency and if the child is being adopted by a person other than the child's stepparent, grandparent, aunt, or uncle by birth, marriage, or prior adoption, the person or entity who places the child for adoption shall file the report with the department, which shall retain the copies for 99 years from the date of the adoption.

§ 162.0065. Editing Adoption Records in Department Placement

Notwithstanding any other provision of this chapter, in an adoption in which a child is placed for adoption by the Department of Protective and Regulatory Services, the department is not required to edit records to protect the identity of birth parents and other persons whose identity is confidential if the department determines that information is already known to the adoptive parents or is readily available through other sources, including the court records of a suit to terminate the parent-child relationship under Chapter 161.

§ 162.007. Contents of Health, Social, Educational, and Genetic History Report

(a) The health history of the child must include information about:

(1) the child's health status at the time of placement;

(2) the child's birth, neonatal, and other medical, psychological, psychiatric, and dental history information;

(3) a record of immunizations for the child; and

(4) the available results of medical, psychological, psychiatric, and dental examinations of the child.

(b) The social history of the child must include information, to the extent known, about past and existing relationships between the child and the child's siblings, parents by birth, extended family, and other persons who have had physical possession of or legal access to the child.

(c) The educational history of the child must include, to the extent known, information about:

(1) the enrollment and performance of the child in educational institutions;

(2) results of educational testing and standardized tests for the child; and

(3) special educational needs, if any, of the child.

(d) The genetic history of the child must include a description of the child's parents by birth and their parents, any other child born to either of the child's parents, and extended family members and must include, to the extent the information is available, information about:

(1) their health and medical history, including any genetic diseases and disorders;

(2) their health status at the time of placement;

(3) the cause of and their age at death;

(4) their height, weight, and eye and hair color;

(5) their nationality and ethnic background;

(6) their general levels of educational and professional achievements, if any;

(7) their religious backgrounds, if any;

(8) any psychological, psychiatric, or social evaluations, including the date of the evaluation, any diagnosis, and a summary of any findings;

(9) any criminal conviction records relating to a misdemeanor or felony classified as an offense against the person or family or public indecency or a felony violation of a statute intended to control the possession or distribution of a substance included in Chapter 481, Health and Safety Code; and

(10) any information necessary to determine whether the child is entitled to or otherwise eligible for state or federal financial, medical, or other assistance.

§ 162.008. Filing of Health, Social, Educational, and Genetic History Report

(a) This section does not apply to an adoption by the child's:

(1) grandparent;

(2) aunt or uncle by birth, marriage, or prior adoption; or

(3) stepparent.

(b) A petition for adoption may not be granted until the following documents have been filed:

(1) a copy of the health, social, educational, and genetic history report signed by the child's adoptive parents; and

(2) if the report is required to be submitted to the bureau of vital statistics under Section 162.006(e), a certificate from the bureau acknowledging receipt of the report.

(c) A court having jurisdiction of a suit affecting the parent-child relationship may by order waive the making and filing of a report under this section if the child's biological parents cannot be located and their absence results in insufficient information being available to compile the report.

§ 162.0085. Criminal History Report Required

(a) In a suit affecting the parent-child relationship in which an adoption is sought, the court shall order each person seeking to adopt the child to obtain that person's own criminal history record information. The court shall accept under this section a person's criminal history record information that is provided by the Department of Protective and Regulatory Services or by a licensed child-placing agency that received the information from the department if the information was obtained not more than one year before the date the court ordered the history to be obtained.

(b) A person required to obtain information under Subsection (a) shall obtain the information in the manner provided by Section 411.128, Government Code.

Cross Reference

TEX. GOV'T CODE ANN. § 411.128. Access to Criminal History Record Information: Person Seeking To Adopt Child.

---

§ 162.009. Residence With Petitioner

(a) The court may not grant an adoption until the child has resided with the petitioner for not less than six months.

(b) On request of the petitioner, the court may waive the residence requirement if the waiver is in the best interest of the child.

Comment

Waiver of the six months residence of the child with the prospective adoptive parents is commonplace. Moreover, quite often the requisite time period has been met before the adoption petition is filed.

---

§ 162.010. Consent Required

(a) Unless the managing conservator is the petitioner, the written consent of a managing conservator to the adoption must be filed. The court may waive the requirement of consent by the managing conservator if the court finds that the consent is being refused or has been revoked without good cause. A hearing on the issue of consent shall be conducted by the court without a jury.

(b) If a parent of the child is presently the spouse of the petitioner, that parent must join in the petition for adoption and further consent of that parent is not required.

(c) A child 12 years of age or older must consent to the adoption in writing or in court. The court may waive this requirement if it would serve the child's best interest.

Leading Case

In re M.T., 21 S.W.3d 925 (Tex. App.—Beaumont 2000, no pet.) (DFPS refusal to consent to foster parent adoption withheld without good cause)

---

§ 162.011. Revocation of Consent

At any time before an order granting the adoption of the child is rendered, a consent required by Section 162.010 may be revoked by filing a signed revocation.

§ 162.012. Direct or Collateral Attack

(a) Notwithstanding Rule 329, Texas Rules of Civil Procedure, the validity of an adoption order is not subject to attack after six months after the date the order was signed.

(b) The validity of a final adoption order is not subject to attack because a health, social, educational, and genetic history was not filed.

Comment

Subsection (a) shortens the time to attack directly or collaterally an adoption order, similar to termination matters, § 161.211. The reference to Rule 329, Texas Rules of Civil Procedure ensures that the six month time frame also applies to actions based on citation by publication.

---

§ 162.013. Abatement or Dismissal

(a) If the sole petitioner dies or the joint petitioners die, the court shall dismiss the suit for adoption.

(b) If one of the joint petitioners dies, the proceeding shall continue uninterrupted.

(c) If the joint petitioners divorce, the court shall abate the suit for adoption. The court shall dismiss the petition unless the petition is amended to request adoption by one of the original petitioners.

Comment

Given the automatic abatement and potential dismissal, and given the waiting time and expense of an infant adoption, prospective adoptive parents who decide to divorce may wish to delay filing that action until after an adoption is complete. Whether that is fair to the child is problematic.

---

§ 162.014. Attendance at Hearing Required

(a) If the joint petitioners are husband and wife and it would be unduly difficult for one of the petitioners to appear at the hearing, the court may waive the attendance of that petitioner if the other spouse is present.

(b) A child to be adopted who is 12 years of age or older shall attend the hearing. The court may waive this requirement in the best interest of the child.

§ 162.015. Race or Ethnicity

(a) In determining the best interest of the child, the court may not deny or delay the adoption or otherwise discriminate on the basis of race or ethnicity of the child or the prospective adoptive parents.

(b) This section does not apply to a person, entity, tribe, organization, or child custody proceeding subject to the Indian Child Welfare Act of 1978 (25 U.S.C. Section 1901 et seq.). In this subsection "child custody proceeding" has the meaning provided by 25 U.S.C. Section 1903.

Comment

This section clearly states that race or ethnicity is not to be considered in the placement of a child for adoption. Federal law, however, creates an exception for Native American children, *see* Indian Child Welfare Act, 25 U.S.C. 1901, et seq.

---

§ 162.016. Adoption Order

(a) If a petition requesting termination has been joined with a petition requesting adoption, the court shall also terminate the parent-child relationship at the same time the adoption order is rendered. The court must make separate findings that the termination is in the best interest of the child and that the adoption is in the best interest of the child.

(b) If the court finds that the requirements for adoption have been met and the adoption is in the best interest of the child, the court shall grant the adoption.

(c) The name of the child may be changed in the order if requested.

Comment

Not only must all procedural requirements be met, but the court must also find that adoption is in the child's best interest.

---

§ 162.017. Effect of Adoption

(a) An order of adoption creates the parent-child relationship between the adoptive parent and the child for all purposes.

(b) An adopted child is entitled to inherit from and through the child's adoptive parents as though the child were the biological child of the parents.

(c) The terms "child," "descendant," "issue," and other terms indicating the relationship of parent and child include an adopted child unless the context or express language clearly indicates otherwise.

(d) Nothing in this chapter precludes or affects the rights of a biological or adoptive maternal or paternal grandparent to reasonable possession of or access to a grandchild, as provided in Chapter 153.

Comment

The adoptive parents are legally substituted in toto for the biological parents. This includes inheritance rights from the adoptive parents and the collateral relatives. Under Section 161.206(b), however, an adopted child retains the right to inherit from the biological parents "unless the court otherwise provides."

---

§ 162.018. Access to Information

(a) The adoptive parents are entitled to receive copies of the records and other information relating to the history of the child maintained by the department, licensed child-placing agency, person, or entity placing the child for adoption.

(b) The adoptive parents and the adopted child, after the child is an adult, are entitled to receive copies of the records that have been edited to protect the identity of the biological parents and any other person whose identity is confidential and other information relating to the history of the child maintained by the department, licensed child-placing agency, person, or entity placing the child for adoption.

(c) It is the duty of the person or entity placing the child for adoption to edit the records and information to protect the identity of the biological parents and any other person whose identity is confidential.

(d) At the time an adoption order is rendered, the court shall provide to the parents of an adopted child information provided by the bureau of vital statistics that describes the functions of the voluntary adoption registry under Subchapter E. The licensed child-placing agency shall provide to each of the child's biological parents known to the agency, the information when the parent signs an affidavit of relinquishment of parental rights or affidavit of waiver of interest in a child. The information shall include the right of the child or biological parent to refuse to participate in the registry. If the adopted child is 14 years old or older the court shall provide the information to the child.

§ 162.019. Copy of Order

A copy of the adoption order is not required to be mailed to the parties as provided in Rules 119a and 239a, Texas Rules of Civil Procedure.

§ 162.020. Withdrawal or Denial of Petition

If a petition requesting adoption is withdrawn or denied, the court may order the removal of the child from the proposed adoptive home if removal is in the child's best interest and may enter any order necessary for the welfare of the child.

§ 162.021. Sealing File

(a) The court, on the motion of a party or on the court's own motion, may order the sealing of the file and the minutes of the court, or both, in a suit requesting an adoption.

(b) Rendition of the order does not relieve the clerk from the duty to send information regarding adoption to the bureau of vital statistics as required by this subchapter and Chapter 108.

§ 162.022. Confidentiality Maintained by Clerk

The records concerning a child maintained by the district clerk after entry of an order of adoption are confidential. No person is entitled to access to the records or may obtain information from the records except for good cause under an order of the court that issued the order.

§ 162.023. Adoption Order From Foreign Country

(a) Except as otherwise provided by law, an adoption order rendered to a resident of this state that is made by a foreign country shall be accorded full faith and credit by the courts of this state and enforced as if the order were rendered by a court in this state unless the adoption law or process of the foreign country violates the fundamental principles of human rights or the laws or public policy of this state.

(b) A person who adopts a child in a foreign country may register the order in this state. A petition for registration of a foreign adoption order may be combined with a petition for a name change. If the court finds that the foreign adoption order meets the requirements of Subsection (a), the court shall order the state registrar to:

(1) register the order under Chapter 192, Health and Safety Code; and

(2) file a certificate of birth for the child under Section 192.006, Health and Safety Code.

§ 162.024. Repealed.

§ 162.025. Placement by Unauthorized Person; Offense

(a) A person who is not the natural or adoptive parent of the child, the legal guardian of the child, or a child-placing agency licensed under Chapter 42, Human Resources Code, commits an offense if the person:

(1) serves as an intermediary between a prospective adoptive parent and an expectant parent or parent of a minor child to identify the parties to each other; or

(2) places a child for adoption.

(b) It is not an offense under this section if a professional provides legal or medical services to:

(1) a parent who identifies the prospective adoptive parent and places the child for adoption without the assistance of the professional; or

(2) a prospective adoptive parent who identifies a parent and receives placement of a child for adoption without the assistance of the professional.

(c) An offense under this section is a Class B misdemeanor.

Comment

This section addresses concerns about the brokering of Texas children for adoption. Under its provisions children may be placed for adoption only by a parent (natural or adoptive), legal guardian, or licensed child placing agency (including DFPS). Any other person who places a child for adoption commits a criminal offense. Additionally, except for licensed agencies, serving as an intermediary between a biological and prospective adoptive parent is illegal. Providing medical or legal services to a parent or adoptive parent does not violate the law, provided that the doctor or lawyer does not bring the parties together in the first place.

Lawyers handling adoptions should also review § 25.09, Penal Code. Unless the advertiser is a licensed agency, advertising is prohibited in the public media, including the Internet, for the placement of a child or to obtain a child for adoption. Additionally, § 162.107 establishes a criminal offense for violating the provisions of the Interstate Compact on the Placement of Children. The ICPC is mandatory reading for lawyers who choose to handle adoption matters.

SUBCHAPTER B. INTERSTATE COMPACT ON THE PLACEMENT OF CHILDREN

Introductory Comment

Issues regarding this compact between states, commonly referred to as the ICPC, arise frequently in litigation involving an allegedly abused and neglected child. For example, placement of the child with relatives residing in another state triggers an ICPC inquiry—at least, it is supposed to do so. A question could be asked, "What is the ICPC doing in the Adoption chapter? Isn't is really primarily related to CPS cases involving a SAPCR for termination?" True. Perhaps its placement was designed to keep company with the Adoption Compact and the other DFPS subchapters that follow, *infra*.

Interestingly, a Westlaw® search in 2010 identified exactly seven reported cases between 1989 and 2009 involving the ICPC, two of which were reported only in Westlaw®.

CLE/Other Legal Publication

Interstate Compact on Placement of Children and the Indian Child Welfare Act: What You Don't Know CAN Hurt You. Dewey D. Britt, Jr., 2009 Adv. Fam. L.

Leading Cases

Rodriguez v. Lutheran Social Services of Texas, Inc., 814 S.W.2d 153 (Tex. App.—San Antonio 1991, writ denied) (testimony did not convincingly show that ICPC not involved)

Broyles v. Ashworth, 782 S.W.2d 31 (Tex. App.—Fort Worth 1989, no writ) (mother's revocation of relinquishment did not entitle her, as "sending agency" to custody of children placed with TMC's)

---

§ 162.101. Definitions

In this subchapter:

(1) "Appropriate public authorities," with reference to this state, means the executive director.

(2) "Appropriate authority in the receiving state," with reference to this state, means the executive director.

(3) "Compact" means the Interstate Compact on the Placement of Children.

(4) "Executive head," with reference to this state, means the governor.

§ 162.102. Adoption of Compact; Text

The Interstate Compact on the Placement of Children is adopted by this state and entered into with all other jurisdictions in form substantially as provided by this subchapter.

INTERSTATE COMPACT ON THE PLACEMENT OF CHILDREN

ARTICLE I. PURPOSE AND POLICY

It is the purpose and policy of the party states to cooperate with each other in the interstate placement of children to the end that:

(a) Each child requiring placement shall receive the maximum opportunity to be placed in a suitable environment and with persons or institutions having appropriate qualifications and facilities to provide a necessary and desirable degree and type of care.

(b) The appropriate authorities in a state where a child is to be placed may have full opportunity to ascertain the circumstances of the proposed placement, thereby promoting full compliance with applicable requirements for the protection of the child.

(c) The proper authorities of the state from which the placement is made may obtain the most complete information on the basis on which to evaluate a projected placement before it is made.

(d) Appropriate jurisdictional arrangements for the care of children will be promoted.

ARTICLE II. DEFINITIONS

As used in this compact:

(a) "Child" means a person who, by reason of minority, is legally subject to parental, guardianship, or similar control.

(b) "Sending agency" means a party state, officer, or employee thereof; a subdivision of a party state, or officer or employee thereof; a court of a party state; a person, corporation, association, charitable agency, or other entity which sends, brings, or causes to be sent or brought any child to another party state.

(c) "Receiving state" means the state to which a child is sent, brought, or caused to be sent or brought, whether by public authorities or private persons or agencies, and whether for placement with state or local public authorities or for placement with private agencies or persons.

(d) "Placement" means the arrangement for the care of a child in a family free or boarding home or in a child-caring agency or institution but does not include any institution caring for the mentally ill, mentally defective, or epileptic or any institution primarily educational in character, and any hospital or other medical facility.

ARTICLE III. CONDITIONS FOR PLACEMENT

(a) No sending agency shall send, bring, or cause to be sent or brought into any other party state any child for placement in foster care or as a preliminary to a possible adoption unless the sending agency shall comply with each and every requirement set forth in this article and with the applicable laws of the receiving state governing the placement of children therein.

(b) Prior to sending, bringing, or causing any child to be sent or brought into a receiving state for placement in foster care or as a preliminary to a possible adoption, the sending agency shall furnish the appropriate public authorities in the receiving state written notice of the intention to send, bring, or place the child in the receiving state. The notice shall contain:

(1) the name, date, and place of birth of the child;

(2) the identity and address or addresses of the parents or legal guardian;

(3) the name and address of the person, agency, or institution to or with which the sending agency proposes to send, bring, or place the child;

(4) a full statement of the reasons for such proposed action and evidence of the authority pursuant to which the placement is proposed to be made.

(c) Any public officer or agency in a receiving state which is in receipt of a notice pursuant to Paragraph (b) of this article may request of the sending agency, or any other appropriate officer or agency of or in the sending agency's state, and shall be entitled to receive therefrom, such supporting or additional information as it may deem necessary under the circumstances to carry out the purpose and policy of this compact.

(d) The child shall not be sent, brought, or caused to be sent or brought into the receiving state until the appropriate public authorities in the receiving state shall notify the sending agency, in writing, to the effect that the proposed placement does not appear to be contrary to the interests of the child.

ARTICLE IV. PENALTY FOR ILLEGAL PLACEMENT

The sending, bringing, or causing to be sent or brought into any receiving state of a child in violation of the terms of this compact shall constitute a violation of the laws respecting the placement of children of both the state in which the sending agency is located or from which it sends or brings the child and of the receiving state. Such violation may be punished or subjected to penalty in either jurisdiction in accordance with its laws. In addition to liability for any such punishment or penalty, any such violation shall constitute full and sufficient grounds for the suspension or revocation of any license, permit, or other legal authorization held by the sending agency which empowers or allows it to place or care for children.

ARTICLE V. RETENTION OF JURISDICTION

(a) The sending agency shall retain jurisdiction over the child sufficient to determine all matters in relation to the custody, supervision, care, treatment, and disposition of the child which it would have had if the child had remained in the sending agency's state, until the child is adopted, reaches majority, becomes self-supporting, or is discharged with the concurrence of the appropriate authority in the receiving state. Such jurisdiction shall also include the power to effect or cause the return of the child or its transfer to another location and custody pursuant to law. The sending agency shall continue to have financial responsibility for support and maintenance of the child during the period of the placement. Nothing contained herein shall defeat a claim of jurisdiction by a receiving state sufficient to deal with an act of delinquency or crime committed therein.

(b) When the sending agency is a public agency, it may enter into an agreement with an authorized public or private agency in the receiving state providing for the performance of one or more services in respect of such case by the latter as agent for the sending agency.

(c) Nothing in this compact shall be construed to prevent a private charitable agency authorized to place children in the receiving state from performing services or acting as agent in that state for a private charitable agency of the sending state; nor to prevent the agency in the receiving state from discharging financial responsibility for the support and maintenance of a child who has been placed on behalf of the sending agency without relieving the responsibility set forth in Paragraph (a) hereof.

ARTICLE VI. INSTITUTIONAL CARE OF DELINQUENT CHILDREN

A child adjudicated delinquent may be placed in an institution in another party jurisdiction pursuant to this compact but no such placement shall be made unless the child is given a court hearing on notice to the parent or guardian with opportunity to be heard, prior to his being sent to such other party jurisdiction for institutional care and the court finds that:

(1) equivalent facilities for the child are not available in the sending agency's jurisdiction; and

(2) institutional care in the other jurisdiction is in the best interest of the child and will not produce undue hardship.

ARTICLE VII. COMPACT ADMINISTRATOR

The executive head of each jurisdiction party to this compact shall designate an officer who shall be general coordinator of activities under this compact in his jurisdiction and who, acting jointly with like officers of other party jurisdictions, shall have power to promulgate rules and regulations to carry out more effectively the terms and provisions of this compact.

ARTICLE VIII. LIMITATIONS

This compact shall not apply to:

(a) the sending or bringing of a child into a receiving state by his parent, stepparent, grandparent, adult brother or sister, adult uncle or aunt, or his guardian and leaving the child with any such relative or nonagency guardian in the receiving state; or

(b) any placement, sending, or bringing of a child into a receiving state pursuant to any other interstate compact to which both the state from which the child is sent or brought and the receiving state are party, or to any other agreement between said states which has the force of law.

ARTICLE IX. ENACTMENT AND WITHDRAWAL

This compact shall be open to joinder by any state, territory, or possession of the United States, the District of Columbia, the Commonwealth of Puerto Rico, and, with the consent of congress, the government of Canada or any province thereof. It shall become effective with respect to any such jurisdiction when such jurisdiction has enacted the same into law. Withdrawal from this compact shall be by the enactment of a statute repealing the same, but shall not take effect until two years after the effective date of such statute and until written notice of the withdrawal has been given by the withdrawing state to the governor of each other party jurisdiction. Withdrawal of a party state shall not affect the rights, duties, and obligations under this compact of any sending agency therein with respect to a placement made prior to the effective date of withdrawal.

ARTICLE X. CONSTRUCTION AND SEVERABILITY

The provisions of this compact shall be liberally construed to effectuate the purposes thereof. The provisions of this compact shall be severable and if any phrase, clause, sentence, or provision of this compact is declared to be contrary to the constitution of any party state or of the United States or the applicability thereof to any government, agency, person, or circumstance is held invalid, the validity of the remainder of this compact and the applicability thereof to any government, agency, person, or circumstance shall not be affected thereby. If this compact shall be held contrary to the constitution of any state party thereto, the compact shall remain in full force and effect as to the remaining states and in full force and effect as to the state affected as to all severable matters.

§ 162.103. Financial Responsibility for Child

(a) Financial responsibility for a child placed as provided in the compact is determined, in the first instance, as provided in Article V of the compact. After partial or complete default of performance under the provisions of Article V assigning financial responsibility, the executive director may bring suit under Chapter 154 and may file a complaint with the appropriate prosecuting attorney, claiming a violation of Section 25.05, Penal Code.

(b) After default, if the executive director determines that financial responsibility is unlikely to be assumed by the sending agency or the child's parents, the executive director may cause the child to be returned to the sending agency.

(c) After default, the department shall assume financial responsibility for the child until it is assumed by the child's parents or until the child is safely returned to the sending agency.

§ 162.104. Approval of Placement

The executive director may not approve the placement of a child in this state without the concurrence of the individuals with whom the child is proposed to be placed or the head of an institution with which the child is proposed to be placed.

§ 162.105. Placement in Another State

A juvenile court may place a delinquent child in an institution in another state as provided by Article VI of the compact. After placement in another state, the court retains jurisdiction of the child as provided by Article V of the compact.

§ 162.106. Compact Authority

(a) The governor shall appoint the executive director of the Department of Protective and Regulatory Services as compact administrator.

(b) The executive director shall designate a deputy compact administrator and staff necessary to execute the terms of the compact in this state.

§ 162.107. Offenses; Penalties

(a) An individual, agency, corporation, or child-care facility that violates a provision of the compact commits an offense. An offense under this subsection is a Class B misdemeanor.

(b) An individual, agency, corporation, child-care facility, or child-care institution in this state that violates Article IV of the compact commits an offense. An offense under this subsection is a Class B misdemeanor. On conviction, the court shall revoke any license to operate as a child-care facility or child-care institution issued by the department to the entity convicted and shall revoke any license or certification of the individual, agency, or corporation necessary to practice in the state.

SUBCHAPTER C. INTERSTATE COMPACT ON ADOPTION AND MEDICAL ASSISTANCE

§ 162.201. Adoption of Compact; Text

The Interstate Compact on Adoption and Medical Assistance is adopted by this state and entered into with all other jurisdictions joining in the compact in form substantially as provided under this subchapter.

INTERSTATE COMPACT ON ADOPTION AND MEDICAL ASSISTANCE

ARTICLE I. FINDINGS

The legislature finds that:

(a) Finding adoptive families for children for whom state assistance is desirable, under Subchapter D, Chapter 162, and assuring the protection of the interest of the children affected during the entire assistance period require special measures when the adoptive parents move to other states or are residents of another state.

(b) The provision of medical and other necessary services for children, with state assistance, encounters special difficulties when the provision of services takes place in other states.

ARTICLE II. PURPOSES

The purposes of the compact are to:

(a) authorize the Department of Protective and Regulatory Services, with the concurrence of the Health and Human Services Commission, to enter into interstate agreements with agencies of other states for the protection of children on behalf of whom adoption assistance is being provided by the Department of Protective and Regulatory Services; and

(b) provide procedures for interstate children's adoption assistance payments, including medical payments.

ARTICLE III. DEFINITIONS

In this compact:

(a) "Adoption assistance state" means the state that signs an adoption assistance agreement in a particular case.

(b) "Residence state" means the state in which the child resides by virtue of the residence of the adoptive parents.

(c) "State" means a state of the United States, the District of Columbia, the Commonwealth of Puerto Rico, the Virgin Islands, Guam, the Commonwealth of the Northern Mariana Islands, or a territory or possession of or a territory or possession administered by the United States.

ARTICLE IV. COMPACTS AUTHORIZED

The Department of Protective and Regulatory Services, through its executive director, is authorized to develop, participate in the development of, negotiate, and enter into one or more interstate compacts on behalf of this state with other states to implement one or more of the purposes of this compact. An interstate compact authorized by this article has the force and effect of law.

ARTICLE V. CONTENTS OF COMPACTS

A compact entered into under the authority conferred by this compact shall contain:

(1) a provision making the compact available for joinder by all states;

(2) a provision for withdrawal from the compact on written notice to the parties, with a period of one year between the date of the notice and the effective date of the withdrawal;

(3) a requirement that protections under the compact continue for the duration of the adoption assistance and apply to all children and their adoptive parents who on the effective date of the withdrawal are receiving adoption assistance from a party state other than the one in which they reside and have their principal place of abode;

(4) a requirement that each case of adoption assistance to which the compact applies be covered by a written adoption assistance agreement between the adoptive parents and the state child welfare agency of the state that provides the adoption assistance and that the agreement be expressly for the benefit of the adopted child and enforceable by the adoptive parents and the state agency providing the adoption assistance; and

(5) other provisions that are appropriate for the proper administration of the compact.

ARTICLE VI. OPTIONAL CONTENTS OF COMPACTS

A compact entered into under the authority conferred by this compact may contain the following provisions, in addition to those required under Article V of this compact:

(1) provisions establishing procedures and entitlement to medical, developmental, child-care, or other social services for the child in accordance with applicable laws, even if the child and the adoptive parents are in a state other than the one responsible for or providing the services or the funds to defray part or all of the costs thereof; and

(2) other provisions that are appropriate or incidental to the proper administration of the compact.

ARTICLE VII. MEDICAL ASSISTANCE

(a) A child with special needs who resides in this state and who is the subject of an adoption assistance agreement with another state is entitled to receive a medical assistance identification from this state on the filing in the state medical assistance agency of a certified copy of the adoption assistance agreement obtained from the adoption assistance state. In accordance with rules of the state medical assistance agency, the adoptive parents, at least annually, shall show that the agreement is still in effect or has been renewed.

(b) The state medical assistance agency shall consider the holder of a medical assistance identification under this article as any other holder of a medical assistance identification under the laws of this state and shall process and make payment on claims on the holder's account in the same manner and under the same conditions and procedures as for other recipients of medical assistance.

(c) The state medical assistance agency shall provide coverage and benefits for a child who is in another state and who is covered by an adoption assistance agreement made by the Department of Protective and Regulatory Services for the coverage or benefits, if any, not provided by the residence state. The adoptive parents acting for the child may submit evidence of payment for services or benefit amounts not payable in the residence state and shall be reimbursed for those amounts. Services or benefit amounts covered under any insurance or other third-party medical contract or arrangement held by the child or the adoptive parents may not be reimbursed. The state medical assistance agency shall adopt rules implementing this subsection. The additional coverage and benefit amounts provided under this subsection are for services for which there is no federal contribution or services that, if federally aided, are not provided by the residence state. The rules shall include procedures for obtaining prior approval for services in cases in which prior approval is required for the assistance.

(d) The submission of a false, misleading, or fraudulent claim for payment or reimbursement for services or benefits under this article or the making of a false, misleading, or fraudulent statement in connection with the claim is an offense under this subsection if the person submitting the claim or making the statement knows or should know that the claim or statement is false, misleading, or fraudulent. A person who commits an offense under this subsection may be liable for a fine not to exceed $10,000 or imprisonment for not more than two years, or both the fine and the imprisonment. An offense under this subsection that also constitutes an offense under other law may be punished under either this subsection or the other applicable law.

(e) This article applies only to medical assistance for children under adoption assistance agreements with states that have entered into a compact with this state under which the other state provides medical assistance to children with special needs under adoption assistance agreements made by this state. All other children entitled to medical assistance under adoption assistance agreements entered into by this state are eligible to receive the medical assistance in accordance with the laws and procedures that apply to the agreement.

ARTICLE VIII. FEDERAL PARTICIPATION

Consistent with federal law, the Department of Protective and Regulatory Services and the Health and Human Services Commission, in connection with the administration of this compact or a compact authorized by this compact, shall include the provision of adoption assistance and medical assistance for which the federal government pays some or all of the cost in any state plan made under the Adoption Assistance and Child Welfare Act of 1980 (Pub. L. No. 96–272), Titles IV-E and XIX of the Social Security Act, and other applicable federal laws. The Department of Protective and Regulatory Services and the Health and Human Services Commission shall apply for and administer all relevant federal aid in accordance with law.

§ 162.202. Authority of Department of Protective and Regulatory Services (sic) [*since 2003 is the Department of Family and Protective Services*]

The Department of Protective and Regulatory Services, with the concurrence of the Health and Human Services Commission, may develop, participate in the development of, negotiate, and enter into one or more interstate compacts on behalf of this state with other states to implement one or more of the purposes of this subchapter. An interstate compact authorized by this article has the force and effect of law.

§ 162.203. Compact Administration

The executive director of the Department of Protective and Regulatory Services shall serve as the compact administrator. The administrator shall cooperate with all departments, agencies, and officers of this state and its subdivisions in facilitating the proper administration of the compact and any supplemental agreements entered into by this state. The executive director and the commissioner of human services shall designate deputy compact administrators to represent adoption assistance services and medical assistance services provided under Title XIX of the Social Security Act.

§ 162.204. Supplementary Agreements

The compact administrator may enter into supplementary agreements with appropriate officials of other states under the compact. If a supplementary agreement requires or authorizes the use of any institution or facility of this state or requires or authorizes the provision of a service by this state, the supplementary agreement does not take effect until approved by the head of the department or agency under whose jurisdiction the institution or facility is operated or whose department or agency will be charged with rendering the service.

§ 162.205. Payments by State

The compact administrator, subject to the approval of the chief state fiscal officer, may make or arrange for payments necessary to discharge financial obligations imposed on this state by the compact or by a supplementary agreement entered into under the compact.

§ 162.206. Penalties

A person who, under a compact entered into under this subchapter, knowingly obtains or attempts to obtain or aids or abets any person in obtaining, by means of a wilfully false statement or representation or by impersonation or other fraudulent device, any assistance on behalf of a child or other person to which the child or other person is not entitled, or assistance in an amount greater than that to which the child or other person is entitled, commits an offense. An offense under this section is a Class B misdemeanor. An offense under this section that also constitutes an offense under other law may be punished under either this section or the other applicable law.

SUBCHAPTER D. ADOPTION SERVICES BY THE DEPARTMENT OF PROTECTIVE AND REGULATORY SERVICES (sic) [in 2003 became the *DEPARTMENT OF FAMILY AND PROTECTIVE SERVICES*]

§ 162.301. Definitions

In this subchapter:

(1) "Adoption assistance agreement" means a written agreement, binding on the parties to the agreement, between the department and the prospective adoptive parents that specifies the nature and amount of any payment, services, or assistance to be provided under the agreement and stipulates that the agreement will remain in effect without regard to the state in which the prospective adoptive parents reside at any particular time.

(2) "Child" means a child who cannot be placed for adoption with appropriate adoptive parents without the provision of adoption assistance because of factors including ethnic background, age, membership in a minority or sibling group, the presence of a medical condition, or a physical, mental, or emotional disability.

(3) "Department" means the Department of Protective and Regulatory Services.

§ 162.302. Adoption Assistance Program

(a) The department shall administer a program designed to promote the adoption of children by providing information to prospective adoptive parents concerning the availability and needs of the children, assisting the parents in completing the adoption process, and providing adoption assistance necessary for the parents to adopt the children.

(b) The legislature intends that the program benefit children residing in foster homes at state or county expense by providing them with the stability and security of permanent homes and that the costs paid by the state and counties for foster home care for the children be reduced.

(c) The program shall be carried out by licensed child-placing agencies or county child-care or welfare units under rules adopted by the department.

(d) The department shall keep records necessary to evaluate the program's effectiveness in encouraging and promoting the adoption of children.

(e) It is the intent of the legislature that the department in providing adoption services, when it is in the children's best interest, keep siblings together and whenever possible place siblings in the same adoptive home.

§ 162.303. Dissemination of Information

The department, county child-care or welfare units, and licensed child-placing agencies shall disseminate information to prospective adoptive parents concerning the availability and needs of children for adoption and the existence of adoption assistance for parents who adopt them. Special effort shall be made to disseminate the information to families that have lower income levels or that belong to disadvantaged groups.

§ 162.304. Financial and Medical Assistance

(a) The department shall enter into adoption assistance agreements with the adoptive parents of a child as authorized by Part E of Title IV of the federal Social Security Act, as amended (42 U.S.C. Section 673).

(b) The adoption of a child may be subsidized by the department. The need for and amount of the subsidy shall be determined by the department under its rules.

(b–1) The department shall pay a $150 subsidy each month for the premiums for health benefits coverage for a child with respect to whom a court has entered a final order of adoption if the child:

(1) was in the conservatorship of the department at the time of the child's adoptive placement;

(2) after the adoption, is not eligible for medical assistance under Chapter 32, Human Resources Code; and

(3) is younger than 18 years of age.

(b–2) The executive commissioner of the Health and Human Services Commission shall adopt rules necessary to implement Subsection (b–1), including rules that:

(1) limit eligibility for the subsidy under that subsection to a child whose adoptive family income is less than 300 percent of the federal poverty level;

(2) provide for the manner in which the department shall pay the subsidy under that subsection; and

(3) specify any documentation required to be provided by an adoptive parent as proof that the subsidy is used to obtain and maintain health benefits coverage for the adopted child.

(c) In addition to the subsidy under Subsection (b), the department may subsidize the cost of medical care for a child. The department shall determine the amount and need for the subsidy.

(d) The county may pay a subsidy under Subsection (b) or (c) if the county is responsible for the child's foster care at the time of the child's adoptive placement.

(e) If the child is receiving supplemental security income from the federal government, the state may pay the subsidy regardless of whether the state is the managing conservator for the child.

(f) Subject to the availability of funds, the department shall work with the Health and Human Services Commission and the federal government to develop a program to provide medical assistance under Chapter 32, Human Resources Code, to children who were in the conservatorship of the department at the time of adoptive placement and need medical or rehabilitative care but do not qualify for adoption assistance.

(g) The executive commissioner of the Health and Human Services Commission by rule shall provide that the maximum amount of the subsidy under Subsection (b) that may be paid to an adoptive parent of a child under an adoption assistance agreement is an amount that is equal to the amount that would have been paid to the foster parent of the child, based on the child's foster care service level on the date the department and the adoptive parent enter into the adoption assistance agreement. This subsection applies only to a child who, based on factors specified in rules of the department, the department determines would otherwise have been expected to remain in foster care until the child's 18th birthday and for whom this state would have made foster care payments for that care. Factors the department may consider in determining whether a child is eligible for the amount of the subsidy authorized by this subsection include the following:

(1) the child's mental or physical disability, age, and membership in a sibling group; and

(2) the number of prior placement disruptions the child has experienced.

(h) In determining the amount that would have been paid to a foster parent for purposes of Subsection (g), the department:

(1) shall use the minimum amount required to be paid to a foster parent for a child assigned the same service level as the child who is the subject of the adoption assistance agreement; and

(2) may not include any amount that a child-placing agency is entitled to retain under the foster care rate structure in effect on the date the department and the adoptive parent enter into the agreement.

Text of subsec. (i) effective until Jan. 1, 2012

(i) A child for whom a subsidy is provided under Subsection (b–1) for premiums for health benefits coverage and who does not receive any other subsidy under this section is not considered to be the subject of an adoption assistance agreement for any other purpose, including for determining eligibility for the exemption from payment of tuition and fees for higher education under Section 54.2111, Education Code.

Text of subsec. (i) effective Jan. 1, 2012

(i) A child for whom a subsidy is provided under Subsection (b–1) for premiums for health benefits coverage and who does not receive any other subsidy under this section is not considered to be the subject of an adoption assistance agreement for any other purpose, including for determining eligibility for the exemption from payment of tuition and fees for higher education under Section **54.367** ~~54.2111~~, Education Code.

Amended by Acts 2011, 82nd Leg., ch. 359 (S.B. 32), § 11, eff. Jan. 1, 2012.

§ 162.3041. Continuation of Assistance after Child's 18th Birthday

(a) The department shall, in accordance with department rules, offer adoption assistance after a child's 18th birthday to the child's adoptive parents under an existing adoption assistance agreement entered into under Section 162.304 until:

(1) the first day of the month of the child's 21st birthday if the department determines, as provided by department rules, that:

(A) the child has a mental or physical disability that warrants the continuation of that assistance;

(B) the child, or the child's adoptive parent on behalf of the child, has applied for federal benefits under the supplemental security income program (42 U.S.C. Section 1381 et seq.), as amended; and

(C) the child's adoptive parents are providing the child's financial support; or

(2) if the child does not meet the requirements of Subdivision (1), the earlier of:

(A) the date the child ceases to regularly attend high school or a vocational or technical program;

(B) the date the child obtains a high school diploma or high school equivalency certificate;

(C) the date the child's adoptive parents stop providing financial support to the child; or

(D) the first day of the month of the child's 19th birthday.

(a–1) Notwithstanding Subsection (a), if the department first entered into an adoption assistance agreement with a child's adoptive parents after the child's 16th birthday, the department shall, in accordance with rules adopted by the executive commissioner of the Health and Human Services Commission, offer adoption assistance after the child's 18th birthday to the child's adoptive parents under an existing adoption agreement until the last day of the month of the child's 21st birthday, provided the child is:

(1) regularly attending high school or enrolled in a program leading toward a high school diploma or high school equivalency certificate;

(2) regularly attending an institution of higher education or a postsecondary vocational or technical program;

(3) participating in a program or activity that promotes, or removes barriers to, employment;

(4) employed for at least 80 hours a month; or

(5) incapable of doing any of the activities described by Subdivisions (1)–(4) due to a documented medical condition.

(b) In determining whether a child meets the requirements of Subdivision (a)(1), the department may conduct an assessment of the child's mental or physical disability or may contract for the assessment to be conducted.

(c) The department and any person with whom the department contracts to conduct an assessment under Subsection (b) shall:

(1) inform the adoptive parents of the child for whom the assessment is conducted of the application requirement under Subsection (a)(1)(B) for federal benefits for the child under the supplemental security income program (42 U.S.C. Section 1381 et seq.), as amended;

(2) provide assistance to the adoptive parents and the child in preparing an application for benefits under that program; and

(3) provide ongoing consultation and guidance to the adoptive parents and the child throughout the eligibility determination process for benefits under that program.

(d) If the legislature does not appropriate sufficient money to provide adoption assistance to the adoptive parents of all children described by Subsection (a), the department shall provide adoption assistance only to the adoptive parents of children described by Subsection (a)(1). The department is not required to provide adoption assistance benefits under Subsection (a–1) unless the department is specifically appropriated funds for purposes of that subsection.

§ 162.305. Funds

The department and other state agencies shall actively seek and use federal funds available for the purposes of this subchapter.

§ 162.306. Postadoption Services

(a) The department may provide services after adoption to adoptees and adoptive families for whom the department provided services before the adoption.

(b) The department may provide services under this section directly or through contract.

(c) The services may include financial assistance, respite care, placement services, parenting programs, support groups, counseling services, crisis intervention, and medical aid.

§ 162.307. Repealed.

§ 162.308. Race or Ethnicity

(a) The department, a county child-care or welfare unit, or a licensed child-placing agency may not make an adoption placement decision on the presumption that placing a child in a family of the same race or ethnicity as the race or ethnicity of the child is in the best interest of the child.

(b) Unless an independent psychological evaluation specific to a child indicates that placement with a family of a particular race or ethnicity would be detrimental to the child, the department, county child-care or welfare unit, or licensed child-placing agency may not deny, delay, or prohibit the adoption of a child because the department, county, or agency is attempting to locate a family of a particular race or ethnicity.

(c) This section does not prevent or limit the recruitment of minority families as adoptive families, but the recruitment of minority families may not be a reason to delay placement of a child with an available family of a race or ethnicity different from that of the child.

(d) A state or county employee who violates this section is subject to immediate dismissal. A licensed child-placing agency that violates this section is subject to action by the licensing agency as a ground for revocation or suspension of the agency's license.

(e) A district court, on the application for an injunction or the filing of a petition complaining of a violation of this section by any person residing in the county in which the court has jurisdiction, shall enforce this section by issuing appropriate orders. An action for an injunction is in addition to any other action, proceeding, or remedy authorized by law. An applicant or petitioner who is granted an injunction or given other appropriate relief under this section is entitled to the costs of the suit, including reasonable attorney's fees.

§ 162.309. Advisory Committee on Promoting Adoption of Minority Children

(a) An advisory committee on promoting the adoption of and provision of services to minority children is established within the department.

(b) The committee is composed of 12 members appointed by the board of the Department of Protective and Regulatory Services. The board shall appoint to the committee individuals who in the aggregate have knowledge of and experience in community education, cultural relations, family support, counseling, and parenting skills and education. At least six members must be ordained members of the clergy.

(c) A committee member serves for a two-year term and may be appointed for additional terms.

(d) A member of the committee receives no compensation but is entitled to reimbursement for actual and necessary expenses incurred in performing the member's duties under this section.

(e) The committee shall elect one member to serve as presiding officer. The presiding officer serves for a two-year term and may be elected for additional terms.

(f) The department shall set the time and place of the first committee meeting. The committee shall meet at least quarterly.

(g) The department shall pay the expenses of the committee and shall supply necessary personnel and supplies.

(h) To promote the adoption of and provision of services to minority children, the committee shall:

(1) study, develop, and evaluate programs and projects relating to community awareness and education, family support, counseling, parenting skills and education, and reform of the child welfare system;

(2) consult with churches and other cultural and civic organizations; and

(3) report to the department at least annually the committee's recommendations for department programs and projects that will promote the adoption of and provision of services to minority children.

(i) On receiving the committee's recommendations, the department may adopt rules to implement a program or project recommended under this section. The department may solicit, accept, and use gifts and donations to implement a program or project recommended by the committee.

(j) The department shall report to the legislature not later than November 1 of each even-numbered year following the first year in which it receives recommendations under this section regarding committee recommendations and action taken by the department under this section.

(k) The recruitment of minority families may not be a reason to delay placement of a child with an available family of a race or ethnicity different from that of the child.

SUBCHAPTER E. VOLUNTARY ADOPTION REGISTRIES

§ 162.401. Purpose

The purpose of this subchapter is to provide for the establishment of mutual consent voluntary adoption registries through which adoptees, birth parents, and biological siblings may voluntarily locate each other. It is not the purpose of this subchapter to inhibit or prohibit persons from locating each other through other legal means or to inhibit or affect in any way the provision of postadoptive services and education, by adoption agencies or others, that go further than the procedures set out for registries established under this subchapter.

§ 162.402. Definitions

In this subchapter:

(1) "Administrator" means the administrator of a mutual consent voluntary adoption registry established under this subchapter.

(2) "Adoptee" means a person 18 years of age or older who has been legally adopted in this state or another state or country.

(3) "Adoption" means the act of creating the legal relationship of parent and child between a person and a child who is not the biological child of that person. The term does not include the act of establishing the legal relationship of parent and child between a man and a child through proof of paternity or voluntary legitimation proceedings.

(4) "Adoption agency" means a person, other than a natural parent or guardian of a child, who plans for the placement of or places a child in the home of a prospective adoptive parent.

(5) "Adoptive parent" means an adult who is a parent of an adoptee through a legal process of adoption.

(6) "Alleged father" means a man who is not deemed by law to be or who has not been adjudicated to be the biological father of an adoptee and who claims or is alleged to be the adoptee's biological father.

(7) "Authorized agency" means a public agency authorized to care for or to place children for adoption or a private entity approved for that purpose by the department through a license, certification, or other means. The term includes a licensed child-placing agency or a previously licensed child-placing agency that has ceased operations and has transferred its adoption records to the bureau or an agency authorized by the department to place children for adoption and a licensed child-placing agency that has been acquired by, merged with, or otherwise succeeded by an agency authorized by the department to place children for adoption.

(8) "Biological parent" means a man or woman who is the father or mother of genetic origin of a child.

(9) "Biological siblings" means persons who share a common birth parent.

(10) "Birth parent" means:

(A) the biological mother of an adoptee;

(B) the man adjudicated or presumed under Chapter 151 to be the biological father of an adoptee; and

(C) a man who has signed a consent to adoption, affidavit of relinquishment, affidavit of waiver of interest in child, or other written instrument releasing the adoptee for adoption, unless the consent, affidavit, or other instrument includes a sworn refusal to admit or a denial of paternity. The term includes a birth mother and birth father but does not include a person adjudicated by a court of competent jurisdiction as not being the biological parent of an adoptee.

(11) "Central registry" means the mutual consent voluntary adoption registry established and maintained by the bureau under this subchapter.

(12) "Department" means the Department of Protective and Regulatory Services.

(13) "Registry" means a mutual consent voluntary adoption registry established under this subchapter.

(14) "Bureau" means the bureau of vital statistics.

Editors' Note: *The correct reference for Subsection (10)(B) is found in the Uniform Parentage Act, § 160.204*

---

§ 162.403. Establishment of Voluntary Adoption Registries

(a) The bureau shall establish and maintain a mutual consent voluntary adoption registry.

(b) Except as provided by Subsection (c), an agency authorized by the department to place children for adoption and an association comprised exclusively of those agencies may establish a mutual consent voluntary adoption registry. An agency may contract with any other agency authorized by the department to place children for adoption or with an association comprised exclusively of those agencies to perform registry services on its behalf.

(c) An authorized agency that did not directly or by contract provide registry services as required by this subchapter on January 1, 1984, may not provide its own registry service. The bureau shall operate through the central registry those services for agencies not permitted to provide a registry under this section.

§ 162.404. Requirement to Send Information to Central Registry

An authorized agency that is permitted to provide a registry under this subchapter or that participates in a mutual consent voluntary adoption registry with an association of authorized agencies shall send to the central registry a duplicate of all information the registry maintains in the agency's registry or sends to the registry in which the agency participates.

§ 162.405. Determination of Appropriate Registry

(a) The administrator of the central registry shall determine the appropriate registry to which an applicant is entitled to apply.

(b) On receiving an inquiry by an adoptee, birth parent, or sibling who has provided satisfactory proof of age and identity and paid all required inquiry fees, the administrator of the central registry shall review the information on file in the central index and consult with the administrators of other registries in the state to determine the identity of any appropriate registry through which the adoptee, birth parent, or sibling may register.

(c) Each administrator shall, not later than the 30th day after the date of receiving an inquiry from the administrator of the central registry, respond in writing to the inquiry that the registrant was not placed for adoption by an agency served by that registry or that the registrant was placed for adoption by an agency served by that registry. If the registrant was placed for adoption by an agency served by the registry, the administrator shall file a report with the administrator of the central registry including:

(1) the name of the adopted child as shown in the final adoption decree;

(2) the birth date of the adopted child;

(3) the docket number of the adoption suit;

(4) the identity of the court that granted the adoption;

(5) the date of the final adoption decree;

(6) the identity of the agency, if any, through which the adopted child was placed; and

(7) the identity, address, and telephone number of the registry through which the adopted child may register as an adoptee.

(d) After completing the investigation, the administrator of the central registry shall issue an official certificate stating:

(1) the identity of the registry through which the adoptee, birth parent, or biological sibling may apply for registration, if known; or

(2) if the administrator cannot make a conclusive determination, that the adoptee, birth parent, or biological sibling is entitled to apply for registration through the central registry.

§ 162.406. Registration Eligibility

(a) An adoptee who is 18 years of age or older may apply to a registry for information about the adoptee's birth parents and biological siblings.

(b) A birth parent who is 18 years of age or older may apply to a registry for information about an adoptee who is a child by birth of the birth parent.

(c) An alleged father who is 18 years of age or older and who acknowledges paternity but is not, at the time of application, a birth father may register as a birth father but may not otherwise be recognized as a birth father for the purposes of this subchapter unless:

(1) the adoptee's birth mother in her application identifies him as the adoptee's biological father; and

(2) additional information concerning the adoptee obtained from other sources is not inconsistent with his claim of paternity.

(d) A biological sibling who is 18 years of age or older may apply to a registry for information about the person's adopted biological siblings.

(e) Only birth parents, adoptees, and biological siblings may apply for information through a registry.

(f) A person, including an authorized agency, may not apply for information through a registry as an agent, attorney, or representative of an adoptee, birth parent, or biological sibling.

§ 162.407. Registration

(a) The administrator shall require each registration applicant to sign a written application.

(b) An adoptee adopted or placed through an authorized agency may register through the registry maintained by that agency or the registry to which the agency has delegated registry services or through the central registry maintained by the bureau.

(c) Birth parents and biological siblings shall register through:

(1) the registry of the authorized agency through which the adoptee was adopted or placed; or

(2) the central registry.

(d) The administrator may not accept an application for registration unless the applicant:

(1) provides proof of identity as provided by Section 162.408;

(2) establishes the applicant's eligibility to register; and

(3) pays all required registration fees.

(e) A registration remains in effect until the 99th anniversary of the date the registration is accepted unless a shorter period is specified by the applicant or the registration is withdrawn before that time.

(f) A registrant may withdraw the registrant's registration in writing without charge at any time.

(g) After a registration is withdrawn or expires, the registrant shall be treated as if the person has not previously registered.

(h) A completed registry application must be accepted or rejected before the 46th day after the date the application is received. If an application is rejected, the administrator shall provide the applicant with a written statement of the reason for the rejection.

§ 162.408. Proof of Identity

The rules and minimum standards of the Texas Board of Health for the bureau must provide for proof of identity in order to facilitate the purposes of this subchapter and to protect the privacy rights of adoptees, adoptive parents, birth parents, biological siblings, and their families.

§ 162.409. Application

(a) An application must contain:

(1) the name, address, and telephone number of the applicant;

(2) any other name or alias by which the applicant has been known;

(3) the age, date of birth, and place of birth of the applicant;

(4) the original name of the adoptee, if known;

(5) the adoptive name of the adoptee, if known;

(6) a statement that the applicant is willing to allow the applicant's identity to be disclosed to a registrant who is eligible to learn the applicant's identity;

(7) the name, address, and telephone number of the agency or other entity, organization, or person placing the adoptee for adoption, if known, or, if not known, a statement that the applicant does not know that information;

(8) an authorization to the administrator and the administrator's designees to inspect all vital statistics records, court records, and agency records, including confidential records, relating to the birth, adoption, marriage, and divorce of the applicant or to the birth and death of any child or sibling by birth or adoption of the applicant;

(9) the specific address to which the applicant wishes notice of a successful match to be mailed;

(10) a statement that the applicant either does or does not consent to disclosure of identifying information about the applicant after the applicant's death;

(11) a statement that the registration is to be effective for 99 years or for a stated shorter period selected by the applicant; and

(12) a statement that the adoptee applicant either does or does not desire to be informed that registry records indicate that the applicant has a biological sibling who has registered under this subchapter.

(b) The application may contain the applicant's social security number if the applicant, after being advised of the right not to supply the number, voluntarily furnishes it.

(c) The application of a birth parent must include:

(1) the original name and date of birth or approximate date of birth of each adoptee with respect to whom the parent is registering;

(2) the names of all other birth children, including maiden names, aliases, dates and places of birth, and names of the birth parents;

(3) each name known or thought by the applicant to have been used by the adoptee's other birth parent;

(4) the last known address of the adoptee's other birth parent; and

(5) other available information through which the other birth parent may be identified.

(d) The application of a biological sibling must include:

(1) a statement explaining the applicant's basis for believing that the applicant has one or more biological siblings;

(2) the names, including maiden and married names, and aliases of all the applicant's siblings by birth and adoption and their dates and places of birth, if known;

(3) the names of the applicant's legal parents;

(4) the names of the applicant's birth parents, if known; and

(5) any other information known to the applicant through which the existence and identity of the applicant's biological siblings can be confirmed.

(e) An application may also contain additional information through which the applicant's identity and eligibility to register may be ascertained.

(f) The administrator shall assist the applicant in filling out the application if the applicant is unable to complete the application without assistance, but the administrator may not furnish the applicant with any substantive information necessary to complete the application.

§ 162.410. Repealed.

§ 162.411. Fees

(a) The costs of establishing, operating, and maintaining a registry may be recovered in whole or in part through users' fees charged to applicants and registrants.

(b) Each registry shall establish a schedule of fees for services provided by the registry. The fees shall be reasonably related to the direct and indirect costs of establishing, operating, and maintaining the registry.

(c) A fee may not be charged for withdrawing a registration.

(d) The fees collected by the bureau shall be deposited in a special fund in the general revenue fund. Funds in the special fund may be appropriated only for the administration of the central registry.

(e) The administrator may waive users' fees in whole or in part if the applicant provides satisfactory proof of financial inability to pay the fees.

§ 162.412. Supplemental Information

(a) A registrant may amend the registrant's registration and submit additional information to the administrator. A registrant shall notify the administrator of any change in the registrant's name or address that occurs after acceptance of the application.

(b) The administrator does not have a duty to search for a registrant who fails to register a change of name or address.

§ 162.413. Counseling

The applicant must participate in counseling for not less than one hour with a social worker or mental health professional with expertise in postadoption counseling after the administrator has accepted the application for registration and before the release of confidential information.

§ 162.414. Matching Procedures

(a) The administrator shall process each registration in an attempt to match the adoptee and the adoptee's birth parents or the adoptee and the adoptee's biological siblings.

(b) The administrator shall determine that there is a match if the adult adoptee and the birth mother or the birth father have registered or if a biological sibling has registered.

(c) To establish or corroborate a match, the administrator shall request confirmation of a possible match from the bureau. If the agency operating the registry has in its own records sufficient information through which the match may be confirmed, the administrator may, but is not required to, request confirmation from the bureau. The bureau may confirm or deny the match without breaching the duty of confidentiality to the adoptee, adoptive parents, birth parents, or biological siblings and without a court order.

(d) To establish a match, the administrator may also request confirmation of a possible match from the agency, if any, that has possession of records concerning the adoption of an adoptee or from the court that granted the adoption, the hospital where the adoptee or any biological sibling was born, the physician who delivered the adoptee or biological sibling, or any other person who has knowledge of the relevant facts. The agency, court, hospital, physician, or person with knowledge may confirm or deny the match without breaching any duty of confidentiality to the adoptee, adoptive parents, birth parents, or biological siblings.

(e) If a match is denied by a source contacted under Subsection (d), the administrator shall make a full and complete investigation into the reliability of the denial. If the match is corroborated by other reliable sources and the administrator is satisfied that the denial is erroneous, the administrator may make disclosures but shall report to the adoptee, birth parents, and biological siblings involved that the match was not confirmed by all information sources.

§ 162.415. Repealed.

§ 162.416. Disclosure of Identifying Information

(a) When a match has been made and confirmed to the administrator's satisfaction, the administrator shall mail to each registrant, at the registrant's last known address, by fax or registered or certified mail, return receipt requested, delivery restricted to addressee only, a written notice:

(1) informing the registrant that a match has been made and confirmed;

(2) reminding the registrant that the registrant may withdraw the registration before disclosures are made, if desired; and

(3) notifying the registrant that before any identifying disclosures are made, the registrant must:

(A) sign a written consent to disclosure that allows the disclosure of identifying information about the other registrants to the registrant and allows the disclosure of identifying information about the registrant to other registrants;

(B) participate in counseling for not less than one hour with a social worker or mental health professional who has expertise in postadoption counseling; and

(C) provide the administrator with written certification that the counseling required under Subdivision (B) has been completed.

(b) Identifying information about a registrant shall be released without the registrant's having consented after the match to disclosure if the registrant is dead, the registrant's registration was valid at the time of death, and the registrant had in writing specifically authorized the postdeath disclosure in the registrant's application or in a supplemental statement filed with the administrator.

(c) Identifying information about a deceased birth parent may not be released until each surviving child of the deceased birth parent is an adult or until each child's surviving parent, guardian, managing conservator, or legal custodian consents in writing to the disclosure.

(d) The administrator shall prepare and release written disclosure statements identifying information about each of the registrants if the registrants complied with Subsection (a) and, before the 60th day after the date notification of match was mailed, the registrant or registrants have not withdrawn their registrations.

(e) If the administrator establishes that a match cannot be made because of the death of an adoptee, birth parent, or biological sibling, the administrator shall promptly notify the affected registrant. The administrator shall disclose the reason why a match cannot be made and may disclose nonidentifying information concerning the circumstances of the person's death.

§§ 162.417, 162.418. Repealed.

§ 162.419. Registry Records Confidential

(a) All applications, registrations, records, and other information submitted to, obtained by, or otherwise acquired by a registry are confidential and may not be disclosed to any person or entity except in the manner authorized by this subchapter.

(b) Information acquired by a registry may not be disclosed under freedom of information or sunshine legislation, rules, or practice.

(c) A person may not file or prosecute a class action litigation to force a registry to disclose identifying information.

§ 162.420. Rulemaking

(a) The Texas Board of Health shall make rules and adopt minimum standards for the bureau to:

(1) administer the provisions of this subchapter; and

(2) ensure that each registry respects the right to privacy and confidentiality of an adoptee, birth parent, and biological sibling who does not desire to disclose the person's identity.

(b) The bureau shall conduct a comprehensive review of all rules and standards adopted under this subchapter not less than every six years.

(c) In order to provide the administrators an opportunity to review proposed rules and standards and send written suggestions to the Texas Board of Health, the board shall, before adopting rules and minimum standards, send a copy of the proposed rules and standards not less than 60 days before the date they take effect to:

(1) the administrator of each registry established under this subchapter; and

(2) the administrator of each agency authorized by the department to place children for adoption.

§ 162.421. Prohibited Acts; Criminal Penalties

(a) This subchapter does not prevent the bureau from making known to the public, by appropriate means, the existence of voluntary adoption registries.

(b) Information received by or in connection with the operation of a registry may not be stored in a data bank used for any purpose other than operation of the registry.

(c) A person commits an offense if the person knowingly or recklessly discloses information from a registry application, registration, record, or other information submitted to, obtained by, or otherwise acquired by a registry in violation of this subchapter. This subsection may not be construed to penalize the disclosure of information from adoption agency records. An offense under this subsection is a felony of the second degree.

(d) A person commits an offense if the person with criminal negligence causes or permits the disclosure of information from a registry application, registration, record, or other information submitted to, obtained by, or otherwise acquired by a registry in violation of this subchapter. This subsection may not be construed to penalize the disclosure of information from adoption agency records. An offense under this subsection is a Class A misdemeanor.

(e) A person commits an offense if the person impersonates an adoptee, birth parent, or biological sibling with the intent to secure confidential information from a registry established under this subchapter. An offense under this subsection is a felony of the second degree.

(f) A person commits an offense if the person impersonates an administrator, agent, or employee of a registry with the intent to secure confidential information from a registry established under this subchapter. An offense under this subsection is a felony of the second degree.

(g) A person commits an offense if the person, with intent to deceive and with knowledge of the statement's meaning, makes a false statement under oath in connection with the operation of a registry. An offense under this subsection is a felony of the third degree.

§ 162.422. Immunity From Liability

(a) The bureau or authorized agency establishing or operating a registry is not liable to any person for obtaining or disclosing identifying information about a birth parent, adoptee, or biological sibling within the scope of this subchapter and under its provisions.

(b) An employee or agent of the bureau or of an authorized agency establishing or operating a registry under this subchapter is not liable to any person for obtaining or disclosing identifying information about a birth parent, adoptee, or biological sibling within the scope of this subchapter and under its provisions.

(c) A person or entity furnishing information to the administrator or an employee or agent of a registry is not liable to any person for disclosing information about a birth parent, adoptee, or biological sibling within the scope of this subchapter and under its provisions.

(d) A person or entity is not immune from liability for performing an act prohibited by Section 162.421.

SUBCHAPTER F. ADOPTION OF AN ADULT

§ 162.501. Adoption of Adult

The court may grant the petition of an adult residing in this state to adopt another adult according to this subchapter.

Comment

An adoption of one adult by another is almost invariably intended to affect inheritance rights. The only duty of the court is to confirm that all adults involved have agreed to the adoption. The adult adoption process is sometimes used by same sex couples to cross adopt each other to affect standing of one partner if the other partner is a parent of a child.

CLE/Other Legal Publication

Common law and same sex marriages, adult adoptions, maternity tests, and other unusual topics. Sam M. "Trey" Yates, III., 2009 So. Tex. Fam. L. Conf.

Leading Cases

Lehman v. Corpus Christi Nat'l Bank, 668 S.W.2d 687 (Tex. 1984) (adult adoptees have same inheritance rights as child adoptees)

Hagman v. Hagman, 886 S.W.2d 398 (Tex. App.—Dallas 1994, writ denied) (person adopted as an adult qualifies as "bodily issue" under will)

---

§ 162.502. Jurisdiction

The petitioner shall file a suit to adopt an adult in the district court or a statutory county court granted jurisdiction in family law cases and proceedings by Chapter 25, Government Code, in the county of the petitioner's residence.

§ 162.503. Requirements of Petition

(a) A petition to adopt an adult shall be entitled "In the Interest of ________, An Adult."

(b) If the petitioner is married, both spouses must join in the petition for adoption.

§ 162.504. Consent

A court may not grant an adoption unless the adult consents in writing to be adopted by the petitioner.

§ 162.505. Attendance Required

The petitioner and the adult to be adopted must attend the hearing. For good cause shown, the court may waive this requirement, by written order, if the petitioner or adult to be adopted is unable to attend.

§ 162.506. Adoption Order

(a) The court shall grant the adoption if the court finds that the requirements for adoption of an adult are met.

(b) Notwithstanding that both spouses have joined in a petition for the adoption of an adult as required by Section 162.503(b), the court may grant the adoption of the adult to both spouses or, on request of the spouses, to only one spouse.

§ 162.507. Effect of Adoption

(a) The adopted adult is the son or daughter of the adoptive parents for all purposes.

(b) The adopted adult is entitled to inherit from and through the adopted adult's adoptive parents as though the adopted adult were the biological child of the adoptive parents.

(c) The adopted adult may not inherit from or through the adult's biological parent. A biological parent may not inherit from or through an adopted adult.

SUBCHAPTER G. MISCELLANEOUS PROVISIONS

§ 162.601. Incentives for Licensed Child-Placing Agencies

(a) Subject to the availability of funds, the Department of Protective and Regulatory Services shall pay, in addition to any other amounts due, a monetary incentive to a licensed child-placing agency for the completion of an adoption:

(1) of a child, as defined by Section 162.301, receiving or entitled to receive foster care at department expense; and

(2) arranged with the assistance of the agency.

(b) The incentive may not exceed 25 percent of the amount the department would have spent to provide one year of foster care for the child, determined according to the child's level of care at the time the adoption is completed.

(c) For purposes of this section, an adoption is completed on the date on which the court issues the adoption order.

§ 162.602. Documentation to Accompany Petition for Adoption or Annulment or Revocation of Adoption

At the time a petition for adoption or annulment or revocation of adoption is filed, the petitioner shall also file completed documentation that may be used by the clerk of the court, at the time the petition is granted, to comply with Section 192.009, Health and Safety Code, and Section 108.003.

SUBTITLE C. JUDICIAL RESOURCES AND SERVICES

Chapter

★★★

CHAPTER 201. ASSOCIATE JUDGE

SUBCHAPTER A. ASSOCIATE JUDGE

SUBCHAPTER B. ASSOCIATE JUDGE FOR TITLE IV–D CASES

SUBCHAPTER C. ASSOCIATE JUDGE FOR CHILD PROTECTION CASES

SUBCHAPTER D. ASSOCIATE JUDGE FOR JUVENILE MATTERS [New]

Editors' Note: *This chapter contains guest commentary by: J. Andrew Hathcock, Associate Judge, Travis County, formerly Child Protection Court of Central Texas; Charles G. Childress, Clinical Professor (retired), Children's Rights Clinic, University of Texas Law School, and former Chief Attorney, Field Operations, Legal Division, Texas Department of Family and Protective Services (then DPRS, now DFPS); Alicia Gray Key, Deputy Attorney General and IV–D Director, and H. Patrick Sullivan, Deputy Director for Federal and State Operations, Child Support Division, Office of the Attorney General of Texas respectively identified as (J.A.H.; C.G.C.; or A.G.K. & H.P.S.).*

SUBCHAPTER A. ASSOCIATE JUDGE

Introductory Comment

As the population of Texas exploded over the last two decades of the 20th Century, the legislature did not adequately respond to the increasing demands on the judicial system by creating new district courts or providing for additional county courts-at-law to exercise family law jurisdiction.

Given the vastly increased use of alternative dispute resolution techniques, in retrospect this may have been a wise course to follow. In any event, the legislature enacted statutes that authorized counties to employ associate judges to assist with an ever expanding family law caseload. The elected judges were given both appointment authority and the duty of supervision. What began as a simple program of adding a judge or two to assist in crowded metropolitan counties has grown exponentially into a comprehensive, statewide judicial system with three separate categories of associate judges.

Interestingly, the three types of associate judges have similar, but not identical powers to decide cases that come before them. For example, general jurisdiction associate judges (Subchapter A) may render temporary orders and agreed or default orders but all other orders recommended and signed by an associate judge must be ratified by the referring court. An associate judge for child protection cases (Subchapter C) may render and sign any order except a final order after a trial on the merits. Further, a final order recommended by an associate judge takes effect without ratification by the referring court if a de novo hearing is not requested. Finally, very few of the actions of associate judges handling Title IV–D child support cases (Subchapter B, formerly known as a child support masters) require ratification by a district judge.

CLE/Other Legal Publication

Practice before an associate judge—temporary orders. Charla F. Moore. 2007 ADV. FAM. L.

Leading Cases

State ex rel. Latty v. Owens, 907 S.W.2d 484 (Tex. 1995) (although de novo hearing not held as required, district court's inadvertent adoption of master's recommendation is final appealable order)

In re F.A.V., 284 S.W.3d 929 (Tex. App.—Dallas 2009, no pet.) (trial court did not abuse discretion by reversing sanction of striking pleadings imposed by associate judge)

In re M.K.R., 216 S.W.3d 58 (Tex. App.—Fort Worth 2007, no pet.) (associate judge's report of contempt approved and ordered by trial court—separate document not required)

In re T.S., 191 S.W.3d 736 (Tex. App.—Houston [14th Dist.] 2006, pet. denied) (report by associate judge based on jury verdict still subject to de novo hearing by district court)

Kennedy v. Kennedy, 125 S.W.3d 14 (Tex. App.—Austin, 2003, no pet.) (trial court could not adopt and approve entirety of associate judge's order before hearing former wife's de novo appeal—conditional approval required within 72 hours only to continue incarceration)

In re A.J.L., 108 S.W.3d 414 (Tex. App.—Fort Worth 2003, pet. denied) (former stepfather's standing to pursue modification of biological parents' custody order within power of associate judge to decide)

In re D.J.M., 114 S.W.3d 637 (Tex. App.—Fort Worth 2003, pet. denied) (waiving record before associate judge means record absent of needed information for sufficiency of evidence review)

In re W.G.S., 107 S.W.3d 624 (Tex. App.—Corpus Christi 2002, no pet.) (failure to appeal to referring court resulting in approval of associate judge's report does not deprive party of right to appeal)

In re N.R.C., 94 S.W.3d 799 (Tex. App.—Houston [14th Dist.] 2002, no pet.) (failure to appeal associate judge's sanctions to trial court doesn't preclude appeal to Court of Appeals)

Robles v. Robles, 965 S.W.2d 605 (Tex. App.—Houston [1st Dist.] 1998, no writ) (associate judge adequately provided parties with notice of substance of report)

---

§ 201.001. Appointment

(a) A judge of a court having jurisdiction of a suit under this title or Title 1 or 4 may appoint a full-time or part-time associate judge to perform the duties authorized by this chapter if the commissioners court of a county in which the court has jurisdiction authorizes the employment of an associate judge.

(b) If a court has jurisdiction in more than one county, an associate judge appointed by that court may serve only in a county in which the commissioners court has authorized the associate judge's appointment.

(c) If more than one court in a county has jurisdiction of a suit under this title or Title 1 or 4 the commissioners court may authorize the appointment of an associate judge for each court or may authorize one or more associate judges to share service with two or more courts.

(d) If an associate judge serves more than one court, the associate judge's appointment must be made with the unanimous approval of all the judges under whom the associate judge serves.

(e) This section does not apply to an associate judge appointed under Subchapter B or C.

§ 201.002. Qualifications

(a) Except as provided by Subsection (b), to be eligible for appointment as an associate judge, a person must meet the requirements and qualifications to serve as a judge of the court or courts for which the associate judge is appointed.

(b) To be eligible for appointment as an associate judge under Subchapter B or C, a person must meet the requirements and qualifications established under those subchapters.

§ 201.003. Compensation

(a) An associate judge shall be paid a salary determined by the commissioners court of the county in which the associate judge serves.

(b) If an associate judge serves in more than one county, the associate judge shall be paid a salary as determined by agreement of the commissioners courts of the counties in which the associate judge serves.

(c) The associate judge's salary is paid from the county fund available for payment of officers' salaries.

(d) This section does not apply to an associate judge appointed under Subchapter B or C.

§ 201.004. Termination of Associate Judge

(a) An associate judge who serves a single court serves at the will of the judge of that court.

(b) The employment of an associate judge who serves more than two courts may only be terminated by a majority vote of all the judges of the courts which the associate judge serves.

(c) The employment of an associate judge who serves two courts may be terminated by either of the judges of the courts which the associate judge serves.

(d) This section does not apply to an associate judge appointed under Subchapter B or C.

§ 201.005. Cases That May Be Referred

(a) Except as provided by this section, a judge of a court may refer to an associate judge any aspect of a suit over which the court has jurisdiction under this title or Title 1 or 4 including any matter ancillary to the suit.

(b) Unless a party files a written objection to the associate judge hearing a trial on the merits, the judge may refer the trial to the associate judge. A trial on the merits is any final adjudication from which an appeal may be taken to a court of appeals.

(c) A party must file an objection to an associate judge hearing a trial on the merits or presiding at a jury trial not later than the 10th day after the date the party receives notice that the associate judge will hear the trial. If an objection is filed, the referring court shall hear the trial on the merits or preside at a jury trial.

(d) The requirements of Subsections (b) and (c) shall apply whenever a judge has authority to refer the trial of a suit under this title, Title 1, or Title 4 to an associate judge, master, or other assistant judge regardless of whether the assistant judge is appointed under this subchapter.

Comment

An associate judge may preside at a jury trial, including a trial for termination of parental rights, unless a party objects or the referring court determines that the associate judge should not handle the case. *(C.G.C.)*

---

§ 201.006. Order of Referral

(a) In referring a case to an associate judge, the judge of the referring court shall render:

(1) an individual order of referral; or

(2) a general order of referral specifying the class and type of cases to be heard by the associate judge.

(b) The order of referral may limit the power or duties of an associate judge.

§ 201.007. Powers of Associate Judge

(a) Except as limited by an order of referral, an associate judge may:

(1) conduct a hearing;

(2) hear evidence;

(3) compel production of relevant evidence;

(4) rule on the admissibility of evidence;

(5) issue a summons for:

(A) the appearance of witnesses; and

(B) the appearance of a parent who has failed to appear before an agency authorized to conduct an investigation of an allegation of abuse or neglect of a child after receiving proper notice;

(6) examine a witness;

(7) swear a witness for a hearing;

(8) make findings of fact on evidence;

(9) formulate conclusions of law;

(10) recommend an order to be rendered in a case;

(11) regulate all proceedings in a hearing before the associate judge;

(12) order the attachment of a witness or party who fails to obey a subpoena;

(13) order the detention of a witness or party found guilty of contempt, pending approval by the referring court as provided by Section 201.013;

(14) without prejudice to the right of appeal under Section 201.015, render and sign:

(A) a final order agreed to in writing as to both form and substance by all parties;

(B) a final default order;

(C) a temporary order; or

(D) a final order in a case in which a party files an unrevoked waiver made in accordance with Rule 119, Texas Rules of Civil Procedure, that waives notice to the party of the final hearing or waives the party's appearance at the final hearing;

(15) take action as necessary and proper for the efficient performance of the associate judge's duties; and

(16) sign a final order that includes a waiver of the right of appeal pursuant to Section 201.015.

(b) An associate judge may, in the interest of justice, refer a case back to the referring court regardless of whether a timely objection to the associate judge hearing the trial on the merits or presiding at a jury trial has been made by any party.

(c) An order described by Subsection (a)(14) that is rendered and signed by an associate judge constitutes an order of the referring court.

(d) An answer filed by or on behalf of a party who previously filed a waiver described in Subsection (a)(14)(D) shall revoke that waiver.

Comment

The legislature has conferred ever-broader judicial powers on associate judges. Formerly, the findings and recommendations of an associate judge became an order of the referring court only when the referring court signed an order conforming to the associate judge's report. Amendments in 2003 eliminated that requirement with respect to agreed and default final orders. The 2005 amendments did the same for temporary orders, whether agreed or resulting from a contested hearing. A final order other than an agreed or default order, recommended and signed by an associate judge, still must be ratified by the referring court. *See* § 201.013(b), *infra*.

By an amendment in 2007, an associate judge may render a final order in a case in which a party files a written waiver of citation that also waives notice of final hearing or waives the party's appearance at the final hearing. A subsequently filed answer revokes the waiver. A party has the right to request a de novo hearing from any order rendered by an associate judge.

Subsection (b) permits the associate judge to refer a case back to the presiding court "in the interest of justice" even if no party objects. For example, if it is clear that a request for a de novo hearing to the referring court is inevitable no matter how the associate judge may rule, justice, or at least judicial economy, may best be served by having the case tried by the district judge. Parties may, however, waive the right to request a de novo hearing to the referring court, without waiving the right to seek relief from an appellate court. *See* § 201.015(g) and § 201.016(a), *infra*. *(J.A.H.)*

§ 201.008. Attendance of Bailiff

A bailiff may attend a hearing by an associate judge if directed by the referring court.

§ 201.009. Court Reporter; Record

(a) A court reporter may be provided during a hearing held by an associate judge appointed under this chapter. A court reporter is required to be provided when the associate judge presides over a jury trial or a contested final termination hearing.

(b) A party, the associate judge, or the referring court may provide for a reporter during the hearing, if one is not otherwise provided.

(c) Except as provided by Subsection (a), in the absence of a court reporter or on agreement of the parties, the record may be preserved by any means approved by the associate judge.

(d) The referring court or associate judge may tax the expense of preserving the record under Subsection (c) as costs.

(e) On a request for a de novo hearing, the referring court may consider testimony or other evidence in the record in addition to witnesses or other matters presented under Section 201.015.

Comment

A court reporter is required when an associate judge presides over a jury trial or a contested termination hearing. An associate judge may hear an uncontested termination—e.g., one based on voluntary affidavits of relinquishment, or by default—without a court reporter. The record may be made by any means approved by the associate judge, usually electronic recording. On the de novo hearing, the referring court may consider the record made at the hearing before the associate judge (whether by a court reporter or by other means), along with any additional evidence presented by the parties, to support the proposed judgment.

In 2007 the legislature made a number of changes to the terminology used in this chapter. Most notable is replacing "an appeal" of an associate judge's proposed order or judgment with "a request for de novo hearing" before the referring court. This appropriately reserves the term "appeal" to an appellate review under § 201.016, *infra*. *(J.A.H., C.G.C., A.G.K., & H.P.S.)*

§ 201.010. Witness

(a) A witness appearing before an associate judge is subject to the penalties for perjury provided by law.

(b) A referring court may fine or imprison a witness who:

(1) failed to appear before an associate judge after being summoned; or

(2) improperly refused to answer questions if the refusal has been certified to the court by the associate judge.

§ 201.011. Report

(a) The associate judge's report may contain the associate judge's findings, conclusions, or recommendations and may be in the form of a proposed order. The associate judge's report must be in writing in the form directed by the referring court.

(b) After a hearing, the associate judge shall provide the parties participating in the hearing notice of the substance of the associate judge's report, including any proposed order.

(c) Notice may be given to the parties:

(1) in open court, by an oral statement or a copy of the associate judge's written report, including any proposed order;

(2) by certified mail, return receipt requested; or

(3) by facsimile transmission.

(d) There is a rebuttable presumption that notice is received on the date stated on:

(1) the signed return receipt, if notice was provided by certified mail; or

(2) the confirmation page produced by the facsimile machine, if notice was provided by facsimile transmission.

(e) After a hearing conducted by an associate judge, the associate judge shall send the associate judge's signed and dated report, including any proposed order, and all other papers relating to the case to the referring court.

Comment

It is common practice for an associate judge to make a "report or recommendation" in the form of an order. This procedure leaves no doubt about the "substance of the associate judge's report." It also conforms to the increasing use of the associate's order by the referring court to constitute the final court action subject to appellate appeal or other post-trial review. *(C.G.C.)*

---

§ 201.012. Notice of Right to De Novo Hearing Before Referring Court

(a) Notice of the right to a de novo hearing before the referring court shall be given to all parties.

(b) The notice may be given:

(1) by oral statement in open court;

(2) by posting inside or outside the courtroom of the referring court; or

(3) as otherwise directed by the referring court.

§ 201.013. Order of Court

(a) Pending a de novo hearing before the referring court, a proposed order or judgment of the associate judge is in full force and effect and is enforceable as an order or judgment of the referring court, except for an order providing for the appointment of a receiver.

(b) Except as provided by Section 201.007(c), if a request for a de novo hearing before the referring court is not timely filed or the right to a de novo hearing before the referring court is waived, the proposed order or judgment of the associate judge becomes the order or judgment of the referring court only on the referring court's signing the proposed order or judgment.

(c) An order by an associate judge for the temporary detention or incarceration of a witness or party shall be presented to the referring court on the day the witness or party is detained or incarcerated. The referring court, without prejudice to the right to a de novo hearing provided by Section 201.015, may approve the temporary detention or incarceration or may order the release of the party or witness, with or without bond, pending a de novo hearing. If the referring court is not immediately available, the associate judge may order the release of the party or witness, with or without bond, pending a de novo hearing or may continue the person's detention or incarceration for not more than 72 hours.

Comment

An agreed order or a default judgment signed by the associate judge may "become the order of the referring court" without the signature of the referring court under § 201.007(c).

The language in Subsection (c) permits temporary detention, or release on bond, of a person found guilty of contempt of court pending an appeal to the referring court. Before adoption of this provision, some associate judges ordered a contemnor to report for jail on a specific date after the referring court would have time to sign the commitment order. Not surprisingly, many of those so ordered failed to return. Other associate judges immediately transferred the contemnor to the referring court for "approval" of the order, thus denying the contemnor three days to consider whether to request a de novo appeal. This section sets a 72 hour deadline for the referring court to either approve the detention or order release of the contemnor, and makes clear that the contemnor continues to have a right to de novo review without regard to the interim actions. *(C.G.C.)*

§ 201.014. Judicial Action on Associate Judge's Proposed Order or Judgment

(a) Unless a party files a written request for a de novo hearing before the referring court, the referring court may:

(1) adopt, modify, or reject the associate judge's proposed order or judgment;

(2) hear further evidence; or

(3) recommit the matter to the associate judge for further proceedings.

(b) Regardless of whether a party files a written request for a de novo hearing before the referring court, a proposed order or judgment rendered by an associate judge in a suit filed by the Department of Family and Protective Services that meets the requirements of Section 263.401(d) is considered a final order for purposes of Section 263.401.

Comment

Subsection (b), added in 2007, ensured that a request for a de novo hearing—and certainly the granting of that request—would not jeopardize the status of the associate judge's proposed order in a child protection case filed by DFPS as a "final" order. A similar safeguard was provided under § 201.2041, *infra*. Of course, to be deemed a "final" order in the first place, the associate judge's order was required to conform to the requirements of § 263.401(d). Unfortunately, also in 2007, the same legislature repealed § 263.401(d) and deleted the requirement for a final order in Chapter 263, which complicates the analysis. The court must now "commence the trial on the merits" within the time limit, making the "final order" issue irrelevant. The question now is whether the commencement of the trial before the associate judge is sufficient under the statute. *(J.A.H., H.P.S. & C.G.C.)*

§ 201.015. De Novo Hearing Before Referring Court

(a) A party may request a de novo hearing before the referring court by filing with the clerk of the referring court a written request not later than the seventh working day after the date the party receives notice of the substance of the associate judge's report as provided by Section 201.011.

(b) A request for a de novo hearing under this section must specify the issues that will be presented to the referring court.

(c) In the de novo hearing before the referring court, the parties may present witnesses on the issues specified in the request for hearing. The referring court may also consider the record from the hearing before the associate judge, including the charge to and verdict returned by a jury.

(d) Notice of a request for a de novo hearing before the referring court shall be given to the opposing attorney under Rule 21a, Texas Rules of Civil Procedure.

(e) If a request for a de novo hearing before the referring court is filed by a party, any other party may file a request for a de novo hearing before the referring court not later than the seventh working day after the date the initial request was filed.

(f) The referring court, after notice to the parties, shall hold a de novo hearing not later than the 30th day after the date on which the initial request for a de novo hearing was filed with the clerk of the referring court.

(g) Before the start of a hearing by an associate judge, the parties may waive the right of a de novo hearing before the referring court in writing or on the record.

(h) The denial of relief to a party after a de novo hearing under this section or a party's waiver of the right to a de novo hearing before the referring court does not affect the right of a party to file a motion for new trial, motion for judgment notwithstanding the verdict, or other post-trial motion.

(i) A party may not demand a second jury in a de novo hearing before the referring court if the associate judge's proposed order or judgment resulted from a jury trial.

Comment

When associate judges were first recognized in the Family Code, one immutable principle was that any party could "appeal" the associate judge's "report," then "recommendation," and even later "proposed order." The time limit was "filing a notice of appeal within three days" after receiving notice of the associate judge's order or of the substance of the A.J.'s report or recommendation. This relatively short timeframe was extended to seven working days as of September 1, 2007. This corresponds to the time period under Subsection (e) for the filing of a de novo hearing request by another party after the initial request for a de novo hearing was filed. The word "appeal" for this de novo review has been dropped from the Code, so that "appeal" now refers to review by the courts of appeal, not the supervising district court.

The record, made by a court reporter or by electronic means, and any jury charge and verdict may be considered as part of the de novo review. A party may file a motion for new trial or other post-trial motions when an associate judge has presided, but if the presiding judge's signature is not required because the order was agreed or by default, the time to file such motions or a notice of appeal runs from the date the order was signed by the associate judge. See § 201.016, *infra*.

Subsection (i) prohibits parties from requesting a second jury on the request of a de novo hearing from an associate judge's order based on a jury verdict. *(C.G.C., J.A.H., A.G.K. & H.P.S.)*

§ 201.016. Appellate Review

(a) A party's failure to request a de novo hearing before the referring court or a party's waiver of the right to request a de novo hearing before the referring court does not deprive the party of the right to appeal to or request other relief from a court of appeals or the supreme court.

(b) Except as provided by Subsection (c), the date an order or judgment by the referring court is signed is the controlling date for the purposes of appeal to or request for other relief from a court of appeals or the supreme court.

(c) The date an agreed order or a default order is signed by an associate judge is the controlling date for the purpose of an appeal to, or a request for other relief relating to the order from, a court of appeals or the supreme court.

Comment

Because an agreed order or default order rendered and signed by an associate judge constitutes an order of the referring court (§ 201.007, *supra*), the date on which an associate judge signs such an order is the controlling date in an appeal to an appellate court (skipping the de novo step). Since appeals of termination orders (and conservatorship orders involving DFPS under Chapter 263) are accelerated appeals, the deadline for filing a notice of appeal is 20 days after the default or agreed order is signed by the associate judge or 20 days after the referring court's order following de novo review. Post-trial motions, such as a motion for new trial do not affect this appellate deadline. *See* § 109.002(a) and § 263.405. *(C.G.C., A.G.K. & H.P.S.)*

§ 201.017. Immunity

An associate judge appointed under this subchapter has the judicial immunity of a district judge. All existing immunity granted an associate judge by law, express or implied, continues in full force and effect.

§ 201.018. Visiting Associate Judge

(a) If an associate judge appointed under this subchapter is temporarily unable to perform the judge's official duties because of absence or illness, injury, or other disability, a judge of a court having jurisdiction of a suit under this title or Title 1 or 4 may appoint a visiting associate judge to perform the duties of the associate judge during the period of the associate judge's absence or disability if the commissioners court of a county in which the court has jurisdiction authorizes the employment of a visiting associate judge.

(b) To be eligible for appointment under this section, a person must have served as an associate judge for at least two years.

(c) Sections 201.001 through 201.017 apply to a visiting associate judge appointed under this section.

(d) This section does not apply to an associate judge appointed under Subchapter B.

SUBCHAPTER B. ASSOCIATE JUDGE FOR TITLE IV–D CASES

Introductory Comment

Initially, the corps of judicial officers who specialize in establishing, enforcing, and modifying child support orders were known as "child support masters." The term "child support master" had been used in Texas family law since 1987 when the state instituted a system of child support masters in response to a federal mandate under the Child Support Enforcement Amendments of 1984 that states use an administrative or quasi-judicial process for expeditiously handling cases being enforced by their Title IV–D child support enforcement agencies. The use of "Master" was derived from the "Masters in Chancery" provided under Rule 171, Texas Rules of Civil Procedure who may be appointed "for good cause" by a court to conduct hearings, take evidence, and make a report of findings to the referring court "in exceptional cases." While in many ways child support masters resembled administrative hearing officers, they clearly belonged to the judicial branch of government. Effective Sept. 1, 2003, the legislature has remedied the nomenclature imbalance between these judges and other appointed judges by eliminating the term "master" from the code and substituting "associate judge." The legislative intent obviously was to create uniformity of nomenclature with respect to the judicial officers who hear cases upon referral from a court. Notwithstanding this effort, the old terminology is occasionally still heard.

The renamed "associate judges for Title IV–D cases" preside over all cases prosecuted by the Attorney General of Texas, as the state's designated Title IV–D agency (Chapter 231 *infra*). While in many ways child support masters resembled administrative hearing officers, they clearly belonged to the judicial branch of government. The child support A.J.'s, together with the "cluster-court" associate judges described in the following subchapter, are unique in Texas jurisprudence because: (1) their caseloads are extremely specialized; (2) they are appointed by the presiding judges of the administrative judicial regions; and, (3) they may be appointed to serve in more than one court. While in most respects the powers and duties of an associate judge specializing in child support mirror those of an associate judge with general family law jurisdiction as described in Subchapter A, significantly fewer actions taken by a child support associate judge require ratification by a referring court.

As of June 30, 2010, the Office of Court Administration employs 43 associate judges and 41 administrative assistants to hear and dispose of Title IV-D child support establishment and enforcement cases and paternity cases within the expedited time frames established by Chapter 201.110 of the Texas Family Code. The Office of the Attorney General (OAG) provides purchasing and on-site technical (computer) support. *(A.G.K. & H.P.S.)*

CLE/Other Legal Publications

Navigating the Attorney General maze. Cynthia J. Barela & April Palmer, 2008 UT FAM. L. FRONT LINES

*Practice Before an Associate Judge—Temporary Orders.*Charla F. Moore. 2007 ADV. FAM. L.

Understanding the AG and CPS. Rhonda F. Hunter. 2007 ADV. FAM. L.

Navigating the Attorney General's child support enforcement program. Alicia G. Key, 2007 UT DEFINITIVE SAPCR

Cross References

IV–D Child Support Enforcement. 42 U.S.C.A. § 651 *et seq.*, § 666(a)(2) (expedited processes); *see* 45 C.F.R. § 303.101

§ 201.101. Authority of Presiding Judge

(a) The presiding judge of each administrative judicial region, after conferring with the judges of courts in the region having jurisdiction of Title IV–D cases, shall determine which courts require the appointment of a full-time or part-time associate judge to complete each Title IV–D case within the time specified in this subchapter.

(b) The presiding judge may limit the appointment to a specified time period and may terminate an appointment at any time.

(c) An associate judge appointed under this subchapter may be appointed to serve more than one court. Two or more judges of administrative judicial regions may jointly appoint one or more associate judges to serve the regions.

(d) If the presiding judge determines that a court requires an associate judge for Title IV–D cases, the presiding judge shall appoint an associate judge for that purpose. Except as provided under Subsection (e), if an associate judge is appointed for a court under this subchapter, all Title IV–D cases shall be referred to the associate judge by a general order for each county issued by the judge of the court for which the associate judge is appointed, or, in the absence of that order, by a general order issued by the presiding judge who appointed the associate judge. Referral of Title IV–D cases may not be made for individual cases or case by case.

(e) If a county has entered into a contract with the Title IV–D agency under Section 231.0011, enforcement services may be directly provided by county personnel as provided under Section 231.0011(d), including judges and associate judges of the courts of the county.

Comment

Normally all IV–D cases are referred to the associate judge under a general order of the referring court. Subsection (e), however, carves out an exception for courts in those counties in which, by local rule and a contract with the Title IV–D agency, all new support orders are automatically subject to IV–D services unless the obligee in a case specifically declines the services. This exception enables judges to retain in their courts such cases as they choose, while turning the others over to the associate judge for Title IV–D cases. *(A.G.K. & H.P.S.)*

§ 201.102. Application of Law Governing Associate Judges

Subchapter A applies to an associate judge appointed under this subchapter, except that, to the extent of any conflict between this subchapter and Subchapter A, this subchapter prevails.

§ 201.1021. Qualifications

(a) To be eligible for appointment under this subchapter, a person must be and be:

(1) eligible for assignment under Section 74.054, Government Code, because the person is named on the list of retired and former judges maintained by the presiding judge of the administrative region under Section 74.055, Government Code; or

(2) licensed to practice law in this state and have been a practicing lawyer in this state, or a judge of a court in this state who is not otherwise eligible under Subdivision (1), for the four years preceding the date of appointment.

(b) An associate judge appointed under this subchapter shall during the term of appointment reside in the administrative judicial region, or a county adjacent to the region, in which the court to which the associate judge is appointed is located. An associate judge appointed to serve in two or more administrative judicial regions may reside anywhere in the regions.

§ 201.103. Designation of Host County

(a) The presiding judges of the administrative judicial regions by majority vote shall determine the host county of an associate judge appointed under this subchapter.

(b) The host county shall provide an adequate courtroom and quarters, including furniture, necessary utilities, and telephone equipment and service, for the associate judge and other personnel assisting the associate judge.

(c) An associate judge is not required to reside in the host county.

§ 201.104. Powers of Associate Judge

(a) On the motion of a party or the associate judge, an associate judge may refer a complex case back to the judge for final disposition after the associate judge has recommended temporary support.

(b) An associate judge may render and sign any order that is not a final order on the merits of the case.

(c) An associate judge may recommend to the referring court any order after a trial on the merits.

(d) Only the referring court may hear and render an order on a motion for postjudgment relief, including a motion for a new trial or to vacate, correct, or reform a judgment.

(e) Notwithstanding Subsection (d) and subject to Section 201.1042(g), an associate judge may hear and render an order on:

(1) a suit to modify or clarify an existing child support order;

(2) a motion to enforce a child support order or revoke a respondent's community supervision and suspension of commitment;

(3) a respondent's compliance with the conditions provided in the associate judge's report for suspension of the respondent's commitment; or

(4) a motion for postjudgment relief, including a motion for a new trial or to vacate, correct, or reform a judgment, if neither party has requested a de novo hearing before the referring court.

Comment

Subsection (b) provides that a pretrial or temporary order rendered by the associate judge need not be ratified by the referring court.

Subsection (d) states that only the referring court may hear and act on post judgment motions for a new trial or to vacate, correct, or reform a judgment. A 2009 amendment to Subsection (e) extends this authority to an associate judge if there has been no request for a de novo hearing before the referring court. In addition, under Subsection (e) an associate judge may hear post-judgment motions and render orders with respect to contempt or modification of final child support orders. There is, then, very little that an associate judge may not do, although an associate judge's order or judgment for enforcement by contempt or immediate incarceration must be ratified by the referring court, as provided under § 201.1041(b). *(A.G.K. & H.P.S.)*

§ 201.1041. Judicial Action on Associate Judge's Proposed Order or Judgment

(a) If a request for a de novo hearing before the referring court is not timely filed or the right to a de novo hearing before the referring court is waived, the proposed order or judgment of the associate judge, other than a proposed order or judgment providing for enforcement by contempt or the immediate incarceration of a party, shall become the order or judgment of the referring court by operation of law without ratification by the referring court.

(b) An associate judge's proposed order or judgment providing for enforcement by contempt or the immediate incarceration of a party becomes an order of the referring court only if:

(1) the referring court signs an order adopting the associate judge's proposed order or judgment; and

(2) the order or judgment meets the requirements of Section 157.166.

(c) Except as provided by Subsection (b), a proposed order or judgment of the associate judge is in full force and effect and is enforceable as an order or judgment of the referring court pending a de novo hearing before the referring court.

Comment

A party may file a request for a de novo hearing before the referring court on most proposed orders or judgments of the associate judge, including those to establish paternity, establish or modify support, or to reduce unpaid child support to judgment. If a request for de novo hearing is not timely made, or if the right to file a request has been waived, such proposed orders or judgments become enforceable court orders without the necessity of signature or ratification by the referring court. An associate judge's proposed order of contempt or immediate enforcement, however, must be ratified by the referring court. *(A.G.K. & H.P.S.)*

§ 201.1042. De Novo Hearing Before Referring Court

(a) Except as provided by this section, Section 201.015 applies to a request for a de novo hearing before the referring court.

(b) The party requesting a de novo hearing before the referring court shall file notice with the clerk of the referring court not later than the seventh working day after the date the associate judge signs the proposed order or judgment.

(c) A respondent who timely files a request for a de novo hearing on an associate judge's proposed order or judgment providing for incarceration shall be brought before the referring court not later than the first working day after the date on which the respondent files the request for a de novo hearing. The referring court shall determine whether the respondent should be released on bond or whether the respondent's appearance in court at a designated time and place can be otherwise assured.

(d) If the respondent under Subsection (c) is released on bond or other security, the referring court shall condition the bond or other security on the respondent's promise to appear in court for a de novo hearing at a designated date, time, and place, and the referring court shall give the respondent notice of the hearing in open court. No other notice to the respondent is required.

(e) If the respondent under Subsection (c) is released without posting bond or security, the court shall set a de novo hearing at a designated date, time, and place and give the respondent notice of the hearing in open court. No other notice to the respondent is required.

(f) If the referring court is not satisfied that the respondent's appearance in court can be assured and the respondent remains incarcerated, a de novo hearing shall be held as soon as practicable, but not later than the fifth day after the date the respondent's request for a de novo hearing before the referring court was filed, unless the respondent or, if represented, the respondent's attorney waives the accelerated hearing.

(g) Until a de novo hearing is held under this section and the referring court has signed an order or judgment or has ruled on a timely filed motion for new trial or a motion to vacate, correct, or reform a judgment, an associate judge may not hold a hearing on the respondent's compliance with conditions in the associate judge's proposed order or judgment for suspension of commitment or on a motion to revoke the respondent's community supervision and suspension of commitment.

Comment

The caption to this section does not describe the entirety of its contents. Subsections (a) and (b) are innocuous enough, merely providing for appeal and notice. But the remaining subsections are designed to implement the associate judge's recommendation for contempt and incarceration. Read together, Subsections (c) and (f) rather clearly indicate that an associate judge may order a respondent to be held in custody until the next working day, at which time the respondent must be "brought before the referring court" for a hearing on whether he "should be released."

An obligor who is incarcerated by the associate judge cannot obtain immediate release by filing a request for de novo hearing before the referring court on an appeal of the associate judge's proposed order. This procedure follows the § 157.105 release hearing that the court conducts after an obligor is arrested on a capias for failure to appear. Under Subsection (g), the associate judge may not hold a hearing on a respondent's compliance with conditions in the associate judge's order for suspension of commitment or on a motion to revoke community supervision and suspension of commitment if: (1) a timely filed request for a de novo hearing before the referring court's is pending; or, (2) the referring court has rendered an order for a new trial or post judgment relief. The intent is to achieve an orderly process and to avoid conflicting actions by the associate judge and the referring court. *(C.G.C., A.G.K. & H.P.S.)*

Leading Cases

In re T.S., 191 S.W.3d 736 (Tex. App.—Houston [14th Dist.] 2006, pet. denied) (report by associate judge based on jury verdict still subject to appeal to district court)

Phagan v. Aleman, 29 S.W.3d 632 (Tex. App.—Houston [1st Dist.] 2000, no pet.) (appeal from child-support master's recommended order absolutely entitled to de novo hearing)

Attorney General v. Orr, 989 S.W.2d 464 (Tex. App.—Austin 1999, no pet.) (notice of appeal requires de novo hearing by district court—which is new and independent action with all attributes of original civil action)

---

§ 201.105. Compensation of Associate Judge

(a) An associate judge appointed under this subchapter is entitled to a salary to be determined by a majority vote of the presiding judges of the administrative judicial regions. The salary may not exceed 90 percent of the salary paid to a district judge as set by the General Appropriations Act.

(b) The associate judge's salary shall be paid from county funds available for payment of officers' salaries or from funds available from the state and federal government as provided by this subchapter.

§ 201.106. Child Support Court Monitor and Other Personnel

(a) The presiding judge of an administrative judicial region or the presiding judges of the administrative judicial regions, by majority vote, may appoint other personnel, including a child support court monitor for each associate judge appointed under this subchapter, as needed to implement and administer the provisions of this subchapter.

(b) The salaries of the personnel and court monitors shall be paid from county funds available for payment of officers' salaries or from funds available from the state and federal government as provided by this subchapter.

§ 201.1065. Duties of Child Support Court Monitor

(a) A child support court monitor appointed under this subchapter shall monitor child support cases in which the obligor is placed on probation for failure to comply with the requirements of a child support order.

(b) In monitoring a child support case, a court monitor shall:

(1) conduct an intake assessment of the needs of an obligor that, if addressed, would enable the obligor to comply with a child support order;

(2) refer an obligor to employment services offered by the employment assistance program under Section 302.0035, Labor Code, if appropriate;

(3) provide mediation services or referrals to services, if appropriate;

(4) schedule periodic contacts with an obligor to assess compliance with the child support order and whether additional support services are required;

(5) monitor the amount and timeliness of child support payments owed and paid by an obligor; and

(6) if appropriate, recommend that the court:

(A) discharge an obligor from or modify the terms of the obligor's community supervision; or

(B) revoke an obligor's community supervision.

§ 201.1066. Supervision of Associate Judges

The office of court administration shall assist the presiding judges in:

(1) monitoring the associate judges' compliance with job performance standards and federal and state laws and policies;

(2) addressing the training needs and resource requirements of the associate judges;

(3) conducting annual performance evaluations for the associate judges and other personnel appointed under this subchapter based on written personnel performance standards adopted by the presiding judges; and

(4) receiving, investigating, and resolving complaints about particular associate judges or the associate judge program under this subchapter based on a uniform process adopted by the presiding judges.

§ 201.107. State and Federal Funds

(a) The office of court administration may contract with the Title IV–D agency for available state and federal funds under Title IV–D and may employ personnel needed to implement and administer this subchapter. An associate judge, a court monitor for each associate judge, and other personnel appointed under this subchapter are state employees for all purposes, including accrual of leave time, insurance benefits, retirement benefits, and travel regulations.

(b) The presiding judges of the administrative judicial regions, state agencies, and counties may contract with the Title IV–D agency for available federal funds under Title IV–D to reimburse costs and salaries associated with associate judges, court monitors, and personnel appointed under this subchapter and may also use available state funds and public or private grants.

(c) The presiding judges and the Title IV–D agency shall act and are authorized to take any action necessary to maximize the amount of federal funds available under the Title IV–D program.

§ 201.108. Repealed.

§ 201.1085. Repealed.

§ 201.109. Repealed.

§ 201.110. Time for Disposition of Title IV–D Cases

(a) Title IV–D cases must be completed from the time of successful service to the time of disposition within the following time:

(1) 75 percent within six months; and

(2) 90 percent within one year.

(b) Title IV–D cases shall be given priority over other cases.

(c) A clerk or judge may not restrict the number of Title IV–D cases that are filed or heard in the courts.

Comment

This section reflects the requirements of federal law for the expedited processing of Title IV–D cases, as provided by 42 U.S.C. 666(a)(2), 45 C.F.R. 303.101). *(A.G.K. & H.P.S.)*

---

§ 201.111. Time to Act on Associate Judge's Proposed Order or Judgment That Includes Recommended Finding of Contempt

(a) Not later than the 10th day after the date an associate judge's proposed order or judgment recommending a finding of contempt is signed, the referring court shall:

(1) adopt, modify, or reject the proposed order or judgment;

(2) hear further evidence; or

(3) recommit the matter for further proceedings.

(b) The time limit in Subsection (a) does not apply if a party has filed a written request for a de novo hearing before the referring court.

§ 201.112. Limitation on Law Practice by Certain Associate Judges

A full-time associate judge appointed under this subchapter may not engage in the private practice of law.

§ 201.113. Visiting Associate Judge

(a) If an associate judge appointed under this subchapter is temporarily unable to perform the associate judge's official duties because of absence resulting from family circumstances, illness, injury, disability, or military service, or if there is a vacancy in the position of associate judge, the presiding judge of the administrative judicial region in which the associate judge serves or the vacancy occurs may appoint a visiting associate judge for Title IV–D cases to perform the duties of the associate judge during the period the associate judge is unable to perform the associate judge's duties or until another associate judge is appointed to fill the vacancy.

(b) A person is not eligible for appointment under this section unless the person has served as a master or associate judge under this chapter, a district judge, or a statutory county court judge for at least two years before the date of appointment.

(c) A visiting associate judge appointed under this section is subject to each provision of this chapter that applies to an associate judge serving under a regular appointment under this subchapter. A visiting associate judge appointed under this section is entitled to compensation to be determined by a majority vote of the presiding judges of the administrative judicial regions through use of funds under this subchapter. A visiting associate judge is not considered to be a state employee for any purpose.

(d) Section 2252.901, Government Code, does not apply to the appointment of a visiting associate judge under this section.

Comment

If an associate judge becomes unable to perform the judge's official duties (because of illness, injury, retirement, or some other similar event), the presiding judge of an administrative region may fill the vacancy by appointing a retired or former associate judge to serve as a "visiting associate judge." However, because this section and Section 201.208, *supra*, provide that a "visiting associate judge is not considered to be a state employee for any purpose," OCA must hire visiting associate judges as contractors. TEX. GOV'T CODE § 2252.901, specifically prohibits a state agency from contracting with a former employee for a one year period following the employee's last date of employment with the agency. This prohibition complicated the hiring of visiting associate judges.

In 2005, the legislature added Subsection (d) to exempt visiting associate judges from the Government Code prohibition in order to allow the presiding judges to appoint (and OCA to contract with) retired or former child protection and child support associate judges as visiting associate judges regardless of when they were last employed by OCA. *(A.G.K. & H.P.S.)*

SUBCHAPTER C. ASSOCIATE JUDGE FOR CHILD PROTECTION CASES

Introductory Comment

This subchapter establishes a system parallel to the associate judges who specialize in Title IV–D child support cases; here the goal is to establish and fund associate judges to handle child protection cases filed by the Department of Family and Protective Services, a.k.a. DFPS or CPS in its local guise. These courts were started with federal grant funds through the Court Improvement Project. The pilot projects were called "Cluster Courts" because they clustered the child protection cases in several counties into one docket. Some are still called cluster courts, although most are called child protection courts. The associate judges created under this subchapter are state employees paid by the Office of Court Administration and are appointed and supervised by the presiding judges of the administrative judicial regions (similar to the IV–D associate judges, *supra*). There are seventeen of these specialized courts serving half of Texas' 254 counties. *(J.A.H.)*

CLE/Other Legal Publications

Child Evidentiary Issues and Child Testimony in CPS Cases. Hon. J. Andrew Hathcock, 2009 ADV. FAM. L.

Practice Before an Associate Judge—Temporary Orders. Charla F. Moore, 2007 ADV. FAM. L.

Leading Case

In re T.D.S.T., 287 S.W.3d 926 (Tex. App.—Amarillo 2009, no pet.) and Garza v. Texas Dept. of Family and Protective Services, 212 S.W.3d 373 (Tex. App.—Austin 2006, no pet.) (A.J.'s report is rendition of final order under § 263.401)

§ 201.201. Authority of Presiding Judge

(a) The presiding judge of each administrative judicial region, after conferring with the judges of courts in the region having family law jurisdiction and a child protection caseload, shall determine which courts require the appointment of a full-time or part-time associate judge to complete **cases under Subtitle E** ~~each case within the times specified in Chapters 262 and 263~~.

(b) The presiding judge may limit the appointment to a specified period and may terminate an appointment at any time.

(c) An associate judge appointed under this subchapter may be appointed to serve more than one court. Two or more judges of administrative judicial regions may jointly appoint one or more associate judges to serve the regions.

(d) If the presiding judge determines that a court requires an associate judge, the presiding judge shall appoint an associate judge. If an associate judge is appointed for a court, all child protection cases shall be referred to the associate judge by a general order for each county issued by the judge of the court for which the associate judge is appointed or, in the absence of that order, by a general order issued by the presiding judge who appointed the associate judge.

(e) This section does not limit the jurisdiction of a court to issue orders under **Subtitle E** ~~Chapter 262 or 263~~.

Amended by Acts 2011, 82nd Leg., ch. 377 (S.B. 283), § 1, eff. June 17, 2011.

§ 201.202. Application of Law Governing Associate Judges

Except as provided by this subchapter, Subchapter A applies to an associate judge appointed under this subchapter.

§ 201.2021. Qualifications

(a) To be eligible for appointment under this subchapter, a person must be and be:

(1) eligible for assignment under Section 74.054, Government Code, because the person is named on the list of retired and former judges maintained by the presiding judge of the administrative region under Section 74.055, Government Code; or

(2) licensed to practice law in this state and have been a practicing lawyer in this state, or a judge of a court in this state who is not otherwise eligible under Subdivision (1), for the four years preceding the date of appointment.

(b) An associate judge appointed under this subchapter shall during the term of appointment reside in the administrative judicial region, or a county adjacent to the region, in which the court to which the associate judge is appointed is located. An associate judge appointed to serve in two or more administrative judicial regions may reside anywhere in the regions.

§ 201.203. Designation of Host County

(a) Subject to the approval of the commissioners court of the proposed host county, the presiding judges of the administrative judicial regions by majority vote shall determine the host county of an associate judge appointed under this subchapter.

(b) The host county shall provide an adequate courtroom and quarters, including furniture, necessary utilities, and telephone equipment and service, for the associate judge and other personnel assisting the associate judge.

(c) An associate judge is not required to reside in the host county.

§ 201.204. General Powers of Associate Judge

(a) On the motion of a party or the associate judge, an associate judge may refer a complex case back to the referring court for final disposition after recommending temporary orders for the protection of a child.

(b) An associate judge may render and sign any pretrial order.

(c) An associate judge may recommend to the referring court any order after a trial on the merits.

Comment

Time was associate judges did not have the power to render judgment. Since 2003, associate judges for child protection cases have had the authority to render and sign any order except for an order after a trial on the merits, and may recommend any order after a trial on the merits. Such an order recommended by an associate judge takes effect without ratification by the referring court if a de novo appeal is not requested. *See* § 201.2041, below. This simplifies life in the rural areas served by associate judges for child protection cases where a District Judge is not always readily available to countersign orders. (*J.A.H.*)

---

§ 201.2041. Judicial Action on Associate Judge's Proposed Order or Judgment

(a) If a request for a de novo hearing before the referring court is not timely filed or the right to a de novo hearing before the referring court is waived, the proposed order or judgment of the associate judge becomes the order or judgment of the referring court by operation of law without ratification by the referring court.

(b) Regardless of whether a de novo hearing is requested before the referring court, a proposed order or judgment rendered by an associate judge that meets the requirements of Section 263.401(d) is considered a final order for purposes of Section 263.401.

Comment

As noted extensively in Subchapters A and B, a number of changes to the terminology used in this chapter were made in 2007. Most notable is replacing "an appeal" of an associate judge's "recommendation" with "a request for de novo hearing" before the referring court of an A.J.'s "proposed order or judgment." These changes seek to achieve a consistent use of terminology. Temporary orders in a case become orders of the referring court by operation of law without ratification under this section.

A final agreed or default order is effective for purposes of post-judgment motions and the appellate timetable on the date signed by the associate judge. *See* § 201.016(c) above. The statute is silent on exactly when the appellate timetable begins to run in a contested case in which the referring court's signature is not required because a timely request for de novo hearing was not filed. Starting the appellate clock on the date the associate judge signs a proposed final judgment, given the 20 day deadline for notice of appeal is problematic at best, and a trap for the unwary at worst. Arguably, the associate judge's order "becomes" a judgment of the referring court at the expiration of the seven day de novo period. *See* §§ 201.007, 201.013. Note that no appellate court has yet addressed this issue. Thus, if a de novo hearing is not requested, a smart and cautious practitioner should file a notice of appeal within 20 days after the associate judge signs the proposed order. *(C.G.C.)*

---

§ 201.2042. De Novo Hearing Before Referring Court

(a) Except as provided by this section, Section 201.015 applies to a request for a de novo hearing before the referring court.

(b) The party requesting a de novo hearing before the referring court shall file notice with the referring court and the clerk of the referring court.

Comment

Section 201.015 requires that notice of request for a de novo hearing must be filed with the referring court. This section requires the notice to be filed with both the referring court and the clerk of the referring court. Since in rural counties the judges, both the sitting district judges and the associate judges, are circuit riders, a notice sent to the judge might not get timely processed and put on a docket. Best practice would always be to notify the department's attorney, the judges and the clerk. Supposedly there are some things that go without saying; apparently this is not one of them. *(C.G.C.)*

---

§ 201.205. Compensation of Associate Judge

(a) An associate judge appointed under this subchapter is entitled to a salary as determined by a majority vote of the presiding judges of the administrative judicial regions. The salary may not exceed 90 percent of the salary paid to a district judge as set by the state General Appropriations Act.

(b) The associate judge's salary shall be paid from county funds available for payment of officers' salaries subject to the approval of the commissioners court or from funds available from the state and federal governments as provided by this subchapter.

§ 201.206. Personnel

(a) The presiding judge of an administrative judicial region or the presiding judges of the administrative judicial regions, by majority vote, may appoint personnel as needed to implement and administer the provisions of this subchapter.

(b) The salaries of the personnel shall be paid from county funds available for payment of officers' salaries subject to the approval of the commissioners court or from funds available from the state and federal governments as provided by this subchapter.

§ 201.2061. Supervision of Associate Judges.

The office of court administration shall assist the presiding judges in:

(1) monitoring the associate judges' compliance with any applicable job performance standards, uniform practices adopted by the presiding judges, and federal and state laws and policies;

(2) addressing the training needs and resource requirements of the associate judges;

(3) conducting annual performance evaluations for the associate judges and other personnel appointed under this subchapter based on written personnel performance standards adopted by the presiding judges; and

(4) receiving, investigating, and resolving complaints about particular associate judges or the associate judge program under this subchapter based on a uniform process adopted by the presiding judges.

§ 201.207. State and Federal Funds; Personnel

(a) The office of court administration may contract for available state and federal funds from any source and may employ personnel needed to implement and administer this subchapter. An associate judge and other personnel appointed under this subsection are state employees for all purposes, including accrual of leave time, insurance benefits, retirement benefits, and travel regulations.

(b) The presiding judges of the administrative judicial regions, state agencies, and counties may contract for available federal funds from any source to reimburse costs and salaries associated with associate judges and personnel appointed under this section and may also use available state funds and public or private grants.

(c) The presiding judges and the office of court administration in cooperation with other agencies shall take action necessary to maximize the amount of federal money available to fund the use of associate judges under this subchapter.

§ 201.208. Assignment of Judges and Appointment of Visiting Associate Judges

(a) This chapter does not limit the authority of a presiding judge to assign a judge eligible for assignment under Chapter 74, Government Code, to assist in processing cases in a reasonable time.

(b) If an associate judge appointed under this subchapter is temporarily unable to perform the associate judge's official duties because of absence resulting from family circumstances, illness, injury, disability, or military service, or if there is a vacancy in the position of associate judge, the presiding judge of the administrative judicial region in which the associate judge serves or the vacancy occurs may appoint a visiting associate judge to perform the duties of the associate judge during the period the associate judge is unable to perform the associate judge's duties or until another associate judge is appointed to fill the vacancy.

(c) A person is not eligible for appointment under this section unless the person has served as a master or associate judge under this chapter, a district judge, or a statutory county court judge for at least two years before the date of appointment.

(d) A visiting associate judge appointed under this section is subject to each provision of this chapter that applies to an associate judge serving under a regular appointment under this subchapter. A visiting associate judge appointed under this section is entitled to compensation, to be determined by a majority vote of the presiding judges of the administrative judicial regions, through use of funds under this subchapter. A visiting associate judge is not considered to be a state employee for any purpose.

(e) Section 2252.901, Government Code, does not apply to the appointment of a visiting associate judge under this section.

§ 201.209. Limitation on Law Practice by Associate Judge

An associate judge appointed under this subchapter may not engage in the private practice of law.

SUBCHAPTER D. ASSOCIATE JUDGE FOR JUVENILE MATTERS

§ 201.301. Applicability.

Text of section effective Jan. 1, 2012, if H.B. 79 of the First Called Session of the 82nd Legislature becomes law. At time of publication, Texas Governor Rick Perry had yet to take action on this bill, which was enrolled and sent to the governor on June 29, 2011.

This subchapter applies only to an associate judge appointed under this subchapter and does not apply to a juvenile court master appointed under Subchapter K, Chapter 54, Government Code.

Added by Acts 2011, 82nd Leg., 1st C.S. (H.B. 79), Sec. 6.03, eff. Jan. 1, 2012.

§ 201.302. Appointment

Text of section effective Jan. 1, 2012, if H.B. 79 of the First Called Session of the 82nd Legislature becomes law. At time of publication, Texas Governor Rick Perry had yet to take action on this bill, which was enrolled and sent to the governor on June 29, 2011.

(a) A judge of a court that is designated as a juvenile court may appoint a full-time or part-time associate judge to perform the duties authorized by this chapter if the commissioners court of a county in which the court has jurisdiction has authorized creation of an associate judge position.

(b) If a court has jurisdiction in more than one county, an associate judge appointed by that court may serve only in a county in which the commissioners court has authorized the appointment.

(c) If more than one court in a county has been designated as a juvenile court, the commissioners court may authorize the appointment of an associate judge for each court or may authorize one or more associate judges to share service with two or more courts.

(d) If an associate judge serves more than one court, the associate judge's appointment must be made as established by local rule, but in no event by less than a vote of two-thirds of the judges under whom the associate judge serves.

Added by Acts 2011, 82nd Leg., 1st C.S. (H.B. 79), Sec. 6.03, eff. Jan. 1, 2012.

§ 201.303. Qualifications

Text of section effective Jan. 1, 2012, if H.B. 79 of the First Called Session of the 82nd Legislature becomes law. At time of publication, Texas Governor Rick Perry had yet to take action on this bill, which was enrolled and sent to the governor on June 29, 2011.

To qualify for appointment as an associate judge under this subchapter, a person must:

(1) be a resident of this state and one of the counties the person will serve;

(2) have been licensed to practice law in this state for at least four years;

(3) not have been removed from office by impeachment, by the supreme court, by the governor on address to the legislature, by a tribunal reviewing a recommendation of the State Commission on Judicial Conduct, or by the legislature's abolition of the judge's court; and

(4) not have resigned from office after having received notice that formal proceedings by the State Commission on Judicial Conduct had been instituted as provided in Section 33.022, Government Code, and before final disposition of the proceedings.

Added by Acts 2011, 82nd Leg., 1st C.S. (H.B. 79), Sec. 6.03, eff. Jan. 1, 2012.

§ 201.304. Compensation

Text of section effective Jan. 1, 2012, if H.B. 79 of the First Called Session of the 82nd Legislature becomes law. At time of publication, Texas Governor Rick Perry had yet to take action on this bill, which was enrolled and sent to the governor on June 29, 2011.

(a) An associate judge shall be paid a salary determined by the commissioners court of the county in which the associate judge serves.

(b) If an associate judge serves in more than one county, the associate judge shall be paid a salary as determined by agreement of the commissioners courts of the counties in which the associate judge serves.

(c) The associate judge's salary is paid from the county fund available for payment of officers' salaries.

Added by Acts 2011, 82nd Leg., 1st C.S. (H.B. 79), Sec. 6.03, eff. Jan. 1, 2012.

§ 201.305. Termination

Text of section effective Jan. 1, 2012, if H.B. 79 of the First Called Session of the 82nd Legislature becomes law. At time of publication, Texas Governor Rick Perry had yet to take action on this bill, which was enrolled and sent to the governor on June 29, 2011.

(a) An associate judge who serves a single court serves at the will of the judge of that court.

(b) The employment of an associate judge who serves more than two courts may only be terminated by a majority vote of all the judges of the courts which the associate judge serves.

(c) The employment of an associate judge who serves two courts may be terminated by either of the judges of the courts which the associate judge serves.

(d) To terminate an associate judge's employment, the appropriate judges must sign a written order of termination. The order must state:

(1) the associate judge's name and state bar identification number;

(2) each court ordering termination; and

(3) the date the associate judge's employment ends.

Added by Acts 2011, 82nd Leg., 1st C.S. (H.B. 79), Sec. 6.03, eff. Jan. 1, 2012.

§ 201.306. Cases That May Be Referred

Text of section effective Jan. 1, 2012, if H.B. 79 of the First Called Session of the 82nd Legislature becomes law. At time of publication, Texas Governor Rick Perry had yet to take action on this bill, which was enrolled and sent to the governor on June 29, 2011.

(a) Except as provided by this section, a judge of a juvenile court may refer to an associate judge any aspect of a juvenile matter brought:

(1) under this title or Title 3; or

(2) in connection with Rule 308a, Texas Rules of Civil Procedure.

(b) Unless a party files a written objection to the associate judge hearing a trial on the merits, the judge may refer the trial to the associate judge. A trial on the merits is any final adjudication from which an appeal may be taken to a court of appeals.

(c) A party must file an objection to an associate judge hearing a trial on the merits or presiding at a jury trial not later than the 10th day after the date the party receives notice that the associate judge will hear the trial. If an objection is filed, the referring court shall hear the trial on the merits or preside at a jury trial.

(d) The requirements of Subsections (b) and (c) apply when a judge has authority to refer the trial of a suit under this title, Title 1, or Title 4 to an associate judge, master, or other assistant judge regardless of whether the assistant judge is appointed under this subchapter.

Added by Acts 2011, 82nd Leg., 1st C.S. (H.B. 79), Sec. 6.03, eff. Jan. 1, 2012.

§ 201.307. Methods of Referral

Text of section effective Jan. 1, 2012, if H.B. 79 of the First Called Session of the 82nd Legislature becomes law. At time of publication, Texas Governor Rick Perry had yet to take action on this bill, which was enrolled and sent to the governor on June 29, 2011.

(a) A case may be referred to an associate judge by an order of referral in a specific case or by an omnibus order.

(b) The order of referral may limit the power or duties of an associate judge.

Added by Acts 2011, 82nd Leg., 1st C.S. (H.B. 79), Sec. 6.03, eff. Jan. 1, 2012.

§ 201.308. Powers of Associate Judge

Text of section effective Jan. 1, 2012, if H.B. 79 of the First Called Session of the 82nd Legislature becomes law. At time of publication, Texas Governor Rick

Perry had yet to take action on this bill, which was enrolled and sent to the governor on June 29, 2011.

(a) Except as limited by an order of referral, an associate judge may:

(1) conduct a hearing;

(2) hear evidence;

(3) compel production of relevant evidence;

(4) rule on the admissibility of evidence;

(5) issue a summons for:

(A) the appearance of witnesses; and

(B) the appearance of a parent who has failed to appear before an agency authorized to conduct an investigation of an allegation of abuse or neglect of a child after receiving proper notice;

(6) examine a witness;

(7) swear a witness for a hearing;

(8) make findings of fact on evidence;

(9) formulate conclusions of law;

(10) recommend an order to be rendered in a case;

(11) regulate proceedings in a hearing;

(12) order the attachment of a witness or party who fails to obey a subpoena;

(13) order the detention of a witness or party found guilty of contempt, pending approval by the referring court; and

(14) take action as necessary and proper for the efficient performance of the associate judge's duties.

(b) An associate judge may, in the interest of justice, refer a case back to the referring court regardless of whether a timely objection to the associate judge hearing the trial on the merits or presiding at a jury trial has been made by any party.

Added by Acts 2011, 82nd Leg., 1st C.S. (H.B. 79), Sec. 6.03, eff. Jan. 1, 2012.

§ 201.309. Referees

Text of section effective Jan. 1, 2012, if H.B. 79 of the First Called Session of the 82nd Legislature becomes law. At time of publication, Texas Governor Rick Perry had yet to take action on this bill, which was enrolled and sent to the governor on June 29, 2011.

(a) An associate judge appointed under this subchapter may serve as a referee as provided by Sections 51.04(g) and 54.10.

(b) A referee appointed under Section 51.04(g) may be appointed to serve as an associate judge under this subchapter.

Added by Acts 2011, 82nd Leg., 1st C.S. (H.B. 79), Sec. 6.03, eff. Jan. 1, 2012.

§ 201.310. Attendance of Bailiff

Text of section effective Jan. 1, 2012, if H.B. 79 of the First Called Session of the 82nd Legislature becomes law. At time of publication, Texas Governor Rick Perry had yet to take action on this bill, which was enrolled and sent to the governor on June 29, 2011.

A bailiff may attend a hearing by an associate judge if directed by the referring court.

Added by Acts 2011, 82nd Leg., 1st C.S. (H.B. 79), Sec. 6.03, eff. Jan. 1, 2012.

§ 201.311. Witness

Text of section effective Jan. 1, 2012, if H.B. 79 of the First Called Session of the 82nd Legislature becomes law. At time of publication, Texas Governor Rick Perry had yet to take action on this bill, which was enrolled and sent to the governor on June 29, 2011.

(a) A witness appearing before an associate judge is subject to the penalties for perjury provided by law.

(b) A referring court may fine or imprison a witness who:

(1) failed to appear before an associate judge after being summoned; or

(2) improperly refused to answer questions if the refusal has been certified to the court by the associate judge.

Added by Acts 2011, 82nd Leg., 1st C.S. (H.B. 79), Sec. 6.03, eff. Jan. 1, 2012.

§ 201.312. Court Reporter; Record

Text of section effective Jan. 1, 2012, if H.B. 79 of the First Called Session of the 82nd Legislature becomes law. At time of publication, Texas Governor Rick Perry had yet to take action on this bill, which was enrolled and sent to the governor on June 29, 2011.

(a) A court reporter may be provided during a hearing held by an associate judge appointed under this subchapter. A court reporter is required to be provided when the associate judge presides over a jury trial or a contested final termination hearing.

(b) A party, the associate judge, or the referring court may provide for a reporter during the hearing if one is not otherwise provided.

(c) Except as provided by Subsection (a), in the absence of a court reporter or on agreement of the parties, the record may be preserved by any means approved by the associate judge.

(d) The referring court or associate judge may assess the expense of preserving the record as costs.

(e) On a request for a de novo hearing, the referring court may consider testimony or other evidence in the record, if the record is taken by a court reporter, in addition to witnesses or other matters presented under Section 201.317.

Added by Acts 2011, 82nd Leg., 1st C.S. (H.B. 79), Sec. 6.03, eff. Jan. 1, 2012.

§ 201.313. Report

Text of section effective Jan. 1, 2012, if H.B. 79 of the First Called Session of the 82nd Legislature becomes law. At time of publication, Texas Governor Rick Perry had yet to take action on this bill, which was enrolled and sent to the governor on June 29, 2011.

(a) The associate judge's report may contain the associate judge's findings, conclusions, or recommendations and may be in the form of a proposed order. The associate judge's report must be in writing and in the form directed by the referring court.

(b) After a hearing, the associate judge shall provide the parties participating in the hearing notice of the substance of the associate judge's report, including any proposed order.

(c) Notice may be given to the parties:

(1) in open court, by an oral statement or by providing a copy of the associate judge's written report, including any proposed order;

(2) by certified mail, return receipt requested; or

(3) by facsimile.

(d) A rebuttable presumption exists that notice is received on the date stated on:

(1) the signed return receipt, if notice was provided by certified mail; or

(2) the confirmation page produced by the facsimile machine, if notice was provided by facsimile.

(e) After a hearing conducted by an associate judge, the associate judge shall send the associate judge's signed and dated report, including any proposed order, and all other papers relating to the case to the referring court.

Added by Acts 2011, 82nd Leg., 1st C.S. (H.B. 79), Sec. 6.03, eff. Jan. 1, 2012.

§ 201.314. Notice of Right to De Novo Hearing; Waiver

Text of section effective Jan. 1, 2012, if H.B. 79 of the First Called Session of the 82nd Legislature becomes law. At time of publication, Texas Governor Rick Perry had yet to take action on this bill, which was enrolled and sent to the governor on June 29, 2011.

(a) An associate judge shall give all parties notice of the right to a de novo hearing to the judge of the referring court.

(b) The notice may be given:

(1) by oral statement in open court;

(2) by posting inside or outside the courtroom of the referring court; or

(3) as otherwise directed by the referring court.

(c) Before the start of a hearing by an associate judge, a party may waive the right of a de novo hearing before the referring court in writing or on the record.

Added by Acts 2011, 82nd Leg., 1st C.S. (H.B. 79), Sec. 6.03, eff. Jan. 1, 2012.

§ 201.315. Order of Court

Text of section effective Jan. 1, 2012, if H.B. 79 of the First Called Session of the 82nd Legislature becomes law. At time of publication, Texas Governor Rick Perry had yet to take action on this bill, which was enrolled and sent to the governor on June 29, 2011.

(a) Pending a de novo hearing before the referring court, a proposed order or judgment of the associate judge is in full force and effect and is enforceable as an order or judgment of the referring court, except for an order providing for the appointment of a receiver.

(b) If a request for a de novo hearing before the referring court is not timely filed or the right to a de novo hearing before the referring court is waived, the proposed order or judgment of the associate judge becomes the order or judgment of the referring court only on the referring court's signing the proposed order or judgment.

(c) An order by an associate judge for the temporary detention or incarceration of a witness or party shall be presented to the referring court on the day the witness or party is detained or incarcerated. The referring court, without prejudice to the right to a de novo hearing provided by Section 201.317, may approve the temporary detention or incarceration or may order the release of the party or witness, with or without bond, pending a de novo hearing. If the referring court is not immediately available, the associate judge may order the release of the party or witness, with or without bond, pending a de novo hearing or may continue the person's detention or incarceration for not more than 72 hours.

Added by Acts 2011, 82nd Leg., 1st C.S. (H.B. 79), Sec. 6.03, eff. Jan. 1, 2012.

§ 201.316. Judicial Action on Associate Judge's Proposed Order or Judgment

Text of section effective Jan. 1, 2012, if H.B. 79 of the First Called Session of the 82nd Legislature becomes law. At time of publication, Texas Governor Rick Perry had yet to take action on this bill, which was enrolled and sent to the governor on June 29, 2011.

Unless a party files a written request for a de novo hearing before the referring court, the referring court may:

(1) adopt, modify, or reject the associate judge's proposed order or judgment;

(2) hear additional evidence; or

(3) recommit the matter to the associate judge for further proceedings.

Added by Acts 2011, 82nd Leg., 1st C.S. (H.B. 79), Sec. 6.03, eff. Jan. 1, 2012.

§ 201.317. De Novo Hearing

Text of section effective Jan. 1, 2012, if H.B. 79 of the First Called Session of the 82nd Legislature becomes law. At time of publication, Texas Governor Rick Perry had yet to take action on this bill, which was enrolled and sent to the governor on June 29, 2011.

(a) A party may request a de novo hearing before the referring court by filing with the clerk of the referring court a written request not later than the seventh working day after the date the party receives notice of the substance of the associate judge's report as provided by Section 201.313.

(b) A request for a de novo hearing under this section must specify the issues that will be presented to the referring court. The de novo hearing is limited to the specified issues.

(c) Notice of a request for a de novo hearing before the referring court shall be given to the opposing attorney in the manner provided by Rule 21a, Texas Rules of Civil Procedure.

(d) If a request for a de novo hearing before the referring court is filed by a party, any other party may file a request for a de novo hearing before the referring court not later than the seventh working day after the date the initial request was filed.

(e) The referring court, after notice to the parties, shall hold a de novo hearing not later than the 30th day after the date the initial request for a de novo hearing was filed with the clerk of the referring court.

(f) In the de novo hearing before the referring court, the parties may present witnesses on the issues specified in the request for hearing. The referring court may also consider the record from the hearing before the associate judge, including the charge to and verdict returned by a jury, if the record was taken by a court reporter.

(g) The denial of relief to a party after a de novo hearing under this section or a party's waiver of the right to a de novo hearing before the referring court does not affect the right of a party to file a motion for new trial, a motion for judgment notwithstanding the verdict, or other posttrial motions.

(h) A party may not demand a second jury in a de novo hearing before the referring court if the associate judge's proposed order or judgment resulted from a jury trial.

Added by Acts 2011, 82nd Leg., 1st C.S. (H.B. 79), Sec. 6.03, eff. Jan. 1, 2012.

§ 201.318. Appellate Review

Text of section effective Jan. 1, 2012, if H.B. 79 of the First Called Session of the 82nd Legislature becomes law. At time of publication, Texas Governor Rick

Perry had yet to take action on this bill, which was enrolled and sent to the governor on June 29, 2011.

(a) A party's failure to request a de novo hearing before the referring court or a party's waiver of the right to request a de novo hearing before the referring court does not deprive the party of the right to appeal to or request other relief from a court of appeals or the supreme court.

(b) Except as provided by Subsection (c), the date an order or judgment by the referring court is signed is the controlling date for the purposes of appeal to or request for other relief from a court of appeals or the supreme court.

(c) The date an agreed order or a default order is signed by an associate judge is the controlling date for the purpose of an appeal to, or a request for other relief relating to the order from, a court of appeals or the supreme court.

Added by Acts 2011, 82nd Leg., 1st C.S. (H.B. 79), Sec. 6.03, eff. Jan. 1, 2012.

§ 201.319. Judicial Immunity

Text of section effective Jan. 1, 2012, if H.B. 79 of the First Called Session of the 82nd Legislature becomes law. At time of publication, Texas Governor Rick Perry had yet to take action on this bill, which was enrolled and sent to the governor on June 29, 2011.

An associate judge appointed under this subchapter has the judicial immunity of a district judge.

Added by Acts 2011, 82nd Leg., 1st C.S. (H.B. 79), Sec. 6.03, eff. Jan. 1, 2012.

§ 201.320. Visiting Associate Judge

Text of section effective Jan. 1, 2012, if H.B. 79 of the First Called Session of the 82nd Legislature becomes law. At time of publication, Texas Governor Rick Perry had yet to take action on this bill, which was enrolled and sent to the governor on June 29, 2011.

(a) If an associate judge appointed under this subchapter is temporarily unable to perform the judge's official duties because of absence or illness, injury, or other disability, a judge of a court having jurisdiction of a suit under this title or Title 1 or 4 may appoint a visiting associate judge to perform the duties of the associate judge during the period of the associate judge's absence or disability if the commissioners court of a county in which the court has jurisdiction authorizes the employment of a visiting associate judge.

(b) To be eligible for appointment under this section, a person must have served as an associate judge for at least two years.

(c) Sections 201.001 through 201.017 apply to a visiting associate judge appointed under this section.

Added by Acts 2011, 82nd Leg., 1st C.S. (H.B. 79), Sec. 6.03, eff. Jan. 1, 2012.

CHAPTER 202. FRIEND OF THE COURT

Introductory Comment

This chapter authorizes county governments and trial courts to initiate voluntary "friend of the court" programs. The concept is derived from the system for enforcing child support and visitation employed in Michigan. The basic principle is that the attorney (or the domestic relations office appointed to act in that capacity) does not represent any of the parties, nor represent the child. Rather, a duty is owed to the court to ensure that all aspects of its orders are enforced and appropriate under the existing circumstances. Generally, both child support and visitation are subject to enforcement motions filed by the friend of the court. Similarly, a petition to modify support or possession may seek an increase or decrease in the support order, or to modify the terms of visitation in an appropriate manner (as viewed by the friend of the court). Texas courts have embraced the program in a wide variety of ways, ranging from a case-by-case appointment of an attorney to enforce support to a general appointment of an individual with a courthouse office and staff to perform that function.

Leading Case

In re Office of Attorney General, 257 S.W.3d 695 (Tex. 2008) (TRO directing OAG to remit child-support payments to private company was void)

---

§ 202.001. Appointment

(a) After an order for child support or possession of or access to a child has been rendered, a court may appoint a friend of the court on:

(1) the request of a person alleging that the order has been violated; or

(2) its own motion.

(b) A court may appoint a friend of the court in a proceeding under Part D of Title IV of the federal Social Security Act (42 U.S.C. Section 651 et seq.) only if the Title IV–D agency agrees in writing to the appointment.

(c) The duration of the appointment of a friend of the court is as determined by the court.

(d) In the appointment of a friend of the court, the court shall give preference to:

(1) a local domestic relations office;

(2) a local child support collection office;

(3) the local court official designated to enforce actions as provided in Chapter 159; or

(4) an attorney in good standing with the State Bar of Texas.

(e) In the execution of a friend of the court's duties under this subchapter, a friend of the court shall represent the court to ensure compliance with the court's order.

Comment

Subsection (e) makes clear that the duty of the friend of the court is to represent the court and not one of the parties or the child.

---

§ 202.002. Authority and Duties

(a) A friend of the court may coordinate nonjudicial efforts to improve compliance with a court order relating to child support or possession of or access to a child by use of:

(1) telephone communication;

(2) written communication;

(3) one or more volunteer advocates under Chapter 107;

(4) informal pretrial consultation;

(5) one or more of the alternate dispute resolution methods under Chapter 154, Civil Practice and Remedies Code;

(6) a licensed social worker;

(7) a family mediator; and

(8) employment agencies, retraining programs, and any similar resources to ensure that both parents can meet their financial obligations to the child.

(b) A friend of the court, not later than the 15th day of the month following the reporting month:

(1) shall report to the court or monitor reports made to the court on:

(A) the amount of child support collected as a percentage of the amount ordered; and

(B) efforts to ensure compliance with orders relating to possession of or access to a child; and

(2) may file an action to enforce, clarify, or modify a court order relating to child support or possession of or access to a child.

(c) A friend of the court may file a notice of delinquency and a request for a writ of income withholding under Chapter 158 in order to enforce a child support order.

Comment

The friend of the court is implicitly directed to engage in a wide range of nonjudicial activities in an effort to settle a case prior to seeking enforcement by more conventional means. Subsection (b) is the key, authorizing the friend of court to keep track of compliance by monitoring payments, in cooperation with whomever serves as the court's registry, and to take action independently when compliance falls below 100 percent (a lofty goal).

---

§ 202.003. Duty of Local Offices and Officials to Report

A local domestic relations office, a local registry, or a court official designated to receive child support under a court order shall, if ordered by the court, report to the court or a friend of the court on a monthly basis:

(1) any delinquency and arrearage in child support payments; and

(2) any violation of an order relating to possession of or access to a child.

§ 202.004. Access to Information

A friend of the court may arrange access to child support payment records by electronic means if the records are computerized.

§ 202.005. Compensation

(a) A friend of the court is entitled to compensation for services rendered and for expenses incurred in rendering the services.

(b) The court may assess the amount that the friend of the court receives in compensation against a party to the suit in the same manner as the court awards costs under Chapter 106.

(c) A friend of the court or a person who acts as the court's custodian of child support records, including the clerk of a court, may apply for and receive funds from the child support and court management account under Section 21.007, Government Code.

(d) A friend of the court who receives funds under Subsection (c) shall use the funds to reimburse any compensation the friend of the court received under Subsection (b).

CHAPTER 203. DOMESTIC RELATIONS OFFICES

Introductory Comment

This chapter authorizes county governments voluntarily to provide services for families, courts, and county departments at county expense. Over time, the range of services has grown significantly. Originally DRO's were best known for their roles in recording and enforcing child support, providing marriage counseling, and representing abused and neglected children. As of 2007, the list of powers and duties expanded into alternative dispute resolution and parenting coordinator services, *see* § 203.004.

§ 203.001. Definitions

In this chapter:

(1) "Administering entity" means a commissioners court, juvenile board, or other entity responsible for administering a domestic relations office under this chapter.

(2) "Domestic relations office" means a county office that serves families, county departments, and courts to ensure effective implementation of this title.

§ 203.002. Establishment of Domestic Relations Office

A commissioners court may establish a domestic relations office.

§ 203.003. Administration

(a) A domestic relations office shall be administered:

(1) as provided by the commissioners court; or

(2) if the commissioners court does not otherwise provide for the administration of the office, by the juvenile board that serves the county in which the domestic relations office is located.

(b) The administering entity shall appoint and assign the duties of a director who shall be responsible for the day-to-day administration of the office. A director serves at the pleasure of the administering entity.

(c) The administering entity shall determine the amount of money needed to operate the office.

(d) A commissioners court that establishes a domestic relations office under this chapter may execute a bond for the office. A bond under this subsection must be:

(1) executed with a solvent surety company authorized to do business in the state; and

(2) conditioned on the faithful performance of the duties of the office.

(e) The administering entity shall establish procedures for the acceptance and use of a grant or donation to the office.

§ 203.004. Powers and Duties

(a) A domestic relations office may:

(1) collect and disburse child support payments that are ordered by a court to be paid through a domestic relations registry;

(2) maintain records of payments and disbursements made under Subdivision (1);

(3) file a suit, including a suit to:

(A) establish paternity;

(B) enforce a court order for child support or for possession of and access to a child; and

(C) modify or clarify an existing child support order;

(4) provide an informal forum in which alternative dispute resolution is used to resolve disputes under this code;

(5) prepare a court-ordered social study under Chapter 107;

(6) represent a child as an amicus attorney, an attorney ad litem, or a guardian ad litem in a suit in which:

(A) termination of the parent-child relationship is sought; or

(B) conservatorship of or access to a child is contested;

(7) serve as a friend of the court;

(8) provide predivorce counseling ordered by a court;

(9) provide community supervision services under Chapter 157;

(10) provide information to assist a party in understanding, complying with, or enforcing the party's duties and obligations under Subdivision (3);

(11) provide, directly or through a contract, visitation services, including supervision of court-ordered visitation, visitation exchange, or other similar services;

(12) issue an administrative writ of withholding under Subchapter F, Chapter 158; and

(13) provide parenting coordinator services under Chapter 153.

(b) A court having jurisdiction in a proceeding under this title, Title 3, or Section 25.05, Penal Code, may order that child support payments be made through a domestic relations office.

(c) A domestic relations office may:

(1) hire or contract for the services of attorneys to assist the office in providing services under this chapter; and

(2) employ community supervision officers or court monitors.

§ 203.005. Fees and Charges

(a) The administering entity may authorize a domestic relations office to assess and collect:

(1) an initial operations fee not to exceed $15 to be paid to the domestic relations office on each filing of an original suit, motion for modification, or motion for enforcement;

(2) in a county that has a child support enforcement cooperative agreement with the Title IV–D agency, an initial child support service fee not to exceed $36 to be paid to the domestic relations office on the filing of an original suit;

(3) a reasonable application fee to be paid by an applicant requesting services from the office;

(4) a reasonable attorney's fee and court costs incurred or ordered by the court;

(5) a monthly service fee not to exceed $3 to be paid annually in advance by a managing conservator and possessory conservator for whom the domestic relations office provides child support services;

(6) community supervision fees as provided by Chapter 157 if community supervision officers are employed by the domestic relations office;

(7) a reasonable fee for preparation of a court-ordered social study;

(8) in a county that provides visitation services under Sections 153.014 and 203.004 a reasonable fee to be paid to the domestic relations office at the time the visitation services are provided;

(9) a fee to reimburse the domestic relations office for a fee required to be paid under Section 158.503(d) for filing an administrative writ of withholding;

(10) a reasonable fee for parenting coordinator services; and

(11) a reasonable fee for alternative dispute resolution services.

(b) The first payment of a fee under Subsection **(a)(5)** ~~(a)(4)~~ is due on the date that the person required to pay support is ordered to begin child support, alimony, or separate maintenance payments. Subsequent payments of the fee are due annually and in advance.

(c) The director of a domestic relations office shall attempt to collect all fees in an efficient manner.

(d) The administering entity may provide for an exemption from the payment of a fee authorized under this section if payment of the fee is not practical or in the interest of justice. Fees that may be exempted under this subsection include fees related to:

(1) spousal and child support payments made under an interstate pact;

(2) a suit brought by the Texas Department of Human Services;

(3) activities performed by the Department of Protective and Regulatory Services or another governmental agency, a private adoption agency, or a charitable organization; and

(4) services for a person who has applied for or who receives public assistance under the laws of this state.

(e) A fee authorized by this section for providing child support services is part of the child support obligation and may be enforced against both an obligor and obligee by any method available for the enforcement of child support, including contempt.

Amended by Acts 2011, 82nd Leg., ch. 1341 (S.B. 1233), § 10, eff. June 17, 2011.

§ 203.006. Fund

(a) As determined by the administering entity, fees collected or received by a domestic relations office shall be deposited in:

(1) the general fund for the county in which the domestic relations office is located; or

(2) the office fund established for the domestic relations office.

(b) The administering entity shall use the domestic relations office fund to provide money for services authorized by this chapter.

(c) A domestic relations office fund may be supplemented as necessary from the county's general fund or from other money available from the county.

§ 203.007. Access to Records; Offense

(a) A domestic relations office may obtain the records described by Subsections (b), (c), (d), and (e) that relate to a person who has:

(1) been ordered to pay child support;

(2) been designated as a conservator of a child;

(3) been designated to be the father of a child;

(4) executed an acknowledgment of paternity;

(5) court-ordered possession of a child; or

(6) filed suit to adopt a child.

(b) A domestic relations office is entitled to obtain from the Department of Public Safety records that relate to:

(1) a person's date of birth;

(2) a person's most recent address;

(3) a person's current driver's license status;

(4) motor vehicle accidents involving a person;

(5) reported traffic-law violations of which a person has been convicted; and

(6) a person's criminal history record information.

(c) A domestic relations office is entitled to obtain from the Texas Workforce Commission records that relate to:

(1) a person's address;

(2) a person's employment status and earnings;

(3) the name and address of a person's current or former employer; and

(4) unemployment compensation benefits received by a person.

(d) To the extent permitted by federal law, a domestic relations office is entitled to obtain from the national directory of new hires established under 42 U.S.C. Section 653(i), as amended, records that relate to a person described by Subsection (a), including records that relate to:

(1) the name, telephone number, and address of the person's employer;

(2) information provided by the person on a W-4 form; and

(3) information provided by the person's employer on a Title IV-D form.

(e) To the extent permitted by federal law, a domestic relations office is entitled to obtain from the state case registry records that relate to a person described by Subsection (a), including records that relate to:

(1) the street and mailing address and the social security number of the person;

(2) the name, telephone number, and address of the person's employer;

(3) the location and value of real and personal property owned by the person; and

(4) the name and address of each financial institution in which the person maintains an account and the account number for each account.

(f) An agency required to provide records under this section may charge a domestic relations office a fee for providing the records in an amount that does not exceed the amount paid for those records by the agency responsible for Title IV-D cases.

(g) The Department of Public Safety, the Texas Workforce Commission, or the office of the secretary of state may charge a domestic relations office a fee not to exceed the charge paid by the Title IV-D agency for furnishing records under this section.

(h) Information obtained by a domestic relations office under this section that is confidential under a constitution, statute, judicial decision, or rule is privileged and may be used only by that office.

(i) A person commits an offense if the person releases or discloses confidential information obtained under this section without the consent of the person to whom the information relates. An offense under this subsection is a Class C misdemeanor.

(j) A domestic relations office is entitled to obtain from the office of the secretary of state the following information about a registered voter to the extent that the information is available:

(1) complete name;

(2) current and former street and mailing address;

(3) sex;

(4) date of birth;

(5) social security number; and

(6) telephone number.

CHAPTER 204. CHILD SUPPORT COLLECTION BY PRIVATE ENTITY

§ 204.001. Applicability

This chapter applies only to a commissioners court or domestic relations office of a county that did not have the authority to contract with a private entity to receive, disburse, and record payments or restitution of child support on January 1, 1997.

§ 204.002. Authority to Contract

A county, acting through its commissioners court or domestic relations office, may contract with a private entity to:

(1) enforce, collect, receive, and disburse:

(A) child support payments;

(B) other amounts due under a court order containing an order to pay child support; and

(C) fees, including fees provided by this chapter;

(2) maintain appropriate records, including records of child support and other amounts and fees that are due, past due, paid, or delinquent;

(3) locate absent parents;

(4) furnish statements to parents accounting for payments that are due, past due, paid, or delinquent;

(5) send billings and other appropriate notices to parents;

(6) perform any duty or function that a local registry is authorized to perform;

(7) perform any duty or function in connection with the state case registry; or

(8) provide another child support or visitation enforcement service authorized by the commissioners court, including mediation of disputes related to child support or visitation.

§ 204.003. Terms and Conditions of Contract

The commissioners court or domestic relations office shall include all appropriate terms and conditions in the contract that it determines are reasonable to secure the services of a private entity as provided by this chapter, including:

(1) provisions specifying the services to be provided by the entity;

(2) the method, conditions, and amount of compensation for the entity;

(3) provisions for the security of funds collected as child support, fees, or other amounts under the contract or that otherwise provide reasonable assurance to the county of the entity's full and faithful performance of the contract;

(4) provisions specifying the records to be kept by the entity, including any records necessary to fully account for all funds received and disbursed as child support, fees, or other amounts;

(5) requirements governing the inspection, verification, audit, or explanation of the entity's accounting or other records;

(6) the county's right to terminate the contract on 30 days' notice to the private entity if the private entity engages in an ongoing pattern of child support enforcement that constitutes wilful

and gross misconduct subjecting delinquent obligors to unconscionable duress, abuse, or harassment;

(7) provisions permitting an obligor and obligee to jointly waive the monitoring procedure, if not required by law, by written request approved by order of the court having jurisdiction of the suit in which the child support order was issued; and

(8) provisions for the disclosure or nondisclosure of information or records maintained or known to the entity as a result of contract performance, including a requirement for the private entity to:

(A) disclose to any child support obligor that the private entity is attempting to enforce the obligor's child support obligation; and

(B) make no disclosure of the information or records other than in furtherance of the effort to enforce the child support order.

§ 204.004. Funding

(a) To provide or recover the costs of providing services authorized by this chapter, a commissioners court, on its behalf or on behalf of the domestic relations office, may:

(1) provide by order for the assessment and collection of a reasonable fee at the time a party files a suit affecting the parent-child relationship;

(2) provide by order for the assessment and collection of a fee of $3 per month at a time specified for payment of child support;

(3) provide by order for the assessment and collection of a late payment fee of $4 per month to be imposed if an obligor does not make a payment of child support in full when due;

(4) accept or receive funds from public grants or private sources available for providing services authorized by this chapter; or

(5) use any combination of funding sources specified by this subsection.

(b) The commissioners court, on its behalf or on behalf of the domestic relations office, may:

(1) provide by order for reasonable exemptions from the collection of fees authorized by Subsection (a); and

(2) require payment of a fee authorized by Subsection (a)(2) annually and in advance.

(c) The commissioners court may not charge a fee under Subsection (a)(2) if the amount of child support ordered to be paid is less than the equivalent of $100 per month.

(d) The fees established under Subsection (a) may be collected by any means provided for the collection of child support. The commissioners court may provide by order, on its behalf or on behalf of the domestic relations office, for the manner of collection of fees and the apportionment of payments received to meet fee obligations.

§ 204.005. Cumulative Effect of Chapter

A power or duty conferred on a county, county official, or county instrumentality by this chapter is cumulative of the powers and duties created or conferred by other law.

SUBTITLE D. ADMINISTRATIVE SERVICES

★★★

CHAPTER 231. TITLE IV–D SERVICES

SUBCHAPTER A. ADMINISTRATION OF TITLE IV–D PROGRAM

SUBCHAPTER B. SERVICES PROVIDED BY TITLE IV–D PROGRAM

SUBCHAPTER C. PAYMENT OF FEES AND COSTS

SUBCHAPTER D. LOCATION OF PARENTS AND RESOURCES

Editors' Note: *This chapter contains guest commentary by Alicia Gray Key, Deputy Attorney General and IV–D Director and H. Patrick Sullivan, Deputy Director for Federal and State Operations, Child Support Division, Office of the Attorney General of Texas identified as (A.G.K. & H.P.S.).*

Introductory Comment

Under the Child Support Enforcement Amendments of 1984, Congress required states to adopt expedited procedures for child support enforcement, whether by judicial or administrative processes or some combination of the two, in order to meet federal time frames for establishing and enforcing support obligations in cases enforced by state Title IV–D agencies. Moreover, the 1984 Act imposed a number of "statutorily prescribed procedures" (for example, mandatory income withholding for support) which all states had to institute as a condition for receiving federal matching funds for the operation of their IV–D child support enforcement programs. The federal Family Support Act of 1986 extended the use of expedited processes to paternity establishment, added state law requirements, and mandated the development of automated systems for data management and case processing by state Title IV–D agencies. The child support enforcement provisions of the Personal Responsibility and Work Opportunity Act of 1996 (PRWORA) enlarged the authority of state Title IV–D agencies through the use of expedited administrative procedures, expanded the role of automated systems in support enforcement, and compelled greater uniformity of family law and legal processes among the states. *(A.G.K. & H.P.S.)*

CLE/Other Legal Publications

Navigating the Attorney General maze. Cynthia J. Barela & April Palmer, 2008 UT FAM. L. FRONT LINES

Navigating the Attorney General's child support enforcement program. Alicia G. Key, 2007 UT DEFINITIVE SAPCR

Understanding the AG and CPS. Rhonda F. Hunter. 2007 ADV. FAM. L.

Leading Cases

Blessing v. Freestone, 520 U.S. 329, 117 S.Ct. 1353 (1997) (applicants for child support enforcement do not have cause of action against IV–D agency for inadequate services)

In re A.M., 192 S.W.3d 570 (Tex. 2006) (A.G. has standing to defend against obligor's assertion of statutory offsets and counter-claims, even when obligee defaults)

Office of Attorney General v. Lee, 92 S.W.3d 526 (Tex. 2002) (A.G. not required to pay any portion of appellate filing fee)

SUBCHAPTER A. ADMINISTRATION OF TITLE IV–D PROGRAM

§ 231.001. Designation of Title IV–D Agency

The office of the attorney general is designated as the state's Title IV–D agency.

§ 231.0011. Development of Statewide Integrated System for Child Support and Medical Support Enforcement

(a) The Title IV–D agency shall have final approval authority on any contract or proposal for delivery of Title IV–D services under this section and in coordination with the Texas Judicial Council, the Office of Court Administration of the Texas Judicial System, the federal Office of Child Support Enforcement, and state, county, and local officials, shall develop and implement a statewide integrated system for child support and medical support enforcement, employing federal, state, local, and private resources to:

(1) unify child support registry functions;

(2) record and track all child support orders entered in the state;

(3) establish an automated enforcement process which will use delinquency monitoring, billing, and other enforcement techniques to ensure the payment of current support;

(4) incorporate existing enforcement resources into the system to obtain maximum benefit from state and federal funding; and

(5) ensure accountability for all participants in the process, including state, county, and local officials, private contractors, and the judiciary.

(b) Counties and other providers of child support services shall be required, as a condition of participation in the unified system, to enter into a contract with the Title IV–D agency, to comply with all federal requirements for the Title IV–D program, and to maintain at least the current level of funding for activities which are proposed to be included in the integrated child support system.

(c) The Title IV–D agency may contract with any county meeting technical system requirements necessary to comply with federal law for provision of Title IV–D services in that county. All new cases in which support orders are entered in such county after the effective date of a monitoring contract shall be Title IV–D cases. Any other case in the county, subject to federal requirements and the agreement of the county and the Title IV–D agency, may be included as a Title IV–D case. Any obligee under a support order may refuse Title IV–D enforcement services unless required to accept such services pursuant to other law.

(d) Counties participating in the unified enforcement system shall monitor all child support registry cases and on delinquency may, subject to the approval of the Title IV–D agency, provide enforcement services through:

(1) direct provision of services by county personnel;

(2) subcontracting all or portions of the services to private entities or attorneys; or

(3) such other methods as may be approved by the Title IV–D agency.

(e) The Title IV–D agency may phase in the integrated child support registry and enforcement system, and the requirement to implement the system shall be contingent on the receipt of locally generated funds and federal reimbursement. Locally generated funds include but are not limited to funds contributed by counties and cities.

(f) The Title IV–D agency shall adopt rules to implement this section.

(g) Participation in the statewide integrated system for child support and medical support enforcement by a county is voluntary, and nothing in this section shall be construed to mandate participation.

(h) This section does not limit the ability of the Title IV–D agency to enter into an agreement with a county for the provision of services as authorized under Section 231.002.

Comment

The "Integrated Child Support System" (ICSS) described under this section was established under provisions of S.B. 793 enacted by the 74th Texas Legislature in 1995 and operates under certain federal waivers—in particular a waiver from the federal requirement that in non-public assistance cases the services of the Title IV-D agency may be provided only on the written application of an individual seeking those services. In those counties which voluntarily participate in the ICSS new child support orders are made Title IV-D cases by operation of law without the necessity of a written application, although custodial parents are provided the opportunity to decline IV-D services.

The ICSS is intended to be a "self-starting" enforcement system in which support orders are monitored for payment from the outset, with immediate enforcement action being triggered by any delinquency—the supposition being that such a system is more efficient, productive, and cost-effective than a complaint-driven system which requires an obligee to file an application for services before any enforcement action may take place, usually after significant arrearages have accrued. The system has proved its worth in the small number of Texas counties in which it has operated over the years. Its continued operation, however, will rest with those in the federal bureaucracy who every five years renew the needed waivers. *(H.P.S.)*

§ 231.0012. Child Support Enforcement Management

The person appointed by the attorney general as the person responsible for managing the Title IV-D agency's child support enforcement duties shall report directly to the attorney general.

§ 231.0013. Dedication of Funds

Appropriations made to the Title IV-D agency for child support enforcement may be expended only for the purposes for which the money was appropriated.

§ 231.002. Powers and Duties

(a) The Title IV–D agency may:

(1) accept, transfer, and expend funds, subject to the General Appropriations Act, made available by the federal or state government or by another public or private source for the purpose of carrying out this chapter;

(2) adopt rules for the provision of child support services;

(3) initiate legal actions needed to implement this chapter; and

(4) enter into contracts or agreements necessary to administer this chapter.

(b) The Title IV–D agency may perform the duties and functions necessary for locating children under agreements with the federal government as provided by 42 U.S.C. Section 663.

(c) The Title IV–D agency may enter into agreements or contracts with federal, state, or other public or private agencies or individuals for the purpose of carrying out the agency's responsibilities under federal or state law. The agreements or contracts between the agency and other state agencies or political subdivisions of this or another state, including a consortia of multiple states, and agreements or contracts with vendors for the delivery of program services are not subject to Chapter 771 or 783, Government Code.

(d) Consistent with federal law and any international treaty or convention to which the United States is a party and that has been ratified by the United States Congress, the Title IV–D agency may:

(1) on approval by and in cooperation with the governor, pursue negotiations and enter into reciprocal arrangements with the federal government, another state, or a foreign country or a political subdivision of the federal government, state, or foreign country to:

(A) establish and enforce child support obligations; and

(B) establish mechanisms to enforce an order providing for possession of or access to a child rendered under Chapter 153;

(2) spend money appropriated to the agency for child support enforcement to engage in international child support enforcement; and

(3) spend other money appropriated to the agency necessary for the agency to conduct the agency's activities under Subdivision (1).

(e) The Title IV–D agency may take the following administrative actions with respect to the location of a parent, the determination of parentage, and the establishment, modification, and enforcement of child support and medical support orders required by 42 U.S.C. Section 666(c), without obtaining an order from any other judicial or administrative tribunal:

(1) issue an administrative subpoena, as provided by Section 231.303, to obtain financial or other information;

(2) order genetic testing for parentage determination, as provided by Chapter 233;

(3) order income withholding, as provided by Chapter 233, and issue an administrative writ of withholding, as provided by Chapter 158; and

(4) take any action with respect to execution, collection, and release of a judgment or lien for child support necessary to satisfy the judgment or lien, as provided by Chapter 157.

(f) The Title IV–D agency shall recognize and enforce the authority of the Title IV–D agency of another state to take actions similar to the actions listed in this section.

(g) The Title IV–D agency shall develop and use procedures for the administrative enforcement of interstate cases meeting the requirements of 42 U.S.C. Section 666(a)(14) under which the agency:

(1) shall promptly respond to a request made by another state for assistance in a Title IV–D case; and

(2) may, by electronic or other means, transmit to another state a request for assistance in a Title IV–D case.

(h) Repealed by Acts 2009, 81st Leg., ch. 164, § 3.

(i) The Title IV–D agency may provide a release or satisfaction of a judgment for all or part of the amount of the arrearages assigned to the Title IV–D agency under Section 231.104(a).

Comment

PRWORA required states to have laws providing the IV–D agency with authority to take specific administrative actions without the necessity of any other judicial or administrative order. This section lists those administrative actions, as well as other federal mandates relating to administrative enforcement of interstate cases and authorizes the IV–D agency to enter into multi-state consortia for interstate enforcement. It also includes specific provisions for international enforcement of child support and custody orders.

Federal law does not require the IV–D agency to enforce custody and access rights and, therefore, does not authorize federal matching funds for any enforcement actions relating to custody and access. This section authorizes the attorney general to pursue the establishment of reciprocal arrangements with foreign nations for the enforcement of both child support and custody and access rights to the extent that federal law and international treaties allow and specific funds are appropriated.

The IV–D agency provides child support enforcement services upon the request of any foreign country which the secretaries of the U.S. Departments of State and of Health and Human Services "declare" to be a reciprocating country for enforcement purposes. States on their own may enter into reciprocal agreements for support enforcement with foreign countries that are not the subject of a declaration. The IV–D agency must treat any request from a foreign reciprocating country in the same manner as an interstate request and may not charge a requesting country or foreign obligee any fee for services, although the agency may attempt to recover fees from the obligor.

Subsection (d) is quite unusual in its scope. The agency is authorized to negotiate and recognize foreign nations or their political subdivisions for reciprocal enforcement of child support orders. Texas has done so with a large number of Canadian provinces and European nations. *(A.G.K. & H.P.S.)*

Subsection (i) codifies under this section's enumeration of the powers and duties of the IV–D agency the authority of the agency, identified under § 157.272, to "forgive" support arrearages assigned to the state (§ 231.104 *infra*). The agency may not, of course, compromise or release a judgment of support arrearages owed a custodial parent. *(A.G.K. & H.P.S.)*

Repealed in 2009, former subsection (h) specified that the IV-D agency "shall enforce" by filing a child support lien under a specified fact circumstances. This was a bit too much micromanagement by statute.

---

§ 231.003. Forms and Procedures

The Title IV–D agency shall by rule promulgate any forms and procedures necessary to comply fully with the intent of this chapter.

§ 231.004. Repealed.

§ 231.005. Biennial Report Required

(a) The Title IV–D agency shall report to the legislature each biennium on:

(1) the effectiveness of the agency's child support enforcement activity in reducing the state's public assistance obligations; **and**

(2) the use and effectiveness of all enforcement tools authorized by state or federal law or otherwise available to the agency~~; and(3) the progress and impact of the Title IV D agency's efforts to use private contractors to perform Title IV D program functions~~.

(b) The agency shall develop a method for estimating the costs and benefits of the child support enforcement program and the effect of the program on appropriations for public assistance.

Amended by Acts 2011, 82nd Leg., ch. 990 (H.B. 1781), § 2, eff. June 17, 2011.

§ 231.006. Ineligibility to Receive State Grants or Loans or Receive Payment on State Contracts

(a) A child support obligor who is more than 30 days delinquent in paying child support and a business entity in which the obligor is a sole proprietor, partner, shareholder, or owner with an ownership interest of at least 25 percent is not eligible to:

(1) receive payments from state funds under a contract to provide property, materials, or services; or

(2) receive a state-funded grant or loan.

(a–1) Repealed by Acts 2007, 80th Leg., ch. 972, § 65(1).

(b) A child support obligor or business entity ineligible to receive payments under Subsection (a) remains ineligible until:

(1) all arrearages have been paid;

(2) the obligor is in compliance with a written repayment agreement or court order as to any existing delinquency; or

(3) the court of continuing jurisdiction over the child support order has granted the obligor an exemption from Subsection (a) as part of a court-supervised effort to improve earnings and child support payments.

(c) A bid or an application for a contract, grant, or loan paid from state funds must include the name and social security number of the individual or sole proprietor and each partner, shareholder, or owner with an ownership interest of at least 25 percent of the business entity submitting the bid or application.

(d) A contract, bid, or application subject to the requirements of this section must include the following statement:

"Under Section 231.006, Family Code, the vendor or applicant certifies that the individual or business entity named in this contract, bid, or application is not ineligible to receive the specified grant, loan, or payment and acknowledges that this contract may be terminated and payment may be withheld if this certification is inaccurate."

(e) If a state agency determines that an individual or business entity holding a state contract is ineligible to receive payment under Subsection (a), the contract may be terminated.

(f) If the certificate required under Subsection (d) is shown to be false, the vendor is liable to the state for attorney's fees, the costs necessary to complete the contract, including the cost of advertising and awarding a second contract, and any other damages provided by law or contract.

(g) This section does not create a cause of action to contest a bid or award of a state grant, loan, or contract. This section does not impose a duty on the Title IV-D agency to collect information to send to the comptroller to withhold a payment to a business entity. The Title IV-D agency and other affected agencies are encouraged to develop a system by which the Title IV-D agency may identify a business entity that is ineligible to receive a state payment under Subsection (a) and to ensure that a state payment to the entity is not made. This system should be implemented using existing funds and only if the Title IV-D agency, comptroller, and other affected agencies determine that it will be cost-effective.

(h) This section does not apply to a contract between governmental entities.

(i) The Title IV-D agency may adopt rules or prescribe forms to implement any provision of this section.

(j) A state agency may accept a bid that does not include the information required under Subsection (c) if the state agency collects the information before the contract, grant, or loan is executed.

Comment

This section casts a broad net to constrain delinquent child support obligors who might otherwise be eligible to apply for or receive state funds from contracts, loans, and grants. *(H.P.S.)*

§ 231.007. Debts to State

(a) A person obligated to pay child support in a case in which the Title IV-D agency is providing services under this chapter who does not pay the required support is indebted to the state for the purposes of Section 403.055, Government Code, if the Title IV-D agency has reported the person to the comptroller under that section properly.

(b) The amount of a person's indebtedness to the state under Subsection (a) is equal to the sum of:

(1) the amount of the required child support that has not been paid; and

(2) any interest, fees, court costs, or other amounts owed by the person because the person has not paid the support.

(c) The Title IV-D agency is the sole assignee of all payments, including payments of compensation, by the state to a person indebted to the state under Subsection (a).

(d) On request of the Title IV-D agency:

(1) the comptroller shall make payable and deliver to the agency any payments for which the agency is the assignee under Subsection (c), if the comptroller is responsible for issuing warrants or initiating electronic funds transfers to make those payments; and

(2) a state agency shall make payable and deliver to the Title IV-D agency any payments for which the Title IV-D agency is the assignee under Subsection (c) if the comptroller is not responsible for issuing warrants or initiating electronic funds transfers to make those payments.

(e) A person indebted to the state under Subsection (a) may eliminate the debt by:

(1) paying the entire amount of the debt; or

(2) resolving the debt in a manner acceptable to the Title IV-D agency.

(f) The comptroller or a state agency may rely on a representation by the Title IV-D agency that:

(1) a person is indebted to the state under Subsection (a); or

(2) a person who was indebted to the state under Subsection (a) has eliminated the debt.

(g) Except as provided by Subsection (h), the payment of workers' compensation benefits to a person indebted to the state under Subsection (a) is the same for the purposes of this section as any other payment made to the person by the state. Notwithstanding Section 408.203, Labor Code, an order or writ to withhold income from workers' compensation benefits is not required before the benefits are withheld or assigned under this section.

(h) The amount of weekly workers' compensation benefits that may be withheld or assigned under this section may not exceed 50 percent of the person's weekly compensation benefits. The comptroller or a state agency may rely on a representation by the Title IV–D agency that a withholding or assignment under this section would not violate this subsection.

(i) Section 403.055(d), Government Code, does not authorize the comptroller to issue a warrant or initiate an electronic funds transfer to pay the compensation or remuneration of an individual who is indebted to the state under Subsection (a).

(j) Section 2107.008(h), Government Code, does not authorize a state agency to pay the compensation or remuneration of an individual who is indebted to the state under Subsection (a).

(k) In this section, "compensation," "state agency," and "state officer or employee" have the meanings assigned by Section 403.055, Government Code.

§ 231.008. Disposition of Funds

(a) The Title IV–D agency shall deposit money received under assignments or as fees in a special fund in the state treasury. The agency may spend money in the fund for the administration of this chapter, subject to the General Appropriations Act.

(b) All other money received under this chapter shall be deposited in a special fund in the state treasury.

(c) Sections 403.094 and 403.095, Government Code, do not apply to a fund described by this section.

§ 231.009. Payment of Penalties

From funds appropriated for the Title IV–D agency, the agency shall reimburse the Texas Department of Human Services for any penalty assessed under Title IV–A of the federal Social Security Act (42 U.S.C. Section 651 et seq.) that is assessed because of the agency's administration of this chapter.

§ 231.010. Cooperation With Department of Protective and Regulatory Services

(a) In this section, "department" means the Department of Protective and Regulatory Services.

(b) To the extent possible, the Title IV-D agency shall:

(1) provide to the department access to all of the Title IV-D agency's available child support locating resources;

(2) allow the department to use the Title IV-D agency's child support enforcement system to track child support payments and to have access to the agency's management reports that show payments made;

(3) make reports on Title IV-E, Social Security Act (42 U.S.C. Section 670 et seq.), foster care collections available to the department in a timely manner; and

(4) work with the department to obtain child support payments for protective services cases in which the department is responsible for providing care for children under temporary and final orders.

§ 231.011 Repealed.

§ 231.012. Child Support Work Group

(a) The director of the Title IV–D agency may convene a work group representing public and private entities with an interest in child support enforcement in this state to work with the director in developing strategies to improve child support enforcement in this state.

(b) The director of the Title IV–D agency shall appoint the members of the work group after consulting with appropriate public and private entities.

(c) The work group shall meet as convened by the director of the Title IV–D agency and consult with the director on matters relating to child support enforcement in this state, including the delivery of Title IV–D services.

(d) A work group member or the member's designee may not receive compensation but is entitled to reimbursement for actual and necessary expenses incurred in performing the member's duties under this section.

(e) The work group is not an advisory committee as defined by Section 2110.001, Government Code. Chapter 2110, Government Code, does not apply to the work group.

§ 231.013. Information Resources Steering Committee

(a) The Title IV–D agency shall create an information resources steering committee to:

(1) oversee information resource project development for the Title IV–D agency;

(2) make strategic prioritization recommendations;

(3) facilitate development of accurate information for the director of the Title IV–D agency; and

(4) perform other functions as determined by the director of the Title IV–D agency.

(b) The steering committee must include a senior management executive representing each significant function of the Title IV–D agency. The steering committee may include a person representing:

(1) counties; or

(2) a vendor contracting with the Title IV–D agency.

(c) The director of the Title IV–D agency shall appoint the members of the steering committee after consulting with the Department of Information Resources.

§ 231.014. Personnel

The director of the Title IV–D agency shall provide to the employees of the Title IV–D agency, as often as necessary, information regarding the requirements for employment under this title, including information regarding a person's responsibilities under applicable laws relating to standards of conduct for state employees.

§ 231.015. Insurance Reporting Program

(a) In consultation with the Texas Department of Insurance and representatives of the insurance industry in this state, including insurance trade associations, the Title IV–D agency by rule shall operate a program ~~to improve the enforcement of child support, including the use of child support liens under Chapter 157. The program shall provide for procedures, including data matches,~~ under which **insurers** ~~insurance companies~~ shall cooperate with the Title IV–D agency in identifying obligors who owe child support arrearages **and** ~~or who~~ are subject to liens for child support arrearages to intercept certain ~~liability~~ insurance settlements or awards for claims in satisfaction of the arrearage amounts.

(b) An **insurer** ~~insurance company~~that provides information or responds to a notice of child support lien or levy under Subchapter G, Chapter 157, or acts in good faith to comply with procedures established by the Title IV–D agency under this section is not liable for those acts under any law to any person.

Amended by Acts 2011, 82nd Leg., ch. 508 (H.B. 1674), § 12, eff. Sept. 1, 2011.

SUBCHAPTER B. SERVICES PROVIDED BY TITLE IV–D PROGRAM

§ 231.101. Title IV–D Child Support Services

(a) The Title IV–D agency may provide all services required or authorized to be provided by Part D of Title IV of the federal Social Security Act (42 U.S.C. Section 651 et seq.), including:

(1) parent locator services;

(2) paternity determination;

(3) child support and medical support establishment;

(4) review and adjustment of child support orders;

(5) enforcement of child support and medical support orders; and

(6) collection and distribution of child support payments.

(b) At the request of either the obligee or obligor, the Title IV-D agency shall review a child support order once every three years and, if appropriate, adjust the support amount to meet the requirements of the child support guidelines under Chapter 154.

(c) Except as notice is included in the child support order, a party subject to a support order shall be provided notice not less than once every three years of the party's right to request that the Title IV-D agency review and, if appropriate, adjust the amount of ordered support.

(d) The Title IV-D agency may review a support order at any time on a showing of a material and substantial change in circumstances, taking into consideration the best interests of the child.

(e) The Title IV-D agency shall distribute a child support payment received by the agency from an employer within two working days after the date the agency receives the payment.

Comment

The federal Family Support Act of 1988 required states, on pain of loss of federal matching funds for their IV–D programs, to have procedures for the periodic review and, as needed, adjustment of child support amounts in orders being enforced by the IV–D agency in order to ensure that the support amounts remain consistent with state child support guidelines. This section incorporates the federal review and adjustment requirements, as amended by PRWORA. Reviews must be conducted by the IV-D agency on a three year cycle in public assistance cases, but only at the request of either the obligee or obligor in other IV-D cases. This automatic review process does not preclude, however, a review at any time on a showing of a material and substantial change of circumstances, subject to the best interests of the child. *(A.G.K. & H.P.S.)*

§ 231.102. Eligibility for Child Support Services

The Title IV–D agency on application or as otherwise authorized by law may provide services for the benefit of a child without regard to whether the child has received public assistance.

§ 231.103. Application and Service Fees

(a) The Title IV–D agency may:

(1) charge a reasonable application fee;

(2) charge a $25 annual service fee; and

(3) to the extent permitted by federal law, recover costs for the services provided in a Title IV–D case.

(b) An application fee may not be charged in a case in which the Title IV–D agency provides services because the family receives public assistance.

(c) An application fee may not exceed a maximum amount established by federal law.

(d) Repealed by Acts 2007, 80th Leg., ch. 972, § 65(3).

(e) The Title IV–D agency may impose and collect a fee as authorized by federal law for each request for parent locator services under Section 231.101(a).

(f) The state disbursement unit established and operated by the Title IV–D agency under Chapter 234 may collect a monthly service fee of $3 in each case in which support payments are processed through the unit.

(g) The Title IV–D agency by rule shall establish procedures for the imposition of fees and recovery of costs authorized under this section.

(g–1) A fee authorized under this section for providing child support enforcement services is part of the child support obligation if the obligor is responsible for the fee, and may be enforced against the obligor through any method available for the enforcement of child support, including contempt.

(h) The attorney general child support application and service fee account is an account in the general revenue fund in the state treasury. The account consists of all fees and costs collected under this section. The Title IV–D agency may only use the money in the account for agency program expenditures.

Comment

Federal law (42 U.S.C. 654(6)) requires a state's IV–D agency to charge an application fee for services in cases in which the applicant is not a recipient of public assistance, and it authorizes the agency to charge other appropriate fees and to recover administrative costs for providing services in these cases. In 2003 and again in 2007, the legislature specifically identified under this section the various fees that the agency may levy, including a $25 annual service fee on IV–D nonpublic assistance cases mandated by the federal Deficit Reduction Act of 2005. Although under the federal funding scheme any fees and costs recovered by the IV–D must be shared with the federal government, under Subsection (h) the amounts retained by the state must be reinvested in the IV–D program, thereby producing additional federal matching funds for the operation of the program. In 2007, Subsection (g–1) was added to make any fees for which the obligor may be responsible under this section part of the child support obligation and enforceable as such. *(A.G.K. & H.P.S.)*

§ 231.104. Assignment of Right to Support

(a) To the extent authorized by federal law, the approval of an application for or the receipt of financial assistance as provided by Chapter 31, Human Resources Code, constitutes an assignment to the Title IV-D agency of any rights to support from any other person that the applicant or recipient may have personally or for a child for whom the applicant or recipient is claiming assistance.

(b) An application for child support services is an assignment of support rights to enable the Title IV–D agency to establish and enforce child support and medical support obligations, but an assignment is not a condition of eligibility for services.

§ 231.105. Notice of Change of Payee

(a) Child support payments for the benefit of a child whose support rights have been assigned to the Title IV-D agency under Section 231.104 shall be made payable to the Title IV-D agency and transmitted to the state disbursement unit as provided by Chapter 234.

(b) If a court has ordered support payments to be made to an applicant for or recipient of financial assistance or to an applicant for or recipient of Title IV-D services, the Title IV-D agency shall, on providing notice to the obligee and the obligor, direct the obligor or other payor to make support payments payable to the Title IV-D agency and to transmit the payments to the state disbursement unit. The Title IV-D agency shall file a copy of the notice with the court ordering the payments and with the child support registry. The notice must include:

(1) a statement that the child is an applicant for or recipient of financial assistance, or a child other than a recipient child for whom Title IV-D services are provided;

(2) the name of the child and the caretaker for whom support has been ordered by the court;

(3) the style and cause number of the case in which support was ordered; and

(4) instructions for the payment of ordered support to the agency.

(c) On receipt of a copy of the notice under Subsection (b), the clerk of the court shall file the notice in the appropriate case file.

Comment

Under federal law, an application for, or receipt of, public assistance constitutes an assignment to the state of rights to child support. Similarly, under state law an approved application for IV–D services in non-public assistance cases constitutes an assignment of support rights. Where there is such an assignment in a IV–D case, a court order has been needed in order to redirect support payments to the IV–D agency. Under PRWORA, the agency itself must have the authority, without the requirement of a court order, to effect a change of payee if there is an assignment of support or if support payments (as in the case of all income withholding) are required to be made to the new state disbursement unit under Chapter 234. Using the administrative procedures, the agency itself may direct any payor of support to send payments directly to the agency and notify the court ordering the support and the local support registry of this change. *(A.G.K. & H.P.S.)*

§ 231.106. Notice of Termination of Assignment

(a) On termination of support rights to the Title IV-D agency, the Title IV-D agency shall, after providing notice to the obligee and the obligor, send a notice of termination of assignment to the obligor or other payor, which may direct that all or a portion of the payments be made payable to the agency and to other persons who are entitled to receive the payments.

(b) The Title IV–D agency shall send a copy of the notice of termination of assignment to the court ordering the support and to the child support registry, and on receipt of the notice the clerk of the court shall file the notice in the appropriate case file. The clerk may not require an order of the court to terminate the assignment and direct support payments to the person entitled to receive the payment.

Comment

The IV–D agency must send notice of any termination of assignment of support rights to the obligee, the obligor, and to the appropriate court and local registry. The notice may redirect support payments to a payee other than the agency, although in most instances it will not because of the PRWORA requirement that, with limited exceptions, income withholding be made through the state disbursement unit. *(A.G.K. & H.P.S.)*

§ 231.107. Certificate of Assignment or of Termination of Assignment

If an abstract of judgment or a child support lien on support amounts assigned to the Title IV-D agency under this chapter has previously been filed of record, the agency shall file for recordation, with the county clerk of each county in which such abstract or lien has been filed, a certificate that a notice of change of payee or a notice of termination of assignment has been issued by the agency.

Comment

A lien for child support under Chapter 157 attaches when a lien notice or abstract of judgment is filed with the clerk of a county in which the obligor resides, has nonexempt real or personal property, or in which the court having continuing jurisdiction is located. The certification of an assignment of support rights to the state protects that assignment in the event of foreclosure of the lien or an action to release the lien. *(A.G.K. & H.P.S.)*

§ 231.108. Confidentiality of Records and Privileged Communications

(a) Except as provided by Subsection (c), all files and records of services provided under this chapter, including information concerning a custodial parent, noncustodial parent, child, and an alleged or presumed father, are confidential.

(b) Except as provided by Subsection (c), all communications made by a recipient of financial assistance under Chapter 31, Human Resources Code, or an applicant for or recipient of services under this chapter are privileged.

(c) The Title IV–D agency may use or release information from the files and records, including information that results from a communication made by a recipient of financial assistance under Chapter 31, Human Resources Code, or by an applicant for or recipient of services under this chapter, for purposes directly connected with the administration of the child support, paternity determination, parent locator, or aid to families with dependent children programs. The Title IV–D agency may release information from the files and records to a consumer reporting agency in accordance with Section 231.114.

(d) The Title IV–D agency by rule may provide for the release of information to public officials.

(e) The Title IV-D agency may not release information on the physical location of a person if:

(1) a protective order has been entered with respect to the person; or

(2) there is reason to believe that the release of information may result in physical or emotional harm to the person.

(f) The Title IV–D agency, by rule, may provide for the release of information to persons for purposes not prohibited by federal law.

(g) The final order in a suit adjudicating parentage is available for public inspection as provided by Section 160.633.

Comment

For the most part the provisions of this section reflect the confidentiality requirements of federal law with respect to the operation of state IV–D programs. (*See* 42 U.S.C. § 654(26).) *(A.G.K. & H.P.S.)*

---

§ 231.109. Attorneys Representing State

(a) Attorneys employed by the Title IV–D agency may represent this state or another state in an action brought under the authority of federal law or this chapter.

(b) The Title IV–D agency may contract with private attorneys, other private entities, or political subdivisions of the state to provide services in Title IV–D cases.

(c) The Title IV–D agency shall provide copies of all contracts entered into under this section to the Legislative Budget Board and the Governor's Office of Budget and Planning, along with a written justification of the need for each contract, within 60 days after the execution of the contract.

(d) An attorney employed to provide Title IV-D services represents the interest of the state and not the interest of any other party. The provision of services by an attorney under this chapter does not create an attorney-client relationship between the attorney and any other party. The agency shall, at the time an application for child support services is made, inform the applicant that neither the Title IV–D agency nor any attorney who provides services under this chapter is the applicant's attorney and that the attorney providing services under this chapter does not provide legal representation to the applicant.

(e) An attorney employed by the Title IV–D agency or as otherwise provided by this chapter may not be appointed or act as an amicus attorney or attorney ad litem for a child or another party.

§ 231.110. Authorization of Service

The provision of services by the Title IV–D agency under this chapter or Part D of Title IV of the federal Social Security Act (42 U.S.C. Section 651 et seq.) does not authorize service on the agency of any legal notice that is required to be served on any party other than the agency.

§ 231.111. Disqualification of Agency

A court shall not disqualify the Title IV–D agency in a legal action filed under this chapter or Part D of Title IV of the federal Social Security Act (42 U.S.C. Section 651 et seq.) on the basis that the agency has previously provided services to a party whose interests may now be adverse to the relief requested.

§ 231.112. Information on Paternity Establishment

On notification by the state registrar under Section 192.005(d), Health and Safety Code, that the items relating to the child's father are not completed on a birth certificate filed with the state registrar, the Title IV–D agency may provide to:

(1) the child's mother and, if possible, the man claiming to be the child's biological father written information necessary for the man to complete an acknowledgment of paternity as provided by Chapter 160; and

(2) the child's mother written information:

(A) explaining the benefits of having the child's paternity established; and

(B) regarding the availability of paternity establishment and child support enforcement services.

§ 231.113. Enforcement of Support Obligations in Public Assistance Cases

To the extent possible, the Title IV–D agency shall enforce a child support obligation in a case involving a child who receives financial assistance under Chapter 31, Human Resources Code, not later than the first anniversary of the date the agency receives from the Texas Department of Human Services the information the department is required to provide to assist in the enforcement of that obligation.

§ 231.114. Reports of Child Support Payments to Consumer Reporting Agencies

(a) The Title IV–D agency shall make information available in accordance with this section to a consumer reporting agency regarding the amount of child support owed and the amount paid by an obligor in a Title IV–D case.

(b) Before disclosing the information to consumer reporting agencies, the Title IV–D agency shall send the obligor a notice by mail to the obligor's last known address. The notice must include:

(1) the information to be released, including the amount of the obligor's child support obligation and delinquency, if any, that will be reported;

(2) the procedure available for the obligor to contest the accuracy of the information; and

(3) a statement that the information will be released if the obligor fails to contest the disclosure before the 30th day after the date of mailing of the notice.

(c) If the obligor does not contest the disclosure within the period specified by Subsection (b), the Title IV–D agency shall make the information available to the consumer reporting agency.

(d) The Title IV–D agency shall regularly update the information released to a consumer reporting agency under this section to ensure the accuracy of the released information.

(e) The Title IV–D agency may charge a consumer reporting agency a reasonable fee for making information available under this section, including all applicable mailing costs.

(f) In this section:

(1) "Consumer reporting agency" means any person that regularly engages in whole or in part in the practice of assembling or evaluating consumer credit information or other information on consumers for monetary fees, for dues, or on a cooperative nonprofit basis, to furnish consumer reports to third parties.

(2) "Obligor" means any person required to make payments under the terms of a support order for a child.

(3) "Title IV–D case" means a case in which services are being provided by the Title IV–D agency under Part D of Title IV of the federal Social Security Act (42 U.S.C. Section 651 et seq.) seeking to locate an absent parent, determine parentage, or establish, modify, enforce, or monitor a child support obligation.

§ 231.115. Noncooperation by Recipient of Public Assistance

(a) The failure by a person who is a recipient of public assistance under Chapter 31, Human Resources Code, to provide accurate information as required by Section 31.0315, Human Resources Code, shall serve as the basis for a determination by the Title IV–D agency that the person did not cooperate with the Title IV–D agency.

(b) The Title IV–D agency shall:

(1) identify the actions or failures to act by a recipient of public assistance that constitute noncooperation with the Title IV–D agency;

(2) adopt rules governing noncompliance; and

(3) send noncompliance determinations to the Texas Department of Human Services for immediate imposition of sanctions.

(c) In adopting rules under this section that establish the basis for determining that a person has failed to cooperate with the Title IV–D agency, the Title IV–D agency shall consider whether:

(1) good cause exists for the failure to cooperate;

(2) the person has failed to disclose the name and location of an alleged or probable parent of the child, if known by the person, at the time of applying for public assistance or at a subsequent time; and

(3) the person named a man as the alleged father and the man was subsequently excluded by parentage testing as being the father if the person has previously named another man as the child's father.

§ 231.116. Information on Internet

The Title IV-D agency shall place on the Internet for public access child support information to assist the public in child support matters, including application forms, child support collection in other states, and profiles of certain obligors who are in arrears in paying child support.

Comment

The intent of this provision is to advertise the availability of IV–D services, as well as to identify delinquent obligors to be reported for a reward; *see* § 231.309, which authorizes the agency to make an offer of rewards for information. *(A.G.K. & H.P.S.)*

§ 231.1165. Information on Service of Citation

The Title IV-D agency shall update the agency's child support automated system to inform the parties in a suit of the service of citation in the suit not later than the first business day after the date the agency receives notice that citation has been served. The information required by this section must be available by telephone and on the Internet.

Comment

The intent of this section is to save an obligee in a IV–D case from being required to make special arrangements to attend a child support hearing, or from making an unnecessary trip to the courthouse only to learn that the obligor has not been successfully served a citation requiring appearance. Unfortunately, often the IV–D agency itself does not learn of an unsuccessful attempt at service until its attorneys arrive for a hearing. *(A.G.K. & H.P.S.)*

§ 231.117. Unemployed and Underemployed Obligors

(a) The Title IV-D agency shall refer to appropriate state and local entities that provide employment services any unemployed or underemployed obligor who is in arrears in court-ordered child support payments.

(b) A referral under Subsection (a) may include:

(1) skills training and job placement through:

(A) the Texas Workforce Commission; or

(B) the agency responsible for the food stamp employment and training program (7 U.S.C. Section 2015(d));

(2) referrals to education and literacy classes; and

(3) counseling regarding:

(A) substance abuse;

(B) parenting skills;

(C) life skills; and

(D) mediation techniques.

(c) The Title IV-D agency may require an unemployed or underemployed obligor to complete the training, classes, or counseling to which the obligor is referred under this section. The agency shall suspend under Chapter 232 the license of an obligor who fails to comply with the requirements of this subsection.

(d) A court or the Title IV–D agency may issue an order that requires the parent to either work, have a plan to pay overdue child support, or participate in work activities appropriate to pay the overdue support.

§ 231.118. Service of Citation

(a) The Title IV–D agency may contract with private process servers to serve a citation, a subpoena, an order, or any other document required or appropriate under law to be served a party.

(b) For the purposes of Rule 103 of the Texas Rules of Civil Procedure, a person who serves a citation or any other document under this section is authorized to serve the document without a written court order authorizing the service.

(c) Issuance and return of the process shall be made in accordance with law and shall be verified by the person serving the document.

§ 231.119. Ombudsman Program

(a) The Title IV–D agency shall establish an ombudsman program to process and track complaints against the Title IV–D agency. The director of the Title IV–D agency shall:

(1) designate an employee to serve as chief ombudsman to manage the ombudsman program; and

(2) designate an employee in each field office to act as the ombudsman for the office.

(b) The Title IV–D agency shall develop and implement a uniform process for receiving and resolving complaints against the Title IV–D agency throughout the state. The process shall include statewide procedures to inform the public and recipients of Title IV–D services of the right to file a complaint against the Title IV–D agency, including the mailing addresses and telephone numbers of appropriate Title IV–D agency personnel responsible for receiving complaints and providing related assistance.

(c) The ombudsman in each field office shall ensure that an employee in the field office responds to and attempts to resolve each complaint that is filed with the field office. If a complaint cannot be resolved at the field office level, the ombudsman in the field office shall refer the complaint to the chief ombudsman.

(d) The Title IV–D agency shall maintain a file on each written complaint filed with the Title IV–D agency. The file must include:

(1) the name of the person who filed the complaint;

(2) the date the complaint is received by the Title IV–D agency;

(3) the subject matter of the complaint;

(4) the name of each person contacted in relation to the complaint;

(5) a summary of the results of the review or investigation of the complaint; and

(6) an explanation of the reason the file was closed, if the agency closed the file without taking action other than to investigate the complaint.

(e) The Title IV–D agency, at least quarterly until final disposition of the complaint, shall notify the person filing the complaint and each person who is a subject of the complaint of the status of the investigation of the complaint unless the notice would jeopardize an undercover investigation.

(f) The Title IV–D agency shall provide to the person filing the complaint and to each person who is a subject of the complaint a copy of the Title IV–D agency's policies and procedures relating to complaint investigation and resolution.

§ 231.120. Toll-free Telephone Number for Employers

The Title IV–D agency shall maintain a toll-free telephone number at which personnel are available during normal business hours to answer questions from employers responsible for withholding child support. The Title IV–D agency shall inform employers about the toll-free telephone number.

§ 231.121. Availability of Brochures

The Title IV-D agency shall ensure that all Title IV-D brochures published by the agency are available to the public at courthouses where family law cases are heard in the state.

Comment

Federal law already requires the IV–D agency to publicize agency services available to the public. This section prescribes a specific way of publicizing such services on the apparent assumption that parties in family law cases will have either the time for, or interest in, browsing brochures in a courthouse hallway. *(A.G.K. & H.P.S.)*

---

§ 231.122. Monitoring Child Support Cases; Enforcement

The Title IV–D agency shall monitor each Title IV–D case from the date the agency begins providing services on the case. If a child support obligor in a Title IV–D case becomes more than 60 days delinquent in paying child support, the Title IV–D agency shall expedite the commencement of an action to enforce the child support order.

Comment

This provision attempts to put the IV–D agency on a very short leash. As persons knowledgeable about the subject would be quick to point out, "60 days in arrears ain't nothing." This mandate to expedite an action to enforce child support orders after such a short term of nonpayment seems more than a little idealistic. It's anybody's guess whether this will have any real impact; the guess here is "unlikely."

This section was taken from a voluminous 2005 measure designed to overhaul the state's protective services. At best, it is superfluous inasmuch as the Title IV–D agency is subject to far more stringent federal requirements for monitoring and enforcing child support obligations. *(A.G.K. & H.P.S.)*

---

§ 231.123. Cooperation With Volunteer Income Tax Assistance Programs

(a) In order to maximize the amount of any tax refund to which an obligor may be entitled and which may be applied to child support and medical support obligations, the Title IV–D agency shall cooperate with volunteer income tax assistance programs in the state in informing obligors of the availability of the programs.

(b) The Title IV–D agency shall publicize the services of the volunteer income tax assistance programs by distributing printed materials regarding the programs and by placing information regarding the programs on the agency's Internet website.

(c) The Title IV–D agency is not responsible for producing or paying the costs of producing the printed materials distributed in accordance with Subsection (b).

Comment

Added by the legislature in 2005, this section requires the Title IV–D program to cooperate with the Volunteer Tax Assistance Program (VITA) operated by local communities across the state in collaboration with the Internal Revenue Service. The purpose of VITA is to provide free federal income tax preparation assistance to low-income and other eligible taxpayers so that they may take advantage of all eligible tax credits, especially the Earned Income Tax Credit (EITC). The mandated involvement of the Title IV–D agency with VITA under this section is based on the supposition that many low-income child support obligors do not take advantage of federal tax credits when filing their income tax and, therefore, do not maximize the amount of their federal income tax refunds which may be intercepted by the Title IV–D agency for payment of past-due child support. *(A.G.K. & H.P.S.)*

§ 231.124. Child Support Arrearages Payment Incentive Program

(a) The Title IV–D agency may establish and administer a payment incentive program to promote payment by obligors who are delinquent in satisfying child support arrearages assigned to the Title IV–D agency under Section 231.104(a).

(b) A program established under this section must provide to a participating obligor a credit for every dollar amount paid by the obligor on interest and arrearages balances during each month of the obligor's voluntary enrollment in the program. In establishing a program under this section, the Title IV–D agency by rule must prescribe:

(1) criteria for a child support obligor's initial eligibility to participate in the program;

(2) the conditions for a child support obligor's continued participation in the program;

(3) procedures for enrollment in the program; and

(4) the terms of the financial incentives to be offered under the program.

(c) The Title IV–D agency shall provide eligible obligors with notice of the program and enrollment instructions.

Added by Acts 2011, 82nd Leg., ch. 508 (H.B. 1674), § 13, eff. Sept. 1, 2011.

Comment

In 2001, the 77th Texas Legislature amended the Family Code to add § 157.262 under which the court, with the agreement of the Title IV-D agency, could hold in abeyance the enforcement of child support arrearages (including interest) assigned to the state if the child support obligor complied with a number of conditions. On the expiration of the support order, the court could again with the agreement of the Title IV-D agency reduce the amount of the assigned arrears. This attempt to negotiate arrears proved to have significant limitations, the chief one being the inability of either the court or the agency to monitor fully the several conditions an obligor was required to meet. Also, any reduction by the court of the amount of the arrearages would only occur on the expiration of the support order, which could be many years out.

In 2011, the 82th legislature repealed § 157.262 and added this section authorizing the Title IV-D agency to establish a program—similar to programs operating in a number of other states—to promote payment of arrears assigned to the state. Through voluntary enrollment in this program, obligors will be given a matching credit (in an amount determined by the agency) for every dollar they pay towards arrears during each month of enrollment. This credit will, however, be conditioned on their fully and timely meeting any current support obligation. The intent of the program is, then, to encourage payment not only of support arrears, but also of current support. Unlike the repealed program, fulfillment of the conditions for participation in the new program can be immediately monitored through payment records. *(A.G.K. & H.P.S.)*

SUBCHAPTER C. PAYMENT OF FEES AND COSTS

§ 231.201. Definitions

In this subchapter:

(1) "Federal share" means the portion of allowable expenses for fees and other costs that will be reimbursed by the federal government under federal law and regulations regarding the administration of the Title IV–D program.

(2) "State share" means the portion of allowable expenses for fees and other costs that remain after receipt of the federal share of reimbursement and that is to be reimbursed by the state or may be contributed by certified public expenditure by a county.

§ 231.202. Authorized Costs and Fees in Title Iv–d Cases

In a Title IV–D case filed under this title, including a case filed under Chapter 159, the Title IV–D agency shall pay only the following costs and fees:

(1) filing fees and fees for issuance and service of process as provided by Chapter 110 of this code and by Sections 51.317(b)(1), (2), and (3) and (b–1), 51.318(b)(2), and 51.319(2), Government Code;

(2) fees for transfer as provided by Chapter 110;

(3) fees for the issuance and delivery of orders and writs of income withholding in the amounts provided by Chapter 110;

(4) the fee for services provided by sheriffs and constables, including:

(A) a fee authorized under Section 118.131, Local Government Code, for serving each item of process to each individual on whom service is required, including service by certified or registered mail; and

(B) a fee authorized under Section 157.103(b) for serving a capias;

(5) the fee for filing an administrative writ of withholding under Section 158.503(d);

(6) the fee for issuance of a subpoena as provided by Section 51.318(b)(1), Government Code; and

(7) a fee authorized under a local rule for the electronic filing of documents with a clerk.

Comment

In 1991 the legislature authorized payment to the counties of the filing costs and service fees in cases enforced by the IV–D agency. Since that enactment, federal funds (equal to 66 percent of total costs and fees) have been passed through to counties, with the balance to be paid either by the counties or through specific appropriation made to the attorney general for that purpose. Subsequent amendments to the Family Code have expanded the categories of fees and costs in IV–D cases eligible for reimbursement, subject, however, to certain limitations imposed by federal regulations. Section 158.503(d) authorizes a fee for filing an administrative writ of withholding issued by the IV–D agency, thereby providing counties with further income for a ministerial act of little consequence. *(A.G.K. & H.P.S.)*

Counties receive payment for filing costs and service fees in cases enforced by the IV–D agency. Federal funds (equal to 66 percent of total costs and fees) are passed through to counties, with the balance to be paid either by the counties or through specific appropriation made to the attorney general for that purpose. Subsequent amendments to the Family Code expanded the categories of fees and costs in IV–D cases eligible for reimbursement. *(A.G.K. & H.P.S.)*

§ 231.2025. Contingency Fees

The Title IV-D agency may pay a contingency fee in a contract or agreement between the agency and a private agency or individual authorized under Section 231.002(c).

§ 231.203. State Exemption From Bond Not Affected

This subchapter does not affect, nor is this subchapter affected by, the exemption from bond provided by Section 6.001, Civil Practice and Remedies Code.

§ 231.204. Prohibited Fees in Title IV-D Cases

Except as provided by this subchapter, an appellate court, a clerk of an appellate court, a district or county clerk, sheriff, constable, or other government officer or employee may not charge the

Title IV-D agency or a private attorney or political subdivision that has entered into a contract to provide Title IV-D services any fees or other amounts otherwise imposed by law for services rendered in, or in connection with, a Title IV-D case, including:

(1) a fee payable to a district clerk for:

(A) performing services related to the estates of deceased persons or minors;

(B) certifying copies; or

(C) comparing copies to originals;

(2) a court reporter fee, except as provided by Section 231.209;

(3) a judicial fund fee;

(4) a fee for a child support registry, enforcement office, or domestic relations office;

(5) a fee for alternative dispute resolution services; and

(6) a filing fee or other costs payable to a clerk of an appellate court.

Comment

The services for which the IV–D agency may be charged fees are enumerated under § 231.202, *supra*. The list of services under this section for which the agency may not be charged fees is, of course, not intended to be exclusive or limiting. Even if it is not identified in this list, a fee not specifically required elsewhere in law to be paid by the IV–D agency may not be assessed against the agency. *(A.G.K. & H.P.S.)*

---

§ 231.205. Limitations on Liability of Attorney General for Authorized Fees and Costs

(a) The Title IV–D agency is liable for a fee or cost under this subchapter only to the extent that an express, specific appropriation is made to the agency exclusively for that purpose. To the extent that state funds are not available, the amount of costs and fees that are not reimbursed by the federal government and that represent the state share shall be paid by certified public expenditure by the county through the clerk of the court, sheriff, or constable. This section does not prohibit the agency from spending other funds appropriated for child support enforcement to provide the initial expenditures necessary to qualify for the federal share.

(b) The Title IV–D agency is liable for the payment of the federal share of reimbursement for fees and costs under this subchapter only to the extent that the federal share is received, and if an amount is paid by the agency and that amount is disallowed by the federal government or the federal share is not otherwise received, the clerk of the court, sheriff, or constable to whom the payment was made shall return the amount to the agency not later than the 30th day after the date on which notice is given by the agency.

§ 231.206. Restriction on Fees for Child Support or Registry Services in Title IV–D Cases

A district clerk, a county child support registry or enforcement office, or a domestic relations office may not assess or collect fees for processing child support payments or for child support services from the Title IV–D agency, a managing conservator, or a possessory conservator in a Title IV–D case, except as provided by this subchapter.

§ 231.207. Method of Billing for Allowable Fees

(a) To be entitled to reimbursement under this subchapter, the clerk of the court, sheriff, or constable must submit one monthly billing to the Title IV–D agency.

(b) The monthly billing must be in the form and manner prescribed by the Title IV–D agency and be approved by the clerk, sheriff, or constable.

§ 231.208. Agreements for Reimbursement in Lieu of Fees

(a) The Title IV–D agency and a qualified county may enter into a written agreement under which reimbursement for salaries and certain other actual costs incurred by the clerk, sheriff, or constable in Title IV–D cases is provided to the county.

(b) A county may not enter into an agreement for reimbursement under this section unless the clerk, sheriff, or constable providing service has at least two full-time employees each devoted exclusively to providing services in Title IV–D cases.

(c) Reimbursement made under this section is in lieu of all costs and fees provided by this subchapter.

§ 231.209. Payment for Services Not Affected by This Subchapter

Without regard to this subchapter and specifically Section 231.205, the Title IV–D agency may pay the costs for:

(1) the services of an official court reporter for the preparation of statements of facts;

(2) the costs for the publication of citation served by publication; and

(3) mileage or other reasonable travel costs incurred by a sheriff or constable when traveling out of the county to execute an outstanding warrant or capias, to be reimbursed at a rate not to exceed the rate provided for mileage or other costs incurred by state employees in the General Appropriations Act.

§ 231.210. Authority to Pay Litigation Expenses

(a) The Title IV–D agency may pay all fees, expenses, costs, and bills necessary to secure evidence and to take the testimony of a witness, including advance payments or purchases for transportation, lodging, meals, and incidental expenses of custodians of evidence or witnesses whose transportation is necessary and proper for the production of evidence or the taking of testimony in a Title IV–D case.

(b) In making payments under this section, the Title IV–D agency shall present vouchers to the comptroller that have been sworn to by the custodian or witness and approved by the agency. The voucher shall be sufficient to authorize payment without the necessity of a written contract.

(c) The Title IV–D agency may directly pay a commercial transportation company or commercial lodging establishment for the expense of transportation or lodging of a custodian or witness.

§ 231.211. Award of Cost Against Nonprevailing Party in Title IV–D Case

(a) At the conclusion of a Title IV–D case, the court may assess attorney's fees and all court costs as authorized by law against the nonprevailing party, except that the court may not assess those amounts against the Title IV–D agency or a private attorney or political subdivision that has entered into a contract under this chapter or any party to whom the agency has provided services under this chapter. Such fees and costs may not exceed reasonable and necessary costs as determined by the court.

(b) The clerk of the court may take any action necessary to collect any fees or costs assessed under this section.

Comment

The trial court is authorized to award fees and costs in IV–D cases against the nonprevailing party—meaning the obligor. One litigant, the attorney general, a.k.a. the State of Texas, is exempt from the payment of those fees even if the government fails to prevail (thereby saving the taxpayers cash at the expense of the private party, which is what sovereign immunity is all about).

SUBCHAPTER D. LOCATION OF PARENTS AND RESOURCES

§ 231.301. Title IV–D Parent Locator Services

(a) The parent locator service conducted by the Title IV–D agency shall be used to obtain information for:

(1) child support establishment and enforcement purposes regarding the identity, social security number, location, employer and employment benefits, income, and assets or debts of any individual under an obligation to pay child or medical support or to whom a support obligation is owed; or

(2) the establishment of paternity.

(b) As authorized by federal law, the following persons may receive information under this section:

(1) a person or entity that contracts with the Title IV–D agency to provide services authorized under Title IV–D or an employee of the Title IV–D agency;

(2) an attorney who has the duty or authority, by law, to enforce an order for possession of or access to a child;

(3) a court, or an agent of the court, having jurisdiction to render or enforce an order for possession of or access to a child;

(4) the resident parent, legal guardian, attorney, or agent of a child who is not receiving public assistance; and

(5) a state agency that administers a program operated under a state plan as provided by 42 U.S.C. Section 653(c).

§ 231.302. Information to Assist in Location of Persons or Property

(a) The Title IV-D agency of this or another state may request and obtain information relating to the identity, location, employment, compensation, benefits, income, and property holdings or other assets of any person from a state or local government agency, private company, institution, or other entity as necessary to establish, modify, or enforce a support order.

(b) A government agency, private company, institution, or other entity shall provide the information requested under Subsection (a) directly to the Title IV-D agency, without the requirement of payment of a fee for the information, and shall, subject to safeguards on privacy and information security, provide the information in the most efficient and expeditious manner available, including electronic or automated transfer and interface. Any individual or entity disclosing information under this section in response to a request from a Title IV-D agency may not be held liable in any civil action or proceeding to any person for the disclosure of information under this subsection.

(c) To assist in the administration of laws relating to child support enforcement under Parts A and D of Title IV of the federal Social Security Act (42 U.S.C. Sections 601–617 and 651–669):

(1) each licensing authority shall request and each applicant for a license shall provide the applicant's social security number;

(2) each agency administering a contract that provides for a payment of state funds shall request and each individual or entity bidding on a state contract shall provide the individual's or entity's social security number as required by Section 231.006, Family Code; and

(3) each agency administering a state-funded grant or loan program shall request and each applicant for a grant or loan shall provide the applicant's social security number as required by Section 231.006, Family Code.

(d) This section does not limit the right of an agency or licensing authority to collect and use a social security number under another provision of law.

(e) Except as provided by Subsection (d), a social security number provided under this section is confidential and may be disclosed only for the purposes of responding to a request for information from an agency operating under the provisions of Part A or D of Title IV of the federal Social Security Act (42 U.S.C. Sections 601 et seq. and 651 et seq).

(f) Information collected by the Title IV-D agency under this section may be used only for child support purposes.

(g) In this section, "licensing authority" has the meaning assigned by Section 232.001.

Comment

In 1996 PRWORA significantly expanded the access of state IV–D agencies to various kinds of information useful in child support enforcement. As part of the certification requirements under the Family Support Act of 1988, the IV–D agency's automated system must electronically interface with, among other information sources, the state agencies responsible for administering public assistance and unemployment and workers' compensation programs, the state agencies maintaining property records, vital records, corrections records, and motor vehicle records, and consumer credit reporting bureaus. Under PRWORA, without the necessity of any other court or administrative order and preferably by automated means, the IV–D agency of this or another state must be able to access information from any state or local agency, private company, institution, or any other entity possessing information needed for support enforcement purposes. This includes information from public or private employers about employment, compensation, and benefits and, by administrative subpoena, information appearing in customer records of public utilities and cable companies and information on the assets and liabilities of obligees and obligors maintained in records of financial institutions. Although access to, and release of, information must be subject to appropriate security safeguards and privacy protections, the greatly expanded disclosure of confidential or otherwise sensitive information, particularly through automated data exchanges, increases opportunities for the inappropriate or unauthorized use of the information, not to mention data error.

PRWORA also mandated that states have laws and procedures for the recordation of social security numbers on applications for driver's, professional, recreational, and marriage licenses, on records relating to divorce decrees, support orders, and paternity acknowledgments, and on death certificates. *(A.G.K. & H.P.S.)*

§ 231.303. Title IV-D Administrative Subpoena

(a) The Title IV-D agency of this state or another state may issue an administrative subpoena to any individual or private or public entity in this state to furnish information necessary to carry out the purposes of child support enforcement under 42 U.S.C. Section 651 et seq. or this chapter.

(b) An individual or entity receiving an administrative subpoena under this section shall comply with the subpoena. The Title IV-D agency may impose a fine in an amount not to exceed $500 on an individual or entity that fails without good cause to comply with an administrative subpoena. An alleged or presumed father or a parent who fails to comply with a subpoena without good cause may also be subject to license suspension under Chapter 232.

(c) A court may compel compliance with an administrative subpoena and with any administrative fine for failure to comply with the subpoena and may award attorney's fees and costs to the Title IV-D agency in enforcing an administrative subpoena on proof that an individual or organization failed without good cause to comply with the subpoena.

(d) An individual or organization may not be liable in a civil action or proceeding for disclosing financial or other information to a Title IV-D agency under this section. The Title IV-D agency may disclose information in a financial record obtained from a financial institution only to the extent necessary:

(1) to establish, modify, or enforce a child support obligation; or

(2) to comply with Section 233.001, as added by Chapter 420, Acts of the 75th Legislature, Regular Session, 1997.

Comment

This section complies with the requirement of PRWORA that the IV–D agency have the authority to issue an administrative subpoena and to impose sanctions for failure to comply with a subpoena. Under this section, the real authority for compelling compliance lies with the court, although on its own the agency, following procedures under Chapter 232, may suspend a license of a presumed or alleged father or a parent who fails to comply with an administrative subpoena. The agency's subpoena power may be particularly valuable in gaining access to information on the location and assets of absent parents. *(A.G.K. & H.P.S.)*

§ 231.304. Repealed.

§ 231.305. Memorandum of Understanding on Child Support for Children Receiving Public Assistance

(a) The Title IV–D agency and the Texas Department of Human Services by rule shall adopt a memorandum of understanding governing the establishment and enforcement of court-ordered child support in cases involving children who receive financial assistance under Chapter 31, Human Resources Code. The memorandum shall require the agency and the department to:

(1) develop procedures to ensure that the information the department is required to collect to establish and enforce child support:

(A) is collected from the person applying to receive the financial assistance at the time the application is filed;

(B) is accurate and complete when the department forwards the information to the agency;

(C) is not information previously reported to the agency; and

(D) is forwarded to the agency in an expeditious manner;

(2) develop procedures to ensure that the agency does not duplicate the efforts of the department in gathering necessary information;

(3) clarify each agency's responsibilities in the establishment and enforcement of child support;

(4) develop guidelines for use by eligibility workers and child support enforcement officers in obtaining from an applicant the information required to establish and enforce child support for that child;

(5) develop training programs for appropriate department personnel to enhance the collection of information for child support enforcement;

(6) develop a standard time, not to exceed 30 days, for the department to initiate a sanction on request from the agency;

(7) develop procedures for agency participation in department appeal hearings relating to noncompliance sanctions;

(8) develop performance measures regarding the timeliness and the number of sanctions resulting from agency requests for noncompliance sanctions; and

(9) prescribe:

(A) the time in which the department is required to forward information under Subdivision (1)(D); and

(B) what constitutes complete information under Subdivision (1)(B).

(b) The Title IV–D agency and the Texas Department of Human Services shall review and renew or modify the memorandum not later than January 1 of each even-numbered year.

§ 231.306. Maximizing Medical Support Establishment and Collection by the Title IV–D Agency

(a) On the installation of an automated child support enforcement system, the Title IV–D agency is strongly encouraged to:

(1) maximize the collection of medical support; and

(2) establish cash medical support orders for children eligible for medical assistance under the state Medicaid program for whom private insurance coverage is not available.

(b) In this section, "medical support" has the meaning assigned by Section 101.020.

§ 231.307. Financial Institution Data Matches

(a) The Title IV-D agency shall develop a system meeting the requirements of federal law (42 U.S.C. Sections 666(a)(4) and (17)) for the exchange of data with financial institutions doing business in the state to identify an account of an obligor owing past-due child support and to enforce support obligations against the obligor, including the imposition of a lien and a levy and execution on an obligor's assets held in financial institutions as required by federal law (42 U.S.C. Section 666(c)(1)(G)).

(b) The Title IV-D agency by rule shall establish procedures for data matches authorized under this section.

(c) The Title IV–D agency may enter into an agreement with one or more states to create a consortium for data matches authorized under this section. The Title IV–D agency may contract with a vendor selected by the consortium to perform data matches with financial institutions.

(d) A financial institution providing information or responding to a notice of child support lien **or levy** provided under Subchapter G, Chapter 157, or otherwise acting in good faith to comply with the Title IV–D agency's procedures under this section may not be liable under any federal or state law for any damages that arise from those acts.

(e) In this section:

(1) "Financial institution" has the meaning assigned by Section 157.311; and

(2) "Account" has the meaning assigned by Section 157.311.

(f) A financial institution participating in data matches authorized by this section may provide the Title IV-D agency an address for the purpose of service of notices or process required in actions under this section or Subchapter G, Chapter 157.

(g) This section does not apply to an insurer subject to the reporting requirements under Section 231.015.

Amended by Acts 2011, 82nd Leg., ch. 508 (H.B. 1674), § 14, eff. Sept. 1, 2011.

Comment

PRWORA requires the IV–D agency to establish a system, using automatic processes to the extent possible, under which financial institutions doing business in the state provide the agency each quarter with information on obligors who have accounts in the institutions and whom the agency has identified as being delinquent in support payments. Although at the time only one state has had any experience in executing such data matches, Congress mandated the process as a support enforcement "tool" for all states. Presumably once the assets of a delinquent obligor have been located, the IV–D agency will be able to move quickly to impose and execute a child support lien on those assets up to the amount of support arrearages. On receiving a lien notice, the institution is not to be held liable for encumbering and surrendering assets in complying with a lien. To meet the federal mandate fully, however, the IV–D agency must enter into agreements with not only all banks in the state, but also with all credit unions, benefit associations, insurance companies, safe deposit companies, mutual funds, and any other entity that offers a financial "account." Because this is an intrastate system, accounts which an obligor might maintain outside the state will not necessarily be detected. States can, however, expand their search through multi-state consortia. Moreover, the federal Office of Child Support Enforcement provides a mechanism through the Federal Parent Locator Service for matching state data on delinquent child support obligors with account information in multi-state financial institutions. *(A.G.K. & H.P.S.)*

§ 231.308. Public Identification of Certain Obligors

(a) The Title IV-D agency shall develop a program to identify publicly certain child support obligors who are delinquent in the payment of child support. The program shall include the displaying of photographs and profiles of obligors in public and private locations. The Title IV-D agency shall use posters, the news media, and other cost-effective methods to display photographs and profiles of certain obligors who are in arrears in paying child support. The Title IV-D agency shall divide the state into at least six regions for local identification of certain child support obligors who are delinquent in the payment of child support.

(b) The Title IV-D agency may not disclose information under this section that is by law required to remain confidential.

Comment

The use of a "most wanted" program not only serves to highlight the problem of nonsupport; it also results in the arrest of obligors who have sought to evade their child support responsibilities. *(A.G.K. & H.P.S.)*

§ 231.309. Rewards for Information

(a) The Title IV-D agency may offer a reward to an individual who provides information to the agency that leads to the collection of child support owed by an obligor who is delinquent in paying support.

(b) The Title IV-D agency shall adopt rules providing for the amounts of rewards offered under this section and the circumstances under which an individual providing information described in Subsection (a) is entitled to receive a reward.

(c) A reward paid under this section shall be paid from the child support retained collections account.

Comment

If the IV–D agency exercises the reward option, it must balance the size of the rewards it may be able to offer against other operating costs; both rewards and ongoing agency expenses come from the same account. *(A.G.K. & H.P.S.)*

CHAPTER 232. SUSPENSION OF LICENSE

Editors' Note: *This chapter contains guest commentary by: Alicia Gray Key, Deputy Attorney General and IV–D Director; and H. Patrick Sullivan, Deputy Director for State and Federal Operations, Child Support Division, Office of the Attorney General of Texas; identified respectively as (A.G.K. & H.P.S.).*

Introductory Comment

As a child support enforcement remedy, this chapter provides for the suspension of a business, occupational, professional, recreational, or driver's license of an obligor who: (1) is in arrears in an amount equal to, or greater than, the total support due for 90 days; (2) has been provided an opportunity to make payments towards the arrears under an agreed or court-ordered repayment plan; and, (3) has failed to comply with the plan. The purpose of the statute is not to suspend licenses, but to compel compliance with child support orders—perhaps after other means of compliance have been attempted and exhausted. Just the threat of license suspension, however, may be enough to get a recalcitrant obligor to make timely and full payments or, where there are arrearages, to agree to, and comply with, a repayment plan. The effect of the statute is similar to that of coercive civil contempt; the penalty of license suspension is contingent on failure to comply either with the agreed or court-ordered repayment of the support arrearages.

The Texas statute is designed to provide both an administrative and a judicial process. In non-IV–D cases, a petition for license suspension is filed with the court of continuing jurisdiction or the court in which a child support order has been registered. In IV–D cases, the IV–D agency may handle cases through hearings conducted by an administrative law judge or through the judicial process as provided in non-IV–D cases. Either way, the determination of whether or not to suspend a license is left with the tribunal, not with the licensing agency. Only after an order suspending a license has been rendered is the licensing authority required to act. This means that a new license may not be denied for failure to pay child support, but, once issued, a license may be suspended.

While the federal requirement with respect to the license suspension applies only to child support enforcement, the use of this enforcement mechanism has been expanded to include the enforcement of a court order pertaining to the possession of, or access to, a child.

The license suspension process specifically includes the denial of renewal of a license. *See* § 232.001(1)(B) and § 232.0135. *(A.G.K., & H.P.S.)*

Leading Case

In re M.E.G., 48 S.W.3d 204 (Tex. App.—Corpus Christi 2001, no pet.) (A.G. authorized to suspend obligor's licenses if he failed to pay the arrearage)

CLE/Other Legal Publication

See annotations, Chapter 157, Enforcement, *supra*.

---

§ 232.001. Definitions

In this chapter:

(1) "License" means a license, certificate, registration, permit, or other authorization that:

(A) is issued by a licensing authority;

(B) is subject before expiration to renewal, suspension, revocation, forfeiture, or termination by a licensing authority; and

(C) a person must obtain to:

(i) practice or engage in a particular business, occupation, or profession;

(ii) operate a motor vehicle on a public highway in this state; or

(iii) engage in any other regulated activity, including hunting, fishing, or other recreational activity for which a license or permit is required.

(2) "Licensing authority" means a department, commission, board, office, or other agency of the state or a political subdivision of the state that issues or renews a license or that otherwise has authority to suspend or refuse to renew a license.

(3) "Order suspending license" means an order issued by the Title IV–D agency or a court directing a licensing authority to suspend or refuse to renew a license.

(4) "Subpoena" means a judicial or administrative subpoena issued in a parentage determination or child support proceeding under this title.

§ 232.002. Licensing Authorities Subject to Chapter

Unless otherwise restricted or exempted, all licensing authorities are subject to this chapter.

Comment

In 2007, the legislature mercifully did away with the ever growing, ever changing list of state licensing authorities subject to the provisions of this chapter. Almost every session added new agencies to the list, or replaced the name of an existing state agency with its new name. The wisdom of simplifying the matter by making all licensing authorities subject to the chapter unless otherwise restricted or exempted finally became apparent; two pages of the code were happily reduced to a single sentence. *(A.G.K. & H.P.S.)*

---

§ 232.0021. Application of Chapter to Texas Lottery Commission

With respect to the Texas Lottery Commission, this chapter applies only to a lottery ticket sales agent license issued under Chapter 466, Government Code.

§ 232.0022. Suspension or Nonrenewal of Motor Vehicle Registration

(a) The Texas Department of Motor Vehicles is the appropriate licensing authority for suspension or nonrenewal of a motor vehicle registration under this chapter.

(b) The suspension or nonrenewal of a motor vehicle registration under this chapter does not:

(1) encumber the title to the motor vehicle or otherwise affect the transfer of the title to the vehicle; or

(2) affect the sale, purchase, or registration of the motor vehicle by a person who holds a general distinguishing number issued under Chapter 503, Transportation Code.

Comment

This section, added by the legislature in 2007, largely states the obvious but does provide welcomed assurances to car dealers that they may go about their business. Vehicle registration does not affect the nature or status of a vehicle title, and the suspension or nonrenewal of a vehicle registration under this chapter affects only the operation of a vehicle by the delinquent obligor in whose name the vehicle is registered. *(A.G.K. & H.P.S.)*

§ 232.003. Suspension of License

(a) A court or the Title IV-D agency may issue an order suspending a license as provided by this chapter if an individual who is an obligor:

(1) owes overdue child support in an amount equal to or greater than the total support due for three months under a support order;

(2) has been provided an opportunity to make payments toward the overdue child support under a court-ordered or agreed repayment schedule; and

(3) has failed to comply with the repayment schedule.

(b) A court or the Title IV-D agency may issue an order suspending a license as provided by this chapter if a parent or alleged parent has failed, after receiving appropriate notice, to comply with a subpoena.

(c) A court may issue an order suspending license as provided by this chapter for an individual for whom a court has rendered an enforcement order under Chapter 157 finding that the individual has failed to comply with the terms of a court order providing for the possession of or access to a child.

Comment

The order suspending a license with respect to a support arrearage may be rendered only if the obligor has had an opportunity to meet a repayment plan and has failed to do so. The plan itself need not have been ordered or agreed to prior to the filing of a petition for license suspension. With respect to suspending a license for failure to comply with a subpoena, the only requirement is that a subpoena was duly served.

While originally intended as an enforcement remedy in child support cases, Subsection (c) extends license suspension to the enforcement of a court order providing for the possession of, or access to, a child. Amending language in other sections of the chapter to extend the use of license suspension might incorrectly suggest that the IV–D agency may enforce rights of possession or access. This, however, is not an activity for which the agency receives a subsidy under federal law. So, for the purposes of this chapter, only the court will enforce visitation and custody rights through license suspension. *(A.G.K. & H.P.S.)*

§ 232.004. Petition for Suspension of License

(a) A child support agency or obligee may file a petition to suspend, as provided by this chapter, a license of an obligor who has an arrearage equal to or greater than the total support due for three months under a support order.

(b) In a Title IV–D case, the petition shall be filed with the Title IV–D agency, the court of continuing jurisdiction, or the tribunal in which a child support order has been registered under Chapter 159. The tribunal in which the petition is filed obtains jurisdiction over the matter.

(c) In a case other than a Title IV-D case, the petition shall be filed in the court of continuing jurisdiction or the court in which a child support order has been registered under Chapter 159.

(d) A proceeding in a case filed with the Title IV-D agency under this chapter is governed by the contested case provisions of Chapter 2001, Government Code, except that Section 2001.054 does not apply to the proceeding. The director of the Title IV-D agency or the director's designee may render a final decision in a contested case proceeding under this chapter.

Comment

License suspension is a remedy available to private as well as public child support enforcement agencies. The only requirement for filing a petition with respect to child support is that there be an arrearage equal to an amount due for 90 or more days; there is no need for a repayment plan to be in existence at the time of filing. Although this section does not specifically identity failure to comply with a subpoena as a basis for filing a petition, that may be inferred from other sections of the statute. *(A.G.K. & H.P.S.)*

§ 232.005. Contents of Petition

(a) A petition under this chapter must state that license suspension is required under Section 232.003 and allege:

(1) the name and, if known, social security number of the individual;

(2) the name of the licensing authority that issued a license the individual is believed to hold; and

(3) the amount of arrearages owed under the child support order or the facts associated with the individual's failure to comply with:

(A) a subpoena; or

(B) the terms of a court order providing for the possession of or access to a child.

(b) A petition under this chapter may include as an attachment a copy of:

(1) the record of child support payments maintained by the Title IV-D registry or local registry;

(2) the subpoena with which the individual has failed to comply, together with proof of service of the subpoena; or

(3) with respect to a petition for suspension under Section 232.003(c):

(A) the enforcement order rendered under Chapter 157 describing the manner in which the individual was found to have not complied with the terms of a court order providing for the possession of or access to a child; and

(B) the court order containing the provisions that the individual was found to have violated.

Comment

Although the contents of the petition may identify a single type of license issued by a licensing authority, the effect of a final order is the suspension of any type of license issued by the licensing authority that may be available to the delinquent obligor. *See* § 232.001(i), *supra*. In 2009, the legislature made the matter clearer by amending Subsection (a)(2) to require that the petition only identify the licensing authority believed to have issued a license to the obligor. *(A.G.K. & H.P.S.)*

§ 232.006. Notice

(a) On the filing of a petition under Section 232.004, the clerk of the court or the Title IV-D agency shall deliver to the individual:

(1) notice of the individual's right to a hearing before the court or agency;

(2) notice of the deadline for requesting a hearing; and

(3) a hearing request form if the proceeding is in a Title IV-D case.

(b) Notice under this section may be served:

(1) if the party has been ordered under Chapter 105 to provide the court and registry with the party's current mailing address, by mailing a copy of the notice to the respondent, together with a copy of the petition, by first class mail to the last mailing address of the respondent on file with the court and the state case registry; or

(2) as in civil cases generally.

(c) The notice must contain the following prominently displayed statement in boldfaced type, capital letters, or underlined:

"AN ACTION TO SUSPEND ONE OR MORE LICENSES ISSUED TO YOU HAS BEEN FILED AS PROVIDED BY CHAPTER 232, TEXAS FAMILY CODE. YOU MAY EMPLOY AN ATTORNEY TO REPRESENT YOU IN THIS ACTION. IF YOU OR YOUR ATTORNEY DO NOT REQUEST A HEARING BEFORE THE 21ST DAY AFTER THE DATE OF SERVICE OF THIS NOTICE, AN ORDER SUSPENDING YOUR LICENSE MAY BE RENDERED."

Comment

Subsection (b)(1) reflects the due process presumption under § 105.006(f), for the delivery of notice and service of process and comports with provisions for the delivery of a notice of a motion for enforcement under § 157.065. *(A.G.K. & H.P.S.)*

§ 232.007. Hearing on Petition to Suspend License

(a) A request for a hearing and motion to stay suspension must be filed with the court or Title IV-D agency by the individual not later than the 20th day after the date of service of the notice under Section 232.006.

(b) If a request for a hearing is filed, the court or Title IV-D agency shall:

(1) promptly schedule a hearing;

(2) notify each party of the date, time, and location of the hearing; and

(3) stay suspension pending the hearing.

(c) In a case involving support arrearages, a record of child support payments made by the Title IV-D agency or a local registry is evidence of whether the payments were made. A copy of the record appearing regular on its face shall be admitted as evidence at a hearing under this chapter, including a hearing on a motion to revoke a stay. Either party may offer controverting evidence.

(d) In a case in which an individual has failed to comply with a subpoena, proof of service is evidence of delivery of the subpoena.

§ 232.008. Order Suspending License for Failure to Pay Child Support

(a) On making the findings required by Section 232.003, the court or Title IV-D agency shall render an order suspending the license unless the individual:

(1) proves that all arrearages and the current month's support have been paid;

(2) shows good cause for failure to comply with the subpoena or the terms of the court order providing for the possession of or access to a child; or

(3) establishes an affirmative defense as provided by Section 157.008(c).

(b) The court or Title IV-D agency may stay an order suspending a license conditioned on the individual's compliance with:

(1) a reasonable repayment schedule that is incorporated in the order;

(2) the requirements of a reissued and delivered subpoena; or

(3) the requirements of any court order pertaining to the possession of or access to a child.

(c) An order suspending a license with a stay of the suspension may not be served on the licensing authority unless the stay is revoked as provided by this chapter.

(d) A final order suspending license rendered by a court or the Title IV-D agency shall be forwarded to the appropriate licensing authority by the clerk of the court or Title IV-D agency. The clerk shall collect from an obligor a fee of $5 for each order mailed.

(e) If the court or Title IV-D agency renders an order suspending license, the individual may also be ordered not to engage in the licensed activity.

(f) If the court or Title IV-D agency finds that the petition for suspension should be denied, the petition shall be dismissed without prejudice, and an order suspending license may not be rendered.

Comment

Although the caption states the subject is the order suspending a license, that is true only for the first clause of Subsection (a). In fact, the primary focus of the section is on the means whereby a suspension order may be stayed. Subsections (a) and (b) provide five different reasons for a stay, including full payment and the obligor's compliance with a repayment plan in the case of a support arrearage, or compliance with a reissued subpoena in the case of noncompliance with a subpoena. Subsequent failure to comply with either a repayment plan or a new subpoena may result in a revocation of the stay under § 232.012.

Subsection (a) provides that an obligor is not subject to license suspension if the obligor establishes as an affirmative defense that he was incapable of complying with the order because he lacked the ability to pay the court-ordered support, he has no property that could be sold or otherwise used to pay the support, and that he unsuccessfully attempted to borrow to pay the support and knows of no other means to legally borrow or otherwise obtain the amount needed to pay. *(A.G.K. & H.P.S.)*

---

§ 232.009. Default Order

The court or Title IV-D agency shall consider the allegations of the petition for suspension to be admitted and shall render an order suspending the license of an obligor without the requirement of a hearing if the court or Title IV-D agency determines that the individual failed to respond to a notice issued under Section 232.006 by:

(1) requesting a hearing; or

(2) appearing at a scheduled hearing.

Comment

License suspension is virtually automatic if an individual fails to respond to notice of a suspension action by timely requesting a hearing or appearing at a requested hearing. *(A.G.K. & H.P.S.)*

---

§ 232.010. Review of Final Administrative Order

An order issued by a Title IV-D agency under this chapter is a final agency decision and is subject to review under the substantial evidence rule as provided by Chapter 2001, Government Code.

Comment

In reviewing an agency decision with respect to the suspension of a license the reviewing court must determine whether a reasonable basis exists in the record for that decision, not whether it was the correct decision. *(A.G.K. & H.P.S.)*

---

§ 232.011. Action by Licensing Authority

(a) On receipt of a final order suspending license, the licensing authority shall immediately determine if the authority has issued a license to the individual named on the order and, if a license has been issued:

(1) record the suspension of the license in the licensing authority's records;

(2) report the suspension as appropriate; and

(3) demand surrender of the suspended license if required by law for other cases in which a license is suspended.

(b) A licensing authority shall implement the terms of a final order suspending license without additional review or hearing. The authority may provide notice as appropriate to the license holder or to others concerned with the license.

(c) A licensing authority may not modify, remand, reverse, vacate, or stay an order suspending license issued under this chapter and may not review, vacate, or reconsider the terms of a final order suspending license.

(d) An individual who is the subject of a final order suspending license is not entitled to a refund for any fee or deposit paid to the licensing authority.

(e) An individual who continues to engage in the business, occupation, profession, or other licensed activity after the implementation of the order suspending license by the licensing authority is liable for the same civil and criminal penalties provided for engaging in the licensed activity without a license or while a license is suspended that apply to any other license holder of that licensing authority.

(f) A licensing authority is exempt from liability to a license holder for any act authorized under this chapter performed by the authority.

(g) Except as provided by this chapter, an order suspending license or dismissing a petition for the suspension of a license does not affect the power of a licensing authority to grant, deny, suspend, revoke, terminate, or renew a license.

(h) The denial or suspension of a driver's license under this chapter is governed by this chapter and not by the general licensing provisions of Chapter 521, Transportation Code.

(i) An order issued under this chapter to suspend a license applies to each license issued by the licensing authority subject to the order for which the obligor is eligible. The licensing authority may not issue or renew any other license for the obligor until the court or the Title IV-D agency renders an order vacating or staying an order suspending license.

Comment

Some licensing authorities issue more than one type of license. Subsection (i) clarifies that the ordered suspension of license applies to any type of license that the licensing authority may issue to the obligor. *(A.G.K. & H.P.S.)*

---

§ 232.012. Motion to Revoke Stay

(a) The obligee, support enforcement agency, court, or Title IV-D agency may file a motion to revoke the stay of an order suspending license if the individual who is subject of an order suspending license does not comply with:

(1) the terms of a reasonable repayment plan entered into by the individual;

(2) the requirements of a reissued subpoena; or

(3) the terms of any court order pertaining to the possession of or access to a child.

(b) Notice to the individual of a motion to revoke stay under this section may be given by personal service or by mail to the address provided by the individual, if any, in the order suspending license. The notice must include a notice of hearing. The notice must be provided to the individual not less than 10 days before the date of the hearing.

(c) A motion to revoke stay must allege the manner in which the individual failed to comply with the repayment plan, the reissued subpoena, or the court order pertaining to possession of or access to a child.

(d) If the court or Title IV-D agency finds that the individual is not in compliance with the terms of the repayment plan, reissued subpoena, or court order pertaining to possession of or access to a child, the court or agency shall revoke the stay of the order suspending license and render a final order suspending license.

Comment

The second chance given an individual through the opportunity, provided under § 232.008, to comply with a repayment plan for support arrearages or a reissued subpoena is voided if the individual fails to comply with the plan or reissued subpoena. *(A.G.K. & H.P.S.)*

---

§ 232.013. Vacating or Staying Order Suspending License

(a) The court or Title IV–D agency may render an order vacating or staying an order suspending an individual's license if:

(1) the individual has:

(A) paid all delinquent child support or has established a satisfactory payment record;

(B) complied with the requirements of a reissued subpoena; or

(C) complied with the terms of any court order providing for the possession of or access to a child; or

(2) the court or Title IV–D agency determines that good cause exists for vacating or staying the order.

(b) The clerk of the court or Title IV-D agency shall promptly deliver an order vacating or staying an order suspending license to the appropriate licensing authority. The clerk shall collect from an obligor a fee of $5 for each order mailed.

(c) On receipt of an order vacating or staying an order suspending license, the licensing authority shall promptly issue the affected license to the individual if the individual is otherwise qualified for the license.

(d) An order rendered under this section does not affect the right of the child support agency or obligee to any other remedy provided by law, including the right to seek relief under this chapter. An order rendered under this section does not affect the power of a licensing authority to grant, deny, suspend, revoke, terminate, or renew a license as otherwise provided by law.

Comment

With respect to child support enforcement, the purpose of license suspension is to compel compliance with the support obligation by requiring the obligor to pay all delinquent support or to submit to a repayment plan before the suspension is lifted. There may, however, be circumstances in which the suspension order should be stayed or vacated (*e.g.,* the parties have reunited). Subsection (a)(2) allows the court or IV–D agency to make a "good cause" determination in any case. *(A.G.K. & H.P.S.)*

In 2011, the legislature expanded the provisions under this section to include the initial issuance of a license to an obligor who is delinquent in paying child support for six or more months. This addition, then, brings full circle the imposition of license sanctions under this chapter: issuance, renewal, and suspension. The extent to which the denial of issuance—or of renewal—of a license works fully as an enforcement mechanism depends on the extent to which effective data matches are achieved between the Title IV-D agency and the several dozens of licensing authorities in the state—no small undertaking—and, as noted above, the cooperation of licensing authorities in observing the process laid out in this section. *(A.G.K. & H.P.S.)*

---

§ 232.0135. Denial of License Issuance or Renewal

(a) A child support agency, as defined by Section 101.004, may provide notice to a licensing authority concerning an obligor who has failed to pay child support for six months or more that requests the authority to refuse to accept an application for **issuance of a license to the obligor or** renewal of **an existing** ~~the~~license of the obligor.

(b) A licensing authority that receives the information described by Subsection (a) shall refuse to accept an application for **issuance of a license to the obligor or** renewal of **an existing**

~~the~~license of the obligor until the authority is notified by the child support agency that the obligor has:

(1) paid all child support arrearages;

(2) established with the agency a satisfactory repayment schedule or is in compliance with a court order for payment of the arrearages;

(3) been granted an exemption from this subsection as part of a court-supervised plan to improve the obligor's earnings and child support payments; or

(4) successfully contested the denial of **issuance or** renewal of license under Subsection (d).

(c) On providing a licensing authority with the notice described by Subsection (a), the child support agency shall send a copy to the obligor by first class mail and inform the obligor of the steps the obligor must take to permit the authority to accept the obligor's application for license **issuance or** renewal.

(d) An obligor receiving notice under Subsection (c) may request a review by the child support agency to resolve any issue in dispute regarding the identity of the obligor or the existence or amount of child support arrearages. The agency shall promptly provide an opportunity for a review, either by telephone or in person, as appropriate to the circumstances. After the review, if appropriate, the agency may notify the licensing authority that it may accept the obligor's application for **issuance or** renewal of license. If the agency and the obligor fail to resolve any issue in dispute, the obligor, not later than the 30th day after the date of receiving notice of the agency's determination from the review, may file a motion with the court to direct the agency to withdraw the notice under Subsection (a) and request a hearing on the motion. The obligor's application for license **issuance or** renewal may not be accepted by the licensing authority until the court rules on the motion. If, after a review by the agency or a hearing by the court, the agency withdraws the notice under Subsection (a), the agency shall reimburse the obligor the amount of any fee charged the obligor under Section 232.014.

(e) If an obligor enters into a repayment agreement with the child support agency under this section, the agency may incorporate the agreement in an order to be filed with and confirmed by the court in the manner provided for agreed orders under Chapter 233.

(f) In this section, "licensing authority" does not include the State Securities Board.

Amended by Acts 2011, 82nd Leg., ch. 508 (H.B. 1674), §§ 15, 16, eff. Sept. 1, 2011.

Comment

This section lays out an administrative process that may be used by any "child support agency," which would include, in addition to the Title IV–D agency itself, any county officer (e.g., a county or district attorney) or county that executes a cooperative agreement with the IV–D agency to provide child support enforcement services. It also includes a domestic relations office. *See* § 101.004. The basic elements in the process for denial of renewal of license (which includes a motor vehicle registration) are similar to those for the suspension of a license, except that for denial of renewal the obligor must owe past due support for six or more months, rather than just three months. The intent in the use of the new enforcement tool is the same as in the use of license suspension: not to suspend or deny renewal of an obligor's license, but to compel the obligor's compliance with a support order. As in license suspension, the obligor has an opportunity to pay up past due support or to enter into a repayment agreement in order to avoid the penalty. The degree to which this new enforcement remedy is effective will depend greatly on the cooperation of licensing authorities in following the requirements of the process.

Two features of the section are especially noteworthy. First, if an obligor successfully contests an action to deny renewal of a license but the obligor has already paid the authority an administrative service fee (*see* § 232.014), the child support agency that brought the action must reimburse the obligor the amount of the fee. Second, the only licensing authority not subject to this section is the State Securities Board because, so it argued, the process authorized under the section could significantly impede the Board's ability to license out of state securities traders to do business in the state. Of course, the exemption under this section does not affect the fact that the Board, along with all other licensing authorities in the state, is subject to the license suspension provision of the chapter. *(A.G.K. & H.P.S.)*

---

§ 232.014. Fee by Licensing Authority

(a) A licensing authority may charge a fee to an individual who is the subject of an order suspending license or of an action of a child support agency under Section 232.0135 to deny **issuance or** renewal of license in an amount sufficient to recover the administrative costs incurred by the authority under this chapter.

(b) A fee collected by the Texas Department of Motor Vehicles or the Department of Public Safety shall be deposited to the credit of the state highway fund.

Amended by Acts 2011, 82nd Leg., ch. 508 (H.B. 1674), § 17, eff. Sept. 1, 2011.

§ 232.015. Cooperation Between Licensing Authorities and Title IV–D Agency

(a) The Title IV-D agency may request from each licensing authority the name, address, social security number, license renewal date, and other identifying information for each individual who holds, applies for, or renews a license issued by the authority.

(b) A licensing authority shall provide the requested information in the form and manner identified by the Title IV-D agency.

(c) The Title IV-D agency may enter into a cooperative agreement with a licensing authority to administer this chapter in a cost-effective manner.

(d) The Title IV-D agency may adopt a reasonable implementation schedule for the requirements of this section.

(e) The Title IV-D agency, the comptroller, and the Texas Alcoholic Beverage Commission shall by rule specify additional prerequisites for the suspension of licenses relating to state taxes collected under Title 2, Tax Code. The joint rules must be adopted not later than March 1, 1996.

§ 232.016. Rules, Forms, and Procedures

The Title IV-D agency by rule shall prescribe forms and procedures for the implementation of this chapter.

CHAPTER 233. CHILD SUPPORT REVIEW PROCESS TO ESTABLISH OR ENFORCE SUPPORT OBLIGATIONS

Editors' Note: *This chapter contains guest commentary by: Alicia Gray Key, Deputy Attorney General and IV–D Director; and H. Patrick Sullivan, Deputy Director for State and Federal Operations, Child Support Division, Office of the Attorney General of Texas; identified respectively as* (A.G.K. & H.P.S.).

Introductory Comment

This chapter provides an administrative method to deal with child support matters. The process has been amended many times since it was first authorized. Originally, the legislature created a quasi administrative "expedited agreed order" process for use by child support agencies, including county domestic relations offices and the Office of the Attorney General as the IV–D agency. The purpose was to encourage agreed orders that could be ratified by the court without the necessity of a hearing.

The elaborate "child support review process" requires negotiation conferences in the agency's office to attempt informal resolution of the issues. That process gave the child support agency the authority to issue child support review orders with or without the agreement of the parties.

Administrative procedures, including administrative parentage testing orders and administrative subpoenas comply with the requirements of PRWORA. The use of the child support review process is specifically restricted to the IV–D agency.

Successive legislative revisions of the process have removed some of the earlier mandatory forms and procedures, resulting in greater flexibility in agreed cases. Detailed financial affidavits and mandatory negotiation conferences, for example, are no longer required. The process continues to allow for judicial review of an agency decision, requires the agency to petition the court for confirmation of the review order, and permits the parties to request a court hearing on any issue raised in the review order. *(A.G.K. & H.P.S.)*

CLE/Other Legal Publications

Navigating the Attorney General maze. Cynthia J. Barela & April Palmer, 2008 UT FAM. L. FRONT LINES

Navigating the Attorney General's child support enforcement program. Alicia G. Key, 2007 UT DEFINITIVE SAPCR

§ 233.001. Purpose

(a) The purpose of the procedures specified in the child support review process authorized by this chapter is to enable the Title IV-D agency to take expedited administrative actions to establish, modify, and enforce child support and medical support obligations, to determine parentage, or to take any other action authorized or required under Part D, Title IV, of the federal Social Security Act (42 U.S.C. Section 651 et seq.), and Chapter 231.

(b) A child support review order issued under this chapter and confirmed by a court constitutes an order of the court and is enforceable by any means available for the enforcement of child support obligations under this code, including withholding income, filing a child support lien, and suspending a license under Chapter 232.

Comment

Once the review order is confirmed by a court, it is the operative order of the court and is enforceable by any means, including contempt. *(A.G.K. & H.P.S.)*

§ 233.002. Agreements Encouraged

To the extent permitted by this chapter, the Title IV-D agency shall encourage agreement of the parties.

§ 233.003. Bilingual Forms Required

A notice or other form used to implement administrative procedures under this chapter shall be printed in both Spanish and English.

§ 233.004. Interpreter Required

If a party participating in an administrative proceeding under this chapter does not speak English or is hearing impaired, the Title IV-D agency shall provide for interpreter services at no charge to the party.

§ 233.005. Initiating Administrative Actions

An administrative action under this chapter may be initiated by issuing a notice of child support review under Section 233.006 or a notice of proposed child support review order under Section 233.009 or 233.0095 to each party entitled to notice.

§ 233.006. Contents of Notice of Child Support Review

(a) The notice of child support review issued by the Title IV-D agency must:

(1) describe the procedure for a child support review, including the procedures for requesting a negotiation conference;

(2) inform the recipient that the recipient may be represented by legal counsel during the review process or at a court hearing; and

(3) inform the recipient that the recipient may refuse to participate or cease participation in the child support review process, but that the refusal by the recipient to participate will not prevent the completion of the process or the filing of a child support review order.

(b) In addition to the information required by Subsection (a), the notice of child support review may inform the recipient that:

(1) an affidavit of financial resources included with the notice must be executed by the recipient and returned to the Title IV-D agency not later than the 15th day after the date the notice is received or delivered; and

(2) if the requested affidavit of financial resources is not returned as required, the agency may:

(A) proceed with the review using the information that is available to the agency; and

(B) file a legal action without further notice to the recipient, except as otherwise required by law.

Comment

The process begins when the agency notifies the parties, either by personal service or first class mail, that a review will take place. The agency has the option, rather than the mandate, to include a financial affidavit to be completed by the parties with the notice. *(A.G.K. & H.P.S.)*

§ 233.007. Service of Notice

(a) A notice required in an administrative action under this chapter may be delivered by personal service or first class mail on each party entitled to citation or notice as provided by Chapter 102.

(b) This section does not apply to notice required on filing of a child support review order or to later judicial actions.

Comment

A 2009 amendment to 102.009 specifically exempts notices served in actions under this chapter from the requirements of service of citation under the Texas Rules of Civil Procedure. The procedures under the review process do provide for personal notice to the parties, of course, but not in the manner and following the same timeframes prescribed for service of citation in civil cases generally. *(H.P.S.)*

§ 233.008. Administrative Subpoena in Child Support Review

In a child support review under this chapter, the Title IV-D agency may issue an administrative subpoena authorized under Chapter 231 to any individual or organization believed to have financial or other information needed to establish, modify, or enforce a support order.

§ 233.009. Notice of Proposed Child Support Review Order; Negotiation Conference

(a) After an investigation and assessment of financial resources, the Title IV-D agency may serve on the parties a notice of proposed child support review order in enforcing or modifying an existing order.

(b) The notice of proposed child support review order shall state:

(1) the amount of periodic payment of child support due, the amount of any overdue support that is owed as an arrearage as of the date of the notice, and the amounts that are to be paid by the obligor for current support due and in payment on the arrearage owed;

(2) that the person identified in the notice as the party responsible for payment of the support amounts may contest the notice order on the grounds that:

(A) the respondent is not the responsible party;

(B) the dependent child is no longer entitled to child support; or

(C) the amount of monthly support or arrearage is incorrectly stated; and

(3) that, if the person identified in the notice as the party responsible for payment of the support amounts does not contest the notice in writing or request a negotiation conference to discuss the notice not later than the 15th day after the date the notice was delivered, the Title IV-D agency may file a child support review order for child support and for medical support for the child as provided by Chapter 154 according to the information available to the agency.

(c) The Title IV-D agency may schedule a negotiation conference without a request from a party.

(d) The Title IV-D agency shall schedule a negotiation conference on the timely request of a party.

(e) The agency may conduct a negotiation conference, or any part of a negotiation conference, by telephone conference call, by video conference, as well as in person and may adjourn the conference for a reasonable time to permit mediation of issues that cannot be resolved by the parties and the agency.

(f) Notwithstanding any other provision of this chapter, if the parties have agreed to the terms of a proposed child support review order and each party has signed the order, including a waiver of the right to service of process as provided by Section 233.018, the Title IV-D agency may immediately present the order and waiver to the court for confirmation without conducting a negotiation conference or requiring the production of financial information.

Comment

If a child support obligation already exists, the agency may have sufficient information in its files to calculate a judgment for arrears or a modification of the current support amount. In such a case, the proposed order is mailed to begin the review process. Although procedures exist for scheduling and conducting formal negotiation conferences, the conference may be omitted in agreed cases. *(A.G.K. & H.P.S.)*

§ 233.0095. Notice of Proposed Child Support Review Order in Cases of Acknowledged Paternity

(a) If an individual has signed the acknowledgment of paternity as the father of the child or executed a statement of paternity, the Title IV–D agency may serve on the parties a notice of proposed child support review order.

(b) The notice of proposed child support review order shall state:

(1) the amount of periodic payment of child support due;

(2) that the person identified in the notice as the party responsible for payment of the support amounts may only contest the amount of monthly support; and

(3) that, if the person identified in the notice as the party responsible for payment of the support amounts does not contest the notice in writing or request a negotiation conference to discuss the notice not later than the 15th day after the date the notice was delivered, the Title IV–D agency may file the child support order for child support and for medical support for the child as provided by Chapter 154 according to the information available to the agency.

(c) The Title IV–D agency may schedule a negotiation conference without a request from a party.

(d) The Title IV–D agency shall schedule a negotiation conference on the timely request of a party.

(e) The Title IV–D agency may conduct a negotiation conference, or any part of a negotiation conference, by telephone conference call, by video conference, or in person and may adjourn the conference for a reasonable time to permit mediation of issues that cannot be resolved by the parties and the agency.

(f) Notwithstanding any other provision of this chapter, if paternity has been acknowledged, the parties have agreed to the terms of a proposed child support review order, and each party has signed the order, including a waiver of the right to service of process as provided by Section 233.018, the Title IV-D agency may immediately present the order and waiver to the court for confirmation without conducting a negotiation conference or requiring the production of financial information.

Comment

This section expressly permits the use of the child support review process if paternity has been acknowledged. *See* Chapter 160 [*Uniform Parentage Act*]. In such a case, the process may be employed as an expeditious way to obtain a court order for support, possession or access, and conservatorship. In agreed cases, the formalities of the negotiation conference and the production of financial records may be omitted. *(A.G.K. & H.P.S.)*

---

§ 233.010. Notice of Negotiation Conference; Failure to Attend Conference

(a) The Title IV-D agency shall notify all parties entitled to notice of the negotiation conference of the date, time, and place of the conference not later than the 10th day before the date of the conference.

(b) If a party fails to attend the scheduled conference, the agency may proceed with the review and file a child support review order according to the information available to the agency.

§ 233.011. Rescheduling Negotiation Conference; Notice Required

(a) The Title IV-D agency may reschedule or adjourn a negotiation conference on the request of any party.

(b) The Title IV-D agency shall give all parties notice of a rescheduled conference not later than the third day before the date of the rescheduled conference.

§ 233.012. Information Required to be Provided at Negotiation Conference

At the beginning of the negotiation conference, the child support review officer shall review with the parties participating in the conference information provided in the notice of child support review and inform the parties that:

(1) the purpose of the negotiation conference is to provide an opportunity to reach an agreement on a child support order;

(2) if the parties reach an agreement, the review officer will prepare an agreed review order to be effective immediately on being confirmed by the court, as provided by Section 233.024;

(3) a party does not have to sign a review order prepared by the child support review officer but that the Title IV–D agency may file a review order without the agreement of the parties;

(4) the parties may sign a waiver of the right to service of process;

(5) a party may **file a** request **for** a court hearing on a nonagreed order **not later than** ~~at any time before~~ the 20th day after the date a **copy of the** petition for confirmation of the order is **delivered to the party**;~~filed~~ and

(6) a party may file a motion for a new trial **not later than** ~~at any time before~~the 30th day after an order is confirmed by the court.

Amended by Acts 2011, 82nd Leg., ch. 508 (H.B. 1674), § 18, eff. Sept. 1, 2011.

Comment

If the parties reach an agreement, they may also sign a waiver of the right to service of the subsequent petition to confirm the order. The order is then presented to the court, and becomes effective immediately upon being confirmed. Any party who does not agree or who does not attend the conference is entitled to personal service of the petition to confirm and a copy of the order, and may request a court hearing within 20 days. *(A.G.K. & H.P.S.)*

§ 233.013. Determining Support Amount; Modification

(a) The Title IV-D agency may use any information obtained by the agency from the parties or any other source and shall apply the child support guidelines provided by this code to determine the appropriate amount of child support.

(b) If it has been three years since a child support order was rendered or last modified and the amount of the child support award under the order differs by either 20 percent or $100 from the amount that would be awarded under the child support guidelines, the Title IV-D agency shall file an appropriate child support review order, including an order that has the effect of modifying an existing court or administrative order for child support without the necessity of filing a motion to modify.

(c) Notwithstanding Subsection (b), the Title IV–D agency may, at any time and without a showing of material and substantial change in the circumstances of the parties, file a child support review order that has the effect of modifying an existing order for child support to provide medical support for a child if the existing order does not provide health care coverage for the child as required under Section 154.182.

Amended by Acts 2011, 82nd Leg., ch. 508 (H.B. 1674), § 19, eff. Sept. 1, 2011.

Comment

Subsection (c), added in 2011, authorizes a significant exception to the grounds for modification of child support specified under both § 156.401 and Subsection (b) of this section. (*See supra* § 156.401(a-2) for a conforming amendment made in 2011.) The need for this exception arises in public assistance cases referred to the Title IV-D agency in which the court has failed to provide for medical support in child support orders, as required under § 154.182(b-2), when the child is enrolled in a government medical assistance or health plan. In such cases the Title IV-D agency is both unable to collect cash medical support for lack of a medical support provision and unable to modify the support order to include this provision because there has been no change in the circumstances of the parties or the child and it has not been three years since the rendition of the order. *(A.G.K. & H.P.S.)*

§ 233.014. Record of Proceedings

(a) For the purposes of this chapter, documentary evidence relied on by the child support review officer, including an affidavit of a party, together with the child support review order is a sufficient record of the proceedings.

(b) The Title IV-D agency is not required to make any other record or transcript of the negotiation conference.

§ 233.015. Issuance of Child Support Review Order or Finding That No Order Should be Issued; Effect

(a) If a negotiation conference does not result in agreement by all parties to the child support review order, the Title IV-D agency shall render a final decision in the form of a child support review order or a determination that the agency should not issue a child support review order not later than the fifth day after the date of the negotiation conference.

(b) If the Title IV-D agency determines that the agency should not issue a child support order, the agency shall immediately provide each party with notice of the determination by personal delivery or by first class mail.

(c) A determination that a child support order should not be issued must include a statement of the reasons that an order is not being issued and a statement that the agency's determination does not affect the right of the Title IV-D agency or a party to request any other remedy provided by law.

Comment

The child support review process is designed to handle routine cases. If a review officer becomes aware of domestic violence or some other complicating factor, the officer may decide that no order should be issued. The agency would still have the right to petition the court for any appropriate remedy in the case. *(A.G.K. & H.P.S.)*

§ 233.016. Vacating Child Support Review Order

(a) The Title IV-D agency may vacate a child support review order at any time before the order is filed with the court.

(b) A new negotiation conference, with notice to all parties, may be scheduled or the Title IV-D agency may make a determination that a child support review order should not be issued and give notice of that determination as provided by this chapter.

§ 233.017. Contents of Child Support Review Order

(a) An order issued under this chapter must be reviewed and signed by an attorney of the Title IV-D agency and must contain all provisions that are appropriate for an order under this title, including current child support, medical support, a determination of any arrearages or retroactive support, and, if not otherwise ordered, income withholding.

(b) A child support review order providing for the enforcement of an order may not contain a provision that imposes incarceration or a fine or contains a finding of contempt.

~~(c) A child support review order that establishes or modifies an amount of previously ordered support must include the findings required by Section 154.130.~~

(d) A child support review order that is not agreed to by all the parties may specify and reserve for the court at the confirmation hearing unresolved issues relating to conservatorship or possession of a child.

Amended by Acts 2011, 82nd Leg., ch. 508 (H.B. 1674), § 25, eff. Sept. 1, 2011.

Comment

Although the order, once confirmed, thereafter is enforceable by contempt, the child support review order itself may not include a finding of contempt or a provision for a fine or incarceration. *(A.G.K. & H.P.S.)*

§ 233.018. Additional Contents of Agreed Child Support Review Order

(a) If a negotiation conference results in an agreement of the parties, each party must sign the child support review order and the order must contain as to each party:

(1) a waiver by the party of the right to service of process and a court hearing;

(2) the mailing address of the party; and

(3) the following statement printed on the order in boldfaced type, in capital letters, or underlined:

"I ACKNOWLEDGE THAT I HAVE READ AND UNDERSTAND THIS CHILD SUPPORT REVIEW ORDER. I UNDERSTAND THAT IF I SIGN THIS ORDER, IT WILL BE CONFIRMED BY THE COURT WITHOUT FURTHER NOTICE TO ME. I KNOW THAT I HAVE A RIGHT TO REQUEST THAT A COURT RECONSIDER THE ORDER BY FILING A MOTION FOR A NEW TRIAL AT ANY TIME BEFORE THE 30TH DAY AFTER THE DATE OF THE CONFIRMATION OF THE ORDER BY THE COURT. I KNOW THAT IF I DO NOT OBEY THE TERMS OF THIS ORDER I MAY BE HELD IN CONTEMPT OF COURT."

(b) If a negotiation conference results in an agreement on some but not all issues in the case, the parties may sign a waiver of service along with an agreement to appear in court at a specified date and time for a determination by the court of all unresolved issues. Notice of the hearing is not required.

§ 233.019. Filing of Agreed Review Order

(a) The Title IV-D agency shall file an agreed child support review order and a waiver of service signed by the parties with the clerk of the court having continuing jurisdiction of the child who is the subject of the order.

(b) If there is not a court of continuing jurisdiction, the Title IV-D agency shall file the agreed review order with the clerk of a court having jurisdiction under this title.

(c) If applicable, an acknowledgment of paternity or a written report of a parentage testing expert and any documentary evidence relied upon by the agency shall be filed with the agreed review order as an exhibit to the order.

(d) A child support order issued by a tribunal of another state and filed with an agreed review order as an exhibit to the agreed review order shall be treated as a confirmed order without the necessity of registration under Subchapter G, Chapter 159.

Comment

Subsection (d) enables the IV–D agency to use the review process more efficiently in interstate cases by eliminating the necessity of first registering a foreign order for enforcement, as normally required under UIFSA (Chapter 159), if the parties have agreed to a review order. The foreign order can simply be attached as an exhibit to the agreed review order and together be filed with the court for confirmation. *See* § 233.024. *(A.G.K. & H.P.S.)*

---

§ 233.020. Contents of Petition for Confirmation of Nonagreed Order

(a) A petition for confirmation of a child support review order not agreed to by the parties:

(1) must include the final review order as an attachment to the petition; and

(2) may include a waiver of service executed under Section 233.018(b) and an agreement to appear in court for a hearing.

(b) Documentary evidence relied on by the Title IV–D agency, including, if applicable, an acknowledgment of paternity or a written report of a parentage testing expert, shall be filed with the clerk as exhibits to the petition, but are not required to be served on the parties. The petition must identify the exhibits that are filed with the clerk.

§ 233.021. Duties of Clerk of Court

(a) On the filing of an agreed child support review order or of a petition for confirmation of a nonagreed order issued by the Title IV-D agency, the clerk of court shall endorse on the order or petition the date and time the order or petition is filed.

(b) In an original action, the clerk shall endorse the appropriate court and cause number on the agreed review order or on the petition for confirmation of a nonagreed order.

(c) The clerk shall deliver by personal service a copy of the petition for confirmation of a nonagreed review order and a copy of the order, to each party entitled to service who has not waived service.

(d) A clerk of a district court is entitled to collect in a child support review case the fees authorized in a Title IV-D case by Chapter 231.

§ 233.022. Form to Request a Court Hearing on Nonagreed Order

(a) A court shall consider any responsive pleading that is intended as an objection to confirmation of a child support review order not agreed to by the parties, including a general denial, as a request for a court hearing.

(b) The Title IV-D agency shall:

(1) make available to each clerk of court copies of the form to request a court hearing on a nonagreed review order; and

(2) provide the form to request a court hearing to a party to the child support review proceeding on request of the party.

(c) The clerk shall furnish the form to a party to the child support review proceeding on the request of the party.

§ 233.023. Time to Request a Court Hearing

A party may file a request for a court hearing not later than the 20th day after the date the petition for confirmation of a nonagreed child support review order is delivered to the party.

§ 233.024. Confirmation of Agreed Order

(a) On the filing of an agreed child support review order signed by all parties, together with waiver of service, the court shall sign the order not later than the third day after the filing of the order. The court may sign the order before filing the order, but the signed order shall immediately be filed.

(b) On confirmation by the court, the Title IV-D agency shall immediately deliver to each party a copy of the signed agreed review order.

Comment

The ratification by the court of an agreed child support review order is intended to be a simple process. If the parties have all signed the order and waived service, the court is to confirm the order, without the necessity of hearing or any other action by the court, "not later than the third day after the filing of the order." *(A.G.K. & H.P.S.)*

§ 233.025. Effect of Request for Hearing on Nonagreed Order; Pleading

(a) A request for hearing or an order setting a hearing on confirmation of a nonagreed child support review order stays confirmation of the order pending the hearing.

(b) At a hearing on confirmation, any issues in dispute shall be heard in a trial de novo.

(c) The petition for confirmation and the child support review order constitute a sufficient pleading by the Title IV-D agency for relief on any issue addressed in the petition and order.

(d) The request for hearing may limit the scope of the de novo hearing by specifying the issues that are in dispute.

§ 233.026. Time for Court Hearing

(a) When a timely request for a court hearing has been filed as provided by Section 233.023, the court shall hold a hearing on the confirmation of a child support review order that has not been agreed to by the parties not later than the 30th day after the date the request was filed.

(b) A court may not hold a hearing on the confirmation of a nonagreed child support review order if a party does not timely request a hearing as provided by Section 233.023.

(c) If the court resets the time of the hearing, the reset hearing shall be held not later than the 30th day after the date set for the initial hearing.

Comment

A hearing on the confirmation of a nonagreed child support review order is contingent upon a timely request being made by a party. If no such request has been received by the court, the court may not on its own hold a hearing on the order but must sign the review order as an order of the court "not later than the 30th day after the date the petition for confirmation was delivered to the last party entitled to service" (§ 233.0271, *infra*). *(A.G.K. & H.P.S.)*

---

§ 233.027. Order After Hearing; Effect of Confirmation Order

(a) After the hearing on the confirmation of a nonagreed child support review order, the court shall:

(1) if the court finds that the order should be confirmed, immediately sign a confirmation order and enter the order as an order of the court;

(2) if the court finds that the relief granted in the child support review order is inappropriate, sign an appropriate order at the conclusion of the hearing or as soon after the conclusion of the hearing as is practical and enter the order as an order of the court; or

(3) if the court finds that all relief should be denied, enter an order that denies relief and includes specific findings explaining the reasons that relief is denied.

(b) On the signing of a confirmation order by the judge of the court, the child support review order becomes a final order of the court.

(c) If the party who requested the hearing fails to appear at the hearing, the court shall sign a confirmation order and enter the order as an order of the court.

Comment

If a party who has not agreed to the review order timely requests a court hearing, the court conducts a trial de novo on any issue in dispute. The court has wide discretion to confirm the proposed order, enter a different order, or deny all relief. The failure of the requesting party to appear at the hearing results in an automatic confirmation of the nonagreed order by the court. *(A.G.K. & H.P.S.)*

---

§ 233.0271. Confirmation of Nonagreed Order Without Hearing

(a) If a request for hearing has not been timely received, the court shall confirm and sign a nonagreed child support review order not later than the 30th day after the date the petition for confirmation was delivered to the last party entitled to service.

(b) The Title IV-D agency shall immediately deliver a copy of the confirmed nonagreed review order to each party, together with notice of right to file a motion for a new trial not later than the 30th day after the date the order was confirmed by the court.

§ 233.028. Special Child Support Review Procedures Relating to Establishment of Parentage

(a) If the parentage of a child has not been established, the notice of child support review delivered to the parties must include an allegation that the recipient is a biological parent of the child. The notice shall inform the parties that:

(1) not later than the 15th day after the date of delivery of the notice, the alleged parent of the child shall either sign a statement of paternity or an acknowledgment of paternity or deny in writing that the alleged parent is the biological parent of the child;

(2) either party may request that scientifically accepted parentage testing be conducted to assist in determining the identities of the child's parents;

(3) if the alleged parent timely denies parentage of the child, the Title IV-D agency shall order parentage testing; and

(4) if the alleged parent does not deny parentage of the child, the Title IV-D agency may conduct a negotiation conference.

(b) If all parties agree to the child's parentage, the agency may file an agreed child support review order as provided by this chapter.

(c) If a party denies parentage, the Title IV-D agency shall order parentage testing and give each party notice of the time and place of testing. If either party fails or refuses to participate in administrative parentage testing, the Title IV-D agency may file a child support review order resolving the question of parentage against that party. The court shall confirm the child support review order as a temporary or final order of the court only after an opportunity for parentage testing has been provided.

(d) If genetic testing identifies the alleged parent as the parent of the child and the results of a verified written report of a genetic testing expert meet the requirements of Chapter 160 for issuing a temporary order, the Title IV-D agency may conduct a negotiation conference to resolve any issues of support and file with the court a child support review order.

(e) If the results of parentage testing exclude an alleged parent from being the biological parent of the child, the Title IV-D agency shall issue and provide to each party a child support review order that declares that the excluded person is not a parent of the child.

(f) Any party may file a petition for confirmation of a child support review order issued under this section.

Comment

This section authorizes the IV–D agency to order parentage testing. The alleged father is first given the opportunity to sign an acknowledgment of paternity, or to request testing. Testing is scheduled and paid for by the agency, but in the event of a "positive" result, an order establishing parentage will likely include an order that the father reimburse the state for the cost of testing. The alleged father who fails to submit to testing is subject to the entry of a default order resolving the issue. In 2009, the legislature amended 160.103(a) to eliminate a potential conflict between procedures under Chapter 160 (Uniform Parentage Age) and the procedures authorized for the establishment of parentage under this chapter. *(A.G.K. & H.P.S.)*

§ 233.029. Administrative Procedure Law Not Applicable

The child support review process under this chapter is not governed by Chapter 2001, Government Code.

CHAPTER 234. STATE CASE REGISTRY, DISBURSEMENT UNIT, AND DIRECTORY OF NEW HIRES

SUBCHAPTER A. UNIFIED STATE CASE REGISTRY AND DISBURSEMENT UNIT

SUBCHAPTER B. STATE DIRECTORY OF NEW HIRES

Editors' Note: *This chapter contains guest commentary by: Alicia Gray Key, Deputy Attorney General and IV–D Director; and H. Patrick Sullivan, Deputy Director for State and Federal Operations, Child Support Division, Office of the Attorney General of Texas; identified respectively as* (A.G.K. & H.P.S.).

Introductory Comment

Among the major child support enforcement mandates of the federal "Personal Responsibility and Work Opportunity Reconciliation Act of 1996" (PRWORA) are requirements for the establishment and operation of a state case registry of support orders, a state disbursement unit for support collection and distribution, and a state directory of new hires. All three of these operations are integral to the automated system of the IV–D agency, the Office of the Texas Attorney General, Child Support Division.

The IV–D agency is specifically required under PRWORA to establish, as an integrated component of its automated system, a case registry containing records of all child support orders being enforced by the agency and all other orders rendered or modified in the state on or after October 1, 1998. The system must also be capable of electronic data exchanges with other state and federal data bases.

The state case registry required by PRWORA must maintain not only full records in all IV–D cases, but also house abstracts of support orders in non-IV–D cases, using standardized data elements prescribed by the federal Department of Health and Human Services. Information in the case registry must be shared with a national case registry within the Federal Parent Locator Service, as well as with other state agencies and the registries of other states. Information in the case registry must be shared with a national case registry within the Federal Parent Locator Service, as well as with other state agencies and the registries of other states.

Under PRWORA, there must be a centralized state unit responsible for collecting and disbursing support in all IV–D cases and in all other cases subject to income withholding. This State Disbursement Unit provides a central, single location to which employers in the state shall remit income withheld for child support. As a result of the implementation of the State Disbursement Unit, the work of local registries will be significantly reduced once the unit is fully operational. Although the federal law originally required full implementation by October, 1999, many states, including Texas, took much longer to convert payment processing in existing cases to the unit. To the extent possible, the disbursement unit must use automated procedures, electronic processes, and computer technology to receive and identify payments, disburse collections, and provide information to a parent, upon request, on the status of payments. In IV–D cases, the agency's automated system must be used to assist in the disbursement of support collections, transmitting income withholding notices and orders to employers or other income sources, monitoring payments for the identification of any delinquencies, and taking appropriate enforcement actions when payment delinquencies occur. Under § 234.007, when the State Disbursement Unit was implemented, local courts were notified to include in orders for income withholding that payments should be directed to the unit. A notice of place of payment will be filed by the IV–D agency to redirect payments from the local registry (district clerk or domestic relations office) to the State Disbursement Unit and this notice will be sent to the obligor, obligee, employer and court.

The state directory of new hires required under PRWORA contains information on all new hires reported by all public and private employers doing business in the state and may be operated either within or outside the Title IV–D agency's automated system, although the directory must interface with the state case registry within the IV–D automated system. Using the W–4 or equivalent form, employers are required to report to the directory certain information on each new employee within 20 days of hiring. This information may be transmitted by mail, electronically, or magnetically, and multi state employers may designate one state to which to report all new hire information. Federal employers must report directly to a national new hire directory within the federal Parent Locator Service. Within 7 days of receipt, information in the state directory must be automatically matched with records in the state case registry to identify obligors for whom income withholding orders or notices need to be issued and to issue those orders or notices. Information in the state directory is also transmitted to the national directory to be compared with data in the national case registry and is made available to the IV–D agency for its purposes, as well as to the state-operated Income and Eligibility and Verification System (IEVS) and the state employment security agency (SESA) for the purpose of verifying eligibility for public assistance benefits (including cash welfare, Medicaid, and food stamps) and unemployment compensation benefits.

Together, these three databases are at the core of what PRWORA envisions as a complex, fully interactive, intrastate and interstate automated information network through which rapid data matches will take place between the state IV–D agency and other state agencies, among the case registries and locator services of all states, and between state databases and federal sources in and through the expanded Federal Parent Locator Service. Successful performance of the mandates for child support enforcement that PRWORA places upon the states is predicated upon the expansion of both state and federal computer systems to create a continuous loop of information concerning not just IV–D cases, but all child support cases, within the state and nationwide. *(A.G.K. & H.P.S.)*

SUBCHAPTER A. UNIFIED STATE CASE REGISTRY AND DISBURSEMENT UNIT

§ 234.001. Establishment and Operation of State Case Registry and State Disbursement Unit

(a) The Title IV-D agency shall establish and operate a state case registry and state disbursement unit meeting the requirements of 42 U.S.C. Sections 654a(e) and 654b and this subchapter.

(b) The state case registry shall maintain records of child support orders in Title IV–D cases and in other cases in which a child support order has been established or modified in this state on or after October 1, 1998.

(c) The state disbursement unit shall:

(1) receive, maintain, and furnish records of child support payments in Title IV–D cases and other cases as authorized by law;

(2) forward child support payments as authorized by law;

(3) maintain records of child support payments made through the state disbursement unit; and

(4) make available to a local registry each day in a manner determined by the Title IV–D agency the following information:

(A) the cause number of the suit under which withholding is required;

(B) the payor's name and social security number;

(C) the payee's name and, if available, social security number;

(D) the date the disbursement unit received the payment;

(E) the amount of the payment; and

(F) the instrument identification information.

(d) A certified child support payment record produced by the state disbursement unit is admissible as evidence of the truth of the information contained in the record and does not require further authentication or verification.

Comment

This section authorizes the state IV–D agency to establish and operate the federally mandated state case registry and state disbursement unit without articulating procedural details which will be left to agency rules. Under this section, the disbursement unit and case registry are, to the extent possible, a unified enterprise, located within the IV–D agency's statewide system. *(A.G.K. & H.P.S.)*

§ 234.002. Integrated System for Child Support and Medical Support Enforcement

The statewide integrated system for child support and medical support enforcement under Chapter 231 shall be part of the state case registry and state disbursement unit authorized by this subchapter.

Comment

This section authorizes the incorporation of the "Integrated Child Support System" (ICSS) under § 231.0011 into the state case registry. *(A.G.K. & H.P.S.)*

§ 234.003. Expired

§ 234.004. Contracts and Cooperative Agreements

(a) The Title IV-D agency may enter into contracts and cooperative agreements as necessary to establish and operate the state case registry and state disbursement unit authorized under this subchapter.

(b) To the extent funds are available for this purpose, the Title IV-D agency may enter into contracts or cooperative agreements to process through the state disbursement unit child support collections in cases not otherwise eligible under 42 U.S.C. Section 654b.

§ 234.005. Expired

§ 234.006. Rulemaking

The Title IV–D agency may adopt rules in compliance with federal law for the operation of the state case registry and the state disbursement unit.

§ 234.007. Notice of Place of Payment

(a) The Title IV–D agency shall notify the courts that the state disbursement unit has been established. After receiving notice of the establishment of the state disbursement unit, a court that orders income to be withheld for child support shall order that all income withheld for child support be paid to the state disbursement unit.

(b) In order to redirect payments from a local registry to the state disbursement unit after the date of the establishment of the state disbursement unit, the Title IV–D agency shall issue a notice of place of payment informing the obligor, obligee, and employer that income withheld for child support is to be paid to the state disbursement unit.

(c) A copy of the notice under Subsection (b) shall be filed with the court of continuing jurisdiction and with the local child support registry.

(d) The notice under Subsection (b) must include:

(1) the name of the child for whom support is ordered and of the person to whom support is ordered by the court to be paid;

(2) the style and cause number of the case in which support is ordered; and

(3) instructions for the payment of ordered support to the state disbursement unit.

(e) On receipt of a copy of the notice under Subsection (b), the clerk of the court shall file the notice in the appropriate case file.

(f) The notice under Subsection (b) may be used by the Title IV–D agency to redirect child support payments from the state disbursement unit of this state to the state disbursement unit of another state.

Comment

Subsection (f) provides for the redirection of support payments to an obligee who has moved from Texas to another state. *See* § 159.319(b). The notice of place of payment required under this section may be used by the IV–D agency to ensure that support payments paid to the Texas state disbursement unit are promptly redirected to the disbursement unit of the state to which the obligee has relocated. *(A.G.K. & H.P.S.)*

---

§ 234.008. Deposit, Distribution, and Issuance of Payments

(a) Not later than the second business day after the date the state disbursement unit receives a child support payment, the state disbursement unit shall distribute the payment to the Title IV–D agency or the obligee.

(b) The state disbursement unit shall deposit daily all child support payments in a trust fund with the state comptroller. Subject to the agreement of the comptroller, the state disbursement unit may issue checks from the trust fund.

(c) to (e) Repealed by Acts 2007, 80th Leg., ch. 972, § 65(5).

Comment

The IV–D agency is authorized to charge a monthly service fee of $3.00 in each case, IV–D or non IV–D, in which support payments are processed through the disbursement unit. How this fee will be assessed is left to the agency's rulemaking authority.

The purpose of the fee is to help offset costs incurred by the disbursement unit in processing income withholding and other support payments in non IV–D cases that receive only registry services. The fee is retained by the disbursement unit from monthly collections that exceed the amount of the fee itself and is separate from, and in addition to, any fee that may be charged in non IV–D cases handled by a domestic relations office. *See* § 203.005. *(A.G.K. & H.P.S.)*

---

§ 234.009. Official Child Support Payment Record

(a) The record of child support payments maintained by a local registry is the official record of a payment received directly by the local registry.

(b) The record of child support payments maintained by the state disbursement unit is the official record of a payment received directly by the unit.

(c) After the date child support payments formerly received by a local registry are redirected to the state disbursement unit, a local registry may accept a record of payments furnished by the state disbursement unit and may add the payments to the record of payments maintained by the local registry so that a complete payment record is available for use by the court.

(d) If the local registry does not add payments received by the state disbursement unit to the record maintained by the registry as provided by Subsection (c), the official record of child support payments consists of the record maintained by the local registry for payments received directly by the registry and the record maintained by the state disbursement unit for payments received directly by the unit.

§ 234.0091. Administrative Review of Child Support Payment Record

(a) On request, the state disbursement unit shall provide to an obligor or obligee a copy of the record of child support payments maintained by the unit. The record must include the amounts and dates of all payments received from or on behalf of the obligor and disbursed to the obligee.

(b) An obligor or obligee may request that the Title IV–D agency investigate an alleged discrepancy between the child support payment record provided by the state disbursement unit under Subsection (a) and the payment records maintained by the obligor or obligee. The obligor or obligee making the request must provide to the Title IV–D agency documentation of the alleged discrepancy, including a canceled check or other evidence of a payment or disbursement at issue.

(c) The Title IV–D agency shall respond to a request under Subsection (b) not later than the 20th day after the date the agency receives the request. If, after an investigation, the agency determines that the child support payment record maintained by the state disbursement unit should be amended, the state disbursement unit shall immediately make the required amendment to the record and notify the obligor or obligee who made the request under Subsection (b) of that amendment.

Comment

On request of an obligor or obligee, the state disbursement unit is to provide "timely information on the current status of support payments" processed through the unit, 42 U.S.C. 654B(b)(4). This section goes beyond the federal requirement by enabling an obligor or obligee to challenge any discrepancy between the official payment record produced by the disbursement unit and the record of the obligor or obligee with respect to payment or receipt of support processed through the unit. Inasmuch as the IV–D agency is responsible for the operation of the disbursement unit, it must promptly investigate an alleged discrepancy upon receipt of supporting evidence from the obligor or obligee and, if warranted, immediately make appropriate changes in the payment record. *(A.G.K. & H.P.S.)*

---

§ 234.010. Direct Deposit and Electronic Benefits Transfer of Child Support Payments

(a) The state disbursement unit authorized under this chapter may make a direct deposit of a child support payment to an obligee by electronic funds transfer into an account with a financial institution maintained by the obligee. It is the responsibility of the obligee to notify the state disbursement unit of:

(1) the existence of an account;

(2) the appropriate routing information for direct deposit by electronic funds transfer into an account; and

(3) any modification to account information previously provided to the state disbursement unit, including information that an account has been closed.

(b) Except as provided by Subsection (d), the state disbursement unit shall deposit a child support payment by electronic funds transfer into a debit card account established for the obligee by the Title IV–D agency if the obligee:

(1) does not maintain an account with a financial institution;

(2) fails to notify the state disbursement unit of the existence of an account maintained with a financial institution; or

(3) closes an account maintained with a financial institution previously used to accept direct deposit of a child support payment without establishing a new account and notifying the state disbursement unit of the new account in accordance with Subsection (a).

(c) The Title IV–D agency shall:

(1) issue a debit card to each obligee for whom a debit card account is established under Subsection (b); and

(2) provide the obligee with instructions for activating and using the debit card.

(c–1) Chapter 604, Business & Commerce Code, does not apply to a debit card issued under Subsection (c).

(d) An obligee may decline in writing to receive child support payments by electronic funds transfer into an account with a financial institution or a debit card account and request that payments be provided by paper warrants if the obligee alleges that receiving payments by electronic funds transfer would impose a substantial hardship.

(e) A child support payment disbursed by the state disbursement unit by electronic funds transfer into an account with a financial institution maintained by the obligee or into a debit card account established for the obligee under Subsection (b) is solely the property of the obligee.

Comment

This section was totally revised in 2009. The use of electronic funds transfer for payment of support collections had become well established by 2009. This section broadly lays out the procedures for direct deposit of collection of a support order, either into an obligee's bank account (if one exists) or into a child support debit card account established for the obligee by the Title IV-D agency. The use of electronic funds transfer for support payments appears to be a safer way of disbursing collections than the issuance of a paper warrant, which could be lost or stolen. It also is clearly a way to eliminate the costs to the state of issuing paper warrants. This fact did not escape the attention of the Legislative Budget Board, which in a January, 2009 issued a set of recommendations on state government effectiveness and efficiency. Subsection (d) does provide an opportunity for an obligee to request the continuation of payment by paper warrants if the obligee alleges in writing that electronic funds transfer of support collections would impose "substantial hardship." Note that the obligee must opt-out, not opt-in, which leaves electronic transfer as the default mode of delivery of the child support collected.

Subsection (e) provides an important and greatly needed clarification; once properly disbursed by the unit, a support collection is the property of the obligee and no longer a dollar amount for which the state can be held accountable. This subsection tied into an amendment to §72.101, Property Code; an undisbursed collection held by the unit or a local registry pending identification or location of the proper owner may not be deemed abandoned property subject to escheat. The effect of these amendments is, on the one hand, the protection of a support collection as the personal property of the obligee up to the time of disbursement. On the other hand, it grants protection against liability of the government for any amount properly disbursed. *(A.G.K. & H.P.S.)*

§ 234.011. Repealed.

§ 234.012. Release of Information From State Case Registry

Unless prohibited by a court in accordance with Section 105.006(c), the state case registry shall, on request and to the extent permitted by federal law, provide the information required under Sections 105.006 and 105.008 in any case included in the registry under Section 234.001(b) to:

(1) any party to the proceeding;
(2) an amicus attorney;
(3) an attorney ad litem;
(4) a friend of the court;
(5) a guardian ad litem;
(6) a domestic relations office;
(7) a prosecuting attorney or juvenile court acting in a proceeding under Title 3; or
(8) a governmental entity or court acting in a proceeding under Chapter 262.

Comment

In 2007 the legislature repealed Chapter 235, which had provided procedures for releasing information on cases recorded in the state case registry to certain individuals. It also provided for the inclusion, on application, of cases in the registry that are not required by federal law to be included. For ten years the provisions making up the chapter had lain fallow (originally as part of Chapter 233, then renumbered as Chapter 235 in 1999). The legislature decided that the usefulness of the chapter had been found wanting. This section is an attempt to salvage that part of the chapter that may be of some use—the release of information to authorized individuals and entities—although that too may ultimately found to be of little or no value. *(A.G.K. & H.P.S.)*

SUBCHAPTER B. STATE DIRECTORY OF NEW HIRES

Introductory Comment

This section authorized the IV–D agency to develop and operate the new hires directory in cooperation with the Texas Workforce Commission, although other state agencies will necessarily be involved because of the electronic interfaces the directory must have with entities administering public welfare and workers' compensation programs. Federal law does not require the IV–D agency to house the directory, although the sort of linkage the directory must have with the case registry and the national directory of new hires within the Federal Parent Locator Services argued for the agency's custodianship of the directory. Because of the complexity of federal statutory requirements and the paucity of federal regulatory guidance, procedural details for the operation of the directory are left to the IV–D agency's rulemaking authority. *(A.G.K. & H.P.S.)*

§ 234.101. Definitions

In this subchapter:

(1) "Employee" means an individual who is an employee within the meaning of Chapter 24 of the Internal Revenue Code of 1986 (26 U.S.C. Section 3401(c)). The term does not include an employee of a state agency performing intelligence or counterintelligence functions if the head of the agency has determined that reporting employee information under this subchapter could endanger the safety of the employee or compromise an ongoing investigation or intelligence activity.

(2) "Employer" has the meaning given that term by Section 3401(d) of the Internal Revenue Code of 1986 (26 U.S.C. Section 3401(d)) and includes a governmental entity and a labor organization, as that term is identified in Section 2(5) of the National Labor Relations Act (29 U.S.C. Section 152(5)), including an entity, also known as a "hiring hall," used by the labor organization and an employer to carry out requirements of an agreement between the organization and an employer described in Section 8(f)(3) of that Act (29 U.S.C. Section 158(f)(3)).

§ 234.102. Operation of New Hire Directory

In cooperation with the Texas Workforce Commission, the Title IV-D agency shall develop and operate a state directory to which employers in the state shall report each newly hired or rehired employee in accordance with the requirements of 42 U.S.C. Section 653a.

§ 234.103. Contracts and Cooperative Agreements

The Title IV-D agency may enter into cooperative agreements and contracts as necessary to create and operate the directory authorized under this subchapter.

§ 234.104. Procedures

The Title IV-D agency by rule shall establish procedures for reporting employee information and for operating a state directory of new hires meeting the requirements of federal law.

§ 234.105. Civil Penalty

(a) In addition to any other remedy provided by law, an employer who knowingly violates a procedure adopted under Section 234.104 for reporting employee information may be liable for a civil penalty as permitted by Section 453A(d) of the federal Social Security Act (42 U.S.C. Section 653a).

(b) The amount of the civil penalty may not exceed:

(1) $25 for each occurrence in which an employer fails to report an employee; or

(2) $500 for each occurrence in which the conduct described by Subdivision (1) is the result of a conspiracy between the employer and an employee to not supply a required report or to submit a false or incomplete report.

(c) The attorney general may sue to collect the civil penalty. A penalty collected under this section shall be deposited in a special fund in the state treasury.

CHAPTER 235. SHARING INFORMATION IN STATE CASE REGISTRY [REPEALED]

CHAPTER 236. COMPETITIVE BIDDING FOR CHILD SUPPORT COLLECTION SERVICES

Editors' Note: *This chapter contains guest commentary by: Alicia Gray Key, Deputy Attorney General and IV–D Director; and H. Patrick Sullivan, Deputy Director for State and Federal Operations, Child Support Division, Office of the Attorney General of Texas; identified respectively as* (A.G.K. & H.P.S.).

Introductory Comment

States are increasingly looking to the private sector for cost-effective ways to deliver some of the services offered by the IV–D agencies, particularly the collection of child support. These provisions authorize the State Council on Competitive Government, under GOV'T CODE ch. 2162, to explore with the IV–D agency possibilities for contracting out appropriate agency services and for recovering from the parties in non-public assistance cases the costs of providing services. The demands of growing caseloads and increasing fiscal constraints are making both the use of private contractors and the recovery of administrative expenditures attractive options to state IV–D programs, but both have their drawbacks. Because of the complexity of federal regulations governing the IV–D program, state agencies have found that they must closely monitor the performance of private contractors to ensure that federal standards and time frames are met. Still, states are finding that certain child support enforcement services can be delivered more efficiently and with increased cost-effectiveness by private contractors than by the public agency because of the private sector's greater flexibility in acquiring and using resources and freedom from bureaucratic procedures. With respect to the recovery of costs, few states have elected either to charge administrative costs against obligees who usually rely on every dollar of collected support or to attempt to recover these costs from obligors who usually do very well just to pay current support fully and timely. Nonetheless, financial exigencies are compelling state IV–D agencies to re-examine their funding mechanisms and to consider equitable ways of charging fees for services in appropriate cases. *(A.G.K. & H.P.S.)*

§ 236.001. Definition

In this chapter, "council" means the State Council on Competitive Government.

§ 236.002. Powers and Duties of Council

(a) The council shall:

(1) establish an initiative called "Kids Can't Wait" to increase child support enforcement;

(2) identify child support enforcement functions performed by the Title IV-D agency that may be competitively bid;

(3) establish guidelines for referral of child support enforcement cases to a contractor;

(4) after consulting with the Title IV-D agency, make recommendations regarding competitive bidding of child support enforcement functions that are identified under Subdivision (2);

(5) consider the benefits of the state's participation in an electronic parent locator network or a similar national service designed to locate parents who owe child support;

(6) study the feasibility of cost recovery options in child support collection actions for children who do not receive public assistance; and

(7) engage in other activities necessary for the administration of this chapter.

(b) The Title IV-D agency shall coordinate with the council regarding competitive bidding of child support enforcement functions identified under this section.

(c) A member of the council may designate an employee of the state agency represented by the member to perform any of the member's powers or duties under this section.

(d) The Title IV-D agency shall cooperate with the council if requested by the council.

~~(e) The council and the Title IV-D agency shall report not later than October 1, 1998, to the presiding officer of each house of the legislature the results of the council's efforts under this section.~~

Amended by Acts 2011, 82nd Leg., ch. 990, (H.B. 1781), § 10(1), eff. June 17, 2011; Acts 2011, 82nd Leg., ch. 1083 (S.B. 1179), § 25(26), eff. June 17, 2011.

Comment

The State Council on Competitive Government is mandated to explore ways to enhance the delivery of state agency services through competitive bidding among agencies and between state agencies and private vendors. This section brings IV–D child support enforcement services into the arena of competitive bidding under the direction of the council. *(A.G.K. & H.P.S.)*

§ 236.003. Child Support Collection Agreement

The Title IV-D agency or a contractor awarded a contract under this chapter to collect child support may enter into an agreement with a person liable for the payment of child support. The agreement may relate to any matter that may be adjudicated by a court, including:

(1) the determination of paternity;

(2) the determination of the amount of child support due;

(3) the method of making child support payments;

(4) the imposition of income garnishment or withholding;

(5) the payment of fees;

(6) the reimbursement of costs; and

(7) other child support enforcement matters permitted by state or federal law.

Comment

The intent of this section is unclear. Under Chapter 233, the IV–D agency may already enter into agreements relating "to any matter that may be adjudicated by a court." But such an agreement would involve both the obligor and obligee and, in the form of an agreed order, would have to be confirmed by the court. This provision suggests that a private child support collection agency could work out agreements with just the obligor (or a presumed or alleged father) concerning matters well beyond, say, a plan to repay arrearages as a condition for avoiding suspension of a license under Chapter 232. The questionable usefulness of this section is matched only by its unintelligibility. *(A.G.K. & H.P.S.)*

SUBTITLE E. PROTECTION OF THE CHILD

Chapter

261. Investigation of Report of Child Abuse or Neglect
262. Procedures in Suit by Governmental Entity To Protect Health and Safety of Child
263. Review of Placement of Children Under Care of Department of Protective and Regulatory Services (sic) [*in 2003 became the Department of Family and Protective Services*].
264. Child Welfare Services
265. Prevention and Early Intervention Services
266. Medical Care and Educational Services for Children in Foster Care

★★★

CHAPTER 261. INVESTIGATION OF REPORT OF CHILD ABUSE OR NEGLECT

SUBCHAPTER A. GENERAL PROVISIONS

§ 261.001. Definitions. **[amended]**
§ 261.002. Central Registry.
§ 261.003. Application to Students in School for Deaf or School for Blind and Visually Impaired.
§ 261.004. Statistics of Abuse and Neglect of Children.

SUBCHAPTER B. REPORT OF ABUSE OR NEGLECT; IMMUNITIES

§ 261.101. Persons Required to Report; Time to Report.
§ 261.102. Matters to be Reported.
§ 261.103. Report Made to Appropriate Agency.
§ 261.104. Contents of Report.
§ 261.105. Referral of Report by Department or Law Enforcement.
§ 261.1055. Notification of District Attorneys.
§ 261.106. Immunities.
§ 261.107. False Report; Criminal Penalty; Civil Penalty.
§ 261.108. Frivolous Claims Against Person Reporting.
§ 261.109. Failure to Report; Penalty.
§ 261.110. Employer Retaliation Prohibited.
§ 261.111. Refusal of Psychiatric or Psychological Treatment of Child.

SUBCHAPTER C. CONFIDENTIALITY AND PRIVILEGED COMMUNICATION

§ 261.201. Confidentiality and Disclosure of Information.
§ 261.202. Privileged Communication.
§ 261.203. Information Relating to Child Fatality.

SUBCHAPTER D. INVESTIGATIONS

§ 261.301. Investigation of Report.

SUBCHAPTER E. INVESTIGATIONS OF ABUSE, NEGLECT, OR EXPLOITATION IN CERTAIN FACILITIES

Editors' Note: *This chapter contains guest commentary by Charles G. Childress, Clinical Professor (retired), Children's Rights Clinic, University of Texas Law School, formerly Chief Attorney, Field Operations, Legal Division, Texas Department of Family and Protective Services, identified as (C.G.C.).*

SUBCHAPTER A. GENERAL PROVISIONS

Introductory Comment

Chapter 261, like Chapters 264 through 266, speaks almost exclusively to the Texas Department of Family and Protective Services and its local units of the Children's Protective Services. These chapters generate very little appellate case law. Indeed, with rare exception, an attorney will seldom have occasion to consult the innumerable directives from the legislature to the agency and its personnel in the extraordinarily detailed provisions contained in this and other chapters.

§ 261.001. Definitions

In this chapter:

(1) "Abuse" includes the following acts or omissions by a person:

(A) mental or emotional injury to a child that results in an observable and material impairment in the child's growth, development, or psychological functioning;

(B) causing or permitting the child to be in a situation in which the child sustains a mental or emotional injury that results in an observable and material impairment in the child's growth, development, or psychological functioning;

(C) physical injury that results in substantial harm to the child, or the genuine threat of substantial harm from physical injury to the child, including an injury that is at variance with the history or explanation given and excluding an accident or reasonable discipline by a parent, guardian, or managing or possessory conservator that does not expose the child to a substantial risk of harm;

(D) failure to make a reasonable effort to prevent an action by another person that results in physical injury that results in substantial harm to the child;

(E) sexual conduct harmful to a child's mental, emotional, or physical welfare, including conduct that constitutes the offense of continuous sexual abuse of young child or children under Section 21.02, Penal Code, indecency with a child under Section 21.11, Penal Code, sexual assault under Section 22.011, Penal Code, or aggravated sexual assault under Section 22.021, Penal Code;

(F) failure to make a reasonable effort to prevent sexual conduct harmful to a child;

(G) compelling or encouraging the child to engage in sexual conduct as defined by Section 43.01, Penal Code, **including conduct that constitutes an offense of trafficking of persons under Section 20A.02(a)(7) or (8), Penal Code, prostitution under Section 43.02(a)(2), Penal Code, or compelling prostitution under Section 43.05(a)(2), Penal Code**;

(H) causing, permitting, encouraging, engaging in, or allowing the photographing, filming, or depicting of the child if the person knew or should have known that the resulting photograph, film, or depiction of the child is obscene as defined by Section 43.21, Penal Code, or pornographic;

(I) the current use by a person of a controlled substance as defined by Chapter 481, Health and Safety Code, in a manner or to the extent that the use results in physical, mental, or emotional injury to a child;

(J) causing, expressly permitting, or encouraging a child to use a controlled substance as defined by Chapter 481, Health and Safety Code; ~~or~~

(K) causing, permitting, encouraging, engaging in, or allowing a sexual performance by a child as defined by Section 43.25, Penal Code**; or**

(L) knowingly causing, permitting, encouraging, engaging in, or allowing a child to be trafficked in a manner punishable as an offense under Section 20A.02(a)(5), (6), (7), or (8), Penal Code, or the failure to make a reasonable effort to prevent a child from being trafficked in a manner punishable as an offense under any of those sections.

(2) "Department" means the Department of Family and Protective Services.

(3) "Designated agency" means the agency designated by the court as responsible for the protection of children.

(4) "Neglect" includes:

(A) the leaving of a child in a situation where the child would be exposed to a substantial risk of physical or mental harm, without arranging for necessary care for the child, and the demonstration of an intent not to return by a parent, guardian, or managing or possessory conservator of the child;

(B) the following acts or omissions by a person:

(i) placing a child in or failing to remove a child from a situation that a reasonable person would realize requires judgment or actions beyond the child's level of maturity, physical condition, or mental abilities and that results in bodily injury or a substantial risk of immediate harm to the child;

(ii) failing to seek, obtain, or follow through with medical care for a child, with the failure resulting in or presenting a substantial risk of death, disfigurement, or bodily injury or with the failure resulting in an observable and material impairment to the growth, development, or functioning of the child;

(iii) the failure to provide a child with food, clothing, or shelter necessary to sustain the life or health of the child, excluding failure caused primarily by financial inability unless relief services had been offered and refused;

(iv) placing a child in or failing to remove the child from a situation in which the child would be exposed to a substantial risk of sexual conduct harmful to the child; or

(v) placing a child in or failing to remove the child from a situation in which the child would be exposed to acts or omissions that constitute abuse under Subdivision (1)(E), (F), (G), (H), or (K) committed against another child; or

(C) the failure by the person responsible for a child's care, custody, or welfare to permit the child to return to the child's home without arranging for the necessary care for the child after the child has been absent from the home for any reason, including having been in residential placement or having run away.

(5) "Person responsible for a child's care, custody, or welfare" means a person who traditionally is responsible for a child's care, custody, or welfare, including:

(A) a parent, guardian, managing or possessory conservator, or foster parent of the child;

(B) a member of the child's family or household as defined by Chapter 71;

(C) a person with whom the child's parent cohabits;

(D) school personnel or a volunteer at the child's school; or

(E) personnel or a volunteer at a public or private child-care facility that provides services for the child or at a public or private residential institution or facility where the child resides.

(6) "Report" means a report that alleged or suspected abuse or neglect of a child has occurred or may occur.

(7) "Board" means the Board of Protective and Regulatory Services.

(8) "Born addicted to alcohol or a controlled substance" means a child:

(A) who is born to a mother who during the pregnancy used a controlled substance, as defined by Chapter 481, Health and Safety Code, other than a controlled substance legally obtained by prescription, or alcohol; and

(B) who, after birth as a result of the mother's use of the controlled substance or alcohol:

(i) experiences observable withdrawal from the alcohol or controlled substance;

(ii) exhibits observable or harmful effects in the child's physical appearance or functioning; or

(iii) exhibits the demonstrable presence of alcohol or a controlled substance in the child's bodily fluids.

Amended by Acts 2011, 82nd Leg., ch. 1 (S.B. 24), § 4.03, eff. Sept. 1, 2011.

Comment

A good example of the dichotomy between the legal perspective and the viewpoint of the personnel of DFPS is the at subtle disconnect in terminology in Chapter 161, Termination of the Parent-Child Relationship, and Chapters 261 through 266. The latter constantly refer to "abuse" and "neglect" of children. Section 261.001 provides extended definitions of those terms, enactment of which was urged on the legislature by the agency to assist its personnel to identify the factual patterns that should elicit action by them. Interestingly, the terms "child abuse and neglect" play almost no part in Chapter 161, the statutory text guiding litigation of termination of parental rights as a potential result of child abuse or neglect, nor does Chapter 101, Definitions, explain the concepts. The grounds for termination of parental rights rather attempt to describe in textual terms the conduct that would warrant that most severe of penalties on the civil side of the docket.

---

§ 261.002. Central Registry

(a) The department shall establish and maintain in Austin a central registry of reported cases of child abuse or neglect.

(b) The department may adopt rules necessary to carry out this section. The rules shall provide for cooperation with local child service agencies, including hospitals, clinics, and schools, and cooperation with other states in exchanging reports to effect a national registration system.

(c) The department may enter into agreements with other states to allow for the exchange of reports of child abuse and neglect in other states' central registry systems. The department shall use information obtained under this subsection in performing the background checks required under Section 42.056, Human Resources Code. The department shall cooperate with federal agencies and shall provide information and reports of child abuse and neglect to the appropriate federal agency that maintains the national registry for child abuse and neglect, if a national registry exists.

§ 261.003. Application to Students in School for Deaf or School for Blind and Visually Impaired

This chapter applies to the investigation of a report of abuse or neglect of a student, without regard to the age of the student, in the Texas School for the Deaf or the Texas School for the Blind and Visually Impaired.

§ 261.004. Statistics of Abuse and Neglect of Children

(a) The department shall prepare and disseminate statistics by county relating to the department's activities under this subtitle and include the information specified in Subsection (b) in an annual report available to the public.

(b) The department shall report the following information:

(1) the number of initial phone calls received by the department alleging abuse and neglect;

(2) the number of children reported to the department as having been abused and neglected;

(3) the number of reports received by the department alleging abuse or neglect and assigned by the department for investigation;

(4) of the children to whom Subdivision (2) applies:

(A) the number for whom the report was substantiated;

(B) the number for whom the report was unsubstantiated;

(C) the number for whom the report was determined to be false;

(D) the number who did not receive services from the department under a state or federal program;

(E) the number who received services, including preventative services, from the department under a state or federal program; and

(F) the number who were removed from the child's home during the preceding year;

(5) the number of families in which the child was not removed, but the child or family received services from the department;

(6) the number of children who died during the preceding year as a result of child abuse or neglect;

(7) of the children to whom Subdivision (6) applies, the number who were in foster care at the time of death;

(8) the number of child protective services workers responsible for report intake, assessment, or investigation;

(9) the response time by the department with respect to conducting an initial investigation of a report of child abuse or neglect;

(10) the response time by the department with respect to commencing services to families and children for whom an allegation of abuse or neglect has been made;

(11) the number of children who were returned to their families or who received family preservation services and who, before the fifth anniversary of the date of return or receipt, were the victims of substantiated reports of child abuse or neglect, including abuse or neglect resulting in the death of the child;

(12) the number of cases pursued by the department in each stage of the judicial process, including civil and criminal proceedings and the results of each proceeding; and

(13) the number of children for whom a person was appointed by the court to represent the best interests of the child and the average number of out-of-court contacts between the person and the child.

(c) The department shall compile the information specified in Subsection (b) for the preceding year in a report to be submitted to the legislature and the general public not later than February 1 of each year.

SUBCHAPTER B. REPORT OF ABUSE OR NEGLECT; IMMUNITIES

Introductory Comment

This subchapter imposes a duty on everyone, from ordinary citizens to relatives, teachers, doctors, lawyers, and religious officers, to report suspected child abuse or neglect under penalty of criminal prosecution for failure to do so. In fact, prosecutions are extremely rare but occasionally occur.

Leading Cases

DeShaney v. Winnebago County Dept. Social Services, 489 U.S. 189, 103 L.Ed.2d 249, 109 S.Ct. 998 (1989) (U.S. Const. does not mandate tort liability of caseworkers who fail to rescue abused child after report)

Perry v. S.N., 973 S.W.2d 301 (Tex. 1998) (statutory duty to report child abuse does not create cause of action based on negligence per se)

Mattix–Hill v. Reck, 923 S.W.2d 596 (Tex. 1996) (DHS caseworker doesn't inflict intentional emotional distress on parent)

Scott v. Butcher, 906 S.W.2d 14 (Tex. 1995) (failure to report suspected child sexual abuse not negligence per se, but fact question of duty arises)

Gates v. Texas Dept. of Family and Protective Services, 252 S.W.3d 90 (Tex. App.—Austin 2008, no pet.) (TDFPS does not have exclusive jurisdiction to determine child abuse cases and must grant hearing once a party requests it)

B.K. v. Cox, 116 S.W.3d 351 (Tex. App.—Houston [14th Dist.] 2003, no pet.) (doctor performing court-ordered psychological exams entitled to claim derived judicial immunity in mother's suit for failure to report abuse)

Walker v. Pollock, 981 S.W.2d 226 (Tex. App.—Houston [1st Dist.] 1998, no pet.) (doctor who misdiagnosed child's medical status protected from civil liability—child abuse allegation was trigger for examination)

Blum v. Julian, 977 S.W.2d 819 (Tex. App.—Fort Worth 1998, no pet.) (licensed counselor report of suspected sexual abuse privileged in absence of bad faith or malice)

Marshall v. Sackett, 907 S.W.2d 925 (Tex. App.—Houston [1st Dist.] 1995, no writ) (CPS program director immune when makes good faith investigation of alleged medical neglect even if refusal of treatment based on religious beliefs)

Gonzalez v. Avalos, 866 S.W.2d 346 (Tex. App.—El Paso 1993, writ dism'd w.o.j., 907 S.W.2d 443 (Tex. 1995)) (DFPS supervisor not entitled to immunity when failed to investigate abuse allegations)

Albright v. Texas Department of Human Services, 859 S.W.2d 575 (Tex. App.—Houston [1st Dist.] 1993, no writ) (social worker acting in good faith with reasonable cause to investigate abuse allegation is immune from personal liability)

§ 261.101. Persons Required to Report; Time to Report

(a) A person having cause to believe that a child's physical or mental health or welfare has been adversely affected by abuse or neglect by any person shall immediately make a report as provided by this subchapter.

(b) If a professional has cause to believe that a child has been abused or neglected or may be abused or neglected, or that a child is a victim of an offense under Section 21.11, Penal Code, and the professional has cause to believe that the child has been abused as defined by Section 261.001 or 261.401, the professional shall make a report not later than the 48th hour after the hour the professional first suspects that the child has been or may be abused or neglected or is a victim of an offense under Section 21.11, Penal Code. A professional may not delegate to or rely on another person to make the report. In this subsection, "professional" means an individual who is licensed or certified by the state or who is an employee of a facility licensed, certified, or operated by the state and who, in the normal course of official duties or duties for which a license or certification is required, has direct contact with children. The term includes teachers, nurses, doctors, day-care employees, employees of a clinic or health care facility that provides reproductive services, juvenile probation officers, and juvenile detention or correctional officers.

(c) The requirement to report under this section applies without exception to an individual whose personal communications may otherwise be privileged, including an attorney, a member of the clergy, a medical practitioner, a social worker, a mental health professional, and an employee of a clinic or health care facility that provides reproductive services.

(d) Unless waived in writing by the person making the report, the identity of an individual making a report under this chapter is confidential and may be disclosed only:

(1) as provided by Section 261.201; or

(2) to a law enforcement officer for the purposes of conducting a criminal investigation of the report.

Comment

Subsection (a) imposes a broad duty to report child abuse or neglect on *every person who has "cause to believe" a child has been abused or neglected*. Notwithstanding the fact that the meaning of "a person" in this context is crystal clear, in the past there was considerable debate over the definition of person, advanced primarily by attorneys. Thanks to definitive action by the legislature on behalf of child victims, any possible controversy about the comprehensive sweep of the duty to report has been eliminated.

Subsection (b) requires *"a professional who has cause to believe"* a child has been abused or neglected or may be abused or neglected, must report that belief in an expeditious manner, i.e., "not later than the 48th hour after the professional first suspects that the child has been or may be abused or neglected ...." Professionals include a wide variety of occupations, including teachers, nurses, doctors, juvenile probation, juvenile detention and correctional officers, and the employees of a clinic or other health care facility providing "reproductive services." The standard for reporting is not certainty, nor preponderance of the evidence, nor even the lower standard established for CPS intervention into a family as stated in § 262.104, "personal knowledge of facts that would lead a person of ordinary prudence and caution to believe that there is an immediate danger to the physical health or safety of the child." Rather, *for a professional to report to CPS the key verb is "suspects,"* based on "cause to believe" the child "has been or may be" abused or neglected.

For those who noticed that attorneys/lawyers did not make the list of professionals in subsection (b), read on. Subsection (c) clearly states that the attorney client privilege does not exempt a lawyer from the duty of reporting child abuse or neglect, no matter how or from whom the lawyer has "cause to believe." The attorney client privilege is testimonial in nature, *see*, § 261,202. Thus, when a lawyer learns of abuse from any source, including a client, the attorney must report possible abuse or neglect of a child, but may not be required to testify to the exact communications with a client. This requirement is carefully explained in Tex. Atty. Gen. Op. DM–458. Moreover, the legislature has rejected all efforts to soften or limit the requirement. In point of fact, the subsection overrides all important privileged communications in order to protect children, including priest penitent, doctor patient, etc. Note also that the general requirement in subsection (a) mandating lay persons to report if a child "has been adversely affected" by abuse or neglect, gives way in (b) and (c) to the professional's duty to report "cause to believe" that a child "may be abused or neglected" in the future.

The identity of the person making the report is strictly protected. In some cases this has forced the department to black out (redact) this information from the documents even though the identity of the reporter is, or may be, known, or the reporter has no concern about his or her identity being known to the alleged perpetrator. Under subsection (d), the reporter may waive in writing this confidentiality right.

Leading Cases

Perry v. S.N., 973 S.W.2d 301 (Tex. 1998) (failure to report child abuse does not create a new tort)

Bordman v. State, 56 S.W.3d 63 (Tex. App.—Houston [14th Dist.] 2001, pet. refused) (defendant may not rely on a clergy communication privilege to exclude confession that he sexually assaulted his three children)

Blum v. Julian, 977 S.W.2d 819 (Tex. App.—Fort Worth 1998, no pet.) (licensed counselor report of suspected sexual abuse privileged in absence of bad faith or malice)

§ 261.102. Matters to be Reported

A report should reflect the reporter's belief that a child has been or may be abused or neglected or has died of abuse or neglect.

§ 261.103. Report Made to Appropriate Agency

(a) Except as provided by Subsections (b) and (c) and Section 261.405, a report shall be made to:

(1) any local or state law enforcement agency;

(2) the department;

(3) the state agency that operates, licenses, certifies, or registers the facility in which the alleged abuse or neglect occurred; or

(4) the agency designated by the court to be responsible for the protection of children.

(b) A report may be made to the Texas Youth Commission instead of the entities listed under Subsection (a) if the report is based on information provided by a child while under the supervision of the commission concerning the child's alleged abuse of another child.

(c) Notwithstanding Subsection (a), a report, other than a report under Subsection (a)(3) or Section 261.405, must be made to the department if the alleged or suspected abuse or neglect involves a person responsible for the care, custody, or welfare of the child.

Comment

A person wishing to report child abuse or neglect may report to law enforcement officers, other state agencies, or the Department of Family and Protective Services [DFPS] on a 24–hour toll free number, ***1–800–252–5400***. The department has an on-line reporting system for professionals and others reporting in situations where a response is not needed in less than 24 hours, at http://www.txabusehotline.org/. The reporter is not required to determine whether the abuser is "responsible for the care, custody, or welfare of the child" before making the report. Other provisions in this chapter require that the department refer cases to law enforcement or the appropriate agency if it is determined that the alleged perpetrator is not a caretaker.

Under subsection (b) and § 261.409, the Texas Youth Commission is the primary investigative agency when the information is provided by a child in TYC custody "concerning the child's alleged abuse of another child." Section 261.405 tasks the Texas Juvenile Probation Commission with the duty to investigate abuse in juvenile facilities, except for a facility operated solely for children committed to TYC. Rather obviously, the 2007 scandal regarding sexual abuse of inmates in TYC by staff personnel raised a fox in the henhouse issue with respect to TYC self-investigation. *(C.G.C.)*

§ 261.104. Contents of Report

The person making a report shall identify, if known:

(1) the name and address of the child;

(2) the name and address of the person responsible for the care, custody, or welfare of the child; and

(3) any other pertinent information concerning the alleged or suspected abuse or neglect.

§ 261.105. Referral of Report by Department or Law Enforcement

(a) All reports received by a local or state law enforcement agency that allege abuse or neglect by a person responsible for a child's care, custody, or welfare shall be referred immediately to the department or the designated agency.

(b) The department or designated agency shall immediately notify the appropriate state or local law enforcement agency of any report it receives, other than a report from a law enforcement agency, that concerns the suspected abuse or neglect of a child or death of a child from abuse or neglect.

(c) In addition to notifying a law enforcement agency, if the report relates to a child in a facility operated, licensed, certified, or registered by a state agency, the department shall refer the report to the agency for investigation.

(c–1) Notwithstanding Subsections (b) and (c), if a report under this section relates to a child with mental retardation receiving services in a state supported living center as defined by Section 531.002, Health and Safety Code, or the ICF–MR component of the Rio Grande State Center, the department shall proceed with the investigation of the report as provided by Section 261.404.

(d) If the department initiates an investigation and determines that the abuse or neglect does not involve a person responsible for the child's care, custody, or welfare, the department shall refer the report to a law enforcement agency for further investigation. If the department determines that the abuse or neglect involves an employee of a public primary or secondary school, and that the child is a student at the school, the department shall orally notify the superintendent of the school district in which the employee is employed about the investigation.

(e) In cooperation with the department, the Texas Youth Commission by rule shall adopt guidelines for identifying a report made to the commission under Section 261.103(b) that is appropriate to refer to the department or a law enforcement agency for investigation. Guidelines adopted under this subsection must require the commission to consider the severity and immediacy of the alleged abuse or neglect of the child victim.

Comment

This section requires cooperation among law enforcement agencies, the department, and licensing agencies to ensure that reports of child abuse are properly investigated. As a result of the "fight night" scandal involving persons with mental retardation, the 2009 legislature added subsection (c-1) to this section and substantially rewrote the investigation guidelines in § 261.404, below. The legislation also increased the penalty for failure to report these facility abuses in § 261.109. Subsection (e) requires TYC, in cooperation with the department, to develop rules to guide the referral process for cases that may come under the TYC self-investigation provisions of § 261.103(b). *(C.G.C.)*

§ 261.1055. Notification of District Attorneys

(a) A district attorney may inform the department or designated agency that the district attorney wishes to receive notification of some or all reports of suspected abuse or neglect of children who were in the county at the time the report was made or who were in the county at the time of the alleged abuse or neglect.

(b) If the district attorney makes the notification under this section, the department or designated agency shall, on receipt of a report of suspected abuse or neglect, immediately notify the district attorney as requested and the department or designated agency shall forward a copy of the reports to the district attorney on request.

§ 261.106. Immunities

(a) A person acting in good faith who reports or assists in the investigation of a report of alleged child abuse or neglect or who testifies or otherwise participates in a judicial proceeding arising from a report, petition, or investigation of alleged child abuse or neglect is immune from civil or criminal liability that might otherwise be incurred or imposed.

(b) Immunity from civil and criminal liability extends to an authorized volunteer of the department or a law enforcement officer who participates at the request of the department in an investigation of alleged or suspected abuse or neglect or in an action arising from an investigation if the person was acting in good faith and in the scope of the person's responsibilities.

(c) A person who reports the person's own abuse or neglect of a child or who acts in bad faith or with malicious purpose in reporting alleged child abuse or neglect is not immune from civil or criminal liability.

Leading Cases

Chaney v. Corona, 103 S.W.3d 608 (Tex. App.—San Antonio 2003, pet. denied) (school principal had reasonable basis for reporting teacher for suspected child abuse committed on student; immunity statute applies)

State v. Harrod, 81 S.W.3d 904 (Tex. App.—Dallas 2002, pet. refused) (mother failed to immediately report sexual abuse of her daughters, criminal immunity statute doesn't apply)

B.K. v. Cox, 116 S.W.3d 351 (Tex. App.—Houston [14th Dist.] 2003, no pet.) (doctor performing court ordered psychological exams entitled to claim derived judicial immunity in mother's suit for failure to report abuse)

Walker v. Pollock, 981 S.W.2d 226 (Tex. App.—Houston [1st Dist.] 1998, no pet.) (doctor who misdiagnosed child's medical status protected from civil liability—child abuse allegation was trigger for examination)

Albright v. Texas Department of Human Services, 859 S.W.2d 575 (Tex. App.—Houston [1st Dist.] 1993, no writ) (social worker acting in good faith with reasonable cause to investigate abuse allegation is immune from personal liability)

§ 261.107. False Report; Criminal Penalty; Civil Penalty

(a) A person commits an offense if, with the intent to deceive, the person knowingly makes a report as provided in this chapter that is false. An offense under this subsection is a state jail felony unless it is shown on the trial of the offense that the person has previously been convicted under this section, in which case the offense is a felony of the third degree.

(b) A finding by a court in a suit affecting the parent-child relationship that a report made under this chapter before or during the suit was false or lacking factual foundation may be grounds for the court to modify an order providing for possession of or access to the child who was the subject of the report by restricting further access to the child by the person who made the report.

(c) The appropriate county prosecuting attorney shall be responsible for the prosecution of an offense under this section.

(d) The court shall order a person who is convicted of an offense under Subsection (a) to pay any reasonable attorney's fees incurred by the person who was falsely accused of abuse or neglect in any proceeding relating to the false report.

(e) A person who engages in conduct described by Subsection (a) is liable to the state for a civil penalty of $1,000. The attorney general shall bring an action to recover a civil penalty authorized by this subsection.

Comment

Historically, the criminal penalties provided by this section for a false report, or for failure to report under § 261.109, have seldom been enforced. The exact extent of the problem of false reporting is completely unknown because the agency does not even attempt to track how many cases it refers to county or district attorneys for possible prosecution. The agency does keep records, of course, on its caseload. In fiscal 2006 over 500,000 calls were made to CPS. Over 75% of the reports of abuse or neglect were labeled "unconfirmed." That label is of no assistance in identifying false reports, however, due to the wide variety of facts that result in that disposition of the investigation. Two things are known about the frequency of the criminal offense "false report." First, spokespersons in the field report that there are "some instances." Second, there has been only one reported appellate case sustaining a conviction since the 1995 recodification. Notwithstanding the rarity of the offense, in 2005 the legislature increased the criminal law sanction for false reporting. Punishment for the offense is heightened from Class A misdemeanor to state jail felony. Whether perpetrators will be additionally deterred is as unknown as the census of the wrongdoers.

Subsection (b) permits the making of a false report to be used as a ground for restricting access by the accuser to the child. A party contemplating making a claim of a false report must also consider the risk that a court may award damages to the reporter if the claim of false report is determined to be frivolous under § 261.108. The net effect of these conflicting provisions may discourage litigation on either side of the issue.

Subsections (d) and (e) add attorney's fees and a monetary "civil penalty" to the mix.

Leading Case

Harvey v. State, 97 S.W.3d 162 (Tex. App.—Houston [14th Dist.] 2002, pet. ref'd) (second jury found false report of child abuse; assessed maximum sentence—one year and $4,000 fine)

§ 261.108. Frivolous Claims Against Person Reporting

(a) In this section:

(1) "Claim" means an action or claim by a party, including a plaintiff, counterclaimant, cross-claimant, or third-party plaintiff, requesting recovery of damages.

(2) "Defendant" means a party against whom a claim is made.

(b) A court shall award a defendant reasonable attorney's fees and other expenses related to the defense of a claim filed against the defendant for damages or other relief arising from reporting or assisting in the investigation of a report under this chapter or participating in a judicial proceeding resulting from the report if:

(1) the court finds that the claim is frivolous, unreasonable, or without foundation because the defendant is immune from liability under Section 261.106; and

(2) the claim is dismissed or judgment is rendered for the defendant.

(c) To recover under this section, the defendant must, at any time after the filing of a claim, file a written motion stating that:

(1) the claim is frivolous, unreasonable, or without foundation because the defendant is immune from liability under Section 261.106; and

(2) the defendant requests the court to award reasonable attorney's fees and other expenses related to the defense of the claim.

§ 261.109. Failure to Report; Penalty

(a) A person commits an offense if the person has cause to believe that a child's physical or mental health or welfare has been or may be adversely affected by abuse or neglect and knowingly fails to report as provided in this chapter.

(b) An offense under this section is a Class A misdemeanor, except that the offense is a state jail felony if it is shown on the trial of the offense that the child was a person with mental retardation who resided in a state supported living center, the ICF–MR component of the Rio Grande State Center, or a facility licensed under Chapter 252, Health and Safety Code, and the actor knew that the child had suffered serious bodily injury as a result of the abuse or neglect.

Leading Cases

Porter v. State, 121 S.W.3d 404 (Tex. App.—Amarillo 2003, pet. refused) (day care operator failed to report child abuse when her employees inadvertently left small child alone in van for over an hour)

State v. Harrod, 81 S.W.3d 904 (Tex. App.—Dallas 2002, pet. refused) (mother failed to immediately report sexual abuse of her daughters, criminal immunity statute doesn't apply)

White v. State, 50 S.W.3d 31 (Tex. App.—Waco 2001, pet. refused) (ex-wife convicted for failure to report abuse of her former step-daughter by her ex-husband)

§ 261.110. Employer Retaliation Prohibited

(a) In this section, "professional" has the meaning assigned by Section 261.101(b).

(b) An employer may not suspend or terminate the employment of, or otherwise discriminate against, a person who is a professional and who in good faith:

(1) reports child abuse or neglect to:

(A) the person's supervisor;

(B) an administrator of the facility where the person is employed;

(C) a state regulatory agency; or

(D) a law enforcement agency; or

(2) initiates or cooperates with an investigation or proceeding by a governmental entity relating to an allegation of child abuse or neglect.

(c) A person whose employment is suspended or terminated or who is otherwise discriminated against in violation of this section may sue for injunctive relief, damages, or both.

(d) A plaintiff who prevails in a suit under this section may recover:

(1) actual damages, including damages for mental anguish even if an injury other than mental anguish is not shown;

(2) exemplary damages under Chapter 41, Civil Practice and Remedies Code, if the employer is a private employer;

(3) court costs; and

(4) reasonable attorney's fees.

(e) In addition to amounts recovered under Subsection (d), a plaintiff who prevails in a suit under this section is entitled to:

(1) reinstatement to the person's former position or a position that is comparable in terms of compensation, benefits, and other conditions of employment;

(2) reinstatement of any fringe benefits and seniority rights lost because of the suspension, termination, or discrimination; and

(3) compensation for wages lost during the period of suspension or termination.

(f) A public employee who alleges a violation of this section may sue the employing state or local governmental entity for the relief provided for by this section. Sovereign immunity is waived and abolished to the extent of liability created by this section. A person having a claim under this section may sue a governmental unit for damages allowed by this section.

(g) In a suit under this section against an employing state or local governmental entity, a plaintiff may not recover compensatory damages for future pecuniary losses, emotional pain, suffering, inconvenience, mental anguish, loss of enjoyment of life, and other nonpecuniary losses in an amount that exceeds:

(1) $50,000, if the employing state or local governmental entity has fewer than 101 employees in each of 20 or more calendar weeks in the calendar year in which the suit is filed or in the preceding year;

(2) $100,000, if the employing state or local governmental entity has more than 100 and fewer than 201 employees in each of 20 or more calendar weeks in the calendar year in which the suit is filed or in the preceding year;

(3) $200,000, if the employing state or local governmental entity has more than 200 and fewer than 501 employees in each of 20 or more calendar weeks in the calendar year in which the suit is filed or in the preceding year; and

(4) $250,000, if the employing state or local governmental entity has more than 500 employees in each of 20 or more calendar weeks in the calendar year in which the suit is filed or in the preceding year.

(h) If more than one subdivision of Subsection (g) applies to an employing state or local governmental entity, the amount of monetary damages that may be recovered from the entity in a suit brought under this section is governed by the applicable provision that provides the highest damage award.

(i) A plaintiff suing under this section has the burden of proof, except that there is a rebuttable presumption that the plaintiff's employment was suspended or terminated or that the plaintiff was otherwise discriminated against for reporting abuse or neglect if the suspension, termination, or discrimination occurs before the 61st day after the date on which the person made a report in good faith.

(j) A suit under this section may be brought in a district or county court of the county in which:

(1) the plaintiff was employed by the defendant; or

(2) the defendant conducts business.

(k) It is an affirmative defense to a suit under Subsection (b) that an employer would have taken the action against the employee that forms the basis of the suit based solely on information, observation, or evidence that is not related to the fact that the employee reported child abuse or neglect or initiated or cooperated with an investigation or proceeding relating to an allegation of child abuse or neglect.

(*l*) A public employee who has a cause of action under Chapter 554, Government Code, based on conduct described by Subsection (b) may not bring an action based on that conduct under this section.

(m) This section does not apply to a person who reports the person's own abuse or neglect of a child or who initiates or cooperates with an investigation or proceeding by a governmental entity relating to an allegation of the person's own abuse or neglect of a child.

Comment

Virtually everyone having cause to believe that a child is being abused or neglected has a duty to report the abuse and cooperate with an investigation. However, until 2001 there was no specific protection for teachers, day-care employees or others from retaliation by an employer for making a report or for cooperating with an investigation. This section prohibits employer retaliation against an employee who in good faith reports child abuse or neglect or cooperates with an investigation of such a report. *(C.G.C.)*

§ 261.111. Refusal of Psychiatric or Psychological Treatment of Child

(a) In this section, "psychotropic drug" means a substance that is:

(1) used in the diagnosis, treatment, or prevention of a disease or as a component of a medication; and

(2) intended to have an altering effect on perception, emotion, or behavior.

(b) The refusal of a parent, guardian, or managing or possessory conservator of a child to administer or consent to the administration of a psychotropic drug to the child, or to consent to any other psychiatric or psychological treatment of the child, does not by itself constitute neglect of the child unless the refusal to consent:

(1) presents a substantial risk of death, disfigurement, or bodily injury to the child; or

(2) has resulted in an observable and material impairment to the growth, development, or functioning of the child.

SUBCHAPTER C. CONFIDENTIALITY AND PRIVILEGED COMMUNICATION

Introductory Comment

The only privileged communications recognized by this chapter are those between an attorney and client. This testimonial privilege protects confidential communications; it is not a blanket privilege that immunizes an attorney from responsibility to report injury to a child caused by abuse or neglect.

Leading Cases

Bordman v. State, 56 S.W.3d 63 (Tex. App.—Houston [14th Dist.] 2001, pet. refused) (defendant may not assert clergy communication privilege to exclude his confession of sexual assault of his children)

Texas Dept. Human Serv. v. Benson, 893 S.W.2d 236 (Tex. App.—Austin 1995, writ denied) (child abuse report is confidential; court voids agency policy regarding second reports and professionals, but governmental immunity applies to agency)

§ 261.201. Confidentiality and Disclosure of Information

(a) Except as provided by Section 261.203, the following information is confidential, is not subject to public release under Chapter 552, Government Code, and may be disclosed only for purposes consistent with this code and applicable federal or state law or under rules adopted by an investigating agency:

(1) a report of alleged or suspected abuse or neglect made under this chapter and the identity of the person making the report; and

(2) except as otherwise provided in this section, the files, reports, records, communications, audiotapes, videotapes, and working papers used or developed in an investigation under this chapter or in providing services as a result of an investigation.

(b) A court may order the disclosure of information that is confidential under this section if:

(1) a motion has been filed with the court requesting the release of the information;

(2) a notice of hearing has been served on the investigating agency and all other interested parties; and

(3) after hearing and an in camera review of the requested information, the court determines that the disclosure of the requested information is:

(A) essential to the administration of justice; and

(B) not likely to endanger the life or safety of:

(i) a child who is the subject of the report of alleged or suspected abuse or neglect;

(ii) a person who makes a report of alleged or suspected abuse or neglect; or

(iii) any other person who participates in an investigation of reported abuse or neglect or who provides care for the child.

(b–1) On a motion of one of the parties in a contested case before an administrative law judge relating to the license or certification of a professional, as defined by Section 261.101(b), or an educator, as defined by Section 5.001, Education Code, the administrative law judge may order the disclosure of information that is confidential under this section that relates to the matter before the administrative law judge after a hearing for which notice is provided as required by Subsection (b)(2) and making the review and determination required by Subsection (b)(3). Before the department may release information under this subsection, the department must edit the information to protect the confidentiality of the identity of any person who makes a report of abuse or neglect.

(c) In addition to Subsection (b), a court, on its own motion, may order disclosure of information that is confidential under this section if:

(1) the order is rendered at a hearing for which all parties have been given notice;

(2) the court finds that disclosure of the information is:

(A) essential to the administration of justice; and

(B) not likely to endanger the life or safety of:

(i) a child who is the subject of the report of alleged or suspected abuse or neglect;

(ii) a person who makes a report of alleged or suspected abuse or neglect; or

(iii) any other person who participates in an investigation of reported abuse or neglect or who provides care for the child; and

(3) the order is reduced to writing or made on the record in open court.

(d) The adoptive parents of a child who was the subject of an investigation and an adult who was the subject of an investigation as a child are entitled to examine and make copies of any report, record, working paper, or other information in the possession, custody, or control of the state that pertains to the history of the child. The department may edit the documents to protect the identity of the biological parents and any other person whose identity is confidential, unless this information is already known to the adoptive parents or is readily available through other sources, including the court records of a suit to terminate the parent-child relationship under Chapter 161.

(e) Before placing a child who was the subject of an investigation, the department shall notify the prospective adoptive parents of their right to examine any report, record, working paper, or other information in the possession, custody, or control of the state that pertains to the history of the child.

(f) The department shall provide prospective adoptive parents an opportunity to examine information under this section as early as practicable before placing a child.

(f–1) The department shall provide to a relative or other individual with whom a child is placed any information the department considers necessary to ensure that the relative or other individual is prepared to meet the needs of the child. The information required by this subsection may include information related to any abuse or neglect suffered by the child.

(g) Notwithstanding Subsection (b), the department, on request and subject to department rule, shall provide to the parent, managing conservator, or other legal representative of a child who is the subject of reported abuse or neglect information concerning the reported abuse or neglect that would otherwise be confidential under this section if the department has edited the information to protect the confidentiality of the identity of the person who made the report and any other person whose life or safety may be endangered by the disclosure.

(h) This section does not apply to an investigation of child abuse or neglect in a home or facility regulated under Chapter 42, Human Resources Code.

(i) Notwithstanding Subsection (a), the Texas Youth Commission shall release a report of alleged or suspected abuse or neglect made under this chapter if:

(1) the report relates to a report of abuse or neglect involving a child committed to the commission during the period that the child is committed to the commission; and

(2) the commission is not prohibited by Chapter 552, Government Code, or other law from disclosing the report.

(j) The Texas Youth Commission shall edit any report disclosed under Subsection (i) to protect the identity of:

(1) a child who is the subject of the report of alleged or suspected abuse or neglect;

(2) the person who made the report; and

(3) any other person whose life or safety may be endangered by the disclosure.

(k) Notwithstanding Subsection (a), an investigating agency, other than the department or the Texas Youth Commission, on request, shall provide to the parent, managing conservator, or other legal representative of a child who is the subject of reported abuse or neglect, or to the child if the child is at least 18 years of age, information concerning the reported abuse or neglect that would otherwise be confidential under this section. The investigating agency shall withhold information under this subsection if the parent, managing conservator, or other legal representative of the child requesting the information is alleged to have committed the abuse or neglect.

(*l*) Before a child or a parent, managing conservator, or other legal representative of a child may inspect or copy a record or file concerning the child under Subsection (k), the custodian of the record or file must redact:

(1) any personally identifiable information about a victim or witness under 18 years of age unless that victim or witness is:

(A) the child who is the subject of the report; or

(B) another child of the parent, managing conservator, or other legal representative requesting the information;

(2) any information that is excepted from required disclosure under Chapter 552, Government Code, or other law; and

(3) the identity of the person who made the report.

Comment

The Open Records Act does not apply to files or records of the department relating to an investigation or to services provided as a result of that investigation. The specific provisions of this section also limit the discretion of the department to respond to certain kinds of discovery; a court order is required for release of unredacted records. Protection for the confidentiality of caretakers, such as foster parents, is crucial when the release of information might endanger their lives or safety. Subsection (h) clarifies that this provision does not apply to licensing investigations, which are controlled by federal and state confidentiality provisions under Tex. Hum. Res. Code Ann. chs. 40 and 48. Subsections (i) and (j) relate to TYC self-investigations. Subsection (k) requires disclosure of certain information to the parent, managing conservator or legal representative of the child subject of the investigation unless the requestor is also the alleged perpetrator. Subsection (*l*) requires the department to redact "personally identifiable information about" a minor victim or witness, the identity of the reporter, and any other information exempt from disclosure under the Open Records Act, or other law. *(C.G.C.)*

§ 261.202. Privileged Communication

In a proceeding regarding the abuse or neglect of a child, evidence may not be excluded on the ground of privileged communication except in the case of communications between an attorney and client.

Comment

Read together with § 261.101, this provision confirms the fact that the attorney-client privilege is strictly testimonial when abuse or neglect of a child is involved.

§ 261.203. Information Relating to Child Fatality

(a) Not later than the fifth day after the date the department receives a request for information about a child fatality with respect to which the department is conducting an investigation of alleged abuse or neglect, the department shall release:

(1) the age and sex of the child;

(2) the date of death;

(3) whether the state was the managing conservator of the child at the time of the child's death; and

(4) whether the child resided with the child's parent, managing conservator, guardian, or other person entitled to possession of the child at the time of the child's death.

(b) If, after a child abuse or neglect investigation is completed, the department determines a child's death was caused by abuse or neglect, the department shall promptly release the following information on request:

(1) the information described by Subsection (a), if not previously released to the person requesting the information;

(2) for cases in which the child's death occurred while the child was living with the child's parent, managing conservator, guardian, or other person entitled to possession of the child:

(A) a summary of any previous reports of abuse or neglect of the deceased child or another child made while the child was living with that parent, managing conservator, guardian, or other person entitled to possession of the child;

(B) the disposition of any report under Paragraph (A);

(C) a description of the services, if any, that were provided by the department to the child or the child's family as a result of any report under Paragraph (A); and

(D) the results of any risk or safety assessment completed by the department relating to the deceased child; and

(3) for a case in which the child's death occurred while the child was in substitute care with the department or with a residential child-care provider regulated under Chapter 42, Human Resources Code, the following information:

(A) the date the substitute care provider with whom the child was residing at the time of death was licensed or verified;

(B) a summary of any previous reports of abuse or neglect investigated by the department relating to the substitute care provider, including the disposition of any investigation resulting from a report;

(C) any reported licensing violations, including notice of any action taken by the department regarding a violation; and

(D) records of any training completed by the substitute care provider while the child was placed with the provider.

(c) If the department is unable to release the information required by Subsection (b) before the 11th day after the date the department receives a request for the information or the date the investigation of the child fatality is completed, whichever is later, the department shall inform the person requesting the information of the date the department will release the information.

(d) After receiving a request for information required by Subsection (b), the department shall notify and provide a copy of the request to the attorney ad litem for the deceased child, if any.

(e) Before the department releases any information under Subsection (b), the department shall redact from the records any information the release of which would:

(1) identify:

(A) the individual who reported the abuse or neglect; or

(B) any other individual other than the deceased child or an alleged perpetrator of the abuse or neglect;

(2) jeopardize an ongoing criminal investigation or prosecution;

(3) endanger the life or safety of any individual; or

(4) violate other state or federal law.

(f) The executive commissioner of the Health and Human Services Commission shall adopt rules to implement this section.

SUBCHAPTER D. INVESTIGATIONS

§ 261.301. Investigation of Report

(a) With assistance from the appropriate state or local law enforcement agency as provided by this section, the department or designated agency shall make a prompt and thorough investigation of a report of child abuse or neglect allegedly committed by a person responsible for a child's care, custody, or welfare. The investigation shall be conducted without regard to any pending suit affecting the parent-child relationship.

(b) A state agency shall investigate a report that alleges abuse or neglect occurred in a facility operated, licensed, certified, or registered by that agency as provided by Subchapter E. In conducting an investigation for a facility operated, licensed, certified, registered, or listed by the department, the department shall perform the investigation as provided by:

(1) Subchapter E; and

(2) the Human Resources Code.

(c) The department is not required to investigate a report that alleges child abuse or neglect by a person other than a person responsible for a child's care, custody, or welfare. The appropriate state or local law enforcement agency shall investigate that report if the agency determines an investigation should be conducted.

(d) The department shall by rule assign priorities and prescribe investigative procedures for investigations based on the severity and immediacy of the alleged harm to the child. The primary purpose of the investigation shall be the protection of the child. The rules must require the department, subject to the availability of funds, to:

(1) immediately respond to a report of abuse and neglect that involves circumstances in which the death of the child or substantial bodily harm to the child would result unless the department immediately intervenes;

(2) respond within 24 hours to a report of abuse and neglect that is assigned the highest priority, other than a report described by Subdivision (1); and

(3) respond within 72 hours to a report of abuse and neglect that is assigned the second highest priority.

(e) As necessary to provide for the protection of the child, the department or designated agency shall determine:

(1) the nature, extent, and cause of the abuse or neglect;

(2) the identity of the person responsible for the abuse or neglect;

(3) the names and conditions of the other children in the home;

(4) an evaluation of the parents or persons responsible for the care of the child;

(5) the adequacy of the home environment;

(6) the relationship of the child to the persons responsible for the care, custody, or welfare of the child; and

(7) all other pertinent data.

(f) An investigation of a report to the department that alleges that a child has been or may be the victim of conduct that constitutes a criminal offense that poses an immediate risk of physical or sexual abuse of a child that could result in the death of or serious harm to the child shall be conducted jointly by a peace officer, as defined by Article 2.12, Code of Criminal Procedure, from the appropriate local law enforcement agency and the department or the agency responsible for conducting an investigation under Subchapter E.

(g) The inability or unwillingness of a local law enforcement agency to conduct a joint investigation under this section does not constitute grounds to prevent or prohibit the department from performing its duties under this subtitle. The department shall document any instance in which a law enforcement agency is unable or unwilling to conduct a joint investigation under this section.

(h) The department and the appropriate local law enforcement agency shall conduct an investigation, other than an investigation under Subchapter E, as provided by this section and Article 2.27, Code of Criminal Procedure, if the investigation is of a report that alleges that a child has been or may be the victim of conduct that constitutes a criminal offense that poses an immediate risk of physical or sexual abuse of a child that could result in the death of or serious harm to the child. Immediately on receipt of a report described by this subsection, the department shall notify the appropriate local law enforcement agency of the report.

Comment

This section requires cooperation between the department and law enforcement agencies in serious abuse cases. The primary purpose of a DFPS investigation is to protect the child, not to develop a criminal case against the perpetrator. Subsection (b) provides that licensing investigations are conducted under provisions of the TEX. HUM. RES. CODE ANN., as well as Chapter 261, Subchapter E. Required standards of care are different; for example, corporal punishment may be "reasonable discipline" when administered by a parent, but is not permitted in licensed child care facilities. *(C.G.C.)*

Leading Cases

DeShaney v. Winnebago County Dept. Social Services, 489 U.S. 189, 103 L.Ed.2d 249, 109 S. Ct. 998 (1989) (U.S. Const. does not mandate tort liability of caseworkers who fail to rescue abused child after report)

Department of Protective and Regulatory Services v. Schutz, 101 S.W.3d 512 (Tex. App.—Houston [1st Dist.] 2002, no pet.) (parents operating foster home could not seek relief from neglect finding in district court prior to exhausting administrative remedies)

§ 261.3011. Joint Investigation Guidelines and Training

(a) The department shall, in consultation with the appropriate law enforcement agencies, develop guidelines and protocols for joint investigations by the department and the law enforcement agency under Section 261.301. The guidelines and protocols must:

(1) clarify the respective roles of the department and law enforcement agency in conducting the investigation;

(2) require that mutual child protective services and law enforcement training and agreements be implemented by both entities to ensure the integrity and best outcomes of joint investigations; and

(3) incorporate the use of forensic methods in determining the occurrence of child abuse and neglect.

(b) The department shall collaborate with law enforcement agencies to provide to department investigators and law enforcement officers responsible for investigating reports of abuse and neglect joint training relating to methods to effectively conduct joint investigations under Section 261.301. The training must include information on interviewing techniques, evidence gathering, and testifying in court for criminal investigations, as well as instruction on rights provided by the Fourth Amendment to the United States Constitution.

Comment

Child abuse and neglect involves both the criminal and the civil side of the legal docket. In the past decade or so there has been a growing awareness that cooperation between law enforcement officers and CPS caseworkers at the local level is essential to serve both public interests. Prosecution and conviction of defendants, especially those committing felonies against children, must be balanced with the protection of children and their permanent placement. This chapter is designed to improve the methods for achieving the desired goal of cooperation in the joint efforts to attack abuse and neglect.

§ 261.3012. Completion of Paperwork

An employee of the department who responds to a report that is assigned the highest priority in accordance with department rules adopted under Section 261.301(d) shall identify, to the extent reasonable under the circumstances, forms and other paperwork that can be completed by members of the family of the child who is the subject of the report. The department employee shall request the assistance of the child's family members in completing that documentation but remains responsible for ensuring that the documentation is completed in an appropriate manner.

§ 261.3013. Case Closure Agreements Prohibited

(a) Except as provided by Subsection (b), on closing a case, the department may not enter into a written agreement with a child's parent or another adult with whom the child resides that requires the parent or other adult to take certain actions after the case is closed to ensure the child's safety.

(b) This section does not apply to an agreement that is entered into by a parent or other adult:

(1) following the removal of a child and that is subject to the approval of a court with continuing jurisdiction over the child;

(2) as a result of the person's participation in family group conferencing; or

(3) as part of a formal case closure plan agreed to by the person who will continue to care for a child as a result of a parental child safety placement.

(c) The department shall develop policies to guide caseworkers in the development of case closure agreements authorized under Subsections (b)(2) and (3).

Added by Acts 2011, 82nd Leg., ch. 598 (S.B. 218), § 1, eff. Sept. 1, 2011.

§ 261.3015. Flexible Response System

(a) In assigning priorities and prescribing investigative procedures based on the severity and immediacy of the alleged harm to a child under Section 261.301(d), the department shall establish a flexible response system to allow the department to make the most effective use of resources by investigating serious cases of abuse and neglect and by screening out less serious cases of abuse and neglect if the department determines, after contacting a professional or other credible source, that the child's safety can be assured without further investigation. The department may administratively close the less serious cases without providing services or making a referral to another entity for assistance.

(a–1) For purposes of Subsection (a), a case is considered to be a less serious case of abuse or neglect if the circumstances of the case do not indicate an immediate risk of abuse or neglect that could result in the death of or serious harm to the child who is the subject of the case.

(b) The classification under the flexible response system of a case may be changed as warranted by the circumstances.

(c) The department may implement the flexible response system by establishing a pilot program in a single department service region. The department shall study the results of the system in the region in determining the method by which to implement the system statewide.

§ 261.3016. Training of Personnel Receiving Reports of Abuse and Neglect

The department shall develop, in cooperation with local law enforcement officials and the Commission on State Emergency Communications, a training program for department personnel who receive reports of abuse and neglect. The training program must include information on:

(1) the proper methods of screening reports of abuse and neglect; and

(2) ways to determine the seriousness of a report, including determining whether a report alleges circumstances that could result in the death of or serious harm to a child or whether the report is less serious in nature.

§ 261.3019. Expired

§ 261.302. Conduct of Investigation

(a) The investigation may include:

(1) a visit to the child's home, unless the alleged abuse or neglect can be confirmed or clearly ruled out without a home visit; and

(2) an interview with and examination of the subject child, which may include a medical, psychological, or psychiatric examination.

(b) The interview with and examination of the child may:

(1) be conducted at any reasonable time and place, including the child's home or the child's school;

(2) include the presence of persons the department or designated agency determines are necessary; and

(3) include transporting the child for purposes relating to the interview or investigation.

(b–1) Before the department may transport a child as provided by Subsection (b)(3), the department shall attempt to notify the parent or other person having custody of the child of the transport.

(c) The investigation may include an interview with the child's parents and an interview with and medical, psychological, or psychiatric examination of any child in the home.

(d) If, before an investigation is completed, the investigating agency believes that the immediate removal of a child from the child's home is necessary to protect the child from further abuse or neglect, the investigating agency shall file a petition or take other action under Chapter 262 to provide for the temporary care and protection of the child.

(e) An interview with a child conducted by the department during the investigation stage shall be audiotaped or videotaped. An interview with a child alleged to be a victim of physical abuse or sexual abuse conducted by an investigating agency other than the department shall be audiotaped or videotaped unless the investigating agency determines that good cause exists for not audiotaping or videotaping the interview in accordance with rules of the agency. Good cause may include, but is not limited to, such considerations as the age of the child and the nature and seriousness of the allegations under investigation. Nothing in this subsection shall be construed as prohibiting the investigating agency from audiotaping or videotaping an interview of a child on any case for which such audiotaping or videotaping is not required under this subsection. The fact that the investigating agency failed to audiotape or videotape an interview is admissible at the trial of the offense that is the subject of the interview.

(f) A person commits an offense if the person is notified of the time of the transport of a child by the department and the location from which the transport is initiated and the person is present at the location when the transport is initiated and attempts to interfere with the department's investigation. An offense under this subsection is a Class B misdemeanor. It is an exception to the application of this subsection that the department requested the person to be present at the site of the transport.

Comment

Subsection (b–1) is another in a long line of directives to CPS workers to act with consideration and respect when dealing with the parents of allegedly abused and neglected children. Whether attempts to notify the parents prior to CPS transporting the child after a report of abuse will succeed is problematic. Obviously, the issue only arises if the parent is not present when the department decides to take temporary physical custody of the child. Ordinarily, this will involve a pick up at the child's school or daycare facility. In these circumstances, it means that an attempt to notify will be unavailing if the parent is at work or out and about on one of those adventures parents often take. Nonetheless, a statutory requirement to give parents notice of CPS actions is not unprecedented, *see*, § 262.109. This has the ring of a common courtesy requirement.

§ 261.3021. Casework Documentation and Management

Subject to the appropriation of money for these purposes, the department shall:

(1) identify critical investigation actions that impact child safety and require department caseworkers to document those actions in a child's case file not later than the day after the action occurs;

(2) identify and develop a comprehensive set of casework quality indicators that must be reported in real time to support timely management oversight;

(3) provide department supervisors with access to casework quality indicators and train department supervisors on the use of that information in the daily supervision of caseworkers;

(4) develop a case tracking system that notifies department supervisors and management when a case is not progressing in a timely manner;

(5) use current data reporting systems to provide department supervisors and management with easier access to information; and

(6) train department supervisors and management on the use of data to monitor cases and make decisions.

§ 261.3022. Child Safety Check Alert List

(a) Subject to the availability of funds, the Department of Public Safety of the State of Texas shall create a child safety check alert list as part of the Texas Crime Information Center to help locate a family for purposes of investigating a report of child abuse or neglect.

(b) If the child safety check alert list is established and the department is unable to locate a family for purposes of investigating a report of child abuse or neglect, after the department has exhausted all means available to the department for locating the family, the department may seek assistance under this section from the appropriate county attorney, district attorney, or criminal district attorney with responsibility for representing the department as provided by Section 264.009.

(c) If the department requests assistance, the county attorney, district attorney, or criminal district attorney, as applicable, may file an application with the court requesting the issuance of an ex parte order requiring the Texas Crime Information Center to place the members of the family the department is attempting to locate on a child safety check alert list. The application must include a summary of:

(1) the report of child abuse or neglect the department is attempting to investigate; and

(2) the department's efforts to locate the family.

(d) If the court determines after a hearing that the department has exhausted all means available to the department for locating the family, the court shall approve the application and order the appropriate law enforcement agency to notify the Texas Crime Information Center to place the family on a child safety check alert list. The alert list must include:

(1) the name of the family member alleged to have abused or neglected a child according to the report the department is attempting to investigate;

(2) the name of the child who is the subject of the report;

(3) a code identifying the type of child abuse or neglect alleged to have been committed against the child;

(4) the family's last known address; and

(5) the minimum criteria for an entry as established by the center.

§ 261.3023. Law Enforcement Response to Child Safety Check Alert

(a) If a law enforcement officer encounters a person listed on the Texas Crime Information Center's child safety check alert list who is alleged to have abused or neglected a child, or encounters a child listed on the alert list who is the subject of a report of child abuse or neglect the department is attempting to investigate, the officer shall request information from the person or the child regarding the child's well-being and current residence.

(b) If the law enforcement officer determines that the circumstances described by Section 262.104 exist, the officer may take possession of the child without a court order as authorized by that section if the officer is able to locate the child. If the circumstances described by Section 262.104 do not exist, the officer shall obtain the child's current address and any other relevant information and report that information to the department.

§ 261.3024. Removal from Child Safety Check Alert List

(a) A law enforcement officer who locates a child listed on the Texas Crime Information Center's child safety check alert list who is the subject of a report of child abuse or neglect the department is attempting to investigate and who reports the child's current address and other relevant information to the department under Section 261.3023 shall report to the Texas Crime Information Center that the child has been located.

(b) If the department locates a child described by Subsection (a) through a means other than information reported by a law enforcement officer under Subsection (a), the department shall report to the Texas Crime Information Center that the child has been located.

(c) On receipt of notice under this section that a child has been located, the Texas Crime Information Center shall remove the child and the child's family from the child safety check alert list.

§ 261.303. Interference With Investigation; Court Order

(a) A person may not interfere with an investigation of a report of child abuse or neglect conducted by the department or designated agency.

(b) If admission to the home, school, or any place where the child may be cannot be obtained, then for good cause shown the court having family law jurisdiction shall order the parent, the person responsible for the care of the children, or the person in charge of any place where the child may be to allow entrance for the interview, examination, and investigation.

(c) If a parent or person responsible for the child's care does not consent to release of the child's prior medical, psychological, or psychiatric records or to a medical, psychological, or psychiatric examination of the child that is requested by the department or designated agency, the court having family law jurisdiction shall, for good cause shown, order the records to be released or the examination to be made at the times and places designated by the court.

(d) A person, including a medical facility, that makes a report under Subchapter B shall release to the department or designated agency, as part of the required report under Section 261.103, records that directly relate to the suspected abuse or neglect without requiring parental consent or a court order. If a child is transferred from a reporting medical facility to another medical facility to treat the injury or condition that formed the basis for the original report, the transferee medical facility shall, at the department's request, release to the department records relating to the injury or condition without requiring parental consent or a court order.

(e) A person, including a utility company, that has confidential locating or identifying information regarding a family that is the subject of an investigation under this chapter shall release that information to the department on request. The release of information to the department as required by this subsection by a person, including a utility company, is not subject to Section 552.352, Government Code, or any other law providing liability for the release of confidential information.

Comment

This section permits the department or agency investigating child abuse allegations to gather necessary information concerning the child, and prohibits interference with the investigation. Subsections (b) and (c) permit a court "for good cause shown" to order access to the child or release of relevant records as well as examination of a child reported to have been abused.

Subsection (d) makes clear that records immediately related to the report may be released as part of the report without a court order. Both the Medical Practices Act [art. 4495b, Sec. 5.08 (h)(1)] and the TEX. HEALTH & SAFETY CODE ANN. [§ 241.153(9)] provide that medical records may be released to governmental agencies as authorized or required by law. It had been unclear whether "any other pertinent information" under § 261.104 included medical records related to the report. The amendment makes clear that a doctor who reports a spiral bone fracture may show the x ray picture to an investigator without waiting for a court order or consent of the possibly abusive or negligent parents. Subsection (e) provides liability protection for utility companies and others that provide locating or identifying information about families that are subject to the investigation. *(C.G.C.)*

---

§ 261.3031. Failure to Cooperate With Investigation; Department Response

(a) If a parent or other person refuses to cooperate with the department's investigation of the alleged abuse or neglect of a child and the refusal poses a risk to the child's safety, the department shall seek assistance from the appropriate county attorney or district attorney or criminal district attorney with responsibility for representing the department as provided by Section 264.009 to obtain a court order as described by Section 261.303.

(b) A person's failure to report to an agency authorized to investigate abuse or neglect of a child within a reasonable time after receiving proper notice constitutes a refusal by the person to cooperate with the department's investigation. A summons may be issued to locate the person.

§ 261.3032. Interference with Investigation; Criminal Penalty

(a) A person commits an offense if, with the intent to interfere with the department's investigation of a report of abuse or neglect of a child, the person relocates the person's residence, either temporarily or permanently, without notifying the department of the address of the person's new residence or conceals the child and the person's relocation or concealment interferes with the department's investigation.

(b) An offense under this section is a Class B misdemeanor.

(c) If conduct that constitutes an offense under this section also constitutes an offense under any other law, the actor may be prosecuted under this section or the other law.

§ 261.304. Investigation of Anonymous Report

(a) If the department receives an anonymous report of child abuse or neglect by a person responsible for a child's care, custody, or welfare, the department shall conduct a preliminary investigation to determine whether there is any evidence to corroborate the report.

(b) An investigation under this section may include a visit to the child's home and an interview with and examination of the child and an interview with the child's parents. In addition, the department may interview any other person the department believes may have relevant information.

(c) Unless the department determines that there is some evidence to corroborate the report of abuse, the department may not conduct the thorough investigation required by this chapter or take any action against the person accused of abuse.

§ 261.305. Access to Mental Health Records

(a) An investigation may include an inquiry into the possibility that a parent or a person responsible for the care of a child who is the subject of a report under Subchapter B has a history of medical or mental illness.

(b) If the parent or person does not consent to an examination or allow the department or designated agency to have access to medical or mental health records requested by the department or agency, the court having family law jurisdiction, for good cause shown, shall order the examination to be made or that the department or agency be permitted to have access to the records under terms and conditions prescribed by the court.

(c) If the court determines that the parent or person is indigent, the court shall appoint an attorney to represent the parent or person at the hearing. The fees for the appointed attorney shall be paid as provided by Chapter 107.

(d) A parent or person responsible for the child's care is entitled to notice and a hearing when the department or designated agency seeks a court order to allow a medical, psychological, or psychiatric examination or access to medical or mental health records.

(e) This access does not constitute a waiver of confidentiality.

Comment

This section applies only to parents or caretakers of a child reported to have been abused or neglected. The court may, prior to the filing of a SAPCR, order access to the medical records of the parent or caretaker to determine if there is a history of medical or mental illness that may bear upon the probability of abuse or neglect. Subsection (c) mandates that if the parent or caretaker is indigent, an attorney must be appointed for that person. *(C.G.C.)*

---

§ 261.306. Removal of Child From State

(a) If the department or designated agency has reason to believe that a person responsible for the care, custody, or welfare of the child may remove the child from the state before the investigation is completed, the department or designated agency may file an application for a temporary restraining order in a district court without regard to continuing jurisdiction of the child as provided in Chapter 155.

(b) The court may render a temporary restraining order prohibiting the person from removing the child from the state pending completion of the investigation if the court:

(1) finds that the department or designated agency has probable cause to conduct the investigation; and

(2) has reason to believe that the person may remove the child from the state.

§ 261.307. Information Relating to Investigation Procedure

(a) As soon as possible after initiating an investigation of a parent or other person having legal custody of a child, the department shall provide to the person:

(1) a summary that:

(A) is brief and easily understood;

(B) is written in a language that the person understands, or if the person is illiterate, is read to the person in a language that the person understands; and

(C) contains the following information:

(i) the department's procedures for conducting an investigation of alleged child abuse or neglect, including:

(a) a description of the circumstances under which the department would request to remove the child from the home through the judicial system; and

(b) an explanation that the law requires the department to refer all reports of alleged child abuse or neglect to a law enforcement agency for a separate determination of whether a criminal violation occurred;

(ii) the person's right to file a complaint with the department or to request a review of the findings made by the department in the investigation;

(iii) the person's right to review all records of the investigation unless the review would jeopardize an ongoing criminal investigation or the child's safety;

(iv) the person's right to seek legal counsel;

(v) references to the statutory and regulatory provisions governing child abuse and neglect and how the person may obtain copies of those provisions; and

(vi) the process the person may use to acquire access to the child if the child is removed from the home;

(2) if the department determines that removal of the child may be warranted, a proposed child placement resources form that:

(A) instructs the parent or other person having legal custody of the child to:

(i) complete and return the form to the department or agency; and

(ii) identify in the form three individuals who could be relative caregivers or designated caregivers, as those terms are defined by Section 264.751; and

(B) informs the parent or other person of a location that is available to the parent or other person to submit the information in the form 24 hours a day either in person or by facsimile machine or e-mail; and

(3) an informational manual required by Section 261.3071.

(b) The child placement resources form described by Subsection (a)(2) must include information on the periods of time by which the department must complete a background check.

§ 261.3071. Informational Manuals

(a) In this section:

(1) "Designated caregiver" and "relative caregiver" have the meanings assigned those terms by Section 264.751.

(2) "Voluntary caregiver" means a person who voluntarily agrees to provide temporary care for a child:

(A) who is the subject of an investigation by the department or whose parent, managing conservator, possessory conservator, guardian, caretaker, or custodian is receiving family-based safety services from the department;

(B) who is not in the conservatorship of the department; and

(C) who is placed in the care of the person by the parent or other person having legal custody of the child.

(b) The department shall develop and publish informational manuals that provide information for:

(1) a parent or other person having custody of a child who is the subject of an investigation under this chapter;

(2) a person who is selected by the department to be the child's relative or designated caregiver; and

(3) a voluntary caregiver.

(c) Information provided in the manuals must be in both English and Spanish and must include, as appropriate:

(1) useful indexes of information such as telephone numbers;

(2) the information required to be provided under Section 261.307(a)(1);

(3) information describing the rights and duties of a relative or designated caregiver;

(4) information regarding the relative and other designated caregiver program under Subchapter I, Chapter 264; and

(5) information regarding the role of a voluntary caregiver, including information on how to obtain any documentation necessary to provide for a child's needs.

§ 261.308. Submission of Investigation Report

(a) The department or designated agency shall make a complete written report of the investigation.

(b) If sufficient grounds for filing a suit exist, the department or designated agency shall submit the report, together with recommendations, to the court, the district attorney, and the appropriate law enforcement agency.

(c) On receipt of the report and recommendations, the court may direct the department or designated agency to file a petition requesting appropriate relief as provided in this title.

(d) The department shall release information regarding a person alleged to have committed abuse or neglect to persons who have control over the person's access to children, including, as appropriate, the Texas Education Agency, the State Board for Educator Certification, the local school board or the school's governing body, the superintendent of the school district, or the school principal or director if the department determines that:

(1) the person alleged to have committed abuse or neglect poses a substantial and immediate risk of harm to one or more children outside the family of a child who is the subject of the investigation; and

(2) the release of the information is necessary to assist in protecting one or more children from the person alleged to have committed abuse or neglect.

(e) On request, the department shall release information about a person alleged to have committed abuse or neglect to the State Board for Educator Certification if the board has a reasonable basis for believing that the information is necessary to assist the board in protecting children from the person alleged to have committed abuse or neglect.

§ 261.309. Review of Department Investigations

(a) The department shall by rule establish policies and procedures to resolve complaints relating to and conduct reviews of child abuse or neglect investigations conducted by the department.

(b) If a person under investigation for allegedly abusing or neglecting a child requests clarification of the status of the person's case or files a complaint relating to the conduct of the department's staff or to department policy, the department shall conduct an informal review to clarify the person's status or resolve the complaint. The immediate supervisor of the employee who conducted the child abuse or neglect investigation or against whom the complaint was filed shall conduct the informal review as soon as possible but not later than the 14th day after the date the request or complaint is received.

(c) If, after the department's investigation, the person who is alleged to have abused or neglected a child disputes the department's determination of whether child abuse or neglect occurred, the person may request an administrative review of the findings. A department employee in administration who was not involved in or did not directly supervise the investigation shall conduct the review. The review must sustain, alter, or reverse the department's original findings in the investigation.

(d) Unless a civil or criminal court proceeding or an ongoing criminal investigation relating to the alleged abuse or neglect investigated by the department is pending, the department employee shall conduct the review prescribed by Subsection (c) as soon as possible but not later than the 45th day after the date the department receives the request. If a civil or criminal court proceeding or an ongoing criminal investigation is pending, the department may postpone the review until the court proceeding is completed.

(e) A person is not required to exhaust the remedies provided by this section before pursuing a judicial remedy provided by law.

(f) This section does not provide for a review of an order rendered by a court.

§ 261.310. Investigation Standards

(a) The department shall by rule develop and adopt standards for persons who investigate suspected child abuse or neglect at the state or local level. The standards shall encourage professionalism and consistency in the investigation of suspected child abuse or neglect.

(b) The standards must provide for a minimum number of hours of annual professional training for interviewers and investigators of suspected child abuse or neglect.

(c) The professional training curriculum developed under this section shall include:

(1) information concerning:

(A) physical abuse and neglect, including distinguishing physical abuse from ordinary childhood injuries;

(B) psychological abuse and neglect;

(C) available treatment resources; and

(D) the incidence and types of reports of child abuse and neglect that are received by the investigating agencies, including information concerning false reports;

(2) law–enforcement–style training, including training relating to forensic interviewing and investigatory techniques and the collection of physical evidence; and

(3) training regarding applicable federal law, including the Adoption and Safe Families Act of 1997 (Pub. L. No. 105–89) and the Child Abuse Prevention and Treatment Act (Pub. L. No. 93–247) and its subsequent amendments by the Keeping Children and Families Safe Act of 2003 (Pub. L. No. 108–36).

(d) The standards shall:

(1) recommend that videotaped and audiotaped interviews be uninterrupted;

(2) recommend a maximum number of interviews with and examinations of a suspected victim;

(3) provide procedures to preserve evidence, including the original recordings of the intake telephone calls, original notes, videotapes, and audiotapes, for one year; and

(4) provide that an investigator of suspected child abuse or neglect make a reasonable effort to locate and inform each parent of a child of any report of abuse or neglect relating to the child.

(e) The department, in conjunction with the Department of Public Safety, shall provide to the department's residential child-care facility licensing investigators advanced training in investigative protocols and techniques.

§ 261.3101. Forensic Investigation Support

The department shall, subject to the availability of money:

(1) employ or contract with medical and law enforcement professionals who shall be strategically placed throughout the state to provide forensic investigation support and to assist caseworkers with assessment decisions and intervention activities;

(2) employ or contract with subject matter experts to serve as consultants to department caseworkers in all aspects of their duties; and

(3) designate persons who shall act as liaisons within the department whose primary functions are to develop relationships with local law enforcement agencies and courts.

§ 261.311. Notice of Report

(a) When during an investigation of a report of suspected child abuse or neglect a representative of the department or the designated agency conducts an interview with or an examination of a child, the department or designated agency shall make a reasonable effort before 24 hours after the time of the interview or examination to notify each parent of the child and the child's legal guardian, if one has been appointed, of the nature of the allegation and of the fact that the interview or examination was conducted.

(b) If a report of suspected child abuse or neglect is administratively closed by the department or designated agency as a result of a preliminary investigation that did not include an interview or examination of the child, the department or designated agency shall make a reasonable effort before the expiration of 24 hours after the time the investigation is closed to notify each parent and legal guardian of the child of the disposition of the investigation.

(c) The notice required by Subsection (a) or (b) is not required if the department or agency determines that the notice is likely to endanger the safety of the child who is the subject of the report, the person who made the report, or any other person who participates in the investigation of the report.

(d) The notice required by Subsection (a) or (b) may be delayed at the request of a law enforcement agency if notification during the required time would interfere with an ongoing criminal investigation.

§ 261.312. Review Teams; Offense

(a) The department shall establish review teams to evaluate department casework and decision-making related to investigations by the department of child abuse or neglect. The department may create one or more review teams for each region of the department for child protective services. A review team is a citizen review panel or a similar entity for the purposes of federal law relating to a state's child protection standards.

(b) A review team consists of at least five members who serve staggered two-year terms. Review team members are appointed by the director of the department and consist of volunteers who live in and are broadly representative of the region in which the review team is established and have expertise in the prevention and treatment of child abuse and neglect. At least two members of a review team must be parents who have not been convicted of or indicted for an offense involving child abuse or neglect, have not been determined by the department to have engaged in child abuse or neglect, and are not under investigation by the department for child abuse or neglect. A member of a review team is a department volunteer for the purposes of Section 411.114, Government Code.

(c) A review team conducting a review of an investigation may conduct the review by examining the facts of the case as outlined by the department caseworker and law enforcement personnel. A review team member acting in the member's official capacity may receive information made confidential under Section 40.005, Human Resources Code, or Section 261.201.

(d) A review team shall report to the department the results of the team's review of an investigation. The review team's report may not include confidential information. The findings contained in a review team's report are subject to disclosure under Chapter 552, Government Code. This section does not require a law enforcement agency to divulge information to a review team that the agency believes would compromise an ongoing criminal case, investigation, or proceeding.

(e) A member of a review team commits an offense if the member discloses confidential information. An offense under this subsection is a Class C misdemeanor.

§ 261.3125. Child Safety Specialists

(a) The department shall employ in each of the department's administrative regions at least one child safety specialist. The job responsibilities of the child safety specialist must focus on child abuse and neglect investigation issues, including reports of child abuse required by Section 261.101, to achieve a greater compliance with that section, and on assessing and improving the effectiveness of the department in providing for the protection of children in the region.

(b) The duties of a child safety specialist must include the duty to:

(1) conduct staff reviews and evaluations of cases determined to involve a high risk to the health or safety of a child, including cases of abuse reported under Section 261.101, to ensure that risk assessment tools are fully and correctly used;

(2) review and evaluate cases in which there have been multiple referrals to the department of child abuse or neglect involving the same family, child, or person alleged to have committed the abuse or neglect; and

(3) approve decisions and assessments related to investigations of cases of child abuse or neglect that involve a high risk to the health or safety of a child.

§ 261.3126. Colocation of Investigators

(a) In each county, to the extent possible, the department and the local law enforcement agencies that investigate child abuse in the county shall colocate in the same offices investigators from the department and the law enforcement agencies to improve the efficiency of child abuse investigations. With approval of the local children's advocacy center and its partner agencies, in each county in which a children's advocacy center established under Section 264.402 is located, the department shall attempt to locate investigators from the department and county and municipal law enforcement agencies at the center.

(b) A law enforcement agency is not required to comply with the colocation requirements of this section if the law enforcement agency does not have a full-time peace officer solely assigned to investigate reports of child abuse and neglect.

(c) If a county does not have a children's advocacy center, the department shall work with the local community to encourage one as provided by Section 264.402.

§ 261.313. [Blank]

§ 261.314. Testing

(a) The department shall provide testing as necessary for the welfare of a child who the department believes, after an investigation under this chapter, has been sexually abused, including human immunodeficiency virus (HIV) testing of a child who was abused in a manner by which HIV may be transmitted.

(b) Except as provided by Subsection (c), the results of a test under this section are confidential.

(c) If requested, the department shall report the results of a test under this section to:

(1) a court having jurisdiction of a proceeding involving the child or a proceeding involving a person suspected of abusing the child;

(2) a person responsible for the care and custody of the child as a foster parent; and

(3) a person seeking to adopt the child.

§ 261.315. Removal of Certain Investigation Information From Records

(a) At the conclusion of an investigation in which the department determines that the person alleged to have abused or neglected a child did not commit abuse or neglect, the department shall notify the person of the person's right to request the department to remove information about the person's alleged role in the abuse or neglect report from the department's records.

(b) On request under Subsection (a) by a person whom the department has determined did not commit abuse or neglect, the department shall remove information from the department's records concerning the person's alleged role in the abuse or neglect report.

(c) The board shall adopt rules necessary to administer this section.

§ 261.316. Exemption From Fees for Medical Records

The department is exempt from the payment of a fee otherwise required or authorized by law to obtain a medical record from a hospital or health care provider if the request for a record is made in the course of an investigation by the department.

SUBCHAPTER E. INVESTIGATIONS OF ABUSE, NEGLECT, OR EXPLOITATION IN CERTAIN FACILITIES

§ 261.401. Agency Investigation

(a) Notwithstanding Section 261.001, in this section:

(1) "Abuse" means an intentional, knowing, or reckless act or omission by an employee, volunteer, or other individual working under the auspices of a facility or program that causes or may cause emotional harm or physical injury to, or the death of, a child served by the facility or program as further described by rule or policy.

(2) "Exploitation" means the illegal or improper use of a child or of the resources of a child for monetary or personal benefit, profit, or gain by an employee, volunteer, or other individual working under the auspices of a facility or program as further described by rule or policy.

(3) "Neglect" means a negligent act or omission by an employee, volunteer, or other individual working under the auspices of a facility or program, including failure to comply with an individual treatment plan, plan of care, or individualized service plan, that causes or may cause substantial emotional harm or physical injury to, or the death of, a child served by the facility or program as further described by rule or policy.

(b) Except as provided by Section 261.404, a state agency that operates, licenses, certifies, registers, or lists a facility in which children are located or provides oversight of a program that serves children shall make a prompt, thorough investigation of a report that a child has been or may be abused, neglected, or exploited in the facility or program. The primary purpose of the investigation shall be the protection of the child.

(c) A state agency shall adopt rules relating to the investigation and resolution of reports received as provided by this subchapter. The Health and Human Services Commission shall review and approve the rules of agencies other than the Texas Department of Criminal Justice, Texas Youth Commission, or Texas Juvenile Probation Commission to ensure that those agencies implement appropriate standards for the conduct of investigations and that uniformity exists among agencies in the investigation and resolution of reports.

(d) The Texas School for the Blind and Visually Impaired and the Texas School for the Deaf shall adopt policies relating to the investigation and resolution of reports received as provided by this subchapter. The Health and Human Services Commission shall review and approve the policies to ensure that the Texas School for the Blind and Visually Impaired and the Texas School for the Deaf adopt those policies in a manner consistent with the minimum standards adopted by the Health and Human Services Commission under Section 261.407.

Comment

Children in institutional settings are not only dependent on staff for personal care and protection, they are vulnerable to financial exploitation as well as abuse or neglect. "Exploitation" of a child is part of the prohibited conduct that must be investigated. The definitions of "abuse," "exploitation," and "neglect" incorporate the rules and policies of the affected agencies. *(C.G.C.)*

---

§ 261.402. Investigative Reports

(a) A state agency shall prepare and keep on file a complete written report of each investigation conducted by the agency under this subchapter.

(b) A state agency shall immediately notify the appropriate state or local law enforcement agency of any report the agency receives, other than a report from a law enforcement agency, that concerns the suspected abuse, neglect, or exploitation of a child or the death of a child from abuse or neglect. If the state agency finds evidence indicating that a child may have been abused, neglected, or exploited, the agency shall report the evidence to the appropriate law enforcement agency.

(c) A state agency that licenses, certifies, or registers a facility in which children are located shall compile, maintain, and make available statistics on the incidence of child abuse, neglect, and exploitation in the facility.

(d) A state agency shall compile, maintain, and make available statistics on the incidence of child abuse, neglect, and exploitation in a facility operated by the state agency.

§ 261.403. Complaints

(a) If a state agency receives a complaint relating to an investigation conducted by the agency concerning a facility operated by that agency in which children are located, the agency shall refer the complaint to the agency's board.

(b) The board of a state agency that operates a facility in which children are located shall ensure that the procedure for investigating abuse, neglect, and exploitation allegations and inquiries in the agency's facility is periodically reviewed under the agency's internal audit program required by Chapter 2102, Government Code.

§ 261.404. Investigations Regarding Certain Children with Mental Illness or Mental Retardation

(a) The department shall investigate a report of abuse, neglect, or exploitation of a child receiving services:

(1) in a facility operated by the Department of Aging and Disability Services or a mental health facility operated by the Department of State Health Services;

(2) in or from a community center, a local mental health authority, or a local mental retardation authority;

(3) through a program providing services to that child by contract with a facility operated by the Department of Aging and Disability Services, a mental health facility operated by the Department of State Health Services, a community center, a local mental health authority, or a local mental retardation authority;

(4) from a provider of home and community-based services who contracts with the Department of Aging and Disability Services; or

(5) in a facility licensed under Chapter 252, Health and Safety Code.

(b) The department shall investigate the report under rules developed by the executive commissioner of the Health and Human Services Commission with the advice and assistance of the department, the Department of Aging and Disability Services, and the Department of State Health Services.

(c) If a report under this section relates to a child with mental retardation receiving services in a state supported living center or the ICF–MR component of the Rio Grande State Center, the department shall, within one hour of receiving the report, notify the facility in which the child is receiving services of the allegations in the report.

(d) If during the course of the department's investigation of reported abuse, neglect, or exploitation a caseworker of the department or the caseworker's supervisor has cause to believe that a child with mental retardation described by Subsection (c) has been abused, neglected, or exploited by another person in a manner that constitutes a criminal offense under any law, including Section 22.04, Penal Code, the caseworker shall immediately notify the Health and Human Services Commission's office of inspector general and promptly provide the commission's office of inspector general with a copy of the department's investigation report.

(e) The definitions of "abuse" and "neglect" prescribed by Section 261.001 do not apply to an investigation under this section.

(f) In this section:

(1) "Community center," "local mental health authority," "local mental retardation authority," and "state supported living center" have the meanings assigned by Section 531.002, Health and Safety Code.

(2) "Provider" has the meaning assigned by Section 48.351, Human Resources Code.

§ 261.405. Investigations in Juvenile Justice Programs and Facilities

(a) In this section:

(1) "Juvenile justice facility" means a facility operated wholly or partly by the juvenile board, by another governmental unit, or by a private vendor under a contract with the juvenile board, county, or other governmental unit that serves juveniles under juvenile court jurisdiction. The term includes:

(A) a public or private juvenile pre-adjudication secure detention facility, including a holdover facility;

(B) a public or private juvenile post-adjudication secure correctional facility except for a facility operated solely for children committed to the Texas Youth Commission; and

(C) a public or private non-secure juvenile post-adjudication residential treatment facility that is not licensed by the Department of Protective and Regulatory Services or the Texas Commission on Alcohol and Drug Abuse.

(2) "Juvenile justice program" means a program or department operated wholly or partly by the juvenile board or by a private vendor under a contract with a juvenile board that serves juveniles under juvenile court jurisdiction. The term includes:

(A) a juvenile justice alternative education program;

(B) a non-residential program that serves juvenile offenders under the jurisdiction of the juvenile court; and

(C) a juvenile probation department.

(b) A report of alleged abuse, neglect, or exploitation in any juvenile justice program or facility shall be made to the Texas Juvenile Probation Commission and a local law enforcement agency for investigation.

(c) The Texas Juvenile Probation Commission shall conduct an investigation as provided by this chapter if the commission receives a report of alleged abuse, neglect, or exploitation in any juvenile justice program or facility.

(d) In an investigation required under this section, the investigating agency shall have access to medical and mental health records as provided by Subchapter D.

(e) As soon as practicable after a child is taken into custody or placed in a juvenile justice facility or juvenile justice program, the facility or program shall provide the child's parents with:

(1) information regarding the reporting of suspected abuse, neglect, or exploitation of a child in a juvenile justice facility or juvenile justice program to the Texas Juvenile Probation Commission; and

(2) the commission's toll-free number for this reporting.

Comment

This section designates the TJPC as the primary investigative agency in local "juvenile justice" facilities except those operated by the Texas Youth Commission and residential treatment facilities licensed by DFPS or the Texas Commission on Alcohol and Drug Abuse. TJPC is also given access to medical and mental health records on the same terms as the department. *(C.G.C.)*

---

§ 261.406. Investigations in Schools

(a) On receipt of a report of alleged or suspected abuse or neglect of a child in a public or private school under the jurisdiction of the Texas Education Agency, the department shall perform an investigation as provided by this chapter.

(b) The department shall send a copy of the completed report of the department's investigation to the Texas Education Agency, the State Board for Educator Certification, the local school board or the school's governing body, the superintendent of the school district, and the school principal or director, unless the principal or director is alleged to have committed the abuse or neglect, for appropriate action. On request, the department shall provide a copy of the report of investigation to the parent, managing conservator, or legal guardian of a child who is the subject of the investigation and to the person alleged to have committed the abuse or neglect. The report of investigation shall be edited to protect the identity of the persons who made the report of abuse or neglect. Other than the persons authorized by the section to receive a copy of the report, Section 261.201(b) applies to the release of the report relating to the investigation of abuse or neglect under this section and to the identity of the person who made the report of abuse or neglect.

(c) Nothing in this section may prevent a law enforcement agency from conducting an investigation of a report made under this section.

(d) The Board of Protective and Regulatory Services shall adopt rules necessary to implement this section.

Comment

The department is required to investigate allegations of abuse or neglect in schools. In practice, the requirement to redact from the reports all individuals who "provided information" for the report has not been followed because it would be impossible to write a report without identifying any of the informants. *(C.G.C.)*

§ 261.407. Minimum Standards

(a) The Health and Human Services Commission by rule shall adopt minimum standards for the investigation under Section 261.401 of suspected child abuse, neglect, or exploitation in a facility.

(b) A rule or policy adopted by a state agency or institution under Section 261.401 must be consistent with the minimum standards adopted by the Health and Human Services Commission.

(c) This section does not apply to a facility under the jurisdiction of the Texas Department of Criminal Justice, Texas Youth Commission, or Texas Juvenile Probation Commission.

§ 261.408. Information Collection

(a) The Health and Human Services Commission by rule shall adopt uniform procedures for collecting information under Section 261.401, including procedures for collecting information on deaths that occur in facilities.

(b) The department shall receive and compile information on investigations in facilities. An agency submitting information to the department is responsible for ensuring the timeliness, accuracy, completeness, and retention of the agency's reports.

(c) This section does not apply to a facility under the jurisdiction of the Texas Department of Criminal Justice, Texas Youth Commission, or Texas Juvenile Probation Commission.

§ 261.409. Investigations in Facilities Under Texas Youth Commission Jurisdiction

The board of the Texas Youth Commission by rule shall adopt standards for:

(1) the investigation under Section 261.401 of suspected child abuse, neglect, or exploitation in a facility under the jurisdiction of the Texas Youth Commission; and

(2) compiling information on those investigations.

§ 261.410. Report of Abuse by other Children

(a) In this section:

(1) "Physical abuse" means:

(A) physical injury that results in substantial harm to the child requiring emergency medical treatment and excluding an accident or reasonable discipline by a parent, guardian, or managing or possessory conservator that does not expose the child to a substantial risk of harm; or

(B) failure to make a reasonable effort to prevent an action by another person that results in physical injury that results in substantial harm to the child.

(2) "Sexual abuse" means:

(A) sexual conduct harmful to a child's mental, emotional, or physical welfare; or

(B) failure to make a reasonable effort to prevent sexual conduct harmful to a child.

(b) An agency that operates, licenses, certifies, or registers a facility shall require a residential child-care facility to report each incident of physical or sexual abuse committed by a child against another child.

(c) Using information received under Subsection (b), the agency that operates, licenses, certifies, or registers a facility shall, subject to the availability of funds, compile a report that includes information:

(1) regarding the number of cases of physical and sexual abuse committed by a child against another child;

(2) identifying the residential child-care facility;

(3) regarding the date each allegation of abuse was made;

(4) regarding the date each investigation was started and concluded;

(5) regarding the findings and results of each investigation; and

(6) regarding the number of children involved in each incident investigated.

CHAPTER 262. PROCEDURES IN SUIT BY GOVERNMENTAL ENTITY TO PROTECT HEALTH AND SAFETY OF CHILD

SUBCHAPTER A. GENERAL PROVISIONS

SUBCHAPTER B. TAKING POSSESSION OF CHILD

SUBCHAPTER C. ADVERSARY HEARING

SUBCHAPTER D. EMERGENCY POSSESSION OF CERTAIN ABANDONED CHILDREN

Editors' Note: *This chapter contains guest commentary by Charles G. Childress, Clinical Professor (retired), Children's Rights Clinic, University of Texas Law School, formerly Chief Attorney, Field Operations, Legal Division, Texas Department of Family and Protective Services, identified as (C.G.C.).*

Introductory Comment

This chapter authorizes police, juvenile probation officers, and caseworkers from DFPS to take possession of a child in an emergency. This may be done with either the prior approval of a judicial officer, or without such an order if the situation warrants immediate state intervention to rescue a child from dangerous circumstances. Because actions taken under Chapter 262 are all temporary in nature, limited case law developed until the 2008 Fifth Circuit decision in the *Gates* case discussed below.

It appears that the practices and procedures in place in the various counties vary considerably, but to an unknown degree. Since a substantial part of the foster care funding for children taken into the care of DFPS under this chapter comes from the federal government, many of the provisions in this chapter have been updated over the years to comply with changing federal mandates and interpretations, most notably the requirements of the Adoption and Safe Families Act of 1997, 42 U.S.C.A. 678 *et seq.* This chapter also contains substantive and procedural guidance for cases in which prior notice to the parent or caretaker and a hearing before removal may be provided without undue danger to the child.

In general, Chapter 262 provides very specific directions to Children's Protective Services (CPS) regarding a child allegedly abused or neglected by the child's caretaker. As such, the chapter generates very little appellate law, thanks to the rule that temporary orders are not appealable. That proposition was certainly called into question by Gates v. Texas Dept. of Protective & Regulatory Services, 537 F.3d 404 (5th Cir. 2008). In that case the federal circuit court extensively renewed the investigative procedures employed by DFPS caseworkers in response to allegations of child abuse or neglect. In the case itself, the court found that a summary judgment in favor of the agency was warranted. More importantly, however, the court found that exigent circumstances in the case did not justify warrantless entry into the parents' home and that the process was subject to the constraints on search and seizure of the Fourth Amendment.

In April 2008, the Texas Department of Protective and Human Services secured an ex parte order removing over 400 children from a compound operated by the Fundamentalist Church of the Latter Day Saints of Jesus Christ. This action sparked national news coverage as the largest child custody proceeding in the history of the United States. At the hearing for temporary orders, after two days of testimony, the trial court issued a temporary order placing all of the children in foster care around the state. A writ of mandamus was sought to reverse this ruling. The Austin Court of Appeals reversed the trial court and ordered the children released. The court held the Department had failed to meet its burden of proof under Section 262.201(b)(1), and ordered the district to vacate its temporary orders granting the Department custody. *In re* Steed, 2008 WL 2132014 (Tex. App.—Austin 2008, orig. proceeding) (mem. op.). The ruling was challenged by writ of mandamus to the Texas Supreme Court, which in a 6–3 per curiam ruling held:

> "Having carefully examined the testimony at the adversary hearing and the other evidence before us, we are not inclined to disturb the court of appeals' decision. On the record before us, removal of the children was not warranted. The Department argues without explanation that the court of appeals' decision leaves the Department unable to protect the children's safety, but the Family Code gives the district court broad authority to protect children short of separating them from their parents and placing them in foster care." *In re* Texas Dept. of Family and Protective Services, 255 S.W.3d 613, 615 (Tex. 2008).

Ultimately, all of the children were returned to the custody of their mothers or other relatives. The long term effect of this case is impossible to predict. Will it embolden more challenges to the state's effort to remove children from parents? Will it cause the state to more carefully screen those cases where the evidence is equivocal? Doubtlessly, this decision and its aftermath will be discussed for a long time to come. *(C.G.C.)*

See Chapters 161 and 263 for CLE/Other Legal Publications.

Leading Cases

Baltimore City Dept. Social Services v. Bouknight, 493 U.S. 549, 110 S.Ct. 900, 107 L.Ed.2d 992 (1990) (custodial parent ordered by the court to produce the child may not claim the Fifth Amendment privilege against self-incrimination to resist the order)

Moore v. Sims, 442 U.S. 415, 60 L.Ed.2d 994, 99 S.Ct. 2371 (1979), reversing Sims v. State Dept. of Public Welfare, 438 F. Supp. 1179 (S. D. Tex. 1977) (Texas emergency procedures found unconstitutional by three judge panel, reversed and remanded to dismiss on Younger grounds)

In re Texas Dept. of Family and Protective Serv., 255 S.W.3d 613 (Tex. 2008)(allegation of sexual abuse of post pubescent girls did not warrant trial court's temporary order to remove all 468 children from allegedly polygamous FLDS ranch—return all children ordered)

Gates v. Texas Dept. of Protective & Regulatory Services, 537 F.3d 404 (5th Cir. 2008) (Fourth Amendment applicable to investigation of alleged child abuse or neglect)

Black v. Dallas County Child Welfare Unit, 835 S.W.2d 626 (Tex. 1992) (award of attorney's fees against governmental unit for its frivolous and unreasonable actions)

Gates v. Texas Dept. of Family and Protective Services, 252 S.W.3d 90 (Tex. App.—Austin 2008, no pet.) (TDFPS does not have exclusive jurisdiction to determine child abuse cases and must grant hearing once a party requests it)

In re M.C.M., 57 S.W.3d 27 (Tex. App.—Houston [1st Dist.] 2001, no pet.) (without considering the time during which the case is stayed, a termination suit must be resolved within the time remaining on the 18 month statutory deadline)

Albright v. Texas Department of Human Services, 859 S.W.2d 575 (Tex. App.—Houston [1st Dist.] 1993, no writ) (social worker acting in good faith with reasonable cause to investigate abuse allegation is immune from personal liability)

***See* Chapters 161 and 263 and Accompanying CD–ROM for Cases Linked to Westlaw and Additional Leading Cases**

Cross Reference

Adoption Assistance and Child Welfare Act of 1980. 42 U.S.C.A. §§ 671–675

SUBCHAPTER A. GENERAL PROVISIONS

§ 262.001. Authorized Actions by Governmental Entity

(a) A governmental entity with an interest in the child may file a suit affecting the parent-child relationship requesting an order or take possession of a child without a court order as provided by this chapter.

(b) In determining the reasonable efforts that are required to be made with respect to preventing or eliminating the need to remove a child from the child's home or to make it possible to return a child to the child's home, the child's health and safety is the paramount concern.

Comment

The state, acting through DFPS or its various law enforcement agencies, has the authority and the power to rescue a child and to file a SAPCR seeking managing or possessory conservatorship or a termination of parental rights. Subsection (b) establishes that the paramount concern in protective services cases is to be the child's health and safety. *(C.G.C.)*

§ 262.002. Jurisdiction

A suit brought by a governmental entity requesting an order under this chapter may be filed in a court with jurisdiction to hear the suit in the county in which the child is found.

§ 262.003. Civil Liability

A person who takes possession of a child without a court order is immune from civil liability if, at the time possession is taken, there is reasonable cause to believe there is an immediate danger to the physical health or safety of the child.

Comment

The immunity from civil liability seems to require an objective standard of reasonableness rather than subjective good faith by the actor.

Leading Cases

DeShaney v. Winnebago County Dept. Social Services, 489 U.S. 189, 103 L.Ed.2d 249, 109 S.Ct. 998 (1989) (U.S. Const. does not mandate tort liability of caseworkers who fail to rescue abused child after report)

Gonzalez v. Avalos, 866 S.W.2d 346 (Tex. App.—El Paso 1993), writ dism'd w.o.j., 907 S.W.2d 443 (Tex. 1995) (DFPS supervisor not entitled to immunity when failed to investigate abuse allegations)

Albright v. Texas Department of Human Services, 859 S.W.2d 575 (Tex. App.—Houston [1st Dist.] 1993, no writ) (social worker acting in good faith with reasonable cause to investigate abuse allegation is immune from personal liability)

§ 262.004. Accepting Voluntary Delivery of Possession of Child

A law enforcement officer or a juvenile probation officer may take possession of a child without a court order on the voluntary delivery of the child by the parent, managing conservator, possessory conservator, guardian, caretaker, or custodian who is presently entitled to possession of the child.

§ 262.005. Filing Petition After Accepting Voluntary Delivery of Possession of Child

When possession of the child has been acquired through voluntary delivery of the child to a law enforcement officer or juvenile probation officer, the law enforcement officer or juvenile probation officer taking the child into possession shall cause a suit to be filed not later than the 60th day after the date the child is taken into possession.

§ 262.006. Living Child After Abortion

(a) An authorized representative of the Department of Protective and Regulatory Services may assume the care, control, and custody of a child born alive as the result of an abortion as defined by Chapter 161.

(b) The department shall file a suit and request an emergency order under this chapter.

(c) A child for whom possession is assumed under this section need not be delivered to the court except on the order of the court.

§ 262.007. Possession and Delivery of Missing Child

(a) A law enforcement officer who, during a criminal investigation relating to a child's custody, discovers that a child is a missing child and believes that a person may flee with or conceal the child shall take possession of the child and provide for the delivery of the child as provided by Subsection (b).

(b) An officer who takes possession of a child under Subsection (a) shall deliver or arrange for the delivery of the child to a person entitled to possession of the child.

(c) If a person entitled to possession of the child is not immediately available to take possession of the child, the law enforcement officer shall deliver the child to the Department of Protective and Regulatory Services. Until a person entitled to possession of the child takes possession of the child, the department may, without a court order, retain possession of the child not longer than five days after the date the child is delivered to the department. While the department retains possession of a child under this subsection, the department may place the child in foster home care. If a parent or other person entitled to possession of the child does not take possession of the child before the sixth day after the date the child is delivered to the department, the department shall proceed under this chapter as if the law enforcement officer took possession of the child under Section 262.104.

Comment

A law enforcement officer investigating a criminal offense related to child custody must take possession of the child if the officer believes that a person may flee with or conceal the child, and must deliver the child to a person entitled to possession or to DFPS. The department has five days to locate and deliver the child to a caretaker. If no caretaker can be found within that time, a court order must be obtained giving the department conservatorship. Neither state nor federal foster care payments are available for the cost of care of a child unless a legal proceeding is filed. This section, and a parallel provision in § 262.110, reduce county exposure for these costs by limiting the time a child may be kept by DFPS without a court order. *(C.G.C.)*

§ 262.008. Abandoned Children

(a) An authorized representative of the Department of Protective and Regulatory Services may assume the care, control, and custody of a child:

(1) who is abandoned without identification or a means for identifying the child; and

(2) whose identity cannot be ascertained by the exercise of reasonable diligence.

(b) The department shall immediately file a suit to terminate the parent-child relationship of a child under Subsection (a).

(c) A child for whom possession is assumed under this section need not be delivered to the court except on the order of the court.

Comment

If a child is abandoned without identification, the DFPS is mandated to take custody of the child and immediately file a SAPCR for termination. Procedural complications abound, of course, when there is no identification of the child. Service of citation to the abandoning person (presumably the parent, but not assuredly so), is problematic, to say nothing of the termination of the rights of the other parent, whose consent cannot be inferred. Moreover, because the identities of the parents are unknown, none of the shortcuts for citation, e.g., waiver or failure to register with the paternity registry, are applicable. Thus, it appears that service by publication will be necessary. Assuming the mystery of the child's parentage remains unsolved, termination under § 161.001(1)(G) is authorized.

§ 262.009. Temporary Care of Child Taken Into Possession

An employee of or volunteer with a law enforcement agency who successfully completes a background and criminal history check approved by the law enforcement agency may assist a law enforcement officer or juvenile probation officer with the temporary care of a child who is taken into possession by a governmental entity without a court order under this chapter until further arrangements regarding the custody of the child can be made.

§ 262.010. Child With Sexually Transmitted Disease

(a) If during an investigation by the Department of Family and Protective Services the department discovers that a child younger than 11 years of age has a sexually transmitted disease, the department shall:

(1) appoint a special investigator to assist in the investigation of the case; and

(2) file an original suit requesting an emergency order under this chapter for possession of the child unless the department determines, after taking the following actions, that emergency removal is not necessary for the protection of the child:

(A) reviewing the medical evidence to determine whether the medical evidence supports a finding that abuse likely occurred;

(B) interviewing the child and other persons residing in the child's home;

(C) conferring with law enforcement;

(D) determining whether any other child in the home has a sexually transmitted disease and, if so, referring the child for a sexual abuse examination;

(E) if the department determines a forensic interview is appropriate based on the child's age and development, ensuring that each child alleged to have been abused undergoes a forensic interview by a children's advocacy center established under Section 264.402 or another professional with specialized training in conducting forensic interviews if a children's advocacy center is not available in the county in which the child resides;

(F) consulting with a department staff nurse or other medical expert to obtain additional information regarding the nature of the sexually transmitted disease and the ways the disease is transmitted and an opinion as to whether abuse occurred based on the facts of the case;

(G) contacting any additional witness who may have information relevant to the investigation, including other individuals who had access to the child; and

(H) if the department determines after taking the actions described by Paragraphs (A)-(G) that a finding of sexual abuse is not supported, obtaining an opinion from the Forensic Assessment Center Network as to whether the evidence in the case supports a finding that abuse likely occurred.

(b) If the department determines that abuse likely occurred, the department shall work with law enforcement to obtain a search warrant to require an individual the department reasonably believes may have sexually abused the child to undergo medically appropriate diagnostic testing for sexually transmitted diseases.

Added by Acts 2011, 82nd Leg., ch. 598 (S.B. 218), § 2, eff. Sept. 1, 2011.

SUBCHAPTER B. TAKING POSSESSION OF CHILD

§ 262.101. Filing Petition Before Taking Possession of Child

An original suit filed by a governmental entity that requests permission to take possession of a child without prior notice and a hearing must be supported by an affidavit sworn to by a person with personal knowledge and stating facts sufficient to satisfy a person of ordinary prudence and caution that:

(1) there is an immediate danger to the physical health or safety of the child or the child has been a victim of neglect or sexual abuse and that continuation in the home would be contrary to the child's welfare;

(2) there is no time, consistent with the physical health or safety of the child, for a full adversary hearing under Subchapter C; and

(3) reasonable efforts, consistent with the circumstances and providing for the safety of the child, were made to prevent or eliminate the need for the removal of the child.

Comment

This provision provides both the substantive and pleading requirements when removal of a child is to be made pursuant to court order, but without prior notice to the parents to give them an opportunity for a hearing. Stripped to its essentials, the petition must be supported by an affidavit showing: (1) summary removal of the child is justified by a present risk to the child, or because of past offenses of abuse or neglect; (2) failure to remove would not be in the child's best interest; (3) the immediacy of the situation prevents notice to the parents of the ex parte hearing; and, (4) steps were taken to avoid the removal, which failed. Federal financial participation in foster care funding requires that the court find that "continuation in the home would be contrary to the child's welfare" and that "reasonable efforts" were made to prevent or eliminate the need for removal. As noted above, the child's health and safety is the paramount concern. Depending on the circumstances, relatively minimal efforts, such as asking the reporter about potential relative placements, may be all that can reasonably be expected; in other cases, where alternatives to removal are readily apparent, those alternatives must be explored. *(C.G.C.)*

§ 262.1015. Removal of Alleged Perpetrator; Offense

(a) If the department determines after an investigation that child abuse has occurred and that the child would be protected in the child's home by the removal of the alleged perpetrator of the abuse, the department shall file a petition for the removal of the alleged perpetrator from the residence of the child rather than attempt to remove the child from the residence.

(a–1) Notwithstanding Subsection (a), if the Department of Family and Protective Services determines that a protective order issued under Title 4 provides a reasonable alternative to obtaining an order under that subsection, the department may:

(1) file an application for a protective order on behalf of the child instead of or in addition to obtaining a temporary restraining order under this section; or

(2) assist a parent or other adult with whom a child resides in obtaining a protective order.

(b) A court may issue a temporary restraining order in a suit by the department for the removal of an alleged perpetrator under Subsection (a) if the department's petition states facts sufficient to satisfy the court that:

(1) there is an immediate danger to the physical health or safety of the child or the child has been a victim of sexual abuse;

(2) there is no time, consistent with the physical health or safety of the child, for an adversary hearing;

(3) the child is not in danger of abuse from a parent or other adult with whom the child will continue to reside in the residence of the child;

(4) **the parent or other adult with whom the child will continue to reside in the child's home is likely to:**

(A) make a reasonable effort to monitor the residence; and

(B) report to the department and the appropriate law enforcement agency any attempt by the alleged perpetrator to return to the residence; and

(5) the issuance of the order is in the best interest of the child.

(c) The order shall be served on the alleged perpetrator and on the parent or other adult with whom the child will continue to reside.

(d) A temporary restraining order under this section expires not later than the 14th day after the date the order was rendered.

(e) A temporary restraining order under this section and any other order requiring the removal of an alleged perpetrator from the residence of a child shall require that the parent or other adult with whom the child will continue to reside in the child's home make a reasonable effort to monitor the residence and report to the department and the appropriate law enforcement agency any attempt by the alleged perpetrator to return to the residence.

(f) The court shall order the removal of an alleged perpetrator if the court finds that the child is not in danger of abuse from a parent or other adult with whom the child will continue to reside in the child's residence and that:

(1) the presence of the alleged perpetrator in the child's residence constitutes a continuing danger to the physical health or safety of the child; or

(2) the child has been the victim of sexual abuse and there is a substantial risk that the child will be the victim of sexual abuse in the future if the alleged perpetrator remains in the residence.

(g) A person commits an offense if the person is a parent or other person with whom a child resides, the person is served with an order containing the requirement specified by Subsection (e), and the person fails to make a reasonable effort to monitor the residence of the child or to report to the department and the appropriate law enforcement agency an attempt by the alleged perpetrator to return to the residence. An offense under this section is a Class A misdemeanor.

(h) A person commits an offense if, in violation of a court order under this section, the person returns to the residence of the child the person is alleged to have abused. An offense under this subsection is a Class A misdemeanor, except that the offense is a felony of the third degree if the person has previously been convicted under this subsection.

Amended by Acts 2011, 82nd Leg., ch. 222 (H.B. 253), § 2, eff. Sept. 1, 2011; Acts 2011, 82nd Leg., ch. 598 (S.B. 218), § 3, eff. Sept. 1, 2011.

Comment

DFPS may seek an order removing an alleged perpetrator of child abuse from the home if the agency "determines" that the child can be protected in the home by a parent or other adult. Finding a fact situation in which the alleged perpetrator is ordered to leave will probably continue to be "a good idea" honored in theory, but avoided in practice. After all, what if the respondent doesn't stay away as ordered and the child is abused again? How will that read in the newspapers?

---

§ 262.102. Emergency Order Authorizing Possession of Child

(a) Before a court may, without prior notice and a hearing, issue a temporary restraining order or attachment of a child in a suit brought by a governmental entity, the court must find that:

(1) there is an immediate danger to the physical health or safety of the child or the child has been a victim of neglect or sexual abuse and that continuation in the home would be contrary to the child's welfare;

(2) there is no time, consistent with the physical health or safety of the child and the nature of the emergency, for a full adversary hearing under Subchapter C; and

(3) reasonable efforts, consistent with the circumstances and providing for the safety of the child, were made to prevent or eliminate the need for removal of the child.

(b) In determining whether there is an immediate danger to the physical health or safety of a child, the court may consider whether the child's household includes a person who has:

(1) abused or neglected another child in a manner that caused serious injury to or the death of the other child; or

(2) sexually abused another child.

(c) If, based on the recommendation of or a request by the department, the court finds that child abuse or neglect has occurred and that the child requires protection from family violence by a member of the child's family or household, the court shall render a temporary order under Chapter 71 for the protection of the child. In this subsection, "family violence" has the meaning assigned by Section 71.004.

Comment

Before issuing an ex parte order for removal of a child the court must find that the specific requirements of Subsection (a) have been met. If these prerequisites are not met, the court may order notice and set an adversary hearing under this chapter without granting ex parte relief. On rare occasion that may actually happen in some counties.

Chapter 262 provides three options for intervention by DFPS into a family: (1) emergency removal prior to obtaining a court order; (2) removal after obtaining an ex parte order; or, (3) removal after notice and hearing. Because the procedure for obtaining a court order is listed first, it may be presumed that prior judicial approval is the first option that should be considered. The department's affidavit must show facts sufficient to "satisfy a person of ordinary prudence and caution that there is an immediate danger to the physical health or safety of the child or the child has been a victim of sexual abuse." Although this standard is similar to the "probable cause" requirement for a search warrant in a criminal law context, the language used here is unique, and is intended to require only that through the exercise of "ordinary prudence and caution" the trial court be "satisfied" that the action is necessary.

In order to qualify the child for federal foster care funding the court must find both that DFPS made reasonable efforts under the circumstances to prevent or eliminate the need for removal, and that continuing in the home would be contrary to the child's welfare. Although under federal law the court may make the "reasonable efforts to prevent removal" finding after, but not more than 60 days after, the initial removal, the "contrary to welfare" finding must be made at the time of removal. It is much easier to include both required findings in the same order, especially because failure of the court to make the required finding could result in loss of all eligibility for foster care funding for the entire time the child spends in substitute care. DFPS is careful to ensure that its temporary orders contain a recitation of the federally required findings. *(C.G.C.)*

§ 262.103. Duration of Temporary Restraining Order and Attachment

A temporary restraining order or attachment of the child issued under this chapter expires not later than 14 days after the date it is issued unless it is extended as provided by the Texas Rules of Civil Procedure.

§ 262.104. Taking Possession of a Child in Emergency Without a Court Order

(a) If there is no time to obtain a temporary restraining order or attachment before taking possession of a child consistent with the health and safety of that child, an authorized representative of the Department of Family and Protective Services, a law enforcement officer, or a juvenile probation officer may take possession of a child without a court order under the following conditions, only:

(1) on personal knowledge of facts that would lead a person of ordinary prudence and caution to believe that there is an immediate danger to the physical health or safety of the child;

(2) on information furnished by another that has been corroborated by personal knowledge of facts and all of which taken together would lead a person of ordinary prudence and caution to believe that there is an immediate danger to the physical health or safety of the child;

(3) on personal knowledge of facts that would lead a person of ordinary prudence and caution to believe that the child has been the victim of sexual abuse;

(4) on information furnished by another that has been corroborated by personal knowledge of facts and all of which taken together would lead a person of ordinary prudence and caution to believe that the child has been the victim of sexual abuse; or

(5) on information furnished by another that has been corroborated by personal knowledge of facts and all of which taken together would lead a person of ordinary prudence and caution to believe that the parent or person who has possession of the child is currently using a controlled substance as defined by Chapter 481, Health and Safety Code, and the use constitutes an immediate danger to the physical health or safety of the child.

(b) An authorized representative of the Department of Family and Protective Services, a law enforcement officer, or a juvenile probation officer may take possession of a child under Subsection (a) on personal knowledge or information furnished by another, that has been corroborated by personal knowledge, that would lead a person of ordinary prudence and caution to believe that the parent or person who has possession of the child has permitted the child to remain on premises used for the manufacture of methamphetamine.

Comment

If prior judicial approval is not feasible, this section provides that a CPS caseworker, a juvenile probation officer, or a law enforcement officer may take immediate possession of a child in danger, subject to a prompt—almost invariably ex parte—judicial hearing. Although the statute seems to clearly discourage "emergency rescue" if prior notice and hearing, or at least a prior ex parte order, is feasible without endangering the child, the exact nature of the emergency is determined by the worker or officer at the scene. According to the DFPS Child Protection Services Handbook, a caseworker should consider emergency removal only if other options for protecting the child are ruled out. But, official policy and actual practice are not always congruent.

If a child is "rescued" without prior judicial approval, a post removal hearing is required "no later than the first working day after the child is taken into possession." Under supposedly extraordinary circumstances the time for the ex parte hearing may be extended to three days. By permitting this hearing to be ex parte, the statute allows the common practice of eliciting the requisite judicial approval without notice to the parents. The statute requires that the ex parte order be based upon a review of a sworn petition or affidavit; most courts seldom require sworn testimony. Although theoretically the burden of proof is on the state, it is very difficult for the court, in the absence of the parent or other caretaker, to choose to do anything other than continue possession of the child with the state until a full adversary hearing can be held as required by § 202.201. *(C.G.C.)*

§ 262.1041. Release of Child by Law Enforcement or Juvenile Probation Officer

(a) A law enforcement or juvenile probation officer who takes possession of a child under this chapter may release the child to:

(1) a child-placing agency licensed by the Department of Family and Protective Services under Chapter 42, Human Resources Code, if the agency is authorized by the department to take possession of the child;

(2) the Department of Family and Protective Services; or

(3) any other person authorized by law to take possession of the child.

(b) A child-placing agency or other authorized person who takes possession of a child under this section shall:

(1) immediately notify the Department of Family and Protective Services that the agency or other authorized person has taken possession of the child; and

(2) with the assistance of the law enforcement or juvenile probation officer who releases the child to the agency or other authorized person, complete a form prescribed by the Department of

Family and Protective Services that contains basic information regarding the child and the circumstances under which the officer took possession of the child and promptly submit the completed form to the department.

§ 262.105. Filing Petition After Taking Possession of Child in Emergency

(a) When a child is taken into possession without a court order, the person taking the child into possession, without unnecessary delay, shall:

(1) file a suit affecting the parent-child relationship;

(2) request the court to appoint an attorney ad litem for the child; and

(3) request an initial hearing to be held by no later than the first working day after the date the child is taken into possession.

(b) If the Department of Protective and Regulatory Services files a suit affecting the parent-child relationship required under Subsection (a)(1) seeking termination of the parent-child relationship, the department shall file the suit not later than the 45th day after the date the department assumes the care, control, and custody of a child under Section 262.303.

§ 262.106. Initial Hearing After Taking Possession of Child in Emergency Without Court Order

(a) The court in which a suit has been filed after a child has been taken into possession without a court order by a governmental entity shall hold an initial hearing on or before the first working day after the date the child is taken into possession. The court shall render orders that are necessary to protect the physical health and safety of the child. If the court is unavailable for a hearing on the first working day, then, and only in that event, the hearing shall be held no later than the first working day after the court becomes available, provided that the hearing is held no later than the third working day after the child is taken into possession.

(b) The initial hearing may be ex parte and proof may be by sworn petition or affidavit if a full adversary hearing is not practicable.

(c) If the initial hearing is not held within the time required, the child shall be returned to the parent, managing conservator, possessory conservator, guardian, caretaker, or custodian who is presently entitled to possession of the child.

(d) For the purpose of determining under Subsection (a) the first working day after the date the child is taken into possession, the child is considered to have been taken into possession by the Department of Protective and Regulatory Services on the expiration of the five-day period permitted under Section 262.007(c) or 262.110(b), as appropriate.

Comment

An initial hearing generally must be held on the first working day after a child is taken into the possession of the department under § 262.104. If the child is taken into possession with intent to return home, the hearing must be held on the day after expiration of the five days allowed for locating parents or custodians. *(C.G.C.)*

§ 262.107. Standard for Decision at Initial Hearing After Taking Possession of Child Without a Court Order in Emergency

(a) The court shall order the return of the child at the initial hearing regarding a child taken in possession without a court order by a governmental entity unless the court is satisfied that:

(1) there is a continuing danger to the physical health or safety of the child if the child is returned to the parent, managing conservator, possessory conservator, guardian, caretaker, or custodian who is presently entitled to possession of the child or the evidence shows that the child has been the victim of sexual abuse on one or more occasions and that there is a substantial risk that the child will be the victim of sexual abuse in the future;

(2) continuation of the child in the home would be contrary to the child's welfare; and

(3) reasonable efforts, consistent with the circumstances and providing for the safety of the child, were made to prevent or eliminate the need for removal of the child.

(b) In determining whether there is a continuing danger to the physical health or safety of a child, the court may consider whether the household to which the child would be returned includes a person who has:

(1) abused or neglected another child in a manner that caused serious injury to or the death of the other child; or

(2) sexually abused another child.

Comment

To qualify the child for federal foster care funding, the court must find that the current conditions in the home are such that continuation of the child in the home would be contrary to the child's welfare, as well as that reasonable efforts were made to prevent or eliminate the need for removal of the child. *(C.G.C.)*

§ 262.108. Unacceptable Facilities for Housing Child

When a child is taken into possession under this chapter, that child may not be held in isolation or in a jail, juvenile detention facility, or other secure detention facility.

§ 262.109. Notice to Parent, Conservator, or Guardian

(a) The department or other agency must give written notice as prescribed by this section to each parent of the child or to the child's conservator or legal guardian when a representative of the Department of Protective and Regulatory Services or other agency takes possession of a child under this chapter.

(b) The written notice must be given as soon as practicable, but in any event not later than the first working day after the date the child is taken into possession.

(c) The written notice must include:

(1) the reasons why the department or agency is taking possession of the child and the facts that led the department to believe that the child should be taken into custody;

(2) the name of the person at the department or agency that the parent, conservator, or other custodian may contact for information relating to the child or a legal proceeding relating to the child;

(3) a summary of legal rights of a parent, conservator, guardian, or other custodian under this chapter and an explanation of the probable legal procedures relating to the child; and

(4) a statement that the parent, conservator, or other custodian has the right to hire an attorney.

(d) The written notice may be waived by the court at the initial hearing:

(1) on a showing that:

(A) the parents, conservators, or other custodians of the child could not be located; or

(B) the department took possession of the child under Subchapter D; or

(2) for other good cause.

Comment

This section requires DFPS to provide a notice of removal to the parent or caretaker when it takes physical custody of a child under Chapter 262. The legislative necessity of enacting a statutory directive on this matter does not represent a high point of bureaucratic sensitivity. In the agency's defense, however, it has developed a comprehensive form to give the required notice to what may be a frantic parent who has arrived home only to find a left-alone child missing.

The court may, but is not required to, waive the required written notice under special circumstances, such as: (1) the inability to locate the parent or caretaker; (2) the child is an abandoned infant delivered to an emergency care provider under Subchapter D; or, (3) for other "good cause." By its terms, this section requires the written notice to be given by law enforcement officers, juvenile probation officers, and "designated emergency infant care providers," all of whom are authorized to take possession of a child under this chapter. *(C.G.C.)*

§ 262.1095. Information Provided to Relatives and Certain Individuals; Investigation

(a) When the Department of Family and Protective Services or another agency takes possession of a child under this chapter, the department:

(1) shall provide information as prescribed by this section to each adult the department is able to identify and locate who:

(A) is related to the child within the third degree by consanguinity as determined under Chapter 573, Government Code, or is an adult relative of the alleged father of the child who the department determines is most likely to be the child's biological father; and

(B) is identified as a potential relative or designated caregiver, as defined by Section 264.751, on the proposed child placement resources form provided under Section 261.307; and

(2) may provide information as prescribed by this section to each adult the department is able to identify and locate who has a long-standing and significant relationship with the child.

(b) The information provided under Subsection (a) must:

(1) state that the child has been removed from the child's home and is in the temporary managing conservatorship of the department;

(2) explain the options available to the individual to participate in the care and placement of the child and the support of the child's family;

(3) state that some options available to the individual may be lost if the individual fails to respond in a timely manner; and

(4) include, if applicable, the date, time, and location of the hearing under Subchapter C, Chapter 263.

(c) The department is not required to provide information to an individual if the individual has received service of citation under Section 102.009 or if the department determines providing information is inappropriate because the individual has a criminal history or a history of family violence.

(d) The department shall use due diligence to identify and locate all individuals described by Subsection (a) not later than the 30th day after the date the department files a suit affecting the parent-child relationship. In order to identify and locate the individuals described by Subsection (a), the department shall seek information from:

(1) each parent, relative, and alleged father of the child; and

(2) the child in an age-appropriate manner.

(e) The failure of a parent or alleged father of the child to complete the proposed child placement resources form does not relieve the department of its duty to seek information about the person under Subsection (d).

Added by Acts 2011, 82nd Leg., ch. 1071 (S.B. 993), § 2, eff. Sept. 1, 2011.

§ 262.110. Taking Possession of Child in Emergency With Intent to Return Home

(a) An authorized representative of the Department of Protective and Regulatory Services, a law enforcement officer, or a juvenile probation officer may take temporary possession of a child without a court order on discovery of a child in a situation of danger to the child's physical health or safety when the sole purpose is to deliver the child without unnecessary delay to the parent, managing conservator, possessory conservator, guardian, caretaker, or custodian who is presently entitled to possession of the child.

(b) Until a parent or other person entitled to possession of the child takes possession of the child, the department may retain possession of the child without a court order for not more than five days. On the expiration of the fifth day, if a parent or other person entitled to possession does not take possession of the child, the department shall take action under this chapter as if the department took possession of the child under Section 262.104.

§ 262.111. Repealed by Acts 2001, 77th Leg., ch. 849, § 10, eff. Sept. 1, 2001.

§ 262.112. Expedited Hearing and Appeal

(a) The Department of Protective and Regulatory Services is entitled to an expedited hearing under this chapter in any proceeding in which a hearing is required if the department determines that a child should be removed from the child's home because of an immediate danger to the physical health or safety of the child.

(b) In any proceeding in which an expedited hearing is held under Subsection (a), the department, parent, guardian, or other party to the proceeding is entitled to an expedited appeal on a ruling by a court that the child may not be removed from the child's home.

(c) If a child is returned to the child's home after a removal in which the department was entitled to an expedited hearing under this section and the child is the subject of a subsequent allegation of abuse or neglect, the department or any other interested party is entitled to an expedited hearing on the removal of the child from the child's home in the manner provided by Subsection (a) and to an expedited appeal in the manner provided by Subsection (b).

§ 262.113. Filing Suit Without Taking Possession of Child

An original suit filed by a governmental entity that requests to take possession of a child after notice and a hearing must be supported by an affidavit sworn to by a person with personal knowledge and stating facts sufficient to satisfy a person of ordinary prudence and caution that:

(1) reasonable efforts have been made to prevent or eliminate the need to remove the child from the child's home; and

(2) allowing the child to remain in the home would be contrary to the child's welfare.

Comment

This section specifies pleading requirements when it is not necessary to remove a child prior to notice and hearing, but family preservation efforts have failed and continuation in the home would be contrary to the child's welfare. Note that there is no requirement of immediate danger to the child when the removal is made after prior notice and full adversary hearing. The "reasonable efforts" and "contrary to welfare" provisions track federal foster care standards, and must be established for federal financial participation in the cost of foster care. *(C.G.C.)*

---

§ 262.114. Evaluation of Identified Relatives and other Designated Individuals; Placement

(a) Before a full adversary hearing under Subchapter C, the Department of Family and Protective Services must perform a background and criminal history check of the relatives or other designated individuals identified as a potential relative or designated caregiver, as defined by Section 264.751, on the proposed child placement resources form provided under Section 261.307. The department shall evaluate each person listed on the form to determine the relative or other designated individual who would be the most appropriate substitute caregiver for the child and must complete a home study of the most appropriate substitute caregiver, if any, before the full adversary hearing. Until the department identifies a relative or other designated individual qualified to be a substitute caregiver, the department must continue to explore substitute caregiver options. The time frames in this subsection do not apply to a relative or other designated individual located in another state.

(a–1) At the full adversary hearing under Section 262.201, the department shall, after redacting any social security numbers, file with the court:

(1) a copy of each proposed child placement resources form completed by the parent or other person having legal custody of the child;

(2) a copy of any completed home study performed under Subsection (a); and

(3) the name of the relative or other designated caregiver, if any, with whom the child has been placed.

(a–2) If the child has not been placed with a relative or other designated caregiver by the time of the full adversary hearing under Section 262.201, the department shall file with the court a statement that explains:

(1) the reasons why the department has not placed the child with a relative or other designated caregiver listed on the proposed child placement resources form; and

(2) the actions the department is taking, if any, to place the child with a relative or other designated caregiver.

(b) The department may place a child with a relative or other designated individual identified on the proposed child placement resources form if the department determines that the placement is in the best interest of the child. The department may place the child with the relative or designated individual before conducting the background and criminal history check or home study required under Subsection (a). The department shall provide a copy of an informational manual required under Section 261.3071 to the relative or other designated caregiver at the time of the child's placement.

(c) The department shall consider placing a child who has previously been in the managing conservatorship of the department with a foster parent with whom the child previously resided if:

(1) the department determines that placement of the child with a relative or designated caregiver is not in the child's best interest; and

(2) the placement is available and in the child's best interest.

Comment

The legislature continues to push DFPS to identify, locate, evaluate and, if at all possible, place the child with a relative or other caregiver outside the foster care system. In 2005 the legislature amended § 261.307 to require the development and use of a "proposed child placement resources form." Each parent was "required" to identify "three individuals who could be relative caregivers or designated caregivers," as possible placements when the department is considering removal of a child. Moreover, this section requires the department to perform background and criminal history checks, complete a home study, unless the proposed placement was out of state, and to place the child "if the department determines that the placement is in the best interest of the child." All of this was to occur prior to the 14 day adversary hearing. The department was also given authority to place the child with the designated caregiver before completing the background and criminal history checks or the home study.

The 2009 legislature added subsection (a-1) requiring the department to file with the court a copy of each child placement resources form provided by the a parent, a copy of any completed home study and the name of the relative or designated caregiver with whom the child was placed. Subsection (a-2) requires the department to file an explanation of why such a placement was not made and what actions, if any, the department is taking to place the child with a relative or other designated caregiver. These changes emphasize the legislative intent that the child's placement outside of foster care should be a significant issue for the court and the parties at the adversary hearing.

Subsection (c) requires the department to consider placing a child returning to foster care with the child's previous foster parents when a relative or other designated caregiver is not available or appropriate. *(C.G.C.)*

SUBCHAPTER C. ADVERSARY HEARING

§ 262.201. Full Adversary Hearing; Findings of the Court

(a) Unless the child has already been returned to the parent, managing conservator, possessory conservator, guardian, caretaker, or custodian entitled to possession and the temporary order, if any, has been dissolved, a full adversary hearing shall be held not later than the 14th day after the date the child was taken into possession by the governmental entity.

(b) At the conclusion of the full adversary hearing, the court shall order the return of the child to the parent, managing conservator, possessory conservator, guardian, caretaker, or custodian entitled to possession unless the court finds sufficient evidence to satisfy a person of ordinary prudence and caution that:

(1) there was a danger to the physical health or safety of the child which was caused by an act or failure to act of the person entitled to possession and for the child to remain in the home is contrary to the welfare of the child;

(2) the urgent need for protection required the immediate removal of the child and reasonable efforts, consistent with the circumstances and providing for the safety of the child, were made to eliminate or prevent the child's removal; and

(3) reasonable efforts have been made to enable the child to return home, but there is a substantial risk of a continuing danger if the child is returned home.

(c) If the court finds sufficient evidence to satisfy a person of ordinary prudence and caution that there is a continuing danger to the physical health or safety of the child and for the child to remain in the home is contrary to the welfare of the child, the court shall issue an appropriate temporary order under Chapter 105. The court shall require each parent, alleged father, or relative of the child before the court to complete the proposed child placement resources form provided under Section 261.307 and file the form with the court, if the form has not been previously filed with the court, and provide the Department of Family and Protective Services with information necessary to locate any other absent parent, alleged father, or relative of the child. The court shall inform each parent, alleged father, or relative of the child before the court that the person's failure to submit the proposed child placement resources form will not delay any court proceedings relating to the child. The court shall inform each parent in open court that parental and custodial rights and duties may be subject to restriction or to termination unless the parent or parents are willing and able to provide the child with a safe environment. If the court finds that the child requires protection from family violence by a member of the child's family or household, the court shall render a protective order under Title 4 for the child. In this subsection, "family violence" has the meaning assigned by Section 71.004.

(d) In determining whether there is a continuing danger to the physical health or safety of the child, the court may consider whether the household to which the child would be returned includes a person who:

(1) has abused or neglected another child in a manner that caused serious injury to or the death of the other child; or

(2) has sexually abused another child.

(e) The court shall place a child removed from the child's custodial parent with the child's noncustodial parent or with a relative of the child if placement with the noncustodial parent is inappropriate, unless placement with the noncustodial parent or a relative is not in the best interest of the child.

(f) When citation by publication is needed for a parent or alleged or probable father in an action brought under this chapter because the location of the parent, alleged father, or probable father is unknown, the court may render a temporary order without delay at any time after the filing of the action without regard to whether notice of the citation by publication has been published.

(g) For the purpose of determining under Subsection (a) the 14th day after the date the child is taken into possession, a child is considered to have been taken into possession by the department on the expiration of the five-day period permitted under Section 262.007(c) or 262.110(b), as appropriate.

Comment

The "full adversary hearing" terminology appears nowhere else in the Family Code, nor anywhere else in Texas statutes for that matter. Details regarding the exact nature of a "full adversary hearing" are left to local practice. In fact, it is clear that the reality of full adversary hearings has extreme variations across the state. In some counties the hearings are routinely conducted in a formal manner, with witnesses sworn, testifying in the witness box, and subject to direct and cross examination. Although this format is probably available in most, if not all, counties, some hearings stand in very sharp contrast with the preceding description. For example, in some counties the hearing are more conversational as the judge tries to fashion a workable scheme to protect the child while minimizing the disruption in the child's life. One such procedure is locally known as the "semicircle of justice" because all those interested array themselves in that formation before the bench and explain their positions (unsworn). Thus, the attorney representing the state, the CPS caseworkers, the parent(s) and their attorney(s), interested relatives and other persons who may provide a placement, the child's ad litem attorney, a CASA may all be present in the semicircle.

Without regard to the format of the full adversary hearing, the state has the burden of proving its right to retain possession of a child because of a continuing danger. Again the test is "satisfy a person of ordinary prudence and caution." In this section, the decision-maker is a judge rather than a caseworker, law enforcement officer, or juvenile probation officer as was the case when the child was taken into protection. Findings that "reasonable efforts" were made to allow the child to return home are also required to assure federal foster care funding. Obviously, such efforts would be of no avail if the court finds that there is a substantial risk of a continuing danger if the child is returned home.

The term "full adversary hearing" is intended to contrast with the *ex parte* hearings described in §§ 262.101, .102, .104, .106. and .112, in which "proof may be by sworn petition if a full adversary hearing is not practicable." As a practical matter (if only for the convenience of the state), those hearing are virtually always ex parte (the "may be ex parte" greatly understates the frequency). Practitioners sometimes refer to the full adversary hearing as the "fourteen day" hearing, because it is mandated to be held within 14 days after the child is taken into possession. It is not unusual for the mandate to be delayed, however, and the full adversary hearing to be continued because of difficulties with achieving service on respondent parents or the natural delay caused by the appointment of counsel for indigent parents.

Subsection (c) continues the efforts to avoid expensive foster care by requiring the court to direct the parents to complete and file the proposed child placement resources form, if it has not previously been filed. The form is described and required to be produced as soon as possible after initiating an investigation...." by § 261.307. Experience has shown that parents are sometimes reluctant to "involve" their relatives—and thus let them know about the abuse, neglect or substance abuse. It is therefore up to the court to make sure the matter is addressed. In addition to child placement resources, the court must assist DFPS by requiring each parent, alleged father or relative at the hearing to provide information necessary to locate absent alleged fathers, parents or relatives of the child.

Subsection (c) also requires the court to provide parents their first warning to reform their ways or risk losing their child.

As noted above, the "full adversary hearing" must be held within 14 days after the child is taken into possession, whether the ex parte order was issued before or after the child was taken into possession of the state. However, for purposes of the permanency deadlines under Chapter 263, the critical date is the date an order granting DFPS temporary managing conservatorship (TMC) is rendered, not the date the department came into possession of the child. TMC may have been granted in the ex parte orders under Subchapter B, or might not be granted until the conclusion of the adversary hearing.

If the court finds "sufficient evidence to satisfy a person of ordinary prudence and caution that there is a continuing danger to the physical health or safety of the child and for the child to remain in the home is contrary to the welfare of the child, the court shall issue an appropriate temporary order under Chapter 105." Section 105.001(a) provides that the court may "make a temporary order, including the modification of a prior temporary order, for the safety and welfare of the child, including an order: (1) for the temporary conservatorship of the child; (2) for the temporary support of the child; (3) restraining a party from disturbing the peace of the child or another party; (4) prohibiting a person from removing the child beyond a geographical area identified by the court; or (5) for payment of reasonable attorney's fees and expenses." § 105.001(a).

Consistent with this broad authority, subsection (e) requires the court to "place a child removed from the child's custodial parent with the child's noncustodial parent or with a relative of the child if placement with the noncustodial parent is inappropriate, unless placement with the noncustodial parent or a relative is not in the best interest of the child."

The court may render temporary orders binding on the parent or custodian before the court without regard to whether notice of citation by publication has been published. § 262.201(f). It should be kept in mind, however, that parties not before the court and who have not been served are not bound by the orders, and can request a hearing if they later appear in the case. *(C.G.C.)*

Leading Cases

In re S.P., 168 S.W.3d 197 (Tex. App.—Dallas 2005, no pet.) (if return to parent not appropriate, placement of child with suitable adult relative is preferred at full adversary hearing although best interest trumps)

In re J.M.C., 109 S.W.3d 591 (Tex. App.—Fort Worth 2003, no pet.) (14 day hearing requirement is procedural, not jurisdictional)

In re E.D.L., 105 S.W.3d 679 (Tex. App.—Fort Worth 2003, rev. denied) (14–day deadline for "full adversary hearing" not jurisdictional, but is enforceable by mandamus; statute designed to generate temporary orders pending final adjudication)

CLE/Other Legal Publications

See CLE/Legal Publications in Chapters 161 and 162, *infra*.

Temporary orders. Gary L. Nickelson, 2009 Fam. L. Boot Camp

SAPCR issues at temporary order hearings. K. Nicole Voyles, Beth A. Poulos & Richard T. Sutherland, 2009 Marriage Dissolution

Trial and presentation at temporary order hearings. Larry E. Noll, Suzanne Hansen Wooten, Coye Conner, Jr., Ronald E. Massingill, Michelle May O'Neil & Rick Robertson, 2009 Marriage Dissolution

---

§ 262.2015. Aggravated Circumstances

(a) The court may waive the requirement of a service plan and the requirement to make reasonable efforts to return the child to a parent and may accelerate the trial schedule to result in a final order for a child under the care of the department at an earlier date than provided by Subchapter D, Chapter 263, if the court finds that the parent has subjected the child to aggravated circumstances.

(b) The court may find under Subsection (a) that a parent has subjected the child to aggravated circumstances if:

(1) the parent abandoned the child without identification or a means for identifying the child;

(2) the child is a victim of serious bodily injury or sexual abuse inflicted by the parent or by another person with the parent's consent;

(3) the parent has engaged in conduct against the child that would constitute an offense under the following provisions of the Penal Code:

(A) Section 19.02 (murder);

(B) Section 19.03 (capital murder);

(C) Section 19.04 (manslaughter);

(D) Section 21.11 (indecency with a child);

(E) Section 22.011 (sexual assault);
(F) Section 22.02 (aggravated assault);
(G) Section 22.021 (aggravated sexual assault);
(H) Section 22.04 (injury to a child, elderly individual, or disabled individual);
(I) Section 22.041 (abandoning or endangering child);
(J) Section 25.02 (prohibited sexual conduct);
(K) Section 43.25 (sexual performance by a child);
(L) Section 43.26 (possession or promotion of child pornography); ~~or~~
(M) Section 21.02 (continuous sexual abuse of young child or children);
(N) Section 43.05(a)(2) (compelling prostitution); or
(O) Section 20A.02(a)(7) or (8) (trafficking of persons);

(4) the parent voluntarily left the child alone or in the possession of another person not the parent of the child for at least six months without expressing an intent to return and without providing adequate support for the child;

(5) the parent's parental rights with regard to another child have been involuntarily terminated based on a finding that the parent's conduct violated Section 161.001(1)(D) or (E) or a substantially equivalent provision of another state's law;

(6) the parent has been convicted for:

(A) the murder of another child of the parent and the offense would have been an offense under 18 U.S.C. Section 1111(a) if the offense had occurred in the special maritime or territorial jurisdiction of the United States;

(B) the voluntary manslaughter of another child of the parent and the offense would have been an offense under 18 U.S.C. Section 1112(a) if the offense had occurred in the special maritime or territorial jurisdiction of the United States;

(C) aiding or abetting, attempting, conspiring, or soliciting an offense under Subdivision (A) or (B); or

(D) the felony assault of the child or another child of the parent that resulted in serious bodily injury to the child or another child of the parent; or

(7) the parent's parental rights with regard to two other children have been involuntarily terminated.

(c) On finding that reasonable efforts to make it possible for the child to safely return to the child's home are not required, the court shall at any time before the 30th day after the date of the finding, conduct an initial permanency hearing under Subchapter D, Chapter 263. Separate notice of the permanency plan is not required but may be given with a notice of a hearing under this section.

(d) The Department of Protective and Regulatory Services shall make reasonable efforts to finalize the permanent placement of a child for whom the court has made the finding described by Subsection (c). The court shall set the suit for trial on the merits as required by Subchapter D, Chapter 263, in order to facilitate final placement of the child.

Amended by Acts 2011, 82nd Leg., ch. 1 (S.B. 24), § 4.04, eff. Sept. 1, 2011.

Comment

As required by the Adoption and Safe Families Act, 42 U.S.C.A. 678 *et seq.*, this section provides a definition of the "aggravated circumstances" which will justify a waiver of the general directive to the department to preserve the family and return the child to it. If such efforts are waived, the case must be put on a fast track to permanency. *(C.G.C.)*

§ 262.202. Identification of Court of Continuing, Exclusive Jurisdiction

If at the conclusion of the full adversary hearing the court renders a temporary order, the governmental entity shall request identification of a court of continuing, exclusive jurisdiction as provided by Chapter 155.

§ 262.203. Transfer of Suit

(a) On the motion of a party or the court's own motion, if applicable, the court that rendered the temporary order shall in accordance with procedures provided by Chapter 155:

(1) transfer the suit to the court of continuing, exclusive jurisdiction, if any;

(2) if grounds exist for mandatory transfer from the court of continuing, exclusive jurisdiction under Section 155.201, order transfer of the suit from that court; or

(3) if grounds exist for transfer based on improper venue, order transfer of the suit to the court having venue of the suit under Chapter 103.

(b) Notwithstanding Section 155.204, a motion to transfer relating to a suit filed under this chapter may be filed separately from the petition and is timely if filed while the case is pending.

(c) Notwithstanding Sections 6.407 and 103.002, a court exercising jurisdiction under this chapter is not required to transfer the suit to a court in which a parent has filed a suit for dissolution of marriage before a final order for the protection of the child has been rendered under Subchapter E, Chapter 263.

Comment

The court with jurisdiction under Chapter 262 may hear and decide mandatory transfer cases. If the facts establish that the child has resided for six months or longer in the county in which the suit for protection of the child has been filed, it is not necessary to return to the former court of continuing jurisdiction for a hearing. The Chapter 262 court may also transfer the case to the court of continuing jurisdiction or to a court with venue. A motion to transfer may be filed separately from the petition at any time before final judgment.

Subsection (c) prevents a parent from filing for divorce in a different county as a tactic to delay or derail a child protection case. The suit affecting the parent child relationship will not be transferred until a final order for the protection of the child has been entered. *(C.G.C.)*

---

§ 262.204. Temporary Order in Effect Until Superseded

(a) A temporary order rendered under this chapter is valid and enforceable until properly superseded by a court with jurisdiction to do so.

(b) A court to which the suit has been transferred may enforce by contempt or otherwise a temporary order properly issued under this chapter.

Comment

Any Texas court with jurisdiction to hear a SAPCR has authority to render an order under Chapter 262 for the protection of a child. Such orders continue in force until superseded by the court with proper venue or continuing jurisdiction, if that should prove to be a court other than one taking the emergency action.

---

§ 262.205. Hearing When Child Not in Possession of Governmental Entity

(a) In a suit requesting possession of a child after notice and hearing, the court may render a temporary restraining order as provided by Section 105.001. The suit shall be promptly set for hearing.

(b) After the hearing, the court may grant the request to remove the child from the parent, managing conservator, possessory conservator, guardian, caretaker, or custodian entitled to possession of the child if the court finds sufficient evidence to satisfy a person of ordinary prudence and caution that:

(1) reasonable efforts have been made to prevent or eliminate the need to remove the child from the child's home; and

(2) allowing the child to remain in the home would be contrary to the child's welfare.

(c) If the court orders removal of the child from the child's home, the court shall:

(1) issue an appropriate temporary order under Chapter 105; and

(2) inform each parent in open court that parental and custodial rights and duties may be subject to restriction or termination unless the parent is willing and able to provide a safe environment for the child.

(d) If citation by publication is required for a parent or alleged or probable father in an action under this chapter because the location of the person is unknown, the court may render a temporary order without regard to whether notice of the citation has been published.

(e) Unless it is not in the best interest of the child, the court shall place a child who has been removed under this section with:

(1) the child's noncustodial parent; or

(2) another relative of the child if placement with the noncustodial parent is inappropriate.

(f) If the court finds that the child requires protection from family violence by a member of the child's family or household, the court shall render a protective order for the child under Title 4.

Comment

This section provides a framework for an adversary hearing when prior removal of the child has not been necessary. The court may enjoin the parents from removing the child from the jurisdiction of the court, or render other appropriate restraining orders short of placing the child in the possession of the department as part of the "show cause" order setting the hearing. Upon hearing, the court must determine whether reasonable efforts have been made to prevent or eliminate the need to remove the child from the child's home, and whether allowing the child to remain in the home would be contrary to the child's welfare. These standards mirror federal requirements for foster care payments. However, there is no requirement that the department show an immediate danger to the child under this section. Rather the test is only that the circumstances are such that allowing the child to remain in the home would be contrary to the child's welfare. The court has authority to render temporary orders and a duty to advise the parents that their rights may be further restricted or terminated. The court also has a duty to place the child with the non-custodial parent or a relative unless placement outside the foster care system is not in the child's best interest. If the court grants temporary managing conservatorship to the department, the case must be resolved within one year in accordance with the case processing time frames for reaching permanency under Chapter 263. *(C.G.C.)*

SUBCHAPTER D. EMERGENCY POSSESSION OF CERTAIN ABANDONED CHILDREN

Introductory Comment

The provisions of this subchapter and the related Penal Code statute are commonly known as the "Baby Moses Law" (abandonment in bull rushes is optional). The intent of this subchapter is to encourage parents not to abandon infants in unsafe places by establishing "designated emergency infant care providers" that may take possession of the infant, provide care, and deliver the child to DFPS. The parent cannot be detained and is exempt from prosecution under TEX. PEN. CODE § 22.041. The parent is not exempt from prosecution for injury to the child or from termination of parental rights based on the voluntary abandonment, *see* § 161.001(S). *(C.G.C.)*

§ 262.301. Definitions

In this chapter:

(1) "Designated emergency infant care provider" means:

(A) an emergency medical services provider;

(B) a hospital; or

(C) a child-placing agency licensed by the Department of Protective and Regulatory Services under Chapter 42, Human Resources Code, that:

(i) agrees to act as a designated emergency infant care provider under this subchapter; and

(ii) has on staff a person who is licensed as a registered nurse under Chapter 301, Occupations Code, or who provides emergency medical services under Chapter 773, Health and Safety Code, and who will examine and provide emergency medical services to a child taken into possession by the agency under this subchapter.

(2) "Emergency medical services provider" has the meaning assigned that term by Section 773.003, Health and Safety Code.

§ 262.302. Accepting Possession of Certain Abandoned Children

(a) A designated emergency infant care provider shall, without a court order, take possession of a child who appears to be 60 days old or younger if the child is voluntarily delivered to the provider by the child's parent and the parent did not express an intent to return for the child.

(b) A designated emergency infant care provider who takes possession of a child under this section has no legal duty to detain or pursue the parent and may not do so unless the child appears to have been abused or neglected. The designated emergency infant care provider has no legal duty to ascertain the parent's identity and the parent may remain anonymous. However, the parent may be given a form for voluntary disclosure of the child's medical facts and history.

(c) A designated emergency infant care provider who takes possession of a child under this section shall perform any act necessary to protect the physical health or safety of the child. The designated emergency infant care provider is not liable for damages related to the provider's taking possession of, examining, or treating the child, except for damages related to the provider's negligence.

§ 262.303. Notification of Possession of Abandoned Child

(a) Not later than the close of the first business day after the date on which a designated emergency infant care provider takes possession of a child under Section 262. 302, the provider shall notify the Department of Protective and Regulatory Services that the provider has taken possession of the child.

(b) The department shall assume the care, control, and custody of the child immediately on receipt of notice under Subsection (a).

§ 262.304. Filing Petition after Accepting Possession of Abandoned Child

A child for whom the Department of Protective and Regulatory Services assumes care, control, and custody under Section 262.303 shall be treated as a child taken into possession without a court order, and the department shall take action as required by Section 262.105 with regard to the child.

§ 262.305. Report to Law Enforcement Agency; Investigation

(a) Immediately after assuming care, control, and custody of a child under Section 262.303, the Department of Protective and Regulatory Services shall report the child to appropriate state and local law enforcement agencies as a potential missing child.

(b) A law enforcement agency that receives a report under Subsection (a) shall investigate whether the child is reported as missing.

§ 262.306. Notice

Each designated emergency infant care provider shall post in a conspicuous location a notice stating that the provider is a designated emergency infant care provider location and will accept possession of a child in accordance with this subchapter.

§ 262.307. Reimbursement for Care of Abandoned Child

The department shall reimburse a designated emergency infant care provider that takes possession of a child under Section 262.302 for the cost to the provider of assuming the care, control, and custody of the child.

§ 262.308. Confidentiality

(a) All identifying information, documentation, or other records regarding a person who voluntarily delivers a child to a designated emergency infant care provider under this subchapter is confidential and not subject to release to any individual or entity except as provided by Subsection (b).

(b) Any pleading or other document filed with a court under this subchapter is confidential, is not public information for purposes of Chapter 552, Government Code, and may not be released to a person other than to a party in a suit regarding the child, the party's attorney, or an attorney ad litem or guardian ad litem appointed in the suit.

(c) In a suit concerning a child for whom the Department of Family and Protective Services assumes care, control, and custody under this subchapter, the court shall close the hearing to the public unless the court finds that the interests of the child or the public would be better served by opening the hearing to the public.

(d) Unless the disclosure, receipt, or use is permitted by this section, a person commits an offense if the person knowingly discloses, receives, uses, or permits the use of information derived from records or files described by this section or knowingly discloses identifying information concerning a person who voluntarily delivers a child to a designated emergency infant care provider. An offense under this subsection is a Class B misdemeanor.

§ 262.309. Search for Relatives Not Required

The Department of Family and Protective Services is not required to conduct a search for the relatives of a child for whom the department assumes care, control, and custody under this subchapter.

CHAPTER 263. REVIEW OF PLACEMENT OF CHILDREN UNDER CARE OF DEPARTMENT OF PROTECTIVE AND REGULATORY SERVICES (sic) [*in 2003 became the Department of Family and Protective Services*].

SUBCHAPTER A. GENERAL PROVISIONS

SUBCHAPTER B. SERVICE PLAN

SUBCHAPTER C. STATUS HEARING

SUBCHAPTER D. PERMANENCY HEARINGS

SUBCHAPTER E. FINAL ORDER FOR CHILD UNDER DEPARTMENT CARE

SUBCHAPTER F. PLACEMENT REVIEW HEARINGS

SUBCHAPTER G. EXTENDED JURISDICTION AFTER CHILD'S 18TH BIRTHDAY

Editors' Note: *In 2003 an amendment to Tex. Gov't Code. § 531.001(4)(J), changed the name of the Department of Protective and Regulatory Services, a.k.a. DPRS, to its current name of the Department of Family and Protective Services, a.k.a. DFPS. This change is also codified in Family Code § 261.001 and § 264.001. For legislation enacted in 2005 and thereafter, however, the Texas Legislative Council decided to correct the name of the agency only when amending or adding statutes to the Family Code that make reference to the agency, and not to make hundreds of corrections throughout the Code. Applying this general rule and failing to correctly amend the title of the major chapter relating to the trial of CPS cases seems both wrongheaded and just plain wrong.*

Editors' Note: *This chapter contains guest commentary by Charles G. Childress, Clinical Professor (retired), Children's Rights Clinic, University of Texas Law School, formerly Chief Attorney, Field Operations, Legal Division, Texas Department of Family and Protective Services, identified as (C.G.C.).*

Introductory Comment

This chapter provides for judicial review of the circumstances of children under the care of the Texas Department of Family and Protective Services [DFPS] to prevent children from being "lost in the welfare system."

In 1997 landmark legislation mandating a basic one year deadline for lawsuits in which the state intervenes in a family was enacted in an attempt to accelerate placement of children and to prevent them from languishing in the "care of the state." In termination or conservatorship suits filed by DFPS, the clock starts ticking on the date the court makes its temporary order appointing DFPS as the child's temporary managing conservator. As the basic rule, the court has until the first Monday after the first anniversary of that temporary order to commence the trial on the merits, § 263.401, *infra*. Of course, the basic rule has exceptions, one six months extension of the one year deadline is permitted, supposedly under strict terms. If the trial does not "commence" by the one year deadline, or within 18 months if the court grants an extension, the DFPS suit must be dismissed.

The court must schedule a status hearing at 60 days and permanency hearings at 120 day intervals thereafter, i.e., at six months, ten months, and 14 months. The hearings must address not only the needs of the child and the progress toward achieving a permanent placement for the child, but the progress of the parties toward getting the case to trial before the one-year deadline.

Even after a final judgment is rendered, the statute seeks to move the child to permanency outside the foster care system; permanent managing conservatorship with the department is the last, and least acceptable option. An appeal, if one is filed, must be accelerated, *see* § 263.405. The court must continue to monitor progress toward adoption or permanent placement in other than a foster home. *(C.G.C.)*

CLE/Other Legal Publications

Interventions in CPS cases. Robin Camille Matthews, 2011 Adv. Fam. L.

Undocumented and abused children. Pamela Kemp Parker, 2011 Adv. Fam. L.

Educational needs of children in foster care. Joy Surratt Baskin, 2011 Adv. Fam. L.

Beyond D & E—a look at the other 18 grounds for termination of parental rights. Valeria Lee Brock, 2011 Adv. Fam. L.

Dismissal dates, extraordinary circumstances, when trial on the merits commences—§263.401 TFC. Phil N. Vanderpool, 2011 Adv. Fam. L.

Termination/adoption: primer on Texas termination and adoption. Victor H. Negron Jr., 2011 U.T. Parent–Child Relationships: Basics

Legal ramifications of emotional abuse. Shelby Moore, 2010 Adv. Fam. L.

Parentage testing and child support in CPS cases. Alicia G. Key, 2010 Adv. Fam. L.

AG and CPS. Frederick S. Adams, Jr. & Alicia G. Key, 2010 Adv. Fam. L. Drafting

Youth aging out—extended foster care—foster care redesign. Phoebe Knauer & Mary Christine Reed, 2011 Adv. Fam. L.

Cross-over youth in CPS cases and juvenile cases. Dustin Rynders, 2011 Adv. Fam. L.

[CPS] Case law update. Michael C. Shulman & Trevor A. Woodruff, 2010 Adv. Fam. L.

Constitutional rights of children. Barbara J. Elias-Perciful, 2010 Adv. Fam. L.

Selected issues in parentage and termination. Ellen A. Yarrell, 2010 Adv. Fam. L.

Representing the parent in CPS cases. Thomas E. Stanton, 2010 Adv. Fam. L.

Mediation in CPS cases: ethical considerations. Karin Bonicoro, Pam Coffey & Dale A. Rabe, Jr., 2010 Adv. Fam. L.

Legal ramifications of emotional abuse. Shelby Moore, 2010 Adv. Fam. L.

Foster children and their attorneys ad litem: Resources for Children in Care. Carole Hurley, 2010 Adv. Fam. L.

What do you do with a 263.405 hearing? Sandra D. Hachem, 2010 Adv. Fam. L.

Navigating through CPS: concerns to anticipate. Lon M. Loveless, 2010 U.T. Parent–Child Rel.

Ethical when representing issues for the appointed attorney children. Charles G. Childress, 2009 Adv. Fam. L.

Child evidentiary issues and child testimony in CPS cases. Hon. J. Andrew Hathcock, 2009 Adv. Fam. L.

CPS perspectives. Charles G. Childress, 2009 U.T. Parent–Child Rel.

The Impact of Domestic Violence on the Child. Jeana Lungwitz, 2009 Adv. Fam. L.

Nuts and bolts of appointments, protective orders, and working with CPS. Hon. Judy Warne, Hon. Meca Walker, & Amy Allen, 2010 and 2009 So. Tex. Fam. L. Conf.

Navigating the CPS system. Jack W. Marr, 2007 U.T. Definitive SAPCR

Leading Cases

See case citations following § 263.401 and § 263.405, *supra*.

Baltimore City Dept. Social Services v. Bouknight, 493 U.S. 549, 110 S.Ct. 900, 107 L.Ed.2d 992 (1990) (a custodial parent ordered by the court to produce the child may not claim the Fifth Amendment privilege against self-incrimination to resist the order)

Moore v. Sims, 442 U.S. 415, 60 L.Ed.2d 994, 99 S.Ct. 2371 (1979), reversing Sims v. State Dept. of Public Welfare, 438 F. Supp. 1179 (S. D. Tex. 1977), *rev'd*, 442 U.S. 415, 60 L.Ed.2d 994, 99 S.Ct. 2371 (1979) (Texas emergency procedures found unconstitutional by three judge panel, reversed on *Younger* grounds)

Gates v. Texas Dept. of Protective & Regulatory Services, 537 F.3d 404 (5th Cir. 2008) (Fourth Amendment applicable to investigation of alleged child abuse or neglect)

See Accompanying CD–ROM for Cases Linked to Westlaw and Additional Leading Cases.

Cross Reference

Adoption Assistance and Child Welfare Act of 1980. 42 U.S.C.A. §§ 421, 671–675.

SUBCHAPTER A. GENERAL PROVISIONS

§ 263.001. Definitions

(a) In this chapter:

(1) "Department" means the Department of Family and Protective Services.

(2) "Child's home" means the place of residence of at least one of the child's parents.

(3) "Household" means a unit composed of persons living together in the same dwelling, without regard to whether they are related to each other.

(4) "Substitute care" means the placement of a child who is in the conservatorship of the department or an authorized agency in care outside the child's home. The term includes foster care, institutional care, adoption, placement with a relative of the child, or commitment to the Texas Youth Commission.

(b) In the preparation and review of a service plan under this chapter, a reference to the parents of the child includes both parents of the child unless the child has only one parent or unless, after due diligence by the department in attempting to locate a parent, only one parent is located, in which case the reference is to the remaining parent.

§ 263.002. Review of Placements by Court

In a suit affecting the parent-child relationship in which the department or an authorized agency has been appointed by the court or designated in an affidavit of relinquishment of parental rights as the temporary or permanent managing conservator of a child, the court shall hold a hearing to review:

(1) the conservatorship appointment and substitute care; and

(2) for a child committed to the Texas Youth Commission, the child's commitment in the Texas Youth Commission or release under supervision by the Texas Youth Commission.

§ 263.003. Information Relating to Placement of Child

(a) Except as provided by Subsection (b), not later than the 10th day before the date set for a hearing under this chapter, the department shall file with the court any document described by Sections 262.114(a–1) and (a–2) that has not been filed with the court.

(b) The department is not required to file the documents required by Subsection (a) if the child is in an adoptive placement or another placement that is intended to be permanent.

§ 263.004. Repealed.

§ 263.005. Enforcement of Family Service Plan

The department shall designate existing department personnel to ensure that the parties to a family service plan comply with the plan.

§ 263.006. Warning to Parents

At the status hearing under Subchapter C and at each permanency hearing under Subchapter D held after the court has rendered a temporary order appointing the department as temporary managing conservator, the court shall inform each parent in open court that parental and custodial rights and duties may be subject to restriction or to termination unless the parent or parents are willing and able to provide the child with a safe environment.

Comment

The warning to parents required by this section is a critical aspect of the permanency statute. Even if the current expectation of the department is reunification of the family, there should be a concurrent alternative plan of termination and adoption or permanent managing conservatorship with a relative or other suitable adult if the parents cannot or will not provide the child with a safe home. The court is responsible for reminding the parents and all parties of this fact in open court at each review hearing. *(C.G.C.)*

---

§ 263.007. Foster Children's Bill of Rights

Text of section as added by Acts 2011, 82nd Leg., ch. 791 (H.B. 2170), § 1. See, also, § 263.007 as added by Acts 2011, 82nd Leg., ch. 1071 (S.B. 993), § 3.

(a) In this section:

(1) "Agency foster group home," "agency foster home," "facility," "foster group home," and "foster home" have the meanings assigned by Section 42.002, Human Resources Code.

(2) "Foster care" means the placement of a child who is in the conservatorship of the department or an authorized agency and in care outside the child's home in an agency foster group home, agency foster home, foster group home, foster home, or another facility licensed or certified under Chapter 42, Human Resources Code, in which care is provided for 24 hours a day.

(3) "Foster children's bill of rights" means the rights described by Subsection (b).

(b) It is the policy of this state that each child in foster care be informed of the child's rights provided by state or federal law or policy that relate to:

(1) abuse, neglect, exploitation, discrimination, and harassment;

(2) food, clothing, shelter, and education;

(3) medical, dental, vision, and mental health services, including the right of the child to consent to treatment;

(4) emergency behavioral intervention, including what methods are permitted, the conditions under which it may be used, and the precautions that must be taken when administering it;

(5) placement with the child's siblings and contact with members of the child's family;

(6) privacy and searches, including the use of storage space, mail, and the telephone;

(7) participation in school-related extracurricular or community activities;

(8) interaction with persons outside the foster care system, including teachers, church members, mentors, and friends;

(9) contact and communication with caseworkers, attorneys ad litem, guardians ad litem, and court-appointed special advocates;

(10) religious services and activities;

(11) confidentiality of the child's records;

(12) job skills, personal finances, and preparation for adulthood;

(13) participation in a court hearing that involves the child;

(14) participation in the development of service and treatment plans;

(15) if the child has a disability, the advocacy and protection of the rights of a person with that disability; and

(16) any other matter affecting the child's ability to receive care and treatment in the least restrictive environment that is most like a family setting, consistent with the best interests and needs of the child.

(c) The department shall provide a written copy of the foster children's bill of rights to each child placed in foster care in the child's primary language, if possible, and shall inform the child of the rights described by the foster children's bill of rights:

(1) orally in the child's primary language, if possible, and in simple, nontechnical terms; or

(2) for a child who has a disability, including an impairment of vision or hearing, through any means that can reasonably be expected to result in successful communication with the child.

(d) A child placed in foster care may, at the child's option, sign a document acknowledging the child's understanding of the foster children's bill of rights after the department provides a written copy of the foster children's bill of rights to the child and informs the child of the rights described by the foster children's bill of rights in accordance with Subsection (c). If a child signs a document acknowledging the child's understanding of the foster children's bill of rights, the document must be placed in the child's case file.

(e) An agency foster group home, agency foster home, foster group home, foster home, or other facility in which a child is placed in foster care shall provide a copy of the foster children's bill of rights to a child on the child's request. The foster children's bill of rights must be printed in English and in a second language.

(f) The department shall promote the participation of foster children and former foster children in educating other foster children about the foster children's bill of rights.

(g) The department shall develop and implement a policy for receiving and handling reports that the rights of a child in foster care are not being observed. The department shall inform a child in foster care and, if appropriate, the child's parent, managing conservator, or guardian of the method for filing a report with the department under this subsection.

(h) This section does not create a cause of action.

Added by Acts 2011, 82nd Leg., ch. 791 (H.B. 2170), § 1, eff. Sept. 1, 2011.

§ 263.007. Report Regarding Notification of Relatives

Text of section as added by Acts 2011, 82nd Leg., ch. 1071 (S.B. 993), § 3. See, also, § 263.007 as added byActs 2011, 82nd Leg., ch. 791 (H.B. 2170), § 1.

Not later than the 10th day before the date set for a hearing under Subchapter C, the department shall file with the court a report regarding:

(1) the efforts the department made to identify, locate, and provide information to the individuals described by Section 262.1095;

(2) the name of each individual the department identified, located, or provided with information; and

(3) if applicable, an explanation of why the department was unable to identify, locate, or provide information to an individual described by Section 262.1095.

Added by Acts 2011, 82nd Leg., ch. 1071 (S.B. 993), § 3, eff. Sept. 1, 2011.

SUBCHAPTER B. SERVICE PLAN

§ 263.101. Department to File Service Plan

Not later than the 45th day after the date the court renders a temporary order appointing the department as temporary managing conservator of a child under Chapter 262, the department or other agency appointed as the managing conservator of a child shall file a service plan.

Comment

The requirement that DFPS present a comprehensive service plan to the court within 45 days of its appointment as temporary managing conservator is intended to expedite the processing of cases and speed final determinations by focusing the department's attention on long-range planning for the children at an early stage. *(C.G.C.)*

§ 263.1015. Service Plan Not Required

A service plan is not required under this subchapter in a suit brought by the department for the termination of the parent-child relationship for a child who has been abandoned without identification and whose identity cannot be determined.

Comment

Developing a plan of services for parents who abandon an unidentified or unidentifiable child would truly be a pointless act.

§ 263.102. Service Plan; Contents

(a) The service plan must:

(1) be specific;

(2) be in writing in a language that the parents understand, or made otherwise available;

(3) be prepared by the department or other agency in conference with the child's parents;

(4) state appropriate deadlines;

(5) state whether the goal of the plan is:

(A) return of the child to the child's parents;

(B) termination of parental rights and placement of the child for adoption; or

(C) because of the child's special needs or exceptional circumstances, continuation of the child's care out of the child's home;

(6) state steps that are necessary to:

(A) return the child to the child's home if the placement is in foster care;

(B) enable the child to remain in the child's home with the assistance of a service plan if the placement is in the home under the department's or other agency's supervision; or

(C) otherwise provide a permanent safe placement for the child;

(7) state the actions and responsibilities that are necessary for the child's parents to take to achieve the plan goal during the period of the service plan and the assistance to be provided to the parents by the department or other authorized agency toward meeting that goal;

(8) state any specific skills or knowledge that the child's parents must acquire or learn, as well as any behavioral changes the parents must exhibit, to achieve the plan goal;

(9) state the actions and responsibilities that are necessary for the child's parents to take to ensure that the child attends school and maintains or improves the child's academic compliance;

(10) state the name of the person with the department or other agency whom the child's parents may contact for information relating to the child if other than the person preparing the plan; and

(11) prescribe any other term or condition that the department or other agency determines to be necessary to the service plan's success.

(b) The service plan shall include the following statement:

TO THE PARENT: THIS IS A VERY IMPORTANT DOCUMENT. ITS PURPOSE IS TO HELP YOU PROVIDE YOUR CHILD WITH A SAFE ENVIRONMENT WITHIN THE REASONABLE PERIOD SPECIFIED IN THE PLAN. IF YOU ARE UNWILLING OR UNABLE TO PROVIDE YOUR CHILD WITH A SAFE ENVIRONMENT, YOUR PARENTAL AND CUSTODIAL DUTIES AND RIGHTS MAY BE RESTRICTED OR TERMINATED OR YOUR CHILD MAY NOT BE RETURNED TO YOU. THERE WILL BE A COURT HEARING AT WHICH A JUDGE WILL REVIEW THIS SERVICE PLAN.

(c) If both parents are available but do not live in the same household and do not agree to cooperate with one another in the development of a service plan for the child, the department in preparing the service plan may provide for the care of the child in the home of either parent or the homes of both parents as the best interest of the child requires.

(d) The department or other authorized entity must write the service plan in a manner that is clear and understandable to the parent in order to facilitate the parent's ability to follow the requirements of the service plan.

(e) Regardless of whether the goal stated in a child's service plan as required under Subsection (a)(5) is to return the child to the child's parents or to terminate parental rights and place the child for adoption, the department shall concurrently provide to the child and the child's family, as applicable:

(1) time-limited family reunification services as defined by 42 U.S.C. Section 629a for a period not to exceed the period within which the court must render a final order in or dismiss the suit affecting the parent-child relationship with respect to the child as provided by Subchapter E; and

(2) adoption promotion and support services as defined by 42 U.S.C. Section 629a.

(f) The department shall consult with relevant professionals to determine the skills or knowledge that the parents of a child under two years of age should learn or acquire to provide a safe placement for the child. The department shall incorporate those skills and abilities into the department's service plans, as appropriate.

(g) To the extent that funding is available, the service plan for a child under two years of age may require therapeutic visits between the child and the child's parents supervised by a licensed psychologist or another relevant professional to promote family reunification and to educate the parents about issues relating to the removal of the child.

§ 263.103. Original Service Plan: Signing and Taking Effect

(a) **The original service plan shall be developed jointly by the child's parents and a representative of the department or other authorized agency, including informing the parents of their rights in connection with the service plan process. If a parent is not able or willing to participate in the development of the service plan, it should be so noted in the plan.**

(a–1) Before the **original** service plan is signed, the child's parents and the representative of the department or other **authorized** agency shall discuss each term and condition of the plan.

(b) The child's parents and the person preparing the **original** service plan shall sign the plan, and the department shall give each parent a copy of the service plan.

(c) If the department or other authorized agency determines that the child's parents are unable or unwilling to **participate in the development of the original service plan or** sign the ~~service~~ plan, the department may file the plan without the parents' signatures.

(d) The **original service** plan takes effect when:

(1) the child's parents and the appropriate representative of the department or other authorized agency sign the plan; or

(2) the **court issues an order giving effect to** ~~department or other authorized agency files~~ the plan without the parents' signatures.

(e) The **original** service plan is in effect until amended by the court **or as provided under Section 263.104**.

Amended by Acts 2011, 82nd Leg., ch. 598 (S.B. 218), § 4, eff. Sept. 1, 2011.

§ 263.104. Amended Service Plan

(a) The service plan may be amended at any time. **The department shall work with the parents to jointly develop any amendment to the service plan, including informing the parents of their rights in connection with the amended service plan process.**

(b) The amended service plan supersedes the previously filed service plan and takes effect when:

(1) the child's parents and the appropriate representative of the department or other authorized agency sign the plan; or

(2) the department or other authorized agency determines that the child's parents are unable or unwilling to sign the amended plan and files it without the parents' signatures.

(c) **A parent may file a motion with the court at any time to request a review and modification of the amended service plan** ~~The amended service plan remains in effect until amended by the court~~.

(d) An amended service plan remains in effect until:

(1) superseded by a later-amended service plan that goes into effect as provided by Subsection (b); or

(2) modified by the court.

Amended by Acts 2011, 82nd Leg., ch. 598 (S.B. 218), § 5, eff. Sept. 1, 2011.

§ 263.105. Review of Service Plan; Modification

(a) The service plan currently in effect shall be filed with the court.

(b) The court shall review the plan at the next required hearing under this chapter after the plan is filed.

(c) The court may modify an original or amended service plan at any time.

Acts 2011, 82nd Leg., ch. 1071 (S.B. 993), §§ 4, 5, eff. Sept. 1, 2011.

§ 263.106. Court Implementation of Service Plan

After reviewing the original or any amended service plan and making any changes or modifications it deems necessary, the ~~The~~ court **shall incorporate the original and any amended service plan into the orders of the court and** may render **additional** appropriate orders to implement or require compliance with an original or amended service plan.

Amended by Acts 2011, 82nd Leg., ch. 598 (S.B. 218), § 6, eff. Sept. 1, 2011.

SUBCHAPTER C. STATUS HEARING

§ 263.201. Status Hearing; Time

(a) Not later than the 60th day after the date the court renders a temporary order appointing the department as temporary managing conservator of a child, the court shall hold a status hearing to review the child's status and the service plan developed for the child.

(b) A status hearing is not required if the court holds an initial permanency hearing under Section 262.2015 **and makes findings required by Section 263.202** before the date a status hearing is required by this section.

(c) The court shall require each parent, alleged father, or relative of the child before the court to submit the proposed child placement resources form provided under Section 261.307 at the status hearing, if the form has not previously been submitted.

Amended by Acts 2011, 82nd Leg., ch. 1071 (S.B. 993), § 6, eff. Sept. 1, 2011.

Comment

The status review hearing must be held not later than 60 days after the appointment of DFPS as temporary managing conservator of the child. If a status hearing is not held because the parents have been found guilty of subjecting the child to "aggravated circumstances," the case will be on an even faster track. The court has only 30 days after the order under § 262.2015 to hold the initial permanency hearing. *(C.G.C.)*

---

§ 263.202. Status Hearing; Findings

(a) If all **persons** ~~parties~~ entitled to citation and notice **of a status hearing** under this chapter were not served, the court shall make findings as to whether:

(1) the department or other agency has exercised due diligence to locate all necessary persons, **including an alleged father of the child, regardless of whether the alleged father is registered with the registry of paternity under Section 160.402**; and

(2) **the child and** each ~~custodial~~ parent, alleged father, or relative of the child before the court **have** ~~has~~ furnished to the department all available information necessary to locate **an** ~~another~~ absent parent, alleged father, or relative of the child through exercise of due diligence.

(b) Except as **otherwise** provided by **this subchapter** ~~Subsection (e)~~, a status hearing shall be limited to matters related to the contents and execution of the service plan filed with the court. The court shall review the service plan that the department or other agency filed under this chapter for reasonableness, accuracy, and compliance with requirements of court orders and make findings as to whether:

(1) a plan that has the goal of returning the child to the child's parents adequately ensures that reasonable efforts are made to enable the child's parents to provide a safe environment for the child; ~~and~~

(2) the child's parents have reviewed and understand the ~~service~~ plan and have been advised that unless the parents are willing and able to provide the child with a safe environment, even with the assistance of a service plan, within the reasonable period of time specified in the plan, the parents' parental and custodial duties and rights may be subject to restriction or to termination under this code or the child may not be returned to the parents;

(3) the plan is reasonably tailored to address any specific issues identified by the department or other agency; and

(4) the child's parents and the representative of the department or other agency have signed the plan.

(b–1) After reviewing the service plan and making any necessary modifications, the court shall incorporate the service plan into the orders of the court and may render additional appropriate orders to implement or require compliance with the plan.

~~(c) The court shall advise the parties that progress under the service plan will be reviewed at all subsequent hearings, including a review of whether the parties have acquired or learned any specific skills or knowledge stated in the service plan.~~

~~(d) If a service plan with respect to a parent has not been filed with the court, the court shall consider whether to waive the service plan under Section 262.2015.~~

(e) At the status hearing, the court shall make a finding as to whether the court has identified the individual who has the right to consent for the child under Section 266.003.

(f) The court shall review the report filed by the department under Section 263.007 and inquire into the sufficiency of the department's efforts to identify, locate, and provide information to each adult described by Section 262.1095(a). The court shall order the department to make further efforts to identify, locate, and provide information to each adult described by Section 262.1095(a) if the court determines that the department's efforts have not been sufficient.

(g) The court shall give the child's parents an opportunity to comment on the service plan.

(h) If a proposed child placement resources form as described by Section 261.307 has not been submitted, the court shall require each parent, alleged father, or other person to whom the department is required to provide a form to submit a completed form.

Amended by Acts 2011, 82nd Leg., ch. 1071 (S.B. 993), §§ 7, 9, eff. Sept. 1, 2011.

Comment

The court is directed to inquire at the status hearing whether parents or other parties have provided information necessary to locate an alleged father, an absent parent, or a relative of the child, and inquire into the department's efforts to locate and provide information to relatives. As usual, it is left to the court to decide what action, if any, should be taken. Subsection (b) makes clear that the parties may not use the status hearing to relitigate the issues that the court decided at the full adversary hearing, i.e., the removal of the child from the home. However, the court is directed to review the reasonableness, adequacy and compliance of the service plan with prior orders and statutory requirements, review the sufficiency of the department's efforts to identify, locate and provide information the parents and relatives, and make "appropriate" orders to implement an appropriate service plan. The court may not waive a service plan, although if the parents are totally uncooperative, the plan may be implemented without their signatures. *(C.G.C.)*

§ 263.203. Appointment of Attorney Ad Litem; Admonishments

(a) The court shall advise the parties of the provisions regarding the mandatory appointment of an attorney ad litem under Subchapter A, Chapter 107, and shall appoint an attorney ad litem to represent the interests of any person eligible if the appointment is required by that subchapter.

(b) The court shall advise the parties that progress under the service plan will be reviewed at all subsequent hearings, including a review of whether the parties have acquired or learned any specific skills or knowledge stated in the plan.

Added by Acts 2011, 82nd Leg., ch. 1071 (S.B. 993), § 8, eff. Sept. 1, 2011.

SUBCHAPTER D. PERMANENCY HEARINGS

Introductory Comment

Review hearings held during the time that DFPS has placed the child in temporary foster care are named "permanency" hearings to distinguish them from "placement review" hearings, which are held after a final judgment is rendered. The federal government does not make this distinction, and requires that the state continue to seek true permanency for the child both before and after a "final" order is rendered on the original petition. This semantic distinction apparently fits the definition of "without a difference." *(C.G.C.)*

---

§ 263.301. Notice

(a) Notice of a permanency hearing shall be given as provided by Rule 21a, Texas Rules of Civil Procedure, to all persons entitled to notice of the hearing.

(b) The following persons are entitled to at least 10 days' notice of a permanency hearing and are entitled to present evidence and be heard at the hearing:

(1) the department;

(2) the foster parent, preadoptive parent, relative of the child providing care, or director of the group home or institution where the child is residing;

(3) each parent of the child;

(4) the managing conservator or guardian of the child;

(5) an attorney ad litem appointed for the child under Chapter 107;

(6) a volunteer advocate appointed for the child under Chapter 107; and

(7) any other person or agency named by the court to have an interest in the child's welfare.

(c) If a person entitled to notice under Chapter 102 or this section has not been served, the court shall review the department's or other agency's efforts at attempting to locate all necessary persons and requesting service of citation and the assistance of a parent in providing information necessary to locate an absent parent.

§ 263.302. Child's Attendance at Hearing

The child shall attend each permanency hearing unless the court specifically excuses the child's attendance. A child committed to the Texas Youth Commission may attend a permanency hearing in person, by telephone, or by videoconference. The court shall consult with the child in a developmentally appropriate manner regarding the child's permanency plan, if the child is four years of age or older and if the court determines it is in the best interest of the child. Failure by the child to attend a hearing does not affect the validity of an order rendered at the hearing.

Comment

Mandating the child's attendance unless excused states the obverse of the former statute which allowed the court to "dispense with the attendance of the child." The child is, after all, the focus of these permanency plans and hearings. Although the court controls the extent of the child's participation, his or her presence puts a human face on what might otherwise appear bureaucratic or perfunctory. A child in custody for a juvenile offense with the Texas Youth Commission may participate in person, by telephone or by videoconference. While the child's absence won't invalidate the results of the hearing, the sense of the statute is that ordinarily the child should attend.

---

§ 263.3025. Permanency Plan

(a) The department shall prepare a permanency plan for a child for whom the department has been appointed temporary managing conservator. The department shall give a copy of the plan to each person entitled to notice under Section 263.301(b) not later than the 10th day before the date of the child's first permanency hearing.

(b) In addition to the requirements of the department rules governing permanency planning, the permanency plan must contain the information required to be included in a permanency progress report under Section 263.303.

(c) The department shall modify the permanency plan for a child as required by the circumstances and needs of the child.

(d) In accordance with department rules, a child's permanency plan must include concurrent permanency goals consisting of a primary permanency goal and at least one alternate permanency goal.

§ 263.3026. Permanency Goals; Limitation

(a) The department's permanency plan for a child may include as a goal:

(1) the reunification of the child with a parent or other individual from whom the child was removed;

(2) the termination of parental rights and adoption of the child by a relative or other suitable individual;

(3) the award of permanent managing conservatorship of the child to a relative or other suitable individual; or

(4) another planned, permanent living arrangement for the child.

(b) If the goal of the department's permanency plan for a child is to find another planned, permanent living arrangement for the child, the department shall document that there is a compelling reason why the other permanency goals identified in Subsection (a) are not in the child's best interest.

§ 263.303. Permanency Progress Report

(a) Not later than the 10th day before the date set for each permanency hearing other than the first permanency hearing, the department or other authorized agency shall file with the court and provide to each party, the child's attorney ad litem, the child's guardian ad litem, and the child's volunteer advocate a permanency progress report unless the court orders a different period for providing the report.

(b) The permanency progress report must:

(1) recommend that the suit be dismissed; or

(2) recommend that the suit continue, and:

(A) identify the date for dismissal of the suit under this chapter;

(B) provide:

(i) the name of any person entitled to notice under Chapter 102 who has not been served;

(ii) a description of the efforts by the department or another agency to locate and request service of citation; and

(iii) a description of each parent's assistance in providing information necessary to locate an unserved party;

(C) evaluate the parties' compliance with temporary orders and with the service plan;

(D) evaluate whether the child's placement in substitute care meets the child's needs and recommend other plans or services to meet the child's special needs or circumstances;

(E) describe the permanency plan for the child and recommend actions necessary to ensure that a final order consistent with that permanency plan, including the concurrent permanency goals contained in that plan, is rendered before the date for dismissal of the suit under this chapter;

(F) with respect to a child 16 years of age or older, identify the services needed to assist the child in the transition to adult life; and

(G) with respect to a child committed to the Texas Youth Commission or released under supervision by the Texas Youth Commission:

(i) evaluate whether the child's needs for treatment and education are being met;

(ii) describe, using information provided by the Texas Youth Commission, the child's progress in any rehabilitation program administered by the Texas Youth Commission; and

(iii) recommend other plans or services to meet the child's needs.

(c) A parent whose parental rights are the subject of a suit affecting the parent-child relationship, the attorney for that parent, or the child's attorney ad litem or guardian ad litem may file a response to the department's or other agency's report filed under Subsection (b). A response must be filed not later than the third day before the date of the hearing.

Comment

In its permanency progress report DFPS must either recommend that its suit be dismissed, i.e., that the child be returned home, or that the suit continue. In addition to a focus on the child's needs and possible family services, DFPS must provide its calculation of the dismissal date and include information about barriers to the plan to bring the case to trial before the dismissal date, such as problems with service of citation and other locate problems. All parties and the child's advocates are entitled to a copy of the report 10 days prior to the hearing, and may file a written response to correct or challenge the report. The responses, if filed, should be filed at least three days before the hearing. In actual practice. The 10–day deadline is often missed, which ordinarily has little consequence beyond a justified complaint being lodged without eliciting a sanction.*(C.G.C.)*

§ 263.304. Initial Permanency Hearing; Time

(a) Not later than the 180th day after the date the court renders a temporary order appointing the department as temporary managing conservator of a child, the court shall hold a permanency hearing to review the status of, and permanency plan for, the child to ensure that a final order consistent with that permanency plan is rendered before the date for dismissal of the suit under this chapter.

(b) The court shall set a final hearing under this chapter on a date that allows the court to render a final order before the date for dismissal of the suit under this chapter. Any party to the suit or an attorney ad litem for the child may seek a writ of mandamus to compel the court to comply with the duties imposed by this subsection.

Comment

Consistent with the one-year deadline for temporary foster care, the first permanency hearing is to be held within 180 days after the appointment of DFPS as temporary managing conservator. Subsection (b) gives the department, the parents, and the child an enforceable right to obtain a timely trial setting in order to dispose of the case within the required time-frames. *(C.G.C.)*

§ 263.305. Subsequent Permanency Hearings

A subsequent permanency hearing before entry of a final order shall be held not later than the 120th day after the date of the last permanency hearing in the suit. For good cause shown or on the court's own motion, the court may order more frequent hearings.

Comment

Permanency hearings are timed to bring the case to the attention of the court several times before the absolute dismissal date deadline. Except when the "monitored return to parent" provision, § 263.403, comes into play, the deadline for any case for the first permanency hearing is about 180 days before the "Monday next" one-year deadline in the case. On this schedule, the second permanency hearing will be about 120 days later, which will be approximately 60 days prior to the one-year deadline. If an extension is granted, there will be a hearing at 420 days. If there is to be yet another permanency hearing, it must be held before the 540–day mark, which is the drop-dead deadline of 18 months. *(C.G.C.)*

Leading Cases

In re L.S.C., 169 S.W.3d 758 (Tex. App.—Dallas 2005, no pet.) (after one year time limitation for final order exceeded, DFPS should have been dismissed as party to suit)

In re N.V.D., 102 S.W.3d 268 (Tex. App.—Beaumont 2003, no pet.) (failure to conduct permanency review hearing within 120 days of prior permanency review harmless error; mother partially responsible)

---

§ 263.306. Permanency Hearings: Procedure

(a) At each permanency hearing the court shall:

(1) identify all persons or parties present at the hearing or those given notice but failing to appear;

(2) review the efforts of the department or another agency in:

(A) attempting to locate all necessary persons;

(B) requesting service of citation; and

(C) obtaining the assistance of a parent in providing information necessary to locate an absent parent, alleged father, or relative of the child;

(3) review the efforts of each custodial parent, alleged father, or relative of the child before the court in providing information necessary to locate another absent parent, alleged father, or relative of the child;

(4) return the child to the parent or parents if the child's parent or parents are willing and able to provide the child with a safe environment and the return of the child is in the child's best interest;

(5) place the child with a person or entity, other than a parent, entitled to service under Chapter 102 if the person or entity is willing and able to provide the child with a safe environment and the placement of the child is in the child's best interest;

(6) evaluate the department's efforts to identify relatives who could provide the child with a safe environment, if the child is not returned to a parent or another person or entity entitled to service under Chapter 102;

(7) evaluate the parties' compliance with temporary orders and the service plan;

(8) determine whether:

(A) the child continues to need substitute care;

(B) the child's current placement is appropriate for meeting the child's needs, including with respect to a child who has been placed outside of the state, whether that placement continues to be in the best interest of the child; and

(C) other plans or services are needed to meet the child's special needs or circumstances;

(9) if the child is placed in institutional care, determine whether efforts have been made to ensure placement of the child in the least restrictive environment consistent with the best interest and special needs of the child;

(10) if the child is 16 years of age or older, order services that are needed to assist the child in making the transition from substitute care to independent living if the services are available in the community;

(11) determine plans, services, and further temporary orders necessary to ensure that a final order is rendered before the date for dismissal of the suit under this chapter;

(12) if the child is committed to the Texas Youth Commission or released under supervision by the Texas Youth Commission, determine whether the child's needs for treatment, rehabilitation, and education are being met; and

(13) determine the date for dismissal of the suit under this chapter and give notice in open court to all parties of:

(A) the dismissal date;

(B) the date of the next permanency hearing; and

(C) the date the suit is set for trial.

(b) The court shall also review the service plan, permanency report, and other information submitted at the hearing to:

(1) determine:

(A) the safety of the child;

(B) the continuing necessity and appropriateness of the placement;

(C) the extent of compliance with the case plan;

(D) the extent of progress that has been made toward alleviating or mitigating the causes necessitating the placement of the child in foster care; and

(E) whether the department has made reasonable efforts to finalize the permanency plan that is in effect for the child, including the concurrent permanency goals for the child; and

(2) project a likely date by which the child may be returned to and safely maintained in the child's home, placed for adoption, or placed in permanent managing conservatorship.

Comment

Procedures for permanency hearings focus on the one-year time limit for temporary foster care, as well as on the child's current placement and prospects for being placed in a safe and permanent home. The court evaluates the efforts of the department and other parties to locate and serve necessary parties (a potential barrier to meeting the deadline), and to identify relatives who might care for the child. The court may remove the child from foster care and place the child with a parent or nonparent who can provide a safe environment consistent with the child's best interests. However, unless the department is removed as temporary managing conservator, placement outside foster care does not stop the clock on the permanency deadline.

A monitored placement with the parent under § 263.403, with the department maintaining temporary managing conservatorship, can toll the running of the time limit for up to six months. But, the monitored placement order must be carefully drafted in exact compliance with the statute. *See In re* Neal, 4 S.W.3d 443 (Tex. App.—Houston [1st Dist.] 1999, orig. proceeding). If the child remains in foster care with the clock still ticking, the court must determine what else needs to be done to ensure that the time limit is met. And, just to make sure that all parties get the message that there is a deadline coming up, the court must warn the parents, as required by § 263.006, that their rights may be terminated and give all parties notice of the upcoming dismissal date, the next permanency hearing, and the setting of a trial on the merits.

Subsection (b) conforms to 42 U.S.C.A. § 675(5)(B), to ensure that all federal permanency review requirements of the Adoption and Safe Families Act of 1997 are brought to the attention of the court and addressed. *(C.G.C.)*

§ 263.307. Factors in Determining Best Interest of Child

(a) In considering the factors established by this section, the prompt and permanent placement of the child in a safe environment is presumed to be in the child's best interest.

(b) The following factors should be considered by the court, the department, and other authorized agencies in determining whether the child's parents are willing and able to provide the child with a safe environment:

(1) the child's age and physical and mental vulnerabilities;

(2) the frequency and nature of out-of-home placements;

(3) the magnitude, frequency, and circumstances of the harm to the child;

(4) whether the child has been the victim of repeated harm after the initial report and intervention by the department or other agency;

(5) whether the child is fearful of living in or returning to the child's home;

(6) the results of psychiatric, psychological, or developmental evaluations of the child, the child's parents, other family members, or others who have access to the child's home;

(7) whether there is a history of abusive or assaultive conduct by the child's family or others who have access to the child's home;

(8) whether there is a history of substance abuse by the child's family or others who have access to the child's home;

(9) whether the perpetrator of the harm to the child is identified;

(10) the willingness and ability of the child's family to seek out, accept, and complete counseling services and to cooperate with and facilitate an appropriate agency's close supervision;

(11) the willingness and ability of the child's family to effect positive environmental and personal changes within a reasonable period of time;

(12) whether the child's family demonstrates adequate parenting skills, including providing the child and other children under the family's care with:

(A) minimally adequate health and nutritional care;

(B) care, nurturance, and appropriate discipline consistent with the child's physical and psychological development;

(C) guidance and supervision consistent with the child's safety;

(D) a safe physical home environment;

(E) protection from repeated exposure to violence even though the violence may not be directed at the child; and

(F) an understanding of the child's needs and capabilities; and

(13) whether an adequate social support system consisting of an extended family and friends is available to the child.

(c) In the case of a child 16 years of age or older, the following guidelines should be considered by the court in determining whether to adopt the permanency plan submitted by the department:

(1) whether the permanency plan submitted to the court includes the services planned for the child to make the transition from foster care to independent living; and

(2) whether this transition is in the best interest of the child.

SUBCHAPTER E. FINAL ORDER FOR CHILD UNDER DEPARTMENT CARE

§ 263.401. Dismissal After One Year; Extension

(a) Unless the court has commenced the trial on the merits or granted an extension under Subsection (b), on the first Monday after the first anniversary of the date the court rendered a temporary order appointing the department as temporary managing conservator, the court shall dismiss the suit affecting the parent-child relationship filed by the department that requests termination of the parent-child relationship or requests that the department be named conservator of the child.

(b) Unless the court has commenced the trial on the merits, the court may not retain the suit on the court's docket after the time described by Subsection (a) unless the court finds that extraordinary circumstances necessitate the child remaining in the temporary managing conservatorship of the department and that continuing the appointment of the department as temporary managing conservator is in the best interest of the child. If the court makes those findings, the court may retain the suit on the court's docket for a period not to exceed 180 days after the time described by Subsection (a). If the court retains the suit on the court's docket, the court shall render an order in which the court:

(1) schedules the new date on which the suit will be dismissed if the trial on the merits has not commenced, which date must be not later than the 180th day after the time described by Subsection (a);

(2) makes further temporary orders for the safety and welfare of the child as necessary to avoid further delay in resolving the suit; and

(3) sets the trial on the merits on a date not later than the date specified under Subdivision (1).

(c) If the court grants an extension but does not commence the trial on the merits before the required date for dismissal under Subsection (b), the court shall dismiss the suit. The court may not grant an additional extension that extends the suit beyond the required date for dismissal under Subsection (b).

(d) Repealed by Acts 2007, 80th Leg., ch. 866, § 5.

Comment

Texas children can no longer be kept in temporary foster care indefinitely, as once was true. The threat of mandatory dismissal of the department's suit has forced DFPS to accelerate its own assessment process and to push the courts for final resolution of the cases.

In 1997 the "dismissal after one year" requirement was instituted thanks to recommendations of the Supreme Court Task Force on Foster Care, chaired by Judge John Specia of San Antonio. The members of the task force believed that generally one year was a sufficient time for parents, or caretakers, to either reform their conduct or suffer the consequences. There was a recognition, however, that in some instances a one-year timeframe would be inadequate to achieve the appropriate result. Thus, in the spirit of compromise, a one-time six month extension was authorized.

Originally the statute was basically silent regarding the standard for the court to apply in ordering an extension. The mere statement that the extension must be in the best interest of the child was, in fact, is no standard at all, other than ceding complete discretion to the trial court.

As long as statutes must be written in the English language, whenever deviation from an absolute rule is contemplated, debate is inevitable. Any formulation will of necessity be subject to "statutory construction." Nonetheless, in 2005 the legislature determined to bring a greater degree of clarity to the always slippery concept of an "exception to the rule." Mandating that an extension should be granted only for "extraordinary circumstances" clearly indicates a stricter application of the time-frame than previously was perceived to have been the norm. The revised test seems to have succeeded in restricting the number of extensions ordered. Obviously, this conclusion will vary from county to county, or from judge to judge; after all, "extraordinary circumstances also will depend on the eye of the beholder.

Subsections (b) and (c) reinforce the trial court's duty to set the trial date before the extended dismissal date. A trial court that still fails to set a final hearing on the merits in a timely manner may face a petition for mandamus under § 263.304. Since 2007 commencement of a trial on the merits, not rendition of a final order before the deadline, is the test for preventing dismissal of the action for exceeding the allowed time for resolution of the case. *(C.G.C.)*

CLE/Other Legal Publications

Educational needs of children in foster care. Joy Surratt Baskin, 2011 ADV. FAM. L.

Dismissal dates, extraordinary circumstances, when trial on the merits commences—§263.401 TFC. Phil N. Vanderpool, 2011 ADV. FAM. L.

Youth aging out—extended foster care—foster care redesign. Phoebe Knauer & Mary Christine Reed, 2011 ADV. FAM. L.

Mediation in CPS cases: ethical considerations. Karin Bonicoro, Pam Coffey & Dale A. Rabe, Jr., 2010 ADV. FAM. L.

What do you do with a 263.405 hearing? Sandra D. Hachem, 2010 ADV. FAM. L.

Ethical when representing issues for the appointed attorney children. Charles G. Childress, 2009 ADV. FAM. L.

Child evidentiary issues and child testimony in CPS cases. Hon. J. Andrew Hathcock, 2009 ADV. FAM. L.

Leading Cases

Gates v. Texas Dept. of Protective and Regulatory Services, 537 F.3d 404 (5th Cir. 2008)(Fourth Amendment applies to warrantless search by CPS in alleged abuse and neglect cases)

In re J.H.G., 302 S.W.3d 304 (Tex.2010) (appellate court may not consider issues not included in points of appeal; remanded on issue raised but not decided) (dismissal date is procedural, not jurisdictional); *accord, In re* Department of Family and Protective Services, 273 S.W.3d 637 (Tex. 2009)

In re J.O.A., 283 S.W.3d 336 (Tex. 2009) (15-day rule for statement of points on appeal unconstitutional as applied, due process requires right to assert ineffective assistance of counsel)

In re Dept. of Family & Protective Services, 273 S.W.3d 637 (Tex. 2009) (termination decreed, new trial purportedly granted by note on docket sheet after one-year time limit without further orders; time to resolve case had expired, case dismissed)

In re Lovito-Nelson , 278 S.W.3d 773 (Tex. 2009) (motion for new trial requires signed order; final SAPCR effective after 75 days)

In re Texas Dept. of Family and Protective Services, 210 S.W.3d 609 (Tex. 2006) (trial court should have dismissed case after one-year deadline passed—because mother had remedy by accelerated appeal, mandamus improper)

In re R.R., 209 S.W.3d 112 (Tex. 2006) (default termination decree reversed, new trial granted *re Craddock* test—CPS had time for new trial or seek 180 day extension)

In re K.A.F., 160 S.W.3d 923 (Tex. 2005) (timeline for accelerated appeal of termination not affected by post-trial motions); *accord In re* J.L., 163 S.W.3d 79 (Tex. 2005) (but new final order from grant of post-trial motion restarts accelerated appeal time frame)

In re T.D.S.T., 287 S.W.3d 268 (Tex. App.—Amarillo 2009, no pet.) and, Garza v. Texas Dept. of Family and Protective Services, 212 S.W.3d 373 (Tex. App.—Austin,2006, no pet.) (A.J.'s report is rendition of final order under § 263.401)

In re J.L.C., 194 S.W.3d 667 (Tex. App.—Fort Worth 2006, motion granted) (mother's request for extension of one year deadline binds her to 18 months maximum for decision)

In re L.S.C., 169 S.W.3d 758 (Tex. App.—Dallas 2005, no pet.) (after one year time limitation for final order exceeded, DPRS should have been dismissed as party to suit)

§ 263.402. Limit on Extension; Waiver

(a) The parties to a suit under this chapter may not extend the deadlines set by the court under this subchapter by agreement or otherwise.

(b) A party to a suit under this chapter who fails to make a timely motion to dismiss the suit under this subchapter waives the right to object to the court's failure to dismiss the suit. A motion to dismiss under this subsection is timely if the motion is made before the trial on the merits commences.

Comment

The parties may not extend the statutory deadlines set by the court by agreement. In addition, a party may not lie behind a log and jump out crying "dismissal" after the department has commenced its case-in-chief at trial. Because either party may compel the court to set the case for trial, a party that fails to seek dismissal before the department commences the trial waives the mandatory dismissal provision. *(C.G.C.)*

Leading Cases

In re J.B.W., 99 S.W.3d 218 (Tex. App.—Fort Worth 2003, rev. denied) (parents waived right to object on appeal to trial court's failure to dismiss termination after statutory time expired—"remedial" statute applied retroactively)

In re Bishop, 8 S.W.3d 412 (Tex. App.—Waco 1999, mand. denied) (order following permanency hearing constituted extension order)

§ 263.403. Monitored Return of Child to Parent

(a) Notwithstanding Section 263.401, the court may retain jurisdiction and not dismiss the suit or render a final order as required by that section if the court renders a temporary order that:

(1) finds that retaining jurisdiction under this section is in the best interest of the child;

(2) orders the department to return the child to the child's parent;

(3) orders the department to continue to serve as temporary managing conservator of the child; and

(4) orders the department to monitor the child's placement to ensure that the child is in a safe environment.

(b) If the court renders an order under this section, the court shall:

(1) include in the order specific findings regarding the grounds for the order; and

(2) schedule a new date, not later than the 180th day after the date the temporary order is rendered, for dismissal of the suit unless a trial on the merits has commenced.

(c) If a child placed with a parent under this section must be moved from that home by the department before the dismissal of the suit or the commencement of the trial on the merits, the court shall, at the time of the move, schedule a new date for dismissal of the suit unless a trial on the merits has commenced. The new dismissal date may not be later than the original dismissal date established under Section 263.401 or the 180th day after the date the child is moved under this subsection, whichever date is later.

(d) If the court renders an order under this section, the court must include in the order specific findings regarding the grounds for the order.

Comment

The permanency clock keeps running as long as the child is out of the home in the temporary conservatorship of DFPS, whether the substitute care is paid foster care or an unpaid relative placement. The only exception to this rule is provided by this section, which permits a monitored placement back with the parents for up to 180 days. If the placement breaks down and the child must be returned to substitute care, the court has until 180 days after the removal or the original dismissal date, whichever is later, to render a final order. If the placement back in the home extends beyond 180 days, both state and federal law require a new removal order meeting the requirements of Chapter 262. Not only is the suit subject to dismissal, but federal foster care funding is not available if the child is removed from the home after 180 days of "monitoring" in the absence of a new removal order. *(C.G.C.)*

---

§ 263.404. Final Order Appointing Department as Managing Conservator Without Terminating Parental Rights

(a) The court may render a final order appointing the department as managing conservator of the child without terminating the rights of the parent of the child if the court finds that:

(1) appointment of a parent as managing conservator would not be in the best interest of the child because the appointment would significantly impair the child's physical health or emotional development; and

(2) it would not be in the best interest of the child to appoint a relative of the child or another person as managing conservator.

(b) In determining whether the department should be appointed as managing conservator of the child without terminating the rights of a parent of the child, the court shall take the following factors into consideration:

(1) that the child will reach 18 years of age in not less than three years;

(2) that the child is 12 years of age or older and has expressed a strong desire against termination or being adopted;

(3) that the child has special medical or behavioral needs that make adoption of the child unlikely; and

(4) the needs and desires of the child.

Comment

Permanent foster care is a poor option for any child. Even a "committed foster parent" cannot guarantee a child the stability that a relative or adoptive family can provide. Thus, the legislature has restated the parental presumption from § 153.131(a), and added a requirement that relative placement be considered before placement with DFPS. Permanent managing conservatorship of a child with the state should clearly be the last option considered. The department is not permitted to set a goal of permanent managing conservatorship to the department, referred to in federal law as "Another Planned, Permanent Living Arrangement," unless there is a documented, compelling reason that reunification, adoption, or permanent managing conservatorship to a relative or other suitable individual are not in the child's best interest. § 263.3026. *(C.G.C.)*

§ 263.405. Appeal of Final Order

(a) An appeal of a final order rendered under this subchapter is governed by the **procedures** ~~rules of the supreme court~~ for accelerated appeals in civil cases **under the Texas Rules of Appellate Procedure** ~~and the procedures provided by this section~~. The appellate court shall render its final order or judgment with the least possible delay.

(b) **A final order rendered under this subchapter must contain the following prominently displayed statement in boldfaced type, in capital letters, or underlined: "A PARTY AFFECTED BY THIS ORDER HAS THE RIGHT TO APPEAL. AN APPEAL IN A SUIT IN WHICH TERMINATION OF THE PARENT-CHILD RELATIONSHIP IS SOUGHT IS GOVERNED BY THE PROCEDURES FOR ACCELERATED APPEALS IN CIVIL CASES UNDER THE TEXAS RULES OF APPELLATE PROCEDURE. FAILURE TO FOLLOW THE TEXAS RULES OF APPELLATE PROCEDURE FOR ACCELERATED APPEALS MAY RESULT IN THE DISMISSAL OF THE APPEAL."** ~~Not later than the 15th day after the date a final order is signed by the trial judge, a party who intends to request a new trial or appeal the order must file with the trial court:(1) a request for a new trial; or(2) if an appeal is sought, a statement of the point or points on which the party intends to appeal.~~

~~(b-1) The statement under Subsection (b)(2) may be combined with a motion for a new trial.~~

(c) **The supreme court shall adopt rules accelerating the disposition by the appellate court and the supreme court of an appeal of a final order granting termination of the parent-child relationship rendered under this subchapter.** ~~A motion for a new trial, a request for findings of fact and conclusions of law, or any other post-trial motion in the trial court does not extend the deadline for filing a notice of appeal under Rule 26.1(b), Texas Rules of Appellate Procedure, or the deadline for filing an affidavit of indigence under Rule 20, Texas Rules of Appellate Procedure.~~

~~(d) The trial court shall hold a hearing not later than the 30th day after the date the final order is signed to determine whether:~~

~~(1) a new trial should be granted;~~

~~(2) a party's claim of indigence, if any, should be sustained; and~~

~~(3) the appeal is frivolous as provided by Section 13.003(b), Civil Practice and Remedies Code.~~

~~(e) If a party claims indigency and requests the appointment of an attorney, the court shall require the person to file an affidavit of indigency and shall hear evidence to determine the issue of indigency. If the court does not render a written order denying the claim of indigence or requiring the person to pay partial costs before the 36th day after the date the final order being appealed is signed, the court shall consider the person to be indigent and shall appoint counsel to represent the person.~~

~~(f) The appellate record must be filed in the appellate court not later than the 60th day after the date the final order is signed by the trial judge, unless the trial court, after a hearing, grants a new trial or denies a request for a trial court record at no cost.~~

~~(g) The appellant may appeal the court's order denying the appellant's claim of indigence or the court's finding that the appeal is frivolous by filing with the appellate court the reporter's record and clerk's record of the hearing held under this section, both of which shall be provided without advance payment, not later than the 10th day after the date the court makes the decision. The appellate court shall review the records and may require the parties to file appellate briefs on the issues presented, but may not hear oral argument on the issues. The appellate court shall render appropriate orders after reviewing the records and appellate briefs, if any.~~

~~(h) Except on a showing of good cause, the appellate court may not extend the time for filing a record or appellate brief.~~

~~(i) The appellate court may not consider any issue that was not specifically presented to the trial court in a timely filed statement of the points on which the party intends to appeal or in a statement combined with a motion for new trial. For purposes of this subsection, a claim that a judicial decision is contrary to the evidence or that the evidence is factually or legally insufficient is not sufficiently specific to preserve an issue for appeal.~~

Amended by Acts 2011, 82nd Leg., ch. 75 (H.B. 906), §§ 4, 5, eff. Sept. 1, 2011.

Comment

Whether or not termination is granted, CPS cases are accelerated appeals under the Texas Rules of Appellate Procedure. A notice of appeal must be filed within 20 days after the judgment is signed. Unlike an ordinary appeal, a motion for new trial or other post-trial motion does not extend the deadline for filing a notice of accelerated appeal.

A final order in a CPS case must include the statutory notice specified in subsection (b) that any appeal must comply with the rules applicable to accelerated appeals and failure to follow the rules may result in dismissal of the appeal. Effective September 1, 2011, the detailed trial-level procedures formerly provided by this section are repealed. *(C.G.C.)*

On July 2, 2010, Justice Nathan Hecht, speaking for the court, issued a declaration that this section, as applied to the father whose parental rights had been terminated, was a denial of his constitutional rights to due process. On more than one occasion, the accelerated timetable for perfecting appeals has served as a trap for the unwary, denying an appeal on strictly, and onerous, procedural grounds.

Given the nature of a biennial legislative process, luckily the erroneous statute capable of unconstitutional application was corrected in less than a year. (Lucky because a similar decision in an odd numbered July would be forced to languish for nearly two years.)

The new version of § 263.405 retains the principle of an accelerated for a termination of parental rights, but in a far more transparent fashion that establishes a more reasonable approach to the difficulties involved in combining relative speed with understandable rules, as follows:

(1) the accelerated appeals are subject to the usual rules under the Texas Rules of Appellate Procedure;

(2) yet another prominent warning is formulated in order to give fair notice of the rule and the consequences for failure to comply;

(3) the 15 day time frame to seek a new trial or to appeal, identifying point or points to be asserted, is deleted;

(4) the supreme court is directed to adopt rules to assure accelerating the disposition of the case by the appellate system;

(5) deletes the most of the extraordinary details formerly found in the section to wit: (b-1) (relating to providing for authorizing the combination of a statement of the point or points on which a party intends to appeal with a motion for a new trial, (d) (relating to requiring the trial court to hold a hearing not later than the 30th day after the date the final order is signed), (e) (relating to

requiring a party to file an affidavit of indigency), (f) (relating to the filing of the appellate record), (g) (relating to the reporter's record and the clerk's record), (h) (relating to prohibiting the appellate court from extending the time for filing a record or appellate brief except on a showing of good cause), and (i) (relating to prohibiting the appellate court from considering any issue not specifically timely presented to the trial court.

Effective September 1, 2011, the detailed trial-level procedures formerly provided by this section are repealed.

Caveat: the caselaw cited below should be subjected to strict scrutiny given the sweeping revision of the statute. *(C.G.C. & J.J.S.)*

Leading Cases

In re B.G., 317 S.W.3d 250 (Tex. 2010) (accelerated timetable for perfecting appeals of termination of parental rights under this section violated father's due process rights; failure to timely file statement of appellate points cannot be basis for denying indigent parent's right to appellate record)

In re J.H.G., 302 S.W.3d 304 (Tex.2010) (appellate court may not consider issues not included in points of appeal; remanded on issue raised but not decided) (dismissal date is procedural, not jurisdictional); accord, In re Department of Family and Protective Services, 273 S.W.3d 637 (Tex.2009)

In re J.O.A., 283 S.W.3d 336 (Tex. 2009) (ineffective assistance of counsel claim may be raised on appeal despite failure to include it in statement of points; § 263.405(i) unconstitutional as applied when construed as precluding parent from raising alleged insufficiency of the evidence)

In re Dept. of Family & Protective Services, 273 S.W.3d 637 (Tex. 2009) (termination decreed; new trial granted after one-year time limit had passed without further orders being rendered—time to resolve case expired, so case dismissed)

In re M.N., 262 S.W.3d 799 (Tex. 2008) (fairness permits trial court to extend time to file statement of points of appeal for good cause shown)

In re K.C.B., 251 S.W.3d 514 (Tex. 2008) (statement of points on appeal may be supplemented for consideration of merits)

In re M.C.T., 250 S.W.3d 161 (Tex. App.—Fort Worth 2008, no pet.) (15–day filing requirement for a statement of points of appeal violates separation of powers provision of the Texas Constitution)

See Accompanying CD–ROM for Cases Linked to Westlaw and Additional Leading Cases.

---

§ 263.406. Court Information System

The Office of Court Administration of the Texas Judicial System shall consult with the courts presiding over cases brought by the department for the protection of children to develop an information system to track compliance with the requirements of this subchapter for the timely disposition of those cases.

§ 263.407. Final Order Appointing Department as Managing Conservator of Certain Abandoned Children; Termination of Parental Rights

(a) There is a rebuttable presumption that a parent who delivers a child to a designated emergency infant care provider in accordance with Subchapter D, Chapter 262:

(1) is the child's biological parent;

(2) intends to relinquish parental rights and consents to the termination of parental rights with regard to the child; and

(3) intends to waive the right to notice of the suit terminating the parent-child relationship.

(a–1) A party that seeks to rebut a presumption in Subsection (a) may do so at any time before the parent-child relationship is terminated with regard to the child.

(b) If a person claims to be the parent of a child taken into possession under Subchapter D, Chapter 262, before the court renders a final order terminating the parental rights of the child's parents, the court shall order genetic testing for parentage determination unless parentage has previously been established. The court shall hold the petition for termination of the parent-child relationship in abeyance for a period not to exceed 60 days pending the results of the genetic testing.

(c) Before the court may render an order terminating parental rights with regard to a child taken into the department's custody under Section 262.303, the department must:

(1) verify with the National Crime Information Center and state and local law enforcement agencies that the child is not a missing child; and

(2) obtain a certificate of the search of the paternity registry under Subchapter E, Chapter 160, not earlier than the date the department estimates to be the 30th day after the child's date of birth.

Comment

Proof that the parent has voluntarily delivered the child to a designated emergency infant care provider under § 262.302, the so called "Baby Moses Law," creates a rebuttable presumption in a termination suit. This section provides a further presumption of parental consent to that termination. If an alleged father or the mother appears after a child has been safely delivered to an emergency care provider and seeks to rebut the presumption and oppose the termination, any necessary genetic testing must be done within 60 days. The department must check with the National Crime Information Center and the paternity registry to verify that the child is not a "missing child" and that no man has registered for notice of a child born about the time of the surrendered infant. This section is far removed from Chapter 161, which establishes the grounds for termination of parental rights. *(C.G.C.)*

Voluntary delivery of an infant child to a designated emergency infant care provider under § 262.302, the so called "Baby Moses Law," creates crucial rebuttable presumptions in a suit for termination of the parents. These include that the parents are unknown and that one of them is the person who delivered the child (invariably the mother). This section provides a further presumption of parental consent to that termination.

If a person, or persons, appear claiming to be the father or the mother after a child has been safely delivered to an emergency care provider seeking to rebut the presumption and oppose the termination, necessary genetic testing must be done within 60 days. Also the department must check with the National Crime Information Center and the paternity registry to verify that the child is not a "missing child," and that no man has registered for notice of a child born about the time of the surrendered infant.

Unfortunately, this section is rather far removed from Chapter 161, which establishes the grounds for termination of parental rights, which runs some risk of it being lost in the shuffle.

SUBCHAPTER F. PLACEMENT REVIEW HEARINGS

Introductory Comment

Section 153.375 requires a non-parent managing conservator other than DFPS to file an annual report of the child's welfare with the court. DFPS, however, must provide detailed information to the court for review of the child's situation every six months. *(C.G.C.)*

§ 263.501. Placement Review After Final Order

(a) If the department has been named as a child's managing conservator in a final order that does not include termination of parental rights, the court shall conduct a placement review hearing at least once every six months until the child becomes an adult.

(b) If the department has been named as a child's managing conservator in a final order that terminates a parent's parental rights, the court shall conduct a placement review hearing not later than the 90th day after the date the court renders the final order. The court shall conduct additional placement review hearings at least once every six months until the date the child is adopted or the child becomes an adult.

(c) Notice of a placement review hearing shall be given as provided by Rule 21a, Texas Rules of Civil Procedure, to each person entitled to notice of the hearing.

(d) The following are entitled to not less than 10 days' notice of a placement review hearing and are entitled to present evidence and be heard at the hearing:

(1) the department;

(2) the foster parent, preadoptive parent, relative of the child providing care, or director of the group home or institution in which the child is residing;

(3) each parent of the child;

(4) each possessory conservator or guardian of the child;

(5) the child's attorney ad litem and volunteer advocate, if the appointments were not dismissed in the final order; and

(6) any other person or agency named by the court as having an interest in the child's welfare.

(e) The licensed administrator of the child-placing agency responsible for placing the child is entitled to not less than 10 days' notice of a placement review hearing.

(f) The child shall attend each placement review hearing unless the court specifically excuses the child's attendance. A child committed to the Texas Youth Commission may attend a placement review hearing in person, by telephone, or by videoconference. The court shall consult with the child in a developmentally appropriate manner regarding the child's permanency or transition plan, if the child is four years of age or older. Failure by the child to attend a hearing does not affect the validity of an order rendered at the hearing.

(g) A court required to conduct placement review hearings for a child for whom the department has been appointed permanent managing conservator may not dismiss a suit affecting the parent-child relationship filed by the department regarding the child while the child is committed to the Texas Youth Commission or released under the supervision of the Texas Youth Commission, unless the child is adopted or permanent managing conservatorship of the child is awarded to an individual other than the department.

Comment

The court must hold a placement review hearing within 90 days if parental rights have been terminated, and thereafter at least every six months on all cases until the child is adopted, the final order is modified and the child placed in the permanent managing conservatorship of someone other than the department, or the child becomes an adult. Federal law requires these reviews be held at least once per year as a condition of federal funding for the substitute care. To ensure that the department is not the only potential source of information for the court, notice of the hearing must be given at least 10 days in advance to adults having regular contact or ongoing relationships with the child. These requirements apply to youth in the juvenile justice system, and subsection (g) prohibits the trial court from dismissing the department's case simply because the youth has been committed to TYC. *(C.G.C.)*

---

§ 263.502. Placement Review Report

(a) Not later than the 10th day before the date set for a placement review hearing, the department or other authorized agency shall file a placement review report with the court and provide a copy to each person entitled to notice under Section 263.501(d).

(b) For good cause shown, the court may order a different time for filing the placement review report or may order that a report is not required for a specific hearing.

(c) The placement review report must identify the department's permanency goal for the child and must:

(1) evaluate whether the child's current placement is appropriate for meeting the child's needs;

(2) evaluate whether efforts have been made to ensure placement of the child in the least restrictive environment consistent with the best interest and special needs of the child if the child is placed in institutional care;

(3) contain a transition plan for a child who is at least 16 years of age that identifies the services and specific tasks that are needed to assist the child in making the transition from substitute care to adult living and describes the services that are being provided through the Transitional Living Services Program operated by the department;

(4) evaluate whether the child's current educational placement is appropriate for meeting the child's academic needs;

(5) identify other plans or services that are needed to meet the child's special needs or circumstances;

(6) describe the efforts of the department or authorized agency to place the child for adoption if parental rights to the child have been terminated and the child is eligible for adoption, including efforts to provide adoption promotion and support services as defined by 42 U.S.C. Section 629a and other efforts consistent with the federal Adoption and Safe Families Act of 1997 (Pub. L. No. 105–89); ~~and~~

(7) for a child for whom the department has been named managing conservator in a final order that does not include termination of parental rights, describe the efforts of the department to find a permanent placement for the child, including efforts to:

(A) work with the caregiver with whom the child is placed to determine whether that caregiver is willing to become a permanent placement for the child;

(B) locate a relative or other suitable individual to serve as permanent managing conservator of the child; and

(C) evaluate any change in a parent's circumstances to determine whether:

(i) the child can be returned to the parent; or

(ii) parental rights should be terminated; **and**

(8) with respect to a child committed to the Texas Youth Commission or released under supervision by the Texas Youth Commission:

(A) evaluate whether the child's needs for treatment and education are being met;

(B) describe, using information provided by the Texas Youth Commission, the child's progress in any rehabilitation program administered by the Texas Youth Commission; and

(C) recommend other plans or services to meet the child's needs.

(d) If the goal of the department's permanency plan for a child is to find another planned, permanent living arrangement, the placement review report must document a compelling reason why adoption, permanent managing conservatorship with a relative or other suitable individual, or returning the child to a parent are not in the child's best interest.

Amended by Acts 2011, 82nd Leg., ch. 91 (S.B. 1303), § 9.002, eff. Sept. 1, 2011.

Comment

In preparation for the placement review hearing, the department reports on the child's needs and placement and, if parental rights have been terminated, its efforts to locate an adoptive home.

The department must continue to have permanency goals for each child in foster care. Subsection (c)(7) requires that, for a child in the permanent managing conservatorship of the department without termination of parental rights, the placement review report must describe the efforts of the department to find a permanent placement for the child by: (1) working with the caregiver on whether that caregiver is willing to become a permanent placement for the child; (2) locating a relative or other suitable individual to serve as permanent managing conservator of the child; and (3) evaluating any change in a parent's circumstances to determine whether the child can be returned to the parent or parental rights should be terminated. Subsection (d) requires that the report of the placement review "document a compelling reason why adoption, permanent managing conservatorship with a relative or other suitable individual, or returning the child to a parent are not in the child's best interest" if the proposal is to continue the child in PMC of the department.

---

§ 263.503. Placement Review Hearings; Procedure

(a) At each placement review hearing, the court shall determine whether:

(1) the child's current placement is necessary, safe, and appropriate for meeting the child's needs, including with respect to a child placed outside of the state, whether the placement continues to be appropriate and in the best interest of the child;

(2) efforts have been made to ensure placement of the child in the least restrictive environment consistent with the best interest and special needs of the child if the child is placed in institutional care;

(3) the services that are needed to assist a child who is at least 16 years of age in making the transition from substitute care to independent living are available in the community;

(4) other plans or services are needed to meet the child's special needs or circumstances;

(5) the department or authorized agency has exercised due diligence in attempting to place the child for adoption if parental rights to the child have been terminated and the child is eligible for adoption;

(6) for a child for whom the department has been named managing conservator in a final order that does not include termination of parental rights, a permanent placement, including appointing a relative as permanent managing conservator or returning the child to a parent, is appropriate for the child;

(7) for a child whose permanency goal is another planned, permanent living arrangement, the department has:

(A) documented a compelling reason why adoption, permanent managing conservatorship with a relative or other suitable individual, or returning the child to a parent is not in the child's best interest; and

(B) identified a family or other caring adult who has made a permanent commitment to the child; ~~and~~

(8) the department or authorized agency has made reasonable efforts to finalize the permanency plan that is in effect for the child; and

(9) ~~(7)~~if the child is committed to the Texas Youth Commission or released under supervision by the Texas Youth Commission, the child's needs for treatment, rehabilitation, and education are being met.

(b) For a child for whom the department has been named managing conservator in a final order that does not include termination of parental rights, the court may order the department to provide services to a parent for not more than six months after the date of the placement review hearing if:

(1) the child has not been placed with a relative or other individual, including a foster parent, who is seeking permanent managing conservatorship of the child; and

(2) the court determines that further efforts at reunification with a parent are:

(A) in the best interest of the child; and

(B) likely to result in the child's safe return to the child's parent.

Amended by Acts 2011, 82nd Leg., ch. 91 (S.B. 1303), § 9.003, eff. Sept. 1, 2011.

Comment

Both state and federal law recognize that long term foster care is a poor solution for the child. Federal statutes and regulations refer to these continuing hearings as permanency hearings because foster care is recognized as not being a stable and permanent home for any child. Federal law recognizes adoption, return to the birth family or placement with a permanent custodian outside the foster care system as acceptable; the euphemism for permanent foster care is "another planned, permanent living arrangement (APPLA), and the department must have a "compelling reason" to have that goal. A final order does not close the door on efforts to locate an adoptive home for a child eligible for adoption, nor on efforts to seek a stable permanent placement for every child in foster care. The court may order the department to resume work with a birth parent if parental rights have not been terminated and a relative or other adult is not seeking permanent managing conservatorship of the child. *(C.G.C.)*

SUBCHAPTER G. EXTENDED JURISDICTION AFTER CHILD'S 18TH BIRTHDAY

§ 263.601. Definitions

Text of section effective until H.B. 79 or S.B. 1 of the First Called Session of the 82nd Legislature becomes law. At time of publication, Texas Governor Rick Perry had yet to take action on these bills, which were sent to the governor on June 29, 2011.

In this subchapter:

(1) "Foster care" means a voluntary residential living arrangement with a foster parent or other residential child-care provider that is:

(A) licensed by the department or verified by a licensed child-placing agency; and

(B) paid under a contract with the department.

(2) "Guardianship services" means the services provided by the Department of Aging and Disability Services under Subchapter E, Chapter 161, Human Resources Code.

(3) "Institution" means a residential facility that is operated, licensed, registered, certified, or verified by a state agency other than the department. The term includes a residential service provider under a Medicaid waiver program authorized under Section 1915(c) of the federal Social Security Act that provides services at a residence other than the young adult's own home.

(4) "Young adult" means a person between 18 and 21 years of age who:

(A) was in the conservatorship of the department on the day before the person's 18th birthday; and

(B) after the person's 18th birthday, resides in foster care or receives transitional living services from the department.

Added by Acts 2009, 81st Leg., ch. 96, § 1, eff. May 23, 2009.

§ 263.601. Definitions

Text of section effective if H.B. 79 or S.B. 1 of the First Called Session of the 82nd Legislature becomes law. At time of publication, Texas Governor Rick Perry had yet to take action on these bills, which were sent to the governor on June 29, 2011.

In this subchapter:

(1) "Foster care" means a voluntary residential living arrangement with a foster parent or other residential child-care provider that is:

(A) licensed **or approved** by the department or verified by a licensed child-placing agency; and

(B) paid under a contract with the department.

(2) "Guardianship services" means the services provided by the Department of Aging and Disability Services under Subchapter E, Chapter 161, Human Resources Code.

(3) "Institution" means a residential facility that is operated, licensed, registered, certified, or verified by a state agency other than the department. The term includes a residential service provider under a Medicaid waiver program authorized under Section 1915(c) of the federal Social Security Act that provides services at a residence other than the young adult's own home.

(3–a) "Trial independence period" means a period of not less than six months, or a longer period as a court may order not to exceed 12 months, during which a young adult exits foster care with the option to return to foster care under the continuing extended jurisdiction of the court.

(4) "Young adult" means a person between 18 and 21 years of age who:

(A) was in the conservatorship of the department on the day before the person's 18th birthday; and

(B) after the person's 18th birthday, resides in foster care or receives transitional living services from the department.

Amended by Acts 2011, 82nd Leg., 1st C.S. (H.B. 79), § 11.01, eff. Jan. 1, 2012; Acts 2011, 82nd Leg., 1st C.S. (S.B. 1), § 63.01, eff. Sept. 28, 2011.

§ 263.602. Extended Jurisdiction

Text of section effective until H.B. 79 or S.B. 1 of the First Called Session of the 82nd Legislature becomes law. At time of publication, Texas Governor Rick Perry had yet to take action on these bills, which were sent to the governor on June 29, 2011.

(a) A court that had continuing, exclusive jurisdiction over a young adult may, at the young adult's request, render an order that extends the court's jurisdiction over the young adult as provided by this subchapter.

(b) The extended jurisdiction of the court terminates on the earlier of:

(1) the young adult's 21st birthday; or

(2) the date the young adult withdraws consent to the extension of the court's jurisdiction in writing or in court.

Added by Acts 2009, 81st Leg., ch. 96, § 1, eff. May 23, 2009.

§ 263.602. Extended Jurisdiction

Text of section effective if H.B. 79 or S.B. 1 of the First Called Session of the 82nd Legislature becomes law. At time of publication, Texas Governor Rick Perry had yet to take action on these bills, which were sent to the governor on June 29, 2011.

(a) A court that had continuing, exclusive jurisdiction over a young adult **on the day before** ~~may, at~~ the young adult's **18th birthday continues to have extended** ~~request, render an order that extends the court's~~ jurisdiction over the young adult **and shall retain the case on the court's docket while the young adult remains in extended foster care and during a trial independence period described** ~~as provided~~ by this **section** ~~subchapter~~.

(b) **A court with extended jurisdiction over a young adult who remains in extended foster care shall conduct extended foster care review hearings every six months for the purpose of reviewing and making findings regarding:**

(1) whether the young adult's living arrangement is safe and appropriate and whether the department has made reasonable efforts to place the young adult in the least restrictive environment necessary to meet the young adult's needs;

(2) whether the department is making reasonable efforts to finalize the permanency plan that is in effect for the young adult, including a permanency plan for independent living;

(3) whether, for a young adult whose permanency plan is independent living:

(A) the young adult participated in the development of the plan of service;

(B) the young adult's plan of service reflects the independent living skills and appropriate services needed to achieve independence by the projected date; and

(C) the young adult continues to make reasonable progress in developing the skills needed to achieve independence by the projected date; and

(4) whether additional services that the department is authorized to provide are needed to meet the needs of the young adult. ~~The extended jurisdiction of the court terminates on the earlier of:~~

~~(1) the young adult's 21st birthday; or~~

~~(2) the date the young adult withdraws consent to the extension of the court's jurisdiction in writing or in court.~~

(c) Not later than the 10th day before the date set for a hearing under this section, the department shall file with the court a copy of the young adult's plan of service and a report that addresses the issues described by Subsection (b).

(d) Notice of an extended foster care review hearing shall be given as provided by Rule 21a, Texas Rules of Civil Procedure, to the following persons, each of whom has a right to present evidence and be heard at the hearing:

(1) the young adult who is the subject of the suit;

(2) the department;

(3) the foster parent with whom the young adult is placed and the administrator of a child-placing agency responsible for placing the young adult, if applicable;

(4) the director of the residential child-care facility or other approved provider with whom the young adult is placed, if applicable;

(5) each parent of the young adult whose parental rights have not been terminated and who is still actively involved in the life of the young adult;

(6) a legal guardian of the young adult, if applicable; and

(7) the young adult's attorney ad litem, guardian ad litem, and volunteer advocate, the appointment of which has not been previously dismissed by the court.

(e) If, after reviewing the young adult's plan of service and the report filed under Subsection (c), and any additional testimony and evidence presented at the review hearing, the court determines that the young adult is entitled to additional services, the court may order the department to take appropriate action to ensure that the young adult receives those services.

(f) A court with extended jurisdiction over a young adult as described in Subsection (a) shall continue to have jurisdiction over the young adult and shall retain the case on the court's docket until the earlier of:

(1) the last day of the:

(A) sixth month after the date the young adult leaves foster care; or

(B) 12th month after the date the young adult leaves foster care if specified in a court order, for the purpose of allowing the young adult to pursue a trial independence period; or

(2) the young adult's 21st birthday.

(g) A court with extended jurisdiction described by this section is not required to conduct periodic hearings for a young adult during a trial independence period and may not compel a young adult who has exited foster care to attend a court hearing.

Amended by Acts 2011, 82nd Leg., 1st C.S. (H.B. 79), § 11.02, eff. Jan. 1, 2012; Acts 2011, 82nd Leg., 1st C.S. (S.B. 1), § 63.02, eff. Sept. 28, 2011.

§ 263.6021. Voluntary Extended Jurisdiction for Young Adult Receiving Transitional Living Services

Text of section effective if H.B. 79 or S.B. 1 of the First Called Session of the 82nd Legislature becomes law, which were both sent to the governor on June 29, 2011.

(a) Notwithstanding Section 263.602, a court that had continuing, exclusive jurisdiction over a young adult on the day before the young adult's 18th birthday may, at the young adult's request, render an order that extends the court's jurisdiction beyond the end of a trial independence period if the young adult receives transitional living services from the department.

(b) The extended jurisdiction of the court under this section terminates on the earlier of:

(1) the young adult's 21st birthday; or

(2) the date the young adult withdraws consent to the extension of the court's jurisdiction in writing or in court.

(c) At the request of a young adult who is receiving transitional living services from the department and who consents to voluntary extension of the court's jurisdiction under this section, the court may hold a hearing to review the services the young adult is receiving.

(d) Before a review hearing scheduled under this section, the department must file with the court a report summarizing the young adult's transitional living services plan, services being provided to the young adult under that plan, and the young adult's progress in achieving independence.

(e) If, after reviewing the report and any additional testimony and evidence presented at the hearing, the court determines that the young adult is entitled to additional services, the court may order the department to take appropriate action to ensure that the young adult receives those services.

Added by Acts 2011, 82nd Leg., 1st C.S. (H.B. 79), § 11.03, eff. Jan. 1, 2012; Acts 2011, 82nd Leg., 1st C.S. (S.B. 1), § 63.03, eff. Sept. 28, 2011.

§ 263.603. Extended Jurisdiction to Determine Guardianship

Text of section effective until H.B. 79 or S.B. 1 of the First Called Session of the 82nd Legislature becomes law. At time of publication, Texas Governor Rick Perry had yet to take action on these bills, which were sent to the governor on June 29, 2011.

(a) Notwithstanding Section 263.602, if the court believes that a young adult may be incapacitated as defined by Section 601(14)(B), Texas Probate Code, the court may extend its jurisdiction on its own motion without the young adult's consent to allow the department to refer the young adult to the Department of Aging and Disability Services for guardianship services as required by Section 48.209, Human Resources Code.

(b) The extended jurisdiction of the court under this section terminates on the earliest of the date:

(1) the Department of Aging and Disability Services determines a guardianship is not appropriate under Chapter 161, Human Resources Code;

(2) a court with probate jurisdiction denies the application to appoint a guardian; or

(3) a guardian is appointed and qualifies under the Texas Probate Code.

(c) If the Department of Aging and Disability Services determines a guardianship is not appropriate, or the court with probate jurisdiction denies the application to appoint a guardian, the court under Subsection (a) may continue to extend its jurisdiction over the young adult only as provided by Section 263.602.

Added by Acts 2009, 81st Leg., ch. 96, § 1, eff. May 23, 2009.

§ 263.603. Extended Jurisdiction to Determine Guardianship

Text of section effective if H.B. 79 or S.B. 1 of the First Called Session of the 82nd Legislature becomes law. At time of publication, Texas Governor Rick Perry had yet to take action on these bills, which were sent to the governor on June 29, 2011.

(a) Notwithstanding Section **263.6021** ~~263.602~~, if the court believes that a young adult may be incapacitated as defined by Section 601(14)(B), Texas Probate Code, the court may extend its jurisdiction on its own motion without the young adult's consent to allow the department to refer the young adult to the Department of Aging and Disability Services for guardianship services as required by Section 48.209, Human Resources Code.

(b) The extended jurisdiction of the court under this section terminates on the earliest of the date:

(1) the Department of Aging and Disability Services determines a guardianship is not appropriate under Chapter 161, Human Resources Code;

(2) a court with probate jurisdiction denies the application to appoint a guardian; or

(3) a guardian is appointed and qualifies under the Texas Probate Code.

(c) If the Department of Aging and Disability Services determines a guardianship is not appropriate, or the court with probate jurisdiction denies the application to appoint a guardian, the court under Subsection (a) may continue to extend its jurisdiction over the young adult only as provided by Section 263.602 **or 263.6021**.

Amended by Acts 2011, 82nd Leg., 1st C.S. (H.B. 79), § 11.04, eff. Jan. 1, 2012; Acts 2011, 82nd Leg., 1st C.S. (S.B. 1), § 63.04, eff. Sept. 28, 2011.

§ 263.604. Guardian's Consent to Extended Jurisdiction

(a) A guardian appointed for a young adult may request that the court extend the court's jurisdiction over the young adult.

(b) A court that extends its jurisdiction over a young adult for whom a guardian is appointed may not issue an order that conflicts with an order entered by the probate court that has jurisdiction over the guardianship proceeding.

§ 263.605. Continued or Renewed Appointment of Attorney ad Litem, Guardian ad Litem, or Volunteer Advocate

A court with extended jurisdiction under this subchapter may continue or renew the appointment of an attorney ad litem, guardian ad litem, or volunteer advocate for the young adult to assist the young adult in accessing services the young adult is entitled to receive from the department or any other public or private service provider.

§ 263.606. Duties of Attorney or Guardian ad Litem

An attorney ad litem or guardian ad litem appointed for a young adult who receives services in the young adult's own home from a service provider or resides in an institution that is licensed, certified, or verified by a state agency other than the department shall assist the young adult as necessary to ensure that the young adult receives appropriate services from the service provider or institution, or the state agency that regulates the service provider or institution.

§ 263.607. Prohibited Appointments and Orders

(a) The court may not appoint the department or the Department of Aging and Disability Services as the managing conservator or guardian of a young adult.

(b) A court may not order the department to provide a service to a young adult unless the department:

(1) is authorized to provide the service under state law; and

(2) is appropriated money to provide the service in an amount sufficient to comply with the court order and the department's obligations to other young adults for whom the department is required to provide similar services.

§ 263.608. Rights of Young Adult

A young adult who consents to the continued jurisdiction of the court has the same rights as any other adult of the same age.

§ 263.609. Service Review Hearings

Text of section effective until H.B. 79 or S.B. 1 of the First Called Session of the 82nd Legislature becomes law. At time of publication, Texas Governor Rick Perry had yet to take action on these bills, which were sent to the governor on June 29, 2011.

(a) If the court's jurisdiction is extended under this subchapter for a young adult who remains in foster care, the court may hold periodic hearings to review the services provided to the young adult.

(b) At the request of a young adult who is receiving transitional living services from the department, the court may hold a hearing to review the services the young adult is receiving.

(c) Before a review hearing scheduled under this section, the department must provide the court with a copy of:

(1) the young adult's plan of service; and

(2) the voluntary foster care agreement if the young adult is in foster care or the transition plan if the young adult is receiving transitional living services from the department.

(d) The court shall review the plan of service and voluntary foster care agreement or transition plan, as applicable, and shall determine whether the department and any service provider under contract with the department is providing the appropriate services as provided in the plan or agreement.

(e) If the court believes that the young adult is entitled to additional services under the department's rules or policies or under a contract with a service provider, the court may order the department to take appropriate action to ensure that the young adult receives the additional services to which the young adult is entitled.

Added by Acts 2009, 81st Leg., ch. 96, § 1, eff. May 23, 2009.

§ 263.609. ~~Service Review Hearings~~

Repeal of section effective if passage of H.B. 79 or S.B. 1 of the First Called Session of the 82nd Legislature becomes law. At time of publication, Texas Governor Rick Perry had yet to take action on these bills, which were sent to the governor on June 29, 2011.

~~(a) If the court's jurisdiction is extended under this subchapter for a young adult who remains in foster care, the court may hold periodic hearings to review the services provided to the young adult.~~

~~(b) At the request of a young adult who is receiving transitional living services from the department, the court may hold a hearing to review the services the young adult is receiving.~~

~~(c) Before a review hearing scheduled under this section, the department must provide the court with a copy of:~~

~~(1) the young adult's plan of service; and~~

~~(2) the voluntary foster care agreement if the young adult is in foster care or the transition plan if the young adult is receiving transitional living services from the department.~~

~~(d) The court shall review the plan of service and voluntary foster care agreement or transition plan, as applicable, and shall determine whether the department and any service provider under contract with the department is providing the appropriate services as provided in the plan or agreement.~~

~~(e) If the court believes that the young adult is entitled to additional services under the department's rules or policies or under a contract with a service provider, the court may order the department to take appropriate action to ensure that the young adult receives the additional services to which the young adult is entitled.~~

Repealed by Acts 2011, 82nd Leg., 1st C.S. (H.B. 79), § 11.05, eff. Jan. 1, 2012; Acts 2011, 82nd Leg., 1st C.S. (S.B. 1), § 63.05, eff. Sept. 28, 2011.

CHAPTER 264. CHILD WELFARE SERVICES

SUBCHAPTER A. GENERAL PROVISIONS

SUBCHAPTER B. FOSTER CARE

SUBCHAPTER C. CHILD AND FAMILY SERVICES

SUBCHAPTER D. SERVICES TO AT–RISK YOUTH

SUBCHAPTER E. CHILDREN'S ADVOCACY CENTERS

SUBCHAPTER F. CHILD FATALITY REVIEW AND INVESTIGATION

SUBCHAPTER G. COURT–APPOINTED VOLUNTEER ADVOCATE PROGRAMS

SUBCHAPTER H. CHILD ABUSE PROGRAM EVALUATION

SUBCHAPTER H–1. TASK FORCE TO REDUCE CHILD ABUSE AND NEGLECT AND IMPROVE CHILD WELFARE [new]

SUBCHAPTER I. RELATIVE AND OTHER DESIGNATED CAREGIVER PLACEMENT PROGRAM

SUBCHAPTER J. FAMILY DRUG COURT PROGRAM

SUBCHAPTER K. PERMANENCY CARE ASSISTANCE PROGRAM

SUBCHAPTER L. PARENTAL CHILD SAFETY PLACEMENTS [new]

Editors' Note: *This chapter contains guest commentary by Charles G. Childress, Clinical Professor (retired), Children's Rights Clinic, University of Texas Law School, formerly Chief Attorney, Field Operations, Legal Division, Texas Department of Family and Protective Services, identified as (C.G.C.).*

Introductory Comment

The provisions of this chapter are undoubtedly of limited utility to the practicing attorney. It contains the restrictions and mandated actions for DFPS to follow in carrying out its duties as the designated agency for child protection.

SUBCHAPTER A. GENERAL PROVISIONS

§ 264.001. Definitions

In this chapter:

(1) "Department" means the Department of Family and Protective Services.

(2) "Commission" means the Health and Human Services Commission.

(3) "Executive commissioner" means the executive commissioner of the Health and Human Services Commission.

(4) "Residential child-care facility" has the meaning assigned by Section 42.002, Human Resources Code.

§ 264.002. Duties of Department

(a) The department shall:

(1) promote the enforcement of all laws for the protection of abused and neglected children; and

(2) take the initiative in all matters involving the interests of children where adequate provision has not already been made.

(b) The department shall give special attention to the dissemination of information through bulletins and visits, where practical, to all agencies operating under a provision of law affecting the welfare of children.

(c) Through the county child welfare boards, the department shall work in conjunction with the commissioners courts, juvenile boards, and all other officers and agencies involved in the protection of children. The department may use and allot funds for the establishment and maintenance of homes, schools, and institutions for the care, protection, education, and training of children in conjunction with a juvenile board, a county or city board, or any other agency.

(d) The department shall visit and study the conditions in state-supported eleemosynary institutions for children and shall make actions for the management and operation of the institutions that ensure that the children receive the best possible training in contemplation of their earliest discharge from the institutions.

(e) The department may not spend state funds to accomplish the purposes of this chapter unless the funds have been specifically appropriated for those purposes.

§ 264.003. Repealed.

§ 264.004. Allocation of State Funds

(a) The department shall establish a method of allocating state funds for children's protective services programs that encourages and rewards the contribution of funds or services from all persons, including local governmental entities.

(b) Except as provided by this subsection, if a contribution of funds or services is made to support a children's protective services program in a particular county, the department shall use the contribution to benefit that program. The department may use the contribution for another purpose only if the commissioners court of the county gives the department written permission.

(c) The department may use state and federal funds to provide benefits or services to children and families who are otherwise eligible for the benefits or services, including foster care, adoption assistance, medical assistance, family reunification services, and other child protective services and related benefits without regard to the immigration status of the child or the child's family.

§ 264.005. County Child Welfare Boards

(a) The commissioners court of a county may appoint a child welfare board for the county. The commissioners court and the department shall determine the size of the board and the qualifications of its members. However, a board must have not less than seven and not more than 15 members, and the members must be residents of the county. The members shall serve at the pleasure of the commissioners court and may be removed by the court for just cause. The members serve without compensation.

(b) With the approval of the department, two or more counties may establish a joint child welfare board if that action is found to be more practical in accomplishing the purposes of this chapter. A board representing more than one county has the same powers as a board representing a single county and is subject to the same conditions and liabilities.

(c) The members of a county child welfare board shall select a presiding officer and shall perform the duties required by the commissioners court and the department to accomplish the purposes of this chapter.

(d) A county child welfare board is an entity of the department for purposes of providing coordinated state and local public welfare services for children and their families and for the coordinated use of federal, state, and local funds for these services. The child welfare board shall work with the commissioners court.

(e) A county child welfare board is a governmental unit for the purposes of Chapter 101, Civil Practice and Remedies Code.

(f) A county child protective services board member may receive information that is confidential under Section 40.005, Human Resources Code, or Section 261.201 when the board member is acting in the member's official capacity.

(g) A child welfare board may conduct a closed meeting under Section 551.101, Government Code, to discuss, consider, or act on a matter that is confidential under Section 40.005, Human Resources Code, or Section 261.201.

§ 264.006. County Funds

The commissioners court of a county may appropriate funds from its general fund or any other fund for the administration of its county child welfare board. The court may provide for services to and support of children in need of protection and care without regard to the immigration status of the child or the child's family.

§ 264.007. Cooperation With Department of Health and Human Services

The department is the state agency designated to cooperate with the United States Department of Health and Human Services in:

(1) establishing, extending, and strengthening public welfare services for the protection and care of abused or neglected children;

(2) developing state services for the encouragement and assistance of adequate methods of community child welfare organizations and paying part of the cost of district, county, or other local child welfare services in rural areas and in other areas of special need; and

(3) developing necessary plans to implement the services contemplated in this section and to comply with the rules of the United States Department of Health and Human Services under the federal Social Security Act (42 U.S.C. Section 651 et seq.).

§ 264.008. Child Welfare Service Fund

The child welfare service fund is a special fund in the state treasury. The fund shall be used to administer the child welfare services provided by the department.

§ 264.009. Legal Representation of Department

(a) Except as provided by Subsection (b), (c), or (f), in any action under this code, the department shall be represented in court by the county attorney of the county where the action is brought, unless the district attorney or criminal district attorney of the county elects to provide representation.

(b) If the county attorney, district attorney, or criminal district attorney is unable to represent the department in an action under this code because of a conflict of interest or because special circumstances exist, the attorney general shall represent the department in the action.

(c) If the attorney general is unable to represent the department in an action under this code, the attorney general shall deputize an attorney who has contracted with the department under Subsection (d) or an attorney employed by the department under Subsection (e) to represent the department in the action.

(d) Subject to the approval of the attorney general, the department may contract with a private attorney to represent the department in an action under this code.

(e) The department may employ attorneys to represent the department in an action under this code.

(f) In a county with a population of 2.8 million or more, in an action under this code, the department shall be represented in court by the attorney who represents the state in civil cases in the district or county court of the county where the action is brought. If such attorney is unable to represent the department in an action under this code because of a conflict of interest or because special circumstances exist, the attorney general shall represent the department in the action.

Comment

Assigning child abuse and neglect cases to the local criminal prosecutor occasionally may create an awkward situation because the same office will be handling cases on both the civil and criminal sides of the docket. District attorneys don't seem to be bothered, however, by this potential conflict of interest between their assistant D.A.'s.

---

§ 264.0091. Use of Teleconferencing and Videoconferencing Technology

Subject to the availability of funds, the department, in cooperation with district and county courts, shall expand the use of teleconferencing and videoconferencing to facilitate participation by medical experts, children, and other individuals in court proceedings, including children for whom the department, an authorized agency, or a licensed child-placing agency has been appointed managing conservator and who are committed to the Texas Youth Commission.

§ 264.010. Child Abuse Plan; Limitation on Expenditure of Funds

(a) Funds appropriated for protective services, child and family services, and the purchased service system for the department may only be spent on or after March 1, 1996, in a county that provides the department with a child abuse prevention and protection plan. If a plan is not submitted to the department under this section, the department shall document the county's failure to submit a plan and may spend appropriated funds in the county to carry out the department's duties under this subtitle.

(b) A child abuse prevention and protection plan may be submitted by the governing body of a county or of a regional council of governments in which the county is an active participant.

(c) The department may not require a child abuse prevention and protection plan to exceed five double-spaced letter-size pages. The county or council of governments may voluntarily provide a longer plan.

(d) A child abuse prevention and protection plan must:

(1) specify the manner of communication between entities who are parties to the plan, including the department, the Texas Department of Human Services, local law enforcement agencies, the county and district attorneys, members of the medical and social service community, foster parents, and child advocacy groups; and

(2) provide other information concerning the prevention and investigation of child abuse in the area for which the plan is adopted.

§ 264.011. Local Accounts

(a) The department may establish and maintain local bank or savings accounts for a child who is under the managing conservatorship of the department as necessary to administer funds received in trust for or on behalf of the child.

(b) Funds maintained in an account under this section may be used by the department to support the child, including for the payment of foster care expenses, or may be paid to a person providing care for the child.

§ 264.0111. Money Earned by Child

(a) A child for whom the department has been appointed managing conservator and who has been placed by the department in a foster home or child-care institution as defined by Chapter 42, Human Resources Code, is entitled to keep any money earned by the child during the time of the child's placement.

(b) The child may deposit the money earned by the child in a bank or savings account subject to the sole management and control of the child as provided by Section 34.305, Finance Code. The child is the sole and absolute owner of the deposit account.

(c) If a child earns money as described by this section and is returned to the child's parent or guardian, the child's parent or guardian may not interfere with the child's authority to control, transfer, draft on, or make a withdrawal from the account.

(d) In this section, a reference to money earned by a child includes any interest that accrues on the money.

(e) The department may adopt rules to implement this section.

Comment

Children in the care of residential treatment centers are commonly encouraged to earn and manage their own money in order to improve their self-esteem and sense of responsibility. But when these children leave the care of the state and return home, parents or caretakers may undermine those efforts by exercising their parental rights to the child's earnings, i.e., closing the account and spending the money. This section eliminates the ownership and managerial rights of parents to the accumulated earnings of a child who has been returned home after earning money and establishing a bank account while in state custody. The department is required by section 264.016 to ensure that these older children also get and are able to interpret their credit report. H.B. 2170, 82nd Legislature, 2011. *(C.G.C.)*

---

§ 264.012. Burial Expenses for Child in Foster Care

(a) The department shall request that the parents pay reasonable and necessary burial expenses for a child for whom the department has been appointed managing conservator and who dies in foster care, including a request that if the parents have an insurance policy or a bank account for the child, that the parents spend the proceeds from the policy or money in the account on the burial expenses. If the parents cannot pay all or part of the burial expenses, the department shall spend funds appropriated for the child protective services program to pay reasonable and necessary burial expenses for the child.

(a–1) The department shall spend money appropriated for the child protective services program to pay reasonable and necessary burial expenses for a person for whom the department is paying for foster care under Section 264.101(a–1)(2) and who dies while in foster care unless there is money in the person's estate or other money available to pay the person's burial expenses.

(b) The department may accept donations, gifts, or in-kind contributions to cover the costs of any burial expenses paid by the department under this section.

(c) This section does not apply to a foster parent.

§ 264.013. Exchange of Information with other States

Subject to the availability of funds, the department shall enter into agreements with other states to allow for the exchange of information relating to a child for whom the department is or was the managing conservator. The information may include the child's health passport and education passport.

§ 264.014. Provision of Copies of Certain Records

If, at the time a child is discharged from foster care, the child is at least 18 years of age or has had the disabilities of minority removed, the department shall provide to the child, not later than the 30th day before the date the child is discharged from foster care, a copy of:

(1) the child's birth certificate;

(2) the child's immunization records;

(3) the information contained in the child's health passport;

(4) a personal identification certificate under Chapter 521, Transportation Code;

(5) a social security card or a replacement social security card, if appropriate; and

(6) proof of enrollment in Medicaid, if appropriate.

§ 264.0145. Release of Case Record

(a) In this section, "case record" means those files, reports, records, communications, audiotapes, videotapes, or working papers under the custody and control of the department that are collected, developed, or used:

(1) in a child abuse or neglect investigation; or

(2) in providing services as a result of an investigation, including substitute care services for a child.

(b) The department by rule shall establish guidelines that prioritize requests to release case records, including those made by an adult previously in the department's managing conservatorship.

(c) The department is not required to release a copy of the case record except as provided by law and department rule.

Added by Acts 2011, 82nd Leg., ch. 568 (H.B. 3234), § 1, eff. Sept. 1, 2011.

§ 264.015. Training

(a) The department shall include training in trauma-informed programs and services in any training the department provides to foster parents, adoptive parents, kinship caregivers, ~~and~~ department caseworkers, **and department supervisors**. The department shall pay for the training provided under this **subsection** ~~section~~ with gifts, donations, and grants and any federal money available through the Fostering Connections to Success and Increasing Adoptions Act of 2008 (Pub. L. No. 110–351). **The department shall annually evaluate the effectiveness of**

the training provided under this subsection to ensure progress toward a trauma-informed system of care.

(b) The department shall require department caseworkers and department supervisors to complete an annual refresher training course in trauma-informed programs and services.

(c) To the extent that resources are available, the department shall assist the following entities in developing training in trauma-informed programs and services and in locating money and other resources to assist the entities in providing trauma-informed programs and services:

(1) court-appointed special advocate programs;

(2) children's advocacy centers;

(3) local community mental health centers created under Section 534.001, Health and Safety Code; and

(4) domestic violence shelters.

Amended by Acts 2011, 82nd Leg., ch. 371 (S.B. 219), § 1, eff. Sept. 1, 2011.

§ 264.016. Credit Report for Foster Child

The department shall ensure that each child in the permanent managing conservatorship of the department who is 16 years of age or older:

(1) obtains a free copy of the child's credit report in accordance with the Fair and Accurate Credit Transactions Act of 2003 (Pub. L. No. 108–159) each year until the child is discharged from foster care; and

(2) receives information regarding interpreting the report and the procedure for correcting inaccuracies in the report.

Added by Acts 2011, 82nd Leg., ch. 791 (H.B. 2170), § 2, eff. Sept. 1, 2011.

SUBCHAPTER B. FOSTER CARE

§ 264.101. Foster Care Payments

(a) The department may pay the cost of foster care for a child:

(1) for whom the department has initiated a suit and has been named managing conservator under an order rendered under this title, who is a resident of the state, and who has been placed by the department in a foster home or child-care institution, as defined by Chapter 42, Human Resources Code; or

(2) who is under the placement and care of a state agency or political subdivision with which the department has entered into an agreement to reimburse the cost of care and supervision of the child.

(a–1) The department shall continue to pay the cost of foster care for a child for whom the department provides care, including medical care, until the last day of the month in which the child attains the age of 18. The department shall continue to pay the cost of foster care for a child after the month in which the child attains the age of 18 as long as the child is:

(1) regularly attending high school or enrolled in a program leading toward a high school diploma or high school equivalency certificate;

(2) regularly attending an institution of higher education or a postsecondary vocational or technical program;

(3) participating in a program or activity that promotes, or removes barriers to, employment;

(4) employed for at least 80 hours a month; or

(5) incapable of performing the activities described by Subdivisions (1)–(4) due to a documented medical condition.

(a–2) The department shall continue to pay the cost of foster care under:

(1) Subsection (a–1)(1) until the last day of the month in which the child attains the age of 22; and

(2) Subsections (a–1)(2)–(5) until the last day of the month the child attains the age of 21.

(b) The department may not pay the cost of protective foster care for a child for whom the department has been named managing conservator under an order rendered solely under Section 161.001(1)(J).

(c) The payment of foster care, including medical care, for a child as authorized under this subchapter shall be made without regard to the child's eligibility for federally funded care.

(d) The executive commissioner of the Health and Human Services Commission may adopt rules that establish criteria and guidelines for the payment of foster care, including medical care, for a child and for providing care for a child after the child becomes 18 years of age if the child meets the requirements for continued foster care under Subsection (a–1).

(d–1) The executive commissioner may adopt rules that prescribe the maximum amount of state money that a residential child-care facility may spend on nondirect residential services, including administrative services. The commission shall recover the money that exceeds the maximum amount established under this subsection.

(e) The department may accept and spend funds available from any source to pay for foster care, including medical care, for a child in the department's care.

(f) In this section, "child" means a person who:

(1) is under 22 years of age and for whom the department has been appointed managing conservator of the child before the date the child became 18 years of age; or

(2) is the responsibility of an agency with which the department has entered into an agreement to provide care and supervision of the child.

§ 264.1015. Liability of Child's Estate for Foster Care

(a) The cost of foster care provided for a child, including medical care, is an obligation of the estate of the child and the estate is liable to the department for the cost of the care.

(b) The department may take action to recover from the estate of the child the cost of foster care for the child.

§ 264.102. County Contracts

(a) The department may contract with a county commissioners court to administer the funds authorized by this subchapter for eligible children in the county and may require county participation.

(b) The payments provided by this subchapter do not abrogate the responsibility of a county to provide child welfare services.

§ 264.103. Direct Payments

The department may make direct payments for foster care to a foster parent residing in a county with which the department does not have a contract authorized by Section 264.102.

§ 264.104. Parent or Guardian Liability

(a) The parent or guardian of a child is liable to the state or to the county for a payment made by the state or county for foster care of a child under this subchapter.

(b) The cost of foster care for a child, including medical care, is a legal obligation of the child's parents, and the estate of a parent of the child is liable to the department for payment of the costs.

(c) The funds collected by the state under this section shall be used by the department for child welfare services.

§ 264.105. Medical Services Payments

The department shall attempt to maximize the use of federal funding to provide medical care payments authorized by Section 264.101(c) for children for whom the department has been named managing conservator.

§ 264.106. Contracts for Substitute Care and Case Management Services

(a) In this section:

(1) "Case management services" means the provision of services, other than conservatorship services, to a child for whom the department has been appointed temporary or permanent managing conservator and the child's family, including:

(A) developing and revising the child and family case plan, using family group decision-making in appropriate cases;

(B) coordinating and monitoring permanency services needed by the child and family to ensure that the child is progressing toward permanency within state and federal mandates; and

(C) assisting the department in a suit affecting the parent-child relationship commenced by the department.

(2) "Conservatorship services" means services provided directly by the department that the department considers necessary to ensure federal financial participation and compliance with state law requirements, including:

(A) initial placement of a child and approval of all subsequent placements of a child;

(B) approval of the child and family case plan; and

(C) any other action the department considers necessary to ensure the safety and well-being of a child.

(3) "Permanency services" means services provided to secure a child's safety, permanency, and well-being, including:

(A) substitute care services;

(B) medical, dental, mental health, and educational services;

(C) family reunification services;

(D) adoption and postadoption services and preparation for adult living services;

(E) convening family group conferences;

(F) child and family visits;

(G) relative placement services; and

(H) post-placement supervision services.

(4) "Substitute care provider" means:

(A) a child-care institution, a general residential operation, or a child-placing agency, as defined by Section 42.002, Human Resources Code; or

(B) a provider of residential child-care that is licensed or certified by another state agency.

(5) "Substitute care services" means services provided by a substitute care provider to or for a child in the temporary or permanent managing conservatorship of the department or for the child's placement, including the recruitment, training, and management of foster and adoptive homes by a child-placing agency. The term does not include the regulation of facilities under Subchapter C, Chapter 42, Human Resources Code.

(b) The department shall, in accordance with Chapter 45, Human Resources Code:

(1) assess the need for substitute care services throughout the state;

(2) contract with substitute care providers for the provision of all necessary substitute care services when the department determines that entering into a contract will improve services to children and families;

(3) monitor the quality of services for which the department contracts under this section; and

(4) ensure that the services are provided in accordance with federal law and the laws of this state, including department rules and rules of the Department of State Health Services and the Texas Commission on Environmental Quality.

(c) The department shall develop a pilot program for the competitive procurement of case management services in one or more geographic areas of the state. The department shall contract with one or more substitute care providers to provide case management services under the pilot program. The department shall have a goal of privatizing case management services in five percent of the cases in which the department has been appointed temporary or permanent managing conservator of a child.

(d) Repealed by Acts 2007, 80th Leg., ch. 1406, § 54(1).

(e) In addition to the requirements of Section 40.058(b), Human Resources Code, a contract authorized under this section must include provisions that:

(1) enable the department to monitor the effectiveness of the services;

(2) specify performance outcomes;

(3) authorize the department to terminate the contract or impose sanctions for a violation of a provision of the contract that specifies performance criteria;

(4) ensure that a private agency that is providing substitute care or case management services for a child shall provide to the child's attorney ad litem and guardian ad litem access to the agency's information and records relating to the child;

(5) authorize the department, an agent of the department, and the state auditor to inspect all books, records, and files maintained by a contractor relating to the contract; and

(6) the department determines are necessary to ensure accountability for the delivery of services and for the expenditure of public funds.

(f) Repealed by Acts 2007, 80th Leg., ch. 1406, § 54(1).

(g) In determining whether to contract with a substitute care provider, the department shall consider the provider's performance under any previous contract between the department and the provider.

(h) A contract under this section does not affect the rights and duties of the department in the department's capacity as the temporary or permanent managing conservator of a child.

(i) to (k) Repealed by Acts 2007, 80th Leg., ch. 1406, § 54(1).

(*l*) Notwithstanding any other law, the department or an independent administrator may contract with a child welfare board established under Section 264.005, a local governmental board granted the powers and duties of a child welfare board under state law, or a children's advocacy center established under Section 264.402 for the provision of substitute care and case management services in this state if the board or center provided direct substitute care or case management services under a contract with the department before September 1, 2006.

§ 264.1061. Foster Parent Performance

The department shall monitor the performance of a foster parent who has been verified by the department in the department's capacity as a child-placing agency. The method under which performance is monitored must include the use of objective criteria by which the foster parent's performance may be assessed. The department shall include references to the criteria in a written agreement between the department and the foster parent concerning the foster parent's services.

§ 264.1062. Repealed.

§ 264.1063. Monitoring Performance of Substitute Care and Case Management Providers

(a) The department, in consultation with substitute care providers under contract with the department to provide substitute care or case management services, shall establish a quality assurance program that uses comprehensive, multitiered assurance and improvement systems to evaluate performance.

(b) The contract performance outcomes specified in a contract under Section 264.106 must be within the contractor's authority to deliver. The contract must clearly define the manner in which the substitute care or case management provider's performance will be measured and identify the information sources the department will use to evaluate the performance.

§ 264.107. Placement of Children

(a) The department shall use a system for the placement of children in contract residential care, including foster care, that conforms to the levels of care adopted and maintained by the Health and Human Services Commission.

(b) The department shall use the standard application for the placement of children in contract residential care as adopted and maintained by the Health and Human Services Commission.

(c) The department shall institute the use of real-time technology in the department's placement system to screen possible placement options for a child and match the child's needs with the most qualified providers with vacancies.

(d) The department shall ensure that placement decisions are reliable and are made in a consistent manner.

(e) In making placement decisions, the department shall:

(1) consult with the child's caseworker and the child's attorney ad litem, guardian ad litem, or court-appointed volunteer advocate when possible; and

(2) use clinical protocols to match a child to the most appropriate placement resource.

(f) The department may create a regional advisory council in a region to assist the department in:

(1) assessing the need for resources in the region; and

(2) locating substitute care services in the region for hard-to-place children.

(g) If the department is unable to find an appropriate placement for a child, an employee of the department who has on file a background and criminal history check may provide temporary emergency care for the child. An employee may not provide emergency care under this subsection in the employee's residence. The department shall provide notice to the court for a child placed in temporary care under this subsection not later than the next business day after the date the child is placed in temporary care.

§ 264.1071. Placement for Children Under Age Two

In making a placement decision for a child under two years of age, the department shall:

(1) ensure that the child is placed with a person who will provide a safe and emotionally stable environment for the child; and

(2) give priority to a person who will be able to provide care for the child without disruption until the child is returned to the child's parents or the department makes a permanent placement for the child.

§ 264.1075. Assessing Needs of Child

(a) On removing a child from the child's home, the department shall use assessment services provided by a child-care facility, a child-placing agency, or the child's medical home during the initial substitute care placement. The assessment may be used to determine the most appropriate substitute care placement for the child, if needed.

(b) As soon as possible after a child begins receiving foster care under this subchapter, the department shall assess whether the child has a developmental disability or mental retardation. The commission shall establish the procedures that the department must use in making an assessment under this subsection. The procedures may include screening or participation by:

(1) a person who has experience in childhood developmental disabilities or mental retardation;

(2) a local mental retardation authority; or

(3) a provider in a county with a local child welfare board.

§ 264.108. Race or Ethnicity

(a) The department may not make a foster care placement decision on the presumption that placing a child in a family of the same race or ethnicity as the race or ethnicity of the child is in the best interest of the child.

(b) Unless an independent psychological evaluation specific to a child indicates that placement or continued living with a family of a particular race or ethnicity would be detrimental to the child, the department may not:

(1) deny, delay, or prohibit placement of a child in foster care because the department is attempting to locate a family of a particular race or ethnicity; or

(2) remove a child from foster care with a family that is of a race or ethnicity different from that of the child.

(c) The department may not remove a child from foster care with a family that is of a race or ethnicity different from that of the child for the sole reason that continued foster care with that family may:

(1) strengthen the emotional ties between the child and the family; or

(2) increase the potential of the family's desire to adopt the child because of the amount of time the child and the family are together.

(d) This section does not prevent or limit the department's recruitment of minority families as foster care families, but the recruitment of minority families may not be a reason to delay placement of a child in foster care with an available family of a race or ethnicity different from that of the child.

(e) An employee who violates this section is subject to immediate dismissal.

(f) The department by rule shall define what constitutes a delay under Subsections (b) and (d).

(g) A district court, on the application for an injunction or the filing of a petition complaining of a violation of this section by any person residing in the county in which the court has jurisdiction, shall enforce this section by issuing appropriate orders. An action for an injunction is in addition to any other action, proceeding, or remedy authorized by law. An applicant or petitioner who is granted an injunction or given other appropriate relief under this section is entitled to the costs of the suit, including reasonable attorney's fees.

Comment

This section applies to placements of a child in foster care; for related statutes applicable to placements for adoption, *see* § 162.015 and § 162.308.

§ 264.109. Assignment of Support Rights in Substitute Care Cases

(a) The placement of a child in substitute care by the department constitutes an assignment to the state of any support rights attributable to the child as of the date the child is placed in substitute care.

(b) If a child placed by the department in substitute care is entitled under federal law to Title IV-D child support enforcement services without the requirement of an application for services, the department shall immediately refer the case to the Title IV-D agency. If an application for Title IV-D services is required and the department has been named managing conservator of the child, then an authorized representative of the department shall be the designated individual entitled to apply for services on behalf of the child and shall promptly apply for the services.

(c) The department and the Title IV-D agency shall execute a memorandum of understanding for the implementation of the provisions of this section and for the allocation between the department and the agency, consistent with federal laws and regulations, of any child support funds recovered by the Title IV-D agency in substitute care cases. All child support funds recovered under this section and retained by the department or the Title IV-D agency and any federal matching or incentive funds resulting from child support collection efforts in substitute care cases shall be in excess of amounts otherwise appropriated to either the department or the Title IV-D agency by the legislature.

§ 264.110. Adoptive Parent Registry

(a) The department shall establish a registry of persons who are willing to accept foster care placement of a child in the care of the department. The child may be placed temporarily with a person registered under this section pending termination of the parent-child relationship.

(b) A person registered under this section must satisfy requirements adopted by rule by the department.

(c) The department shall maintain a list of persons registered under this section and shall make a reasonable effort to place a child with the first available qualified person on the list if a qualified extended family member is not available for the child.

(d) Before a child may be placed with a person under this section, the person must sign a written statement in which the person agrees to the immediate removal of the child by the department under circumstances determined by the department.

(e) A person registered under this section is not entitled to compensation during the time the child is placed in the person's home but may receive support services provided for the child by the department.

(f) A person registered under this section has the right to be considered first for the adoption of a child placed in the person's home if the parent-child relationship is terminated with regard to the child.

(g) The department may refuse to place a child with a person registered under this section only for a reason permitted under criteria adopted by department rule.

(h) The department shall make the public aware of the existence and benefits of the adoptive parent registry through appropriate existing department communication methods.

§ 264.111. Adoption and Substitute Information

(a) The department shall maintain in the department's central database information concerning children placed in the department's custody, including:

(1) for each formal adoption of a child in this state:

(A) the length of time between the date of the permanency plan decision of adoption and the date of the actual placement of the child with an adoptive family;

(B) the length of time between the date of the placement of the child for adoption and the date a final order of adoption was rendered;

(C) if the child returned to the department's custody after the date a final order of adoption was rendered for the child, the time between the date the final adoption order was rendered and the date the child returned to the department's custody; and

(D) for the adoptive family of a child under Paragraph (C), whether the family used postadoption program services before the date the child returned to the department's custody; and

(2) for each placement of a child in substitute care:

(A) the level of care the child was determined to require;

(B) whether the child was placed in an appropriate setting based on the level of care determined for the child;

(C) the number of moves for the child in substitute care and the reasons for moving the child;

(D) the length of stay in substitute care for the child from the date of initial placement to the date of approval of a permanency plan for the child;

(E) the length of time between the date of approval of a permanency plan for the child and the date of achieving the plan;

(F) whether the child's permanency plan was long-term substitute care;

(G) whether the child's achieved permanency plan was placement with an appropriate relative or another person, other than a foster parent, having standing; and

(H) whether the child was adopted by the child's foster parents.

(b) In addition to the information required in Subsection (a), the department shall compile information on:

(1) the number of families that used postadoption program services to assist in maintaining adoptive placements;

(2) the number of children returned to the department's custody after placement with an adoptive family but before a final adoption order was rendered;

(3) the number of children returned to the department's custody after the date a final order of adoption was rendered for the child;

(4) the number of adoptive families who used postadoption program services before the date a child placed with the family returned to the department's custody;

(5) the percentage of children who were placed in an appropriate setting based on the level of care determined for the child;

(6) the percentage of children placed in a department foster home;

(7) the percentage of children placed in a private child-placing agency;

(8) the number of children whose permanency plan was long-term substitute care;

(9) the number of children whose achieved permanency plan was placement with an appropriate relative or another person, other than a foster parent, having standing;

(10) the number of children adopted by the child's foster parents; and

(11) the number of children whose achieved permanency plan was removal of the disabilities of minority.

(c) The department shall make the information maintained under this section, other than information that is required by law to be confidential, available to the public by computer.

§ 264.112. Report on Children in Substitute Care

(a) The department shall report the status for children in substitute care to the Board of Protective and Regulatory Services at least once every 12 months.

(b) The report shall analyze the length of time each child has been in substitute care and the barriers to placing the child for adoption or returning the child to the child's parent or parents.

§ 264.113. Foster Parent Recruitment

(a) In this section, "faith-based organization" means a religious or denominational institution or organization, including an organization operated for religious, educational, or charitable purposes and operated, supervised, or controlled, in whole or in part, by or in connection with a religious organization.

(b) The department shall develop a program to recruit and retain foster parents from faith-based organizations. As part of the program, the department shall:

(1) collaborate with faith-based organizations to inform prospective foster parents about the department's need for foster parents, the requirements for becoming a foster parent, and any other aspect of the foster care program that is necessary to recruit foster parents;

(2) provide training for prospective foster parents recruited under this section; and

(3) identify and recommend ways in which faith-based organizations may support persons as they are recruited, are trained, and serve as foster parents.

(c) The department shall work with OneStar Foundation to expand the program described by Subsection (b) to increase the number of foster families available for the department and its private providers. In cooperation with the department, OneStar Foundation may provide training and technical assistance to establish networks and services in faith-based organizations based on best practices for supporting prospective and current foster families.

(d) The department shall work with the Department of Assistive and Rehabilitative Services to recruit foster parents and adoptive parents who have skills, training, or experience suitable to care for children with hearing impairments.

§ 264.114. Immunity From Liability

(a) A faith-based organization, including the organization's employees and volunteers, that participates in a program under this chapter is subject to civil liability as provided by Chapter 84, Civil Practice and Remedies Code.

(b) A faith-based organization that provides financial or other assistance to a foster parent or to a member of the foster parent's household is not liable for damages arising out of the conduct of the foster parent or a member of the foster parent's household.

§ 264.115. Returning Child to School

(a) If the department takes possession of a child under Chapter 262 during the school year, the department shall ensure that the child returns to school not later than the third school day after the date an order is rendered providing for possession of the child by the department, unless the child has a physical or mental condition of a temporary and remediable nature that makes the child's attendance infeasible.

(b) If a child has a physical or mental condition of a temporary and remediable nature that makes the child's attendance in school infeasible, the department shall notify the school in writing that the child is unable to attend school. If the child's physical or mental condition improves so that the child's attendance in school is feasible, the department shall ensure that the child immediately returns to school.

§ 264.116. Texas Foster Grandparent Mentors

(a) The department shall make the active recruitment and inclusion of senior citizens a priority in ongoing mentoring initiatives.

(b) An individual who volunteers as a mentor is subject to state and national criminal background checks in accordance with Sections 411.087 and 411.114, Government Code.

(c) The department shall require foster parents or employees of residential child-care facilities to provide appropriate supervision over individuals who serve as mentors during their participation in the mentoring initiative.

(d) Chapter 2109, Government Code, applies to the mentoring initiative described by this section.

§ 264.1165. Mentorship Pilot Program

Text of section effective until September 1, 2011

(a) The department shall establish a pilot program under which the department contracts with a private or nonprofit entity to pair children in foster care in Tarrant County, Denton County, Dallas County, and Collin County who are 14 years of age or older with volunteer adult mentors in order to foster relationships of support and guidance in preparation for the children's transition to adult living.

(b) The private or nonprofit entity selected by the department to administer the program must have a demonstrated record of successfully providing services similar to those provided under the program.

(c) Children in foster care who qualify for participation in the program may participate on a voluntary basis.

(d) An individual who volunteers as a mentor under the program is subject to state and national criminal background checks in accordance with Sections 411.087 and 411.114, Government Code.

(e) The department shall encourage substitute care providers to facilitate participation in the program by a child who chooses to voluntarily participate in the program.

(f) The executive commissioner may adopt rules for the administration of this section.

(g) The department shall report to the lieutenant governor, the speaker of the house of representatives, and the members of the legislature not later than January 1, 2011, on the activities conducted under the pilot program. The report must include the department's recommendations on improvements to the program and whether the program should be continued on a statewide basis.

(h) The department shall contract with a public institution of higher education located in the geographic area served by the pilot program for the institution to conduct an evaluation of the effectiveness of the program. The institution selected to conduct an evaluation under this subsection shall report its findings to the lieutenant governor, the speaker of the house of representatives, and the members of the legislature not later than January 1, 2011. The report must include the institution's:

(1) assessment of the effectiveness of the program; and

(2) recommendations on improvements to the program and whether the program should be continued on a statewide basis.

(i) This section expires September 1, 2011.

§ 264.117. Notice to Attorney Ad Litem

(a) The department shall notify the attorney ad litem for a child in the conservatorship of the department about each event involving the child that the department reports in the child's case file.

(b) The department shall give a child's attorney ad litem written notice at least 48 hours before the date the department changes the child's residential care provider. The department may change the child's residential care provider without notice if the department determines that an immediate change is necessary to protect the child.

§ 264.118. Annual Survey

(a) The department shall **collect and report service and outcome information for certain current and former foster care youth for use in the National Youth in Transition Database as required by 42 U.S.C. Section 677(f) and 45 C.F.R. Section 1356.80 et seq**~~conduct an annual random survey of a sample of children from each region of the state who are at least 14 years of age and who receive substitute care services. The survey must include questions regarding:(1) the quality of the substitute care services provided to the child;(2) any improvements that could be made to better support the child; and(3)any other factor that the department considers relevant to enable the department to identify potential program enhancements~~.

(b) The identity of each child participating in a department survey is confidential and not subject to public disclosure under Chapter 552, Government Code. The department shall adopt procedures to ensure that the identity of each child participating in a department survey remains confidential.

Amended by Acts 2011, 82nd Leg., ch. 598 (S.B. 218), § 7, eff. Sept. 1, 2011.

§ 264.119. Notice of Change of Placement

(a) In this section, "residential child-care facility" and "child-placing agency" have the meanings assigned by Section 42.002, Human Resources Code.

(b) Except in the case of an emergency or as otherwise provided by a court order or agreed to by a residential child-care facility or child-placing agency, the department

must provide written notice to the residential child-care facility and any child-placing agency involved with a child before the department may change the child's residential child-care facility.

(c) The department must provide the notice required under Subsection (b) at least 48 hours before the residential child-care facility is changed.

Added by Acts 2011, 82nd Leg., ch. 724 (H.B. 807), § 1, eff. Sept. 1, 2011.

§ 264.121. Transitional Living Services Program

(a) The department shall address the unique challenges facing foster children in the conservatorship of the department who must transition to independent living by:

(1) expanding efforts to improve transition planning and increasing the availability of transitional family group decision-making to all youth age 14 or older in the department's permanent managing conservatorship, including enrolling the youth in the Preparation for Adult Living Program before the age of 16;

(2) coordinating with the Health and Human Services Commission to obtain authority, to the extent allowed by federal law, the state Medicaid plan, the Title IV–E state plan, and any waiver or amendment to either plan, necessary to:

(A) extend foster care eligibility and transition services for youth up to age 21 and develop policy to permit eligible youth to return to foster care as necessary to achieve the goals of the Transitional Living Services Program; and

(B) extend Medicaid coverage for foster care youth and former foster care youth up to age 21 with a single application at the time the youth leaves foster care; and

(3) entering into cooperative agreements with the Texas Workforce Commission and local workforce development boards to further the objectives of the Preparation for Adult Living Program. The department, the Texas Workforce Commission, and the local workforce development boards shall ensure that services are prioritized and targeted to meet the needs of foster care and former foster care children and that such services will include, where feasible, referrals for short-term stays for youth needing housing.

(a–1) The department shall require a foster care provider to provide or assist youth who are age 14 or older in obtaining experiential life-skills training to improve their transition to independent living. Experiential life-skills training must be tailored to a youth's skills and abilities and may include training in practical activities that include grocery shopping, meal preparation and cooking, using public transportation, performing basic household tasks, and balancing a checkbook.

(b) In this section:

(1) "Local workforce development board" means a local workforce development board created under Chapter 2308, Government Code.

(2) "Preparation for Adult Living Program" means a program administered by the department as a component of the Transitional Living Services Program and includes independent living skills assessment, short-term financial assistance, basic self-help skills, and life-skills development and training regarding money management, health and wellness, job skills, planning for the future, housing and transportation, and interpersonal skills.

(3) "Transitional Living Services Program" means a program, administered by the department in accordance with department rules and state and federal law, for youth who are age 14 or older but not more than 21 years of age and are currently or were formerly in foster care, that assists youth in transitioning from foster care to independent living. The program provides transitional living services, Preparation for Adult Living Program services, and Education and Training Voucher Program services.

(c) At the time a child enters the Preparation for Adult Living Program, the department shall provide an information booklet to the child and the foster parent describing the program and the benefits available to the child, including extended Medicaid coverage until age 21, priority status with the Texas Workforce Commission, and the exemption from the payment of tuition and fees at institutions of higher education as defined by Section 61.003, Education Code. The information booklet provided to the child and the foster parent shall be provided in the primary language spoken by that individual.

(d) The department shall allow a youth who is at least 18 years of age to receive transitional living services, other than foster care benefits, while residing with a person who was previously designated as a perpetrator of abuse or neglect if the department determines that despite the person's prior history the person does not pose a threat to the health and safety of the youth.

(e) The department shall ensure that each youth acquires a certified copy of the youth's birth certificate, a social security card or replacement social security card, as appropriate, and a personal identification certificate under Chapter 521, Transportation Code, on or before the date on which the youth turns 16 years of age. The department shall designate one or more employees in the Preparation for Adult Living Program as the contact person to assist a youth who has not been able to obtain the documents described by this subsection in a timely manner from the youth's primary caseworker. The department shall ensure that:

(1) all youth who are age 16 or older are provided with the contact information for the designated employees; and

(2) a youth who misplaces a document provided under this subsection receives assistance in obtaining a replacement document or information on how to obtain a duplicate copy, as appropriate.

(f) The department shall require a person with whom the department contracts for transitional living services for foster youth to provide or assist youth in obtaining:

(1) housing services;

(2) job training and employment services;

(3) college preparation services;

(4) services that will assist youth in obtaining a general education development certificate; and

(5) any other appropriate transitional living service identified by the department.

§ 264.122. Court Approval Required for Travel Outside United States by Child in Foster Care

(a) A child for whom the department has been appointed managing conservator and who has been placed in foster care may travel outside of the United States only if the person with whom the child has been placed has petitioned the court for, and the court has rendered an order granting, approval for the child to travel outside of the United States.

(b) The court shall provide notice to the department and to any other person entitled to notice in the suit if the court renders an order granting approval for the child to travel outside of the United States under this section.

§ 264.123. Reports Concerning Missing Child

(a) If a child in the department's managing conservatorship is missing from the child's substitute care provider, including a child who is abducted or is a runaway, the department shall notify the following persons that the child is missing:

(1) the appropriate law enforcement agencies;

(2) the court with jurisdiction over the department's managing conservatorship of the child;

(3) the child's attorney ad litem;

(4) the child's guardian ad litem; and

(5) the child's parent unless the parent:

(A) cannot be located or contacted;

(B) has had the parent's parental rights terminated; or

(C) has executed an affidavit of relinquishment of parental rights.

(b) The department shall provide the notice required by Subsection (a) not later than 24 hours after the time the department learns that the child is missing or as soon as possible if a person entitled to notice under that subsection cannot be notified within 24 hours.

(c) If a child has been reported as a missing child under Subsection (a), the department shall notify the persons described by Subsection (a) when the child returns to the child's substitute care provider not later than 24 hours after the time the department learns that the child has returned or as soon as possible if a person entitled to notice cannot be notified within 24 hours.

(d) The department shall make continuing efforts to determine the location of a missing child until the child returns to substitute care, including:

(1) contacting on a monthly basis:

(A) the appropriate law enforcement agencies;

(B) the child's relatives;

(C) the child's former caregivers; and

(D) any state or local social service agency that may be providing services to the child; and

(2) conducting a supervisory-level review of the case on a quarterly basis if the child is 15 years of age or younger to determine whether sufficient efforts have been made to locate the child and whether other action is needed.

(e) The department shall document in the missing child's case record:

(1) the actions taken by the department to:

(A) determine the location of the child; and

(B) persuade the child to return to substitute care;

(2) any discussion during, and determination resulting from, the supervisory-level review under Subsection (d)(2);

(3) any discussion with law enforcement officials following the return of the child regarding the child's absence; and

(4) any discussion with the child described by Subsection (f).

(f) After a missing child returns to the child's substitute care provider, the department shall interview the child to determine the reasons why the child was missing and where the child stayed during the time the child was missing. The department shall report to an appropriate law enforcement agency any disclosure made by a child that indicates that the child was the victim of a crime during the time the child was missing. The department shall make a report under this subsection not later than 24 hours after the time the disclosure is made. The department is not required to interview a missing child under this subsection if, at the time the child returns, the department knows that the child was abducted and another agency is investigating the abduction.

Added by Acts 2011, 82nd Leg., ch. 1130 (H.B. 943), § 1, eff. Sept. 1, 2011.

SUBCHAPTER C. CHILD AND FAMILY SERVICES

§ 264.201. Services by Department

(a) When the department provides services directly or by contract to an abused or neglected child and the child's family, the services shall be designed to:

(1) prevent further abuse;

(2) alleviate the effects of the abuse suffered;

(3) prevent removal of the child from the home; and

(4) provide reunification services when appropriate for the return of the child to the home.

(b) The department shall emphasize ameliorative services for sexually abused children.

(c) The department shall provide or contract for necessary services to an abused or neglected child and the child's family without regard to whether the child remains in or is removed from the family home. If parental rights have been terminated, services may be provided only to the child.

(d) The services may include in-home programs, parenting skills training, youth coping skills, and individual and family counseling.

(e) The department may not provide and a court may not order the department to provide supervision for visitation in a child custody matter unless the department is a petitioner or intervener in the underlying suit.

Comment

Subsection (e) prohibits use of DFPS employees to provide visitation supervision in private cases. The temptation to turn to the child abuse professionals for this service has proven almost irresistible to some trial judges. However, the legislature has never appropriated funds for this service. The limited resources of the department must be devoted to more pressing duties relating to serious child abuse and neglect. *(C.G.C.)*

§ 264.2011. Enhanced In–Home Support Program

(a) To the extent that funding is available, the department shall develop a program to strengthen families through enhanced in-home support. The program shall assist certain low-income families and children in child neglect cases in which poverty is believed to be a significant underlying cause of the neglect and in which the enhancement of in-home support appears likely to prevent removal of the child from the home or to speed reunification of the child with the family.

(b) A family that meets eligibility criteria for inclusion in the program is eligible to receive limited funding from a flexible fund account to cover nonrecurring expenses that are designed to help the family accomplish the objectives included in the family's service plan.

(c) The executive commissioner shall adopt rules establishing:

(1) specific eligibility criteria for the program described in this section;

(2) the maximum amount of money that may be made available to a family through the flexible fund account; and

(3) the purposes for which money made available under the program may be spent.

(d) The department shall evaluate the results of the program to determine whether the program is successful in safely keeping families together. If the department determines that the program is successful, the department shall continue the program to the extent that funding is available.

§ 264.2015. Family Group Conferencing

The department may collaborate with the courts and other appropriate local entities to develop and implement family group conferencing as a strategy for promoting family preservation and permanency for children.

§ 264.202. Standards and Effectiveness

(a) The department, with assistance from national organizations with expertise in child protective services, shall define a minimal baseline of in-home and foster care services for abused or neglected children that meets the professionally recognized standards for those services. The department shall attempt to provide services at a standard not lower than the minimal baseline standard.

(b) The department, with assistance from national organizations with expertise in child protective services, shall develop outcome measures to track and monitor the effectiveness of in-home and foster care services.

§ 264.203. Required Participation

(a) Except as provided by Subsection (d), the court on request of the department may order the parent, managing conservator, guardian, or other member of the subject child's household to:

(1) participate in the services the department provides or purchases for:

(A) alleviating the effects of the abuse or neglect that has occurred; or

(B) reducing the reasonable likelihood that the child may be abused or neglected in the immediate or foreseeable future; and

(2) permit the child and any siblings of the child to receive the services.

(b) The department may request the court to order the parent, managing conservator, guardian, or other member of the child's household to participate in the services whether the child resides in the home or has been removed from the home.

(c) If the person ordered to participate in the services fails to follow the court's order, the court may impose appropriate sanctions in order to protect the health and safety of the child, including the removal of the child as specified by Chapter 262.

(d) If the court does not order the person to participate, the court in writing shall specify the reasons for not ordering participation.

§ 264.204. Community–based Family Services

(a) The department shall administer a grant program to provide funding to community organizations, including faith-based or county organizations, to respond to:

(1) low-priority, less serious cases of abuse and neglect; and

(2) cases in which an allegation of abuse or neglect of a child was unsubstantiated but involved a family that has been previously investigated for abuse or neglect of a child.

(b) The executive commissioner shall adopt rules to implement the grant program, including rules governing the submission and approval of grant requests and the cancellation of grants.

(c) To receive a grant, a community organization whose grant request is approved must execute an interagency agreement or a contract with the department. The contract must require the organization receiving the grant to perform the services as stated in the approved grant request. The contract must contain appropriate provisions for program and fiscal monitoring.

(d) In areas of the state in which community organizations receive grants under the program, the department shall refer low-priority, less serious cases of abuse and neglect to a community organization receiving a grant under the program.

(e) A community organization receiving a referral under Subsection (d) shall make a home visit and offer family social services to enhance the parents' ability to provide a safe and stable home environment for the child. If the family chooses to use the family services, a case manager from the organization shall monitor the case and ensure that the services are delivered.

(f) If after the home visit the community organization determines that the case is more serious than the department indicated, the community organization shall refer the case to the department for a full investigation.

(g) The department may not award a grant to a community organization in an area of the state in which a similar program is already providing effective family services in the community.

(h) For purposes of this section, a case is considered to be a less serious case of abuse or neglect if:

(1) the circumstances of the case do not appear to involve a reasonable likelihood that the child will be abused or neglected in the foreseeable future; or

(2) the allegations in the report of child abuse or neglect:

(A) are general in nature or vague and do not support a determination that the child who is the subject of the report has been abused or neglected or will likely be abused or neglected; or

(B) if substantiated, would not be considered abuse or neglect under this chapter.

§ 264.2041. Cultural Awareness

The department shall:

(1) develop and deliver cultural competency training to all service delivery staff;

(2) increase targeted recruitment efforts for foster and adoptive families who can meet the needs of children and youth who are waiting for permanent homes;

(3) target recruitment efforts to ensure diversity among department staff; and

(4) develop collaborative partnerships with community groups, agencies, faith-based organizations, and other community organizations to provide culturally competent services to children and families of every race and ethnicity.

§ 264.205. Swift Adoption Teams

(a) The department shall develop swift adoption teams to expedite the process of placing a child under the jurisdiction of the department for adoption. Swift adoption teams developed under this section shall, in performing their duties, attempt to place a child for adoption with an appropriate relative of the child.

(b) A swift adoption team shall consist of department personnel who shall operate under policies adopted by rule by the department. The department shall set priorities for the allocation of department resources to enable a swift adoption team to operate successfully under the policies adopted under this subsection.

~~(c) The department shall, using a system of measurement developed by the department, report to the legislature on the success of swift adoption teams in expediting the administrative procedures and the length of time in placing children for adoption. The report shall include recommendations by the department concerning legislation that would enable the department to further improve adoption placements. The department shall report under this section on or before December 1 of each even-numbered year.~~

Amended by Acts 2011, 82nd Leg., ch. 1050 (S.B. 71), § 20, eff. Sept. 1, 2011; Acts 2011, 82nd Leg., ch. 1083 (S.B. 1179), § 25, eff. June 17, 2011.

§ 264.206. Search for Adoptive Parents

(a) The department shall begin its efforts to locate qualified persons to adopt a child, including persons registered with the adoptive parent registry under Subchapter B, at the time the department's permanency plan for the child becomes the termination of the parent-child relationship and adoption of the child.

(b) The department shall report to the court in which the department petitions for termination of the parent-child relationship on the child's adoptability and the department's search for prospective adoptive parents for the child, including information relating to the department's efforts to work with licensed child-placing agencies.

§ 264.207. Department Planning and Accountability

(a) The department shall adopt policies that provide for the improvement of the department's services for children and families, including policies that provide for conducting a home study within four months after the date an applicant is approved for an adoption and documenting the results of the home study within 30 days after the date the study is completed. The policies adopted under this section must:

(1) be designed to increase the accountability of the department to individuals who receive services and to the public; and

(2) assure consistency of services provided by the department in the different regions of the state.

(b) To accomplish the goals stated in Subsection (a), the department shall:

(1) establish time frames for the initial screening of families seeking to adopt children;

(2) provide for the evaluation of the effectiveness of the department's management-level employees in expeditiously making permanent placements for children;

(3) establish, as feasible, comprehensive assessment services in various locations in the state to determine the needs of children and families served by the department;

(4) emphasize and centralize the monitoring and promoting of the permanent placement of children receiving department services;

(5) establish goals and performance measures in the permanent placement of children;

(6) seek private licensed child-placing agencies to place a child in the department's managing conservatorship who has been available for permanent placement for more than 90 days;

(7) provide information to private licensed child-placing agencies concerning children under Subdivision (6);

(8) provide incentives for a private licensed child-placing agency that places a child, as defined by Section 162.301, under Subdivision (6);

(9) encourage foster parents to be approved by the department as both foster parents and adoptive parents;

(10) address failures by the department's service regions in making permanent placements for children in a reasonable time; and

(11) require the department's service regions to participate in the Texas Adoption Resources Exchange.

§ 264.208. Location of Parents

(a) The department shall create a division staffed by personnel trained in locating parents and relatives of children throughout the state.

(b) The department shall use outside contractors and volunteer resources to the extent feasible to perform its responsibilities under this section.

Comment

This section requires the department to establish a "locate" division in order to speed the process to reach a final order and find permanent placements for abused or neglected children. *(C.G.C.)*

SUBCHAPTER D. SERVICES TO AT–RISK YOUTH

§ 264.301. Services for At-Risk Youth

(a) The department shall operate a program to provide services for children in at-risk situations and for the families of those children.

(b) The services under this section may include:

(1) crisis family intervention;

(2) emergency short-term residential care;

(3) family counseling;

(4) parenting skills training;

(5) youth coping skills training;

(6) mentoring; and

(7) advocacy training.

§ 264.302. Early Youth Intervention Services

(a) This section applies to a child who:

(1) is seven years of age or older and under 17 years of age; and

(2) has not had the disabilities of minority for general purposes removed under Chapter 31.

(b) The department shall operate a program under this section to provide services for children in at-risk situations and for the families of those children.

(c) The department may not provide services under this section to a child who has:

(1) at any time been referred to juvenile court for engaging in conduct that violates a penal law of this state of the grade of felony other than a state jail felony; or

(2) been found to have engaged in delinquent conduct under Title 3.

(d) The department may provide services under this section to a child who engages in conduct for which the child may be found by a court to be an at-risk child, without regard to whether the conduct violates a penal law of this state of the grade of felony other than a state jail felony, if the child was younger than 10 years of age at the time the child engaged in the conduct.

(e) The department shall provide services for a child and the child's family if a contract to provide services under this section is available in the county and the child is referred to the department as an at-risk child by:

(1) a court under Section 264.304;

(2) a juvenile court or probation department as part of a progressive sanctions program under Chapter 59;

(3) a law enforcement officer or agency under Section 52.03; or

(4) a justice or municipal court under Article 45.057, Code of Criminal Procedure.

(f) The services under this section may include:

(1) crisis family intervention;

(2) emergency short-term residential care for children 10 years of age or older;

(3) family counseling;

(4) parenting skills training;

(5) youth coping skills training;

(6) advocacy training; and

(7) mentoring.

Comment

Texas DFPS is authorized to provide services to "at-risk" youth, ages 7 to 17, as an option to juvenile proceedings under Title 3.

Subsection (e) lists those who may refer the child and the child's family to DFPS for services. DFPS may not provide services to a child over 10 years of age who has previously been referred to the juvenile court for delinquent conduct that would be a felony offense.

§ 264.303. Commencement of Civil Action for Determination of At-Risk Children

(a) The department may file a civil action to request any district court or county court, other than a juvenile court, to determine that a child is an at-risk child. A person with whom the department contracts to provide services under Section 264.302 may file an action under this section if the department has approved the filing.

(b) Notice of the action must be provided to:

(1) the child;

(2) the parent, managing conservator, or guardian of the child; and

(3) any other member of the child's household who may be affected by an order of the court if the court finds that the child is an at-risk child.

(c) A person served with notice of the action may, but is not required, to file a written answer. Any answer must be filed before the hearing on the action begins.

§ 264.304. Hearing; Determination of At-Risk Child

(a) Unless a later date is requested by the department, the court shall set a date and time for the hearing not later than 30 days after the date the action is filed.

(b) The court is the trier of fact at the hearing.

(c) The court shall determine that the child is an at-risk child if the court finds that the child has engaged in the following conduct:

(1) conduct, other than a traffic offense and except as provided by Subsection (d), that violates:

(A) the penal laws of this state; or

(B) the penal ordinances of any political subdivision of this state;

(2) the unexcused voluntary absence of the child on 10 or more days or parts of days within a six-month period or three or more days or parts of days within a four-week period from school without the consent of the child's parent, managing conservator, or guardian;

(3) the voluntary absence of the child from the child's home without the consent of the child's parent, managing conservator, or guardian for a substantial length of time or without intent to return;

(4) conduct that violates the laws of this state prohibiting driving while intoxicated or under the influence of intoxicating liquor (first or second offense) or driving while under the influence of any narcotic drug or of any other drug to a degree that renders the child incapable of safely driving a vehicle (first or second offense); or

(5) conduct that evidences a clear and substantial intent to engage in any behavior described by Subdivisions (1)–(4).

(d) The court may not determine that a child is an at-risk child if the court finds that the child engaged in conduct violating the penal laws of this state of the grade of felony other than a state jail felony when the child was 10 years of age or older.

§ 264.305. Court Order for Services

(a) Except as provided by Subsection (b), if the court finds that the child is an at-risk child under Section 264.304, the court may order the child, the child's parent, managing conservator, or guardian or any other member of the child's household to participate in services provided by the department under Section 264.302 and contained in a plan approved by the court.

(b) The court may order an at-risk child to participate in services involving emergency short-term residential care only if the court finds that the child engaged in conduct described by Section 264.304(c)(1), (2), (3), or (4).

(c) An order rendered by a court under this section expires not later than six months after the date the order was rendered.

Comment

This section authorizes a court to declare a child to be an "at-risk" child and to order the child, the child's parents, managing conservator, or guardian to participate in services provided by DFPS.

---

§ 264.306. Sanctions

(a) A child who violates a court order under Section 264.305 by failing to participate in services provided by the department engages in conduct indicating a need for supervision and the department shall refer the child to an appropriate juvenile authority for proceedings under Title 3 for that conduct.

(b) A parent, managing conservator, guardian, or other member of the child's household who violates a court order under Section 264.305 by failing to participate in services provided by the department is subject to contempt of court. The court may under its contempt powers impose a community service requirement.

Comment

A child who fails to participate in the services ordered under § 264.305 may be referred by the court for proceedings under Title 3. Additionally, a court has the power to hold in contempt a parent, managing conservator or guardian who fails to participate in such services as ordered by the court.

SUBCHAPTER E. CHILDREN'S ADVOCACY CENTERS

§ 264.401. Definition

In this subchapter, "center" means a children's advocacy center.

§ 264.402. Establishment of Children's Advocacy Center

On the execution of a memorandum of understanding under Section 264.403, a children's advocacy center may be established by community members and the participating entities described by Section 264.403(a) to serve a county or two or more contiguous counties.

§ 264.403. Interagency Memorandum of Understanding

(a) Before a center may be established under Section 264.402, a memorandum of understanding regarding participation in operation of the center must be executed among:

(1) the division of the department responsible for child abuse investigations;

(2) representatives of county and municipal law enforcement agencies that investigate child abuse in the area to be served by the center;

(3) the county or district attorney who routinely prosecutes child abuse cases in the area to be served by the center; and

(4) a representative of any other governmental entity that participates in child abuse investigations or offers services to child abuse victims that desires to participate in the operation of the center.

(b) A memorandum of understanding executed under this section shall include the agreement of each participating entity to cooperate in:

(1) developing a cooperative, team approach to investigating child abuse;

(2) reducing, to the greatest extent possible, the number of interviews required of a victim of child abuse to minimize the negative impact of the investigation on the child; and

(3) developing, maintaining, and supporting, through the center, an environment that emphasizes the best interests of children and that provides investigatory and rehabilitative services.

(c) A memorandum of understanding executed under this section may include the agreement of one or more participating entities to provide office space and administrative services necessary for the center's operation.

§ 264.404. Board Representation

(a) In addition to any other persons appointed or elected to serve on the governing board of a children's advocacy center, the governing board must include an executive officer of, or an employee selected by an executive officer of:

(1) a law enforcement agency that investigates child abuse in the area served by the center;

(2) the child protective services division of the department; and

(3) the county or district attorney's office involved in the prosecution of child abuse cases in the area served by the center.

(b) Service on a center's board by an executive officer or employee under Subsection (a) is an additional duty of the person's office or employment.

§ 264.405. Duties

A center shall:

(1) assess victims of child abuse and their families to determine their need for services relating to the investigation of child abuse;

(2) provide services determined to be needed under Subdivision (1);

(3) provide a facility at which a multidisciplinary team appointed under Section 264.406 can meet to facilitate the efficient and appropriate disposition of child abuse cases through the civil and criminal justice systems; and

(4) coordinate the activities of governmental entities relating to child abuse investigations and delivery of services to child abuse victims and their families.

§ 264.406. Multidisciplinary Team

(a) A center's multidisciplinary team must include employees of the participating agencies who are professionals involved in the investigation or prosecution of child abuse cases.

(b) A center's multidisciplinary team may also include professionals involved in the delivery of services, including medical and mental health services, to child abuse victims and the victims' families.

(c) A multidisciplinary team shall meet at regularly scheduled intervals to:

(1) review child abuse cases determined to be appropriate for review by the multidisciplinary team; and

(2) coordinate the actions of the entities involved in the investigation and prosecution of the cases and the delivery of services to the child abuse victims and the victims' families.

(d) A multidisciplinary team may review a child abuse case in which the alleged perpetrator does not have custodial control or supervision of the child or is not responsible for the child's welfare or care.

(e) When acting in the member's official capacity, a multidisciplinary team member is authorized to receive information made confidential by Section 40.005, Human Resources Code, or Section 261.201 or 264.408.

§ 264.407. Liability

(a) A person is not liable for civil damages for a recommendation made or an opinion rendered in good faith while acting in the official scope of the person's duties as a member of a multidisciplinary team or as a board member, staff member, or volunteer of a center.

(b) The limitation on civil liability of Subsection (a) does not apply if a person's actions constitute gross negligence.

§ 264.408. Use of Information and Records; Confidentiality and Ownership

(a) The files, reports, records, communications, and working papers used or developed in providing services under this chapter are confidential and not subject to public release under Chapter 552, Government Code, and may only be disclosed for purposes consistent with this chapter. Disclosure may be to:

(1) the department, department employees, law enforcement agencies, prosecuting attorneys, medical professionals, and other state **or local** agencies that provide services to children and families; and

(2) the attorney for the child who is the subject of the records and a court-appointed volunteer advocate appointed for the child under Section 107.031.

(b) Information related to the investigation of a report of abuse or neglect under Chapter 261 and services provided as a result of the investigation is confidential as provided by Section 261.201.

(c) The department, a law enforcement agency, and a prosecuting attorney may share with a center information that is confidential under Section 261.201 as needed to provide services under this chapter. Confidential information shared with or provided to a center remains the property of the agency that shared or provided the information to the center.

(d) A videotaped interview of a child made at a center is the property of the prosecuting attorney involved in the criminal prosecution of the case involving the child. If no criminal prosecution occurs, the videotaped interview is the property of the attorney involved in representing the department in a civil action alleging child abuse or neglect. If the matter involving the child is not prosecuted, the videotape is the property of the department if the matter is an investigation by the department of abuse or neglect. If the department is not investigating or has not investigated the matter, the videotape is the property of the agency that referred the matter to the center. If the center employs a custodian of records for videotaped interviews of children, the center is responsible for the custody of the videotape. A videotaped interview may be shared with other agencies under a written agreement.

(d–1) A videotaped interview described by Subsection (d) is subject to production under Article 39.14, Code of Criminal Procedure, and Rule 615, Texas Rules of Evidence. A court shall deny any request by a defendant to copy, photograph, duplicate, or otherwise reproduce a videotape of an interview described by Subsection (d), provided that the prosecuting attorney makes the videotape reasonably available to the defendant in the same manner as property or material may be made available to defendants, attorneys, and expert witnesses under Article 39.15(d), Code of Criminal Procedure.

(e) The department shall be allowed access to a center's videotaped interviews of children.

Amended by Acts 2011, 82nd Leg., ch. 653 (S.B. 1106), § 4, eff. June 17, 2011.

§ 264.409. Administrative Contracts

(a) The department or the office of the attorney general may contract with a statewide organization of individuals or groups of individuals who have expertise in the establishment and operation of children's advocacy center programs. The statewide organization shall provide training, technical assistance, and evaluation services for local children's advocacy center programs.

(b) If the office of the attorney general enters into a contract under this section, the contract must provide that the statewide organization may not spend annually for administrative purposes more than 12 percent of the annual amount appropriated to the office of the attorney general for purposes of this section.

Comment

This provision places the Children's Advocacy Center program with the Attorney General's office. The Attorney General is also the umbrella agency for Court Appointed Volunteer Advocate Programs under Subchapter G. *(C.G.C.)*

---

§ 264.410. Contracts With Children's Advocacy Centers

(a) The statewide organization with which the department or the office of the attorney general contracts under Section 264.409 shall contract for services with eligible centers to enhance the existing services of the programs.

(b) The contract under this section may not result in reducing the financial support a local center receives from another source.

(c) If the attorney general enters into a contract with a statewide organization under Section 264.409, the attorney general by rule shall adopt standards for eligible local centers. The statewide organization shall assist the attorney general in developing the standards.

§ 264.411. Eligibility for Contracts

(a) A public entity that operated as a center under this subchapter before November 1, 1995, or a nonprofit entity is eligible for a contract under Section 264.410 if the entity:

(1) has a signed memorandum of understanding as provided by Section 264.403;

(2) operates under the authority of a governing board as provided by Section 264.404;

(3) has a multidisciplinary team of persons involved in the investigation or prosecution of child abuse cases or the delivery of services as provided by Section 264.406;

(4) holds regularly scheduled case reviews as provided by Section 264.406;

(5) operates in a neutral and physically separate space from the day-to-day operations of any public agency partner;

(6) has developed a method of statistical information gathering on children receiving services through the center and shares such statistical information with the statewide organization, the department, and the office of the attorney general when requested;

(7) has an in-house volunteer program;

(8) employs an executive director who is answerable to the board of directors of the entity and who is not the exclusive salaried employee of any public agency partner; and

(9) operates under a working protocol that includes a statement of:

(A) the center's mission;

(B) each agency's role and commitment to the center;

(C) the type of cases to be handled by the center;

(D) the center's procedures for conducting case reviews and forensic interviews and for ensuring access to specialized medical and mental health services; and

(E) the center's policies regarding confidentiality and conflict resolution.

(b) The statewide organization may waive the requirements specified in Subsection (a) if it determines that the waiver will not adversely affect the center's ability to carry out its duties under Section 264.405. Any waiver that is granted must be identified in the written contract with the center.

SUBCHAPTER F. CHILD FATALITY REVIEW AND INVESTIGATION

§ 264.501. Definitions

In this subchapter:

(1) "Autopsy" and "inquest" have the meanings assigned by Article 49.01, Code of Criminal Procedure.

(2) "Bureau of vital statistics" means the bureau of vital statistics of the Texas Department of Health.

(3) "Child" means a person younger than 18 years of age.

(4) "Committee" means the child fatality review team committee.

(5) "Department" means the Department of Protective and Regulatory Services.

(6) "Health care provider" means any health care practitioner or facility that provides medical evaluation or treatment, including dental and mental health evaluation or treatment.

(7) "Meeting" means an in-person meeting or a meeting held by telephone or other electronic medium.

(8) "Preventable death" means a death that may have been prevented by reasonable medical, social, legal, psychological, or educational intervention. The term includes the death of a child from:

(A) intentional or unintentional injuries;

(B) medical neglect;

(C) lack of access to medical care;

(D) neglect and reckless conduct, including failure to supervise and failure to seek medical care; and

(E) premature birth associated with any factor described by Paragraphs (A) through (D).

(9) "Review" means a reexamination of information regarding a deceased child from relevant agencies, professionals, and health care providers.

(10) "Review team" means a child fatality review team established under this subchapter.

(11) "Unexpected death" includes a death of a child that, before investigation:

(A) appears to have occurred without anticipation or forewarning; and

(B) was caused by trauma, suspicious or obscure circumstances, sudden infant death syndrome, abuse or neglect, or an unknown cause.

§ 264.502. Committee

(a) The child fatality review team committee is composed of:

(1) a person appointed by and representing the state registrar of vital statistics;

(2) a person appointed by and representing the commissioner of the department;

(3) a person appointed by and representing the Title V director of the Department of State Health Services; and

(4) individuals selected under Subsection (b).

(b) The members of the committee who serve under Subsections (a)(1) through (3) shall select the following additional committee members:

(1) a criminal prosecutor involved in prosecuting crimes against children;

(2) a sheriff;

(3) a justice of the peace;

(4) a medical examiner;

(5) a police chief;

(6) a pediatrician experienced in diagnosing and treating child abuse and neglect;

(7) a child educator;

(8) a child mental health provider;

(9) a public health professional;

(10) a child protective services specialist;

(11) a sudden infant death syndrome family service provider;

(12) a neonatologist;

(13) a child advocate;

(14) a chief juvenile probation officer;

(15) a child abuse prevention specialist;

(16) a representative of the Department of Public Safety; and

(17) a representative of the Texas Department of **Transportation**~~Motor Vehicles~~.

(c) Members of the committee selected under Subsection (b) serve three-year terms with the terms of five or six members, as appropriate, expiring February 1 each year.

(d) Members selected under Subsection (b) must reflect the geographical, cultural, racial, and ethnic diversity of the state.

(e) An appointment to a vacancy on the committee shall be made in the same manner as the original appointment. A member is eligible for reappointment.

(f) Members of the committee shall select a presiding officer from the members of the committee.

(g) The presiding officer of the committee shall call the meetings of the committee, which shall be held at least quarterly.

(h) A member of the committee is not entitled to compensation for serving on the committee but is entitled to reimbursement for the member's travel expenses as provided in the General Appropriations Act. Reimbursement under this subsection for a person serving on the committee under Subsection (a)(2) shall be paid from funds appropriated to the department. Reimbursement for other persons serving on the committee shall be paid from funds appropriated to the Department of State Health Services.

Amended by Acts 2011, 82nd Leg., ch. 1290 (H.B. 2017), § 42, eff. Sept. 1, 2011.

§ 264.503. Purpose and Duties of Committee and Specified State Agencies

(a) The purpose of the committee is to:

(1) develop an understanding of the causes and incidence of child deaths in this state;

(2) identify procedures within the agencies represented on the committee to reduce the number of preventable child deaths; and

(3) promote public awareness and make recommendations to the governor and the legislature for changes in law, policy, and practice to reduce the number of preventable child deaths.

(b) To ensure that the committee achieves its purpose, the department and the Department of State Health Services shall perform the duties specified by this section.

(c) The department shall work cooperatively with:

(1) the Department of State Health Services;

(2) the committee; and

(3) individual child fatality review teams.

(d) The Department of State Health Services shall:

(1) recognize the creation and participation of review teams;

(2) promote and coordinate training to assist the review teams in carrying out their duties;

(3) assist the committee in developing model protocols for:

(A) the reporting and investigating of child fatalities for law enforcement agencies, child protective services, justices of the peace and medical examiners, and other professionals involved in the investigations of child deaths;

(B) the collection of data regarding child deaths; and

(C) the operation of the review teams;

(4) develop and implement procedures necessary for the operation of the committee; and

(5) promote education of the public regarding the incidence and causes of child deaths, the public role in preventing child deaths, and specific steps the public can undertake to prevent child deaths.

(d–1) The committee shall enlist the support and assistance of civic, philanthropic, and public service organizations in the performance of the duties imposed under Subsection (d).

(e) In addition to the duties under Subsection (d), the Department of State Health Services shall:

(1) collect data under this subchapter and coordinate the collection of data under this subchapter with other data collection activities; and

(2) perform annual statistical studies of the incidence and causes of child fatalities using the data collected under this subchapter.

(f) The committee shall issue a report for each preventable child death. The report must include findings related to the child's death, recommendations on how to prevent similar deaths, and details surrounding the department's involvement with the child prior to the child's death. Not later than April 1 of each year, the committee shall publish a compilation of the reports published under this subsection during the year, submit a copy of the compilation to the governor, lieutenant governor, speaker of the house of representatives, and department, and make the compilation available to the public. Not later than October 1 of each year, the department shall submit a written response on the compilation from the previous year to the committee, governor, lieutenant governor, and speaker of the house of representatives describing which of the committee's recommendations regarding the operation of the child protective services system the department will implement and the methods of implementation.

(g) The committee shall perform the functions and duties required of a citizen review panel under 42 U.S.C. Section 5106a(c)(4)(A).

§ 264.504. Meetings of Committee

(a) Except as provided by Subsections (b), (c), and (d), meetings of the committee are subject to the open meetings law, Chapter 551, Government Code, as if the committee were a governmental body under that chapter.

(b) Any portion of a meeting of the committee during which the committee discusses an individual child's death is closed to the public and is not subject to the open meetings law, Chapter 551, Government Code.

(c) Information identifying a deceased child, a member of the child's family, a guardian or caretaker of the child, or an alleged or suspected perpetrator of abuse or neglect of the child may not be disclosed during a public meeting. On a majority vote of the committee members, the members shall remove from the committee any member who discloses information described by this subsection in a public meeting.

(d) Information regarding the involvement of a state or local agency with the deceased child or another person described by Subsection (c) may not be disclosed during a public meeting.

(e) The committee may conduct an open or closed meeting by telephone conference call or other electronic medium. A meeting held under this subsection is subject to the notice requirements applicable to other meetings. The notice of the meeting must specify as the location of the meeting the location where meetings of the committee are usually held. Each part of the meeting by telephone conference call that is required to be open to the public shall be audible to the public at the location specified in the notice of the meeting as the location of the meeting and shall be tape-recorded. The tape recording shall be made available to the public.

(f) This section does not prohibit the committee from requesting the attendance at a closed meeting of a person who is not a member of the committee and who has information regarding a deceased child.

§ 264.505. Establishment of Review Team

(a) A multidisciplinary and multiagency child fatality review team may be established for a county to review child deaths in that county. A review team for a county with a population of less than 50,000 may join with an adjacent county or counties to establish a combined review team.

(b) Any person who may be a member of a review team under Subsection (c) may initiate the establishment of a review team and call the first organizational meeting of the team.

(c) A review team may include:

(1) a criminal prosecutor involved in prosecuting crimes against children;

(2) a sheriff;

(3) a justice of the peace or medical examiner;

(4) a police chief;

(5) a pediatrician experienced in diagnosing and treating child abuse and neglect;

(6) a child educator;

(7) a child mental health provider;

(8) a public health professional;

(9) a child protective services specialist;

(10) a sudden infant death syndrome family service provider;

(11) a neonatologist;

(12) a child advocate;

(13) a chief juvenile probation officer; and

(14) a child abuse prevention specialist.

(d) Members of a review team may select additional team members according to community resources and needs.

(e) A review team shall select a presiding officer from its members.

§ 264.506. Purpose and Duties of Review Team

(a) The purpose of a review team is to decrease the incidence of preventable child deaths by:

(1) providing assistance, direction, and coordination to investigations of child deaths;

(2) promoting cooperation, communication, and coordination among agencies involved in responding to child fatalities;

(3) developing an understanding of the causes and incidence of child deaths in the county or counties in which the review team is located;

(4) recommending changes to agencies, through the agency's representative member, that will reduce the number of preventable child deaths; and

(5) advising the committee on changes to law, policy, or practice that will assist the team and the agencies represented on the team in fulfilling their duties.

(b) To achieve its purpose, a review team shall:

(1) adapt and implement, according to local needs and resources, the model protocols developed by the department and the committee;

(2) meet on a regular basis to review child fatality cases and recommend methods to improve coordination of services and investigations between agencies that are represented on the team;

(3) collect and maintain data as required by the committee; and

(4) submit to the bureau of vital statistics data reports on deaths reviewed as specified by the committee.

(c) A review team shall initiate prevention measures as indicated by the review team's findings.

§ 264.507. Duties of Presiding Officer

The presiding officer of a review team shall:

(1) send notices to the review team members of a meeting to review a child fatality;

(2) provide a list to the review team members of each child fatality to be reviewed at the meeting;

(3) submit data reports to the bureau of vital statistics not later than the 30th day after the date on which the review took place; and

(4) ensure that the review team operates according to the protocols developed by the department and the committee, as adapted by the review team.

§ 264.508. Review Procedure

(a) The review team of the county in which the injury, illness, or event that was the cause of the death of the child occurred, as stated on the child's death certificate, shall review the death.

(b) On receipt of the list of child fatalities under Section 264.507, each review team member shall review the member's records and the records of the member's agency for information regarding each listed child.

§ 264.509. Access to Information

(a) A review team may request information and records regarding a deceased child as necessary to carry out the review team's purpose and duties. Records and information that may be requested under this section include:

(1) medical, dental, and mental health care information; and

(2) information and records maintained by any state or local government agency, including:

(A) a birth certificate;

(B) law enforcement investigative data;

(C) medical examiner investigative data;

(D) juvenile court records;

(E) parole and probation information and records; and

(F) child protective services information and records.

(b) On request of the presiding officer of a review team, the custodian of the relevant information and records relating to a deceased child shall provide those records to the review team at no cost to the review team.

(c) This subsection does not authorize the release of the original or copies of the mental health or medical records of any member of the child's family or the guardian or caretaker of the child or an alleged or suspected perpetrator of abuse or neglect of the child which are in the possession of any state or local government agency as provided in Subsection (a)(2). Information relating to the mental health or medical condition of a member of of the child's family or the guardian or caretaker of the child or the alleged or suspected perpetrator of abuse or neglect of the child acquired as part of an investigation by a state or local government agency as provided in Subsection (a)(2) may be provided to the review team.

§ 264.510. Meeting of Review Team

(a) A meeting of a review team is closed to the public and not subject to the open meetings law, Chapter 551, Government Code.

(b) This section does not prohibit a review team from requesting the attendance at a closed meeting of a person who is not a member of the review team and who has information regarding a deceased child.

(c) Except as necessary to carry out a review team's purpose and duties, members of a review team and persons attending a review team meeting may not disclose what occurred at the meeting.

(d) A member of a review team participating in the review of a child death is immune from civil or criminal liability arising from information presented in or opinions formed as a result of a meeting.

§ 264.511. Use of Information and Records; Confidentiality

(a) Information and records acquired by the committee or by a review team in the exercise of its purpose and duties under this subchapter are confidential and exempt from disclosure under the open records law, Chapter 552, Government Code, and may only be disclosed as necessary to carry out the committee's or review team's purpose and duties.

(b) A report of the committee or of a review team or a statistical compilation of data reports is a public record subject to the open records law, Chapter 552, Government Code, as if the committee or review team were a governmental body under that chapter, if the report or statistical compilation does not contain any information that would permit the identification of an individual.

(c) A member of a review team may not disclose any information that is confidential under this section.

(d) Information, documents, and records of the committee or of a review team that are confidential under this section are not subject to subpoena or discovery and may not be introduced into evidence in any civil or criminal proceeding, except that information, documents, and records otherwise available from other sources are not immune from subpoena, discovery, or introduction into evidence solely because they were presented during proceedings of the committee or a review team or are maintained by the committee or a review team.

§ 264.512. Governmental Units

The committee and a review team are governmental units for purposes of Chapter 101, Civil Practice and Remedies Code. A review team is a unit of local government under that chapter.

§ 264.513. Report of Death of Child

(a) A person who knows of the death of a child younger than six years of age shall immediately report the death to the medical examiner of the county in which the death occurs or, if the death occurs in a county that does not have a medical examiner's office or that is not part of a medical examiner's district, to a justice of the peace in that county.

(b) The requirement of this section is in addition to any other reporting requirement imposed by law, including any requirement that a person report child abuse or neglect under this code.

(c) A person is not required to report a death under this section that is the result of a motor vehicle accident. This subsection does not affect a duty imposed by another law to report a death that is the result of a motor vehicle accident.

§ 264.514. Procedure in the Event of Reportable Death

(a) A medical examiner or justice of the peace notified of a death of a child under Section 264.513 shall hold an inquest under Chapter 49, Code of Criminal Procedure, to determine whether the death is unexpected or the result of abuse or neglect. An inquest is not required under this subchapter if the child's death is expected and is due to a congenital or neoplastic disease. A death caused by an infectious disease may be considered an expected death if:

(1) the disease was not acquired as a result of trauma or poisoning;

(2) the infectious organism is identified using standard medical procedures; and

(3) the death is not reportable to the Texas Department of Health under Chapter 81, Health and Safety Code.

(b) The medical examiner or justice of the peace shall immediately notify an appropriate local law enforcement agency if the medical examiner or justice of the peace determines that the death is unexpected or the result of abuse or neglect, and that agency shall investigate the child's death.

(c) In this section, the terms "abuse" and "neglect" have the meaning assigned those terms by Section 261.001.

Comment

Subsection (b) makes clear that even an "expected" death resulting from child abuse or neglect must be reported to law enforcement by the medical examiner or justice of the peace. Tex. Health and Safety Code Ann. § 673.002 requires an autopsy for all unexplained deaths of children 12 months old or younger and requires the Department of Health to develop rules defining Sudden Infant Death Syndrome (SIDS) and to provide reimbursement for required autopsies. *(C.G.C.)*

§ 264.515. Investigation

(a) The investigation required by Section 264.514 must include:

(1) an autopsy, unless an autopsy was conducted as part of the inquest;

(2) an inquiry into the circumstances of the death, including an investigation of the scene of the death and interviews with the parents of the child, any guardian or caretaker of the child, and the person who reported the child's death; and

(3) a review of relevant information regarding the child from an agency, professional, or health care provider.

(b) The review required by Subsection (a)(3) must include a review of any applicable medical record, child protective services record, record maintained by an emergency medical services provider, and law enforcement report.

(c) The committee shall develop a protocol relating to investigation of an unexpected death of a child under this section. In developing the protocol, the committee shall consult with individuals and organizations that have knowledge and experience in the issues of child abuse and child deaths.

SUBCHAPTER G. COURT–APPOINTED VOLUNTEER ADVOCATE PROGRAMS

§ 264.601. Definitions

In this subchapter:

(1) "Abused or neglected child" means a child who is:

(A) the subject of a suit affecting the parent-child relationship filed by a governmental entity; and

(B) under the control or supervision of the department.

(2) "Volunteer advocate program" means a volunteer-based, nonprofit program that:

(A) provides advocacy services to abused or neglected children with the goal of obtaining a permanent placement for a child that is in the child's best interest; and

(B) complies with recognized standards for volunteer advocate programs.

§ 264.602. Contracts With Advocate Programs

(a) The statewide organization with which the attorney general contracts under Section 264.603 shall contract for services with eligible volunteer advocate programs to provide advocacy services to abused or neglected children.

(b) The contract under this section may not result in reducing the financial support a volunteer advocate program receives from another source.

(c) The attorney general shall develop a scale of state financial support for volunteer advocate programs that declines over a six-year period beginning on the date each individual contract takes effect. After the end of the six-year period, the attorney general may not provide more than 50 percent of the volunteer advocate program's funding.

(d) The attorney general by rule shall adopt standards for a local volunteer advocate program. The statewide organization shall assist the attorney general in developing the standards.

(e) The department, in cooperation with the statewide organization with which the attorney general contracts under Section 264.603 and other interested agencies, shall support the expansion of court-appointed volunteer advocate programs into counties in which there is a need for the programs. In expanding into a county, a program shall work to ensure the independence of the program, to the extent possible, by establishing community support and accessing private funding from the community for the program.

(f) Expenses incurred by a volunteer advocate program to promote public awareness of the need for volunteer advocates or to explain the work performed by volunteer advocates that are paid with money from the attorney general volunteer advocate program account under Section 504.611, Transportation Code, are not considered administrative expenses for the purpose of Section 264.603(b).

§ 264.603. Administrative Contracts

(a) The attorney general shall contract with one statewide organization of individuals or groups of individuals who have expertise in the dynamics of child abuse and neglect and experience in operating volunteer advocate programs to provide training, technical assistance, and evaluation services for the benefit of local volunteer advocate programs. The contract shall:

(1) include measurable goals and objectives relating to the number of:

(A) volunteer advocates in the program; and

(B) children receiving services from the program; and

(2) follow practices designed to ensure compliance with standards referenced in the contract.

(b) The contract under this section shall provide that not more than 12 percent of the annual legislative appropriation to implement this subchapter may be spent for administrative purposes by the statewide organization with which the attorney general contracts under this section.

§ 264.604. Eligibility for Contracts

(a) A person is eligible for a contract under Section 264.602 only if the person is a public or private nonprofit entity that operates a volunteer advocate program that:

(1) uses individuals appointed as volunteer advocates or guardians ad litem by the court to provide for the needs of abused or neglected children;

(2) has provided court-appointed advocacy services for at least six months;

(3) provides court-appointed advocacy services for at least 10 children each month; and

(4) has demonstrated that the program has local judicial support.

(b) The statewide organization with which the attorney general contracts under Section 264.603 may not contract with a person that is not eligible under this section. However, the statewide organization may waive the requirement in Subsection (a)(3) for an established program in a rural area or under other special circumstances.

§ 264.605. Contract Form

A person shall apply for a contract under Section 264.602 on a form provided by the attorney general.

§ 264.606. Criteria for Award of Contracts

The statewide organization with which the attorney general contracts under Section 264.603 shall consider the following in awarding a contract under Section 264.602:

(1) the volunteer advocate program's eligibility for and use of funds from local, state, or federal governmental sources, philanthropic organizations, and other sources;

(2) community support for the volunteer advocate program as indicated by financial contributions from civic organizations, individuals, and other community resources;

(3) whether the volunteer advocate program provides services that encourage the permanent placement of children through reunification with their families or timely placement with an adoptive family; and

(4) whether the volunteer advocate program has the endorsement and cooperation of the local juvenile court system.

§ 264.607. Contract Requirements

(a) The attorney general shall require that a contract under Section 264.602 require the volunteer advocate program to:

(1) make quarterly and annual financial reports on a form provided by the attorney general;

(2) cooperate with inspections and audits that the attorney general makes to ensure service standards and fiscal responsibility; and

(3) provide as a minimum:

(A) independent and factual information in writing to the court and to counsel for the parties involved regarding the child;

(B) advocacy through the courts for permanent home placement and rehabilitation services for the child;

(C) monitoring of the child to ensure the safety of the child and to prevent unnecessary movement of the child to multiple temporary placements;

(D) reports in writing to the presiding judge and to counsel for the parties involved;

(E) community education relating to child abuse and neglect;

(F) referral services to existing community services;

(G) a volunteer recruitment and training program, including adequate screening procedures for volunteers;

(H) procedures to assure the confidentiality of records or information relating to the child; and

(I) compliance with the standards adopted under Section 264.602.

(b), (c) Repealed by Acts 2009, 81st Leg., ch. 1224, § 7.

§ 264.608. Report to the Legislature

(a) Before each regular session of the legislature, the attorney general shall publish a report that:

(1) summarizes reports from volunteer advocate programs under contract with the attorney general;

(2) analyzes the effectiveness of the contracts made by the attorney general under this chapter; and

(3) provides information on:

(A) the expenditure of funds under this chapter;

(B) services provided and the number of children for whom the services were provided; and

(C) any other information relating to the services provided by the volunteer advocate programs under this chapter.

(b) The attorney general shall submit copies of the report to the governor, lieutenant governor, speaker of the house of representatives, the Legislative Budget Board, and members of the legislature.

§ 264.609. Rule–Making Authority

The attorney general may adopt rules necessary to implement this chapter.

§ 264.610. Confidentiality

The attorney general may not disclose information gained through reports, collected case data, or inspections that would identify a person working at or receiving services from a volunteer advocate program.

§ 264.611. Consultations

In implementing this chapter, the attorney general shall consult with individuals or groups of individuals who have expertise in the dynamics of child abuse and neglect and experience in operating volunteer advocate programs.

§ 264.612. Funding

(a) The attorney general may solicit and receive grants or money from either private or public sources, including by appropriation by the legislature from the general revenue fund, to implement this chapter.

(b) The need for and importance of the implementation of this chapter by the attorney general requires priority and preferential consideration for appropriation.

§ 264.613. Use of Information and Records; Confidentiality

(a) The files, reports, records, communications, and working papers used or developed in providing services under this subchapter are confidential and not subject to disclosure under Chapter 552, Government Code, and may only be disclosed for purposes consistent with this subchapter.

(b) Information described by Subsection (a) may be disclosed to:

(1) the department, department employees, law enforcement agencies, prosecuting attorneys, medical professionals, and other state agencies that provide services to children and families;

(2) the attorney for the child who is the subject of the information; and

(3) eligible children's advocacy centers.

(c) Information related to the investigation of a report of abuse or neglect of a child under Chapter 261 and services provided as a result of the investigation are confidential as provided by Section 261.201.

SUBCHAPTER H. CHILD ABUSE PROGRAM EVALUATION

§ 264.701. Child Abuse Program Evaluation Committee

(a) The Child Abuse Program Evaluation Committee is established within the Department of Protective and Regulatory Services.

(b) The committee is appointed by the Board of Protective and Regulatory Services and is composed of the following 15 members:

(1) an officer or employee of the Texas Education Agency;

(2) two officers or employees of the Department of Protective and Regulatory Services;

(3) an officer or employee of the Texas Juvenile Probation Commission;

(4) an officer or employee of the Texas Department of Mental Health and Mental Retardation;

(5) an officer or employee of the Health and Human Services Commission;

(6) three members of the public who have knowledge of and experience in the area of delivery of services relating to child abuse and neglect;

(7) three members of the public who have knowledge of and experience in the area of evaluation of programs relating to the prevention and treatment of child abuse and neglect; and

(8) three members of the public who are or have been recipients of services relating to the prevention or treatment of child abuse or neglect.

(c) In appointing members to the committee under Subsection (b)(8), the board shall consider appointing:

(1) an adult who as a child was a recipient of services relating to the prevention or treatment of child abuse or neglect; and

(2) a custodial and a noncustodial parent of a child who is or was a recipient of services relating to the prevention or treatment of child abuse or neglect.

(d) A committee member appointed to represent a state agency or entity serves at the pleasure of the board or until termination of the person's employment or membership with the agency or entity. The public members serve staggered six-year terms, with the terms of three public members expiring on September 1 of each even-numbered year.

(e) A member of the committee serves without compensation. A public member is entitled to reimbursement for travel expenses and per diem as provided by the General Appropriations Act.

(f) The committee shall elect from its members a presiding officer and any other officers considered necessary.

(g) Appointments to the committee shall be made without regard to the race, color, handicap, sex, religion, age, or national origin of an appointee.

(h) The committee shall:

(1) develop and adopt policies and procedures governing the system each state agency uses to evaluate the effectiveness of programs to prevent or treat child abuse or neglect with which the agency contracts;

(2) develop and adopt standard definitions of "child abuse treatment" and "child abuse prevention" to be used in implementing and administering the evaluation system created under this subchapter;

(3) develop and adopt standard models and guidelines for prevention and treatment of child abuse to be used in implementing and administering the evaluation system created under this subchapter;

(4) develop and adopt, in cooperation with each affected state agency, a schedule for each agency's adoption and implementation of the committee's evaluation system that considers each agency's budget cycle;

(5) develop and adopt a standard report form and a reporting schedule for the affected agencies; **and**

(6) develop and adopt objective criteria by which the performance of child abuse programs may be measured after reports under this subchapter are submitted and evaluated.~~; and (7) report annually to the Board of Protective and Regulatory Services, governor, lieutenant governor, and speaker of the house of representatives on the results of the committee's evaluation process~~

(i) In adopting an evaluation system under this subchapter, the committee shall allow the affected agencies as much latitude as possible in:

(1) the methods used to collect the required data; and

(2) the timetable for full implementation of the system, allowing for gradual implementation of the system according to classes of program providers.

(j) Each agency that contracts with a public or private entity for services relating to a program for the prevention or treatment of child abuse or neglect shall adopt and implement the committee's evaluation system and shall report to the committee as required by this subchapter.

Amended by Acts 2011, 82nd Leg., ch. 1050 (S.B. 71), § 1, eff. Sept. 1, 2011; Acts 2011, 82nd Leg., ch. 1083 (S.B. 1179), § 4, eff. June 17, 2011.

SUBCHAPTER H–1. TASK FORCE TO REDUCE CHILD ABUSE AND NEGLECT AND IMPROVE CHILD WELFARE

§ 264.721. Establishment of Task Force

A task force is established under this subchapter to develop a strategy to reduce child abuse and neglect and improve child welfare.

Added by Acts 2011, 82nd Leg., ch. 435 (S.B. 1154), § 1, eff. June 17, 2011.

§ 264.722. Task Force

(a) The task force consists of nine members appointed as follows:

(1) seven members appointed by the governor, two of whom must be appointed from a list of candidates submitted by the speaker of the house of representatives; and

(2) two members appointed by the lieutenant governor.

(b) Members of the task force must be individuals who:

(1) are actively involved in the prevention of child abuse and neglect and the improvement of child welfare; and

(2) represent a diversity of backgrounds.

(c) Appointments to the task force shall be made without regard to the race, color, disability, sex, religion, age, or national origin of the appointee.

(d) A task force member is not entitled to compensation for service on the task force but is entitled to reimbursement for travel expenses as provided by Chapter 660, Government Code, and the General Appropriations Act.

(e) The task force shall elect a presiding officer by a majority vote of the membership of the task force.

(f) The task force shall meet at the call of the presiding officer.

(g) Chapter 2110, Government Code, does not apply to the task force.

Added by Acts 2011, 82nd Leg., ch. 435 (S.B. 1154), § 1, eff. June 17, 2011.

§ 264.723. Task Force Duties

(a) The task force shall identify:

(1) all existing programs in the state relating to reducing child abuse and neglect or improving child welfare; and

(2) the programs described by Subdivision (1) that receive state money.

(b) The task force shall establish a strategy for reducing child abuse and neglect and for improving child welfare in this state. In establishing that strategy, the task force shall:

(1) gather information concerning child safety, child abuse and neglect, and child welfare throughout the state;

(2) receive reports and testimony from individuals, state and local agencies, community-based organizations, and other public and private organizations;

(3) create goals for state policy that would improve child safety, prevent child abuse and neglect, and improve child welfare;

(4) review and revise the strategic plan to accomplish those goals submitted by a previous task force; and

(5) submit the revised strategic plan.

(c) The revised strategic plan submitted under Subsection (b) may include proposals for specific statutory changes, the creation of new programs, and methods to foster cooperation among state agencies and between the state and local governments.

Added by Acts 2011, 82nd Leg., ch. 435 (S.B. 1154), § 1, eff. June 17, 2011.

§ 264.724. Support Agency Duties

The department, the Department of State Health Services, the Texas Department of Criminal Justice, the Texas Youth Commission, the Texas Juvenile Probation Commission, The University of Texas System, and The Texas A&M University System shall:

(1) provide administrative support services to the task force;

(2) coordinate administrative responsibilities with the task force to avoid unnecessary duplication of duties;

(3) share equally the costs of the task force, including reimbursement for travel expenses, administrative expenses, and the costs of publishing the task force's strategic plan; and

(4) each designate a person to serve as the agency liaison with the task force.

Added by Acts 2011, 82nd Leg., ch. 435 (S.B. 1154), § 1, eff. June 17, 2011.

§ 264.725. Consultation With Other Agencies; Private Foundations

(a) The task force shall consult with employees of the department, the Department of State Health Services, the Texas Department of Criminal Justice, the Texas Youth

Commission, the Texas Juvenile Probation Commission, The University of Texas System, and The Texas A&M University System as necessary to accomplish the task force's responsibilities under this subchapter.

(b) The task force shall cooperate as necessary with any other state agency.

(c) The task force may consult with private foundations that have made a substantial commitment to the prevention of child abuse in this state to accomplish the task force's responsibilities under this chapter.

Added by Acts 2011, 82nd Leg., ch. 435 (S.B. 1154), § 1, eff. June 17, 2011.

§ 264.726. Funding; Account

(a) The task force shall review the funding strategies for the task force and develop proposals for expanding the sources of funds available to finance the activities of the task force.

(b) The task force may accept gifts and grants from individuals or private or public organizations and accept federal and local funds to support the task force.

(c) The child abuse reduction task force account is an account in the general revenue fund. Money in the account may be appropriated only to the task force for the purposes of this subchapter. The child abuse reduction task force account is exempt from the application of Section 403.095, Government Code. The account consists of:

(1) gifts and grants to the task force;

(2) money received by the task force from the federal, state, or local government; and

(3) notwithstanding Section 404.071, Government Code, all interest attributable to money held in the account.

Added by Acts 2011, 82nd Leg., ch. 435 (S.B. 1154), § 1, eff. June 17, 2011.

§ 264.727. Submission of Plan

Not later than December 1, 2012, the task force shall submit the strategic plan required by Section 264.723 to the governor, lieutenant governor, and speaker of the house of representatives.

Added by Acts 2011, 82nd Leg., ch. 435 (S.B. 1154), § 1, eff. June 17, 2011.

§ 264.728. Expiration

The task force is abolished and this subchapter expires September 1, 2013.

Added by Acts 2011, 82nd Leg., ch. 435 (S.B. 1154), § 1, eff. June 17, 2011.

SUBCHAPTER I. RELATIVE AND OTHER DESIGNATED CAREGIVER PLACEMENT PROGRAM

§ 264.751. Definitions

In this subchapter:

(1) "Designated caregiver" means an individual who has a longstanding and significant relationship with a child for whom the department has been appointed managing conservator and who:

(A) is appointed to provide substitute care for the child, but is not licensed by the department or verified by a licensed child-placing agency or the department to operate a foster home, foster group home, agency foster home, or agency foster group home under Chapter 42, Human Resources Code; or

(B) is subsequently appointed permanent managing conservator of the child after providing the care described by Paragraph (A).

(2) "Relative" means a person related to a child by consanguinity as determined under Section 573.022, Government Code.

(3) "Relative caregiver" means a relative who:

(A) provides substitute care for a child for whom the department has been appointed managing conservator, but who is not licensed by the department or verified by a licensed child-placing agency or the department to operate a foster home, foster group home, agency foster home, or agency foster group home under Chapter 42, Human Resources Code; or

(B) is subsequently appointed permanent managing conservator of the child after providing the care described by Paragraph (A).

§ 264.752. Relative and other Designated Caregiver Placement Program

(a) The department shall develop and procure a program to:

(1) promote continuity and stability for children for whom the department is appointed managing conservator by placing those children with relative or other designated caregivers; and

(2) facilitate relative or other designated caregiver placements by providing assistance and services to those caregivers in accordance with this subchapter and rules adopted by the executive commissioner.

(b) To the extent permitted by federal law, the department shall use federal funds available under Title IV–E, Social Security Act (42 U.S.C. Section 670 et seq.), to administer the program under this subchapter.

(c) The executive commissioner shall adopt rules necessary to implement this subchapter. The rules must include eligibility criteria for receiving assistance and services under this subchapter.

§ 264.753. Expedited Placement

The department or other authorized entity shall expedite the completion of the background and criminal history check, the home study, and any other administrative procedure to ensure that the child is placed with a qualified relative or caregiver as soon as possible after the date the caregiver is identified.

§ 264.754. Investigation of Proposed Placement

Before placing a child with a proposed relative or other designated caregiver, the department must conduct an investigation to determine whether the proposed placement is in the child's best interest.

§ 264.755. Caregiver Assistance Agreement

(a) The department shall, subject to the availability of funds, enter into a caregiver assistance agreement with each relative or other designated caregiver to provide monetary assistance and additional support services to the caregiver. The monetary assistance and support services shall be based on a family's need, as determined by rules adopted by the executive commissioner.

(b) Monetary assistance provided under this section must include a one-time cash payment of not more than $1,000 to the caregiver on the initial placement of a child or a sibling group. The cash payment must be provided on the initial placement of each child with the caregiver and is provided to assist the caregiver in purchasing essential child-care items such as furniture and clothing.

(c) Monetary assistance and additional support services provided under this section may include:

(1) case management services and training and information about the child's needs until the caregiver is appointed permanent managing conservator;

(2) referrals to appropriate state agencies administering public benefits or assistance programs for which the child, the caregiver, or the caregiver's family may qualify;

(3) family counseling not provided under the Medicaid program for the caregiver's family for a period not to exceed two years from the date of initial placement;

(4) if the caregiver meets the eligibility criteria determined by rules adopted by the executive commissioner, reimbursement of all child-care expenses incurred while the child is under 13 years of age, or under 18 years of age if the child has a developmental disability, and while the department is the child's managing conservator;

(5) if the caregiver meets the eligibility criteria determined by rules adopted by the executive commissioner, reimbursement of 50 percent of child-care expenses incurred after the caregiver is appointed permanent managing conservator of the child while the child is under 13 years of age, or under 18 years of age if the child has a developmental disability; and

(6) reimbursement of other expenses, as determined by rules adopted by the executive commissioner, not to exceed $500 per year for each child.

§ 264.756. Assistance with Permanent Placement

The department shall collaborate with the State Bar of Texas and local community partners to identify legal resources to assist relatives and other designated caregivers in obtaining conservatorship, adoption, or other permanent legal status for the child.

§ 264.757. Coordination with other Agencies

The department shall coordinate with other health and human services agencies, as defined by Section 531.001, Government Code, to provide assistance and services under this subchapter.

§ 264.758. Funds

The department and other state agencies shall actively seek and use federal funds available for the purposes of this subchapter.

§ 264.759. Records of Placements That Fail for Financial Reasons

(a) The department shall record each instance in which a placement under this subchapter is not able to be made solely because the relative or designated caregiver cannot afford to care for the child. The department shall document, if possible, the amount of monetary assistance and reimbursement to which the caregiver would be entitled and the amount of assistance that would have made the placement affordable for the caregiver.

(b) The department shall compile statistics based on the information recorded under this section and shall report annually to the legislature regarding proposed placements that are not made in the preceding year due to financial reasons. The report required under this subsection may be made in conjunction with other reports the department is required to submit to the legislature.

§ 264.760. Eligibility for Foster Care Payments and Permanency Care Assistance

Notwithstanding any other provision of this subchapter, a relative or other designated caregiver who becomes licensed by the department or verified by a licensed child-placing agency or the department to operate a foster home, foster group home, agency foster home, or agency foster group home under Chapter 42, Human Resources Code, may receive foster care payments in lieu of the benefits provided by this subchapter, beginning with the first month in which the relative or other designated caregiver becomes licensed or is verified.

SUBCHAPTER J. FAMILY DRUG COURT PROGRAM

§ 264.801. Family Drug Court Program Defined

In this subchapter, "family drug court program" means a program that has the following essential characteristics:

(1) the integration of substance abuse treatment services in the processing of civil cases in the child welfare system with the goal of family reunification;

(2) the use of a comprehensive case management approach involving department caseworkers, court-appointed case managers, and court-appointed special advocates to rehabilitate a parent who has had a child removed from the parent's care by the department because of suspected child abuse or neglect and who is suspected of substance abuse;

(3) early identification and prompt placement of eligible parents who volunteer to participate in the program;

(4) comprehensive substance abuse needs assessment and referral to an appropriate substance abuse treatment agency;

(5) a progressive treatment approach with specific requirements that a parent must meet to advance to the next phase of the program;

(6) monitoring of abstinence through periodic alcohol or other drug testing;

(7) ongoing judicial interaction with program participants;

(8) monitoring and evaluation of program goals and effectiveness;

(9) continuing interdisciplinary education to promote effective program planning, implementation, and operations; and

(10) development of partnerships with public agencies and community organizations.

§ 264.802. Authority to Establish Program

The commissioners court of a county may establish a family drug court program for persons who:

(1) have had a child removed from their care by the department; and

(2) are suspected by the department or a court of having a substance abuse problem.

§ 264.803. Oversight

(a) The lieutenant governor and the speaker of the house of representatives may assign to appropriate legislative committees duties relating to the oversight of family drug court programs established under this subchapter.

(b) A legislative committee or the governor may request the state auditor to perform a management, operations, or financial or accounting audit of a family drug court program established under this subchapter.

§ 264.804. Participant Payment for Treatment and Services

A family drug court program may require a participant to pay the cost of all treatment and services received while participating in the program, based on the participant's ability to pay.

§ 264.805. Funding

A county creating a family drug court under this chapter shall explore the possibility of using court improvement project funds to finance the family drug court in the county. The county shall also explore the availability of federal and state matching funds to finance the court.

SUBCHAPTER K. PERMANENCY CARE ASSISTANCE PROGRAM

§ 264.851. Definitions

In this subchapter:

(1) "Foster child" means a child who is or was in the temporary or permanent managing conservatorship of the department.

(2) "Kinship provider" means a relative of a foster child, or another adult with a longstanding and significant relationship with a foster child before the child was placed with the person by the department, with whom the child resides for at least six consecutive months after the person becomes licensed by the department or verified by a licensed child-placing agency or the department to provide foster care.

(3) "Permanency care assistance agreement" means a written agreement between the department and a kinship provider for the payment of permanency care assistance benefits as provided by this subchapter.

(4) "Permanency care assistance benefits" means monthly payments paid by the department to a kinship provider under a permanency care assistance agreement.

(5) "Relative" means a person related to a foster child by consanguinity or affinity.

§ 264.852. Permanency Care Assistance Agreements

(a) The department shall enter into a permanency care assistance agreement with a kinship provider who is eligible to receive permanency care assistance benefits.

(b) The department may enter into a permanency care assistance agreement with a kinship provider who is the prospective managing conservator of a foster child only if the kinship provider meets the eligibility criteria under federal and state law and department rule.

(c) A court may not order the department to enter into a permanency care assistance agreement with a kinship provider unless the kinship provider meets the eligibility criteria under federal and state law and department rule, including requirements relating to the criminal history background check of a kinship provider.

(d) A permanency care assistance agreement may provide for reimbursement of the nonrecurring expenses a kinship provider incurs in obtaining permanent managing conservatorship of a foster child, including attorney's fees and court costs. The reimbursement of the nonrecurring expenses under this subsection may not exceed $2,000.

§ 264.8521. Notice to Applicants

At the time a person applies to become licensed by the department or verified by a licensed child-placing agency or the department to provide foster care in order to qualify for the permanency care assistance program, the department or the child-placing agency shall:

(1) notify the applicant that a background check, including a criminal history record check, will be conducted on the individual; and

(2) inform the applicant about criminal convictions that:

(A) preclude an individual from becoming a licensed foster home or verified agency foster home; and

(B) may also be considered in evaluating the individual's application.

Added by Acts 2011, 82nd Leg., ch. 318 (H.B. 2370), § 1, eff. Sept. 1, 2011.

§ 264.853. Rules

The executive commissioner shall adopt rules necessary to implement the permanency care assistance program. The rules must:

(1) establish eligibility requirements to receive permanency care assistance benefits under the program; and

(2) ensure that the program conforms to the requirements for federal assistance as required by the Fostering Connections to Success and Increasing Adoptions Act of 2008 (Pub. L. No. 110–351).

§ 264.854. Maximum Payment Amount

The executive commissioner shall set the maximum monthly amount of assistance payments under a permanency care assistance agreement in an amount that does not exceed the amount of the monthly foster care maintenance payment the department would pay to a foster care provider caring for the child for whom the kinship provider is caring.

§ 264.855. Continued Eligibility for Permanency Care Assistance Benefits after Age 18

If the department first entered into a permanency care assistance agreement with a foster child's kinship provider after the child's 16th birthday, the department may continue to provide permanency care assistance payments until the last day of the month of the child's 21st birthday, provided the child is:

(1) regularly attending high school or enrolled in a program leading toward a high school diploma or high school equivalency certificate;

(2) regularly attending an institution of higher education or a postsecondary vocational or technical program;

(3) participating in a program or activity that promotes, or removes barriers to, employment;

(4) employed for at least 80 hours a month; or

(5) incapable of any of the activities described by Subdivisions (1)–(4) due to a documented medical condition.

§ 264.856. Appropriation Required

The department is not required to provide permanency care assistance benefits under this subchapter unless the department is specifically appropriated money for purposes of this subchapter.

§ 264.857. Deadline for New Agreements

The department may not enter into a permanency care assistance agreement after August 31, 2017. The department shall continue to make payments after that date under a permanency care assistance agreement entered into on or before August 31, 2017, according to the terms of the agreement.

SUBCHAPTER L. PARENTAL CHILD SAFETY PLACEMENTS

§ 264.901. Definitions

In this subchapter:

(1) "Caregiver" means an individual, other than a child's parent, conservator, or legal guardian, who is related to the child or has a long-standing and significant relationship with the child or the child's family.

(2) "Parental child safety placement" means a temporary out-of-home placement of a child with a caregiver that is made by a parent or other person with whom the child resides in accordance with a written agreement approved by the department that ensures the safety of the child:

(A) during an investigation by the department of alleged abuse or neglect of the child; or

(B) while the parent or other person is receiving services from the department.

(3) "Parental child safety placement agreement" means an agreement between a parent or other person making a parental child safety placement and the caregiver that contains the terms of the placement and is approved by the department.

Added by Acts 2011, 82nd Leg., ch. 1071 (S.B. 993), § 1, eff. Sept. 1, 2011.

§ 264.902. Parental Child Safety Placement Agreement

(a) A parental child safety placement agreement must include terms that clearly state:

(1) the respective duties of the person making the placement and the caregiver, including a plan for how the caregiver will access necessary medical treatment for the child and the caregiver's duty to ensure that a school-age child is enrolled in and attending school;

(2) conditions under which the person placing the child may have access to the child, including how often the person may visit and the circumstances under which the person's visit may occur;

(3) the duties of the department;

(4) the date on which the agreement will terminate unless terminated sooner or extended to a subsequent date as provided under department policy; and

(5) any other term the department determines necessary for the safety and welfare of the child.

(b) A parental child safety placement agreement must contain the following statement in boldface type and capital letters: "YOUR AGREEMENT TO THE PARENTAL CHILD SAFETY PLACEMENT IS NOT AN ADMISSION OF CHILD ABUSE OR NEGLECT ON YOUR PART AND CANNOT BE USED AGAINST YOU AS AN ADMISSION OF CHILD ABUSE OR NEGLECT."

(c) A parental child safety placement agreement must be in writing and signed by the person making the placement and the caregiver.

(d) The department must provide a written copy of the parental child safety placement agreement to the person making the placement and the caregiver.

Added by Acts 2011, 82nd Leg., ch. 1071 (S.B. 993), § 1, eff. Sept. 1, 2011.

§ 264.903. Caregiver Evaluation

(a) The department shall develop policies and procedures for evaluating a potential caregiver's qualifications to care for a child under this subchapter, including policies and procedures for evaluating:

(1) the criminal history of a caregiver;

(2) allegations of abuse or neglect against a caregiver; and

(3) a caregiver's home environment and ability to care for the child.

(b) A department caseworker who performs an evaluation of a caregiver under this section shall document the results of the evaluation in the department's case records.

(c) If, after performing an evaluation of a potential caregiver, the department determines that it is not in the child's best interest to be placed with the caregiver, the department shall notify the person who proposed the caregiver and the proposed caregiver of the reasons for the department's decision, but may not disclose the

specifics of any criminal history or allegations of abuse or neglect unless the caregiver agrees to the disclosure.

Added by Acts 2011, 82nd Leg., ch. 1071 (S.B. 993), § 1, eff. Sept. 1, 2011.

§ 264.904. Department Procedures for Closing Case

(a) Before closing a case in which the department has approved a parental child safety placement, the department must develop a plan with the person who made the placement and the caregiver for the safe return of the child to the person who placed the child with the caregiver or to another person legally entitled to possession of the child, as appropriate.

(b) The department may close a case with a child still living with the caregiver in a parental child safety placement if the department has determined that the child could safely return to the parent or person who made the parental child safety placement but the parent or other person agrees in writing for the child to continue to reside with the caregiver.

(c) If the department determines that the child is unable to safely return to the parent or person who made the parental child safety placement, the department shall determine whether the child can remain safely in the home of the caregiver or whether the department must seek legal conservatorship of the child in order to ensure the child's safety.

(d) Before the department may close a case with a child still living in a parental child safety placement, the department must:

(1) determine and document in the case file that the child can safely remain in the placement without the department's supervision;

(2) obtain the written agreement of the parent or person who made the parental child safety placement, if possible;

(3) obtain the caregiver's agreement in writing that the child can continue living in the placement after the department closes the case; and

(4) develop a written plan for the child's care after the department closes the case.

(e) The department is not required to comply with Subsection (d) if the department has filed suit seeking to be named conservator of the child under Chapter 262 and been denied conservatorship of the child.

Added by Acts 2011, 82nd Leg., ch. 1071 (S.B. 993), § 1, eff. Sept. 1, 2011.

§ 264.905. Removal of Child by Department

This subchapter does not prevent the department from removing a child at any time from a person who makes a parental child safety placement or from a caregiver if removal is determined to be necessary by the department for the safety and welfare of the child as provided by Chapter 262.

Added by Acts 2011, 82nd Leg., ch. 1071 (S.B. 993), § 1, eff. Sept. 1, 2011.

§ 264.906. Placement Preference During Conservatorship

If, while a parental child safety placement agreement is in effect, the department files suit under Chapter 262 seeking to be named managing conservator of the child, the department shall give priority to placing the child with the parental child safety placement caregiver as long as the placement is safe and available.

Added by Acts 2011, 82nd Leg., ch. 1071 (S.B. 993), § 1, eff. Sept. 1, 2011.

CHAPTER 265. PREVENTION AND EARLY INTERVENTION SERVICES

Introductory Comment

This chapter establishes a division in DFPS to coordinate prevention and early intervention programs. The department is responsible for managing Services to At–Risk Youth under Chapter 264, Subchapter D. Three other prevention and early intervention programs, the "Communities in Schools" program, the "Parents as Teachers" program, and the "Buffalo Soldier Heritage Program" also are under the direction of the DFPS. The division is also intended to maximize the impact of funding, develop accountability systems and ensure that the State of Texas obtains its share of federal funding. DFPS is given a broad grant of authority to consolidate prevention and early intervention services that already exist within the agency and to add services to the extent existing resources allow.

---

§ 265.001. Definitions

In this chapter:

(1) "Department" means the Department of Family and Protective Services.

(2) "Division" means the prevention and early intervention services division within the department.

(3) "Prevention and early intervention services" means programs intended to provide early intervention or prevent at-risk behaviors that lead to child abuse, delinquency, running away, truancy, and dropping out of school.

§ 265.002. Prevention and Early Intervention Services Division

The department shall operate a division to provide services for children in at-risk situations and for the families of those children and to achieve the consolidation of prevention and early intervention services within the jurisdiction of a single agency in order to avoid fragmentation and duplication of services and to increase the accountability for the delivery and administration of these services. The division shall be called the prevention and early intervention services division and shall have the following duties:

(1) to plan, develop, and administer a comprehensive and unified delivery system of prevention and early intervention services to children and their families in at-risk situations;

(2) to improve the responsiveness of services for at-risk children and their families by facilitating greater coordination and flexibility in the use of funds by state and local service providers;

(3) to provide greater accountability for prevention and early intervention services in order to demonstrate the impact or public benefit of a program by adopting outcome measures; and

(4) to assist local communities in the coordination and development of prevention and early intervention services in order to maximize federal, state, and local resources.

§ 265.003. Consolidation of Programs

(a) In order to implement the duties provided in Section 265.002, the department shall consolidate into the division programs with the goal of providing early intervention or prevention of at-risk behavior that leads to child abuse, delinquency, running away, truancy, and dropping out of school.

(b) The division may provide additional prevention and early intervention services in accordance with Section 265.002.

§ 265.004. Use of evidence–based programs for at–risk families

(a) To the extent that money is appropriated for the purpose, the department shall fund evidence-based programs offered by community-based organizations that are designed to prevent or ameliorate child abuse and neglect. The evidence-based programs funded under this subsection may be offered by a child welfare board established under Section 264.005, a local governmental board granted the powers and duties of a child welfare board under state law, or a children's advocacy center established under Section 264.402.

(b) The department shall place priority on programs that target children whose race or ethnicity is disproportionately represented in the child protective services system.

(c) The department shall periodically evaluate the evidence-based abuse and neglect prevention programs to determine the continued effectiveness of the programs.

CHAPTER 266. MEDICAL CARE AND EDUCATIONAL SERVICES FOR CHILDREN IN FOSTER CARE

SUBCHAPTER A. GENERAL PROVISIONS

SUBCHAPTER A. GENERAL PROVISIONS

§ 266.001. Definitions

In this chapter:

(1) "Commission" means the Health and Human Services Commission.

(2) "Department" means the Department of Family and Protective Services.

(2–a) "Drug research program" means any clinical trial, clinical investigation, drug study, or active medical or clinical research that has been approved by an institutional review board in accordance with the standards provided in the Code of Federal Regulations, 45 C.F.R. Sections 46.404 through 46.407, regarding:

(A) an investigational new drug; or

(B) the efficacy of an approved drug.

(3) "Executive commissioner" means the executive commissioner of the Health and Human Services Commission.

(4) "Foster child" means a child who is in the managing conservatorship of the department.

(4–a) "Investigational new drug" has the meaning assigned by 21 C.F.R. Section 312.3(b).

(5) "Medical care" means all health care and related services provided under the medical assistance program under Chapter 32, Human Resources Code, and described by Section 32.003(4), Human Resources Code.

§ 266.002. Construction with other Law

This chapter does not limit the right to consent to medical, dental, psychological, and surgical treatment under Chapter 32.

§ 266.003. Medical Services for Child Abuse and Neglect Victims

(a) The commission shall collaborate with health care and child welfare professionals to design a comprehensive, cost-effective medical services delivery model, either directly or by contract, to meet the needs of children served by the department. The medical services delivery model must include:

(1) the designation of health care facilities with expertise in the forensic assessment, diagnosis, and treatment of child abuse and neglect as pediatric centers of excellence;

(2) a statewide telemedicine system to link department investigators and caseworkers with pediatric centers of excellence or other medical experts for consultation;

(3) identification of a medical home for each foster child on entering foster care at which the child will receive an initial comprehensive assessment as well as preventive treatments, acute medical services, and therapeutic and rehabilitative care to meet the child's ongoing physical and mental health needs throughout the duration of the child's stay in foster care;

(4) the development and implementation of health passports as described in Section 266.006;

(5) establishment and use of a management information system that allows monitoring of medical care that is provided to all children in foster care;

(6) the use of medical advisory committees and medical review teams, as appropriate, to establish treatment guidelines and criteria by which individual cases of medical care provided to children in foster care will be identified for further, in-depth review;

(7) development of the training program described by Section 266.004(h);

(8) provision for the summary of medical care described by Section 266. 007; and

(9) provision for the participation of the person authorized to consent to medical care for a child in foster care in each appointment of the child with the provider of medical care.

(b) The commission shall collaborate with health and human services agencies, community partners, the health care community, and federal health and social services programs to maximize services and benefits available under this section.

(c) The executive commissioner shall adopt rules necessary to implement this chapter.

§ 266.0031. Expired

§ 266.004. Consent for Medical Care

(a) Medical care may not be provided to a child in foster care unless the person authorized by this section has provided consent.

(b) Except as provided by Section 266.010, the court may authorize the following persons to consent to medical care for a foster child:

(1) an individual designated by name in an order of the court, including the child's foster parent or the child's parent, if the parent's rights have not been terminated and the court determines that it is in the best interest of the parent's child to allow the parent to make medical decisions on behalf of the child; or

(2) the department or an agent of the department.

(c) If the person authorized by the court to consent to medical care is the department or an agent of the department, the department shall, not later than the fifth business day after the date the court provides authorization, file with the court and each party the name of the individual who will exercise the duty and responsibility of providing consent on behalf of the department. The department may designate the child's foster parent or the child's parent, if the parent's rights have not been terminated, to exercise the duty and responsibility of providing consent on behalf of the department under this subsection. If the individual designated under this subsection changes, the department shall file notice of the change with the court and each party not later than the fifth business day after the date of the change.

(d) A physician or other provider of medical care acting in good faith may rely on the representation by a person that the person has the authority to consent to the provision of medical care to a foster child as provided by Subsection (b).

(e) The department, a person authorized to consent to medical care under Subsection (b), the child's parent if the parent's rights have not been terminated, a guardian ad litem or attorney ad litem if one has been appointed, or the person providing foster care to the child may petition the court for any order related to medical care for a foster child that the department or other person believes is in the best interest of the child. Notice of the petition must be given to each person entitled to notice under Section 263.301(b).

(f) If a physician who has examined or treated the foster child has concerns regarding the medical care provided to the foster child, the physician may file a letter with the court stating the reasons for the physician's concerns. The court shall provide a copy of the letter to each person entitled to notice under Section 263.301(b).

(g) On its own motion or in response to a petition under Subsection (e) or Section 266.010, the court may issue any order related to the medical care of a foster child that the court determines is in the best interest of the child.

(h) Notwithstanding Subsection (b), a person may not be authorized to consent to medical care provided to a foster child unless the person has completed a department-approved training program related to informed consent and the provision of all areas of medical care as defined by Section 266.001. This subsection does not apply to a parent whose rights have not been terminated unless the court orders the parent to complete the training.

(i) The person authorized under Subsection (b) to consent to medical care of a foster child shall participate in each appointment of the child with the provider of the medical care.

(j) Nothing in this section requires the identity of a foster parent to be publicly disclosed.

§ 266.0041. Enrollment and Participation in Certain Research Programs

(a) Notwithstanding Section 266.004, a person may not authorize the enrollment of a foster child or consent to the participation of a foster child in a drug research program without a court order as provided by this section, unless the person is the foster child's parent and the person has been authorized by the court to make medical decisions for the foster child in accordance with Section 266.004.

(b) Before issuing an order authorizing the enrollment or participation of a foster child in a drug research program, the court must:

(1) appoint an independent medical advocate;

(2) review the report filed by the independent medical advocate regarding the advocate's opinion and recommendations concerning the foster child's enrollment and participation in the drug research program;

(3) consider whether the person conducting the drug research program:

(A) informed the foster child in a developmentally appropriate manner of the expected benefits of the drug research program, any potential side effects, and any available alternative treatments and received the foster child's assent to enroll the child to participate in the drug research program as required by the Code of Federal Regulations, 45 C.F.R. Section 46.408; or

(B) received informed consent in accordance with Subsection (h); and

(4) determine whether enrollment and participation in the drug research program is in the foster child's best interest and determine that the enrollment and participation in the drug research program will not interfere with the appropriate medical care of the foster child.

(c) An independent medical advocate appointed under Subsection (b) is not a party to the suit but may:

(1) conduct an investigation regarding the foster child's participation in a drug research program to the extent that the advocate considers necessary to determine:

(A) whether the foster child assented to or provided informed consent to the child's enrollment and participation in the drug research program; and

(B) the best interest of the child for whom the advocate is appointed; and

(2) obtain and review copies of the foster child's relevant medical and psychological records and information describing the risks and benefits of the child's enrollment and participation in the drug research program.

(d) An independent medical advocate shall, within a reasonable time after the appointment, interview:

(1) the foster child in a developmentally appropriate manner, if the child is four years of age or older;

(2) the foster child's parent, if the parent is entitled to notification under Section 266.005;

(3) an advocate appointed by an institutional review board in accordance with the Code of Federal Regulations, 45 C.F.R. Section 46.409(b), if an advocate has been appointed;

(4) the medical team treating the foster child as well as the medical team conducting the drug research program; and

(5) each individual who has significant knowledge of the foster child's medical history and condition, including any foster parent of the child.

(e) After reviewing the information collected under Subsections (c) and (d), the independent medical advocate shall:

(1) submit a report to the court presenting the advocate's opinion and recommendation regarding whether:

(A) the foster child assented to or provided informed consent to the child's enrollment and participation in the drug research program; and

(B) the foster child's best interest is served by enrollment and participation in the drug research program; and

(2) at the request of the court, testify regarding the basis for the advocate's opinion and recommendation concerning the foster child's enrollment and participation in a drug research program.

(f) The court may appoint any person eligible to serve as the foster child's guardian ad litem, as defined by Section 107.001, as the independent medical advocate, including a physician or nurse or an attorney who has experience in medical and health care, except that a foster parent, employee of a substitute care provider or child placing agency providing care for the foster child, representative of the department, medical professional affiliated with the drug research program, independent medical advocate appointed by an institutional review board, or any person the court determines has a conflict of interest may not serve as the foster child's independent medical advocate.

(g) A person otherwise authorized to consent to medical care for a foster child may petition the court for an order permitting the enrollment and participation of a foster child in a drug research program under this section.

(h) Before a foster child, who is at least 16 years of age and has been determined to have the capacity to consent to medical care in accordance with Section 266.010, may be enrolled to participate in a drug research program, the person conducting the drug research program must:

(1) inform the foster child in a developmentally appropriate manner of the expected benefits of participation in the drug research program, any potential side effects, and any available alternative treatments; and

(2) receive written informed consent to enroll the foster child for participation in the drug research program.

(i) A court may render an order approving the enrollment or participation of a foster child in a drug research program involving an investigational new drug before appointing an independent medical advocate if:

(1) a physician recommends the foster child's enrollment or participation in the drug research program to provide the foster child with treatment that will prevent the death or serious injury of the child; and

(2) the court determines that the foster child needs the treatment before an independent medical advocate could complete an investigation in accordance with this section.

(j) As soon as practicable after issuing an order under Subsection (i), the court shall appoint an independent medical advocate to complete a full investigation of the foster child's enrollment and participation in the drug research program in accordance with this section.

(k) This section does not apply to:

(1) a drug research study regarding the efficacy of an approved drug that is based only on medical records, claims data, or outcome data, including outcome data gathered through interviews with a child, caregiver of a child, or a child's treating professional;

(2) a retrospective drug research study based only on medical records, claims data, or outcome data; or

(3) the treatment of a foster child with an investigational new drug that does not require the child's enrollment or participation in a drug research program.

(*l*) The department shall annually submit to the governor, lieutenant governor, speaker of the house of representatives, and the relevant committees in both houses of the legislature, a report regarding:

(1) the number of foster children who enrolled or participated in a drug research program during the previous year;

(2) the purpose of each drug research program in which a foster child was enrolled or participated; and

(3) the number of foster children for whom an order was issued under Subsection (i).

(m) A foster parent or any other person may not receive a financial incentive or any other benefit for recommending or consenting to the enrollment and participation of a foster child in a drug research program.

§ 266.005. Parental Notification of Significant Medical Conditions

(a) In this section, "significant medical condition" means an injury or illness that is life-threatening or has potentially serious long-term health consequences, including hospitalization for surgery or other procedures, except minor emergency care.

(b) Except as provided by Subsection (c), the department shall make reasonable efforts to notify the child's parents within 24 hours of:

(1) a significant medical condition involving a foster child; and

(2) the enrollment or participation of a foster child in a drug research program under Section 266.0041.

(c) The department is not required to provide notice under Subsection (b) to a parent who:

(1) has failed to give the department current contact information and cannot be located;

(2) has executed an affidavit of relinquishment of parental rights;

(3) has had the parent's parental rights terminated; or

(4) has had access to medical information otherwise restricted by the court.

§ 266.006. Health Passport

(a) The commission, in conjunction with the department, and with the assistance of physicians and other health care providers experienced in the care of foster children and children with disabilities and with the use of electronic health records, shall develop and provide a health passport for each foster child. The passport must be maintained in an electronic format and use the commission's and the department's existing computer resources to the greatest extent possible.

(b) The executive commissioner shall adopt rules specifying the information required to be included in the passport. The required information may include:

(1) the name and address of each of the child's physicians and health care providers;

(2) a record of each visit to a physician or other health care provider, including routine checkups conducted in accordance with the Texas Health Steps program;

(3) an immunization record that may be exchanged with ImmTrac;

(4) a list of the child's known health problems and allergies;

(5) information on all medications prescribed to the child in adequate detail to permit refill of prescriptions, including the disease or condition that the medication treats; and

(6) any other available health history that physicians and other health care providers who provide care for the child determine is important.

(c) The system used to access the health passport must be secure and maintain the confidentiality of the child's health records.

(d) Health passport information shall be part of the department's record for the child as long as the child remains in foster care.

(e) The commission shall provide training or instructional materials to foster parents, physicians, and other health care providers regarding use of the health passport.

(f) The department shall make health passport information available in printed and electronic formats to the following individuals when a child is discharged from foster care:

(1) the child's legal guardian, managing conservator, or parent; or

(2) the child, if the child is at least 18 years of age or has had the disabilities of minority removed.

§ 266.007. Judicial Review of Medical Care

(a) At each hearing under Chapter 263, or more frequently if ordered by the court, the court shall review a summary of the medical care provided to the foster child since the last hearing. The summary must include information regarding:

(1) the nature of any emergency medical care provided to the child and the circumstances necessitating emergency medical care, including any injury or acute illness suffered by the child;

(2) all medical and mental health treatment that the child is receiving and the child's progress with the treatment;

(3) any medication prescribed for the child and the condition, diagnosis, and symptoms for which the medication was prescribed and the child's progress with the medication;

(4) the degree to which the child or foster care provider has complied or failed to comply with any plan of medical treatment for the child;

(5) any adverse reaction to or side effects of any medical treatment provided to the child;

(6) any specific medical condition of the child that has been diagnosed or for which tests are being conducted to make a diagnosis;

(7) any activity that the child should avoid or should engage in that might affect the effectiveness of the treatment, including physical activities, other medications, and diet; and

(8) other information required by department rule or by the court.

(b) At or before each hearing under Chapter 263, the department shall provide the summary of medical care described by Subsection (a) to:

(1) the court;

(2) the person authorized to consent to medical treatment for the child;

(3) the guardian ad litem or attorney ad litem, if one has been appointed by the court;

(4) the child's parent, if the parent's rights have not been terminated; and

(5) any other person determined by the department or the court to be necessary or appropriate for review of the provision of medical care to foster children.

(c) At each hearing under Chapter 263, the foster child shall be provided the opportunity to express to the court the child's views on the medical care being provided to the child.

§ 266.008. Education Passport

(a) The commission shall develop an education passport for each foster child. The commission, in conjunction with the department, shall determine the format of the passport. The passport may be maintained in an electronic format. The passport must contain educational records of the child, including the names and addresses of educational providers, the child's grade-level performance, and any other educational information the commission determines is important.

(b) The department shall maintain the passport as part of the department's records for the child as long as the child remains in foster care.

(c) The department shall make the passport available to the person authorized to consent to medical care for the foster child and to a provider of medical care to the foster child if access to the foster child's educational information is necessary to the provision of medical care and is not prohibited by law.

(d) The department and the commission shall collaborate with the Texas Education Agency to develop policies and procedures to ensure that the needs of foster children are met in every school district.

§ 266.009. Provision of Medical Care in Emergency

(a) Consent or court authorization for the medical care of a foster child otherwise required by this chapter is not required in an emergency during which it is immediately necessary to provide medical care to the foster child to prevent the imminent probability of death or substantial bodily harm to the child or others, including circumstances in which:

(1) the child is overtly or continually threatening or attempting to commit suicide or cause serious bodily harm to the child or others; or

(2) the child is exhibiting the sudden onset of a medical condition manifesting itself by acute symptoms of sufficient severity, including severe pain, such that the absence of immediate medical attention could reasonably be expected to result in placing the child's health in serious jeopardy, serious impairment of bodily functions, or serious dysfunction of any bodily organ or part.

(b) The physician providing the medical care or designee shall notify the person authorized to consent to medical care for a foster child about the decision to provide medical care without consent or court authorization in an emergency not later than the second business day after the date of the provision of medical care under this section. This notification must be documented in the foster child's health passport.

(c) This section does not apply to the administration of medication under Subchapter G, Chapter 574, Health and Safety Code, to a foster child who is at least 16 years of age and who is placed in an inpatient mental health facility.

§ 266.010. Consent to Medical Care by Foster Child at Least 16 Years of Age

(a) A foster child who is at least 16 years of age may consent to the provision of medical care, except as provided by Chapter 33, if the court with continuing jurisdiction determines that the child has the capacity to consent to medical care. If the child provides consent by signing a consent form, the form must be written in language the child can understand.

(b) A court with continuing jurisdiction may make the determination regarding the foster child's capacity to consent to medical care during a hearing under Chapter 263 or may hold a hearing to make the determination on its own motion. The court may issue an order authorizing the child to consent to all or some of the medical care as defined by Section 266.001. In addition, a foster child who is at least 16 years of age, or the foster child's attorney ad litem, may file a petition with the court for a hearing. If the court determines that the foster child lacks the capacity to consent to medical care, the court may consider whether the foster child has acquired the capacity to consent to medical care at subsequent hearings under Section 263.503.

(c) If the court determines that a foster child lacks the capacity to consent to medical care, the person authorized by the court under Section 266.004 shall continue to provide consent for the medical care of the foster child.

(d) If a foster child who is at least 16 years of age and who has been determined to have the capacity to consent to medical care refuses to consent to medical care and the department or private agency providing substitute care or case management services to the child believes that the medical care is appropriate, the department or the private agency may file a motion with the court requesting an order authorizing the provision of the medical care.

(e) The motion under Subsection (d) must include:

(1) the child's stated reasons for refusing the medical care; and

(2) a statement prepared and signed by the treating physician that the medical care is the proper course of treatment for the foster child.

(f) If a motion is filed under Subsection (d), the court shall appoint an attorney ad litem for the foster child if one has not already been appointed. The foster child's attorney ad litem shall:

(1) discuss the situation with the child;

(2) discuss the suitability of the medical care with the treating physician;

(3) review the child's medical and mental health records; and

(4) advocate to the court on behalf of the child's expressed preferences regarding the medical care.

(g) The court shall issue an order authorizing the provision of the medical care in accordance with a motion under Subsection (d) to the foster child only if the court finds, by clear and convincing evidence, after the hearing that the medical care is in the best interest of the foster child and:

(1) the foster child lacks the capacity to make a decision regarding the medical care;

(2) the failure to provide the medical care will result in an observable and material impairment to the growth, development, or functioning of the foster child; or

(3) the foster child is at risk of suffering substantial bodily harm or of inflicting substantial bodily harm to others.

(h) In making a decision under this section regarding whether a foster child has the capacity to consent to medical care, the court shall consider:

(1) the maturity of the child;

(2) whether the child is sufficiently well informed to make a decision regarding the medical care; and

(3) the child's intellectual functioning.

(i) In determining whether the medical care is in the best interest of the foster child, the court shall consider:

(1) the foster child's expressed preference regarding the medical care, including perceived risks and benefits of the medical care;

(2) likely consequences to the foster child if the child does not receive the medical care;

(3) the foster child's prognosis, if the child does receive the medical care; and

(4) whether there are alternative, less intrusive treatments that are likely to reach the same result as provision of the medical care.

(j) This section does not apply to emergency medical care. An emergency relating to a foster child who is at least 16 years of age, other than a child in an inpatient mental health facility, is governed by Section 266.009.

(k) This section does not apply to the administration of medication under Subchapter G, Chapter 574, Health and Safety Code, to a foster child who is at least 16 years of age and who is placed in an inpatient mental health facility.

(*l*) Before a foster child reaches the age of 16, the department or the private agency providing substitute care or case management services to the foster child shall advise the foster child of the right to a hearing under this section to determine whether the foster child may consent to medical care. The department or the private agency providing substitute care or case management services shall provide the foster child with training on informed consent and the provision of medical care as part of the Preparation for Adult Living Program.

TEXAS CONSTITUTION AND RELATED TEXAS LAW

As amended through the 82nd Legislature, First Called Session (2011)

***Editors' Note**: Texas attorneys involved in family law practice encounter a wide variety of issues involving an enormous spectrum of law other than that contained in the Texas Family Code, including a wide variety of state and federal law. Beginning with our first edition in 1981, this publication has recognized this truism by including selected provisions from other Texas Codes and the United States Code, a.k.a. U.S.C. or U.S.C.A. Interestingly, as the Family Code grew to its present massive proportions the space devoted to other law diminished in order to limit the size of the book to a reasonable degree. Over the years, that has been something of a losing battle.*

The time has come to take more dramatic action for the benefit of our readers. Luckily modern technology has been on our doorstep for the past few years, but we have not taken full advantage of the world of electronic delivery of information. We hope the following decision is but the first step in reducing the bulk of the print version of Sampson & Tindall's Texas Family Code Annotated, while increasing the overall utility of the entire package. To the end, ***A LIST OF THE relevant sections of Related TEXAS Law for family law purposes IS set forth below; The full text OF THOSE STATUTES AND OTHER MATERIALS is found on the Accompanying CD-ROM.***

Texas Constitution of 1876

Article 1. Bill of Rights

§ 3a. Equality under the law.

§ 32. Marriage.

Article 16. General Provisions

§ 15. Separate and community property of husband and wife.

§ 28. Garnishment of wages.

§ 49. Protection of personal property from forced sale.

§ 50. Homestead; protection from forced sale; mortgages, trust deeds and liens.

§ 51. Amount of homestead; uses.

§ 52. Descent and distribution of homestead; restrictions on partition.

Texas Civil Practice and Remedies Code

On the ACCOMPANYING CD-ROM the editors are pleased to provide the ADR materials related to Family Law from McGehee's Texas Civil Practice & Remedies Code Annotated (2010). The author, Diane Feiler McGehee, is of council with the Houston firm of McGehee, Chang, Barnes.

Chapter 154. Alternative Dispute Resolution Procedures.

Subchapter A. General provisions

§ 154.001. Definitions

§ 154.002. Policy

Texas Code of Criminal Procedure

Chapter 5. Family Violence Prevention Act [Chapter in full].

Chapter 7A. Protective Order for Victim of Sexual Assault [Chapter in full].

Art. 7A.01. Application for Protective Order.

Art. 7A.02. Temporary Ex Parte Order.

Art. 7A.03. Required Findings; Issuance of Protective Order.

Art. 7A.04. Application of Other Law.

Art. 7A.05. Conditions Specified by Order.

Art. 7A.06. Warning on Protective Order.

Art. 7A.07. Duration of Protective Order.

Chapter 14. Arrest Without Warrant [Selected article].

Art. 14.03. [214] [261] [249] Authority of peace officers.

Chapter 17. Bail [Selected articles].

Art. 17.29. Accused liberated.

Art. 17.291. Further detention of certain persons.

Art. 17.292. Magistrate's Order for Emergency Protection.

Art. 17.293. Delivery of Order for Emergency Protection to Other Persons.

Chapter 42. Judgment and Sentence [Selected article].

Art. 42.23. Notification of Court of Family Violence Conviction.

Chapter 56. Rights of Crime Victims [Selected article].

Art. 56.11. Notification to Victim or Witness of Release or Escape of Defendant.

Art. 56.42. Limits on Compensation.

Texas Government Code

Title 2. Judicial Branch

Chapter 74. Court Administration Act [Selected section].

§ 74.053. Objection to Judge Assigned to a Trial Court.

Texas Penal Code

On the ACCOMPANYING CD–ROM the editors are pleased to provide the materials related to Family Law from Kinkeade & McColloch's Texas Penal Code Annotated (2010–2011). The authors are The Honorable Ed Kinkeade, U.S. District Judge for the Northern District of Texas, and S. Michael McColloch, of McColl & McColloch, Dallas.

Chapter 25. Offenses Against the Family [Full chapter].

§ 25.01. Bigamy.

§ 25.02. Prohibited Sexual Conduct.

§ 25.03. Interference with Child Custody.

§ 25.031. Agreement to Abduct from Custody.

§ 25.04. Enticing a Child.

§ 25.05. Criminal Nonsupport.

§ 25.06. Harboring Runaway Child.

§ 25.07. Violation of Protective Order or Magistrate's Order.

§ 25.071. Violation of Protective Order Preventing Offense Caused by Bias or Prejudice.

§ 25.08. Sale or Purchase of Child.

§ 25.09. Advertising for Placement of Child.

§ 25.10. Interference with Rights of Guardian of the Person.

Chapter 38. Obstructing Governmental Operation [Selected section].

§ 38.112. Violation of Protective Order Issued on Basis of Sexual Assault

Chapter 42. Disorderly Conduct and Related Offenses [Selected sections].

§ 42.062. Interference With Emergency Telephone Call

§ 42.07. Harassment.

§ 42.072. Stalking.

Chapter 46. Weapons [Selected sections].

§ 46.04. Unlawful Possession of Firearm.

§ 46.06. Unlawful Transfer of Certain Weapons.

§ 46.13. Making a Firearm Accessible to a Child.

TEXAS PROBATE CODE

On the ACCOMPANYING CD–ROM the editors are pleased to provide the Probate Code materials related to Family Law from Johanson's Probate Code Annotated (2011). The author, Professor Stanley M. Johanson, is the Fannie Coplin Regents Chair in Law at the School of Law, The University of Texas at Austin.

CHAPTER II. Descent and Distribution

CHAPTER XI. Nontestamentary Transfers

CHAPTER II. DESCENT AND DISTRIBUTION

§ 37. Passage of Title Upon Intestacy and Under a Will.

§ 37A. Means of Evidencing Disclaimer or Renunciation of Property or Interest Receivable From a Decedent.

§ 37B. Assignment of Property Received from a Decedent.

§ 37C. Satisfaction of Devise.

§ 38. Persons Who Take Upon Intestacy.

§ 39. No Distinction Because of Property's Source.

§ 40. Inheritance by and From an Adopted Child.

§ 41. Matters Affecting and Not Affecting the Right to Inherit.

§ 42. Inheritance Rights of Children.

§ 43. Determination of Per Capita and Per Stirpes Distribution.

§ 44. Advancements.

§ 45. Community Estate.

§ 46. Joint Tenancies.

§ 47. Requirement of Survival by 120 Hours.

§ 47A. Marriage Voidable Based on Mental Incapacity.

CHAPTER IV. EXECUTION AND REVOCATION OF WILLS

§ 69.Will Provisions Made Before Dissolution of Marriage.

§ 69A. Changing Wills.

CHAPTER XI. NONTESTAMENTARY TRANSFERS

PART 1. MULTIPLE–PARTY ACCOUNTS

§ 436. Definitions.

§ 437. Ownership as Between Parties and Others.

§ 438. Ownership During Lifetime.

§ 438A. Convenience Account.

§ 438B. Convenience Signer on Other Accounts.

§ 439. Right of Survivorship.

§ 439A. Uniform Single–Party or Multiple–Party Account Form.

§ 440. Effect of Written Notice to Financial Institution.

§ 441. Accounts and Transfers Nontestamentary.

§ 442. Rights of Creditors; Pledge of Account.

§ 443. Protection of Financial Institutions.

§ 444. Payment on Signature of One Party.

§ 445. Payment of Joint Account After Death or Disability.

TEXAS PROPERTY CODE

On the ACCOMPANYING CD–ROM the editors are pleased to provide the Property Code materials related to Family Law from Beyer's Texas Property Code Annotated (2011). The author, Professor Gerry W. Beyer, is the Governor Preston E. Smith Regents Professor of Law the Texas Tech School of Law.

Chapter 41. Interests in Land.

Chapter 42. Personal Property.

§ 42.005. Child Support Liens.

Chapter 92. Residential Tenancies.

§ 92.016. Right to Vacate and Avoid Liability Following Family Violence. [new]

§ 92.017. Right to Vacate and Avoid Liability Following Certain Decisions Related to Military Service. [new]

Texas Rules of Civil Procedure.

Texas Rules of Evidence.

Related Federal Law

Selected Statutory, Regulatory and Treaty Provisions

As amended through the First Session of the 112th Congress, Public Law 112-20

***Editors' Note**: Texas attorneys involved in family law practice encounter a wide variety of issues involving an enormous spectrum of law other than that contained in the Texas Family Code, including a wide variety of state and federal law. Beginning with our first edition in 1981, this publication has recognized this truism by including selected provisions from the United States Code, a.k.a. U.S.C. or U.S.C.A. Interestingly, as the Family Code grew to its present massive proportions the space devoted to other law diminished in order to limit the size of the book to a reasonable degree. Over the years, that has been something of a losing battle.*

The time has come to take more dramatic action for the benefit of our readers. Luckily modern technology has been on our doorstep for the past few years, but we have not taken full advantage of the world of electronic delivery of information. We hope the following decision is but the first step in reducing the bulk of the print version of Sampson & Tindall's Texas Family Code Annotated, while increasing the overall utility of the entire package. To the end, ***A LIST OF THE relevant sections of Related FEDERAL Law for family law purposes IS set forth below; The full text OF THOSE STATUTES AND OTHER MATERIALS is found on the Accompanying CD–ROM****.*

NOTE: THE SWITCH FROM THE BOOK TO THE CD–ROM FOR RELATED FEDERAL LAW HAS ENABLED US TO MASSIVELY EXPAND OUR COVERAGE OF FEDERAL LAW.

YOUR COMMENTS ARE REQUESTED REGARDING THIS CHANGE IN PRESENTATION.

Special Immigrant Juvenile Status

U.S.C.A. TITLE 8. ALIENS AND NATIONALITY

§ 1101. Definitions.

(a) (27) (J) (defining special immigrant juvenile status).

§ 1182. Inadmissible aliens

(a) (related to SIJS inadmissibility)

§ 1255. Adjustment of status on nonimmigrant to that of person admitted for permanent residence

(h) (adjustment status)

Military Retirement and Insurance Benefits

U.S.C.A. Title 10: Armed Forces

10 U.S.C.A. 1408. Payment of retired or retainer pay in compliance with court orders

10 U.S.C.A. 1431. Election of annuity: Members of armed forces .

10 U.S.C.A. 1432. Election of annuity: Former members of armed forces

10 U.S.C.A. 1434. Kinds of annuities that may be elected

10 U.S.C.A. 1435. Eligible beneficiaries

10 U.S.C.A. 1437. Payment of annuity

10 U.S.C.A. 1440. Annuities not subject to legal process

10 U.S.C.A. 1444a. Regulations regarding payment of annuity to a representative payee

10 U.S.C.A. 1447. Definitions

10 U.S.C.A. 1448. Application of Plan

10 U.S.C.A. 1448a. Election to discontinue participation: One-year opportunity after second anniversary. of commencement of payment of retired pay

10 U.S.CA. 1450. Payment of annuity: beneficiaries

10 U.S.C.A. 1451. Amount of annuity .

10 U.S.C.A. 1456 to 1460b. Repealed.

10 U.S.C.A. 1475. Death gratuity: Death of members on active duty or inactive duty training and of certain other persons

10 U.S.C.A. 1476. Death gratuity: Death after discharge or release from duty or training

10 U.S.C.A. 1477. Death gratuity: Eligible survivors

10 U.S.C.A. 1478. Death gratuity: amount

10 U.S.C.A. 1479. Death gratuity: Delegation of determinations, payments

10 U.S.C.A. 1480. Death gratuity: Miscellaneous provisions

10 U.S.CA. 1485. Dependents of members of armed forces

Bankruptcy

U.S.C.A. Title 11: Bankruptcy

11 U.S.C.A. 101. Definitions

11 U.S.C.A. 362. Automatic stay

11 U.S.C.A. 502. Allowance of claims or interest13

11 U.S.C.A. 503. Allowance of administrative expenses

11 U.S.C.A. 506. Determination of secured status

11 U.S.C.A. 507. Priorities

11 U.S.C.A. 522. Exemptions

11 U.S.C.A. 523. Exceptions to discharge

11 U.S.C.A. 524. Effect of discharge

11 U.S.C.A. 541. Property of the estate

11 U.S.C.A. 707. Dismissal of a case or conversion to a case under chapter 11 or 13

11 U.S.C.A. 727. Discharge

11 U.S.C.A. 1307. Conversion or Dismissal

11 U.S.C.A. 1328. Discharge

Federal Criminal Law

U.S.C.A. Title 18: Crimes and Criminal Procedure

Child Support Recovery Act (CSRA)

Chapter—11A–Child Support

§ 228. Failure To Pay Legal Child Support Obligations.

The International Parental Kidnapping Crime Act of 1993 (IPKCA)

Chapter 55. Kidnapping

§ 1204—International Parental Kidnapping.

Sexual Exploitation of Children

18 U.S.C.A. 2243. Sexual abuse of a minor or ward

18 U.S.C.A. 2251. Sexual exploitation of children

18 U.S.C.A. 2251A. Selling or buying of children

18 U.S.C.A. 2252. Certain activities relating to material involving the sexual exploitation of minors

18 U.S.C.A. 2252A. Certain activities relating to material constituting or containing child pornography

18 U.S.C.A. 2253. Criminal forfeiture

18 U.S.C.A. 2254. Civil forfeiture

18 U.S.C.A. 2255. Civil remedy for personal injuries

18 U.S.C.A. 2256. Definitions for chapter

18 U.S.C.A. 2257. Record keeping requirements

18 U.S.C.A. 2257A. Record keeping requirements for simulated sexual conduct

18 U.S.C.A. 2258. Failure to report child abuse

18 U.S.C.A. 2259. Mandatory restitution

18 U.S.C.A. 2260. Production of sexually explicit depictions of a minor for importation into the United States

18 U.S.C.A. 2260A. Penalties for registered sex offenders

Violence Against Women Act (VAWA)

18 U.S.C.A. 2261. Interstate domestic violence

18 U.S.C.A. 2261A. Stalking

18 U.S.C.A. 2262. Interstate violation of protection order

18 U.S.C.A. 2263. Pretrial release of defendant

18 U.S.C.A. 2264. Restitution

18 U.S.C.A. 2265. Full Faith and Credit Given to Protection Orders.

18 U.S.C.A. 2265A. Repeat offenders.

18 U.S.C.A. 2266. Definitions.

Indian Child Welfare Act of 1978

U.S.C.A. Title 25: Indians

CHAPTER 21—INDIAN CHILD WELFARE

Indian Child Welfare Act of 1978 (ICWA)

18 U.S.C.A. 1901. Congressional Findings.

18 U.S.C.A. 1902. Congressional Declaration of Policy.

18 U.S.C.A. 1903. Definitions.

18 U.S.C.A. 1911. Indian Tribe Jurisdiction over Indian Child Custody Proceedings.

18 U.S.C.A. 1912. Pending Court Proceedings.

18 U.S.C.A. 1913. Parental Rights; Voluntary Termination.

18 U.S.C.A. 1914. Petition to Court of Competent Jurisdiction To Invalidate Action upon Showing of Certain Violations.

18 U.S.C.A. 1915. Placement of Indian Children.

18 U.S.C.A. 1916. Return of Custody.

18 U.S.C.A. 1917. Tribal Affiliation Information and Other Information of Protection of Rights from Tribal Relationship; Application of Subject of Adoptive Placement; Disclosure by Court.

18 U.S.C.A. 1918. Reassumption of Jurisdiction over Child Custody Proceedings.

18 U.S.C.A. 1919. Agreements Between States and Indian Tribes.

18 U.S.C.A. 1920. Improper Removal of Child from Custody; Declination of Jurisdiction; Forthwith Return of Child: Danger Exception.

18 U.S.C.A. 1921. Higher State or Federal Standard Applicable To Protect Rights of Parent or Indian Custodian of Indian Child.

18 U.S.C.A. 1922. Emergency Removal or Placement of Child; Termination; Appropriate Action.

18 U.S.C.A. 1923. Effective Date.

Foreign Travel

U.S.C.A. Title 22: Foreign Relations and Intercourse

22 U.S.C.A. 213. Application for passport; verification by oath of initial passport.

Federal Income Tax

U.S.C.A. Title 26: Internal Revenue Code

26 U.S.C.A. 61. Gross income defined.

26 U.S.C.A. 66. Treatment of Community Income.

26 U.S.C.A. 71. Alimony and Separate Maintenance Payments.

26 U.S.C.A. 121. Exclusion of Gain from Sale of Principal Residence.

26 U.S.C.A. 152. Dependent Defined.

26 U.S.C.A. 215. Alimony, etc., Payments.

26 U.S.C.A. 401. Qualified pension, profit-sharing, and stock bonus plans

26 U.S.C.A. 408. Individual retirement accounts

26 U.S.C.A. 414. Definitions and special rules

26 U.S.C.A. 1041. Transfers of Property Between Spouses or Incident to Divorce.

26 U.S.C.A. 2516. Certain property settlements

26 U.S.C.A. 6015. Relief From Joint and Several Liability on Joint Return.

26 C.F.R. 1.6015.0–1.6015.9 (67 FR 47278–01)

26 U.S.C.A. 7703. Determination of marital status

Full Faith and Credit

U.S.C.A. Title 28: Judiciary and Judicial Procedure

28 U.S.C.A. 1738A. Full Faith and Credit Given to Child Custody Determinations. (*Parental Kidnapping Prevention Act*) *(PKPA)*

28 U.S.C.A. 1738B. Full Faith and Credit for Child Support Orders *(FFCCSOA)*.

28 U.S.C.A. 1738C. Certain Acts, Records, and Proceedings and the Effect Thereof. (*Defense of Marriage Act*) *(DOMA)*

HIPAA

29 U.S.C.A. Title 29. Labor

CHAPTER 18. EMPLOYEE RETIREMENT INCOME SECURITY PROGRAM (ERISA)

Subchapter I. Protection of Employee Benefit Rights

Subtitle A–General Provisions

Health Insurance Portability and Accountability Act of 1996 (HIPAA)

Part 7–Group Health Plan Requirements

Subpart A–Requirements Relating to Portability, Access:, and Renewability

29 U.S.C.A. 1181. Increased portability through limitation on preexisting condition exclusions.

29 U.S.C.A. 1182. Prohibiting discrimination against individual participants and beneficiaries based on health status.

29 U.S.C.A. 1183. Guaranteed renewability in multiemployer plans and multiple employer welfare arrangements.

Subpart B–Other Requirements

29 U.S.C.A. 1185.Standards relating to benefits for mothers and newborns.

29 U.S.C.A. 1185a.Parity in application of certain limits to mental health or substance use disorder benefits.

29 U.S.C.A. 1185b.Required coverage for reconstructive surgery following mastectomies.

29 U.S.C.A. 1185c.Coverage of dependent students on medically necessary leave of absence.

Subpart C–General Provisions

29 U.S.C.A. 1191.Preemption; State flexibility; construction.

29 U.S.C.A. 1191a. Special rules relating to group health plans.

29 U.S.C.A. 1191b.Definitions.

29 U.S.C.A. 1191c.Regulations.

Social Security

U.S.C.A. Title 42: Social Security

42 U.S.C.A. 402. Old-age and survivors insurance benefit payments

42 U.S.C.A. 407. Assignment; amendment of section

42 U.S.C.A. 416. Additional definitions

Temporary Assistance for Needy Families (TANF)

U.S.C.A. Title 42. PUBLIC Health and Welfare

CHAPTER 7–SOCIAL SECURITY

SUBCHAPTER IV–GRANTS TO STATES FOR AID AND SERVICES TO NEEDY FAMILIES WITH CHILDREN AND FOR CHILD–WELFARE SERVICES

PART A–BLOCK GRANTS TO STATES FOR TEMPORARY ASSISTANCE FOR NEEDY FAMILIES (TANF)

42 U.S.C.A. 604. Use of grants.

42 U.S.C.A. 605. Administrative provisions.

42 U.S.C.A. 606. Federal loans for State welfare programs.

42 U.S.C.A. 607. Mandatory work requirements.

42 U.S.C.A. 608. Prohibitions; requirements.

42 U.S.C.A. 609. Penalties.

42 U.S.C.A. 611. Data collection and reporting.

42 U.S.C.A. 612. Direct funding and administration by Indian tribes.

42 U.S.C.A. 613. Research, evaluations, and national studies.

42 U.S.C.A. 614. Study by the Census Bureau.

42 U.S.C.A. 618. Funding for child care.

Child welfare Services

PART B–CHILD AND FAMILY SERVICES

Subpart 1–Stephanie Tubbs Jones Child Welfare Services Program

42 U.S.C.A. 620. Repealed.

42 U.S.C.A. 621. Purpose.

42 U.S.C.A. 622. State plans for child welfare services.

42 U.S.C.A. 623. Allotments to States.

42 U.S.C.A. 624. Payment to States.

42 U.S.C.A. 625. Limitations on authorization of appropriations.

Child Support Enforcement

U.S.C.A. Title 42: The Public Health and Welfare

CHAPTER 7 SOCIAL SECURITY.

SUBCHAPTER IV GRANTS TO STATES FOR AID AND SERVICES TO NEEDY FAMILIES WITH CHILDREN AND FOR CHILD–WELFARE SERVICES

PART D CHILD SUPPORT AND ESTABLISHMENT OF PATERNITY

42 U.S.C.A. 653. Federal Parent Locator Service

42 U.S.C.A. 653a. State Directory of New Hires

42 U.S.C.A. 654. State plan for child and spousal support

42 U.S.C.A. 654b. Collection and disbursement of support payments

42 U.S.C.A. 655. Payments to States.

42 U.S.C.A. 656. Support obligation as obligation to State; amount; discharge in bankruptcy

42 U.S.C.A. 657. Distribution of collected support.

42 U.S.C.A. 659. Consent by the United States to income withholding, garnishment.

42 U.S.C.A. 659a. International support enforcement

42 U.S.C.A. 660. Civil action to enforce child support obligations; jurisdiction of district courts

42 U.S.C.A. 663. Use of Federal Parent Locator Service in connection with enforcement or determination of child custody in cases of parental kidnaping of child

42 U.S.C.A. 664. Collection of past-due support from Federal tax refunds

42 U.S.C.A. 665. Allotments from pay for child and spousal support owed by members of uniformed services on active duty .

42 U.S.C.A. 666; Requirement of statutorily prescribed procedures to improve effectiveness of child support enforcement

42 U.S.C.A. 667. State guidelines for child support awards

42 U.S.C.A. 668. Encouragement of States to adopt simple civil process for voluntarily acknowledging paternity and a civil procedure for establishing paternity in contested cases

42 U.S.C.A. 669. Collection and reporting of child support enforcement data

42 U.S.C.A. 669a. Nonliability for financial institutions providing financial records to State child support enforcement agencies in child support cases similar proceedings for enforcement of child support and alimony obligations.

PART E—FEDERAL PAYMENTS FOR FOSTER CARE AND ADOPTION ASSISTANCE

42 U.S.C.A. 671. State plan for foster care and adoption assistance.

42 U.S.C.A. 672. Foster care maintenance payments program.

42 U.S.C.A. 673. Adoption and guardianship assistance program.

42 U.S.C.A. 673b. Adoption incentive payments.

42 U.S.C.A. 673c. Timely interstate home study incentive payments.

42 U.S.C.A. 674. Payments to States.

42 U.S.C.A. 675. Definitions.

42 U.S.C.A. 676. Administration.

42 U.S.C.A. 677. John H. Chafee Foster Care Independence Program.

42 U.S.C.A. 679b. Annual report.

42 U.S.C.A. 679c. Programs operated by Indian tribal organizations.

Fostering Connections to Success and Increasing Adoptions Act of 2008 (PL 110–351)

International Child Abduction Remedies Act *(ICARA)*

U.S.C.A. Title 42: The Public Health and Welfare

42 U.S.C.A. 11601. Findings and Declarations.

42 U.S.C.A. 11602. Definitions.

42 U.S.C.A. 11603. Judicial Remedies.

42 U.S.C.A. 11604. Provisional Remedies.

42 U.S.C.A. 11605. Admissibility of Documents.

42 U.S.C.A. 11606. United States Central Authority.

42 U.S.C.A. 11607. Costs and Fees.

42 U.S.C.A. 11608. Collection, Maintenance, and Dissemination of Information.

42 U.S.C.A. 11608a. Office of Children's Issues.

42 U.S.C.A. 11609. Interagency Coordinating Group.

42 U.S.C.A. 11610. Authorization of Appropriations.

Hague Convention on the Civil Aspects of International Child Abduction

International Adoption of Children

U.S.C.A. Title 42: Public Health and Welfare

42 U.S.C.A. 14901. Findings and purposes

42 U.S.C.A. 14902. Definitions

42 U.S.C.A. 14911. Designation of central authority

42 U.S.C.A. 14912. Responsibilities of the Secretary of State

42 U.S.C.A. 14913. Responsibilities of the Attorney General

42 U.S.C.A. 14914. Annual report on inter country adoptions

42 U.S.C.A. 14921. Accreditation or approval required in order to provide adoption services in cases subject to the Convention

42 U.S.C.A. 14922. Process for accreditation and approval; role of accrediting entities

42 U.S.C.A. 14923. Standards and procedures for providing accreditation or approval

42 U.S.C.A. 14924. Secretarial oversight of accreditation and approval

U.S.C.A. Title 42: The Public Health and Welfare

42 U.S.C.A. 679a. National Adoption Information Clearinghouse

Servicemembers Civil Relief Act *(SCRA)*

U.S.C.A. Title 50 Appendix: War and National Defense

50 U.S.C.A. App. 511. Definitions.

50 U.S.C.A. App. 512. Jurisdiction and applicability of Act.

50 U.S.C.A. App. 513. Protection of persons secondarily liable.

50 U.S.C.A. App. 514. Extension of protections to citizens serving with allied forces.

50 U.S.C.A. App. 515. Notification of benefits.

50 U.S.C.A. App. 515a. Information for members of the armed forces and their dependents on rights and protections of the Servicemembers Civil Relief Act.

50 U.S.C.A. App. 516. Extension of rights and protections to reserves ordered to report for military service and to persons ordered to report for induction.

50 U.S.C.A. App. 517. Waiver of rights pursuant to written agreement.

50 U.S.C.A. App. 518. Exercise of rights under Act not to affect certain future financial transactions.

50 U.S.C.A. App. 519. Legal representatives.

50 U.S.C.A. App. 521. Protection of servicemembers against default judgments.

50 U.S.C.A. App. 522. Stay of proceedings when servicemember has notice.

50 U.S.C.A. App. 523. Fines and penalties under contracts.

50 U.S.C.A. App. 524. Stay or vacation of execution of judgments, attachments, and garnishments.

50 U.S.C.A. App. 525. Duration and term of stays; codefendants not in service.

50 U.S.C.A. App. 526. Statute of limitations.

50 U.S.C.A. App. 527. Maximum rate of interest on debts incurred before military service.

50 U.S.C.A. App. 581. Inappropriate use of Act.

50 U.S.C.A. App. 582. Certificates of service; persons reported missing.

50 U.S.C.A. App. 583. Interlocutory orders.

50 U.S.C.A. App. 591. Anticipatory relief.

50 U.S.C.A. App. 592. Power of attorney.

50 U.S.C.A. App. 593. Professional liability protection.

22 C.F.R. § 51.28. Minors

26 C.F.R. 1.71–1. Alimony and separate maintenance payments; income to wife or former wife

26 C.F.R. 1.71–1T. Alimony and separate maintenance payments (temporary)

26 C.F.R. 1. 152–4T. [Reserved by 73 FR 37804]

26 C.F.R. 1.215–1. Periodic alimony, etc., payments

26 C.F.R. 1.215–1T. Alimony, etc., payments (temporary)

26 C.F.R. 1.1041–1T. Treatment of transfer of property between spouses or incident to divorce (temporary)

26 C.F.R. 1.6015.0. Table of contents

26 C.F.R. 1.6015.1. Relief from joint and several liability on a joint return

26 C.F.R. 1.6015.2. Relief from liability applicable to all qualifying joint filers

26 C.F.R. 1.6015.3. Allocation of liability for individuals who are no longer married, are legally separated, or are not members of the same household

26 C.F.R. 1.6015.4. Equitable relief

26 C.F.R. 1.6015.5. Time and manner for requesting relief

26 C.F.R. 1.6015.6. Nonrequesting spouse's notice and opportunity to participate in administrative proceedings

26 C.F.R. 1.6015.7. Tax Court review

26 C.F.R. 1.6015.8. Applicable liabilities

26 C.F.R. 1.6015.9. Effective date

General Index

Section numbers refer to the Texas Family Code unless otherwise noted.

Editors' Note: If you cannot find a subject covered in the index, please notify John J. Sampson at jsampson@law.utexas.edu, or Harry L. Tindall at htindall@tindallengland.com. Our goal is to provide a user-friendly index. For example, a lawyer called to observe that the "emancipation" statutes were not listed in the index. The addition of that term to the index with a cross reference to ch. 42, Removal of Disabilities of Minority, cured the problem.

We are very proud of our index because it is between 25% and 50% the length of other indices with which we compete and has elicited many positive comments for its usability. Thus, we think our index is less frustrating than the others. However, this publication has an infinitely more important feature for ease of use. The accompanying CD-ROM provides instant word search. To coin a phrase, to find something in the Family Code or Related Texas and Federal materials, just Google S&T.

†